The Rorschach: A Comprehensive System, in two volumes
  *by John E. Exner, Jr.*
Theory and Practice in Behavior Therapy
  *by Aubrey J. Yates*
Principles of Psychotherapy
  *by Irving B. Weiner*
Psychoactive Drugs and Social Judgment: Theory and Research
  *edited by Kenneth Hammond and C. R. B. Joyce*
Clinical Methods in Psychology
  *edited by Irving B. Weiner*
Human Resources for Troubled Children
  *by Werner I. Halpern and Stanley Kissel*
Hyperactivity
  *by Dorothea M. Ross and Sheila A. Ross*
Heroin Addiction: Theory, Research and Treatment
  *by Jerome J. Platt and Christina Labate*
Children's Rights and the Mental Health Profession
  *edited by Gerald P. Koocher*
The Role of the Father in Child Development
  *edited by Michael E. Lamb*
Handbook of Behavioral Assessment
  *edited by Anthony R. Ciminero, Karen S. Calhoun, and Henry E. Adams*
Counseling and Psychotherapy: A Behavioral Approach
  *by E. Lakin Phillips*
Dimensions of Personality
  *edited by Harvey London and John E. Exner, Jr.*
The Mental Health Industry: A Cultural Phenomenon
  *by Peter A. Magaro, Robert Gripp, David McDowell, and Ivan W. Miller III*
Nonverbal Communication: The State of the Art
  *by Robert G. Harper, Arthur N. Wiens, and Joseph D. Matarazzo*
Alcoholism and Treatment
  *by David J. Armor, J. Michael Polich, and Harriet B. Stambul*
A Biodevelopmental Approach to Clinical Child Psychology: Cognitive Controls and Cognitive Control Theory
  *by Sebastiano Santostefano*
Handbook of Infant Development
  *edited by Joy D. Osofsky*
Understanding the Rape Victim: A Synthesis of Research Findings
  *by Sedelle Katz and Mary Ann Mazur*
Childhood Pathology and Later Adjustment: The Question of Prediction
  *by Loretta K. Cass and Carolyn B. Thomas*
Intelligent Testing with the WISC-R
  *by Alan S. Kaufman*
Adaptation in Schizophrenia: The Theory of Segmental Set
  *by David Shakow*
Psychotherapy: An Eclectic Approach
  *by Sol L. Garfield*
Handbook of Minimal Brain Dysfunctions
  *edited by Herbert E. Rie and Ellen D. Rie*
Handbook of Behavioral Interventions: A Clinical Guide
  *edited by Alan Goldstein and Edna B. Foa*
Art Psychotherapy
  *by Harriet Wadeson*
Handbook of Adolescent Psychology
  *edited by Joseph Adelson*
Psychotherapy Supervision: Theory, Research and Practice
  *edited by Allen K. Hess*

*Continued on back*

HANDBOOK OF
INNOVATIVE
PSYCHOTHERAPIES

# OTHER BOOKS BY RAYMOND CORSINI

**AUTHORED**

*Methods of Group Psychotherapy*

*Roleplaying in Business and Industry* (with Robert Blake and Malcolm Shaw)

*Roleplaying in Psychotherapy*

*The Family Council* (with Rudolf Dreikurs and Shirley Gould)

*The Practical Parent* (with Genevieve Painter)

*Roleplaying: a Handbook for Group Facilitators*
(with Robert Blake, Malcolm Shaw, and Jane Mouton)

*Give In or Give Up* (with Clinton Phillips)

*Adlerian Psychology: Theory and Practice* (with Guy Manaster)

**EDITED**

*Critical Incidents in Psychotherapy* (with Stanley Standal)

*Adlerian Family Counseling* (with Ray Lowe, Manford Sonstegard, and Rudolf Dreikurs)

*Critical Incidents in Teaching* (with Daniel Howard)

*Critical Incidents in School Counseling* (with Vincent Calia)

*Critical Incidents in Nursing* (with Loretta Bermosk)

*Current Psychotherapies*

*Current Personality Theories*

*Great Cases in Psychotherapy* (with Dan Wedding)

*Alternative Educational Systems* (with Edward Ignas)

*Theories of Learning* (with George Gazda)

*Educational Systems Around the World* (with Edward Ignas)

# HANDBOOK OF INNOVATIVE PSYCHOTHERAPIES

*Edited by*

RAYMOND J. CORSINI

A WILEY-INTERSCIENCE PUBLICATION

JOHN WILEY & SONS, New York • Chichester • Brisbane • Toronto • Singapore

*Library of Congress Cataloging in Publication Data:*

Main entry under title:

Handbook of innovative psychotherapies.

(Wiley series on personality processes ISSN 0195-4008)
Includes bibliographical references and index.
1. Psychotherapy.    I. Corsini, Raymond J.
RC480.5.H276    616.89′14    80-29062
ISBN 0-471-06229-4

Printed in the United States of America

10 9 8 7 6 5 4 3

**To Kleo**

# Series Preface

This series of books is addressed to behavioral scientists interested in the nature of human personality. Its scope should prove pertinent to personality theorists and researchers as well as to clinicians concerned with applying an understanding of personality processes to the amelioration of emotional difficulties in living. To this end, the series provides a scholarly integration of theoretical formulations, empirical data, and practical recommendations.

Six major aspects of studying and learning about human personality can be designated: personality theory, personality structure and dynamics, personality development, personality assessment, personality change, and personality adjustment. In exploring these aspects of personality, the books in the series discuss a number of distinct but related subject areas: the nature and implications of various theories of personality; personality characteristics that account for consistencies and variations in human behavior; the emergence of personality processes in children and adolescent; the use of interviewing and testing procedures to evaluate individual differences in personality; efforts to modify personality styles through psychotherapy, counseling, behavior therapy, and other methods of influence; and patterns of abnormal personality functioning that impair individual competence.

IRVING B. WEINER

*University of Denver*
*Denver, Colorado*

# Preface

The *Handbook of Innovative Psychotherapies* contains a disciplined, authoritative, concise, and readable account of 64 major innovative approaches to psychotherapy in current use.

Consider the term *disciplined* in the preceding sentence. Every chapter in this book follows the same outline: *definition; history; current status; theory; methodology; applications; case example; summary;* and *references.*

Every author was given (a) a minimum and maximum number of pages for his or her chapter, (b) a minimum and maximum number of pages for each of the nine sections, and (c) explicit instructions as to what the contents of each section was to be.

These instructions were given in an attempt to achieve *comparability* and *uniformity,* so that any reader would be able to obtain a complete account of each of the therapeutic approaches and to make comparisons between the various systems. Thus, if one were interested in comparing the theories of the first system in this book and the last system, all one would have to do is look up the section called "Theory" in each of these two chapters.

In discussing the subject of *authoritativeness* with some of the innovators of the various approaches in this book, I constantly was informed that they felt that their systems often had not been presented correctly by others. This complaint is common also to proponents of the better established or "standard" systems, such as Adler's Individual Psychotherapy. One of my goals was to present an authoritative account of each system and I determined that this could best be presented by the innovators of the systems. Accordingly, most of the reports in this book are by the founders of the particular approaches. When this was not possible, for any of several reasons—e.g.: Meditation is over 3000 years old; the developer of Primary Relationship Therapy is dead; the major innovators of two systems in this book refused to participate—I then attempted to locate the next most qualified person, and if possible asked that individual to have his or her chapter reviewed by qualified others.

By and large, I believe the reader will find an authoritative account of every system covered.

Too often the typical book or major articles about the various systems of psychotherapy cover in too much depth what I am not interested in learning, and spend too little time on what I want to know. I assume that the typical busy practitioner or harried student who comes to this book wants hard facts plainly written, not a lot of useless words. And so *conciseness* was one of my major goals as editor.

This was achieved in two major ways: First, as already explained, the authors had to cover specific areas within an allotted space; and second, I used my editorial pencil quite liberally. Overall, interestingly enough, the authors accepted this excising quite well, especially when I removed what I consider my enemies: adjectives and adverbs. One will find very few "verys" in this book. The result is that there is a lot of meat and very little fat in these accounts.

While all the areas mentioned thus far were important factors in adding to the book's *readability,* there was still another important task that I faced as editor: to "plane down" the manuscript so that it would read as though written by one person: to have a uniform style. In essence, while editing the various chapters, I reworked them, if possible, as though I had written them and was going over my own first draft. My own style of writing tends to be simple, my sentences tend to be short, and my vocabulary tends to be limited. I don't like to use a lot of punctuation.

And so I would change semicolons to periods. I would take out adverbs and adjectives. I would excise self-aggrandizing statements. I would blue-pencil repetitions. And in general, I tried to achieve the utmost simplicity and clarity.

As the reader will discover, this was not always possible, and at least three of the chapters in this book are quite difficult to understand. But the reader can be certain that I: (a) tried to get the authors to strive for greater clarity and; (b) attempted myself to achieve this through editing. But I did not succeed in all cases. However, were anyone to criticize me for the difficulty of any of the chapters, my retort would be: "You should have seen them before editing!"

As the reader can see by examining the List of Psychotherapies following the Preface, some 250 systems of psychotherapy are noted. A baker's dozen of them, found in another book that I edited,* may be considered the major standard systems; the other systems may be considered innovative. My task was to make the best selection from this rather formidable, although certainly only partial, list of all the approaches to psychotherapy in existence.

My criteria for inclusion were simple. I defined a system as a therapeutic approach that had a logically coordinated relationship between its theory and its procedures, and at least one of them had to be novel. That is to say, either the underlying concepts about modifying human nature and human behavior

*Current Psychotherapies.* Itasca, Ill.: F. E. Peacock, 1973/1979.

had to be novel or the procedures had to be unusual—or both had to be somewhat different from standard systems.

Still, I was forced to make value judgments about the importance of the various approaches. My selection will not satisfy all readers; another editor would no doubt formulate a different set of chapters to be included. Consequently, to any critic who may wonder about inclusions versus noninclusions, I can say:

1.  I did make an attempt to locate as many systems as possible and to locate the innovators of these systems, but I was not as successful as I might have been.

2.  In some cases, possible contributors were indifferent or even hostile (one innovator had his lawyer threaten to sue me and the publisher if his system were included in this book).

3.  In some cases (two) authors did not meet certain deadlines, and withdrew even after I indicated my willingness to extend the deadline.

As I employ it, the term *innovative* need not mean "new" in the sense of being recently developed but rather "new" in the sense of being relatively unknown to people like myself. Consequently, included are systems that are quite old—such as Meditation, which has been in existence as a therapeutic method for well over 3000 years—as well as Art Therapy and Dance Therapy, which probably are just as old. I would have liked to have included Trigant Burrow's Phyloanalysis, my own first system of psychotherapy, but I could not locate anyone to write the chapter, since this system appears to have disappeared from use.

My standards for calling a system *innovative* were subjective. If the system seemed trivial I rejected it on the grounds of not being "major"; if the theory or the procedures seemed too similar to other systems, I did not consider the approach truly "innovative." Although other editors might have made different choices, but it appears to me at this time that every single chapter has at the very least one major innovative element.

It is my judgment that the typical reader will find some chapters so innovative as to be considered absurd or even dangerous—but in all cases, I am convinced that the authors were passionately sincere in their beliefs about the fundamental value of their views and procedures.

Finally, *what is psychotherapy?* Frankly, I don't know whether I can define the term. Beyond saying that it is a formal way of operating based on some theory and coordinated procedures for changing the behavior, the thinking, and the feelings of individuals in ways desired either by the individual in question or by others, there is little I can add.

To illustrate: There are two other realms of thinking and acting that can be distinguished from psychotherapy; one is education, the other is religion. But a system such as Multiple Impact Therapy may be considered education and a system such as Mutual Need Therapy might be considered religion.

Or how about the realm of exercise or of aesthetics? Dance Therapy and Art Therapy pose problems of classification.

The reader will probably find such systems as Aesthetic Realism, the Body Therapies, Naikan, Natural High Therapy, Poetry Therapy, Radical Psychiatry, Rebirthing, Transcendence Therapy, and Z-Process Attachment Therapy difficult to classify, since each contains features that might preclude their clear-cut classification as psychotherapy.

In addition, there are several chapters in this book, each innovative and about psychotherapy, that even I would have trouble classifying as psychotherapy—yet they are among the most important chapters to be found. I refer to Comprehensive Relaxation Training, Crisis Management, Feminist Therapy, Mainstreaming, and Stress Management.

### Uses of This Book

While it is certain that this comprehensive account of 66 innovative psychotherapies will have different values for different people, I believe it will provide reference material for at least four different audiences.

I see this book as most valuable for people who make a living, totally or partially, as counselors and therapists, who deal primarily with people having difficulty adjusting to themselves and/or to others, who are struggling to find peace and success. These counselors and therapists often need help themselves to better understand human nature and how to help others. Frequently people in these professions are trapped, as it were, by their training and their experiences, and just don't know how to extend themselves. For such individuals, the *Handbook of Innovative Psychotherapies* should provide, as it did for me, many new ideas, and may encourage them to experiment and to find out more about other approaches.

A second important group who would want to use this book as a text would be students preparing for careers as psychiatrists, psychologists, social workers, school counselors, or practitioners in other helping professions, and whose training has been limited to one approach. Often the approach that one is indoctrinated in has not been chosen by the student. Thus, a student may go to this particular university or may attend that particular training institute—for any of a variety of reasons having nothing to do with a desire to study a particular kind of counseling or psychotherapy. While indoctrination in one system, rather than a shotgun approach, is probably the best way of training new professionals, it frequently happens that the approach one is trained in is just not the right system for that new professional. What happens then is that the new counselor or therapist enters the real world ill-equipped, following a theory or using a methodology that, while entirely legitimate, may not be the right one for him or her.

This happened to me: I operated for about three years in one way, then changed to another approach for about ten years, and then, finally, found a system that was compatible with my own particular personality.

And this is precisely what happened to

most innovators. It is my impression that a number of psychotherapy innovators—including Carl Rogers, J. L. Moreno, Albert Ellis, and Eugene Gendlin—found whatever they were originally trained in not compatible with their essential personality. They then developed systems of operating that were appropriate with their uniqueness.

Certainly this has been the case with those contributors with whom I am personally acquainted—Jack Annon, George Bach, Paul Bindrim, George Gazda, Nira Kefir, Arthur Lerner, Lew Losoncy, Walter O'Connell, Harry Olson, Paul Pedersen, Will Schutz, John Watkins, and Robert Zaslow. Their preferred method of operating and their manifest personalities are congruent. Each of these people is a primary innovator and each has developed, in my judgment, a system entirely congruent with his or her manifest personalities.

For the student or the person newly entering into this exciting field of counseling/psychotherapy, I offer this advice: In this book are a considerable number of systems over and beyond those you already know or have been trained in. Learn about these systems and experience them vicariously, for one of them may really be the very best system for you.

A third group for whom this book will be of value are those who make referrals and who may want to know more about a particular psychotherapist's theory and practices. Say that you are a physician and you have a patient in constant tension, or a social worker faced with a client with a particular kind of problem, and you would like to refer this person to someone. An examination of the titles of the various chapters may lead you to some systems. Or even better, reading the various definitions may enable you to zero in on some methods that will intuitively appear to you as suitable for your patient. In an institution, there may be a desire to establish some procedure to deal with a variety of clients. Thus, in a rehabilitation hospital, for example, Gazda's Multiple Impact Training may seem the

system of choice, or in a prison consideration might be given to Immediate Therapy. Or, in a school, students may be taught Meditation.

Finally, of course, this book can be employed as a kind of encyclopedia for spot information about a particular system or for ideas about how to treat a particular problem.

## Comments about the Therapies

At one point I attempted to classify every system in this book in some sort of multiple category, such as client-control, directed to the unconscious, future-oriented, and so forth, but the reactions of the chapter authors were mixed regarding the value of my categorization. Additionally, my classification of some systems differed radically from the authors' own classification; thus I decided against including this classification system.

However, I can assure the reader that the systems in this book vary considerably with respect to the following dimensions: *control*—some are client-centered, some therapist-centered, and some are mixed; *awareness*—some are directed to conscious awareness, some to the unconscious, and some are mixed; *temporality*—some of the approaches go into the past, some into the present, and some are future-oriented; *range* (of results)—some systems aim for limited results, while some have grander aspirations of changing the whole personality; *focus*—some systems fix on cognition, some on emotions, and some on behavior, while other systems go for combinations of these three; *view of humans*—some systems see the human being as strictly determined, some as having free will, and some as determined by a combination of heredity, environment, and self; *operations*—some of the systems are very limited in their operations, some are varied, and some are quite wide.

In other words, an extreme range of theories and procedures is to be found in this book: Some systems may be considered very simple, some very complicated; some very conservative, some quite radical; some appear to be of the commonsense variety, while some appear to be just plain foolish; some systems appear to be combinations of what others have thought of or done, while others appear to be completely new; some systems should be acceptable in the most fundamentalist of social agencies, while some systems couldn't get in the front door. But all of the systems are in one way or another innovative—and each should have some impact on the careful reader.

RAYMOND J. CORSINI

*Honolulu, Hawaii*
*February 1981*

# List of Psychotherapies

In the list below, generally speaking, the word *Psychotherapy* is understood to follow the term shown. Thus, in the first term, *Action,* the full name of the therapy is *Action Psychotherapy.* In other cases, the full name is given, Thus—*Adaptational Psychodynamics.* There are several points to be considered in going over the list. In some cases, the system of therapy is general and possibly even vague. This may be the case, for example, in *Art Therapy.* In some cases, a particular theory may have had several names. This is true of *Non-directive Therapy, Client-Centered Therapy* and *Person-Centered Therapy* all being different names for the same conceptualization.

I had thought of trying to tie the name of the various therapies with their innovators, but this was too much of a problem: trying to find out, for example, who developed PLOMP (or even what it was) was beyond my capacity. Also, there are instances of the same name serving two quite different therapies. George Gazda, for example, gave the name *Multiple Impact Therapy* to a system he developed and then learned someone else had previously used the term and so he changed the name of his system to *Multiple Impact Training.*

Some purists might dispute whether some of the systems here included, such as *Arica* or *Scientology* are therapeutic systems; but then, some will question whether *Psychoanalysis* is. This listing is very inclusive and not exclusive.

Names capitalized, such as ADLERIAN, represent systems not in this book but which are to be found in my *Current Psychotherapies;* names italicized, such as *Actualizing* are those systems to be found in this book.

| | |
|---|---|
| Action | Assertion-structured |
| Active | Assertiveness Training |
| Actualism | Assumption Centered |
| *Actualizing* | Atase |
| Adaptational Psychodynamics | Attitude |
| ADLERIAN | Autochthonous |
| *Aesthetic Realism* | *Autogenic Training* |
| Alexander Technique | Aversion |
| Alphagenics | Aversive |
| ANALYTICAL | BEHAVIORAL |
| Anger Provocation | Behavioral Counseling |
| Anxiety Management Training | Behavioral Family |
| *Aqua-Energetics* | Bibliotherapy |
| *Art* | Biocentrics |
| Arica | Bioenergetics |

*Biofeedback*
Body Awareness
*Body*
Breakthru Dreaming
Breathing
*Brief*
Character Analysis
Choices
Client-Centered
Clinical Behavior
Clinical Biofeedback
Cognitive
*Cognitive Behavior*
Communication
*Comprehensive Relaxation*
Concentrative Movement
*Conditioned Reflex*
*Conflict Resolution*
Confrontation
Conjoint Family
Coping Skills Training
Course in Miracles
*Covert Conditioning*
Covert Desensitization
Creative
*Creative Aggression*
Creative Problem Solving
*Crisis Intervention*
Cybernetics
*Dance —*
Dance—Mime
Dance—Movement
Dasein Analysis
Depth
Direct Decision
*Direct Psychoanalysis*
Directive
Directed Reverie
Eclectics
Ego Directive
*Ego State*
*Eidetics*
Emotive Reconstructive
Encounter
*Encouragement*
Esoteric
Erhard Seminar Training
Eutonia
Existential

Existential Analytic
EXPERIENTIAL
Experiential Family
Expressive
FAMILY
Family Contact
Fantasy
Feeling
Feldenkrais
*Feminist*
*Fixed Role*
*Focusing*
Formative Spirituality
Free Painting
*Functional*
General Semantics
GESTALT
Gestalt Attitude
Go-between Process
*Holistic Education*
Humanistic
HUMAN  POTENTIAL
Hydropsychotherapy
Hypnosis
Hypnobehavioral
Hypnography
Illumination
Imagery
*Immediate*
*Impass/Priority*
Implicit
Implosive
Insight
Intense Feeling
Intensive Journal
*Integratative*
*Integrity Groups*
*Interpersonal Process Recall*
Logotherapy
*Mainstreaming*
Marathon
Medical moralizations
*Meditation*
Mental Movements
Milieu
*Morita*
Movement
Multimedia
*Multimodal*

*Multiple Family*
Multiple Impact
*Multiple Impact Training*
*Mutual Need*
Music
*Naikan*
Natural
*Natural High*
Neobehavioral
Neo-Reichian
Network
*New Identity Process*
Neuro-Linguistics
Nirvana
Non-directive
*Non-directive Psychoanalysis*
Non-rational
Nude
Objective
Objectivism
Open Door
Open Education
Open Encounter
Open Ended
Operant Group
*Orgone*
Past Lives
PERSON CENTERED
*Personal constructs*
Personal Science
Philotherapy
Philosophic
Phyloanalysis
Piagetian
*Plissit*
Plomp
*Poetry*
Polarity
Positive
*Primal*
*Primary Relationships*
Priorities
*Provocative*
PSYCHOANALYSIS
Psychobiological
Psychocybernetics
Psychodelics
PSYCHODRAMA
*Psycho-Imagination*

Psychomotor
Psychosocial
Psychosomatics
*Psychosynthesis*
*Radical*
*Radix*
Rage reduction
Rational
RATIONAL-EMOTIVE
Realativity
REALITY
*Rebirthing*
Redecision
*Reevaluation*
Regressive
Reichian
Re-grief
Relationships
Regressive
Reparenting
Role
Role Construct
Rolfing
Round Table
Scientology
Scream
Sector
Self
Self Analysis
Self Hypnosis
*Self Image*
Self Instructional Training
Self-talk
Semantic
Sensor Awareness
Sentics
Separation
*Sex*
Sleep
*Social Influence*
Social Learning
Social Modeling
Stress Innoculation Training
*Stress management*
Structural Integration
*Structured Learning*
Syntetics
Systematic Relaxation
T Groups

# *Acknowledgments*

As can be imagined, a great many people assisted me directly and indirectly in the preparation of this book. Some of them, such as the librarians at the University of Hawaii and at the Library of Congress, must be anonymous since I never knew their names. However, I would like to emphasize that for this book as well as for all others I have worked on, I have always found librarians more than willing to be of help.

My greatest appreciation is to my wife, Dr. Kleona Rigney, to whom I dedicate this book. She was of help in many areas—from doing clerical work to reading the systems and giving opinions, as well as helping with chores that were my responsibility.

I am appreciative to Robert Lawless of Wiley-Interscience, who first accepted this book and who advised and encouraged me; to Herb Reich, my editor at Wiley-Interscience, who improved my book considerably; and to Walter J. Maytham III, the publisher, whose advice I value.

Among others who assisted me from time to time and in different ways were: Elinor Brown, Mary Cade, Donna DeNeeve, William R. Dinker, Albert Ellis, George Okazaki, Arnold Schwartz, Alan Simpkins, and Dan Wedding.

Most of all, I, along with the readers of this book, should be appreciative of the authors of the chapters, all of them busy people, who accepted the assignment to write a chapter and who (for the most part) cooperated cheerfully in my various demands to generate a disciplined work.

The ultimate purpose of the *Handbook of Innovative Psychotherapies* is to further psychotherapy as a science, a profession, and a means of improving human living. I offer this book with the hope that its purpose will be at least partially fulfilled.

R.J.C.

# Contents

# Contributors

Jack R. Adams-Webber, Ph.D.
Brock University
Ontario, Canada

Camilla M. Anderson, M.D.
Private practice, Psychiatry
405 West Main Street
Sidney, Montana

Jack S. Annon, Ph.D.
Private practice, Psychotherapy
1380 Lusitana Street, Suite 909
Honolulu, Hawaii

George R. Bach, Ph.D.
Institute of Group Psychotherapy
Los Angeles, California

Elworth F. Baker, M.D.
Private practice
200 East End Avenue
New York, New York

Martha Baird, B.A.
Aesthetic Realism Foundation
New York, New York

Avis K. Bennett, M.A.
Boston College
Chestnut Hill, Massachusetts

Paul Bindrim, Ph.D.
Private practice, Psychotherapy
2000 Cantana Drive
Hollywood, California

Patricia A. Boger
University of Florida
Gainesville, Florida

Heide F. Brenneke
Autogenic therapist
1935 East Calhoun Street
Seattle, Washington

Laura S. Brown, Ph.D.
University of Washington
Seattle, Washington

Daniel M. Casriel, M.D.
Private practice, Psychiatry
47 East 51st Street
New York, New York

Joseph R. Cautela, Ph.D.
Boston College
Chestnut Hill, Massachusetts

Richard J. Corriere, Ph.D.
Clinic for Functional Counseling and
Psychotherapy
Los Angeles, California

Raymond J. Corsini, Ph.D.
Private practice, Psychotherapy
140 Niuki Circle
Honolulu, Hawaii

Martha Crampton, M.A.
Private practice, Psychosynthesis
Redding, Connecticut

Arnold E. Dahlke, Ph.D.
Foundation for the Rechanneling of
Emotions and Education
Beverly Hills, California

Diane Duggan, M.S.
Registered Dance Therapist
149 West 4th Street
New York, New York

Franz R. Epting, Ph.D.
University of Florida
Gainesville, Florida

Frank Farrelly, A.C.S.W.
Private practice, Psychotherapy
1414 East Washington
Suite 104
Madison, Wisconsin

Albert G. Forgione, Ph.D.
Massachusetts Psychological Center
Boston, Massachusetts

John P. Foreyt, Ph.D.
Baylor College of Medicine
Houston, Texas

Barbara L. Forisha, Ph.D.
University of Michigan
Dearborn, Michigan

George M. Gazda, Ed.D.
University of Georgia
Athens, Georgia

Darryl L. Gentry, M.S.W.
Private practice, Psychotherapy
3713 Heathrow Drive
Winston Salem, North Carolina

Dianne Gerard, M.S.W.
University of Hawaii
Honolulu, Hawaii

N. Jane Gershaw, Ph.D.
Veterans Administration Medical Center
Syracuse, New York

John S. Gillis, Ph.D.
Oregon State University
Corvallis, Oregon

Arnold P. Goldstein, Ph.D.
Syracuse University
Syracuse, New York

G. Ken Goodrick, Ph.D.
University of Houston
Houston, Texas

Sophie T. Goren
Mainstreaming technician
University of Southern California
School of Medicine
Los Angeles, California

Barry Green, Ph.D.
Institute of Psycho-Structural Balancing
1122 4th Avenue
San Diego, California

James L. Greenstone, Ed.D.
Marriage and Family Counselor
8609 Northwest Plaza Drive
Suite 440A
Dallas, Texas

Joseph T. Hart, Ph.D.
University of Southern California
Psychology Research & Service Center
Los Angeles, California

Reed Holmberg, R.N., M.A.
Massachusetts Psychology Center
Boston, Massachusetts

James R. Iberg, Ph.D.
Private practice, Psychotherapy
5321 South Woodlawn
Chicago, Illinois

Eve Jones, Ph.D.
Los Angeles City College
Los Angeles, California

Charles S. Jordan, Ph.D.
Medical University of South Carolina
Charlestown, South Carolina

Norman I. Kagan, Ph.D.
Michigan State University
East Lansing, Michigan

Werner Karle, Ph.D.
Center for Feeling Therapy
7165 Sunset Boulevard
Los Angeles, California

Nira Kefir, Ph.D.
Alfred Adler Institute
Tel Aviv, Israel

Dennis O. Kirkman
Denver Primal Center
Denver, Colorado

Charles B. Kreitzberg, Ph.D.
Multimodal Therapy Institute
Kingston, New Jersey

Jesse Lair, Ph.D.
Montana State University
Bozeman, Montana

Eugene E. Landy, Ph.D.
Foundation for the Rechanneling of
Emotions and Education
Beverly Hills, California

Arnold A. Lazarus, Ph.D.
Rutgers University
Piscataway, New Jersey

Arthur Lerner, Ph.D.
Los Angeles City College
Los Angeles, California

Myra Levick, M.Ed.
Hahnemann Medical College
Philadelphia, Pennsylvania

Sharon B. Leviton, B.A.
Southwestern Academy of Crisis Interveners
Dallas, Texas

Nechama Liss-Levinson, Ph.D.
Brooklyn College
Brooklyn, New York

George Lockwood, M.A.
840 Fred R.D. #21
Lansing, Michigan

Lew Losoncy, Ed.D.
Institute for Personal and Organizational
Development
Reading, Pennsylvania

Stephanie N. Lynch, Ph.D.
Clinical psychologist
19 Muzzey Street
Lexington, Massachusetts

Richard McQuellon, M.A.
Michigan State University
East Lansing, Michigan

Scott Matthews, Ph.D.
Northern Michigan University
Marquette, Michigan

Werner M. Mendel, M.D.
University of Southern California School
of Medicine
Los Angeles, California

Dan Montgomery, Ph.D.
Southern California College
Costa Mesa, California

Arthur Nelson, M.D.
Private practice, Psychiatry
71 Park Avenue
New York, New York

Walter E. O'Connell, Ph.D.
Veterans Administration Center
Houston, Texas

Harry A. Olson, Ph.D.
Private practice, Psychology
313 Main Street
Reisterstown, Maryland

Genevieve Painter, Ed.D.
Private practice, Psychology
2333 Kapiolam
Honolulu, Hawaii

I. H. Paul, Ph.D.
City University of New York
New York, New York

Paul B. Pedersen, Ph.D.
Cultural Learning Institute
East-West Center
Honolulu, Hawaii

E. Lakin Phillips, Ph.D.
George Washington University
Washington, D.C.

John W. Raasoch, M.D.
Monadrock Family and Mental
Health Service
Keane, New Hampshire

Ellen Reiss, B.A.
Aesthetic Realism Foundation
New York, New York

David K. Reynolds, Ph.D.
TODO Institute
Los Angeles, California

Joan Roberts, Ph.D.
Private practice, Psychotherapy
313 Main Street
Reisterstown, Maryland

John N. Rosen, M.D.
Private practice, Psychotherapy
144 East Oakland Avenue
Doylestown, Pennsylvania

Andrew Salter, B.S.
Private practice, Psychotherapy
903 Park Avenue
New York, New York

Valerie J. Sasserath, Ph.D.
Multimodel Therapy Institute
Kingston, New Jersey

Robert F. A. Schaef, Ph.D.
Denver Primal Center
Denver, Colorado

Will C. Schutz, Ph.D.
Private practice, Psychotherapy
Box 259
Muir Woods, California

Lynn Segal, M.S.W.
Mental Research Institute
Palo Alto, California

Anees A. Sheikh, Ph.D.
Marquette University
Milwaukee, Wisconsin

Joseph E. Shorr, Ph.D.
Institute for Psycho-Imagination Therapy
Los Angeles, California

Everett L. Shostrom, Ph.D.
Private practice, Psychotherapy
205 West 20th Street
Santa Ana, California

Robert P. Sprafkin, Ph.D.
Veterans Administration Medical Center
Syracuse, New York

Hugh A. Storrow, M.D.
University of Kentucky Medical Center
Lexington, Kentucky

Claude Steiner, Ph.D.
Private practice, Psychology
2901 Piedmont Avenue
Berkeley, California

Alan C. Turin, Ph.D.
Private practice, Psychology
19 Muzzy Street
Lexington, Massachusetts

Barbara Ungashick
Denver Primal Center
Denver, Colorado

Walter J. Urban, Ph.D.
Research psychoanalyst
6320 Drexel Street
Los Angeles, California

Adrian van Kaam, Ph.D.
Dusquesne University
Pittsburgh, Pennsylvania

Anthony J. Vattano, Ph.D.
University of Illinois
Urbana, Illinois

Sally Vernon, M.A.
Private practice, Psychotherapy
2333 Kapiolam
Honolulu, Hawaii
Honolulu, Hawaii

Roger N. Walsh, M.D., Ph.D.
University of California Medical School
Irvine, California

Elaine Warburton, M.Ed.
Radix Institute
Ojai, California

Helen H. Watkins, M.A.
University of Montana
Missoula, Montana

John G. Watkins, Ph.D.
University of Montana
Missoula, Montana

Robert W. Zaslow, Ph.D.
San José State University
San José, California

HANDBOOK OF
INNOVATIVE
PSYCHOTHERAPIES

# CHAPTER 1

# *Actualizing Therapy*

EVERETT L. SHOSTROM and DAN MONTGOMERY

*One of my long-term and long-held goals is to write the definitive book on psychotherapy. In this book I will combine everything that I know from both my own experience and the experience of others to generate the final system of psychotherapy. Everett Shostrom and Dan Montgomery beat me to it in their chapter on Actualizing Therapy, but then so have Hart, and Sprafkin and Lazarus.*

*Actualizing Therapy is intended to be the final therapy, combining all theories of known value—a synthetic supersystem, if you will, of the best of all known theories and procedures. Such a therapy is not a mere piecing together of unrelated elements but is a true creation, in the same sense that an artist assembles into meaningful patterns unrelated items.*

*I believe an eclectic system of this type will eventually be the therapeutic system of the future. At the present time we are all like the blind men of Hindustani, each clearly seeing a part of the elephant; eventually, I expect, the elephant will be put together, and there will be one final system of psychotherapy—and of personality theory. This position will, of course, be rejected by proponents of single-mode theories and therapies, but in my judgment Actualizing Therapy is a step in the direction that we must eventually go to really become a profession based on science.*

Actualizing Therapy employed in an individual or group setting is a system for helping people to get in touch with themselves. A basic tenet of Actualizing Therapy is that most people are other-directed rather than inner-directed (Riesman, 1950). They look to the outside—to authorities and people they respect—for "shoulds," "have tos" and "musts," not realizing that they could better learn to live from within: to trust their own thoughts, feelings, and bodies. Experiencing one's self within and expressing one's self without: This is the process of actualization.

Actualizing Therapy incorporates a creative synthesis from many schools of theory and practice in psychotherapy that focus on body, mind, and feelings. From Buber (1951) and Allport (1937, 1961) comes the emphasis on achieving one's "particularity." From Maslow (1954) comes the emphasis on self-actualizing as a reasonable goal of psychotherapy. From Leary (1957) and Satir (1966) comes the emphasis on the feeling polarities of anger—love and strength—weakness as core structures in the personality.

The goal of Actualizing Therapy is to restore a client's trust in his own being, and to aid him to become rhythmic and expressive on the feeling polarities in verbal, feeling, and bodily ways. Replacing survival tactics with actualizing growth responses enables the client to handle problems of living with creative self-expression, interpersonal effectiveness, commitment to values, and choice of one's mission in life.

1

## HISTORY

Actualizing Therapy emerged through the close friendship of Everett Shostrom, the senior author of this chapter, and Abraham Maslow. Maslow (1954) proposed self-actualization as a reasonable goal of therapy. Shostrom (1976) designed a system of concepts and techniques capable of assisting a client along the journey of actualizing.

The theoretical underpinnings of Actualizing Therapy came from research at the Institute of Personality Assessment at Berkeley by Leary, Barron, MacKinnon, and Coffey (Leary, 1957). Factor analysis of personality traits on a sample of over 5000 cases showed that two dynamic polarities form the core of personality: anger—love and strength—weakness. Other polarities, such as masculinity—femininity, dominance—submission, and independence—dependence, were also found to be significant. For simplicity and to provide key reference points of latitude and longitude in the domain of feelings, anger—love, strength—weakness were chosen by Shostrom to be the core elements of Actualizing Therapy.

These "compass points of the self" correspond to Maslow's classic research on personality (1954), where he found that actualizing people express tender love and anger with ease, and that they are competent and strong, yet keenly aware of weaknesses.

In 1962 Shostrom collaborated with Maslow to produce the *Personal Orientation Inventory* (POI; Shostrom, 1963), the first assessment procedure for measuring actualizing tendencies. POI introduced a scientific research orientation to Actualizing Therapy, and research over the past 16 years has shown that persons completing Actualizing Therapy are more synergistically balanced on the four polarities.

An important dimension to the historical evolution of theory and technique of Actualizing Therapy is the close personal association of Shostrom with founders of other schools of psychotherapy. This association came about primarily through a series of films Shostrom produced on each of the following persons and their theories: Abraham Maslow, Rollo May, Carl Rogers, Victor Frankl, Albert Ellis, Fritz Perls, Alexander Lowen, and Arnold Lazarus. In addition to these films, Shostrom produced several films of a more philosophical nature with Paul Tillich, Alan Watts, and Ashley Montague.

Actualizing Therapy is a creative synthesis. From Rogers (1951) comes the focus on a client's feelings and the importance of nonjudgmental warmth between client and therapist. From Perls (1969) comes the focus on the client's awareness in the here and now. From Ellis (1962) comes the view of therapy as the process of revising assumptions about life. And from Lowen (1975) comes the focus on the client's body as a primary tool for diagnosis and therapy.

Taken together, the creative synthesis puts equal importance on thinking, feeling and bodily aspects of being.

In 1976 Shostrom's most comprehensive work, *Actualizing Therapy: Foundations for a Scientific Ethic,* was published. The book includes verbatim transcripts, lists of films on Actualizing Therapy, therapeutic techniques, and a full range of tests known collectively as the Actualizing Assessment Battery.

In 1979 the *Growth Process Inventory* (GPI) was published. The GPI measures survival patterns taken from Lowen's bioenergetic character types, and also reveals actualizing growth tendencies on the dimensions of anger, love, strength, weakness, and trust. The GPI represents Shostrom's latest efforts to build a system that reveals actualizing tendencies as well as pathology, and that supports healthy intra- and interpersonal functioning.

## CURRENT STATUS

Shostrom is director of the Institute of Actualizing Therapy in Santa Ana, California, where he and Dan Montgomery are engaged in research, writing, and therapy. Shostrom is Distinguished Professor of Psychology at the United States International University, where Actualizing Therapy is a part of the professional psychology curriculum.

The roots of Actualizing Therapy are found in two publications, the *Personal Orientation Inventory* (Shostrom, 1963) and *Therapeutic Psychology* (Brammer and Shostrom, 1977), a textbook now in its third edition currently used in 200 colleges and universities. The POI has generated over 250 published studies and is currently being used in therapeutic, educational, industrial, and religious settings.

The most comprehensive book available for studying Actualizing Therapy is *Actualizing Therapy: Foundations for a Scientific Ethic* (Shostrom 1976b).

With its emphasis on normal human growth, Actualizing Therapy has also found expression in popular literature. *Man, the Manipulator* (Shostrom, 1967) continues to be a best-seller, having sold nearly 2 million copies. *Healing Love* (Shostrom and Montgomery, 1978) integrates actualizing principles with religious thought.

In addition to books and tests, Shostrom has produced two historically significant films on psychotherapy. The first, *Three Approaches to Psychotherapy I* (the "Gloria" film), features Rogers, Perls, and Ellis working with the same client, and has received world-wide attention. A more recent film, *Three Approaches to Psychotherapy II* (the "Kathy" film), features Rogers, Shostrom, and Lazarus working with the same client. The film received the American Personnel and Guidance Association award for the most outstanding film of 1979.

## THEORY

Actualizing Therapy is based on a model of becoming an actualizing person rather than curing a state of illness or merely solving immediate life problems.

Figure 1, the central model of Actualizing Therapy, is systematically explained throughout this section. For a more compre-hensive treatment of the model, the reader is referred to Shostrom's *Actualizing Therapy* (1976).

Traditionally psychotherapy has steered away from the suggestion of universal values. However, the polarities of anger—love, strength—weakness seem to us to come close to a concept of universal values that support personal growth and interpersonal fulfillment through the journey of life.

The advantage of the actualizing model in Figure 1 is that it shows how growth is arrested and how growth can be restored: The model joins a system of malfunction with a system of healthy functioning.

Notice that the thickness of the circles changes as one moves from the outer, actualizing level into the inner, progressively more constricted rings of manipulation, character disorder, and psychoses. The broken line of the outermost circle shows that the facade or "public self" of the actualizing person functions as a semipermeable membrane, allowing the person to be in constant touch with his own core (the area inside the circle) and to express himself freely along the polar vectors of anger—love, strength—weakness. The arrows form figure-eights between the opposing polarities, showing that the actualizing person is not only expressive of his core self but also sensitive to emotional, intellectual, and physical information received from others. The person takes these inputs into his core for consideration of a genuine response.

A good analogy for an actualizing life style is the human heart. The constant movement of expansion and contraction suggests the dynamic rhythm of the polarities. A person dies physically when the heart stops pulsating. A person dies emotionally when the polarities of anger, love, strength, and weakness are constricted. Without vivid, pulsating feelings, the person becomes insensitive to his own core as well as to the needs and feelings of others.

Bleuler (1940) has said that schizophrenia is the inability to modulate affect. Actualizing Therapy holds that actualizing includes the *ability* to modulate affect fully. If

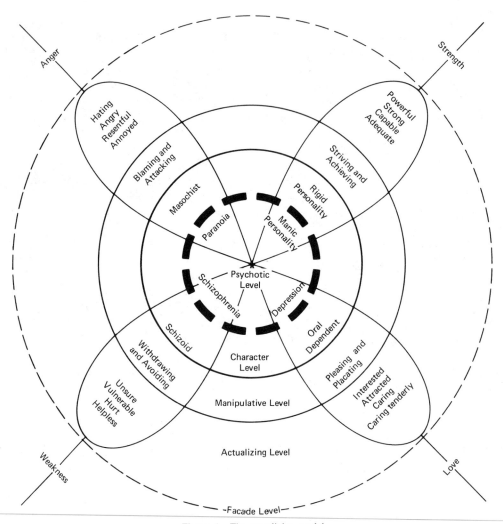

Figure 1   The actualizing model.

schizophrenia is the major mental disorder—and it allegedly accounts for 90 percent of the people in mental hospitals—then it is logical to define actualizing as the opposite of schizophrenia. Indeed the data of Fox, Knapp, and Michael (1968), based on the POI, demonstrates that hospitalized schizophrenics are extemely low on all scales of actualizing. The actualizing person, in contrast, develops the capacity for a "full feeling repertoire," as shown in Figure 2.

Actualizing does not mean arriving at a final state of full emotional awareness and perfect self-expression. Rather, it connotes an attitude of openness to what one is feeling, coupled with a willingness to express those feelings in actualizing ways. One learns compassion for one's limitations and takes comfort in one's manipulative tendencies, knowing that growth is a process that requires commitment, patience, and self-acceptance. "Effortless effort" describes the paradox of actualizing growth. In the actualizing spectrum of Figure 2, the ability to modulate affect enables a person to sometimes move in a "maxi-swing" to points of intense feeling at the very ends of the polarities, but more often to be sensitive to more subtle, milder levels of emotional expression shown as "mini-swings".

The journey of life involves enhancing emotional sensitivity. As one becomes more "at home" with one's self and more "in touch" with others, there arises a new and more accurate picture of reality. From this vantage point options become visible that were once obscure; elasticity and flexibility increase one's satisfaction in living. Actualizing behavior emerges out of being finely tuned to one's own and others' needs, desires, and feelings.

Grace and trust are interlocking concepts at the heart of Actualizing Therapy. The ex-perience of grace—of knowing that we are loved and lovable—allows us to lay down our defenses, come out of our hiding places, and be what we are. The experience of grace generates trust. When trust energizes the core of our being, we are able to risk expression of natural feelings that come spontaneously with involvement and interest in living. We are able to be on the outside ("public self") what we feel within (core). But trust in our cores does not always prevail. Emotional traumas, deprivations in childhood, wrong teachings about life, and limitations placed on us by circumstances can result in fear, not trust, dominating our inner cores.

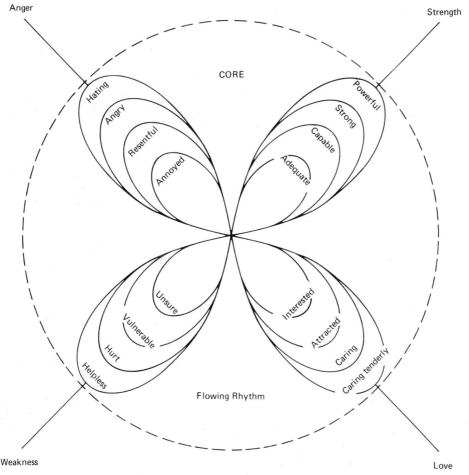

Figure 2  The actualizing spectrum.

Fear brings resistance to experiencing and expressing feelings. Fear causes us to constrict our feelings, rigidify our behavior, and lose our sensitivity. Increasing amounts of fear make a person more defensive, more desperate, and more emotionally numb. Fear is similar to cold; too much fear causes our cores to freeze and become inactive.

In Actualizing Therapy we seek to invite a distressed person back into the warmth of human encounter to "thaw out" his or her core. We do this through vigorous action techniques that mobilize the person's core feelings and that move him or her from indifference to caring, from apathy to full feeling. Psychopathology may be understood in terms of limited or distorted attempts to actualize. Manipulative behavior, character disorders, and psychotic states (see Figure 1) represent survival tactics for trying to get along in the world when one has been hurt and frightened. Therapy is a system of rebirth where the individual reexperiences fears and finds the strength to trust his or her core in spite of negative influences from life.

We define the core as an untouched, perfectly preserved sense of self. The core may be threatened, resulting in core pain, but it can never be destroyed. Individual therapy enables the client to make contact with repressed core pain. The client expresses intense feelings of rage, terror, shame, or longing that reside in the core as residue from past betrayals or rejections. In time the person is invited into group therapy, where he or she has a laboratory for interpersonal relationships. In a group the client works through ancillary feelings of embarrassment or guilt by learning to admit his or her manipulations. The client becomes free to experiment with experiencing and expressing the feeling polarities in the "here-and-nowness" of the group. *Dependence* in asking for help becomes *independence* as the client becomes more expressive at the core level. Finally, the client understands what it means to be *interdependent:* to be strong and yet vulnerable; to be autonomous and yet surrender to one's feelings of love for others.

## Levels of Psychopathology

As shown in Figure 1, we seek to understand pathology against the background of healthy functioning. Healthy functioning is based on trust in one's core; pathology is based on fear.

To understand how fear works to constrict the core, we use the analogy of the amoeba, a tiny one-celled organism. If the amoeba is repeatedly pricked by a pin, it permanently contracts itself to survive the attack. If a person is threatened psychologically or physically, especially early in life when basic character is being formed, he or she learns to contract bodily musculature and constrict awareness and expression of feeling. Control rather than trust comes to characterize the person's behavior. The stronger the inner fear and accompanying core pain, the more rigid and defensive the life style. Core pain is defined as a person's reaction to the denial of his fundamental right to exist and to express his being in satisfying ways. At the deepest level of the core, there is hurt and pain reflected in the feelings: Why wasn't I loved, given freedom to be, the right to exist?

Unresolved core pain yields defensive, survival-oriented behaviors that can be understood as the person's creative, yet self-defeating, attempts to get along in a world that is perceived as basically hostile. The behaviors can be predicted for each level of fearful constriction by understanding the specific way in which the person was invalidated by physical or psychological threats, early in life. Efforts to control his organismic responses to life (feelings, thoughts, and bodily responses) as well as fearful calculation in relationships to others are the basis for his immobility ("stuckness") and problems. The *manipulative level* of behavior is common to everyone. Manipulative patterns are based on a more normal level of fear and occasional calculating rather than feelingful responses to others. Persons stuck at the manipulative level are usually not suffering enough to seek professional psychotherapy, but they can benefit from principles of Actualizing Therapy presented in an educational or religious context.

At the *character level* the person is more tightly walled from life. There is a greater use of defense mechanisms to ward off inner core pain. Perception, affect, and cognition are more rigid. The person does not learn from experiences in life, and tends to respond to new events or relationships in stereotypic ways that reflect contamination from unresolved childhood conflicts. The person stuck at the character level is the one most likely to seek psychotherapy. Although he may have little or no insight into his problems (usually construing them as the work of fate, bad luck, or some other party), he knows that he is suffering. This suffering may be understood as a positive force that compels the person to get out of the straitjacket of survival tactics and surrender to the rhythm of growth and actualizing available to everyone.

The *psychotic level* of fearful constriction is the drastic "Custer's last stand" of a person who is being torn to pieces by unresolved core conflicts. The feelings of terror, rage, longing, or apathy finally overwhelm the person's rigid ego control, and the personality disintegrates. The process is symbolized by the thick, broken line at the center of Figure 1.

It must be emphasized that only certain character traits or psychotic behaviors (those most exemplary of behavior on the anger-love, strength—weakness continuum) are described here. While actualizing theory does not purport to account for all character or psychotic behavior, it does explain much pathological behavior as abortive attempts at actualizing: It joins a theory of malfunction with one of healthy functioning.

In actualizing theory it is assumed that energy is present at all personality levels, energy that provides the motivational force impelling the person to action. The more energy invested in fortifying the facade, repressing core pain, and utilizing survival behavior tactics, the less that is available for actualizing growth. Repressed feelings re-

quire energy investment in chronically tensed musculature.

The actualizing process, then, consists of aiding the person to become aware of core pain, to express feelings that have been rigidly held back, to experiment with actualizing behaviors, body awareness, and feeling expression on the four polarities, to develop a sense of core trust in being oneself, and to use newfound energies for effective and satisfying living.

## METHODOLOGY

### General Techniques

Therapy is as much an art as it is a science. The artistic dimension comes from the therapist's ability to orchestrate the client's awareness in feeling, thinking, and bodily aspects of being, so as to transform rigidity to movement, defensiveness to growth. The following techniques are therapeutic tools for facilitating awareness and change: (1) reflection of feeling; (2) reflection of experience; (3) therapist self-disclosure; (4) interpretation; (5) body awareness; and (6) value clarification.

*Reflection of Feeling* This is the re-expression, in fresh words, of the essential attitudes (not so much the content) expressed by the client. To reflect different dimensions of the total gestalt of the client's feelings, the therapist may focus on the client's self-feelings, the client's feelings toward others, or the client's feelings about the situation(s) in which he finds himself.

*Reflection of Experience* This involves observing the posture, gestures, tone of voice, breathing, facial expression, and eye contact of the client *while* he is expressing himself, and feeding certain information back to him as it happens in order to expand his awareness of what his body is doing. This technique is effective for focusing on contradictions between what the client says he feels and what the therapist sees his total organism saying. For example, the person who says he is not angry yet shortens his breath and doubles his fists can benefit from experiential feedback.

*Disclosure of the Therapist's Feelings*  The client is thus provided with a real human encounter. The therapist needs courage to express his own percepts of the client, as well as to discuss his own weaknesses and defenses candidly. In so doing he models a basic tenet of Actualizing Therapy: Owning your weaknesses is a precursor of actualizing your strengths.

*Interpretation*  This is an attempt by the therapist to present the client with a hypothesis about relationships or meanings for the client's consideration. Interpretation brings a fresh look at behavior, a new frame of reference, or a revised outlook on life. Other uses of intellectual interpretation include clarifying the client's problems, gathering relevant information, exploring alternative solutions in order to set therapeutic goals, clarifying values, trying out a therapeutic plan with periodic reevalation in light of new information and changing circumstances, providing the client with cognitive understanding of therapeutic experiences, and generalizing growth processes in the client to new life situations. Further techniques for the intellectual approach to therapy can be found in the works of Krumboltz and Thoresen (1969), Brammer and Shostrom (1977), and Lazarus (1971).

*Body Awareness Techniques*  Such techniques involve giving attention to the body and what it is expressing at the moment. To be able to feel fully requires that one get in touch with the body. Actualizing Therapy focuses on three aspects of body work: learning to breathe fully from the diaphragm, learning to relax body musculature, and learning to express oneself bodily on the feel-

ing polarities. The following are ways in which body exercises help people to develop contact with the polar dimensions of anger, love, strength, and weakness.

To facilitate expression of *anger*, the therapist can engage the client in role playing a "family argument." The therapist says "yes," and the client is asked to say "no" while reflecting on past experiences of being required to do something he did not want to do. The technique is to go back and forth, gradually increasing volume and bodily participation. The client has a safe opportunity to experience the bodily dimensions of anger, and to become more comfortable in self-, assertion and interpersonal confrontation. A second technique is to allow the client to beat a couch with a tennis racket. This desensitizes the person's fear of angry self-expression and facilitates an integrated expression of anger through the body-feelings-mind. It also allows for the release of rage or other strong negative feelings stored in body musculature from painful past experiences.

Feelings for the *love* polarity can be elicited through two exercises. In the first exercise the therapist and client work together to feel their caring for one another by warmly saying "yes" instead of "no." The therapist may be himself or he may role play a person to whom the client wants to evoke tender feelings, for instance, the client's mother or father. The exercise may bring a desire to touch or hug, which is appropriate in that it helps the client express caring in a physical way. The second exercise is "facial touch." The therapist role plays a mother or father and the client surrenders to feelings of being a child once again. The therapist says, "I'd like you to close your eyes now and I'm going to touch your face. I'd like you to feel that I'm your father (mother)." With that the therapist begins gently touching and outlining the brow, eyes, nose, cheeks, mouth, and chin. While tracing the client's face the therapist makes positive comments typical of those parents make when they are gazing tenderly at and gently touching their children. This physical and verbal expression of tenderness can be a very meaningful demonstration of the importance of caring. The exercise often brings tears to the client's eyes and awakens strong caring feelings.

On the *strength* polarity we have found that stamping one's feet firmly into the ground gives a real sense of feeling one's strength. By stamping his feet until he begins to feel the muscle strain in calves and thighs, the client will enhance his feeling of self-support. A second exercise, helpful for demonstrating strong resistance to being manipulated by one's environment, is to lie on a couch with both knees up, pounding the couch with both fists and saying, ''I won't give up!''

A technique for getting into touch with one's *weakness* is to stand in front of a couch, bent forward, with all weight on one's feet. The feet should be about 15 inches apart, with toes turned slightly inward. The fingers touch the floor out in front for balance. The knees are bent forward and then slowly brought back so that they begin to tremble. The vibration brings a tingling sensation in the feet and legs. Respiration begins to deepen. When standing this way becomes painful, the client is told to fall backward onto the couch. The point of the exercise is to experience falling (which represents one's weakness dimension, or ''fall-ability'') and surrendering to one's weakness. In a second exercise to get in touch with one's vulnerability the client is asked to stand with feet about 30 inches apart and hands on hips. The therapist then grasps the client's arms at the elbow and pushes him forward and down. As the client slowly lets himself down to the floor, he experiences deep feelings of vulnerability and surrender. The ability to surrender to one's feelings of weakness and vulnerability is central to Actualizing Therapy. To surrender is to accept one's losses. The fear of falling is related to the fear of surrendering to another, especially parents and others who have manipulated one. As individuals overcome their fear of falling,

they give in more readily to their bodies and their feelings.

These and other body-awareness techniques can be found in Lowen (1977), Schutz (1973), and Shostrom (1976b).

*Value Clarification* This involves ''prioritizing'' one's values. Priorities are statements of one's needs, wants, and desires at any one moment. Priorities also involve a wide perspective of future goals and past learning experiences. A practical method of choosing priorities is asking the client to periodically arrange the concerns and commitments most important to his life. A ''priority recital'' enlightens the client as to how to invest himself and as to what changes he needs to make to act on future goals or present desires. The actualizing person eventually develops a system in which he or she is constantly aware of priorities and changes, ready to act in terms of committed values. Operating from core values brings creativity, flexibility, and joy.

## Manipulative Analysis

In addition to general techniques, analysis of manipulation is an important part of Actualizing Therapy. Manipulations are patterns of survival by which people adapt to their environments without having to feel. As the client talks, the therapist begins to see a pattern emerging in which the individual is utilizing one or more manipulative patterns (see Figure 1, Manipulative Level). Once the pattern becomes clear, the manipulations are analyzed from the standpoint of short-term and long-range ''effects.'' For example, manipulations are most often used for controlling, exploiting, or seducing others, for avoiding situations, or for structuring time. These tactics provide short-term gains. However the long-term effect can be shown to be self-defeating in that the manipulative behaviors alienate the individual from others and keep him or her immature and dependent.

A second method to explore the client's manipulative patterns is for the therapist to role play the client and to ask the client to role play significant other people in his or her life. In this way the client sees mirrored back to him the particular ways in which he seeks to control others. He also experiences the frustration, confusion, and hurt that he normally dishes out to others. This technique can provide an experience of surprising self-discovery as well as lead to greater empathy and understanding toward people clients have formerly manipulated.

Actualizing Therapy helps the client develop a sense of worth by showing him that his manipulative behavior was a creative but self-defeating attempt to survive in a world that has manipulated him. He discovers that manipulative tactics can be transformed into actualizing behavior. For instance, blaming and attacking can be changed into the more healthy expressions of anger: asserting and confronting. Withdrawing and avoiding can be changed into feeling vulnerable and empathizing. The therapist encourages the development and practice of the new actualizing behaviors, and gently points out when the client regresses to former manipulative patterns.

A further technique of manipulative analysis is based on Perl's (1973) approach of "gestalt shuttling." A person whose personality is fragmented by polarization operates in an either/or manner. He plays nice guy or bully; he is weak or strong. In Actualizing Therapy the client learns to encompass both ends of his polarities in more direct and satisfying ways. In the shuttling technique the therapist places an empty chair in front of the client and has the client project onto the empty chair the parts of his own personality that he tends to disown and deny. By switching back and forth between chairs and expressing himself through a dialogue between the polarities, the client establishes better contact with both ends of the continuum. He learns to appreciate each of the polarities: to be both caring *and* assertive, vulnerable *and* strong.

## Character Analysis

When the therapist sees that a client's problems are deeply rooted in historical experiences, character analysis becomes an appropriate technique. Character styles, which are complex systems of negative muscular defenses, are originally adopted to withstand early manipulations by parents and other significant people.

Each level of personality (see Figure 1) has significant feelings associated with it, and these feelings become the focus of psychotherapy at the character level. It should be noted that feelings are avoided at the level of manipulation, whereas they become defensive or hostile at the character level. Feelings expressed at the character level have become lodged in the muscle structure as masochistic spite and rage, oral longing and bitterness, schizoid terror and hostility, and rigid betrayal and rejection.

To facilitate expression of these significant core feelings locked into each character style, we use an approach derived from Lowen (1975). The client lies on a couch, mattress, or pad, and assumes the passive role characteristic of a child in a crib.

The therapist, through the technique of character dialogue, plays the role of parents or significant others who manipulated the client earlier in life through discounting the client's feelings: rejecting, abandoning, or making excessive demands. This dialogue causes angry, hurt, and rageful feelings—character feelings—to be loosened and expressed openly. The client lies on the couch, kicks his legs, pounds his hands, and shouts "no!" many times in refutation of such parental patterns:

SCHIZOID CLIENT:   I AM! (core need: to feel his existence)

THERAPIST   (leaning over client and expressing the original parental response):   You are nothing! (or) We don't want you! (or) I wish you weren't here! (or) I wish you were never born!

SCHIZOID CLIENT:   No! No! No! I hate you!

ORAL CLIENT: I NEED YOU! (core need: to feel wanted)

THERAPIST: Your needs don't matter! (or) There are other people around here besides you! (or) Forget it, you're not important!

ORAL CLIENT: No! No! No! I don't need you!

MASOCHISTIC CLIENT: I WANT TO BE FREE! (core need: to feel free)

THERAPIST: We understand. (or) Don't worry about us. (or) Just remember all we've done for you. (or) Respect your parents!

MASOCHISTIC CLIENT: No! No! No! Get off my back!

RIGID CLIENT: I WANT YOUR LOVE! (core need: to feel love)

THERAPIST: Of course, you know I love you. (or) Stop pestering me! (or) Don't sit so close! (or) Don't touch yourself there (genital area)!

RIGID CLIENT: No! No! No! I don't need your love!

In the above character dialogues it is important for the client to take a stand against parental demands by saying "no." Being able to stand up for one's self breaks the pattern of dependence and generates feelings of self-confidence. In later sessions, as the client becomes more independent, he is directed by the therapist to a new character dialogue that focuses on the fulfillment of client needs. This time the client stands on his own two feet, face to face with the therapist (who is role playing the parent figure), and asks for what he needs. The therapist, as he hears the genuine expression of need in an adult fashion, responds to the request for fulfillment by the client.

SCHIZOID CLIENT: Please believe in me. I need you.

THERAPIST (reaching toward client): I believe in you. I support you.

ORAL CLIENT: Please help me.

THERAPIST: I want to help you.

MASOCHISTIC CLIENT: I want to be free. Please respect me.

THERAPIST: I want you to be free. I do respect you.

RIGID CLIENT: Please love me.

THERAPIST: I do love you. I do care.

The power of this exercise is the emotional bond that is recreated between the client and a parent figure. In this way the client reestablishes trust in his or her core needs for self-affirmation, support from others, freedom to be, and love.

As the client gives in to the spontaneous body movements that express original core needs, integration of body and feelings takes place. This process takes time, however, and may require repeated attempts. After integration of body and feelings, realistic acceptance of losses takes place. At the character level the schizoid person accepts his aloneness and the reality of his existence. The oral person accepts that his longing will never be fully filled. The masochist gives up his feelings of hostility and spite and accepts limited freedom. The rigid person accepts his betrayal and heartbreak, and surrenders to his need for love. All become more lovable and loving in spite of their hurt and losses. By understanding their historical development, by accepting losses as well as strengths, and by becoming genuinely expressive of thoughts, feelings, and body, clients find a new harmony within and a courage to grow in the world rather than merely survive.

## APPLICATIONS

A study by Shostrom and Riley (1968) confirms the hypothesis that experienced, seasoned therapists tend to be creative synthesizers. Creative synthesis means that a therapist may use a combination of techniques, or different single techniques, for different clients. For example, the psychologist might choose to use several different approaches with one client. Or the therapist might use one model (such as Gestalt Therapy, Rational-Emotive Therapy, or Behavior Modification) throughout the duration of one client's therapy, but use a different approach with another client.

The strength of Actualizing Therapy is its creative synthesis of many therapeutic systems around the central framework of self-actualization as the comprehensive goal of psychotherapy.

Those who choose therapy are more often people who are hurting inside even though they are not "sick" in the old-fashioned psychiatric sense. In fact, Actualizing Therapy has been used most successfully with normal or mildly disturbed persons [referred to in the *Diagnostic and Statistical Manual* (1980) as those with "character disorders"]. Actualizing Therapy has not been used extensively with psychotics or strongly neurotic populations.

When used for individual or group psychotherapy in the clinical setting, the *Personal Orientation Inventory* provides an objective measure of the client's level of actualizing as well as positive guidelines for growth during therapy. In a study relating changes in POI scores to stages of Actualizing Therapy, Shostrom and Knapp (1966) found that all POI scales significantly differentiated a sample of psychiatric outpatients beginning therapy from those in advanced stages of the psychotherapeutic progress.

The technical instruments of Actualizing Therapy are a set of psychological inventories known as the *Actualizing Assessment Battery* (AAB; Shostrom, 1976). These instruments measure the dynamics of *intra-* and *inter*personal functioning. The recognition of patterns in the person's historical development, coupled with an understanding of the major survival or growth systems that he or she presently uses, is important in launching Actualizing Therapy and in suggesting directions that clients can take in their personal journey of actualizing. In addition to its usefulness in individual therapy,

we believe that the AAB is an important research tool for exploring the positive effects of therapy. Inventories from the AAB, including the newly developed *Growth Process Inventory* (Shostrom, 1979), are used to measure survival and actualizing patterns in a wide variety of populations including college students, church congregations, delinquents, alcoholics, teachers, hospitalized psychotics, and nominated actualizing persons.

Many psychologists and clergymen have been conducting "marriage enrichment workshops" (Bustanoby, 1974), in which they use the AAB as a basis for discussion of the health or "wellness" of the marriage partners. The AAB is particularly suited to workshops of this kind because it provides a quick evaluation of the actualizing status of the individuals themselves, by means of the *Personal Orientation Inventory* (Shostrom, 1963), and of the actualizing status of the relationship, as measured by the *Caring Relationship Inventory* (Shostrom, 1966) and the *Pair Attraction Inventory* (Shostrom, 1970).

Actualizing Therapy has potential for broad use, even though it is an eclectic system, because the basics can be taught in a two- or three-week workshop to clinicians, counselors, pastoral counselors, and teacher counselors who have had a minimum of formal training in psychotherapy.

## CASE EXAMPLE

Joe comes to the office of an Actualizing Therapist from a crisis that developed the night before. His fiancee, Karen, has broken their engagement. Joe expresses fear of losing Karen. He says that an on-again, off-again pattern has characterized his dating relationships in adolescence and now as an adult. He feels sure that he could persuade her to come back, but knows that this would not really change the pattern. What he hopes to gain in therapy is deeper insight into the roots of his problem and some kind of genuine change in his relationships with women.

In exploring the historical roots to Joe's problems, the therapist asks him about the relationship between his mother and father. Immediately a clue jumps out as Joe responds: "Mother was always disappointed in Father. He never lived up to her demands; she complained a lot about him."

The therapist senses that Joe may have become the mother's substitute husband—that her frustrated marital energies may have been displaced into heavy yokes to be born by Joe.

The therapist explores how Joe's mother related to him. Joe replies, "She always told me that I was her good little soldier. I tried to make her happy by pleasing her with my achievements. I didn't rebel because she always made me feel guilty if I disappointed her. It was as though I had to be the good boy that my father wasn't."

The therapist suggests to Joe that perhaps he felt betrayed by his mother's lack of love and resentful at her many demands. Joe gets more in touch with core feelings of fear and anger.

"I didn't realize it then," he says, "but I was a childhood Dr. Jeckyl and Mr. Hyde. I felt so much pressure to be a good little boy that I had to deny anything that didn't fit the picture—especially sexual feelings, which were taboo to mother. I busied myself trying to do everything she wanted. I wanted her love, but she never really gave it to me."

The therapist asks if Joe sees a connection between his past relationship with his mother and his present problems with Karen. Joe makes a discovery. "I guess I start out being afraid of every woman I date. Then I try to impress them with my achievements. And I always feel guilty and uncomfortable with my sexual feelings. Most of all I'm afraid that she will somehow get control of me like Mother had." The therapist zeroes in on the obvious: "Joe, you're on-again, off-again pattern with Karen and with other women you have dated has been your way of keeping distance in your relationships. No woman scores a home run with you because

you keep sending her back to first base. When you feel the threat of too much intimacy, you call 'foul.' So you constantly keep the woman off balance and achieve your need to control and limit the depth of the relationship."

In terms of actualizing theory, the therapist sees Joe's problems as having to do with getting stuck on the strength polarity in early childhood. Joe's survival tactics for coping with a demanding, smothering mother involved learning to strive and achieve in order to meet her expectations for perfection. Joe now complains of rheumatism in his spine, which is probably related to having too much "backbone"—stiffening his back in order to appear responsible. Joe avoids the other polarities of anger, love, and weakness, because he would have to give up his tactic of controlling others by making them admire him because of his achievements. Most of all he avoids surrendering to tender, loving feelings. Having been controlled by his mother in childhood, he is determined to control women (i.e., Karen) by avoiding genuine intimacy and by striving to impress them instead.

Joe's present behavior is a creative but misdirected attempt to avoid the pain of betrayal. The therapist helps Joe to see how he can form a more satisfying bond with Karen by learning to affirm his freedom yet risk *yielding* to loving feelings. This is the basis for transforming manipulative coping patterns into actualizing growth patterns.

In the second and third sessions the therapist focuses on different aspects of Joe's problems by taking the part of Joe's mother, by playing Karen, and by representing warring factions of Joe's own personality. The explorations are done through psychodramas, gestalt shuttling techniques, and guided fantasy. Joe makes more and more progress in working through the impasse that has blocked his actualizing development. He realizes that getting a doctorate, becoming a professor, and writing seven books have not enabled him to break free of his fear of rejection and betrayal by women. He is glad for his professional development, yet he realizes that it was in part a compulsive attempt to find love and approval in safe ways that excluded his emotions and his sexuality. He could get the praise of students and readers, while keeping them at arm's length. The full impact of Joe's growing awareness comes when he says during a fourth session: "I have really succeeded in getting people's attention, but I find that I'm a very lonely person because I never commit myself to anyone. I've overdeveloped by intellect in order to keep in control. And I've left my feelings and my body out in the cold."

Indeed, Joe's body becomes a vital part of therapy during sessions 4 through 8 because his body reflects the conflicts he is wrestling with. Bioenergetic techniques are used to mobilize his breathing and to enhance his sensitivity to sexual feelings. A series of exercises is repeated for several weeks to help break down muscular tension in his back, jaw, shoulders, and pelvis. These exercises release a flood of new vitality and bodily excitement. Joe comments week by week that he has more energy than ever before.

Joe reports several dreams of an erotic nature, but feels less threatened by them. Because the therapist views sexual feelings, fantasies, and dreams as normal, Joe's embarrassment and self-consciousness begin to change to a sense of adventure and enjoyment in regard to his sexuality. The mind is finally being connected to the heart and genitals—a process that has been severely blocked by a stern mother and a demanding superego.

In his relationship with Karen, Joe feels less concerned with always pleasing her and more concerned with expressing his needs, desires, and values. Yet, ironically, it is through his newfound freedom to assert himself that he finds the ability to surrender to genuine loving feelings for Karen.

The therapist accentuates new experiences with Karen by having Joe become more aware of all the feeling polarities, getting

personal experience in surrendering to each one. Especially in group therapy, which he joins in his fourth week, Joe has ample opportunities to experience and express love, anger, strength, and weakness at different times and in various combinations. The group members persist in not accepting his controlling and distancing tactics, expressing instead their desire that he be more vulnerable and involved.

The therapist augments Joe's learning in group therapy by helping him finish working through the "unfinished business" with his mother in individual therapy. In a later session the therapist asks Joe to stand with his back against a door, knees bent forward, and to surrender to the feeling of weakness that develops in his legs. This position helps recapture the original feelings of helplessness that Joe had in the early years of his life. But it gives him an opportunity to choose a new, more actualizing response in place of the old tactic of cutting off his feelings and stiffening his back. The therapist coaches Joe: "Tell your mother that you want her to love you for yourself. Tell her that you're not a god, but that you're human too—that you have sexual feelings and desires. Tell her that you have the right to make mistakes—to be "fallable"—and that you are not going to feel embarrassed about it any more. Tell her that you love her but you are not going to bow down to her. Let yourself express whatever you feel."

As Joe surrenders to the bioenergetic process, he begins to cry. The second time through he gets very angry. The third time he gets in touch with his own strength, and feels a deep relief in just being able to be himself—whatever that may be. The therapist has Joe go through the exercise one last time, this time addressing Karen instead of his mother. As the integration of past and present, and of body and feelings, is being accomplished, the therapist gives Joe more homework: "I want you to think about some good things about your father and I want you to think of some bad things about your mother.'' The therapist is seeking to break down the stereotypic perception that made a goddess out of mother and a devil out of father.

Further sessions with Joe involve a greater awareness of the constrictions in his body, particularly in the pelvis, where chronic muscular tension has cut off the flow of sexual feelings, just as his mother had wanted it to. At one point the muscles of the chest are massaged while Joe leans backward over a breathing stool. The tensed chest muscles have been a part of Joe's armor to defend himself against his own tender feelings from the heart. Learning to loosen up and feel sensations in the areas of heart and solar plexis helps Joe be in better contact with his core, and to establish more trust in the ''Inner Supreme Court'' that supports him in making choices from his whole being.

Another assignment the therapist gives Joe is designed to help him work through his perfectionism. The therapist says, ''Did you ever experience yourself as a student getting nine out of ten questions right on a test, and still feeling like a failure?'' Joe answers that he did. The therapist says, ''On a scale of one to ten, how do you rate yourself as a human being?'' Joe replies, ''Well, before I started therapy I guess I rated myself about nine—always better than other people, but never good enough to be perfect. But now I'm starting to think of myself as more of a six or seven.''

The therapist gives Joe the following homework: ''Keep thinking all week about yourself as a six or seven and think of everyone you meet as about the same. This will help to 'humanize' your perception of people. It will help you break the old pattern of seeing authority figures as nines and tens and everyone else as twos and threes. You need to get rid of more of your fear of people and feel more at home with them instead.''

Joe is giving up the rigid protective shell of his survival orientation from childhood. The first fruits of actualizing are in the warm and positive responses he gets from others when he comes across as more human and vulnerable. This change in attitude comes as a surprise to Joe, because he has spent his life trying to get people to like and respect him but has consistently failed because no one likes a showoff and a prude.

Joe feels that he has worked through his most troublesome problems after eight individual sessions. The therapist agrees, but reminds him that growth comes slowly and he will need to further develop his actualizing orientation to life. The therapist suggests that Joe continue to attend group therapy for several more months to consolidate his gains and to support his growth.

## SUMMARY

In Actualizing Therapy we believe that the most effective way to aid clients in making wise and satisfying choices is to work through core conflicts and core pain that block awareness and growth.

Since the core is the center of one's existence, a key process is to enable clients to get acquainted with their core characteristics. This includes accepting that they are to some extent disabled by painful childhood experiences, and learning to surrender to the feelings of terror, rage, longing, or betrayal that they have formerly denied. When clients let go of their rigid defense strategies and give in to painful core feelings, they move through the impasse from manipulating to actualizing.

The presence of a supportive therapist or group makes it safe for the clients to experience strong negative feelings without constricting themselves or distorting reality. In experiencing core pain in an honest and direct way, clients find that it passes through them (emotional catharsis) and that they lose their fear of feeling. Releasing strong negative feelings from the core results in the emergence of strong positive feelings such as trust, harmony, and confidence. Thus clients come to be more ''at home'' with all that they are, the good and the bad, the negative and the positive, the manipulative and the actualizing. They learn compassion and the ability to forgive themselves and others for inevitable mistakes that occur in living.

In individual Actualizing Therapy, the emphasis is on the bodily and the intellectual dimension of each client's personality and value system. Group therapy is a miniature society in which interpersonal expression of emotion becomes a primary focus. Individual therapy is analogous to a lecture-discussion in college; group therapy is the laboratory session. Each is necessary for total learning.

In the laboratory of the group clients are afforded the opportunity to try out a new "stance" in life, to express values to which they are committing themselves, and to expand their awareness and expression of the feeling-polarities.

Individual and group work also seek to uncover a person's deepest needs at the core level and satisfy those needs. Most people have their physiological and safety needs met, but their love needs have been ignored or exploited. Fear can be replaced by trust in one's core as individual or group therapy helps a person to surrender to needs for love and to have these needs satisfied in direct, realistic ways. As this happens, the person becomes more free to move on to esteem needs and self-actualizing needs. Actualizing needs are nurtured by developing a style of emotional expression and interpersonal trust based on honesty, awareness, freedom, creativity, and mission.

A basic tenet of Actualizing Therapy is that energy released from core conflicts becomes immediately available for growth and creative living. Availability of energy for growth, coupled with learning to express oneself along the feeling polarities, offers clients a wide spectrum of actualizing possibilities. Being what you are (awareness of character structure) and becoming all you can be (trust in the core and self-expression along the polarities) are the heart and soul of Actualizing Therapy.

# REFERENCES

Allport, G. W. *Personality: A psychological interpretation*. New York: Holt, 1937.

Allport, G. W. *Patterns and growth in personality*. New York: Holt, 1961.

Bleuler, E. Cited in J. F. Brown, *Psychodynamics of abnormal behavior*. New York: McGraw-Hill, 1940.

Brammer, L. M. and Shostrom, E. L. *Therapeutic psychology: Fundamentals of actualizing counseling and therapy* (3rd ed.). Englewood Cliffs, N. J.: Prentice-Hall, 1977.

Buber, M. *The way of man*. Chicago: Wilcox and Follett, 1951.

Bustanoby, A. The pastor and the other woman. *Christianity Today*, August 30, 1974, pp. 7–10.

Ellis, A. *Reason and emotion in psychotherapy*. Seacaucus, N. J.: Lyle Stuart, 1962.

Fox, J., Knapp, R. R., and Michael, W. B. Assessment of self-actualization of psychiatric patients: Validity of the Personal Orientation Inventory. *Educational and Psychological Measurement*, 1968, **28**, 565–569.

Krumboltz, J. D. and Thoreson, C. E. *Behavioral counseling: Cases and techniques*. New York: Holt, 1969.

Lazarus, A. A. *Behavior therapy and beyond*. New York: McGraw-Hill, 1971.

Leary, T. *Interpersonal diagnosis of personality*. New York: Ronald Press, 1957.

Lowen, A. *Bioenergetics*. New York: Coward, 1975.

Maslow, A. H. *Motivation and personality*. New York: Harper & Row, 1954.

Perls, F. S. *Gestalt therapy verbatim*. Lafayette, Calif: Real People Press, 1969.

Perls, F. S. *The gestalt approach and eyewitness to therapy*. Ben Lomand, Calif.: Science and Behavior Books, 1973.

Riesman, D. *The lonely crowd*. Garden City, N. Y.: Doubleday, 1950.

Rogers, C. R. *Client-centered therapy*. Boston: Houghton Mifflin, 1951.

Satir, V. *Conjoint family therapy*. Palo Alto, Calif.: Science and Behavior Books, 1966.

Schutz, W. C. *Elements of encounter: A bodymind approach*. Big Sur, Calif.: Joy Press, 1973.

Shostrom, E. L. *Personal orientation inventory*. San Diego: EdITS/Educational and Industrial Testing Service, 1963.

Shostrom, E. L. *Caring relationship inventory*. San Diego: EdITS/Educational and Industrial Testing Service, 1966.

Shostrom, E.L. *Man, the manipulator*. Nashville: Abingdon, 1967.

Shostrom, E. L. *Pair attraction inventory*. San Diego: EdITS/Education and Industrial Testing Service, 1970.

Shostrom, E. L. *Actualizing assessment battery*. San Diego: EdITS/Educational and Industrial Testing Service, 1976a.

Shostrom, E. L. *Actualizing Therapy: Foundations for a scientific ethic*. San Diego: EdITS, 1976a.

Shostrom, E. L. *Growth process inventory*. San Diego: EdITS/Educational and Industrial Testing Service, 1979.

Shostrom, E. L., and Knapp, R. R. The relationship of a measure of self-actualization (POI) to a measure of pathology (MMPI) and to therapeutic growth. *American Journal of Psychotherapy*, 1966, **20**, 193–202.

Shostrom, E. L., and Montgomery, D. *Healing love*. Nashville: Abingdon, 1978.

Shostrom, E. L. and Riley, C. Parametric analysis of psychotherapy. *Journal of Consulting and Clinical Psychology*, 1968, **32**, 628–632.

# CHAPTER 2

# *Aesthetic Realism*

MARTHA BAIRD and ELLEN REISS

*One of the more unusual of the innovative psychotherapies in this book is Aesthetic Realism. I first learned of Aesthetic Realism while watching a David Susskind show on television. Four men on the show said that they had changed their sexual preferences from homosexuality to heterosexuality and gave credit to Eli Siegel, not only for this changeover but also for larger and grander personal changes. In my subsequent reading of Siegel's works, it appeared that he had, on his own, come to an understanding of life that was not only unique but also clearly related to the mind-boggling concept of complementarity in physics, in which two antithetical concepts are considered true at the same time. To quote Warren Weaver\*:*

The idea of the valid use of two contradictory viewpoints is by no means restricted to physics. As [Niels] Bohr emphasized, there are numerous pairs of contradictory concepts (*love* and *hate*, for example; *practical* and *ideal; intuitive* and *logical*) that, when held jointly and used appropriately, give us a more complete and satisfying description that can be achieved otherwise.

*The devotion of Eli Siegel's students is impressive. Martha Baird, Siegel's widow, has been an indefatigable proponent of the value and validity of Aesthetic Realism. She and representatives of the Aesthetic Realism Foundation are convinced that the press has been unfair to her late husband and his ideas, and her letters invariably end with the phrase "victim of the press," reflecting her belief that Aesthetic Realism has been unacknowledged. I am happy to give this rather unusual system further exposure.*

Aesthetic Realism is a philosophy, founded by Eli Siegel (1902–1978), who defined it in these words:

Aesthetic Realism is a way of seeing the world and oneself that says: One, the purpose of everyone is to like the world; Two, the way to like the world and the things in it is to see both as the aesthetic oneness of opposites; Three, the greatest danger for a person is to have contempt for the world and what is in it, despite their aesthetic structure. (Siegel, in Atherton et al., 1979)

*Warren Weaver, The religion of a scientist. In L. Rosen (Ed.) *Religions of America*, New York: Simon & Schuster, 1975, p. 301.

Another form of the definition: Aesthetic Realism is the study of how "the world, art, and self explain each other: each is the aesthetic oneness of opposites" (Siegel, in van Griethuysen et al., 1969, p. 1).

The purpose of Aesthetic Realism is to describe the world; it is education. Yet for 38 years, as people have learned from Aesthetic Realism how to see the world (which includes Spinoza, the Rocky Mountains, and one's uncle), as they have learned that in every work of art is an answer in outline to one's own problems, as they have learned about the greatest damager of mind, contempt—the desire in every person to be superior to all things—they have come to a feeling of ease and excitement about life, which every person hopes for.

## HISTORY

In a sense, Aesthetic Realism began formally with the first Aesthetic Realism lesson given by Eli Siegel in October 1941, in New York City. In another sense, it began in 1924, with his poem "Hot Afternoons Have Been in Montana," which won the *Nation* Poetry Prize in 1925 and brought fame to its 22-year-old author. In the February 25, 1925, *Baltimore Sun,* Siegel described his purpose in that poem—a purpose that came to be the clear, kind, comprehensive philosophic structure of Aesthetic Realism: "In 'Hot Afternoons' I tried to take many things that are thought of usually as being far apart and foreign and to show, in a beautiful way, that they aren't so separate and that they do have a great deal to do with each other."

This purpose was met by anger on the part of the literary establishment, anger at the scope and power of this poem by a young, unknown writer. Years later William Carlos Williams said that "Hot Afternoons" stood for "the new," which the "fixed, sclerotic mind" resents (Baird & Reiss, 1970, p. 8). This resentment of Eli Siegel for what he saw and said was to continue for the next half century.

From 1925 to 1941, Siegel, while engaged in literary work, was studying the world and people, developing Aesthetic Realism. He read widely and deeply, but his knowledge was never only bookish. One of the strongest influences on him was the great English literary critic George Saintsbury, whom he saw as interested in and fairest to the most things. Siegel often cited Coleridge as foreshadowing Aesthetic Realism, especially in Chapter 14 of the *Biographia Literaria* (1817), with his description of the poetic imagination as that which "reveals itself in the balance or reconciliation of opposite or discordant qualities" (1967, pp. 2, 12). In his development of Aesthetic Realism, as in the philosophy itself, Siegel combined the utmost erudition and a tremendous interest in life as it took place on streets, in coffee shops, at jobs, in politics, at parties. Central to Aesthetic Realism is seeing that poetry and sanity are the same.

Siegel knew thoroughly the materialistic philosophers—Holbach, Hobbes, La Mettrie—and the subtleties of pessimistic and skeptical thought. In coming to an affirmative view of reality, he did not skip over the arguments against it. The philosopher he cared most for was probably Kant. He also studied the English idealist Thomas Hill Green and the German philosophers Fichte, Hegel, and Schelling. He gave, in the 1950s, a series of lectures on William James; he esteemed Josiah Royce and had a liking for Croce. He was critical of Santayana, Dewey, Wittgenstein, and the logical positivists. But all this does not convey the quality of Eli Siegel's mind or of Aesthetic Realism. He saw philosophy in children, in doings in the kitchen; he was humorous and loved the everyday. People he talked to were affected by him as by no one else: by his vast knowledge, his honesty and kindness, and his critical uncompromising attitude.

The first Aesthetic Realism lesson was given in 1941. As Siegel described it:

Aesthetic Realism, as taught by an individual, arose from requests from people in my poetry classes who asked if they could talk to me privately. In my talks on poetry, I mentioned often the fact that what makes a good poem is like what can make a good life. This I see as still true, for poetry is a mingling of intensity and calm, emotion and logic. (1979)

By 1943 he was giving many lessons to individuals. His students all learned of him through word of mouth; he never had any institutional backing. He gave a poetry class once a week, and in 1944 he began a series of philosophic lectures presenting the formal basis of Aesthetic Realism. Throughout the years persons learned about the universe, culture, economics, and science as their own lives were talked about at lessons. And they learned about their own deepest purposes and feelings as Eli Siegel lectured on such subjects as Goethe's *Faust,* the Compromise of 1850, Alexander the Great, Vermeer, Thomas Aquinas, Donatello. The fact that the largest and most intellectual matters are seen as inextricably one with the most pulsatingly personal distinguishes Aesthetic Realism from all other thought, and is why people who study it come to see their own lives with pride—a pride respectful of the universe.

Among the students of Aesthetic Realism were artists, photographers, actors, writers, and teachers who saw increasingly that what they were learning was new, and that it had enormous power and value. Yet there was a staggering discrepancy between the value of Aesthetic Realism and the recognition it received. One explanation of this discrepancy appears in the editors' introduction to *The Press Boycott of Aesthetic Realism:*

Persons in authority . . . do not wish to learn something new and central about their chosen fields, and about their own feelings and purposes from something that does not flatter the ego. . . . *The one reason for the boycott of Aesthetic Realism is terror of respect.* (Baird & Reiss, 1978, p. xi).

The following is a chronological list of some events in the history of Aesthetic Realism.

1945    Eli Siegel writes *Definitions, and Comment: Being a Description of the World,* presenting the philosophic basis of Aesthetic Realism (published 1978–1979). One hundred thirty-four terms are defined.

1946    Publication of *The Aesthetic Method in Self-Conflict* and *Psychiatry, Economics, Aesthetics* by Siegel (1976a). Formation of the Society for Aesthetic Realism by persons who believed Aesthetic Realism was true and should be better known. Sheldon

Kranz the first man to change from homosexuality through Aesthetic Realism.

1950    Siegel lectures on *Hamlet* and Shakespeare's *Sonnets;* evidence in Shakespeare that beauty is the making one of opposites.

1951    William Carlos Williams's letter about the poetry of Eli Siegel: "He belongs in the very first rank of our living artists" (Baird & Reiss, 1970, p. 6). For the history of Williams and Aesthetic Realism, see *The Williams-Siegel Documentary,* (Baird & Reiss, 1970).

1954    Establishment of Definition Press for the publication of works on Aesthetic Realism.

1955    Opening of the Terrain Gallery at 20 West 16th Street, New York City; Dorothy Koppelman, Director. First catalogue, *Is Beauty the Making One of Opposites?,* contained fifteen questions by Siegel. Many public discussions by artists of these questions in relation to specific works of art. For details of the press boycott of the Terrain Gallery, see Chaim Koppelman in *The Press Boycott* (Baird & Reiss, 1978).

1957    *Hot Afternoons Have Been in Montana: Poems* by Siegel, with a letter by William Carlos Williams, published by Definition Press; nominated for National Book Award in 1958.

1963    *Shakespeare's Hamlet: Revisited, A Critical Play from the Play* by Siegel, presented by Ted van Griethuysen, Anne Fielding, Rebecca Thompson.

1968    Publication of *James and the Children: A Consideration of Henry James's "The Turn of the Screw"* by Siegel and of *Hail, American Development,* poems by Siegel. Production of a film, *People Are Trying to Put Opposites Together,* directed by Ken Kimmelman, with Siegel conducting an Aesthetic Realism class; shown on

WNET, Channel 13, in New York City.

1969   Publication of *Aesthetic Realism: We Have Been There—Six Artists on the Siegel Theory of Opposites,* essays on acting, art, photography, by Ted van Griethuysen, Dorothy Koppelman, David Bernstein, Chaim Koppelman, Lou Bernstein, and Anne Fielding.

1970   Publication of *The Williams-Siegel Documentary,* edited by Martha Baird and Ellen Reiss; and of *Goodbye Profit System* by Siegel.

1971   Appearance on the *David Susskind Show* of four men who changed from homosexuality through study of Aesthetic Realism: Sheldon Kranz, Ted van Griethuysen, Roy Harris, and Tom Shields. Publication of their book, *The H Persuasion.* First Aesthetic Realism consultations, in which students of Eli Siegel teach others what they have learned.

1973   Beginning of *The Right of Aesthetic Realism to Be Known (TRO),* a weekly newsletter used to counter the refusal of the press to report news of Aesthetic Realism. Establishment of the Aesthetic Realism Foundation, Inc., a tax-exempt educational organization.

1975   First statement by Siegel, in *TRO* 133, that contempt causes insanity.

1978   Publication in February of *The Press Boycott of Aesthetic Realism: Documentation,* edited by Martha Baird and Ellen Reiss. Death of Eli Siegel on November 8.

1979   Continuation at the Aesthetic Realism Foundation of the work of Siegel by Aesthetic Realism consultants and students, with classes for consultants and consultants-in-training conducted by Class Chairman Ellen Reiss. Projected publication of Siegel's Aesthetic Realism text, *Self and World.*

## CURRENT STATUS

Aesthetic Realism is now chiefly taught at the Aesthetic Realism Foundation, in New York City, N.Y., by a faculty of 45 consultants. The quality of this Aesthetic Realism education can be seen in the following description of Aesthetic Realism consultants, given by Eli Siegel in 1975:

The junction of knowledge and ethics in every instance of a consultant has been clear—in such a manner that a person listening to the consultant would be listening to someone who had both perceptive and ethical strength. . . . A person is an Aesthetic Realism consultant who, while seeing Aesthetic Realism as true, is interested in both science and art as living things; and sees teaching as going along with learning every day. . . . An Aesthetic Realism consultant must care for both the old and new; must be able to see what is alive and useful in the past, and also be aware that the past can any day be seen in some new fashion. (1975b)

This union of knowledge and ethics, the past and the immediate present, is in seminars given each Thursday by one of the consultation trios, and in Saturday-night dramatic presentations that show Aesthetic Realism in all its variety. The seminars and presentations are open to the public. As with Siegel's early lessons, a person's life is met directly by Aesthetic Realism through individual consultations with a trio of consultants.

Among the seminars are *Consultation with Three,* which talks to men about homosexuality; *The Three Persons* and *First Person Plural,* which talk to young women; *The Young Mind,* which talks to boys of from 12 to 18; *There Are Wives,* which is addressed to wives in particular; and *Each And All* trios, whose makeup and functions are flexible.

Classes in the Aesthetic Realism way of seeing poetry, literature, acting, photography, marriage, drawing, anthropology, dance, and music take place at the foundation. There are also classes for children in poetry and "Learning to Like the World."

The literature of Aesthetic Realism has great variety—in keeping with the variety of reality, which it is Aesthetic Realism's purpose to be true to.

For persons out of town, consultations can take place via telephone; and people have said their lives have changed across a continent.

## THEORY

Aesthetic Realism begins not with personality but with reality, the cause of all selves.

In an article in the September 24, 1944, *Baltimore Sun* Donald Kirkley described Eli Siegel's purpose in the time between the writing of "Hot Afternoons" and the formation of Aesthetic Realism:

He thought all knowledge was connected—that geology was connected with music, and poetry with chemistry, and history with sports. Since, as he saw it, all knowledge was one, he wished to find something, or some principle, unifying all the various manifestations of reality as these manifestations took the form of specific studies.

Siegel found that unifying principle: "The world, art, and self explain each other: each is the aesthetic oneness of opposites." Other philosophies have dealt with opposites (the Greek cosmologists, Hegel, the Chinese), but the Aesthetic Realism way of seeing the opposites differs from these.

Some of the differences are the following:

1. Aesthetic Realism says all the opposites are present in every item of reality. Sameness and difference, rest and motion, oneness and manyness, cause and effect, substance and form are together in: the Pacific Ocean, one's great-aunt Miranda, Mozart, a daisy, a typewriter, a kiss, one's annoyance at 4 P.M. This means that one's own most private feelings are related, as structure, to every item in the universe. The realization of this has enabled people to feel free.

2. Aesthetic Realism sees the relation of opposites in reality as aesthetic—which means it has value, beauty.

3. Aesthetic Realism says: "All beauty is a making one of opposites"; and in that statement by Eli Siegel is the criterion for beauty that the history of aesthetics has looked for. When the permanent and mobile opposites of the world are felt as one by an individual concerned with a specific object, art comes to be: in dance, in drama, in painting, in music, in literature. When the everpresent opposites are not seen as having a deep purpose in common, there is unsuccessful art. There is also unfortunate life.

4. Every instance of the art of the world is an explanation of the questions of people—the abiding questions and the immediate ones. In seeing this, Siegel has done two mighty things: He has shown why art is necessary, and he has enabled people to be happy. In "Aesthetic Realism: A Summary" (1944), he wrote:

. . . everybody is after freedom and security. You can't play off one against the other as many people try to do. So you have to have both. In aesthetics (which is the real dialectics of the world), and only there, do you have both at once. In a Beethoven symphony, for example, there is a feeling of freedom but also a feeling of accuracy, of security. There isn't freedom at one time and security at another. The symphony is freedom and security, abandon and logic, *simultaneously.* (1976a, p. 3)

This describes what every person desires; it also says each person has a right to desire it, and that its realization is possible.

As to the human mind, the subject of the present book, Siegel described the main question of every person in his preface to *The Aesthetic Method in Self-Conflict* (1946):

In our method, the problem of problems, the major, constant, underlying, inevitable thing to organize, deal with sensibly, is: Self and World. However philosophical this phrase may sound, it concerns everyone in the U.S. census or any other census or possible census. Everyone is confronted with, has, the job of: I and All That. (1976a, p. 5)

He says of these continuous opposites in each person:

There is a deep and "dialectic" duality facing every human being, which can be put this way: How is he to be entirely himself, and yet be fair to that world which he does not see as himself? (1976a, p. 9)

The meaning and answer to that question is the study of Aesthetic Realism. The deepest desire of every person, according to Aesthetic Realism, is to like the world on an honest basis. The world, Siegel used to say, is "what begins where your fingertips end."

Aesthetic Realism shows in many ways that a person's opinion of himself—his pride or shame, his ease or nervousness—arises from how just he is to the world. It shows with rigorous logic and also charm that we have an attitude to the whole world all the time, an attitude that affects every specific thing we do: the way we shake someone's hand or construct an English sentence. In "An Outline of Aesthetic Realism," Siegel writes about food:

A child grows from 12 pounds to 80 pounds through making the world himself. In eating anything, we assimilate the world; that is, the world becomes like ourselves. The fact that we need food in order to have the strength to complain of the world is one of the great signs that the world is more friendly than we know. (1976b)

In Aesthetic Realism, Siegel has explained that in every person what most interferes with happiness, pride, ease, intelligence, width, sanity, is contempt, the "disposition in every person to think he will be for himself by making less of the outside world" (Siegel, 1968b, p. xii). Siegel came to see that contempt was the central cause of every human evil: war, poverty, insanity, ignorance, boredom, cruelty. Throughout his years of teaching Aesthetic Realism, he described contempt in its massiveness and intricacy. In Aesthetic Realism lessons he fought contempt in individuals with kind imagination, power, and often humor. One description of

contempt and its consequences is in *James and the Children: A Consideration of Henry James's "The Turn of the Screw"* (Siegel, 1968b). Here Siegel comments on the children in the James story:

If we are not interested in the feelings of others, in the feelings walking about as people walk, sitting as people sit, lying down as people lie down—we may be either deceived by them or cruel to them.

From evil seen and unseen in man, beginning where he begins, we have the fall of Madrid. (p. viii)

In the autumn of 1975, in the weekly journal *The Right of Aesthetic Realism to Be Known (TRO)*, Eli Siegel stated for the first time: "Contempt causes insanity." This statement represented the culmination of years of thought. He showed that qualitites frequently observed in the insane, and to some extent in all people, such as "flight from reality"; "alienation from reality"; dullness, apathy; irritation and anger—including destructive anger; phobias and fears, are forms of contempt. He wrote: "All anger would like to become contempt. Anger has pain in it, but contempt is inward bliss; repose; some quietude. . . . How pleasing it is to say to something we once feared, 'Pooh, I'm not afraid of you' " (1975a). Every week for the next three years, Siegel wrote essays in *TRO* giving evidence that contempt causes insanity.

To provide some notion—really a faint one—of the scope of Aesthetic Realism, we quote three sections from "An Outline of Aesthetic Realism."

Education Is for Liking the World.—Since the purpose of life itself is to like the world as much as can be, it is clear that education in all its diversity is for the purpose of liking the world. (Siegel, 1976b)

This way of seeing education has been hugely successful in practice in elementary schools, high schools, and colleges, including New York's South Bronx—an area in which educators have despaired of being useful.

Sex Is Either.—Sex is either a means of having the world just the way we want it—that is, having contempt for it; or it can be the means of making the ordinary things of the world take on more meaning. Sex, therefore, is always either for contempt or respect. The chief thing wrong with sex is that it so easily can be used as a means of ecstatic revenge on a world which we see as not having been good to us. Sex often is revenge, not expression. (Siegel, 1976b)

Aesthetic Realism is against the psychoanalytic emphasis on sex. Reality caused sex; sex did not cause reality. Our attitude to the world affects the way we see the body of another. This has been shown clearly and dramatically in the change of persons from homosexuality through the study of Aesthetic Realism. This will be described later.

The following paragraph on economics is an explanation of that which is bewildering economists now. Aesthetic Realism is not political as such, but it sees economics as chiefly an ethical and aesthetic matter. Among Eli Siegel's earliest writing is "The Complete Socialism" (1923), reprinted in 1969 as part of *Modern Quarterly Beginnings of Aesthetic Realism: 1922–1923*. Siegel never deviated from the idea expressed there that the earth should be owned by all the people living on it.

Economics Has Made for Bad Power.—Economics has made for bad power in the history of the world and of America. At no time should a person have had to depend on another person for the chance to be productive; that is, to work. The way men have got jobs or given them through the years has been unjust or unethical. In May 1970, I said the protest against the way jobs were had and profits were made had become more conscious in the world. There will be no economic recovery in the world until economics itself, the making of money, the having of jobs, becomes ethical; is based on good will rather than on the ill will which has been predominant for centuries. (Siegel, 1976b, p. 27)

We believe it can be discerned from what has been said that Aesthetic Realism is the oneness of large praise of a person and sharp criticism. It sees a person as having two desires, always present: to be just to the world and to be superior to it. Students of Aesthetic Realism have felt an enormous gratitude to Eli Siegel and his thought: This is because we met the criticism we yearned for and found it to be the same as love.

## METHODOLOGY

Aesthetic Realism consultations are a principal way of studying Aesthetic Realism, for it is through give and take, critical questions and answers about one's life, that one comes to a conviction that a body of knowledge outside one's self is actually true about one's very self.

The beginning of all consultations is in the lessons given by Eli Siegel from 1941 to 1977, which are the most valuable part of the education of each Aesthetic Realism consultant. Many of these lessons were recorded; some have been transcribed and published. More will be. They are invaluable for their knowledge of the human heart and how to know it.

Eli Siegel said he could not give lessons if he did not have good will and a desire to know the person he talked to. He always did. He never dismissed contemptuously any person or thing. His desire to know was subtle and delightful, and he was untiring in the pursuit of evil. It is impossible to show the wealth in Aesthetic Realism lessons in a short space, but a quotation from one lesson may give a taste of their quality, for it has the poetic way of putting things that was characteristic of Eli Siegel. This is quoted in *TRO* number 321 and is from the Aesthetic Realism lesson of Jessica Throckmorton, published by the Terrain Gallery in 1971.

Siegel was describing what he called "the awful feeling 'These people think they know me! And they've left out something!'" Then he said to Miss Throckmorton:

I'm struggling, in dim afternoon, up the Jessica Throckmorton mountainside. I hope it has some use. But the last thing I would say is something that puts things into a symmetrical shape with a string around it. (Baird, 1971)

And Jessica Throckmorton, who thought people had dealt cruelly with her, felt that at last someone was trying to be kind.

The Aesthetic Realism consultations given by trios of consultants at the Aesthetic Realism Foundation will be described by Rebecca Thompson, consultant with *First Person Plural,* a trio that deals with the questions of women.

## AESTHETIC REALISM CONSULTATIONS

### by Rebecca Thompson

Consultations are the continuation, in principle, of the Aesthetic Realism lessons given by Eli Siegel. They are the education of a person in how to like the world and the opposition to this: contempt. These two opposite and organic motions are constant and simultaneous in every person. The conflict between the two takes thousands of individual forms.

A consultee speaks for an hour with three consultants, in an atmosphere at once formal and casual. Our method is one of critical questions and answers. The purpose is to have a person see his or her questions and feelings, however intricate, as objects that can be studied in relation to the whole world.

Every woman that *First Person Plural* speaks with, takes the world in her individual way; however, there are necessary, general questions of Aesthetic Realism that everyone hears—ethical questions that are also beautiful. Some are:

1.  What do you have most against yourself?
2.  Do you see the world—that is, everything not immediately yourself—as friendly, unfriendly, or indifferent?
3.  Has anyone known you really—seen you as you are to yourself?
4.  Can you see a man or woman any better than you see the world as such?
5.  Do you use your family to have contempt for the world or respect for it?

The material of everyone's life is different, yet one factor is constant: No person likes himself or herself sufficiently, because the way reality is seen is not good enough. So we have these beginning questions that honor the sameness and difference of every self.

We might ask a young woman: Are you as passionately interested in good will, in having your boyfriend's relation to other people and things as good as possible, as you are in having him care for *just you*? We have asked a college instructor in grammar: "Do you see any relation between how the preposition 'of' is used in a sentence and being 'of' a person in sex?" A college student, who had a question, among others, about food, was asked: "Do you want to use food to conquer the world, grab it, or use food as a means of knowing the world?"

A central principle of Aesthetic Realism is: "The resolution of conflict in self is like the making one of opposites in art" (Siegel, 1976a, p. 3). This is deeply true of consultations. For example, both men and women have been stirred, felt less isolated, and understood contempt better as they felt themselves described in these musical lines of the nineteenth-century poet Christina Rossetti, from "Who Shall Deliver Me?":

> All others are outside myself;
> I lock my door and bar them out,
> The turmoil, tedium, gad-about.
> I lock my door upon myself,
> And bar them out; but who shall wall
> Self from myself, most loathed of all?
> (1909, vol. 1, p. 283)

And humor is present in many ways. Aesthetic Realism loves humor in its truest sense. Many a pessimistic person has heard this maxim from Eli Siegel's book *Damned Welcome*: "A pessimist is a person who finds an oyster in a pearl" (1972, p. 26).

Assignments are given, such as: Write a soliloquy of your father when he was your age; Describe three objects exactly and ask what opposites are there. Aesthetic Realism texts are assigned, as well as biographies and the great novels of the world.

The ongoing, lifetime assignment given seems simple, but has a profound effect: *In a complete sentence, write down one thing you like every day.* This one assignment has made minds more integrated.

More will be said of the effectiveness of consultations. Meanwhile, people have said that through Aesthetic Realism consultations they feel understood for the first time in their lives. This already makes an impersonal world closer to one, more likable.

## APPLICATIONS

In the publication *Questions & Answers about Aesthetic Realism* is the following dialogue:

- Is Aesthetic Realism for everybody?
- Yes. If a person can be happier, he can use Aesthetic Realism. (Siegel, 1976c, p. 3)

We believe that in time, Aesthetic Realism will be studied by professionals in medicine, social work, criminology, the treatment of drug addiction, insanity, alcoholism—in other words, by those dealing with the worst afflictions of mankind. If Aesthetic Realism were studied respectfully, we believe there is not a situation on earth it couldn't improve. It should be taught universally and become part of everyone's education, the way music is, or grammar.

In the meantime, here are some of the ways Aesthetic Realism has changed people's lives for the better:

1. It makes a person feel known, understood, as he or she never believed possible; and as a result, no longer lonely. This has been attested to hundreds of times.

2. For this reason, and because a person also learns to see the world in a new way—as an aesthetic structure—Aesthetic Realism gives people an increased sense of life, a belief in its meaning.

3. There is more honest kindness in the family. The family agony of devotion and resentment changes to warmth and respect as people learn to use relatives to help them like the world "from which all families come."

4. Children like the world more.

5. After studying Aesthetic Realism, people have been able to stop taking drugs.

6. People have stopped being alcoholics.

7. People care for reading more.

8. People become more expressive.

9. Anger and depression are felt less.

10. Aesthetic Realism's teaching that the purpose of marriage, in every detail, is to like the world has made marriages deeper, more interesting, kinder. It has enabled people to stay married. Violence in marriages has been stopped. See *The Press Boycott of Aesthetic Realism,* pages 53–56 (Baird & Reiss, 1978), for a more detailed account.

11. Aesthetic Realism can change homosexuality. This will be told of in the next section.

## CASE EXAMPLE

Perhaps the most dramatic success of Aesthetic Realism is in changing homosexuality to heterosexuality. To date 142 persons—134 men, 8 women—have changed sexuality through the study of Aesthetic Realism. This has not been reported in the press. It is frequently written that homosexuality is thought to be unchangeable. Most of the persons who changed from homosexuality through Aesthetic Realism have made their names public and have asked to be interviewed by the press—so far, unavailingly. In 1978 they placed a large advertisement, with 50 signatures, in the *New York Times*. In 1979 the ad was repeated in the *New York Times*, the *Washington Post*, and the *Los Angeles Times*. There was no response from the press.

It may at first be hard to believe that a condition that seems organic and is often thought to be innate can change through the principle of aesthetics, through a reseeing of those abstract opposites, sameness and difference. But this is what has happened. And logically, sameness and difference is what homosexuality is about: the preference for what is sexually the same as oneself, not what is different.

Aesthetic Realism sees the cause of homosexuality as contempt for the world, which in homosexual men becomes contempt for women.

The first person to change from homosexuality was Sheldon Kranz, in 1946. Eli Siegel tells about how he saw this in an essay he wrote in April 1978, "The Homosexual Story." He says:

But I did not make much of this, for the essential purpose of Aesthetic Realism was to have a person see the world differently and like it more. Besides, in the 1940s, there was not the national furor over homosexuality that took place later. (1979)

In 1961 a second man changed: Ted van Griethuysen, actor and Fulbright scholar. In 1968, there was Roy Harris, of Tuscaloosa, Alabama.

In 1971 these three were the first men in history to say publicly they had changed from homosexuality. They said it first on New York City's Channel 13, and then on network television on the *David Susskind Show*. This was not reported in the press, but mail and telephone response was such that *Consultation With Three*, a consultation trio, was formed so that Kranz, van Griethuysen, and Harris could talk to homosexual men and teach them what they themselves had learned through lessons with Eli Siegel. In that same year their book, *The H Persuasion*, was published.

In 1975 *Consultation With Three* and Hector Smith, who also changed from homosexuality, appeared on the Tom Snyder television show; again there was no report in the press.

In *The Press Boycott of Aesthetic Realism* (1978), Sheldon Kranz states that of the men who have had seven or more consultations with *Consultation With Three*, "which we see as the minimum number of hours necessary to understand some of the basic principles of Aesthetic Realism, 84 per cent have said they have changed" (Baird & Reiss, 1978, pp. 8–9).

The story of one man who changed from homosexuality, James Gordon of St. Louis, will be told in his own words. We quote a paper by Gordon given at the Aesthetic Realism Foundation in June 1979. Gordon was then an Aesthetic Realism consultant in the teaching trio *The Masculine Inquiry*.

## YES, WE HAVE CHANGED

### by James Gordon

When I met Aesthetic Realism at 27 years of age, cynicism and fear were in a chaotic, harmful relation in me. I was hard and bitter, certain that I had all the facts about this world and that they didn't come to much. Yet I was so frightened. I thought my mind was gone. There had been much sex, all kinds of drugs, trouble with the law, a suicide attempt. Two years of psychotherapy found me little improved. I was plagued with insomnia and hallucinations. In an early consultation, I described my mind as a sieve. I would try to read and an hour later I couldn't remember the name of the book.

I felt driven by sex and so very scared; yet I was looking desperately for something. I met it in the kindness of *Consultation With Three* on April 24, 1971, across a consultation table. I had never met anyone who said they changed from homosexuality; these three men did, and said I could change too.

Aesthetic Realism describes the cause of homosexuality as contempt of the world, not liking it sufficiently, which changes into a contempt for women. When I first heard this, it made me angry. I didn't feel how I saw the world had anything to do with my sexual preference, and certainly I did not have contempt for women! Why, I loved women; they were my best friends. I could spend hours with the women I knew, advising them how best to be with their boyfriends and husbands. They saw my advice as invaluable. "I just have this sex question, that's all," I told *Consultation With Three*. "And besides, contempt seems like such a harsh word. I will admit, though," I added, "I don't like the world very much."

*Consultation With Three* asked: Is one person you've used not to like the world your mother? Did you conquer her early?

JG:   My mother and I have been very close. She always tried to make me feel good about myself.

CWT:   Did she care for you more than she cared for your father?

JG:   Oh, yes!

CWT:   Did you also feel that your mother was silly in giving you so much affection?

JG:   Sometimes it did seem a bit excessive.

CWT:   Could this affect the way you see all women? Are all women pushovers?

JG:   Somewhat, yes.

CWT:   Is that contempt? Could the sense of friendliness towards women that you feel be associated in your mind with scorn, contempt, and the ability to manage them?

JG:   Wow, maybe!

My consultations continued and I learned about my father also. For as long as I could remember, I did not like Clarence Gordon. I saw him as stony and indifferent. But with all the criticisms I had of him, all that I saw wrong with him, I had a secret respect and admiration for him. My father didn't seem to be moved by anything; and in this world, I thought that was a smart way to be.

As important as any assignment I did in consultations was the biography I wrote of Clarence Gordon. *Consultation With Three* insisted I see him as an object. I was asked to read Mr. Siegel's poem "Ralph Isham, 1753 and Later" in preparation. When I read these lines:

What was he to himself?
There, there is something
(Siegel, 1957, p. 8)

*Consultation With Three* stopped me and asked if I thought I could ask that question about my father and have a sincere desire to know. "I'll

try," I said, "I'll try." I present now a short excerpt from that assignment, done three months after my first consultation:

Dad knew how much the family valued Catholicism. He converted, partly to please us and partly in the hope of attaining an inner peace he had never been able to find. I remember distinctly being proud of him on the day he was baptized, but something in me (I'm learning now this is the desire for contempt) would not let me show how affected I was. I acted as if it didn't mean a thing. I remember his hurt look as I ran outside to play, following the church ceremony, without a word. After this, the physical fights between my father and me became more violent, and I eventually left home.

I know now that I have contributed to my father's feeling bad about himself. He wanted to be a good father, but he didn't have the knowledge. I owe my seeing of this to Aesthetic Realism, and I want to thank Eli Siegel for enabling me to have good will for my father and the world.

I knew homosexuality was changing in me. I had used my father to like the world and I was happier.

In all, I had 17 consultations, two a month for eight months. Today, eight years later, I am a very different person. I have not repressed homosexuality; I am not bisexual. I am deeply and permanently changed. Aesthetic Realism does not involve years of psychological therapy or aversion techniques; it is satisfying to the intellectual being of a person, to his dignity; and it meets the everyday hopes of a man.

As a consultant now and a member of *The Masculine Inquiry*, I teach men how to like the world. This need is a universal one, and it transcends a person's sexual orientation. It is a high point in my life that I, who once had such a narrow picture of women, can now be a member of a trio teaching other men about the depth and beauty of women.

That Eli Siegel came to a way of seeing the world that can permanently change homosexuality is something that must be known by the American people. I had the great honor to study in classes with him in the years following my change. When I heard Eli Siegel lecture about the world or talk to a specific person about the questions that can trouble him, I knew I was hearing a consistently honest man—I was in the presence of greatness.

Eli Siegel, more than anyone I have ever met, was impelled by the desire to know and understand the nature of man and the world he is in. Because of this, hundreds of lives are better. Because of this, over 140 persons have permanently changed from homosexuality. Eli Siegel's thought has a right to be known by America. This should begin now.

## SUMMARY

Aesthetic Realism, currently taught by a faculty of 45 at the Aesthetic Realism Foundation, New York City, through individual consultations, public seminars, and classes, was developed by one man: Eli Siegel. Unaided, and in fact boycotted, by the press and the literary and academic establishments, Siegel gave shape to a body of thought unprecedented in its scope. Aesthetic Realism is about, literally and with abundance of details, every aspect of the world.

No other philosophy has been able, for example, to define the nature of the poetic line; to explain the current economic situation with a basis in the whole of world history; and also, through questions and answers, to help a girl feel at last she could be proud of the way she thought about her mother, to have people feel that the most tormenting matters of their personal lives were finally understood.

A classic summary of the ideas of Aesthetic Realism has been given by Siegel:

1. Every person is always trying to put together opposites in himself.
2. Every person in order to respect himself has to see the world as beautiful or good or acceptable.
3. There is a disposition in every person to think he will be for himself by making less of the outside world.
4. All beauty is a making one of opposites, and the making one of opposites is what we are going after in ourselves.

The first statement describes the essential structure of self, which, according to Aesthetic Realism, is similar to the structure of earth and the structure of beauty. His students have seen Siegel explain the central aspect of man by asking a person to make a fist and then open the hand: closed and open, concentration and expansion, belligerence and welcoming are opposites, and yet they are in the same hand. We would like our generosity to be at one with our selfishness, our toughness to be equivalent to our sweetness, our activity to have the same purpose as our resting, in the same way that the hand that opens is the very hand that made a fist.

In his second statement, Siegel describes the deepest desire of every person: to like the world. This is our greatest need at every moment of our life. We breathe, we eat, we read in order to like the world. When we turn away from this central need, we have guilt and are permeatingly frustrated. Eli Siegel has explained that the greatest repression is not of sex but of our desire to like and respect the outside world. Therefore, this assignment is part of the Aesthetic Realism education of every person: *write, every day, a sentence about one thing you liked.*

The third statement is a definition of contempt, and in it Siegel has isolated, as a scientist isolates the cause of a disease, the great cause of suffering in self (including nervousness, loneliness, and insanity); it is also the cause of pain in social and domestic life, and the cause of international unkindness and war: "Contempt causes insanity." This statement is revolutionary and has been meticulously documented (Baird and Reiss, 1978).

In his fourth statement, Siegel has, for the first time in the history of aesthetics, explained what art is, and why it is not a luxury or a "help" but is a necessity for every life. He writes, for example, of how Aesthetic Realism began: "In my talks on poetry, I mentioned often the fact that what makes a good poem is like what can make a good life. This I see as still true, for poetry is a mingling of intensity and calm, emotion and logic" (1979).

Since Aesthetic Realism was founded in 1941, it has been boycotted by the press for a reason we have come to see as terror of respect. The world scope and permeating personal meaning of Aesthetic Realism can make the ego of a person shudder, for one has to reeducate oneself deeply in studying it. Eli Siegel was punished for this throughout his life, and for being great while not being a member of the establishment.

In "On the Dying of Eli Siegel: A Letter of Regret to the American Press," the students of Aesthetic Realism describe the injustice with which we ourselves met Eli Siegel and Aesthetic Realism, even as we felt life-giving gratitude. There are hundreds of people who want to tell of the specific good effects of Aesthetic Realism in their own lives: This includes over 140 persons who have changed from homosexuality. There are hundreds of people who have seen and felt that Aesthetic Realism is true, beautiful, charming, endlessly inclusive, terrifically personal, humorous, serious, strict, flexible, and kind. Eli Siegel was all these, and was true to his thought always. No other approach to mind, in our estimation, encompasses what Aesthetic Realism does.

Because the prose of Eli Siegel has been quoted extensively throughout this chapter, it seems well to include a summary of Aesthetic Realism as given in a poem. Aesthetic Realism arose from poetry; and here is, in a strict Petrarchan sonnet, what Aesthetic Realism is.

### Aesthetic Realism

If true, it has been true for many years:
A man must like the world; or try with all
His honest might for this.—What unheard brawl
Between the self with its contempt and fears;
And all that's different! One's self appears
So warm. Therefore, it's right to have a wall
Between the warm and what we darkly call
The cold outside—the puzzling cause of tears.

The harshness and the kindness, though, are one.
The self is cozy hearth and yards of ice.
Aesthetics is the distant warming sun
And cold beneath our feet. The real knocks twice.
The self is point and wide circumference.
The self is lightsomeness of consequence.

(Siegel, 1977)

The understanding of what is in these fourteen lines has had this effect on people's lives: They feel there is something honest and beautiful in this world, something they can love with their keenest mind always. It is Aesthetic Realism, and it stands for the world itself.

## REFERENCES

Atherton, W. et al. We have changed from homosexuality. *New York Times,* May 3, 1979, p. B 12.

Baird, M. (Ed.). *The two selves of Jessica Throckmorton: Aesthetic Realism lesson with Eli Siegel.* New York: Terrain Gallery, 1971.

Baird, M. and Reiss, E. (Eds.). *The Williams-Siegel documentary.* New York: Definition Press, 1970.

Baird, M. and Reiss, E. (Eds.). *The press boycott of Aesthetic Realism: Documentation.* New York: Definition Press, 1978.

*Baltimore Sun* unsigned article [Poem by Baltimorean chosen from 4000 for annual prize] February 2, 1925, p. 16.

Coleridge, S. T. *Biographia literaria (1817).* London: Oxford University Press, 1967. 2 vols.

Kirkley, D. Poet who wrote "Hot afternoons." *Baltimore Sun,* September 24, 1944, p.A 3.

Kranz, S. (Ed.). *The H persuasion: How persons have permanently changed from homosexuality through the study of Aesthetic Realism with Eli Siegel.* New York: Definition Press, 1971.

Rossetti, C. *The poetical works of Christina G. Rossetti.* Boston: Little, Brown 1909. 2 vols.

Siegel, E. *Is beauty the making one of opposites?* New York: Terrain Gallery, 1955.

Siegel, E. *Hot afternoons have been in Montana: Poems.* New York: Definition Press, 1957.

Siegel, E. *Hail, American development.* New York: Definition Press, 1968a.

Siegel, E. *James and the children: A consideration of Henry James's "The turn of the screw."* New York: Definition Press, 1968b.

Siegel, E. *The Modern Quarterly beginnings of Aesthetic Realism, 1922–1923.* New York: Definition Press, 1969.

Siegel, E. *Goodbye profit system.* New York: Definition Press, 1970.

Siegel, E. *Damned welcome: Aesthetic Realism maxims.* New York: Definition Press, 1972.

Siegel, E. Contempt hurts mind. *The Right of Aesthetic Realism to Be Known (TRO),* October 15, 1975a, 133.

Siegel, E. On Aesthetic Realism consultants. Unpublished letter. July 26, 1975b.

Siegel, E. *The aesthetic method in self-conflict, accompanied by Psychiatry, economics, aesthetics*. New York: Definition Press, 1976a.

Siegel, E. An outline of Aesthetic Realism. In full-page advertisement of Aesthetic Realism Foundation. *New York Times,* August 16, 1976b, p. 27.

[Siegel, E.] *Questions & answers about Aesthetic Realism*. New York: Aesthetic Realism Foundation, 1976c.

Siegel, E. "Aesthetic Realism," Unpublished poem, 1977.

Siegel, E. Contempt causes insanity: CLXXXIII. The homosexual story. *The Right of Aesthetic Realism to Be Known,* April 25, 1979, 316.

Siegel, E. "Definitions, and comment: Being a description of the world." In *The Right of Aesthetic Realism to Be Known,* October 11, 1978–August 1, 1979, 289–339,

Students of Aesthetic Realism. On the dying of Eli Siegel: A letter of regret to the American press from the Students of Aesthetic Realism, 1979.

van Griethuysen, T. et al. *Aesthetic Realism: We have been there—six artists on the Siegel theory of opposites*. New York: Definition Press, 1969.

# CHAPTER 3

# *Aqua-Energetics*

PAUL BINDRIM

> *Paul Bindrim is one of those controversial individuals who sees life clearly but quite differently from others. He joins the ranks of people such as J. L. Moreno, Fritz Perls, and Wilhelm Reich, who each had the ability to upset others. When I circulated a list of names of contributors to all contributors, only Bindrim's name drew comments. Some years ago when I was invited to be the presenter at a workshop on group psychotherapy in Southern California, out of an attendance of some 200 people with a dozen workshops going, Bindrim attracted at least 100, with the other 11 professionals having to share the remaining 100.*
>
> *Of the several other systems that have an organic similarity—Rebirthing, for example—Aqua-Energetics, Bindrim's system, is probably the best developed both in theory and in process. It is based on some new and old concepts, and resembles in some ways both Primal Therapy and Z-Process. I believe the typical reader will enjoy and benefit from this account, learning new concepts, which, after all, is the primary purpose of this book.*

Aqua-Energetics is a method of transformation that increases the aliveness of the individual by opening neuromuscular blocks that inhibit the breathing process and impede the flow of life energy. With the increase of aliveness, symptoms are cured, realistic life adjustments are established, self-actualization and creativity displace dependency, and the first stages of enlightenment reduce the normal anxieties about the nature of life and death.

Central to the process is group work in a body-temperature pool, which facilitates the relaxation of chronic muscle tension (body armor), thereby restoring the natural breathing process. Since restricted breathing is the mechanism through which emotion is repressed, the reversal of this process leads to the spontaneous discharge of repressed emotion and lessens the crippling effect that past traumatic episodes have had on the character structure.

The womblike environment of the pool facilitates regression. This regression enables the participant to discharge repressed emotion from recent traumatic events and then from progressively earlier ones that have had a more profound effect on the shaping of personality. Finally the individual experiences difficulty in breathing, accompanied by the feeling of imminent death, and reexperiences even earlier painful events often associated with birth that have cut him off from the core of his being and his sense of unity with life. When these emotions are discharged, he is reunited with his deepest self and experiences a state of inner bliss. This reestablishment of his true identity allows him to be sufficiently detached from his past traumas and his identification with them so that they may now be easily reexperienced and readily discharged.

Support is provided by individual weekly sessions. A holistic approach is employed based on the integration of a variety of therapies covering the six vectors through which people grow (intellectual, interpersonal, fantasy, biochemical, transpersonal, and neuromuscular).

## HISTORY

### Precursors

Since Aqua-Energetics is a highly integrated system which has drawn procedures from many disciplines, a wide range of seemingly disassociated precursors enter into the therapeutic process.

The concept that man fell from grace by committing the original sin of intellectually separating life into good and evil components, and therefore no longer knows his true spiritual nature, has been expressed in the Judeo-Christian Garden of Eden myth. In oriental philosophies man lived in a world of sin and illusion called Maya, and this eventually led to sickness, old age, and death. The regaining of his enlightened state required that he allow this portion of himself to die that he might be reborn. The concept that psychological death precedes rebirth or enlightenment is found in all of the world's great religions. In Buddhism it is referred to as the ''Great Death'' preceding enlightenment. In the Judeo-Christian concept it is termed death and resurrection. In the mushroom cults of Central America the participant dies in order to return to the source and regain his soul.

Water for purposes of purification has been employed in spiritual rituals, such as baptism. Wilhelm Reich (Raknes, 1970) claimed that water absorbed negative energy, and he employed it in designing a therapeutic device called the DOR-buster. The practice of calming disturbed patients by placing them in tubs of water was formerly a commonly employed therapeutic technique.

Breathing techniques had been used in many systems of yoga to circulate *prana*, or life energy, for healing purposes and to activate the *kundalini*. Mesmer had termed this form of energy *mesmeric fluid*. Reich (1968) called it *orgone* and attempted to facilitate

its flow by softening chronic muscle tension (body armor).

The fact that human beings can gain momentary states of greater self-actualization during peak experiences and can evaluate life more effectively from this enlightened perspective was inherent in the work of Maslow (1964).

Although the concepts of biological evolution maintained that the cortex is the human beings primary organ of adaptability and survival, the assumption that this does not constitute overspecialization with its inherent handicaps appeared to be debatable. However, it was also apparent that humans could voluntarily retreat from the use of their overspecialized cortex to reprogram this organ by means of the nonintellectual therapies that characterized the humanistic psychology movement.

The use of behavioristic desensitization had proven effective.

Group interaction in a marathon format was a widely employed procedure.

### Beginnings

Aqua-Energetics emerged experientially. Aside from its use in hydrotherapy for calming disturbed patients, a search of the literature indicates that water had never been used as a psychotherapeutic device.

In the beginning I was not committed to any theoretical system. My basic criteria was to do the best that I could for the people with whom I was working. If process A produced better results than process B, process B was discarded and process A became part of my format.

I had been exploring Maslow's concept that during a peak experience an individual is in a temporary state of self-actualization. I hypothesized if this peak state could be evoked in the course of a therapy session, the individual would then be able to see himself with greater than normal clarity and could benefit therapeutically. While Maslow (1964) and Jung (1933) both claimed that states of heightened consciousness only occurred spontaneously and could not be induced, I found that I could foster their occurrence by asking a participant to relive a prior peak experience while in light hypnosis. I discovered that sensory saturation through stimulating the participant simultaneously with the things that he or she most enjoyed to touch, smell, taste, hear, and see—facilitated this process. When a participant was in this transient state of self-actualization, I would ask him to extend a recent dream beyond the point at which it had ended. The meaning of the dream, as well as the possible solutions to the problems it revealed, often became clear spontaneously. The method proved effective, but had a weakness. Because each individual required different peak stimuli, it could not be used in a group setting.

I therefore looked for a universal peak stimulus and found that camping out in a primitive natural setting worked for almost everyone. This, however, had the disadvantage of requiring participants to travel to reach the appropriate setting. In the meantime I had experienced group nudity and found that it gave me the same lift I experienced in nature. I experimented with nudity in therapy groups and found that it worked, but again there was a drawback. People were reluctant to remove their clothing. Realizing that many of us had enjoyed skinny-dipping as youngsters, I circumvented this block by having the group engage in nude swimming. Since people preferred warm water to cold, I quickly learned to heat the pool. As warm water relaxed them, it became apparent that they also enjoyed being held, while floating on their backs, and rocked. I complied in order to heighten their pleasure.

I was amazed at what happened then. Out of their increasing depths of relaxation and pleasure frequently came sudden and unexplainable volcanic eruptions of anger, fear, and grief. I wrote to Maslow in 1968, expressing my amazement at the intensity of the abreaction, which was new to me, and the degree of agony that was harbored in the human soul. Neurotic symptoms lessened and participants became more self-actualized after these outbursts of intense irrational emotion. I therefore encouraged this "cra-

ziness" by having the group hold their arms and legs so they could not injure themselves or others. Thus they were relieved of all responsibility for their actions. A few years later Janov (1970) described this phenomenon and called it "The Primal Scream."

The emotional trauma that participants discharged first came from recent painful events and then from progressively earlier ones. Meanwhile their behavior in the pool became increasingly more infantile. Their cries finally resembled those of newborn babies and their mouths made sucking movements resembling nursing. I responded by providing "mothers" who held and rocked them, and fed them with baby bottles. In this respect I followed the concepts that Harlow (1962) had arrived at in his experiments with mothering apes. Skin contact seemed to be of the greatest importance and I discovered that if I massaged tense musculature, the participants' discharge of traumatic emotion was further facilitated.

It then occurred to me that my clients were growing rapidly while I was remaining static even though I had undergone Psychoanalysis, Jungian analysis, LSD sessions, Psychosynthesis, and three years of Gestalt work with Fritz Perls. I wanted someone to work with me along the lines I had developed. Thanks to Alexander Lowen, I discovered Bioenergetics and found that his procedures, at least to some degree, paralleled mine. This led to personal therapy with Philip Curcuruto, and to taking training programs in both Reichian and Bioenergetic therapies. These gave me not only the personal transformation I was seeking, but also the knowlege of a valuable technology that I could then employ in the pool.

At this point I gained a more comprehensive understanding of what I was doing, and a few theoretical concepts began to emerge. Some participants seemed to run through their prior traumas repeatedly, as in Primal Therapy, and grew slowly. Others went through the experience of dying, followed by a state of partial enlightenment, after which they ran through their prior traumas, seemed to be done with them, and grew rapidly. They also seemed to be experiencing an inner joy. They were like newborn babies in adult bodies. Within a year's time, most radically changed their social relationships and occupational pursuits to those they more deeply enjoyed. Apparently a new sense of self based on the enlightenment experience partially freed them from their neurotic ego-identifications. The theoretical construct of the individual, which I will describe in detail later, emerged as the rationale for this phenomenon.

It became apparent that an integrated and balanced method of therapy could be developed by selectively drawing from a variety of therapeutic schools as long as all the six vectors through which people grow were included.

The theory that humans could withdraw from their overspecialized cortex, which threatened their existence, and rely on their subcortical capacities to regain a sense of direction and to reprogram the cortex also emerged.

I then discovered that the pool process worked almost as effectively when bathing suits were worn as when the group was nude. I therefore no longer considered nudity to be indispensable, worked with bathing suits unless the entire group preferred nudity, and changed the name from the Nude Marathon to Aqua-Energetics. This made the procedure useful to institutions that would not become involved with nudity and for participants who found nudity too threatening.

More recently I have been experimenting with a breathing technique described by Leonard Orr (Orr & Ray, 1977) that seems to be effective in establishing a new sense of self by allowing hyperventilation to open the neuromuscular blocks while discouraging abreaction. Only occasional assistance is provided through massage.

## CURRENT STATUS

Over the past 12 years, 6000 persons, mostly professionals, have experienced my workshops. Many have trained with me and employed aspects of my system in their growth

centers and private practices. Consider the following examples.

William Swartley changed the name of the process to Primal Encounter and employed it in his growth center at Mays Landing, New Jersey, where I conducted 43 training sessions. He later formed the International Primal Association, a group of about 100 professionals to whom he taught this procedure. They practice in various parts of the country and emphasize the use of the pool to induce primal experience.

Michel Bernet conducts Aqua-Energetic groups in Connecticut, calling the process Pool Therapy. Two-thirds of the time is spent in the group room working through the problems that emerge in the pool.

Marie Courie is my co-therapist on the East Coast, running sessions and practicing in Washington, D.C.

Leonard Orr, who recently discovered aspects of the Aqua-Energetic method independently, called it Rebirthing and conducts workshops at centers in various locations. He emphasizes overcoming the birth trauma and draws heavily on metaphysical concepts rather than using psychotherapeutic procedures.

I regularly conduct Aqua-Energetic sessions and professional training groups in Hollywood, California, assisted by my co-therapist, Helaine Harris. I also give training sessions for professionals in Paris.

Although there are many articles and one-chapter descriptions of my work in a number of professional volumes, they deal with the early phases under the title of the Nude Marathon and are quite superficial. The best of these chapters is by Elliott and is found in a work titled *Confrontation,* (1971) edited by Blank, Gottsegen, and Gottsegen.

At present the only major works on Aqua-Energetics are the following three unpublished dissertations: Bindrim (1975), "Outcome Research and Analysis of the Nude Marathon as an Application of Reichian Concepts to Group Therapy; Harris (1979), "A Handbook for Aqua-energetics"; and Wheatley (1974), "Effects of Nude Marathon Regression Therapy on Interpersonal and Intrapersonal Change in Self-Selected Subjects: Psychological Nudism or Psychic Strip-tease?''

A 90-minute documentary on Aqua-Energetics was released in Canada, titled *Out of Touch* (Bindrim, 1971).

## THEORY

Increasing the aliveness of the participant is the main objective in Aqua-Energetics as well as the criteria for progress in the course of the therapy. This is achieved by increasing the flow of life energy. The final result of this increase in aliveness is the reunifying of the individual with the core of his being, his true self. Since this center is united with all life and is his source of life energy, this also constitutes a return to his place in the universe. In the fullest sense, this is a death and rebirth process in which the false sense of self or ego dies and true self-identity is born.

In Aqua-Energetics, the core of the individual (Figure 1) is called the *self*. When the

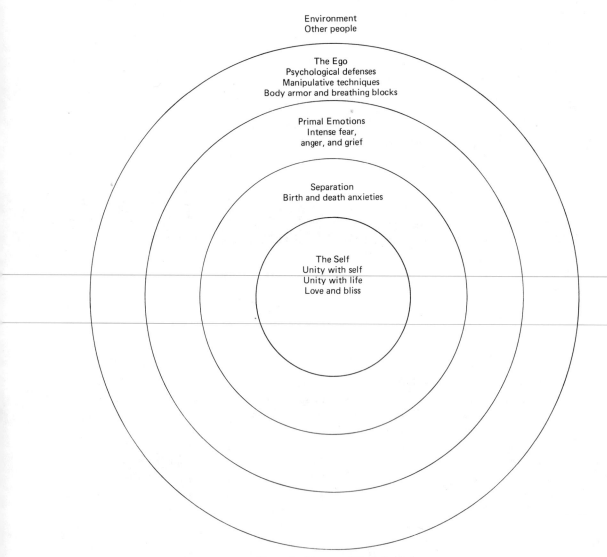

Figure 1   Diagram of the individual.

individual is centered in the self, he experiences the full flow of life energy as love and bliss. He feels unified both with his own nature and with all of life. He is fully alive.

Prior to birth, the individual is in this state of being and is both a distinct individual and an inextricable part of his mother through his umbilical cord, the life-support system. If this sense of unity is terminated abruptly and painfully by the premature cutting of the cord or by intense prenatal or postnatal trauma, the newborn infant will feel a threat to his life. He will feel separated from his source, and the resultant existential anxiety over his aloneness and his ultimate death and extinction will become a fundamental aspect of his personality from the moment of his birth.

This separation is indicated by the second ring from the center in the figure and is responsible for the so-called untreatable existential anxieties. His reaction to the loss of his place in the universe and the imminence of his eventual extinction gives rise to the intense primal emotions of grief, anger, and fear, indicated by ring three.

To avoid these intensely painful emotions and anxieties and to replace the feelings of bliss, unity, and love, which he has lost, he tries to gain substitute satisfactions from his environment and the people in it. For example, when he experiences his death anxiety and the uncertainties of life, he may compensate by accumulating wealth and attempting to enjoy the temporary security that it brings. If he feels lonely and unloved because the separation blocks his access to his core and his internal sense of unity and love, he may try to please people to gain companionship and love.

These game-playing processes, which are aimed at gaining substitute satisfactions, constitute his psychological defenses. To carry out these social manipulations, the individual must inhibit the natural discharge of his emotions in order to fake the reactions that society requires. To repress emotion, he must control his breathing, which he does through tightening his musculature. Thus, the psychological defenses carry with them a parallel system of chronic muscle tension and restricted breathing, which Reich called *body armor*.

Since the individual, cut off from his center, can only believe that he is the ongoing embodiment of his past experiences, he becomes identified with his defenses, manipulations, and body armor. In short, he believes that he is the ego that is composed of this configuration. If he is to return to his center and a state of inner bliss, he must give up his ego-identification, allowing what he believes himself to be to die. He must also pass through and experience the intense primal emotions of fear, anger, and grief, as well as his death anxiety, which are part and parcel of the original separation.

If his ego defenses are strong and his concept of himself greatly distorted, this experience cannot be achieved until his defenses are weakened by permitting the discharge of emotion that has been repressed through body armor and breathing constrictions. Thus, the Reichian and primal processes of discharge, described by Janov (1970), are a preparation for the return to the self.

Therapies that retrain behavior or function primarily on the intellectual vector reorganize the defensive systems of the ego so that they function more effectively in gaining substitute satisfactions. This further impairs the individual's chances of returning to his core. While these therapies may seem to be temporarily beneficial, in the long run they do not result in liberation and are like preparing better meals for the inmates on death row. For the participant who believes he is the ego and who, therefore, stands condemned to death at birth, these therapies cannot circumvent his gut feeling of aloneness and despair.

For most participants Aqua-Energetics is only the beginning of the journey of the return to the self. But even a brief encounter with the intrinsic nature of one's being can be enormously helpful. Even the partial experience of the real self greatly lessens the grip of the ego and facilitates the discharge of past traumatic experiences.

To use an analogy, an individual gripped by a horror movie he is watching knows he has a separate identity, and it is only this fact that prevents him from panicking and running to the nearest exit. It is also this fact that results in his becoming bored with the second or third showing of the film and eventually results in his becoming totally detached and leaving the theater. In a like manner, the horror film of our past can be disregarded more readily when we know who we are.

Aqua-Energetics first increases the aliveness of the individual through hyperventilation and the weakening of body armor, permitting repressed emotion to be discharged and traumatic episodes to be desensitized, thus weakening ego-identification and permitting the individual to move closer to his center and a new identity. Once this new identity has been even partially experienced, the process is greatly accelerated. As the individual's dependency upon his environment and the substitute satisfactions it provides is lessened, his increased freedom gives him the capacity to create through his environment, and he is able to change his life in line with his newfound values. His energy level is greatly increased, and even his appearance changes to the extent that he may not be recognized by old friends who have not seen him for some time.

It should not be assumed that the individual who has established a partial new identity is unable to cope with life because of the loss of his ego defenses. These defenses are not lost. It is only the significance of the situation that has changed. The defenses may be used at any time, but they are no longer compulsively needed to gain satisfactions from the environment, since the feeling of love and unity now arise from within the individual.

Nor is Aqua-Energetics an instantaneous process of enlightenment. If it were, the individual would find himself a totally displaced person in an environment that he created while under the domination of his ego. Life changes gradually, and the therapy progresses in harmony with the growth of the individual and his life circumstances.

From this viewpoint, neurosis arises out of existential anxieties based on aloneness and the fear of death. When substitute satisfactions gained from the environment are insufficient to compensate the individual for the loss of his centeredness, he tries to increase them by altering his natural behavior to fit the culture. He uses his cortex to repress his emotional energy through body armor and restricted breathing. This reduces his aliveness and he enters a state of hibernation, which is the neurosis.

A bear hibernates and reduces its aliveness when its food supply is low, thereby preserving the animal's existence. The human being does the same thing when substitute gratifications are inadequate. With the coming of spring, the bear regains its aliveness. The human being, on the other hand, does not realize that the impossible circumstances of his birth and infancy are no longer operant. He must be awakened by another person, the therapist. In Aqua-Energetics, the therapist's role is like that of a gardener who attempts to restore vitality to plants with water and fertilizer and then is fascinated as each plant evolves in its own way in terms of its own nature. Symptom cure, better adjustment, and self-actualization, although not being the goals of the therapy, occur as by-products when aliveness is increased.

## Evolutionary Concepts Applies to Psychotherapy

According to biological evolution, the organisms that survived geological changes in the environment and competitive struggles for the food supply did so by altering their physical structures to adjust to the prevailing conditions. For example, one species of deer grew longer antlers in order to fight more effectively. When the area became wooded at a later time, this species could not move between the trees and became extinct. This type of biological adjustment is an example of overspecialization, since the organism could not retreat from its prior commitment and so did not survive.

Human beings are thought to be at the top of the evolutionary pyramid because the adjustments they made were adaptable rather than overspecialized. To extend his reach in battle, man developed the sword, the gun, and the rocket, all of which could be readily discarded if they were no longer useful. The development and use of these tools, which made physical changes unnecessary, are attributed to the cortex, considered a human being's chief organ of adaptability.

But the cortex may prove to be an example of overspecialization rather than adaptability. What other animal enjoys the glories of insanity, war, and potential thermonuclear extinction, all products of the cortex? It is far easier to push a button cortically, release a rocket, and kill a million people whom you have never seen than it is to kill five subcortically in hand-to-hand combat. The cortex, indisputably the most recent improvement on the species, has, like all new developments, mechanical or biological, its inherent bugs that need to be worked out.

This can be done by relying on backup systems. For example, the pneumatic tire is an improvement on the steel rim of the covered wagon. But, like everything new, it has its problems, including blowouts. When a blowout occurs, the passenger's life is saved because the car can roll on the steel rim of the wheel. Humans can do much the same thing in dealing with their cortical blowouts if they are wise enough to depend on subcortical functions, which, although less evolved, are time-tested and dependable. The "touchie-feelie" subcortical aspects of humanistic psychology are an attempt to rely on earlier evolutionary emergents to handle the bugs that still exist in the cortex. These principles have worked where the more analytical approach failed because one buggy cortex cannot effectively analyze another buggy cortex. The human being's unique ability and saving grace lie in the fact that he can at times withdraw from using his cortex and rely on his less evolved but more dependable subcortical functions in reprogramming his biological computer. This theoretical construct of relying on earlier emergent backup systems is basic to the dynamics of Aqua-Energetics described in the equilibrium equation.

## The Equilibrium Equation

In Aqua-Energetics, an attempt is made to increase the flow of life energy, the pleasure that the individual experiences, the spontaneity of his expression, and the life energy charge. In Table 1 the methods used to increase each of these are listed directly below them. These four factors are shown in an equilibrium equation since the increase of any one of them automatically increases all of them.

For example, if the energy flow is increased by relaxing body armor, the individual experiences this as pleasurable. It also increases his expression, since it facilitates the discharge of repressed emotion. When this happens, the individual's life energy charge increases; this can be detected by the fact that he looks more alive. If, on the other hand, we increase the pleasure he is experiencing, he will relax his body armor, which increases life energy flow. His repressed emotions will also be permitted to come into expression, as when an individual who is deriving deep pleasure from an experience in nature or listening to a beautiful piece of music suddenly begins to cry. If the life energy charge is increased—when a person encounters a holy man or deeply loving individual, for instance—he will experience deep pleasure and perhaps fall apart as his repressed emotion surfaces.

The therapist may therefore work with any one or all of these factors simultaneously, as he deems appropriate.

## Vectors of Human Growth

There are six basic vectors through which humans grow: the rational, the neuromuscular, the interpersonal, the fantasy, the transpersonal, and the biochemical vector. A therapeutic procedure must cover each of these vectors to be maximally effective. Most schools of psychotherapy cover only

**Table 1. Increasing Aliveness through the Equilibrium Equation**[a]

| Energy Flow ⇌ | Pleasure ⇌ | Expression ⇌ | Life Energy Charge ⇌ | Aliveness |
|---|---|---|---|---|
| Relaxing body armor by means of: | Increasing pleasure by means of: | Encouraging expression by means of: | Increasing the life energy charge by means of: | Goal of therapy |
| 1. Breathing | 1. Floating on your back in warm water while experiencing gentle support | 1. Working in whichever one of the six vectors is appropriate for you | 1. Releasing negative energy and allowing it to be absorbed in the water of the pool | |
| 2. Moving | 2. Having body contact with others | 2. Relying on your evolutionary backup systems to bypass the inhibitory cortical functions of your central nervous system by: | 2. Opening to the positive energy being released by other participants who have already been worked with | |
| 3. Permitting massage | 3. Being rocked | a. allowing your autonomic nervous system to take over, permitting vegetative responses to occur such as vomiting, shivering, and so forth. | | |
| | 4. Experiencing sensory saturation with peak stimuli | b. allowing yourself to be driven into expression by permitting yourself to feel emotional pain rather than inhibiting it | | |
| | 5. Engaging in guided peak fantasies | c. trusting your holders to protect you so that you can permit the irrational expression of your rage, fear, and grief to occur—in a sense allowing yourself to go crazy | | |
| | 6. Feeding from baby bottles | d. entering your fantasies and permitting regression to occur to progressively earlier ages and traumas | | |
| | 7. Experiencing the love and concern of the group | | | |

[a]The equation is an equilibrium reaction, since increasing any one of the four factors by the procedures listed below it will automatically increase the other three. The therapist may therefore work with any one or all of these factors simultaneously, as is deemed appropriate.

one or two of these vectors. It is therefore essential that, in the development of a therapeutic procedure, techniques from a number of schools be integrated so that all vectors of human growth are covered.

In Aqua-Energetics, the components of the rational vector are drawn from Psychoanalysis and Behavior Therapy. The neuromuscular vector is based upon Bioenergetics and Reichian therapy. The fantasy vector is based upon Hypnotherapy. The transpersonal vector draws from Zen meditation, yoga, Judeo-Christian concepts, Jungian psychology, and Psychosynthesis. The biochemical vector employs hyperventilation and the dynamics of LSD therapy. The interpersonal vector draws from Encounter, Gestalt Therapy, Psychodrama, and Conjoint Family Therapy.

## METHODOLOGY

The Aqua-Energetic marathon is a 20- to 24-hour session for 12 to 20 participants. The facilities required are a carpeted meeting room and a pool kept at 93° to 94° Fahrenheit located where high noise levels will not be objectionable. Whenever possible, a natural setting is preferable.

The marathon is divided into the following four phases, which follow each other in sequence.

*Phase 1*   The first phase begins at 5 P.M. and consists of six or seven hours of verbal and nonverbal encounter and interaction to cultivate a reasonably intimate group by encouraging participants to move from game playing to authentic relationships. The therapist may use any techniques with which he feels comfortable for this purpose. During this period the therapist also acquaints the participants with the theory and dynamics of the pool process to enable them to gain the most from the experience and function responsibly in a group. The following points are covered:

1. Participants are shown how to protectively hold the person being worked with as he floats on his back in waist-deep water. Four persons face in the same direction he is facing and hook arms around each thigh above the knees and around each arm above the elbows while the opposite hand grasps the ankle or wrist respectively. A fifth person supports the head of the person being worked with. Since the holders are responsible for protecting the participant, he is free to move and express intense feelings with complete safety. This is perhaps the only situation in therapy and in life in which a person can totally let go with safety, that is, literally go crazy.

2. The participants are told that while being worked with they may suddenly be gripped by intense and irrational emotions and that they are to allow these feelings to be expressed verbally and with their bodies.

3. They are told that they may suddenly experience intense physical reactions in their bodies, which generally precede explosive emotional outbursts. They are instructed to go along with these feelings and permit their intensification and expression. These may take the form of vomiting, tingling, the cramping of musculature, clonic states of partial paralysis, difficulty in breathing, and the feeling of imminent death.

4. They are informed that the key to the process is to permit it to happen; when these negative energies are allowed to discharge by expression, the unplesant feelings first become neutral and then pleasurable. Pain, whether emotional or physical, is caused mainly by people's own resistance to the natural expression of their emotions.

5. They are shown how to hyperventilate, allowing no pause between the in and out breaths, and are instructed how to breathe, using both their stomachs and chests.

6.  They are informed that massage will be used to assist them in relaxing chronically tense musculature and that this may be somewhat uncomfortable until body armor is released.

7.  They are made aware that they may experience energy flowing through their bodies or go into altered states of consciousness and that these experiences can be extremely pleasurable. They are not to become frightened, but to simply realize that they are becoming more alive and experiencing new dimensions of life for the first time.

8.  They are told that they are in complete control of the process at all times and that if they say "Stop!" we will comply immediately.

9.  They are informed that they may regress into childhood or into infancy and that they are to allow this to happen; we will be there to take care of them.

10. They are also informed that they may experience intense imagery relating to their childhood. They are to share this with the therapist and work with these introjects through internalized psychodrama under his guidance.

11. They are told that they do not have to work in the pool and that participation in any activity is up to them and should only be undertaken when they feel ready.

*Phase 2.* Phase 2 begins with a group meditation at midnight and consists of six hours during which there is no verbal communication. This allows tensions that have arisen during the interactions in Phase 1 to intensify. It also permits the participants to renew their energy with a few hours of rest. A light breakfast is served at 6 A.M.

*Phase 3.* This phase follows breakfast and consists of six hours of continous work in the pool. Throughout this phase there is no verbalization except between the therapist and the person with whom he is working.

To begin the session, participants stand in two facing rows, an arm's length apart. One by one they are floated down this human conveyor while being gently supported and rocked by people on either side. Underwater speakers play interuterine sounds. Since water is a stiffer medium than air, this results in not only an auditory effect, but also a physical massage, which reduces the rigidity of body armor, allowing the participants to feel pleasure. During their second turn at being passed, participants are asked to hyperventilate.

Suddenly volcanic eruptions of the emotions that have been repressed by body armor and restricted breathing begin to occur. When this happens to an individual, he is floated on his back and held by five persons. This provides the security that he needs in order to completely let go. The process proceeds spontaneously, with the therapist encouraging the participant to let go and to express whatever he is feeling with his voice and body. If he restricts his breathing, he is encouraged to continue full hyperventilation. He may also be asked to make movements that will release his body armor. Musculature that is chronically cramped and sensitive to the touch may be massaged. These areas vary from person to person, but they generally correspond to tensions found in the body types described by Lowen (1958), who correlated them with psychoanalytic theory.

Whatever can be done to intensify the phenomena that are occurring is appropriate so long as it does not inject extraneous materials. If the participant, in his fantasy, experiences traumatic events out of the past, these may be worked with using internalized Psychodrama, Gestalt techniques, or with the therapist or a group member playing the role of the introject. Recordings may also be employed to heighten the desensitization process. For example, in the case of a woman who was trapped in a building during a bombing and later taken to a concentration camp, the sounds of bombs exploding were played through underwater speakers while the therapist imitated a Nazi officer shouting commands to his troops.

When recent traumatic episodes have been desensitized, earlier ones surface and are worked with. This follows the COEX system described by Grof (1975). When the process of emotional discharge occurs effectively, it is either followed by a state of relaxation and pleasurable experience or by the surfacing of another emotion related to the traumatic episodes. In this regard anger, fear, and grief are a triad. Whichever emotion is being expressed, one of the other two is usually being repressed. It can, at times, be heard in the overtone of the emotion being expressed and needs to be discharged.

Periods of intense physical and emotional discharge will be followed by a brief state of exhaustion during which the participant is allowed to rest and is comforted by being held, rocked, and allowed to experience the pleasurable sensations of the peak stimuli he has brought with him to the session.

These peak stimuli are not only used during the resting cycle but also employed to coax out repressed emotions and to help the individual enter a blissful state after he has effectively discharged traumatic material.

When regression to infancy occurs, a good mother selected from the group treats the participant as an infant, holding him, rocking him, and feeding him with a baby bottle. It is not unusual for a participant who has experienced oral deprivation to take two or three bottles and then peacefully fall asleep in her arms. This constitutes a process of reconditioning on a most basic level of personality. Within a week or two, it may result in the elimination of overeating, smoking, alcoholism, excessive talking, and other orally dependent forms of behavior. In a like manner, other psychoanalytically defined neurotic states are worked with through regression and resolved by satisfying the unmet childhood needs and redirecting the fixated energy.

A wide range of physical reactions may occur, including vomiting, difficulty in breathing, painful clonic contractions most common in the hands, numbness, paralysis, shivering, and tingling, among others. These phenomena occur when the life energy flow has been increased by hyperventilation and then encounters the body armor blocks. Since these reactions generally precede the discharge of repressed painful emotion, the participant is encouraged to continue his breathing and express his emotions.

Physical reactions may also accompany the discharge of birth trauma, a phenomenon often accompanied by diffuse pain throughout the body, choking sensations along with the profuse discharge of mucus, and the feeling of imminent death. Intense primal fear is experienced by participants, and they require the utmost support. When they break through, breathing becomes deep, rhythmic, and effortless. An energy flow that goes throughout the body and enters the head is experienced. Often there is a burst of extreme joy over being alive. The participant enters into an indescribable state of bliss and experiences a new sense of being. To some degree he seems to have transcended the existential anxieties related to aloneness and death and experiences a new identity that is united with all life. His joy and love are contagious, and they facilitate the work of the other group members. In subsequent sessions, he may rapidly run off past traumatic episodes as though he were discarding an old movie film in which he no longer has any interest. Over the next year, profound changes occur in his life and in his appearance so that at times friends do not recognize him or spontaneously comment on how much better he looks.

Since this remarkable phenomenon is the most valuable aspect of Aqua-Energetics, I am experimenting with a procedure that seems to bring it about in one out of five participants in the first pool session. Instead of abreacting to painful physical and emotional experiences, the participant is instructed to concentrate on his breathing and to direct the breath through the emotional or physical areas of distress. If, over a period of time, the breath alone does not relieve the discomfort, the therapist massages the painful areas that are blocked by body armor. Difficulty in breathing is experienced and moves progressively upward from the stomach to the chest, and finally to the throat. When the throat block dissolves, the energy enters the head and the fear of imminent death changes into the experience of joy and bliss. This process is slow and somewhat painful, taking from one to three hours, and can only be practiced by persons who are not overcome by the need to abreact. For most participants, some abreaction and desensitization apparently must occur before they are able to tolerate this procedure.

Most participants undergoing the usual type of abreaction work for 20 to 60 minutes. The work generally ends when the particpant has desensitized the traumatic material with which he is working and feels in a state of peace and relaxation. Stopping the procedure before the cycle is complete is contraindicated.

*Phase 4.* Phase 4 begins at one in the afternoon when the participants leave the pool and continues from two to four hours. Lunch is served buffet style without interrupting the group process. Since the pool experience at times has a dreamlike quality and tends to fade from memory, it is important that it be reinforced by verbalization. Group members are asked to share their experience, relate the new insights that they have had to their present lives, and accept playback from other members of the group. This work can be further enriched by Gestalt and Psychodrama techniques when appropriate.

*Variations of format.* This format may be varied as long as pool sessions, Phase 3, are immediately followed by integrative sessions, Phase 4. Workshops may be conducted for a series of days or even a week, as long as this sequence is followed each day.

*Nudity option.* Since Aqua-Energetics works almost as well with bathing suits on as it does in the nude, wearing bathing suits makes the process useful to institutions and to participants who are not ready to explore nudity and who would not attend if it were mandatory. However, since nudity is distinctly helpful to some persons and therefore adds to the value of the session, it should be used whenever there are no objections. A blind ballot is taken to free the participant from group pressure; if no one objects, nudity becomes optional, with some group members going nude and others wearing bathing suits. If, however, even one person objects, the session is run clothed and the identity of the person objecting is not revealed.

## APPLICATIONS

Because of the broad nature of Aqua-Energetic procedures, when properly applied, they are suitable for all persons whose health will permit them to exercise and who are capable of functioning in a group. This includes all individuals on the growth path from those who are seeking symptom cure, to those who want better adjustment in life, to people interested in self-actualization, and finally to those who are seeking enlightenment.

In actual practice many individuals who accomplish initial, lesser goals, such as symptom cure, become aware of their own potential to achieve higher goals, such as self-actualization, and continue the therapy. Others stop when they have attained their first objective.

To illustrate the wide range of applicability, I will discuss a few areas in which this method is useful.

### Body-Image Problems

Drawings made of the self before and after an Aqua-Energetic session usually show a profound change for the better in body image. Since these problems often concern the penis in the male and the breasts in the female, areas that are normally clothed, they can only be effectively handled in a nude session. It is pointless to talk about what one cannot observe or to attempt to desensitize an individual to negative conepts about an organ that cannot be exposed. When the organ in question is reasonably normal, Gestalt desensitization techniques and the consensus of the group are usually sufficient to alter the individual's point of view. When this does not happen, the problem is usually a deeper psychological one, as when a man who feels he lacks masculinity attributes this to a penis that is normal but which he sees as being too short. The body-image work then allows the underlying problem to be seen and worked with.

In instances where there is a real deformity, such as a mastectomy, the participant learns that while no one thinks the scar is beautiful, she is more than her scarred tissue. Before the 24 hours is up, she discovers to her delight that she is fully accepted despite this imperfection. Aqua-Energetic sessions should follow all breast surgeries to handle the psychological trauma that otherwise can render a woman emotionally blocked and sexually inexpressive for the remainder of her life.

## Sexual Problems

In the early days of the nude marathon, I wondered why, when we prohibited overt sexual expression in the session, about 80 percent of the participants reported improved sexual functioning a month later in the post-session. It soon became appparent that, without knowing it, we were following the Masters and Johnson (1966) concept of sensate focus enabling people to enjoy sensuality through body contact and massage in an atmosphere in which the threat inherent in sexual performance or compliance is eliminated. Since sensuality is fundamental to sexuality,

it is natural that an improvement occurred in this area.

In addition, blocks to sexual functioning have their neuromuscular component, which are resolved by Reichian techniques. The increase in life energy that accompanies this process further stimulates sexuality. If the new self-identity is experienced, tantric fusion becomes possible and replaces the ordinary sexual goal of reaching a climax with that of union and Reichian orgasm.

Conditions such as premature ejaculation, identity confusion, impotence, frigidity, exhibitionism, and masochism, among others, have yielded to this approach. When dealing with sexual problems, the session should be run in the nude.

## Drug Abuse

One of the most effective approaches to the elimination of reliance upon drugs is to enable participants to have a transpersonal experience without the use of drugs that exceeds the ecstatic level obtained through the use of chemical substances. Since the turned-on state is the natural state in the healthy child and is only lost as body armor accumulates and blocks life energy, it reoccurs as soon as these blocks are dissolved. This natural turn-on is more enjoyable than a drug turn-on since it is free of the toxic effects of the chemical materials, does not end when the drug wears off, and does not interfere with the pursuit of normal activities. When this natural turn-on occurs, participants may discover, to their amazement, that the chemical substances that formerly gave them a high no longer work and, in fact, produce a negative effect.

## Alcoholism

The alcoholic is usually a person whose character structure overemphasizes conformity and who suppresses self-expression through body armor. When these blocks are removed, he no longer has to relax them with alcohol. In addition, the transpersonal experience, which has long been recognized by Alcoholics Anonymous as the key to sobriety, happens in Aqua-Energetic sessions.

## Psychotics

Aqua-Energetics is an effective method for working with psychotics in remission who are being maintained by medication. Medication is terminated prior to the pool session. The pool allows the psychotic to freely express the full extent of his diffuse rage and fear without damaging himself or others. In addition, the womblike effect of the warm water permits him to undergo the profound regression necessary to deal with the early traumatic episodes that are responsible for the disturbance. Skin contact, which occurs in the pool, is basic in reaching the psychotic since the later evolutionary emergents of hearing and seeing often become hallucinatory. Rather than blocking his psychotic experience with medication, in the pool session he is encouraged to go even deeper into them until a resolution is reached.

Confirming the psychotic's cosmic experiences rather than denying them usually leads to better rapport. A degree of empathy should be established with the therapist in this way prior to the session in the pool. The individual should only be worked with in an Aqua-Energetic session if he does so at his own volition. Forcing a psychotic to participate will produce an escape into psychosis from which he will not voluntarily return. By following this principle, I have never had a participant enter a psychosis in the pool that did not resolve itself within an hour or two, leaving him in better shape then when we began.

Working with psychotics calls for a high level of skill and should not be attempted by a neophyte therapist. The possibility that this method could be of value in working with psychotics when they are first brought to a mental hospital before institutionalization adds to the problem should be explored.

## Repressed Violence

There is no psychotherapeutic method more suited to the discharge of hostility by participants who cannot be trusted to control or direct their rage than Aqua-Energetics. Even the most powerful male can be adequately restrained by putting two holders on each limb. The possibility that this method could be of value in working with prison inmates who have been convicted of crimes of violence should be explored.

## CASE EXAMPLE

Karen, 30 years of age, came to work with me from Belgium, along with her husband during his two-month summer vacation. They have been married seven years and have a two-year-old baby. Karen's reason for entering therapy is: "I want to be more than what I am, which is nothing." She is an emaciated woman with a death-mask face and eyes that suck at me when I look at her. She has been in a deep depression for years and tells me that all she wants to do is to die. She tried substitute teaching for a few months, which she did not like, and since then has been unemployed.

When her father refused to allow her to continue living at home, she married Charles. She states, "I would have married anyone who would take the place of my parents and deal with my problems." She complains of being so weak that she never likes to do anything. She sleeps most of the day. Occasionally she cooks a meal. She resents her two-year-old child and does not take care of him, leaving this to her husband. She says, "Sex is a real drag. I feel more distant from Charles when we make love than when we don't. Even masturbating myself is not worth the bother."

She insists that her husband remain with her all the time except when he is working and refuses to let him pursue his studies in art. When he is away, she panics. Recently she has not even been able to answer the telephone. She is a perfect example of an oral type as described by Lowen (1958) with schizophrenic aspects.

I have a few private sessions with her, which are uneventful, and then she attends the Aqua-Energetic workshop. In the pool she wants to be worked with but stretches out like a soggy doormat and does absolutely nothing for herself. When asked to forcefully hyperventilate, her breathing is hardly perceptible. She is totally unresponsive to her peak stimuli or to my attempts at massaging areas in which she has body armor. She does not even resist, but turns her head away to ignore what is happening.

I notice that the only life in her body is a periodic clenching of her jaws. This is the earliest way in which an infant can express hostility and is the last vestige of her own anger. If I can get this to intensify and spread throughout her body, she may be on the road out of her depression. I massage her jaws to open the body armor and let more energy flow into her jaw muscles. The clenching of her jaws increases, and breathing deepens.

On a hunch, I thrust a baby bottle into her mouth. At first she tries to ignore it, neither sucking on nor biting it. I massage her jaw muscles some more and try the baby bottle again. This time she grasps the nipple with her teeth and violently tears it out of the bottle. Her breathing becomes more intense. I replace the bottle with a towel and ask her to grip it with her teeth while I pull. She does this and, when I pull, fury enters her face, and she hangs on like a bulldog, but the rest of her body is limp. I suggest that she let the anger pour into the rest of her body and let it move. I continue to pull on the towel she is gripping with her jaws. Gradually she allows the anger to enter her body and begins to move her arms and legs. Suddenly she bursts into a fury of flailing and kicking and pushing her holders all over the pool. She has let go of the towel and is shouting and screaming. The discharge goes on for about five minutes. I allow her to rest, rock her, stimulate her with her peak stimuli,

and then repeat the process. Again I begin with the towel, which she grips with her jaws until her fury expresses itself throughout her body.

Now she is regressing. The sounds she is emitting become more like those of a baby. She goes into a fetal position. The holders and I allow her to do this. Her body makes spasmodic movements that are somewhat discoordinated, like an infant being born. Gradually she comes out of the fetal posture. Her mouth is now making sucking sounds and movements. I sense that the anger discharge I got earlier is a reaction to not being properly nursed. I ask a woman in the group who had the ability to mother to hold her head. Again I try the baby bottle. Again it is rejected. Somehow I must retrain Karen at this early level so that she can learn to accept what she needs and then reach out for what she wants in her present life. But how can I bring this about?

I notice that her thumb is extending from her hand in a strange manner and moving toward her mouth. I pick up the cue and put her thumb in her mouth. She sucks it vigorously. Obviously she is not prepared to trust anyone else to feed her and must do it for herself. Gradually I replace the thumb with the baby bottle; she grasps the bottle, feeding herself. I ask the substitute mother to hold her and to hold the baby bottle at the same time that Karen is holding it, to rock her, and to mother her. Gradually Karen allows her substitute mother to hold the bottle and finally removes her own hand. Over a period of an hour she drinks three bottles of milk. Her face becomes increasingly alive. There is joy in her eyes.

I suggest that the substitute mother gradually enable her to stand in the pool while holding her. When this is attempted, Karen screams hysterically and clutches the substitute mother. The substitute mother assures her that she will not leave, but that Karen may enjoy feeling her feet on the ground. Over the next half hour she is gradually able to accomplish this without panicking.

Now it is time to teach her to walk. Again she screams and panics and clutches the substitute mother. Over the next half hour she is gradually able to accomplish this and walks while holding her mother.

Now it is time for her to walk and stand alone. Again she panics at the thought of not having physical contact with her mother. The substitute mother stands a foot away from her, and Karen takes her first hesitant steps. Gradually she begins to walk freely and enjoys the feeling of her feet on the ground. She is standing and walking on her own. She enjoys the accomplishment and begins to jump up and down and dance. Her expression is totally changed. The death mask is replaced with the vitality of joy.

I then see Karen in weekly private sessions. She is a changed person. Instead of a deprived baby, she now resembles an adolescent who wants to experience the world. She is fed up with depending upon her husband. Instead of being unable to drive, she now is fighting with him to see who will get the use of the family car.

I have also been working with her husband. He stated, "I married her because no one else would want me and I needed a woman who would be absolutely dependent upon me in order to feel secure." But now he has also changed. For the first time in his life he feels that he can pick a woman whom he really wants. He tries it and, to his amazement, the woman is also interested in him. We have a conjoint session, and they decide that they both want to have the freedom to date. Karen goes jogging in the morning, meets another jogger, and dates him. She finds that now she is turned on sexually and enjoys intercourse. She becomes increasingly more fed up with depending upon her husband financially and decides to become free of this parental substitute by getting a job. Although she has no working papers, she talks an owner of a Belgian restaurant into hiring her as a waitress. This has all happened during two months of her summer vacation, and it is now time for her husband to go back to work. She wants to stay in this country for a while longer and would like to send Charles back to Belgium with their child. When the chips are down, she chickens out. She decides to go back to Belgium with him.

I have a sinking feeling, knowing that she needs the experience of independent living before she can possibly make a go of her marriage. If she returns to Belgium at this point, it will not work. I am afraid that she will regress into her old dependencies. However, I have learned not to advise or intervene. So I say very little. Inwardly I doubt that she will have the courage to come back to the States on her own. They leave for Belgium together.

To my amazement, two weeks later she walks into my office. She explains that she could not stand her old way of life and had to return to the States. She has bought a car, is living with friends, and has a job. She neither has the money for further therapy nor does she feel the need of it.

A year later both Karen and Charles come in for sessions during his summer vacation. The marriage is still continuing, although they are both dating a variety of people and enjoying the new experience. They are exploring the human potential movement and going to workshops all over the country.

The dramatic change that took place in Karen after the Aqua-Energetic workshop causes me to conclude that her regression to infancy made it possible for her to have the experience of receiving what she needed, namely nourishment from another human being. Along with this she learned that she could stand on her own feet and enjoy the process. These learning experiences were then translated into a changed attitude toward life. As she reached out, people responded and this, in turn, led to a new way of relating.

## SUMMARY

The Aqua-Energetic marathon is a 20- to 24-hour session for 12 to 20 participants that takes place in a carpeted room and in a body-temperature pool. It is a method of transformation that increases the aliveness of the individual by opening the neuromuscular blocks that inhibit the breathing process and impede the flow of life energy. With the increase of vitality, symptoms are cured, realistic life adjustments are established, self-actualization and creativity displace dependency, and existential anxiety is lessened by varying degrees of enlightenment.

Aqua-Energetics evolved out of the nude marathon, created by the writer in 1967, when it was discovered that wearing bathing suits did not detract from the process. Nudity is currently employed only when there is complete group consensus or when it is helpful in body-image work and with sexual problems.

Central to the process is group work in a body-temperature pool that creates an atmosphere of enormous love and trust, permitting closeness and emotional intimacy and making it possible for some dramatic therapeutic changes to occur that years of conventional therapy or psychoanalysis were not able to achieve.

Research conducted by Paul Wheatley (1974) at the California School of Professional Psychology compared the results attained in Aqua-Energetic marathons with those of traditional encounter marathons. He administered Shostrom's *Personal Orientation Inventory* (POI) before, after, and five months following each marathon.

Wheatley, in summarizing his findings, states, "Nude marathon regression therapy obviously facilitates more significant long-term changes than the traditional encounter marathons analyzed." (1974).

Referring to the honeymoon effect in which apparent gains made in a marathon are lost as time goes on, he states:

One fascinating characteristic of the long-term results is that, in general, test scores for participants in the more traditional encounter marathons decreased while test scores for the nude marathon participants showed several significant increases within the five months following the marathon. 1974 (p. 82)

He concludes:

This would seem to indicate that nude marathon regression therapy is a form of psychotherapy that reaches the depths of interpersonal and/or intrapersonal dynamics to such an extent that significant personal growth continues to occur for some time following the actual marathon experience. (1974, p. 82)

Referring to the statistically significant scores on the POI scales, he states:

Nude marathon participants learn to like themselves better and begin to rely more on themselves as primary reference points. They show an increased ability to be themselves and to desire relationships with others. This desire for relationship is characterized by an increased ability to make intimate contact with others and may be complimented by an increased ability to view constructively the nature of mankind without regard for encumbering sex role stereotypes. Nude marathon participants clearly increase their ability to live in the present, making more efficient use of their time and generally increase their affirmation of self-actualizing values (1974, pp. 113–114)

The body-temperature pool helps to relax chronic muscle tension (body armor) and thus restores the natural breathing process. Since restricted breathing is the mechanism through which emotion is repressed, the reversal of this process leads to the spontaneous discharge of repressed emotion and the desensitization of past traumatic episodes.

The womblike environment of the pool also facilitates regression and thus the discharge of progressively earlier painful events that have had increasingly more profound effects on the shaping of the personality.

Some participants terminate therapy when their goal of symptom cure or better adjustment is achieved. Others continue the process. As their aliveness increases, about 50 percent of this group find that their ego-identification begins to lessen and a new sense of self is born. This is a profound experience for the participant, which carries with it an understanding of his own nature and his unity with all life that cannot be conveyed in words. He enters a state of bliss and is filled with love and energy.

Past traumas and their effect on his personality fall away. He no longer depends upon his environment for emotional sustenance and therefore is free to function creatively. If his occupation is laborious rather than pleasurable, he soon changes it and finds a way of doing what he enjoys. To his surprise, this usually results in better pay.

Sexuality becomes an ecstatic experience in which he enjoys tantric union and the Reichian orgasm, making his former orientation toward attaining a climax seem as worn out as masturbation.

Being in touch with the source of his own energy, he is thoroughly alive. His appearance becomes more youthful and may be so profoundly changed that individuals who have not seen him in the last year at times do not recognize him.

He becomes highly intuitive and his psychic abilities unfold. This is a natural turn-on characterized by the qualities of aliveness that we enjoy in children. It is free of the toxic aspect and the temporary quality of a drug high. Although it varies in degree, it is continuous. It increases the participant's efficiency in life rather than impairing it.

Most of these changes occur spontaneously, and the participant is more aware of the increasing beauty of his world than of his personal growth. Since these changes occur quite rapidly, the average participant is aware of his improvement after having attended four private sessions and one Aqua-Energetic marathon. As a result, he does not have to make major commitments of time and money before knowing whether the process will prove helpful.

Pool sessions occur once a month and are supported by individual weekly sessions. A holistic approach is employed throughout based on the integration of a variety of therapies that cover the six vectors through which people grow (intellectual, interpersonal, fantasy, biochemical, transpersonal, and neuromuscular).

Aqua-Energetic workshops are suitable for all persons in reasonably good health who are capable of working in groups. There are no contraindications if the procedure is properly carried out, and to the best of my knowledge, I have had no negative results using this procedure. This method is spreading rapidly. Over 6000 persons have experienced such workshops in the last 12 years. Many professionals use Aqua-Energetic procedures under different names, such as Rebirthing and Primal Encounter.

## REFERENCES

Bindrim, P. *Out of touch*. Documentary film produced by Aisa Films, Canada, 1971.

Bindrim, P. "Outcome research and analysis of the nude marathon as an application of Reichian concepts to group therapy." Ph.D Dissertation, International College, Los Angeles, California, 1975.

Elliott, J. The nude marathon in a conversation with Paul Bindrim. In L. Blank, G. B. Gottsegen, and M. G. Gottsegen (Eds.), *Confrontation*. New York: Macmillan, 1971.

Grof, S. *Realms of the human unconscious: Observations from LSD research*. New York: Viking Press, 1975.

Harlow, H. F. Social deprivation in monkeys. *Scientific American*, 1962, **207**, 136–146.

Harris, H. "*A handbook for aqua-energetics.*" Masters Thesis, Californa State University, Northridge, 1979.

Janov, A. *The primal scream—primal therapy: The cure for neurosis*. New York: Putnam Sons, 1970.

Jung, C. G. *Modern man in search of soul*. Trans. by W. S. Dell and C. F. Baynes. New York: Harcourt 1933.

Lowen, A. *Language of the body*. London: Collier Macmillan, 1958.

Maslow, A. H. *Religious values and peak-experience*. Columbus: Ohio State University Press, 1964.

Masters, W. and Johnson, V. *Human sexual response*. Boston: Little, Brown, 1966.

Orr, L. and Ray, S. *Rebirthing in the new age*. Millbrae, Calif. Celestial Arts, 1977.

Raknes, O. *Wilhelm Reich and orgonomy*. Baltimore, Penguin, 1970.

Reich, W. *The discoverry of the orgone: The function of the orgasm*. New York: Farrar, Straus, 1968.

Wheatley, P. M. "*Effects of nude marathon regression therapy on interpersonal and intrapersonal change in self-selected subjects: Psychological nudism or psychic strip-tease?*" Ph.D Dissertation, California School of Professional Psychology, Los Angeles, 1974.

# CHAPTER 4

# Art Therapy

MYRA LEVICK

*We humans, in our basic wisdom about ourselves, tend to find ways to "cure" ourselves when we are troubled. One of the most common of ways to divert ourselves from problems, to get relaxed and in touch with others, to express our feelings, is through aesthetic productions. Just as music and dance and poetry have been employed consciously by professionals in therapeutic fields, so too art has been used for psychotherapeutic purposes.*

*In the following chapter, Myra Levick explains how the production of art becomes psychotherapy. Experts in Art Therapy are able to use this means of expression for release, for understanding, and for greater adjustment to life.*

*Art has a diagnostic as well as a curative value. Surely one who has problems of adjustment is likely to show evidence of this through imaginative creative productions. As a matter of fact, a clever and well-trained art therapist may be able to understand the nature of a troubled person's difficulties through examination of his or her projections. As this chapter demonstrates, we can see progress through paintings.*

*Naturally, for this therapy—as well as for all other forms of therapy—the quality of the treatment is a function of the sensitivity of the therapist and the nature of the client's problems.*

Art Therapy as a discipline has been growing rapidly over the last 20 years, and its definition has evolved over the years. Fink, Goldman, and Levick (1967) define Art Therapy as "that discipline which combines elements of psychotherapy with untapped sources of creativity and expression in the patient;" Levick (1967) a "prescribed substitution of creative activity to replace neurotic symptoms and to strengthen defenses successfully by the patient before illness becomes acute, and establish a prescribed relationship with the therapist."

The current definition as described by the American Art Therapy Association is as follows:

Art therapy provides the opportunity for non-verbal expression and communication. Within the field there are two major approaches. The use of art as therapy implies that the creative process can be a means both of reconciling emotional conflicts and of fostering self-awareness and personal growth. When using art as a vehicle for psychotherapy, both the product and the associative references may be used in an effort to help the individual find a more compatible relationship between his inner and outer worlds.

Art therapy like art education may teach technique and media skills. When art is used as therapy the instruction provides a vehicle for self-expression, communication and growth. Less product oriented, the art therapist is more concerned with the individual's inner experience. Process, form, content, and/or associations become important for what each reflects about personality development, personality traits and the unconscious.

## HISTORY

### Precursors

Ernest Harms, founder and former editor of the *International Journal of Art Psychotherapy*, traced the healing effects of the arts (in this case, music) back to biblical sources that describe how David tried to cure King Saul's depression by playing the harp (Harms, 1976). Emil Kraeplin, in 1912, and Eugen Bleuler, in 1918, also suggested that drawings of patients be considered in making diagnosis. Hans Printzhorn, in the early 1970's, spurred outstanding psychopathologists to use the art expressions of their patients to diagnose their pathological conditions. Emanuel Hammer states: "From these causal diagnostic beginnings, a great number of systematic diagnostic methods have been developed which today we call tests; and the method has been designed as a projective technique" (in Harms, 1975, pp. 241–244).

In 1925 Nolan D. C. Lewis began to use free painting with adult neurotics (see Naumburg, 1947). Max Stern described free painting in psychoanalysis with adult neurotics and stated that one of the reasons that this modality has not been generally adopted may be due to part to a lack of understanding in the use of this technique and results (see Fink, Goldman, & Levick, 1967).

### Beginnings

"Art therapy as a profession was first defined in America in the writings of Margaret Naumburg" (Levick, 1973). Naumburg dates her awareness of the relationship between children's drawings and psychotherapy to her early years of experience as director and art teacher of the Walden School, which she founded in 1915. She became convinced that the free art expression of children represented a symbolic form of speech basic to all education. As the years passed, she concluded that this "form of spontaneous art expression was also basic to psychotherapeutic treatment" (Naumburg, 1966, p. 30).

Under the direction of Nolan D. C. Lewis, she initiated an experimental research program in the use of spontaneous art in therapy with behavior-problem children at the New York State Psychiatric Unit. The results of the study were first published in 1947. In 1958 graduate courses in the principle and methods of her concept of dynamically oriented Art Therapy were instituted at New York University. Her prolific writings, lectures, and seminars throughout the country spearheaded growing interest in the field and stimulated mental health professionals and educators to question and explore the possibilities of a broader conceptual framework in the application of art as a diagnostic and therapeutic tool.

Subsequent art therapists, some trained by Naumburg, added significant impetus to the development of this modality and should be mentioned briefly. Eleanor Ulman originally defined her profession as an art teacher. She received some training in art education through lectures and seminars at the Washington School of Psychiatry and a series of lectures on Art Therapy by Naumburg. In the early 1950s she took a position in a psychiatric clinic. She later worked at the District of Columbia General Hospital where Bernard Levy, chief psychologist, taught her the principles of diagnosis (Ulman, 1966). In 1961 she published the first issue of the *Bulletin of Art Therapy*, which has continued to be a major publication in the field.

Ben Ploger has been both an art teacher and art therapist. He began teaching art in 1935, and is currently professor and chairman, Department of Fine Arts, Delgado College, New Orleans. In the early 1960s he was persuaded by a psychiatric nurse to volunteer to teach art to mentally disturbed nuns cloistered in the religious unit of the De Paul Hospital. He soon began to introduce and implement his own particular expertise throughout the hospital and was made director of art psychotherapy there in 1966 (reported in personal communication to the author).

In 1950 Edith Kramer initiated and for

nine years conducted an Art Therapy program at Wiltwick School for Boys, New York City. Her first book, *Art Therapy in a Children's Community*, was written in 1958. Kramer is widely known as a lecturer and teacher in the field, and is currently on the faculty of the graduate program of art therapy at New York University.

During World War II, Don Jones, a conscientious objector, volunteered for duty at Marlboro State Hospital, New Jersey. In a letter to this writer he stated, "Having had an art background before, I immediately became intrigued by the many graphic productions and projections of patients which literally covered the walls of some rooms and of passageways between different buildings." In 1950, a number of psychiatrists and social workers from the Menninger Clinic were his students in painting classes at Kansas University. He was soon introduced to Karl Menninger and shared with him a manuscript and paintings reflecting his wartime experiences. This resulted in his being employed as an art therapist at Menninger's Foundation, and marked the beginning of the Art Therapy program at the institution. Jones remained there until 1966, and since then has been director of the Adjunctive Therapy Department, Harding Hospital, Worthington, Ohio, and is a past president of the American Art Therapy Association.

This writer received a bachelor of fine arts degree in painting in 1963 and was planning to pursue training in art history. However, I answered a provocative job advertisement for a trained artist to work with mental patients in the first open inpatient unit in a general hospital in Philadelphia and spent the next five years in intensive in-service psychiatric training with the staff under the direction of the late Morris J. Goldman. An Art Therapy program was implemented, and I wrote several papers in collaboration with Goldman and Paul Jay Fink, about experiences with Art Therapy. During that time I also attended graduate school and in 1967 received a masters degree in educational psychology from Temple University. That same year Goldman became director of the Hahnemann Community Health Center, Philadelphia, and within a few months he and Fink, then director of education and training, Department of Psychiatry, Hahnemann Medical College and Hospital, proposed the first graduate training program in Art Therapy in the world. I was appointed director.

In 1968 Hahnemann Medical College and Hospital hosted a lecture series in Art Therapy and a reception for practicing art therapists throughout the country. At that meeting an ad hoc committee was elected to develop guidelines for the organization of the National Art Therapy Association. The committee members were Elinor Ulman; Don Jones; Felice Cohen, a well-known art therapist at Texas Research Institute in Houston; Robert Ault, an art therapist at the Menninger Foundation, who had been trained by Don Jones and who replaced Jones when he left Menninger; and this writer. In 1969 the American Art Therapy Association (AATA) was officially launched into existence at Louisville, Kentucky.

The art therapists mentioned here reflect only a small number of the highly competent men and women who were ultimately responsible for establishing Art Therapy as a profession in the United States and abroad.

## CURRENT STATUS

The American Art Therapy Association has designated professional entry into the field at the masters or graduate level training in institute or clinical programs. Graduate training must include didactic and practicum experience, but the emphasis may vary depending on the facility in which the student is trained. A masters degree from an academic institution or a certificate of completion from an institute or clinical program is supported by the American Art Therapy Association as professional qualification for entry into the field.

Undergraduate programs that provide basic areas of fine arts and the behavioral and social sciences in preparation for graduate training is also supported by the American Art Therapy Association. These two areas are prerequisites for specializied Art Therapy training, which includes a knowledge of history, theory, and the practice of Art Therapy itself.

Guidelines and criteria for Art Therapy training and clinical training are available from the American Art Therapy Association, in Baltimore, Maryland.

Numerous academic institutions, clinics, and institutes currently train art therapists, and other institutions provide undergraduate course work in preparation for graduate training. A list of available programs and whom to write to for information is available upon request from the American Art Therapy Association.

Procedures for program approval were instituted in 1978, and the first group of programs meeting these requirements were announced in November of 1979.

There are three classifications of members in the association: (1) active membership, which is open to all persons "who are or have been actively engaged in the therapeutic use of art" (AATA pamphlet, 1970); (2) associate membership, which is available to volunteers or individuals who "may or may not be engaged in the therapeutic use of art, who wish to support the program of the Association" (AATA pamphlet); (3) student membership for students involved in Art Therapy training.

The association has also developed specific standards for registration; art therapists who have met these standards receive a certificate of registration by the AATA and may use the initials *ATR*. Currently there are approximately 1800 members of the association.

In 1974 Linda Gantt and Marilyn Strauss Schmal prepared a comprehensive, annotated bibliography of literature in the field of Art Therapy from 1940 to 1973 through a grant from the National Institute of Mental Health. There are two major publications in the field: *The American Journal of Art Therapy* (previously *Journal of Art Therapy*) and *The Arts in Psychotherapy: An International Journal*.

Art therapists work in public and private institutions treating a variety of mental disorders, and in public and private schools for the learning disabled child, and the mentally and physically handicapped child and adult.

Art Therapy is practiced with individuals, groups and/or families and, more recently, the terminally ill and physically disabled.

## THEORY

Not all practicing art therapists view human beings' behavior as a product of unconscious thoughts and feelings. Current training in the field embraces many orientations; therefore, it follows that the philosophy of art therapists coming from theoretical frameworks such as Behavior Modification, Gestalt, Client-Centered, Humanistic, and so forth, would be different from that originally put forth by Naumburg.

"Most drawings of the emotionally disordered express problems involving certain polarities, e.g., life-death, male-female, father-mother, love-hate, activity versus passivity, space rhythm, color, some being specialized and others being generalized in composition" (Naumburg, 1947, p. v).

The psychoanalytic approach to ego mechanisms of defense is the basis for treatment methods in Art Therapy (Naumburg, 1966). Naumburg maintains that spontaneous art expression releases unconscious material; that the transference relation between patient and therapist plays an important role in the therapeutic process. Further, the encouragement of free association in pictures closely allies dynamic Art Therapy to psychoanalytic therapy (Ulman, 1961).

More recent proponents of Naumburg's original premise maintain that the patient's artistic productions, like the dream brought to the analyst, cannot be interpreted without the patient's associations. Condensation, displacement, symbolism and secondary elaboration, components of dreams and graphic productions, plus the patient's associations, provide more information than is often observable in the clinical setting (Fink, 1967).

In 1958 a second theory of Art Therapy was formulated by Edith Kramer. While recognizing the unconscious as a determinant for the human being's behavior, she believes that the very act of creating is healing; that the *art* in therapy provides a means of widening the range of human experience by "creating equivalents for such experiences" (Ulman, 1961, p. 13).

Kramer places great emphasis on the process of sublimation and feels that the arts are to be highly valued in the treatment process of the mentally ill. She clearly identifies her role with patients as different from that of the art teacher, in that in teaching art the process takes precedence over the product (Ulman, 1961).

The art therapists who have adopted the Naumburg ideology are viewed as psychotherapists by the followers of the Kramer ideology; the art therapists who, like Kramer, place emphasis on the healing quality of the creative process are viewed as art teachers (Ulman, 1961). The current literature, which consists primarily of case studies, reflects a wide variety of theoretical concepts somewhere between Naumburg and Kramer. Many of these theoretical formulations and methodology have evolved as the result of the many graduate training programs that have been established throughout this country in the past eight years. As was briefly suggested above, a number of pioneers in the field developed their own unique Art Therapy theories based on years of experience rather than on a single theoretical frame of reference. There are no longer just two accepted, divergent viewpoints, but many valid frames of reference that lead to as many valid goals.

For those dynamically oriented art therapists, the goal is to allow a transference relationship to develop so that through the patients' associations to their spontaneous drawings insights into conflictural areas of the psyche may be uncovered. In the process of making verbal what was nonverbal, conscious what was unconscious, the art psychotherapist makes connections and clarifications in an effort to help the patient interpret his or her own symbolic images.

In placing emphasis on the healing aspect of the creative process, the goal of Art Therapy is to provide a means, according to Kramer "wherein experiences can be chosen, varied, repeated at will" (Ulman, 1961, p. 13). It also provides an opportunity to reexperience conflict, resolve and integrate the resolution.

This writer was trained in a psychoanalytically oriented milieu but years of experience as a therapist and educator have demonstrated that the most valid goal is that which is consistent with the needs of the patient/client regardless of theoretical orientation.

In summary, a list of goals all art therapists should keep in mind includes: (1) providing a means for strengthening the ego; (2) providing a cathartic experience; (3) providing a means to uncover anger; (4) offering an avenue to reduce guilt; (5) facilitating a task to develop impulse control; (6) introducing an experience to help develop the ability to integrate and relate; and (7) helping patients/clients use art as a new outlet during an incapacitating illness (Levick, 1967).

## METHODLOGY

The clinical application of Art Therapy encompasses the hospitalized child and adult, psychotic and neurotic populations voluntarily seeking some form of psychiatric intervention or treatment, prison populations, mentally retarded populations, learning disabled children, troubled couples and families, and, more recently, those individuals manifesting emotional problems resulting from physical illnesses such as chronic kidney disease, cancer, hemophilia, asthma, diabetes, and neurological diseases.

Art Therapy sessions may be conducted on a one-to-one basis, in small or large groups, and with families. They may be held in the art therapist's office, the classroom, the dining room of an inpatient unit, or the basement of a general hospital. The locale is contingent on the needs and ideology of the director or administrator of the institution that employs an art therapist or the orientation and style of the art therapist in private practice.

Specific methods and techniques vary for the very reasons mentioned above. However, it is generally accepted within the profession that the art therapist must have a sound knowledge of and considerable experience with all art media to carry out treatment goals in the Art Therapy session. For example, fingerpaint, oil paints, and clay are tactile media that foster the compulsion to smear. If the treatment goal is to provide structure toward helping the patient gain internal controls, these supplies would be detrimental. A more productive choice of media might be felt-tip markers or crayons.

Patients who need to be encouraged to communicate with others but cannot do so verbally often benefit from some form of group mural activity.

For the child who is withdrawn or who has a behavior problem because of a specific learning disability, the first accepted, valued drawing by the art therapist/teacher may be the first step toward self-acceptance.

For all patients/clients, Art Therapy, a nonverbal form of communication, provides a way to gain distance from disturbing thoughts and feelings. For the psychotic patient, it often helps to separate fantasy from fact; for the severely neurotic patient, it may help connect feelings and thoughts.

For troubled families, Art Therapy may dispel family myths and uncover denied scapegoating. Unhealthy alliances can be confronted and changed, and healthy separation of generations and consequent individuation can be reinforced.

Drawings done by chronic, long-term, in-

articulate patients often serve as the only means of evaluating prognosis, establishing treatment goals, and determining discharge procedures.

The length of therapy varies according to the setting in which it is conducted and the orientation of the therapist. For example, in a short-term hospital unit, Art Therapy would be consistent with the treatment goals of the milieu. In a one-to-one situation where the art therapist has a therapeutic contract with the patient, the length of therapy would reflect both the needs of the patient and the therapist's particular clinical orientation.

## APPLICATIONS

In this writer's experience, Art Therapy has demonstrated its efficacy with a variety of populations diagnosed with an equal variety of mental disorders. The most prevalent of these is schizophrenia, and this is probably due to the fact that the schizophrenic patient, suffering an acute episode, is usually in a severe state of regression and "seems compelled to express himself compulsively and continually through any art media" (Levick, 1975). Spontaneous drawings and associations are elicited and used to gain a better understanding of areas of conflict. "The art therapist offers the patient clarifications, connections, confrontations, and interpretations depending on the patient's capacity to handle the material being expressed" (Levick, 1975).

There is a need for caution in providing oil paints for the older adult schizophrenic patient. This medium may foster regression and thus overwhelm the patient. The following, however, is a case in which the therapist devised a method to prevent regression for the schizophrenic patient and yet provide encouragement:

A man in his early 30s, who had previously demonstrated some artistic talent, communicated that he wished to paint in oils. On his own, he obtained the medium and was later observed in great distress. He had stopped painting with the brush and had begun painting with his fingers directly on the canvas and seemed unable to stop. In reviewing the situation with him, it became clear that to refuse to allow him to use this medium would only create more frustration and reinforce his feelings of inadequacy. Therefore, it was suggested that he conceptualize his ideas first in pastels on paper, then copy his own drawing in oil paint. In this way, he established some structure thus avoiding regression and fulfilling his wish to progress to a more difficult medium. (Levick, 1975),

Many mental patients who have been hospitalized for years have learned that "doing something is good for them." Art Therapy can provide an activity that may alleviate anxiety, and is useful in situations where verbalization cannot be elicited—in fact, it is not necessary. Patient gratification is obtained in the act of participating in the creative process. Art Therapy also provides a form of resocialization for the chronic patient who often feels isolated from society.

The involutional-depressed patient usually resists any request to perform a task that might reflect his feelings of helplessness and inadequacy. The art therapist must be cognizant of this and not offer any activity or project that would cause frustration or anxiety. The art therapist must keep in mind too that if electroconvulsive therapy (ECT) is given, there will be a transitory memory loss. Therefore, to engage such a patient in any activity, the goals must be tasks that will foster ego enhancement. One such patient who was encouraged to draw or paint anything he wanted with the art therapist acting as teacher obtained considerable gratification from his experience. Though he had no conscious awareness of hostile feelings, he projected these onto a painting of a ferocious fish, which he proudly carried home with him when he was discharged from the hospital (Levick, 1975). Therapeutic gratification was obtained through externalization of hostility.

Obsessive-compulsive neurotic patients rely heavily on their ability to intellectualize

and often resist involvement in an activity, particularly a nonverbal one, such as drawing or painting. Here too the art therapist must be skilled in therapeutic techniques in order to establish a therapeutic relationship. With this type of patient it is sometimes helpful to draw projecting thoughts and ideas onto the same piece of paper in a shared experience. Mirroring as a means of confrontation can be particularly useful here. For example, a young woman reported a dream. When asked how she felt upon awakening, she said she was very depressed. The art therapist asked her to draw these feelings; the patient took brush in hand, dipped into the paint, and furiously put strokes of vivid color across the paper. The art therapist proceeded to mirror this demonstration and then asked the patient to describe the therapist's actions and product. The patient could not avoid recognizing that this reflected anger, not depression, and recognized her own anger, even though it was still somewhat removed from conscious awareness. These kinds of interactions cut through lengthy obsessive verbalizations and facilitate the ability of the obsessive-compulsive patient to get in touch with feelings that can then be expressed in an acceptable way.

There are numerous articles in the literature describing work with alcoholics, prisoners, and physically and emotionally handicapped children. A great deal of work has been done with families using the Art Therapy evaluation designed by the late Hanna Kwiatkowska many years ago. This evaluation is used widely throughout the country by art therapists working with various different kinds of populations, both child and adult. The evaluation consists of six tasks (Kwiatkowska, 1967) and provides a considerable amount of data about individual ego strengths and weaknesses and family interactions. Often data elicited through the Art Therapy evaluation will provide direction for future therapeutic interventions.

This writer was asked to evaluate a family who was facing the real problem of dealing with the terminal illness of their 19-year-old son. This young man, whose illness had first been discovered when he was 14, had had his leg amputated and wore a prosthesis, which he handled very well. In the evaluation, the parents and children (another daughter, aged 23) were asked to draw family members. The father, who had originally protested that he could not draw, finally proceeded to draw family members—all without completed lower limbs. During this evaluation, this and other sensitive issues were not pointed out. However, after the family recognized the need for therapy and reviewed their evaluation with the therapist, the father's drawing of the family suggested the direction, not just for the father, but for the entire family in the therapeutic process. It soon became obvious that one way of denying their son's illness was to act as if they too had physical problems; this was initially manifested in the father's representing all family members with incomplete lower limbs.

Greater awareness on the part of educators of learning disabilities has reinforced early writings by Kramer (1958) and Naumburg (1966) regarding the knowledge that can be gained of developmental sequences and intrapsychic conflicts from children's drawings. Kramer, Naumburg, and other well-known art therapists have demonstrated that spontaneous drawings of both children and adults reveal normal and pathological evidence of fears, fantasies, thoughts, and affects stimulated by internal and external pressures, ego strengths, and weaknesses, id derivatives, and normal and abnormal defensive mechanisms (Levick et al., 1979).

The trained art therapist can, by studying children's drawings, "guide the therapeutic team in pinpointing developmental, motoric, perceptual, or emotional problems that may interfere with learning" (Levick et al., 1979, p. 364).

Little has been published regarding the use of Art Therapy with the learning disabled. Levick et al. (1979) provide a list of unpublished theses that address this problem from several different viewpoints. These references are cited in a book on learning disa-

bilities (Levick et al. 1979). The reader is referred to the references listed at the end of the chapter and particularly to *Art Therapy: A Bibliography* (Gannt & Strauss, 1974) for further information.

## CASE EXAMPLE

The following case example reflects the training of this writer in dynamic and psychoanalytic theory. Naumburg (1966 p. 8) states that "in art therapy, transference is not only expressed verbally but also projected in many pictures." It is her conclusion that this transference relationship in Art Therapy is more easily dealt with through the use of spontaneous images which are associated to the patient who then can more readily understand original "objectification of his conflicts which may have begun in his earliest family relationships" (Naumburg, 1966, p. 8).

The following case* is followed over a period of two years through examples of transference and countertransference manifestations in drawings. Naturally, these specific drawings are taken out of context of the therapeutic process. Most of these drawings represent the patient's spontaneous graphic therapy. Some, done jointly by the patient and this writer, were precipitated by crisis situations in the therapeutic process and were invaluable in quickly bringing into consciousness transference and countertransference feelings. Hopefully this will not interfere with perceiving how the drawing facilitated the therapeutic process.

Figure 1 is introduced to demonstrate that C from the beginning used a tree to represent primarily father—male, water—mother. Struggling at that time with his own self-concept, he said the face was both mother and himself with a "blind man's stare." At that early session he recalled "hiding in a

*Reprinted by courtesy of the *International Journal of Art Psychotherapy*, 1975.

Figure 1

tree watching people'' and that ''he loves to be in water.''

For this therapist, the picture and the associations suggested that the patient could intellectually and graphically identify male versus female, but emotionally could not identify himself. As these symbols, in many different combinations and variations, continued to appear, this became obvious to the patient and he recognized them as the real issue of therapy, which was initially described as ''fear of going back to college.''

Four months into therapy the patient was manifesting resistance by relating the fantasy that to ''be close to a woman stimulated his fear of hurting a woman which made him think of wanting to hurt his mother.'' Finally, his interpretation was that ''not revealing too much in therapy was a way of sparing me his rage.'' My understanding of this (not interpreted then) was that as he spared me (mother) his rage, he also spared me (mother) the love that he was even more fearful of expressing. So I suggested we draw each other, to provide us both with the op-

portunity to obtain distance from feelings while sharing a ''safe'' experience. Figure 2 is his drawing of me, which we both recognized bore a greater resemblance to Botticelli's Madonna than to me. I pointed out that the Madonna of that period represented the ''good'' and ''bad'' woman—mother and prostitute (Canaday, 1958). He quickly recognized that his mixed feelings for mother were being projected onto me. My drawing of him (Figure 3) also surprised us. I drew him as a boy of about 8 to 10 years of age with closed eyes and tight mouth. He didn't like being seen as a ''little boy who wouldn't look''; but I had to recognize that perhaps I didn't want to ''see'' that the ''hurt little boy'' was also a grown man. The following month he was in the process of winding up his affairs at work prior to starting college and was concerned about his capacity to maintain a relationship with a female coworker whom he really liked. I suggested he draw her. Figure 4 reveals a much older looking person than his friend, one who ''had done a lot of living.'' Her hair (naturally

Figure 2

dark) is depicted as redbrown (like mine). The ice blue in the picture is a color he had associated with his mother. This picture represents the parataxic distortions discussed above, those people in our everyday lives to whom transferential feelings are connected. C had sexual fantasies about her but also wanted to think of her as a sister: therefore in his mind the fantasies were bad. When it was pointed out that in fact he had not permitted himself to really know her. After this had been brought into consciousness, he was later able to maintain the friendship of this young woman without letting his fantasies or fears interfere. This drawing technique was successfully employed several times to help him deal with a few other people in social and work groups he obviously had strong ambivalent feelings about.

During a session a month later, he became aware he was "being very resistant." It must be remembered the young man was very sophisticated in psychological terminology. He decided to "draw his resistance." Figure 5 is a picture that became very significant and one we both referred to in later sessions.

Although he had planned to draw a representation of his avoidance of important matters, he was momentarily stunned when he recognized that what he had drawn was like a cross-section of a cavern with a little figure trying to get in. It took little interpretation on my part for him to see that his "resistance" was indicative of his fear of getting close, and in his words "the wish to be born from me." At that time he was very depressed and asked for another session several days later. He experienced a frightening dream about a nun he remembered from his childhood. She had actually been very nice to him, but in the dream she was trying to seduce him. Figure 6 is his drawing of the nun (as in the dream). After many association, including the nun representing me, and reviewing the last sessions and drawings manifesting his "fighting me," we concluded that "therapy" was the seduction; the white face with red eyes and red mouth was like a newborn baby taking its first breath of air. He recalled being told his own birth was a difficult one and that his mother was very

Figure 3

Figure 4

Figure 5

Figure 6

ill "because of him." He then equated getting well with being born and being rejected.

During the next month he reported a dream in which he said I was realistically represented for the first time. In one of the dream sequences he said I was standing on a veranda with a German soldier in civilian clothes and my dress changed from salmon color to white. There were many aspects to this dream, but in terms of transference he made the following associations: His maternal grandmother had insisted on being buried in a salmon color dress; his mother had worn a salmon color dress to his high school graduation and he had danced with her; he once wanted to be like Siegfried, the German idol. I asked him to draw me and the man in the dream. Unconsciously he drew the "couple" in the exact position of himself and his mother in a photograph taken at the time of his graduation. (He had shown me this picture along with several others in an early session of therapy.) When I pointed out this obvious connection, he readily acknowl-

edged it, but added that he thought changing the color of my dress (in his dream) was the beginning of his efforts to "separate me from mother."

Several months later he was again very depressed and resistant. Finally, feeling very frustrated, I suggested we draw together. He agreed and he began to draw a "yellow" island (Figure 7). (In the past C had reported a fantasy of taking me to the "Canary Islands" and had dreamed of being on a "yellow island.") It should also be noted here that the rug in my office is a yellow shag rug. I put in a tree and three houses. He placed a man in a boat in the water and a small indistinct figure on the ground. He stopped, said "we were finished" and that "he felt good about the picture." He realized that both figures were him representing his uncertainty about transferring to a school abroad for the coming winter and interrupting therapy. In that session he decided if he went he would find a "substitute" for me (a "good mother"). I realized that in the drawing I provided both mother (houses) and father (tree) symbols for him to relate to and identify with.

During the following months C vacillated between progression and regression, exhilaration and depression. In the spring, 15 months after he had started therapy, he decided not to go abroad to school and met someone from another state who invited him to move there and attend college. He completed the first year of college with high grades, gave up all current plans to transfer to another local college, and informed me he was moving away within two weeks. The last session was so acutely painful for both patient and therapist that I again suggested a joint drawing to try to aid, at least nonverbally, his separation anxiety (Figure 8). He drew a bridge with three arches underneath. I converted the arches into houses with open doorways. He placed an object at each end of the bridge, perched there precariously, and said one was himself, the other

me. In the center he placed a rose. The rose had appeared in pictures before and at that time we understood it to represent a male symbol presented to a woman. He told me he liked the picture, and he left therapy and the city—again taking flight from mother (therapist) and seeking refuge with another "substitute." I realized that I had graphically left the "doors" open for him to return.

C wrote to me during the next nine months, first describing how "happy" he was. Finally realizing that this represented another "flight," he became very depressed and returned to the city. He asked if I would resume therapy. Since I had certainly "left the doors open" we had our first session several weeks after his return. He was obviously at a loss for words, so from past experience I quickly suggested a joint drawing "to see where we both were." Figure 9 shows two figures. I had started the one on the right. It was very clear to me as soon as I drew it that while I extended my hand

Figure 7

Figure 8

Figure 9

I did not know what role I was to assume. He drew himself, and, as he described it, "he was holding on but turning away from me and closing his eyes."

A month later, depressed, anxious about plans to get an apartment and to reapply to college in the fall, he spontaneously drew two heads that he said represented himself, consciously aware of the split. To him it represented the fear of what he must now do in therapy—define his identity. The barren tree underneath, he said, was the mother he could no longer look to for support. He must now control his feelings about the past and his behavior in the future. In discussing this with my supervisor, we concluded it also represented his awareness of having to deal with me as a woman and his rage toward his mother. Intellectually and to some degree emotionally he had separated me from mother.

In the next several months he made considerable progress in therapy that was primarily reality oriented, dealing with prob-

lems at work, new acquaintances, getting in touch with old friends, and preparing for college in the fall. In May 1975 he asked me to draw with him. Unlike previous times we both began at the same time—he on the left side, I on the right (Figure 10).

I wanted to do a thatched hut, but instead found myself doing the outline of a house and an incomplete figure next to it. He drew the palm tree, moved in front of me and completed my figure with hair, hands, running feet. He then put a figure climbing his tree. Together we put coconuts in, and I put two more incomplete figures in. He finished the figures (making them look scared) and put a chimney and smoke on my house, which he decided looked more like an island church. Finally, while I put in the green background, he put in the path connecting the tree and my figure, excluding the other figures. Both C and I were pleased with this picture. For him it implied he could now determine his own relationships. He could accept or reject people and places and even

Figure 10

"add" to them, like the chimney on my house. While I did not make the interpetation, his subsequent pictures indicated he knew he now had to act on his new awareness. He was obviously as afraid of this as he was excited, and began to talk about termination. Picking up on his need to "control" the course of termination, I confronted him with his fears about the future, and he admitted he was "afraid of continuing in therapy, but not sure why." It seemed clear he was again resisting and it was agreed we would meet once a month for the next few months. Pictures done during two of these sessions represented C at a crossroad, not sure which road to take. In one picture in which he placed me facing him (Figure 11), it is difficult to determine if he is saying good-bye or hello.

In August, just four days prior to the time I was to leave for vacation, C learned of the death of his father. I saw C, at his request, spoke to him before I left, and he made an appointment for several days after my return. C did not wait until I returned. He had again taken flight, unable to deal with the real loss and the symbolic counterpart—termination of therapy, as manifested in Figure 11.

I did not hear from C for two and one-half years following this flight. Then I received a call from him announcing that he was back in the city briefly and asking whether I would see him. This visit took place shortly thereafter in my office. C reported that the past two and one-half years had been filled with many gratifications, many anxieties, and even some acute depressive periods. He also reported that he had made up his mind, when he recognized that his leaving reflected another flight, that he needed to begin to deal with some of his problems on a more mature level and "use what he had learned in therapy through our long relationship."

In summary, the patient did begin to cope during his two and one-half year absence from therapy, had enrolled in another uni-

Figure 11

versity, and was preparing for graduation. He also had applied for a scholarship at a well-known Eastern college for a masters degree and had been accepted. He has communicated through letters and occasional visits with me and he has now completed the first year of his graduate program in art.

The material presented here graphically demonstrates the utilization of Art Therapy to facilitate the awareness of transference and countertransference feelings and their connections to early childhood experiences through associations to the drawings. In dealing with such issues as fear of closeness and separation, I found my own spontaneous drawings communicated therapeutic distance and support more quickly than any verbal expressions. In training art therapists, bringing these transferential feelings to consciousness through drawings facilitates the student therapists' awareness of their own responses and sharpens their recognition of these manifestations in their patients' drawings.

## SUMMARY

In terms of a body of literature and scientific documentation, Art Therapy is a young profession. As more and more graduate students are required to write a thesis as part of their programs, it is hoped that this growing body of literature will answer the need for more scientific documentation.

Frequently at this time papers written by art therapists are not accepted by other professional journals unless co-authored with a member of that discipline. However, graduate programs and national registration standards based on graduate training have made considerable progress in promoting recognition of what this writer believes to be a valid therapeutic modality.

In recent years art therapists have presented papers at national and international conferences of the American Psychiatric Association, the International Child Psychiatry Conference, and the National and International Society for the Psychopathology of Expression.

"The similarity between this methodology of art therapy and psychoanalytic psychology provides the art therapist with an enormous amount of clinical information which implies a greater appreciation for this modality as a diagnostic and therapeutic process" (Vaccaro, 1973).

There are those who criticize the use of art as a vehicle for psychotherapy and deem that it remain in the background of the mental health sciences as an *adjunctive therapy*. This chapter has addressed the beginnings and the growth of this "new" therapy as it struggles toward autonomy and recognition by all involved in the helping professions.

As stated above, true scientific documentation has not been forthcoming. This writer even questions if this documentation is possible in a profession that deals with human thoughts and feelings. The most valid documentation, however, are the pictures made by the patients/clients, appropriately translated by the trained and skilled Art Therapist. The therapist can then help the patient/client to see, to understand the meaning of his graphic production, own it and either accept or change the discovered emotional content toward self-awareness and growth.

The field [Art Therapy] has grown from the efforts of a very small group of pioneers, who from different educational, geographic backgrounds eventually communicated with each other and so many others, to demonstrate that which Anna Freud said to Erik Erikson, "Psychoanalysis may need people who make others see." (Coles, 1970, p. 000)

## REFERENCES

Coles, R. *Erik H. Erikson, the growth of his work.* Boston: Little, Brown, 1970.

Fink, P. J. Art as a language. *Journal of Albert Einstein Medical Center, 1967,* **15,** 143–150.

Fink, P. J., Goldman, M. J. and Levick, M. F. Art therapy, a new discipline. *Pennsylvania Medicine,* 1967, **70,** 60–66.

Gantt, L. and Schmal, M. S. *Art therapy—a bibliography, January 1940–June 1973*. Maryland: National Institute of Mental Health, 1974.

Harms, E. The development of modern art therapy. *Leonardo*, 1975, **8**, 241–244.

Kramer, E. Art therapy at Wiltwyck School. *School Arts*, 1958a, **58**, 5–8.

Kramer, E. *Art therapy in a children's community*. Sringfield, Ill.: Charles C. Thomas, 1958b.

Kwiatkowska, H. The use of families' art productions for psychiatric evaluation. *Bulletin of Art Therapy*, 1967, **6**, 52–69. [With discussion by N. L. Paul, 69–72.]

Levick, M. F. The goals of the art therapist as compared to those of the art teacher. *Journal of Albert Einstein Medical Center*, 1967, **15**, 157–170.

Levick, M. R. Family art therapy in the community. *Philadelphia Medicine*, 1973, **69**, 257–261.

Levick, M. F. Transference and countertransference as manifested in graphic productions. *International Journal of Art Psychotherapy (U.S.A.)*, 1975, **2**, 203–224.

Levick, M. F. Art in psychotherapy. In J. Masserman (ed.)., *Current Psychotherapies*. New York: Grune & Stratton, 1975.

Levick, M. F., Dulicai, D., Briggs, C. and Billock, L. The creative arts therapies. In William Adamson & K. Adamson (Eds.). *A Handbook for specific learning disabilities*. New York: Gardner Press, 1979.

Naumburg, M. *Studies of free art expression in behavior of children as a means of diagnosis and therapy*. New York: Coolidge Foundation, 1947.

Naumburg, M. *Dynamically oriented art therapy: Its principals and practice*. New York: Grune & Stratton, 1966.

Ulman, E. Art therapy: Problems of definition. *Bulletin of Art Therapy*, 1961, **1**, 10–20.

Ulman, E. Therapy is not enough—the contribution of art to general hospital psychiatry. *Bulletin of Art Therapy*, 1966, **6**, 13–21.

Vaccaro, V. M. Specific aspects of the psychology of art therapy. *International Journal of Art Psychotherapy (U.S.A.)* 1973, **1**, 81–89.

# CHAPTER 5

# *Autogenic Training*

HEIDE F. BRENNEKE

*Autogenic Training is a procedure that most psychotherapists have heard about but don't quite understand. I was lucky to find Heide Brenneke, who was willing to explain the process in this book.*

*As the perceptive reader will note, this procedure has many elements in common with a variety of other systems, such as Biofeedback, Rebreathing, Psycho-Imagination, and Stress Management; but at the same time it adds some new elements.*

*Autogenic Training is used much more in Europe than the United States, and so far it has not penetrated too deeply into the understanding of American therapists. Some of the concepts may be difficult to understand at first, but essentially Autogenic Training seems to seek to establish a state somewhere between full consciousness and the oblivion of sleep and hypnosis. In this intermediate state, one's unconscious is more accessible—according to the theory.*

*Another important element of Autogenic Training is that after one has learned the process, the therapy itself is and should be independent of a therapist. In effect, one enters this altered state of consciousness to let the growth force within get to work to rectify the various insults the body and the mind have suffered in the past, to attain self-healing.*

Autogenic Training is a psychophysiologic form of psychotherapy that works with the body and the mind simultaneously. Through passive concentration on autogenic formulas the trainee self-induces an altered state of consciousness in which he or she learns to manipulate the bodily functions through the mind, resulting in the normalization of both bodily and mental states.

In other words, self-regulatory mechanisms, such as homeostasis and recuperative and self-normalizing processes, are promoted through the concentration of autogenic formulas. These results are diametrically opposed to stress.

Autogenic Training is often used in conjunction with medical forms of treatment in psychophysiologic illnesses such as chronic constipation, bronchial asthma, peptic ul-

cers, hypertension, and sleep disorders.

Behavior disorders and motor disturbances such as anxiety, insecurity, neurotic reactions, stuttering, cramping, and nervous twitching are effectively treated through the practice of Autogenic Training.

## HISTORY

Autogenic Training is based on studies of sleep and hypnosis as conducted by Oskar Vogt, neuropathologist of the Berlin Neuro-Biological Institute during the years from 1894 to 1903. Vogt observed that many of his patients were able to put themselves into a state similar to a hypnotic one after they had experienced his hypnosis treatment. They learned to control stress, tension, and fatigue in this manner and were also able to eliminate symptoms such as headaches, backaches, and so forth.

In 1905 J. H. Schultz began to explore a method that could enhance the therapeutic values of hypnosis without causing unfavorable passivity and dependence on the part of the patient. Schultz observed the sensations patients would experience under hypnosis— such as relaxation, warmth and heaviness in the limbs or in the entire body—and based his standard formulas on these findings. Corresponding effects observed by patients were added to the training formulas to influence heart and breathing rates and to control warmth to the solar plexus and coolness to the forehead.

Most research in Autogenic Training has been done in Germany. Beginning in 1960 much research has been published in the English language by Wolfgang Luthe, probably the foremost authority in Autogenic Training today.

In recent years interest in Autogenic Training has increased in the United States; however, this interest is still mostly confined to the medical arena and strongly emphasizes stress reduction.

## CURRENT STATUS

Many practitioners today, like myself, are not members of the medical profession. The use of Autogenic Training has become the basis for an eclectic approach to psychotherapy with practitioners drawing from Western as well as Eastern disciplines. It is becoming more and more apparent that Autogenic Training is not confined to the body and the mind alone. There have been many reports of spiritual experiences while in the autogenic state.

This writer is not aware of any training center in the United States where interested persons could study. A great number of practitioners are of German background, and most of the training happens on a one-to-one

basis. The International Committee on Autogenic Therapy is based in Canada.

The most comprehensive book on Autogenic Training to date is Wolfgang Luthe's *Autogenic Training,* (1969a).

## THEORY

Stress and tension are necessary to effective living and for survival. However, when stress becomes more powerful than the ability to handle it, it becomes a danger to health. The human body reacts to stress in a manner that is useful to primitive living, where a balance between stress—fight or flight—and restoration is assured.

Not only are there today pressures for survival, jobs, human relationships, and structuring of time, but for many individuals there is also constant sensory overstimulation. In addition many people ingest chemicals such as caffeine, alcohol, drugs, and food additives, which affect the autonomic nervous system, on a regular basis. Addiction to many of the sensory stimulants and/or chemicals is based on physical dependencies they generate.

Autogenic Training is based on the fact that the autonomic nervous system can be voluntarily controlled, and stress therefore reduced at command. The autonomic nervous system is divided into the sympathetic and the parasympathetic nervous systems, which have opposing functions. In general, the sympathetic nervous system is concerned with energy expenditure, while the parasympathetic nervous system is concerned with restorative processes. For example, while under sympathetic nervous system control, there occurs vasoconstriction of the lacrimal, parotid, and submaxillary glands, copious sweating, increased heart and breathing rates, secretion of epinephrine and norepinephrine by the medulla of the suprarenal gland, and so forth. Blood pressure increases and digestion is decreased due to contraction of the stomach and inhibition of glandular secretions in the stomach, intestines, and pancreas.

When under parasympathetic nervous system control the processes are reversed: The lacrimal, parotid, and submaxillary glands are stimulated to produce copious secretions high in enzyme content, sweating stops, the heart and breathing rates slow down, there is no known effect on the suprarenal gland, blood pressure decreases due to vasodilation in the peripheral blood system, and digestion is increased due to secretion of enzymes and increased peristalsis (Jacob & Francone, 1974).

All relaxation and all meditative states increase the functions of the parasympathetic nervous system, with the rare exception of paradoxic phenomena resulting from autogenic discharges (Luthe, 1962; Luthe, Jus, & Geissmann, 1962).

Through the continued practice of Autogenic Training, a state of parasympathetic nervous system control can be induced on command and stress levels reduced so that the basis for psychophysiologic illnesses such as hypertension, ulcers, colitis, headaches, migraines, backaches, and so forth, is weakened or eliminated.

The above description covers stress reduction. Though valuable, the benefits of Autogenic Training only begin here. Through passive concentration the trainee pays attention to internal processes to the exclusion of outside stimuli, generating a kind of stimulus deprivation similar to hypnosis. He or she can enter an altered state of consciousness in which consciously held beliefs can be explored, set aside, and the mind be allowed to expand beyond its accustomed limits.

The trainee, working on his or her own at this point, can have spontaneous access to various experiences from the unconscious and can possibly have spontaneous spiritual experiences. Examples are visualizations of colors, faces, objects, memories of possibly unresolved past events, feelings of pleasure and contentment based on either body sensations or verbal concepts, and so forth.

From this point the trainee can enter what Schultz calls the "interrogatory attitude" in which answers from the unconscious can be expected to problems that the trainee may or may not be aware of. Schultz also discusses "Nirvana Therapy" (Schultz, 1932; Schultz & Luthe, 1962) applied in situations of stimulus deprivation, desperate situations, or in clinically hopeless cases.

If the trainee works with a therapist, the process becomes admittedly less autogenic. Based on the theory that the creativity of a trainee in an altered state of consciousness is greatly increased, and that information produced is less inhibited than when the individual is in a fully conscious state, the therapist will ask questions for the purpose of clarification in problem areas. The therapist will also encourage the directing of self-healing energy to areas of disease or stress, will prompt visualizations, and will attempt to establish new behavior and/or thinking patterns.

Autogenic Training is still limited by the assumptions of the therapist and his or her insights into the areas in need of exploration and change. But due to the lack of verbal interaction between therapist and client, the trainee's conscious mind does not act as censor and the unconscious has free play to bring new experiences into conscious awareness.

As it is easier to receive answers from the unconscious in a meditative state, so is it easier to teach the unconscious new patterns in an altered state of consciousness. The unconscious often retains patterns long after they are needed, sometimes limiting the client's potential to a paralyzing degree. The autogenic state can be used to explore these beliefs and to abandon those of no further purpose.

Beliefs that limit a person and cause problems are often those not consciously acknowledged because they are "unbelievable"—that is, archaic, unevolved, embarrassing—or they are beliefs a person has adopted from an outside source without checking their relevance to personal essential understanding.

Problems are kept alive through selective negative memory about how "things are and always have been and therefore always will be." In a meditative state the unconscious can be encouraged to focus on selective positive memories and to visualize alternative behaviors and feelings, thus gradually training a new set of expectations.

Affirmations should follow new understanding, provided that they evolve from an exploration and take into account the state of the present reality so as not to overextend credibility.

## METHODOLOGY

The room used for Autogenic Training should be pleasantly warm and quiet. Metabolism slows down in deep relaxation and trainees often begin to feel cold. If the training lasts for more than three to five minutes a light blanket will assure comfort. If the horizontal position is assumed, a pillow under the knees for people with lower back problems or a small pillow for general comfort is recommended.

A calm, pleasant voice and proper timing by the practitioner greatly improve the success for the relaxation response.

Three different positions are recommended for clients in Autogenic Training:

1. The horizontal posture, not recommended if the trainee has a tendency to go to sleep.
2. The armchair posture.
3. A simple sitting or cabbie posture.

In the first two postures the legs are kept slightly apart, the arms on the side of the body or resting separately on the armrest, the head in alignment with the spine. In the third posture the legs are separate, the forearms are resting on the thighs, hands hanging without contact, the neck is relaxed with the head hanging slightly forward. The weight in this posture is in the pelvis.

As the concept of passive concentration

and voluntary manipulation of body functions, essential to Autogenic Training, is foreign to many people in Western cultures, a few preliminary exercises are used to establish that experience. Passive concentration is nongoal oriented, is not concerned with outcome or performance.

There are an endless variety of exercises to familiarize the trainee with the experience of passive concentration and voluntary control over functions often believed to be not controllable.

The following are a few examples of directions and information given in Autogenic Training.

*Breathing Exercise.* Become aware of your breathing. Do not change anything, just notice the parts in your body that are affected by your breath and allow yourself to be carried by that breath. Become aware of any changes that may occur, and follow these changes without value judgment and censoring. Then begin to change your breath in the following manner. On your next inhalation first fill your abdomen, then your chest; as you exhale deplete your chest first and then your abdomen. Now a wavelike motion occurs, up on inhalation, down on exhalation.

Now concentrate on the exhalation, making sure that every amount of air is expelled, allowing a natural pause at its termination. You will notice that your next inhalation becomes automatically deeper. Now with each exhalation allow the tensions and pains to drain from your body. With every inhalation take in all the feelings you would like to experience, such as happiness, relaxation, contentment, joy. Now if indeed you were able to evoke these feelings, become aware of doing that by just thinking about them.

Cancellation: Then allow your breath to become more natural again—more shallow.

*Body Inventory.* Without looking for it, actively allow that part of your body that is the most tense or painful at any given moment to come into your awareness. Then explore it. Notice its size, shape, depth, the kind of pain or tension it is—sharp or dull. Look at its color, its texture, and notice its emotional content. Often the pain or tension will disappear and a new place will come into your awareness. Then proceed with the same exploration in another area.

*Left-Right Balance.*    Become aware of your left side and compare it with your right side. Notice any differences. If one side is shorter than the other, pretend that you are made of some elastic material and that without any actual movement you can stretch this material to the extent that it will match the other side. If one side is lower than the other, imagine that you are filled with some liquid and then allow that liquid to swish around in your body until the level is equalized.

The trainee is once more reminded of his active participation in the use of the Autogenic Training method and at this point the peace formulas may be introduced, such as:

1.  I am calm and quiet.
2.  Nothing around me is of any importance.
3.  My thoughts pass like clouds in the summer sky.

When on occasion the discrepancy between the actual state of mind of the trainee and the statement is too great, a process formula should be adopted, such as:

As I am lying (sitting) here I am getting calmer and quieter. The peace formulas are designed to:

1.  Trigger a relaxation response.
2.  Acknowledge the fact that there are outside interferences, but that at this moment they are of no consequence.
3.  Acknowledge that there are thoughts coming through the awareness at all times, but that the trainee chooses not to pay active attention to them for the moment.

Luthe (1969a) suggests that subjects need to practice the standard formulas for between

four to ten months advancing only to each consecutive step after mastery of the preceding one. Many practitioners today introduce all basic formulas at the very beginning, and experience has proven that most subjects will accomplish the different states within a very short time.

As Luthe (1969a) points out, "a sensation of heaviness may or may not occur, and . . . many changes of bodily functions occur which one cannot feel." It is also important for the patient to know that according to experimental observations, the exercises are effective as long as they are performed correctly, even if one does not feel anything at all.

The six standard autogenic exercises are introduced:

1.  My right hand is heavy. (Left-handed persons begin with their left hand.)
2.  My right hand is warm.*
3.  My heartbeat is calm and regular.
4.  My breathing is calm and regular. It breathes me.
5.  My solar plexus is flowingly warm.
6.  My forehead is light and cool.†

The practice session may be interrupted at this point or any time the therapist or client sees fit, or the autogenic state may be used for further work.

The following are a few suggestions of explorations that are likely to occur in subsequent training sessions.

*To Train Visualization*

1.  In front of your inner eye allow a color to appear and then observe this color,

---

*After the second formula a generalization phenomenon occurs in which all limbs become warm and heavy on a regular basis. At times it may be indicated for the therapist to help this generalization process along by suggesting each limb's heaviness and warmth specifically. This is especially useful in a group session where verbal feedback is inappropriate.

†Vascular dilation in the head leads to headaches. This formula assures vascular contraction.

watch its possible changes. After several minutes the therapist will suggest that this color recede and disappear (the procedure to follow to cancel all suggestions).

2.  In front of your inner eye, without deciding who it is going to be, allow the face of someone you love appear. Then observe the face, experiencing it in every detail possible.

Both visualization explorations can be taken further by asking questions as to emotional content, symbolism, and dialogue.

To combine a visualization with "reframing and anchoring," the following exercise may be introduced.

The therapist tells the client, "In front of your inner eye (awareness), without deciding what it is going to be, allow the memory of a beautiful experience to emerge and relive it in every detail possible. See it, hear it, feel it, smell it, allowing as much information to surface as possible, including parts that you are now experiencing for the first time." After a few minutes the therapist asks the client to extract the basic feeling from this experience and to describe it with one or two concepts. Concentrating on these concepts, retaining the feeling, the client is then asked to make contact between his left (right for left-handed persons) thumb, index, and middle fingers in order to anchor the feelings in the body. The exercise is terminated at this point with the suggestion that at any time in the future when the feeling that was just experienced is desired, the trainee can trigger it by making the contact in his or her hand.

To use the above as a basis for reframing, the exercise can be continued by suggesting that the trainee in the imagination move ahead in time to an event anticipated with some anxiety and to go back and forth between the pleasant past experience and the future one until he or she can move through the entire anticipated event without feelings of anxiety, drawing power and positive feelings from the past event whenever necessary.

*Toward Healing of Physical Problems.* The trainee is asked to become aware of an area in the body that he or she is concerned about. The therapist might say:

"In front of your inner eye (awareness) allow an image to appear that shows you the cause of onset of this problem. Then look at the sequence of events that have kept this problem alive until today. Now entertain the possibility that on occasion—and maybe only very rarely—there is something good that comes out of having this problem. On occasion you may get something either from yourself or from someone else that you would not receive if you did not have this particular physical problem. Allow an image or a thought to come into your awareness that will show you the payoff. Now ask your unconscious to show you an alternate way, a more constructive way to receive the same payoff. Find another alternative, and another. Follow this with an affirmation.

"Now for the moment, knowing that you have this problem, set it aside and imagine that it does not exist—just for the moment. Then go back into your past and remember the times that you were free from this concern. Continue to look back and focus on all the times that you were free of any complaint regarding this area. Feel it, see yourself in the circumstances, and hear yourself.

"Now visualize yourself without it today—what you would do, what would there be instead. See yourself very clearly, hear yourself talking about yourself, feel yourself with that new-found health.

"Then concentrate on the area in your body that you have had the concern about and allow all your energy to merge there for a moment, allow all your concentration, all your love to concentrate in this one place. Notice the warmth and the energy expanding the area, clearing it of all restrictions and pain. Allow a white light to surround that part of your body, imagining it to heal you. Now allow the white light to expand and surround your entire body. Retain a feeling of health and well-being."

*Behavior and Emotional Pattern Changes.* A similar process is followed in relationship to behavior and emotional patterns that are no longer useful to the person. The trainee is clued in to the feeling that precedes the behavior, and alternative behavior responses are explored. When the emotion itself is the problem, the underlying belief is explored as well as the reaction that follows, which is the attempt at regaining balance.

After several sessions in which processes similar to the above have been used, the therapist encourages spontaneous problem solving without step-by-step guidance. This is accomplished by asking the trainee to focus on a problem area and to ask the unconscious to bring up new ways of dealing with it. The client is encouraged to access information in as many modes as are available (visual, auditory, or kinesthetic). Some persons are able to recall the process of exploration after the session, others will be aware of some solution without remembering the actual process, and a third group will not remember anything but will realize some time later that the problem no longer exists or has changed significantly enough that it can be handled.

This is a time when the therapist reminds group participants once more not to make comparisons: Every person's process is unique. There is no right or wrong and there is no goal; each and every process is an expansion of the conscious mind, valid in itself.

Each session ends with a general visualization and with general affirmations. Participants are asked to visualize themselves the way they want to be and with what they want to have in their lives. For the moment all known reality is set aside.

This kind of visualization can be viewed as an affirmation in itself. However, verbal affirmations seem to work well with many clients. In contrast to affirmations used as part of the process of specific explorations, these ending affirmations are expansive, such as:

1.  I have the wisdom to know what is right for me.
2.  With every day that passes I am getting a greater feeling of well-being, safety, and security.
3.  I am learning to say good-bye to . . .

4.  Every time that I relax I go deeper, faster.
5.  I am learning that I have a perfect right to all my feelings.
6.  I am learning to picture myself the way I want to be.
7.  I am learning to replace_____with _____ .
8.  I love myself unconditionally.
9.  I am prosperous and happy in my work.
10.  I live a full and rich life.

It needs to be stressed that affirmations will (1) change spontaneously and (2) lose their impact because the process of change is already underway.

To conclude a session and to cancel the autogenic state the practitioner asks participants to:

1.  Give a thought to coming back.
2.  Increase the breathing rate.
3.  Move and stretch your body.
4.  At your own pace open your eyes and come back to the room.

Proper cancellation of the autogenic state is important before moving about. Sudden interruption tends to induce an anxiety state.

When practicing alone the trainee follows the same procedure. With the help of a timer set for one or two minutes longer than the planned session the client can train his or her own internal clock to conclude the session after a predetermined interval.

*Frequency and Procedure of Practice.*    Students are instructed to practice the six standard exercises (see above) a minimum of three times a day for between 5 and 20 minutes. Frequent practice allows the student to reach the autogenic state more quickly and therefore benefit from it even at sudden demand. Frequent practice also encourages a more natural interchange between conscious and unconscious processes.

Ideal times for practice are early in the

morning before leaving the house; in the middle of the day, even when there appears to be no time to practice or when there is a shift in activity; and in the evening bèfore going to sleep.

If the evening session is done in bed it should not be terminated in the usual fashion by stretching and moving around to get back into muscle control and breathing. The trainee should just allow himself or herself to go from the autogenic state directly to sleep.

The following structure is recommended should the trainee wish to use Autogenic Training as a problem-solving technique:

In the morning session the trainee looks ahead to the day by allowing priorities to emerge or programming the kind of day he or she would like to experience, thus programming events to fit the expectation.

In the middle of the day at a time of need for rest or where there is a shift in activity, the session is extended to a longer period of time and concentrates mostly on relaxation, allowing anything to emerge that occurs spontaneously, using an interrogatory attitude.

The evening session is used to review the day and to look at any unfinished business, either positive or negative.

All three sessions should include a brief, positive visualization and affirmations that seem relevant.

Autogenic Training can be practiced under adverse conditions once one is firmly established in quiet surroundings.

## APPLICATIONS

Autogenic Training can be practiced by any person who is suggestible, has the motivation to be helped, and has established trust with the practitioner.

To the extent that Autogenic Training is used with the six standard exercises alone it will benefit anyone, since it reduces stress and allows the trainee to induce parasympathetic nervous system control. In practicing Autogenic Training with the first six

standard exercises the trainee will spontaneously achieve other benefits in terms of problem solving, clarity of direction, and overall better access to the unconscious.

Autogenic Training is especially indicated in cases of psychophysiologic illnesses such as headaches, migraines, ulcers, colitis, and aches and pains that have no apparent organic origin, and for clients who suffer from states of anxiety and insecurity. This latter group reports the most rapid positive results.

If trainees use Autogenic Training mostly as a tool for personal development, physiological benefits still occur, and the spontaneous benefits mentioned above are easily evoked and increased through the interrogatory attitude. Autogenic Training is less effective if the client has strong dependency needs and is not yet willing to take responsibility for his or her own life and health.

Psychotic states and certain heart diseases are contraindications for Autogenic Training. It is advised that anyone with a heart problem have permission of the attending physician to participate.

On occasion either the heart or breathing formula is contraindicated and deleted if it produces anxiety in the trainee. It may then be assumed that the remaining exercises and the generalized relaxation reponse will automatically reduce the heart and breathing rate.

## CASE EXAMPLE

My work with Autogenic Training has mostly been with groups and experiential with the exception of occasional blood pressure readings. Therefore, I am restricting myself to reporting verbal feedback on the changes participants experience after they have practiced Autogenic Training over a period of time (anywhere from two weeks to several years).

Most of the persons I have worked with have had previous psychotherapy treatments and use Autogenic Training as a self-help tool to stress management, general well-being, mind expansion, and for continued personal development. The results of using Autogenic Training are expressed most frequently as follows:

1.  A generalized sense of peace even when the training is not actually being practiced.
2.  A greater awareness of body tensions developing and a more rapid way of letting go of them even though the trainee may at that point not choose to practice Autogenic Training.
3.  An increase in frequency and vividness of remembered dreams, and sudden insights that seem to come from the unconscious while the trainee is in a waking state. These insights may occasionally be spiritual in nature.
4.  Problems are solved with less anxiety and, to a certain extent, automatically, with more relaxation and more trust attributed to the belief that the unconscious mind will lead to the resolve of the problem, by drawing from previously unavailable information.
5.  Frequency of headaches, pains, aches, and migraines is greatly reduced and in some cases eliminated. Sufferers from colitis and ulcers report a decrease in symptoms.
6.  Blood pressure frequently drops 10 to 25 percent systolically, 5 to 10 percent diastolically (Schultz & Luthe, 1959; Luthe, 1960).

To summarize the results of extended practice of Autogenic Training: Trainees sense a greater power to cope with both their physical and their emotional problems and find easier access to their mental processes as they train their unconscious to participate and interact increasingly with their conscious minds.

Marie B., age 33, summarizes what is possible with the Autogenic Training method.

Initially she came to learn Autogenic Training to help her cope with the stress resulting from her Ph.D. program in nursing. She was an easy subject to work with as she thoroughly enjoyed the autogenic state and, after being introduced to the standard formulas, was able to induce it quickly.

In the process of working with her over a period of two months, one session per week, the following problems emerged and were subsequently successfully worked through.

Four months prior to her mentioning it she was diagnosed as having a breast lump. The attending physician was not sure whether it was malignant, and based on her age assumed that it was not. However, neither was the lump clearly a fibro-adenoma. It was irregular in shape and had characteristics of several different kinds of lumps. He decided to wait for another two months before taking a biopsy or excising it.

Marie was frightened that it was cancer. She was asked to set her fear aside each day for a few minutes while practicing autogenics and to imagine herself and her health to be stronger than the lump: to imagine dissolving it through the powers of her mind and to have the cells be absorbed by her bloodstream and destroyed by her immune system. Then she was asked to visualize herself healthy, without the breast lump, to hear herself talking to her friends about no longer having it, to feel her breast without the lump, and to bathe herself in a white light.

The lump disappeared within three days. This was confirmed by her physician. Marie was convinced that her practice dissolved the lump, although there is clearly no proof that this indeed was the case.

After one of the sessions Marie reported the following:

I saw myself in my relationship with my husband the way I have experienced my mother: using withdrawal of affection as punishment for not receiving the kind of attention that I wanted. This has been a problem for a while. I have been feeling out of touch with my ability to be a loving person. I have tried very hard to be loving and it has not felt sincere. During this session I visualized myself being loving and then began to experience that love and caring.

The following week she reported that her love had stayed with her for the entire time and that her husband had commented on the difference in her and in their relationship. As of this writing, a couple of months later, Marie has continued to stay in touch with her own lovingness, apparently having eliminated her punitive behavior of the past. She said that even though the awareness was not new, her ability to change her behavior was something that she had not experienced before the internal process during the Autogenic Training session. She felt that she now reowned a part of herself.

Asked for some general comments about the results of her practicing Autogenic Training, in addition to many of the points listed at the beginning of this section, Marie listed the following:

1.  Using the white light around my body whenever needed makes me feel less vulnerable physically.
2.  It is easier for me to focus on my work.
3.  I feel that I have found a structure for a more positive approach to my life that I did not find in the more traditional therapy that I have had.

## SUMMARY

Autogenic Training differs from other therapies in that it is intended as a self-help tool. It is healing to the body, calming to the mind, and plays a major role in disease prevention. Through health affirmations and visualizations it concentrates on well-being and the ability to heal oneself, taking the focus away from Western preoccupation with symptoms.

The unconscious mind is a teacher with limitless resources. It is neither restricted to form or education. There is no way to ever outgrow this teacher.

In the last analysis each person needs to find the answers to his or her own problems. Often the way to resolve one's problems is blocked by consciously held barriers. Au-

togenic Training removes these barriers; the only skills necessary are those of questioning and attentive observation.

Autogenic Training uses a holistic approach and is easily and quickly learned because it utilizes processes that are natural and innate to humans. Last but not least, it is reinforcing because it is a pleasant and painless way to personal development.

## REFERENCES

Jacob, S. W. and Francone, C. A. *Structure and function in man*. Philadelphia: W. B. Saunders, 1974.

Lindemann, H. *Relieve tensions the autogenic way*. New York: Wyden, 1973.

Luthe, W. Physiological and psychodynamic effects of autogenic training. In B. Stokvis (Ed.), *Topical problems of psychotherapy*. New York: S. Jarger, 1960.

Luthe, W. The clinical significance of various forms of autogenic abreaction. In *Proceedings of the Third International Congress of Psychiatry*, Montreal 1961. Toronto: University of Toronto Press, 1962.

Luthe, W. Autogenic training: Method, research, and application in Medicine. in C. T. Tart (Ed.), *Altered states of consciousness*. New York: Wiley, 1969a.

Luthe, W. *Autogenic therapy*. New York: Grune & Stratton, 1969b.

Luthe, W., Jus, A. and Geissmann, P. Autogenic state and autogenic shift: Psychophysiologic and neurophysiologic aspects. *Acta Psychother.*, 1962.

Schultz, J. *Das autogene training*. Stuttgart: Thieme Verlag, 1932.

Schultz, J. and Luthe, W. *Autogenic Training: A psychophysiologic approach in psychotherapy*. New York: Grune & Stratton, 1959.

Schultz, J. and Luthe, W. Autogenic training. In *Proceedings of the Third International Congress of Psychiatry*, Montreal, 1961. Toronto: University of Toronto Press, 1962.

# CHAPTER 6

# *Biofeedback Therapy*

ALBERT G. FORGIONE and REED HOLMBERG

*If, assuming a holistic position relative to psychology, we agree that individuals are essentially unitary and that there is not body and mind, but rather body/mind, the two being aspects of the same thing, then we are monists, and we are forced to say that the mind is the body and the body is the mind. In my judgment, most of us in the field of psychotherapy philosophically are monists but practically are dualists—a contradiction that probably deserves fuller explanation, but this is not the time or place.*

*In any event, in some of the systems here considered, there is emphasis on the body: in Orgone Therapy and in Rebirthing, for example, as well as in other systems concerned with physical relaxation.*

*One of the most important theoretical advances in psychology and medicine has to do with feedback generally and biofeedback specifically. As Forgione states, it is doubtful that Biofeedback will emerge as a full therapy on its own, but there seems to be no question that in the eventual eclectic psychotherapy of the future, when practitioners will be properly trained (as none are today), Biofeedback will be an essential procedure. Eventually also, the doctor of the mind will be a hybrid, knowledgeable about many more things than current practitioners—and much less knowledgeable about things that most practitioners study nowadays.*

Biofeedback is a therapeutic method of forming information loops that allows the patient, the therapist, or both to observe and modify internal psychophysiological events while they are in process. Every biofeedback application involves the amplification (usually electronic) of a physiological event followed by the processing of the amplified signal and the presentation of this information to sense receptors and associated central nervous system networks originally designed for detection of stimuli in the external environment (Figure 1). According to demand characteristics of the therapeutic situation or instruction, the perceived information is either directly modified by the patient or used as a guide for other mediational activity, such as relaxation training, to recondition reactive patterns of physiological activity.

## HISTORY

### Precursors

Self-regulation, the practice of voluntary modification of one's own physiological activity, motor behavior, or conscious processes, has been an endeavor of human beings for ages. It is impossible to date the origin of Zen and yoga meditation. But in this country, biofeedback may be traced to an almost humorous beginning. Bair, in 1901, found that subjects acquired the ability to wiggle their ears only if they received feedback information. His biofeedback instrument was a system of levers and a kymograph (Stoyva, 1978).

In Europe a movement had begun that was to merge years later with this insignificant

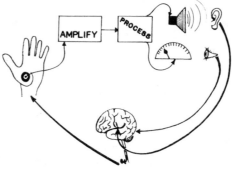

Figure  1

beginning. In 1879 Romain Vigouroux, a disciple of Charcot, commented on the changes in skin resistance in insensitive areas of hysterics. Ten years later Charles Féré reported that the resistance of the skin to the passage of electrical current would vary as a function of cognitive activity and sensory stimulation. Almost simultaneously it was observed that the skin exhibited electrical potentials to mental and external stimulation. This electrodermatological response was initially known as the Tarchanoff reflex after its discoverer, and later, the skin potential response (SPR). However, Féré's method was adoped by American psychologists and was labeled the galvanic skin response (GSR). Only lately has it been appropriately termed the skin resistance response (Venables & Christie, 1973). These early observations of physiological parameters varying in relationship with a psychological condition initiated the emergence of psychophysiology as a discipline of its own.

The turn of the century was a time of great excitement and discovery, relating mental events to body processes on the one hand and to unconscious processes on the other (Ellenberger, 1970). By 1933 Hans Berger reported that the alpha rhythm was blocked by startle. The electroencephalogical investigation of emotion began (Lindsley, 1970). Armed with these tools, psychologists began to add to the body of knowledge relating physiological activity to dimensions of experience. The discipline of psychophysiology had been established.

As early as 1917, Edmond Jacobson (1967) began to apply a technique called progressive relaxation to insomnia and other tension states. Jacobson, a researcher in muscle physiology, proceeded from the point of view that the reduction of proprioceptive impulses from the muscles was associated with and could result in a systemic condition of relaxation. This concept was to later be the rationale for electromyographic (EMG) Biofeedback.

## Beginnings

Biofeedback seemed to burst on the scene in the mid-1960s. Its appearance, however, resulted from the convergence of three directly related disciplines: electrical engineering, learning theory, and psychophysiology. Moreover, Behavior Therapy, as a more active mode of therapy demanding objective validation of behavioral change, was challenging the established, interpretive psychoanalytic therapies. There developed a tendency to more actively involve the patient in his therapy rather than to wait passively for insight to occur. The far-reaching impact of psychophysiology was that private physiological correlates of emotion and mental events were becoming social events with the aid of electronic instrumentation. The therapist could now record and interpret internal events of the patient with a more objective eye and intervene immediately with reinforcement not possible with the more interpretative techniques. The facility of the consciousness of both the patient and the therapist to deny emotional content [due to the crude human interoceptive sensory system (Gannon, 1977) in combination with motivational distortion of perception] was bypassed. Relevant physiological information could now be objectively presented to the finely sensitive exteroceptors. With correlates of emotion being perceived as external events, they were more difficult to deny and more directly subjected to cognitive and conscious strategies.

Before Biofeedback, the attainment of self-knowledge of psychophysiological events and their modification by self-regulation were available only to the yogi who devoted years of self-discipline and meditation to develop interoceptive sensitivity. By combining his technology and knowledge of conditioning, modern humans have extended their potential capabilities beyond those of even the most sophisticated yogi. For example, Basmajian (1963) showed that single motor units could be differentially controlled by EMG feedback.

Following the publication of Basmajian's work, Thomas Budzynski (1979) and Johann Stoyva (1979) developed a technique using EMG feedback for inducing relaxation in the treatment of tension headache. In the middle 1960s the results of operant cardiovascular conditioning experiments with animals appeared in the literature. At the same time correlations began to be published between emotional set, consciousness, and the amount of alpha waves in the electroencephalogram (EEG) of human subjects (Basmajian, 1979). By 1979 there were so many workers in the field that the Biofeedback Research Society was formed (later renamed the Biofeedback Society of America).

In retrospect, probably the first biofeedback device was the human being himself. The early mesmerists were convinced that a magnetic field emanated from the hands to influence cures and induce the crisislike trance. Neurohypnology, later to be known as hypnosis, was a more respectable label for the same phenomenon, albeit that the trance was more somnolent. In these inter-

actions the hypnotist conveys a set or expectancy to the subject, then proceeds to reinforce successive approximations to the posture and relaxed states approaching "sleep" that constitute the definition of "hypnotic state." The hypnotist, subtly and at times unknowingly, is guided in his administration of suggestions, tone of voice, and challenging by the overt motor responses and physiological indicators (breathing rate, muscle tonus, eye roll) that the subject emits. In a similar tradition, a technique called Autogenic Training was developed in which statements of body condition are repeated over and over as the patient searches his body for interoceptive feedback of approximation to the suggested condition (Schultz & Luthe, 1959). Although these two trends in psychology are not directly related to the development of Biofeedback as it is known today, they represent the tradition of behavioral control by reinforcement from which Biofeedback emerged.

## CURRENT STATUS

With the present emphasis on relaxation training and skill training in psychology, Biofeedback in various forms is finding increasing use by psychologists in private practice and hospital settings. The applications are not restricted to those of the Behavior Therapy tradition. Adler and Adler (1979) have reviewed its use in general psychiatry from a tradition of psychodynamic therapy. More medically oriented workers are increasingly applying Biofeedback to caridovascular disorders, rehabilitation, spacticity control, and psychosomatic disorders (Basmajian, 1979). Over the past five years, dental applications of EMG Biofeedback have also begun to appear in the literature (Carlsson, Gale, & Ohman, 1975), and dental school curriculum now includes classes in Biofeedback (Forgione, 1979).

The premature flurry of interest and publicity that alpha feedback caused in the late 1960s has all but died. Although alpha feedback is still used by some clinicians in combination with other techniques to achieve relaxation, other biofeedback techniques find more general use. Listed in order of popularity, electromyographic, electrodermal, thermal, and caridiovascular feedback are used today.

There are numerous state biofeedback societies affiliated with the Biofeedback Society of America. *Biofeedback and Self-Regulation* is the official journal of the society. The society offers numerous courses for professionals at various locations throughout the country each year. Currently, Biofeedback is the topic of increasing interest in Europe. The Annual European Congress of Behavior Therapy, offered extensive biofeedback training courses in 1979 for the first time.

A wide variety of books is available for those wishing to learn about Biofeedback. Since 1972, Aldine Publishing Company (Chicago) has published an annual, edited by leaders in the field. The title is *Biofeedback & Self-Control*. The leading texts are those by Brown (1977), Wickramasekera (1976), and Basmajian (1979). Dental and oral applications are not sufficiently covered in these texts, but the interested reader will find adequate treatment of these topics by Rugh, Perlis, and Disraeli (1977).

## THEORY

Because Biofeedback only recently emerged from its laboratory background, functional relationships are being established in the field. The behavior therapeutic orientation tends to emphasize *that* a technique works and the *degree* to which it works rather than *how* or *why* it works. For example, statements such as "The biofeedback instrument is symbolically in a very special relationship with the patient; it can be seen as a nurturing or withholding mother, connected by an 'umbilical cord' (electrode leads) and responding sensitively to his every shift in feeling" (Adler & Adler, 1979) may allow Biofeedback to be integrated into psychoanalytic

theory, but they add little to the knowledge of change on a behavioral or physiological level.

In order to facilitate understanding of the theoretical bases of biofeedback applications, we will first relate its use to shape lowered arousal states to the established relaxation techniques. Next we will outline the uses of Biofeedback to clarify its meaning. We will then comment upon the theoretical issues that biofeedback use must recognize and the challenge it presents.

From the moment of conception, the cells of the body develop according to a tripartite design: the ectoderm into the neurological system, the mesoderm into the muscles of movement, and the endoderm into the gut and associated glands. This tripartite design is reflected in many ways as one studies psychology. In social psychology, for example, an attitude is defined as an interrelated system of three components (see Schwartz & Shapiro, 1973).

1. *The Cognitive Component:* Beliefs of the individual (evaluative) that attribute good and bad qualities to an object; beliefs about the appropriate or inappropriate ways of responding to an object; and perceptual sets that orient the individual in particular ways to external and internal information such as memory and feelings.

2. *The Action Tendency Component:* Behavorial readiness is associated with the cognitive component: to attack or flee an object associated with a negative attitude, to affiliate with, orient to, reward and support an object associated with a positive attitude.

3. *The Feeling Component:* Emotions or body-marshaling responses of the automatic nervous system are elicited by the object or thoughts of the object.

Lang (1971), recognizing the three body systems, captured the importance of direct, multimodal therapy and the indicated points of application for Biofeedback.

We will need to confine ourselves to measurable behaviors in all systems, and discover the laws that determine their interaction. The data suggest that we must deal with each behavior system [on] its own terms. Thus, a patient who reports anxiety, fails to cope or perform effectively under stress, and evidences autonomic activity that varies widely from the practical energy demands of the situation, needs to receive treatment for all these disorders. He should be administered a treatment directed simultaneously at shaping verbal sets (so as to reduce reported stress over the variety of situations in which it appears), assisted in building effective coping bahaviors and practicing them in appropriate contexts, and finally, administered a program for attenuating autonomic arousal and excessive muscle tonus, with the goal of reducing the distraction and interference of peripheral physiological feedback. In short, psychotherapy should be a vigorous multisystem training program tailored to the unique behavioral topography presented by the patient. (p. 109)

In agreement with Lang, it is fortunate that frequently success in the control of one system eventually appears to result in change throughout the other systems of response. Either by insight, relief from aversive feedback from the autonomic system, or the learning of a new active coping behavior such as assertion, changes in the presenting complaint may occur. However, reinforcement of appropriate levels of functioning in the other two systems may be necessary to ensure durability for the psychological change. In cases where resistance to change occurs, direct modification of the interfering system may be productive. It is an error to assume that the three systems of every patient always act as a coordinated whole.

A concept that influences many treatment strategies in learning-based therapies (and many others as well) is that reduction in the motive state underlying (or consistently evoking) a behavior will facilitate a change in that behavior.

Anxiety is a motive state that does any of the following:

1. Causes discomfort in its physiological expression.

2. Results in dysfunction of organ systems (psychosomatics).

3. Disrupts or distorts cognitive and perceptual functions.

4. Consistently triggers inappropriate sets of overt behaviors or inhibited behaviors (tension).

Any or all of these consequences render the patient feeling powerless in the face of the emotion. Over the years, psychologists have employed relaxation techniques to assist in behavorial change or reduce anxiety levels in patients.

The major relaxation techniques are classified in the tripartite scheme in Figure 2. The basis for classification is the principal target of the relaxation technique. All central techniques involve the focus of perception in a single noncritical way. In this fashion, conflicting thought patterns and emotional tendencies are diminished. Generalized, systemic patterns appropriate to the relaxing suggestion, mantra, or image are then reinforced (Patel, 1977). With the autonomic techniques, the breath patterns are employed to modify emotional reactive patterns both directly (physiologically) and indirectly by focusing the consciousness on maintaining paced patterns as in diaphragmatic breathing or engaging in breathing rituals as in the yogic pranayama (Scholander & Simmons, 1964; Harris et al., 1976). Autogenic training employs focused concentration on suggestions of autonomic modification (the hands warm, the stomach calm) and the concentration of the awareness upon interoceptive sensations of change in the desired direction. Autogenic training has been applied to the other systems (Luthe & Blumberg, 1977). The striated muscles of the somatic-motor systems are the principal focus of modification for the Jacobsonian muscle relaxation, yogic body positions (asana), and hot bath and massage techniques.

Biofeedback applications will be classified according to this scheme in the "Applications" section of this chapter.

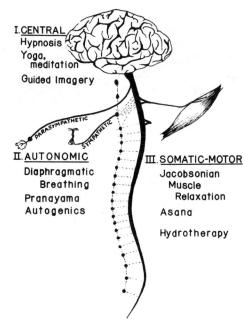

Figure 2

As a psychophysiological method, Biofeedback is particularly suited to assist in emotional change or to help modify the resultants of emotional discharge. It has, however, been employed in at least three different ways by therapists. It will be helpful to outline these uses so that we can focus upon only the important theoretical issues at this stage in its development.

First, as a psychophysiological technique, it can provide a *diagnostic baseline* (Fair, 1979) from which improvement or failure can be measured. In the establishment of the diagnostic baseline, the unique behavioral topography of the patient to stressful events is analyzed. The differential loading of central process (i.e., obsessional thoughts of panic), somatic-motor (tension, muscle spasm, and related symptoms such as dizziness resulting from temporomandibular joint syndrome), or autonomic (racing heart, hyperventilation, sweatiness, hot flushes) systems can be determined by verbal report and correlations with autonomic and EMG readings. The monitoring of the SPR or GSR

concurrent with the administration of a standard fear inventory or a stimulus hierarchy will also reveal the degree of concordance between subjective report and physiological arousal (Katkin & Deitz, 1973).

The second use of Biofeedback is for the benefit of the therapist. Objective physiological data obtained over the period of psychological or behavioral intervention serves as important feedback *to the therapist* in determining the course of analysis or the efficacy of treatment. The therapist can integrate biofeedback information with verbal reports by the patient and his own inference. Because the data are objective, Biofeedback can reduce biased observations of the patient and the therapist. In short, it can provide additional data to make interpretations more robust. The most common application of Biofeedback as a guide to the therapist is in relaxation training. A cue function for the patient is a variation of this second use. As a reinforcement for task performance, feedback information is invaluable *to the patient* in relaxation training either with a specific relaxation technique or in the shaping of low arousal states by sequential criteria (Stoyva, 1979). With more traditional psychotherapy, Sedlacek (1975) and Toomim and Toomim (1975) have reported on the GSR's value in guiding *both the therapist and patient* to relevant content and reducing resistance to threatening material.

The third use of Biofeedback is most familiar to the public: either as a relaxation technique itself or as a method modifying a specific body function directly or indirectly. When the biofeedback application itself is employed as the relaxation technique, it is assumed that reduction of physiological activity in the targeted area and system will result in ''relaxation'' of the other systems of the body. For example, it is currently common to employ frontalis placement EMG in training of relaxation. Muscle feedback relaxation alone shows some promise in treatment conditions such as chronic anxiety (Raskin, Johnson, & Rondestvedt, 1973; Townsend, House, & Addario, 1975). It is reasonable to expect, however, that results would be superior if an autonomic response were employed in addition to EMG in these studies.

There are two major theoretical issues that must be dealt with in biofeedback training.* The first is *what is being trained* and the second is how the learned controls are to be transferred to the patient's everyday life without the benefit of the feedback instrument. The two issues are necessarily intertwined, but it is not necessary to answer the first to establish the necessary and sufficient conditions for the second.

Lazarus (1975) proposed that the self-regulation of somatic disturbances cannot be isolated from the larger context of the person's adaptive interaction with his environment. This adaptive interaction is constantly being mediated by social and psychological processes. In short, Biofeedback should be viewed as one facet in the treatment of the total person. What mediates biofeedback effects will be an open question for some time. Lazarus reviewed some of the possibilities:

1.  The relaxation process could serve as a means of developing attention strategies incompatible with those fixating on the stress-producing sources of tension.
2.  The trained, relaxed psychological state is simply incompatable with tension or chronic arousal.

It is not easy to define relaxation. Often relaxation is operationally defined as a low reading on the one psychophysiological dimension modified. This practice can be misleading since individuals as a group show both stimulus-response *specificity,* the tendency for different stimuli to produce unique patterns of autonomic activity, and response *stereotypy,* an idiosyncratic response pattern to all stimuli (Sternbach, 1966). The use of multiple measures to define relaxation and anxiety states is strongly indicated (Tyrer & Lader, 1976). Using our tripartite scheme, an operational definition of relaxation would have to include an EEG criterion such as the presence of alpha waves, an autonomic criterion such as spontaneous SPR activity within an envelope $\pm 0.3$ mV, and a EMG criterion such as frontalis activity below $3 \mu V$.

Out of recognition of a need to train all body systems in a pattern of relaxation, most recent suggestions for biofeedback training in the clinic include at least two peripheral psychophysiological responses in addition to cognitive strategies (Stoyva, 1979; Fair, 1979).

Epstein and Blanchard (1977) have pointed out that recently emphasis has shifted from the factors that mediate the observed changes in behavior to the factors that are important in continued control. Although a strategy may be learned when feedback is

---

*For the reader interested in the detailed anatomical and physiological basis for Biofeedback, [a chapter] by Wolf (1979) will provide information beyond the scope of this section.

available, it is most important that the patient continue control of the physiologic response when feedback is removed. It has been proposed that feedback training sensitizes the patient to detect sensory changes associated with the criterion values of the physiologic response, but few studies test for this possibility. Self-control is not automatically produced when feedback is removed. Epstein and Blanchard state that self-maintenance is dependent on three factors. First, the patient must be able to discriminate when to impliment self-control procedures. Second, he or she must be able to discriminate changes in physiological activity that indicate success and serve as self-reinforcement, and third, the choice of reinforcer should be appropriate to maintain self-control over long periods of time.

Another issue often neglected in biofeedback research is the higher order learning that contributes to a sense of mastery over emotion or pain. As the patient views a physiological process varying according to some coping strategy he or she employs, the former sense of powerlessness diminishes. In addition, the patient learns that there are degrees to physiological processes and emotion, and that it is possible to discriminate differences in degree. Whether these factors act as organizing influences in the behavioral changes effected by Biofeedback Therapy is yet to be determined. Lazarus (1975) suggests that biofeedback studies provide a powerful tool to resolve the basic psychological questions concerning the modes of self-regulation of emotion that are available to individuals under different environmental contexts. A review of the advances in biofeedback research ten years hence will determine whether this tool was, in fact, wisely used.

An excellent paper by Meichenbaum (1976) discusses the possible role of cognitions in each of the various phases of biofeedback training. The interested reader will find his discussion an excellent amplification of the points made in this chapter.

## METHODOLOGY

There are three critical points in the biofeedback loop pictured in Figure 1 at which artifact or other confounding variables may intrude. The first is the interface between body surface and electrode. This point poses little problem in EMG and the majority of biofeedback applications, but is of major consequence in GSR and SPR applications (see Venables & Christie, 1973). With dry electrodes common in less expensive GSR devices, for example, special care must be taken because pressure variations against the electrode lead to variable contact area, causing resistance to vary independent of skin physiology.

The second point of artifact is the type of electronic instrument used and the processed signal displayed. Again, the electrodermal applications have been the source of some problems. As mentioned earlier, American psychologists opted for the GSR rather than the SPR in their early research. This has led to some confusion. The traditional application of electrodermal monitoring in clinical settings is to use the tonic (base-level) GSR as an index of emotional level so that in relaxation training, the goal is to raise the tonic resistance. However, GSR fluctuates (phasic activity) on this base level either spontaneously or to specific stimuli. Phasic drops in resistance may occur to a number of stimuli or to mental events that are not aversive. It was only recently proposed that the recovery wave of the phasic GSR was diagnostic of aversiveness. Former studies using only the magnitude of the drop in resistance had found mixed results. This led some workers to suggest that electrodermal phasic responses were of little value in the study of anxiety. In light of the recent analysis of the recovery limb of the GSR, these suggestions must be reevaluated along with the earlier negative findings. Had the SPR been used, this confusion might not have resulted.

The SPR is composed of a negative and a positive component. The positive component is monotonically related to increases in noxious stimulation and aversiveness (Raskin, Kotses, & Bever, 1969; Forgione, 1972). Some biofeedback instruments, such as the SPR by Cyborg Corporation, allow the clinician to immediately distinguish between positive and negative components of the SPR. Tonic levels, then, are easily monitored by a simple GSR device. Frequency of response (another index of arousal) may also be measured with this type of instrument. Should any inferences wished to be drawn from phasic activity, however, the SPR or laboratory-quality GSR with paper record must be used. The type of instrument, then affects the information available and the inferences that may be drawn. Another typical problem encountered in the area of what is being monitored and the type of feedback used appears with EMG feedback. Alexander, French, and Goodman (1975) have shown that different effects can be obtained if frontalis EMG feedback is trained with auditory or visual signals. It seems that if the eyes are used, interaction from the muscles of this system can render frontalis area muscle control difficult. With auditory feedback, these muscle systems are not active and feedback signals are more representative of relaxation. This type of research clarifies many methodological issues. For example, Shannon, Goldman, and Lee (1978) compared three feedback techniques in training blood-pressure control. They found the technique that provided the maximal information with the shortest latency to be superior.

The third point of possible artifact in the biofeedback loop, the detection of signal variations and processing of the signal by cortical activity, is most difficult to define and control. In this step, expectancy, set, patient motivation, and instructions are critical variables that can be controlled only in part by the skills of the therapist. For example, Meyers and Craighead (1978) found that instructions significantly affected GSR baselevel. It is within this domain that clinical judgment must be exercised as to whether Biofeedback is to be used as the principal form of therapy or as an adjunct to a broader psychological approach.

The most common psychological biofeedback operation is aimed at modifying chronic states of elevated emotional tone, aversive sensory consequents of the elevated emotional condition in a particular body area (tension headache or racing heart), or the physiological resultant of these states (high blood pressure). Medical operations aim at either rehabilitation of a body function impaired by trauma such as muscle reeducation or modifying neurological states such as epilepsy (see Basmajian, 1979).

Regardless of the instrumentation, the setting requires a comfortable reclining chair in a sound-attenuated room with constant temperature and lighting. A therapist is always present in the early sessions for instruction and coaching. Once patient instruction has occurred, the patient can usually manage his own sessions or be minimally supervised by a technician. Obtained values are always charted so that an objective record of progress is available. Response rates may also be tallied in an automated fashion with more sophisticated systems. With the advent of more inexpensive GSR and EMG portable devices, home practice with instruments on loan is finding greater popularity. Home care offers many advantages, not the least of which is that it requires the patient to take the time out of his or her day to practice in a setting that may have many cues of arousal.

During the first office session, it is customary to give the patient a rationale for using relaxation training in the treatment program. The therapist then usually explains the role of Biofeedback, applying the instrument to himself to demonstrate its use and desensitize the patient to electronic instrumentation. The first session usually ends with an audio tape being made for the patient to use to practice relaxation at home before the next scheduled session.

Because of variations in the physiological expression of response to stress among patients, the second session is usually devoted to obtaining a physiological profile (Fair, 1979) to assess stability or lability of at least two response systems under rest and moderate stress. Some individuals, for example, show maximum response to stress in the somatic-motor system while others show predominantly autonomic responsivity. Still others will show combined somatic-motor and autonomic responses. Based upon this information, the therapist will select a sequence of instrument applications to teach the patient control of his or her response to stressors (Stoyva, 1979). To assist in the assessment of somatic-motor tension locations in the body, the Davicon Corporation has developed a dual-channel EMG device. Rather than requiring electrode paste and adhesive discs, the electrodes themselves contain miniature amplifiers. This innovation allows instantaneous readings to be taken with dry electrodes and permits multiple test sites to be measured in a short period of time. Often, guided by EMG feedback, the patient can be shown that simple postural changes will significantly reduce tension levels in the body.

Although it has been customary to employ only one feedback instrument to one body system (either GSR or EMG frontalis), the use of multiple instruments providing feedback for at least two body systems is finding greater popularity (Naliboff & Johnson, 1978). For example, one technique that has been employed at our facility over the past five years is SPR-contingent EMG biofeedback training. Temporomandibular joint patients are treated for facial pain resulting from tension in the muscles of the jaw, a common source of headache also called the myofascial pain dysfunction syndrome (Laskin, 1969). The technique was devised to allow immediate detection of those patients who "do combat" with the EMG device. This technique is based upon the assumption that sympathetic arousal both impedes the learning process and blocks fine internal per-

ception. It later became apparent that the technique facilitated EMG training even in those patients who were positively motivated. The patient is instructed to reduce SPRs until responses of less than $\pm 0.5$ mV occur. The trigger of the feedback device is set to produce silence for responses of this magnitude. As long as the SPR feedback is silent, attention can be devoted to frontalis EMG reduction. If GSR feedback is employed, EMG training occurs only in the presence of decreasing conductance levels (increasing resistance). In this manner arousal states that might interfere with relaxation training are immediately brought to the patient's attention.

EMG feedback training continues until the patient can reliably maintain frontalis muscle tension at or below $2\mu V$ for extended periods of time. At that time attention is usually devoted to strengthening coping behaviors to extend the gains made in the clinic to real life and protect the new levels of emotional behavior.

## APPLICATIONS

Specific biofeedback applications are classified in Figure 3 according to the tripartite scheme used for relaxation techniques discussed earlier. The principal forms of EEG feedback for central process modification are alpha, theta, and sensorimotor rhythm (Sterman, MacDonald, & Stone, 1974; Brown, 1977; Ancoli & Kamiya, 1978). For autonomic modification, SPR and GSR are the electrodermal applications while heart rate (HR) and blood pressure (BP) are general cardiovascular applications. Blood volume (BV) and the longer delayed skin temperature (TEMP) are autonomic applications that may be used for relaxation or in the treatment of migraine (head and hand locations) and Raynaud's disease. Since the autonomic system affects numerous body sites, a variety of biofeedback applications may be used to monitor its activity. Generally, the electrodermatological instruments are used in relax-

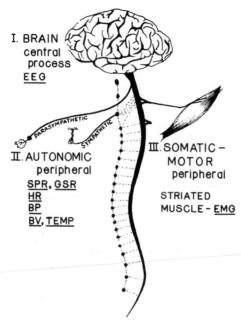

I. BRAIN
central
process
EEG

II. AUTONOMIC
peripheral
SPR, GSR
HR
BP
BV, TEMP

III. SOMATIC –
MOTOR
peripheral

STRIATED
MUSCLE – EMG

PARASYMPATHETIC

SYMPATHETIC

Figure  3

ation training for short delay of reinforcement applications, and finger temperature is used for longer delay applications. For general relaxation training, frontalis EMG feedback is the most popular (Budzynski, 1979). It must be remembered that the frontalis placement of feedback electrodes provides an index of numerous muscle groups of the head (e.g., temporalis, corrugator, and eye muscles among others).

Biofeedback has been applied to so many specific problems that they cannot be exhaustively summarized herein. We will only highlight the most successful applications that have received the bulk of research attention in the past several years. The order of our review will be determined by our evaluation of frequency of clinical application during this period.

In 1974 Blanchard and Young critically reviewed the clinical applications of Biofeedback to that date. The reviewers were impressed with the rapid results of direct muscle feedback in the treatment of hemiplegia, which was refractory to traditional neuromuscular rehabilitation. The evidence

at that time also strongly supported the use of EMG feedback for the elimination of tension headache and of subvocal speech while reading. By 1974 only one study using EMG to assist relaxation training (Raskin, Johnson, & Rondestvedt, 1973) was worthy of note by these reviewers. Interestingly, in that study reports of anxiety were not diminished, but relief of anxiety-mediated symptoms such as tension headache and insomnia did occur. The negative finding substantiates Lang's statement, cited earlier, that the perception of anxiety and the verbal patterns of reporting must also be given therapeutic attention. All systems do not necessarily spontaneously change with change in one body system.

By 1976 Hutchings and Reinking reported that EMG-assisted relaxation procedures were the method of choice for the treatment of tension headache when compared to autogenic-relaxation training. Currently, in the treatment of tension headache, EMG feedback is the most firmly established of all biofeedback applications for problems that involve a psychological etiology (Budzynski, 1978, 1979; Scott, 1979). Direct muscle Biofeedback is also firmly established in physical medicine and rehabilitation (Fernando & Basmajian, 1978; Basmajian, 1979).

The Biofeedback Society of America published a series of reports in 1978 (Stoyva, 1978) to address the issues of accountability and a sound research basis for clinical applications. In this series of reports are summarized the principal applications of Biofeedback: (1) psychophysiologic disorders, (2) vasoconstrictive syndromes, (3) gastrointestinal disorders, (4) vascular headache, (5) muscle-contraction headache and (6) dysfunctions in the domain of physical medicine and rehabilitation.

The general findings of these reports (tension headache was cited above) were that for vascular headache, temperature and EMG feedback alone or in combination may be more therapeutic than EEG alpha feedback. Research, however, is still needed to ascertain how biofeedback and relaxation techniques can be most effectively combined. Peripheral vasoconstrictive syndromes have received some attention using blood volume and temperature feedback. A review article published after the Task Force Reports will be of value to the reader interested in Raynaud's disease (Sappington, Fiorito, & Brehony, 1979).

An area of intense current research is heart rate and blood pressure feedback. Although it does not seem to be a widely used application among clinicians, it may soon be as demand from the medical community increases. There are many complex issues in this area of Biofeedback. Williamson and Blanchard (1979), in a pair of articles, review these issues and the results of research published since 1972.

An application gaining increasing interest from psychologists is temporomandibular joint pain (Laskin, 1969; Carlsson, Gale, & Ohman, 1975; Rugh, Perlis, & Disraeli, 1977; Fernando & Basmajian, 1978). The diagnostic classification is misleading because pain arising from the interaction of personality style, stress, and occlusal disharmony can cause a variety of physical reactions other than jaw-joint pain (unilateral head pain, dizziness, nausea, neck pain, arm and upper back pain, for example) that are stress related and may reinforce neurotic behavior patterns. EMG and relaxation training are the principal behavioral treatments. It is interesting to note that Schwartz, Greene, and Laskin (1979) found the Minnesota Multiphasic Personality Inventory (MMPI) profile of patients suffering from temporomandibular joint pain to be similar to the MMPI profile of low-back-pain patients. Patients with significantly elevated scores were nonresponsive to treatment. Gessel (1975) had predicted that with increasing severity of the pain syndrome, broader therapeutic approaches would be necessary to treat associated depression. Nouwen and Solinger (1979) found that in the EMG feedback treatment of low-back-pain patients, improvement with feedback must be protected by training self-control in daily life.

In the majority of biofeedback applications, control of targeted physiological processes and relief from discomfort have been clearly demonstrated. Workers in the field must now apply their attention to integrating their treatment with existing therapies or devising treatment strategies of their own to promote self-control outside the clinic. In addition, attention must be given to treating other emotional states. Although anxiety and related behaviors have been found to be very responsive to feedback applications, depression has been found to be rather refractory. For example, Biofeedback has been effective with sleep-onset insomnia, but early-waking insomnia, consistent with depression, has not been successfully treated. Depression often accompanies stress-related disorders of long standing. It was seen early as a complicating factor in the treatment of temporomandibular joint pain (Gessel, 1975) and migraine. Often drug dependency is also a factor in disorders of long standing. Diamond and Franklin (1975) treated 119 drug-habituated patients with combined TEMP and EMG feedback and found improvement in only 48 patients. Multimodal therapy may hold promise for these more severely afflicted, resistant patients. For the present, however, Biofeedback has the advantage that, as a short-term, specific therapy, it can be applied to a large number of patients. Patients refractory to this initial screening may then be assigned to the more time-consuming therapeutic approaches.

## CASE EXAMPLE

A single, 28-year-old female nurse presented complaints of constant unilateral headache that at times involved her neck, shoulder, and upper back. There were periods of nausea and excessive pain while chewing, which seriously affected her diet. Repeated medical examinations produced negative findings. She reported being tense and almost constantly frustrated with her inability to express herself. She was quiet and constantly avoided eye contact during the first three hours of assessment. She had been treated with Valium (15–25 mg./day) with some success after a dentist had ground her teeth down in an attempt to treat her. Paper-and-pencil tests verified the clinical impression that the patient was hypersocialized, hypervigilant, obsessive, and compulsive about ordering her environment. She was both anxious and depressed. She lived in an apartment, one floor above her controlling mother and explosive, alcoholic father. The fear of social contact with males interacted with her nausea, severely limiting her social life. Superficial muscular observations revealed that the muscles of the right side of her face, jaw, and shoulder were painful to touch. Bilateral EMG analysis with surface electrodes showed disproportionately elevated readings on the right side. Episodes of day and nocturnal teeth clenching followed difficult days at work or with the family. These episodes led to sharp increases in pain upon awakening.

The treatment strategy was formulated to aim initially for relief of the pain resulting from her temporomandibular joint problem. The nausea was tentatively seen as being related to her oral problem. It was expected that once this diminished, her eating habits would improve. When these basic problems were under reasonable control, it was planned that the broader issues could be approached therapeutically.

A soft vinyl night guard was fabricated by a dentist to minimize the traumatic effects of her nocturnal clenching behavior. (The dentist was discouraged from grinding down her dentition further, since equilibration of dentition with muscles in spasm might have further complicated her conditon.)

Five 20-minute sessions of bilateral EMG feedback of masseter muscle activity combined with training in diaphragmatic breathing resulted in a 50 percent reduction of pain intensity ratings. Working in cooperation with the dentist, a plastic mouthplate was then constructed (Gelb, 1977) and equilibrated with the aid of bilateral EMG feedback to give balance to the muscles of jaw closure.

At that time relaxation training, guided by GSR feedback, was initiated. It immediately became apparent that the patient would allow herself to relax only to a point at which she could still maintain awareness of her environment. As the GSR base level (resistance) increased, there would occur immediate drops in resistance. In an almost stepwise fashion, the increase in resistance would occur to a point, followed by a large drop. Upon questioning, the patient revealed that she was afraid to "let go and relax." She was then assured that she could use the GSR as a guide to let go in little steps to prove to herself that she would not lose control. With this titrated approach, she gradually desensitized herself to relaxation. Interestingly, once she was assured that she had some control and had demonstrated it to herself using the GSR signal, she abreacted feelings of anger at her father. The resurgence of muscular pain that followed subsided over the next two weeks with the help of EMG biofeedback training. Thereafter, pain reports reflected a reduction to 25 percent of original levels and the nausea did not reoccur. With changed diet and increasing involvement in relaxation exercises, her interpersonal communication skills improved. Assertion training was then combined with the relaxation training to protect her gains. Bilateral EMG levels were stabilized at low equal levels and pain-free days began to occur two months into treatment. Within six months she had moved from her parents' house, pain free. She was referred to a psychotherapist to obtain support during her transition to independent life and to further resolve her conflicting feelings about her parents and herself. A one-year follow-up indicated that she was dating and profiting from her psychotherapy. The mouthplate was worn only when she felt tension beginning in her jaw muscles (one hour per week on the average). She remained pain free with the exception of two minor episodes of pain, which were of short duration.

## SUMMARY

The case example reveals the interdisciplinary nature of Biofeedback Therapy. Although not all applications are as complex as the case reported, it should be clear that a great number of patients seeking psychotherapy or medical treatment present a complex of interrelated problems that may not be adequately treated by one discipline alone. It is doubtful that Biofeedback will emerge as a therapy on its own, but its influence may result in expansion of existing therapeutic approaches. At present it is most comfortable in the camp of the behavior therapies that gave it birth, but the dynamic and phenomenological therapies may soon find uses for this new modality. For it holds a promise of contributing a dimension of objectivity to those, more traditional, therapies forced by lack of technological advances at the time of their development to rely mainly upon inference and verbal analysis.

Biofeedback carries a message that has far-reaching implications for psychotherapy. The therapist and the patient must recognize and deal with the body and its involvement in thought and emotion. The body processes, once the domain of medicine, have already begun to be subsumed under the disciplines of behavioral medicine and psychology. Hopefully, cooperation rather than territorial confrontation will take place as psychology and medicine coverage with the advancement of knowledge.

## REFERENCES

Adler, C. S. and Adler, S. M. Strategies in general psychiatry. In J. V. Basmajian (Ed.), *Biofeedback—principles and practice for clinicians*. Baltimore: Williams & Wilkins, 1979.

Alexander, A. B., French, C. A. and Goodman, N. J. A comparison of auditory and visual feedback in biofeedback assisted muscular relaxation training. *Psychophysiology*, 1975, **12**, 119–123.

Ancoli, S. and Kamiya, J. Methodological issues in alpha biofeedback training. *Biofeedback and Self-Regulation*, 1978, **3**, 159–183.

Bair, J. H. Development of voluntary control. *Psychological Review*, 1901, **8**, 474–510.

Basmajian, J. V. Conscious control of individual motor units. *Science*, 1963, **141**, 440–441.

Basmajian, J. V. Introduction: Principles and background. In J. V. Basmajian (Ed.), *Biofeedback—principles and practice for clinicians*. Baltimore: Williams & Wilkins, 1979.

Blanchard, E. B. and Young, L. D. Clinical applications of biofeedback training: A review of evidence. *Archives of General Psychiatry*, 1974, **30**, 573–589.

Brown, B. B. *Stress and the art of biofeedback*. New York: Harper & Row, 1977.

Budzynski, T. H. Biofeedback in the treatment of muscle-contraction (tension) headache. *Biofeedback and Self-Regulation*, 1978, **3**, 409–434.

Budzynski, T. H. Biofeedback strategies in headache treatment. In J. V. Basmajian (Ed.), *Biofeedback—principles and practice for clinicians*. Baltimore: Williams & Wilkins, 1979.

Carlsson, Sven G., Gale, Elliot N. and Ohman, Alf. Treatment of temporomandibular joint syndrome with biofeedback training. *Journal of the American Dental Association*, 1975, **91**, 602–605.

Diamond, S. and Franklin, M. Autogenic training and biofeedback in treatment of chronic headache problems in adults. In W. Luthe and F. Antonelli (Eds.), *Therapy in psychosomatic medicine.* Proceedings of the 3rd Congress of the International College of Psychosomatic Medicine, Rome, 1975.

Ellenberger, H. F. *The discovery of the unconscious.* New York: Basic Books, 1970.

Epstein, L. H. and Blanchard, E. B. Biofeedback, self-control and self-management. *Biofeedback and Self-Regulation,* 1977, **2**, 201–211.

Fair, P. L. Biofeedback strategies in psychotherapy. In J. V. Basmajian (Ed.), *Biofeedback—principles and practice for clinicians.* Baltimore: Williams & Wilkins, 1979.

Fernando, C. K. and Basmajian, J. V. Biofeedback in physical medicine and rehabilitation. *Biofeedback and Self-Regulation,* 1978, **3**, 435–455.

Forgione, A. G. Human discriminated avoidance and associated electrophysiological behaviors under schedules with different contingency probabilities. *Dissertation Abstracts,* 1972, **33(4)** (order no. 72-25273; 398 pages).

Forgione, A. G. Psychology and psychostomatology. Paper delivered at the 9th European Congress of Behavior Therapy. Paris, 1979.

Gannon, L. The role of interoception in learned visceral control. *Biofeedback and Self-Regulation,* 1977, **2**, 337–347.

Gelb, H. *Clinical management of head, neck and TMJ dysfunction.* Philadelphia: W. B. Saunders, 1977.

Gessel, A. H. Electromyographic biofeedback and tricyclic antidepressants in myofascial pain-dysfunction syndrome: Psychological predictors of outcome. *Journal of the American Dental Association,* 1975, **91**, 1049.

Harris, V. A., Katkin, E. S., Lick, J. R. and Habberfield, T. Paced respiration as a technique for the modification of autonomic response to stress. *Psychophysiology,* 1976, **13**, 386–391.

Hutchings, D. F. and Reinking, R. H. Tension headaches: What form of therapy is most effective? *Biofeedback and Self-Regulation,* 1976, **2**, 183–190.

Jacobson, E. *Biology of emotions.* Springfield, Ill.: Charles C Thomas, 1967.

Katkin, E. S. and Deitz, S. R. Systematic desensitization. In W. F. Prokasy and D. C. Raskin (Eds.), *Electrodermal activity in psychological research.* New York: Academic Press, 1973.

Lang, P. The application of psychophysiological methods to the study of psychotherapy and behavior modification. In A. E. Bergin and S. L. Garfield (Eds.), *Handbook of psychotherapy and behavior change.* New York: Wiley, 1971.

Laskin, D. M. Etiology of the pain-dysfunction syndrome. *Journal of the American Dental Association,* 1969, **79**, 147.

Lazarus, R. S. A cognitively oriented psychologist looks at biofeedback. *American Psychologist,* 1975, **30**, 553–561.

Lindsley, D. B. The role of nonspecific reticuo-thalamo-cortical systems in emotion. In P. Black (Ed.), *Physiological correlates of emotion.* New York: Academic Press, 1970.

Luthe, W. and Blumberg, S. R. Autogenic therapy. In E. D. Wittkower and H. Warnes (Eds.), *Psychosomatic medicine: Its clinical applications.* Hagerstown, MD: Harper & Row, 1977.

Meichenbaum, D. Cognitive factors in biofeedback therapy. *Biofeedback and Self-Regulation.* 1976, **1**, 201–216.

Meyers, A. W. and Craighead, W. E. Adaptation periods in psychophysiological research. *Behavior Therapy,* 1978, **9**, 355–362.

Naliboff, B. D. and Johnson, H. J. Finger pulse amplitude and frontalis EMG biofeedback effects of single- and two-system training. *Biofeedback and Self-Regulation,* 1978, **3**, 133–143.

Nouwen, A. and Solinger, J. W. The effectiveness of EMG biofeedback training in low back pain. *Biofeedback and Self-Regulation,* 1979, **4**, 103–111.

Patel, C. H. Biofeedback-aided relaxation and meditation in the management of hypertension. *Biofeedback and Self-Regulation,* 1977, **2**, 1–41.

Raskin, M., Johnson, G. and Rondestvedt, J. W. Chronic anxiety treated by feedback-induced muscle relaxation. *Archives of General Psychiatry,* 1973, **28**, 263–267.

Raskin, D. C., Kotses, H. and Bever, J. Autonomic indicators of orienting and defensive reflexes. *Journal of Experimental Psychology,* 1969, **80**, 423–433.

Rugh, J. D., Perlis, D. B. and Disraeli, R. I., (Eds.). *Biofeedback in dentistry: Research and clinical applications.* Phoenix: Semantodontics, 1977.

Sappington, J. T., Fiorito, E. M. and Brehony, K. A. Biofeedback as therapy in Raynaud's disease. *Biofeedback and Self-Regulation,* 1979, **4**, 155–169.

Scholander, T. and Simmons, R. A conditioning procedure to increase the influence of the respiratory cycle upon electrodermal activity. *Journal of Psychosomatic Research,* 1964, **7**, 295–300.

Schultz, J. H. and Luthe, W. *Autogenic training.* New York: Grune & Stratton, 1959.

Schwartz, G. E. and Shapiro, D. Social psychophysiology. In W. F. Prokasy and D. C. Raskin (Eds.), *Electrodermal Activity in Psychological Research.* New York: Academic Press, 1973.

Schwartz, R. A., Greene, C. S. and Laskin, D. M. Personality characteristics of patients with myofascial pain-dysfunction (MPD) syndrome unresponsive to conventional therapy. *Journal of Dental Research,* 1979, **58**, 1435.

Scott, D. S. A comprehensive treatment strategy for muscle contraction headaches. *Journal of Behavior Therapy and Experimental Psychiatry*, 1979, **10**, 35–40.

Sedlacek, K. "GSR biofeedback in clinical practice (Tape T23)." Biomonitoring Applications, 270 Madison Avenue, New York, NY, 1975.

Shannon, B. J., Goldman, M. S. and Lee, R. M. Biofeedback training of blood pressure: A comparison of three feedback techniques. *Psychophysiology*, 1978, **15**, 53–59.

Sterman, M. B., MacDonald, L. R. and Stone, R. K. Biofeedback training of the sensorimotor electroencephalogram rhythm in man: Effects on epilepsy. *Epilepsia*, 1974, **15**, 395–416.

Sternbach, R. A. *Principles of psychophysiology.* New York: Academic Press, 1966.

Stoyva, J. Editorial. *Biofeedback and Self-Regulation,* 1978, **3**, 329.

Stoyva, J. M. Guidelines in the training of general relaxation. In J. V. Basmajian (Ed.), *Biofeedback—principles and practice for clinicians.* Baltimore: Williams & Wilkins, 1979.

Toomim, M. K. and Toomim, H. GSR biofeedback in psychotherapy: Some clinical observations. *Psychotherapy: Theory, Research and Practice,* 1975, **12,(1)**, 33–38.

Townsend, R. E., House, J. F. and Addario, D. A comparison of biofeedback-mediated relaxation and group therapy in the treatment of chronic anxiety. *American Journal of Psychiatry,* 1975, **132**, 598–601.

Tyrer, P. J. and Lader, M. H. Central and peripheral correlates of anxiety: A comparitive study. *Journal of Nervous and Mental Disease,* 1976, **162**, 99–104.

Venables, P. H. and Christie, M. J. Mechanisms, instrumentation, recording techniques and quantification of responses. In W. F. Prokasy and D. C. Raskin (Eds.), *Electrodermal activity in psychological research.* New York: Academic Press, 1973.

Vigouroux, R. Sur le rôle de la résistance électrique des tissus dans l'électrodiagnostic. *Société de Biologie comptes rendus des séances,* 1879, **31**, 336–339.

Wickramasekera, I., (Ed.). *Biofeedback, behavior therapy and hypnosis: Potentiating the verbal control of behavior for clinicians.* Chicago: Nelson-Hall, 1976.

Williamson, D. A. and Blanchard, E. B. Heart rate and blood pressure feedback I. A review of recent experimental literature. II. A review and integration of recent theoretical models. *Biofeedback and Self-Regulation,* 1979, **4**, 1–50.

Wolf, S. L. Anatomical and physiological basis for biofeedback. In J. V. Basmajian (Ed.), *Biofeedback—principles and practice for clinicians.* Baltimore: Williams & Wilkins, 1979.

# CHAPTER 7

# Body Therapies

BARRY GREEN

*My own biases are such that I have trouble accepting Body Therapies as psychotherapies except through indirection. Here's what I mean: If someone massages me, and if I am convinced that that person is acting because of his or her feeling about me, then it is my perception of the actions that can affect me rather than the actions themselves. Thus, if we could imagine a robot that would give exactly the same manipulations that Body Therapist Dr. Milton Trager would do, the person being massaged would feel good because of the manipulation; however, if a human performed the massage, the recipient would feel good as well as cared for, important, valuable. I was given a short "tragerizing" session and realize that it was the intimacy of the contact rather than the mere physical contact that was important to me.*

*I believe that the beneficial effects of Body Therapies are not completely explained by contact of body to body. In the case example, in Barry Green's excellent chapter, we find that the first five sessions were a kind of "icebreaker" through massage, but in the sixth conventional cognitive psychotherapy took over.*

*Instead of using this fact—that conventional psychotherapy eventually played a major part in Body Therapies—to negate the utility of Body Therapies, it should be recognized that perhaps they are important because they may defeat the common enemy all we therapists have—resistance. It may be that the laying-on of hands works to break through the patient's resistance. If so, these body contacts have value.*

Body Therapy is a process for creating a clarification of the body-mind-emotions-spirit through techniques applied to or learned by the body. Body Therapy encompasses both ancient Eastern traditions of spirituality and cosmology along with contemporary Western neuromuscular and myofascial systems of skeletostructural and neuro-skeleto reorganization. Body Therapy recognizes that the entire body is the vehicle for the Perfect Being that lies within all. This is the meaning of the Chinese concept Su Wen ("Perfect channel")—when there is no trauma in the body or the psyche, then the Being that is the human birthright manifests itself. Body Therapy postulates that the traumas absorbed by the psyche from "false un-

derstanding" are simultaneously absorbed as traumas in specific areas of the body. Body Therapy works to facilitate clarification of these traumas through the use of physical manipulations, movement awareness training, energy-flow balancing, and emotional release techniques.

## HISTORY

The history of Body Therapy dates back to the formation of Eastern culture. There are records of the ancient Chinese and Mongolians using body-oriented therapies for achieving physical and psychological well-being. Ancient Indians and Tibetans practiced numerous forms of "yogas" for the purification of the body-mind-emotions-spirit. The Japanese and Chinese developed the martial arts for both defense and for personal evolution of the Inner Self. These body-psyche disciplines and "yogas" such as Tai Chi, Zen, Taoism, Tantra, and Samurai that have existed for more than 400 years are still an integral part of the societies and cultures from which they arose.

The Eastern traditions put forth the concept that the human being was a reflection, a mirror, of the cosmos. The macrocosm seen outside of man was the same as the microcosm found inside of man. Just as the ancient scientists and sages plotted out the external natural phenomena, they also plotted out the internal natural phenomena. The Chinese described this internal map as the Acupuncture system of energy paths known as meridians of *Chi* energy. The Tibetans and Indians described another flow of internal energy they call *Kundalini* that rose up in two channels on either side of the spine and activated focal points of body-psyche energy called *Chakras*. All the ancient systems described the effects of balance or imbalance, flow or restriction; they all prescribed techniques, exercises, and therapeutic methods for achieving the optimal condition of body-mind-emotion-spirit. This optimal condition would achieve total harmony for the individual, total unity within himself and with his surroundings, Nature. The ancients saw this optimal condition as the state of Enlightenment, Self-Realization. They called this state *samahdi, nirvana,* the tau, and *fana.*

This concept as the body being the vehicle for the body-mind-emotions-spirit reached the West with the Hellenistic Greeks. "Sound mind, sound body" was the axiom for the Hellenistics. Though not as internally oriented as the Orientals, the Greeks paid homage to the body and its unity with the mind. The body was recognized as a part of the being until the coming of the Victorian era, when the body was viewed as being disgraceful. It was covered, considered im-

moral, and discarded as a "vehicle" for awareness and growth.

It was not until the age of science that the body was again used as a method for unifying the being. In the beginning of the twentieth century Wilhelm Reich observed that clinical patients with emotional disturbances all demonstrated severe postural distortions. His observations uncovered more connections between the body-psyche and led to the development fo the Reichian school of Body Therapy. Reich's observations were the foundation for his system of character analysis and therapeutic method known as Vegetotherapy. The muscular holding patterns Reich called character armor. The armor was manifest in one or more of seven rings occurring in horizontal planes from the head to the pelvis. Every armored area blocked the flow of vital energy, or *orgone*. To break up the armoring would directly affect and change the neurotic character and body structure.

Following Reich came another pioneer in the field of Body Therapy, Moshe Feldenkrais. Feldenkrais postulated that the human organism began its process of growth and learning with only one built-in response, the "fear of falling." All other physical and emotional responses were learned as the human organism grew and explored. As the child grew he learned how to function physically and learned any concomitant emotions that accompanied the event or the physical learning. As Feldenkrais (1949) stated:

Thus many of our failings both physical and mental need not be considered as diseases to be cured, or as unfortunate traits of character. They are acquired from faulty learning. Actions repeated habitually for a number of years mold even the bones. (p. 152)

To attain the full potential of the body-mind-emotions-spirit there must be, according to Feldenkrais (1949), "re-education of the kinesthetic sense and resetting of it to the normal course of self adjusting improvement of all muscular activity" (p. 155). This would "directly improve breathing, digestion, and the sympathetic and parasympathetic balance, as well as the sexual function, all linked together with the emotional experience" (p. 156). For Feldenkrais, reeducation of the body and its functioning was the essence for creating unity of the being.

Following the work of Reich and Feldenkrais came the contemporary schools and systems of Body Therapy. These include the deep fascial tissue manipulations performed by those of the Rolf school, the emotional release work of Primal Therapy and Rebirthing, and the movement work of Matthias Alexander, Judith Aston, Milton Trager, and Oscar Aguado.

## CURRENT STATUS

Body Therapies are now a rapidly growing system. There are an indeterminate number of practitioners in the varying special schools and combined approaches. What was once a "new age" approach to health and well-being of the body-psyche is now becoming a part of the mainstream. Rolfing^sm has become a nationally known system; the Eastern body-psyche disciplines such as Yoga, Aikido, and Tai Chi Chuan are increasingly more popular; and Acupuncture is now a part of many Western medical practices.

Many schools of varying size and prominence exist, as well as many publications in the four areas of Body Therapy: physical manipulation, movement awareness training, energy-flow balancing, and emotional release techniques. This chapter will describe the current status of some of the major institutes in these four areas.

In the area of physical manipulations, the Rolf Institute operates its only training facility out of Boulder, Colorado. At the time of publication, 212 certified practitioners were listed by the institute. The Rolf process has been described in the two books by Ida Rolf, *Rolfing* (1977) and *Ida Rolf Speaks* (1978) and in Don Johnson's book, *The Protean Body* (1977). A quarterly bulletin, *The*

*Bulletin of Structural Integration,* is available along with cassettes, films, and magazine reprints from the Rolf Institute.* Other schools offering deep tissue-physical manipulations are Postural Integration^sm, the Soma^sm Institute, Orthasomatics^sm, the Institute of Psycho-Structural Balancing^sm, the Lomi School, and the Arica Institute, Inc.

In the area of movement awareness training, the Feldenkrais technique has approximately 75 practitioners trained by Moshe Feldenkrais. The theoretical foundations of the work are explained in Feldenkrais's book, *Body and Mature Behavior,* (1949), and techniques of the system are given in his *Awareness Through Movement* (1972). Other publications include *The Case of Nora* by Feldenkrais (1977), *Somatics Magazine,* and a soon-to-be released basic manual. The main school is located in Israel; the American branch, the Feldenkrais Guild, is located in San Francisco. The Aston-Patterning™, process of movement awareness, lists 33 practitioners and offers training courses. The Trager Psychophysical Integration process is currently operating with approximately 400 practitioners. The work is taught by Dr. Milton Trager and a small staff of qualified teachers at various locations around the country and abroad. For information about trainings or certified practitioners, contact the Trager Association. The Aguado system of movement awareness, known as "the Form," is taught by Oscar Aguado and a small staff of qualified teachers at various locations throughout the country. Teacher training is scheduled to begin in the fall of 1980. Two books are available by Aguado, *The Form* and *Gravity, the Nether Side of Paradise* (1978).

In the area of energy-flow balancing, two of the major schools associated with Chinese and Indian systems of energy balancing are the New England School of Acupuncture and the Polarity Institute—Alive Fellowship. In this country, the oldest licensed school teach-

---

*Addresses of these various training institutes are to be found in the appendix.

ing Chinese systems of energy balancing is the New England School of Acupuncture. At the time of writing there were approximately 120 graduates of the school. Three unpublished works, available only through the school, by the principal instructor, Dr. James Tin Yau So are featured. The Indian system of energy balancing is taught by the Polarity Institute—Alive Fellowship. The fellowship offers residential programs of one, seven, and nine weeks along with individual and group trainings in Santa Barbara, San Francisco, and Seattle. At the time of writing 129 people had completed the practitioner level of training with the fellowship. The fellowship utilizes the three main works of its founder, Dr. Randall Stone: The *Energy, Vitality Balance,* and *Polarity Therapy.* Tapes and pamphlets are available as well as free brochures and a bimonthly newsletter.

In the area of emotional release the International Bioenergetics Institute, with its headquarters in New York City, lists 40 certified practitioners. Besides the main headquarters, numerous training facilities are located throughout the country and abroad. A bulletin, "Energy and Character," is published in England. Numerous books on Bioenergetics have been published by Alexander Lowen. These include *Bioenergetics* (1975a), *Depression and the Body* (1972), *The Language of the Body* (1958), *Pleasure* (1970), *The Betrayal of the Body* (1969), and *Love and Orgasm* (1975b). Another method of emotional release is the Rebirthing process. The Theta House of San Francisco offers Rebirthing training at three levels. At the time of writing, there were 10 to 12 certified practitioners. Rebirthing is described in the work of Leonard Orr and Sandra Ray, *Rebirthing in the New Age* (1977). Along with this work and free brochures, a monthly newsletter is also published.

In addition to the various training courses listed above, a state-approved degree program emphasizing Body Therapy is now available through the University for Humanistic Studies in San Diego. At the time of

this writing the state had given full approval to the bachelor and master of arts programs in counseling psychology with an emphasis in Body Therapy. This program meets the marriage, family, and child counseling license requirements for the state of California. This program is held in conjunction with the Institute of Psycho-Structural Balancing, also in San Diego.

## THEORY

The following theory of personality is taken from the eclectic Body Psychology program known as Psycho-Structural Balancing[sm], taught by the writer. Psycho-Structural Balancing[sm], recognizes personality as the development of ego states from the initial state of pure Essence. According to the Eastern traditions, at approximately the seventh month of gestation, the Spirit (the Essence, the Soul, the Divine) enters into the organism and the human being is present. In this state there is total bliss, total purity, no ego, no negativity, no personality. In this state the new being repeats internally the sound 'so' ham,'' a mantramic repetition that means "That I am" (Murtananda, 1978,) As birth occurs, the new being begins to repeat internally another mantramic phrase, "ko ham," which means "Who am I?" Now, out of the womb and into the world, the baby begins a learning process to discover its identity. Continually repeating its internal mantramic phrase, "ko ham," it seeks through experience to learn how to do, how to love, and how to be. Having no predetermined patterns or knowledge, it adopts from external inputs. Mainly these external inputs come from the two main role models, mother and father.

Let us stop at this point and reconstruct the above graphically. As the Spirit enters the new baby, it achieves that state of pure awareness and bliss and declares "That" to itself as it repeats internally "So' ham," "That I am." This we consider the state of

Essence, Pure Being. We will call this level 1 and represent it as pure diamond. (See Figure 1.)

As birth occurs, the new baby changes its internal mantramic phrase and asks, "Ko ham?" "Who am I?" Here it begins a learning process, taking in information from, in the early years, the key role models, mother and father. If the parents are blessed with clarity, purity, and unconditional, real love, then the child remains in level 1, the state of pure Being. If the parents pass on wrong understanding and negative love to the child, then the child develops another system of being that we call level 2, shown as encircling the diamond level. (See Figure 2.)

Level 2 begins to cover the diamond level with false knowledge and negative love. False knowledge we will call the ego states, the *maya* or illusions of reality. Negative love is the ego love, such as giving to get, or "see-saw" love (I love you, I hate you, I love you . . . ) or guilt-motivated love. The child, in its need for love and acceptance, adopts the patterns and traits of the parents and/or surrogates. When these patterns and traits are not "true knowledge," *viveka* in the Indian terminology, the child develops a second layer that is the state of the ego personality, level 2. The ego begins to cover the Essence, to hide and obscure it from awareness. As the false knowledge is ac-

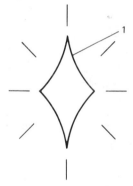

Figure 1

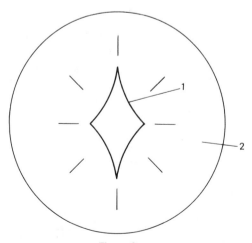

Figure 2

quired, it creates a trauma in the psyche, and at the same time it creates a concomitant trauma in the body. The trauma is stored in the psyche as the level 2 state of being, and it is stored in the body as tension and blockage of the flow of life energy.

The maps of "body psychology" have given correlations of which area of the body stores the different emotional traumas. For instance, the Arica Chua K'a map describes the knees as storing the fear of death and the perineum storing the fear of insecurity. Thus as the false knowledge and understanding created a trauma in the "psyche," it created a corresponding trauma in the body.

To summarize level 2, as the new being enters the world at birth it is not certain of who it is, it is not certain of its birthright, its Essential Being. The child has lost contact with the true knowledge of the mantram "So' ham," "That I am." As it enters the world it asks, "Who am I?" As the child questions and receives answers, all of the false knowledge causes trauma in the psyche and the body, and the ego personality begins to develop and operate. This is the level of all the negative traits, programs, and admonitions that are basically imprinted from the mother and father.

The final level of personality is the social front, or the second ego personality level.

Graphically this is a second ring around the diamond. (See Figure 3.) This level begins to develop between the ages of four and seven. Here the child realizes that the negativity of level 2 is socially unacceptable and adapts a social front, a mask to cover the negativity.

Thus the personality is a process of learning and adapting the learned negative traits. To change is not to get better. In this model Divine Perfection is always present, but it is covered, hidden by layers of wrong understanding, negativity. Each person needs to be in the state of level 1, the level of the diamond. All the clarity, brilliance, radiance, strength, beauty, and preciousness of the being is there in the diamond level. Remove the obstacles, the blocks in the psyche and the body, and the diamond being that lies within will be present and manifest. There will then be no blocks in the psyche; Pure Love and Pure Wisdom will manifest. There will then be no blocks in the body; pure Energy will manifest.

## METHODOLOGY

This section will give a brief description of four categories of Body Therapy methods and then focus on this writer's eclectic system.

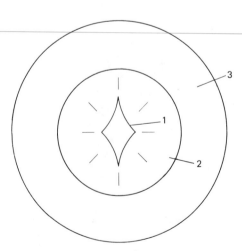

Figure 3

The four systems include physical manipulation systems such as the connective tissue work of the Rolf school and the deep tissue release systems such as the Arica Chua K'a; energy-balancing systems such as Chinese Acupuncture and Acupressure, Polarity, and Jin Shin Jystu; emotional release systems such as Bioenergetics, Primal, and Rebirthing; and movement awareness systems such as Aston, Feldenkrais, Trager, and Aguado. Many of the systems overlap and encompass aspects of the others. The categorization is based on the main feature of the method.

Under the aspect of physical manipulation, a number of systems, including the school of Ida Rolf, employ connective tissue manipulation to posturally reintegrate and align the body. In a typical format the client undergoes a series of sessions, each approximately lasting one hour, in which the practitioner uses his or her fingers, knuckles, fist, or elbows to stretch, lengthen, separate, and organize the connective tissue planes of the body. The practitioner has the client move various areas as the stroke or pressure is applied. This assures that the intergration and organization occurs at a functional as well as a static level. The connective tissue being worked with are the fascial tissue, the encasing tissue of the various muscles, muscle groups, and compartments of the entire body. The other major form of therapeutic physical manipulation focuses on the muscle tissue. As the muscle tissue experiences trauma, it binds up and develops waste deposits within the tissue. Through the application of direct compression or by deep strokes, the tissue can be opened and the particles broken up to be removed by the blood flow. The practitioner applies pressure with the hand, fingers, knuckles, fist, elbow, and feet to accomplish the release of tension and holding patterns.

The energy-balancing systems recognize various patterns of energy flow in the body and seek to balance and harmonize these flows. The Oriental systems, such as Acupuncture and Jin Shyn, use the system of 12 major pathways called *meridians* with trigger points located on those pathways, the acupuncture points. These and other systems based on the meridians test for the excess or deficiency of energy in each of the major pathways. They then utilize various techniques to balance each meridian and the entire system of meridians. The meridians can be tested by: reading the 12 different pulses located above the radial artery of both wrists; testing the strength of various muscle groups associated with each meridian; and checking correspondences to the Chinese Five Element Theory. These correspondences include the client's preference to tastes, colors, weather, time of day, emotional condition, sound of voice, and so forth. When the imbalances are determined, the practitioner manipulates the various points separately or in combination to balance the meridian flows. This manipulation can consist of the use of needles, sound, heat, color, moxabustion (burning of an herb near the point), or hands to create a circuit, or flow, between two points. The Indian systems such as Polarity and Arica Vortex$^{sm}$ work with another set of energy channels. These channels include the different levels of the body, such as the gross, the subtle, and the astral, and the "psychic channels" of the body, the *nadis*. The Vortex system presses on various pressure points that open up the flow in the *nadis*, and the Polarity system holds areas of the body to promote a flow or circuit.

The emotional release systems such as Bioenergetics, Primal, and Rebirthing utilize control of breath to promote an emotional release. Often the practitioner will also apply pressure to different areas of the body to facilitate the emotional release, such as on the sides of the neck or throat. The Bioenergetics system utilizes different exercises or movements to facilitate an opening of one or more areas. The Primal system may utilize an acting-out, or psychodrama, approach to facilitate emotional release. And the Rebirthing method utilizes immersion in water to simulate the womb for promoting emotional release.

The movement awareness systems work

with reeducating the body and the nervous system. All involve various movements, both gentle and conscious, to allow an experience of correct body functioning. The Trager system utilizes gentle shaking, stretching, and rocking to allow a release and a relearning. In the Feldenkrais system, which is a training, educational system, there is no hands-on application by the practitioner or the trainer; it is also a client system, with the practitioner performing the subtle movements. The Aston and the Aguado systems are also training systems wherein the client is taught correct movement. The Aguado system differs from the above systems in that it is a dance form as well as a movement awareness system. In all the systems the new knowledge releases the old patterns of physical and emotional learning and replaces them with right functioning of the body and psyche.

The following is a detailed description of an eclectic system of Body Therapy, Psycho-Structural Balancing[sm], taught and practiced by the writer. Basically the system is designed to clarify and open the body-psyche so that the image and concept of a "clear channel" is present.

Physically this means relating to the body as a mechanical structure and as a living system of energy. As a mechanical structure the body is seen as the skeletal frame supporting, moving, and protecting the life-support systems within. The body is evaluated for proper gravitational alignment and the joints are checked for freedom and range of movement, elasticity, binding, and material buildup. Also evaluated are the relative proportions of body parts, that is, shin to thigh, limbs to torso, head to body, top to bottom portions of body, front to back, and so on. The other major evaluation of the physical body is intrinsic to extrinsic. This is checking the balance between the deep subtle movers of the skeleton and the gross external movers of the skeleton. Evaluation of the final extrinsic layer of the body, the skin, also occurs.

The body is then evaluated for its organization and development of three major ares

relating to body-mind connections. The first area is the legs and pelvis, from the feet to the solar plexus. This area is important to the concept of being connected to the ground. The pelvis is the foundation upon which the support system, the legs, are attached. The practitioner utilizes an appropriate combination of physical manipulations and/or movement awareness systems to release the holding patterns in the belly, pelvis, and legs to achieve a self-supporting lower center. This could include techniques from the circulatory massage systems such as Swedish or Esalen; deep tissue compression releases, such as the Arica Chua K'a; fascial tissue releases such as the Ida Rolf system, skin releases such as the Arica techniques; martial arts exercises such as from Tai Chi; and movement awareness techniques such as from Feldenkrais, Trager, Aguado, or Trepidations.

The second area relates to the chest and diaphragm regions, including the arms and shoulder girdle. This is seen as the area involved with reaching out and connecting with the world. The ability to fully breathe and have full and free movement of the arms and shoulders is the goal of working with this area. Along with the above mentioned techniques would be Arica Psychocalisthenics[sm], deep breathing exercises, and chanting.

The third area relates to the head and shoulders. This area corresponds to the proper plane of physical reference for the head, the "intellect". The metaphor of having one's head sit squarely on one's shoulders applies. All of the above mentioned technologies for manipulations apply to this area.

Methodology for dealing with the "psyche" includes discharging the trauma, the emotional "charge," by understanding how the false knowledge was learned and then replacing the false knowledge with "right understanding." Understanding how the false knowledge was acquired is the first step. This requires a remembering of the event(s) in which the pattern and programs were learned. A memory of the first learning of the trait is the desired goal. Then the release of the emotional "charge" is facilitated. The breathing releases from Primal and Rebirthing processes are used along with verbal facilitation. When the recollection of the learning process and the discharge of the trauma associated with the trait are accomplished, the client replaces the false knowledge with its opposite, "right understanding." This is done through the writing of the affirmative opposite that corresponds to the negative pattern. A self-support regime is developed so that the client can be aware of when the negative trait is operating, can "witness" without the emotional "charge" formerly associated with the trait the mind as it brings the trait up. The final operation is a remembering of the basic goal of the process, the "right understanding" of the diamond state, the "I am That" awareness. For example, should the trait "You'll never make anything of yourself" come up, the process would be for the client to understand that this is the pattern operating, remember where the pattern came from (father repeated it from ages 4 to 20), and to then focus on the awareness of "I am not that," but rather "I am That," "I am a reflection of That which created me"—that is, "Who I am is always Perfect." The connecting of the body and the psyche occurs by having the client prepare for each of the coming sessions. The client is informed at theend of each session what the next session will deal with in the body and psyche. Clients should spend the time between sessions recalling their childhood and the earliest occurrences of negative programs associated with the area to be worked on. Then at the beginning of the session they can give feedback on their memory and report their feelings. From there the physical manipulations and/or movement awareness work proceeds. If emotions begin to surface during the course of the physical work, the practitioner facilitates their release. At the end of the session the practitioner and client descuss what has occurred, and the practitioner suggests exercises

breathing, meditation, or a combination of these to enhance further opening and/or maintenance of the area. Along with work on the specific areas, a regular regimen of conscious exercises, such as Arica Psychocalisthentics[sm], Tai Chi, Feldenkrais, Aguado, or yoga, plus meditation and chanting, is recommended for the positive nourishment and growth of the body and psyche.

## APPLICATIONS

The systems of Body Therapy are applicable to those who are willing to undergo the process. With voluntary acceptance, Body Therapy is applicable to all. Many practitioners in the different schools of Body Therapy deal with the incurably ill, the psychotic and mentally disturbed, alcoholics, the elderly, and infants. Yet the largest area of participants in Body Therapy are not in the high-pathology categories. Up to this time, most people seek Body Therapy as a self-development process.

Body Therapy is especially dynamic and recommended when mental therapies are at an impasse, for it is very powerful in creating movement and opening in the psyche. The deep physical manipulation systems and the emotional release systems are suggested for this purpose. However, those with heart conditions are excluded from these two Body Therapy systems. Those with heart conditions can benefit from the energy-flow systems, such as Acupuncture, Polarity, Jin Shyn, or Arica Vortex[sm]. All of the systems directly relate to the cause of the impasse, and work to break up the blockage and restore the flow of energy to the psyche and the body.

Depression, despair, rage, and anger are worked with dynamically in the emotional release systems, the deep body manipulations, and the energy-flow systems. Discharging the emotional energy around these conditions can often bring immediate relief and resolution.

Since the therapist and the client are in physical contact with each other, Body Therapy is especially applicable for those needing to be touched lovingly. This holds true particularly in the system of Rebirthing and the hands-on movement awareness systems such as Trager, Alexander, or the table work of Feldenkrais.

As already mentioned, for someone to receive full benefit from the Body Therapy, he or she must accept the treatment voluntarily. The psyche must be willing to change. Without the permission of the psyche, the body will not be receptive. This is not to say that results will not occur. They will. Work such as the Rolfing process or the Acupuncture system will definitely have an effect without total agreement from the client. Yet the full effectiveness will be a function of the psyche and the body opening, receiving, and desiring to change.

This writer believes that when the obstacles of creditability are removed from the professional community of psychology, Body Therapy will be as widely utilized as the Freudian ''slip.'' It is direct, effective, immediate, long lasting, and grounded in the sciences of anatomy, physiology, spirituality, and mechanics.

## CASE EXAMPLE

The following is a case history of a male, X. X participated in 20 sessions over an eight-month period. The first eight sessions focused primarily on deep tissue physical manipulations; the remaining 12 combined physical tissue work with emotional release and processing work.

X was 32 at the time of therapy. He was employed as a night-shift security officer. X was 6 feet 3 inches tall, 225 pounds, and considerably top-heavy. His postural deviations included a collapsed chest, head pushed forward, lordosis, holding in the right quadratus lumborum, holding in the gluteals and rotators of the femur, holding across the groin and pubis, lack of skeletal support from

the legs, and elevation of the left shoulder. Movement at the pelvis and hip socket was severely limited. X described his energy level as ''very low,'' and he had difficulty relaxing. Sexually, X's energy had been decreasing, and he had difficulty with maintaining an erection. X was in a period of ''confusion, disorientation, and stuck.'' Relations were reported as ''sour'' with both friends and lovers. His work environment created an attitude of hostility. He reported frequent use of drugs and alcohol. Fear of others' judgment, criticism, and general paranoia were also reported. Insecurity was often reported during session feedback, along with accompanying frustration.

X's family history included a violent, alcoholic father in the law enforcement field. The father, self-righteous, highly judgmental, critical, and lacking in sensitivity or warmth, administered numerous physical beatings along with verbal abuse. The mother was physically absent, occupied with work. She was permissive to the extreme, in contrast to the father's rigid, authoritarian discipline. The older sister was physically and mentally antagonistic. X had few friends and was often harassed by peers and elders. He did poorly in school and operated in a fantasy world through adolescence, wanting escape.

The first five sessions of therapy dealt with opening the physical blocks and increasing the flow of energy and vitality. The Chinese Acupuncture meridians were evaluated through pulse reading, muscle testing, and the Five Element Theory correspondences. Acupuncture points and reflex points were palpated to increase energy flow and balance. These five sessions also included deep tissue release and strokes in the chest, feet and legs, pelvis, lumbar, and back areas.

In session 6 specific work with negative programs and traits began. In this session X reported decisions to stop alcohol and drug abuse and that he had given notice of his resignation from work. He reported awareness of and dissatisfaction with roleplaying along with more physical strength and vitality. He expressed a desire to take care of himself and that his attitudes were changing. The diamond and two levels of ego personality were described to X. Deeper physical work was begun, including the abdomen and ribs.

Sessions 7 and 8 focused on negative childhood programming. X brought to the sessions memories of how traits were taught along with how he demonstrated these same traits in his adult life. X was aware of his adoption of his father's self-destructive traits and hostilities, as well as of his adoption of his mother's "poor me" martyrdom. More deep tissue work was done along with skin "rolling," consisting of a lifting and rolling of the skin. Though X squirmed and winced, he did not vocalize. The *Om* mantra was suggested for daily practice.

It was then agreed that a period of assimilation would occur. X returned to therapy eight weeks later. At this time it was agreed that more work with the psyche was necessary. For the following 12 weeks X remembered scenes from childhood dealing with his major negative emotional traits that corresponded to his major body tension patterns. He wrote out the traits and scenes from childhood that demonstrated how he learned the traits. He then compared his childhood programming with his adult behavior. This created awareness of his adoption of the traits. Several of the sessions dealt with use of psychodrama for the release of the emotional charge. Throughout the 12 weeks X was on a daily routine of Tai Chi Chuan, Arica Psyhcocalisthenicsˢᵐ, meditation on the *Hamsa* mantra, and chanting of the *Om Namah Shivaya* mantra. Besides the two psychodrama sessions for releasing anger, there were also two "primal" type emotional release sessions that included deep tissue work to encourage emotional release. After release of the anger and resentment, X went through a process of "recycling" the negative emotional traits into positive affirmations. He then examined how he could be his own positive "parent" and nourish himself and his psyche with positivity.

Male X has stopped his use of drugs and alcohol to anesthetize his emotions. He has broken off with a previous circle of friends and is involving himself with nourishing relationships. Currently in a Master's level university program in order to acquire skills for a professional career, he has begun a search for work that is satisfying and nourishing both financially, physically, and emotionally. He has created a routine of maintenance for his body and psyche and is vital and enthusiastic about his future.

X has greatly diminished his tendency to "head trip" and now expresses his emotional reactions more openly. The physical blockage at the pelvis has noticeably opened, as demonstrated by X's ability to maintain a "half-lotus" sitting posture, formerly an unbearable task.

## SUMMARY

The writer believes that Body Therapies contribute many unique features and benefits to the field of psychotherapy. To begin with, Body Therapies seek to integrate the body-mind-emotions-spirit, dealing with each aspect as well as the whole being. This is particularly true in the holistic systems of Body Therapy such as Psycho-Structural Balancingˢᵐ, Polarity, and Acupuncture. These holistic systems believe that the health and well-being of the individual is a function of the health and well-being of the balanced body-mind-emotions-spirit, not just the elimination of psychopathological traits. Just as an iceberg shows only a fraction of its total, the holistic Body Therapies believe that the psychological and/or emotional pathologies and imbalances are only a symptom or part of the entire problem and imbalance. Thus I believe that the Body Therapies are a more thorough and complete process for the achievement of well-being and realization of the human potential.

The second aspect that Body Therapies contribute to the field is the principle and concept of energy. Acupuncture and the energy-flow systems most utilize this concept. Einstein proved to the Western world what the Eastern world had known for thousands of years: Energy and matter are interchangeable. The body is energy manifesting as matter. Emotions are energy, the mind is energy, the spirit is energy. Energy can be worked with. It can be measured and correlated, such as in the Acupuncture and Five Element Theory work. Thus in the Body Therapy systems the various disciplines often utilize the principles of energy (the modern Quantum ideas) for dealing with the achievement of well-being. Though this perhaps ventures into the field of parapsychology, I believe that this dealing directly with the *prima mater* of life, the very energies that make up our being, is a powerful contribution to the field. The insertion of an acupuncture needle to balance a flow of energy, the connecting of two energy-flow points with the hands, the releasing of an emotionally "charged" tension pattern in the body—all these are powerful and direct methods of facilitating the growth and therapy process.

This leads into the aspect that is perhaps the most powerful contribution of the Body Therapies. The Body Therapies are very direct, producing immediate and often dramatic results. The outcomes of Rolfing, Primal Therapy, Rebirthing, Bioenergetics, and others certainly attests to this. Additionally, the duration of the Body Therapy systems is relatively short. Very few body system treatments continue for as long as a year.

The last factor is probably the most significant feature of Body Therapies; the therapists place their hands on the body. The act of touching is sorely lacking in many therapies, but it is the mainstay of most body systems. This direct connection, the act of touching, in whatever modality or approach it may take, may be the ingredient that leads to the wonders of the personal unfolding.

## REFERENCES

Aguada, O., and Zucker, D. *The form*. South Laguna, Calif.: The School of the Form, 1977.

Aguado, O., and Zucker, D. *Gravity the nether side of paradise*. South Laguna, Calif.: The School of the Form, 1978.

Connelly, D. *Traditional Acupuncture, the law of the five elements*. Columbia, Md.: The Center for Traditional Acupuncture, 1975.

Dychtwald, K. *Body-mind*. New York: Jove, 1978.

Feldenkrais, M. *Body and mature behavior*. New York: International Universities Press, 1949.

Feldenkrais, M. *Awareness through movement*. New York: Harper & Row, 1972.

Feldenkrais, M. *The case of Nora*. New York: Harper & Row, 1977.

Ichazo, O. *Arica psychocalisthenics*. New York: Simon & Schuster, 1976.

Johnson, D. *The protean body*. New York: Harper & Row, 1977.

Kurtz, R., and Prestera, H. *The body reveals*. New York: Harper & Row, 1976.

Lowen, A. *The language of the body*. New York: Collier, 1958.

Lowen, A. *The Betrayal of the Body*. New York: Collier, 1969.

Lowen, A. *Pleasure*. New York: Penguin, 1970.

Lowen, A. *Depression and the body*. New York: Pelican, 1972.

Lowen, A. *Bioenergetics*. New York: Penguin, 1975a.

Lowen, A. *Love and Orgasm*. New York: Collier, 1975b.

Mann, W. E. *Orgone, Reich and eros*. New York: Simon & Schuster, 1973.

Muktananda, S. *I am that*. Oakland, Calif.: S.Y.D.A. Foundation, 1978.

Orr, L. and Ray, S. *Rebirthing in the new age*. Millbrae, Calif.: Celestial Arts, 1977.

Reich, W. *Character analysis*. New York: Orgone Institute Press, 1949.

Rolf, I. *Rolfing*. Santa Monica, Calif.: Dennis Landman, 1977.

Rolf, I. *Ida Rolf speaks*. New York: Harper & Row, 1978.

So, J. T. Y. "A complete course in acupuncture," 3 vols. Unpublished.

Stone, R. *Energy*. Unlisted.

Stone, R. *Vitality balance*. Unlisted.

Stone, R. *Polarity therapy*. Unlisted.

# CHAPTER 8

# Brief Therapy I

DARRYL L. GENTRY

*Here we have the first of two sets of identically titled chapters. In both cases, it was my decision that the two systems were important enough, and there were enough divergent points of view within each of the systems, to call for two expressions. As the reader will soon see the versions by Darryl Gentry and Lynn Segal complement one another.*

*Brief Therapy may be seen as a system within a system: It is one of the several new and exciting ways of looking at families, especially communication within families. It has, almost paradoxicallly, a close relationship with Behavior Therapy in that close attention is paid to small overt changes as indicative of broader conceptual changes. In practice it also has some relationship with J. L. Moreno's Psychodrama (such as family sculpting) and in avoidance of concern with insight. It might almost be correct to say that Brief Therapy as viewed by Gentry is a kind of social engineering, concerned with changes and not with explanations.*

*The emphasis in this and the next chapter is on results; understandings, causes, and the like should not concern us—they are merely epiphenomena. In this sense, these two chapters represent a revolutionary way of viewing making changes in families and, by extension, in people.*

Brief Therapy, a communication and systems approach to the treatment of psychiatric symptoms, postulates that psychopathology in a person persists only when it is repeatedly reinforced in the course of social interaction between the person and other significant individuals. A social problem is met with an attempted solution that maintains and perpetuates that problem to the point of symptomatic behavior. The course of treatment rests with the therapist who changes the behavior being used to maintain and perpetuate the symptoms regardless of their origin, nature, or duration.

## HISTORY

### Precursors

The philosophic origins of Brief Therapy go back to the first systematic study of the behavioral effects of paradox in human communication, which was conducted by Gregory Bateson, Don Jackson, Jay Haley, and John Weakland in 1952. They became known as the Palo Alto Group.

In 1956 the group published what is considered to be a classic paper, "Toward a Theory of Schizophrenia" based on Bertrand Russell's Theory of Logical Types. The central thesis of this theory is that there is a discontinuity between a class and its members. The class cannot be a member of itself, nor can one of the members represent the class, because the term used for the class is of a different level of abstraction than the terms used for its members. The team hypothesized that when this type of discontinuity is not respected in interpersonal relationships, paradoxes of the Theory of Logical Types appear with pathological consequences. Schizophrenia was considered to be a "conflict of logical types," the result of characteristic repetitive patterns of communication. The double-bind theory was a form of paradoxical communication mostly found in the families of schizophrenic patients. Subsequent work found the theory to be generally applicable to other types of pathological communication, including nonpsychotic interpersonal relationships (Watzlawick, Weakland, & Fisch, 1974).

Basic to the double-bind theory is the fact that communication is more than the transmission of information, but is a complex series of messages (verbal and nonverbal) that take place in an interpersonal relationship. In addition, any single message is best understood by its social context. Furthermore, the complexity of just one specific message, involving multiple channels of communication (words, tone, facial expression) can increase the chance for incongruent messages in social relationships. Communication is viewed as conveying both report (information) and command (influence). The Palo Alto Group recognized the potential power inherent in communicatiion to shape and organize human behavior (Weakland, 1979).

The group recognized early that the double-bind theory involved a cybernetic or circular model of causality rather than a linear model of causalilty (Weakland, 1979). Bateson (1959) viewed the family as a social system that is error-activated to maintain a steady state against change. Jackson (1957) observed that family members of psychiatric patients often developed symtomatic behaviors shortly after the identified patient improved in therapy. He postulated that these sudden changes in behavior and also the patient's illness were homeostatic mechanisms, operating to seek restoration or maintenance of the status quo.

The double-bind theory in its orignial statement was the beginning of the behavioral-interactional view of problems. This epistemological view stated that the behavior of any part (individual) of the system (family) is governed and understood by reference to the present system and the functioning of the present system, not the past history of the system. Emphasis was not placed on *why* or *how* a problem developed, but how a problem persists in the course of repetitive social

interaction within a social system. Psychopathology was viewed as ongoing observable behavior dependent mainly on the maintenance of patterns of repeated reinforcement of social interaction in the here and now. Furthermore, it consisted of communication that was pervasively interactive and systematic among people (Weakland, 1979).

The behavioral-interactional view resulted in a major shift in psychiatric thinking that brought about a new conceptualization of problems. The unit of research and therapy moved away from the individual (intrapsychic) to a more social (interactional/interpersonal) point of view (Haley, 1976).

The group worked together on the double-bind-theory project from 1952 to 1962 and published numerous books and articles in the area of schizophrenia, hypnosis, and therapy. Toward the end of the project, Don Jackson formed the Mental Research Institute. Jackson and Weakland, along with a different group of people, continued studying the behavioral-interactional view of problems with families. About this same time (1963), Haley published *Strategies of Psychotherapy,* which expressed his version of the communication view of the double-bind theory. *Strategies* denotes a style of directive therapy that emphasizes a dyadic view.

Subsequent material has been published by Watzlawick, Beavin, and Jackson (1967) and by Lederer and Jackson (1968) that further elaborates on the behavioral-interactional view of problems.

## Beginnings

In the years 1962 to 1966, John Weakland, Paul Watzlawick, Richard Fisch, and Arthur Bodin were studying and treating a wide variety of psychiatric symptoms with the communication and systems model of family therapy. The team frequently experienced frustration when "logic" and "commonsense" methods made symptoms go from bad to worse. At the same time they became intrigued when so-called "illogic" and "uncommonsense" approaches improved symptomatic behavior. These "gimmicky interventions" led the team to start questioning their own methodologies. The team started to reevaluate from the behavioral-interactional view everything they had believed, learned, and practiced. This led to the development of the Brief Therapy Center of the Mental Research Institute under the direction of Richard Fisch, M.D. Since 1967 the group has been developing this style of directive therapy.

The team has always been interested in the hypnotic work of Milton H. Erickson. His method has had a direct impact on the techniques and interventions of Brief Therapy. First, Erickson relabels what people do in a positive way to encourage change. And second, he moves to change behavior through implicit and indirect influence.

The theoretical basis for Brief Therapy is directly related to the original statement of the double-bind theory, especially the principles of Russell's Theory of Logical Types and the theory of cybernetics. In 1974 the team published *Change: Principles of Problem Formation and Problem Resolution* and "Brief Therapy: Focused Problem Resolution," which attempted to conceptualize the theory and practical application of their approach.

Brief Therapy was first used by Gentry in 1972. He has found this approach to be most effective and efficient in treating a wide variety of psychiatric symptoms in children and adults. Furthermore, he has found that patients treated with Brief Therapy make significant improvements after as few as five to ten sessions. In addition, similar rapid results have been noticed in patients whose symptomatic behavior had been previously unsuccessfully treated by a variety of past therapies. The Brief Therapy Center and other therapists have claimed similar results.

## CURRENT STATUS

The Brief Therapy Center operates as a research and training facility. The center was originally funded by grants from the Luke B. Hancock Foundation and matching funds from the T. B. Walker and the Robert C. Wheeler foundations. When the grants were terminated, the center was forced to reduce the time spent treating families and had to operate on a voluntary basis.

The center offers Brief Therapy workshops (usually three times a year) to selected professionals such as physicians, psychologists, social workers, clergy, guidance counselors, graduate students, and a variety of mental health workers. Besides the introductory workshops, the center offers an advanced long-term training program for those individuals who have completed the basic workshop. The training is predominantly clinical, involving direct and indirect supervision and consultation of treatment. The course consists of a minium of five hours per week for a period of nine months and is limited to ten trainees per year. In addition, the Brief Therapy Center has provided off-site one- and two-day workshops throughout the United States, in Canada, Mexico, and Europe.

In 1975 the Nathan W. Ackerman Institute in New York City formed a special project designed to study and practice Brief Therapy. Its main focus was to experiment with various Brief Therapy techniques for treating families of symptomatic children. This institute also offers residential workshops, off-site training, and consultation in Brief Therapy.

Most of the books and articles published on this subject have been written by the staff members of the Brief Therapy Center. Since the initial publication of the *Change* by Watzlawick, Weakland, and Fisch (1974), many other Brief Therapy books and articles have been published by authors from the center. Watzlawick's *The Language of Change* (1978) and Weakland and Herr's *Counseling Elders and Their Families* are two of the most recent works. Weakland, Fisch, and Lynn Segal are currently working on a "how-to" Brief Therapy book scheduled to be published in 1980. Among the Brief Therapy articles are reports by: Fisch, Watzlawick, Weakland, and Bodin, 1972; Fisch,

1977; Watzlawick and Coyne, 1980; Weakland, Fisch, Watzlawick, and Bodin, 1974; Weakland and Fisch, 1976; and Weakland, 1977, 1979. To this day there are limited publications on Brief Therapy authored by professionals not directly associated with the center. This is most likely because the approach is still relatively new and has not gained widespread acceptance. These publications have been primarily case reports (Gentry, 1978; Kagan, 1980; Palazzoli et al., 1974; Papp, 1977). A further influence has been Palazzoli, Cecchin, Prata, and Boscolo's book (1978), which illustrates the theoretical and practical application of Brief Therapy techniques in the treatment of severely psychotic patients.

Relevant to this type of therapy, paradoxical techniques, a major form of intervention, constitutes the most important form of intervention used in Brief Therapy. There have been a number of books and articles written about these techniques (L'Abate & Weeks, 1978).

## THEORY

Little attention has been given to a theory of personality within the Brief Therapy model. Brief Therapy entertains the position that life is just "one damn difficulty after another and promises to remain so." Furthermore, the manner in which a person handles a specific lilfe difficulty will determine whether he or she turns the difficulty into a problem, often interfering with life activities and relationships in impasses or crises to the point of symptomatic behavior. However, special situations over which people have little control, such as illness and accidents, can lead to problems. The kind of problems psychotherapists normally treat have developed from the "normal" transitional steps that run throughout the family life cycle. These major transitions include: a couple having decided to change the voluntary status of their relationship to the commitment of marriage; a couple experiencing the intensification of their marital commitment when the first child

is born; a couple having to share their autonomy with other authority figures when the child enters school, and with the child himself and his peers during adolescence; a couple having to return to a dyadic relationship after the children leave home; a couple experiencing the intensification of the dyadic relationship at the time of retirement; and last, the return to a single life at the death of one spouse (Weakland et al., 1974). Haley (1973) provides a complete account of the specific transitional periods inherent in the family life cycle.

Most individuals run into trouble in several ways by either placing an overemphasis or an underemphasis on their difficulties of living. "Overemphasis" occurs when a person views a "normal" life difficulty as a problem.

For example, most individuals experience sexual performance difficulties throughout the course of their lives. If a person accepts this difficulty as a "normal" part of life, it will usually spontaneously correct itself. However, if the person accepts the situation as a "special" problem that requires some forced "attempted solution," then it will most likely persist and become symptomatic behavior. The person with the sexual problem is said to be attempting to arrange spontaneous behavior (sexual performance), which places him in a "be spontaneous" paradox (Gentry, 1978).

"Underemphasis" occurs when a person views an everyday difficulty as no difficulty at all. For example, a couple that accepts their marriage as "one made in heaven" is denying the existence of difficulties inherent in any marriage and is increasing the likelihood of developing symptomatic behavior. Also, these difficulties can be compounded further, when two or more people hold similar inappropriate views or opposite inappropriate views; both reciprocally reinforce the mishandling of a difficulty to the point of symptomatic behavior (Weakland et al., Bodin, 1974).

The manner in which a person approaches a life difficulty will be based on his values, beliefs, commitments, and the views that are held dear—that is, his motivations. Therefore, a person's belief system will influence the way he perceives the nature of his difficulty; his relationships with other people (including the therapist); and the direction and handling of his difficulties. However, a person's belief system is not the only way a difficulty can be turned into a problem. For example, many cultural expectations that have been passed down from generation to generation influence a person's inappropriate handling of a life difficulty. One such cultural myth suggests that the best advice to give a depressed person is to cheer him up and point out all he has to live for. Unfortunately, this only leads to more depression.

A person's belief system and cultural expectations are often defined by society as "commonsense" and "logical" solutions to life difficulties. Therefore, the individual will have the tendency to persist repeatedly at his attempted solutions despite the obvious failure or worsening of the problem. Very few people can give up their solutions simply because of the strong social commitment and investment in their actions (Weakland, 1977).

The basic assumptions that therapists make regarding the nature of psychopathology and the handling of it will determine their specific psychotherapeutic methods. Any theory of psychotherapy is essentially a set of assumptions. Whether explicit or implicit, these assumptions dictate the therapist's approach with patients.

The basic assumptions underlying Brief Therapy may be stated quite simply. Brief Therapy focuses on clearly defined symptoms. Accordingly, it postulates that psychopathology in a person (except clearly organic problems) persists only when it is repeatedly reinforced in the course of social interaction and communication between the identified patient and his significant others, not the result of some conflict between his unconscious impulses and his conscious thinking and values. This view involves a cybernetic or circular model of causality as

opposed to a linear model. Therefore, emphasis is on the behavior creating the problem, not the origin of the problem. Based on this view it is unimportant why or how a problem developed, but how the symptomatic behavior is maintained and perpetuated in the course of social interaction between the patient and often his significant others within a social system. Furthermore, psychopathology represents just one aspect of the total system and reflects some dysfunction in the system. This affects the manner in which the brief therapist approaches symptomatic behavior, including the target of intervention, goals of treatment, and creating change in the system.

Basically, this is the positive feedback or vicious-circle concept of psychopathology. From a cybernetic point of view, it is those vicious circles, involving a positive feedback loop, that connect the social problem to the attempted solution and that cause the problem to persist to the point of symptomatic behavior. As stated previously, psychopathology is the result of a person's mishandling of an everyday difficulty. Only when the difficulty is handled in a manner that persistently reinforces it, rather than resolving it, will symptoms develop (Weakland, 1979).

Brief Therapy focuses on current observable behavior and social interaction. Therefore, the brief therapist avoids bringing into the patient's awareness the influence of his past upon current functioning and does not attempt to elicit or explore childhood experiences, but focuses upon the patient's present circumstances and the functional value of his symptoms (Gentry, 1973, 1978). The therapist's basic task becomes one of applying specific strategies and interventions. When applied, these are designed to interdict the misguided solutions being pursued by the identified patient and often his significant others; and to replace the inappropriate solutions with more appropriate solutions. These are usually in the form of an opposite or incompatible behavior. From a cybernetic point of view, this "symptom resolution" consists primarily of substituting more appropriate behavior patterns so as to interrupt the vicious positive feedback loops.

Brief Therapy entertains the idea that a small change in the system can produce positive and beneficial repercussions throughout the entire system. Applied to human problems, this means a small, but significant, change in a person's problem can lead to further self-induced changes in his or her problem, and to other areas in that person's life. Therefore, the probability of effecting positive change is far greater when the therapeutic focus is on the least-important change desired by the patient. Finally, the opportunity for change is just as great for chronic problems as acute problems. The principal difference is only in the length of time a person has been struggling inappropriately with an everyday difficulty (Weakland et al., 1974).

According to the cybernetic view, a change at any point in the system will produce positive results. Therefore, Brief Therapy does not assume that everyone in the family system or other systems, for that matter, is interested in resolving the problem. It entertains the idea that change in a problem is more likely to occur when working with those who are interested in making change. As a point of fact, an early assessment of the party or parties in the system who are most distressed by the problem is most likely to offer the best leverage for change in the system (Weakland, 1977, 1979).

Two theories have been considered important in the development of specific interventions used in Brief Therapy to create behavior change in a social system. First, Group Theory provides a type of framework for thinking about behavior change that can occur within a given system which itself remains unchanged. This is called first-order change. A good example of first-order change is the type that Jackson (1957) observed with family members who developed symptoms soon after the identified patient's symptoms improved. The secondary theory is called the Theory of Logical Types. This theory provides a type of framework for thinking about behavior change that changes the system itself, which is called second-order change. Second-order change is best illustrated in the following example: A few years ago, a well-known radio announcer was in a broadcasting studio with his engineer prerecording a commercial for a leading boat company. Halfway through the commercial the announcer mispronounced a word. He and the engineer began to laugh, and the announcer was unable to complete the commercial. He tried to start from the beginning, only to find himself laughing at the point where he originally found himself in trouble. He tried to repeat the word over to himself and to take short pauses before attempting to complete the commercial. This continued for approximately six minutes before he was able to make spontaneously two interventions that disrupted the positive feedback loop, this in turn allowing him to successfully complete the commercial. What he did was to take off his glasses prior to beginning the commercial and add another word (not the one mispronounced) to the commercial. As the reader can see, the announcer made two interventions outside the system (announcer and engineer) that enabled the system to undergo change.

Thus, first-order change is said to be based on commonsense and logical solutions, while second-order change is based on illogical and paradoxical solutions. Brief Therapy is the application of second-order change interventions and techniques to problems. Furthermore, paradoxical and reframing interventions are viewed as the most powerful and elegant form of second-order change (Watzlawick, Weakland, & Fisch, 1974). These two interventions are discussed in the following section.

## METHODOLOGY

The traditional approach to laying the groundwork for treatment with most psychotherapies has been to schedule an appointment, take a history, and establish guidelines for therapy. However, with Brief Therapy, there is one additional and important step in laying the groundwork for treatment. This step consists of the therapist making an early assessment either by phone or during the initial interview as to who in the family system (or other systems) is most concerned about the problem, since that person is likely to offer the best leverage for change in the system. The reader may consider this an obvious point, but it is one of the most overlooked factors in the therapy process today. Furthermore, all subsequent steps in Brief Therapy will rest on this foundation.

Since Brief Therapy is considered a system, all the various steps in therapy are interrelated and interdependent. Therefore, the entire course of therapy rests on three fundamental pieces of clinical information. In most cases, the therapist will gather this information in the initial interview. This initial interview is considered crucial because it sets the tone for the entire course of therapy.

First, the therapist is to elicit from the patient clear and specific information about the nature of the presenting problem. Since the Brief Therapy focus is symptom resolution, the therapist will want to know the exact problem with which the patient wants help. Furthermore, this information is to focus on ongoing observable behavior. By asking the patient to state the nature of the presenting problem, the therapist exercises a Brief Therapy principle, "start where the patient is at."

Second, the therapist is to elicit clear, explicit, and specific information about how the patient and often the significant others are attempting to prevent or resolve the problem. Furthermore, many people view their solutions to problems as commonsense and logical, and feel a certain commitment and investment in their actions. From a cybernetic point of view, it is those vicious circles, involving a positive-feedback loop that connects the social problem to the attempted solution, that cause the problem to persist. It is the goal of Brief Therapy to interrupt those attempted solutions through specific strate-

gies and interventions. Since the therapy is to change behavior, rather than provide the patient with insight and understanding, the therapist avoids sharing his or her own ideas and opinions regarding the attempted solutions being used by the patient and significant others to maintain and perpetuate the symptomatic behavior.

Third, the therapist is to formulate with the patient the anticipated therapy goal in explicit, clear, and specific behavior terms. This is to prevent any confusion on the patient's part during future therapy sessions. In addition, the therapist should establish the least change desired in the problem as well as a caution that "we move slowly" regarding any improvement in the problem. Setting the goal of treatment states the nature of the therapy and implicitly produces a problem-solving context. Furthermore, the injunctions "go slowly" and "least change" within a Brief Therapy context, paradoxically promote rapid improvement by decreasing the patient's anxiety concerning change and increasing his or her motivation to disprove the therapist's pessimistic stance. It is the Brief Therapy objective to establish the above information by the end of the initial interview; however, the process can sometimes take awhile longer. Finally, the therapist is to establish a 10-session contract with the patient, which creates an important positive expectation set for rapid behavioral change (Gentry, 1978).

Hopefully, by the second session the therapist has gained a clear understanding of the behavior creating the problem and the different behavior needed to resolve the symptoms.

As stated previously, Brief Therapy uses specific strategies and interventions designed to interdict the misguided solutions being pursued. Specifically, the interventions are designed to replace the attempted solution with an opposite or incompatible behavior. As a general rule, two interventions that provide the best possible leverage for change are *behavioral prescription* and *reframing*. Both interventions consist of comments, suggestions, and prescriptions that run counter to those positions generally defined as commonsense or logical (Weakland et al., 1974).

The first technique is frequently called *paradoxical directives* or *symptom prescription,* and examples of it have been cited elsewhere (L'Abate & Weeks, 1978). Paradoxical directives are used frequently with a wide variety of symptoms that are the result of a person's attempts to arrange spontaneous behavior, which place him or her in a "be spontaneous" paradox. For example, people who complain of a circumscribed physical symptom, such as headaches, sexual problems, attacks of anxiety, and so forth, are encouraged to continue their symptomatic behavior in order to lessen such behavior or bring it under control. In addition, the therapist can have the person plan or perform the symptom at a specific time and place. A rationale can be given that if the patient can succeed in making it worse, he or she will at least suffer less from a feeling of helpless lack of control. Paradoxical directives usually result in a decrease of the symptomatic behavior. However, even an increase in symptoms suggests that the patient is following the therapist's directions, proving to himself that change is possible. By binding the patient in a therapeutic paradox, the therapist creates a situation that promotes progress no matter which alternative the patient decides to choose. Even just asking the patient to study the problem can be effective. It is impossible for a patient to be curious about his symptom and arrange spontaneous behavior at the same time. Paradoxical directives can also be applied to patients who show unusually rapid or dramatic improvement in their symptoms. The suggestion to them to have a relapse and the conditions for it constitute a technique designed to deal effectively with their apprehension concerning change. Brief Therapy states that rapid improvement in some patients might increase a person's apprehension about change; relapse intervention meets this problem by paradoxically redefining any relapse as a step forward in therapy. By placing the patient in a "be spon-

taneous" paradox, one of two events can happen: Either he has the relapse, or he does not produce one, in which case either event demonstrates self-control over the problem (Gentry, 1978; Weakland et al., 1974). Finally, paradoxical directives can be effective with people who come into therapy with a feeling of hopelessness and pessimism. By encouraging the patient to be more pessimistic than ever, the therapist redefines what has been implicit (uncertainty about being helped) as explicit, whereby the patient can examine and challenge this feeling of hopelessness and pessimism for himself. This same principle holds true for people who enter therapy depressed. By asking the patient to feel worse than he really is, the therapist redefines the patient's rock-bottom state as not having reached bottom, implying that since he can feel worse, his condition is changeable (Weakland, 1979).

In order for Brief Therapy to be efficient and effective, the therapist must distinguish and understand the patient's particular language. A person's language will include all the values, beliefs, commitments, and views that are held dear,—that is, his or her motivations.

Just being aware of the patient's language will tell the therapist what to avoid with the patient. Therefore, the therapist must learn to use each patient's own language, since the patient is likely to accept the therapist's ideas if they ideas mirror his or her own. It is very unlikely that patients will describe their language on direct questioning. This information is best obtained during the course of discussion about the nature of the presenting problem and the life events associated with the problem.

A second major form of intervention that addresses this issue is called *reframing*. Reframing simply means offering to the patient in his or her own language an alternative solution to the problem, one that is likely to be accepted. The acceptance of it will lead to subsequent beneficial action. To reframe, then, means to offer patients more appropriate solutions to their problems in their own language so that the solutions seem logical and appropriate to them, thereby making it possible for them to try new ways to deal more effectively with their problem. Reframing is based on one of Erickson's most basic rules: "Take what the patient is bringing you." He accepts all the patient's behavior and makes full use of the behavior in assisting in the process of change. A good example of reframing would in the case of parents with an uncooperative and rebellious teenager, complaining that their child's behavior is a basic threat to their parental authority. It should be pointed out that in this case, the parents are expressing a need to feel control over the child. By understanding this, the therapist can now reframe the parents' behavior (attempted solutions). It can be explained to them that their behavior has been minimizing their control of the child. Now positive suggestions of alternative methods (appropriate solutions) can be explained to them that will maximize their authority over the child. (Watzlawick, Weakland, & Fisch, 1974).

As stated previously, Brief Therapy views problems as the by-product of social interaction from within a given system. Therefore, the influence of an entire system can be accomplished by appropriate changes in any member of the system. The treatment aim is to focus on whoever seems most accessible to change, thereby providing the best leverage for change in the system. It is not unusual for Brief Therapy interventions to be used with someone other than the identified patient. For example, after seeing the entire family, the therapist may choose to treat the parents to help them find more appropriate solutions in handling their problem child. In other cases, where there is a marital problem, the therapist may choose to work with just one member (Weakland et al., 1974).

A few brief comments regarding the termination of treatment are in order. First, people are given maximum credit for any improvement in therapy. However, the therapist will note any problems still unresolved. Second, patients are reminded that Brief Therapy is intended to create a small change in their life situation, a life change to build on for the future. Some individuals refuse to accept any improvement in therapy. With these people, it is best to play down any positive improvement in treatment and to express serious doubt about improvement in the future. Third, there are some patients who are unsure and apprehensive about termination. The therapist can reassure them that therapy is available if they should experience some problem at a later time. In all of these cases, the interventions are the same—to increase therapeutic influence beyond therapy (Weakland et al., 1974).

The interventions used in Brief Therapy are designed to influence behavior in order to bring about rapid improvement in the symptomatic behavior. It is important that the brief therapist choose his or her interventions carefully and assume full responsibility for their consequences (Weakland et al., 1974).

## APPLICATIONS

Brief Therapy postulates that a major problem may arise from an ordinary life difficulty that has been mishandled by people in a system of social interaction. Most often the system will involve a patient and his family, although other systems (school, work, and so forth) may become involved. The premise that problems are the result of difficulties between people in a system of social interaction does not necessarily limit problems to the family system; however, it can have much greater implications for larger and complex systems of social interaction, such as organizations. Therefore, Brief Therapy principles can be applied to problem formation and problem resolution regardless of the size of the social system involved. Problems of a national or global level such as poverty, crime, aging, prejudice, race relations, and addiction (such as to drugs, alcohol, and tobacco) could all be dealt with.

Accordingly, problems between powerful groups of an economic, racial, or political nature could also be resolved. The only difference between national and global systems, as opposed to smaller systems, will be in the number of people and subsystems involved in the problem. Still, there is no reason to think that Brief Therapy cannot be just as effective with larger systems as it has been with smaller ones. Brief Therapy does accept the fact that there are certain problems—usually of a physical origin—beyond the reach of human intervention. However, according to Brief Therapy, larger problems are similar to smaller ones; that is, they both are the result of some commonsense or logical solution to a life difficulty that inappropriately reinforces the difficulty to the point of problematic behavior. Based on the aforementioned assumption, it is evident that the illogical and uncommonsense techniques of Brief Therapy could be applied to the total spectrum of human problems (Watzlawick, Weakland, & Fisch, 1974).

Specific individual conditions such as depression, anxiety, learning disabilities, hyperactivity, psychosis, delinquency, marital conflicts, alcohol abuse, psychosomatic illness, and sexual dysfunction are all treated successfully by the application of Brief Therapy. Other areas treated successfully are eating difficulties, identity crisis, maladjustment, school or work difficulties, and a variety of family difficulties.

As mentioned earlier, Brief Therapy is strictly symptom-oriented. Therefore, the success of treatment is usually determined by the resolution of a specific problem (behavioral change), often determined by patient and therapist as the goal of therapy. Brief Therapy success has been mostly determined through case reports and follow-up studies.

A strong example of the aforementioned is that of a six-year follow-up research study at the Brief Therapy Center, which found Brief Therapy to be successful in terms of achieving limited but significant goals related to the patient's main complaints in about three-fourths of 97 cases. Treatment had been limited to a maximum of 10 one-hour sessions, usually at weekly intervals, and involved mostly marital and family problems. The patients varied in race, socioeconomic background, age (5 to 60), and education. Also included were problems that were acute and chronic in nature. These included school and work difficulties; identity crises; marital, family, or sexual problems; delinquency; alcohol abuse; eating problems; anxiety; depression; and schizophrenia (Weakland et al., 1974).

Another area to which Brief Therapy has been applied successfully is the severely psychotic patient. In 1972 the Institute of Family Study of Milan, Italy, under the leadership of Mara Palazzoli and a team of three psychiatrists, applied Brief Therapy techniques to 15 families, 5 of which presented children age 5 to 7 with serious psychotic behavior; 10 of which presented subjects between 10 and 22 who had been diagnosed as acute schizophrenics of recent onset and had received no institutional treatment. Their findings have been reported in *Paradox and Counterparadox* (Palazzoli et al., 1978).

## CASE EXAMPLE

The following case report was selected for several reasons. First, it demonstrates how the success of therapy does not necessarily have to focus on the person with the symptom, but only with those individuals who are involved in the problem and who offer the best leverage for behavioral change. Therefore, the focus of treatment becomes one of strategic choice: Who in the system is likely to be most open for change in the system? Second, the case illustrates how a rather small change in a problem can lead to further and progressive improvement.

### Background

The identified patient, whom I shall call Jill D, was a 15-year-old female originally referred to a child guidance clinic at the suggestion of the family pediatrician because of concerns that included uncooperativeness and rebelliousness at home, as well as a history of school failure, her association with an undesirable peer group, suspected drug abuse, poor self-image, and suicidal threats. Shortly after initial contact with the clinic, the entire family was treated in an insight-oriented Family Therapy modality. After approximately five months of Family Therapy, Jill's parents threatened to terminate treatment because they saw no significant improvement in their daughter's symptomatic behavior. The family was immediately referred to me for Brief Therapy. I agreed to see them and elected to work with a female cotherapist in order to train her in the Brief Therapy approach. We met with Jill and her parents for exactly one session and noticed the following: In talking with Jill, she appeared to be a pretty, shy, and sensitive girl with a depressed appearance. She was the oldest child of five. Her parents were an attractive couple and presented themselves as being happily married. In conversation, Mr. D, age 38, appeared to be a person with an extreme need to control, and he enjoyed his authoritarian position in the family. We observed that Mrs. D, age 34, appeared to be a compulsive person with tendencies toward overinhibition, perfection, and self-doubt. She had an extreme sense of obedience and obligation to people. The family was viewed as being overprotective; the parents' behavior resulted in the identified patient having few extrafamilial relationships and activities. Because Jill was vehemently opposed to returning to the clinic, therapy focused on working exclusively with the parents.

**Treatment**

There were five sessions of one hour each. During our first session with the parents, both expressed concerns that reiterated those stated at the time of referral to the clinic. The parents felt completely out of control of their daughter's behavior.

We asked them to tell us the minimum change they desired to see in Jill's behavior as a result of therapy. Mrs. D stated that she would like her daughter to be more honest and to stop telling stories. Mr. D stated that he would like Jill to be more self-reliant and to choose friends more carefully. Both agreed that therapy should deal with these issues. A contract was then established between therapists and parents in which it was agreed that both would work together on the problem, and that treatment would terminate at the end of 10 sessions. In addition, we suggested to them that "we move slowly" in regard to any improvement in the problem.

Next we focused on discussing the different ways the parents had been attempting to handle or resolve the problem. Specifically, the parents were asked to describe in detail what they had been doing to try to correct the situation. It turned out that each had been trying to improve by using reasoning or restrictions.

From our point of view, the parents were maintaining and perpetuating the problem by some basic means of hassling, exhorting, threatening, discussing, and reasoning with their child. They perceived their daughter's behavior as most threatening to them, a challenge to their parental authority. These assumptions about the parents would provide the foundation for later interventions chosen by us to create change in the problem.

Earlier I said that interventions need to be reframed in the patient's particular language. A reframing intervention was used during our second session. It was explained to the parents that their behavior seemed to minimize the control and influence they had over Jill's behavior. For example, their specific actions either tried to bring the daughter up to their level of understanding or brought them down to her level of understanding. Either way, it placed them both at a disadvantage in maximizing control over their daughter. Mrs. D immediately took exception with this interpretation. She claimed to have extrasensory communication that let her know exactly when her daughter was going to misbehave. We immediately realized that her behavior implied a sense of control and influence over Jill's behavior; Mrs. D was obviously resisting our suggestion that she had no control over Jill's behavior. We then shared with Mr. and Mrs. D a clinical paper taken from a psychiatric journal (Fisch, 1973). The article stated that prior to the use of language, human beings communicated on a nonverbal level. The author theorized that prior to the development of language humans had an instinctive receiving and sending mechanism that enabled them to receive and send messages to people. However, since the inception of language, humans have ceased using this unique skill. Both therapists suggested to Mrs. D that she seemed to possess the unique skill of receiving and sending messages. Furthermore, if she could receive messages from Jill, then it seemed logical that she could send them as well. A suggestion was made to her that this unique "radar-sonar" system might prove to be more effective in dealing with her daughter's behavior. After all, her verbal communication had been ineffective in dealing with Jill's behavior. The couple laughed, and Mrs. D agreed to test this method with their daughter. They left the session looking forward to two weeks at the beach with Jill and their other children.

By explaining this information to Mrs. D, the therapists utilized her belief (language) in magical thinking. This illustrates Brief Therapy's idea that by fully accepting all of the parents' behavior the therapists avoid the phenomenon of resistance and make full use of the parents' skills in assisting in the process of change (Saposnek, 1980). Our acceptance of Mrs. D's belief helped her to stop overreacting, thereby decreasing her anxiety and increasing her self-confidence with Jill.

When the parents returned for the third session, they stated there was significant improvement in the identified patient's symptomatic behavior. Mrs. D felt that she was becoming less involved in the girl's behavior and confessed that she had not received any messages from Jill that she was going to misbehave. The parents were encouraged to continue the therapy task until the next session.

The parents continued to report improvement in Jill's behavior in the fourth session. Mrs. D was quite eager to share with us how her "radar-sonar" system had worked with Jill. According to Mrs. D, Jill had asked them if she could visit a girl friend. Mrs. D immediately received a message from her that she was "up to something." Mrs. D sent a message requesting that her daughter be back home in one hour. Jill returned home within the requested time. We were pleased with Mrs. D's behavior and encouraged her to continue dealing with Jill in this manner. Mr. D was extremely pleased with treatment and was finding himself less involved, due to Jill's improved behavior. He also found himself being more supportive of his wife's behavior with Jill.

In session 5, the concluding session, both parents continued to report positive changes in their daughter's behavior. The parents were told that they need not report to the clinic for further therapy although 10 sessions had been projected originally. They appeared extremely pleased with this decision. We briefly reviewed the course of treatment with them and emphasized that they could contact the clinic if Jill's symptoms recurred.

## Follow-Up

Since that time, the parents have resumed their "normal" routine, and a 12-month follow-up has revealed specific positive changes in Jill's behavior. The parents considered her to be a much happier person at home and in school. In point of fact, Jill brought home a report card with all passing grades for the first time since the third grade. In addition, she was associating with a more desirable peer group and had a part-time job as a cashier after school. Our follow-up evaluation revealed further positive changes with the parents. Both felt that their relationship had improved since therapy. The parents were no longer in disagreement over Jill's behavior. As for Jill, the follow-up had denoted no subsequent symptomatic behavior.

## SUMMARY

Brief Therapy, a communication and systems model of Family Therapy, is different from most schools of family psychotherapy. Unlike most Family Therapies, Brief Therapy does not view symptomatic behavior as representing a dysfunctional fundamental aspect of the total family system that requires a complete reorganization of that system, but it believes that just one aspect of the total family system is dysfunctional. Often a change or modification in that part of the system alone is required.

This major theoretical difference separates Brief Therapy from most family approaches in two very important areas. First, Brief Therapy entertains the idea that small changes in overt behavior are sufficient to initiate positive and beneficial repercussions throughout the entire family system. Secondly, Brief Therapy assumes the position that change can occur at any point in the system. Therefore, it is not necessary to treat the entire family system.

However, like most Family Therapies, Brief Therapy also views symptomatic behavior as a by-product of dysfunctional social interaction and communication among people within a social system, not the result of some conflict between a person's unconscious impulses and his conscious thinking and values. Still, unlike most Family Therapies, it avoids promoting "insight" to families about these dysfunctional patterns of communication and social interaction in the family. Furthermore, Brief Therapy avoids asking the question of why a problem develops, because in doing so it would lead to a search for deeper problems, weaknesses, and limitations in patients. Instead, it accentuates the positive qualities a person brings into therapy.

Brief Therapy postulates that the kind of problems people bring to psychotherapists are often the outcome of a person's, and frequently his significant others', response to an "everday life difficulty" that has been badly mishandled with an attempted solution that perpetuates and maintains the life difficulty to the point of symptomatic behavior. The course of therapy rests with the therapist who applies specific strategies and interventions designed to interdict the misguided solutions being pursued by the patient and often his significant others and to replace them with more appropriate solutions to life difficulties. Paradoxical strategies and reframing are the two most important interventions used in the application of Brief Therapy to problems.

The success of Brief Therapy will rest upon the following four principles. (1) First, we define the presenting problem in terms of actual behavior occurring in the here and now. (2) Second, we formulate an early assessment as to who in the family (or other systems) is most concerned about the problem and therefore offers the greatest leverage for change in the system. (3) Third, we concentrate on the behavior that is serving to perpetuate and maintain the symptomatic behavior (those inappropriate solutions being used) and not the origin of the symptom. (4) Last, we assist the patient with more appropriate solutions to his problem, using *his own language* so that these new solutions will seem logical and appropriate to him. Thereby, we make it acceptable for the patient to try new ways of dealing more effectively with the problem.

The principles of Brief Therapy have enormous implications for those working in overextended social agencies. For example, it is a common fact today that many social agencies have a long waiting list and a shortage of personnel. Brief Therapy could shorten the length of treatment, thereby increasing the number of patients seen without reducing the quality of services. This could have a great impact on the waiting-list problem. In addition, Brief Therapy is a rather pragmatic approach to therapy and could be taught to a great number of lay therapists.

Brief Therapy could make it possible for agencies to hire additional personnel to meet the demanding needs of the community.

Finally, there is the possibility that some will view, and even reject, the strategies and interventions used in Brief Therapy as being too manipulative. Brief Therapy's position regarding this matter is simple: Influence is inherent in all human relationships. The therapist is no exception and must be regarded as an expert in human influence in order to assist people who come to him for help. Even those therapies that follow a certain course of action or practice direct, open and honest communicataion with patients are influencing behavior. The brief therapist accepts whatever influence will help his or her patient and assumes full responsibility for the outcome of treatment.

## REFERENCES

Bateson, G. *Raven*. Stanford, Calif.: Stanford University Press, 1959.

Bateson, G., Jackson, D., Haley, J. and Weakland, J. "Toward a Theory of Schizophrenia." *Behavioral Science,* 1956, **1,** 251–264.

Fisch, Richard. Personal communication. February 1973.

Fisch, Richard. "Sometimes it's better for the right hand not to know what the left hand is doing." In P. Papp (Ed.), *Family therapy*. New York: Gardner Press, 1977.

Fisch, R., Watzlawick, P., Weakland, J. and Bodin, A. "On unbecoming family therapists." In A. Ferber, M. Mendelson, and A. Rapier (Eds.), *The book of family therapy*. New York: Science House, 1972.

Gentry, D. L. "Directive therapy techniques in the treatment of migraine headaches: A case study." *Psychotherapy: Theory, Research and Practice,* 1973, **10,** 308–311.

Gentry, D. L. "The treatment of premature ejaculation through brief therapy." *Psychotherapy: Theory, Research and Practice,* 1978, **15,** 32–34.

Haley, J. *Strategies of psychotherapy*. New York: Grune & Stratton, 1963.

Haley, J. *Uncommon therapy: Psychiatric techniques of Milton H. Erickson, M.D.* New York: Norton, 1973.

Haley, J. *Problem-Solving Therapy*. San Francisco: Jossey-Bass, 1976.

Jackson, D. D. "The Question of family homeostasis." *Psychiatric Quarterly* (supplement), 1957, **31,** 79–90.

Kagan, R. M., "Using Redefinition and Paradox with Children in Placement Who Provoke Rejection." *Child Welfare,* 1980, *59,* 551–559.

L'Abate, L. and Weeks, G. "A bibliography of paradoxical methods in psychotherapy of family systems." *Family Process,* 1978, **17,** 95–98.

Lederer, W.J. and Jackson, D. D. *The mirages of marriage*. New York: Norton, 1968.

Palazzoli, M. S., Boscolo, M., Cecchin, G. and Prata, G., "The treatment of children through brief therapy of their parents." *Family Process,* 1974, **13,** 429–442.

Palazzoli, M. S., Cecchin, G., Prata, G. and Boscolo, M. *Paradox and counterparadox*. New York: Jason Aronson, 1978.

Papp, P. (Ed.). *Family therapy: Full-length case studies*. New York: Gardner Press, 1977.

Saposnek, D. T., "Aikido: A Model for Brief Strategic Therapy." *Family Process,* 1980, *19,* 227–237.

Watzlawick, Paul. *The language of change*. New York: Basic Books, 1978.

Watzlawick, P., Beavin, J. and Jackson, D. D. *Pragmatics of human communication*. New York: Norton, 1967.

Watzlawick, P., & Coyne, J. C., "Depression Following Stroke: Brief, Problem-Focused Family Treatment." *Family Process,* 1980, *19,* 13–17.

Watzlawick, P., Weakland, J. and Fisch, R., *Change: Principles of problem resolution*. New York: Norton, 1974.

Weakland, J. H. "OK you've been a bad mother." In P. Papp (Ed.), *Family Therapy*. New York: Gardner Press, 1977.

Weakland, J. H. "The double-bind Theory." *Journal of Child Psychiatry,* 1979, **18,** 54–66.

Weakland, J., Fisch, R., Watzlawick, P. and Bodin, A. "Brief therapy: Focused problem resolution." *Family Process,* 1974, **13,** 141–167.

Weakland, J. and Fisch, R. "Brief therapy." In D. M. Ross and S. A. Ross (Eds.), *Hyperactivity*. New York: Wiley, 1976.

Weakland, J. and Herr, J. *Counseling elders and their families*. New York: Springer, 1979.

Weakland, J. H., Fisch, R. and Segal, L. *Brief therapy*. Forthcoming.

# CHAPTER 9

# Brief Therapy II*

LYNN SEGAL

*Some people see Brief Therapy (perhaps because of its name) as a somehow abbreviated and therefore superficial version of existing techniques, or as a first-aid or stop-gap measure based on the principles of some existing major school of therapy, employed only when circumstances do not (or not yet) permit real, long-term therapy.*

*In the following contribution, Lynn Segal presents the basis of a therapeutic approach, as developed by the Mental Research Institute (MRI) in Palo Alto. The approach's brevity is not due to the simplification of an established form of therapy but because it is based on a different conceptualization of problem formation and problem resolution, that is, on a different scientific paradigm.*

*The MRI takes an interactional rather than an intrapsychic view, in contrast to some of the older therapies. It investigates problems within the interpersonal context in which they occur and perpetuate themselves. Brief Therapy emerges as the technique of choice within the systems-oriented frame of reference of Family Therapy—a field approach of the gestalt variety.*

*Nothing in this approach denies the importance of past experience as the "cause" of present attitudes, expectations, problems, and the like, but Brief Therapy sees insight as an epiphenomenon rather than a necessity for change.*

*Brief Therapy shares some important concepts with Ericksonian hypnotherapy, behavior therapy, and the work of strategic family therapists—Salvatore Minuchin, Jay Haley, and Mara Selvini; but nevertheless it is a complete, unitary system with its own well-developed rationale.*

Brief Therapy (BT) is a generically based system for solving human problems, especially the kind brought to psychotherapists and counselors. While BT is most recognized in the field of family treatment, it has been used successfully with individuals, couples, and larger social organizations.

BT represents a new way of conceptualizing human problems and a different set of therapeutic techniques based upon this conceptualization (Watzlawick & Weakland, 1977). Most often short-term treatment is associated with crisis intervention or some type of "holding action" until long-term treatment can begin. By contrast, the brief therapist assumes that the goals of psychotherapy can be reached quicker and more effectively as a consequence of the premises he or she holds regarding human problems—how they arise and what is necessary to resolve them.

---

*Although this chapter represents the work of the Brief Therapy Project, Mental Research Institute, Palo Alto, the author is solely responsible for its presentation.

## HISTORY

### Precursors

The seminal ideas underlying BT were originally introduced into psychiatric thinking by Ruesch and Bateson (1951). Together, they began sketching the outline of a new epistemology based on the theories of cybernetics, communication, and systems research.

In 1956 the Bateson group—including John Weakland, Jay Haley, and Don Jackson—published the well-known article "Toward a Theory of Schizophrenia" (Bateson et al., 1956). Although this publication is primarily known for the "double-bind" theory of schizophrenia, it also stands as a landmark for viewing psychiatric problems as communicative behavior, maintained and structured by social interaction, rather than disease entities that reside inside a person.

The Mental Research Institute (MRI) was formed by Don Jackson in 1959 for the purpose of exploring how these new interactional insights might be applied to psychiatric treatment. Joined by Haley, Weakland, and other notables in the family therapy movement including Paul Watzlawick and Virginia Satir, the California Family Therapy Movement got its formal start. Although there were many differences between institute members, they all agreed on a number of basic assumptions: (1) while one family member exhibited pathology—the identified patient—the problem underlying these symptoms resided in the way the family functioned as a group; (2) this group behavior was understood as a rule-governed system, exhibiting homeostasis, feedback, redundancy, and other cybernetic principles; and (3) treating the family meant changing their interactive behavior, that is, changing their patterns of communication.

### Beginnings

MRI's Brief Therapy Project began in 1967 for the purpose of seeing what might be done to alleviate patients' presenting complaints, limiting treatment to 10 one-hour sessions.

All the project members were practicing family therapists with a special interest in the work of Jay Haley (1963) and Dr. Milton H. Erickson (Haley, 1967), known for his unique treatment techniques and rapid cures.

Our research design incorporated a number of features still in use today. We work as a team. One member does the interviewing while the rest look on from an observation room equipped with a sound system, one-way mirror, and audio tape recorder. The two rooms are connected by a telephone, permitting observers to phone in suggestions and corrections to the identified therapist while the interview is in progress.

Patients are not screened prior to treatment, and each case is seen for a maximum of 10 sessions. Following each hour of treatment, time is spent discussing the pros and cons of the interview and the best way to proceed during the next session. Follow-up questions are formulated immediately after the last interview and presented to the patient(s) three and twelve months after the last session by a project member other than the identified therapist.

## CURRENT STATUS

The Brief Therapy Project is now in its thirteenth year of operation, and interest in our work continues to grow. We have presented our approach at conferences, workshops, and seminars across the United States, South America, and the major cities of Europe. The Introductory Brief Therapy Workshop, given three times a year at the Mental Research Institute, Palo Alto, California, continues to draw an international attendance. In September of 1979, the first intensive, nine-month workshop in BT was offered; 10 participants were accepted to treat their own cases in front of the class as part of their training.

The major written presentation of our theory, *Change: Principles of Problem Formation and Problem Resolution* (Watzlawick et al., 1974), has stirred quite an interest in the international psychiatric community and is now published in nine languages, including Japanese and Hebrew.

BT is now used in a wide variety of settings: psychiatric hospitals and clinics, corrections and protective services, social service agencies, and educational and physical health services. It is probably safe to say that one can find BT used in most settings that deal with human problems.

## THEORY

Being pragmatists, we assume that theories are neither truth nor even the approximation of truth. A theory is merely a set of assumptions or working hypotheses that have heuristic value—in the case of therapeutic theories, to facilitate the solving of human problems. From this perspective, theories are like different human languages. Although most, if not all, do an equally good job as representational systems, some languages are better than others for solving a specific problem. "Street language" may be better in a hostage negotiation situation, while proper English would be more useful for a scientific presentation. However, it makes no sense to say that any one language is closer to the truth or reality than any other (Weakland, 1976).

Basic to the Brief Therapy viewpoint is the belief that behavior—"normal" or problematic—is maintained and structured by interaction with other people, usually family members. But interaction could also include friends, colleagues, or other professional helpers.

Human problems develop by mishandling of normal life difficulties that are predictable occurrences in the course of a person's lifetime. Such difficulties include accidents, loss of work, natural disasters, disturbances in one's usual routines, and transitions in the family life cycle: courtship to marriage, birth of the first child, when the children start attending school and reach the teen years, when all the children leave home, and loss of a spouse through death or divorce.

There are three basic ways difficulties are mishandled: (1) by ignoring or denying that anything is wrong and not taking action; (2) by attempting to resolve difficulties that need not or cannot be solved, only endured until they pass; and (3) by taking action but the wrong kind—the most common form of mishandling observed in our clinical practice.

Difficulties are not generally mishandled on purpose or for some unconscious gain. Rather, when people or families have a problem, they go about attempting to deal with it in a manner that is consistent with their frame of reference, that is, their view of reality and what they believe to be the right way to behave. Their "attempted solutions" are maintained because they are considered logical, necessary, or the "only thing to do." When such problem-solving efforts fail, the patient and his or her family are most likely to interpret the failure as confirmation of the problem's severity. This is then followed by more-of-the-same solutions, creating a self-perpetuating system of interaction. The patient is like a man caught in quicksand. The more he struggles, the more he sinks; the more he sinks, the more he struggles.

Although there are many different ways people take "wrong action" to solve a problem, four basic patterns have been repeatedly observed in our clinical practice (Fisch et al., 1975).

*Attempting to Be Spontaneous Deliberately.* This pattern is found in cases involving sleep disorders, sexual difficulties, substance abuse, blocks in creative endeavors, and when a person tries to force himself or others to have a particular emotional feeling.

It is assumed that most people will occasionally have difficulty with bodily functioning or performance, and feelings wax and wane. If such difficulties are seen as normal life difficulties that self-correct with time, all would be well. But once a person sets about deliberate correction, he or she risks the possibility of getting caught in the paradoxical predicament of attempting to force spontaneous behavior. The patient-to-be may try to force himself to sleep, be potent, or cheer himself up and feel happy. When such methods as willpower, reasoning, or positive thinking fail to bring about the desired response, more of the same is tried, setting the stage for a full-fledged problem.

*Seeking a No-Risk Method Where Some Risk Is Inevitable.*   This inappropriate way of solving problems is often found in the areas of work and dating. For instance, the shy single male may try to avoid the risks of rejection or failure when attempting to make new female friends. He becomes so concerned with finding the perfect opening gambit that he never begins a conversation with someone of the opposite sex. Similarly, the single, the salesman, or the jobseeker can all run into another variation of this pattern by *trying too hard* to make a good impression. In doing so, they only alienate the very people they are trying to impress.

*Attempting to Reach Interpersonal Accord Through Argument.*   The popularization of psychology and the human potential movement has led to the erroneous belief that all problems can be solved by discussion and sharing of one's feelings. Many families with marital or child-parent problems come to treatment presenting their problem as "we can't communicate." Many of these marital problems arise when one or both partners define the normal fluctuations of closeness or comfort they feel with each other as evidence of a relationship problem. This is then discussed, and their therapeutic chat degenerates into an argument, which is then interpreted as confirmation of their false assumption—something is wrong with the marriage. This leads to further discussion accompanied by a heightened awareness of the relationship, which makes their interaction even more awkward and uncomfortable. They create the very "reality" they wish to avoid.

*Attracting Attention by Attempting to Be Left Alone.*   Many problems defined as paranoia arise from this solution. A person gets started in this problem when he defines some teasing or harassment by others as insidious, indicating a lack of esteem that others have for him. The attempted solution may range from emotional or physical withdrawal to inquiry about the "persecution" or counterattacks. In either case, these solutions are likely to bring on more attention from others. If the person withdraws, others may seek him out to find out what is wrong. If the patient retaliates, this just sets off a pattern of escalating hostilities.

In short, the theory and techniques of Brief Therapy rest on two major assumptions:

regardless of their basic origins and etiology—if, indeed, that can ever be reliably determined—the kinds of problems people bring to psychotherapists PERSIST only if they are maintained by ongoing current behavior of the patient and others with whom he interacts. Correspondingly, if such problem-maintaining behavior is appropriately changed or eliminated, the problem will be resolved or vanish, regardless of its nature, origin, or duration. (Weakland et al., 1974, p. 144)

## METHODLOGY

Given our view of problems and *how* they persist, the tasks of treatment become clear: (1) obtain an operational definition of the problem and the behavior that maintains it; (2) devise a plan to interdict the attempted solution; (3) implement the plan, revising or proceeding as necessary; and (4) termination.

### Case Management

Most therapists would agree that warmth, empathy, trust, and patient involvement are important elements in a good therapeutic relationship. The brief therapist is also concerned with an additional set of relationship issues that permit him or her to exercise the best clinical judgment throughout the course of treatment.

More specifically, the therapist needs room to maneuver—the freedom to ask questions and obtain necessary information, choose which family members will be interviewed, select interventions, and gain the necessary leverage to see that they are carried out.

Given the limitations of space, it is impossible to begin explaining how this is carried out. The following list simply outlines some of the therapist's main procedures for maximizing his or her maneuverability: obtaining clear, specific information from the patient; using qualifying statements to avoid being pinned down until he or she decides what is the best position to take vis-à-vis the patient; taking time and not being pressured into intervening prematurely because of patient pressure; and using the "one-down" position, explained later in this chapter.

## Data Collection

Treatment begins by simply asking the patient "What brought you in today?" Related questions focus on the referral source, why treatment was sought at this time, and how the problem is getting in the way of the patient's life, that is, what the problem is stopping the patient from doing or making him do unwillingly. This last question serves as a useful barometer of patient distress and provides additional clarification of the presenting complaint.

Next, an assessment is made of the problem-maintaining behavior. We ask how the patient and others have been dealing with the problem and how they have deliberately attempted to solve it—what exactly do they say and do?

Last, the goal of treatment is clarified, emphasizing minimal change on the grounds that there are only 10 sessions in which to work. The therapist might say: "What, at the very least, would you like to see accomplished as a result of our efforts, and what concrete indicators might serve as signposts to indicate this?"

When collecting data, the brief therapist will phrase questions and clarifying remarks with an eye to obtaining descriptions of interaction that resemble the script of a stage play. For instance, if the patient says, "I

really let her have it," the therapist will ask, "What exactly did you say? Then what did she say or do?"

Data collection usually takes from one to three interviews. During this period, other family members might be interviewed, alone or with the identified patient, asking them the same basic questions. This permits the therapist to assess which family member is a "customer" for treatment—the one who really wants to get down to the business of problem solving—and what positions the family members hold about the problem and its treatment, "positions" denoting their beliefs, opinions, and feelings. Since BT utilizes a systems perspective, we have the option of working with family members other than the identified patient to change the attempted solution (see case example).

## Case Planning

The first task of planning is determining the logic, rule, or basic thrust of the attempted solutions. By studying the various individual solutions, the therapist seeks to derive their common denominator as seen from the next higher level of abstraction. In this sense, we seek to uncover the "rule" underlying the system of problem solving, for it is here that change usually needs to take place.

For example, a person who becomes anxious when speaking in public may try any or all of the following solutions: practicing in front of a mirror, practicing relaxation exercises, making extensive notes and outlines, or taking medication. While each solution is different, they share the common denominator of trying to make a perfect presentation.

The basic solution serves as a guide, telling the therapist what in general might be done to resolve things, and, more important, what to stay away from: What remarks or directives are the "mine field"—those comments or directives that are simply a variation of the same basic solution. In the case of the anxious public speaker, the mine field would be any intervention that implies it would help him make a perfect presentation.

The easiest way to avoid the mine field is to select an intervention which is 180 degrees out from the basic solution. With the anxious speaker, many different behaviors fulfill this condition. The patient could: (1) announce to the audience that he is nervous; (2) make a mistake on purpose; (3) act as if he forgot what he was saying and ask the audience for help; or (4) drop his note cards in the middle of his talk. Each of these behaviors represents a 180-degree shift from the attempted solution.

Obviously, getting the patient to carry out such assignments is not easy. From his perspective, this advice would appear to only make things worse. Therefore, the therapist must frame directives in a way that makes sense to the patient, and the information for such framing is derived from what has been learned from the patient's positions. Any of the following framings might be suitable for having a patient make a mistake on purpose: (1) as a method of in vivo desensitization; (2) exaggerating a problem as a way of learning how one does it; or (3) as a special exercise designed to stimulate insight. Some patients are simply intrigued with the question "Do you know how to give a really bad presentation?" And with some cases, we might use an intervention called "the devil's pact." The patient must agree to follow the therapist's assignment without knowing the basis for it or discussing it once it has been presented. The assignment is either carried out or treatment is terminated.

Ideally, the new therapeutic assignment seeks two objectives: to influence the patient to carry out a new solution that is not a variation on the basic solution, and, in doing so, to give up solutions that perpetuate the problem. For example, Erickson is reported to have cured an insomniac by convincing him to wax the kitchen floor during bedtime hours. From our perspective, this assignment fulfills both BT objectives: It stops the patient from trying to force himself to sleep by making himself stay up and wax the floor.

Although much time and effort goes into case planning, such a formulation is not treated as sacred or irreversible. The treatment plan is simply a working hypothesis for bringing about change, and it will be pursued, modified, or replaced, depending on its usefulness.

## Interventions

It is assumed that the therapist is always influencing the patient as a consequence of the communication process and the context in which it takes place. However, there are points in treatment when the therapist makes a deliberate and concerted effort to use his or her influence to reach a particular objective of treatment.

*Changing the Patient's View.* Although we don't believe insight is useful in resolving problems, if a patient's view of his or her problem is changed—not brought into line with reality—trying out a new solution can become easier. Similarly, a different view of the problem can make it *more difficult* for the patient to continue using the same old solutions that are perpetuating the problem. This technique is called *reframing*—"to change the conceptual and/or emotional setting or viewpoint in relation to which a situation is experienced and to place it in another frame which fits the 'facts' of the same situation equally well or even better, and thereby changes its entire meaning" (Watzlawick et al., 1974).

For instance, if a husband who resorts to physical abuse during marital fights accepts the reframing that he is making a loyal sacrifice for his wife by meeting her unconscious need for punishment, it puts him in a dilemma that is therapeutically useful. Since his abuse is defined as a positive gift, he must find new ways to retaliate. The therapist can capitalize on this by suggesting that he "kill her" with kindness.

Similarly, a salesman who came to treatment because he felt his stuttering impeded his work performance benefited greatly when his speaking difficulty was reframed as an advantage, distinguishing him in a positive fashion from the stereotype of the fast, smooth-talking salesman who usually turned off many prospective customers. His acceptance of this new view left him more relaxed about his impediment, resulting in less effort to inhibit it and an improved ability to speak without stuttering. As Shakespeare wrote, ''There is nothing either good or bad, thinking makes it so.''

*Putting the Patient at Ease.*   Patients are more likely to accept new ideas, try out assignments, and give more complete information if the treatment ambience is low-keyed. At the beginning of the first interview, it will be suggested that everyone use first names. Traditional therapeutic techniques, such as the pregnant pause and requesting that the patient vebalize his affect, are rarely used, so that the treatment interview is more likely to resemble a normal conversation. All of these notions stem from the basic idea of ''one-downmanship,'' with the therapist using a number of tactics to diminish the implied distance between himself and the patient. Rather than seeming to be a person with no problems and total understanding, the therapist portrays himself as another human being with frailties and limitations of his own.

When collecting information, the one-down position is used for clarification purposes. We are likely to say, ''Would you please go over that again? Unfortunately, I am one of those people who have to hear things about five times before I get it. Please bear with me.''

In the later stages of treatment, when new ideas or directives are presented, they are framed as ''not very important'' or ''just some small thing that might be of some help.'' At times one of the most useful therapeutic comments is instructing the patient to ''go slow.'' If the patient returns for a session reporting progress, we will probably comment that while we share the patient's satisfaction, it would be wise not to move too rapidly because change always makes waves.

*Motivation.*   There are many ways of motivating the client to behave differently, depending on his or her opinions, beliefs, and attitudes. The angry and frustrated parent can be given assignments that allow him to harmlessly and therapeutically vent his feelings, while caretakers will be instructed to be even more helpful and sacrificing. The curious and insight-oriented can be motivated to try out novel ideas, to see what new things they can learn, while the resistive patient will be encouraged not to change.

*Homework.*   Assuming that therapeutic change takes place between sessions, many of our interventions are in the form of homework assignments that instruct the patient to take new action vis-à-vis the problem. Directives are in the form of small, concrete, specific tasks to be carried out once or twice before the next session. During the early stages of treatment, the patient's homework might be to formulate a goal of treatment or to decide which of his or her problems needs the most attention.

One of the most interesting classes of directives is called the *paradoxical injunction*, more commonly known as *symptom prescriptions*. These are particularly appropriate in cases where the attempted solution takes the form of attempting to force spontaneity. In trying to force his or her symptom, the patient must give up all the solutions used to eliminate it. Our director, Dr. Richard Fisch, rapidly resolved a patient's complaint of premature ejaculation by instructing the marital couple to return home with a stop watch; the wife was told to time the speed of her husband's ejaculation so that, ostensibly, Dr. Fisch could have the necessary data needed to formulate a diagnosis. (The request for additional information was simply a cover story to make the assignment seem reasonable to the couple.) By attempting to carry out the assignment, all problem-engendering solutions were dropped, and much to the couple's surprise, the husband no longer ejaculated quickly. From the patients' perspective, treatment was over before it really began.

## Termination

The brevity of patient contact and emphasis on action rather than insight or expression of feelings make for a relatively simple termination process. In most cases, the subject is not even broached until the last session or the one just preceding it. Basically, we look for three criteria in the patient's report that would indicate that he or she is ready to terminate: (1) a small but significant dent has been made in the problem; (2) the change appears durable; and (3) the patient implies or states that he can handle things on his own.

When wrapping up a case, the course of treatment is briefly reviewed, giving the patient credit for what has been accomplished. Patients are also cautioned against believing that the problem is solved forever. We predict that they will face this or a similar life difficulty again, and that how things go will depend upon how they deal with it.

Some patients are hesitant about terminating treatment, and in these cases we are likely to frame termination as a necessary vacation from treatment, giving them time to digest and incorporate the gains made into their daily lives. They are warned that any further change would be counterproductive, and that the best thing to do now is to "put things on the back burner and let them simmer." In three months they will be contacted for a progress report.

Finally, with resistive or negative patients, any improvement will be challenged as inconsequential or temporary, and the therapist will predict that things will probably get worse. As in all our work, every phase of treatment utilizes therapeutic strategy based upon the needs of the particular case.

## APPLICATIONS

Given the generic nature of this approach, Brief Therapy can be applied to a wide variety of problems. Thus it makes little difference if the presenting complaint is a family problem, a classical psychiatric symptom, a behavior difficulty, or some physiological difficulty such as the nausea that accompanies chemotherapy. In each case the therapist will seek to interrupt the vicious cycle of problem-solution interaction and bring about useful and desirable change.

BT can be particularly useful in dealing with economically disadvantaged clients. Historically, this population has not taken to long-term treatment, analytic approaches and nondirective therapists. These clients also prove difficult for the family therapist who insists that all family members attend each therapeutic interview. By its very nature and design, BT circumvents many of these problems: Treatment is of a short duration; the therapist speaks the language of the clients; directives and suggestions are a large part of the therapeutic procedure; and family problems are addressed without treating the entire family.

In institutional settings, many of the therapeutic problems stem from the fact that the patients are involuntary. Since BT is basically concerned with interaction between people, it is adaptable to such settings by focusing on how to change the staff's behavior (the staff, in this sense, is the customer for treatment) in order to change the behavior of the patient. For instance, a local juvenile holding facility was having a discipline problem with a 13-year-old boy who broke regulations. The usual procedure for this was confinement to his room and loss of privileges. In this particular case, however, the boy would tear apart the room, yelling, banging, and disrupting the rest of the unit. The staff had tried a number of things to quiet him, including putting him in an isolation cell, but he continued to make a disturbance that stirred up the rest of the boys. The staff decided that something was terribly wrong with the boy and called Dr. Fisch to make a psychiatric consultation. Dr. Fisch suggested the following BT type of solution, which worked quite well with this case. The next time the boy was confined to his room and started yelling, the counselor, in a loud, clear voice, called all the other boys to the door outside his room and said, "Johnny is banging and yelling again. I know it's disturbing, but there is nothing we can do to stop it. But since he is doing it, we might as well have a contest. I'm going to pass out slips of paper and pencils, and I want each of you to write your name and guess how long Johnny will bang. The winner gets a Coke." (On this unit, a Coke was a fairly good prize.) The unit counselor reported that the banging only lasted 10 minutes instead of two or three hours. Also, although it wasn't suggested but certainly was made to order, one of the boys had gone to the door and asked Johnny if he would bang for another five minutes so he could win the Coke. This really put an end to things. Subsequently, it was reported that the banging had stopped and Johnny was making a better adjustment to his stay.

One of the most common problems in medical work is patient compliance and cooperation. As illustrated in institutional work, the interpersonal framework allows one to intervene in such problems without necessarily interviewing the identified patient. The author and a colleague, as part of a doctoral thesis, treated five families where the husband had had a major heart attack but continued to engage in high-risk behavior—smoking, poor diet, overwork, and no exercise. Furthermore, each of these identified patients had so irritated their cardiologists and rehabilitation workers that, for the most part, they had given up on these patients. In some cases the men would have nothing more to do with any physician. Taking advantage of our interactional model, we worked with the wives of these patients. Although our cases were limited to five interviews, we were successful in changing the behavior of these women vis-à-vis their husband's high-risk behavior with small but significant positive results.

Finally, BT is seen as a skill or craft that can be passed on to others. Teaching and supervision are enhanced by the close translation of theory into practice, clearly defined

tasks of treatment, a consistent way of evaluating the data, and specific techniques for influencing the client to change. Supervision, using BT theory as a way of understanding the treatment problems faced by the supervisee, lends itself to a process where the supervisee can become more responsible for evaluating his own treatment problems, how he has been handling them (his solutions to the problems), and what he might have to do differently to get the case moving.

## CASE EXAMPLE

### Problem

Mr. and Mrs. Jones entered treatment because their 15-year-old daughter, Jan, was misbehaving. She was cutting classes, staying out late at night, refusing to do things with the rest of the family (which included three siblings—14, 12, and 11 years of age), and making constant demands for money, clothing, and a variety of other things. Both parents emphatically agreed that she "had a knack for breaking you down" with her constant demands, which led to their giving in to her requests.

### Attempted Solutions

The parents had dealt with her misbehavior in a variety of ways, primarily by reasoning and by restricting her to the house. They had tried sending Jan to live with her uncle who "was good with kids," but her misbehavior persisted and she was sent home. On one occasion Mr. Jones had her picked up by the police and kept in juvenile hall overnight, but this had no positive effect on her behavior.

### Interventions

*Session 1.* Since the parents gave such clear information and seemed quite united about their goals and methods, the therapist felt more secure about intervening even more rapidly than is our custom. He ended the first session by taking the position that they might "give her some of her own medicine" by acting unreasonable themselves when she began nagging them. Not wanting to commit himself fully, he suggested they think about this during the next week but *not* put their thinking into action. This assignment subtly suggests that they continue reasoning with her, even though it was identified as unworkable. However, if they were to think about what else they might say in the midst of struggling with her, they could not really deal with her in the same old way. What they did with this directive would also indicate their compliance to therapeutic directives and how such action affected the family system.

*Session 2.*   During the first half of the second interview, the daughter (the identified patient) was seen with her parents. The therapist concluded his contact with her by explaining that she had an amazing power over her parents by nagging them until they gave in to her wishes. She would be foolish to give this up, even if it meant "walking around in a chronic state of rage, or taking an occasional trip to juvenile hall. You'll get used to this." She was sent to the waiting room on the note that the only thing left for the therapist to do was to teach her parents to get used to this.

The therapist's statements to Jan simultaneously accomplished three objectives: (1) It aversively suggested that she continue misbehaving no matter what the cost; (2) the manner in which this was said implied that the therapist was in a coalition with the parents, increasing their compliance with treatment; and (3) the message also implied that Jan's main strategy was to break down the parents by nagging, which only works because they try to reason with her unreasonableness and eventually give in to her demands.

The remainder of the session was devoted to working with the parents. Mrs. Jones still seemed to be operating from a position of

power she could not enforce. However, she did report backing off from her usual solution of trying to reason with Jan. Given her positive response to the suggestions made in session 1, we decided to take things a step further.

It was explained to Mrs. Jones that words were her weakest weapon in dealing with Jan, and that much more could be accomplished by teaching her a very important lesson in life—one hand washes the other. To do this, the therapist explained the technique of *benevolent sabotage*. Any requests made of Jan were to be made as follows: "There is something I would like you to do. I can't make you do it, but I wish you would." This would only be said once. If there was no compliance, benevolent sabotage was to be employed. For example, Mrs. Jones could be late in picking Jan up for an important appointment or could somehow put her favorite white blouse in with the colored wash. When confronted about any of this, Mrs. Jones was to apologize and say, "I'm sorry, I don't know what's wrong with me." To make this behavior even more believable, Mrs. Jones was instructed to tell Jan that in the remaining part of the interview, she learned about some of her own personal problems and was feeling depressed. Her own self-absorption would now implicitly explain some of the mistakes she made that affected Jan's well-being.

Benevolent sabotage served two purposes. It harmlessly channeled Mrs. Jones's anger and frustration into an avenue that did not escalate hostilities, while implicitly steering her away from her usual way of dealing with the problem: reasoning and threats.

*Session 3.*   Parents reported that Jan was "in tears all week because no one would fight with her." Mrs. Jones had made one request in the prescribed manner, and Jan complied, so there was no need to use benevolent sabotage. However, the assignment had made the parents realize that they were continuing to make life easy for Jan on a noncontingent basis.

During this session, they asked for advice concerning Jan's birthday. They could not decide if they should buy her a present, especially the $35.00 pair of leather boots she had been requesting. Earlier in treatment, Mrs. Jones had complained that Jan would not wash her bras out by hand, resulting in frequent replacement at considerable cost. After a bit of figuring in the observation room, the following intervention was offered. They were to purchase four $8.00 bras, have them gift-wrapped, and present them to Jan for her birthday. If she balked at this, they were to apologize and explain they thought she had wanted them.

Mrs. Jones said that Jan's nagging was on the decline. But, at times, she would attempt to get her back into the same old game of arguing. This was dealt with by instructing the parents in another technique called *collusion*. The next time Jan attempted to engage her mother in an argument when her father was home, he was to enter the room, pull a nickel out of his pocket, and give it to her. If she asked what the nickel was for, he was simply to say, ''I felt like it.'' Then both parents were to leave the room without saying another word.

Collusion is similar to benevolent sabotage in distracting the parents from their usual verbal responses, which are not working, thereby breaking the redundancy of the system. Since the parents complained that ''Jan was just too damn sure of herself,'' the assignment was *framed* as a way of ''injecting her with a healthsome dose of insecurity.''

*Session 4.* The parents continued reporting improvement. Mr. Jones laughingly told how he gave Jan a nickel and the experience left her bewildered. They also presented the bras to her, and when she opened the present she said in a faint, disappointed voice, ''Four bras, that would have been the same price as the boots I wanted.'' The parents apologized immediately, explaining that they thought she would have liked them because now she wouldn't have to wash them

out by hand. Jan said ''thank you'' and quietly left the room.

During the last week they reported that Jan was more relaxed, taking her time eating at the dinner table and watching television with the family. Mr. Jones told how she had used her allowance to buy her mother some candy and warned the other children not to eat it. The parents couldn't get over the change in her. The therapist warned them—dangers of improvement—that if they continued dealing with her successfully, they would find it difficult to see her leave the home in a few years. He suggested that they might want to reverse her progress and directed them to bring about a *planned relapse* by taking one occasion to deal with her in their old way: reasoning and threats.

*Session 5.* Mr. and Mrs. Jones found it difficult to bring about a relapse (a desired outcome from the fourth session). Jan continued to improve, staying at home more and showing a renewed interest in her sewing. Mrs. Jones: ''She's a much happier person; I can't believe it.''

*Three-Month Follow-Up Interview.* The parents reported that Jan's behavior was ''much better.'' There was less fighting and arguing, and she complied with simple requests. The parents had felt sufficiently confident to take a weekend trip, leaving her in charge of the other children. Everything had gone well. Mrs. Jones reported no need to act helpless or to use benevolent sabotage. There was no further treatment.

*Twelve-Month Follow-Up Interview.* Jan's behavior continued to improve. She has acted more considerate, giving up her room to visiting relatives. She has shown more concern and respect for her siblings, and, in return, they have done small favors for her. Her school grades have risen from the F–D range to C's and B's. The parents socialize more on their own, and there was no further treatment.

## SUMMARY

The psychotherapy industry is in the midst of a real crisis. Both practitioners and researchers are discouraged by the poor results of psychotherapy outcome studies; third-party payers are beginning to protest the spiraling cost of mental health services, while the demand for treatment continues to rise; and rumor has it that a national health insurance plan would not be financially feasible if it included psychiatric coverage.

Brief Therapy will not solve all of these problems, but the implications and consequences of our work do point in the right direction. Short-term treatment is cost effective, allowing the therapist to treat a greater number of patients within a given time frame. The generic nature of Brief Therapy permits the therapist to treat a wide variety of problems without devoting time, energy, and money for unnecessary, specialized training—Marital Therapy, Child Therapy, and so forth. The nature of the interviewing process and the directive stance make BT highly appropriate for the economically disadvantaged patient, who wants to discuss his or her presenting complaint and expects some concrete, understandable advice. Finally, BT is more easily and quickly taught to others. It utilizes a minimum of theory, which translates directly into a key number of practice principles and techniques. Supervision would also become a more efficient enterprise, defined as a professional relationship where the supervisee learns to refine the skills of the craft rather than working on his or her personal problems or mental health.

## References

Bateson, G., Jackson, D., Haley, J. and Weakland, J. Toward a theory of schizophrenia. *Behavioral Science*, 1956, **1**, 251–264.

Fisch, R., Weakland, J., Watzlawick, P., Segal, L., Hoebel, F. and Deardorff, M. *"Learning brief therapy: An introductory manual."* Unpublished training manual, Mental Research Institute, Palo Alto, Calif. 1975.

Haley, J. *Strategies of psychotherapy.* New York: Grune & Stratton, 1963.

Haley, J. (Ed.). *Advanced techniques of hypnosis and therapy: Selected papers of Milton H. Erickson, M.D.* New York: Grune & Stratton, 1967.

Ruesch, R. & Bateson, G. *Communication: The social matrix of psychiatry.* New York: Norton, 1951.

Watzlawick, P. and Weakland, J. (Eds.) *The interactional view.* New York: Norton, 1977.

Watzlawick, P., Fisch, R., Weakland, J. and Bodin, A. On unbecoming family therapists. In A. Ferber et al. (Eds.), *The book of family therapy.* New York: Science House, 1971.

Watzlawick, P., Weakland, J. and Fisch, R. *Change: Principles of problem formation and problem resolution.* New York: Norton, 1974.

Weakland, J. Communication, theory and clinical change. In P. Guerin (Ed.), *Family therapy, theory and practice.* New York: Gardner Press, 1976.

Weakland, J., Fisch, R., Watzlawick, P., and Bodin, A. Brief therapy: Focused problem resolution. *Family Process*, 1974, *13*, 141–168.

# CHAPTER 10

# Cognitive Behavior Therapy*

JOHN P. FOREYT and G. KEN GOODRICK

*In the early years of psychotherapy there were three major trends: therapies based on (a) instincts (Freud), (b) mysticism (Jung), and (c) common sense (Adler). For quite a while, various innovators of psychotherapies modified one of these three approaches, combining them, altering them, and so forth. In 1924, Mary Cover Jones introduced something brand-new in psychotherapy when retraining a fearful child:* conditioning. *Since then a considerable number of psychotherapeutic researchers and clinicians have become behavior modifiers, bringing with them various concepts and procedures from the laboratory. Among the major individuals in this trend have been Andrew Salter, Hans Eysenck, and Joseph Wolpe.*

*While these procedures, if they are strictly employed, are excellent for symptom removal from the "mindless"—from infants who ruminate (as treated by Sajwaj, Libet, and Agras), the mentally ill (as treated by Atthowe and Krasner), or the very young (as treated by Jones), these procedures are not feasible in dealing with intact adults. And so was born what is a semantic and possibly a logical contradiction: Cognitive Behavior Therapy. Behavior modifiers began to consider the mind—they had to assume the existence of and to deal with cognition, and so they attempted to bring their strict laboratory-type thinking to general psychotherapeutic problems. This chapter by Foreyt and Goodrick is an excellent account of what is going on in this exciting field.*

*Cognitive Behavior Therapy* refers to a set of principles and procedures that share the assumption that cognitive processes affect behavior and that these processes can be changed through cognitive and behavioral techniques. It is different from traditional insight therapy in that specific here-and-now cognitions are targeted for change through specific procedures, such as modeling or imaginal techniques, rather than emphasizing the past as a cause for current difficulties. "Cognitions" include beliefs and belief systems, thoughts, and images. "Cognitive processes" include ways of evaluating and organizing information about the environment and self, ways of processing information for coping or problem solving, and ways of predicting and evaluating future events.

## HISTORY

Behavior Therapy has always claimed conditioning and learning theories as its theoretical underpinnings. Results of many of the early behavior case studies published in the 1960s in *Behaviour Research and Therapy* and the *Journal of Applied Behavior Analysis* were attributed to respondent and operant conditioning. As more and more graduate students began to experiment with behavioral techniques, it became readily apparent that many patients' problems were far more complex than earlier studies implied. The con-

*Supported by the Heart, Lung, and Blood Institute, National Institute of Health, Grants no. HL17269 and 1T32 HL09258-01A1.

ditioning models seemed inadequate to explain complex human learning.

Interest in self-control and self-regulatory processes in the late 1960s within Behavior Therapy helped shift behavior therapists' beliefs in environmental determinism (i.e., one's life is primarily shaped by one's external environment) to one of reciprocal determinism in which a person is not a passive product of his environment but an active participant in his development (Mahoney & Arnkoff, 1978). Also in the 1960s many behavior therapists began to investigate more fully their clients' thoughts. The work of Joseph Cautela in particular served to increase research interest in covert processes. Cautela's technique of covert sensitization was particularly important because of its use of aversive imagery for effecting behavioral change.

Albert Ellis's (1979) Rational-Emotive Therapy, based on the assumption that specific cognitions (irrational beliefs) were the cause of maladaptive behavior and negative affect, began to be read and discussed within the behavioral field. Aaron T. Beck's (1976) Cognitive Therapy, which focused on cognitive styles associated with depression, was also influential with many behavior therapists.

The publication in 1969 of Albert Bandura's *Principles of Behavior Modification* was a significant event for many behavior therapists searching for more integrative models, in that he presented theoretical interpretations of the mechanisms of both operant and classical conditioning along with emphasizing the importance of cognitive mediational processes in the regulation of behavior. With the publication of Bandura's book, interest in thoughts and feelings increased. Conditioning models of human behavior began to give way to models emphasizing cognitive mediational processes. This trend was evident in the reinterpretation of systematic desensitization, originally conceptualized by Wolpe as a counterconditioning procedure, but now viewed by some as involving cognitive mediational processes

such as expectation, coping strategies, and imagery. The cognitive interpretation of desensitization led to such specific therapies as covert modeling (Cautela, 1971), coping skills training (Goldfried, 1971), and anxiety management training (Suinn & Richardson, 1971).

A number of influential books have followed Bandura's. One of his students, Michael Mahoney, has been a major force in the Cognitive Therapy movement. Several of his books, including *Cognition and Behavior Modification* (Mahoney, 1974), have helped define the field. He is also editor of the movement's journal, *Cognitive Therapy and Research*. The first issue was published in March 1977.

## CURRENT STATUS

The recent focus on cognitive mechanisms in therapy, formerly explained by simple classical and operant conditioning principles, is not a passing fad. However, to insure its durability, Cognitive Behavior Therapy must continue to maintain a scientific approach in terms of strategy and methodology, as Behavior Therapy has tried to do. Its evaluation must rely on careful observation, hypothesis testing, and replication. At present there is a paucity of empirical data to support cognitive learning theory as applied to therapeutic change.

The major tasks facing Cognitive Behavior Therapy today include:

a. the development of more reliable methods for assessing cognitive phenomena;

b. the refinement and extension of knowledge regarding the causal impact of cognitive phenomena on other categories of experience (behaviors, feelings, etc.);

c. the identification of parameters that influence the development, maintenance, or change of particular cognitive patterns;

d. the incorporation of those parameters into pragmatic therapy procedures; and

e. a continuing reappraisal of the assumptions

and adequacy of the perspective. (Mahoney, 1977a, p. 10)

If Cognitive Behavior Therapy can successfully deal with these issues, it will undoubtedly become a major force within clinical psychology during the next few years. However, despite its acceptance among many therapists, not all behaviorally oriented researchers welcome this new hybrid. For example, Eysenck (1979), a staunch S-R theorist, warns that "Although cognitive theories seem fashionable at the moment among some behaviour therapists who should know better . . . being fashionable is not the same as being correct, or useful, or in line with the evidence." He feels that "Cognitive theory, *per contra*, does not even exist as a 'theory' that could meaningfully be criticized or tested; it is an aspiration, born of mentalistic preconceptions, in search of hypotheses."

Wolpe (1978, p. 442) points out that "Behavior therapists have deliberately influenced their patients' thinking ever since formal behavior therapy of the neuroses came into existence"; because of this he feels that cognitive approaches to therapy have always been integrated with the behavioral techniques. "Thought," writes Wolpe, "obeys the same 'mechanistic' laws as motor or autonomic behavior" (p. 438). The principles of conditioning are sufficient to account for cognition, and overt behavior is a sufficient indicator of this conditioning.

Despite its critics, judging from its rapidly growing popularity (cf. Kendall & Hollon, 1979), the current status of Cognitive Behavior Therapy is healthy indeed.

## THEORY

When behavior therapists began to apply laws of animal learning to humans, several discrepancies became apparent. Reinforcement or punishment could be applied before or after the target behaviors; the timing was not found to be critical as with animals. In some cases the undesirable behaviors could be "rewarded" and yet the result of therapy was a reduction in their frequency (Meichenbaum, 1976). All the counterconditioning models for systematic desensitization failed to explain why none of their components seemed essential (Murray & Jacobson, 1978). In war some very powerful contingencies have been applied without success to change the behavior of POWs, and it is doubtful that traditional Behavior Therapy techniques could be used to make a fashion model put on 40 pounds if such a gain would jeopardize her career. The reason for all this is that, according to social learning theory (Bandura, 1969, 1977), behavior is not automatically under the control of external contingencies. Rather, humans learn how to satisfy their primary and acquired needs by using contingency information to select behaviors that they expect will lead to desired outcomes based on past experience. According to this theory, therapeutic techniques must produce in the patient an expectation that change will occur and a clear understanding of goals. This expectation is a function of the patient's belief in his or her own ability to perform the required behaviors necessary for therapeutic change, and the belief that the therapeutic procedure will be effective (Bandura, 1977).

Thus the critical processes in therapy are viewed as cognitively mediated. In the same way, social learning theory posits that the critical processes maintaining maladaptive behavior are also cognitive. A person behaves in a maladaptive fashion because, through an abnormal learning process, one expects one can't change, or cope, or avoid feelings of anxiety or depression. The goal of therapy, then, is to change the patient's faulty evaluation of future outcomes, either by changing the way environmental information is processed or by training the patient in skills that will allow him or her to expect desired behavioral outcomes, or by doing both.

Mahoney and Arnkoff (1978) have noted that the cognitive learning perspective includes a wide variety of principles and procedures that have not been tied together into an integrative model. They do feel that there are some common assumptions used by cognitive learning theorists:

1. Humans develop adaptive and maladaptive behavior and affective patterns through cognitive processes (selective attention, symbolic coding, etc.).
2. These cognitive *processes* can be functionally activated by *procedures* that are generally isomorphic with those of the human learning laboratory (although there may be other procedures which activate the cognitive processes as well).
3. The resultant task of the therapist is that of a diagnostician-educator who assesses maladaptive cognitive processes and subsequently arranges learning experiences that will alter cognitions and the behavior and affect patterns with which they correlate. (Mahoney & Arnkoff, 1978, p. 692)

Some claim that cognitions play a primary or even an exclusive role in the formation of maladaptive processes. They argue that therapeutic change can be achieved solely through cognitive change. However, given that the relationships among cognition, behavior, and affect are not and may never be well understood, and that the critical factors in successful therapy remain largely unspecified, it is of little use now to try to develop anything more than preliminary hypotheses. What may be ultimately important in theory development in this area is how the theory determines the way the therapist communicates the cognitive explanation of the presenting problem to the patient. The explanation must make sense to the patient and obviously lead to strategies for change that make sense and are feasible in terms of the patient's perceived self-efficacy. Fortunately, the ways theorists are now viewing cognitions and their therapeutic methods can be easily understood and accepted by patients since the approach does not deviate from commonsense notions of the relations among thoughts, feelings, and behaviors.

From various conceptualizations of the role of cognitions in the development of maladaptive behaviors (Meichenbaum, 1976) have come at least 10 cognitive learning therapies. These have been categorized by Mahoney and Arnhoff (1978) into therapies involving *cognitive restructuring, coping skills,* and *problem solving.* These therapies are summarized in Table 1. Therapies that conceptualize cognitions as behavior use covert conditioning, discussed by Cautela in Chapter 14 of this volume.

The three cognitive restructuring therapies conceptualize cognitions as either part of a behavioral chain, as a thinking style, or as a belief system, depending upon the therapeutic approach. Rational-Emotive Therapy has been around for over 20 years, and is well known to most readers. It therefore will not be discussed in this chapter. For an excellent review of the therapy, one of the first and probably the most popular of the Cognitive Behavior Therapies, see the recent chapter by Ellis (1979).

*Self-Instructional Training* (Meichenbaum, 1977) views cognitions as self-instructions used in the development of response patterns. These cognitions verbally encode the information storage for stimulus saliency, proper sequence, and the topology of the behavioral sequence. If the encoding process was faulty, the learned behavior will be maladaptive. This theory derives from developmental studies of children who use vocal self-instructions to help themselves develop skills. It follows that new instructions provided by the therapist can be used to develop more appropriate skills.

As the skill is acquired, the self-instructions fade from awareness; the skill is performed "automatically," or without conscious verbal processes. However, the person behaves *as if* he were following instructions. This is an important distinction, since the current treatment methodology stresses to the patient that he is behaving *as if* there was a cognitive distortion or deficit, rather than stressing assessment of these distortions or deficits, which may or may not be part of the patient's awareness. This issue will be discussed in the "Methodology" section.

**Table 1.  Cognitive Therapies**

| Therapy | Theoretical Basis | Diagnosis/Assessment | Treatment | Applications |
|---|---|---|---|---|
| | | COGNITIVE RESTRUCTURING | | |
| Rational-Emotive Therapy (RET) (Ellis, 1979) | Cognitions comprise an irrational belief system. Problems stem from preoccupation with what others think about patient. Deviations from perfection and total love are interpreted as terrible catastrophies. | *Cognitive:* Irrational beliefs inferred from patient's reported affective response to life situations. | *Cognitive:* Persuasion, rational modeling, thought monitoring. | Has been used for depression, phobias, assertiveness. |
| | | *Affective:* Negative affect due to irrational evaluation of personal outcomes. *Behavioral:* Behaviors restricted to limit negative affect (depression, anxiety). | *Behavioral:* Behavioral performance assignments. | |
| Self-Instructional Training (SIT) (Meichenbaum, 1977) | Behavior and emotions are controlled by self-instructional speech, which is internalized in childhood. Idiosyncratic thought patterns may develop, which are maladaptive. Cognitions are viewed as part of the response chain leading to behavior, which later leave awareness as behaviors become automatic. | *Cognitive:* Cognitions leading to maladaptive behavior have become automatic and unconscious. | *Cognitive:* Learn new self-instructions for new coping skills. Use appropriate imagery for problem solving. | Promising results with impulsive children, test anxiety, creativity enhancement. Some work with schizophrenics. |
| | | *Affective:* Performance anxiety. *Behavioral:* Aggression, hyperactivity, impulsiveness. | *Behavioral:* Practice coping skills with modeling, desensitization. | |

137

**Table 1.** (Continued)

| Therapy | Theoretical Basis | Diagnosis/Assessment | Treatment | Applications |
|---------|-------------------|----------------------|-----------|--------------|
| Cognitive Therapy (Beck, 1976) | Cognitions comprise irrational thinking styles. Distorted thinking causes selective attention to and inaccurate prediction of consequences. May lead to distorted imagery of consequences. | *Cognitive:* Patient makes arbitrary inferences that reflect on himself negatively, exaggerates importance of events, disregards essential features of life situation. Dichotomous reasoning, overgeneralization of failures, distorted images. | *Cognitive:* Recognize and monitor cognitions. Self-examine thinking style while performing homework tasks. Practice adaptive thinking. | Promising results with depression. Possible use with psychiatric population. |
| | | *Affective:* Depression caused by negative view of self and opportunities for improvement due to distorted thinking style applied to problems. | *Affective:* Test relation between cognition and affect. | |
| | | *Behavioral:* Restricted behavior characteristic of depression, anxiety. | *Behavioral:* Homework assignments, graded tasks. | |
| | | COPING SKILLS | | |
| Covert Modeling (Cautela, 1971) | Mentally rehearsing target behaviors allows patient to learn sequence of events and train his affective responses to develop ability to act in stressful situations. Allows forming of adaptive self-statements (as in SIT) while practicing being relaxed. | *Cognitive:* Anticipated anxiety and stress prevents careful cognitive planning needed to cope with situation. | *Cognitive:* Rehearse target performance mentally. | Promising results for phobias, unassertiveness. May not be so effective as behavioral rehearsal. |
| | | *Affective:* Phobias and unassertiveness. | *Affective:* Relaxation induced during mental rehearsal. | |
| | | *Behavioral:* Restricted behavior characteristic of anxiety avoidance. | | |

**Table 1. (Continued)**

| Therapy | Theoretical Basis | Diagnosis/Assessment | Treatment | Applications |
|---|---|---|---|---|
| Coping Skills Training (Goldfried, 1971) | Patient can learn to regulate anxiety by imagining increasingly threatening events, attempting to cope with the anxiety, and relax it away: similar to systematic desensitization but with active coping imagery. | *Cognitive:* No cognitive skills to cope with anxiety. | *Cognitive:* Patient goes through hierarchy of threatening imagery of problem situations, tries out coping strategies that may decrease anxiety, SIT. | Test anxiety, indecisiveness. |
| | | *Affective:* Unable to cope with situations due to excessive anxiety. *Behavioral:* Stress avoidance. | *Affective:* Relaxation during cognitive learning. *Behavioral:* Role play threatening situations. | |
| Anxiety Management Training (Suinn & Richardson, 1971) | Patient learns to apply relaxation training as an active coping skill in various imaginary scenes. Training generalizes to problem situations. | *Cognitive:* No cognitive skills to cope with anxiety. | *Cognitive:* Relaxation and other coping skills applied during anxiety-causing imaginary scenes. A variety of scenes is used to promote generalizability of skills. | Anxiety control. Too few studies to evaluate effectiveness. |
| | | *Affective:* Unable to cope with situations due to excessive anxiety. *Behavioral:* Stress avoidance. | | |
| Stress Inoculation (Meichenbaum, 1977) | Patient's inability to cope with stress caused by inaccurate appraisal of situation, lack of specific skills (relaxation, cognitive self-statements), lack of experience in dealing with stressful situations. | *Cognitive:* Lack of realistic evaluation of stressful situations. | *Cognitive:* Patient educated about the causes of his anxiety reaction: maladaptive self-statements replaced with adaptive ones. | A few promising studies. May help cope with anger, pain, performance anxieties. |

**Table 1.** (Continued)

| Therapy | Theoretical Basis | Diagnosis/Assessment | Treatment | Applications |
|---|---|---|---|---|
| | | *Affective:* Anxiety under stress; excessive anger. | *Affective:* Learn physiological responses to stress. Relaxation training. | |
| | | *Behavioral:* Inappropriate behavior under stress or stress avoidance. | *Behavioral:* Learn coping behaviors. Rehearse coping skills in stressful situation. | |
| | | PROBLEM SOLVING | | |
| Behavioral Problem Solving (D'Zurilla & Goldfried, 1971; Spivak, Platt, & Shure, 1976) | Emotionally disturbed and deviant persons are deficient in problem-solving ability, perceive fewer alternative behavioral responses to situations that are often antisocial. They have inaccurate expectancies about the results of their behaviors. | *Cognitive:* Poor problem-solving ability. Lack means-end imagery. | *Cognitive:* Learn how to specify problems, generate alternate solutions, and select best solution. | Some early work with emotionally disturbed children, psychiatric patients, disruptive children. |
| | | *Behavioral:* Disturbed and antisocial behaviors. | *Behavioral:* Test and verify selected solution. | |
| Personal Science (Mahoney, 1977a,b) | Personal problems are viewed as scientific problems. Skills taught parallel scientific research skills such as problem specification, data collection and interpretation, selecting hypothetical solution, experimenting, analyzing results, and revising or replacing hypotheses. | *Cognitive:* Poor problem-solving skills. | *Cognitive:* Self-monitoring means-end thinking, evaluation skills. | Paucity of empirical studies. |

*Cognitive Therapy* (Beck, 1976) sees the cause of depression and other mood disorders as the result of an irrational thinking style that leads the patient to interpret reality in a way that reflects negatively on both his self-evaluation and expected outcomes of behavior. The patient makes arbitrary inferences, exaggerates the importance of events, disregards essential features of a life situation, overgeneralizes failures, and may see things as either all good or all bad, with no middle ground. His imagery of expected outcomes may be distorted; the image may involve unrealistically negative or threatening events. The goal of therapy is to encourage more adaptive thinking through self-examination of cognitive style.

*Covert Modeling Therapy* (Cautela, 1971) assumes that persons are unable to cope with the anxiety and stress of certain situations because the anticipated anxiety or stress blocks adaptive, cognitively mediated strategies for coping. According to this theory of coping skills, a person can be helped to develop strategies for coping by rehearsing mentally the target behaviors he or she will need for an adaptive performance. While this therapy was originally theoretically couched in terms of covert conditioning, Mahoney and Arnkoff (1978) view it as a Coping Skills Therapy, since the images produced by mental rehearsal provide a vicarious learning experience, with the patient serving as his own model. During an imaginal sequence, the patient can "try out" and evaluate coping strategies before being faced with a real situation. Thus this therapy is similar to self-instructional training, in that the patient develops a plan of action that is verbally encoded while at the same time learning stress-coping techniques such as relaxation and meditation.

*Coping Skills Training* (Goldfried, 1971) is similar to covert modeling: The patient imagines a stressful situation and imagines coping with the anxiety. However, in Coping Skills Training the imaging occurs in a hierarchical sequence of events according to increasing anxiety, as is done in systematic desensitization. At each stage more anxiety is tolerated through the use of relaxation techniques to cope with the arousal caused by the images.

*Anxiety Management Training* (Suinn & Richardson, 1971) theorizes that anxiety responses to stressful situations can also serve as discriminative stimuli, and that these can be used in turn as cues for using coping strategies such as relaxation or altered cognitions of success or competency feelings. In this way coping skills become a response to anxiety as they are presumed to be in well-adjusted persons. As in Covert Modeling and

Coping Skills Training, imagination of anxiety-arousing events are used. Again, the theory is that learning of skills can take place during imagined sequences. This theory was developed in part on the notion that people imagine future events in daydreaming, dreaming, fantasizing, or purposeful planning in order to predict how best to behave and what to expect.

Meichenbaum's (1977) *Stress Inoculation Training* is based on the theory that a fear or anxiety reaction involves a person's awareness of heightened physiological arousal and a set of anxiety-engendered thoughts and images. The anxiety state can therefore be alleviated by training in relaxation and changing the anxious thoughts and feelings. These coping techniques are rehearsed and then tried out in actual stressful analogue situations, such as unpredictable electric shock. These activities are supposed to result in the development of a cognitive set to resist stressors. This development occurs in controlled clinical settings so that the person can develop skills without being overwhelmed by stressors. The use of small doses of stress to build resistance is similar to disease immunization.

The *Problem-solving Therapies* are based on the idea that problem solving requires a battery of cognitive skills, such as being able to see means-ends relationships to generate alternative solutions and to predict the results of possible solutions. Abnormal behaviors or emotional disturbance are viewed as resulting from inadequate problem-solving skills (D'Zurilla & Goldfried, 1971), especially as applied to social skills. Antisocial behavior may result from either inadequate appreciation for what is socially acceptable or an inability to find a solution that has an acceptable outcome. Problem-solving skills differences have been found between "normal" and "deviant" populations of preschoolers, emotionally disturbed children, adolescents, and institutionalized psychiatric patients (Spivack, Platt, & Shure, 1976).

Another therapy based on problem-solving theory is Mahoney's (1977b) *"Personal Sci-*

*ence''* approach. It posits that there are seven subskills needed for successful adjustment through problem solving:

1. Specify general problem.
2. Collect information.
3. Identify causes or patterns.
4. Examine options.
5. Narrow options and experiment.
6. Compare data.
7. Extend, revise, or replace.

Theoretically the learning of these generalizable skills will allow a patient to select an appropriate and uniquely individual solution to his or her personal problems.

## METHODOLOGY

The methodology of cognitive learning theory involves identifying and changing specific cognitive processes as they relate to problems of affect and behavior. Cognitions are now seen to play an important or essential role in behavior therapy (Bandura, 1969, 1977; Wolpe, 1978), but are largely left labeled as nonspecific factors. Cognitive Learning Therapy made these cognitive processes specific. The emphasis in therapy is to deal with here and now, goal-oriented cognitions in a systematic fashion using the social learning principles of modeling and rehearsal with self-awareness and relaxation training.

Whereas there are several different theoretical conceptualizations of how cognitions play a role in behavior and affect, the current trend in the study of psychotherapy is to explain how a methodology as applied elicits a common set of cognitive processes that are thought to be necessary for successful change. Table 2 depicts the four cognitive processes associated with change, along with the general procedures of Cognitive Learning Therapy that are thought to elicit them. The concepts depicted can be found in greater

detail in Murray and Jacobson (1978) and in Meichenbaum (1976).

The first goal of therapy is to develop an expectation that help is available and that treatment will be effective. In Cognitive Learning Therapy this is achieved by helping the patient develop an awareness of maladaptive cognition-behavior-affect patterns. This can be done by having the patient self-monitor the thoughts, feelings, and behaviors that occur before, during, and after particular problem situations or moods. A self-monitoring recording sheet can be provided to the patient for this purpose. Through therapist interpretation and the patient's own analysis, an agreement can be reached on an explanation of the patient's problems in terms of the inappropriate cognitions associated with them. This mutual understanding provides the patient with a tangible reason for his problems. Rather than thinking he is going crazy, the patient now can identify the problem and see what needs to be changed. Together with his feeling of confidence in the therapist, this leads to an expectation that a successful outcome is possible. This in turn provides the motivation to continue treatment.

There are many techniques available to bring out cognitive information. Direct and indirect questions, correct or purposefully incorrect paraphrasing, or repeating the last words of a sentence may help the patient talk about cognitions. If these methods seem inadequate, additional anxiety-reducing, rapport-establishing techniques may be needed. The patient's cognitive self-awareness can be enhanced if the therapist can recognize recurring themes and point these out frequently.

If the patient fails to report a self-awareness of the kinds of maladaptive cognitions the therapist is looking for, then an alternative strategy is to tell the patient that the maladaptive cognitions associated with his problems have become automatic. It is explained that the maladaptive thinking that led to present patterns has faded from conscious-

**Table 2.    Cognitive Learning Therapy Methodology**

| Therapeutic Process | Therapeutic Procedure | Procedural Examples |
|---|---|---|
| Expectation of help | Develop awareness of maladaptive cognition-behavior-affect patterns. Patient and therapist agree on a cognitive explanation of the problem that gives meaning to maladaption and prospect of a modality for change. | Self-monitor thoughts, feelings, and behaviors. Therapist offers interpretations, cognitive modeling. |
| Correction of maladaptive cognitions | Develop set of cognitions and behaviors that will replace the maladaptive ones. | Therapist guides patient in generating new cognitions and behaviors or suggests them. |
| Developing competencies in dealing with social living | Practice using new cognitions as they apply to social situations. | Patient uses imagery to practice dealing with situations. Analogue situations or *in vivo* experience in controlled situations serve as training episodes. |
| Changes in cognitions about self | As a result of new cognitions and training, patient reassesses *self-efficacy* in dealing adaptively with cognitions and situations. | Patient self-monitors behaviors and cognitions during practice sessions and is helped by therapist to interpret practice as evidence of increased self-efficacy to deal with former problem areas. |

ness in the same way that thinking associated with tying a shoe no longer occurs past childhood. Thus the patient is viewed as behaving *as if* he were still guided by cognitions. This sets the framework and rationale for Cognitive Therapy, and gives meaning to the presenting problem. Some therapists may be more forceful in imposing their ideas about which kinds of cognitions need to be involved in therapy, as do rational-emotive therapists (Ellis, 1979), while others allow the patient to take an active role in selecting critical cognitive patterns and directions for change, as do cognitive therapists such as Beck (1976). The crucial criterion for a successful assessment of cognitions is that their role seems plausible to the patient in explaining his problem (Meichenbaum, 1976).

Once the patient and therapist agree upon a set of maladaptive cognitions as explana-tory of the maladaptive patterns, it remains to develop a new set of cognitions that can be understood to predispose the patient to change. It is assumed that the patient is rational enough to distinguish, with the therapist's help, between healthful and unhealthful patterns in cognition, affect, and behavior. The therapist can guide the patient using examples and by reinforcing constructive suggestions from the patient. The goal is to develop a new set of cognitions that the patient can readily perceive as leading to more adaptive patterns.

The third common process in therapeutic change is the development of the competencies needed to overcome the patient's limitations. In Cognitive Therapy, this involves practice in using the new set of cognitions. This practice is achieved either through imaginal performance, analogue situations, or *in vivo* experience. In some therapies (e.g., Anxiety Management Training), the new adaptive cognitive techniques are developed and tested during imaginal experience. Since heightened anxiety is thought to interfere with cognitive processes, practice usually occurs under conditions of relaxation. The goal is for the patient to report adequate cognitive control through a sequence of behaviors and feelings associated with former problem situations. This means that at each stage he is telling himself how to cope, what to do, and how to evaluate his behavior and its consequences.

While the results of cognitive practice may allow the patient to recite a complete sequence of adaptive, cognitive coping strategies, it may be necessary for the patient to acquire actual experience in using these new cognitive powers. This can be understood in terms of the last process necessary for therapeutic change: a change in the patient's cognitions about himself. The most important change is a sense of self-efficacy in dealing with his problem areas. Recent research in Cognitive Behavior Therapies tends to support Bandura's (1977) theory of self-efficacy, which states that treatments using direct behavioral intervention should be more effective in increasing self-efficacy than methods using purely cognitive techniques. In self-instructional training, rehearsal of self-instructions alone was found to be less effective than rehearsal with an opportunity to use the practiced cognitions in an actual stress situation (Meichenbaum, 1976). The methodology may thus need to include direct behavioral experience, with an emphasis on using new cognitions as a guide but not as a cause for therapeutic change. The patient must not only realize that he knows *how* to perform (cognitively), but that he actually *can* perform (behaviorally). The therapist can help the patient interpret his performance as evidence of his increased self-efficacy to deal with problems.

These general methodological principles have been applied to a number of therapeutic techniques (shown in Table 1). These techniques can be roughly categorized in terms of the types of target problems they address. Cognitive Learning Therapies deal with three broad areas: anxiety-stress reactions, depressive mood disorders, and social competencies. The methodologies for Stress Inoculation and Cognitive Therapy, two of the more promising techniques, are given here as examples.

## Stress Inoculation

The procedures used in Stress Inoculation Training have been described by Meichenbaum (1977). He has divided the therapeutic sequence into three phases. In the educational phase the therapist and client conceptualize the client's stress problem. The second phase involves training the client in various coping skills. The third phase finds the client practicing these skills during exposure to actual stress. These three phases incorporate the four processes for therapeutic change discussed above (Table 2).

In the educational phase the therapist must explain to the client, in lay terms, how his stressful reaction is the result of easily understood processes. A behavioral assessment is taken to discover the extent to which behavior is restricted by stress reactions, such as a particular phobia. The client describes his thoughts and feelings when placed in a stressful situation; to help in this, the client can close his eyes and imagine going through a typical stressful episode. The therapist then describes the anxiety reaction to stresss in terms of a Schachterian model of emotional arousal. According to this model, the client's fear is caused both by perceived increases in physiological functions associated with fear, such as rapid heart rate, sweaty palms, and bodily tension, and by a set of anxiety-causing thoughts reflecting helplessness, panic, embarrassment, or fears of becoming insane. Meichenbaum (1977) points out that the scientific validity of such a model is less crucial than its plausibility for the client, since the important goal of the educational phase is to lay the conceptual groundwork for intervention.

In the last part of the educational phase, the therapist instructs the client to view the stress problem as a series of manageable phases rather than a single overpowering gestalt. This series includes preparation for stress, confrontation with the stressor, the possibility of being overwhelmed, and self-reinforcement after coping successfully. The possibility of being overwhelmed is included so that it is an expected possibility, a battle lost, but not the war.

In the rehearsal phase, the therapist trains the client in coping techniques involving direct action or in cognitive techniques. Direct actions the client can take include becoming knowledgeable about stressful situations or phobic objects, planning alternative escapes, and relaxation induction. Increased knowledge should minimize any misconceptions and reduce the overwhelming perception of the stressor. Knowing that escape routes are available should make confronting the stressor less frightening. Relaxation allows fear reaction reduction through control of physiological responses.

In the assessment, maladaptive cognitions are pointed out to the client. These thoughts now become the cues for the use of coping techniques. Cognitive coping involves learning self-statements that help adaptively to assess the situation, control negative thoughts and images, and to recognize and relabel physiological arousal. Self-statements also include convincing oneself to confront the stressor, to cope with the fear, and to self-evaluate performance. Self-statements in each of these categories are generated by the client for his particular problem.

In the third phase of Stress Inoculation Training, the direct action and cognitive coping skills are applied in actual stress situations. The therapist exposes the client to ego- or pain-threatening stressors. These stressors do not include the phobic situation but may include unpredictable electric shock, imagined stress sequences, or stress-inducing films. During these stress situations, the client is urged to try out a variety of coping techniques learned during the rehearsal phase. The client will eventually develop an armamentarium of coping skills suited to his perceived needs and abilities.

## Cognitive Therapy of Depression

One of the founders of Cognitive Therapy, Beck (1976) has described his approach to the treatment of depression. Depressed patients see themselves as "losers"; therapy is designed to make them feel like winners. The therapist will first select several target problems, which can be emotional, motivational, cognitive, behavioral, or physiological. Each target problem is formulated at three levels: in terms of abnormal behavior, such as inertia; in terms of motivational disturbances, such as wanting to escape; and in terms of cognitions of hopelessness and defeat.

For inertia, the patient is told that keeping busy will make him feel better. The therapist and patient can design a daily activity schedule to fill up each day. These behaviors should not be challenging. However, *graded task assignments* are made so that the patient is motivated to perform a series of tasks of increasing difficulty, which are related to the alleviation of a target problem. If difficulty is increased slowly, the patient should meet with a series of successes. The therapist can provide feedback about success to insure that the patient is coming to think of himself as a winner. This cognitive change is really more important than the behavioral change, since it is thought to be the critical factor in reversing the depressive cycle of failure and negative self-evaluation.

The patient can keep an account of all his daily activities, and put an "M" by the ones he feels he has mastered and a "P" by the ones that give some pleasure. Beck (1976) feels this *self-monitoring* and *self-evaluation* procedure is useful in helping depressed persons realize their success potential and to focus on the pleasurable aspects of their lives, which they may fail to perceive as such.

For *cognitive reappraisal,* the patient and therapist review the relations between depressive cognitions and symptoms. The patient self-monitors thoughts, feelings, and behaviors that occur before, during, and after problem situations. In order to change maladaptive cognitive processes, the therapist can have the patient consider alternative explanations of experiences to show that there are other ways to interpret events besides those that reflect negatively on the self. Alternative strategies for problem solving are suggested since a depressed person may have become rigid in using unsuccessful techniques. The closed belief system involving negativism toward the world and the self is challenged; the therapist questions the reasons for such beliefs, and debates the patient, bringing out evidence to the contrary where applicable. Cognitive rehearsal involves having the patient imagine experiencing a sequence of events related to a problem area. Perceived obstacles and conflicts are thus brought up for discussion, and cognitive reappraisal and problem-solving techniques are used to work through them.

This brief description of two modes of Cognitive Learning Theory gives one a general idea of the procedures used. While more structured and specific than traditional insight therapies, Cognitive Learning Therapies require more interpersonal perception skills than does strict Behavior Therapy. These skills are more an "art" than a science, since cognitive assessment and theory are not developed to the point of easy replication. The techniques and theory may never become a "science" due to the epistemological problems associated with discerning others' thoughts and the relation between thoughts and observable behavior.

## APPLICATIONS

The Cognitive Learning Therapies represent a broad array of procedures that can be applied to virtually all psychological problems.

However, treatments have thus far been fairly limited in populations and extremely limited in terms of demonstrated successes. Table 1 outlines some of the applications for each type of Cognitive Learning Therapy.

Self-Instructional Training (cf. Meichenbaum, 1977) has been used with hyperactive and impulsive children to help them perform more slowly and accurately. It has also been used with some successes for children who are socially withdrawn, schizophrenics (see "Methodology" section), and for increasing the problem-solving ability of college students.

Beck's (1976) Cognitive Therapy has shown preliminary promise with severely depressed patients when compared with tricyclic medication (Rush et al., 1977). In this study, the Cognitive Therapy group improved more rapidly and had less dropout from treatment. Three-fourths of the cognitive group showed marked or complete remission of symptoms; less than one-fourth of the drug group did. Beck (1976) claims that procedures that change cognitions and behaviors are more effective in alleviating depression than nondirective and supportive treatments.

Covert Modeling has shown some promise in the treatment of phobias and unassertiveness, but doubts have been expressed about its efficacy compared with therapies using actual motoric rehearsal (Mahoney & Arnkoff, 1978).

Coping Skills Training has been used with test anxiety and to reduce indecisiveness (Goldfried, 1971). Anxiety Management Training (Suinn & Richardson, 1971) has not yet received enough critical scrutiny to evaluate its effectiveness with various populations. Stress Inoculation appears promising for dealing with anger, pain, and performance anxieties (Meichenbaum, 1977).

Behavioral Problem Solving (D'Zurilla & Goldfried, 1977) has been used successfully with preschool students, emotionally disturbed children, adolescents, psychiatric inpatients, and delinquents. Finally, the Personal Science approach (Mahoney, 1977b) has been used with obese adults.

## CASE EXAMPLE

Barbara was a 29-year-old white female referred by her minister because of increasing depression. On the first visit she appeared so distraught and unkempt that she was asked to see a psychiatrist, who admitted her to a hospital. There she was first given a psychological evaluation to assess the nature and degree of her depression. Testing was also initiated in order to assess possible organic components since she complained of constant headaches and dizziness.

She described her depression as being the result of several traumatic incidents that occurred during the previous year. She interpreted these events as having a catastrophic effect on her ability to cope. Included were the birth of her second child, her husband's involvement in a near-fatal accident, and the death of her father. She evaluated the circumstances of the accident and death in a way that caused her to have deep guilt feelings. She used alcohol to help control her nerves, but she believed she had become too dependent upon it and wanted to give up its use altogether. Apparently she had depressive reactions following the births of both of her children. She never worked, dropping out of college in her junior year to get married and become a housewife. Her husband was a conductor for a railroad. Prior to his accident he was rather demanding and domineering with his wife.

She reported a considerable degree of sleep disturbance. She also reported having little or no appetite. Her libido had been below average since the birth of her second child approximately one year ago. During the testing she was depressed and anxious.

Test results showed her to be functioning in the average range of intelligence. The errors she made were nonspecific and seemed more closely related to motivational or attentional deficits than to organic factors. Scores on tests measuring her concentration and memory were below average. Apparently she was unable to concentrate on those tasks that involved some form of information processing. The deterioration of her performance toward the end of each task seemed due to her inability to concentrate.

The most significant affect expressed in her test productions was a pervasive sense of depression. Her Minnesota Multiphasic Personality Inventory profile indicated substantial psychopathology. *T*-scores were elevated above 70 on six of the 10 clinical scales, with peaks on *D, Pt,* and *Hy.* Her score on the Beck Depression Inventory was 35, suggesting severe depression. Her projective test productions suggested a sense of apathy and a profound lack of energy in dealing with environmental situations. She also showed a tendency to withdraw from others even on an informal basis. Associated with her apathy and lack of energy were ruminations and preoccupations. It was as if all of her energy was directed toward a ruminative train of thought in which she was preoccupied with the things she felt she had done wrong in her life. The latter particularly related to her husband's accident and her father's death. Along with the feelings of guilt were poor self-esteem and low feelings of self-worth.

Her ruminations also indicated a considerable amount of concern about her own bodily functioning and a preoccupation with death. It seemed that her recent situational experiences had focused her attention on her own frailty. Her ruminations about these matters had drained her emotionally to the point where she was no longer able to carry out her normal routine. Test results indicated that her bodily preoccupation was focused upon dysfunction rather than wholeness. These concerns seemed almost obsessional in that they represented a significant investiture of energy and occupied much of her time. She tended to perceive even harmless events in such terms.

Her affective productions appeared to be related to strong dependency needs. In particular, she viewed males as being able to cope with most situations, being strong and capable. The recent traumatic events had served to point out to her the fragility of human nature in general and her confidence in men in particular. Her faith in a strong, domineering father figurehead had been shaken to the point that she felt insecure and helpless. In fact, she reported that since his accident, her husband had been more open rather than demanding and domineering. She had, in a sense, lost the strong father figure that she had in her husband as well as having lost her own father. This insecurity that she felt in relation to those upon whom she was dependent was apparently heightened by her own perceptions of her inability to cope with normal routine. Not only did she feel helpless in coping with the situation, but she also had no one upon whom she could depend. Believing that one must "make one's own future," she had little or no hope of obtaining her expectations or goals for the future.

Associated with and probably secondary to her depression was a complete lack of trust in others. She experienced interpersonal relations as being particularly demanding in terms of the effort and energy required of her. Her ruminations and preoccupations with her own insecurity and helplessness precluded her expending the necessary energy to maintain satisfactory interpersonal relationships.

At the time of her hospitalization, Barbara's condition in terms of inability to cope with her conflicts had progressively deteriorated. She was at the point where she wanted to be alone and not have much to do with other people. She spent most of her time in ruminative thoughts that were destructive in the sense that they simply fed her depressed affect. Her sense of helplessness and hopelessness precluded any efforts on her part to cope with her situation. Test results suggested that her somatic complaints represented a psychophysiological reaction to the tension she was experiencing in her life. Her test productions of depression, helplessness, and dependency were consistent with those involved in a psychophysiological process. Diagnoses were: depressive neurosis, psychophysiologic disorder, and habitual excessive drinking.

During Barbara's two weeks in the hospital, her therapy involved attempts at restructuring her thinking and behavior in a systematic manner. Although the traumatic episodes of the past year were discussed and dealt with, the primary focus was on the here-and-now. The primary goal of the patient sessions was a transformation of Barbara's distorted thinking patterns. Each session consisted of discussing her feelings, thoughts, and attitudes, pointing out that her current behavioral patterns were a direct consequence of her mental set. Considerable time was spent demonstrating the irrationality of many of her beliefs.

After discharge she was seen in therapy twice a week for the next two months. She was asked to keep comprehensive records of the thoughts that went through her mind in response to events that upset her. Sessions were spent going over her records, discussing in detail the interrelationship of her thoughts to the events, determining whether they were realistic and reasonable. Faulty cognitions were analyzed, and Barbara was taught to restructure her thoughts in more reasonable ways.

Barbara was then seen weekly for 11 months. Each session dealt with Barbara's faulty beliefs, substituting more correct interpretations of her experiences. Her guilt over the death of her father required considerable discussion and restructuring. For example, her father had quietly been seeing another woman for at least one year when Barbara accidentally found out about it. She told her mother about her father's affair and firmly believed that this disclosure was the cause of her father's death. The illogic of this belief was pointed out to her. First, she had no real evidence that her mother had told her father that she knew of his affair. Second, her father had had a long history of serious heart trouble. Third, the affair occurred several years before her father's death, so it was doubtful that Barbara's disclosure to her mother would have an effect on her father years later.

About six months into therapy, she joined Alcoholics Anonymous. As her negative view of herself lessened, her poor relationship with her husband became clearer. A letter she wrote to him illustrates her feelings.

Dear Bill,

Let me tell you about *me*—as a person. Two years ago I was a poor, pitiful (no sympathy, please) alcoholic. I had drunk myself completely out of reality and my mental state was almost completely insane. During the last year of my drinking we had Tommy, more responsibility for me (I couldn't handle what I already had). I started drinking morning, noon, and night. Then came your near-fatal accident, and Daddy's death.

I knew I could stand no more drinking after being in the hospital, but knew nothing of the hell to follow. By "hell" I mean what I have had to go through in order to grow and learn these past two years trying to rebuild my life, facing reality, becoming a *whole* person again (really for the first time). God has given me this second chance to live again soberly and I pray everyday for the will to live each day sober and trying to do His will for me, trying to do the right things. I'm not trying to sound like a saint. I fail a lot; I simply pray for the will to keep on trying, even with my faults to keep on honestly trying for a better life, the right kind of life.

I have come a long way, with a long way to go. Don't we all have to keep on trying to live a better life? If not, what would be the purpose of living?

I know I'm still confused about many things. But one thing is clear to me now. I have my life to live (faults, failures, whatever), you have your life to live. I want to live my life *with* you, but not *for* you. I used to have no life (my fault), and lived completely trying to please you. Only I've never really pleased you very much. No wonder, for in trying to be what you wanted, I made myself completely miserable, and grew to resent you terribly. I was your doormat, but I let myself become this; in lots of ways you are not to blame. If I had been a stronger, more independent person when we married, I would never have let this happen, but I was basically insecure, very dependent, and yes, had even then a drinking problem which of course I never admitted then. Then we got married and I had to try to deal with this, and with a man who has a "large ego" (as you put it).

Several weeks ago I was not trying to hurt you when I asked if you wanted to separate. It was because you seemed so miserable with everything I did or said. I am what I am—a person with faults, and whether you can take me as I am with faults and ideas that may conflict with yours is up to you. I am willing to grow, try to understand you, and to change, even when I may not agree with your feelings; in other words, to respect your feelings and you as a person, but you must be willing to do this same thing for me.

Eventually the couple divorced. Barbara is still seen in therapy once a month. She has recently purchased a home for herself and her two children, and has taken a job as secretary-receptionist for a small oil exploration firm, her first job. She has not had a drink of alcohol for two years; she goes to AA at least once a week. She is dating but does not feel she is ready for marriage at this time.

At the time of this writing it has been almost three years since Barbara began treatment. She is continuing to function fully, no longer experiencing significant depression, and on the whole seems to be enjoying her life.

## SUMMARY

Cognitive processes are becoming scientifically respectable within Behavior Therapy. Learning is no longer being seen as solely the result of conditioning; rather, cognitive, emotional, and social learning processes are being emphasized. There has been a shift from a position of environmental determinism—one's life is primarily shaped by our external environment—to one of a reciprocal determinism—one's life is the result of a continual interaction between organism and environment. The person is not a passive product of his environment but rather an active participant in shaping his development. Cognitive processes allow persons to analyze current environmental information, compare it with the past, make predictions, and plan and evaluate strategies in accordance with their current and long-range needs. Cognitive Therapy tries to correct deficits and errors in these processes, using a wide variety of persuasive and behavioral techniques.

Since Cognitive Behavior Therapy is based on social learning theory, it is amenable to experimental validation. Techniques used by cognitive behavior therapists have their roots in basic research, and they are specific enough that their effectiveness can be empirically tested. Cognitive behavior therapists emphasize the importance of an operationally and methodologically sound approach to treating clients. The ultimate goal of Cognitive Behavior Therapies is to provide clients with the skills for regulating their own behaviors. Although cognitive processes are important mechanisms of human functioning, cognitive behavior therapists rely on behavioral and emotional procedures to effect change. While arguments concerning the primacy of cognitions over emotions or behavior persist, the future may find therapy directed at global life skills, which involve cognitive, emotional, and behavioral skills in interaction. Therapies that emphasize cognitive processes may be at an advantage since therapist-patient communication for effective problem solving takes place essentially in a cognitive (verbal) domain. Behavioral problems may require behavioral practice, emotional problems may require emotional practice, and cognitive deficits may require cognitive practice. But all problems will require a cognitive understanding of the therapeutic process on the part of the patient.

Whether Cognitive Behavior Therapy will continue to grow and prosper will ultimately depend on the empirical evidence and the refinement of cognitive assessment techniques. The next few years will undoubtedly be exciting ones for the Cognitive Therapy approach.

# REFERENCES

Bandura, A. *Principles of behavior modification*. New York: Holt, 1969.

Bandura, A. Self-efficacy: Towards a unifying theory of behavior change. *Psychological Review*, 1977, **84**, 191–215.

Beck, A. T. *Cognitive therapy and the emotional disorders*. New York: International Universities Press, 1976.

Cautela, J. R. Covert conditioning. In A. Jacobs and L. B. Sachs (Eds.), *The psychology of private events: Perspectives on covert response systems*. New York: Academic Press, 1971.

D'Zurilla, T. J. and Goldfried, M. R. Problem solving and behavior modification. *Journal of Abnormal Psychology*, 1971, **78**, 107–126.

Ellis, A. Rational-emotive therapy. In R. Corsini (Ed.), *Current psychotherapies*, 2nd ed. Itasca, Ill.: F.E. Peacock, 1979.

Eysenck, H. J. Behavior therapy and the philosophers. *Behaviour Research and Therapy*, 1979, **17**, 511–514.

Goldfried, M. R. Systematic densensitization as training in self-control. *Journal of Consulting and Clinical Psychology*, 1971, **37**, 228–234.

Kendall, P. C. and Hollon, S. D. (Eds.). *Cognitive-behavioral interventions: Theory, research, and procedures*. New York: Academic Press, 1979.

Mahoney, M. J. *Cognition and behavior modification*. Cambridge, Mass.: Ballinger, 1974.

Mahoney, M. J. Reflections on the cognitive-learning trend in psychotherapy. *American Psychologist*, 1977a, **32**, 5–13.

Mahoney, M. J. Personal science: A cognitive learning therapy. In A. Ellis and R. Grieger (Eds.), *Handbook of rational-emotive therapy*. New York: Springer, 1977b.

Mahoney, M. J. and Arnkoff, D. B. Cognitive and self-control therapies. In S. L. Garfield and A. E. Bergin (Eds.), *Handbook of psychotherapy and behavior change: An empirical analysis*, 2nd ed. New York: Wiley, 1978.

Meichenbaum, D. Toward a cognitive theory of self-control. In G. E. Schwartz and D. Shapiro (Eds.), *Consciousness and self-regulation: Advances in research*, vol 1. New York: Plenum, 1976.

Meichenbaum, D. *Cognitive-behavior modification: An integrative approach*. New York: Plenum, 1977.

Murray, E. J. and Jacobson, L. I. Cognition and learning in traditional and behavioral therapy. In S. L. Garfield and A. E. Bergin (Eds.), *Handbook of psychotherapy and behavior change: An empirical analysis*, 2nd ed. New York: Wiley, 1978.

Rush, A. J., Beck, A. T., Kovacs, M. and Hollon, S. Comparative efficacy of cognitive therapy and pharmacotherapy in the treatment of depressed outpatients. *Cognitive Therapy and Research*, 1977, **1**, 17–37.

Spivack, G., Platt, J. J. and Shure, M. D. *The problem-solving approach to adjustment*. San Francisco: Jossey-Bass, 1976.

Suinn, R. M. and Richardson, F. Anxiety management training: A nonspecific behavior therapy program for anxiety control. *Behavior Therapy*, 1971, **2**, 498–510.

Wolpe, J. Cognition and causation in human behavior and its therapy. *American Psychologist*, 1978, **33**, 437–446.

# CHAPTER 11

# Comprehensive Relaxation Training*

ALAN C. TURIN and STEPHANIE N. LYNCH

*A considerable number of dimensions or modalities could be considered when one attempts to classify the various psychotherapies. Thus, for example, Psychonanalysis could be seen as a method that concentrates on the intellect, the cognitive functions, with insight being a primary goal; Client-Centered Therapy could be seen as primarily relating to feelings with self-acceptance as a major goal; and Psychodrama could be seen as a system relating to behavior with assertiveness as a goal.*

*However, in all systems, one major goal is relaxation, calming down, reducing tension. This is a primary reason for the enormous number of pills prescribed for tension reduction, and a primary reason for smoking, alcohol consumption, and drug taking, licit and illicit.*

*One common method of relaxation is to do something (or nothing, as the case may be) with the body to attempt to achieve peace through body work of some kind. In the following chapter, Alan Turin and Stephanie Lynch explain a systematic system of relaxation, which can be a primary method of treatment or which can be used along with any other method of psychotherapy. Relatively simple, having commonsense principles, CRT is a technique all psychotherapists should know.*

Comprehensive Relaxation Training (CRT) is a unique "package" approach to relaxation training developed by Alan C. Turin. A CRT program includes prerecorded relaxation cassettes for home use, brief relaxation exercises, and abstinence from a variety of substances in common foods, beverages, and medicines that can increase stress and work against relaxation.

CRT is useful in the treatment (or prevention) of a variety of stress-related problems, including migraine and tension headaches, anxiety, and insomnia. In addition, some patients report spontaneous improvement in areas such as personal relations, mood, and general feelings of being able to cope. CRT may also be helpful to some individuals in reducing the risk of heart attack and stroke.

CRT may be employed as a primary therapy or used adjunctively, incorporated into other psychological or medical therapies. The entire CRT system can be taught by mental or medical health professionals to patients with no prior experience in relaxation training within four to six hours.

## HISTORY

There is now a large body of research on behavioral techniques developed for or adapted to the treatment of stress-related disorders such as headache, anxiety, insomnia, and hypertension. A common thread running through many of these techniques is that

*Since this writing, effectiveness of the CRT program has been further enhanced by the addition of a more extensive dietary component. For information, write to Dr. Turin directly (19 Muzzey Street, Lexington, MA 02173) and include a self-addressed, stamped envelope.

some form of relaxation training is the major therapeutic element. The symptoms are often thought to be triggered by hyperarousal of the sympathetic branch of the autonomic nervous system or of the musculoskeletal system. In relaxation training, the individual is trained to lower his or her arousal level either on a short-term basis, to modify response to stressful situations, or to maintain lower physiologic arousal throughout the day.

Perhaps the oldest of the relaxation methodologies is meditation, and the most popular branch of this teaching is Transcendental Meditation. Here the individual is instructed to sit in a quiet environment and to repeat a brief phrase or word to himself, thus reducing external and internal stimuli and allowing relaxation to occur. Herbert Benson (1976) modified this technique by asking the learner to repeat the word "one" to himself, to sit comfortably, and to allow intrusive thoughts to pass by. Autogenic Training, as developed by Schultz and Luthe (1969), uses more elaborate phrases and essentially self-hypnotic suggestions for relaxation.

Jacobson (1938) and Wolpe (1969) have each developed active methods for relaxation training and for helping individuals to identify excessive levels of muscle tension through deliberate relaxation or tension and then relaxation of muscles. Hypnotic and self-hypnotic techniques often employ relaxation suggestions, taking advantage of both the relaxing effects of the trance induction and the individual's heightened suggestability while in the trance. Biofeedback, which measures physiologic parameters associated with arousal, presents information about these physiologic responses to the learner in the form of lights, sounds, or meter readings. Persons can then learn to control highly subtle musculoskeletal and automonic responses if given moment-by-moment feedback to aid their learning.

The parameter chosen for measurement usually corresponds to the nervous system thought to be most highly correlated with the symptom (i.e., muscle relaxation biofeed-

back for individuals with muscle tension headaches). Feedback of other parameters is also often provided to assist the individual in learning general relaxation. Many practitioners use more traditional relaxation training methods such as relaxation tapes in addition to biofeedback, and a recent review of research suggests that relaxation training alone is as effective as the combination of relaxation training plus biofeedback (Silver & Blanchard, 1978). This strongly suggests that the induction and maintenance of low arousal (relaxation) is the primary therapeutic ingredient in biofeedback training for stress-related problems.

Caffeine, once felt to be a safe, mild central nervous system stimulant, has come under increasing suspicion as an agent in anxiety neurosis (Greden, 1974) and other stress-related disorders. Recent findings (Robertson et al., 1978) suggest that in many people, ingestion of even small amounts of caffeine leads to a dramatic increase in adrenaline and noradrenaline levels in the body, producing physiological effects similar to those caused by severe external stressors.

Sympathomimetic drugs also produce the effects of increased adrenaline levels, by introducing chemicals that act like adrenaline into the body. Careful examination of chemical components of drugs, particularly those with reported side effects such as "nervousness," reveals a surprising amount of caffeine and sympathomimetics among those drugs commonly prescribed for individuals with stress-related symptoms. Caffeine, for example, which is present in many pain-relieving drugs, may be useful when taken during individual migraine or tension headache attacks. However, it is often prescribed at daily maintenance levels. This can increase arousal on a long-term basis, often inducing stress-related problems such as anxiety, insomnia, irritability, and, at times, even more headaches, in a truly vicious circle.

The CRT program is designed, in part, to take into account the fact that no relaxation program can function at maximum effectiveness if trainees are ingesting caffeine, sympathomimetics, or other substances that work against relaxation in foods, beverages, and medicine.

## CURRENT STATUS

The CRT system was developed in the context of Turin's group practice of clinical psychology. In that practice the system has been used with over 400 patients either as a primary therapy or as an adjunct to individual, marital, or family psychotherapy.

(CRT is a service mark of Alan C. Turin, Ph.D. However the letters CRT are used in this text to simply indicate any program organized along similar lines.)

Much of the empirical support for the combination of relaxation training with abstinence from stimulants is set forth in a review paper (Turin & Sawyer, 1979) on the antagonistic effects of caffeine and relaxation training.

A systematic (controlled) case study (Turin, Nirenburg, & Mattingly, 1979) shows some of the effects of CRT on one patient's mood. In this study the patient's anxiety and depression decreased.

A thorough exposition of CRT methods, theory, and practice is presented in the book *No More Headaches!* (Turin, forthcoming).

CRT relaxation tapes are now available to mental and physical health professionals (Turin, 1979), and separate manuals for patients and professionals are in preparation. The manuals outline the rationale for CRT both as a treatment for stress-related problems and as a tool for the maintenance of a healthy life style. They include detailed information on how and when to use the CRT tapes, and how and when to do a variety of brief relaxation exercises. In addition, extensive information is included on which substances in hundreds of common foods, beverages, and medications can increase

stress and work against relaxation. It is hoped that all materials will be available by the time this book is published.

## THEORY

The human organism's stress responses are influenced by many factors, including environment, internally generated cognitions, chemicals ingested or breathed, genetic and social history, and personality dynamics. The stress-related disorder and its attendant physical and/or psychological pain, effects on self-esteem, and interference with accustomed life style and social relationships can be self-perpetuating. As the patient begins to feel increasing helplessness, the seeking of secondary gain becomes more important as a primary coping strategy, and it becomes more and more difficult for the patient to operate effectively on the environment. As disability from a stress-related disorder continues, several processes may occur. For example, pain or anxiety, with attendant depression, exhaustion, and other effects may preclude continuation of work and activities so that the patient faces reduced sources of self-esteem and gratification. Interpersonal relationships often deteriorate as the patient becomes increasingly helpless and preoccupied with symptoms. Reactive depression may reach clinical proportions and fuel further difficulties. Certain medications' side effects, such as depression, irritability, and drowsiness, may further preclude maintenance of life style. Narcotic and analgesic prescriptions are particularly dangerous in that relief from pain and escape from difficulties are highly desirable to many patients, and dependence is likely to occur with some. Caffeine provides a temporary subjective lift, although its long-term effects may exacerbate many symptoms.

Any or all of the above problems may have the effect of producing anxiety and its physiologic correlates, leaving the individual in a heightened state of arousal, where even relatively mild situational occurrences may cause or exacerbate symptoms. The goals of the CRT program are to bring the patient into a lower, healthier state of arousal and to teach him or her to modify responses to stress.

Acute and chronic stress are directly or indirectly related to a broad variety of physical and psychological ills, ranging from headaches and anxiety to nervous breakdown and perhaps even stroke and heart attack. Relaxation training generally, and CRT specifically, provides a way to reduce, counteract, or prevent some of the negative effects of stress and stress-related problems.

In many cases, CRT can function as a primary therapy.* Many anxiety neurotics, headache patients, insomniacs, and so forth, have been so improved with CRT alone that they have felt no need for further medical or psychological help. In many other cases, however, CRT is not sufficient as a total therapy unto itself, but can be helpful in the context of ongoing medical or psychological treatment. For example, many patients are referred for CRT only, while their other medical and/or psychological needs are attended to by the referring professional.

The dynamics and severity of stress-related disorders vary tremendously. One way to examine these disorders is to note the degree to which psychological dysfunction determines the nature and severity of symptoms. In the case of tension headache, for example, CRT alone (after medical screening) might provide sufficient relief. However, a more complicated case of tension headache might require not only CRT but also individual, couple, or family psychotherapy and medication.

CRT is utilized not only to teach lowering of arousal and modification of responses to stressful events, but also to boost mood and self-esteem by training individuals to modify the symptoms directly by themselves. For

example, use of relaxation techniques, review of arousal-increasing foods, drinks, and medications, and consultation with patients' physicians regarding the use of these substances often results in a rapid, at times dramatic, change in symptom frequency and severity. Such direct symptom relief often brings additional benefits since the patient can begin to resume his or her accustomed activities and interpersonal roles. The vicious circle of despair, isolated social contacts, preoccupation with symptoms, and reactive depression and anxiety may be reversed. Finally, psychotherapy can shift from a focus on stress-related symptoms to helping the patient regain the skills and attitudes necessary for development of a more satisfying, less stressful life style.

A basic theoretical thrust of the CRT program is that in order to treat a stress-related symptom, one must first help the patient to reduce the stress itself.

## METHODOLOGY

Typically, administration of the entire CRT program involves about four to six sessions, each about 50 minutes long. Patients are educated as to the general role of stress in symptom development and maintenance; it is made explicit that hyperarousal of nervous system functioning can be responsible for or involved in the production of various stress-related problems (i.e., tension headaches, insomnia, migraine).

It is explained that with CRT, persons are helped to maintain generally relaxed levels of arousal, so they are less likely to experience symptoms. They are also provided with techniques to relax on an as-needed basis to handle various specific, perhaps unpredicted, stressors as they occur. As with any acute stressful situation, the emergence of the symptom may be handled by relaxation, in order to blunt or abort the effect of the episode and prevent it from leading to full-blown symptom formation.

For these purposes, individuals are trained

*CRT is never to be used instead of necessary medical treatment.

in relaxation techniques and taught to avoid ingesting substances that can increase stress and work against relaxation. A complete explanation is given about these substances and their effects of increasing adrenaline and noradrenaline levels and increasing muscle tension. It is also explained that medications are adjusted only by consultation with the patient's physician.

Patients listen to a series of two prerecorded relaxation techniques, playing one of the tapes at least twice per day. The timing of the tape playing is to some extent dependent on the nature and timing of the occurrence of symptoms. The second step in relaxation training consists of brief relaxation exercises that can be used at any time without a tape recorder. These exercises can be used either to augment general relaxation or to combat specific stressors or episodes of symptom eruption. The brief relaxation exercises are to be practiced several times throughout each day, and, as with the tapes, are to be used regardless of symptom occurrence, since a major purpose of such a program is to provide the maintenance of a state of generalized low arousal as a method of prevention rather than simply to correct or alleviate symptoms once they occur. Systematic reviews are made of progress during the program, and brief relaxation exercises are tailored to the needs of the individual patient. A detailed review of a typical course of treatment is as follows:

During the first session, a review is made of the symptom(s), past and current, and whatever earlier therapeutic efforts have been made. Patients are referred for medical consultation if appropriate, often to rule out possibilities such as brain tumor, temporomandibular joint dysfunction syndrome, or borderline hypoglycemia, but to screen other physical problems as well. The role of stress in producing and maintaining symptoms is explained, as well as the role of CRT in reducing stress and stress-related problems. The patient is given a form for keeping a daily record of symptom activity, medication, and relaxation practice sessions at home. In addition, the patient is to keep a three-day diary of all foods, drinks, and medications ingested.

During the second session, a complete review is made of foods, drinks, and medications containing substances that can increase arousal and interfere with relaxation. These substances include (but are not limited to) caffeine in commonly recognized sources such as coffee, tea and cola drinks as well as in less commonly recognized sources such as pain, diet, and other medications, and coffee- and chocolate-flavored products such as coffee ice cream. It is explained that sympathomimetic substances, which act like adrenaline to increase stress, are found in a variety of common prescription and nonprescription medications, such as many asthma, sinus, weight-loss, and allergy medications, as well as in some common headache and pain medications. All current foods and medications are evaluated in this light, and the patient is urged to abstain from these substances, with the physician's consent.

During the third session, the patient is introduced to the first CRT tape, which is a 15-minute muscle tension-relaxation exercise plus passive relaxation imagery. The trainee is shown the various physical movements required (i.e., how to tense the various muscles involved) and informed that this is the first of many approaches to relaxation, that it may not be particularly effective when played in the office during the session due to the newness of the experience and the inhibiting presence of the therapist. He or she is further advised that the best way a person can help himself or herself to relax is not to worry about relaxing successfully, but to simply experience the tape noncritically. For example, when the tape says "your arms feel heavy," one is to imagine that one's arms feel heavy, rather than worrying whether the arms actually feel heavy or not. The patient is instructed to play the tape at least twice daily, at appropriate times and in appropriate settings, and to record the times of practice and levels of relaxation achieved pre- and post-tape.

During the fourth session, the patient is introduced to the second 15-minute relaxation tape, which is more passive and "hypnotic" in nature, and rich with relaxation imagery. In some cases, tapes are first experienced in the office so that in the unlikely event that problems arise, they will occur in the presence of a trained therapist. This tape is used at home in the same manner as the first tape.

During the fifth sesion, progress is reviewed and the patient is introduced to brief relaxation techniques. Several techniques may be offered for the individual to experiment with, with an eye toward continuing regular use of the technique or techniques found easiest and most relaxing.

During the sixth session, all techniques, procedures, and therapeutic results are reviewed. The treatment is terminated or recommendations are made for continued or additional therapeutic efforts if and as appropriate.

## APPLICATIONS

CRT may be useful in four major areas:

1.  As a primary treatment for mental and physical stress-related problems such as nervous tension, anxiety, migraine and tension headaches, insomnia, and other conditions where either physical or mental stress is a known or suspected factor, and medical causes have been ruled out by a physician.
2.  As an adjunct conducted concurrently with medical or individual, marital, group, or family therapy.
3.  As a method of prevention for individuals at risk of either the stress-related problems mentioned above, or the more ominous problems such as heart attack and stroke.
4.  As a tool for healthy individuals to maintain and enhance a relaxed life style with all its attendant benefits.

As a primary treatment for stress-related problems, CRT can fill a substantial void in most present medical and psychological treatments. Typically, a medical approach to stress-related problems involves prescription for medications such as tranquilizers and painkillers. Oftentimes, the medications bring as many problems—such as depression, drowsiness, dependence—as they resolve. Also, physicians often advise patients to "slow down and take it easy," an action many patients find difficult or impossible to implement without training in specialized techniques such as CRT. Typical psychological approaches, on the other hand, ignore the physiological underpinnings of stress-related problems by focusing almost exclusively on cognitive and emotional intra- and interpersonal issues. A person whose system is "speeding" needs help in slowing down that aspect of his or her physiology that is triggering stress-related symptoms. In the absence of such an approach, the patient is often left feeling personally inadequate for being unable to achieve adequate insight or psychological growth to shed his or her headaches, anxiety, and so forth. In addition to providing the symptom relief and improved mood that come with naturally induced relaxation, CRT enables the patient to change from being essentially a passive victim ministered to by others to a person who actively employs techniques to accomplish his or her own therapeutic results. A patient who can exert some direct control over the results of his or her own treatment not only gains in terms of symptom relief but in the invaluable and therapeutic sense of control over one's own life.

As an adjunct to individual, couple, group, and family psychotherapy, CRT is useful in a variety of ways. Since most individuals in pschotherapy are under at least some intra- and interpersonal stress, CRT can relieve that component of such stress that is amplified and intensified by excess physiological arousal. For example, the patient who drinks coffee to "calm his nerves" as a result of conflict with his or her spouse is more likely to overrespond and be quick to misinterpret anything said by his or her partner in a negative way. With relaxation comes the perspective of tempered and considered judgment. An opportunity to interrupt what would otherwise become a vicious circle of ever expanding conflict thus arises.

As a method of prevention for individuals at risk of stress-related symptoms, CRT has considerable, possibly even lifesaving, potential. CRT is not only useful in preventing everyday stress-related problems such as headache and anxiety, but it may also prove useful in preventing heart attack and stroke. Individuals who exhibit the so-called Type A behavior pattern (urgent time sense, competitive, etc.) are at increased risk of coronary artery disease and heart attack (Friedman and Rosenman, 1975.) Individuals are also at increased risk of stroke from either sustained or transient upward surges of blood pressure. By slowing down one's physiological and emotional levels of general arousal, and providing techniques to maintain or reintroduce low arousal in the face of sudden arousing stimuli, CRT may ultimately help decrease the mortality and morbidity associated with these two major problems.

Finally, CRT can be used as a tool for healthy individuals to maintain and enhance a relaxed life style. Millions of perfectly healthy people have benefited from relaxation training, meditation, and so forth. Millions of others would benefit from abstinence from substances in foods, beverages, and medications that cause them to be nervous, "hyper," or otherwise overaroused without knowing why. CRT combines the best of each of these elements, with the effect of a more relaxed, less pressured life style.

## CASE EXAMPLE

Jenny was referred to Turin by her physician for biofeedback and psychotherapy for multiple functional problems. At the time of referral, Jenny was 35, married, and a housewife with three young children. Jenny suffered both muscle contraction ("tension") and migraine headaches. The tension headache was always with her, and it was experienced as a dull "band" around her head, accompanied by constant neck pain. Superimposed on her tension headaches were migraine headaches, quite severe in nature, that occurred for about one week every two months or so. The throbbing migraine pain was felt in and behind her right eye and at her right temple. The stabbing pain and its attendant nausea, vomiting, and malaise drove Jenny to her bed during these attacks, and a housekeeper had to be hired to attend to the children.

Jenny also suffered what she referred to as "little heart attacks and angina." These were experienced as almost constant pains in her ribcage and left collarbone, neck, shoulder, arm, and wrist. In addition, she frequently experienced a "bulging, pressure" sensation in her abdomen. She was extremely nervous and subject to terror in a variety of circumstances. For example, she would frequently begin to go shopping, panic, and drive straight home as quickly as possible. She described herself as someone who always went at full speed: "It seems like all day I go—go—go. I never stop. I never get enough done."

Her typical method of dealing with her symptoms was to speed more. She would race around the house with her vacuum cleaner, cleaning frantically. She attempted to be so busy that she would forget her symptoms, stopping only to drink coffee so that she could "calm my nerves and prevent headache."

Jenny drank six to ten cups of coffee a day and received additional caffeine in some of her headache medications. Since she initially refused to discontinue her coffee drinking, CRT training began with the relaxation tapes and brief exercises. Her response to this component of the program included diminished headache and chest pain. She commented that the tape had

really kind of changed my whole life. I even had

people waiting for me twice. I never do that. While I'm listening to the tape, I can diminish all pain. It feels like the effect stays with me for hours. I've been very successful at slowing down and taking things more calmly. Like my kid had a football accident, and for once I didn't rush him off to the hospital for x-rays.

Encouraged by this initial response, Jenny agreed to gradually phase her coffee drinking down to zero. At the next session, she commented: "What a difference! My insides have been jumping up and down all the time, and now they're sleeping. I didn't dust as hard, and I didn't kill the bed so hard while I was making it. Now I can finally sit in a chair without moving."

Jenny experienced a futher reduction in symptoms, often going for days with no pains of any kind at all. Her "little heart attacks and angina" were now described as occasional "twinges." There was a visible, qualitative change in her appearance as she sat quiet and composed in the chair.

The possibility of further psychotherapy was explored, but both Jenny and the therapist agreed that it did not seem necessary. A year later, a postcard from Jenny informed the therapist that things were going fine, all headaches and pains were well under control, and that she never intended to touch caffeine again.

## SUMMARY

Traditionally psychological and medical therapies for patients with present or potential stress-related problems have ignored the therapeutic possibilities of naturally induced and maintained states of reduced physiological arousal. In behavior therapy, techniques such as relaxation training and biofeedback training have provided methods to begin filling that gap. However, several problems limit the power and availability of such techniques as generally practiced, including:

1. Need for expensive equipment.

2. Need for specialized training and knowledge over and above general training in psychology, psychiatry, medicine, and so forth.

3. Variation in training techniques (i.e., some systems emphasize either general relaxation or relaxation in the face of specific stressors, but not both. Also, some employ either muscle tense-relax methods or "hypnotic" imagery, but not both).

4. Failure to consider the effects of substances that increase stress and prevent or disrupt relaxation. These are present in hundreds of common prescription and nonprescription medications, foods, and beverages, and can easily sabotage an otherwise elegant relaxation program.

5. Limited availability to those who could benefit, due to requirements for specialized training for treatment providers.

The CRT program is designed as a package, easily integrated into the practices of professionals who are already competent in fields such as psychology, psychiatry, medicine, social work, and nursing. The combination of tape and nontape, tense-relax and "hypnotic," extended and brief relaxation exercises, as well as abstinence from the many common foods and medicines that work against relaxation provides a complete "package" approach to low-arousal therapeutics.

Biofeedback and relaxation training have already produced a burgeoning literature documenting their successes in the treatment of stress-related problems, including nervous tension, anxiety, insomnia, migraine and tension headaches, hyperactivity, hypertension, and type A (coronary-prone) behavior pattern.

CRT combines and extends the main therapeutic ingredients of biofeedback and relaxation training, and adds the neglected component of abstinence from substances that increase stress and work against relaxation. Results with over 400 patients suggest that the method may equal and exceed the demonstrated results of biofeedback and relaxation training as generally practiced.

CRT is a brief-therapy package, which can be taught in four to six sessions. It can be easily learned and taught by professionals who are already competent in their own health/mental health profession, but have no special training in low-arousal therapy methods.

CRT can be used as a primary treatment or prevention method for stress-related problems. It can be comfortably integrated into or used adjunctively to other psychological or medical therapies. Finally, CRT can bring the benefits of a quieter, more relaxed life style to perfectly healthy individuals.

## REFERENCES

Benson, H. *The relaxation response*. New York: Avon, 1976.

Friedman, M. and Rosenman, R. *Type A behavior and your heart*. Greenwich, Conn.: Fawcett, 1975.

Greden, J. F. Anxiety or caffeinism. A diagnostic dilemma. *American Journal of Psychiatry*, 1974, **131**, 1089–1093.

Jacobson, E. *Progressive relaxation*. Chicago: University of Chicago Press, 1938.

Robertson, D., Frolick, J., Carr, R., Watson, J., Hollifield, J., Shand, D. and Oates, J. Effects of caffeine on plasma renin activity, catecholamines and blood pressure. *New England Journal of Medicine*, 1978, **298 (4)**, 181–186.

Shultz, J. and Luthe, W. *Autogenic methods*, vol. 1 New York: Grune & Stratton, 1969.

Silver, B. V. and Blanchard, E. B. Biofeedback and relaxation training in the treatment of psychophysiological disorders: Or are the machines really necessary? *Journal of Behavioral Medicine*, 1978, **1 (2)**, 217–239.

Turin, A. C. *No more headaches!* Boston: Houghton Mifflin, forthcoming.

Turin, A. "Comprehensive Relaxation Training (CRT)." Cassettes, patient manuals, and therapist manuals, 1979.

Turin, A. C., Nirenberg, J. and Mattingly, M. Effects of comprehensive relaxation training (CRT) on mood: A preliminary report on relaxation training plus caffeine cessation. *The Behavior Therapist*, July/August 1979, **2 (4)**, 20–21.

Turin, A. and Sawyer, D. *Physiological and psychological effects of caffeine and relaxation training: Implications for the treatment of stress-related problems*. Submitted for publication, 1979.

Wolpe, J. *The practice of behavior therapy*. New York: Pergamon, 1969.

## CHAPTER 12

# Conditioned Reflex Therapy

ANDREW SALTER

*Andrew Salter occupies an unusual position in the history of psychotherapy. While he is one of the most gifted writers in the field and one of the pioneers—indeed, the pioneer of modern behavioristic psychotherapy—the literature has generally accorded him a low-key position relative to the development of behavioristic psychotherapy. For example, in a book I edited,\* the only mention of Salter is by Albert Ellis in Ellis's chapter on his own system of Rational-Emotive Therapy.*

*Salter, in his youth, was strongly affected by the writings of Jacques Loeb, the eminent physiologist, having been introduced to these writings by Paul de Kruif, the author of the classic* Microbe Hunters *and* Hunger Fighters. *De Kruif's admiration of Salter's work is noted in a quote in the chapter summary, as well as by the fact that de Kruif dedicated his book* The Male Hormone *to Salter.*

*For a broad philosophical understanding of the meaning of the behavioristic position, stretching beyond the more limited writings of current authors, the reader is invited to an intellectual treat by a seminal writer of landmark publications in psychotherapy.*

Maladjustment is a learning process, and so is psychotherapy. Maladjustment is malconditioning, and psychotherapy is reconditioning. The individual's problems are a result of his social experiences, and by changing his techniques of social relations, we change his personality. Experience is not only the best teacher, it is the only teacher. We are not especially concerned with giving the individual stratified knowledge of his past—called "probing." What concerns us is giving him reflex knowledge for his future—called "habits." (Salter, 1949, p.316)

Conditioned Reflex Therapy is based on the laboratory findings of Pavlov, Bechterev, Watson, and their successors. Of particular interest are Pavlov's conceptions of inhibition, excitation, and disinhibition. Mental health is based on a balance between inhibition and excitation, and psychotherapy is a process of disinhibition. "Assertion" is

the term that has become attached to certain aspects of excitation.

Conditioned Reflex Therapy has a broader conception of maladaptive symptoms than its behavioral descendants, and has found that the removal of many subtle manifestations of inhibition results in a posttreatment patient who is truly happy, and not just phobia-free or more socially adept.

## HISTORY

I majored in psychology at college, and when I discovered hypnotism I was fascinated by it—the unconditioned response of all psychology majors. The thoroughly behaviorist

\*Corsini, R. J. (Ed.). *Current Psychotherapies.* Itasca, Ill.: F. E. Peacock, 1973/1979.

approach of Clark L. Hull (1933) in *Hypnosis and Suggestibility* made complete sense to me, and still does. In essence, Hull held that words spoken by the hypnotist are conditioned stimuli that result in ideomotor reactions in the hypnotic subject.

Influenced by Hull I wrote "Three Techniques of Autohypnosis" (1941). This explained three autohypnotic techniques in a self-control paradigm, and is the pioneer paper in the field (see Goldfried & Merbaum, 1973). These techniques were applied to such problems as stage fright, overeating, insomnia, and smoking.

From Hull it was a short step for me to Watson, Pavlov, and Bechterev. Hypnosis was essentially a manifestation of Pavlov's "second signal system," that is, words. Just as sounds associated with meat came to produce salivation in Pavlov's dogs even when there was no meat present, so are words verbally conditioned bells waiting to be rung in human beings. When the appropriate word bells ring, the subject responds with "heavy" or "light" feelings, for instance. This theoretical position was developed in my *What Is Hypnosis* (1944).

Extremely early in my professional career it struck me that on the human level Pavlov's *inhibition* could well be the holding back of emotional reactions; and Pavlov's "excitation," on the human level, could be called *assertion*.

Here is a verbatim extract from the diary a young woman patient kept for me. The entry is dated January 3, 1942.

When I left your place on Saturday I was wondering just what I could do the following day along the lines you suggested. I arrived at the subway entrance, and the stairs were blocked by a crowd of people saying goodbye to each other. Some were going to go down the stairs, and the others had come with them as far as the subway to see them off. I knew they wouldn't be standing there long, and my first thought was to wait until they were through. But then I thought, "Why wait until tomorrow to start asserting yourself. Here's a perfect set-up for you." So I just said "Excuse me," and poked my nose right into the crowd. The people broke apart and I proceeded on my way. (Score 1.)

Why my interest in Pavlov? It must be relevant that when I was a child, my parents (whom I loved very dearly) would speak Russian to each other when they didn't want me to understand, and that I was brought up three houses away from a Russian Greek Orthodox church.

From my writings it is clear that besides being influenced by Pavlov, Bechterev, Hull, and Watson, my thinking was also affected by W. H. Gantt, E. R. Guthrie, N. R. F. Maier, Jules E. Masserman, and O. H. Mowrer.

But there is another person whose work affected me profoundly, even though my writings contain only a single reference to him. This person was Jacques Loeb, the great physiologist. One of his researchers at the Rockefeller Institute had been Paul de Kruif, later the author of the classic *Microbe Hunters*. De Kruif became my dear friend and Dutch uncle, and would often lecture me on Loeb. I listened with delight and read, and reread, a great deal of Loeb.

Jacques Loeb lives on as Dr. Max Gottlieb in Sinclair Lewis's *Arrowsmith*—a book for which de Kruif was Lewis's scientific adviser, and in which de Kruif's wife, Rhea, was the model for Leora, the heroine. Years later, de Kruif dedicated his book *The Male Hormone* to me.

## CURRENT STATUS

In 1959 Eysenck (p. 67) listed the 10 criteria that differentiate behavior therapy from psychoanalysis. My *Conditioned Reflex Therapy* (1949), which had appeared ten years earlier, was the first book or article in any language to embody Eysenck's ten criteria, some of which are that Behavior Therapy:

1. Is "based on consistent, properly formulated theory leading to testable deductions."

2. Is "derived from experimental studies . . ."
3. "Considers symptoms as unadaptive conditioned responses" that are "evidence of faulty learning."
4. "Treatment of neurotic disorders is concerned with habits existing at *present* . . ."
5. Interpretation of symptoms, dreams, acts, and so forth . . . "is irrelevant."

Because *Conditioned Reflex Therapy* was the first and pioneer work on Behavior Therapy, its ideas, perspective, and techniques were almost completely absorbed into the mainstream of Behavior Therapy—operant approaches excluded. The influence of *Conditioned Reflex Therapy* is visible, for instance, in the second book ever written on Behavior Therapy—Wolpe's *Psychotherapy by Reciprocal Inhibition* (1958).

In Patterson's (1966, p. 173) astringent words, "Wolpe's psychotherapy by reciprocal inhibition appears to be a more sophisticated application of the approach used by Salter."

Or as Reyna said:

Despite differences in theory, there are many practical similarities between Wolpe's methods and those of Salter (1944, 1949) who earlier applied conditioning principles to the full spectrum of neurotic behaviors . . . . Salter's case studies show a wide range of techniques, which include "excitation" and the external instigation of a variety of assertive and relaxation responses incompatible with previous behaviors. (Wolpe, Salter, & Reyna, 1964, p. 174).

In Fensterheim and Baer's (1975, p. 23) clear words: "Andrew Salter . . . founded modern behavior therapy."

It may well be that Hullian theory can explain why I have never felt the drive to give courses or felt the goal gradient acceleration as I sped from city to city evangelizing for Behavior Therapy. In any event, I have contented myself with watching the growth of Behavior Therapy, and with the footnotes and mentions of my work that I have encountered.

Kazdin's classic work, *History of Behavior Modification* (1978), includes a thorough review and evaluation of my work and its historical setting. In Kazdin's words:

Cases reported in *Conditioned Reflex Therapy* include applications of techniques closely resembling systematic desensitization, self-control, behavioral rehearsal, and covert conditioning based upon imagery . . . . Fuller versions of techniques initiated by Salter are still being employed by contemporary practitioners of behavior modification. (p. 174)

The interested reader will find fuller explanations of Conditioned Reflex Therapy in *Conditioned Reflex Therapy* (Salter, 1949) and *The Conditioning Therapies* (Wolpe, Salter, & Reyna, 1964; see Chapter 2).

## THEORY

The personality of the individual is the result of the interaction of heredity and environment. Heredity provides the organism with such instinctual patterns as may exist, but these instincts soon become modified by the individual's experiences.

The individual learns an elaborate collection of emotional responses to people and things, and develops elaborate rationalizations for his or her attitudes and behaviors. The individual sees the new through the glasses of the old, and distorts the new accordingly, and proceeds to integrate it into his or her nervous system.

Heredity provides the phonograph, but environment builds the record library of the brain. Not only is it impossible to choose your relatives, but you cannot even choose yourself.

Just as Pavlov's dog learned to salivate when the bell rang, so does the baby learn that certain behavior on his part brings certain responses from those around him, and he gets conditioned quite as involuntarily. If each act of the child is met with a motherly "don't," equivalent to punishing the dog when he salivates, the child will inhibit his emotions, and withdraw into himself. In Pavlovian terms, the flow of saliva when the bell was rung to signal the appearance of meat is an example of an *excitatory reflex*. But if the bell is rung again and again, and not followed by meat, or the dog is punished, the saliva stops flowing, and this is an *inhibitory reflex*.

The newborn infant's behavior is excitatory. It acts without restraint. If we were not to interfere in any way except to gratify its physical needs, it would continue in its excitatory path. But we begin early to inhibit the child, and that is how the trouble begins.

People are surprised that babies learn when so young. The question is "Are babies stimulus receivers?" If they are, then learning has to take place. In fact, the child is the megaphone of his training, and he never does anything to his parents that they didn't do to him in the first place.

The basis of life is excitation. The creatures that survive in the jungle are those that slink and jump and kill. The polite and inhibited ones crouch behind a tree and are soon dead. The human species could never have survived if it were inhibited.

This is not palatable to most of us. Man, the talking primate, insists on clinging to his illusions despite overwhelming evidence to the contrary. We do not like to be reminded that, evolutionarily speaking, we are merely stomachs that grew more complicated.

But the human animal, intelligent as it may be, can no more think its way out of an emotional problem than the monkey in the zoo. Man can only be trained out of it. We are no better than our equipment, and our equipment is primitive. There is nothing objective about an animal's reactions. The human being is bounded by the human body. We are composed of jungle stuff, and ours is a monkey culture. Our troubles are caused by deviations into civilization, which is a fraud perpetrated on evolution. *Homo sapiens* has convinced himself that he is a dancing bear. Consequently, he can only lose his balance.

In the beginning was the gut, and the gut was law, and it is still so. It is the dog part of the human being that gets out of order,

the part we keep telling ourselves we should be a little above, but we never are. The dog part runs by the dog rules. Everything is natural, under the circumstances. The twisted, unhappy person is normal, based on what happened to him. No one does what he should. He only does what he can, because that is what he has been conditioned to do. People are no more naturally one way or another than a piece of marble is naturally the Venus de Milo. Early environment is the sculptor's chisel.

Nothing is ever wrong in the individual's "should" department. It is the "able to" department that causes the difficulty. We live up to our conditioning, not our ideals.

I am always suspicious of the words "like to" or "don't like to." The inhibitory person does not "like" to talk, and the excitatory one does not "like" to keep quiet. An individual's philosophy of life is the product of his feeling-training. His philosophy changes with his emotional reeducation.

Only the drilling into the human tissues of healthy habits will yield "good" thinking and feeling. We are meat in which habits have taken up residence. We are a result of the way other people have acted to us. We are the reactions. Having conditioned reflexes means carrying about pieces of past realities.

We do not control ourselves. We are constantly being controlled by our habit patterns. What we deprecate as present irrelevancies are the imprints of past relevancies. We think with our habits, and our emotional training determines our thinking. Consciousness is like a moving picture. The emotional patterns of infancy are projected into awareness. We sit in the audience, and insist we're in the projection booth.

We have only the volition given by our habits. Where there is a conditioned reflex, there is no free will. Our "willpower" is dependent on our previously learned reflexes. If they are inadequate, the individual will bemoan his lack of "guts" and deprecate himself, though he is not at all to blame. Everybody is a carpenter using the only tools he ever had.

We feel by doing, and we do by feeling. We do not act because of intellectual reasons. Our reasons grow from our emotional habits. The important point about conditioning is that it is not at all an intellectual process. Whether we like it or not, the braincase has been permeated by the viscera. Life would be impossible if we had to think in order to breathe, feel, digest, blink, and keep our hearts beating.

Personality is not a question of logic. It is a question of feeling. Many bright people are as dull as dishwater. It is their emotional training that makes the difference.

Children are interesting because they are emotionally outgoing. A childish childhood is a happy childhood. The baby is born free, but his parents soon put him in chains. The tragedy of the drama of psychology is that all of the villains have friendly faces.

Excitation is a basic law of life, and neurosis is the result of the inhibition of natural impulses. I have also said, as can only be obvious in our daily life, that much of our activity is not logically motivated.

When we pause to consider what we have done when we felt happiest, we will recognize that we spoke without thinking. We expressed our innermost feelings. We did not waste time and energy percolating. We acted in an excitatory fashion.

People ask, "What are the roots of my troubles? How did I get this way?" They really mean, "How, in my childhood, was I robbed of my natural excitation? Where and how was this emotional component dwarfed, twisted, misdirected, or minimized?" *Hundreds of different causes produce the same fundamental deprivation of excitation.*

Causes such as the following are easy enough to determine, but they do nothing except satisfy our intellectual curiosity. I take them at random from my files:

1. Excessively well-mannered English family.
2. Unhappily married parents. A drunken father.

3. "Both my parents are quiet and reserved."
4. A mother-bound only child.
5. A psychopathic father. Great love one moment, overwhelming rage the next.
6. A more able older brother.
7. Brought up in an orphanage.

Finding and exploring the situations that have caused the psychological difficulty do nothing to facilitate the cure. A judge is interested in who is to blame for an automobile accident. The physician is concerned with healing the wounds of the injured. Psychiatry and psychoanalysis play the part of the judge, although they insist they are cast for the role of the physician.

Man's physical and emotional equipment is the same as it was ages ago. Yet modern man finds himself enmeshed in a web of constraining social forms with which he has more and more been required to conform, belying his essential nature, and denying that the human is, now as then, an animal—predatory, sadistic, craving, and emotional. From here springs conflict between artificial and natural, which overlooks the fact that man is a talking primate.

Living in society necessitates inhibition, but modern training goes too far when it teaches children to be polite at all times, not to contradict others, not to interrupt, not to be selfish, and always to consider other people's feelings. A well-adjusted person is like a housebroken dog. He has the basic inhibitions to permit him to live in society, but none extra to interfere with his happiness.

It will be objected that even the animals have their inhibitions. Doesn't the tiger crouch quietly before he leaps? If he went through the underbrush in an excitatory fashion, wouldn't the other animals run away? True. Nevertheless, excitation is the meat of the jungle, while inhibition is the salt and pepper.

Following a set pattern, bowing to artificial vogue, conforming to a standardized mold, smothers excitation. This characterizes the inhibitory "types"—gentlemen-of-the-old-school, chivalrous colonels, well-brought-up boys, "officers and gentlemen," stoics, and ascetics. Every chink in their emotional armor, with a few approved exceptions, is plugged with a socially originated inhibition.

At first thought it might appear that a return to excitation would produce a world inhabited by undisciplined brutes, yet nothing could be further from the truth. Only the predominantly inhibited person is selfish, since he is constantly preoccupied with himself. The inhibitory person's consideration for others is merely a burned child's dread of the fire. He has no thought for others, because he does not have the ability to look outwardly upon those around him. He doesn't love, although he wants to be loved. There is no love without involvement, and he remains in his own shell. He has been conditioned against expressing the emotions of love. He is afraid of other people; he is afraid of responsibility; he is afraid to make decisions. His fears may express themselves in a show of aggression, egocentricity, and a lack of consideration. This type of inhibited person also worries constantly, and he is as maladjusted as his overpolite and shy brother. His suffering is equally intense.

A person has feelings of frustration and conflict when his psychological skills are inadequate to solve the problem that confronts him. It is as if he were trained to open doors, and it is not so much that the emotional lock before him is a new one as that the keys of inhibition are made of putty.

As we modify *behavior,* we modify the self-concept of the individual and the individual's emotional status. Behavior change precedes the change in the self-concept.

To change the way a person feels and thinks about himself, we must change the way he acts toward others. In short, just as the individual's private feelings of low self-esteem, shyness, and inadequacy were caused by earlier social experiences, so will new social experiences alter these personal feelings. Through Conditioned Reflex Therapy the individual is taught to interact socially in an excitatory fashion and not in an inhibitory fashion. Altering the individual's behavior alters the individual's self-image. One is a reflection of the other.

And, simultaneously, the individual's feelings of self-worth and social adequacy rise.

## METHODOLOGY

The primary purpose of Conditioned Reflex Therapy is to alter the patient's psychological tilt from inhibition to excitation. Inhibitory feelings and inhibitory behavior are neurotic. Excitatory behavior is healthy.

Six techniques will do much to increase the individual's level of excitation. They are so interdependent and comingled that by practicing any one of them, the individual is, in effect, learning all of the others.

The first discipline (for that is what it is) I have called *feeling-talk.* It means the deliberate utterance of spontaneously felt emotions. "Thank heavens, today is Friday and the weekend is here" illustrates feeling-talk. However, saying merely "Today is Friday" would be dry fact-talk, and would do nothing to help emotional reconstruction. Man is the word-using animal, and his basic means for excitation is through speech. In a sense, feeling-talk means only to be emotionally outspoken, and is an aspect of small-talk.

My techniques of feeling-talk, rebaptized *assertion,* have attained much professional—and popular—acceptance. All too often I have found that calling feeling-talk "assertion" has resulted in an emphasis on the negative and the critical, and a soft-pedaling of the many other notes on the feeling-talk keyboard. And I must say that I have found too many of the advocates of assertion to be rather brassy, which is not the point of assertion at all.

Here are some examples of the side of assertion that I have found has been neglected by many of its advocates.

| Remark | Type of Feeling-Talk |
|---|---|
| 1. I like the soup. | Like |
| 2. I like that snow scene. It makes me feel cool to look at it. | Like |
| 3. That shade of green is perfect for you. | Praise |
| 4. You did a marvelous job, Miss Jones. | Praise |
| 5. Today is Friday, I thought it would never get here. | Relief |
| 6. I can hardly wait until he gets here. | Impatience |
| 7. My feet hurt. | Discomfort |
| 8. What a wonderful time we had. | Enjoyment |
| 9. The desk set was just what I needed. | Appreciation |
| 10. I cleaned out the poker game. | Self-praise |
| 11. I wonder what happens in the next installment. | Curiosity |
| 12. It was the most extraordinary thing I had seen in a long time. | Amazement |
| 13. Say it again. I like it. | Desire for approbation |
| 14. I'm just dying to meet him. | Anticipation |
| 15. There's nothing to it. I'll take care of it right away. | Confidence |
| 16. This was a real good meal. | Contentment |
| 17. I think the dessert was a mistake. | Regret |
| 18. Darling, I love you with all my heart. | Love |
| 19. Good grief, I feel terrible about that! | Anguish |
| 20. Today is Friday. The week went fast. | Surprise |
| 21. Now, that was stupid of me! | Self-criticism |

Our golden rule is emotional truth, even if it means risking expediency. There is no harm in honoring social amenities and ethical conventions when they do not oppose our feelings. But we must forego premeditated utterances and say what we feel when we feel it. When a cat feels happy, it purrs. When a dog has its paw stepped on, it howls. Let the inhibitory go and do likewise.

Animals also show emotion on their faces. The inhibitory person need not snarl like a tiger nor grin like a Cheshire cat that has read Dale Carnegie. However, he should furrow his brow when he is vexed, and wear a long face. Be emotionally Gallic is my counsel. I have named this second practice *facial talk*.

Our third rule of conduct is to *contradict and attack*. When you* differ with someone, do not simulate agreability. Instead, externalize feeling, and contradict on an unprovable emotional basis. At first blush, this would seem to obstruct intelligent controversy. Actually, it only means interspersing emotional content among bare facts.

The next, and fourth, technique to keep in mind is the *deliberate* use of the word *I* as much as possible. "I like this . . ." "I read that book and . . ." "I want . . ." "I heard . . ." This will not make you appear priggish. It will sound natural. Somebody told one of my patients who was practicing this: "You know, you're conceited, but somehow I don't mind it from you."

The fifth discipline is to *express agreement when you are praised*. When someone says, "That's a fine suit you're wearing," do not remain expressionless. Do not shrug your shoulders and say, "It's nothing." Nor be satirical and say, "Of course, I'm wonderful." Instead, if you believe the compliment at all, say something like, "Thank you. It's my favorite suit. Gives me big shoulders, doesn't it?"

When Dr. Smith congratulates me on my success with Jones, I answer, "Thank you, Doctor. You know, he may consider himself fortunate that you were wide-awake enough to have sent him to see me." Notice that I have praised not only myself but also the

---

*I have retained some of my across-the-desk language.

physician. When you reflect praise like a mirror, the giver of the compliment will not deny it. The recipient, finding his self-praise accepted by the environment, develops increased emotional freedom. This is excellent self-conditioning. *Praise of self should also be volunteered,* and with straightforward naivete.

*Improvisation* is our sixth and last rule of conduct. Don't plan. Live for the next minute, and that's 59 seconds too long. This applies to what you are going to buy, where you are going to visit, and what you are going to say. Daydreaming is a sign of incomplete doing, and improvisation stops it. In order to build this spontaneity do not waste time Monday thinking about Tuesday and Wednesday. Live *now,* and tomorrow will take care of itself, even though we need more foresight than the grasshopper in the fable.

There are six typical procedures used in Conditioned Reflex Therapy.

The first series of procedures is addressed to increasing the excitatory level of the patient. These techniques were discussed above. In the words of Davison and Neale (1978, p. 497) Salter is "the originator of assertion training."

Another important technique introduced in *Conditioned Reflex Therapy* (1949) has been termed *behavior rehearsal*. This simply means going over with the patient future social encounters and discussing what to do and say if "they" say or do this—or, more probably—that. The therapist can play either the patient's role or that of the other participant in the projected encounter.

Behavior rehearsal is an important technique because of the *social* orientation of Conditioned Reflex Therapy. We view the patient's *social interactions* as the *primary source* of the patient's current inhibitions. And this is true despite the individual's having learned his or her inhibitions in the remote past.

The third technique used in Conditioned Reflex Therapy has become known as *systematic desensitization*. It was introduced in case 3 in my *Conditioned Reflex Therapy* (1949). The patient

listened with interest to my explanation of verbal conditioning, and next I told him to practice turning his feeling of claustrophobia on and off, and conditioning relaxation to it . . .

. . . My plan was for him to establish a link between controlling his senses and feeling good. I also told him to take care not to make his claustrophobia stronger than his feelings of well-being, or the conditioning would increase his discomfort.

Systematic desensitization, of course, is now one of the most widely used Behavior Therapy techniques. I did not invent desensitization only for use in phobias, but also for use as a technique of anxiety reduction in social and sexual relations.

From my *Three Techniques of Autohypnosis* (1941) to its attenuated and varied forms described in my *What Is Hypnosis* (1944) and *Conditioned Reflex Therapy* (1949), techniques of *self-control* are an important factor in Conditioned Reflex Therapy. As long as increasing the excitatory level of the patient remains our primary concern, teaching the patient techniques of self-control will be "getting at the roots" and will be quite helpful.

Teaching the patient to relax through *self-verbalizations* before entering (or while in) uncomfortable situations is another point emphasized in Conditioned Reflex Therapy. While this now seems a rather obvious point, as concern with self-instruction training and self-verbalization is now an important area of Behavior Therapy, historically it was not always thus.

I conclude this list of the primary techniques of Conditioned Reflex Therapy by mentioning the use of *covert conditioning based on imagery*. Imagery, as a provider of stimuli for use in conditioning, of course, is the essence of what has come to be called *systematic desensitization*. It is worth mentioning that elaborate lists of stimuli are quite unnecessary in teaching desensitization. Regulating the *duration* of the patient's imagery, and regulating the imaginary *distance* the patient is from a *single* high anxiety stimulus, is usually satisfactory.

Covert conditioning in the therapist's office (or the patient's home) to imagined anxious stimuli produces important benefits to the patient. And mobilizing covert conditioning in the presence of the actual anxiety-inducing stimuli—in an awkward social situation, for instance—is also extremely helpful. What is particularly interesting is that there is laboratory evidence that bonafide conditioning can take place as a result of a subject's juxtaposition of two imagined stimuli.

## APPLICATIONS

Conditioned Reflex Therapy has shown excellent results with the entire spectrum of neurotic disorders. The phobias, anxiety, shyness, obsessive-compulsions, most insomnias and psychosomatic disorders—including migraine and *psychosomatic* coronary conditions—respond excellently to Conditioned Reflex Therapy. As for insufficient assertiveness in interpersonal relations, Conditioned Reflex Therapy should be considered the treatment of choice.

Long before Masters and Johnson, Conditioned Reflex Therapy was using most of their methods in the successful treatment of varied sexual dysfunctions. As Fensterheim (1974, p. 16) wrote, with historical precision and a graceful pun: "We can trace the beginnings of these treatment methods to the seminal work of Salter . . . (1949)." The successful treatment of impotence is often a simple achievement via Conditioned Reflex Therapy. The treatment of poor orgasmic function in women calls for somewhat more effort, but here too the prognosis is usually excellent.

I have found that Conditioned Reflex Therapy is extremely efficacious in overcoming the work blocks of the creative, and I have some remarkable case histories of writers, musicians, and actors and actresses.

Particularly interesting to me have been patients with clusters of symptoms that are clearly neurotic but that defy easy categorization.

Before considering the limitations of Conditioned Reflex Therapy, I should mention that I have noticed that in recent years my caseload includes many fewer alcoholics, stutterers, and homosexuals. My explanation is simply that there has been a tremendous development of different therapies for alcoholism and stuttering, and that most—not all—homosexuals now consider themselves to be quite normal.

The limitations of Conditioned Reflex Therapy are essentially as follows:

Neither the highly defensive (I call them "yes, but-ers,") nor the highly paranoid will respond to Conditioned Reflex Therapy. Nor will such persons respond to any other forms of psychotherapy. Such persons can be spotted in a session or two, and certainly with the help of the Minnesota Multiphasic Personality Inventory.

Mild depressions are quite amenable to Conditioned Reflex Therapy, but as I have written elsewhere:

Assertion trainers should be extremely cautious with depressed clients. In a way, treating depressed clients is an "orange sorting" problem. We have a conveyor belt with holes, and certain sizes of oranges can fall through the holes and larger sizes move on. We can handle certain kinds of clients. Certain other kinds of oranges have to go to people who can give medication and who can use biochemical approaches in treatment. As you talk to a client, and you see, quite correctly, the things that are making the person so depressed ("If she only realized thus and so about her husband," or "That situation with her mother isn't really thus and so"), you may be absolutely correct in your explanation. Nevertheless, your skills will not necessarily keep this person from going into an even deeper depression which really needs institutionalization. The fact that you can correctly see the psychogenesis of the situation does not mean that it can be treated by anybody's assertive, psychotherapeutic, or behavioral techniques." (Salter, 1977, pp. 35–36)

Any therapist who treats unmedicated schizophrenics should be aware that a core of the symptomatology will remain inaccessible until the patient is appropriately medicated.

I have done fairly well with sociopaths if their pathology is relatively mild and if their histories are not malignant.

In general, then, Conditioned Reflex Therapy is well-suited for all of the problems psychoanalysts believe they can treat and many of the problems analysts do not treat.

And Conditioned Reflex Therapy is so much faster and efficacious than arthritically crippled psychoanalysis! Now Conditioned Reflex Therapy and Behavior Therapy in general have reached such a level of acknowledged successful results that only the psychiatrically illiterate would dismiss them as being good only for phobias and mild neuroses.

As Charles Kettering once said to Paul de Kruif, "Remember, Paul, there is no such thing as an incurable disease. The disease has no objection to being cured."

## CASE EXAMPLE

Mrs. R. H. is a blonde, attractive woman of 34. She tells me she is a professional pianist, and recites a series of formidable credits. Now, however, she plays the piano poorly. She was in an automobile accident, and has had surgery on both shoulders and on her arms. After a year of recuperation and physiotherapy she is playing the piano again, but her skill is as a shadow of her former self. In addition, the third finger of her right hand is uncontrollable. It feels numb and she cannot use it at will.

She has recently consulted two eminent neurosurgeons, considering neurosurgery to be the only solution for the problem of the third finger of her right hand. Intensive work-ups resulted in the same conclusion from each of the neurosurgeons: "I can't find any physical basis for this malfunction."

"Do you mean it's all in her head?" her husband asked the second neurosurgeon.

"I don't know" was the answer. "Perhaps she should see a psychoanalyst."

Her husband did not have a high opinion of psychoanalysis and holed himself up in a nearby university library. In the course of

his reading he ran across my writings. I was the person to see. My brand of hypnotism would solve his wife's problem, and he particularly liked my book on psychoanalysis (Salter, 1952).

Before commencing physiotherapy, Mrs. R. H. had been very hopeful about its results, and some months earlier had signed contracts for a series of recitals. Could I restore sensation and control to her numb, uncontrollable finger in time for her first concert, which was four weeks away?

"Maybe," I said, "if the doctors you saw are right. But wouldn't you run out of here without bothering to open the door and go out through the wall like a Mickey Mouse character if I promised you that I could help you? And in four weeks at that?"

She laughed weakly.

I advised her to cancel all of her scheduled concerts. "If everything goes as well as I hope, you'll have all the concerts you want. Your credentials are quite impressive."

My reason for telling her to cancel her schedule was simple. I felt that the achievement pressure of her schedule could seriously inhibit our therapy. Mrs. R. H. agreed to do as I advised.

While I could have immediately gone to work on efforts to restore her finger function, I felt that this would have been superficial treatment. If we succeeded, that would have been the end of the matter. But this would have been unfair to Mrs. R. H., when the repertoire of Conditioned Reflex Therapy has so much more to offer. Besides, more thorough treatment would maximize the possibilities of success in the treatment of her finger condition—which in itself is reason enough for taking such an approach. Borrowing a pharmacological term from Arnold Lazarus (which he uses in another connection), I would say that I advocate "broad spectrum" *personality changes*.

I shall discuss my treatment of the numb-fingered pianist in four parts, as follows:

1. The use of the Minnesota Multiphasic Personality Inventory (MMPI).
2. Preliminary phases—getting the history,

particularly the present circumstances of the patient's life.

3. Deciding on the goals of treatment.
4. Carrying out the goals of treatment.

I like to have my patients take the MMPI after the first session with me so that I have the scores waiting for their second session. The significant scores of this patient were as follows: depression, 90th percentile; psychopathic, 90th percentile; paranoid, 80th percentile; masculinity-femininity, 15th percentile; hypochondria, 33rd percentile.

In short, the patient was somewhat depressed, somewhat rebellious (not amoral), and hypersensitive. The literature considers the low score on masculinity-femininity to be a sign of almost masochistic passivity. There were no signs whatever of any psychotic tendencies.

These scores correlated fully with my clinical impressions. What was also interesting and encouraging was that her "hypochondria" score was in approximately the 33rd percentile, verifying my clinical impression that she was not at all hypochondriacal. No "secondary gain" nonsense here.

My second concern was getting the patient's history, particularly the present circumstances of her life. I also asked details about the accident and about her ruminations regarding music and her malfunctioning finger. All this helped me to determine the third phase, the goals of treatment. These were: (1) restoration of function in her finger; (2) restoration of a feeling of relaxation about music; (3) increasing the patient's level of excitation (i.e., assertion) in her personal and professional life.

In *carrying out the goals of treatment* I often mixed objectives in my consultations with her. But it is possible to describe my techniques separately.

"Forget hypnotism," I told her. "My first task with you is to get you out of the trance you've been in for years." She found my comment quite amusing, and not inaccurate.

The reader will recall that the third finger on the patient's right hand was both numb and without any control. The difficulties, therefore, were both sensory and motor in character. Relaxation, self-control, and covert conditioning were used to attack the problems of the finger. I taught the patient how to induce relaxation of her arms and fingers. I also queried her on her personal experiences with warmth and cold in her hands, and had her imagine these actual experiences (covert conditioning) in her fingers. She also practiced this (quite well) at home. In addition, to try to get at the motor aspects of her finger difficulty, I had her practice (successfully) imagining lightness and heaviness in her hands and fingers—more covert conditioning.

I did not tell her that I had done this exact type of covert conditioning with another woman some years before my pianist patient was born. In that case we were also dealing with the sequelae of an automobile accident, but then the woman's feet were like thin sticks that were completely paralyzed and did not respond to lit matches or ice cubes. By having that patient, for instance, recall childhood memories of her family gathered around a roaring, crackling fire, she was able to summon up feelings of warmth in her feet. Her thrill when we first achieved this is one of the most exciting moments of my professional career. I did not mention this patient to my pianist patient because I did not want to suggest any new symptoms to her.

At the same time I was teaching my patient to relax her entire body and to "feel relaxed about music." I felt that music was a source of excessive pressure to her, just like the need to perform successfully is to a man with impotence. This process of desensitization to the pressure to practice and to concertize could only help her finger.

I devoted a great deal of effort to increasing the patient's level of excitation in her personal and professional life. These areas included:

1. Her marriage. This was the second mar-

riage for both the patient and her husband.

2. The problems caused by the admixture of her children, her husband's children, and their children.

3. Her mother—a tough, driving woman. Her father—important for his nonimportance.

4. Her husband's ex-wife, the mother of the patient's stepchildren, who lived in a nearby community and was a chronic source of frustration.

5. Her musical career.

What was particularly helpful was that the patient's remarriage was a happy one.

I taught the patient the six assertive disciplines mentioned at the beginning of my section on methodology, some simple behavior rehearsal and densensitization techniques, and that completed the strategies.

After four sessions the patient's finger— and her attitude—were fine. Her finger had recovered completely, with no additional physiotherapy, and her emotional level had become completely transformed for the better.

The point may well be raised that covert conditioning alone might have solved the finger problem and that the "broad spectrum" personality changes were a result of the improvement in the finger. If not, they were not that necessary.

However, I think that not to give a patient the maximum improvement that is possible through Conditioned Reflex Therapy is cruel and unfair, and gives support to psychoanalytic criticisms of behavioral treatment.

To respond to any possible criticism of my belief that each patient is entitled to as much improvement as possible, I shall quote from a review written by a music critic.

After her fifth session with me my patient decided to go on a tour as the piano accompanist of a famous violinist. She had been playing perfectly for some weeks, and I wanted her to get her feet wet in a subordinate position before venturing to resume her solo concertizing.

After her first appearance on this tour, a review of the concert appeared in a local paper, one of the most important newspapers in the country. The review had a four-column head: PIANIST OUTSHINES SOLOIST. Then the review went on to say:

"The norm for concerts featuring instrumental soloists is for the piano accompanist to be far beneath the level of accomplishment of the soloist. Yesterday's ———— Hall recital was an exception. William A—— played with pianist R— — H————. Although A—— was the soloist, H— — [the pianist] provided the backbone as strongly as an orchestra does in a concerto. . . .

H—— played with the piano fully open and used the instrument with imagination, tapping its resources expertly.

She is definitely a soloist in her own right. Her ability to shape long movements and independently *assert the character of the music is beyond that of even the greatest accompanists living.* . . ." (Italics added. Note the word "assert".)

I find it difficult to believe that this review ever would have been written if I had "only fixed my patient's finger." It was my total therapy that elicited Mrs. R. H.'s greater expressiveness, and that greater expressiveness in turn elicited this review and the incredible headline.

My pianist's employer, of course, was most unhappy—but it worked out well and besides, that's another story.

## SUMMARY

I would be less than candid not to admit to a feeling of pride that my book *Conditioned Reflex Therapy* has been called "a landmark of the order of Darwin's *Origin of Species*" (de Kruif, 1949); one of the "landmarks in the history of psychology" (Sahakian, 1968); one of the "landmarks in the history of clinical psychology" (Nawas, 1972). And at more length, it has been said: "The books by Salter, Wolpe, Keller and Schoenfeld, and Skinner are landmarks in the history of behavior modification . . .'' (Kazdin, 1978). And the thinking and techniques of *Conditioned Reflex Therapy* certainly permeate Behavior Therapy, which gives me a great deal of satisfaction.

But what gives me the greatest professional satisfaction is one detail that distinguishes Conditioned Reflex Therapy from its descendants. Since Conditioned Reflex Therapy has a broader conception of maladaptive symptoms than its behavioral descendants, its objective is not just to eliminate the, for instance, claustrophobia or agoraphobia that brought the patient to treatment, but also to teach the patient to become a *broadly functioning* and *broadly feeling* human being.

The efforts of therapy should indeed be directed toward symptom removal, but with Conditioned Reflex Therapy's broader conception of symptoms, the removal of many of the subtle manifestations of inhibition results in a posttreatment patient who is truly happy, and not just phobia-free or more socially adept.

The results of behaviorally oriented therapy has too often been to rid the patients of the distressing symptoms that brought them to treatment—which is fine—but the behavior therapist should realize that patients almost always also suffer from debilitating symptoms with which they are not particularly concerned.

The Pavlovian concepts of inhibition, excitation, and disinhibition need refurbishing in the light of newer neurological findings. Nevertheless, the fact that I have eliminated claustrophobia and agoraphobia *solely* by increasing the patient's level of excitation (read "assertion") certainly calls for serious reflection.

This means, clearly, that excitation (or assertion) is by no means indicated solely for problems of defective social interaction—a misapprehension that still clouds the perceptions of the vast majority of behavior therapists.

The historical record now shows that Behavior Therapy has advanced far beyond psy-choanalytic therapy. The time has come to make Behavior Therapy still more liberating and self-fulfilling to the patient than it now is, and this, I believe, is the promise of Conditioned Reflex Therapy.

## References

Davison, G. C. and Neale, J. M. *Abnormal psychology, 2nd ed.* New York: Wiley, 1978.

de Kruif, P. Jacket copy. *Conditioned reflex therapy,* New York: Farrar, Straus, 1949.

Eysenck, H. J. Learning theory and behaviour therapy. *Journal of Mental Science,* 1959, **105**, 61–75.

Fensterheim, H. Behavior therapy of the sexual variations. *Journal of Sex and Marital Therapy,* 1974, **1**, 16–28.

Fensterheim, H. and Baer, J. *Don't say yes when you want to say no.* New York: Dell, 1975.

Goldfried, M. R. and Merbaum, M. (Eds.). *Behavior change through self-control.* New York: Holt, 1973.

Hull, C. L. *Hypnosis and suggestibility.* New York: Appleton, 1933.

Kazdin, A. E. *History of behavior modification: Experimental foundations of contemporary research.* Baltimore, Md.: University Park Press, 1978.

Nawas, M. M. Landmarks in the history of clinical psychology from its early beginnings through 1971. *Journal of Psychology,* 1972, **82**, 91–110.

Patterson, C. H. *Theories of counseling and psychotherapy.* New York: Harper & Row, 1966.

Sahakian, W. S. *History of psychology.* Itasca, Ill.: F. E. Peacock, 1968.

Salter, A. Three techniques of autohypnosis. *Journal of General Psychology,* 1941, **24**, 423–438.

Salter, A. *What is hypnosis: Studies in auto and hetero conditioning.* New York: R. R. Smith, 1944; Farrar, Straus, 1955.

Salter, A. *Conditioned reflex therapy: The direct approach to the reconstruction of personality.* New York: Farrar, Straus, 1949; Capricorn Books-Putnam, 1961.

Salter, A. *The case against psychoanalysis.* New York: Holt, 1952; Harper & Row, 1972.

Salter, A. On assertion. In R. E. Alberti (Ed.), *Assertiveness: Innovations, applications, issues.* San Luis Obispo, Calif.: Impact Publishers, 1977.

Wolpe, J. *Psychotherapy by reciprocal inhibition.* Stanford, Calif.: Stanford University Press, 1958.

Wolpe, J., Salter, A. and Reyna, L. J. (Eds.). *The conditioning therapies: The challenge in psychotherapy.* New York: Holt, 1964.

# CHAPTER 13

# *Conflict Resolution Therapy*

E. LAKIN PHILLIPS

*One of the important individuals in the field of psychotherapy is E. Lakin Phillips, who has been following his particular path for a long time. He assumes broad-gauge position in terms of theory and of operations. In his general approach, he falls into the same category, more or less, as a number of other broad-gauge theorists and practitioners who have written chapters for this book, including Anderson, Hart, Lazarus, Paul, Shostrom, and Urban. According to Conflict Resolution Therapy it is a therapy sufficient unto itself; the same position is taken by the authors referred to above in regard to their therapies and also by the big three of psychotherapy: Freud, Jung, and Adler.*

*Similar to a number of other theorists, notably those in Gestalt Psychotherapy, Phillips centers his attention on the concept of conflict. Another aspect of this theory is the notion that all conflicts essentially are the result of social factors. Still another element, practically unique among theorists is the concept of gradients.*

*This chapter is likely to induce in the careful reader a desire to know more about Conflict Resolution Therapy, since it will provoke considerable speculation and possibly conflict.*

*Conflict resolution therapy* consists of a number of aspects:

1. It is behavioral, locating variables in the person-environment interaction.
2. It asserts that conflict is basic to psychopathology.
3. The approach aspects of the conflict paradigm relate to what the person asserts.
4. The person moves through cycles of asserting, having needs met (or failing this effort, thereby giving rise to avoidance aspects of the conflict paradigm).
5. The organism is constantly in interaction with the environment and learns and changes in this way.
6. Unresolved conflicts provide the need for psychotherapy (or any other behavior-change effort) and provide the impetus for theories of personality and psychopathology.
7. Conflict resolution is a skill that can be taught, for it exists primarily in the area of social exchange, thereby showing the importance of social skills.
8. The psychotherapist becomes specialized in identifying conflicts and in assisting the patient resolve them through known or to-be-learned social skills that have consequences for how the patient feels about him or herself and how he or she functions.

Psychotherapy is seen as an enterprise based on interaction between a "helper" and a "helpee" (or group of the same) in the service of conflict resolution; this, in turn, may take one or more of four directions: reducing/increasing approach behavior (assertions) and/or reducing/increasing avoidance behaviors. Although there are many therapies and many ways to solve problems, they all distill down to one or more of these four. Conflicts may also be thought of as discrepancies between given (observed) and desired (predicted, sought-after) states. The use of the term *conflict* facilitates patient-therapist communication (better than scientific or other unique language) and identifies problems and places problem solving more easily within the person's grasp.

## HISTORY

The early emphasis on assertions arose in the context of carrying out therapy, both individual and group, among children, and collateral therapy with parents. I found myself asking parents, "What is the child 'saying' in his behavior as he refuses to get dressed, sasses you frequently, avoids concentrating on his schoolwork in the light of reasonable expectations, and so on?" This question helps to focus on the child's *behavior,* what he was asserting vis-à-vis his environment, and did not invite obscure, covert, or abstract explanations or theories. If the child did not respect the parent's (or teacher's) strictures, then that was subject to therapeutic discussion. "He's just running rings around me, and I'm letting him get away with it," the parent might aver. Or: "If we arrange things so Johnnie has to get his schoolwork done *before* he goes out to play, then I'll have less trouble, it would seem," a mother surmises.

As to adults, their assertions might be less obvious, but yet they could be ferreted out: "You want your wife to *know* already your preferences—it makes you angry to have to tell her," I might say to a male adult discussing the ups and downs of his marital situation. Or: "You're telling me your boss does not appreciate how hard you work and what you've done for the office," I might point out to a female secretary. "You're asserting that it doesn't matter—you'll just work your fingers to the bone and say nothing, but complain here," might be added.

The early role of an assertion-structured emphasis was important in showing the patient a number of characteristics of his or her behavior: The problem was in part something he or she was *doing*—assertions had consequences for the patient in the environment. Assertions giving difficulty could be compared with other assertions wherein there resulted more effective relationships and problem solving. Assertions were "owned" by the behaving person. By clarifing this more ready and effective behavior change resulted and clients' emotions became less split off from their actions. It also shortened therapy (Phillips & Wiener, 1966) as the focus was on observable and manageable behaviors.

As has been indicated, this is a behavioral viewpoint and the stage was already set for me to be strongly influenced by the behavior modification movement that became articulate by the early 1960s (although precursors were already observable). I felt the behavioral movement was so rich in resources for behavior change that I abandoned for some time the emphasis on conflict and looked more to reinforcement contingencies as the pivotal concept in behavior change. I still think that the notion of contingencies is fundamental, but have recently begun to see that conflict is itself an expresson of a set of contingencies. One can pivot therapeutic discussion either on contingencies or on conflict and perhaps net the same results in the effort to plan and carry out behavior change. But as far as communicating with the patient is concerned, I think the notion of conflict is more readily understandable and engages patient participation more openly.

At the time of my early writing (Phillips, 1956; Phillips & Haring, 1959; Haring & Phillips, 1962; Phillips & Johnston, 1954; Phillips, Wiener & Haring, 1962; Phillips & Wiener, 1972), other psychologists were promulgating similar notions (Ellis, 1962; Rotter, 1954), and the neo-Freudians were emphasizing the social context more (Fromm, 1947; Sullivan, 1947). There was at that time, then, a great upsurge in therapeutic ideas taking one away from the original depth notions to more present-oriented and more behavior-change-oriented procedures, even though behavior modification, as such, was not yet articulated. Krasner (1971) has pointed out how many strands of influence converged to make up present-day Behavior Modification, the work of innovative therapists playing no minor part of this activity. However, Behavior Modification was much broader than any of these therapeutic innovations, as it applied readily to a wide range of disabilities where environmental contingencies were pivotal and did not depend on verbal exchange between patient and therapist or conceptualizations such as conflict theory.

Today my theory combines my original one plus influences exerted by behavior change concepts and techniques. Conflict is reemphasized and seen as of paramount importance in the verbal exchange between patient and therapist and in the monitoring of many changes carried out with handicapped individuals. The armanentarium of behavior change techniques (Phillips, 1977; Haring & Phillips, 1972), varied and multiple as they are, can be seen as ways to overcome conflict. Conflict theory gives clarity and greater simplicity to our notions of anxiety and its role in therapy (Phillips, 1978, 1979), and should, in time, influence personality theory by making it more straightforward, more behavioral, and more able to be researched.

## CURRENT STATUS

As indicated earlier, the present "system" of Conflict Resolution Therapy is and has been in flux. First it was posited on conflict theory, then it emphasized the newer behavior modification developments, and now it is returning to conflict theory but melding it with behaviorial principles. The latter development has included an emphasis on social skills training and development as one outcome of the emphasis on behavioral techniques (Phillips, 1978, 1980). Behavioral techniques have been very salutary, but they have also been criticized as being too narrow and as paying too little attention to feelings, emotions, and attitudes. I believe this criticism of behavioral intervention to be true, but it can be adequately answered by an emphasis on a "holistic" approach arising out of social skills training.

Social skills are important in several ways. They embrace such cogent and salient techniques as assertiveness training, approach behaviors, conversational skills, and the like. In fact, social skills training is a composite of the skills needed to interact in reciprocal, complementary, and functional ways with others. It acknowledges the importance of social (and reciprocal) reinforcement and is ultimately based on learning principles that presumably apply to social situations as well as to other learning tasks.

Social skills are also task oriented—they point to specific behaviors that the person needs in order to get what he or she wants from human interaction—regard, attention, affection, respect, reciprocity, and the handling of aversive interactions and negative emotions. Social skills are the media by which social intercourse is carried out.

Social skills also account for much of the subjectivity (as contrasted with objectivity) in human interaction. That is, they can account for private events, covert states, and the "mental activity" that characterize so much of our lives and so much of the concern in psychotherapy. Most of the concern that patients present to their therapists are ruminations (thoughts, feelings, images) that arise out of conflicts with their environments. If we deal effectively with another person or event, we tend to see the interaction completed, and we move on to other segments of our lives. If, however, we experience conflict with the other person, or circumstance, we mull it over, even ruminate, self-abnegate, attribute blame and ulterior purposes to the other(s); these reactions make up much of the "mental life" of the patient. The reason these private events proliferate, I assert, is due to faults or deficits in problem-solving and social skills. As improved social skills help overcome the heretofore frustrating social interactions, the more the ruminations give way to overt social reinforcement and personal satisfaction. Social skills are the bridge between a satisfactory "inner life" and a well-functioning social life. Social skills minimize or solve the social interaction problems (conflicts) that give rise to the subject matter of psychotherapy, abnormal psychology, and psychiatry.

There is, then, emerging an integration of the areas of conflict, behavior modification (in the sense of techniques), and social skills training (Phillips, 1980). The patient presents his or her conflicts (the presenting complaints are conceptualized in this way); these conflicts, in turn, account for the subjective experiences of the patient because they are, in addition, comments on and signs of social skills lacks and competencies. Some of the therapeutic intervention consists in explaining conflicts and proposing ways of resolving conflicts, some of it revolves around relating the subjective (ruminative) presentations of the patient to these conflicts and to social skills needs, and some of it puts the emphasis directly on social skills development. The therapist could summarize this chain of events by saying to a patient: "No wonder you feel miserable, you're in continual conflict about what to do about your relationships with the opposite sex, wherein you lack the skills to approach, select, sustain, and mutually enjoy these relationships." Such a conceptualization may appear oversimplified, but it is not. In the conflict resolution effort there are many subtle problems in relating the efforts to experiences the patient reports and, in turn, to the social competencies the patient exhibits in this complex chain of activities. Getting these all together becomes the therapeutic task and should, if successful, lead the patient to better feelings and social interactions.

My emphasis in writing and researching about psychotherapy has not been to produce a system, a following, or seek disciples; but

to offer conceptual models of use to everyone, and to point out that people proffering superficially different therapies were, in fact, doing about the same thing, and even had to be doing closely similar things if they were to get results. The proliferation of various kinds of psychotherapy is not based on substantive differences in subject matter but in the selection of variables and in conceptualization. Albert Ellis wants people to be rational about their lives and their self-evaluations—these people are in conflict, lack social skills, and are preoccupied with their inner lives, or else they would not present the "irrationality" they do. The Gestaltists are direct and confrontive and challenge the reasons people give for their behavior and, in effect, point to conflicts and social skills deficits. Transactional therapists talk about the way people act as if they were parents, children, or adults; in their inappropriate behaviors patients display conflicts, social skills lacks, an escapsulation in their inner life, and self-abnegation. And so on throughout all or most psychotherapies. Many therapies locate the significant variables in the psyche, but when you observe or read about what the therapists *do*, you recognize that they concentrate on behavior, they deal with social skills adequacies. They try to help resolve conflicts.

One can learn to do therapy the way I propose by, of course, reading my books and articles (Phillips, 1956, 1977, 1978, 1979, 1980; Phillips & Wiener, 1966) and by looking into earlier work with children, both exceptional and normal (Phillips, Wiener, & Haring, 1962; Phillips & Wiener, 1972; Haring & Phillips, 1962, 1972).

One outgrowth of my viewpoint has been the development of Writing Therapy (Phillips & Wiener, 1966; Phillips, 1977; Phillips, Gershenson, & Lyons, 1977). I believe that what we ordinarily call interpersonal relations in psychotherapy is not pivotal; face-to-face interactions are not needed for therapeutic change to occur. Writing Therapy challenges the age-old assumption of face-to-face relationships. What is called for, in

Writing Therapy as elsewhere, is problem solving, conflict resolution, skill development. These may be pursued by a writing modality as well as, or perhaps even better than, face-to-face encounters that include a host of extraneous matters that often obfuscate change.

Nearly all of my early ideas were worked out in Parent-Child Therapy (what is today called "Family Therapy") that put an emphasis on behavior, on the assertions children (and parents) were living by, on conflict resolution, and on skill development on the parts of parents and children (an early emphasis was placed on a child's responsibility skills, on participation in family life, on sharing, and on social skills competencies.)

## THEORY

The theory of what is today called Conflict Resolution Therapy passed through several stages of development before reaching its present stage. My first contacts were with psychoanalytically trained clinicians—psychologists and psychiatrists—and I underwent an analysis with a well-known Freudian analyst in the Minneapolis-St. Paul area (while attending the University of Minnesota) after World War II and again later at the Washington School of Psychiatry. I later judged these analyses as moderately helpful. However, in my studies I was interested in experimental analogues of so-called clinical and personality phenomena, having been influenced here by the group at Yale—N. E. Miller, John Dollard, O. H. Mowrer, R. R. Sears, and so forth—who also tried to make bridges between experimental psychology (especially Hullian learning theory) and psychoanalysis. They took the latter as more or less given and attempted independent validation via experimental paradigms. Judson Brown's work on conflict grew out of Neal Miller's work, and these studies impressed me considerably. I saw a basis for Freudian psychology in independent, hard-nosed experimental work—*except* the former did not hold up well, and thus I gradually jettisoned the whole Freudian notion of depth, repression, defense mechanisms, and so forth. Extracted from this attempted amalgamation of Freud with the psychologist's experimental laboratory was the fundamental nature of conflict (its measureable approach and avoidance characteristics) and its apparent generalizability (relevance) for the human case. Conflict, then, became the central issue in my thinking, and all the Freudian structure came tumbling down. Conflict theory and its experimental roots could stand on its own two feet, and we could start anew to build relevance for therapy, for diagnosis, to understand anxiety, to apply to the whole gamut of clinical psychology. I felt at this point I had hold of a conceptualization that was theoretically meaningful and reasonably clear, empirically well grounded, and clinically salient. That constituted a meaningful package.

These ideas were embraced in my book on psychotherapy (Phillips, 1956), which was four or five years in the making. While working on that book and developing the theory, I continued to work mainly with parent-child cases, but gradually got more and more involved with adult therapy. It was not as easy to apply the notions to adults as it was to parent-child relations, as the latter's actions were much more observable and the presumed motives more transparent. The most important idea among those I promulgated at this time—other than recognizing the salience of conflict theory—was the notion of *assertion*. People dealt with the environment by asserting themselves, not by denying or defending, not by working from unconscious motives; even though the assertion had more meaning than met the eye. Fundamentally and most simply put, people assert themselves. They may be wrong in these assertions (who is ever right even most of the time?), or they may arrive at them through some temporizing, or compromising their cross purposes, or under the undue influence of others, or out of prejudice, or whatnot. But assertions they were! People behave.

If these assertions could be identified, weighed out as to their relevance, their pros and cons, one should be a long way toward understanding and changing behavior. I soon learned that "understanding" behavior did not mean much; this was mostly verbal accountability, and had nothing to do with accountability in the real world. Confrontation had to interpose itself: What people asserted had to be judged by the consequences of their actions, not by their "justifications" and "good intentions." The consequences were judged by the person (the patient) and by the impact on the environment, including others. I believe—and I say this modestly—the notion of consequences was present in my thinking before it became articulated via Behavior Modification. I had already been greatly influenced by cybernetics, and if any point of view emphasizes consequences it is the notion of the feedback loop derived from cybernetics. I saw its relevance for clinical phenomena, especially in the fact that cybernetics emphasized the redundant, repetitive, circular nature of phenomena. Thus some amalgamation between learning theory, cybernetics, and clincial phenomena were realized and developed.

In these ways the whole notion of the unconscious, defense, and all the paraphernalia of Freudian and other depth psychologies were, I believed (and still do) sidestepped. We could have a conceptualization and a clinical practice that dealt with observables, with potential observables, and enrich our understanding and control in the process. I felt that the ultimate test was whether or not behavior changed. Explanation, understanding, all aside: *Did behavior change?* became the most important criterion.

My early formulations were too verbal, too dependent upon verbal communication between patient and client. Even though much of my work was with children who, of course, communicate in many ways other than verbally, I did not grasp fully the possibilities of the need for techniques and be-

havioral control through other than verbal means until I was impacted by the Behavior Modification movement. I had used what later came to be called "time out" by having parents and teachers isolate youngsters from the classroom, or in parts of the home, when their behavior was out of control. I used successive approximations in teaching parents and teachers to help children overcome learning problems, achievement problems, and the like, but I saw it as just a natural extension of ways to control the assertions of the child that were usually shortsighted and unilateral. The Behavior Modification movement enabled me to put these and other techniques into a larger perspective, and to see the possibilities of many, many more techniques (see my 1977 publication for a list of over 60 of them). Behavior Modification did not change the direction of my thinking—it extended it to encompass more possibilities, and it refined it through a better understanding of reinforcement contingencies. I had always used the latter without so naming it: Saying to parents, "You hold up what the child wants until you get what you want," meaning, of course, a contingent arrangement that was reinforcing to and highly effective for both participants.

As to personality of the developing child, the theory held that as the parent or teacher molded the assertions of the child, the child became socialized and learned to achieve, to gain satisfaction from achievement, and to develop mastery over the environment. One's personality, then, grew with these successes. On the other hand, if the child's assertions often misfired, were unrealistic, overambitious, then avoidance characteristics developed, perhaps resulting in poor motivation, indecisiveness, oppositional behavior, and delayed social skills development. Assertions valued by the family, the school, and society often resulted in conflict situations that called for "therapy."

Children or adults who were balanced and integrated persons were those whose assertions had a high probability of being confirmed or readjusted if they were not confirmed. One moved through life on the basis of the feedback from having assertions confirmed, be they about school, social relations, success in love, family, or vocational areas. Every new challenge was an assertion test; every failure was also an assertion test as it required reevaluation.

Assertions were conceived of more broadly than just observing a child try to put a toy together, solve an arithmetic problem, or deal with another person. Assertions were beliefs, predictions about what would happen to a person if he or she did so-and-so; they covered our "mental life" as well as observables. In therapy the therapist helped the patient make these covert and subtle and implied assertions (usually called assumptions, attitudes, emotional predispositions, etc.) more articulate and attempted to trace them to their consequences. Seeing that assertions did not "pay off" led to changing them, lowering them, reapproaching them, abandoning them, and so on. Personality was the product of the vast repertoire of assertions and their consequences.

I never saw any great purpose in building a "personality" theory. What science and technology both require are a minimal number of heuristic concepts and operations. We tend to confine these conceptualizations to limited areas of knowledge—atomic theory, intelligence theory, social interaction theory, and so on—and when we do we get better results. Overall personality theory may be an illusion; let us go with limited accounts of circumscribed areas, based on nuclear concepts, empirically grounded, that have a heuristic impact.

Personality, then, develops and changes in ways related to how assertions are handled, their consequences. My approach to psychotherapy is to identify and change these assertions where needed; and to point to other areas of assertion that are functional for the person and use these as models of change *and* stability. Naturally the picture of assertions changes with age: The baby makes assertions mainly about hunger, pain, fatigue, and simple activity. As the range of

behavior increases, assertions about ever newer and widely expanding possibilities develop. Handling the child's assertions is not the same as harnessing him or her with restraints or oversocializing him or her to the point of teaching timidity; but, rather, such handling means to help the child assert with confidence and with positively reinforcing results. Moreover, it is important for the child to learn that assertions vis-à-vis the world can be revised and that life consists in great part in making such revisions; this flexibility allows for better relationships with others, more effective mastery over the environment, and the avoidance of undue expectations (assertions about how the world *ought* to be, how it *ought* to treat the person).

Adults in psychotherapy generally present assertions that embrace inordinate expectations: They expect their every wish to be fulfilled, expect to be understood just because they are who they are, expect to achieve their grandest hopes, and expect the world to kowtow to them. When stated this way, it is obvious that these are faulty assumptions about people and the world; these assertions are unconfirmable, giving rise to intense and often prolonged conflict. Their outcomes make up the subject matter of psychotherapy, personality theory, and much social behavior. If we know that we can change these outcomes via therapeutic effort, we have, in effect, a personality theory without trying to encompass everything.

The modification of self-concepts, emotional states, and behavior follow from changing one's assertions. Whereas the frustrated and conflicted assertion nets distress, self-abnegation, depression, preoccupation, anger, and resentment (all strong emotions), assertions that are confirmed net self-esteem, confidence, happiness, optimism, cooperative attitudes, and gainful achievement. An adult who experienced successful therapy averred at the end: "Now I can set my goals and really achieve them without so much turmoil. I used to gain nothing and spend all my time fretting about it." This patient had tried to "favorably impress" everyone he met, tended to project himself too forcefully on others, tended to monopolize interactions—in short, he asserted propositions that were untenable; he lacked social skills. A child who was belligerent and tended to attack others in school sessions and asserted demands at home that others indulged learned to interact more fairly and equally with others when teachers and parents stopped acceding to his whims, stopped lecturing him about his behavior, and set limits he could achieve with satisfaction and consistent performance. The teacher said of the lad: "Why, I've never seen a child change so much so soon by doing such simple things to and with him—and his mother and father agree." An adolescent girl presented herself in therapy as "having no good relationships with boys," despite the fact she was attractive, musically talented, and displayed an apparent willingness to cooperate with others. She was asserting that the boys "ought to like me, since I try so hard to like and please them." Indeed! She overdid the matter; like an overanxious hostess, she turned off others with her oversolicitousness. Her assertions were "I try so hard to please, why don't you try to please me and recognize my efforts toward you?" This was more than most people wanted; they disconfirmed her assertions, placing her in conflict after conflict in redundantly ample supply.

Did these three person's personalities change? Yes, to some extent, but there was no general "overhaul" of their personality makeup. They changed certain pivotal behaviors—assertions about limited relationships with others—which took them off the losing list and put them on the winning list. Were there self-esteem changes? Yes. Behavior changes? Undoubtedly. They are easily observable. Emotional changes in the sense of moving into more positive feelings? Certainly. They are available from the persons themselves and from observing them.

Personality origins are those determining assertions that go far and wide in the person's life, determining more generalized attitudes of a positive or negative nature, leading to confident interactions or to ambivalent and ineffectual outcomes. Given a personality inventory, many patients would show up depressed, ruminating, lacking social confidence, underachieving, fantasy-ridden about great achievements in lieu of ordinary social reinforcement. Their personality sketches or psychometric evaluations, depth interview results, and so forth, would emphasize the negative and failing aspects of their makeup. Given the therapeutic changes cited above, the personality assessment pictures would change and there would be a more positive and confident thrust to their lives.

## METHODOLOGY

One of the interesting points about many types of psychotherapy is that you cannot tell from the name of the therapy how it operates, what its principle variables are, or how it identifies peoples' problems. This point, made before, will be elaborated here.

In reference to how Conflict Resolution Therapy works, it is important to show that conflicts are, indeed, the central notion insofar as communicating with the patient is concerned, and also in the broader conceptual sense. It is peoples' conflicts that bring them to therapy: They cannot achieve their ends, they vacillate, they feel they are handicapped or taken advantage of by others, they feel they are too dependent upon the opinions and support of others; or people presenting themselves for therapy may be overly assertive to the point of aggressively turning off others when they mean only to influence, make friends, or be respected and admired.

Whatever they do, whatever they assert, the end results are not satisfying. In short, they are in conflict. Usually the person presenting him- or herself for therapy has reached an impasse, seemingly has "tried everything," is at the "end of the rope" in trying to solve problems. The old saying of "trying so hard but failing so miserably" applies to most people who seek therapeutic help (unless, of course, they are there at the behest of the others—courts, spouses, parents—and even then there is a notable conflict with some aspect of their environment).

A patient may not come in, sit down, and then say, "I'm in conflict; I need Conflict Resolution Therapy." A person will first tell how distressed he or she is, and what seem to be the reasons (in current living) for the problems. After listening to a male patient, age 35, with marital problems, I said, "It seems from what you say that you and your wife are involved in many conflicts; where do you think the best place is to start working on them? Which ones might yield first?" Here the notion of conflict is already introduced and becomes meaningful to the patient or client. Everyone knows what conflict is, even though they do not think about or care about the intricacies of conflict; they are looking for *resolution*. The skill of the therapist is activated at the point of divining ways of resolving the conflicts.

From the standpoint of Conflict Resolution Therapy, the therapy progresses through essentially three phases. The first is the presentation of the difficulties clients see as important, how they feel about themselves and their plight, and a general muck-and-mire report on the unwelcome and untoward state of things in life. These recitations contain many clues as to how the problems (conflict) might be resolved, how they interrelate with one another, and how capable and ready the person is to start to work on the distressful situations. Many therapists have considered this first phase the definitive one, the one that requires the most therapeutic skill, and the one that most therapies consider the nature of human distress. For example, Rogers's armamentarium of therapeutic skills, such as attentive listening, empathy, unconditional acceptance, are all geared to hearing out the patient, understanding and empathizing with his or her plight. Rogers believes that this high state of rapport will allow the patient to sort out feelings and move toward solutions. In Rogers's view, this whole process is facilitated if the therapist is the right kind of person.

However, a second phase of therapeutic change also occurs. This one goes beyond the immediate recognition and empathic relationships proffered by the therapist; it organizes, conceptualizes, and sets in readiness a phase that signals active change efforts on the patient's part. If parent-child problems are involved, once the general characteristics of their conflict are understood and assessed, there is need for active change on the part of the parent (perhaps on the part of the child, depending upon particulars), and the therapist may help set up this change effort. The reason for this phase is to show that given behaviors can account for the distress reported in the first phase, and other (new) behaviors can promote change. Even though the patient or client is terribly distressed, repetition of this state of affairs need not be endless; if therapy is to be economical and teach self-control and self-discipline to the patient, change occurs very quickly.

The therapist's skills are at a premium here. He or she has suggestions (techniques) that can be employed to reduce the distress that is based on the conflicts noted earlier. Also, as change is promoted, new conflicts arise as old ones are settled. A dynamic state of affairs is put into operation as change efforts are activated. More interaction between therapist and patient occurs; the patient is more active out of therapy; the patient may display many behaviors in therapy typical of his or her general problem status; and therapy may reach critical levels during this active period. For example, one male patient was attempting to more effectively contact females in order to assert himself, overcome shyness, and test out his readiness for a more enduring relationship. As he tried to be more assertive, he was at first awkward, easily discouraged, and sometimes experienced outright rejection by females. He vacillated many times between trying harder and giving up, between attempts to develop social skills and just bulldozing his way (as he put it). Attraction to females kept him renewing his effort; therapist help in approach and conversational skills were useful; but he was not always reinforced to his level of expectation and so his approximations toward a more satisfactory relationship were gradual, halting, and sometimes discouraging. Conflict was present every time he called a woman, asked one to dance, went to one's home for a "date," and whenever he had to make conversation if his partner fell into a silent period even momentarily.

Active role playing was helpful at this second stage. He used the phone to simulate calls to women, then made real calls—in the therapist's office. He wrote down a series of topics (later memorized) that he could use as a conversational base. He took dancing lessons to become more proficient. He noted male-female conversations on radio, television, and in the movies and tried to extract model examples for his own use, which he also rehearsed in therapy. As his approach skills increased, he gained confidence, identified more women he might like to go out with, developed more freedom in talking with women and others, and found he could tell jokes with aplomb ("I had never even tried to tell a joke before!" he said). Once he began to experience some success in these social interactions (upgrading the approach aspect of the conflict paradigm, developing social skills that aided his approach to women), he thought of ways on his own to foster social interaction. The therapy-learned skills had proliferated into wider social areas.

The third phase of therapeutic change has already been anticipated—the patient's "taking over," on his or her own, developing initiative for change, directing and controlling him/herself, and acting independently. The therapist is faded out and therapy moves to its ending point. The presenting symptoms have largely disappeared, or occur infrequently and are brought under control, and the person develops a problem-solving stance that exudes confidence. Conflicts have been resolved for the most part, and when they do occur (as they do for all of us throughout life) they are understood and a modus operandi is available for working on them.

The second phase of therapy sets the stage for some differences between the present conflict resolution position and that of other therapists. Consonant with a problem-solving effort, much energy goes into getting the patient active in solving problems. A number of techniques achieve this end. The patient is asked to keep a log of "ups" and "downs" in his or her daily life. This log has several advantages: It provides a record of feelings and experiences that have impact, it is grist for the therapy mill, it points up recurrent themes, it documents change, it points to needed work, it deals with both success and discouragement in the patient's efforts to change, and it ties the daily life to time with the therapist. During this phase the relationships between feelings and other behavior are elucidated (feelings are behavior), with a view to discerning antecedent and consequent events and to showing that feelings can be brought under control through the control of other related behaviors. The here-and-now emphasis affords continual testing of the patient's avowed intent to change, the regrouping of effort often needed, the checking out of the therapist's contribution in the way of suggestions, hypotheses, and his or her readiness to reinforce appropriately the client's efforts. This is a productive time with the therapist sometimes as active as the patient. There is an emphasis on "meaning" being determined by outcome and outcome being provided by a variety of routes to expressed goals. This kind of program energizes the patient, and even though the road to change is a rocky one, enough successes occur to encourage change.

The therapist should be flexible in suggesting problem-solving actions for the patient to try out. Most people's success in life depends in part upon flexibility in approaching goals and solving problems. The patient who has not heretofore achieved this success (lacking social skills) needs to learn flexible approaches, hence one objective of thereapy is to teach resourcefulness. Therapy emulates successful, everyday living; it doesn't have to promote total personality reorganization or discover hidden secrets from the past.

## APPLICATIONS

The conflict resolution viewpoint in psychotherapy grew out of my work with children and parents and the work of others doing animal research involving the conflict paradigm. Its application, therefore, would seem most appropriate for children and parents, for families generally. As children grow and move into socialization, they naturally run into conflicts with others: parents, peers, teachers, other authorities, rules and regulations at school, on playgrounds, and so forth. During the middle childhood period children become cognizant of rules, games, and formal procedures, the structures of which are both confining (conflictful) and challenging. Much of the time in a child's life, he or she is in conflict with extant rules and regulations (going to bed, amount of television watched, getting schoolwork done, sharing, meeting demands of parents, utilizing opportunities for social growth gainfully, etc.). If one could sum up in a single sentence what many parent-child and family conflict are like, it might be epitomized by the parental statement, "I can't get him to do (or not do) what I want." Equally cogent would be the child's version: "I want (or don't want) to do that—I wish they'd leave me alone."

In therapy parents often need the help of outsiders in order to feel right about what they intuitively think is best for the child. Children are often willful and "play dirty" to get their way. Parents usually want to be reasonable and become unfair and oppressive more often with exasperation than due to initially ill intentions. Bringing out the sincere but often ineffectual assertions of the parents vis-à-vis the child are all part of the therapeutic enterprise. In turn, it is common in therapy with the child to let the child vent his or her anger and resentment from feeling unduly constrained and finding ways of negotiating with parents so that both their ends are met.

If therapists could first work with parents and children, they might learn the simpler versions of conflict theory and resolution and develop a set of paradigms of value when they shift to the more subtle, elusive, and complicated adult. Much of the child's behavior is easily "seen through"—his or her motives are transparent, feelings are worn on the sleeve, and the child is direct and unequivocal in expressing needs and wants. Adults are much more roundabout, not only out of social decorum and the vast network of reflected feelings about what they think of others and what others think of them, but also out of a desire to get their ends achieved with low cost/benefit ratios involved. Adults carry hidden agendas; children almost never do.

The therapist can turn him- or herself to listening to the adult's complaints and learn to ferret out from the often excessively complicated language the simple declarative sentences that occur now and then that spell conflict. "You're really ticked off because the people at the office seem to ignore you, or at least not include you spontaneously in their conversations, coffee klatches, and the like," I said to a woman patient who spent 20 minutes describing the whole social terrain of her office, with many side excursions into the personalities and presumed motivations of members of this group. After a young college student had spent 25 minutes describing how he was unable to concentrate on his schoolwork, I said, "I think you pick inappropriate times and places for study, and try to follow the antics of others at the same time, resulting in unproductive study efforts, and then you attribute this state of affairs to some flaw in your makeup, some brain damage, some emotional block, or any other way to escape the responsibility of studying more efficiently." Such instances could be multiplied endlessly. People like to think their "case" is unusual, hard to fathom, a challenge possibly beyond the therapist; they entertain these notions partly out of conceit, partly because they do not know how to get to the nub of the problem, and partly because they like to talk about themselves. All this makes interesting listening, but it may not change behavior, the real task of therapy.

Adolescents fall in between children and adults in their candidness, and in my experience are more likely to offer both very rewarding or very grudging cooperation; the latter occurs when they are persuaded by others to engage in therapy usually due to some problem with conduct, rather than having developed some motives on their own. While challenging to work with—finding reasons why they might become involved in their own right rather than just acquiescing to authority or openly opposing authority— they often fail to respond to face-to-face therapy but need group settings, Writing Therapy, or some extant institutional setting (preferably not a punitive one) in order to "bring out the best" for them.

Various types of handicapped individuals—retardates, autistic, physically handicapped (orthopedic), cerebral palsy cases, and the like—may respond to verbal therapy if their levels of communication and self-control are sufficient to enable discourse with a therapist in face-to-face settings to operate constructively. More often, however, these individuals—depending on the degree of impairment—need a total environmental rearrangement—a kind of prosthetic environment—utilizing behavioral principles to bring about changes in their behavior. In the more severe cases verbal communication may be limited to sets of instructions and to verbal/social reinforcement. Here one has moved a considerable distance away from verbal, face-to-face psychotherapy to environmental rearrangements and restructuring that use the same principles but change the modality away from verbal communication. These severely handicapped individuals are the least amenable to psychotherapy in the conflict-resolution sense promulgated here; however, their teachers, parents, or other monitors may need help in dealing with the conflict presented by their charges (in dealing with oppositional behavior, low motivation, extreme dependence on others owing to having been "waited on" throughout their lives, etc.). Many times teachers who work in schools for severely handicapped children need therapy for their own frustrations and conflicts in dealing with their charges. The teacher's ability to see him-/or herself in conflict with the child, with the institutional goals, with parental expectations, constitutes the grist for the therapy mill in these cases.

In essence, the more verbally communicative and the more the verbal skills of the patient can match those of the therapist, the more Conflict Resolution Therapy can be of direct benefit in the manner described herein. As the therapy employed moves away from a verbal, face-to-face communication model, the more other modalities are needed; the conflict-resolution aim is changed from the patient and therapist per se to the control of the environment as the chief modifier of conflict.

## CASE EXAMPLE

Al (a pseudonym) was a 27-year-old graduate student who presented four problem areas in the intake interview. He was thoughtful and systematic in his presentation. He had undergone two years of psychotherapy as an undergraduate and again following a hospitalization during his senior year. He had been diagnosed previously as depressed. His four problem areas were: severe biting of fingernails; depression; conflicts with his roommate, a part-time student who worked nights in a restaurant; and concern over his future; he was to graduate within four months.

Al said that his first concern was his nails as he felt they looked bad and "it shows terribly" to others. He was unable to stop the nail biting in his previous therapy and he had tried what he called "home remedies," meaning he had put bitter substances on his nails and had worn gloves when in his room studying. We decided to begin immediately on some measures of control of this problem, and to work gradually on the other ones, planning to start programs for each of them in the upcoming interviews. The therapy was time-limited by natural circumstances—Al leaving school upon graduation.

Some explanation of the fingernail-biting regimen was discussed. He was asked to occupy his hands when reading, studying, watching television, or engaging in other relatively passive endeavors by pacing himself with a ruler and holding a book with the other hand. When watching television, he would work on needlepoint (a hobby) or do some sketching (another hobby) on a pad held in his lap. He was never to be without gainful activity for his hands. He was to was to wash his hands often enough to keep his hands and nails clean and use clippers to trim the nails and cut back the cuticles (they too had been torn into the quick as part of the nail biting). Since fingernails grow relatively rapidly, upon Al's return for his second interview a week later, he was able to proudly display signs of growth. I reinforced him generously and asked him if problems had developed in trying out these measures of self-control. He had "slipped" a time or two he said, but quickly caught himself and instead of finishing the biting of the nails, he used the clippers to trim off the uneven part. He had the most trouble controlling the biting when he watched television, but he worked on this problem by watching only for specific, limited programs, usually news programs of 15 to 30 minutes, rather than sitting before the set for hours as he had previously done. Within a month Al's nails were grown back, they were clean and kept trimmed, and there were no torn cuticles. He was extremely proud of this achievement.

The second problem area—depression—revolved around the heretofore lack of control over his nail biting, hence with improvement in that area he was less depressed. As part of working on depression, Al kept a daily log of "ups" and "downs" in moods,

usually one-sentence entries in a notebook he carried with him. The log included a brief statement of his distress—"I get this piercing thought now and then that I don't know what I'm going to do when I graduate," or "I had a fight with Abe [his roomate] about his turning on the TV too loud when he comes home from his restaurant job at midnight"—and similar concerns. The concern for the future was real as he had no job prospects; hence, together we outlined procedures for him to get up a resume, file it at the university employment office, write friends who might know of jobs locally and in other cities (he had majored in foreign service, and was seeking a clerical job or low-level policy job in the government or in some private concern that had overseas contacts), and to begin interviewing people in foreign service and international trade and import-export businesses (he was proficient in French).

When Al came in for his fourth interview, he said, "Now I feel at least that I'm getting someplace—my nails are fully grown out now and I think I'm getting along with my postgraduation plans." He recited several things he had done in the way of making contacts, having interviews, pursuant to employment. He averred that things with his roommate were not better, however, and both of them were considering moving. We attempted to work out a set of agreements between him and his roommate to minimize conflict between them, but he said his roommate was often "tipsy" when he came home at midnight or later and therefore did not keep his agreement to keep the television turned down or respect other of Al's wishes around the apartment. Al began to feel he should make plans and take direct action to move. Much of the discussion centered on how to implement these plans, the cost, inconvenience, and the benefits.

The third and fourth problems—conflict with roommate and plans for a job after graduation—merged into one, as he did not want to move unless it was compatible with job prospects and he didn't know what he could afford for an apartment until his job prospects and salary were clear. He essentially merged these two problems as he interviewed for jobs.

The above description of the problems Al presented are bare-bones accounts. If one could hear the tapes made of the interviews, one would hear more references to conflict with himself, in regard to the nail biting, feeling depressed, and to his roommate (an open and flagrant conflict at times). His "image" of himself was not one that included unsightly hands and chewed nails; he felt it embarrassing to eat in the presence of others, especially women, who would observe his nails and cuticles. He also previously turned down social activities due to "not feeling up to it" as part of his depression and embarrassment over his hands and nails. In everything he tried to do and in opportunities he was confronted with—at the time of beginning therapy—he was in conflict. We addressed this issue as an open one and talked about how continuing conflict was disabling, depressing, angering, and self-deprecating. We talked about how to reduce each of the conflicts, which ones were within his direct control, which depended upon others, and which conflicts would take time to resolve. The whole conceptualization was around conflict resolution, and each symptom or complaint had a reference to this conceptualization. The articulation of the conflicts he faced also helped him to see that he needed social skills in order to feel less self-conscious, less depressed, especially in the presence of others, at social gatherings, in class, and in job interviews.

In a sense, rules were developed to aid Al at all these junctures. The handling of the nail biting was based on a set of procedures, or "rules." His preparation for interviews was based on procedures that optimized his interview skills (including preparing his resumé); at first he went for interviews for jobs of lesser attraction to him so there was not so much at stake and so he could map out the range of anticipated questions, learn to ask the right questions, and develop poise.

Upon leaving school four months and 15 interviews after beginning therapy, he offered this account of his experience:

Well, I certainly licked—so far, anyhow—the nail biting and I feel very good about it. The depression is less and when I do get depressed I seem to know what it is about and what to do. The roommate problem was never solved there in the apartment, but it will be only a week until I move. I have an interim job with the library for the summer and while I pursue what I really want—it takes a lot of time to get a foreign service job.

Al felt his therapy had been "very successful" and as he put it: "In my earlier therapy we tried to find out where everything came from—my depression, you know—and did nothing about each day's living. We were much more practical here, and I think the conflict notion helped me to understand a lot more."

## SUMMARY

The preceding account of Conflict Resolution Therapy describes some of the developments that bring this point of view up to date. In the development of the theory, there has been constant change in one sense, yet the notion of conflict (somewhat modified for a while under the impact of the early days of Behavior Modification) has remained important throughout. More recently the importance of conflict and conflict resolution have been reemphasized and have included the relevance of social skills training as an integral part of psychotherapy. The social skills training has the simultaneous advantage of capitalizing on the individual's assertiveness (approach behaviors) and reducing anxiety and avoidance behaviors through social reinforcement. Much of Behavior Modification is put to the task of teaching and reinforcing social skills (social approach behaviors, assertiveness, conversational skills, handling aversiveness, expressing feelings such as anger and positiveness, etc.). These social skills not only help to resolve conflict that brings the person to psychotherapy, they generalize to other social situations, increase the repertoire, and move the individual in positive directions toward others. Subsuming these concepts and therapeutic operations is the notion of feedback loops from cybernetics, which recognizes among other things the recurrent or cyclic nature of behavior. The patterns that characterize disturbed, untoward, or unwanted behavior can be described in loop terms, intervention strategies can be planned, and these strategies are then integrated into the repertoire and behavioral economy of the person who is changing his or her behavior.

Conflict Resolution Therapy attempts to present a rationale that is broad and that refers to how disturbances are initiated (through conflict), how they are maintained (through feedback loops), and how they are changed (through altering the loops or, in behavior modification terms, altering the contingencies). The strategies and contingent changes are seen primarily as social skills in which approach behaviors form the working basis of change as well as preserve the integrity of the person from whom change can be encouraged.

Besides wanting to do effective and efficient therapy, I am interested in presenting as coherent a conceptual account of therapy as possible. I believe that in naming therapy (that is, giving it a ''brand'' name) and in describing variables, many therapies fail to take a broad look at the whole gamut of theory and practice that underlies any kind of psychotherapy. This gamut, of course, includes how the disturbed behavior is activated, maintained, and changed. Somehow therapeutic theory must account not only for what the promulgator of a given therapy asserts is important, but for the theory and practice of other therapies as well. Therapies are probably more alike than they are different, but to look at the names of therapies is to encounter semantic confusion and lost opportunities for conceptual clarification.

Even when research is done on one or more aspects of therapy, there is still little additional clarification. I see psychoanalytic (depth) therapies emphasizing reducing the avoidance gradient, behavior therapies emphasizing approach conditions, and most other therapies falling in between. Much needed is clarity as to when therapies are promoting change via the approach or avoidance tendencies, and relating how these choices deal with social skills/assertiveness and with anxiety (anxiety in the present conflict resolution terms would point to avoidance, inhibition, vacillation, and negative appraisals of one's behavior, all of which inhibit conflict resolution, problem solving, and the development of social skills). Most therapies center on pathology, on distress, on symptoms, and erect causal accounts of how pathology arises and what it means; Conflict Resolution Therapy sees psychopathology as a byproduct of conflict. If any therapy is to reduce conflict, it must do so by either the approach or avoidance gradient route. Conflict Resolution Therapy stressess the approach (or assertion, or social skills development) route, which I believe to be the most heuristic, empirically grounded, and clinically economical way to proceed.

## REFERENCES

Ellis, A. *Reason and emotion in psychotherapy*. New York: Lyle Stuart, 1962.

Fromm, E. *Man for himself: An inquiry into the psychology of ethics*. New York: Rinehart, 1947.

Haring, N. G. and Phillips, E. L. *Educating emotionally disturbed children*. New York: McGraw-Hill, 1962.

Haring, N. G. and Phillips, E. L. *Analysis and modification of classroom behavior*. Englewood Cliffs, N.J.: Prentice-Hall, 1972.

Krasner, L. Behavior therapy. In P. H. Munssen (Ed.), *Annual Review of Psychology*. Palo Alto, Calif.: Annual Reviews, 1971.

Phillips, E. L. *Psychotherapy: A modern theory and practice*. Englewood Cliffs, N.J.: Prentice-Hall, 1956.

Phillips, E. L. *Counseling and psychotherapy: A behavioral approach*. New York: Wiley-Interscience, 1977.

Phillips, E. L. *The social skills basis of psychopathology: Alternatives to abnormal psychology and psychiatry.* New York: Grune & Stratton, 1978.

Phillips, E. L. Where now, and whither, behavior modification? *Journal of Nervous and Mental Disease,* 1979, **167**, 317–320.

Phillips, E. L. Social skills instruction as adjunctive/alternative to psychotherapy. In W. T. Singleton (Ed.), *Analysis of Social Skills.* New York: Plenum, 1980.

Phillips, E. L. and Haring, N. G. Results from special techniques for teaching emotionally disturbed children. *Exceptional Children,* 1959, **26**, 64–67.

Phillips, E. L., Gershenson, J. and Lyons, G. D. On time-limited writing therapy. *Psychological Reports,* 1977, **41**, 707–712.

Phillips, E. L. and Johnston, M. H. S. Theory and development of short-term parent-child psychotherapy. *Psychiatry,* 1954, **10**, 267–275.

Phillips, E. L., Wiener, D. N. and Haring, N. G. *Discipline, achievement and mental health.* Englewood Cliffs, N.J.: Prentice-Hall, 1962.

Phillips, E. L. & Wiener, D. N. *Short-term psychotherapy and structured behavior change.* New York: McGraw-Hill, 1966.

Phillips, E. L. & Wiener, D. N. *Discipline, achievement and mental health,* 2nd ed. Englewood Cliffs, N.J.: Prentice-Hall, 1972.

Rotter, J. B. *Social learning and clinical psychology.* Englewood Cliffs, N.J.: Prentice-Hall, 1954.

Sullivan, H. S. *Conceptions of modern psychiatry.* Washington, D.C.: W. A. White Psychiatric Foundation, 1947.

# CHAPTER 14

# *Covert Conditioning*

JOSEPH R. CAUTELA and AVIS K. BENNETT

*Cautela and Bennett present a rather interesting paradox in this chapter. As behaviorists, if they agree with J. B. Watson and B. F. Skinner, they essentially deny the importance of (but not the existence of) what we ordinarily call "the mind"—that is, thoughts and feelings. Indeed they write, "both [Watson and Skinner] felt that scientific quantification of covert behavior was unreliable and unneccessary."*

*Yet what do we find? These two avowed behaviorists (Cautela is head of the doctoral program in Behavior Modification at Boston College) essentially stress exactly what Watson and Skinner attempted to eliminate—covert behavior! In short, the chapter is about phenomenology—the mind—imagination!*

*The importance of this may not be apparent at first. To call this paradoxical behavior or to label these authors phenomenologists rather than Behavior Modifiers (with capital letters, since all therapists are behavior modifiers with small letters) misses the point. Cautela realizes that a true psychotherapy of intact adults requires an admission that there is a mind, that people can and do think, that they can visualize, and that they can imagine, he also understands that in the battlefield of the mind important changes can occur that will later manifest themselves in overt behavior, so that thought and emotion, rather than simply being an epiphenomenon, must be given status of independence.*

*This is one of the most scholarly of the chapters and well worth close reading.*

Covert Conditioning involves both a concept and a set of procedures. Broadly defined, Covert Conditioning is the modification of covert processes in a manner similar to the way in which overt behavior is modified by operant conditioning techniques. In the covert conditioning procedure, the client is asked to imagine performing a behavior that is considered undesirable. The client is then asked to imagine a consequence designed to increase or decrease the probability of that behavior. These procedures are labeled covert sensitization (Cautela, 1967), covert reinforcement (Cautela, 1970a), covert extinction (Cautela, 1971a), covert negative reinforcement (Cautela, 1970b), covert response cost (Cautela, 1976), and covert modeling (Bandura, 1970; Cautela, 1971b). They are analogous to the operant conditioning procedures of punishment, positive reinforcement, extinction, negative reinforcement, response cost, and modeling (conceptualized within the operant framework).

Through the use of Covert Conditioning, an individual can learn to take responsibility for changing unwanted habits, learn new strategies to enhance future interactions, and generally increase adaptive functioning through the use of his or her creative imagination. Covert Conditioning facilitates the resolution of conflict through change in the environment (covert and overt) rather than through resolution of intrapsychic conflicts underlying the problem behavior.

## HISTORY

The human capacity to produce imagery has excited people throughout the millennia. From the earliest expression of imagination in cave drawings, human imagery has inspired the ages. Certainly the Renaissance could be viewed as the origination of the written word designed to evoke imagery, for masters such as Shakespeare, Spencer, and Chaucer seemed to display consummate psychological skill in kindling the imaginations of the world at that time (Singer, 1974).

Although early Christianity negated the importance of imagery, religious figures such as St. Theresa of Avila and St. John of the Cross viewed imagination as a bridge to knowledge of the essence of God (Peers, 1951). That kind of thinking seemed to emanate directly from the philosophy of Plato, who espoused a theory of forms, that is, he felt that innate ideas led to a higher realm where intelligible beings gained true knowledge (Watson, 1971). The influence of innate ideas, or inner experience, and the development of psychology as a separate field followed from that philosophical position.

With the advent of European psychology, the awareness of one's imaginative creativity and its inherent resource as a purveyor of behavior had a profound impact on psychoanalytic practice. Applying their analysis of imagery to the assessment of psychological processes, Freud and Jung wove symbolic interpretation into the core of European and early American psychology (Kazdin, 1978). However, the use of imagery in behaviorism has developed independent of the European tradition.

The origin of behaviorism was characterized by the development of an objective psychology based essentially on precise definitions of stimulus and response. Indeed, Watson (1919) led American psychologists far away from the study of inner experience by labeling thinking as subvocal speech. Skinner (1953) agreed with Watson that mentalistic concepts had no value in the scientific study of psychology and what psy-chologists needed to investigate were overt behavioral reactions such as speech and physical movements. Neither Watson nor Skinner denied that people have thoughts and images, but both felt that scientific quantification of covert behavior was unreliable and unnecesary (Watson, 1971).

The major impetus for the widespread introduction of imagery in American psychology was the emergence of Wolpe's (1958) systematic desensitization. Wolpe sanctioned the investigation of covert processes when he conceptualized systematic desensitization as a therapeutic procedure to modify phobic behavior. It was the first imagery-based procedure that embraced the tenets of behaviorism; that is, the method itself was sufficiently precise and repeatable so that it lent itself to experimental investigation.

Since Wolpe's initial contribution, which can be explained via a Pavlovian or respondent conditioning model, other psychologists from various theoretical orientations within a learning theory framework have investigated the process of imagery manipulation. Stampfl and Levis (1967) developed implosive therapy (a procedure designed to flood a person with aversive imagery) based on Mowrer's (1960) two-factor theory of fear. Bandura's (1970) social learning theory of modeling stems from a mediational-contiguity model, while Homme's (1965) coverant control therapy, in which specific thoughts are made contingent upon the performance of target behaviors to be increased or decreased, and Cautela's (1973a) Covert Conditioning are aligned with an operant orientation.

Still other behaviorists such as Meichenbaum (1974) and Mahoney (1974) subscribe to a somewhat different conceptual model in which faulty cognitive patterns (e.g., talking to oneself), problem solving, and imagining are viewed as mediators of behavior. These investigators label themselves cognitive behavior modifiers rather than learning theorists.

While systematic desensitization emerged in 1958 as a technique designed to eliminate *avoidance* behaviors (e.g., phobias), no parallel technique was advanced to eliminate maladaptive *approach* behaviors (e.g., addictive behaviors, socially inappropriate sexual behaviors). Covert Conditioning began to take shape in 1966 both as a vehicle for therapy and as a research instrument to investigate the elimination of maladaptive approach and avoidance behaviors. At that time, evidence was accumulating that punishment procedures utilizing shock could supress behaviors such as stealing, sexually deviant behavior, and addiction (Kuchner & Sandler, 1966). Cautela (1967) reported that the sequential pairing of a behavior a client wished to eliminate (alcoholism) with an aversive event (vomiting) in imagination led to a decrease in the overt behavior of drinking. Cautela labeled that proedure *covert sensitization*. The term "covert" was used because both the undesirable response and the aversive stimulus took place only in the imagination. The word "sensitization" was used because the purpose was to build up an avoidance to the undesirable response. The conceptualization of covert sensitization as an operantly based imagery procedure followed after the development of covert reinforcement. From that beginning, several imagery-based techniques (utilizing the underpinnings of operant conditioning) were developed by Cautela and have been applied to diverse behavioral disorders and populations.

## CURRENT STATUS

A recent search of the literature (McCullough, 1978) indicated that the years 1966 to 1978 yielded more than 400 studies investigating the effectiveness of covert conditioning procedures either through single-case design methods, group studies, or anecdotal case reports. Of these studies, 70 experiments and 49 dissertations were suficiently rigorous to allow analysis of outcome data. These studies compared covert conditioning techniques to theoretical strategies that stemmed from other than an operant base—for example, hypnosis, positive self statements, expectancy instructions. The majority of studies reviewed focused on three procedures: covert sensitization, covert reinforcement, and covert modeling. However, additional studies on other procedures (covert extinction, covert negative reinforcement, and covert response cost) were included in the final evaluation.

The effectiveness of covert sensitization on maladaptive behaviors including alcoholism, smoking, overeating, and socially censured sexual behaviors was investigated. Research in covert modeling and covert reinforcement was reported in areas of phobia, attitude change, test anxiety, and pain reduction. An overall analysis of the research revealed that 52 percent of the studies demonstrated significant differences. Thirty-three percent of the results were in the expected direction, while 15 percent showed no differences between control groups and covert conditioning groups (McCullough, 1978).

A cogent review of Cautela's covert modeling as one of many imagery-based techniques has been presented by Kazdin (1978). While Kazdin reported a number of therapy outcome studies demonstrating the efficacy of covert modeling in reducing "subphobic" fears of college students (e.g., fears of rats or harmless snakes), he suggested that future research should emphasize more serious clinical problems.

In reviews and evaluations, of the efficacy of Covert Conditioning is usually granted but there is some question about the adequacy of theoretical underpinnings. Investigators suggest further delineation of precise variables affecting behavior change.

Two recent studies (Bennett & Cautela, 1979) investigated the forward conditioning procedure, covert reinforcement, and a backward conditioning procedure, reciprocal inhibition, on the modification of a pain response. This was done by reversing the order of presentation of the reinforcement scene and a cognitive strategy; for example, in forward conditioning reinforcement followed presentation of the cognitive strategy and in backward conditioning reinforcement preceded the cognitive strategy. Each treatment procedure was effective in relieving pain. However, in a group design, subjects utilizing the covert reinforcement procedure reported significantly reduced pain when compared to subjects practicing the reciprocal inhibition procedure. Similarly, in the single-case designs, the operant procedure seemed more effective since people tolerated the pain for longer periods of time. These results suggest that when the response to be modified is an anxiety response, such as pain, an operant interpretation may be parsimonious as a reciprocal inhibition explanation. In a test where the response to be modified was not an anxiety response but the modification of pronoun usage (Ascher, 1973), the effectiveness of covert reinforcement may have been due to operant principles only.

In a survey of behavior therapists conducted to determine what behavioral treatment procedures are commonly used, covert conditioning procedures were often mentioned (Wade, Baker, & Hartmann, 1979). Compared to 13 other behavioral strategies, covert conditioning techniques were reported to be the sixth most frequently used.

Covert Conditioning has also been reported to be a paradigm that can be utilized along with other treatment modalities. In an anecdotal report, Singer (1974) described the effectiveness of covert sensitization as an adjunct to a psychoanalytic approach. Since the tendency toward voyeurism in Singer's client persisted despite considerable insight about his life style, covert sensitization was introduced. Singer noted that within a few days of practice, instances of voyeurism had declined and within a few months had completely disappeared.

Covert Conditioning has been described in many standard texts on Behavior Therapy. A detailed elaboration of the procedures and how to use them can be found in *Covert Conditioning*, by Upper and Cautela (forth-

coming). Further, most college-level courses in Behavior Modification include material on Covert Conditioning. Currently, Cautela teaches the assumptions of Covert Conditioning in various courses in his position as professor at Boston College and as head of the doctoral program in Behavior Modification.

## THEORY

Within the covert conditioning model, three general categories of behavior must be considered: covert psychological behavior (thoughts, feelings, and images), covert physiological behavior (heart rate, pulse, brain waves), and overt behavior. These categories are not mutually exclusive but are interactive and interdependent processes.

A number of important assumptions underlying these categories of behavior form the basis for the efficacy of Covert Conditioning. The first major assumption is that of homogeneity. The concept of homogeneity assumes a functional equivalence in overt and covert behavior; that is, overt and covert processes are similarly important in the explanation, maintenance, and modification of behavior. The second assumption may be called the interaction hypothesis. It states that covert and overt behaviors influence each other—for example, a visual cue signals the thought "I am afraid" and heart rate increases, or a person leaning over notices blood rush to the head and says, "I feel dizzy." The third assumption is that all categories of behavior obey the same laws of learning; that is, all covert levels of behavior, thoughts, images, and physiological responses may be reinforced or punished in the same manner as overt behavior. While in a broad sense generalizations and empirical findings concerning all learning apply to Covert Conditioning, an operant learning framework was chosen because of evidence indicating that all three categories of behavior respond to operant conditioning techniques (Cautela & McCullough, 1978).

The theoretical position of Covert Conditioning depends on the aforementioned assumptions. Since Covert Conditioning is based on a learning theory paradigm, therapeutic effectiveness depends on strict adherence to the model. The operant methodology underlying each covert conditioning technique is presented in Table 1. Integral to the theory is the necessity of the individual to achieve and perform qualitative imagery. Factors such as image quality—for example, level of pleasantness or aversion, emotional arousal, clarity of imagery, and the amount of practice—all contribute to therapeutic improvement. The covert conditioning procedures could be impeded for some individuals if tension level is high or if they have interfering images. Relaxation training (Jacobsen, 1938) is taught to help reduce this interference.

The theoretical underpinnings of Covert Conditioning demand that a certain level of aversion be experienced with covert sensitization and covert negative reinforcement and a certain level of pleasantness be experienced with covert reinforcement. At least a minimum level of clarity and sufficient practice are needed to insure conditioning effects. If the ability to use imagery is deemed inadequate for conditioning, clients are given practice in the office as well as assigned more practice at home.

Central to the efficacy of therapeutic progress and inherent in the covert conditioning system is the notion of a general level of reinforcement. Cautela has described the general level of reinforcement as being directly related to the number and quality of reinforcing and aversive situations a person experiences per unit of time. The writers' experience in clinical practice and use of the daily reinforcement survey schedule (Cautela, 1977b) indicates that the lower the level of reinforcement, the more susceptible one is to the effects of aversive stimulation.

The theoretical position of Covert Conditioning encourages the removal of a reinforcer in maladaptive approach behaviors, such as cigarette smoking and alcoholism. Since the elimination of reinforcing experiences is highly resistant to change, the implementation of covert and overt reinforcement must be increased prior to and along with treatment. Covert reinforcement varies along a continuum that includes: (1) anticipation of a reinforcing event; (2) experience of that event; (3) retrieval of the event through the memory or use of memory aids, such as snapshots of the events.

**Table 1. Covert Conditioning Methodology**

| | | | | |
|---|---|---|---|---|
| *Covert Positive Reinforcement* | | | | |
| (R) imagine making a response | → (S) | imagine a reinforcing event | → (R) | increase in response rate |
| *Covert Negative Reinforcement* | | | | |
| (S) imagine aversive events | → (R) | terminate S by imagining R to be increased | → (R) | increase in response rate |
| *Covert Sensitization* | | | | |
| (R) imagine making a response | → (S) | imagine an aversive event | → (R) | decrease in response rate |
| *Covert Extinction* | | | | |
| (R) imagine making a response | → (S) | imagine the reinforcing stimulus-maintaining behavior is withheld | → (R) | decrease in response rate |
| *Covert Response Cost* | | | | |
| (R) imagine making a response | → (S) | imagine the removal of a positive reinforcer | → (R) | decrease in response rate |
| *Covert Modeling* | | | | |
| (R) imagine a model making the response | → (S) | imagine the model is receiving pleasant or aversive consequences | → (R) | decrease or increase in response rate, depending on consequences |

Adherence to the theoretical system of the covert operant paradigm can lead an individual, through the production of his or her imagery, to countercondition old behavior, learn new response patterns, and gain self-control.

In order to optimize the use of covert conditioning procedures as a therapeutic system, an understanding of operant technology is necessary. The following examples represent the methodology described in Table 1.

Since Covert Conditioning assumes that covert behavior follows the same laws as overt behavior, response frequency is affected by the sequential pairing of the response and consequence. The probability of any covert behavior ocurring again is influenced by the covert or overt behavior that follows it; for example, if the consequence is reinforcing, the behavior will increase in probability; if the consequence is punishing, the behavior is likely to decrease.

The underlying assumption across all the techniques is that a decrease in imagining a behavior will decrease the probability that the behavior will be performed overtly. Concomitantly, a decrease in overt behavior should decrease the covert behavioral component.

Experimental investigation of covert conditioning procedures have included presenting the response to be acquired *in vivo* (overtly) and in imagination. Acquisition of a new response was possible under both conditions when followed by imagination of the consequence.

In the following paragraphs, the clinical approach to Covert Conditioning will be summarized and examples of scenes employed in therapy will be presented.

The clinical implementation of covert conditioning procedures must be preceded by a behavioral analysis in order to determine the antecedents and consequences of the behavior to be changed (Cautela, 1968). Further information can be gleaned and a baseline measure taken by asking the client to record the frequency of occurrence, duration of the response, level of intensity, and location where the behavior takes place. This baseline is important because some clients report, ''I'm *always* in pain,'' or ''I *never* sleep.'' Clients are asked to complete the reinforcement survey schedule (RSS) (Cautela & Kastenbaum, 1967) in order to determine which reinforcers are considered the most pleasant to the client. The following rationale is given to clients:

Your behavior occurs because it is maintained by the environment. Whenever you perform that behavior, it is rewarded or punished by other people. There are many studies that indicate that if the consequences of behavior can be manipulated, then the behavior can be increased or decreased in frequency. We have found that just by having people imagine they are performing certain behaviors and then imagine particular consequences, behavior can change in a similar manner. I am going to have you imagine certain scenes, and ask you to imagine you are really there. Try not to imagine that you are simply seeing what I describe; try to use your other senses as well. If in the scene you are sitting in a chair, try to imagine you can feel the chair against your body. If, for example, the scene involves being at a party, try to imagine you can hear people's voices, hear glasses tinkling, and even smell the liquor and food. Now remember, the main point is that you are actually there experiencing everything. You don't see yourself there but are actually there. First let's determine if you can imagine the scene clearly. Close your eyes and try to imagine everything I describe. Ready? Raise your right index finger when the scene is clear.

After patients signal, they are asked if the scene was clear and how they felt about it. If the scene was clear and they could imagine the consequences as described, they are then asked to imagine the scene by themselves. (If there is any difficulty, the scene is repeated by the therapist, with modified or elaborated instructions, depending on what was difficult for the patient to imagine.)

Patients are told that whenever they finish imagining a scene by themselves, they are to indicate this to the therapist by raising the right index finger. At that point the therapist may say ''Shift'' or ''Reinforcement'' to signal the next scene to be imagined. Patients are then asked to practice the scene at least 10 times a day at home.

Types of scenes and covert conditioning strategies to be used are determined by situations that are discovered through the behavioral analysis. Examples of scenes that have been applied to specific behaviors using specific strategies follows.

## Covert Sensitization (CS)

When a client wishes to change a maladaptive approach behavior, such as smoking, overeating, or alcoholism, the treatment of choice is CS. In treating obese clients, the client is asked to imagine:

You have just had your main meal and you are standing around a dessert table with your friends. You reach for your favorite dessert and as you do you notice an unpleasant feeling in your stomach. You start to feel nauseous and sick all over. As you reach for the fork, food particles are welling up in your throat. You try to swallow them back down. Your throat is burning. You place your fork in the dessert and more undigested food comes up in your mouth. It tastes terrible. As you raise the fork to your mouth, you vomit all over your hands, the fork, the pie. Stinking vomit splashes on your friends. Your friends look horrified. You feel even sicker and vomit again. You run away from the table and go wash up. You feel so relieved to be away from the desserts.

## Covert Reinforcement (CR)

Covert reinforcement has been used to modify both maladaptive approach behaviors and maladaptive avoidance behaviors. Consider the preceding example presented in CS in which punishing consequences (vomiting and social disapproval) followed the response to be decreased (dessert eating). A CR procedure could be used to increase the target behavior of not eating dessert:

Imagine you are standing at the dessert table with your friends. As dessert is passed you politely refuse, and feel good about staying on your diet.

Since the procedure is covert reinforcement, the response to be increased is followed by a pleasant scene:

Imagine you are your ideal weight. You look really slim in your favorite color and style. Someone you like says to you, "Gee, you've lost weight. I've never seen you look so good."

Clinical practice has indicated the need for treatment of "urges" to drink or overeat. A covert reinforcement self-control scene is presented:

You are walking toward the refrigerator; as you open the door, you say, "No. I'm not going to snack between meals," and you feel really good about yourself as you walk away from the refrigerator.

## Covert Negative Reinforcement (CNR)

When clients label themselves depressed, they often have difficulty imagining anything pleasurable. If aversive imagery can be imagined more vividly or realistically, therapy may begin by using escape from an aversive situation as a reinforcement for increasing certain behaviors. In CNR, a client is asked to first imagine an aversive situation. When the client signals the imagery is clear, the therapist says, "Shift." It is important that the noxious scene be terminated immediately by imagining the response to be increased. For example, to increase appropriate sexual behavior:

Imagine that you are walking downtown when all of a sudden an unruly mob storms down the street in your direction. People are yelling and pushing and you're being carried along with the crowd. You can smell sweaty bodies. Your own body is being battered from all sides. You feel trapped. There is no way to escape. SHIFT. You are lying on a bed beside your wife. You feel relaxed and comfortable. You're beginning to feel aroused.

## Covert Extinction (CE)

The covert extinction procedure removes the positive reinforcer maintaining the undesirable behavior. In the treatment of chronic cough:

You are eating in a restaurant with friends. The waitress brings your favorite food to the table. It smells and tastes right. You start a coughing spell. Everyone continues to eat and talk as before. No one even notices you are coughing. Your cough subsides and you resume eating.

## Covert Modeling (CM)

Covert modeling can be applied to the modification of a wide gamut of behaviors, but it has been especially useful in the area of assertiveness training.

Imagine you see someone you admire standing in line at the theater. Someone cuts in line in front of him. He looks relaxed and calm as he steps up to the person and says, "This is my place in line." You see him smile and he looks like he feels good about himself as the intruder goes to the back of the line.

## Covert Response Cost (CRC)

In employing covert response cost, a client is asked to imagine the behavior to be decreased followed by the imaginary loss of a positive reinforcer, such as money, jewelry, or a favorite possession. In the treatment of exhibitionism:

Imagine that you are walking toward a group of people. As you get ready to expose yourself, you reach for your wallet and notice it is gone. You feel sick in the pit of your stomach. You don't know what to do since you have no more money.

It must be reemphasized that successful application of the covert conditioning procedures depends on many factors, including (1) increase in general level of reinforcement, (2) composite presentation of procedures, (3) practice in and out of the office, (4) continuing behavioral assessment, and (5) use of other behavioral procedures such as behavioral rehearsals, relaxation training, and contingency contracting.

In clinical practice, more than one procedure is usually presented to each client. For example, in the treatment of drug addiction, the therapist may want to introduce CE ("Imagine you are injecting yourself and there is no rush or high.") CS might be used to reduce the urge to take drugs, and CR could be used to increase alternative behaviors. In addition to these covert conditioning procedures, the client could be taught relaxation to reduce tension, a contingency contract could be developed to enhance reduction in drug taking, and self-control scenes could be an important variable in maintaining the desired behavior ("You are about to shoot up, you change your mind and feel really good about yourself as you throw the needle away").

## Self-Control Triad (SCT)

Cautela has recently developed another therapeutic strategy, the self-control triad (SCT), to be used in conjunction with the covert conditioning procedures. The SCT can be viewed as an important mechanism in empowering the client with strategies for coping and self-control. That is, the triad is useful in altering an established behavior, maintaining a newly learned behavior, and preventing development of another maladaptive behavior.

A composite of three behavioral techniques is comprised in the SCT: thought stopping, relaxation, and covert reinforcement. While the procedure has not been verified experimentally, it has been found effective in private practice. First, a rationale is presented to the client that explains how the use of the SCT prior to, during, or after any anxiety-provoking situation could reduce stress and increase one's capacity to respond appropriately intellectually or emotionally. The procedure is practiced with the therapist as follows:

Clients are asked to close their eyes and to imagine the thought that is distressing them. When the thought is clear, they signal with the index finger. At that signal, the therapist yells, "Stop." Clients usually report that the thought disappeared, and they are then asked to imagine the thought and yell "Stop" to themselves while visualizing a big red stop sign. Next clients are asked to take a deep breath and exhale, feeling a wave of relaxation spread over their whole body. That sequence of imagining the negative thought, yelling "Stop," and then relaxing is paired and practiced by each client.

The third component is CR, imagining a pleasant scene selected from the RSS. When clients are able to "see" and feel the pleasantness of the scene, the whole triad is practiced together: (1) the client imagines the thought to be decreased and yells "Stop" covertly while imagining a red stop sign; (2) the client takes a deep breath and says the word "Relax"; and (3) the client imagines a pleasant scene. Practice usually continues with the client utilizing the imagery both with the eyes open and closed. (One advantage of this procedure is that it can be utilized with no infringement of privacy when others are around.) Homework practice of two sessions a day—for example, 10 trials with the eyes open and 10 trials with the eyes closed—is suggested to each client. Since satiation can occur on any scene, clients are asked to use a different reinforcer for every 20 trials. A useful suggestion is that upon waking each morning, the client choose his or her favored reinforcer for the day. That also insures the ready availability of a scene and precludes the necessity of searching for a reinforcer when an anxious situation occurs.

The SCT can be used in many situations, such as driving in traffic, at the office, at home, and is applicable to maladaptive approach behaviors as well as maladaptive avoidance behaviors. For example, if tension is associated with maladaptive eating habits, yelling "Stop" distracts one from the thought "I need a snack" and reciprocally inhibits the tension through the relaxation and pleasant scene. The pleasant scene reinforces the thought stopping and relaxing, thereby increasing the probability that new behavior will occur in a variety of situations.

Finally, covert conditioning procedures are employed in the daily behavioral assessment of successful and unsuccessful interactions. Clients are asked to review the day's events. If a situation arose when they should have asserted themselves and they didn't, they are asked to imagine they are handling the situation appropriately and then to imagine a pleasant scene (CR).

All the procedures as previously defined and described can now be used by the individual to change, maintain, or develop the desired response in any situation.

## APPLICATIONS

When originally conceived, the covert conditioning procedures were applied mostly to adult clientele in private practice or in outpatient settings. Currently, the procedures are being extended to other populations, such as children, adolescents, and the elderly in a variety of situations, including residential institutions, schools, and hospitals.

The therapeutic intervention of various covert conditioning procedures, both individually and as a composite package, has been applied to cases of dental fear in children, sibling aggression, to increase social interaction in the autistic, and to curb maladaptive behaviors such as hand flapping and inappropriate hitting in the retarded. Covert Conditioning has been reported to reduce the urge to set fires in an adjudicated delinquent (Cautela, 1966), to enhance children's self-concept (Krop, Calhoun, & Verrier, 1971), and has been applied to the modification of organic dysfunction, for example, epilepsy (Cautela, 1973b).

Adolescent problem behaviors such as poor study habits, test anxiety, obsessive sexually deviant thoughts, and inadequate social skills have all been successfully treated by both writers in Cautela's practice.

Recently the procedures were presented in an attempt to enhance physical rehabilitation in special needs children. In some cases, covert reinforcement was practiced to increase level of participation in treatment and to desensitize antecedent stimuli that appeared to increase frequency of handicapped behavior—for example, with a child with a club foot who was more apt to drag the foot when criticized.

Adult populations have experienced many and varied applications of Covert Conditioning. The presentation of a composite package of covert procedures successfully alleviated heroin addiction in a client who had used 20 bags per day for three years (Wisocki, 1973). A Synanon-type treatment had been unsuccessful and the client had felt his chances for rehabilitation were slim. However, the desire to use drugs began to be reduced as the client practiced imagining the various strategies. Gradually the habit of drug addiction was eliminated; a one-year follow-up indicated that treatment gains were maintained and no evidence of addiction was reported.

An unusual application of Covert Conditioning was in the treatment of life-threatening self-injurious behavior (Cautela & Baron, 1973). The client was hospitalized with a diagnosis of schizo-affective. During the time spent planning a behavioral intervention, the client had completely lost the sight in both eyes by poking them and had bitten off a considerable portion of upper lip tissue and some lower lip tissue. After a one-year treatment with Covert Conditioning including training the hospital staff to reinforce appropriate behaviors while extinguishing inappropriate behaviors, the client showed no further self-injurious behavior. During a recent 10-year follow-up, the client reported that he is now married, has graduated from college and law school, and is currently employed as a lawyer for a state agency. There has been no reoccurrence of self-injurious behavior.

As mentioned, Covert Conditioning has been successfully applied in many maladaptive approach behaviors such as overeating (Brunn & Hedburg, 1974), alcoholism (Ashem & Donner, 1968), and sexual deviance (Barlow, Leitenberg, & Agras, 1969). A new area to receive the attention of Covert Conditioning has been the institutionalized elderly. Cautela (forthcoming) has recently developed an elderly reinforcement survey schedule. Theoretically, an increase in the level of reinforcement should contribute to a reduction in depression. Nursing homes and housing areas for the elderly may be able to incorporate covert reinforcement as a self-control measure in a general therapeutic plan, thereby enhancing institutional efficiency and increasing quality of life for the elderly in general.

Covert conditioning procedures now are being applied in the field of behavioral medicine. Besides treatment of persistent cough, epilepsy, and asthma, Cautela (1977b) has described the effectiveness of Covert Conditioning in reducing pain associated with rheumatoid arthritis. A two-year follow-up indicated that the client has remained free from pain or been able to control pain whenever it occurred. There is growing evidence that the interaction of psychological and physiological factors influences susceptibility to and course of the cancer (Cautela, 1977c).

The writers' approach in treating organic dysfunction, such as seizures, has been the same as our approach in treating psychological disorders: A behavioral analysis operationally defines the dysfunction, measures the frequency, duration, and intensity of the disorder, and identifies the antecedents and consequences. Cautela suggests that every client with an organic dysfunction, regardless of type, should receive both a behavioral analysis and treatment as well as a medical diagnosis and treatment.

The authors recently treated a hospitalized client who was stricken with amyotrophic lateral sclerosis, a syndrome marked by muscular weakness leading to paralysis due to degeneration of motor neurons of the spinal cord, medulla, and cortex. The client was completely paralyzed but retained the motor ability to make an eye-blink response as well as some slight thumb movement. Goals in this case were to reduce fear and frustration in the client, family, and the hospital staff. The client was trained to practice calm, healing imagery designed to increase level of reinforcement and demonstrate that he still retained some control over his bodily processes. In order to reduce fear, covert reinforcement was used on the reliability of equipment functioning—for example, a respirator would continue to breathe for him— and thought stopping was introduced to control negative thinking. Compliance to medical regimen was increased by training the staff in principles of reinforcement and extinction. The client was also taught to reinforce the family and staff whenever possible on a nonvocal communicator. The use of CR prior to the introduction of a portable respirator may have aided the client's successful transition in using it. What had originally appeared to the client, family, and hospital staff as an impending terminal illness was gradually reassessed. As the environment became less hostile and more reinforcing, alternatives for living began to be explored. Currently, with assistance from hospital staff and family, the client has been able to make visits home (using the portable respirator) and to attend occasional public functions.

Since the writers' advances in the field of behavioral medicine have been reported anecdotally, good research data is needed to support Cautela's behavioral/medical treatment regimen.

A major consideration and value in the application of covert conditioning procedures to any type of disorder is the idiosyncratic nature of the techniques.

Limitations in effectiveness could result from lack of practice during the session, lack of practice at home, or therapist failure to obtain adequate feedback on imagery assessment. Clients experiencing any difficulty pertaining to practice or those unable to develop appropriate and effective imagery have not in the past been able to achieve successful intervention. In the hospital setting, partic-

ularly if the staff is trained to encourage practice of covert conditioning strategies and to follow the principles of reinforcement as indicated by the behavioral/medical assessment, the probability of success should be increased.

## CASE EXAMPLE

The following example details the successful application of covert conditioning procedures to the treatment of hacking cough and acute dysphonia (hoarseness).

### History

Mary, the client, was a 16-year-old Caucasian female. She was referred by the university hospital for a persistent cough and acute dysphonia.

Mary was first seen early in 1973 by a physician. At that time she reported symptoms and a persistent cough (two weeks' duration). In April the cough appeared again. She was treated with Prednisone and relieved of her symptoms. In September another flare-up began and although for a while she improved greatly with medication, gradually a "deep, barking, brassy" cough developed and her speech was reduced to a "hoarse whisper." Subsequent treatments of various medications for allergies had no effect. On November 12, when symptoms had failed to respond to any treatment, it was decided the problem was not allergic and, after consultation with other physicians, Mary was admitted to the hospital. All tests during a six-day admission were normal. Mary was then referred to a hospital center for children, where she was hospitalized between November 30, 1976, and December 10, 1976, and again from March 4 to 7, 1977. She was tested extensively both times, and no organic basis was established to explain the continuing cough and dysphonia. She was referred to the hospital's psychosomatic unit but chose to see a private psychiatrist. After a number of sessions, Mary felt she wasn't being helped and reported back to the hospital center, where she was referred to these writers for "psychogenic cough."

## Initial Visit

Mary and her mother, Mrs. Y, appeared for the initial consultation with the writers, who were co-therapists. Initially Mary's mother reported that Mary developed symptoms at the same time the mother and Mary's brothers were experiencing allergy attacks that required them to spend time away from work and school. (Mrs. Y works full time on the 11 to 7 A.M. shift as a registered nurse.) Mrs. Y felt Mary's cough was due to an undiscovered organic problem, but was upset by Mary's missing school and family difficulties with facing Mary's whispering and coughing. Mrs. Y reported that Mary's sister thought Mary was faking. However, Mrs. Y also reported hearing Mary cough during the night every night while she was sleeping. When Mary coughed or whispered, Mrs. Y paid a lot of attention to her (e.g., they watched soap operas together when Mary missed school, which was a frequent occurrence, and Mrs. Y kept telling Mary to talk louder and to repeat what she said).

During Mary's interview she reported that her father didn't get along with her mother and didn't participate in their lives even though he lived with them. She was very angry with him and reported that he asked about her cough only once a month. Mrs. Y was concerned about Mary's reported weight loss of 10 pounds, but Mary liked her thin self. She saw her mother as a martyr who had to work all night to keep the family going. Mary didn't get along with her high-achieving sister and had a chronically ill (asthmatic) brother who still wet the bed at the age 13. She reported becoming a "hermit" since her coughing began; she had tutors and no longer attended school, didn't go out with friends, and couldn't talk on the phone much due to the dysphonia. Further, wherever she went, people asked her if she had a cold, and that made her feel uncom-

fortable. The physical symptoms Mary reported were headaches, cough, whispering, itchy eyes and nose, generalized pain, dry throat, and wakefulness at night. Mary was convinced her cough was not psychological, but she reported wanting to be rid of it.

## Assessment

It was hypothesized that Mary's coughing was being maintained by the medical and social attention paid to it and by the avoidance of anxiety associated with her entry into high school. The home environment further added to Mary's symptoms since she was unable to relate assertively with her siblings. Also there was apparently a lot of modeling of illness behavior by observing the asthmatic brother and frequent respiratory infections of the mother.

While one therapist interviewed Mary, her cough was being monitored by the co-therapist. Mary coughed 10 times per minute during a 15-minute interval.

## Intervention

Based on the initial assessment, the therapists decided to use the following procedures:

1. Progressive relaxation (Jacobsen, 1938) and relaxation coupled with imagery:

You are lying on a blanket at the beach. The sun is shining and you feel warm and comfortable. As your fingers slowly sift the sand you feel the warmth of the sun baking into your body. The warm sand is like a comfortable mattress and you feel peaceful and calm. Smell the salt air. Hear the gulls overhead. All the tension is flowing out of your body and you feel more and more relaxed. You can hear the waves lapping at the shore and you feel warm and wonderful, so peaceful, better than ever before.

2. Self-control triad (as previously described): Mary used this procedure in various situations that caused her tension to increase; for example, when her

parents would argue, when her brother would tease her, and before, during, and after exams.

3. Covert sensitization on coughing: After every cough, Mary would imagine an aversive scene. Since Mary had indicated on the covert conditioning aversive scene survey schedule (Cautela, 1976) that she found bees to be very aversive, she was asked to imagine bees swarming all over her face, especially in her nose and ears, as soon as she began to cough.

4. Covert reinforcement and covert modeling on not coughing in public places and for increasing social activities. In covert reinforcement, Mary would imagine she was at the movies with friends, not coughing, feeling relaxed and calm and not even having an urge to cough, followed by a pleasant scene. In covert modeling, Mary would imagine her ideal self was at the movies with friends and she looked happy, peaceful, and calm as she noticed herself smiling because she wasn't coughing. For increasing social activities utilizing covert reinforcement, Mary would practice 10 times a day imagining she was at a public place or talking on the telephone with friends and then imagining a pleasant scene. When covert modeling was the behavioral strategy being practiced, Mary would imagine the same scene by watching her ideal self in a similar situation.

5. Assertiveness training, which was originally formulated within a learning theory framework by Andrew Salter (1949), combined with covert modeling to increase assertive behavior. Covert procedures consisted of instructing Mary to imagine she was in a previous situation where she had failed to speak up but this time she saw herself speak up and then receive a compliment for having asserted herself.

6. Covert extinction on attention paid to

her cough at home and in public places: For example, Mary would imagine she was at home in the midst of her family watching television (a regular family occurrence) and when she coughed, no one paid any attention to her.

7. Desensitization to her parents and siblings by covert reinforcement by having her imagine situations in which she usually felt anxious and overreactional, while she remained relaxed and calm and/or asserted herself appropriately, followed by a reinforcing scene.

8. Health sweep imagery to try to offset her perseveration on physical symptomology. Mary was asked to try to stifle the urge to cough, followed by imagining a soothing, healing liquid moistening her throat, seeping deeply into the tissue, penetrating and relaxing the muscles, leaving her throat feeling relaxed and calm, with no urge to cough, feeling healed.

It was not possible to interview the father and siblings. Therefore, special emphasis was given in training the mother in therapeutic procedures that would extinguish attention to the cough and reinforce family relationships and activities with Mary that didn't center on her cough.

### Goals

The goals agreed upon by Mary and the therapists were that Mary would gradually return to school with a goal of full-time attendance, resume social activities, and be free of the cough.

Mary was seen twice a week, once by the female therapist and once by both therapists. Mary was trained in the use of imagery, given specific procedures as enumerated, and encouraged to keep records. Apparently she practiced consistently for the first few months and kept good records that included counting (using a wrist counter) the number of times she coughed, listing the number of scenes she did on CS, CR, CM, and CE, and rating her relaxation for comfort. Within four weeks, Mary's cough was timed at three per minute, and she was increasing her social contacts through telephone conversations. Then in November a plateau was reached and the writers began assertiveness training, healing imagery (e.g., health sweep and reinforcement of a healthy body), and use of the self-control triad whenever she felt tense in any situation.

In December Mary practiced less, her sister was home from school, her brother and mother were home sick, and her therapy sessions were reduced to once a week because of family illness. In January her visits decreased to one in three weeks and her cough increased to four to five times per minute when timed. Also in January Mary returned to the referring physician; it was suggested that she continue with the behavior therapist since she showed some evidence of "rehabilitation."

A consultation with Mary and her mother at that time about consistently attending therapy and practicing seemed to produce positive results. With resumption of support and practice, Mary's cough decreased to two per minute and persisted at that level until August, when she was specifically asked how she could be close to a boy (e.g., holding and kissing) if she coughed in his face. Two weeks later Mary reported she just "miraculously" stopped coughing one day while she was cleaning the family room with her brother. Coughing symptoms did not reappear. In September she began school on a full-time basis and in October was dismissed from formal treatment but encouraged to continue relaxation. A follow-up in January showed no coughing and an increase in the loudness of Mary's voice.

During another follow-up six months later, Mary reported she was doing well in school, had a boyfriend, and had resumed a schedule of social activities. Mary spoke in a normal tone of voice and reported she rarely coughs, even though she still has allergies.

## SUMMARY

In summary, Covert Conditioning involves theoretical assumptions and a set of specified procedures that can modify both overt and covert behaviors in a manner similar to operant technology. Covert Conditioning has the advantage over some other theoretical systems such as cognitive behavior modification in that the operations are more specifiable. Also, conceptualization within an operant model allows for the investigation and utilization of findings from the vast body of literature in operant conditioning.

The research on the efficacy of Covert Conditioning has as much empirical support as any other set of therapeutic procedures, including Behavior Therapy. Current data indicate that the use of covert conditioning procedures in a wide variety of situations is increasing. Only a few investigations concerning process variables have been conducted.

The results thus far have been equivocal, especially when the dependent variable has been some measure of anxiety.

However, the writers see no inherent limitations of the assumptions or procedures that would preclude the utilization of Covert Conditioning for the modification of any behavior. As long as one is able to follow instructions, any individual is capable of benefiting from covert conditioning procedures whether applied by therapists or when used individually for self-control. In our experience, clients who have learned to use and practice the covert conditioning procedures gain a self-control technology that can be used for the rest of their lives for stress management and the control of any response they feel is undesirable.

While this may appear presumptuous, preliminary explorations into such areas as relaxation, autism, and organic dysfunctions have been encouraging thus far. It is perhaps better to be overly optimistic about the possible utilization of Covert Conditioning than to avoid its application due to some a priori perceived limitations.

# REFERENCES

Ascher, L. M. An experimental analog study of covert positive reinforcement. In R. Rubin, J. Brady, and J. Henderson (Eds.), *Advances in behavior therapy,* vol. 4. New York: Academic Press, 1973.

Ashem, B. and Donner, L. Covert Sensitization with alcoholics: A controlled replication. *Behavior Research and Therapy,* 1968, **6,** 7–12.

Bandura, A. Modeling theory. In W. S. Sahakian (Ed.), *Psychology of learning: Systems, models, and theories.* Chicago: Markham, 1970.

Barlow, D. H., Leitenberg, H. and Agras, W. S. The experimental control of sexual deviation through manipulation of the noxious scene in covert sensitization. *Journal of Abnormal Psychology,* 1969, **74,** 569–601.

Bennett, A. K. and Cautela, J. R. The use of covert conditioning in the modification of pain: Two experimental tests. Paper presented at the meeting of the Association for the Advancement of Behavior Therapy, San Francisco, December 1979.

Brunn, A. C. and Hedberg, A. G. Covert positive reinforcement as a treatment procedure for obesity. *Journal of Consulting Psychology,* 1974, **2,** 117–119.

Cautela, J. R. Behavior therapy and its implications for treatment of the delinquent child. Paper presented to the Division of Youth Services, Boston, 1966.

Cautela, J. R. Covert sensitization. *Psychological Reports,* 1967, **20,** 459–468.

Cautela, J. R. Behavior therapy and the need for behavioral assessment. *Psychotherapy: Theory, Research and Practice,* 1968, **5,** 175–179.

Cautela, J. R. Covert reinforcement. *Behavior Therapy,* 1970a, **1,** 33–50.

Cautela, J. R. Negative reinforcement. *Behavior Therapy and Experimental Psychiatry,* 1970b, **1,** 272–278.

Cautela, J. R. Covert extinction. *Behavior Therapy,* 1971a, **2,** 192–200.

Cautela, J. R. Covert modeling. Paper presented at the meeting of the Association for the Advancement of Behavior Therapy, Washington, D.C., September 1971b.

Cautela, J. R. Covert processes and behavior modification. *Journal of Nervous and Mental Disease,* 1973a, **1,** 157.

Cautela, J. R. Seizures: Controlling the uncontrollable. *Journal of Rehabilitation,* 1973b, May–June, 34–40.

Cautela, J. R. Covert response cost. *Psychotherapy: Theory, Research and Practice,* 1976, **13,** 397–404.

Cautela, J. R. The use of covert conditioning in modifying pain behavior. *Journal of Behavior Therapy and Experimental Psychiatry,* 1977a, **8,** 45–52.

Cautela, J. R. *Behavior analysis forms for clinical intervention.* Champaign, Ill.: Research Press, 1977b.

Cautela, J. R. Toward a Pavlovian theory of cancer. *Nordisk Tidskrift for Behteendeterapi,* 1977c, **6,** 117–147.

Cautela, J. R. The behavioral treatment of geriatric patients with depression. In J. F. Clarkin and H. Glazer (Eds.), *Depression: Behavioral and directive treatment strategies.* New York: Garland Press, forthcoming.

Cautela, J. R. and Baron, M. G. Multifaceted behavior therapy of self-injurious behavior. *Journal of Behavior Therapy and Experimental Psychiatry,* 1973, **4,** 125–131

Cautela, J. R. and Kastenbaum, R. A reinforcement survey schedule for use in therapy training and research. *Psychological Reports,* 1967, **20,** 1115–1130.

Cautela, J. R. and McCullough, L. Covert conditioning: A learning theory perspective on imagery. In J. R. Singer and K. S. Pope (Eds.), *The power of human imagination.* New York: Plenum, 1978.

Homme, L. E. Perspectives in psychology: XXIV. Control of coverants: The operants of the mind. *Psychological Record,* 1965, **15,** 501–511.

Jacobsen, E. *Progressive relaxation.* Chicago: University of Chicago Press, 1938.

Kazdin, A. E. *History of behavior modification.* Baltimore, Md.: University Park Press, 1978.

Krop, H., Calhoun, B. and Verrier, R. Modification of the self-concept of emotionally disturbed children by covert reinforcement. *Behavior Therapy,* 1971, **2,** 201–204.

Kuchner, M. and Sandler, J. Adversion therapy and the concept of punishment. *Behavior Research and Therapy,* 1966, **4,** 179–186.

McCullough, L. The efficacy of covert conditioning. Paper presented at the meeting of the Association for the Advancement of Behavior Therapy, Chicago, November 1978

Mahoney, M. J. *Cognition and behavior modification.* Cambridge, Mass.: Ballinger, 1974.

Meichenbaum, D. *Cognitive behavior modification.* N.J.: General Learning Press, 1974.

Mowrer, O. H. *Learning theory and the symbolic process.* New York: Wiley, 1960.

Peers, E. A. *Handbook to the "life and times of St. Theresa and St. John of the Cross."* London: Burns, Oates, & Washburn, 1951.

Salter, A. *Conditioned reflex therapy.* New York: Farrar, Strauss, 1949.

Singer, J. R. *Imagery and daydream methods in psychotherapy and behavior modification.* New York: Academic Press, 1974.

Skinner, B. F. *Science and human behavior.* New York: Macmillan, 1953.

Stampfl, T. G. and Levis, D. J. Essentials of implosive therapy: A learning-theory based psychodynamic behavioral therapy. *Journal of Abnormal Psychology,* 1967, **23,** 375–412.

Upper, D. and Cautela, J. R. *Covert conditioning*. Boston: Pergamon Press, forthcoming.

Wade, T. C., Baker, T. B. and Hartmann, D. P. Behavior therapist: Self-reported views and practices. *The Behavior Therapist, 1979,* **2**, 3–6.

Watson, J. B. *Psychology from the standpoint of a behaviorist*. Philadelphia: Lippincott, 1919.

Watson, R. I. *The great psychologists*, 3rd ed. New York: Lippincott, 1971.

Wisocki, P. A. The successful treatment of heroin addiction by covert techniques. *Journal of Behavior Therapy and Experimental Psychiatry*, 1973, **4**, 55–61.

Wolpe, J. *Psychotherapy by reciprocal inhibition*. Stanford, Calif.: Standford University Press, 1958.

# CHAPTER 15

## *Creative Aggression*

GEORGE R. BACH

*In meeting again recently with my old friend George Bach and discussing books we had recently completed about marriage, we came to the conclusion that our approaches to marriage and to life were diametrically opposed. George suggested a kind of intellectual contest, a debate before a professional audience, which we may do some day. Although we are good friends, when it comes to psychotherapy we always take opposite positions, probably because of our manifest personalities. George is probably the most assertive person I know: feisty, always ready to respond to anything that seems like an insult. While I am perhaps even more aggressive, my manifest personality is apparently much less contentious. I get my way by seeming to give in while George readily rises to battle.*

*Probably the best procedure for a psychotherapist to use is one that approximates his or her manifest personality. Initiators of psychotherapeutic messages may be saying to the world, "Hey, look at me—be like me!"*

*George Bach's fascinating chapter describes a completely new way of operating psychotherapeutically. Philosophically, I would think its counterpart would be Farrelly's Provocative Therapy (see Chapter 51). Now, a debate between those two would be worth attending!*

*This chapter represents a startlingly innovative and important point of view in ways of dealing with disturbed human relationships.*

Creative Aggression—or CAG for short—is a system of psychotherapy as well as method of self-education designed to radically improve people's skills for maintaining healthy relationships. CAG therapy and educational procedures focus on all forms and manifestations of human aggression: direct-overt, indirect, passive, toward self, directed toward others, individually or in groups, and in every private and social context, such as self-image, sexuality, work, intimacy, coupling, family, neighborhood, and society at large.

Creative Aggression is a direct unimodel form of therapy that changes overt and covert aggressive feelings, attitudes, and actions by direct retraining methods. CAG techniques

offer rituals and exercises that minimize hurtful effects of aggression while maximizing constructive effects. CAG rejects the idea that aggression is primarily a defense mechanism against psychological stress factors such as fear, inferiority, or frustration.

## HISTORY

From the very start of my career as a professional psychologist, research into the possible constructive function of aggression led to the development of an aggression-release oriented cathartic doll-play technique through which young, nice, normal children could enjoyably express their surprisingly intense rage that had been covertly accumulated, instigated by the play-restrictive rules and regulations of their overtly rather peaceful preschool routines (Bach, 1945). It became crystal-clear early in my career that humans, practically from birth, are aggression-prone. It takes very little stress and frustration to instigate aggression, and even in the absence of realistically noxious conditions, humans often seek out opportunities in which to freely and safely enjoy, at times to the point of sadistic excitement (Stoller, 1979), feelings and expressions of aggression and outrage. Observe children at play, or adults in sports and spontaneous role playing.

After working with young children's aggressive play fantasies, I experimented for about a decade with group-therapeutic techniques that focused on the clarification of conflict, aggression, and group tensions developed by the adult members of my then long-term and intensive therapy groups (Bach, 1954). The nonstop weekend marathon therapy group schedule (Bach, 1967a) developed in 1968 by this writer and Fred Stoller provided a setting in which the effectiveness and helpfulness of aggressive-confrontative, member-member, and therapist-member interactions could be systematically compared with nonaggressive modalities of interaction. I observed that marathon group members found critical-aggressive confrontations at least as helpful and often more helpful than supportive forms of interaction. Further clinical experiences with therapy groups revealed that "group tensions" (Bach, 1954) were caused by members' lack of skills to cope with aggression-related acts, such as rejecting others and being rejected, and the fears of intimate involvement, of being unmasked, analyzed, pressured, or brainwashed, of being made to conform to therapist and group norms, and of expressing fears. This amalgam of various fears that arose in the early phases of therapy group life would normally set up fight-or-flight behavior tendencies. However, these tendencies are blocked, or seem to be

blocked, and therefore communicated in indirect, passive, hostile ways of "resistance"—by keeping quiet or talking a lot of "safe," irrelevant nonsense, or being very nice or subordinate to the group leader, performing according to the official "program." These defensive reactions increase rather than reduce the group tension, which also stressfully affects those group therapists unable to deal constructively with the smoldering aggression beneath the group's tension. These group therapeutic experiences led me to develop techniques for the safe channeling of members' aggressions toward each other, toward me, and toward the whole program. These early aggression-release group techniques—such as the encouragement of brutally frank, candid, critical confrontations—resulted not only in a significant lowering of group tension, so that the work of the group could proceed, but, paradoxically, they increased members' affection for each other. This initial finding gradually led to the development of a broad CAG system applicable beyond its birthplace, the intensive therapy group (Bach, 1954).

## CURRENT STATUS

The theory, concepts, terminology, and techniques of the CAG system have been described and explained by this writer in five recent books and in numerous articles, listed in the references. There the reader will find detailed discussions of all aspects of the CAG approach, together with many case illustrations. Systematic research and follow-up studies, statistics, and, of course, limitations and dangers of misapplications are also reported there.

In the field of clinical-professional as well as academic psychology and psychiatry, a strong, theory-buttressed resistance has long prevailed against exploring the constructive, even therapeutic, potential of aggression. Consequently, all other approaches to psychotherapy known to this writer lack the therapeutic utilization of aggression. The wide variety of innovative psychotherapies reported in this volume most likely will prove to be no exception.

When I became a psychotherapist, almost 40 years ago, the traditionally benign, all-understanding, unconditionally accepting stance of therapy teachers and colleagues poorly suited my aggressive-assertive temperament. It also went counter to my dialectic philosophy of life as a constant, albeit at many times most enjoyable, struggle. I developed the CAG system of therapy and education because no one else dealt directly with the management of aggression in both therapists and clients, except in terms of eradicating aggression as an always destructive, irrational, neurotic, or even psychotic defensive behavior pattern. Early on I considered this aggression-demeaning position of my colleagues to be not only unrealistic but actually evasive and incapable of meeting the complaints and concerns of most intelligent people with the fact that aggression and hostility have increased tremendously since the days of Hitler, with no improvement in sight. So I invented my own system of therapy and education, Creative Aggression—CAG. In my lengthy career as a psychologist, I have not softened my often-unpopular stand. It is interesting to note how much more popular acceptance is currently enjoyed by some of my colleagues (Smith, 1978) who took the assertion or impact element out of my original impact theory of aggression—which I taught in workshops since the early sixties and published in 1968 (Bach & Wyden, 1968). CAG, for example, rejects as unnecessarily indirect the broad multimodel approach whereby aggression is supposed to be treated only in the broader context of all other human conditions. CAG accepts, however, that the one context on which aggression training and retraining depends for its effectiveness is caring or goodwill. Paradoxically, the channeled, nonlethal expression of aggression tends to enhance rather than hinder, the growth of love and affection (Bach, 1974b; Eibl-Eibesfeldt, 1974).

In 1967 I published a series of research studies on those interactions marathon growth-group participants had experienced as most and as least helpful (Bach, 1967). The subjects were asked which of the following standard dimensions of group therapy interactions they found most stimulating to growth: (1) identification or modeling; (2) uncritical acceptance, support, and warmth; (3) problem-solving methods; (4) insight meditation; (5 )aggression—critical confrontation; or (6) other write-in dimensions of helpful interaction. Surprisingly, the second item, *acceptance and warmth,* was by no means the preferred choice for the most growth-stimulating interaction experience. This was true even of participants led by group therapists with a nonaggressive Rogerian unconditional-acceptance orientation. (The research design included marathon group leaders of different persuasions.) The fifth item, *aggression—critical confrontation,* was checked and chosen as most helpful more often than acceptance and warmth and as often as the other dimensions of group-therapeutic interaction. This research result, which was confirmed in an independent study by Breeskin (1968), together with the clinical observation of the paradoxical "love effect" stimulated the systematic exploration of utilizing aggression therapeutically.

Eclectically oriented psychotherapists and marriage and family counselors will find it stimulating to integrate CAG techniques with their own approach. This adaptation has not presented a problem as long as the therapist evinces a serious interest in learning how to deal directly with aggression, in all of its positive and negative expressions, phases, and contexts. Competent CAG trainers and supervisors are concentrated in the Los Angeles area in association with the Bach Institute. CAG training is also available in Florida, Canada, and Europe. CAG specialists are sometimes invited to visit clinics, professional associations, and universities throughout the United States and abroad to give intensive CAG training courses for an extended weekend or up to one full semester.

The writer will be happy to direct individuals or organizations interested in obtaining training in CAG to the appropriate resource.

## THEORY

What has concerned me most throughout my career and still baffles me is the stubborn resistance most psychotherapists have to dealing openly with the vicissitudes of human aggression in their work with clients, patients, students, or trainees. They also seem to be reluctant to deal with their own aggression at work and in their private family lives. A fantastic aggression phobia pervades the professional community of understanding, nice therapists dedicated to supporting man's ancient dream of paradisical life on earth, filled with joy and devoid of hostile hassles. This aggression- and conflict-phobic stance by the very profession supposedly dedicated to helping people deal with major emotional and communication problems in a world populated by people filled with rage, terror, and paralyzed by fears of aggression strikes me as almost perverse—like a play from the theater of the absurd. How can our field justify the failure to offer to the public a program of learning how to cope with the major sources of distress in our time: irritation, anger, rage, fear of aggressive exploitation, rape, criminality, and related symptoms of the total mismanagement of aggression? How can anyone make sense, let alone justify, this absurd dance of psychotherapists around "the beast of aggression"? I try to explain this phobia as a symptom of psychology's catering and accommodating to whatever *Zeitgeist* prevails. Today's fashion is narcissism, and professional psychotherapists fashionably cater to it. The "me first" generation goes into psychotherapy to be sanctioned and encouraged in this pursuit of "self-growth," regardless of how much alienation, disruption, rage, and damage it leaves in its wake (Bach & Torbet, 1980). Psychotherapists get paid for, and gain admiration and status for, helping clients to become free, autonomous, to feel okay, to avoid "noxious" friends; to partake more intensely of the joys of sex; to be lost in a self-produced Zen of motorcycling, cooking, tennis, jogging, imagery, trips (with and without drugs); to reach for maximal power and independence; and above all: *to avoid dependency and caring involvements like the plague!* To assist people in these self-growth narcissistic pursuits, psychotherapists have invented hundreds of techniques designed to teach individuals how to do their own thing, how to let everybody else also do his own thing, and how to stay out of the way of others with possibly conflicting interests. I can see how, in the frame of reference of our narcissistic times, the very idea of aggression, anger, and fighting would be painfully dissonant.

The great variety of management and mismanagement of human aggression can be ordered to a dimension starting with the symbols of "Hawk" standing for "mean," overaggressive, hostile behavior, feelings, attitudes, and the symbol of "Dove" standing for overcontrolled, aggression phobic, accommodating, super-nice, peaceful behavior, feelings, and attitudes. Doves suppress or repress their aggression and never learn to fight directly, while driving their associates crazy with their indirect passive-aggressive defenses. Unable to confront, Doves are losers by default. They seek revenge. The Hawks' excessive hostility frightens most stressed creatures away, leaving them isolated on their belligerent perches—targets for rejection.

In our terrorized society, too many Hawks force decent people into an excessively dovish life style—as if trying to defend themselves through victimological passivity. The combination of wanton hostility and ineffectual dovish defenses results in street and family violence and child and spouse abuses, often to the point of murder (Bach, 1980).

Both hawkish and dovish life styles interfere with optimal self-actualization and make the development and maintenance of mutually supportive interactional systems very difficult. Thus, both the Hawk and the Dove need reprogramming in the daily management of anger, aggression, and hostility; to become lovebirds—that is, to live in peace and harmony through love and equality—the touchstone of successful social living.

My early research in human aggression (Bach, 1945) focused on interpersonal frustration rather than influence. For the study of frustration effects, I found the classic frustration-aggression (F-A) hypothesis an adequate and convenient conceptual tool. However, as my research interests broadened to include both frustration and influence ("impact"), the old F-A theory was unable to account for the major facts observable in clinical practice: When involved people fight, they fight not only to "do each other in," as the F-A theory stated, but also to change for the better. True, people may fight to remove frustration, but it is not necessarily to punish or injure the partner who is perceived as the frustrator.

The expression of anger and aggression serves tension-relief or cathartic purposes, as when we emit an insulting swear word upon stepping barefoot on a thumbtack. However, classical F-A theory (which fortunately no longer governs current psychological research in human aggression) did explicitly exclude both influence and catharsis. This limitation rendered the old F-A theory useless for the clinical investigation of human aggression in the life context of real human fight situations where influence, catharsis, and ritual factors determine the intensity and form of aggression. Clinicians can train people to acquire very high tolerance levels for frustrations. But aggressive behavior often occurs without any blocking of goal-directed behavior, that is, frustration, but rather in sheer joy. People fight to provide each other with interest, entertainment, and stimulation, and to reduce the enormous aggression reservoirs that have built up by civilized fight avoidance.

Whether human aggression is innate or nurtured is theoretically interesting but useless in answering the urgent question of how to control aggression. In fact, it seems socially irresponsible to tell people that (a) they are instinctively aggressive or (b) they have been taught to become mean because of bad modeling (usually mother-made) environments. The instinct theories provide a rationale for a general nihilistic acceptance of violence as a cogent hairshirt in human destiny, while the environmental F-A theorists set the irrational and therefore dangerous expectation that frustrations can be effectively removed and that freedom from aggression can be attained by frustration-free life styles.

One good and practical finding of the psychological research relative to F-A theories is that human aggression is modifiable, either by (a) regulating its instigation or (b) channeling its expression.

CAG fight training makes use of both these methods: the instigation of therapeutic fighting is by mutual consent, the expression thereof is governed by mutually agreeable fair-fight rules, and the objective of the fighting is change and catharsis, not injury. Naturally, hurtful words and deeds are part of all fighting, otherwise we would be dealing with assertiveness rather than aggression and merely playing with words, avoiding the sting of aggression.

CAG theory sees aggression as instrumental in producing change in intimate systems. Verbal as well as nonverbal aggression is primarily informative communication about conditions that would further provoke or maximize the injury-inflicting potentiality of aggression, that is, hostility, or abate it. Aggression exchange produces useful information about desirable (tolerable) and intolerable (alienating) positions along the dimensions of intimacy, such as optimal distance (spacing), authority (power hierarchy), and loyalty (territory). In traditional F-A theory, doing injury is the goal response terminating the aggressive sequence, while in CAG theory, effective influence or change is the terminal point of the fight and improvement is the reward or "reinforcement" for it.

## METHODOLOGY

The fight-training system of CAG consists of a number of exercises in aggressive communication. They are divided into two different but interrelated formats. One format is designed to channel hurtful hostilities into mutually acceptable (although intrinsically painful) *rituals*. The second format, called *impacts*, trains partners to influence one another in a forceful manner to stimulate and discover new ways of providing enjoyment and fulfillment in their relationship. In the course of training, the partners have an opportunity to recognize and explore the operationalization of *intimacy* in the context of their relationship.

### Desensitizing Through Rituals

Hostility rituals provide an outlet for the complete, yet safe, expression of accumulated resentments from the past; allow playful, yet dramatic and authentic, expressions of hostility in a manner that makes these expressions informative, emotionally involving, and also enjoyable and entertaining. Rituals also can lead to a display of a great deal of experiential content that has previously been hidden.

External controls are placed on rituals in the form of an appointed time and place, mutual consent, respect for belt lines, and "arms limitation." These limits reduce or eliminate the need for rational control over the content, thus providing a method for bringing into the open previously unconscious, or at least unexpressed, feelings, hopes, and concerns. The experience of acting-out hostilities with structured verbal and extraverbal rituals tends to reduce fear, shame, and guilt over the paradoxical existence of hate in the context of goodwill. Through the procedure of rituals, individuals become desensitized to the expression of hostility and become more receptive to the helpful information that will be offered during the impact encounters.

### Informing Through Impacts

"Fights for change" require a highly structured framework governed by basic rules that include, for example, a preparation for engagement, the necessity of taking turns, active listening, feedback, specificity of issues, reality-oriented reasoning, change-readiness, and so forth.

It should be emphasized that the highly structured communication exercises in either the ritual or the fair-fight formats are meant to be transitional bridging methods, which are highly modified or even abandoned as soon as each couple has discovered its own spontaneously emerging and highly pair-specific strategies and styles of dealing with conflict and aggression.

It seems that partners learn a deeper trust and mutual respect by having gone through these structured and "artificial," often trivial-appearing, exercises together. The mastery of the fight-training system offers the partners freedom from the fears of aggression and gives them the courage to deal henceforth with whatever serious conflicts may emerge in their groping for growth toward ever-deeper levels of intimacy.

### CAG Exercises

The following is a partial list and brief description of exercises in aggressive communication used in fight-training sessions. The typical group consists of from five to eight couples and meets weekly for four hours under the leadership of a fight trainer who coaches each couple as they take their turn in the "hot seat." Group members, in addition to the trainer, score and offer comments about fight style and may suggest "homework assignments." Each couple is encouraged to make a commitment for a minimum of 13 weeks of fight training to master the CAG system and to apply it to everyday living.

*Hostility rituals* usually serve as the starting point of all confrontations. They are cathartic insult exchanges by mutual consent and appointment, with whatever equalizing rules are necessary to allow a couple to express hostility freely while remaining within the structure of one of the rituals. Rules may consist of time limitations (usually one or two minutes), restriction of content, and use by one or both partners of physical aggression by means of "Batacas," soft rubber bats that provide the experience of beating and being beaten, but make it difficult to inflict any serious physical harm.

Rituals are based on the zero-sum game-playing model, with the extra bonus of a double win. Both partners gain by taking turns at having an assured "listening ear" (without defensive retaliation) and an emotional "unloading." In practice, both partners deescalate feelings of rage and give information such as anger-inspiring specifics, frustrations, and unabsorbable hurts. After a *rage-release ritual*, the partners are more able to open avenues that increase the bonding capacity of the relationship. The emotional effect may be compared to lancing a boil or to releasing the steam from a pressure cooker. Rituals put past grievances aside, at least temporarily, and clear the decks for dealing more rationally with current issues of the relationship.

*The haircut* is an expression of anger caused by a current specific hurt by one partner directed at the other. The partner who receives the request ("May I give you a haircut?") has the right to set the time limit, as well as the right to refuse or postpone acceptance. (Each individual must learn to gauge his or her tolerance for listening to rage-release rituals and set appointments and time limits accordingly.) If the "haircut" is accepted, the partner is obliged to listen to a tongue-lashing without defense, for the time contracted. The information disclosed may, at a later time, be the basis for a behavior-change request (fair fight for change).

When permission for a haircut (or any ritual) is denied, the problem arises of what to do with the accumulated rage. A specific homework assignment for each individual early in fight training is to find alternative idiosyncratic rage releases that do not require a listener, such as pounding a pillow, smashing crockery, working out on a punching bag, scrubbing floors, Bataca beatings, and so forth.

*The museum* (gunnysack or shopping list) is a compendium of old grievances accumulated from the start of the pairing relationship. Confrontation of the partners with their separate lists may be an initial assignment for a couple entering fight training. (Each assignment is pair-specific, based on emotional readiness and the "state of the marital union" of the couple.) The museum is used as a base of information for change and growth tasks.

The first step is to determine which items on the "list" or "museum catalogue" are no longer important. These items are given a "burial ceremony" incorporating attitudes of forgiveness and renunciation of their use as partner-punishing weapons. In a court of law, each crime is assigned a suitable and limited punishment that ends at the expiration of the sentence. Too frequently in marital unions the punishment for sins is endless. The burial procedure offers an escape from excessive punishment and a change in the state of the marital union.

The next step is to use the museum list to discover negotiable items of grievance in hierarchical order. Each item may result in the establishment of a *"belt line"* or form the basis for a fight for change. The items are considered one at a time, beginning with the one most immediately practical to negotiate. Dealing with the contents of a couple's museum lists starts the process of unloading the emotional garbage that is suffocating the relationship and creating barriers to intimacy.

*Beltline respect* is the next step. Every person has a limit for his or her tolerance for criticisms, rejection, insults, and putdowns. The CAG system teaches people to (1) openly declare their sensitivities, (2) demand to respect them, and (3) invite the expression of fair criticism—above the belt! In cases where beltlines are so unreasonably high that it becomes impossible to say anything negative, negotiations to readjust the beltline are engaged in.

*Mind reading* is a ritual exercise to see how far away one partner is from the being of the other. Positions are first defined, and the task of each partner is to listen to the other. The next step is an exchange of mind reading: "I think you think . . ." The process becomes a clarification of the living space of each partner, a process of knowing instead of guessing. Mind reading checkouts determine only the state of knowing or not knowing the other at that particular time, and have no predictive value. The term "mind raping" is used for mind reading without checkout; in other words, acting as if the unchecked assumptions about the partner's attitude are true. In extreme mind raping, the victim is told what he feels and any protestations to the contrary are denied or ignored.

## CASE EXAMPLES

In the CAG approach to psychotherapy all presenting complaints are diagnosed as symptoms of the mismanagement of aggression in the life style of the persons seeking consultations. This applies to all four settings of therapy: individual, group, couples, and family. The illustrative cases for this chapter have been chosen from CAG work with married couples; it is regularly proposed that their presenting complaints and conflicts could be most effectively resolved by learning how to fight fair for improvements. As far as their mismanagement of aggression is concerned, most couples fall into one of the following case types of symbiotic destructive communication patterns:

*Case Type I.* Two fight-phobic Doves tend to give up or give in in any conflict situation. They accommodate each other overtly—to keep the peace. *Covertly,* however, they will drive each other crazy, through passive, indirect hostilities (cf. Bach & Deutch, 1979).

*Case Type II.* A "rage-olic," overaggressive Hawk (of either sex) wins and bonds a dovish "victim" who openly suffers abuse while engaging in various covert retaliations, often in either the financial or sexual area.

*Case Type III.* Two hawkish screamers batter each other around in vicious circles, which generates much heat but no light. Knowing each other's tensions buttons, they press them frequently to cause constant pain and stress. Between bouts they "make up," usually in bed.

*Case Type IV.* A peacock-narcissistic self-actualizer is married to an adoring, chicken-sidekick-servant. As in the other case types, these roles may be taken by a member of either sex. One can also describe this Case Type IV as a symbiotic bond between a self-growth-oriented autonomist and a supporting male or woman. As in Case Type I, here too all seems peaceful for a while, but the quiet is one of suppressed resentment rather than true peace, which can only be a valid one as a result of mutually fair fighting for it! The autonomists feel hindered in their self-growth and demand "more space." Thus they are incapable of devotion to a lasting intimacy. The supporting adorers exhaust themselves in a one-way worship that earns mighty few blessings or redeeming rewards. Eventually both tend to develop symptoms of depression, which brings them into therapy.

What is fascinating in all four case types is the strength of their symbiotic bondage, as if they have become addicted to each other—however miserable. And because they do not know how to handle aggression effectively, they would not know how either to fight their way out or how to fight for changes for the better within their relationship.

However, after they have mastered the CAG system, they have the option of "creative exit fights" or staying and constructively fighting out their ongoing conflicts and then enjoying happy periods of real peace.

## APPLICATIONS

Instead of interpreting aggression away and deploring it as undesirable countertransference neurosis, CAG explores attitudes and techniques that encourage therapists to make full and it is hoped constructive use of their own aggression within appropriate therapeutic contexts and sensitive timing. Specific ways in which the psychotherapist both in individual and especially in group psychotherapy can overcome the stereotypical "nice, accepting" artificial role and make full therapeutic use of his or her own aggression has been explained in three previous publications (Bach & Goldberg, 1974, esp. chapter 4; see also Bach, 1974b, and Whitaker, 1962).

### The CAG System Applied to Family Therapy and Education: The Family "Pow-Wow"

Families are taught how to conduct a family fight fairly and constructively. One CAG-trained therapist-counselor-coach with one assistant meets with three to four families for a six-hour pow-wow session, usually from 10:00 A.M. to 4:00 P.M. on a Saturday or Sunday. A series of six pow-wows, two to four weeks apart, with homework practice in between, will enable the average family of goodwill to master the CAG techniques sufficiently to conduct family pow-wows at home on their own, independent of coaches or counselors but with the aid of a guide book (Nicholson & Torbet, 1980).

### Sex Therapy

In spite of the close connection between aggression and sexuality recognized by and long before Freud, people in general and sex therapists in particular do not like to take an openminded look at the fact that aggression and hostility play a decisive role in sexual excitement (Stoller, 1979; Malamuth, Feshbach & Jaffe, 1977). In almost all sex therapies aggression is treated as a no-no; the fact that love fights are recognized by everybody outside the sex therapy establishment as highly erotic is totally ignored. For sex therapy Luree Nicholson (Bach & Nicholson, 1978) and I have adapted several of the CAG techniques and developed new ones, such as "sleeping prince," which encourages macho males with impotency symptoms to let themselves be aggressively attacked by their lovers, who take on the responsibility of "making them." This and other CAG sex therapy techniques, such as bedroom Bataca bat lashings and spankings (Bach & Nicholson, 1978), have, far from encouraging sadomasochistic perversions, served to enrich healthy sexual intimacy and aided in the cure of so-called sexual dysfunctions in both male and female love-making partners. (See Bach & Goldberg, 1974, chapt. 15.) Systematic experiments with Bataca lashings and spankings have been reported by Beier (see Young et al., 1977). Goldberg (1976) has applied CAG theory in his analyses of sex-role stereotypes.

### Problems of Singles

The *CAG Pairing* system of communication training for young as well as more mature single adults has proven to be effective in avoiding the manipulative pitfalls and romantic traps of traditional "nice" courtship habits. The aggressive-affectionate approach of *Pairing* (Bach & Deutsch, 1970) gives new relationships a start and momentum in the direction of developing authentic intimacy in which "love fights" are conducted in manners that enrich rather than weaken the love bond. Currently Steven Harrison is preparing a report of his research comparing effective and ineffective pairing behaviors. His publication will be an updated guide to constructively aggressive pairing. This approach and material have proven popular not only with the single and divorced population but also with college students exposed to pairing education as part of student counseling programs.

## Constructive Divorce

Within the CAG system, I have developed a love separation ritual called *The Unwedding* that helps disenchanted lovers to let go and to utilize the exit stress for learning and growing. The Unwedding and other separation and rejection-related CAG techniques are described and illustrated in two previous publications (Bach & Bernhard, 1971; and Bach, 1974a).

## Depression and Suicidal Tendencies

Dynamically, both reactive and relatively chronic depression can be viewed as either repressed and/or inner-directed mismanaged aggression and rage. Getting depressed personalities interested—through therapy-group contagion—to try out first within the group sanctuary of therapy and then in real-life contexts, impact as well as hostility-type rituals has had some encouraging results (Bach, 1974–75).

## Organizational In-Fighting

Dr. Eric Field and other associates at the Bach Institute are in the process of developing CAG techniques designed to deal with constructive ways of utilizing (rather than dissolving) the irritation, anger, and hostility that inevitably arise whenever people have to depend on each other to function in certain synchronized ways to assure productivity at work. The constructive management of aggression at work is particularly relevant because current racial and feminine assertions create new challenges to harmonious work environments.

## SUMMARY

Creative Aggression—CAG for short—is a system of psychotherapy and emotional education that focuses on utilizing constructively aggressive energy. It is assumed that human aggression—whether innate or ac-

quired—is aroused relatively easily. Once aroused, the forms of expression of aggression will depend on the kind of channeling available. CAG provides aggression-channeling procedures that effectively control or at least minimize lethal hostility and maximize constructive or "impact" forms of aggression, which can be stimulating to growth. The channeling is accomplished through a series of clearly structured hostility rituals and impact exercises.

While CAG principles can be self-taught through the use of popular guidebooks (see references), CAG-trained professional therapists, counselors, and educators apply this approach in training, clinical work, and teaching. CAG procedures are particularly suitable in group settings, such as multiple couple and family therapy. Other areas of application are sex therapy, beyond assertion training, and organizational conflict resolution. A full understanding of both overt and covert levels of human aggression, hopefully, will contribute toward the prevention of the destructive mismanagement of human aggression. The CAG prevention program goes beyond the treatment of overt aggression and focuses on so-called "passive aggression," or indirect hostility, which I have relabeled "crazymaking" (Bach & Deutsch, 1979; Bach & Nicholson, 1977). A clearer knowledge of the patterns and instigators of crazymaking communication holds the promise of reducing the stressfulness of interdependent living.

## REFERENCES

Bach, G. R. *Young children's aggressive play phantasies*. Psychological Monographs 59, no. 272. Washington, D.C.: American Psychological Association, 1945.

Bach, G. R. *Intensive group psychotherapy*. New York: Ronald Press, 1954.

Bach, G. R. Marathon group dynamics II: Dimensions of helpfulness: Therapeutic aggression. *Psychological Reports*, 1967, **20**, 1147–1158.

Bach, G. R. Creative exits: Fight-therapy for divorcees. In Franks and Burtle (Eds.), *Women in therapy*. New York: Brunner/Mazel, 1974a.

Bach, G. R. Fight with me in group therapy. In Wolberg and Araonson (Eds.), *Group Therapy 1974*. New York: International Medical Book Corp., 1974b.

Bach, G. R. The narcissistic core: The "nice" therapist and the suicidal patient. *Voices*, Winter 1974–75, **10**, 61–65.

Bach, G. R. Spouse-killing: The ultimate abuse. *Journal of Contemporary Psychotherapy* (in press), 1980.

Bach, G. R. and Bernhard, Y. *Aggression lab—the fair fight training manual*. Dubuque, Iowa: Kendall/Hunt, 1971.

Bach, G. R. and Deutsch, R. *Pairing*. New York: Wyden Books, 1970.

Bach, G. R. and Deutsch, R. *Stop! You are driving me crazy!* New York: Putnam, 1979.

Bach, G. R. and Goldberg, H. *Creative aggression*. Garden City, N.Y.: Doubleday, 1974.

Bach, G. R. and Nicholson, L. The cradle of crazy-making. *Voices*, 1977, **12**, 33–42.

Bach, G. R. and Nicholson, L. Sex and aggression: Fair fight therapy for lovers. A tape-recorded workshop sponsored by The Institute for the Advancement of Human Behavior. Palo Alto, Calif., October 1978.

Bach, G. R. and Torbet, L. *Who cares?* New York: Delacorte, 1980.

Bach, G. R. and Wyden, P. *The intimate enemy*. New York: Morrow, 1968.

Breeskin, J. The marathon group in the military. Presented at the 16th Annual Air Force Symposium in the Behavioral Sciences, 1968.

Eibl-Eibesfeldt, I. *Love and hate*. New York: Schoken, 1974. Trans. from German *Liebe und Hass*, Munic: Piper, 1970.

Goldberg, H. *The hazards of being male*. New York: New American Library, 1976.

Malamuth, N. M., Feshbach, S., and Jaffe, Y. Sexual arousal and aggression: Recent experiments and theoretical issues. *Journal of Social Issues*, 1977, **33(2)**, 110–133.

Nicholson, L. and Torbet, L. *How to fight fair with your kids and win!* New York: Harcourt, 1980.

Smith, M. Personal communications, 1978–79.

Stoller, R. J. *Sexual excitement, dynamics of erotic life*. New York: Pantheon, 1979.

Whitaker, C. The use of therapists, aggression in psychotherapy. In G. R. Bach (Ed.), *1962 Proceedings, Ninth Annual Conference, Group Psychotherapy Association of Southern California*. 1962, 4–15.

Young, D., Korner, K., Gill, J. D. and Beier, E. G. Beneficial aggression. *Journal of Communications*, 1977, **27(3)**, 100–104.

# CHAPTER 16

# *Crisis Management*

JAMES L. GREENSTONE and SHARON C. LEVITON

*This is perhaps the most "out of line" chapter in the book yet it is, paradoxically, the one that every reader should study most carefully, since the management of crises is something that no practicing therapist can avoid, and is a skill as useful as first aid for those who deal with people's problems.*

*As Greenstone and Leviton indicate, even experienced therapists sometimes fall apart when faced by crises. When faced with a situation that could provoke panic, knowing what to do and when to do it is a most important skill. Understanding the basic principles of Crisis Intervention and Management is a valuable asset to all, especially therapists, since any client or set of clients might go into a crisis period at any time.*

*In addition, the writers of this chapter include a valuable note regarding the dangers of crisis intervention to the professionals involved—a note that has general applicability to all of us who practice the art and science of psychotherapy.*

Crisis Management, or Crisis Intervention, is the skillful intrusion into the life of an individual at that time in the person's life when, because of unusual stress and tension brought on by unexpected and disruptive events of life, the individual is not able to direct his or her life in the way that he or she would normally under noncrisis conditions. This intrusion is for the purpose of defusing a potentially destructive situation before such physical and/or emotional destruction occurs.

A crisis occurs when unusual stress is present in an individual's life that temporarily renders him unable to direct his life as he usually would. Such a level of stress may be reached as the result of a single event, many stressful events occurring at the same time, or from stressful events occuring serially. Crisis-producing events seem to occur for no apparent planned reason. They occur without warning, and usually in a sudden manner.

Crises are self-limiting and will abate without intervention. However, because of the disorganizing and destructive effects on personal functioning that could occur as a result, immediate and skillful intervention is required. Intervener survival addresses the personal needs and concerns of the crisis intervener. Successful and effective intervention into the crises of others may well depend on the degree to which the intervener is prepared to handle his or her own stress, tensions, safety, nutrition, and personal life. Failure to attend to these areas often results in injuries, physical illness, emotional problems, and a high "burnout" rate among professionals.

## HISTORY

Crisis intervention theory was developed by Gerald Caplan (1964) and Erich Lindemann (1944) in the early 1940s. Their purpose was to study persons in actual crisis situations. These included the parents of those who were killed during World War II and of those who were the victims of the Boston Coconut Grove fire. Their work emphasized that individuals under great personal stress could be assisted in regaining their ability to function as they usually did through the skillful intervention of a third party. Since that time, much emphasis has been placed by various authors, theorists, and mental health professionals on providing immediate help to those individuals who are experiencing great distress in their lives (Stratton, 1976; Farberow, 1967; McGee, 1974). Private and community clinics have been established to provide such care on a walk-in basis, with no fixed appointment required. Concern in such intervention centers is on that which can be done at the critical time to help the person in crisis to return to his former level of pre-crisis functioning (Jacobson, 1971). If such assistance is available, the likelihood that the crisis victim will need subsequent psychotherapy due to prolonged maladjustment is reduced (Langsley & Kaplen, 1968).

The phenomenon of crisis has been defined from various aspects. These relate disruptions in a person's life to an increase in experienced stress and tension that does not allow personal functioning to occur as usual (Burns & Dixon, 1974). According to Caplan (1964), life changes that alter usual living patterns can result in states of crisis for those involved. The categories of situational crises and maturational crises have been found useful in understanding these critical times (Aquilena, Messick, & Farrell, 1970).

Crisis intervention and conflict management procedures for police officers have been of major concern for Bard and Zacker (1976). Because the police officer is often the first line of response during crises such as domestic disputes, training was developed to assist the responding officer in providing skillful and immediate aid before such situations could deteriorate into violence and self-destruction (Bard, 1975).

Greenstone and Leviton (1979, 1980) and Rosenbluh (1974) have provided the crisis intervener, regardless of professional or paraprofessional background, with practical, how-to procedures in a wide range of crisis situations. National training conferences sponsored by the Southwestern Academy of Crisis Interveners in Dallas, Texas, and the American Academy of Crisis Interveners in Louisville, Kentucky, also provide this type of interdisciplinary training and approach to Crisis Management.

## CURRENT STATUS

Crisis Management and intervener survival is advocated and taught at the National Training Conference for Crisis Intervention. This conference is sponsored by the Southwestern Academy of Crisis Interveners and, The University of Dallas. Both are located in Dallas, Texas. Courses taught by the American Academy of Crisis Interveners in Louisville, Kentucky, also offers this approach or modifications of it. To date interveners from 30 states and a wide variety of professional backgrounds and concerns, including helping agencies, police departments, volunteer crisis centers, private practice, probation departments, and schools, have been trained.

The Southwestern Academy of Crisis Interveners and the American Academy of Crisis Interveners jointly publish, seminanually *Emotional First Aid: The Journal of Crisis Intervention,* the only journal currently in print that deals exclusively with Crisis Managment. It is abstracted by the American Psychological Association and appears in *Psychological Abstracts.* Additionally, *The Crisis Intervener's Newsletter* is published quarterly. Both the journal and the newsletter are available on a subscription basis or as part of yearly membership in the academies.

## THEORY

Regardless of the crisis, management requires special skills and the adaptation of skills unique to such situations. The skills involved, while based on current psychotherapeutic thought, may in their application vary significantly from the ways that they are employed in routine, weekly counseling sessions. Time becomes the critical difference. In weekly counseling sessions over a long period of time, or even in short-term counseling, it may be possible to work with an individual extensively to achieve problem resolution. The crisis intervener, however, may have only minutes or perhaps seconds to accomplish his or her purpose. To the degree that the crisis is managed, the need for subsequent psychotherapy is reduced. If the intervener is able to prevent additional personality disorganization and deterioration from occurring and to help the victim of crisis effectively mobilize the personal resources possessed during noncrisis times, those usual life-coping skills can take over and effective functioning can be reestablished, at least to the level of precrisis behavior. While some additional psychotherapy and/or support may be needed after successful intervention, it is usually much less intensive and lengthy than if there was no intervention or if it was mishandled. While much is done in most reputable training programs to develop highly skilled psychotherapists, little attention is paid to the importance and the skills of Crisis Management. While related to basic psychotherapeutic intervention, and adaptable to most theoretical approaches, Crisis Intervention constitutes a skill area all of its own, one to which attention must be focused.

In attempting to study a crisis, Rosenbluh (1974) noted that it does not go on forever, and as a result is self-limiting. The individual in crisis will eventually find a solution to the problems experienced, that solution being effective to a greater or lesser degree. Initally there is a marked increase in the state of tension present relative to a particular problem. It is at this time that usual problem-solving methods are attempted. Since these methods have been ineffective and continue to be so, the stress that the victim is under

will again increase and serve to exacerbate the crisis. The victim is often unable to make effective choices about his life or to evaluate the situation. Disorganized behavior often results as inner tensions compete for expression. Bodily complaints may develop, and the victim may react to the situation by violence, at one end of the behavior continuum, or by complete withdrawl, at the other end. Violence may be directed either inwardly or toward others.

The intervener in crisis situations has two major objectives. First, trauma must be reduced wherever and whenever possible and as quickly as possible. Additonally, the intervener can make use of the situation not only to manage the current difficulties, but also to assist the victims of crisis to master future difficulties by the use of more effective and more adaptive coping mechanisms. (Parad, 1965).

Crisis Intervention is an immediate attempt to deal with immediate problems. The major emphasis is to reestablish precrisis functioning and to assist the victim to achieve higher levels of functioning as appropriate and possible within the allowed time frame. The practice of elaborate history taking is deemphasized in Crisis Management. While some history is gathered, the primary emphasis is on the immediate past that surrounds the current crisis. Time, once again, dictates the extent of this exploration. In any event, some historical assessment must occur not only to establish the basis for the crisis, but also to make the most accurate determination regarding disposition and subsequent needs for therapy. Throughout, however, the emphasis of the intervener will be on the immediate situation and the management thereof.

In many other forms of psychotherapy and counseling, the role of the therapist may be nondirective or indirect at best, and there are few time restrictions. Yet in Crisis Management, the role of the intervener may be quite direct and active and the intervention may last only a few minutes. This rapid assistance in helping the victim to regain his precrisis

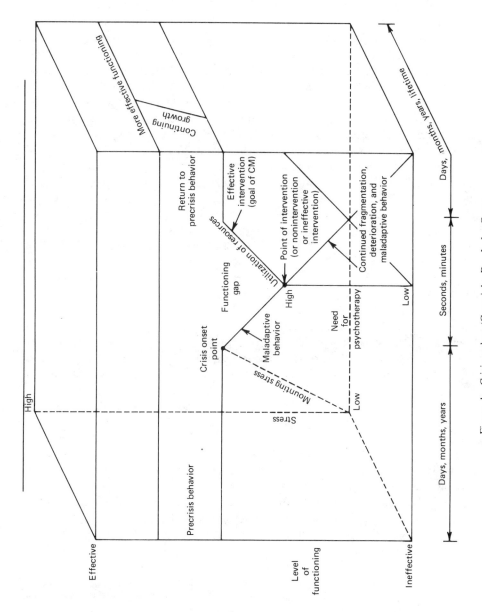

Figure 1  Crisis cube. (Copyright Dr. J. L. Greenstone, 1977. All rights reserved.)

219

efficiency may take the form of both emotional and physical support as needed and as judged to be beneficial. While effective and immediate Crisis Intervention and Management may reduce the need for additional psychotherapy, if further help is needed, the transition to most types of psycotherapy or other treatment is easily accomplished. The value in the use of intervention techniques as an adjunctive mode with most other psychotherapeutic systems can be readily seen. Crisis management procedures can be utilized prior to entrance of the victim into psychotherapy in order to better prepare the individual for the therapeutic relationship. These same procedures are valuable for the patient already involved in ongoing treatment who may experience subsequent crisis that may be detrimental if not immediately and effectively handled.

## METHODOLOGY

The intervener in a crisis situation must ask himself several questions. These include: (1) What problem is the crisis victim experiencing now? (2) What is precipitating the crisis in his life at this particular time? (3) Of the several problems that may surface at this time, which need to be of immediate concern to me, and which can be dealt with later? (4) Which of the problems presented will be most physically or psychologically damaging if not immediately dealt with? (5) Which problems can be most immediately and easily managed? (6) Are there problems that must be managed before other problems can be dealt with? (7) What resources are available both to me and to the victim of crisis that I can utilize as crisis management is attempted? (8) What variables or extraneous factors will hinder the intervention and what can be done to reduce their interference? and (9) What can abe done to implement the most effective Crisis Management possible to defuse a highly volatile situation, and to do it in the shortest realistic amount of time?

The approach to a crisis situation is guided by the need for *immediacy*. The intervener must act *now*. The intervener's aim is to prevent further confusion and disorganization, to relieve the heightened state of anxiety as quickly as possible, and to see that the crisis victim does not hurt himself or others. To this end, intervention begins at the time that the crisis is encountered. The intervener must be ready to act, or in some situations make a decision not to act, at the moment he or she is faced with a person who is experiencing crisis. Little time is available for reflection or discussion of possible approaches. The full measure of the intervener's skill will come to bear at that moment, and the degree to which the intervener is prepared will be reflected in the efficiency of the intervention. Additionally, the intervener needs to know which situations he or she is not willing to enter or is prevented by lack of training from entering. Knowing one's limitations is as important to successful intervention as knowing one's skills.

The second major factor is *control*. Because the victim of a crisis is often not in control of his life at that moment, the intervener must assume control of the total situation to the fullest extent possible, and as circumstances dictate. This may be accomplished by nothing more than the physcial presence of the intervener, which conveys a sense of security and structure, while at other times it may be necessary for the intervener to take control in a more insistent manner. The victim of a crisis is out-of-structure in his life, and he seeks the structure that he lacks. By taking control, the intervener temporarily provides the needed structure. Specific ways of gaining control of a crisis situation will vary depending on the skills and abilities of the particular intervener. Interveners can utilize their own creativity to develop those methods that are effective within the situations with which they are faced. However, regardless of the methods chosen, the attitude of the intervener is of paramount importance. Interveners must convey through being as well as through behavior that control is centered in them. If this is not conveyed, control will not be gained regardless of the specific methods chosen. Persons in crisis will respond to structure and to those who represent it if they sense that it is sincere and not just a manipulative technique.

*Assessment* is the third major factor to consider. An on-the-spot evaluation must be performed. It must be quick while at the same time accurate. It must cover as many critical areas surrounding the crisis as possible to give the intervener as much useful information as possible in the shortest amount of time. The circumstances surrounding the particular crisis will dictate the nature of the assessment. Time, privacy, and other critical factors are some of those influencing circumstances. Simple and direct questions that avoid jargon and complicated verbiage will best serve the intervener and ultimately the victim. Identify, as soon as possible, the precipitating events in the crisis victim's life. Find out how the victim feels; if he or she is afraid; if there are thoughts of harming self or others. Note what actually happened and what the victim's perception is of what happened. Individual perception triggers crisis more often than do facts. Observe what the victim does and does not do; what is said and what is not said. Consider what would be expected under similar circumstances that is not occurring in this situation. Avoid judgment and attend to the nonverbal cues as a source of critical information that can be utilized quickly and efficiently. Such is usually done in regular counseling or therapy. However, under crisis conditions, this must also be done quite rapidly, and what is learned applied with equal speed.

Throughout, the personal attributes of the intervener will often affect the outcome of the intervention as much as any other single factor or combination of factors. A person in a state of crisis will usually respond to someone who seems to be approachable. The warmth, empathy, concern, supportiveness, calmness, steadiness, attentiveness, caring, and willingness to reach out to the victim emotionally, and even physically as needed,

will demonstrate the intervener's approachability. Questions economically stated, and an ear willingly lent, will enhance the cause.

The next step for the intervener is that of *management*. The victim of crisis needs assistance in reestablishing effective methods of handling life in general and the particular problems that specifically led to this crisis episode. Maladaptive behavior must be replaced with more adaptive behavior. Because the goal here is management rather than problem resolution, the regaining of precrisis level functioning efficiency is sufficient. Once this is attained, referral or longer-term psychotherapy may be considered. Attempts at counseling or therapy prior to successful Crisis Management would meet with little success. This cannot be over-emphasized in its importance to ongoing treatment. In Crisis Management, mobilization of personal resources and the resources of significant others in the life of the victim is the central function of intervention.

The intervener can be quite specific in terms of what must be done to accomplish the desired purpose. Reduction of anxiety and diffusing the intensity of the situation can be accomplished first. Sometimes removal of the victim from the crisis scene helps here. Let the victim know that you are there to assist, and to inform the person what can and is being done to help. Remain confident and self-assured during contacts with the victim. While it is usually not helpful to hold out false hope or to lie to a victim, realistic optimism is generally well received. Allow the victim to talk and to tell what happened as desired. Interrupt sparingly, and then only to clarify. Usually, it is best to wait until the victim is finished ventilating to gain clarification. For the purpose of Crisis Intervention, the intervener will be most useful if the short-term nature of the intervention is remembered and emphasized. Concentrate on conveying to the victim how temporary the crisis is rather than dwelling on what may appear to be a chronic situation. If your intervention is successful, the victim will likely be more willing to trust your suggestion for getting help for the ongoing difficulties.

Throughout, maintain a sense of structure and certainty that the victim can hold on to. Give the victim information that he needs to again begin securing his personal life. Repeatedly let the person in crisis know that you believe in his personal ability to control his life, while at the same time, indicate your willingness to provide the necessary support over this short period of chaos. Additionally, seek out, as possible, those significant others who can assist you and the victim to reestablish the control that has been lost. Distinguish those significant others who will aid in your intervention efforts from those who will be unhelpful or even harmful. Consider also those community and individual resources on which you may call if you decide to refer the crisis victim for ongoing care. Certainly, if the victim is currently or has been in psychotherapy, contact the therapist. Such a contact may provide helpful information, while at the same time it will give the therapist useful details if therapy is continued. At this time, medications and the like can also be checked.

The last stage of intervention is that of *referral and follow-up*. Many skillful interventions have been lost at this point. What is done with or for the crisis victim, postcrisis, and how efficiently it is done may mark the difference between the person who lives from crisis to crisis, learning nothing, and the person who utilizes the crisis as a steppingstone to a higher level of functioning efficiency and to the reduced likelihood of repeated crisis episodes. If you plan to continue personally with the victim in long-term psychotherapy, you can use the crisis experience to promote greater insight into the unresolved difficulties that result in this personal stress and chaos. If you intend to refer the victim for treatment, send him or her to someone with whom you have had personal contact or you know is able to work with those who have just experienced crisis. Do all that is necessary to arrange for the smooth transfer from yourself to the receiving ther-

apist. Anticipate difficulties of the crisis victim and try to avoid anything that would keep him or her from getting the additional help needed. Subsequent to the referral, check with the victim and with the new therapist to be sure that successful transition has been accomplished. If there are problems, attempt to resolve them as quickly as possible in order to avoid losing any of the original momentum to get help.

## APPLICATIONS

Crisis Management can be seen as a system that stands alone, or as an adjunct or a preparatory phase to psychotherapy. As a separate system, Crisis Intervention is directed toward those individuals who, because of the unusual stress experienced in their lives at a particular time, cannot direct their lives in the ways that they normally do. Included are those who experience sudden and unexpected disruptions in their usual life routine because of events such as rape, suicidal gestures, domestic disputes, spouse abuse, child abuse, and the like. Also included are those who experience crisis because of certain life changes that they may not be able to handle efficiently, such as marriage, divorce, separation, death or loss of a significant other, encounters with the legal system, promotions or demotions on the job, pregnancy, changes in school status, accidents with or without injury, and job loss. Intervention becomes an immediate aid during these times. The goals of such intervention may be limited. Support, guidance, and assistance is given only to the point that precrisis functioning is reestablished, and at that point the intervention is completed. Additional counseling or assistance may or may not be required. Often there is no such need. When there is, the intervener then makes a referral to the appropriate resource or handles postcrisis therapy himself. While the goals of Crisis Management as a system are limited, they are directed to assist the crisis victim to regain the structure in his life that has been temporarily lost, and to be able again to exercise effective choice regarding available alternatives.

As an adjunct or preparatory phase to psychotherapy, Crisis Management may be used to redirect those critical instances that may be disruptive to the usual course of counseling or therapy. An individual who experiences crisis resulting ostensibly from a singular event, but in reality as the culmination of many unresolved events, clearly may evidence the need for subsequent treatment. Such deep-rooted problems may be seen during the intervention into the immediate situation. Because the victim of a crisis is out-of-structure with life, and because he may be particularly vulnerable during these times, much information regarding previously unresolved crises may be disclosed. In addition, the victim's vulnerability during these times may make him more receptive to suggestions for subsequent psychotherapy. The key to positive outcome seems to be the degree to which the intervener is successful in helping the victim to manage his crisis and the trust level that has been developed. Such success and trust may be related to the recognition on the part of the intervener that the crisis encountered requires a different approach than that usually used in therapy.

Prior to seeking psychotherapeutic treatment, many individuals undergo a crisis. However, by the time of their first appointment, they are usually no longer in a crisis state. Subsequent to beginning the therapeutic process, they may again experience a crisis due to life changes or as a result of awarenesses gained during the therapeutic process. The therapist's recognition of such occurrences, and efficient responses to them, may mean the difference between losing all that has been gained, or being able to continue effectively from that point once the crisis has been managed.

Certain individuals seem more prone to experience crisis in their lives than others. Recognition of such individuals as potential high risks can aid us in working with clients. Those who fall into this category can be noted and some preparation made so as not to be caught off guard should a crisis occur. Individuals who may be somewhat more prone to experience crisis in their lives than others are usually seen as feeling alienated from real and meaningful relationships. They may be the cause of such alienation, and even though social supports may be available, the crisis-prone person is either unable or unwilling to use them. Provocativeness, low self-worth, and difficulty learning from previously made mistakes are also characteristic of the crisis-prone. Their history may reflect ongoing emotional problems that have not been treated, difficulty on the job, marginal income, impulsiveness, marital problems, drug abuse, physical accidents and injuries, and frequent problems with the police or legal system. Lasting bonds are obviously absent for the individual prone to experience crisis, and such a person will sometimes be transient and without a permanent place to live.

Crisis intervention procedures are limited; they focus on the immediate rather than on the long-term problems the individual may experience. In Crisis Management there is no attempt to move beyond the current disruptive and disorganizing event or events experienced. All people who are upset are not necessarily experiencing crisis. The need for accurate recognition is critical to the system. Such limited focus and accurate recognition can be the connerstone to any additional support services, or therapy that may be subsequently given.

### Intervener Survival

Intervener survival addresses the needs and concerns of the intervener as he or she prepares for or actually performs intervention into a crisis situation. It is not sufficient to learn crisis management procedures without also attending to those specific sources of stress and tension that may impinge on the intervener and thereby affect his or her ability to perform the intervention efficiently and effectively. The intervener who experiences a personal crisis while attempting to assist others who are also in crisis is of no help to anyone, least of all himself. Sometimes it is assumed that the trained professional has mastered the areas of concern that may plague less trained, nonprofessionals. This does not seem to be the case at all. Intervener and victim alike are subject to the same or similar stressors; both may fall prey to them.

If we are to be helpful, we must remain truly effective. In our roles as interveners in the crises of others, we may neglect our own needs, our own health and nutrition, our own safety, and our own responsibility for self-direction. We may become so involved in the lives of others that we fail to attend to ourselves. If this occurs, and we fail to place the same value on ourselves that we place on those we want to help, we may soon lose our effectiveness as interveners and cause harm to ourselves. If we neglect concerns for personal safety during interventions into crisis situations, or if we fail to recognize our own experience of stress, allowing it to go unchecked, our productivity and effectiveness will suffer. Conversely, if we are aware of these areas, have spent the necessary time and energy attending to them, and then have taken necessary steps to reduce the intensity of the problems in our own lives, we are better prepared to focus attention on the crisis of others.

One aspect of this personal concern for self is the area of goal setting. All crisis interveners must ask themselves: What are my goals today? What am I doing to accomplish these goals? Have I set realistic goals for myself today? Given the "givens" of my situation, what are my chances for accomplishing these goals? When goals are prioritized within the framework of the present setting, chances of success are increased. Conversely, when goals are set based on what you would like a situation to be, or on what you wish conditions were, then the chances of accomplishing those goals are greatly diminished. Further, when unattainable goals are not recognized as such based

on present circumstances, and responsibility for altering immediate goals is not taken, frustration, stress, and a sense of failure is likely to result both for the intervener and for the crisis victim he or she is trying to assist.

If frustrations are allowed to continue unchecked, stress levels rise as productivity falls. If, however, a decision is made to utilize the givens of the situation and thereby to set goals that are realistic to that situation, much energy is freed that can then be used in more effective ways. Sometimes this process is difficult, because we often set goals higher than we or others can achieve. Alteration of goals may then be seen as a symbol of failure. At that point, it may become easier to blame our feelings of frustration and tension on some outside source. This scapegoat may be the intervener's department, family, or even the crisis victim.

The bottom line is that regardless of how we attempt to disavow ownership for our feelings of frustration, anger, stress, and tension, they remain our personal responsibility. Further, the responsibility for lowering the effect of these stressors also remains ours. Seen in this way, the risk of taking charge in all areas of our lives for our own actions becomes an exciting challenge. The givens of the situation remain the same. What we can change is our assumptions.

## CASE EXAMPLE

Mr. and Mrs. Jones arrived at the therapist's office with their 10-year old daughter, Lisa. The appointment was suggested by the school counselor, who requested that Lisa be evaluated. The presenting problem is Lisa's disruptiveness in the classroom as demonstrated by her refusal to participate when called on, her constant moving about and chattering at inappropriate times, and her constant arguing with her classmates. This pattern began a year ago, and the school's attempts to effect changes in Lisa's behavior have failed. The teacher can no longer manage the situation.

## Phase 1

As Dr. G. receives the family, he notices that Mr. Jones keeps fumbling with his watch and seems to be quite angry. Mrs. Jones seems harassed but apparently is in control. Lisa is sullen. As Dr. G greets each family member, Mr. Jones clearly and angrily announces that the session is unnecessary, that the school is at fault for Lisa's problems, that he sees nothing wrong with what Lisa is doing in school, and that he feels imposed upon both by the school and by having to come to this session. The only reason that he has kept this appointment, he points out, is to pacify his wife's constant nagging. When Dr. G suggests that the family sit down, Mr. Jones insists that he would prefer to stand since he would not be there very long. While Mrs. Jones sits, Lisa remains standing with her father and cuddles him. She glances at her mother with disdain.

Dr. G recognizes that the stage is now set for impending crisis that could prevent any type of problem resolution if not managed properly. Mr. Jones is preoccupied with his own agenda, while Mrs. Jones seems caught in a struggle between her daughter and her husband. Lisa is also experiencing some difficulty in relating effectively to her parents. However, attention to Lisa's problems both at home and at school may well be affected by the way in which the crises of her parents are handled. This family is experiencing the effects of previously unresolved personal and marital problems, and cannot focus on current concerns until the tension is reduced and their crises managed.

At this point Dr. G has several options. He could terminate the session, acquiesing to Mr. Jones's insistence that he does not want to be there anyway. He could suggest that termination will occur unless all sit down and discuss Lisa's problems. Or he could explain that because the school has made a

referral, the focus of the session must be on school-related problems. While all three possibilities are related to the family and its problems in various ways, all three miss recognizing that this family is either already in crisis or about to experience crisis. This crisis situation, if recognized as such, can be managed, and at the same time provide inroads to the other, more extensive problems that require ongoing attention. Attempts to proceed therapeutically without first managing the existing crises may be met with little or no success.

Dr. G attempts to intervene immediately upon recognizing the current situation, and he realizes that Mr. Jones needs immediate attention. He also notices that Lisa will probably take her cues from her father. While Mrs. Jones needs to be acknowledged, she can wait to be heard.

Dr. G assures Mrs. Jones that he will attend to her shortly. He then returns and stands by and with Mr. Jones and Lisa. Mr. Jones explodes his frustration and his anger. He pursues his same theme. Dr. G knows that until these feelings are dealt with, there can be no constructive discussion, and he attends to Mr. Jones and notes several recurrent key phrases that reflect Mr. Jones's concerns. ''I care about my little girl,'' ''I want to do what is right for my child,'' ''I am a good father'' are some of the most obvious. Dr. G works specifically with these concerns and reflects understanding of them and reassurance as to their validity. He builds on these concerns as a way of encouraging Mr. Jones to discuss his daughter's problems in school. The apparent threat to his parenting ability is used to encourage good parenting and problem solving on Lisa's behalf. Mr. Jones has been heard. His integrity as a parent is no longer being questioned. Now he may be more receptive to other concerns.

It is obvious that Dr. G took immediate control by being willing to utilize the momentum of the situation as it was presented rather than trying to restructure it, as might have seemed appropriate at first glance. The session could have easily aborted without this immediate control and intervention.

## Phase 2

Now that Mr. Jones is more agreeable to moving on, Dr. G suggests that they all be seated. At this point he becomes attentive to Lisa. Having observed that Lisa and her father seem very close, and as a result of that closeness may appear to be conspiring against Mrs. Jones, seating is strategically structured with Lisa next to her mother.

Lisa begins to protest. She will either sit beside her father or she will not stay. She begins yelling, and as she does Mrs. Jones, who has been passive until now, accuses Mr. Jones of spoiling the child. She states that he always lets her have her way and is the source of Lisa's present problems at school. She continues that Mr. Jones cares more about what Lisa wants than he does about her. She becomes emotionally distraught and retorts that in the last year, he has spent all of his free time and energy with Lisa. Lisa then rushes to her father and begins laughing.

Dr. G must act quickly to take control again. Where is the greatest need? Because a reasonable degree of trust has already been developed with Mr. Jones, perhaps it can be utilized. Mrs. Jones is becoming progressively more upset, crying and screaming. Lisa continues to laugh at her mother.

Dr. G addresses Lisa first. Feeling that Mr. Jones will support his actions, Dr G calmly and firmly commands Lisa to return to her seat. Lisa looks at her father, and Mr. Jones tells her to do as told. Dr. G tells Lisa that while he is very interested in hearing about her and her problems, this could best be done in a separate session. He suggests that she wait in the outer office while he talks with her parents, and then an appointment will be set for her. Mr. Jones gives support to this proposal and Lisa is taken out of the office by Dr. G.

Attention must now be given to Mrs. Jones. Expression of her feelings and of her concerns are allowed. Subsequent to this ventilation, Dr. G asks for an agreement from both Mr. and Mrs. Jones that they will listen to the concerns and the problems of the other without interruption. Once this setting for dialogue has been established, Dr. G asks one party and then the other to express fully the concerns that each has. Interruptions are prevented as per the agreement. Dr. G serves as the clarifier of what is said, and helps each party to understand specifically what the other has said. When he feels it appropriate, Dr. G begins removing himself from the dialogue, suggesting that Mr. and Mrs. Jones speak to each other without a mediator. Dr. G continues to press for the need for clarity. Additionally, he directs their exploration of possible ways in which to handle the problems that exist between them currently in order to be able to work together to assist Lisa. Just as problems are sharpened to clarity, so are the possible ways of managing them that would thereby allow positive interaction between Mr. and Mrs. Jones on matters of joint concern.

It is apparent that even though the appointment was arranged primarily to examine Lisa's behavior in school, the total family is experiencing crisis. As an attentive, effective intervener, Dr. G begins zeroing in on each person's particular crisis or impending crisis as soon as recognized. For Mr. Jones, the fact that he might be seen as a bad parent by the school, by the counselor, or by his wife precipitated a crisis for him. For Mrs. Jones, the fact that she felt she was constantly competing with her daughter for the attention of her husband, while being mocked by her daughter, created her crisis. For Lisa, the tensions within her family and the power struggles in which she found herself produced constant stress, which she handled alternately through withdrawl and aggressive behavior.

## Phase 3

Dr. G. returns control of the situation to Mr. and Mrs. Jones as soon as they seem to be having some success in working with each other. He suggests that the family use the concerns about Lisa as a foundation for further exploration of the problems expressed during this session. An appropriate appointment is set for Lisa concerning her school problems, and parental cooperation is requested. While nothing has been done yet to resolve Lisa's problems, it is clear that because the crises that existed in this family have been managed, the likelihood that Lisa can be helped is greater than if such intervention had not been made. Additionally, while the crisis management procedures did not solve the ongoing problems between Mr. and Mrs. Jones, the possibility that the Joneses will continue with additional therapy is enhanced.

## SUMMARY

Crisis Intervention involves entering into the life situation of the person who is experiencing crisis, as well as into the lives of significant others (individuals or groups), in order to diminish the effect of that problem or difficulty that has caused the perceived heightened state of tension or stress. In doing so, the intervener will attempt to assist the victim in activating those sources of aid, both personal and social, that can help remove the sense of hopelessness and helplessness that accompanies crisis.

Crisis Intervention has different meanings to different people, depending on the service they offer and their particular professional frame of reference. Table 1 will clarify the specific area of concern addressed herein. As should be quite clear, a distinction is made between psychotherapy, regardless of form, and what is referred to as Crisis Management. It has been the writers' experience that regardless of academic training, most people can be trained to be effective crisis interveners. This includes those with limited or no prior formal professional training. The importance of every therapist's developing these skills and abilities, however, cannot be overemphasized. While most already possess the theoretical background and the capabilities for effective intervention, Crisis Management as an adjunct to the therapeutic function requires a rethinking and an adapting of already acquired skills. To do so may not only save, but also enhance, what might otherwise be a lost therapeutic attempt.

## REFERENCES

Aguilera, D. C., Messick, J. M., and Farrell, M. A. *Crisis intervention: Theory and methodology.* St. Louis: C. V. Mosby, 1970.

**Table 1. Comparison of Psychoanalysis and Short-term Psychotherapy with Crisis Intervention**

| Areas | Psychoanalysis | Short Therapy | Crisis Management |
|---|---|---|---|
| Focus | Past and the unconscious | Past as related to current situation, unconscious | Present. Restore precrisis levels of functioning |
| Role of therapist | Exploratory; Nondirective, passive observer | Indirect, passive observer | Direct, active participant |
| Control | Shared | Shared | Intervener |
| Awareness | Unconscious | Mixed | Conscious |
| Goals | Restructuring the personality | Removal of specific symptoms | Management of immediate crisis situation |
| Range | Limited | Varied | Limited |
| Indications | Neurotic personality patterns | Acute emotional pain and disruptive circumstances | Sudden loss of ability to handle life situations in way usually handled |
| Average length of treatment | Indefinite | One to twenty sessions | Usually only a few sessions, may be no more than one |

Bard, M. *The function of the police in crisis intervention and conflict management: A training guide* (U.S. Department of Justice, Law Enforcement Assistance Administration, National Institute of Law Enforcement and Criminal Justice). Washington, D.C.: U.S. Government Printing Office, 1975.

Bard, M. and Zacker, J. *The police and interpersonal conflict: Third-party intervention approaches.* Washington, D.C.: Police Foundation, 1976.

Burns, J. L. and Dixon, M. C. Telephone crisis intervention and crisis volunteers: Some considerations for training. *American Journal of Community Psychology,* 1974, **2**, 120–125.

Caplan, G. *Symptoms of preventative psychiatry.* New York: Basic Books, 1964

Farberow, N. W. Crisis, disaster and suicide: Theory and therapy. In E. S. Schneiderman (Ed.), *Essays in self-destruction.* New York: Science House, 1967.

Greenstone, J. L. and Leviton, S. *The crisis intervener's handbook,* Volume I. Dallas: Crisis Management Workshops, 1979.

Greenstone, J. L. and Leviton, S. *The crisis intervener's handbook,* Volume II. Dallas: Rothschild Publishing House, 1980.

Jacobson, E. *Depression: Comparative studies of normal, neurotic and psychotic conditions.* New York: International Universities Press, 1971.

Langsley, D. G. and Kaplen, D. M. *The treatment of families in crisis.* New York: Grune & Stratton, 1968.

Lindemann, E. Symptomatology and management of acute grief. *American Journal of Psychiatry,* 1944, **101**, 141–148.

McGee, R. *Crisis intervention in the community.* Baltimore, Md.: University Park Press, 1974.

Parad, H. J. (Ed.) *Crisis intervention: Selected readings.* New York: Family Service Association of America, 1965.

Rosenbluh, E. S. *Techniques of crisis intervention.* Louisville, Ky.: Behavioral Science Services, 1974.

Stratton, J. Law enforcement participation in crisis counseling for rape victims. *The Police Chief,* 1976, **43**, 46–49.

# CHAPTER 17

# *Dance Therapy*

DIANE DUGGAN

> *My general attitude toward psychotherapy is that it is an artificial, undesirable, and awkward way of getting "straightened out," and that in a perfect world people would be able to take care of their own problems or, if they needed assistance, they would get it from friends and family. In short, I see psychotherapy as practiced today as a necessary evil, a "purchase of friendship."*
>
> *How much better would it be to solve one's psychological problems by thinking on one's own, or by discussions with others, or by physical activities, or by social interactions rather than going to a stranger for help. Yet, for many people, professional assistance is the best solution to their problems.*
>
> *In this chapter we can see how a natural form of therapy, dance, can be adapted in a formal manner. Undoubtedly, the reasons for the therapeutic value of dance are complicated. To some extent I imagine that therapy occurs from the physiological effects alone; but probably the more important factor is the interaction with the dance partners, relationships with the therapist, and new disclosures about one's body and one's self. Consequently, the psychotherapeutic values of dance come from several modalities, and while dance, like music, poetry, and other aesthetic procedures, may help because of the pleasure of participation, it has additional, important physiological benefits.*

Dance Therapy is psychotherapeutic use of movement as a process to further the emotional and physical integration of the individual (American Dance Therapy Association, 1972). It is a holistic approach that, in recognition of complex body/mind interaction, deals with disturbances of emotional, cognitive, and physical origin through intervention on a body movement level. Movement is the therapeutic modality that provides a diagnostic tool for assessment and the material for exploration. It also serves as a mode of relationship between client and therapist and is the medium for change.

The dance therapist focuses on expressive, adaptive, and communicative behaviors as manifested by the client's muscle tension, breathing, posture, movement dynamics, and interactions. Through movement expe-

riences the client becomes aware of these behaviors and explores their significance. The movement process aids the client in developing alternate ways of coping with inner impulses and environmental demands, and integrates affective, cognitive, and somatic aspects of being.

Currently there are two separate terms used to designate the profession, Dance Therapy and Movement Therapy. The term "movement" is used by those therapists who wish to avoid connotations of performance and who do not use music but focus on inner sensing by the client. Those who prefer the term "dance" point to its connotation of expressive movement and the integrating aspects of the rhythmic use of body movement, as well as the profession's roots in the creative arts.

## HISTORY

Dance Therapy has roots in both dance and psychology. In dance its roots extend back to ancient times, when dance was used in religious ritual as a means of expressing profound emotion in times of hardship, transition, and celebration. In many cultures dance served a transcendant function, a means of achieving ecstatic communion with the spirit world in an effort to understand and cope with the forces of nature. It figured prominently in healing ceremonies in which shamans danced to exorcise evil spirits.

Dance served a preventive, regulative function as well. Traditional dances affirmed community identity and values through reinforcing cultural movement styles and patterns of interaction. Within the structure of the dance, individuals were afforded a means of releasing tension in a socially accepted manner and of coming to terms with their experience in the larger context of community values.

From the Dark Ages until the twentieth century, dance in Western culture became increasingly formalized and performance oriented, and its expressive, transcendant, and participatory aspects were often ignored. This began to change when Isdora Duncan and the dancer/choreographers who followed her moved away from formalized conventions of ballet toward a modern dance whose style drew on inner feelings for choreographic inspiration. Proponents of modern dance, such as Mary Wigman, influenced the development of many dance therapists.

Rudolf Laban (1960) had a significant impact on the development of Dance Therapy through his Effort/Shape system of movement analysis and observation. Effort/Shape provided a coherent and consistent tool for dealing with movement behavior. It describes not what is done in movement but *how* it is done, thereby emphasizing individual variation in performing the same movement activity. Irmgard Bartenieff brought this system to the United States and trained many dance therapists in movement observation and correctives.

Theoreticians, clinicians, and researchers in psychology also contributed to the field of Dance Therapy. Much of their work was published concurrently with the development of the field. Wilhelm Reich (1949) was particularly influential. In developing the analysis of resistance into character analysis he proposed a functional identity between psyche and soma, relating posture, breathing, and movement to characteristic coping style. He saw psychological defenses manifested physically in the character armor, chronic patterns of muscular tension that attempted to bind energy flow and deaden areas of conflict.

Lowen (1958) furthered Reich's theories in attempting to correlate topological patterns of tension with diagnostic categories. He also developed techniques of intervention that combined verbal analysis with movement activities designed to evoke emotional response and discharge tension.

Schilder (1950) wrote on the body image and the reciprocal interrelationship between psyche and soma. His work gave support to the conception of intervention on a body level in the treatment of emotional problems. Condon's (1968) findings of interactional synchrony and its importance in interpersonal communication has profound implications for the use of rhythmic dance as a therapeutic modality for individuals with severe interpersonal disturbances. Davis (1970) focused on intrapsychic aspects of body movement in her study on hospitalized psychotic individuals. She also studied nonverbal interactions in the therapeutic process (1977)

Marian Chace is generally acknowledged as the originator of Dance Therapy in the United States. A former Denishawn dancer teaching in the Washington, D.C. area, Chace began to gear her classes toward personal expression through movement rather than technique. Psychiatrists in the area heard of her skills and, after referring private clients to her, invited her in 1942 to use dance as a form of therapy with patients at St. Elizabeth's Hospital. Chace's work proved so successful in reaching and motivating nonverbal patients that Dance Therapy was integrated into the regular treatment program at the hospital. After her retirement from St. Elizabeth's, Chace worked at Chestnut Lodge with Freida Fromm-Reichmann and Harry Stack Sullivan.

Another seminal figure in Dance Therapy was Mary Whitehouse. In the 1950s she combined her extensive dance training with Jungian analysis to develop an approach to dance as a means of self-discovery and growth for neurotic individuals. Whitehouse was particularly influential in the development of the profession on the West Coast. Liljan Espenak and Blanche Evan also developed techniques for dance as therapy with the normal neurotic, while Trudi Schoop used dance in the treatment of hospitalized psychotic individuals.

These pioneer clinicians developed into teachers as students sought them out for training and apprenticeships. A growing need for communication and professional development resulted in the formation of the American Dance Therapy Association in 1966. The infant organization had 73 charter members, and Marian Chace was elected the first president.

## CURRENT STATUS

The American Dance Therapy Association (ADTA) is the recognized professional organization for dance therapists, and the great majority of practitioners are members. In 1979 the ADTA had a membership of slightly over 1,000 in the United States and 12 foreign countries. The association promulgates standards for clinical practice and education. A rigorous registry procedure was developed that includes appropriate training plus two years of clinical employment and evidence of integration of training and practice. The association considers registered dance therapists (DTR) to have the minimum level of competency to enable them to engage in private practice or training of dance therapists.

Professional training of dance therapists

occurs on the graduate level. In 1979 there were 10 programs leading to a masters degree in Dance Therapy. All programs include coursework in areas such as dance therapy theory, movement observation, and psychodynamics, as well as a clinical internship.

In addition to these formal training programs, courses and workshops are given throughout the country by dance therapists. These are listed in the ADTA's *Newsletter,* published bimonthly. The ADTA also publishes a free brochure on educational opportunities, listing programs and other ongoing training.

The ADTA holds an annual conference in the fall and encourages regional workshops and conferences throughout the year. The association also publishes literature on the field, including conference proceedings, monographs, the collected papers of Marian Chace, and the *American Journal of Dance Therapy.*

The growing professionalism in the field of Dance Therapy has resulted in its increasing recognition by governmental agencies and the mental health community. Dance Therapy is included in the 1975 Education for All Handicapped Children Act (PL94.142) as a related service. This has resulted in a growing number of dance therapists working in special educational settings. At this time the majority of dance therapists work in mental health settings such as psychiatric hospitals and community mental health centers.

## THEORY

Movement is a fundamental fact of life; all observable human behavior consists of body movement. Movement has intrapsychic, adaptive, and interpersonal significance. A primitive and relatively uncensored expression of inner states, movement is a means of coping with the environment and a communicative link to others. Fundamental, pervasive, and multifaceted, movement lends itself to use within a variety of conceptual frameworks. Bernstein (1979) compiled eight different theoretical approaches written by leading dance therapists. Among these were Jungian, psychoanalytic, gestalt, and transpersonal orientations.

Fundamental to the work of all dance therapists, whatever their theoretical orientation, is a holistic philosophy that recognizes the complex interaction and interdependence of mind and body. Psychological states are manifested somatically in muscle tension, breathing, posture, and movement dynamics. The mind/body relationship is reciprocal, so not only does the mind influence the body, but experience on a body level has an impact on the psyche. The body reflects and affects an individual's feelings of the moment, history, characteristic attitude toward life, and even cultural identity. There is no simple one-to-one body/mind correlation; the relationships are complex and influenced by many variables.

Dance therapists are likely to view development according to their theoretical orientation, but all would agree on the importance of movement in the developmental process. In the earliest stages of development movement is one of the infant's most significant means of acquiring information about the self and the environment. Both the infant's own reflexive and random, undifferentiated movements and the handling the child receives provide sensory input. At this stage all learning is body learning.

Movement stimulates the kinesthetic sense, which, along with touch, is crucial in the development of the body image, the individual's mental representation of his or her body. The influence of the body image is considerable. Its early renditions are thought to provide a basis for the development of the ego (Fisher & Cleveland, 1968). The body image influences perception of the environment by acting as a basic frame of reference for spatial judgments, and it influences acquisition of motor skills through affecting the individual's ability to differentiate, control, and coordinate body parts.

Since human beings are capable of reflexive movement response to tactile stimulation as early as the seventh week after conception,

it is not surprising that individual differences in movement have been identified in infants. Kestenberg (1965 a and b) describes these differences in terms of rhythms of tension flow and looks at them longitudinally, in relation to psychosexual stages, and in the mother-child interaction.

Movement has a profound role in emotional development. The infant's first relationship is based primarily on touch and movement. This relationship forms the prototype for subsequent relationships and affects the individual's self-concept and attitude toward life. In this relationship the infant learns to sense and relate to another through patterns of touch, movement, and bodily rhythms. The infant internalizes aspects of these patterns from the mother and learns to respond, accommodate, and assert, all on a movement level. Deprivation of movement and tactile stimulation at this stage has devastating effects on the individual's ability to relate and to perceive the self positively.

During this preverbal period, all experience is linked to body sensation and movement. Dance therapists believe that the body is a repository of memories of this period and seek to tap them directly through the body. S. Chaiklin (1975) points out that while all existing psychiatric theories acknowledge preverbal levels of development, the techniques for intervention on this level are very limited. Dance Therapy has the advantage of connecting directly with this level through movement and making preverbal material available to the individual without first filtering it through language. In dealing with severely regressed individuals, language may be totally ineffective. Dance Therapy provides a means of establishing a relationship with these individuals on their level, so that work toward higher levels of functioning can begin.

In normal development, patterns of movement, interacting with the environment, are internalized over time, and they integrate with affective and cognitive processes. This integration results in a moving, feeling, thinking being capable of experiencing the full range of human emotions. The individual is aware of inner feelings, able to cope creatively with the demands of the environment, and able to engage in satisfying relationships with other people.

There is no one particular healthy style of movement. It is recognized that each individual has movement preferences that reflect his or her unique personality and also that different cultures value and therefore encourage specific styles of movement. Emphasis in Dance Therapy is placed on awareness of and comfort with one's movement style and on a range of adaptive movement with which to meet the demands of the environment. It is not adaptive, for example, to move loosely, with free flow all the time. At times bound flow is required, as when carrying something extremely fragile.

Dance therapists see in emotional disturbance a pathological split between mind and body that cuts the individual off from his or her body and inner feelings. This split is accomplished through the body, with muscle tension and breathing patterns used to defend against unacceptable internal impulses or environmental threats. Patterns of chronic tension restrict blood flow and sensation in body parts that are related to the source of conflict. This limits body functioning and the amount of energy available to the individual as well. Traditionally psychologists have approached emotional disturbance through verbal intervention. Dance therapists work through body movement to effect awareness and change on a body level and consequently on feeling and cognitive levels as well.

A major focus in Dance Therapy is deepening the individual's ability to experience the self. One aspect of this experiencing occurs on a body level. The dance therapist helps the individual to get in touch with blocked areas and dysfunctional breathing patterns. These may be explored in movement to clarify their significance and the way in which they work for and against the individual. The distortions often speak eloquently of the individual's maladaptations in dealing with inner impulses and environmental demands. The feelings that these distortions repress are also examined, both in movement and verbally, and related to other aspects of the individual's life.

Through nondirected inner sensing, the individual also experiences inner dynamics and states. Ideally, the individual does not direct his or her movement. The movement seems to simply unfold by itself. This unplanned movement may be limited, but if it is inevitable, authentic movement (Whitehouse, 1979) it reveals to the individual inner dynamics as they emerge in direct experiencing.

Alperson (1977) points out that an advantage of the body movement approach to self-awareness is that it does not demand definition prior to expression and therefore potentially limit the experience, as verbalization might. The individual can explore him- or herself directly in a state of flux. From this dynamic state emerge new ways of behaving and perceiving the self and others. The insights resulting from the movement experience are processed verbally to further clarify their personal meanings. Moving before talking prevents the client from being limited at the outset by accustomed ways of thinking about one's self and one's relationships.

The moving person feels him- or herself in the moment as a result of immediate multisensory feedback produced by the movement itself. Such kinesthetic, tactile, vestibular, visual, and auditory stimulation help to strengthen the body image and develop a clearer, more stable sense of self. Movement also promotes physical well-being. Relaxation and corrective techniques reduce muscle tension and bring awareness to deadened areas, diminishing feelings of physical discomfort and increasing vitality. The development of control of the body increases feelings of worth and competence. All of these increase positive feelings about the self, giving the individual a stable base from which to undertake the difficult tasks of self-exploration and change.

Dance is an intrinsically pleasurable activity for most people, especially when there is no pressure to perform or compete.

Rhythmic aspects of dance are particularly important. Snyder (1972) cites research findings that reveal that the body tends to synchronize internal rhythms, such as heartbeat and respiration, with motor activity and with outside rhythms. Rhythmic activities then can produce internal harmony and self-synchrony through synchronizing body rhythms. Rhythm facilitates interaction by creating a feeling of unity among people. The propensity for self-synchronization enables group members to relate to each other in an indirect but intimate and compelling manner as they move together to a common beat. This moving together parallels the interactional synchrony found in normal conversation, and Condon (1968) equates it with communication. For severely disturbed individuals it can provide an experience of belonging and connection with others.

Movement is not only a means of enhancing self-awareness and communication; it is also a medium for organizing and managing internal impulses. Severely disturbed persons may be all too painfully aware of internal impulses, to the point of being overwhelmed by them. Chace (H. Chaiklin, 1975) felt that dance was a powerful means of structuring and reintegration for the individual because it is a way of organizing expressive movement. The actual forming of expressive movement in Dance Therapy involves exercising a degree of mastery over impulses and can enable the severely disturbed individual to make some order of the chaos of his or her feelings.

Movement experiences in the dance therapy session can further aid the individual in managing impulses through the bodily expression of emotion in a safe and supportive environment, which can dispel some of the pain and panic associated with the feelings. This makes emotionally laden situations more manageable and can be a real step toward clarifying feelings, issues, and choices.

Dance Therapy supports change through enhancing the capacity for adaptive response and supporting development of more appropriate coping behaviors. The dance therapist, starting with the individual's movement style and utilizing movement affinities and other techniques, seeks to enlarge his or her movement repertoire, thus affording a greater range of adaptive response to the environment. Opportunities for trying out alternate means of coping and conflict resolution are provided in the sessions. New adaptive behaviors are identified and supported until they are integrated and available to the individual in everyday life.

## METHODOLOGY

Methodology in Dance Therapy varies according to the theoretical orientation of the therapist, the setting, and the type of client. There is considerable variation in the therapist's role as active participant or observer and the amount and type of structure provided. Although many decisions are made on the basis of training and personal style, the most important variable in determining methodology is the type of client. The needs of psychotic individuals are far different from those of functioning neurotic persons. Dance Therapy is flexible enough to adapt to both, emphasizing in some instances formalized structures and in others creative improvisation and inner sensing.

A feature common to the work of all dance therapists is the process orientation. Dance Therapy is not a set of techniques to be used according to the client's diagnostic category, and there is no preset prescription for a dance therapy session. The dance therapist responds to the client's movement behavior in the moment, seeing it as a continuous process of unfolding of the self.

The dance therapist relates movement behavior on the level of intrapsychic and/or interpersonal functioning to the client's history and general therapeutic goals. The therapist may facilitate nondirective exploration of inner sensations or provide structures that support the individual and develop perception of the environment and adaptive response. He or she takes cues on how to proceed from the ongoing nonverbal and verbal feedback of the client. Often methodology will change during the course of therapy as the client's needs change.

Movement, a concrete phenomenon, is transitory and exists only in the moment. To identify discrete and relevant dimensions from the continuous stream of movement behavior, the dance therapist needs a systematized approach to movement observation. For the majority of dance therapists, Laban's (1960) system of Effort/Shape fulfills this need.

In Effort/Shape, movement is viewed as efforts, dynamic qualities that relate to exertion of energy, and shape, which relates to body form in space (Dell, 1970). Effort qualities are seen on continuums between extremes of dynamic qualities in tension flow (free to bound), weight (light to strong), time (sustained to sudden), and space (indirect to direct). Shape is comprised of shape flow (relation to the body itself), directional movement, and shaping (creating or adapting to forms in space).

The use of Effort/Shape gives the dance therapist a language based on movement behavior rather than on psychological constructs. It facilitates observation, analysis, and comparison between individuals and over time of the qualities that give movement its expressive coloration.

Not all dance therapists move with the client. A few take the role of observer, interacting with the client through words rather than active movement. Their decision not to participate in the movement reflects a belief that they may unduly influence the client and distract him or her from awareness of inner impulses. However, many dance therapists function as participant observers, and gear their level of movement involvement to the situation at hand. They may participate in movement while working on interactional issues or when the client needs that support, then function as observer only when the client works on inner sensing.

Other dance therapists, especially those working with severely disturbed persons, nearly always move with their clients. Their focus is often on facilitating connection with the environment rather than inner sensing. They use their body movement to reflect and respond to the client's movements and to engage the client in a nonverbal relationship.

For those dance therapists who move with their clients, the Chacian technique of mirroring is an important therapeutic tool. Mirroring entails picking up and reflecting back to the client essential, characteristic elements of movement behavior. Mirroring serves several functions. First, it establishes a connection between the therapist and the client. The dance therapist literally meets the individual on his or her level by sharing in the actual movement. The client may perceive the therapist as relating to him or her or as an actual part of him- or herself. Mirroring also develops an empathic bond between therapist and client. The dance therapist gains some insight into the individual's feelings because the movement affects the therapist on a feeling level and calls forth associations that the client may or may not share. Finally, the therapist is able to facilitate the development of the specific movement to its fullest expression by picking it up. This development is aimed at increasing the individual's awareness of his or her movement behavior and establishing a connection between the movement and internal states. It also provides a release of energy and, at times, resolution of conflict on a movement level.

The development of movement themes is a major methodological process in the dance therapy session. Here the client experiences him- or herself directly, with meaning and associations unfolding through the movement process. The first step in this process is identifying significant themes. With functioning neurotic clients this can be done by facilitating inner sensing, having the client listen to his or her own body, not moving until the impulse to do so becomes clear. If the impulse is to remain still, this too has meaning and is worked with. Themes can also emerge from suggestions for movement exploration made by the therapist. Exploration of movement polarities, body parts, or entities such as the kinesphere can reveal personal associations for the individual. Such explorations can have significance for the client in clarifying longstanding conflicts and characteristic modes of being in the world.

If at all possible, the development of the movement themes is accomplished by the client, with suggestions and feedback as necessary from the therapist. The purpose is to explore the issue and its meanings for the individual. The direct experience of movement, as opposed to simply talking about it, gives the issue immediacy and brings up associations that may have been forgotten. There is also an opportunity to explore different aspects of the issue and find a resolution on a movement level.

With clients who need more structure and connection to external reality, the therapist picks up recurrent themes as they are manifested in movement. Here the therapist is likely to guide the development through his or her own movement, calling on improvisational skills, a knowledge of the client, and an ability to observe and analyze the movement response. Although the therapist guides this process, the responses of the client determine its direction. As they move, the therapist encourages the client to associate thoughts and feelings with the movements to aid in integrating these facets of the experience and to come to terms with the experience.

The amount of structure in sessions depends largely on the client's ability to structure him- or herself. Music provides structure, as do regular group rituals, such as greetings and warm up exercises. Spatial formations are another way of providing structure. The circle is a favored formation because it allows a continuous, unbroken contact among participants, provides unobstructed vision, and gives everyone a potentially equal standing. Sometimes spatial formations may be used to elicit responses or explore certain issues, as when the therapist

structures dyads or small groups to work on interactional themes. The individual's awareness of his or her response to the situation is highlighted, and he or she receives immediate feedback on the impact on others of his or her characteristic style of relating.

Props are another means of structure available to the dance therapist. A prop such as a stretch rope or piece of fabric can be used to keep a group of severely disturbed individuals together. A ball or other object might be used in greeting rituals or improvisations to direct focus and connect individuals. Props can be especially useful in work with autistic children, who may be able to relate to an object but not to another person. Here the prop serves both as a bridge to facilitate contact and as a defense for the child against too direct contact.

The use of music by dance therapists varies greatly. Some use no music at all, emphasizing internal rhythms and self-awareness. Other dance therapists do use music, but with varying aims. Some look at transference relationships to the music, whether the client fights the music, is dominated by it, or needs it to organize his or her response. Other dance therapists use music specifically to evoke emotional and movement responses and, with severely disturbed clients, to organize movement behavior.

In group work music has a powerfully cohesive effect, especially if it has a clear, definite rhythm. Group rhythmic movement is a means of engaging the total being. The beat promotes a deeply satisfying synchrony, both in terms of the organization of the individual's own internal rhythms and his or her movement in relation to others. This can provide a much-needed experience of contact and unity for persons with severe disturbances in interpersonal relations.

Verbalization plays a role in Dance Therapy in the form of providing suggestions, feedback, support, sharing, and, in some cases, interpretations. Verbal processing of the movement experience is important in aiding the individual to make sense of what has gone on in the session. The therapist uses words carefully, aware that excessive verbalization can dilute the movement experience, while not enough verbalizing may isolate the experience and prevent its application to other aspects of the client's life. Talking in dance therapy sessions engages the cognitive processes and helps to integrate thought, feeling, and action.

Many dance therapists have had training in systems such as progressive relaxation, massage, yoga, and Feldenkrais technique. These techniques are used adjunctively, to supplement the dance therapy process as needed. They do not in themselves constitute dance therapy methodology.

## APPLICATIONS

Dance Therapy lends itself to use with a wide range of client populations because it is based on the fundamental, universal phenomenon of movement and because its methodology is flexible and responsive to the needs of the client. It has been used successfully with clients as diverse as profoundly retarded, multiply handicapped children with minimal voluntary movement and articulate neurotic individuals whose verbal defensiveness had stymied their progress in more traditional forms of psychotherapy.

While there are no apparent limitations to its applicability in terms of client population, Dance Therapy is best used in conjunction with a verbal modality when working with verbal clients. Some dance therapists have had advanced training in psychotherapy. They act as primary therapists, combining verbal and movement techniques in their work. When practitioners have not had advanced training in psychotherapy, Dance Therapy is best used as an adjunctive modality. The dance therapist and verbal therapist should work closely together in this case to maximize their effectiveness.

There seem to be no contraindications for the use of Dance Therapy. As S. Chaiklin points out, the methodology changes to serve the purpose. The dance therapist may be non-

directive in working with clients with strong, intact egos, but can structure sessions with formal, nonemotional patterns for clients with superficial controls who may be frightened by the intensity of feeling. Dance Therapy can be used to stimulate depressed clients or to relax agitated, tense ones. Goals and techniques vary according to its uses.

Dance Therapy has great value in the treatment of autistic children. Much of the work with them occurs on a one-to-one basis. The dance therapist relates to the child on a movement level, mirroring characteristic movements to establish a relationship based on the child's own repertoire. This approach shows an implicit acceptance of the child as he or she is and permits the child the security and gratification of familiar movements in the initial stages of contact. The dance therapist facilitates the child's meaningful exploration of the self and the environment, attempting to establish a coherent body image and enlarge the movement repertoire to develop adaptive coping skills.

Children with learning disabilities benefit from Dance Therapy on several levels. The tactile and kinesthetic stimulation derived through movement activities aid in strengthening the body image and integrating sensory input from other modalities. Movement activities are pleasurable and engage the total child, helping him or her to focus and sustain attention and to control impulsive behavior. The creative, process approach in Dance Therapy emphasizes each child's uniqueness as an asset rather than a liability, and helps to heal self-concepts that have been damaged by repeated failure. Children are helped to work through emotional issues in an atmosphere of support and trust.

Chace's original application of Dance Therapy was with hospitalized psychotic adults, and it is in this context that the treatment has gained perhaps the greatest recognition to date. Dance therapists working with severely disturbed individuals seek to draw them out of self-absorption and fantasy into a greater connectedness with other people and the environment. They typically use music, the circle formation, and other organizing structures to bolster inadequate defenses and support meaningful contact. Movement activities directly enhance body awareness and integration as a prerequisite to clearer perception of the environment. Movement structures organize inner impulses and help to mobilize the emotional and physical resources of the clients.

In work with neurotic clients the dance therapy process is useful in enhancing sensitivity to inner states and personal movement styles. The creative act in movement improvisation provides a means of tapping unconscious feelings and personal imagery, making them available for further exploration. Movement also serves as a medium for developing themes to clarify their meanings and evaluate their impact on adaptive and interpersonal functioning.

Dance Therapy is also being used with good results with the mentally retarded, the aged, blind and deaf persons, anorexic individuals, the criminally insane, and individuals with chronic pain.

## CASE STUDY

Maria, a slender 25-year-old woman, referred herself to a private dance therapy group for "normal neurotic" adults. She chose Dance Therapy because she felt little connection with and control over her body. Maria wore thick glasses, and the corners of her mouth were downturned in what appeared to be a perpetual frown. Although verbal sharing was an important part of the group, Maria was reluctant to reveal herself in this way at first. Much of the information on her came from the initial interview and her movement. After a movement experience, however, Maria was able to share brief but meaningful reactions to her experience.

In movement it became clear that Maria disliked her body. In an exploration of the kinesphere, the area of personal space around the body, she moved almost exclusively in far-reach space, extending her limbs but not drawing them back in recovery. She explored

the space close to her body only at the suggestion of the therapist, and then only briefly. She reported afterward that she had a great deal of trouble moving close to her body and did not want to touch herself.

Nor did she want anyone else to touch her. In neck and back massage activities, which other group members requested, Maria would tirelessly massage her partner but, after enduring a massage in an early session, steadfastly declined to let herself be massaged. She reported that touch was unpleasant for her.

Maria's movements in structured improvisations tended to be large and abrupt, with a sharp, aggressive quality. At one point when the group members were slowly and gently touching hands she became uncomfortable and initiated a light but sharp slapping. In an attempt to engage her aggressiveness through pushing, it became clear that Maria was not connected with her center of weight. She held her pelvis stiffly behind her and gave way almost immediately, unable to mobilize her strength.

In free improvisation the fragility of Maria's control became obvious. She careened wildly through space, making sudden and reckless changes of level with no attempt to protect herself. Her interactions with others were characterized by abrupt beginnings and endings. No matter who had initiated the contact, it was she who controlled and ended the interaction. She showed no accommodation to the shapes or movement dynamics of her partners. After moving in this way she would become tense and withdrawn. She soon admitted that she felt out of control and frightened.

It was clear that Maria had very little sense of her body, and this contributed to her inability to engage her strength and control her movements. She began to concentrate on control in the structured corrective exercise portion of the session. While others in the group focused on awareness, she worked on developing slow, sustained movements, without holding her breath, and gradually began feeling a sense of control.

Free-movement improvisations were replaced by more structured exploration, starting on the floor and sensing the center of weight. After a while Maria began to move in a primitive amoebalike fashion, growing and shrinking from her newfound center. She returned again and again to this, even when the structure was loosened somewhat to give others in the group more space. At one point she reported that she didn't need her eyes because she could explore the space around her with her body. In verbal sharing she began to talk about her negative feelings about her body and her food and cigarette binges. She also spoke of her inability to deal with and even bring up some of these issues in verbal therapy. It had taken her six months to reach this point.

In the next four months Maria developed rapidly. Although she usually began improvisations on the floor to center herself, she came up and gradually began to interact with others. At first she was directly aggressive, beginning to feel and mobilize her strength. This gave way to testing out support from others and then to working out feelings of frustration and rage against her parents. By the summer break she was beginning to move in a dyad with sensitivity and accommodation to her partner.

After the two-month break Maria continued to work in self-initiated dyads, sharing leadership and achieving moments of heightened interactional synchrony, which she reported as being very pleasurable. She reported to the group that she was making progress in her verbal therapy and had controlled her eating, although she had somewhat of a relapse over the Christmas holidays. Maria continued working on mobilizing her strength in movement and began to explore her emerging feelings of sensuality and sexuality.

Maria terminated therapy after a total of 18 months. She was moving out of her parents' house and out of the city. In terms of her movement, she was very much in touch with her body and literally standing on her own two feet. Her relations to others were more genuine and characterized by a real recognition of and accommodation to the other as well as a developing ability to hold her own. Maria's progress in therapy had paralleled the normal sequence of development and provided material for the issues she was dealing with in her verbal therapy: developing a positive sense of self, dealing with aggression, interacting genuinely with others, independence, and sexuality. Dance Therapy was particularly well suited for Maria because of her fundamental lack of connectedness with her body and her difficulty in verbalizing her feelings.

## SUMMARY

Dance Therapy is a powerful and versatile therapeutic modality that lends itself to the treatment of a wide range of client populations. Virtually all people are capable of movement, no matter how limited, and their movement reflects and affects their internal processes. The dance therapist uses the medium of body movement to make a therapeutic relationship and to enhance functioning in emotional, cognitive, and physical areas.

Dance Therapy has a profound impact on the individual because it involves direct experiencing rather than simply talking about experience. Movement taps primitive levels of experience and enables the individual to express feelings that defy words. Personal imagery and repressed feelings that are made available in Dance Therapy provide the basis for further therapeutic exploration verbally and in movement.

Dance is a communicative as well as an expressive modality. Aspects of rhythmic synchrony, spatial formation, and touch create connections among participants in the dance therapy session and foster feelings of contact and belonging.

Body movement is the mode of experience and growth at basic levels of development. Through the recapitulation of normal sequences of development, Dance Therapy promotes behavioral change. It facilitates expansion of the movement repertoire, providing a greater range of adaptive responses.

It also provides support for new adaptive behaviors until they can be fully integrated and available to the individual.

Through its use of body movement to facilitate emotional growth, Dance Therapy engages the total person and provides an experience of integration and wholeness. Whether used as a primary or adjunctive treatment modality, Dance Therapy is a compelling and universally applicable treatment approach. It fosters self-awareness and provides a medium for self-expression, communication, and growth.

## REFERENCES

Alperson, E. D. Experiential movement psychotherapy. *American Journal of Dance Therapy*. 1977, **1(1)**, 8–12.

American Dance Therapy Association. Dance therapy (informational brochure). Columbia, M., 1972.

Bernstein, P. L. (Ed). *Eight theoretical approaches in dance/movement therapy*. Dubuque, Iowa: Kendall/Hunt, 1979.

Chaiklin, H. (Ed). *Marian Chace: Her papers*. Columbia, M. American Dance Therapy Association, 1975.

Chaiklin, S. Dance Therapy. In S. Arieti (Ed.), *American Handbook of Psychiatry*, vol. 5, Basic Books, 1975.

Condon, W. S. Linguistic-kinesic research and dance therapy. *ADTA Combined Third and Fourth Annual Conference Proceedings*. Columbia, M., 1968, 21–42.

Davis, M. A. Movement characteristics of hospitalized psychiatric patients. *ADTA Fifth Annual Conference Proceedings*. Columbia, M. 1970, 25–45.

Davis, M. A., Dulicai, D. and Climenko, J. Movement researcher and movement therapist: A collaboration. *American Journal of Dance Therapy*, 1977, 28–31.

Dell, C. *A primer for movement description*. New York: Dance Notation Bureau, 1970.

Fisher, S. and Cleveland, S. *Body image and personality*, 2nd rev. ed. New York: Dover, 1968.

Kestenberg, J. The role of movement patterns in development: I. Rhythms of movement. *Psychoanalytic Quarterly, 1965a*, **34**, 1–36.

Kestenberg, J. The role of movement patterns in development: II. Flow of tension and effort. *Psychoanalytic Quarterly*, 1965b, **34**, 517–563.

Laban, R. *The mastery of movement*, (2nd rev. ed. L. Ullmann (Ed.) London: MacDonald and Evans, 1960.

Lowen, A. *The language of the body*. New York: Macmillan, 1958.

Reich, W. *Character analysis*. New York: Farrar, Straus, 1949.

Schilder, P. *The image and appearance of the human body*. New York: International Universities Press, 1950.

Snyder, A. F. Some aspects of the nature of the rhythmic experience and its possible therapeutic value. *ADTA Writings on Body Movement and Communication: Monograph 2*. Columbia, M., 1972, 128–149.

Whitehouse, M. S. C. G. Jung and dance therapy: Two major principles. In P. Bernstein (Ed.), *Eight theoretical approaches in dance/movement therapy*. Dubuque, Iowa: Kendall/Hunt, 1979.

# CHAPTER 18

# *Direct Psychoanalysis*

JOHN N. ROSEN

*Many years ago, while still an undergraduate and already interested in psychology, I learned that a neighbor, a woman in her mid-fifties, had a daughter in a state mental hospital. I went along with her to visit her daughter several times. She was a beautiful young woman who talked on and on about "flies buzzing on the window." With a mixture of pity, excitement, wonder, and eventually discouragement, I attempted in all the ways I could think of to draw her out, to get her to communicate, even to just look at me. I never succeeded, never saw or heard of her since, and have often wondered what ever happened to that "crazy" girl.*

*Over the years, I have had, from time to time, in various capacities, the opportunity to deal with those who are frankly insane. Eventually I came to believe that they are helpless and hopeless. But then I would hear of the work of Dr. John Rosen. He was always spoken of in wonder by those who saw what he accomplished, and when I began this book I wrote to him, never really expecting him to accept my invitation to contribute.*

*The reader is now in for a thrilling experience—what follows is a chapter that should be read carefully by all those who wish to understand psychotherapy in its fullest.*

Direct Psychoanalysis utilizes the insights and dynamics established by Freud and his coworkers, but modifies them in an effort to enhance their therapeutic value with a greater emphasis on treatment rather than investigation. It holds that the manifest content of mental illness is analogous to the cry of a baby, which indicates that something is wrong. With the baby, if the disturbance is corrected, the cry stops and the baby regains peace of mind. With the sick patient, if the disturbance is corrected, the symptoms stop. If the mother simply makes observations of the crying baby—for instance, the loudness of the cry, the redness of the baby's face, the writhings of the baby's body, and so forth—it might be excellent research but it would hardly stop the baby's crying. On the other hand, if the mother discovers the reason for the crying and does what has to be done

about it, the crying will stop. In order to listen to the communications of a disturbed person in a meaningful way, a special kind of knowledge is required. The responsibility of the direct psychoanalyst is to understand the meaning of the manifest content. To that end he must spend endless hours listening to and observing his patient.

A direct psychoanalyst assumes the attitude of a benevolent, protecting, and controlling parent to discover the reasons for the disturbance. No drugs, shock, group, or other therapies are used in direct psychoanalysis.

## HISTORY

Early in my medical career I was called upon to do a postmortem examination on two patients who presumably died suddenly of coronary thrombosis. The examination revealed no evidence, either grossly or microscopically, of anatomical pathology that could possibly explain their deaths. Although a pathologist classified these deaths as an "act of God," it was not a satisfactory answer to me at that time. Some colleagues who were working in the field of psychosomatic medicine mentioned the concept of psychological death when I discussed these autopsies with them. They suggested that I read Freud's monograph, *Totem and Taboo*. From that work I learned that anthropologists were familiar with the hysterical death that occurred among primitives when they violated a taboo by either looking at or touching a taboo object.

My interest in psychological medicine mounted rapidly, and I learned much from reading texts on psychosomatic medicine written by Eduardo Weiss, O. Spurgeon English, Flanders Dunbar, George Daniels, and others. Likewise, I noted that the majority of patients in my internal medicine practice showed no evidence of organic pathology but nevertheless were very ill. It was a real challenge to explain why the mind could do this to an individual. My previous attitude in clinical pathological conferences was one of "show me," and the presenter had to be prepared to demonstrate specific pathological changes in the tissue. In this new psychological field of medicine there were no specific pathological changes to be found. Could my two so-called "coronary" deaths be explained on the basis of these new theoretical psychodynamic concepts? I applied to the New York Psychoanalytic Institute for admittance and was granted permission to take courses in psychosomatic medicine and certain other courses based on Freud's teachings. So much of the material dealt with the unconscious that I felt it necessary to explore my own unconscious, and at that point I undertook a personal analysis.

My own analysis, which I consider indispensable, lasted 11 years. The length of time was as much my decision as that of my analyst. My analysis, my reading of Freud and

his coworkers, my study at the Psychoanalytic Institute, and listening to patients convinced me of the importance of understanding the unconscious. In this way one could become familiar with the meaning of the unconscious as manifested at various levels of regression, down to and including the deepest neo-infancy of the schizophrenic.

It became apparent to me and my analyst that I had a special ability to understand manifest psychiatric content and dream material. This was further verified when I successfully treated acute catatonic patients at Brooklyn State Hospital who had hitherto been treated with no results, and who when in the exhaust status would die. From the manifest content of what the patients shouted in their catatonic excitement I was able to understand the nature of their early childhood experiences and could interpret this back to the patients in such a way that they would begin to feel understood. After a considerable amount of this interpreting there came a point when the patients' temperature began to drop, they would break into a profuse sweat, and over the next few days would recover from the severity of the illness and start to function in ways that indicated they were more in touch with reality than before—they were able to take food, have natural sleep, and so forth.

This took place in the early 1940s when the standard treatment was shock therapy, lobotomy, and drugs. I found these procedures interfered with my kind of treatment because they hid the manifest content or made patients so changed by brain damage that they were unreceptive to the kind of communication required for direct psychoanalytic therapy. Although my work was ridiculed by many of my colleagues, I went my own way and complied my own results, continuing to learn more and more about the nature of schizophrenia and all emotional illness from the point of view of etiology.

In 1945 I wrote a paper entitled "The Treatment of Schizophrenic Psychosis by Direct Analytic Therapy," in which I reported on 37 patients. The findings were incredible from the point of experience of psychiatry at that early date. The results were verified by a member of the Massachussets Psychiatric Society; as a result of the favorable reaction of the psychiatric profession to my work, I was called upon by many institutions and societies to lecture and/or demonstrate my method. When I presented my paper, one of the discussants was Dr. Paul Federn. In his review, he coined the phrase "direct psychoanalytic," from which the name "Direct Psychoanalysis" originated for this method of treatment.

## CURRENT STATUS

The various techniques of treatment employed in Direct Psychoanalysis are fully documented in the textbooks I have written (1953, 1962, 1968). There also exists a 22-page bibliography of the articles and books available, not only about Direct Psycho-analysis but also about how we deal with countless manifest behavior patterns that emotionally disturbed patients evidence.

It is rather surprising that after all these years of documentation and evidence of the beneficial effects of Direct Psychoanalysis, a large segment of the psychiatric profession still remains unconvinced. I do not feel that this is any great tragedy because the work of Freud remains equally unconvincing to a large segment of the psychiatric profession.

The method of Direct Psychoanalysis is taught at the Direct Psychoanalytic Institute in Doylestown, Pennsylvania, under the guidance of this writer. There is also a Direct Psychoanalytic Institute in New Delhi, India, under the direction of Dr. Raj Bhatia. Since my textbooks have been translated into Spanish, there has been a remarkable upsurge of interest in Direct Psychoanalysis in the psychiatric profession in Spanish-speaking countries. There are presently direct psychoanalytic institutes in Barcelona, Madrid, and Valencia, as well as in Puerto Rico. Dr. Juan Portuondo is responsible for the creation of the direct psychoanalytic institute in Barcelona and the branches in Madrid and Valencia. The physicians responsible for the

teaching and demonstration of Direct Psychoanalysis in Spain have met with me for implementation of their program. In 1979, 12 doctors who will comprise the faculty of these various institutes came to Doylestown for an intensive two-week seminar. A protocol was created that would deal with who could become a student at the institutes, the arrangement for the students' analysis, and the agreement among the training analysts that the charge for analyzing students would not exceed three dollars per session. An additional part of the training program contained an agreement from those to be trained to the effect that in the future, when they were able to train others, this minimal fee would still remain in force. They will make no distinction between qualified psychologists or qualified physicians in their training. In other words, there will be no prejudice against the training of psychologists and members of closely allied disciplines. The primary method of training will be the apprentice method, in which the direct psychoanalyst will treat patients in the presence of the students. When students are sufficiently qualified, they will then treat patients under the direct observation of the professor.

In 1980 another group of 12 doctors traveled to Doylestown from Nantes, France, for two weeks of intensive training as described above. Under the direction of Messrs. C. Sleeth and M. Guibert, Direct Psychoanalysis is already being studied at the AREFPPI, a research and study center for psychoanalysis.

At the present time, Direct Psychoanalysis and the enthusiasm of all those involved is the basis for an attack against the futility of shock, drugs, and lobotomy. If the enthusiasm existing at this time continues undiminished, there is reason to hope for progress along these lines.

## THEORY

The theory of Direct Psychoanalysis is more a matter of philosophy than physiology in the sense that psychotherapy is much closer to the teachings of the church than it is to the methods embodied in ordinary medical teaching and practice. The mind becomes distorted and distressed through malfunction rather than organic changes. I like to think of the analogy of a child banging on a concert grand piano, which normally produces beautiful music. Under no stretch of the imagination would one think that because the piano is thus malfunctioning something is wrong with the instrument. It is not that there is anything wrong with the mind, but for various reasons, which are our responsibility to discover, the mind in some cases ceases to function the way it is supposed to.

In Direct Psychoanalysis the brain is viewed as neither being damaged nor having hereditary influences that doom it to failure. Our approach, therefore, is seriously weakened by giving the patients "somatic therapy" such as drugs, electric shock, or brain surgery. Drugs interfere with the manifestations of any kind of mental activity, even the psychotic. The manifest content of the illness is viewed as an appeal for help. To respond to this plea we formulate a psychological approach that then becomes the treatment plan. The material uncovered in observing the psychotic patient follows along the lines of the original formulations laid down by Sigmund Freud, Karl Abraham, Paul Federn, Victor Tausk, Bertram Lewis, and others. These concepts have to do with the existence of the id, the ego, and the superego, and with the levels of psychosexual development: namely, the oral, anal, and genital phases, in that order. In psychosis, the degree of maturity achieved in the direction of genital psychosexual level is weak. Considering the genital psychosexual level of development to be evidence of proper maturity, there is a tendency, because of this weakness, for the patient to regress to earlier oral or anal levels. The oral level essentially is demonstrated by deep schizophrenic manifestations, and the anal level is more at the manic-depressive level of regression. In psychotic regression, regression is to the pregenital level. That is, the patient regresses

to the age where the infant is not yet aware of its gender. It knows nothing about sexual development at those very early oral and anal stages.

A tentative prognosis can be reached when evaluating a new patient by taking note of the degree of maturity and success achieved by him prior to the collapse into psychosis. Those patients who were underdeveloped prior to psychosis are the hardest cases to treat and become the least valuable functioning citizens if they recover. However, patients who graduated from college and had become professionals or who were significant members of their community present the best prognosis in terms of reestablishing a mature state from the present state of regression.

Based on the idea that the psychotic becomes a baby again, we have formulated the governing principle of Direct Psychoanalysis: "The therapist must be a loving, omnipotent protector and provider for the patient'. Expressed another way, the therapist must be the idealized mother who now has the responsibility of bringing the patient up all over again." We believe that the cause of schizophrenia is that the individual was raised in an environment in which the maternal instinct was perverted, in the same sense that any other instinct can be perverted. The first mother figure (the real mother or a maternal surrogate) affects the child in the earliest neonatal period. The influence of this person determines the degree to which a healthy ego can develop. There are, however, also genetic factors that must also be taken into consideration. Some patients can withstand psychic trauma better than others. Little is known about these genetic factors. Since they have not given us any clues as to therapeutic progress in clinical experience, we cannot say more about genetic factors than to recognize that they probably exist. But to direct psychoanalysts they exist in the sense that some people can run faster than others, can play tennis better then others, and so forth, depending upon their endowments at birth.

We see no great difference between the dream and the psychotic material. Freud referred to the dream as a psychosis and referred to it as ''the royal road to the unconscious.'' The psychotic process is perhaps a more regal road to the unconscious in the sense that it is relentless and does not end upon awakening. But if awakening can be brought about, so the psychosis can evaporate, like a dream that evaporates in the morning.

We place great store in the concept of the unconscious, being quite convinced that that portion of the mind has lost no memory of early events, both salutory and pathological. The earliest developmental years are recorded in the unconscious part of the mind even if there is little or no hope of recovering consciousness of these memories. We believe that the schizophrenic is reliving memories that the ordinary person cannot recapture. However, we all had a day when we first dressed ourselves or took our first steps by ourselves. We do not have to relearn these experiences because they are indelibly recorded in the unconscious portion of the mind, but to recover these memories is impossible.

We have found that the superego is not derived from the resolution of the Oedipus complex, as the current Freudian theory states. Rather, the superego (ego-ideal?) is formed from the earliest relationships with the mother through the processes of imitation, introjection, incorporation, and identification, much as Freud declared, and it consists of a continuing identification with the early maternal environment. It became apparent to me in the treatment of a schizophrenic patient that ''taking in'' is not only an oral ''taking in,'' in relation only to the mother, but every symbolic equivalent of orality is the means for ''taking in.'' I saw an example of this when a psychotic patient once took her lipstick from her pocketbook during a therapeutic dialogue and painted her eyes as if they were her lips. When I asked her what she was doing, her response was ''I'm taking in a stage show.'' The ''stage show'' was

the breast in the sense of Bert Lewin's description of the breast as the dream screen.

In a psychosis the patient often suffers frustration and even murderous rage directed against himself or the environment. Mainly this rage is a matter of the superego killing the ego or the ego killing the superego as they are locked in a relentless combat for the possession of the psychotic. If the superego cannot tolerate the ego, and vice versa, voices and sights are hallucinated by the psychotic patient. This hallucinatory process is really part of the patient himself, but it seems external and foreign to him. The superego is like a plague of vermin that create an intolerable itch. The psyche attempts to extrude and get rid of this toxic part of itself. This psychological attempt at healing cannot succeed, and as a result the psychosis goes on and on. It is from this understanding of what takes place that we have come to realize that the therapist must adhere to the governing principle of Direct Psychoanalysis.

Further, in our theoretical concept we believe that no person wakes up one morning psychotic, or even neurotic. Rather, the development of any severe mental illness consists of a gradual process that starts at birth in an attempt to struggle with an unincorporable maternal environment. As a result there never occurs a comfortable union between the various components of the psyche, namely the ego, the superego, and the id. Since there is never a union of these forces, the individual never has the strength that would result from this union. In union there is strength. This situation has been described as being like an individual who grows leaning like the Tower of Pisa. The Tower of Pisa remains at a point consistent with not collapsing, but the human being goes on and on in his weakend state, being confronted again and again with unmanagable social demands, as he encounters the demands of mature social living. The demands of puberty, adolescence, dating, mating, matrimony, parenthood, and so forth, are chronologically increasing ones made on the psyche that was weak to begin with. And ultimately one of these demands will bring about a partial or total collapse of the psyche; it seeks a haven in regressing to earlier, less demanding years of life. But there again, in this earliest level of life, which regression seeks to achieve, there still is no peace.

Therefore, since the demands of life are an ongoing experience, there comes a point at which the foundation is so overcome by sufficiently traumatic experiences that the individual collapses. We believe that no one is immune to developing a mental illness and that even the strongest person cannot withstand constant and intolerable psychic pain. In the state of regression that exists in schizophrenia, the unmet needs of the earliest formative years create a developmental vacuum. And as nature abhors a vacuum, it returns to perilous and defeating situations that it now hopes in some way to master but cannot.

Implicit in the story the patient tells us is an idea that might be best described as seeking the mother he once knew. One wonders why the patient invariably deals with a perilous and self-defeating situation created in his mind. It is almost as though he is conditioned to exist just this way. Whereas the healthy mind can construct pleasurable and enjoyable mirages with Garden-of-Eden-like gratifications immediately available (such as these required for a newborn baby), the sick mind will construct terrifying mirages such as mountainous waves in the ocean falling down upon him, causing suffocation and engulfment. Why can't psychotics fantasize pleasure instead of disaster? Through our studies we have been led to believe that they are seeking the rejecting mother they knew; this self-defeating situation is implicit in all psychotic patients.

## METHODOLOGY

Before undertaking treatment a determination must be made of where the patient is on the psychological scale of being healthy to being utterly incapacitated. We believe that the patient goes downward from some neurotic form of defense—such as hysteria,

perverson, psychopathy, and so forth—through various levels of regression at various rates of speed in terms of time, depending upon the patient's genetic characteristics. This regression phenomenon goes down to the beginning of the psychosis, which Direct Psychoanalysts consider to be the manic-depressive phase. From there it goes further down through the levels of schizophrenia, namely, paranoid, hebephrenic, and finally catatonic withdrawal, in that order.

We require an understanding of where the patient is regressed to because for each patient we set up a treatment unit that can be likened to an individual mental hospital, created for the patient's individual needs. We rent a house and staff it with trained assistant therapists who are usually psychologists, sociologists, or those with equivalent academic background. These assistants have personal warmth and a feeling about psychotherapy as a way of life and are not interested in the number of hours per day that they work. These people, like the therapist, become the patient's foster family. They understand that the patient, since he is like a baby, now requires the same kind of care that a mother must supply for the newborn infant, which means 24-hour-a-day, seven day-a-week care. In these treatment units, daily therapeutic dialogue takes place in which the patient and the therapist listen to each other in the presence of assistant therapists. The assistant therapists can then be instructed and made aware of what the therapist sees and is aiming toward. Also, the assistant therapists are able to continue along the lines that the therapist has established for the balance of the 24 hours, so that treatment is continuous and consistent. Like a baby, the psychotic has regressed to earliest infantile levels. He might wet, soil, and be unable to feed or clothe himself. Like a baby, the patient must be cared for night and day.

The therapeutic dialogue uncovers the fact that transference phenomena and intense resistance dominate the scene. This, as in conventional analysis, follows the pattern of repetition compulsion. If transference and resistance are successfully managed, the patient develops a childlike dependence on the therapist, and at this positive phase of therapy, education and discipline can begin.

It is not to be thought that therapeutic dialogue brings about rapid response. Sometimes endless hours of work result in simply a crumb of improvement, but one is not to be discouraged by this slow improvement. If one has patience over the long run, the patient eventually shows improvement and will begin to assert himself. This sign of growth will give added impetus toward the continuation of therapy. Sometimes five years go by before a patient is at the point where education and discipline can begin.

In contrast to the conventional 50-minute hour of orthodox psychoanalysis, we spend as much time as the patient seems to require in terms of understanding of the productions. We have spent as much as five or six hours continuously with one patient. On the other hand we have spent as little as two minutes with a patient if it appeared that he was unable to tolerate any further revelations or insights concerning himself. In other words, the treatment is tailored to meet the needs of the individual patient.

Therapeutic dialogue is not ordinary conversation, but rather a highly specialized kind of communication that requires endless concentration and attention on the part of the therapist. All manner of details of the patient's speech and behavior require this attention. Further, the therapist must have the ability to understand the symbolic meaning of what the patient is saying and what the patient requires from the environment. The patient talks in primary-process language such as is employed in dreams or acts as one acts in dreams. This communication simply disguises the latent content, which tells the true story of what is wrong. Some therapists are more artful and understanding of this type of material than others. Even though a person may not have a particular gift for understanding psychotic communications, a personal analysis will provide 95 percent of what he needs to improve his ability to understand. Therefore, a prerequisite for the therapist to understand the dynamic meaning of what the patient is communicating is a deep personal analysis. The assistant therapists' work is also helped if they also have had a personal analysis. Two of the most useful assistants that I have employed for this type of therapy were young women who had gone through a psychotic episode themselves, had recovered, and were then exposed to further psychoanalysis.

If the therapist grasps quickly the meaning of what the patient is saying and is able to convey such information to the patient in such a way that the patient can comprehend it—and this requires considerable ingenuity on the part of the therapist—then the patient can express an enormous relief. The therapist, in fact, becomes to the patient the heavenly mother originally required or the witch who tortures him constantly. The patient will see the therapist in the light of his needs. In the case of intense negative transferences it is important, very often in self-defense, to remind the patient again and again, "I am not your mother, I am ———." Unwary therapists who are not able to understand the nature of the patient's transference or response—or transference psychosis, as it is more aptly labeled—may become the undeserved victim of what the original parents deserved. It is ill-advised to force treatment on a patient when the patient's behavior becomes aggressive and uncontrolled. There is always the danger of an attack against the therapist.

There are those who feel that success in treatment depends on the personality of the therapist, and that it does not make any difference what he says. We have found this an absolutely false concept. It is necessary to say pertinent things to get the patient to pay attention and to accept the therapist, to incorporate him for the purpose of ultimate identification with the therapist as the benevolent exponent in the governing principal of direct psychoanalysis rather than the "mother he knew." To do this it is not possible to keep suppressing the patient's cry for help but rather to comprehend it and do what is required. This does not mean doing specific things for the patient in terms of meeting conscious demands. What it does require is the utilization of such techniques as will satisfy whatever it is the patient is crying for.

The way to get the patient to understand that you know what his needs are is through direct interpretations. The patient does not consciously understand what he is crying but will appreciate that you understand him when you convey the correct interpretations to him. I have found that wrong interpretations are immaterial. Right interpretations produce the emotional confirmation that we seek.

Correct interpretations lead to understanding and gratification of needs. Mutual understanding and gratifications are probably the basis of all good human relationships. With this newly developed therapeutic relationship comes a parental responsibility on the part of the therapist, who in transference is first the mother and then the father and sometimes either, depending upon circumstances. Having achieved this relationship, the therapist must then teach the patient socially acceptable behavior, as any parent should.

Assuming that all goes well in the matter of understanding the patient's cry, a new kind of relationship develops between the patient's ego and the superego. The superego no longer is telling the patient "You are evil," "You are unworthy," "You should be dead." The environment no longer seems to be noxious to the patient, but if it pursues the governing principal of Direct Psychoanalysis it now hopefully includes all that one experiences from a "good mother." The patient begins to feel loved, cared for, and protected. The deadly schizophrenic nightmare beings to subside and indications of maturing behavior become apparent, much to everyone's gratification.

If a patient is properly and adequately treated, he recovers from his psychosis and now has a kind of psychological integrity that withstands those life events that he could not have tolerated prior to treatment. Such significant events could be the loss of a spouse, parent, sibling, or a traumatic social

event. Ordinarily such events will now produce depression or mourning, which is a healthy reaction, rather than pathological mourning, or psychosis. We find that our treated patients have weathered such occurrences with no more than the usual emotional reactions.

## APPLICATIONS

Direct Psychoanalysis is useful in treating all kinds of emotional disturbances. For the psychotic, we consider the hospital setting the least advisable way to treat. The optimum way to treat a psychotic is to carry out a 24-hour-a-day, seven-day-a-week program under the direction of the therapist who conducts the therapeutic dialogue. The therapeutic dialogue is witnessed by the psychological assistants who themselves are being or have already been analyzed. From the insights obtained from the therapeutic dialogue in terms of understanding the manifest verbalizations, as well as nonverbal communications, they are guided in the continuing therapeutic experience provided for the patient. The assistants must always bear in mind the governing principle of Direct Psychoanalysis, derived from the Christian ethics of brotherly love. Although Christ preached it 2,000 years ago, up until the present time it has never really taken hold of the human race. The governing principle requires benevolent, loving, caring, providing, protecting behavior on the part of the therapist.

Drugs, shock therapy that dulls the brain and make one forget, and lobotomy are interferences in this type of therapy. Some patients who have had more than a thousand electroshock and insulin shock treatments show absolutely no signs of improvement. Patients have been brought to us in such a state of numbness from tranquilizing drugs that they were unresponsive to any therapeutic efforts on our part.

After several years of ingesting a drug such as Valium, even if one discontinues the drug, the detrimental effects can continue. This indicates that the brain is now fixed, and one cannot reverse the process. If a patient is brought to us before any drug, shock, or lobotomies are used as treatment, their psychosis can sometimes be relieved within as short a time as two weeks.

Neurotic patients, particularly those suffering from anxiety hysteria, are the easiest to treat. We have found that hysterics, agrophobics, claustrophobics, and those suffering from various forms of psychosomatic fixations can also sometimes be quickly resolved.

For the conventional analytic case, the analyst, instead of acting like an observer and a researcher, is required to do two things when he understands the meaning of the patient's complaint—the pathological, psychological material that the symptomology covers up—if the patient is sufficiently amenable: (1) educate the patient along the lines of insights uncovered and (2) train the patient in the exercise of discipline. For instance, in treating an alcoholic, if the meaning of the "bottle" is understood in terms of orality, and so forth, the influence of the therapist in the matter of discipline that the patient will ultimately have to exercise is of paramount importance. There is no cure without discipline.

In the conventional training of a psychoanalyst, the student must do no more in relation to the patient than remain a mirror reflecting the patient's behavior back to the patient. When hoping to bring about a recovery from mental illness, this is an exercise in futility.

## CASE EXAMPLE

M.S.B. came to this writer after 16 years in a state hospital, where he had been treated with the usual shock therapy and drugs. His paranoid delusional system, where he had become God, was very well organized and his behavior certainly carried out the concepts of God that fundamentalists would hold to.

He would spend his days marking down the names of countless people, either fictitious or people he had actually known. In beautiful handwriting he would describe them as good, bad, better, best, and under "good" he would give them eternal salvation, under "bad," eternal damnation, and so forth. These long written lists went on endlessly year in and year out.

Although we went into his background history carefully, there was nothing we could find that explained why he had to defend himself by becoming the most powerful personality that the human mind can conceive of, namely, God. As long as he was God he was safe from whatever terrors may have existed in life. But nothing in his history shed any light on the advent of his psychosis, which began with obsessive-compulsive behavior and manic-depressive manifestations at the age of puberty. By the time he was 18 he had developed a full-blown psychosis. The only possible influence found in the history of his background was the separation of his father and mother.

While I believe that a broken home is a devastating experience for a young child, I would not go so far as to state that divorce is sufficient explanation for the development of psychological defenses. Many children of divorced parents, although usually emotionally troubled, can survive this event and become healthy adults.

M.S.B. had a remarkable talent for painting and was given painting materials to occupy himself with. He would create a beautiful scene and then work over it until it was meaningless. He did this again and again and could never finish anything. Some of his paintings were so beautiful that it was a pity that he did not finish them.

The obsessive-compulsive neurosis that he developed was analytically fixated at the anal level. A sublimation of anality would be beautiful paintings or sculpting like those of children's finger paintings, mud pies, and sand castles. The fact that he never could finish his paintings could have been a refusal to supply what his mother wanted, namely, the completion of a bowel movement. Also, if he did it improperly, he would have been the victim of severe punishment, which would also lead to his fear of completion.

It is to be understood that this patient was free from anxiety. There is no doubt that his Godlike defense successfully protected him. All attempts to induce anxiety in him with threats of burning at the stake, as was done to Joan of Arc; or casting aspersions on his belief that he was God by means of logic, ridicule, or various other methods over several years of treatment brought little results. Finally I conceived the idea that perhaps it would be rewarding to shake his paranoid delusion in the hopes of inducing anxiety that might cause him to show some progress—either becoming more psychotic or moving upward to a more mature level.

In order to do this I now acted toward him as though I accepted the fact that he was God. After a period of several weeks of this acceptance, I had occasion to do the following: In a naive way I asked him to demonstrate some of his powers, such as walking on air, which he claimed he could do. When I asked him to show me how he walked on air, he got up on a chair and started to walk, and the force of gravity overcame his powers. He then got up on the table and violently tried to walk off the table on to air, which also failed. At this point it was clear that he was beginning to be very anxious about his belief in himself. The outcome of this was almost a hysterical state of terror. He turned white as a sheet and stood trembling. He pointed to various assistant therapists, claiming that they were "throwing harms in his way." He finally attacked one of them violently.

From this occasion onward, his belief in his delusional system began to come apart. For periods of time he became more and more reasonable and spent more time in reality. He ceased to proclaim "good," "bad," "better," "best," "eternal damnation," and "salvation." He began to show some understanding, although not much, as to why he thought he had to be God. Whereas at first, when threatened if he again said he was

God, he found a clever way to counteract my threat. Now when I said that if he said he was God again I would punish him and I then asked him who he was, he replied, "I am who I am," which indicated that he was beginning to develop some common sense.

About six months after the first occasion that he felt he had lost his power, he became well enough to return to his home for visits with his family. After a period of testing in this way, he was allowed to rent an apartment of his own and to continue his career in painting. Within a year after leaving our hospital he had a show of his art that was so spectacular that it was written up in the *New York Times*. To this date, although he had traveled to Paris and has been living on his own, there has been no recurrence of his delusional system. On a few occasions when he was seen again it was hard to recognize any remnants of his psychotic status. There is every reason to believe that there will be no recurrence.

## SUMMARY

Direct Psychoanalysis is a method of treating seriously disturbed patients, even those generally considered hopelessly insane. Developed by this writer in the early 1940s, the method depends on the insights gained through psychoanalysis as presented by Sigmund Freud. It consists essentially of attempts to communicate with highly disturbed patients by making direct interpretations of their various verbal and nonverbal communications. This writer saw, as did Freud, that psychosis is a withdrawal from reality of seriously psychologically wounded individuals who now have their own logic and who want to avoid relationships with others. They have regressed to various infantile levels of development.

Direct psychoanalysts differ from Freud in that instead of simply making observations, as he did, we introduce ourselves into the equation forcefully in order to make the patient aware of someone in the real world who may become a bridge back to reality.

A direct interpretation aids this process, because it is the way in which the patient gathers that you understand him in the way that he does not understand himself. To quote from a recovered patient's letter, describing his feelings when he was ill: "My mind kept saying, why won't someone listen? Why can't anyone understand me?"

It is not to be inferred that Direct Psychoanalysis is applicable only to deeply regressed psychotics. It has proven most valuable many times in patients suffering from neurosis as well.

The hope of Direct Psychoanalyis is to counter the disarray that the psychoanalytic institutes are in at present. It is tragic that the writings of Martin L. Gross (1978) in *The Psychological Society* and such severe critics as Andrew Salter (1972) in *The Case Against Psychoanalysis* are presently the vogue. This leads to the probable criminal abuse of human beings by those who agree with them in advocating drugs, especially lithium carbonate, which could easily prove fatal, as well as Valium and other tranquilizers. The continuing use of shock therapy, although it has proven again and again not only to be useless in curing a patient with a mental problem but to be harmful, to say nothing of lobotomy, is to be deplored. These methods, extreme examples of man's inhumanity to man, can be countered by showing the rapidity in which knowledgeable therapeutic dialogue can bring about far better results with no physical harm to the patient.

It is heartening that after 40 years of research and treating and teaching there is an ever-increasing flow of colleagues using Direct Psychoanalysis. I do not deny that the critics of conventional psychonalysis have made out a sound case for their hostility. I do feel, however, that throwing out the concepts and contributions of Freud is analogous to throwing out the baby with the bath water.

I am as critical of my psychoanalytic colleagues who sit by and do nothing more than become a mirror reflecting the patient's behavior as I am of those who use the physical therapies so thoughtlessly and uselessly. While at this point in my life I cannot take on the huge task of training that is required, I envision a future in which psychonalysts are trained to do the things that are possible for them to do and a psychoanalytic peace corps of assistant therapists is also trained. They could then perhaps undertake the herculean task of dealing with the problems that exist in state hospitals, where 12,000 patients become the responsibility of a handful of doctors who themselves are hardly equipped to treat even one patient.

In Direct Psychoanalysis, we consider man's humanity to man to be a medicine.

## REFERENCES

*Bibliography of the literature on direct psychoanalysis.* The Direct Psychoanalytic Institute, Doylestown, Pa.

English, O. S. Clinical observations on direct analysis. *Comprehensive Psychiatry*, 1960, **1**, 156–163. Abstracted by D. Prager in *Psychological Abstracts*, 1961, **35**, 510. Reprinted with revisions in *Direct analysis and schizophrenia* ed. by O. S. English, W. W. Hampe, Jr., C. L. Bacon and C. F. Settlage. New York: Grune & Stratton, 1961.

Gross, Martin L. *The psychological society.* New York: Random House, 1978.

Rosen, J. N. The treatment of schizophrenic psychosis by direct analytic therapy. *Psychiatric Quarterly*, 1945.

Rosen, J. N. *Direct analysis: Selected papers.* Doylestown, Pa.: The Doylestown Foundation, 1953.

Rosen, J. N. *Direct psychoanalytic psychiatry.* New York: Grune & Stratton, 1962.

Rosen, J. N. *Selected papers on direct psychoanalysis*, vol. 2. New York: Grune & Stratton, 1968.

Salter, A. *The case against psychoanalysis.* New York: Harper & Row, 1972.

Scheflen, A. E. *A psychotherapy of schizophrenia: Direct analaysis.* Springfield, Ill.: Charles C Thomas, 1961.

## CHAPTER 19

# Ego-State Therapy

JOHN G. WATKINS and HELEN H. WATKINS

*I anticipate greater theoretical controversy over Ego-State Therapy than for any other system in this book. Essentially, John and Helen Watkins state that we all have multiple personalities, different ego states, and that some states are not under the control of others.*

*This controversial position has been in the news in recent years, with various defense lawyers, representing people who have committed hideous crimes, arguing for their clients: (1) yes, X did it, but (2) X cannot be blamed because it was Y (another personality within X) who was actually responsible.*

*In my own 35 years as a clinician I have interviewed in depth some 10,000 people, only one of whom spontaneously stated that he had a multiple personality.*

*And yet Watkins and Watkins make a strong case for their position. I know both of them well—Helen once hypnotized me—and I believe that every reader should put aside any prejudices about the highly controversial issue of multiple personalities and read carefully and sympathetically the following account. Just because a position is not popular does not make it wrong—nor does it make it right.*

Ego-State Therapy holds that perceptions, thoughts, feelings, motor reactions, and experiences are organized into coherent patterns that are relatively more or less discrete from one another. This means that "the ego" is not a unitary phenomenon, but rather is more like a confederation of states. Accordingly, the normal human personality functions like a country that has both a "national" government and subsections (such as states, counties, cities) that retain varying degrees of local autonomy. These "ego states" ("part persons") are separated from each other by boundaries that are more or less permeable.

Each ego state is composed of behavioral and experiential elements organized around some common principle—such as being six years old, dealing with authority figures, protecting the individual from harm, acting as a center of common sense, representing a parental introject, and so forth.

When the boundaries of the ego states are so rigid and impermeable that little or no communication occurs between them, the individual may develop a multiple personality. However, persons also suffer from clashes between *unconscious* ego states that operate like "covert multiple personalities." Special procedures are required to resolve such conflicts.

Ego-State Therapy, accordingly, represents the utilization of group and family therapy techniques for the resolution of conflicts between the various ego states that constitute a "family of self" within a single individual.

## HISTORY

The theoretical conceptions and procedures of Ego-State Therapy are both very old and very new. The question of the personality's unity was considered by St. Augustine in his

*Confessions* (O'Connell, 1969). In the nineteenth century J. C. Reil (1803) asked how it was possible for "the ego to divide itself into persons, who produce things of which he is not aware." Pierre Janet's studies of dissociation (1907) and the classic cases of multiple personality described by Morton Prince (1906) and Boris Sidis (1910) pictured the interaction of ego-states in their pure, overt, and conscious form, hence, when the boundaries between them are rigid and impermeable. We have drawn heavily from the writings of Paul Federn (Weiss, 1952) in the development of our ego-state theory, although we have also extended and modified his conceptions (J.G. Watkins, 1978). Finally, we have incorporated into our treatment methodology many of the hypnoanalytic techniques described by Wolberg (1945), Schneck (1965), Erickson (see Haley, 1973), and others.

What is new in Ego-State Therapy is its integration of both theoretical concepts and treatment strategies drawn from a wide variety of previous therapies. In one sense it is eclectic, but in still another sense we have developed a fairly distinct theory of personality functioning (J. G. Watkins, 1978) and an array of treatment procedures around its theoretical position.

## Beginnings

Although "Ego-State Therapy" began to be used as a name for a body of treatment techniques applied within a specific conception of personality functioning (termed "ego-state theory") only in the mid-1970s, the development of this approach goes back to the experiences of John Watkins during World War II. As Chief Psychologist for the Army's 5,000 bed Welch Convalescent Hospital in Daytona Beach, Florida, he conducted intensive hypnotherapy with people having a wide variety of war neuroses, many exhibiting amnesia and other types of dissociation.

His first case of true Ego-State Therapy involved a patient suffering from a phobia of the dark. Under hypnosis two entities, George, a tough psychopathic personality, and Melvin, a weak personality with a high superego, emerged. These were studied at considerable length by both projective and hypnoanalytic techniques. The case is described in detail in a book on war neuroses (Watkins, 1949).

During the mid-1950s John Watkins treated intensively a multiple-personality patient (the case of M-L), which was reported at the 1958 meeting of the Society for Clinical and Experimental Hypnosis but has not yet been published. This case afforded an opportunity to learn much about the interaction of overt ego states.

In 1968 John Watkins consulted on a fascinating case of multiple personality treated by Dr. Bernauer Newton of Los Angeles. The interactions of the various states in therapy were tape-recorded and filmed. These were edited, the scripts studied exhaustively, and much more learned about dissociative behavior.

Since 1972 the present writers have collaborated in a joint program of research and therapy at the University of Montana. We have increasingly realized that dissociation is not an either/or phenomenon. Not only is dissociation manifested in overt form in true cases of multiple personality, but in "covert" or unconscious form it seems to range on a continuum that extends from normal and neurotic individuals to borderline multiple personalities and even perhaps to psychoses.

Since 1972 Helen Watkins has treated many ego-state problems, both privately and within the University of Montana's Center for Student Development. She is primarily responsible for developing the strategies and innovative therapy techniques to be described herein. Many of her treatment sessions furnished the basic data from which ego-state theory was derived.

John Watkins has concentrated on the intensive treatment of a few true multiple personalities, the experimental investigation of hypnotically induced ego states, and the development of the theory. The system of Ego-State Therapy presented here is thus the evolving product of a joint endeavor.

## CURRENT STATUS

The period of 1973 to 1977 was spent primarily in developing theory, devising therapy techniques, and recording cases. Our findings were transmitted to our colleagues through papers presented at scientific meetings.*

Only recently have we begun publishing these items in article, tape, and book form (J. G. Watkins, 1976, 1977, 1978, 1978a; H. H. Watkins, 1978; J. G. Watkins & H. H. Watkins, 1976, 1979a, 1979b, 1979c). We have also presented courses in Ego-State Therapy at the University of Montana, the International Graduate University in Switzerland, the Florida Institute of Technology, and at a number of workshops.

Several of our students have used ego-state theory as the basis for masters theses and declared dissertations. Many professionals who have taken our courses or workshops have reported to us their current successful work in applying ego-state concepts in their therapy. As yet, however, the ego-state approach is not well known.

## THEORY**

The heart of the problem of dissociation is what is subject and what is object: What is me and what not-me? If my arm is paralyzed, it becomes for me simply an object, an "it," a thing not part of my self. A similar experience occurs in regard to mental processes when a thought, a feeling, or an impulse is banished from awareness through forgetting or repression. If I am not con-

*These meetings included The Society for Clinical and Experimental Hypnosis, 1973, 1974, 1977, 1979; the American Society of Clinical Hypnosis, 1975, 1979; the 3rd Congress of the International College of Psychosomatic Medicine, Rome, 1975; and a presentation of the presidential address, Division 30, The American Psychological Association, 1976.

**For a more complete explanation of ego-state theory, see J. G. Watkins, (1978).

scious of it, I do not own it. It is not experienced as part of "me."

In the case of the paralyzed arm, I can sense it as an object by touching it with my other hand, but it is not felt as being within my own self. I am conscious of its existence but only as something outside of me. Perceptions initiated by stimuli emanating from sources outside my own body are experienced as objects. My thoughts and feelings come from stimuli originating from sources inside "my" body and "my" mind. Normally, I own them as a part of my self.

Sometimes, however, a thought, an emotion, or an entire experience may make its way to consciousness without it being imbued with the feeling of selfness. Then I sense it as a foreign object. I may then tell others that I am *seeing* my dead father, not that I am *thinking* about him. Observers may say that I am psychotic and hallucinating.

Infrequently, an entire segment of an individual's personality will cease to be sensed as part of the self. If this disowned segment is then energized and "activated" (becomes overt and takes over the behavior of the person's body), the individual is diagnosed as having a multiple personality. When the original (and presumably main) personality returns (is reactivated) it may report that it was aware of the disowned segment, but it experienced that other segment as object. It was like perceiving another person in a dream, speaking and behaving in an interaction with one's own self.

Paul Federn (Weiss, 1952) held that a person experiences a part of his body as subject ("my" arm) when it has been cathected that is, invested, with a self energy, which he termed *ego cathexis*. If an idea reaches consciousness and is so cathected, I recognize it as "my" thought. If it comes to awareness without being so ego-cathected, then it is experienced as an object, as if it stems from a source outside my self—like any other "outside" perception. Ego cathexis in Federn's theory represents the essence of self, the experience of self, self itself, pure self without content. Self is viewed as an energy without content. Any physiological or psychological item invested with this energy is then experienced as subject, as a part of "my" body, "my" thoughts, or "my" feelings.

Since all psychological processes require energy for their activation, Federn hypothesized a qualitatively different kind of energy, called *object cathexis,* to energize processes that were experienced as "it," as "not-me." Whether a part of the body or a mental process is experienced as me or not-me will be determined by whether it is invested with ego cathexis or object cathexis.

In the case of a multiple personality, Eve Black (Thigpen & Cleckley, 1957) became activated and overt when the ego cathexis flowed into the dissociated Eve Black personality segment, leaving the Eve White Segment invested only with object cathexis. The "person" then became Eve Black. When the object-cathected contents of Eve White impacted the ego-cathected Eve Black, the secondary personality described Eve White as "she," not "I." As the ego energies returned to the Eve White personality segment, a reversal took place. The experience of subject and object shifted.

## Ego States

Federn held that the *normal* ego was divided (dissociated) into segments that assumed responsibility for different areas of behavior and experience, much as the individuals in a society specialize their contributions through different occupations. These subpatterns of personality he called *ego states.* The normal ego, therefore, is similar to a nation with different geographical areas and jurisdictions such as states, counties, and so forth. The well-adjusted individual has a strong "federal" government, but different ego states enable him to activate certain behaviors when at a party and others when at work.

An ego state may be defined as a body of behaviors and experiences bound together by some common principle or function and separated from other such entities by a more or less permeable boundary. It has a semiautonomous existence within the entire personality. That state in which the largest amount of ego cathexis is invested at any time is said to be "executive." It is the self in "the now," hence, the immediate experience and behavior.

Each ego state is like a "part person." As ego and object energies flow out of one state into another, the new one becomes "executive." The person changes. Perhaps his child self takes over. He plays and is no longer in a working mood. He may not be able to recall the details of work projects when he is in the child state. The partly impermeable boundary between the two states blocks out of awareness many items normally available in the work ego state. Like the person who changes residence, he leaves behind certain contents (memories, abilities, feelings, ideas, or other patterns of behavior). He reacts differently but still experiences himself as "I."

If the boundary between his former state and the new one is rigid and impermeable (like that between East and West Germany), then his new ego state has no contact with his original one. This situation exists in a multiple personality. The difference between the alternation of ego states in the normal individual and in the dissociated personality is simply the relative rigidity or permeability of the boundary between them and the intensity with which the various states are energized.

## Dissociation

Most psychological processes do not appear on an either/or basis. Anxiety, depression, rationalization, learning, and so forth, range themselves on continuums, and we must consider their degree or magnitude. So it is with dissociation. Ego states that are still differentiated from one another may have boundaries so permeable that energies can easily cross from one to the other. However, if they are but lightly energized, the impacts of a substate on the executive state may be below the threshold of awareness. They still, however, play their roles of subject-object to each other, and the individual's overt behavior and conscious experience may be unconsciously influenced. Within the entire person ego states exercise relative degrees of individual autonomy.

## Hypnosis

Hypnosis permits manipulation of ego and object energies. When an arm is hypnotically paralyzed and rendered insensitive, the ego cathexis in it has been removed. When an idea is hypnotically lifted out of repression and once more owned within the self, it is egotized, hence, invested with ego cathexis. Multiple personalities alternate as inner psychodynamic factors divert ego cathexis into and out of the different entities. Through hypnosis we can do the same. Different personalities can be activated in hypnotherapy. Hypnosis is thus both a research and a treatment modality in dealing with ego states.

When normal, hypnotically susceptible individuals are hynotized, it is easy to activate underlying ego states and demonstrate their existence. They can describe themselves, their functions in the psychic economy of the entire person, and their reactions to each other. Each calls itself "I," often gives itself a name, and treats other states and the entire person as object ("he," "she," or "it").

## Hidden Observers

The Hilgards (E. R. Hilgard, 1977; E. R. Hilgard & J. R. Hilgard, 1975) in their Stanford University laboratory have shown that individuals rendered deaf through hypnotic suggestion can still hear at covert levels, and that subjects given suggestions of analgesia continue to "feel" the pain unconsciously. They described the personality entity that had the experience as an underlying "cognitive control system" and termed it "the hidden observer."

We replicated their procedures for initi-ating hypnotic deafness and analgesia and have found that their "hidden observers" are the same phenomena as our covert ego states (J. G. Watkins & H. H. Watkins, 1979a, 1979b).

## Ego States and Multiple Personalities

Equally interesting is a finding not yet published. In the successful treatment of a true multiple personality, the major personalities, Barbara, Ellen, Jennifer, and Mary, were fused not by suggestion but by a laborious hypnoanalytic working-through of the conflicts that originally dissociated them from one another. The patient eventually experienced herself as a whole person, and the separate personalities no longer appeared. She then felt their contents as subject, hence, as belonging to her own self. However, we found that under hypnosis these entities continued to exist as ego states. Their description of their posttreatment functions and roles paralleled those we have found in ego states hypnotically activated in normal subjects who had volunteered for our experimental studies. In other words, the return of these dissociated personalities to the status of normal ego states tended to validate our hypothesis that dissociation is on a continuum, and that the difference between normal and multiple personalities is only a matter of the intensity of cathexis and the permeability of the ego-state boundaries.

## Neuroses

Most psychological theories view neuroses as the result of conflict. It may be between the ego and the id, or the superego and ego, or instincts and defenses, or feelings of inferiority and life plans, or society and individual pleasure drives, and so forth, depending on one's theoretical orientation. The element of conflict between the needs of the individual and the demands of the world, or between opposing drives within the individuals, is an essential part of most theories of neuroses. Their differences lie in which are the two parties to the conflict.

We find that neurotic symptoms and maladaptive behaviors are often the product of a conflict between underlying ego states cognitively dissonant from one another. They differ from each other in needs, motivations, and goals. However, the differences between "covert" ego states may not be as pronounced as between overt multiple personalities since their boundaries are not as impermeable and usually their differential energizings are not as strong. Nevertheless, the conflict is still there, with resulting symptoms and maladaptive behaviors. The focusing effect of the hypnotic modality acts to delineate their differences almost as clearly as if they were true, overt, alternating multiple personalities. We might expect that the somewhat greater permeability of their boundaries (as compared to true, overt multiple personalities) would make the therapeutic resolution of their conflicts and their subsequent integration easier.

Whether overt or covert, the parties to the conflict are ego states, and it is the ego states that must be activated, studied, reconciled, or altered. They become the centers of focus for successful psychotherapeutic intervention. Their respective motivations, needs, goals, and conflicts must be uncovered and satisfactory solutions reached.

## METHODOLOGY

Ego states may be activated either hypnotically or nonhypnotically. The hypnotic modality offers greater "depth" and is preferable when it can be used. A nonhypnotic "chair technique" can be used in many cases, usually in the early stages of therapy. The most productive use of this procedure occurs after the client has described a conflict. An outline of this nonhypnotic technique, using several empty chairs, follows.

### Part I: Discovering Ego States on a Specific Problem

1.  Set the stage by mentioning we all have mixed emotions and that the purpose of the chairs is to separate out the different feelings on the conflict at hand.
2.  Together decide the topic for each ego state by starting out with the words "I feel . . ." Examples of topics might be attitudes toward studying, or a parent, or spouse, or self, or whatever conflict the client brings up.
3.  Have each ego state express its position on the topic while the therapist records verbatim as much as possible.
4.  Have the client move from chair to chair until there are no more ego states to express themselves.

### Part II: Delineating the Characteristics of Each Ego State

1.  While standing together, read off the transcript of each ego state in a voice and tone that approximates the client's rhythm and voice when in that chair.
2.  Next have the client give a simple description of the personality of each ego state without allowing evaluation or negative labeling.
3.  Ask for a title or a name that encapsulates the personality of each ego state for the client.
4.  Then ask: "How old does that part feel to you—older, younger, or contemporary?" If the client gives a noncontemporary age, then say, "What comes to mind when you think of age_____?"
5.  Record these data on the transcript as it is given.

### Part II: Co-Therapist Step

1.  Place the transcript of each ego state on the appropriate chair.
2.  Review the name, age, and a brief description of each ego state as given by the client.
3.  Then, while both therapist and client are standing, looking at all the ego-state chairs with their transcripts, the therapist asks: "How do you see what's going on here?"

## Part IV: Therapist Input

1. After the client describes what is going on in the conflict, the therapist realigns the chairs to follow the description. For example, if the client describes several states as being on one side of the conflict, then the therapist places those chairs side by side, facing those ego-state chairs that are in opposition, and perhaps turning around a chair that seems to be intellectualizing but not directly involved in the conflict.

2. The therapist makes therapeutic interventions by having the client sit in one of the chairs and talk to another ego-state chair. Then the client moves to the addressed chair and replies.

3. It is important for the therapist to follow the client at first and then lead in the direction the client seems to be going. In that way therapist and client stay together, both literally and figuratively.

4. A compromise can be worked out by using one of the ego states as an arbitrator for two other ego states, or by the therapist speaking directly to one of the ego states as the client is sitting in the chair, or by any combination of maneuvers. The sensitivity of the therapist and the flexibility of the client are the only limits. It is essential that the therapist become aware of the needs of each ego state. If needs can be met (e.g., achievement) through a new form of behavior (i.e., encouragement) toward another ego state, then the demanding ego state may be willing to give up a nonproductive behavior (nagging).

5. Ideally, some closure should be accomplished during this session, which usually lasts between one and one-half to two hours. Future sessions might deal with only the core of the conflict, that is, the interaction between two or three ego states that have already been identified during the initial session.

As with all Ego-State Therapy, with or without hypnosis, the purpose is to reduce conflict so that the family of ego states can live together in peace and harmony.

Ego states can also be activated simply by hypnotizing the patient and asking if there is "a part of George that is causing his headaches," or "some part of Mary that is aware of why she can't study," and so forth. "If there is such a part, please come out and say, 'I'm here.' ". Since an underlying ego state may be exerting an influence on the patient that is experienced as object (not-me), the request might be put as follows: "I would like to talk to that part of Ellen that pulled her into a bar last night when she really wanted to go home." Ego states sometimes emerge spontaneously under hypnosis. One ego state may reveal the presence of another one, thus helping the therapist to zero in on a new entity. In one case a cognitive, observing, passive state was asked directly if there was "somebody else" involved in the problem, since everything pointed to an unknown factor unconsciously influencing the total person. Stammering, and with much embarrassment, it said, "Well, yes—there's Mary, but we don't talk about her." Mary was activated and found to be a most angry and vengeful young religious zealot. She was making the patient depressed because she felt the entire person was "sinful." In fact, when her attention was called to the fact that the individual was in danger of committing suicide, she responded with, "She *should* kill herself. She's bad. I won't die with her. I'll go to heaven." This illustrates the concrete thinking that ego states (as "part persons") so often manifest.

Once activated, an ego state is initially interviewed to ascertain how it perceives itself, how it views the entire person and other ego states (if it is aware of them), how long it has been in existence ("When were you born?"), what its function is within the psychic economy of the person, what its motivations and goals are, and so forth. This is like the usual clinical evaluation a patient ordinarily receives, except it is done on each ego state separately. Psychological tests can also be given to each ego state individually. The results usually differ from one state to another—and from the tests administered to the entire, conscious person.

Sometimes ego states appear in the patient's dreams as dream figures. They can be activated by having the person redream the fantasy, much as is done in the Jungian analytic technique of "active imagination." We prefer to do this under hypnosis (Watkins, 1952).

Typically, ego-state therapy sessions are similar to family therapy sessions. One family member speaks, another answers; or the therapist questions one, then another, in an attempt to understand each state's interactions with the others and to mediate conflicts.

Ego states can be influenced by any of the same procedures used by therapists on whole persons: suggestion, ventilation, reflection of feeling, abreaction, reinforcement, desensitization, free association, confrontation, construction, interpretation, and diplomatic negotiation. Any therapeutic technique used by the various theoretical approaches can be utilized in Ego-State Therapy, except that it is applied to ego states rather than to a presumably whole, conscious person.

It is often helpful to bring awareness of ego states and their various roles to the conscious attention of the entire person. Efforts may be made to increase the energizing "cathexis" of constructive states and to reduce the power of unconstructive ones. At other times coalitions of the more constructive entitites are established to control the malevolent ones. However, we have found it unproductive to establish the unconstructive states as enemies and do battle with them. They can mobilize tremendous resistance in thwarting therapeutic efforts. Diplomacy is much better than war.

Negotiation and compromise are particularly desirable when trying to meet the needs of each ego state. An ego state may have an achievement need, a play need, a need to be creative or whatever, but the way the ego state is trying to meet that need may arouse the resistance of another ego state. A good example is an achievement need in one state interfering with the play needs of another, resulting in procrastination. The way the achievement-need ego state (often a parental introject) tries to impose its will on the other (a child state) may be through nagging and

evoking guilt ("you should . . ."). The overt person is usually conscious only of the effects of such inner conflict, such as a feeling of tension, depression, and the inability to accomplish. Apparently we not only introject the significant figures in the process of growing up but also the drama. The conflict between the original parent and child are now replayed within the psyche of the child grown up.

On several occasions we have developed an ego state into a co-therapist. In one case a malevolent ego state, "the Evil One," which so frightened the patient with hallucinatory voices whenever she was approached by men, was changed through the therapist's resonance into a cooperative, constructive entity, renamed "the Dark One" (see H. H. Watkins, 1978). Dark One was taught Wolpian desensitization techniques and, as a co-therapist, successfully carried out the resolution of a phobia in an infantile child state, "Little One." This child state had been frozen (fixated, in psychoanalytic terminology) at the age of one and a half when the patient was isolated in an oxygen tent in the hospital. The alleviation of this phobia in Little One significantly helped the patient to emerge from a life-long schizoid condition and improve her interpersonal relationships.

The technique in this case involved, first, recognition that Dark One was created as a protective entity (when the patient was molested as a three-year-old). Second, the protective needs of the previously malevolent state* were enlisted in the total therapeutic strategy. Dark One was very proud of being taught therapeutic tactics and given treatment responsibilities. His efforts (a "male" state in a female person) were given positive reinforcement and much praise by the therapist.

---

*We have found that most malevolent states were originally established as defenses. It is their manner of protection that has become anachronistic and maladaptive. By resonating with their original protective intentions, they come to accept the therapist and his or her suggestions of more constructive ways of protecting the entire person.

Specific techniques in Ego-State Therapy are derived from many other therapies, directive, behavioral, cognitive, analytic, or humanistic. It is the unit to which they are applied and the modality (hypnotic) in which the transactions are accomplished that is different.

## APPLICATIONS

We have used Ego-State Therapy with a wide variety of clinical syndromes, ranging from simple problems of stopping smoking, weight reduction, and study difficulties, through the various neuroses to borderline schizophrenics—for which we have found it especially effective. We have treated overt multiple personalities by returning them to covert, cooperating ego states, such as we find in normal individuals. Any case involving internal conflicts may be approached in this manner. We have not yet tried it on true schizophrenics, although we are struck by the finding that hallucinations may represent the voices of ego states. This might suggest a new approach to the psychotherapeutic treatment of psychosis.

We have not found any specific conditions in which Ego-State Therapy is contraindicated. However, some patients, especially hypnotically insusceptible subjects, may be resistant to this approach. A few individuals show initial fear at the possibility that they might have more than one "personality." Patients with very rigid personality structures, who have a strong need to be always in control, may not work well in this approach.

Ego-State Therapy often gets at the key conflicts rapidly. However, the opportunity to make faster therapeutic change brings with it the greater danger of making therapeutic blunders. This approach is not for the amateur therapist. The ego-state therapist should be already skilled in other therapeutic procedures—behavioral, cognitive, analytic, or humanistic—should be psychodynamically sophisticated in working with unconscious processes, and preferably should have had training and experience in the field of clinical hypnosis. We believe that a therapist with such a background will find the exploration and treatment of ego-state problems a new and exciting experience. This conceptualization of personality disorders and their treatment is a most challenging one.

The following are excerpts from a recording of a therapy session. If the movement seems too fast, or different states appear to change their attitudes too rapidly, it is due to the fact that space limitations required that many of the "working-through" interactions be deleted.

## CASE EXAMPLE*

This young, divorced woman with two small children could not work effectively when at home. She would frequently spend many hours reading and sitting on a pillow in the corner of her apartment feeling tired and unable to mobilize herself to do her housework. She was also given to frequent bouts with colds and other minor illnesses. A medical examination disclosed no physical findings that could account for her condition. The following are excerpts of Ego-State Therapy from the third session of her treatment. She has been hypnotized and the hypnotic state deepened.

* * * * *

### Therapist's Notes

T:  Deeper and deeper relaxed. And as you lie there on your magic cloud I want to talk to the part of you that's been sitting in the corner of your apartment on the pillows avoiding life and reading. I want to talk to

End of hypnotic induction. Activating the ego state that seems to be causing the pa-

---

*In the following case example, T(therapist) refers to Helen H. Watkins. P refers to patient.

her, and when she's there just say, "I'm here."

P: . . . I'm here.

T: All right. Did I ever talk to you before? . . . You're not sure?

P: Huh-uh.

T: Tell me about yourself.

*New state.*
*Nondirective question.*

P: . . . I'm all in a knot right now, and I feel scared.

T: Oh, you're scared. Do you know what you're scared of?

P: Huh-uh.

T: Oh, you don't know. How old do you feel?

P: Pretty little to be this scared.

*A child state.*

T: Hmm. Pretty little. Is there any particular name that I could call you? . . . You shrug your shoulders. You don't know?

P: Huh-uh.

T: Can I call you The Little One?

P: Suzy.

*State has its own name. Won't just accept any one the therapist suggests.*

T: I wonder what's been happening to you, Suzy? What are you so frightened about?

P (SUZY): There's so much to do.

T: Oh, there's so much to do, and you can't do it all. Is that it? (Suzy now crying). It's just too much. I guess for a little girl that's more than you can handle. Isn't it?

*Child state (Suzy) is feeling too much pressure.*

P (SUZY): Uh-huh.

T: Hmm. Just can't do it all. How come you're expected to do it all? Isn't there somebody else in there who can help you out or are you all by yourself?

*Looking for help from other ego states.*

P (SUZY): Elegant is all busy—Her and Warm.

*Elegant and Warm are two other ego states previously contacted.*

T: Oh, what's Warm been doing?

P (SUZY): I don't know where he's been gone.

T: Oh? He's been gone then, huh?

P (SUZY): I want him back.

*Warm is a "he."*
*Masculine ego states often found in women. (Not sexualized.) Therapist resonating with little Suzy.*

T: You want him back. Okay, I'll see what I can find out for you. I don't think it's fair for anybody as little as you to have to do all that work, and it's just too much for you to handle, isn't it?

P (SUZY): Uh-huh.

T: Do you know how old you are, Suzy?

P (SUZY): About ten.

*Suzy is patient's 10-year-old state.*
*Suzy dismissed. Warm activated.*

T: I see. Okay. Well, I'm going to see what

tient's complaints, for example, "I can't seem to get anything done."

I can do. . . . Suzy, I'd like you to step aside, and now I want to talk to Warm. You step aside, Suzy, and when Warm is there, just say, ''I'm here.''

P: (WARM):  . . . I'm here.

T:  Hi. I haven't talked to you for a long time. How have you been?

P: (WARM):  I think Suzy's right. I've been gone.

Change of voice.

T:  Oh, you heard what she said then, huh?

Warm is aware of Suzy and can hear her. Warm-Suzy is boundary permeable, at least in Warm's direction.

P: (WARM):  Yeah.

T:  Well, why have you been gone?

P: (WARM):  I just didn't feel like I was needed around there.

T:  Well, it's clear that you're needed. Suzy's the one that's been burdened with all the responsibilities. Apparently Elegant is the one who goes to work and does a good job and is occupied with doing things professionally and, then when she comes home Elegant takes a rest. The only one that has to do all the housework is Suzy, and she can't handle all the kids, all the work, she just hides in the corner and reads. She needs you.

Patient's work situation as a professional person has not deteriorated, only her housework. Elegant is effective, but not Suzy.

P: (WARM):  Yeah. . . . I sure needed a break, though.

Warm is not enthusiastic about helping. He has been ''resting'' and leaving responsibilities to little Suzy.

T:  Are you willing to help out Suzy?

P: (WARM):  . . . Yeah.

T:  Does she know that you exist?

P: (WARM):  Yeah.

T:  Okay. I would like you to contact her now internally in any way that you feel is appropriate and tell her whatever you want to say, and say it out loud, but I want you to talk to her.

Therapist wants to get Warm's cooperation and induce a direct conversation between the two states.

P: (WARM):  . . . Suzy, I'm sorry I've been gone so long. I guess I just took a break and forgot to come back. . . . There are things that have to be done, and I'm the one that's there to do them.

T:  Now Suzy;, I'd like you to say anything to Warm that you want to say.

Therapist stimulates this dialogue.

P (SUZY):  I'm mad, hurt. . . .

T:  You just talk to Warm.

P (SUZY):  I'm afraid you're going to go away

Suzy is in conflict. Fear of abandonment,

again, and I don't want to be left with all that stuff. . . . You keep things on an even keel, and I get real angry and . . . I'm scared you'll go away again. I don't really understand why you went away.

T: Warm, why don't you explain it to her. See if you can make sure that she is reassured. Tell her what it was all about, so that she can understand.

anger, then fear that anger will stimulate further abandonment.

P: (WARM):   . . . Suzy . . . I don't really know why I stayed away that long. I wasn't listening, and I feel bad about that. I needed the break when I took it, and things went well, and I know you remember that for a while. Everything went real smoothly . . . but it was really wrong for me to go away that long.

Warm can reduce Suzy's conflict. Every time Suzy speaks she is crying. Warm's voice contrasts. He is not crying. He is now reassuring Suzy and acts like a responsible adult.

T: Do you think that maybe you could take her hand and kind of walk with her, so that she knows that you're in touch with her. Is that okay? . . . And now I would like to talk to Suzy. Suzy, I'd like you to say anything that you want to say in terms of what Warm has just said to you.

Warm has made a commitment to Suzy. Therapist suggests close and reassuring contact between the two states.

P (SUZY):  I feel better about. . . . But I feel like you're going to have to prove to me that you will be there . . . before I can really trust you.

Suzy reassured by Warm but not yet completely trusting.

T:  Actions speak louder than words, huh, Suzy?

P (SUZY):  Yeah, right.

T:  Can you feel Warm's hand in yours? You know one of the things you could do, Suzy, is to not let go of that hand. . . . And now I'd like the two of you just to walk off together because you need to stay together. . . . And now I want to talk to an entirely different part, the part that was puckering up her lips and kept saying in the mirror "I don't want to be here."

Touch represents tangible reassurance.

Existence of another possibly relevant ego state suggested by "puckering" of lips. Noted prior to hypnosis.

P:  Yeah.

T:  Who are you?

P:  Spoiled.

T:  Spoiled, oh, is that your name?

Another new state.
Spoiled—a body of behaviors developed over the years. No specific point of origin. Loaded with anger. Typical behavior of Spoiled under stress is to retreat and sulk.

P (SPOILED):  Yep.

T:  Oh . . . what's your problem?

P (SPOILED):  . . . Everybody's in my way. . . . Then I get distant from everything, cut myself off from everything, put up a wall.

T:  Hmm. Are you connected with any other part inside there? Are you aware of any other part?

P (SPOILED):  . . . I know they are all there.

T:  Who do you know is there?

Are there other ego states relevant to patient's conflict?

P (SPOILED):  One I know especially is the Little Baby that gets L sick.

T:  The Little Baby causes L to get sick?

P (SPOILED):  Yeah.

L is name of patient. Little Baby "causes" patient to get sick?

T:  That wasn't the one that I just talked to?

P (SPOILED):  No, no-no.

T:  Who else do you know?

Any more?

P (SPOILED):  There's somebody else I know.

T:  Mmmm.

P (SPOILED):  It's a big man.

"Big"—important, powerful.

T:  It's a big man?

P (SPOILED):  Yeah. It's not Warm; I know who Warm is.

T:  This is another man.

P (SPOILED):  Yeah. Just standing there.

T:  Find out his name.

P (SPOILED):  . . . He says his name is Dad.

Parental introject.

T:  Oh, I see, his name is Dad. What does he do inside the personality?

P (SPOILED):  . . . I don't know.

T:  Dad, I would like to talk to you.

P (DAD):  Yeah.

T:  I haven't talked to you before. Is that right?

Also new to therapist.

P (DAD):  No.

T:  Ah, can you tell me about yourself?

P (DAD):  Well, I'm a lot like Warm, only I'm older.

Both masculine, but Dad is fatherly.

T:  Oh, I see. What do you tell them, everybody in there? What are the messages you send out?

P (DAD):  . . . A lot of moralities.

T:  Moralities? What kinds of things do you say?

Dad ego state, like patient's father, moralized but didn't really interact with family.

P (DAD):  Well, things about dealing with people, about honesty.

T:  Do you know what's been going on last month?

P (DAD):  . . . Well . . . I've seen a lot of factions. . . . I've seen Spoiled and the Little Baby when . . . and Elegant, they're kind of separate . . . I didn't like saying that but I don't generally get involved in that kind of thing.

T:  It's like you stand on the sidelines and don't get involved in a family squabble.

P (DAD):  Yeah, right.

T:  Is there anything that you could do within that personality to help out instead of standing on the sidelines?

How about doing something, Dad?

P (DAD):  . . . Well, Warm generally does a lot more of the mediating. I don't generally play that role.

Dad wants to remain passive and aloof from family controversies. Therapist pushes Dad to get more involved. She confronts him with his failure to take responsibility.

T:  I think what she could use from you is a little bit more action and not just words, and to get more involved. I get the feeling you've been standing on the sidelines not taking any responsibility for what's going on.

P (DAD):  I didn't see that it was my responsibility.

T:  Why not? . . . It's your family too, you know. You're part of that family . . . and those kids in there need you. You're aware, you said, of Spoiled and the Little Baby. Apparently the Little Baby brings on physical problems, is that right? . . . That's what Spoiled said. Ah, we sure could use you as a healthy force in there to help take care of the kids. You said you were Father, and you're standing on the sidelines. Well, I think they could use Father. They can't handle all the pressure from the world. Spoiled is all upset, and the Little Baby somatizes stress into the body through physical problems. We sure could use you.

Dad nods.

Come on, Dad. Shape up and help out.

P (DAD):  What can I do?

T:  Well, you're a big man, and they are just little, and you seem to be constructive and supportive. I think that they could use your energy and your protection.

He shows signs of constructive change. Therapist reinforces Dad's constructive potential.

P (DAD):  Okay.

T:  Now, I wonder if you could just gather

Let's get better communication between all

them together and have them beside you. Can you do that? All right. You just talk to each one in turn, whatever you wish, and just talk out loud so I can hear you but talk to them.

P (DAD):  . . . I think it's time that I get more involved and take the load off of some of the people, so that we can work a little better . . . Suzy, I want you to know that I'm really proud of what you've done. Even though you fought it a lot. You've done a good job, and you were right to have fought it. . . . Spoiled, I guess I'm here to paddle your butt some, because you can't have things always the way you want them, but also so that you can lean on me . . . and Little One . . . you just need to be held. . . .

T:  Yeah, the Little Baby needs to be held.

P (DAD):  . . . The others of you, Elegant, Warm, I want you to know the commitment I'm making, so that I have a responsibility to you to live up to that commitment as well as to the others.

T:  Now, I'd like anyone who wishes to answer Father to talk to him directly, but do it out loud so I can hear you.

P:  I'm Elegant.

T:  Hi, you're Elegant? All right.

P (ELEGANT):  I just want to say I'm glad, and it's about time. . . .

T:  Maybe there's somebody else. I'd like to hear from the rest of you. . . .

P (ELEGANT):  Warm's shaking his hand.

P:  I'm Suzy.

T:  You're Suzy? All right.

P (SUZY):  I've got two hands to hold.

T:  Oh, two hands to hold, nice.

P (SUZY):  Feels good.

T:  You've got Warm and you're holding on to Father, huh?

P (SUZY):  Yeah.

T:  How about Spoiled? I'd like to hear from you. . . . You're kind of curling up your lips.

P (SPOILED):  (Laughs) Well, I don't like the part about paddling my butt.

T:  (Laughs)

P (SPOILED):  But I guess he's right.

the states. They can then cooperate and form a more unified person. Dad starts to take a strong and nurturing role.

Dad is acting now like a father.

He makes a commitment.

A new source of strength is mobilized in the patient's psychic economy.

The other ego states begin to respond positively.

Elegant still speaking.

Suzy is reassured by contact with Warm on one side and Father on the other.

Sounds like a typical response from an amused preadolescent.

T: I wonder if I could talk to the Little Baby. I know that Father said that all she needs is to be held, and I don't know if she's too little to talk or what, but I'd like to talk to her.

P (LITTLE BABY): . . . Yeah.

A real getting together of the ego-state "family."

T: How do you feel about what's been happening?

P (LITTLE BABY): . . . It's kind of nice to be little and have a lot of power.

Oh-oh. What's this all about?

T: It's nice to be little and have a lot of power?

P (LITTLE BABY): Yeah.

Let's check it out.

T: . . . How do you mean that?

P (LITTLE BABY): I can bring them all down.

T: . . . You can bring them all down. How?

P (LITTLE BABY): Make them sick.

Immature ego states, like real children, often do not realize the consequences of their behavior. They think concretely.

T: Oh, make them sick.

P (LITTLE BABY): . . . When they're ignoring me.

T: Do I hear then, that if Father is willing to hold you and you're not being ignored, that you would have no reason to make them sick?

P (LITTLE BABY): Yeah, that's right, and then I have to give up my power.

T: Well, when you make them sick, you don't get what you want, and you're not happy.

P (LITTLE BABY): Yeah, that's true . . . 'cause if he's sick he can't hold me.

Getting Little Baby to think more realistically.

T: That's right. If he's sick he can't hold you. Then everything falls apart. The whole family falls apart when he gets sick.

P (LITTLE BABY): Yeah.

T: Are you willing to stay with Father and be held?

Getting a commitment from Little Baby.

P (LITTLE BABY): Yeah.

T: Okay. Just one last thing to Father. Father, I really appreciate all the things that you have done. You have gathered together this family so that you have now become the rightful leader, a leader that is not bossy, but one who cooperates, who understands everybody's needs, and who interacts with all members of the family, who makes sure all the children are well taken care of and their

Dad (Father ego state) reinforced on new attitude of mature responsibility for his "family of self."

Therapist continuing to reinforce Dad and summarizing his accomplishments.

needs met. I really appreciate and respect all that you have done today.

P (DAD):   Thank you.

T:   Now, I want to talk to the total personality, and in a moment I'm going to arouse you by counting up to five. You'll be wide awake, fresh and alert. Coming up now at the count of five, coming up one, two, three, four, five.

P:   . . . Thank you.

Removing the hypnosis and reactivating the entire person, L.

\* \* \* \* \*

In this session we see an internal conflict in which various ego states in the patient's personality refuse to take responsibilities. All housework is left to a 10-year-old child state, Suzy, who feels abandoned, tired, and angry. She spends many hours sitting on a pillow in the corner reading.

In addition, an internal "baby" state is resentful that it receives little affection from a father state, Dad (probably an introject of the original father). The angry "Baby" has been revenging itself by creating many minor illness (perhaps by reducing the patient's resistance to colds).

The therapist induces other ego states (Warm, Elegant) to help Suzy with the housework and confronts Father with his failure to assume parental responsibility for the internal "family." He then "holds" the resentful Baby and welds the conflict-ridden "family" into a more cooperating constellation of ego states. They can now meet each other's needs rather than frustrating them. Subsequently, the patient lost her fatigue, acquired a new sense of direction, and was motivated to effective behavior. Her greater physical well-being matched her increased *esprit de corps*.

Greater internal "family harmony" has been established.

defined as a body of behaviors and experiences bound together by a common principle and separated from other such states by a boundary that is more or less permeable. When the boundary between these entities is impermeable, and they are highly energized, they may manifest themselves as multiple personalities. Otherwise, they continue to operate in normal and neurotic individuals like "covert" personalities. Their existence can be clearly demonstrated through hypnosis, although under some conditions they can be activated nonhypnotically.

Like overt multiple personalities, when they emerge (become "executive") they describe themselves as having independent identities. They regard other such states and the entire person as objects, hence, as "he," "she," or "it." Even though their presence may be unconscious to the individual, these clusters of personality can be in conflict with each other. The patient then experiences anxiety and other symptoms. By activating these states, either hypnotically or otherwise, a wide variety of psychotherapeutic techniques (such as suggestion, ventilation, abreaction, reinforcement, desensitization, confrontation, interpretation, and diplomatic negotiation) may be used to resolve their conflicts and bring internal harmony into the patient's psyche. Our experience has been that following such an integration, symptoms and maladaptive behaviors diminish.

Ego-State Therapy is innovative in that it more clearly delineates the parties to internal conflict and focuses upon key elements. The hypnotic trance, like transference in psycho-

## SUMMARY

Ego-State Therapy is the utilization of group and family therapy techniques for the resolution of conflicts between the various "ego states" that constitute a "family of self" within a single individual. An ego state is

analysis, permits a reexperiencing of previously introjected individuals and childhood dramas in the here and now (Watkins, 1954).

Contrary to criticisms we have received that by focusing on ego-state differences we are increasing dissociation, we find that as the various ego states become aware of each other, and through communication and interaction come to understand one another, dissociation is reduced. Their boundaries become more permeable, and our patients become more integrated. Repressed material brought to awareness during psychoanalysis is not created by the analyst; it is simply released by him. So also it is with ego states. We do not create them; we activate them if they are already there. We bring them to the conscious awareness of the entire person and increase their cooperation with each other— thus promoting integration in the individual.

Another criticism is that we create these ego states by suggestion. We are quite aware of the literature on operator influence (Orne, 1969, Rosenthal, 1966) and attempt to guard against it. We do ask for "a part of you" to respond. But we do not give that "part" a name or suggest its content. We are surprised at how often ego-state replies are contrary to our expectations. They show considerable spontaneity and frequently resist our suggestions.

Ego states react in ways similar to entire persons. They can hate, love, fear, and be cooperative or obstructinistic. We are careful not to antagonize any ego state, even malevolent ones. For if one does, the resistance to treatment will almost certainly increase as the offended one sabotages the therapist's efforts. Being only "part persons" and often like children, their thinking may be concrete and childlike. It is necessary to communicate with them in simple language. They are frequently singleminded and attempt to achieve their goals independently without regard for the welfare of the whole individual. They may be quite unaware of the consequences of their actions.

Our therapeutic objective is integrated cooperation between these entities, not their fusion. When ego states are threatened with fusion, hence, with loss of individual identity, their resistance to change is greatly increased. They fight, just as would the geographical states of Montana and Idaho if faced with the threat of a forced merger. They prize their individual identities. However, ego states can accept their role as being relatively autonomous self-governments within a "federal" jurisdiction of the entire personality.

There is room within the normal individual for both differentiation and integration of functions. That these various functions, both constructive and maladaptive, are carried out through organizational patterns of personality that overlap and are separated by boundaries is not surprising. We would also expect that such patterns might sometimes conflict with each other in the accomplishment of their functions, since organisms are imperfect institutions of adaptation.

What is astonishing, however, is that these personality units, when activated, claim identity (personhood) and at least a semiautonomous existence independent of the whole individual. Some of the functions that these subpersonalities carry out have been initiated locally, within that unit or "ego state," as we have called it, and not by the entire person. Its operations then may be in conflict with those of other units and of the complete individual.

It should not be surprising to consider that if personality functions can be separated and differentiated within circumscribed contents and boundaries, the very essence of selfness or personal identity, which is indigenous to a personality, may also be so partitioned off. Thus, other partial identities are created within a single human organism, most of whom (unlike true, dissociated personalities) are covert, not normally observed, yet with differing aims and needs, and with limited degrees of autonomy.

It is not necessary that these subidentities be fused or destroyed. Once these units are understood and their needs met, uncooperative ego states change and become more cognitively consonant to the goals of the entire individual. They take their place as constructive members in an integrated "family of self."

## REFERENCES

Haley, J. *Uncommon therapy: The psychiatric techniques of Milton H. Erickson, M. D.* New York: Norton, 1973.

Hilgard, E. R. *Divided consciousness.* New York: Wiley, 1977.

Hilgard, E. R. and Hilgard, J. *Hypnosis in the relief of pain.* Los Altos, Calif.: Kaufman, 1975.

Janet, P. *The major symptoms of hysteria.* New York: Macmillan, 1907.

O'Connell, R. J. *Saint Augustine's confessions: The odyssey of soul.* Boston: Harvard University Press, 1969.

Orne, M. T. Demand characteristics and the concept of quasi-controls. In R. Rosenthal and R. L. Rosnow (Eds.), *Artifact in behavorial reserach.* New York: Academic Press, 1969.

Prince, M. *The dissociation of a personality.* New York: Longmans-Green, 1906.

Reil, J. C. *Rhapsodien über die Anwendung der psychischen Curmethode auf Geisteszerrüttungen.* Halle: Curt, 1803.

Rosenthal, R. *Experimenter effects in behavioral research.* New York: Appleton, 1966.

Schneck, J. M. *Principles and practice of hypnoanalysis.* Springfield, Ill.: Charles C Thomas, 1965.

Sidis, B. *The psychology of suggestion.* New York: Appleton, 1910.

Thigpen, C. H. and Cleckley, H. M. *Three faces of Eve.* New York: McGraw-Hill, 1957.

Watkins, H. H. Ego-state therapy. In J. G. Watkins, *The therapeutic self.* New York: Human Sciences Press, 1978.

Watkins, J. G. *Hypnotherapy of war neuroses.* New York: Ronald Press, 1949.

Wakins, J. G. Projective hypnoanalysis. In L. M. LeCron (Ed.), *Experimental hypnosis.* New York: Macmillan, 1952.

Watkins, J. G. The affect bridge: A hypnoanalytic technique. *International Journal of Clinical and Experimental Hypnosis,* 1971, **19**, 21–27.

Watkins, J. G. Ego states and the problem of responsibility: A psychological analysis of the Patty Hearst case. *Journal of Psychiatry and Law,* Winter 1976, 471–489.

Watkins, J. G. The psychodynamic manipulation of ego states in hypnotherapy. In F. Antonelli (Ed.), *Therapy in psychosomatic medicine,* vol. 2, *Symposia.* Rome, Italy: International College of Psychosomatic Medicine, 1977.

Watkins, J. G. *The therapeutic self.* New York: Human Sciences Press, 1978.

Watkins, J. G. Ego states and the problem of responsibility II: The case of Patricia W. *Psychiatry and Law,* Winter 1978a, 519–535.

Watkins, J. G. and Watkins, H. H. Hypnoanalytic ego-state therapy. Audio tape no. 97. Orlando, Fla.: American Academy of Psychotherapists Tape Library, 1976.

Watkins, J. G. and Watkins, H. H. Theory and practice of ego-state therapy: A short-term therapeutic approach. In H. Grayson (Ed.), *Short-term approaches to psychotherapy.* New York: Human Sciences Press, 1979a.

Watkins, J. G. and Watkins, H. H. Ego states and hidden observers. *Journal of Altered States of Consciousness,* 1979b, **5**, 3–18.

Watkins, J. G. and Watkins, H. H. I. Ego-states and hidden observers. II. Ego-state therapy: The lady in white and the woman in black. Audio tape. New York: Jeffrey Norton, 1979c.

Weiss, E. (Ed.). *Ego psychology and the psychoses (The writings of Paul Federn).* New York: Basic Books, 1952.

Wolberg, L. R. *Hypnoanalysis.* New York: Grune & Stratton, 1945.

# CHAPTER 20

# *Eidetic Psychotherapy*

ANEES A. SHEIKH and CHARLES S. JORDAN

*I suppose that I overuse the word "unique" in reference to the various systems in this book, but all of the chapters are unique. There are other unique systems that I have not considered including; an example is Past Lives Therapy, the premise of which seemed to me to be absurd. However, a good many of the chapters are very different from anything that the typical, well-trained, eclectic, conservative therapist (as I view myself, incidentally) has experienced. Among these are Aesthetic Realism, Aqua-Energetics, Ego-State Therapy, Focusing, Holistic Education, Interpersonal Process Recall, Morita/Naikan, Natural High, Primary Relationship, Rebirthing, Transcendence Therapy, and Z-Process. Eidetic Psychotherapy joins this distinguished list.*

*The report by Anees Sheikh and Charles Jordan is based on a truly unique conceptualization of what is wrong with people who are maladjusted and how to make readustments. This chapter should be read in conjuction with Shorr's Psycho-Imagination Therapy and Iberg's Focusing. In each case, the emphasis is on the inner experience, the inmost aspect of the individual, and the therapists' behaviors are directed to helping the individual cure himself from within. I believe that most people new to the concept of Eidetics will be gratified to learn about this truly innovative method of psychotherapy.*

Eidetic Psychotherapy is based on the elicitation and manipulation of eidetic images that are posited to act as the self-organizing nuclei in the psyche, to direct personality development, and to restore mind-body wholeness. They are a self-motivated, affect-laden imagery phenomenon with a visual core to which somatic and meaning components are attached. This tridimensional unity displays certain lawful tendencies toward change. The behavior of eidetics is purported to have specific meaningful relations to psychological processes. Every significant event in the developmental course of individuals implants an eidetic in their system. Eidetics are considered to be bipolarly configured, involving ego-positive and ego-negative elements of the experience. It is believed that among other things, a

quasi-separation of the visual cue from other components, fixation on the negative pole of the eidetic, or repression of a significant experience can lead to a variety of symptoms. Eidetic therapists mainly aim to revive the tridimensional unity, shift attention to the neglected pole, and to uncover appropriate healthful experiences through eidetic progression. When original wholeness of the psyche has been mobilized, the therapeutic goal set by Eidetic Therapy is achieved.

## HISTORY

### Precursors

The early work on eidetic imagery was done largely at the Marburg Institute of Psychol-

271

ogy in Germany under E. R. Jaensch in the early 1900's. The Marburg eidetic theory was developed out of experiments in which actual single external objects were presented through single exposures and the subjects projected the resultant images on an external background, usually a gray screen.

The eidetic, as defined by the Marburg School, consisted of a vivid visual image of a presented figure, which usually lingered on for a duration, localized in a space in front of the eyes, positive in color, and usually on the plane where the original figure appeared. The capacity to project such an eidetic was considered to be a rare quality possessed by most children but only a few adults with "photographic" memories. These *eidetikers* could scan the figure they projected continuously during inspection without any interference with the production of an eidetic image. Scanning was considered necessary to generate an image of the entire figure. Upon removal of the actual figure, they could continue to scan their image without loss of details (Jaensch, 1930; Ahsen, 1977a).

In contrast to this type of eidetic imagery which has been labeled "typographic," Müller (1826), Allport (1924), and Ahsen (1965) discussed a form of eidetic imagery that has been termed "structural." It is internal and spontaneously evoked in all individuals. This type of image had also been reported in the Hindu tradition of Vedas and Tantras (Avalon, 1913; Müller, 1888). The internal eidetic is defined as

a normal subjective visual image which is experienced with pronounced vividness: although not necessarily evoked at the time of the experience by an actual situation, it is seen inside of the mind or outside in the literal sense of the word, and this seeing is accompanied by certain somatic events as well as a feeling of meaning; the total experience in all its dimensions excludes the possibility that it is pathological. (Ahsen, 1977b, p. 6)

Allport's (1924) account supports this position. He stated that this category of images "should be understood to exclude both pathological hallucinations and dream images, and to admit those spontaneous images of phantasy which, though possessed of perceptual character, cannot be said to be literally revivals or restorations of any specific previous perception" (Allport, 1924, p. 100).

## Beginnings

Akhter Ahsen was the first to apply the concepts of internal eidetics to a system of psychotherapy. Allport (1924) had laid the groundwork by restoring recognition of the central role of internal eidetics as a normal developmental phenomenon in all children rather than an ontogenetically archaic precursor of memory. However, he failed to recognize the continuing importance of eidetics in adults, perhaps because of his lack of clinical experience with an adult population. Ahsen filled in this important gap. He arrived at an understanding of the role of internal eidetics in consciousness through predominately three avenues: first, via mythic imagery of an eidetic nature that served as a guide in his own personal life; second, through his scholarly knowledge of the role of internal imagery in the evolution of human consciousness as reflected in the psychological, anthropological, and literary works of the East and West; and third, through his observations of the role of the naturally occurring eidetic imagery in symptom formation and resolution in his patients. Ahsen began formulating the concepts of Eidetic Psychotherapy in the late 1950's while in Pakistan. His first systematic presentation of the concepts appeared in 1965. This was followed by a more comprehensive presentation in 1968. In these first two publications Ahsen outlined a theory of personality development and therapeutic change. At the center of this system stand eidetic images, which he claims to have both a genetic and a developmental origin. The genetic eidetic will be discussesd later.

The developmental eidetic image is affect-laden, vivid, repeatable, and universally present. This image pertains to key memories and fantasies associated with basic growth and conflict situations. When this image is elicited, it spontaneously progresses in an independent fashion beyond the bounds of voluntary control. Repeated evocation of this image leads to bypassing resistances and directing the image toward core problems in a self-organizing fashion (Ahsen, 1972, 1974).

The developmental eidetic represents an organismic event made up of a *visual* component—the image (I); a *somatic* pattern—a set of bodily reactions (S); and a *meaning*, including feelings (M). Ahsen refers to this tripartite structure as the eidetic complex, or ISM. The ISM is a semipermanent structure representing developmental events of highly positive or negative emotional value.

While this eidetic is vulnerable to the distortions of the memory process, that is, to fragmentation and overlay of several images, it can be made to regain the clarity through repeated evocation. The eidetic is not necessarily isomorphic with any external event, but is rather a repesentation of an experience, inclusive of the event and the individual's full-scale reaction to it.

Wilder Penfield's (1959) neurological work lends evidence for internal mental images that function in the same manner as Ahsen's ISM. During the course of brain surgery, Penfield observed that there were areas in the cerebral cortex from which a record of the past could be retrieved when stimulated by an electrode. The patients, under local anesthesia, were able to report with full consciousness and high fidelity details of recorded events within the brain. Penfield stated: "It is as though a wire recorder or a strip of cinamatographic film with sound track had been set in motion within the brain. The sights and sounds, and the thoughts, of a former day passed through the man's mind again" (Penfield, 1959, p. 1719).

Both Ahsen and Penfield appear to be describing the same phenomenon: Both deal with internally evoked experiential pictures; both rely on repeated evocation of the problem experiences for elucidation, progressive evolvement, and understanding of the ex-perience; both consider interpretation and change a natural and inalienable part of the reported experiential pictures; both stress the vividness of the image; both have observed that the image has somatic components and attributed meanings, including feeling states; both report the repeatability of the image and the progressive clarity of the image upon repetition. Also, both Ahsen and Penfield agree that the reports of internal images do not necessarily correspond to actual external events; rather, they represent a hybrid produced by a combination of the external events and the psychic events. Both men appear to be interested primarily in the function of the image for the indivdual rather than in trying to separate fact from fiction on the basis of rationality or irrationality.

## CURRENT STATUS

In late 1960's and early 1970's pactitioners of diverse persuasions (see Sheikh, 1978) began to herald Ahsen's Eidetic Psychotherapy as a truly innovative, new approach. G. E. W. Scobie (1974, p. 16) referred to Eidetic Psychotherapy as "one of the most significant developments yet to emerge in psychotherapy since Freud's psychoanalysis," and A. A. Lazarus (1972, p. vii) called Ahsen's work "a milestone in the evolution of a truly integrative and comprehensive system of effective psychotherapy." He further observed that "compared to Akhter's penetrating analysis of imagery formation and eidetic processes, all other clinical uses of imagery appear singularly embryonic" (1972, p. v). More recently, Thomas Hanna stated that eidetic psychotherapy is "a major innovation in the traditions of psychotherapy that is as neurologically informed as it is humanistically and holistically conceived." Eidetic psychotherapy, he continued, "is emphatically *not* a new wrinkle in psychotherapy. It is in fact, a new psychotherapy" (Hanna, 1979, p. 48).

Ahsen outlined the theory and technique of Eidetic Psychotherapy in three major books, *Basic Concepts in Eidetic Psycho-*

*therapy* (1968), *Eidetic Parents Test and Anaysis* (1972), and *Psycheye: Self-analytic Consciousness* (1977a). In addition, over 100 articles by Ahsen and others, published in India, Pakistan, Europe, Canada, South America, and the United States, review or extend the theory and application of Eidetic Psychotherapy.

Most practitioners of Eidetic Psychotherapy have been trained directly by Ahsen and his staff at the Eidetic Analysis Institute in Yonkers, New York, or in workshops sponsored by those trained by him in institutions around various countries. Elitism is noticeably lacking in the education of eidetic therapists; professionals and nonprofessionals alike have been trained in these methodologies, to operate within the limits of their knowledge and skills. Ahsen has been careful to offer ongoing supervision and consultation to those learning Eidetic Psychotherapy methods. Hence there are a fair number of skilled practitioners who can be located through the Eidetic Analysis Institute in New York.

## THEORY

### Origins of Personality

Ahsen's eidetic theory of personality is based upon the assumption that within the individual there is a "biolatent" or genetically endowed tendency toward wholeness. The eidetic image is posited as the synthesizing nucleus within the mind that preserves the encoded descriptions of positive life impressions. Ahsen states: "When a life activity has been traumatically mutilated its original is still available whole and complete in the encoded cell in the form of an arrested picture . . . which can be rejuvenated" (Ahsen, 1977a, p. 51). Hence, the eidetic theory of personality development is based on a biological model of encoded holograms that comprise a library of internal eidetic images. The eidetic image, whether of a genetic or of acquired origin, becomes the transforming

lens through which the processes of image object relations, memories, sensations, feelings, and meaning are transmuted, synthesized, and encoded.

Ahsen's notion of the innate biolatent potential of the ISM resembles the concepts of innate releasing mechanisms (IRM) and innate motor patterns as defined by ethologists. In discussing the concept of an innate releasing schema in the central nervous system, Konrad Lorenz states: "The term schema is misleading, to the extent that it easily gives the false impression that the organism innately possesses an overall picture of an object or situation, whereas in reality, the releasing mechanism never gives rise to more than one quite specific response" (1971, p. 127). Lorenz implies that some visual cue, though not a complete pictorial representation of an external object, may be involved in the IRM. The IRM is triggered by a "releaser" or orienting response in a particular sensory modality, which serves as a stimulus-transmission mechanism. In regard to the importance of visual releasers in humans, Lorenz states:

They are more interesting because the innate releasing mechanisms which respond to them are by far the most differentiated among those so far known. Nowhere is the function of the innate releasing mechanisms as single lock of the response and that of the releaser as the appropriate key so clearly analyzable. (Lorenz, 1971, p. 141)

The selectivity of the IRM serves to insure a biologically appropriate response for a given time, place, and species.

While Ahsen's ISM is not necessarily dependent on external stimuli for evocation, there are many similarities in the internally selective nature of the ISM and IRM. Both the ISM and IRM, when paired with an appropriate external stimulus, result in positive social and evolutionarily adaptive behavior. The ethologists, as well as Ahsen, believe that many social behaviors are guided by the innate parallel processing of the central nervous system and somatic cue functions. The notion of a necessary and sufficient external stimulus to evoke an innate central nervous system and paired somatic response, which occurs, for instance, in the smiling responses in human infants, also is part of both theories. A single visual cue or movement may trigger a complex instinctual response in animals, and it may also do so in humans; Ahsen cites many examples where a familiar object or gesture leads the individual to operate as if the part were the whole.

There are two major differences in Ahsen's and the ethologists' theories: First, the innate ISM in eidetic theory serves as both the IRM and releaser, while these two mechanisms are defined as independent processes by ethologists; second, the internal image has primacy in the ISM, while external stimuli and innate somatic patterns called releasers have primacy in triggering the IRM.

## Image Object Theory of Object Relations

Normal development, according to eidetic theory, is a product of the interaction between innate biological images and the historical images.

In eidetic theory of object relations, it is assumed that an intrapsychic image object is constitutionally present in the organism and experientially present in the consciousness of the child. Even when not seen explicitly by the child, the image object is latently present and becomes accessible when the potential matures with time. When the "reality" ministration or the external mother performs an activicty in conformity with the genetic code (e.g., nursing at the breast), it confirms the original image effect, giving it a memory counterpart which then appears in the historical context. Thus, within this theory, the parental images are treated as a paradigm of primary image objects. (Dolan, 1977, p. 221)

Ahsen's "image object" theory of object relations diametrically opposes the analytical view of "object image" and mental functions. Psychoanalytical object relations theory proposes that the infant starts from chaos and requires parental introjects to establish

reality orientation; Ahsen (1977a), conversely, emphasizes the importance of inner structures over the outside stimuli.

## Psychical Dialectics and Personality Change

Personality development, according to Ahsen, involves a dialectical interaction between the forces of equilibrium and disequilibrium around the bipolar features of mental life. In normal development, the ISM exhibits a bipolar nature that creates "psychical dialectics" between a distinctly positive image and an associated negative image. As time passes, the favorite interpretation of the percept becomes confirmed and emotionally cathected, while the other pole is "dessociated." This dialectical nature of the eidetic is the pivotal point for a healthy development as well as the basis for symptom formation. Dessociation implies a temporary and retrievable loss, while the analytical concept of dissociation implies that the material is repressed and unavailable.

The explanation for image bipolarity and a dialectical process leading to a semipermanent monopolar configuration lies in psychic economics that serve both the equilibrium and nonequilibrium needs of the individual. To maximally utilize the available psychic energy and to accomplish memory storage in an efficient manner, the mind reduces the bipolar configuration of the ISM to a monopolar visual image temporarily dessociated from the somatic and bipolar elements in the original ISM and stored as a point of light. This eidetic image reduced to a point of light can be repeatedly evoked to retrieve the unity of the ISM.

Ahsen believes that the avoidance tendencies of the ego, guided by the reality principle, possibly lead to symptom formation and rigid character structure. Psychically, the development and preservation of self-concepts and identity generated by the ego require that the image pole creating the most cognitive dissonance within the existing personal constructs be ignored or actively rejected. Therefore, confirming one of the poles leads to identity formation through the clustering of internally consistent images. These clusters become the basis of the individual's constructs, or traits, that lead to the modus operandi for selective attention, ego defenses, and more complex patterns of personality. While personality development guided by the rational decisions of the ego has tremendous adaptive value, the costs of linear rationality, used to excess, can be great in terms of lost flexibility and creativity. The adaptive functions of the linear, equilibrium-fixated ego need to be balanced by a nonlinear, nonequilibrium mechanism of self-renewal.

Nonequilibrium forces favor a transition state between the two stable states: the monopolar eidetic image associated with semipermanent personality structures on the one hand, and the bipolar eidetic image associated with the original experience on the other. In close parallel with the nonequilibrium thermodynamics of Prigogine and Nicolis (1972), it is suggested that the dynamic eidetic nucleus has properties that "perturbate" these transition states and result in higher levels of organization within the personality. Thus, the eidetic image may serve as Prigogine's "dissipative structure" that results from "order through fluctuations" and cannot be explained by an equilibrium-seeking tendency of the individual alone.

Thus the "dissipative" nature of the eidetic image may answer the question by Panagiotou and Sheikh (1974): How are old ISM's broken up and new ones created, to avoid inflexible stereotyped generalization of old response patterns? Futhermore, a new ISM created by this process progresses to a stimulation of the dissipative creative properties of a whole sequence of other meaningfully related eidetic images. The orderly progression of this sequence results in the creation of numerous new ISM's and a reordering of existing ones. Through this nonlinear, nonrational process, personality structures are rendered flexible and free to respond to the everchanging new demands of a dy-

namic flow of life within and without the individual.

Pensinger and Paine (1978) suggest that Karl Pribram's neural holograms may be dissipative structures that account for J. H. Schultz's "autogenic discharge" activity, which leads to deautomization of the automotized or semipermanent structures of the personality. While Pribram's neural hologram (1971) seems to explain the manner in which eiditic images are stored, ordered, retrieved, and reordered, Ahsen is careful to avoid a reductionistic neurological view of the eidetic image's structure and function. The concept of the retrieval of the entire hologram from a part of it seems to best correspond to one of Ahsen's "magical laws" of the psyche—that is, *part is whole*. Ahsen gives preeminence to these "magical laws" of the mind at the expense of rational and reductionistic approaches to understanding the manner in which personality change occurs.

## Magical Laws of the Psyche

Ahsen arrived at a group of magical laws of the psyche on the basis of his clinical experience, his anthropological study of magical thinking, and his study of superstition in various cultures. These magical laws of the psyche are: (1) part is whole; (2) contact is unification; (3) imitation is reality; and (4) wish is action. The last three laws are subcategories of the first. Ahsen offers the following brief examples of how these magical laws operate symbolically in everyday activity: (1) I press a switch to put on electricity in the whole house—part is whole; (2) I hold my friend close to me to express my feelings of union—contact is unification; (3) I consult the road map when I go on a drive—imitation is reality; (4) I cannot punish somebody physically, but I wish he would drop dead—wish is action.

## Personality Multiples

Ahsen gives every significant ISM the status of a minipersonality, which he calls a "personality multiple'': ''Under the magical principles every significant state turns out to be active in its own right, seeking its own direction and destiny'' (1968, p. 32). Thus, one's identity is not viewed as a rationally and logically organized whole.

It is Mr. X's one image at a particular time when he was feeling or doing something bearing relevance to his problems of existence. As he was virtually involved tens of thousands of times, he has generated an equal number of personality multiples along this line of action. All these personality multiples are now living, feeling and breathing in him, contending toward the same old aims they completed or left unfinished. They variously live the lives they once incarnated while something in this individual tries to force an illusory unity among them. (Ahsen, 1968, p. 141)

The millions of personality multiples that make up the personality are shaped out of self and others as viewed through parents, brothers and sisters, relatives, animals, and inanimate objects. According to Ahsen, the individual,

formulates theses personality multiples, first of all in a relationship to the mother. Her various significant aspects are welded with relevant visual cues. The personality multiple formed in brothers and sisters usually represents themes of jealousy and death. Significant dresses worn by brothers and sisters under typical situations come to represent these themes. . . . Personality multiples projected in the father usually deal with themes of protection and discipline or his relationship with mother and problems of weaning and transition to his liberating image in the psyche. . . . Personality multiples may also be found projected in various space settings meaningful to the individual. They can be detected in various rooms of the house where the individual lived during early and late childhood. (1968, pp. 142–143)

The personality multiples continue to function unless they are resolved through growth experience or therapy. As discussed above, the eidetic image serves as the ''dissipative structure'' leading to transition states between bipolar and monopolar states that promote the discharge of both the pos-

itive and the negative emotions associated with a personality multiple, or ISM. This results in the neutralization of the emotion of the old personality multiple and the creation of a higher level of organization or a more expansive personality multiple around a new nuclear eidetic.

Ahsen states that the form of identity based on personality multiples ''has no enemies in the repressed to fear and no rationalizations to defend constantly, it being a manifestation of release and openness. It is powerful and dynamic, fearless and all-embracing; it honors categories of living above categories of reasoning'' (1968, p.34). As a therapeutic focus, these personality multiples are excellent vehicles for analysis, communication, and catharsis.

## METHODOLOGY*

In eidetic analysis the diagnostic and therapeutic procedures are inseparably intertwined. Eidetic analytic methods help not only in understanding the underlying dynamics but also in drawing up the therapeutic plan.

Eidetic Analysis by Ahsen and by others who have followed his system indicates that symptoms are largely caused either by dessociation of components, by fixation on the negative pole, or by a partial or complete repression of a significant positive or negative experience. Consequently, the aim of Eidetic Therapy is achieved mainly by the revival of the tripartite unity, by a shift of the ego's attention to the neglected positive pole, which brings about a more balanced and realistic appraisal of the experience, or by the uncovering of the repressed experience through progression of eidetic imagery. Since Ahsen considers an eidetic event in its full intensity to be the psychic equivalent of

*This section is a slightly modified version of a portion of another paper on Eidetic Therapy by Anees A. Sheikh published in J. L. Singer and K. S. Pope (Eds.), *The power of human imagination*, Plenum, 1978. Included with the permission of the publisher.

the corresponding actual event, to reexperience personality multiples in the form of eidetics is to reexperience the individual's history, which thus becomes available for change through eidetic methodology.

There are three main levels in the eidetic psychotherapeutic process. The first level deals with symptoms of a psychosomatic, hysterical, or phobic nature. Next is the developmental level, which pertains primarily to the widespread problems developed in early life with reference to parents. Ahsen has developed two major eidetic tests, the Age Projection Test (1968) and the Eidetic Parents Test (1972), that form the basis for diagnosis and therapy at each of the first two states respectively. Ahsen also reports a third universal symbolic level of analysis that may help individuals to attain a deeper understanding and integration of meanings of psychic contents. However, as he has not yet presented this third level of analysis in detail in his published works, it will not be discussed herein.

Eidetic Psychotherapy begins with symptom composition, which is accomplished through a structured interview during which time the therapist tries to determine the exact nature of the physical (e.g., "I ache all over") as well as the psychological (e.g., "I can't think straight") elements of the symptom complex. The patient is also questioned about the worries or concerns that he or she may entertain about the symptom (e.g., "I am afraid of going crazy"). Worries and concerns about various parts of the body are also recorded. The symptom is composed completely in the language of the patient. Subsequent to the symptom composition, the therapist is ready to administer the Age Projection Test.

## The Age Projection Test

The therapist asks the patient to give his first, middle, and last names, nicknames, and any other names by which he or she has been called since childhood, for these names are assumed to refer to an individual's various identities. Next the patient is asked to pay relaxed attention to what the therapist says. The patient is informed that when the therapist repeats certain words over and over again, he will see an image of himself somewhere in the past:

The salient features of the symptom discovered during symptom composition are now reiterated to the patient in his own words in a repetitious manner. In the course of this repetition, the patient is addressed by his various names alternately. This repetition artificially activates the symptom to an almost unbearable acuteness. At this point five seconds of total silence are allowed to elapse. Suddenly the therapist starts talking about the time when the patient was healthy and happy. As the therapist talks about health in those areas where the symptom now exists, the patient spontaneously forms a self-image subliminally. The patient is now suddenly asked to project a self-image and describe the following: (a) the self-image itself; (b) the clothing on the self-image; (c) the place where it appears; (d) the events occurring during the age projected in the self-image; (e) the events occurring during the year prior to the age projected in the image. (Dolan & Sheikh, 1977, p. 599)

This procedure usually uncovers an event that precipitated the symptom or that began a series of events that eventually led to symptom formation. Once the self-image related to this event is formed, the patient is asked to project it repeatedly until it becomes clear, and then he is interrogated further about the critical period.

If no relevant event is discovered, the last portion of the test, called "Theme Projection," is administered. The patient is told to see the self-image standing before the parents, crying to provoke pity and love. Then the self-image takes off one article of clothing and throws it down before the parents, saying, "Take it away, I don't want to wear it." The image proceeds: One of the parents picks the clothing up and deposits it somewhere. The patient sees where it has been placed, what objects appear to surround it, and what objects stand out. He is then asked to report any direct impressions or memories concerning the object that stands out most in his image.

Alternatively, an important image may evolve spontaneously during the dialogue on imagery between therapist and patient. Ahsen reports, however, that when the Age Projection Test is administered, the meaning and origin of a somatic or quasi-somatic symptom usually become evident. Based on information revealed by the test, a therapeutic image is then constructed, and the patient is asked to project the new image repeatedly. This therapeutic image may work in a variety of ways. It derives its therapeutic effectiveness from the four principles of "magical" functioning. Through these symbolic mechanisms, the image may prompt the release of repressed responses, lead to catharsis of accumulated affect, symbolically satisfy unfulfilled wishes, or correct an imbalanced ego interpretation of events by focusing on hitherto neglected aspects of the experience (Panagiotou & Sheikh, 1974).

In the area of psychosomatic and hysterical symptoms, stunning successes in an astoundingly brief period have been reported using the Age Projection Test. Numerous case histories are now available (Ahsen, 1968; Dolan & Sheikh, 1977; Sheikh, 1978). As these cases demonstrate, the symptom frequently is dispelled during the first session. Even when this occurs, further analysis of basic developmental trends may be undertaken through another important imagery test developed by Ahsen (1972), the Eidetic Parents Test.

## Eidetic Parents Test

In Eidetic Therapy special significance is attached to the patterns of interaction between the patient and his or her parents and the patient's perception of polarities that existed in their relationship. The Eidetic Parents Test (EPT) is designed specifically to uncover eidetics in these areas. The test has been shown to reveal to a significant extent the quality of the familial relationships and their predominant positive and negative

themes. This test is central to eidetic procedure and provides not only the means for identifying areas of conflict, but also the format for therapeutic procedure. The test involves a systematic scrutiny of features of the parental images to determine the exact nature of the interparental and parent-child patterns of interaction. The entire EPT consists of a total of 30 situation images in which various aspects of the parents and the parental relationships are visualized. The first item on the test proceeds in the following manner:

Picture your parents in the house where you lived most of the time, the house that gives you feeling of home.

Where do you see them?

What are they doing?

How do you feel when you see the images?

Any reactions or memories connected with the picture? (Ahsen, 1972, p. 52)

The test includes standard verbatim instructions for presenting the stimuli. Ahsen has left nothing unspecified regarding the administration of the EPT, nor about the constitution of acceptable responses. After the participant has been introduced to eidetics with a brief practice image, the test is administered in a "piecemeal, phrase by phrase enunciation of each item."

Every image is to be repeatedly projected until its essential elements are sharpened and separated from its vague or changing aspects. The participant is encouraged to acquaint himself thoroughly with the eidetic image before he is asked to describe it. It is essential to the effectiveness of the EPT that the participant see the image over and over again, and describe his visual experience thoroughly. The participant is instructed not to force any aspects of the image, but to allow it to grow without any interference. He is encouraged to describe the image in "positive declarative statements."

It should be noted that eidetic responses, unlike dreamlike reveries, are not narrative. The repetitious, piecemeal projection of segments of the response is an important methodological feature in handling eidetics. It helps to construct the rigid sequence of what defines an eidetic area. Any attempt to project in a smooth, narrative fashion leads to a fictional response; the true eidetic, however, is not fictional. It is real: a true projection.

Verbal EPT stimuli are highly structured. The initial presentation of each stimulus permits only a brief response. Repeated projections allow no more latitude in responding; the image unfolds only under the guiding questions of the therapist. This limiting nature of the stimuli and the directiveness of their presentation have afforded Ahsen a rigid basis for comparison between individuals and the possibility of using comparative data for establishing interpretive guidelines.

The faithful reporting of eidetic responses is aided by the fact that they are repeatable to the last detail. The reporting by the patient, however, is complicated by a number of items, and the first response is rarely a pure eidetic. Ahsen has given the name "eidetic matrix" to the group of phenomena elicited during EPT administration. These include (1) the first response, (2) the primary response, (3) the secondary response, (4) the interjected response, (5) the underlying primary response, and (6) the overt behavior.

The first response reflects the participant's initial reaction to the instruction. This may take a variety of forms, including resistance, and, of course, will not always be an eidetic image. The primary response is the true eidetic. It never fails to be repeatable and tends to recur in an almost mechanical manner. It is usually bright and clear, rich in emotional accompaniment, and has a meaning or set of meanings that the individual can usually recognize with some certainty. Any portion of the primary response may be repeated for elaboration or detailed examination. When repeated, it elicits feelings and memories, and after many repetitions, which may be punctuated by resistances and other types of behavior, it may spontaneously be replaced by a new primary that, in turn, through repetition, may give rise to still another primary.

The primaries arising out of repetition of the first primary are termed "underlying primaries." The secondary response, interjected response, and overt behavior are types of reaction that frequently occur between primaries. After a few repetitions, the primary response may suddenly be replaced by material only superficially related to it, such as elements of the individual's ordinary fancy. Such responses are termed "secondary" and are usually used as a defense. Sometimes the individual punctuates the primary response with significant verbal or fantasy material. Ahsen calls this behavior an interjected response and points out that it occasionally contains important depth material of use in structuring therapy. Overt behavior refers primarily to the individual's facial expressions, postures, and other acts that express his attitude toward the imagery experience: For example, he may appear interested, indifferent, or irritated.

Repeated projection of the primary response along with the resultant affective elaboration and eventual replacement of one primary eidetic by another and then another is the crux of the full-length diagnostic-cum-therapeutic technique. It is through this process that actual therapeutic progress is made. The reader will recall that the primary eidetic is accompanied by somatic patterns and affective significations. Repetition of the primary eidetic image results in a fuller experience of these somatic and affective aspects along with the visual component; this process implies the acquisition of a degree of conscious recognition of the connections involved, as well as a rather thorough working-over of the affective reactions. Only when this process has been carried to completion for one eidetic does the therapist begin with another. Thus, each progression or change represents a step forward, a deepening and broadening of understanding and assimilation, an illumination of another aspect of the complex problem that the individual is now prepared to examine.

The experience that emerges in the eidetic treatment often is at variance with the patient's conscious views. For instance, his experience of a parent via the eidetic imagery may differ radically from his conscious opinion of this parent. Generally, this consciousness-imagery-gap (C-I-G), or distortion, is caused by the patient's need to repress a painful experience. Or the distortion may be the result of the parent's brainwashing of the patient.

Once the C-I-G has been uncovered, the next step is to challenge the patient's beliefs and attitudes by confronting him with the contrary perceptions revealed in his eidetics. It is vital to take note of the patient's reactions to this procedure. *Does he deny the existence of a gap, and thus reject change? If he resists, what is the form of his resistance? Does he make an effort to bridge the gap? Is he eager to learn more about the unknown within himself?* The nature of the patient's reactions to the C-I-G clarifies the problem under investigation (Ahsen, 1972).

Recent developments in Eidetic Therapy include Ahsen's (1977a) positive group methods, which can be applied to couples and families. The group methods have been used for inpatients and outpatients (Twente, Turner, & Haney, 1978). Basically this procedure involves a group empathy process by which all members simultaneously work on their own eidetic experiences and offer empathetic responses to the other members' images based on the adoption of the others' content.

There are numerous other eidetic procedures beyond the scope of this chapter. Interested readers are referred to Ahsen's books.

## APPLICATIONS

Eidetic diagnostic and therapeutic procedures can be utilized with all individuals who possess a minimum capacity to form eidetic images. They are best prepared for eidetic work by being exposed to positive images of parents or parent surrogates; for it is important that they are assured they were loved

and accepted when they were children, before exploring negative images. Individuals who persistently resist eidetic images are usually those who are phobic of inner life and emotions. To prepare them for eidetic work, relaxation training and positive nature images have proven to be beneficial.

Patients who report no images can be aided in image formation by the image sculpturing (Jordan, 1975), a process based on recruitment of sensory data from various sensory modalities. One patient who reported no images showed nystagmus of her eyes when closed, a symptom characteristic of individuals who are fearful of their internal states. To aid her in image formation, she was instructed to visualize the activity she enjoyed most. She chose making love to her husband. Instructed to relive any sensory experience involving contact with her husband, she reported first the tactile sensation of her hands on her husband's hairy chest and then the smell of his body. After repetition of these sensory experiences, an image of her husband's face appeared spontaneously, but in tunnel vision. She saw only a vague round image of his nose and eyes and part of his mouth. After further repetition and after she had been instructed to attend to details, the face appeared whole and clear, and this image became progressively richer.

According to the eidetic diagnostic classification system, symptoms often represent a disordered ISM, that is, MIS, MSI, SIM, and SMI. With patients for whom words and meanings (MIS, MSI) or somatization and impulsive discharge of bodily tensions (SIM, SMI) have primacy over images, the therapist enhances the defensive structures and then allows images to appear spontaneously. Once the image grows out of an oververbal description or a somatic response, it is repeated many times, and the therapist points out the simultaneity of image, bodily response, and meaning, and the primacy of the image.

Individuals who are acutely psychotic are usually not capable of sustained focusing on eidetic images, and require supportive care and structure before beginning eidetic work on their own. Eidetic images have been used successfully in treating the extreme splitting and associational problems of schizophrenics, who are known to lack the ability to regenerate experience (Ahsen, 1977a). A continuous series of developmental eidetics over a fairly long period of time often reconstructs a schizophrenic's emotional life and stops and reverses the general splitting process (Sheikh & Panagiotou, 1975). When introduced in a timely manner, Eidetic Psychotherapy can be used successfully with almost all individuals to reevoke the natural flow of eidetic images.

The therapist encourages autonomy and merely serves as a guide in the patient's self-exploration. Initially, while teaching the dialectical method of eidetics, the therapist is quite directive, but the content for therapy flows directly from the patient's consciousness. Excessive transference and dependency are thwarted by the autocatalytic nature of eidetic work, which greatly accelerates therapy.

## CASE EXAMPLE

Mr. Smith, a 34-year-old merchant seaman, suffered from panic attacks characterized by pains in his left shoulder and chest that radiated down his left arm, extreme palmar sweating, and hyperventilation. Frightening hypnagogiclike hallucinations and nightmares also plagued him. These symptoms had begun two years ago following an incident on board ship, in which he had attempted to rescue the first mate, whom he considered to be his closest friend. The rescue attempt was quite heroic: He entered the hull of the ship where his friend had been overcome by gas fumes and attached a harness for hoisting his friend. As he was losing consciousness himself, he heard a loud thud, which upon exploration turned out to have been caused by the falling of the mangled body of his friend. At this point he panicked and ran, but soon he was overcome by gas

fumes and lost consciousness. He was rescued after a nearby ship furnished gas masks. After regaining consciousness, he and the body of his friend were removed by helicopter. He was hospitalized in a foreign port for a mild brain syndrome, attributed to the gas intoxication and his traumatic reaction. By this time, he had begun to blame himself for the death of this friend, even though he was told that the rope hoisting his friend had become snagged and severed during the attempt to pull him to the deck, and that he was in no way responsible for the unfortunate development. After a week's rest, he was flown to the United States where he underwent further hospitalization for his worsening traumatic reaction of quasi-psychotic proportions, marked by nightmares, hallucinations, panic attacks, and self-blame.

While in the hospital, he also began having intrusive daytime reveries. He attempted to relive the accident and particularly to piece together his gas-induced semiconscious moments in the hull of the ship. His failures to reconstruct the accident led to an exacerbation of symptoms and the fixed resolution that he was responsible for his friend's death.

Over the next two years, he consulted three different psychiatrists and two physicians who prescribed muscle relaxants and antianxiety and antipsychotic medication; but none of these reduced his symptoms. During this period, he had tried to return to work on another ship, but he became phobic and incapacitated by panic attacks and was consequently removed from the ship. It is important to note that the panic attacks occurred not only in connection with the phobic stimulus of the ship, but also in other situations.

In the first session of Eidetic Therapy, his symptoms were defined by eliciting eidetic images associated with the accident. Relaxation training was implemented to reduce the extreme tensions, sweating, and hyperventilation episodes associated with his current panic state. Initially his effort was only partially and transiently successful in reducing the symptoms.

In the second session, the Age Projection Test was administered: First the symptoms around his phobia of being on board ship were exacerbated and then he was taken back to a time before the symptoms occurred. He recalled being at home in Jamaica when he was 15 years of age with his mother, combing her hair and pulling out her gray hair for her. When focusing on this image, he became deeply relaxed and the sweating subsided. When associated memories were elicited, he recalled his mother being driven from home by his father and his continuing loyalty to her. Subsequently he commented that he felt responsible for his mother's death. Although he had instructed the shipping company not to inform his mother of his accident, they had ignored his request. He felt certain that the bad news had hastened her death two months later. However, his wife related that his mother had been ill for a year before the accident and that she died six months after his accident. The patient also felt guilty because his extended hospitalization had prevented him from visiting his mother before her death. Although he experienced considerable guilt in regard to his mother, in this session he strongly denied that she had anything to do with his present symptoms. He missed his third appointment due to the increase of his somatic symptoms and the fear that he was going to have a heart attack. It was clear to the therapist that these worsening symptoms represented resistance to admitting the painful core problem: his guilt over his mother's death.

In the third session, the patient's resistance was directly interpreted for him, and he was challenged to experiment further with the positive calming image of combing his mother's hair and pulling out her gray hair. Upon the administration of this image, he again began to have symptom relief: His hands stopped sweating and his muscles began to relax, but the pain in the left side of his chest and in his left shoulder and arm continued. He then reported the image of visiting his mother's grave and talking with her, and in so doing, he developed the con-

viction that she forgave him for not being at her deathbed. Immediately another vague image appeared to him from a recurring dream in which he saw his mother standing at the foot of his bed, saying, "Keep up the good work, son, God loves you." He was asked to repeat this image and these words, but to see his real mother standing in front of him rather than the vague dream image. Upon doing so, all of the pain left first his chest, then his shoulder, arm, and hand, and he felt thoroughly relaxed. He was encouraged to repeat this image in order to see the connection between the positive image of his mother and the disappearance of his symptoms. After he had resolved his guilt over his mother's death, he was able to work through the guilt associated with the death of the first mate and the phobic images related to the ship. He was encouraged to use these positive images if the symptoms recurred. Several weeks later, none of the symptoms that had plagued him for two years had returned.

In this case, as in other cases of the treatment of phobias (Dolan & Sheikh, 1976), and psychosomatic problems (Ahsen, 1968; Sheikh, 1978), a follow-up one or two years later revealed no recurrence of symptoms.

This case graphically illustrates the speed with which the nonlinear process of eidetics identifies the core themes and leads to resolving phobic and panic reactions or other neurotic symptoms. It is to be noted that the patient's earlier attempts at self-treatment through distorted memories and reverie images had failed (Jordan, 1979). It is only through focusing on the eidetic image standing clearly alone or extracted from dreams, hallucinations, memories, and reveries that lasting symptom relief is achieved.

## SUMMARY

Eidetic Psychotherapy represents the most systematic and precise use of the natural images of consciousness in rapidly resolving conflict and promoting creative changes in the personality. Eidetic methods have been successfully employed to treat a wide variety of problems. Psychosomatic disorders seem to respond particularly well to this approach (see Ahsen, 1968; Jordan, 1977; Sheikh, 1978; Sheikh, Richardson, & Moleski, 1979).

Individual and group eidetic therapy methods have also been used extensively by people for their own personal growth. Ahsen's most recent book, *Psycheye: Self-Analytic Consciousness* (1977a), represents the extension of his work in the direction of self-analysis and self-education. He states that "the center of creative and renewal activity in the individual is always his own self, and no high priest of any sort should be allowed to stand between him and that light" (p. vi).

At the core of this process of self-renewal is the eidetic image, which serves as a dissipative structure to promote higher levels of organization and creativity. The eidetic image serves not only to restore the unity of experience seen in the ISM (Image—Somatic pattern—Meaning), but also to dissipate and neutralize the old frozen structures, freeing the individual to respond to the here-and-now demands of life as directed by higher levels of consciousness. While unity is not found among the numerous personality multiples, it is found within the creative experience of the eidetic, which is a reflection of the total unity of consciousness at an ego-transcendent level. This represents the essence of Eidetic Therapy. The eidetic image is a stepping-stone to higher consciousness, a symbol in the service of transcending symbols.

## REFERENCES

Ahsen, A. *Eidetic psychotherapy: A short introduction.* Lahore, Pakistan: Nai Mat Booat, 1965.

Ahsen, A. *Basic concepts in eidetic psychotherapy.* New York: Brandon House, 1968.

Ahsen, A. *Eidetic parents test and analysis.* New York: Brandon House, 1972.

Ahsen, A. Anna O.—patient or therapist? An eidetic view. In V. Franks and V. Burtle (Eds.), *Women in therapy.* New York: Brunner/Mazel, 1974.

Ahsen, A. *Psycheye: Self-analytic consciousness.* New York: Brandon House, 1977a.

Ahsen, A. Eidetics: An overview. *Journal of Mental Imagery,* 1977b, **1,** 5–38.

Allport, G. W. Eidetic imagery. *British Journal of Psychology,* 1924, **15,** 99–120.

Avalon, A. *Tantra of the great liberation.* London: Luzac, 1913.

Dolan, A. T. Eidetic and general image theory of primary image objects and identification processes. *Journal of Mental Imagery,* 1977, **2,** 217–228.

Dolan, A. T. and Sheikh, A. A. Eidetics: A visual approach to psychotherapy. *Psychologia,* 1976, **19,** 210–219.

Dolan, A. T. and Sheikh, A. A. Short-term treatment of phobias through eidetic imagery. *American Journal of Psychotherapy,* 1977, **31,** 595–604.

Hanna, T. Review of Ahsen's books. In *Somatics,* 1979, **6,** 10–11.

Jaensch, E. R. *Eidetic imagery.* New York: Harcourt, 1930.

Jordan, C. S. Image sculpturing. Paper presented at the Eidetic Analysis Institute, Yonkers, N.Y., February 1975.

Jordan, C. S. The assertive person: Assertive training through group eidetics. Paper presented at the American Group Psychotherapy Association Meeting, San Francisco, 1977.

Jordan, C. S. Mental imagery and psychotherapy: European approaches In A. A. Sheikh and J. T. Shaffer (Eds.), *The potential of fantasy and imagination.* New York: Brandon House, 1979.

Lazarus, A. A. Preface. In A. A. Ahsen, *Eidetic parents test and analysis.* New York: Brandon House, 1972.

Lorenz, K. *Studies in animal and human behavior.* Cambridge, Mass.: Harvard University Press, 1971.

Müller, J. *Ueber die phantastische Gesichtserscheinugen.* Coblenz, Germany: Holscher, 1826.

Müller, M. *Natural religion. The Gifford lectures delivered before the University of Glasgow,* 1888.

Panagiotou, N. and Sheikh, A. A. Eidetic psychotherapy: Introduction and evaluation. *International Journal of Social Psychiatry,* 1974, **20,** 231–241.

Penfield, W. The interpretive cortex. *Science,* 1959, **129,** 1719–1725.

Pensinger, W. L. and Paine, D. A. Deautomatization and the autogenic discharge. *Journal of Altered States of Consciousness,* 1978, **3 (4),** 325–335.

Pribram, K. H. *Languages of the brain: Experimental paradoxes and principles in neuropsychology.* Englewood Cliffs, N.J.: Prentice-Hall, 1971.

Prigogine, I. and Nicolis, G. Thermodynamic theory of evolution. *Physics Today,* 1972, **25 (11),** 23–28.

Scobie, G. E. W. Book review of Ahsen, A. Eidetic

parents test and analysis, 1972. *Glasgow Journal of Psychology*, 1974, **12**, 16.

Sheikh, A. A. Eidetic psychotherapy. In J. L. Singer and K. S. Pope (Eds.), *The power of human imagination*. New York: Plenum, 1978.

Sheikh, A. A. and Panagiotou, N. C. Use of mental imagery in psychotherapy: A critical review. *Perceptual and Motor Skills*, 1975, **41**, 555–585.

Sheikh, A. A., Richardson, P. and Moleski, L. M. Psychosomatics and mental imagery. In A. A. Sheikh and J. T. Shaffer (Eds.), *The potential of fantasy and imagination*. New York: Brandon House, 1979.

Twente, G. E., Turner, D. and Haney, J. Eidetics in the hospital setting and private practice: A report on eidetic therapy procedures emplyed with 69 patients. *Journal of Mental Imagery*, 1978, **2**, 275–290.

# CHAPTER 21

# *Encouragement Therapy*

LEW LOSONCY

*Several times I have indicated that there is a connection between a person's manifest personality and his theory of therapy. This is certainly the case with Lew Losoncy, who just bubbles with enthusiasm and who views the whole world with excitement.*

*According to Adlerian theory (and Losoncy, as well as myself and several contributors of this book, is an Adlerian), psychotherapy is mainly a matter of encouragement. Think of it. Is it not true that most people who come for psychotherapy are discouraged, disspirited, defeated, unsure of themselves? Is not fear the common enemy that all psychotherapists face? And is it not courage that we attempt to give people—courage to face life more bravely, to see things as they are, to measure themselves accurately?*

*The essence of this system of therapy is to give clients courage to take an optimistic stance. How Losoncy suggests it be done follows.*

Encouragement Therapy is an optimistic and practical approach to developing responsible, confident, and courageous clients. The main hypothesis is that regardless of which approach therapists use, when all is said and done, the major reason why people change is because they themselves are motivated to change. The primary task in therapy then is to encourage the client's own willingness and determination to change. The raw material for therapy already exists in the client's assets, strengths, resources, and potentially positive life outlook; reorganization is what is required. Reorganization is achieved through developing the client's perceptual alternatives. With fresh perceptions of self, others, and reality, clients begin to recognize the relationship among what they think, what they tell themselves, how they feel, and how they act. This powerful discovery gives them a sense of internal unity, personal control, self-power, and motivation for positive movement. Encouragement Therapy incorporates elements from various schools of humanistic psychotherapies applied in unique ways in each phase of the therapeutic process.

## HISTORY

### Precursors

Bertrand Russell suggested that in the vast realm of the alive human mind there are no limitations. This panoramic vision of human possibilities inspires the thought that somewhere within the client's universe exists a best perceptual and behavioral alternative, regardless of current life circumstances. The therapist, or encourager, continually conveys the theme that the mere fact of being alive represents hope and the possibilities for courageous living. Courageous living reflects the personal belief ''I will determine myself to accept those things that I choose not to change, to move toward changing those things I want to change, and to select my directions with efficiency and courage.'' This, of course, is recognized as a variation of a popular creed.

The value of courageous living has been addressed for centuries. The Stoics, about 2,000 years ago, set the stage for recognizing the importance of the ''human viewer'' in what has become known as the philosophy of Phenomenology. The Stoic Epictetus concluded that ''No man is free who is not master of himself.'' Discouraged people are not free, but rather are slaves to their own perceptual myopia. Encouragers help their clients to regenerate their perceptual and behavioral life alternatives to overcome their discouragement. Alternatives are the gifts of being human, yet these gifts are rarely appreciated by discouraged people who choose to function as part-time humans. The unlimited power of the courageous person to overcome current circumstances was further supported by Epictetus in his comment that ''Men are not disturbed by things, only thinking makes it so.'' Later this theme was echoed by the Roman emperor Marcus Aurelius, who concluded that ''No man is happy who does not make himself so.''

The strongest voice for Phenomenology appeared 18 centuries later in philosopher Immanuel Kant. Kant discussed the differences between noumena and phenomena. Noumena are things that exist on the outside of the mind. Phenomena, however, are what the mind eventually brings home from this complex arrangement of noumena. Thus, while an ''optimistic'' and a ''pessimistic'' perceiver may be exposed to the same noumena, each brings home a different phenomenon. And while both may be in error, it is ultimately the perceiver's phenomenology that influences behavior. It is this phenomenology that stimulates the interest of Encouragement Therapy.

Indebted to the contributions of the Phenomenologists, Encouragement Therapy-turned toward those writers emphasizing active self-determinism and personal responsibility. Alfred Adler, the most impor-tant precursor to Encouragement Therapy, wrote to a pupil:

Do not forget the most important fact that not heredity and not environment are determining factors. Both are giving only the frame and the influences which are answered by the individual in regard to his styled creative power. (Ansbacher & Ansbacher, 1956, p. xxiv)

Encouragement Therapy also drew on the work of the Existentialists. On this issue of personal responsibility, Sartre wrote that ''Man is nothing else but what he makes of himself'' (1957, p. 15). People are viewed as responsible creators of their feelings, thoughts, actions, and life meanings. The best guess of where a person really wants to be in life is where that person *is;* the final proof that the person wants to be somewhere else occurs at the moment that the person sets foot on the new ground (Losoncy, 1981). As Sartre asserted, ''There is no reality except in action'' (1957, p. 32). Courageous living is ultimately measured by action toward stated goals.

### Beginnings

Personality theorist Robert White saw encouragement as the essential ingredient in any efficacious therapeutic process. This comment perhaps was influenced by Alfred Adler, who was the first to recognize the significance of encouragement as a therapeutic tool (1959). Even today the emphasis on encouragement in relationships maintains deep respect in the growing Adlerian following.

One of Adler's pupils, Rudolf Dreikurs, further detailed the techniques and process of encouragement (Dreikurs, 1968; Dreikurs & Grey, 1968; Dreikurs & Soltz, 1967). Dreikurs continually spoke of the importance of encouragement. The first book devoted totally to encouragement was *Encouraging Children to Learn,* co-authored by Don Dinkmeyer and Rudolf Dreikurs in 1963. This book shows how the techniques of encouragement can be applied to enhance learning. Walter O'Connell writes, lectures, and conducts workshops on encouragement, providing some empirical support for its use (O'Connell, 1975; O'Connell & Bright, 1977). O'Connell concludes that encouragement is a lifelong process of expanding self-esteem and social interest. This writer wrote two books devoted solely to encouragement: *Turning People On: How to Be an Encouraging Person* (1977) and *You Can Do It: How to Encourage Yourself* (1980). In essence, I explicated that the process of encouraging others and encouraging oneself is essentially the same. Dinkmeyer and I combined efforts to co-author *The Encouragement Book: On Becoming a Positive Person* (1980), a phase-by-phase and skill-by-skill breakdown of the encouragement process.

Encouragement Therapy incorporates elements from different humanistic schools of psychotherapy. The first phase of encouragement is heavily steeped in the ideas of Carl Rogers (1961), and uses relationship-building skills such as empathy, genuineness, respect, and unconditionality. The second phase of encouragement, or client perceptual expansion, shows the influence largely of Alfred Adler (1959), Albert Ellis (1962), and Charles Zastrow (1979). The third, or action phase of encouragement, can be recognized as being similar to Reality Therapy (Glasser, 1965). The final phase of encouragement is client self-encouragement.

The complete roots and beginnings of encouragement are too numerous to mention, and perhaps even to be aware of. Encouragement Therapy's biggest contribution may be in putting elements of many therapies together in a way that is believed to lead most effectively to client responsibility, confidence, courage, and motivation to change.

## CURRENT STATUS

The Institute for Personal and Organizational Development (IPOD) is a center for the study and teaching of encouragement. Although the institute was formed only in 1978, the ideas on which it is based have been studied and practiced by this writer since the early 1970s. IPOD is devoted to: (1) the scientific study of encouragement; and (2) the teaching and practice of encouragement with individuals, groups, and ultimately, the total community.

Encouragement Therapy has grown out of the Encouragement Training Program offered at the institute. Encouragement Training is a skills approach to encouraging self and others. In its approach, Encouragement Training has drawn from the Human Relations Development Program of Gazda and associates (1973) and Microcounseling as developed by Allen Ivey (1971).

One focus of Encouragement Training (ET) is on the many groups in the community that, despite touching many lives every day, have not been viewed as helping professions. As of this writing, for example, thousands of hairstylists throughout North America have received Encouragement Training. Other groups such as bank tellers, bartenders, secretaries, waitresses, and volunteers have experienced ET as well.

In those professions that are more traditionally viewed as helping professions, ET has recently received widespread popularity. In schools, for example, thousands of teachers, administrators, board members, students, custodians, and cafeteria workers have received ET.

In the criminal justice system, administrators, police officers, guards, caseworkers, social workers, and counselors, as well as prisoners, have been trained.

Encouragement therapists believe that, to have an impact, any program ultimately needs the involvement of the total community.

If our ultimate goal is an encouraging society which will tap everyone's best—and to be encouraging means to be willing to give and take the best in human relationships—then everyone needs to be included, and no longer do the behavioral scientists have a right to hoard all of the human nourishment. (Losoncy, 1981)

Encouragement Therapy is a more in-depth extension of Encouragement Training and is limited to those individuals who already have a background in education, counseling, social work, and related areas. Therapeutic training is conducted in conjunction with an agency, school, or organization. IPOD is in the process of developing formal certificate programs in Encouragement Therapy.

## THEORY

Discouraged people are viewed as being unmotivated to change rather than being incapable of change. The encouragement therapist recognizes that this immobilization makes sense in light of the client's total phenomenology. How can discouragement possibly make sense? First of all, there are many fringe benefits to immobilization, including the comfort found in routine. Change provokes uncertainty and is thus anxiety producing (May, 1977). A second fringe benefit includes social rewards, such as attention and sympathy that the discouraged person receives (Losoncy, 1980). Third, the client has been busy, perhaps for years, selectively gathering beliefs about self, others, and reality, both consciously and unconsciously to support his or her discouragement. It is these personal beliefs that play the song to which the person's emotions and actions dance (Losoncy, 1981).

To remain discouraged, the client needs to keep two themes alive. The first is ''I am not responsible for my life.'' The second is

''I am a worthless and incapable person who has no assets, strengths, or resources.''

This first theme, *irresponsibility,* is seen when the client continually blames other people, the world, or the past for his or her current life. I (1980) distinguish four types of blame: group blame (e.g., the Russians, Society, the Americans); person blame (e.g., ''He hit me first''); thing blame (e.g., ''This weather makes me miserable''); and self-blame (e.g., ''Because I did a rotten thing, I am a rotten person''). Responsibility, as opposed to blaming, involves taking the position that ''I am responsible for moving in a task-involved way to accept or change those things in my life that I choose. It is up to me! What is my first step?''

Irresponsibility might be revealed in the client's talk, emotions, or actions. Encouragement Therapy uses a model such as Table 1 to demonstrate the role of beliefs in life functioning. While each of these components functions interdependently and perhaps simultaneously, Encouragement Therapy takes the position that directly changing beliefs is the most efficient and effective approach. Imagine the impact of a person's courage when he or she starts dancing to the song of responsible as opposed to irresponsible beliefs!

The other discouraging belief is ''I am a worthless and incapable person who has no assets, strengths, or resources.'' This person has chosen a rigid negative identity of self (e.g., ''I'm the kind of person who always . . .'') as well as finalized generalizations about other people and the world (e.g., ''It's a dog-eat-dog world''). In their liability-oriented identity, discouraged people believe they have no chance to win a battle, solve a problem, find a solution, or even move

**Table 1.  Role of Beliefs in Life Functioning**

| Components of Self | Beliefs (Talk) | Emotions | Actions |
| --- | --- | --- | --- |
| Irresponsibility | If only it weren't for . . . | Anger, depression | Immobilization or retaliation |
| Responsibility | It's up to me, wherever I am, to move ahead | Anxiety of possibilities, exhilaration | Courageous movement toward goals |

toward a possible solution. They lack confidence in their own abilities (Dinkmeyer & Losoncy, 1980). Instead of focusing on the constructive steps they could take toward reaching their goals, their energies are consumed contemplating the hazards of failure.

The confident person, contrarily, concludes that "I am a complex bundle of talents and possibilities. I have many resources within me and it is up to me to energize these strengths. I always have the ability to perceive any given situation in many different ways and choose the best one for me." People with this rich vision of life have "perceptual alternatives" (Losoncy, 1977, 1980, 1981). It is at that exact moment when people are generating new perceptual alternatives that their humanness is fully validated. When responsibility and confidence are present, courage, which is risk-taking movement toward stated goals, is more likely to occur. Courage is witnessed at that moment when people hold their nose and jump with total commitment into a fuller self (Losoncy, 1981). On this note, French philosopher Jacques Maritian concluded that "a coward flees backward away from new things while a man of courage flees forward in the midst of new things."

How does this backward movement or discouragement occur? Are humans born discouraged, or do they become discouraged through life experiences?

## Origins and Dynamics of Discouragement

Humans are born partly courageous and partly discouraged. They are courageous to the extent that they willingly take risks to move in new ways within their physiological limitations. Their courage, however, is indiscriminate and irresponsible. They lack responsibility because their needs must be ministered to by others if they are to survive. So it is impossible for the young child to feel that "It's up to me." Despite the fact that they lack responsibility, newborns have the potential of developing confidence through perceived mastery over their environment.

The ideal encouraging atmosphere is one that "invites"* the development of responsibility and nourishes the potential for confidence, without destroying the original energy toward courageous movement.

## Encouraging Responsibility

The most powerful invitations for the development of client courage come from the social environment. Thus, while newborns are incapable of assuming responsibility ("It's up to me"), they have the potential of slowly developing a more responsible outlook. In an environment where children are dominated, are rarely allowed to make decisions, aren't given appropriate responsibility, and don't perceive that their actions can have a direct and positive impact on anything, they feel powerless.

By the same token, children may become irresponsible when they believe that the world revolves around them. Parents symbolically represent what children begin to expect from the world. The more inaccurately parents represent reality, the more likely children will develop discouraging beliefs.

Much discouragement is a result of two basic mistaken beliefs about self, other, and life. The first error is in the failure of people to face and accept reality as it is and the second major mistake is in the failure of people to realize all of the possible alternatives available to them once they face and accept that reality. (Losoncy, 1980)

Responsibility is encouraged by helping people to realize "It's up to me to accept those things I choose not to change, to change those things I select, and to choose courageously and efficiently." The encouragement therapist is a healthy representative

---

*Encouragement Therapy refers to external factors as invitations rather than causes, to be consistent with what I (1980) call S—You—R Psychology. That is, in the end, people's responses are determined by their choice at "You" and are not automatically the result of the stimulus.

of reality who shows how new beliefs, talk, emotions, and actions "make sense."

## Encouraging Confidence

The primary material to encourage already exists within the client's assets, strengths, resources, and potentially positive life outlook. Confident people move forward by vigorously generating fresh perceptions of their possibilities. However, discouraged people, believing that they can't change, focus on their liabilities. Yet, as John Dryden said, "When there is no hope, there can be no endeavor."

Newborns have the potential for confidence through perceived mastery over their environments. Observe the young child's expression the first time he or she successfully uses a spoon without anyone's help! Through their experiences, children begin to conclude "I'm capable at this" or "I'm no good at that." Their identity begins to emerge from their perception of these experiences.

There are numerous ways for children to begin to see themselves as incapable rather than as capable. When they perceive that they are worthwhile only when they perform well and succeed, they begin to lose confidence and shy away from those areas where they see themselves as incapable. This discouraging trend is especially noted at the onset of school, where the focus is on the number of wrong answers rather than the effort made. When heroes, successes, and perfection are valued, the only way to avoid a humiliating defeat is to choose discouragement and give up. The child concludes "I am incapable and have no assets," often generalizing this discouraging conclusion to other areas of life. And how does someone who is incapable act? They don't! Any thought of risking change provokes anxiety and fear of failure. The person buys safety at the cost of life.

Confidence is the feeling of complexity and personal effectiveness and comes from a personal reservoir of perceived past suc-

cesses. As people become sensitive to all of their vast potential to behave in new ways, they are impressed with the personal power constantly within their grasp (Dinkmeyer & Losoncy, 1980).

Through perceptual alternatives offered during therapy, the client develops a new vision of self, others, and reality. The client begins looking at life through new eyes. Consequently, all events are viewed more productively. With the combined feeling of responsibility ("It's up to me") and confidence ("I am complex, capable, and have many strengths, assets, and resources"), the client becomes self-motivated to change.

## Process of Encouragement

As mentioned earlier, Encouragement Therapy incorporates ideas from various schools of humanistic psychotherapy. The therapist's approach changes according to the phase of the process. Phase one of Encouragement Therapy places emphasis on understanding the client's emotions. Since emotions are viewed as the servants to a person's beliefs, understanding how the client feels helps the therapist to identify the underlying discouraging beliefs. In phase two, cognition focusing, clients are invited to recognize the effects of their beliefs on their emotions and actions. This is accomplished by developing their perceptual alternatives, thus enriching their view of self, others, and reality. With these new perceptions, clients become more responsible and confident. When clients internalize these two conclusions of responsibility and confidence, the process moves to phase three, action focusing.

In phase three, the therapist is interested only in action toward stated goals. Here the client explores possibilities, develops plans, makes a commitment, sets goals, acts, and evaluates the action.

The final phase is holistic focusing. With their new feelings, thoughts, and actions, clients recognize the relationship between what they think, say, feel, and do. This powerful discovery gives them a sense of internal unity, personal control, self-power, and motivation for courageous action. They are independent, even of the therapist, and experience what John Mierzwa (1979) calls the ultimate gift of therapy, "freedom."

## METHODOLOGY

The attitudes of encouragement therapists are as important in inviting client change as are the techniques they use. So, before proceeding to a discussion on the skills and techniques of the therapist and the phases of the encouragement process, a few comments on how the encourager views clients are in order.

### Attitudes of the Encouragement Therapist

Psychotherapy is done by therapists who are, beyond everything else, people themselves. Just as the beliefs of clients effect their talk, emotions, and actions, so do the beliefs of therapists effect the encouragement process. So important are the attitudes of the encourager that it is doubtful that one could be successful in motivating clients without a positive view of life. In general, the main difference between clients and therapists is that therapists have more perceptual alternatives, or a richer vision of self, others, and reality. When the perceptual field of the therapist is constricted and closed, the needs of the client are shunted aside. Consequently, much of the work of the therapist is in living life in an open, responsible, and confident way. What are those therapist attitudes that tend to invite client courage?

For the sake of space only a few productive attitudes will be mentioned. A more detailed analysis of therapist attitudes is found in my *Encouragement Therapy: A Positive and Practical Approach to Developing Responsibility, Confidence, and Courage.*

1. Clients are viewed as discouraged rather than as suffering from psychopathology (Mozak & Dreikurs, 1973).

2. Whenever possible, therapists avoid data about clients that may limit their perceptual alternatives regarding their possibilities (Losoncy, 1981).

3. The therapist's job is to make clients stronger and independent, as opposed to weaker and dependent (Rogers, 1961).

4. The therapist's beliefs or expectations about the client play an important role in therapeutic outcome (Losoncy, 1977).

5. While clients are viewed as being responsible for their behaviors, they are not blamed for them (Dinkmeyer & Losoncy, 1980).

6. The therapist's reactions play an important role in inviting or disinviting further client exploration (Festinger, 1954).

7. When therapists are imperfect and vulnerable human beings, clients are given permission to be the same (O'Connell & Bright, 1977).

8. Clients have many strengths, assets, and resources that need to be recognized and communicated to them to develop their confidence (Dinkmeyer & Losoncy, 1980; Losoncy, 1977).

9. The client's interests are important sources of motivation to be used in the therapeutic process. The task is to make the connection between these interests and the client's strengths, assets, and resources (Losoncy, 1981).

### Process of Encouragement

Encouragement Therapy incorporates elements from various schools of psychotherapy, each employed in different phases of the process. Each phase focuses on certain components of the client, uses specific therapist skills, and demands unique approaches to achieve the desired therapeutic outcome for the phase. The client's pace determines movement through the various phases.

***Phase 1.*** This phase consists of relationship building and exploration (affect focusing). The initial phase of Encouragement Therapy draws largely from what has become known as Person-Centered Therapy as developed by Carl Rogers (1961, 1977). The therapist focuses primarily on the emotions of the client in an accepting, nonjudgmental manner. Through empathic understanding, respect, and warmth, the therapist seeks to create a relationship in which the client can be who he or she really is. Total acceptance or unconditional positive regard enables the client to explore nondefensively his or her real underlying concerns. Since the client's first stated problem is often only the tip of the iceberg, attempts to solve this problem are often naive. If the client is understood, and not judged, with this initial problem, he or she is likely to conclude that there is a green light to explore further.

Encouragement therapists also are enthusiastic about the concerns and interests of their clients. If the therapist understands—really understands—what clients are feeling when they proudly present their new idea or their good news, the therapist can hardly be anything but enthusiastic. The encouragement therapist is not afraid of his or her positive emotions and can express them (Dinkmeyer & Losoncy, 1980).

Some approaches used in phase 1 include reflection of feeling, encouraging clients to turn what they have just said into feelings, focusing on the client's interests, and looking for client's claims to fame.

Encouragement Therapy moves from the focusing on affect to the second phase, or cognition focusing, when the therapist concludes that the client feels accepted, understood, and ready to take on the challenges of looking at self, others, and reality in new ways. This second phase has been influenced by Rational Emotive Therapy as developed by Albert Ellis (1962) and by Self-Talk Therapy as discussed by Charles Zastrow (1979).

***Phase 2.*** This phase consists of expanding client perceptions (cognition focusing).

Focusing initially on the client's emotions serves two purposes. First, it helps the client feel understood and accepted. Second, through an understanding of the client's emotions, the therapist gains insights into the client's beliefs. Beliefs—talk—emotions—action. So while the therapist empathizes with the emotions of the client, the goal of phase 2 is to help the client to reach a new, higher-level outlook on these self-defeating negative emotions, such as hurt or anger. Personal responsibility and confidence develop as clients begin to realize that they play a role in creating their misery and they can play a role in pulling themselves out of misery. Personal power is experienced as they come to conclude that their view of life affects how they feel about life.

Perceptual alternatives are the different ways of looking at and giving meaning to any situation (Losoncy, 1977). The therapist invites the development of the client's perceptual alternatives by focusing on the client's strengths, assets, and resources. Both the client and the therapist identify client assets, resources, and potentials. This is the primary material used to develop client confidence to change. Even those characteristics that are at first glance viewed as liabilities can be turned into assets. For example, a stubborn person might also be seen as persistent or determined. Encouragement therapists are similar to talent scouts who are able to envision the potential of clients and who then try to motivate them. They search for "talents in the raw" or "diamonds in the rough." As clients begin to feel that they are complex and have many assets, they are more likely to develop the confidence and courage to change (Dinkmeyer & Losoncy, 1980).

After assets have been internalized and the client's perceptual alternatives are developed, the therapist raises questions to encourage personal responsibility. The therapist asks, "Who or what are you currently blaming that is holding you back from taking personal responsibility for your life?" Other questions might include: "How much of your immobilization is related to how you look at your current circumstances? How many other ways do you think you could look at that? Which way is the most productive? What are your assets? How can you use your assets to overcome your current circumstances to reach your goals?'' And, of course, the bottom-line question is, ''Is your current situation something you choose to change, or do you choose to accept it?'' This is the question that brings the client to the crossroads (Losoncy, 1981).

When clients develop responsibility (''It's up to me'') and confidence (''I am a complex and capable person with many assets''), they are ready for phase 3 of the encouragement process.

**Phase 3.**   This is the phase of planning, commitment, and movement (action focusing). The client has been understood and accepted and has developed a richer vision of self, others, and reality. With this newfound responsibility and confidence, the client is brought to the insight that he or she can only be known by actions. A universe of well-intended thoughts, words, and feelings is not equal to one step in a positive direction (Losoncy, 1981).

Drawing from Reality Therapy (Glasser, 1965) during this phase the therapist focuses on the actual behavior rather than thoughts or feelings. The therapist keeps asking the questions: ''What are you going to do?'' and ''When will you do it?'' The encouragement therapist goes through nine stages in this action phase of the process: (1) exploring all of the perceptual and behavioral alternatives; (2) encouraging the client to develop a plan; (3) encouraging a total client commitment; (4) setting specific goals, which include times and places whenever possible; (5) reaffirming client responsibility and confidence; (6) encouraging client action through effort rather than focusing on success or failure; (7) nourishing client pride or ''celebrating'' the action (in the case of no action, starting again in an earlier phase); (8) task-

involved evaluation of action; and (9) commitment to new action.

**Phase 4.**   This is the freedom phase (holistic focusing). The ultimate goal of Encouragement Therapy is client responsibility and confidence. While this outcome is achieved through the assistance of the therapist, in the end the process is only successful when the client becomes self-encouraging. It is at this point that the client concludes ''It's up to me and I can do it!''

Freedom is the feeling of personal control over one's life. To accomplish this, the therapist focuses on the total person (holism) and helps the client to recognize the relationship between what he or she thinks, says, feels, and does. This enlightening realization gives the client a sense of internal unity, personal control, self-power, and motivation for positive movement. When this goal is achieved, the condition of the central hypothesis of Encouragement Therapy has been met: In the end, the major reason why people change is because they themselves are motivated to change.

## APPLICATIONS

Encouragement Therapy agrees with Gordon Paul's comment on treatment applications. Paul (1967, p.111) asked, ''What treatment, by whom, is most effective for this individual with that specific problem, under which set of circumstances?''

Encouragement procedures might be justified for most nonorganic problems if one's starting point is ''Where are you now and what is your next reasonable step?'' Yet it may not be the most effective and efficient approach. The encouragement therapist is advised to be knowledgeable in many schools of psychotherapy. Keeping in mind Paul's basic question, the encouragement therapist is well aware that no single form of treatment can claim a monopoly on client improvement. Research from emotive, cognitive, and behaviorally oriented approaches has affected Encouragement Therapy, and has become what could be called a school with primary cognitive emphasis but with strong emotive and behavioral components (phases one and three).

In general, Encouragement Therapy is not the most efficient treatment with properly diagnosed, seriously disturbed clients. In this category are included: (1) organic problems; (2) disorders with accompanying hallucinations; and (3) severe depression that leads to an unbending morbid life outlook and failure to internalize resources. Even in the last instance, however, Encouragemnt Therapy proceeds with the first-line hypothesis that movement is possible.

Encouragement Therapy is most effective with the discouraged person who lacks positive motivation. People suffering from what is currently called "existential neurosis," or problems in living, can be assisted to develop meaning and goals in life. Discouraged people who are faced with major life adjustments (return to school, divorce, loss of loved ones) can be helped to develop courage to face these challenges. People lacking confidence in their own abilities can be given new ways of looking at themselves, others, and life that are more productive. Encouragement Therapy has potential for use in the schools with underachievers and timid students. Even school phobics have been sucessfully treated with this therapy. As a matter of fact, Encouragement Therapy groups have been used with students, teachers, administrators, and school board members.

Clients traditionally classified as "psychopaths" have been taught more responsible attitudes and action through encouragement. Clients with drug-related problems as well have been encouraged to develop self-confidence and responsibility to become dependent on self, rather than peers and drugs.

In general, Encouragement Therapy has promise as a treatment procedure in most cases where the client needs responsibility, self-confidence, and more positive and productive ways of looking at self, others, and life.

## CASE EXAMPLE

Eugene was a 16-year-old high school junior with above-average intelligence, but a history of near school failure and repetitive discipline problems. His peers viewed him as the class clown who would take on any illegal challenge in school. His frequent classroom disruptions had his teachers at wits' end, and much of his time was spent in the disciplinarian's office. He was on the verge of being expelled several times, but his charm managed to keep him in school. An excellent football player, if Eugene managed to remain in school for his senior year, he would probably be elected captain of the football team. Eugene had a poor self-concept, referring to himself as an "idiot." He talked freely of being in the bottom fifth of his school class and, at grade time, he would flash his report card to everyone, revealing his failure.

The first therapist who saw Eugene described him primarily as an "attention getter" with psychopathic tendencies. Eugene told the therapist that he had no problems and didn't see why he had to go to a therapist since he wasn't insane. (Before you allow some of the information to limit your perceptual alternatives of Eugene's possibilities, review the list of therapist attitudes in the "Methodology" section. This will provide a background for understanding the handling of the case.)

Another school therapist, F, was aware of his colleague's difficulties in dealing with Eugene and felt he would like to try a new approach in working with the difficult teenager. F felt that to be effective in treating Eugene, he needed to initially win the boy over. (The encouragement therapist believes that to be an effective therapist you need to have the presence and the willingness and cooperation of the client.)

Passing Eugene in the hallway, F enthusiastically patted him on the shoulder, congratulating him on his touchdown the previous weekend. He encouraged Eugene to talk about how it felt, how he accomplished it, and what the coach and the other players said to him about it (empathy, claims to fame). F pointed out to Eugene what a positive contribution his accomplishment made to the school (focus on contribution). F closed the conversation by asking Eugene if he had ever thought of playing college football. Eugene looked astonished at this thought and quickly responded, "Me, go to college? You must be kidding." F empathically answered, "Sounds like you have ruled college out for yourself. I hope whatever you do, Eugene, that you make full use of that unlimited brain that you have. If you'd ever combine your brains with your leadership talents, watch out world!" (empathy, respect, confidence, enthusiasm). F concluded by inviting Eugene to his office if he wanted to talk more about next week's game.

The seeds for an encouraging relationship were planted with the early relationship skills of empathy, warmth, respect, enthusiasm, and claim-to-fame focusing. It was no surprise that Eugene arrived two days later to see F. Part of the dialogue of this first session is included to demonstrate F's use of perceptual alternatives.

F:   You sure have the ability to influence people.

E:   Me? What do you mean?

F:   Well, the other day for example. You had two of your teachers so upset they lost control of themselves.

E:   (Not sure how to respond) Oh? That's a talent?

F:   Sure is. I mean, I believe that if you wanted to, you could probably amass the forces to put this school in a state of attack alert. That's what I mean by influence and by your leadership talents [turning liability into asset]. It must feel good to be that powerful [empathy].

E:   Yes, sometimes I guess. But usually I wind up getting into trouble because nobody understands, and I mean the, uh, stupid rules. I'm always in Mr. G's [principal's] office.

F:   Sure must take a lot out of you constantly defending yourself. Boy, I guess talents can work against people at times. Is there any way you could use your leadership skills that wouldn't wind up giving you more trouble than pleasure? [perceptual alternatives].

E:   (thinking) One way is as captain of the football team. There I could lead and not get into trouble.

F:   Yes, I could see a smile on your face the other day when we talked about football. Football sure means a lot to you [empathy]. I'm looking forward to getting the inside scoop from you on next week's game [you are important and contribute in positive ways].

Another Session:

E:   The other day you said something about me going to college. Were you putting me on? I mean, me and college! Have you looked at my grades?

F:   I've looked beyond your grades. I've looked at you. I've seen what you can do. College success requires intelligence, determination, responsibility, and confidence. You have the intelligence. Playing safety and halfback requires intelligence. Your IQ supports this. And determination—Eugene, when you make up your mind to get something, you get it.

E:   But you said a couple of other things, I think, responsibility and something else.

F:   Yes, responsibility and confidence. Responsibility is using your intelligence in a courageous way. It takes a gutsy person to say "I will take responsibility for everything about me—not blaming anyone else for my life.'' Irresponsibility is just thinking about the moment, not thinking ahead.

E:   (laughs) You know what, Mr. F? The other day when I threw that cherry pie at Mrs. J, it was kind of funny, but I guess I wasn't thinking beyond the moment.

F:   Yes, you probably thought, ''She'll be impressed with this and perhaps will ask me if she should write a recommendation for college for me, huh? [humor]. (Both laugh.) You sure learn fast, Eugene [focus on strength].

E:   (seeing time is up) Can we talk again soon?

When F felt that Eugene had internalized the perceptual alternatives of responsibility and confidence, they discussed the possibility of Eugene's going to college. Eugene had a great fear of being rejected as an applicant. The therapist encouraged Eugene to forget his past record and to say responsibly ''What is my next step?'' Eugene and the therapist continually enumerated his resources (perceptual alternatives), and Eugene was shown how his beliefs and talk (''It would be horrible to be rejected'') affected his actions. More effective beliefs and talk were developed. When Eugene finally made a commitment to apply, the two ''celebrated'' the decision. Eugene concluded that even if he failed, at least he tried (effort focusing).

By early in his senior year, Eugene's grades had increased an average of 15 points, he served as football captain to a winning season, and presented only one major discipline problem. He applied to six colleges and was accepted by two. Five years after his high school graduation, Eugene wrote to F, telling him that he had completed his master's degree in counseling. Eugene wrote, ''Without you, I would still be fighting the world and walking around feeling like the 'idiot'. When you helped me to realize what I could do rather than what I couldn't, my world changed.''

## SUMMARY

The central hypothesis of Encouragement Therapy is that regardless of which approach therapists use, in the end the major reason why clients change is because they themselves are motivated to change. Encouragement therapists seek to motivate client action by developing their responsibility (''It's up to me'') and confidence (''I have strengths and assets and I can do it'').

Responsibility and confidence are nourished by helping the client to look at self, others, and the world in more positive and productive ways. Encouragement Therapy is phenomenological in that a person's vision of things is believed to determine his or her actions. By enriching clients' vision through developing their perceptual alternatives, new emotions and actions are believed to follow. Although Encouragment Therapy is primarily cognitive, emotive and behavioral components are addressed throughout the four phases of encouragement.

This optimistic form of helping can be used with most clients to reorganize those assets that are already present. It is believed that Encouragement Therapy makes an excellent adjunct to any form of psychotherapy, especially at the ''moment of movement'' in the client's life. Wherever successful therapy is done by a therapist, some form of encouragment is present.

## REFERENCES

Adler, A. *Understanding human nature.* New York: Premier Books, 1959.

Ansbacher, H. and Ansbacher, R. (Eds.) *The individual psychology of Alfred Adler.* New York: Basic Books, 1956.

Dinkmeyer, D. and Dreikurs, R. *Encouraging children to learn.* Englewood Cliffs, N.J.: Prentice-Hall, 1963.

Dinkmeyer, D. and Losoncy, L. *The encouragement book: On becoming a positive person.* Englewood Cliffs, N.J.: Prentice-Hall, 1980.

Dreikurs, R. *Psychology in the classroom.* New York: Harper & Row, 1968.

Dreikurs, R. and Grey, L. *Logical consequences*. New York: Meredith, 1968.

Dreikurs, R. and Soltz, V. *Children: The challenge*. New York: Duell, Sloan and Pearle, 1967.

Ellis, A. *Reason and emotion in psychotherapy*. Seacaucus, N.J.: Lyle-Stuart, 1962.

Festinger, L. A theory of social comparison processes. *Human Relations*, 1954, **7**, 117–140.

Gazda, G. et al. *Human relations development*. Boston: Allyn and Bacon, 1973.

Glasser, W. *Reality therapy*. New York: Harper & Row, 1965.

Ivey, A. *Microcounseling*. Springfield, Ill.: Charles C Thomas, 1971.

Losoncy, L. *Turning people on: How to be an encouraging person*. Englewood Cliffs, N.J.: Prentice-Hall, 1977.

Losoncy, L. *Encouragement therapy*. In press, Englewood Cliffs, N.J.: Prentice-Hall, 1981.

Losoncy, L. *You can do it: How to encourage yourself*. Englewood Cliffs, N.J.: Prentice-Hall, 1980.

May, R. *The meaning of anxiety*. New York: Norton, 1977.

Mierzwa, J. Personal communication. August 15, 1979.

Mozak, H. and Dreikurs, R. In R. Corsini (Ed.), *Adlerian psychotherapy*. Itasca, Ill.: F.F. Peacock, 1973.

O'Connell, W. *Action therapy and Adlerian therapy*. Chicago: Alfred Adler Institute, 1975.

O'Connell, W. and Bright, M. *Natural high primer*. Chicago: Alfred Adler Institute, 1977.

Paul, G. Strategy of outcome research in psychotherapy. *Journal of Consulting Psychology*, 1967, **31**, 108–118.

Rogers, C. *On becoming a person*. Boston: Houghton Mifflin, 1961.

Rogers, C. *On personal power*. New York: Delacorte, 1977.

Sartre, J. *Existentialism and human emotion*. New York: Philosophical Library, 1957.

Zastrow, C. *Self-talk therapy*. Englewood Cliffs, N.J.: Prentice-Hall, 1979.

# CHAPTER 22

# Feminist Therapy I

LAURA S. BROWN and NECHAMA LISS-LEVINSON

> *Inclusion of this chapter by Laura Brown and Nechama Liss-Levinson was based primarily on political considerations—my desire to give as much exposure to an increasingly urgent point of view in psychotherapy, to the effect that women are the victims of psychotherapy in several dimensions.*
>
> *Certainly, their conclusions may be argued, and probably the two chapters on Feminist Therapy are most debatable. In reading this chapter and the following one by Barbara Forisha, my opinions kept alternating between "Yes, you are right" and "No, you are wrong." In any case, in order to give not only full exposure but double exposure to this point of view, two chapters are presented.*
>
> *Part of the importance of these two chapters relates to the meaning this viewpoint may have for other natural disaffected groups: homosexuals, alcoholics, the very old—and even the very young!*
>
> *If workers in the field of psychotherapy are generally socially oriented and directed to the creation of a better world, the messages in these two chapters should be attended to carefully.*

Feminist Therapy is a philosophical approach to the conduct of therapy, counseling, and consultation that may incorporate a variety of techniques and methods under its basic tenets. As a developing field, it lacks a formal and universally agreed-upon definition. Most feminist therapists are influenced by the following assumptions:

First, that the personal, and thus the therapeutic, is political. That is, all behaviors and experiences should be viewed in the greater sociopolitical context in which they occur. Experiences are not isolated versions of reality but part of the pattern of socialization deriving from society.

Second, that sexism and sex-role stereotyping limit the options available to both women and men.

Third, that therapists should use the insights of political feminism to create new strategies for intervention and new structures for service delivery that will stand in contrast to those therapies that derive their norms from cultural sexism.

Fourth, that a therapist must be aware of and explicit about her or his personal value systems, particularly those values regarding gender-"appropriate" behavior.

Feminist Therapy draws upon the norms and ethics of political feminism as guides to both theory and action. Thus, feminist therapists have a commitment to developing an egalitarian relationship with clients. A feminist therapist delineates the ways in which the client is affected by the culture, as well

---

Order of authorship was randomly determined. We wish to point out that our authorship of this chapter reflects movement activism rather than any claim to Feminist Therapy "stardom." Proceeds from this chapter benefit the Association for Women in Psychology.

as the ways in which she or he has learned to participate in her or his own oppression. Feminist Therapy is not a particular set of techniques. Rather, it is a set of operating principles that influences the very questions the therapist asks, and the choices made in working with clients.

## HISTORY

Feminist Therapy evolved from the second wave of feminism that began in the mid-1960s. Feminist Therapy is the response elicited by the unnerving realization that many women were being harmed by traditional psychotherapy (Chesler, 1972, Tennov, 1973). Broverman and associates (1970) specifically documented that a double standard of mental health for men and women was held by helping professionals. Chesler (1971) offered a stunning analysis of the similarities between a patriach and the therapist in the traditional therapeutic relationship who reinforced passivity, dependence, and helplessness in women seeking to change. Sex bias was evident in personality theory, clinical assessment, and career counseling (Weisstein, 1970). It was difficult not to find evidence of sex bias under any psychological rock that was overturned.

Response to this critique of traditional therapy was multifaceted. Many therapists, sensitized to feminist values, began to incorporate a feminist perspective in their own work (i.e., sex-role analysis, egalitarian relationships, expanded role options). Lerman (1976) noted that therapists throughout the country were "independently arriving at the same concepts and changing their modes of interaction with clients."

Feminist philosophy advised strength through collective action. Professionals and students worked together to form caucuses both within and outside the traditional mental health establishment (American Psychological Association Committee on Women, Ad Hoc Committees on Women of the Division of Counseling Psychology and Division of Psychotherapy of the American Psycholog-

ical Association, Association for Women in Psychology, National Feminist Therapist Association). These groups all worked to provide: (1) further empirical evidence of sex bias and sexism in psychotherapy; (2) forums for the development of feminist alternatives; (3) contact and support among feminist therapists; (4) dissemination of information and education to consumers of psychotherapy; (5) education of colleagues whose consciousnesses had not yet been raised.

Simultaneously, many women began developing alternative care delivery systems, including feminist therapy collectives, battered wives' shelters, rape crisis centers, and women's peer-support and self-help groups. In these settings, professionals and paraprofessionals worked synergistically. For example, after attention was focused on the problem of rape following the first New York Radical Feminists Rape Speakout in 1970, feminist therapists began consulting with rape crisis centers, writing grants, and training rape counselors. In addition, they educated their own colleagues regarding the destructive rape myths to which many had fallen prey. Interactions among participants in the alternative institutions involved reciprocal sharing of knowledge and skills.

Interest in Feminist Therapy, from both professional and consumer perspectives, grew rapidly. The Association for Women in Psychology developed a Feminist Therapy Roster in 1971, providing the first national listing of feminist therapists. However, there was some ideological confusion as to exactly what Feminist Therapy was.

This confusion reflected a strength of the feminist mental health movement, that is, the lack of hierarchical structure or movement "stars." In the absence of a single spokesperson, there was room for evolution and flexibility in the struggle for self-definition. This struggle took place at conferences, forums, workshops, and in shared discussions. In many publications, practitioners shared their feminist principles in general and consciousness-raising in particular (Brodsky, 1973; Rawlings & Carter, 1977; Mander & Rush, 1974; Miller, 1976; Franks & Burtle,

1974). Certain ideas (i.e., personal is polit-ical, rejection of traditional diagnostic cat-egories) have become both accepted and ex-plicit values within Feminist Therapy. Still, Feminist Therapy is in the process of con-tinual self-evaluation.

Holroyd (1976) noted that a number of changes in global society were concurrent with the women's movement, including:

secularization, population growth, war, socialist theories, urbanization, advances in health care, economic vicissitudes, and perhaps soon [sic!] a guaranteed right to equal treatment under law. (p.23, brackets added)

These, coupled with consumer awareness and changing sexual values, affected both the women's movement and the development of Feminist Therapy.

Feminist therapists utilize ideas and tech-niques from Humanistic Therapy, Behavior Therapy, Radical Psychiatry, and some of the innovative psychotherapies appearing in this volume. However, as will be explicated in the sections on theory and method, it would be incorrect to say that Feminist Ther-apy developed or evolved from any of these other theories.

## CURRENT STATUS

Feminist Therapy has been a grass-roots phe-nomenon. Its practice is widespread, as judged from the numerous local and national listings of feminist therapists advertised in the feminist press. Estimates of the number of feminist therapists come from the mem-bership rosters of the Association for Women in Psychology and the National Feminist Therapist Association. A conservative guess is that there are 2,000 feminist-therapists in the United States and Canada. This group consists primarily of women. Opinion is di-vided as to whether a man can be a feminist therapist. The moderate view is that a man could be a feminist therapist, depending on his sex-role awareness and willingness to examine his own sexism. Some suggest that a male feminist therapist could particularly

meet the needs of men seeking feminist ther-apy.

Feminist Therapy cuts across professional boundaries, embracing nursing, social work, psychology, and psychiatry. In addition to either professional or paraprofessional train-ing, a feminist therapist may include specific life experiences among her or his credentials. This breadth of criteria reflects the belief that an advanced degree should not be regarded as a necessary or sufficient credential. Some, reflecting a more radical viewpoint, note that standard professional training may serve to obscure the issues of women's oppression that are central to a feminist analysis. Thus, a feminist therapist's formal training gener-ally coexists with a raised consciousness re-garding the influence of sexism in traditional psychotherapy as well as in clients' lives.

There is currently one training center for feminist therapists, the Goddard-Cambridge School for Social Change, that offers a mas-ter's degree concentration in Feminist Ther-apy. Courses in the psychology of women, an important data base for feminist thera-pists, are widely available. However, they are primarily at the undergraduate level. Practica and supervision in Feminist Therapy are available at a small but expanding num-ber of psychology graduate programs and schools of social work.

In lieu of formal training programs, fem-inist therapists have developed new ways of teaching and learning from one another. Many graduate programs now offer training in some of the skills that feminist therapists commonly utilize (i.e., life planning, sex-uality counseling, assertion training). There also exists a mutually advantageous relation-ship between feminist social service agencies (i.e., rape crisis centers, lesbian resource centers, shelters for battered women) and individual feminist therapists. Therapists re-ceive training and supervision, and in return offer low-cost services, consultation, and referrals. The National Feminist Therapist Association conducts written symposia in its newsletter, in which therapists respond in print to previously published case examples that demonstrate feminist therapy principles.

Many feminist therapists create their own training. Often this means organizing peer supervision and support, reading books that other feminist therapists have found helpful, or finding a feminist therapist who will offer training, apprenticeship, and supervision. Recently, some feminist therapists have identified the need for more systematic training, and it seems likely that alternative training collectives and other facilities will become more common as Feminist Therapy further spreads its wings.

At this writing, the only publication that deals solely with Feminist Therapy is the newsletter of the National Feminist Therapist Association. Articles of interest to feminist therapists appear regularly in other publications. These include the newsletter of the Association for Women in Psychology, the newsletter of the Division of Psychology of Women of the American Psychological Association, the *Psychology of Women Quarterly,* and *Sex Roles—A Journal of Research,* as well as two journals of the radical psychiatry movement, *State and Mind* and *Issues in Radical Therapy.* Some journals, including the *Journal of Social Issues,* the *Counseling Psychologist,* and the *Journal of the Orthopsychiatric Association,* have published special issues devoted to the topic of feminist or nonsexist psychotherapy. Much information about Feminist Therapy is presented orally rather than published. The major sources of these data include the annual conference on feminist theory, research, and therapy of the Association for Women in Psychology, the Women's Institutes of the Orthopsychiatric Association, organized by the National Feminist Therapist Association, and the paper sessions sponsored by the Division of Psychology of Women at annual American Psychological Association meetings.

## THEORY

Therapy in feminist terms, then, means healing, not helping. It means working in groups to pool information, and building a base of strength.

There are no experts, no authorities. There are no patients, there are no doctors. There are no labels. There are, instead, facilitators; there are organizers. There are clients, there are clues. Feminism does not exclude individual therapy, but it does say no to the traditional therapist-patient model. . . .

It is harmful for women to be treated as sick, weak and isolated. We want to assume responsibility for our own lives, and this can only be done if we are treated as adults by equals. (Mander, 1977, p. 287)

Another important philosophical position which plays a large part in feminist therapy is the tenet of the feminist movement that the "personal is the political." We help the woman client to differentiate between what she has been taught and has accepted as socially appropriate, and what may actually be appropriate for her. Women have been taught to view difficulties arising out of their socially imposed roles as results of their own personal problems. . . .

Where the more usual therapy encourages clients to introspect and thereby learn to know themselves better, feminist therapy helps its clients look outward as well as inward and differentiate clearly what belongs to the society and is being imposed and what is internal. (Lerman, 1976, pp. 379–380)

The theory of Feminist Therapy differs from most theories of psychotherapy and personality development in that it is actually a philosophy or set of values, which can be integrated with almost any other theory or therapy (Lerman, 1976; Rawlings & Carter, 1977). Feminist Therapy may be likened to the rules of fair play in sports. All players must accept these rules, regardless of what particular sport one engages in. In a similar manner, Feminist Therapy is the "rule of fair play" in therapy.

Only orthodox Freudian psychoanalysis is seen as incompatible with the philosophy of Feminist Therapy (American Psychological Association, 1975). Within Feminist Therapy there exist a number of viewpoints, from the more moderate to the most radical philosophy of feminist theory (Deckard, 1979). Within this range, there is the more moderate view that some consider "nonsexist" (versus feminist) therapy (Rawlings & Carter, 1977), as well as the more radical view that feminism as a philosophy is incongruent with the idea of "therapy" as we understand it (Tennov, 1976).

Despite these variations, there are a number of issues on which most writers in the field are in general agreement (Rawlings & Carter, 1977; Lerman, 1976; Brodsky, 1973; Holroyd, 1976). These points include: (1) the egalitarian nature of the therapy relationship; (2) the importance of identifying external sex-role-related determinants of difficulties, and separating these from internally related problems; (3) taking personal responsibility for change; (4) importance of expanded sex-role definitions and options. An excellent summary of the values of the feminist therapist, adapted from Rawlings and Carter (1977) is presented in Table 1, and explicated in detail in the text.

## Origins of Personality

Feminist theory assumes that an individual girl or boy differs no more at birth than any two individuals, regardless of gender, on psychological measures. Variance contributed by biological, particularly neurological, differences is not ignored but is considered of minor importance in early personality development. As children develop, they receive an *un*healthy dose of sex-role socialization, learning "appropriate" gender behaviors from parents, television, picture books, school, newspapers, greeting cards, *ad nauseum* (Deckard, 1979). It is somewhat surprising, considering this massive socialization, that so few psychological sex differences have been documented as children progress into adolescence (Maccoby & Jacklin, 1974). Major differences do appear at the level of adult functioning. Women in our culture achieve less than men (as defined by male standards), work at lower-status jobs for less pay, and have significantly higher rates of depression, phobias, suicide attempts, and schizophrenia. They also receive at least three times as many Valium prescriptions as men (Chesler, 1972). According to

**Table 1. Values of Feminist Therapy**[a]

1. The therapist is aware of her/his own values.[a]
2. There are no prescribed sex-role behaviors.
3. Sex-role reversals in life style are not labeled pathological.
4. Marriage is not regarded as any better an outcome of therapy for a female than for a male.
5. Females are expected to be as autonomous and assertive as males. Males are expected to be as expressive and tender as females.
6. Theories based on anatomical differences are rejected.
7. The inferior status of women is due to their having less political and economic power than men.
8. A feminist therapist does not value an upper- or middle-class client more than a working-class client.
9. The primary source of women's pathology is social, not personal.
10. The focus on environmental stress as a major source of pathology is not used as an escape from individual responsibility.
11. Feminist Therapy is opposed to personal adjustment to social conditions. The goal is social and political change.
12. Other women are not the enemy.
13. Men are not the enemy either.
14. Women must be economically and psychologically autonomous.
15. Relationships of friendship, love, and marriage should be equal in personal power.
16. Major differences between "appropriate" sex-role behaviors must disappear.

[a]Adapted from Rawlings & Carter, 1977, pp. 51–57.
[b]Numbers 1 to 6 are presumed to be values held by both feminist and nonsexist therapists. Numbers 7 to 16 are assumed to be values held specifically by feminist therapists.

feminist theory, these adult differences are mainly attributable to the oppressive roles to which women are assigned and to the discrimination they face in daily life. The personality traits commonly associated with women (slyness, docility, dullness) are also those associated with minority-group status (Hacker, 1951; Rawlings & Carter, 1977). Some feminist therapists are reexamining the interaction between the female body experience (i.e., menstruation, sexuality, pregnancy, menopause) and adult personality development (Mander, 1977; Washbourn, 1977; Bardwick, 1971). This feminist analysis is distinct from previous deterministic literature, which focused on limitations rather than potentialities.

## Diagnosis, or "Doctor, they say I'm a crazy lady"

Tremendous power rests in the hands of those sanctioned by our culture to label people "crazy." According to Szasz (1960), persons are often labeled "sick" (i.e., suffering from some mental illness) when they don't fit in with the roles prescribed by those in power. Feminist analysis, citing historical examples ranging from witch-burning to clitoridectomy, adds that there may be particular punishment for digression from gender-role norms (Chesler, 1972; Wyckoff, 1977; Szasz, 1960).

Feminist theory rejects the use of traditional diagnostic labels, along with the personality tests used to assist the categorization process. Many diagnostic terms applied to women (e.g., "hysterical") have sexist implications and assumptions, and serve to "mystify," or keep the client at a "professional" distance (Wyckoff, 1977). Feminist Therapy views the definition of the problem as the client's privilege (Lerman, 1976; Wyckoff, 1977; Mander, 1977). "The client tells us what her primary problems are. We don't tell her. She tells us what she's doing about them and if and when she thinks she's made progress. We offer validation, support . . ." (Ferson, 1973, p. 192).

Definitions of mental health also imply power, as they identify an ideal toward which the society strives. Evidence has been presented that mental health professionals in our culture endorse a double standad of mental health. The mentally healthy woman is seen as differing from both the healthy adult male and the healthy adult, gender unspecified (Broverman et al., 1970). Initial attempts to modify this attitude resulted in an androcentric model of mental health, which endorsed stereotypic masculine traits as the ideal for all persons (Rawlings & Carter, 1977). Contemporary feminist theorists favor the andro-

gynous model of mental health (Kaplan, 1976; Bem, 1974). In this model, the individual embraces and integrates the positive aspects of both "feminine" and "masculine" roles. For example, a woman, or man, could be both compassionate and assertive, intelligent and nurturant. She or he would be able to respond in a particular situation based on personal needs and immediate situational demands, rather than because of her or his gender (Kaplan, 1976).

## Changing Women/Changing Men

Feminist Therapy views change as the result of awareness and action in a supportive environment. Awareness includes the discovery of the role of sex-role oppression in the development of problems, as well as the sorting out of issues that may not reflect such oppression. It means taking responsibility for change, without blaming oneself. Action may be taken by an individual or a group, on a personal, institutional, or systems level (Wyckoff, 1977; Gluckstern, 1977).

Feminist Therapy can encourage a woman to change both her self-concept and her behavior. Women often begin seeing themselves as competent and powerful. They become self-affirming, caring for themselves both physically and emotionally. They become more assertive and direct in relationships with others. A number of theorists stress three themes that tend to occur in the course of feminist therapy—anger, self-nurturance, and autonomy (Kaplan, 1976; Lerman, 1976; Mander, 1977).

*Anger.* Generally, women are taught to suppress their anger. Its expression has long been socially proscribed; the woman who does voice such sentiments risks being labeled "bitchy," a "nag," or (courtesy of the popularization of psychoanalytic theory) "castrating." Often anger is turned inward, manifesting itself as an immobilizing depression, or in the form of somatic complaints. Or it may seethe unseen as rage, too frightening to acknowledge. Since feminist theory validates the expression of women's anger as an accurate and healthy emotional response to oppression occurring at both the macro- and microlevels (Kaplan, 1976), Feminist Therapy is an excellent approach for women who experience this difficulty. Many clients who come to Feminist Therapy will comment that they have no memory of expressing anger, although they are intensely self-critical. In Feminist Therapy, they may learn new ways of expressing and channeling these feelings. Wyckoff (1977) has suggested that anger can be used as a source of motivation for collective action and social change.

*Self-Nurturance.*   Women in our society are taught to care for others. They have been the nurturant caretakers of their husbands and children. They often assume the nurturing role with friends, other family members, and in the "service" professions, such as nursing or social work. Little time or energy is left for oneself. Women begin to ignore their own needs or assume that they are unimportant. Those who learn the role well are labeled as "martyrs," sacrificing themselves for the sake of others. Feminist Therapy emphasizes the importance of caring for oneself. Healthy development requires that an individual become aware of her or his own needs and desires. In addition, she or he must learn that giving to oneself is not selfish, but self-loving. Through cognitive restructuring and assertiveness training, women can learn the positive aspects of knowing one's own needs and expressing them to others (Jakubowski-Spector, 1973; Mander, 1977; Wyckoff, 1977).

*Autonomy.*   Feminist therapists support women in their striving toward autonomy. Therapists validate the client's own experience; they trust the client's judgment, enhancing her trust in her own perceptions. Women are encouraged to see expanded role options for themselves and enabled to choose without the heavy burdens of role constriction (Lerman, 1976).

Feminist theory emphasizes change in both the personal and institutional/political level (Gluckstern, 1977). Both the process and end results of institutional change may be cause for feminist celebration. For example, both women and men will have clear benefits from the (eventual) passage of the Equal Rights Amendment (ERA). Lerman (unpublished ms.) has suggested its passage as a form of primary prevention for women's psychological functioning. Involvement in the process of passing the ERA may also cause changes in a person's self-concept, and lead to a reevaluation of one's life style. In addition, such activism leads to skills in financial management, organization, and group development.

## METHODOLOGY

Since feminist therapists vary in their theoretical orientation (they may be gestalt, humanistic, behavioral), it follows that they will vary widely in the procedures or techniques they employ. However, Feminist Therapy does make a fundamental contribution in its view of the psychotherapeutic relationship, as well as the notion of what therapy is and who can practice it (Lerman, 1976; Rawlings & Carter, 1977).

Feminist Therapy demands the equalization of power between the client and the therapist. Clients are assumed to be their own best expert. They define their own problems and set their own goals. They are encouraged to take an active consumer stance with regard to their own therapy. The therapist may suggest a contract in the therapy relationship, clearly specifying the rights and responsibilities of each part (Hare-Mustin et al., 1979). Clients have access to their file, as well as any reports or test results (in the rare instance that they are used). The therapist is consistent in the use of nonsexist language, and shuns diagnostic terms, sexist jokes, or offhand, demeaning remarks about women or men (American Psychological Association, 1975).

In dealing with a woman client, the presence of a competent female role model (in the person of the therapist or other group members) is generally viewed as one of the "curative" factors in feminist process of change (Johnson, 1976). Feminist theories suggest that the therapist needs to have a solid base of knowledge, skills, and values regarding women's lives (Oliver & Hill, 1978). Areas that are considered essential include: sex-role stereotyping, rape, lesbianism, female sexual development, widowhood, divorce, motherhood, career development, aging, battered women, minority women, and career counseling.

Feminist Therapy can be done individually, in couple or family counseling (Hare-Mustin, 1979), or in a group, usually composed exclusively of women. Many theorists prefer the group format, stating that it fosters a sense of sisterhood, trust in other women (and oneself), exposure to varying female role models, and development of collective action (Brodsky, 1973).

Although feminist therapists may use practically any approach or technique to aid a woman in reaching her goals, three procedures stand out as particularly helpful in Feminist Therapy.

### Assertiveness Training

Assertiveness involves standing up for one's own rights, without stepping on the rights of others. It involves the clear, direct, and honest communication of one's thoughts, feelings, and opinions (Jakubowski-Spector, 1973). Assertiveness training addresses itself to the three major theoretical issues previously discussed, helping women to express their anger, to develop autonomy, and to give permission for self-nurturance. Training programs involve both cognitive restructuring and behavioral skill components. A number of programs have been developed specifically for women, sometimes focusing on particular areas such as sexual assertiveness or assertiveness in the job interview (Liss-Levinson, Coleman, and Brown, 1975).

### Life Planning

Feminist therapists provide encouragement and resources for women who are seeking financial autonomy (Rawlings & Carter, 1977). Feminist therapists employ nonsexist techniques to aid in career planning, such as the Nonsexist Vocational Card Sort (Dewey, 1977). They provide support for women as they expand their role options, including realistic coping strategies for dealing with role conflicts. Feminist therapists give women skills for planning for their futures and reclaiming power over their own lives.

### Sex-Role Analysis

Feminist therapists encourage women to become aware of ways in which they are constrained by adherence to traditional sex roles.

As women remedy the sex-role constrictions in their behavior, they discover strengths in themselves that they either had been unaware of or had regarded negatively. These strengths provide an important therapeutic base for pursuing rational and rewarding behavioral alternatives. (Rawlings & Carter, 1977, p. 64)

It should be emphasized that the analysis of sex roles does not remove responsibility for change from the individual. Feminist Therapy expands the limitations of therapy. There is a commitment to sharing of knowledge and skills with others. Alternative institutions are often created and staffed by feminist therapists. Feminist therapists are actively pursuing their work when they are involved in the training of volunteers to work at a birth control center, consulting with police on rape counseling techniques, and developing postmastectomy counseling. Feminist therapists support women helping themselves, for example in gynecological self-help groups or through bibliotherapy.

Feminist theory emphasizes social change and collective political action as means of growth and development for the individual, the collective, and the institution (Gluckstern, 1977). Several theorists adjure the therapist to be involved personally in social action also (Rawlings & Carter, 1977; Wyckoff, 1977).

As can be seen, Feminist Therapy can mean different strategies for different persons. An example adapted from Greenspan (1976) may serve to clarify this. Imagine a woman, employed as a secretary, who is angry, feeling that she is being discriminated against by her boss, both by receiving low pay and by being asked to perform menial duties. All feminist therapists would validate her anger (not assuming that it is either symbolic or a "racket"). Some would suggest assertion training as a method to overcome the discrimination and express resentments. Another would suggest additional vocational skills training and a career change. A third would suggest that the woman organize the other clerical workers for a protest or strike. A fourth would support the woman in instituting a complaint against the employer. Feminist Therapy can be powerful and nurturant in a multitude of ways.

## APPLICATIONS

Feminist therapists, when asked who is best helped by Feminist Therapy, have tended to reply that everyone is best helped by it. Most clients who choose feminist therapists are women (i.e., of 200 requests for a national roster of feminist therapists, four came from men). This partly reflects the erroneous belief that feminism, and thus, Feminist Therapy, is at best of no interest and at worst hostile to men. In fact, Feminist Therapy can be particularly helpful to men who are dealing with such issues as exploring the restrictions of the male sex role, getting in touch with tender feelings, developing egalitarian heterosexual relationships, or becoming active and nurturing parents. Many women choose Feminist Therapy because they feel reassured that they won't reexperience some of the more negative aspects of their previous, traditional therapy. One client put it

succinctly to a female feminist therapist: "I can trust you not to make a pass at me and not to try to convince me that I'll make the wrong choice by going back to school."

Feminist Therapy is appropriate for a wide range of client concerns. In general, Feminist Therapy may be seen as the optimal intervention in any case where a client of either gender is restrained from freedom of emotional, relational, or vocational choice by the boundaries of sex roles, or where the client has been directly victimized by the norms of sexist society. It is particularly suggested in cases where available therapeutic alternatives accept the status quo of sex roles as healthy or correct. A number of issues stand out as particularly well-suited to Feminist Therapy. These include the following.

*Power*.  Women's socialization often includes the notion that, except where sexual access is concerned, women lack power. This manifests itself economically (women earn less than men, have less easy access to credit, and so on), as well as interpersonally. This lack of interpersonal power is seen in language and gesture, and through the invasion of personal space (Henley & Freeman, 1976).

Popular culture provides deceptive models of power, such as Morgan's "Total Woman" approach, which exemplifies the notion that women can be powerful only via sexual manipulativeness. Feminist Therapy would be an appropriate context for a woman to challenge her beliefs about her own lack of personal power and to experiment with powerful behavior that falls outside the generally acceptable patterns for women. Therapy here might include assertion training, referring the client to a women's martial arts class or other physical training activity, or fantasy work to explore and expand the client's awareness of her powerful behaviors. Power is linked, for many women, to another issue, sexuality.

*Sexuality*.  Western culture offers women mixed messages about sexuality. Stone

(1976) has hypothesized that as our culture switched from a matriarchal to a patriarchal religion, we proscribed those forms of sexuality associated with the old beliefs. This put a particular onus on women's sexuality, whose expression had been closely interwoven with goddess worship. Our culture has evolved what James (1971) has described as the ''madonna-whore'' continuum, which limits the sexual roles of women to either virgin/mother or sexual/evil. Liss-Levinson and associates (1975) and Carlson and Johnson (1975) have noted that women are socialized to be sexually unassertive, that is, to not know what their sexual needs and limits are, or to lack the social skills to get needs met or limits set. Barbach (1975) has described the ways in which cultural norms help to develop sexual dysfunction in women.

Feminist Therapy explicitly validates all sexual choices for women (Childs, Stocker & Sachnoff, 1976) and views the awareness and expression of sexuality as a right rather than a privilege (Larson, unpublished ms.). Thus, Feminist Therapy offers women an opportunity to explore the bases of their current sexual attitudes, values, and behaviors, as well as to contemplate the options for future sexual choices. Feminist Therapy ethics explicitly prohibit sexual contact between client and therapist. This prohibition is particularly important in light of evidence (Lerman, 1974) that some traditional therapists will ''prescribe'' sexual intercourse as a cure-all for their female clients with sexual concerns. In Feminist Therapy, the client is free to explore the potential of her sexuality without being sexually exploited.

Feminist interventions in the area of sexuality might include assigning readings on the development of cultural norms about sexuality; asking a client to interview her mother or grandmother about sexual attitudes and values; teaching self-pleasuring techniques; introducing body-image work (to confront social stereotypes about sexuality being only for the beautiful); or referring a client to a women's coffeehouse or dance to begin examination of same-sex attractions.

*Victims of Violence.* Feminist Therapy has responded to issues raised by the women's movement regarding violence against women such as rape, molestation, incest, and battering. Rush's statement (1974) that the victim in these cases is not culpable provided an early model for feminist intervention. Feminist Therapy rejects the notions of the ''seductive'' molested child, the ''deserving'' rape victim, the ''antisexual'' mother who ''causes'' her husband's molestation of their children, the battered woman who has ''provoked'' her own beating. These are identified as the explanatory fictions of a sexist society that has encouraged violence against women to such a degree as to consistently blame its victims for its occurrence. Feminist Therapy sees women who have experienced violence as neither deviant nor unusual, but as similar to all women in sexist cultures, any of whom can be a potential victim of violent misogyny.

Feminist Therapy, in contrast to more traditional approaches, gives the victim explicit permission and support for her anger at her assailant. Rage is viewed as an appropriate response; fear and terror are validated as real, not delusional. Women are encouraged to gain support by speaking with others who have shared and coped with similar brutalization. Therapy may also involve political activity aimed at reducing violence against women in the client's neighborhood or city.

*Depression.* Feminist theorists have pointed to the disproportionately high rates of depression in women as an indication that sex-role constraints may socialize women into depressive symptomatology (Chesler, 1972). Bart (1976) has, for example, given a feminist analysis of ''endogenous'' depression in middle-aged women, tying it to a loss of role function, rather than menopausal hormonal changes. Bart has pointed out that for women middle age heralds the loss of work (as a mother, possibly as a wife), the loss of ''beauty,'' and often the loss of sense of self. In this feminist analysis, an emphasis is put on the existence of real and external restraints on behavior within the sex role. Women are taught by the culture to behave in "appropriately" helpless ways only, and models of failed effort are specifically and carefully delineated in popular literature, cinema, and women's magazines (Gornick & Moran, 1971). Bart also ties depression in women to issues of power and self-nurturance. Feminist interventions increase perceived power and focus on the development of self-nurturance. It is not uncommon for depressed women to echo the sentiment expressed by one of Bart's subjects: "I never did anything for myself; I sacrificed for my children." Feminist Therapy might include assertion training, with an emphasis on making self-statements and asking for needs to be met; career counseling to expand the woman's freedom of vocational movement; or specific nurturing exercises aimed at facilitating the client in learning to respond to her own needs. Some feminist therapists have prescribed political organizing as a good intervention for depression in women (Greenspan, 1976). Feminist Therapy eschews the use of drugs and electroshock therapy; depression's biochemical aspects are not ignored, but viewed in context with sociocultural conditions.

The examples given above are illustrative rather than exhaustive. At this time, the precise limitations of a feminist approach to therapy are unclear, and the possibilities for application seem endless. Feminist Therapy has been used with such diverse groups as chemically dependent women, new mothers, obese women, and severely disoriented (i.e., psychotic) women. Feminist approaches have also been used successfully with men, particularly in those cases where the clients are suffering negative effects of oversocialization in the male sex role (i.e., male alcoholics).

Feminist Therapy assumes that there is no value-free therapy, only value-aware therapists. Because of their awareness of their own values, some feminist therapists may place limitations on the clients with whom they choose to work. For example, it is highly unlikely that a feminist therapist would support a client with a clearly sexist agenda in therapy; or a woman who wished to become more like Morgan's "Total Woman"; or a couple where the man wanted the woman to become less assertive and more dependent. In these cases, most feminist therapists would share their value system with their clients, and explore mutually whether such extreme value differences would yield satisfactory therapy for the clients.

## CASE EXAMPLE*

It is difficult to choose a sample of work that characterizes a "typical" case of Feminist Therapy by its content. The case described here is illustrative in terms of the process and philosophy demonstrated by the therapist, rather than because of the specific techniques used. In this case the therapist had been trained in gestalt, TA, and behavior therapy techniques. Prior to including this case in this chapter, the client was consulted and her permission obtained. She was also asked to share her perspective of what had been helpful in therapy, and her views have been integrated into the description below.

The client, C, was a 41-year-old woman, long divorced, the mother of two adolescent sons. She was unique in many respects. A convert to Judaism, she returned to college as the single parent of young children years before that action had become common, and was a professional in the hard sciences. She had previously been in therapy and sought a feminist therapist at this time because of her concern that a more traditional therapist would respond judgmentally to the central issue she wished to explore, her sexual orientation.

In the initial session, the therapist invited C to get sufficient information about the therapist as an individual so that she could feel comfortable working with her. Being open to questions in this way creates a more equal power relationship. A norm is developed that

*The therapist in this case was Laura Brown.

the client can question any of the therapist's interventions without raising suspicion of resistance. The therapist's value system begins to emerge early on; this allows the client a more informed choice of therapy. In the first session, the therapist also shared with the client literature on her rights in therapy, and made available to C the option of interviewing other therapists if she so desired. The therapist was careful to let C know that she was willing to work with her and also would support C in choosing another therapist if C felt that this would better meet her needs. Thus, at the initial contact, the norm of supporting the client's choices began to be developed.

At the time she began therapy, C felt depressed, and she decided to deal first with her depression. Contracting with a client for the agenda of therapy in this way creates a new autonomy for the client. For C, this was a first step in learning to pay attention to her own needs and to assert them with others. As with many women, she had been well socialized to see her desires for nurturance as "selfishness" and as immensely less important than the needs of her children, partners, co-workers, and friends. For example, she had given away a pet she was attached to because her "boyfriend" hadn't liked it. C was, in addition, fearful of loss of approval from others if she withdrew any of her self-sacrificing support from them. In therapy C learned and practiced self-nurturing skills by making requests for nurturing holding from the therapist, by setting the agenda of sessions, and by dealing, in fantasy work, with her expectations about the responses of her significant others to this new focus on herself. Through homework assignments C learned to transfer these skills from the therapy setting to the rest of her environment. Learning to self-nurture led to concurrent cognitive and behavioral changes; C felt less depressed, was less self-critical, and began to act in ways that would increase the support she got from her environment.

As C began to make herself a more clear priority, she decided to shift the focus of therapy to the important but personally threatening issue of her sexual orientation. C reported that she had been aware of her attraction to other women since adolescence, but had always been fearful of attending to that attraction and terrified of the consequences of acting it out. She had a history of relationships with men that were sexually but not emotionally satisfactory; in fact, her relationships mirrored many of her more basic interpersonal concerns. Because of her strong need for approval from others, she feared that acknowledgment and expression of her same-sex feelings would bring general disapproval, and even ostracism, from the people who made up her social support system. She was particularly afraid of being cut off from her religious community, of which she was an active and prominent member. C had energetically avoided her attraction to women (for example, she would not allow her partners, all male, to sexually arouse her manually or orally because, "If I could respond to that, it didn't have to be a man doing it, and I didn't want to know about that").

C was ambivalent about expressing her feelings in therapy. A previous therapist had indicated that they were inappropriate and should be buried (telling her that she could not possibly be a lesbian, as she was heterosexually active and had children). Feminist Therapy could provide a safe setting for C to explore her feelings, as the therapist, in clearly stating her own values, had indicated to C that she viewed all sexual choices, made consciously, as equivalent in health and goodness. C could proceed with therapy, knowing that any choice she made would receive support as a valid option.

In therapy C explored her fantasies of what her life would become if she chose to identify as a lesbian. This exploration included bibliotherapy (*Lesbian/Woman*, by Martin and Lyons, *Our Right to Love*, by Vida), as well as such homework as a visit to the local lesbian resource center to meet and talk with other women who have experienced similar trepidations and conflicts in their own sexuality. C also investigated Jewish groups to find some that would welcome sexual minority members.

Toward the end of therapy C began to take exploratory steps into the lesbian community. She attended a political meeting, went to a rap group at the resource center, and began to feel more socially confident in this novel setting. She ceased to be fearful of her own needs and was sufficiently self-supportive to feel no longer dependent on the approval of others for her actions. She joined an older lesbian's group to facilitate making friends and social contacts who shared life concerns other than sexual orientation, and began to participate in a Jewish group that had many openly lesbian and gay members. She initiated a relationship with a woman she met in the rap group, and was able to utilize this new learning to actualize the skills she had gained in therapy for meeting her own needs in the context of a relationship. C reported that she no longer felt depressed and saw herself as now having coping skills with which to handle occasional emotional lows. Her self-acceptance was mirrored in the positive response that her "coming out" evoked from her children and friends, and in her increasing position of leadership within her newly chosen peer group. Therapy was ended by mutual agreement between client and therapist, with C expressing her satisfaction with therapy and her ability to solve problems on her own.

What made this Feminist Therapy? How did the conduct of this case differ from that deriving from other approaches? Several attitudinal issues stand out. From the beginning, power was invested in the client. The therapist was not mysterious about herself or her values. Of equal importance, she conveyed respect for C's values and choices while maintaining the integrity of her own value system. The therapist provided a model of value-awareness.

C was neither labeled nor diagnosed; she defined her problem and her goals in therapy. The therapist facilitated C's exploration of her needs; she did not tell C what those needs were. By choosing her interventions carefully, the therapist aided C in developing skills that would increase her autonomy and decrease her dependence on others, including the therapist. The therapist clarified the intent of her interventions as therapy progressed; C could thus receive support without feeling that she lacked the data to do for herself what the therapist was doing. A major concern of Feminist Therapy has been to create supportive structures that simultaneously foster independence, that nurture without rescue. The therapist made available to C at all times information about how and why she intervened.

In addition to the ways in which therapy was structured, a feminist approach acted to broaden the focus of intervention. Therapy focused equally on intrapsychic, interpersonal, and sociocultural issues. C was able to view her concerns in terms of both her individual and unique experience and also in the cultural context in which that experience occurred. Without engaging in blaming, she was able to discover the ways in which her life was affected by sexism and the ways in which her concerns were similar to those of other women. The development of this political awareness and sense of community was an integral aspect of therapy. C was able to become autonomous without needing to feel isolated or alienated from other women.

## SUMMARY

Feminist Therapy is a philosophical approach to the conduct of therapy, counseling, and consultation. Feminist Therapy presents a new set of ground rules for the therapeutic experience. These rules were developed from the ideology of political feminism and the women's liberation movement. These values and attitudes may be integrated with almost any other psychological theory or therapy.

Feminist Therapy developed in response to the realization that traditional psychotherapy had generally used a male model of development. Theories pertaining to women were often based on erroneous or sexist assumptions. In addition, the traditional psychotherapist (both male and female) often subtly incorporated societal biases that demean and devalue women.

Feminist Therapy developed at the grassroots level, through the response and raised consciousness of individual therapists, as well as caucuses and groups of therapists working together. Sensitized to the damage done by the imposition of unspoken values, feminist therapists emphasize the awareness of one's own values (particularly with regard to sex and gender issues) and the clear expression of therapist values to the client.

Feminist therapists are aware of the limitations that may be imposed by rigid adherence to sex roles and support an androgynous view of mental health. They are painfully aware of the extent to which individual difficulties may reflect external sex-role bias and discrimination. Feminist therapists help clients sort out the external constraints from the internal ones. They encourage the client to take personal responsibility for changing. However, the therapist role is also expanded so that support is offered to the client for political action aimed at institutional or societal change.

The very process of therapy is affected by feminist principles. The client is viewed as a consumer seeking a service. Contracts are often developed between the client and therapist. Power is shared and reflected in the egalitarian nature of the client-therapist relationship. The therapist is assumed to have particular skills; the client is assumed to be the expert concerning her- or himself. Diagnoses and diagnostic tests are rarely used. The client is a participant in the process.

Issues commonly discussed in Feminist Therapy are anger, self-nurturance, and power and autonomy. As more and more information becomes available concerning the psychology of women, feminist therapists are putting that information to practical use. Feminist therapists have developed new approaches for dealing with problems in sexuality, depression, and victims of violence.

An important point is that not every therapist who is nonsexist in attitude or "respectful" toward women is a feminist therapist. Rather, Feminist Therapy is an active stance toward the development of women (and sometimes, men), taking into account past grievances against women. Feminist Therapy developed in response to the psychological damage previousy inflicted on women, presumably for "their own good."

In a popular novel, *The Women's Room* (French, 1977), one of the characters, Lily, has a "nervous breakdown." She describes her treatment by the traditional mental health establishment to her friend Mira. Her words are fictional, but they reflect the reality experienced by many women.

"Look at me, look what they've done to me," Lily said, but her speech sounded like a song, like wailing controlled and brought into form. "My whole body oozes sweat. I shake all the time. I hate them, those doctors. They don't care what they do to you as long as they can get you out of the office. I'm just a crazy woman, what do they care about me? Mira, I cut down the dosage, but I don't dare stop taking them. I can't go back there, Mira, it will kill me, it will drive me crazy. . . ."

"Carl says I can't do anything right. I don't know, Mira, I try. I clean and clean and clean. If I don't, they'll send me back. And I couldn't stand it, Mira, it's torture, it's medieval, you wouldn't believe what they do to you. Now my memory is gone. . . . Every day they come and get you and take you to that room. . . . Then they give you this shock, oh it's terrible, it's such a violation! They don't care what they do to you, you don't matter, you're just a crazy woman, you have no dignity." (pp. 260–261)

Feminist Therapy vows to give Lily and all women back their dignity.

## REFERENCES

American Psychological Association. Report of the task force on sex bias and sex-role stereotyping in psychotherapeutic practice. *American Psychologist*, 1975, **30**, 1169–1175.

Barbach, L. *For yourself: The fulfillment of female sexuality.* New York: Doubleday, 1975.

Bardwick, J. *Psychology of women: A study of bio-cultural conflicts*. New York: Harper & Row, 1971.

Bart, P. Depression in middle-aged women. In S. Cox (Ed.), *Female psychology: The emerging self*. Palo Alto, Calif.: Science Research Associates, 1976.

Bem, S. The measurement of psychological androgyny. *Journal of Consulting and Clinical Psychology*, 1974, **42**, 155–162.

Brodsky, A. The consciousness-raising group as a model for therapy with women. *Psychotherapy: Theory, Research and Practice*, 1973, **10**, 24–29.

Broverman, I. K., Broverman, D. M., Clarkson, F. E., Rosencrantz, P. S., and Vogel, S. R. Sex-role stereotypes and clinical judgments of mental health. *Journal of Consulting and Clinical Psychology*, 1970, **34**, 1–7.

Carlson, N. and Johnson, D. Sexuality assertiveness training: A workshop for women. *Counseling Psychologist*, 1975, **5**, 53–59.

Chesler, P. Patient and patriarch: Women in the psychotherapeutic relationship. In V. Gornick and B. Moran (Eds.), *Women in sexist society: Studies in power and powerlessness*. New York: Basic Books, 1971.

Chesler, P. *Women and madness*. New York: Doubleday, 1972.

Childs, E., Stocker, E. and Sachnoff, E. Women's sexuality: A feminist view. In S. Cox (Ed.), *Female psychology: The emerging self*. Palo Alto, Calif.: Science Research Associates, 1976.

Deckard, B. *The women's movement*. New York: Harper & Row, 1979.

Dewey, C. Vocational counseling with women: A non-sexist technique. In E. Rawlings and D. Carter (Eds.), *Psychotherapy for women: Treatment toward equality*. Springfield, Ill.: Charles C Thomas, 1977.

Ferson, J. The feminist therapy collective in Philadelphia. Paper presented at the 81st Annual Convention of the American Psychological Association, Montreal, August 1973.

Franks, V. and Burtle, V. *Women in therapy: New psychotherapies for a changing society*. New York: Brunner/Mazel, 1974.

French, M. *The women's room*. New York: Jove/HJB, 1977.

Gornick, V. and Moran, B. *Woman in sexist society*. New York: Basic Books, 1971.

Gluckstern, N. Beyond therapy: Personal and institutional change. In E. Rawlings and D. Carter (Eds.), *Psychotherapy for women: Treatment toward equality*. Springfield, Ill.: Charles C Thomas, 1977.

Greenspan, M. Psychotherapy and women's liberation. Paper presented at the National Conference of Feminist Therapists, Boulder, Colorado, January 1976.

Hacker, H. Women as a minority group. *Social Forces*, 1951, **31**, 67–70.

Hare-Mustin, R. Family therapy from a feminist perspective. *Counseling Psychologist*, 1979, **8**, 19–27.

Hare-Mustin, R., Marecek, J., Kaplan, A., and Liss-Levinson, N. Rights of clients, responsibilities of therapists. *American Psychologist*, 1979, **34**, 3–16.

Henley, N. and Freeman, J. The sexual politics of interpersonal behavior. In S. Cox (Ed.), *Female psychology: The emerging self*. Chicago: Science Research Associates, 1976.

Holroyd, J. Psychotherapy and women's liberation. *Counseling Psychologist*, 1976, **6**, 22–28.

Jakubowski-Spector, P. Facilitating the growth of women through assertive training. *Counseling Psychologist*, 1973, **4**, 75–86.

James, J. *A formal analysis of prostitution: Final report to the division of research*. Olympia, Wash.: Washington State Department of Social and Health Services, 1971.

Johnson, M. An approach to feminist therapy. *Psychotherapy: Theory, Research, and Practice*, 1976, **13**, 72–76.

Kaplan, A. G. Androgyny as a model of mental health for women: From theory to therapy. In S. Kaplan and J. Bean, *Beyond sex-role stereotypes: Readings toward a psychology of androgyny*. Boston: Little, Brown, 1976.

Larson, E. R. S.I.S.T.E.R. Statement of purpose. Unpublished manuscript.

Lerman, H. Sex between client and therapist. Panel discussion, meeting of the Association for Women in Psychology, New Orleans, Louisiana, August 1974.

Lerman, H. What happens in feminist therapy? In S. Cox (Ed.), *Female psychology: The emerging self*. Chicago: Science Research Associates, 1976.

Lerman, H. Caution: Failure to ratify the equal rights amendment may be hazardous to your mental health. Unpublished manuscript.

Liss-Levinson, N., Coleman, E. and Brown, L. A program of sexual assertiveness training for women. *Counseling Psychologist*, 1975, **5**, 74–78.

Maccoby, E. and Jacklin, C. *The psychology of sex differences*. Stanford, Calif.: Stanford University Press, 1974.

Mander, A. Feminism as therapy. In E. Rawlings and D. Carter (Eds.), *Psychotherapy for women: Treatment toward equality*. Springfield, Ill.: Charles C Thomas, 1977.

Mander, A. and Rush, A. *Feminism as therapy*. New York: Randon House, 1974.

Miller, J. *Toward a new psychology of women*. Boston: Beacon Press, 1976.

Oliver, L. and Hill, C. Principles concerning the counseling/therapy of women. Panel discussion at the 86th Annual Convention of the American Psychological Association, Toronto, September 1978.

Rawlings, E. and Carter, D. *Psychotherapy for women: Treatment toward equality*. Springfield, Ill.: Charles C Thomas, 1977.

Rush, F. The sexual abuse of children: A feminist point of view. In N. Cornell and C. Wilson (Eds.), *Rape: The first sourcebook for women*. New York: New American Library, 1974.

Stone, M. *When God was a woman*. New York: Dial Press, 1976.

Szasz, T. The myth of mental illness. *American Psychologist*, 1960, **15**, 113–118.

Tennov, D. *Psychotherapy: The hazardous cure*. New York: Anchor Press, 1976.

Washbourn, P. *Becoming woman: The quest for whole-ness in female experience*. New York: Harper & Row, 1977.

Weisstein, N. Psychology constructs the female. In S. Cox (Ed.), *Female psychology: The emerging self*. Chicago: Science Research Associates, 1976.

Wyckoff, H. Radical psychiatry techniques for solving women's problems in groups. In E. Rawlings and D. Carter (Eds.), *Psychotherapy for women: Treatment toward equality*. Springfield, Ill.: Charles C Thomas, 1977.

# CHAPTER 23

# *Feminist Psychotherapy II*

BARBARA L. FORISHA

*During the course of investigating the need for this book and important systems of psychotherapy, I kept being reminded of the importance of having a chapter on Feminist Psychotherapy. Although I had some doubts that there was any such thing as Feminist Psychotherapy as a system of theory and practice, and felt that the issue was really a political/ethical/professional one rather than a theoretical-procedural matter, I decided that it would be quite valuable to have in this book two points of view on this very sensitive issue.*

*In Barbara Forisha's chapter we obtain glimpses not only of the question of psychotherapy for a special group, that is, women, but also some of the major concepts that a small but relatively powerful group of individuals have about the state of the profession.*

*Since feminist therapy is essentially a political issue, I am positive that many will disagree with the conclusions, and may even, as I do, take umbrage at these views. Nevertheless, these views need to be heard—and at this point I regret that I have no means to permit counterarguments.*

*The essential message that Barbara Forisha expresses—of the need for a genuinely humanistic approach—is one that I am sure all therapists of goodwill will accept.*

Feminist Psychotherapy is both a humanistic therapy and a force for social change. As a humanistic therapy, feminist therapists promote self-awareness, self-affirmation, and personal integration. However, feminists recognize that personal integration, particularly for women, is not encouraged by a sexist society that prescribes differing roles for women and men and that allots the marginal role to women. Thus, in facilitating personal integration in all individuals, feminists come into conflict with societal norms that are seen as creating dysfunctional behavior patterns for all individuals. Feminist Psychotherapy, therefore, turns inward to promote personal integration, but also turns outward to act as a force against the societal, sex-differentiated expectations that discourage personal integration in individuals within the society.

Feminists, therefore, are in accord with most other humanistic schools of thought that affirm the worth of the individual, postulate growth-oriented tendencies in the individual, and believe in the individual's ability to live the process of the complexities of life as a basis for trustworthy decision making. Feminists differ from other schools of therapy, however, in recognizing that no model of mental health encompasses a view of healthy womanhood and that it is incumbent upon therapists to facilitate the development of such a model in individual clients. Such a stance transforms the "personal into the political" and requires that feminist therapists stand against all social forces that attempt to pressure women into those unhealthy behavior patterns that are part of current societal norms.

## HISTORY

Feminist Psychotherapy has developed out of a complex of historical conditions: the marginal status of women, which has made it relatively easy and convenient to label them as "deviant" in times of social stress; the emphasis on finding one's own personhood, which has been popularized by the humanistic movement; and the specific impact of the Women's Movement, which has crystallized the contradictions between societal marginality and the search for personal identity. Each of these will be briefly reviewed in turn.

### Women as Marginal Human Beings

Simone de Beauvoir, in her classic work *The Second Sex* (1953), developed the thesis that throughout history women have always been defined as the "Other" as opposed to men, who are the "One." In most societies, men have embodied (or been conceptualized as embodying) the socially valued traits of that culture. In our own society, such traits are assertion, independence, self-reliance, and other instrumental qualities. As a consequence, other devalued traits have been ascribed to women. Thus women have been conceptualized as embodying the desirable but not highly valued traits of nurturance and receptivity and also the undesirable traits of dependence, emotionality, and submissiveness. In general, women have been viewed, therefore, as demonstrating traits that are outside the mainstream of desirable social norms. As a consequence, women *are* somewhat deviant in times of stress when the "One" can scapegoat the "Other."

Many writers and psychologists have lent support to the thesis that the marginality of women and the narrow definition of appropriate feminine behavior led to psychological distress. Virginia Woolf (1957) suggests that any woman of talent would, historically, have been stifled by the lack of outlets for her gifts. She states that

any woman born with a great gift in the sixteenth century would certainly have gone crazed, shot herself, or ended her days in some lonely cottage outside the village, half witch, half wizard, feared and mocked at. For it needs little skill in psychology to be sure that a highly gifted girl who had tried to use her gift for poetry would have been so thwarted and hindered by other people, so tortured and pulled asunder by her own contrary instincts, that she must have lost her health or sanity to a certainty. (p. 51)

The situation is only somewhat modified today. Osmond, Franks, and Burtle (1974) point out that women today may have more opportunities to use their gifts than previously but are still socially constrained from doing so. They state that medical science has improved the physical status of women so that they now have more leisure and better health, leading to a greater desire to exercise their abilities, yet societal norms have not changed sufficiently to allow them to do so. These changes are, therefore, "a source of stress and strain." Menaker (1974) echoes the same point of view finding that social changes have increased expectations for women without necessarily increasing opportunities for action and that this creates a particular vulnerability in modern women who therefore seek psychotherapeutic help.

In part, the marginality of women explains the fact that women have accounted for greater numbers in the annals of madness. In the sixteenth and seventeenth centuries when mental illness was not yet defined, women were more often burned and drowned as witches than were men. With the redefinition of deviant behavior and the establishment of asylums in the eighteenth century, women were the more frequent inhabitants of these institutions (Osmund, Franks, & Burtle, 1974). In therapeutic settings of the twentieth century, studies show that women are more frequently mentally ill and/or in therapy than men (Gove, 1972) and that the larger group of women in therapy are white, educated, middle-class housewives and mothers (Fabrikant, 1974). Other research studies showed that women comprised two-thirds of the therapeutic population and that women were twice as likely to be perceived as having psychiatric and emotional problems than were men (Locke & Gardner, 1969; Rosen et al., 1972).

Women have received more than their share of attention from psychotherapists, yet psychotherapy has historically been antithetical to the full development of women as human beings. Freud's early insistence that "anatomy is destiny" led him to the conclusion that women are merely defective men and that a women's development is complete at 30 and she has nowhere else to go. Freud's work on hysteria was based primarily on clinical observation of his female clientele, and elaborated on the assumptions that women are remarkably passive and tractable, the mere objects of male desire. Osmund, Franks, and Burtle (1974) state that "The main female characteristic which emerged from the Freudian world appears to have been docility combined perhaps with envy that she was not a man" (p. 13).

Among other early therapists there were, however, glimmerings of a more sympathetic approach to women. Alfred Adler (1927), for one, recognized that many of woman's problems originated in the society in which she lived, which was designed to suit the male:

All our institutions, our traditional attitudes, our laws, our morals, give evidence of the fact that they are determined and maintained by privileged males for the glory of male domination. (p. 123)

Yet in 1931 he could still write that women's problems basically stemmed from insufficient training for their secondary role in life (Janeway, 1975).

The first truly sympathetic approach to women was developed by Karen Horney. Just as did Adler, she realized the implication of living in a society designed for the "One" when one is only the "Other." She wrote in 1926:

Like all sciences and all valuations, the psychology of women has hitherto been considered only from the point of view of men. It is inevitable that the man's position of advantage should cause objective validity to be attributed to his subjective, effective relations to the woman, and . . . the psychology of women hitherto actually represents a deposit of the desires and disappointments of men. An additional and very important factor in the situation is that women have adapted themselves to the wishes of men and felt as if their adaptation were their true nature. That is, they see or saw themselves in the way that their men's wishes demanded of them; unconsciously they yielded to the suggestion of the masculine thought. (pp. 56–57)

Women have allowed themselves to become the "Other," for they have internalized views promulgated by a male world. Yet the options allowed by a traditionally sex-role divided society make it difficult for women to do otherwise. Only recently has the psychotherapeutic emphasis encouraged women as well as men to disentangle themselves from internalized values and "find themselves." The conflict this produces for women, who have little societal support for so doing, has fed the fires of feminism.

**Cultural Emphasis: Finding Oneself**

The growth of humanistic psychology since World War II was spearheaded by the theoretical orientations of Abraham Maslow (1970) and Carl Rogers (1961). In the late 1970s, the humanistic ethic of self-realization has been popularized by many so that the importance of personal growth has become part of mass cultural expectations. Humanists write and speak of individuals "finding themselves" and detaching themselves from societal expectations. This orientation toward human beings emphasizes a present-centeredness, an individually based system of values, and an injunction to utilize one's potential. Within therapeutic relationships these principles are applied by establishing egalitarian relationships in which clients and therapists relate to each other as people, in which openness and transparency are encouraged, and in which the ultimate base for decision-making rests with the client.

Humanistic psychologists have encouraged women as well as men to further their own growth in ways based on an "inner locus of evaluation" rather than on societal norms and thus have provided a theoretical framework for overturning existing societal sex-role stereotypes. However, the humanistic psychologists' focus is inward. There is little awareness of external, sociological forces that hinder full human development, nor is there much emphasis on the differential conditioning of the two sexes. Feminist psychotherapists thus build upon the humanistic theory by adding to the psychological process a sociological emphasis—and challenging the social norms that act against liberation from our conditioning.

## Women, Self, and Society

Feminist psychotherapists have been particularly attuned to the difficulties women and men face in finding themselves in a society that denies to each a full repertoire of human action and feeling. In an oversimplified sense, men have been deprived of the experience of intimacy in the private sphere and women have been deprived of their power and the right to achievement in the public sphere. Neither women nor men have had full opportunity to maximize their capacities to work and to love, a definition of mental health since the time of Freud. The impetus provided by the Women's Movement, however, since the mid-1960s has led to the crystallization of a theoretical, therapeutic and activist school that, to facilitate individual self-realization, is standing against the status quo and the historical heritage that argues that women should possess but half of human traits and the lesser half at that.

## CURRENT STATUS

Feminist Psychotherapy has come of age since the rise of the Women's Movement in the mid-1960s. Many feminist therapists work primarily with problems arising out of the dysfunctional impact of sex-role norms on the personal and professional lives of women and men. Other therapists also have been sensitized to the problems of women and men and have adopted an orientation of "people's liberation," which is compatible with feminist theory.

A number of men as well as women claim to be feminist. This means that men as well as women are working for the liberation of both sexes from traditional patterns of behavior that do not suit the world in which we live. There is, however, considerable controversy over whether men really can be feminist therapists; many women feminists claim that patterns of sexism are so bred into our system that it is not possible for a male, raised in this society, to fully comprehend the problems of growing up female. In an ultimate sense this is no doubt true, and there are some women's issues that are perhaps beyond the understanding of anyone who is not female. Yet the collective failings in male understanding in many cases do no more disservice to specific clients than do the idiosyncratic failings of all therapists who, in some areas, fail to measure up to an unattainable ideal. The cause of human liberation is facilitated from many sources, and none provides the only or the surest source of guidance. Thus many acknowledge that feminist therapists may be male as well as female—and the clientele may also be drawn from both sexes. Yet the orientation remains predominantly female on both sides of the therapeutic relationship.

Recently the general public as well as therapists have been sensitized to the particular difficulties of women in our society. Increasing numbers of individuals, primarily women, are now asking for and selecting therapists with a feminist orientation. This increased popularity of feminist thought must be viewed, however, against the backdrop of the patriarchal system that still dominates therapeutic circles. The larger number of therapists still act out, consciously or unconsciously, the mandates of a male-dominated society. Chesler's (1971, 1972) criticism of the therapeutic system is cogent. She states that the majority of psychologists and psychiatrists are middle-aged, middle-class, married males who see in therapy middle-age, middle-class married females, and who thus perpetuate the very problems from which women are suffering. The problems that women sustain living in relationship to males are then transferred to the therapeutic situation. A therapist, from his own orientation, may urge the woman to accommodate herself to the existing system, both for his own comfort as well as the male(s) with whom she lives. Chesler maintains, in fact, that men (including therapists) drive women crazy by urging them to maintain a submissive role in accord with the status quo. Some of Chesler's claims are supported by research studies that tell of the perplexity and lack of empathetic understanding male therapists demonstrate toward their women patients' complaints and dissatisfactions (see Rice & Rice, 1973).

If, as Karen Horney suggests, the view that men have of women is a record of their desires and disappointments when in the company of women, then men indeed do women an injustice and refuse to perceive them in fully human terms. Several studies done in the last decades document this view. The landmark study by the Brovermans and their colleagues (1970) shows that clinicians (both male and female) tend to see a healthy woman as contrary to all the norms of a healthy person. On the other hand, the healthy person is perceived as a healthy male. This is similar to the conclusions drawn by Neulinger (1968) in an earlier study; he concluded that men chose to see women as nurturant, sensuous playthings.

The result of this view in therapy is that women are urged to support their husbands, take care of their children, and please men. Since many of women's difficulties arise from the fact that they lose their own identity in the process of caring for others, the strong suggestion of further accommodation to oth-

ers can only exacerbate women's malaise. Adjustment to the existing system has historically been detrimental to women, and traditional therapy has generally urged women only to "try harder" to accommodate this system rather than creating one more suited to their needs.

Feminist Psychotherapy thus stands against traditional views of women and society in urging women to find themselves. Feminists also recognize, however, that their stance, though popularly accepted, is still a minority point of view, and the development of new theoretical foundations requires that women work together to counteract the force of traditional institutionalized views of women. Hence in many ways Feminist Psychotherapy is a resocialization to a new system of being and requires the theoretical foundations, the individual examples, and the support networks that can support, strengthen, and expand a nonsexist view in a patriarchal society.

## THEORY

In many ways Feminist Psychotherapy may be viewed as a form of resocialization to a new world—and in part to a world that does not yet exist. As such, Feminist Therapy requires detachment from previous cultural norms, many of which are internalized, and the conscious development of new patterns of behavior based on a new perception of women's needs and capabilities in a changing world. Such resocialization requires an understanding of the realistic options offered by society; an awareness of the learned patterns and internalized norms acquired in previous socialization; a knowledge of self, one's talents, abilities, limitations, and potential for growth; a new theoretical perception encompassing a view of the individual in society; and an interpersonal network that supports the individual's growth-oriented path. Each of these facets of the resocialization process of Feminist Psychotherapy will be explored in the sections that follow.

## Economic and Social Conditions

Contrary to popular mythology, woman's place is no longer in the home but in the workforce, where women are generally overqualified and underpaid (Forisha & Goldman, 1981). Many women must work, as their income is the sole or a necessary part of household survival: There are a large number of single-parent homes headed by women; the climbing divorce rate has left many women in a position where they must expect to work for the rest of their lives; in addition, more women are choosing to remain single or to be married and remain childless, and hence expect to be continuous members of the workforce.

The statistics on work and marriage are indicative of the changing status of woman in our society. Yet societal norms have changed but little. There is some general social support for women in the workforce when they *have* to be there, but there is still very little support for women leaving the nurturing functions traditionally ascribed to them. Thus women who choose to work, or who are overburdened by expectations of both working and caring for husband and/or children, find little support for the conflicts that they face. They are subject to feelings of guilt, inadequacy, and lowered self-esteem. The old model of traditional feminine behavior, for which all women have been socialized, no longer fits the world in which we live.

## Feminine Socialization

Numerous writers have characterized the socialization of women as inculcating docility and responsiveness—traits counterproductive for women who must or who choose to earn their own way in the world. Weisstein (1971), for one, writes:

How are women characterized in our culture, and in psychology? They are inconsistent, emotionally unstable, lacking in a strong conscious or superego, weaker, "nurturant" rather than productive, "intuitive" rather than intelligent, and

if they are at all "normal," suited to the home and family. In short, the list adds up to a typically minority group stereotype of inferiority; if they know their place, which is in the home, they are really quite lovable, happy, childlike, loving creatures. (p. 221)

Freeman (1976) concurs in pointing out that the traits manifested by girls in our society are those attributed to victimized groups by psychologists. Moreover, the victim's traits appear to develop in women as they grow up. They begin healthy and strong but later lose this advantage. As the impact of social expectations takes its toll, girls succumb to the expected attributes of inferiority. Freeman writes: "Girls start off better than boys and end up worse" (p. 139).

In the process of becoming feminine, then, girls become women who have lower self-esteem and less confidence in their ability to act in this world than they had in their early years. Steinman (1974) describes the result of this process:

if for one reason or another, a woman is forced to suppress her need for self-expression, she will experience a loss of self-esteem, she will become less effectual in all spheres of her life. This is true for all women, but it is particularly severe for the educated woman who, in the process of her education, was given high aspirations for personal success in the world of business or the professions. (p. 76)

The resulting picture of the adult women in our society, particularly the educated one, still emphasizes receptivity. The suppression of other areas of self-expression leads to lowered self-esteem. The extremes of this picture are those that, in many ways, resemble the typical clinical picture of hysteria and masochism.

***Hysteria and Masochism.*** Karen Horney (1935, 1950, 1967) was one of the first to comment on the similarity between the socially approved picture of femininity and the occurrence of masochism. She said these clinical pathologies were induced in whole societies by certain sociological factors—all of which occur in modern society. She wrote that masochism in women may appear in any culture-complex in which: expansiveness and sexuality have small outlet; the number of children is restricted; women are assessed as inferior; women are economically dependent on men; women are restricted to the spheres of life that are built chiefly on emotional bonds (family life, religious or charity work); and there is a surplus of marriageable women. In such a setting, as Douglas (1978) writes of nineteenth-century America, suffering may be eulogized because it is one of the few areas in which women can excel.

Similarly, hysteria is closely akin to the normal female personality (Wolowitz, 1972, p. 313). Cox, drawing on the work of Belote (1976), explains this relationship by saying that women escalate to a hysterical pitch when they do not get emotional response from others (i.e., men). Trained to be emotional and responsive, women tend to expect this responsiveness in others. Yet men do not respond to women's needs because they do not think of it and because they do not know how, and other women do not do so either because traditionally their attention has been focused on men. As Cox (1976) concludes, from a feminist point of view, taking into account the patriarchal context, women as a class may become "hysterical" because men as a class do not respond.

The socialization of women may be said, therefore, to lead not only to docility and responsiveness but often to hysteria and masochism. The fact that these behavior patterns are socially induced and yet regarded as pathological are part of the double-bind in which women's traditional socialization leaves them.

### Awareness of Self

The process of women finding out who they are, in therapy, is necessarily interwoven with the social framework in which they live and the internalized view of women as non-assertive, other-oriented, and dependent. Increasing self-awareness thus requires that women differentiate their own needs from those that they have learned "ought to be" their needs, and learn to recognize their own worth and independence. The path to this self-awareness often leads through recognizing one's anger, learning to nurture oneself, and ultimately seeing oneself as an independent person.

*Anger.* Women who have been trained to say yes have trouble saying no. Often the development of anger is necessary in order to break through this conditioning and ultimately seek an integration where one can say both yes and no. The development of the capacity to express anger is a necessary transition toward dismantling overly acquiescent behavior. As women come to disentangle their anger from their hurt, and to give expression to their anger as well as their pain, they may temporarily exaggerate their anger. Yet without this process of differentiation, the road to full humanness is barred. In a feminist poem, "For Witches," Susan Sutheim (1969) writes of this process:

today
i lost my temper.

temper, when one talks of metal
means strong,
perfect.

temper, for humans
means angry
irrational bad.

today i found my temper
i said,
you step on my head
for 27 years you step on my head
and though i have been trained
to excuse you for you inevitable
clumsiness

today i think
i prefer to head to your clumsiness

today i begin
to find
myself

tomorrow
perhaps
i will begin
to find you.

*Self-Nurturance.*   Discovering one's anger is often a necessary part of discovering one's self. Women have gone a long way down the other path of caring for others and disregarding themselves. A recent commentary by Ellen Goodman illustrates the tendency for women to "understand" others rather than to stand up for or defend themselves. In a newspaper column entitled "Understanding Woman," she says that such a woman is a good listener and helps others to put the pieces of their lives back together. However, she might be demonstrating too much of a good thing. Goodman (1979) writes of her "understanding woman":

The last time I saw her I thought about the men in her life. I remember the husband who said he needed space. And she understood.
I remember the guy who was, from time to time, unfaithful. And she understood.
There was also a man who didn't want to get married and have children, after all, he had already been there. And now there is a man who has difficulty relating to her son because, after all, he has a boy the same age in another state. It is all very understandable. (p. 46)

Goodman compares such a woman to a marathon runner, a runner in a sympathy marathon, for which most women have been trained from childhood. Yet she points out that the "understanding woman" has understood too much and asked for too little and "has logged too many miles in other people's shoes."

Feminist therapists then are asking women to *ask* and to take care of themselves, to free themselves from always running in somebody else's place, and to give careful attention to their own course and the facilitation of their own record. For women, trained to excuse the other's inevitable clumsiness, this is often hard to do.

*Independence.*   Both anger and self-nurturance are steps on the way to differentiating oneself from others—in order to better relate to others when the transitional phase has passed. Learning to be angry and to take care of oneself are a part of seeing oneself as an independent person whose fortunes are not always dependent on the whims of others. Yet, traditionally, this has been the experience of women. Virginia Woolf (1957), for example, writes that women have always served as reflections of men rather than independent human beings. She states: "Women have served all these centuries as looking-glasses possessing the magic and delicious power of reflecting the figure of man at twice its natural size." Yet the capacity to mirror another, when it becomes a way of life, precludes an active orientation based on one's own sense of self. Another novelist, in a popular work, has her main character, a nineteenth-century woman, elaborate on this tendency. After the loss of her husband, a young widow writes:

But what will I be without him to tell me how beautiful and bright I am? Are other women as frightened as I am, wondering how much of what they are is merely a reflection of what others see in them? What am I when I am all alone? Am I strong and brave without children to assure me I am, out of their own need? Will I ever believe that I am beautiful and bright out of the sight of a man who loves me? I feel as if I have just been born—cut apart from the sustaining presence that made all my decisions for me and left helpless in the hands of strangers. (Hailey, 1978, p. 77)

The social sciences confirm the novelists' musings. Kaplan (1976) writes that women are socialized to be dependent and must learn to rely on self-evaluation rather than other-evaluation. The work of Bart (1971) illustrates this phenomena in a study of depression in middle-aged women. She finds that the more feminine her subjects were, the more depressed they were apt to become when the children left home. Bart says: "If one's satisfaction, one's sense of worth comes from other people rather than from one's own accomplishments, one is left with an empty shell in place of a self when such people depart."

The necessary struggle for independence is thus a struggle for self-differentiation. Women, embedded in their families and responsive to others in their circle, must come to see themselves as not only related but also separate, as not only responsive but also assertive, as not only together with others but also alone. For if women are to be fully human, they must be all of these, even accepting the loneliness often experienced in the initial steps of creating one's own path.

## Theoretical World View

The world view that supports the feminist orientation is generally based on humanistic theory and incorporates Rogers's (1961) view of fully functioning individuals, Maslow's (1970) self-actualization, Fromm's (1941) spontaneous affirmation, and Horney's (1950) self-realization. This writer (1978a,b) has written of this view as process-oriented, based on a belief on living all of one's experience, allowing one's experience to shape one's sense of self, and seeking a harmonious integration of all parts of self.

Developmentally, this view encompasses a view of human growth as one of differentiation and integration in which new learnings cause new, differentiated behavior that eventually results in a higher integration of valued old and new learnings. Much of the desired integration can be termed androgynous in the sense developed by Bem (1974), and can be interpreted as bringing together characteristics associated with love (the expressive qualities) and those associated with power (the instrumental capacities) in an integration in which the person is both competent and caring, assertive and receptive, able to work and able to play.

The underpinnings of this theory developed by Maslow (1970), Rogers (1961), Fromm (1941), and supported by the developmental work of Erikson (1950) were formulated primarily in regard to male development. The application of a model of process-oriented, androgynous living, when applied to women, is somewhat different and more problematic. The path to full human development, as outlined by the humanists, is not the same for women and for men.

For men, trained to be assertive, competent, and analytical, the path to full human-

ness requires the development and integration of the expressive qualities. Levinson (1978) tells us that in optimum development this occurs for many men during the midlife crisis. Maslow's (1970) examples of self-actualizing individuals also illustrate that high levels of integration occur later in life. For women, however, trained to be receptive, nurturing, and global in thought, the path to full humanness requires the development and integration of the instrumental qualities. To seek a high level of androgynous development, women must, therefore, come to terms with power.

The difficulties that women have in doing so are illustrated in recent research. Analyses of development in educated and gifted women attest to the fact that women evolve at higher levels only with anxiety—and more anxiety than their male peers. In their longitudinal study of gifted individuals, Terman and Oden (1959) report that the gifted adult women have a higher incidence of nervous disorders than found among women in the average population (which is already higher than that of men), whereas gifted adult men have a lower incidence of such disorders than the average male population. Helson (1967) also found that highly gifted women mathematicians were less emotionally secure than their male counterparts. In studies of college students, Marcia and Friedman (1970) and Orlofsky (1977) found that college women struggling toward the achievement of an independent identity were more anxious than a comparable group of men. Finally, Haan (1971) and her colleagues (1968) found that female students of high ethical development were more anxious, moody, and discontented than a similar group of men.

Thus the androgynous, process-oriented model of health, developed from observations of men, is not so readily conceptualized in the case of women. Women who choose to move away from the dysfunctional feminine prescriptions in our society incur heightened anxiety and internal conflict when they seek a resolution that psychologists have argued is more fully human. As Maccoby (1963) states, the predicament of women is something of a "horror story," for if a woman is going to exceed normal, feminine expectations for her behavior, she "must be fleet of foot indeed to scale the hurdles society has erected for her and to remain a whole and a happy person while continuing to follow her intellectual bent." Thus women benefit by seeking external support for their nontraditional venture.

## Resocialization and Support Systems

Women, with the encouragement of feminist psychotherapists, are turning to each other for such support and developing networks that support their new personal and professional choices. Barbara Bunker (1981) writes of the necessity of professional women devoting consciously directed energy into the creation of support systems. Mary Rowe (1981) writes of the creation of such a system within the academic professional world. Feminist collectives in large urban centers are also a wellspring for "networking," for finding the necessary supportive framework for nontraditional choices. It is important to note, however, that the support women are seeking is not the traditional support they relied upon for survival in the traditional, other-oriented feminine model; nor is it the support traditionally offered by women to each other, which vanished when the man came home. Rather, women are seeking from each other the nurturance they have long denied themselves which is also a counterweight to the heavy impact of socialization. The new networks being created, in fact, do for the growing woman what society has traditionally done for the feminine woman—helped her stay in place. Yet the new world view and its supportive networks offers greater promise for the process-oriented, androgynous view of full functioning than the old sex-role differentiated model ever offered—to either women or men. Phyllis Chesler summarized this point of view:

Women whose psychological identities are forged out of concern for their own survival and self-

definition, and who withdraw from or avoid any interactions which do not support this formidable endeavor, need not "give up" their capacity for warmth, emotionality, and nurturance. They do not have to foresake the "wisdom of the heart" and become "men." They need only transfer the primary force of their "supportiveness" to themselves and to each other—and never to the point of self-sacrifice. Women need not stop being tender, compassionate, and concerned with the feelings of others. They must start being tender and compassionate with themselves and with other women. Women must begin to "save" themselves and their daughters before they "save" their husbands and their sons . . . and the whole world. (cited in Cox, 1976, p. 387)

## METHODOLOGY

The basic model for therapeutic transactions in Feminist Therapy may incorporate gestalt, Rogerian, rational emotive, or other humanistic techniques. Underlying the choice of technique, however, is basically a strong belief in the individual worth of the person.

What happens in Feminist Therapy? Lerman (1976) writes that the therapist assumes that the client is competent, that the client has personal power, and that "the personal is political," which means that the conflicts with which the client struggles have both internal and external referents. In general, the therapist stresses the forgotten side of the woman's socialization: issues concerned with power. Feminist Therapy thus is designed to fill in the gaps left in the woman's previous socialization.

Perlstein (1976) points out that the goals of Feminist Therapy are that a woman have access to herself and know her own feelings; that she be aware of and make decisions based on her relation to her own work; that she maintain and develop connections with others that bring meaning and support into her life (but that are not essential to her sense of self), and that she learn to relate to other human beings at the level at which we are all human. Once again, the process-oriented, androgynous view of personhood is emphasized: Women are to learn to relate both to their work and to others from a basic sense of self. In the process, they learn to combine both power and love.

The course of therapy proceeds through several stages, many of which are typical of other schools of therapy.

## 1. INCREASING SELF-AWARENESS

a. *What is it that I want?* versus
b. *What is it that I have learned to want?*

During this phase the client begins to discover her own needs and desires as separate from those needs and desires that she has been conditioned to recognize as hers. Because of the similarities in the conditioning of all women, generally she finds that she seeks some independent expression of self and that she has learned to confuse this with serving others.

## 2. ACCEPTANCE OF SELF-AWARENESS

a. *Is it Okay to want what I want?* versus
b. *Is it only Okay to want what you want?*

The realization of self-felt desires that conflict with the expectations of others is often experienced along with self-derogation ("I am bad because I do not want what you want") and guilt ("I ought to want what you want"). The acceptance of one's own needs as legitimate is often difficult for women who have learned that others' needs (men's and children's) are more important. The acceptance of one's own importance is thus a major step in the therapeutic process.

## 3. STRENGTHENING OF SELF-ACCEPTANCE

a. *I am angry to have been so misled by you* versus
b. *I have been rightly victimized by you.*

The path to acceptance of one's own legitimate needs and desires, for most women, leads through the recognition and expression of anger. Having realized the strength of her own self, women in therapy may still decide to retreat to the familiar position of "victim" and accede to the wishes of others with all the familiar costs. The healthier counterpoint to this is to express the anger that emerges as one realizes the negative effects of the feminine societal model. In the expression of appropriate anger, there is strength; in the channeling of anger, there is power.

## 4. DEVELOPING THE POWER TO ACT

a. *Do I experiment with new alternatives and accept the risks inherent in such experimentation?* versus
b. *Do I stay with the comfortable and familiar?*

The ability to act on one's own, to accept the consequences of one's actions, is difficult for many people but particularly for women who have traditionally traded their independence for economic and social security. If one chooses to live only through others, as women have been trained to do, then one risks only through others; there is always an illusion of security in standing *behind* rather than *alone* (one never catches the first bullet!). Yet, if women are to come into their own as fully independent people, they must be able to stand alone and, reaping the rewards of independence, also risk the penalties.

## 5. RECOGNIZING SOCIETAL RESTRAINTS

At this point, women who have chosen to act on their world run into obstacles, external rather than internal, that may handicap the enactment of their desires. At such a point, a support group of other women often is necessary to sort out the external obstacles from the internal obstacles. A woman who works, for example, may not be promoted because of external sexism rather than personal competence, abilities, and attitudes. Collectively, these external difficulties may be recognized as such. Isolated, the woman may take them into herself and succumb to lowered self-esteem. The acknowledgment of common feminine experience guards against this personal inculpation.

6.  ACCEPTING SOCIETAL RESTRAINTS

The increasing awareness of societal impositions is often met with anger, as is the process of realizing the internalized societal restraints. Beyond anger, however, lies acceptance of the world as it is and the motivation to act for change. This is concomitant with coming to accept oneself, which is the final stage of therapy.

7.  ACCEPTANCE OF SELF, BOTH
    CAPABILITIES AND LIMITATIONS

At this point there is an increasing acceptance of self and others. As in most views of liberation, as stated by Alan Watts (1974), women will have moved beyond their conditioning and beyond hatred of their conditioning. They will have accepted themselves as they are, a composite of both what they have been and what they can be. Both powerful and loving, the fully integrated woman brings together both the reality of what she is and the vision of what she can be. She lives in the present with a view toward the future.

The course of therapy can be described as a process of differentiation—of self and others—and a new integration that brings together the best of the old and the new. The necessary steps in differentiation are somewhat similar for many women as they emphasize power-related issues: anger, self-nurturance, and independence. A similar process occurs in the therapy of men, yet the content generally differs as men learn to differentiate their feelings, to recognize their dependencies and vulnerabilities, and then to achieve an integration with other parts of themselves. For both sexes, the integration brings together power and love.

The process, of course, is never complete, and each new integration is the platform from which further differentiation begins. Yet as

in all development, successful transitions from one plateau to another develop the skills with which to move through the next transition.

## APPLICATIONS

Clients of feminist psychotherapists are most often educated women who are generally the first socioeconomic and sex status to experience the conflicts induced by social change (Forisha, 1978a). However, feminist psychotherapists also number men among their clients. Generally the clientele of a feminine psychotherapist, however, is composed of those who experience conflict between their own personal needs for self-realization and those of the society in which they live—and, as Virginia Woolf reminded us, it is often the gifted women who go crazy first. It is those with the best resources, both internal and external, who are the first to feel the stress involved by the creation of new options.*

In the lives of educated women—and most everybody else—there are often two primary issues. The first involves the woman's relation to her own work, the second her relation to others. Each of these will be examined in turn.

### Women and Work

As Perlstein (1976) pointed out, one of the chief issues in Feminist Psychotherapy is the woman's relation to her work. In the kaleidoscope of human affairs, the woman's relation to *her* work is a new variable that affects the patterns established in all areas of her life—and in the lives of those with whom she lives. Formerly, men were related both to work and family, and women only

---

*Other feminist therapists reject this emphasis and turn their attention largely toward those women who are a subject of oppressive environmental circumstances. The emphasis on the educated woman expressed here is but one of many feminist orientations.

to family. To add to these traditional relationships the relationship of women and work shifts all relationships mentioned above.

What does the introduction of this relationship mean? For many women who have been wives and mothers, it means that they are choosing not to be so any longer—or they fill these roles only part-time. For other women, it means choosing nontraditional relationships based on two-career patterns. For others, it means choosing to stay single. As one working woman said to her friend the other day, "I told him I loved him, but my work came first. I made that perfectly clear to him, but he didn't seem to understand why I couldn't go to New York over the weekend. So we split up . . . and now I'm seeing. . . ."

For women, who are perceived as basing their lives on pleasing others, particularly men, this is a startling new occurrence. The woman above, as many others, is establishing new patterns of relationships in her life based on the premise that her work is important. The relationship of women to work (not just work when there are bills to be paid, or when the husband has departed, or when a child gets sick) has opened up for women a new range of possibilities with enormous ramifications.

Culturally, women are being offered new options—the chance to choose one's work and enjoy it. Yet in a changing society, and a predominantly sexist one, such options always lead to conflict, internal as well as external, and the costs of the new alternatives are often heavy. It is part of the educational process of therapy to point out the options available, the potential rewards, the potential costs, and affirm the fact that women *can* make a choice.

The second input of Feminist Therapy is to help women to sustain the choice once made. In relationship to work, this often involves providing confirmation for the "outsider" (female) on the "inside" (male) world, helping her to see her world and herself with clear eyes and to develop networks of other individuals who can pave the way

or back her up when the "inside" ignores her, chastises her, or threatens to spew her out (Forisha & Goldman, 1981).

## Women and Relationships

Women who relate closely to their work are powerful in the eyes of others in ways women have never been. Women have, of course, always been powerful, but the power was tolerable because they remained in the private sphere and did not intrude into the "real world." The image of the powerful mother figure in juxtaposition with women at work is, at root, terrifying to many men. The assumption of overt and external power by women has rocked the establishment boat and changed the nature of both work and professional relationships.

Therefore, the way in which women are relating to each other and to men is being shifted not only by women's relationship to work but by the increasing perception of power in women. The traditional arrangement in which men know they're powerful (and therefore okay) because they work in the "real world" and women know they are loved (and therefore okay) because they are protected from that world is outdated. Male and female sources of self-esteem have changed, and hence the stability of many relationships is threatened. Individuals are, therefore, in a process of experimentation with new forms of relating to others.

The result is increasing turbulence and uncertainty in relationships. In many cases the immediate rewards are greater, and perhaps the long-term ones (though not enough time has passed yet to really tell); but in many cases the immediate pain is also greater. However, the promise of what may be and the reality of what is may eventually come together in a higher integration of love and power in relationships as well as in one's work. Once again, however, women need each other and profit from the sharing of their collective experience as they try out new forms. The resocialization experience engendered by feminism and its therapeutic offshoots requires both personal growth, theoretical understanding, and collective confirmation of the alternative courses of living.

## CASE EXAMPLES

Each of the three cases below illustrates some of the difficulties with which women are grappling and some of the decisions they are living out. In all cases, these are women, sensitive to the crosscurrents induced by social change, who are seeking to form a process-oriented identity in which they seek to find themselves, to find their work, and to find significant others in their lives. Juanita, though of Latin-American origin, illustrates the full panorama of changes through which women in the United States are passing, whereas Lynne and Aileen are still in transition at different developmental points in their lives. All three cases together illustrate the orientation of many women in feminist psychotherapy today.

Juanita is a very small, dark-haired woman of 30 who, when I first met her, was lost under a mass of long hair. Juanita's small voice, her slouched posture, and her lowered eyes contributed further to a picture of insignificance. Our initial work together revolved around her need to be "bigger" and not feel so at the mercy of others, particularly her husband and three small boys. During our early experience together Juanita became occasionally more bold, grew in intellectual understanding of her own capabilities, and occasionally spoke out for herself.

Six months later Juanita and her husband, John, requested a session in which they could work on their relationship. Juanita had recently entered a university and was no longer totally absorbed in her family's life. John had initially encouraged this move, but was now uncomfortable with Juanita's interest and enthusiasm in school. Juanita, on the other hand, felt that she was still regarded as a little girl by her husband and that she was rarely listened to in any serious sort of way. During this session a cofacilitator and myself monitored and clarified communication between Juanita and John. The session concluded with Juanita enthusiastically beaming at John and saying, "I think you've finally heard me," and John's pleased, but somewhat perplexed, acknowledgment of Juanita's newfound assertion.

A year later Juanita had finished her university education. John had divorced Juanita and was preparing to marry another woman who was traditional in her outlook. During the next year Juanita struggled with the problems of singleness and single parenthood. Her new responsibilities challenged previously untouched resources in herself and she emerged from this time as a vivacious, lively person—with short, curly hair—who knew that she would handle the world. In that year she had not only handled divorce proceedings, school difficulties with her sons, won a custody suit, but had also obtained a professional-level job working with people of Latin origin.

She returned to therapy shortly thereafter to continue her journey into self. During this time her increasing sense of self received additional confirmation, and Juanita finally came to terms with the fact that she was not "small" but as big as she wished to be. In a group session, this conflict came to the surface when Juanita remarked that a superior had praised her for a brilliant piece of work. At that point she ducked down and appeared small—discounting her capacity to do anything noticeable or brilliant. I asked Juanita then to stand up and deliver a speech based on the professional work she had done—and in fact to sell us her services as a consultant for bilingual peoples. She began reluctantly, but soon swung into the spirit of it and astonished all of us, including herself, with her straightforward self-assertion. She stood straighter, her face glowed, and when she concluded she leaped down and hugged everybody, exclaiming "I really can do it!"

Juanita then spent the next few months exploring her relationships with men. A brief and explosive affair surfaced old feelings of dependency and her still present, though latent, desires for return to her formerly married state. In working through this episode,

Juanita came to the conclusion, once again, that her happiness depended on herself and not others, and that this particular affair was a positive and groundbreaking experience for her. She learned that the value of an experience is not measured solely by duration but rather by the quality of the experience itself and what can be learned from it.

Juanita today is still unmarried, involved in an ongoing relationship with a man for whom she cares, and is excited and stimulated by her work. She has achieved, in many ways, the model of healthy womanhood proposed by Lerman (1976): She is aware of self, relates to her work and others, and experiences herself as part of the global connectedness of the universe. The same process is partially revealed in the cases of Lynne and Aileen.

Lynne has been married to a lawyer for over 20 years and is a young-looking, attractive, brilliant mother of teenage children. She dates her transformation from about two years ago when she began reading feminist literature and continuing her college career. She says within two years her husband watched "Gracie Allen at the breakfast table transformed into Gloria Steinem." At the moment she is struggling with her desire to continue this relationship, which was satisfying as long as she continued to be her "old self," and her desire for further exploration of the options she sees opening out before her.

She tends to see these alternatives as mutually exclusive and feels caught on a pendulum. She rushed from her schoolwork and fantasies of romantic entanglements with like-minded intellectuals to a reenactment of her old role serving up carefully prepared four- and five-course dinners for the assembled family. She phrases her alternatives as extremes: either a room of her own (apartment) or continued cooking 24 hours a day. Recently, however, she has come to rephrase her alternatives in more moderate terms, recognizing that the process of change is slow and not always an all-or-nothing proposition. She is still caught by the swinging pendulum, but the swings have diminished now and a

new direction is beginning to evolve that she will most likely act upon in time. Her major decisions are still in the future.

Aileen illustrates another aspect of a woman's search for self. A young and talented single woman, she has "fallen in love" with various men who often treat her badly. My work with Aileen has been to pull back toward herself the strings to her happiness that she has attached to others and to base her own sense of being more firmly in herself. In one session she talked about Jerry, who was "fantastic, intelligent, sensitive, and sexy" and who, nonetheless, periodically disappeared from her life without notice and turned up again at moments that suited his convenience. In the early part of the session, Aileen came to recognize the incongruence of her description of Jerry's character and her recounting of his behavior. Aileen, as many of us, was projecting her desired image of a man upon the nearest likeness of that image, yet the human being is always more complex than the projections.

In the second part of the session, Aileen made a list of all the qualities she felt in herself when she was with Jerry. The list included many of the qualities attributed to Jerry himself: sensitivity, intelligence, and sexiness. Yet Aileen claimed that she *was* these things because she was with Jerry and she lost them—and a desired part of herself—when he was gone. I asked Aileen to reclaim these qualities in herself by telling the group "I am . . . (sensitive, intelligent, sexy, etc.)." Aileen was at that time unable to do so. She claimed sensitivity, and hence the capacity to be hurt, but refused intelligence and sexiness. In succeeding sessions we worked through to the point where she finally could admit, in a straightforward fashion, that she was both sexy and intelligent, and hence could find in herself the resources that she had believed existed due to the benevolent attention of men.

Aileen, like Lynne and Juanita, is seeking herself. Like most women she has learned to find happiness in others and is devastated when those others depart, partly because women have difficulty untangling what belongs to others and what belongs to themselves. The departure of significant others, then, is often experienced as taking part of the self, and devastation and depression are the result. The differentiation of self and another leads to a new integration in which the departure of another is the cause for further awareness and expansion of self rather than the diminishing of self. This is an important step for many women in therapy.

## SUMMARY

Feminist Psychotherapy is directed both inward toward personal growth and outward toward recognition of the impact of social norms. Since many of these norms are seen as handicapping to women, Feminist Psychotherapy often takes a stand against the status quo and is thus a force for social change.

Women have always been deviant by virtue of their marginality. Their marginal status has not encouraged expression of their desire for independence or achievement. Further, the marginal status of women, who remain outsiders in the mainstream of society, has made them easy targets for projection of more severe deviance in times of social stress. The traditional response to women's discomfort with personal and social deviance has been for psychotherapists to urge women back into their marginal role and to remain content with things as they are. The role of Feminist Psychotherapy, since the 1960s, has been to urge women to assert their full individuality, and in doing so challenge the norms that define them as marginal.

The process of Feminist Psychotherapy is, therefore, one of resocialization. Women are urged to grow in the direction of process-oriented, androgynous behavior that presents greater scope for individual talent than do the traditional sex-role norms and that is postulated as an appropriate model of mental health, displacing those based on masculine and feminine role characteristics. The process of therapy involves not only greater awareness of self but greater awareness of

societal norms; not only change in self, but change in society. Because many of the afflictions of women have been suffered collectively, the process of change is also necessarily a collective one in which women are learning to work together both to support personal growth and social action.

Many of the concerns that are brought into Feminist Psychotherapy today revolve around issues that are traditionally associated with power (the ability to *do* things) as opposed to those traditionally associated with love (the capacity to *be* and to *care*). Because of the sex-differentiated socialization in our society, men more often than women have been groomed for the world of power; women have been sequestered in the world of love. Hence, in reclaiming part of their human heritage, women in therapy are coming to grips with power, affirming their own worth, recognizing their anger, and learning to care for themselves and each other. In this way, as in the case examples cited above, women are moving toward a fully functioning integration of love and power, which is pivotal in a model of human health.

## REFERENCES

Adler, A. *Understanding human nature*. New York: Holt, 1927.

Bart, P. Depression in middle-aged women. In V. Gornick and B. Moran (Eds.), *Women in sexist society: Studies in power and powerlessness*. New York: Basic Books, 1971.

Belote, B. Masochistic syndrome, hysterical personalities and the illusion of a healthy woman. In S. Cox (Ed.), *Female Psychology: The emerging self*. Palo Alto, Calif.: Science Research Associates, 1976.

Bem, S. The measurement of psychological androgyny. *Journal of Consulting and Clinical Psychology*, 1974, **2**, 153–62.

Broverman, I. K., Broverman, D. M., Clarkson, F. E., Rosenkrantz, P. S. and Vogel, S. R. Sex-role stereotypes and clinical judgements of mental health. *Journal of Consulting and Clinical Psychology*, 1970, **34**, 1–7.

Bunker, B. Developing support networks. In B. Forisha and B. Goldman (Eds.), *The outsider on the inside: Women and organizations*. Englewood Cliffs, N.J.: Prentice-Hall (forthcoming).

Chesler, P. Patient and patriarch: Women in the psychotherapeutic relationship. In V. Gornick and B.

Moran (Eds.) *Women in sexist society: Studies in power and powerlessness.* New York: Basic Books, 1971.

Chesler, P. *Women and madness.* New York: Avon, 1972.

Cox, S. *Female psychology: The emerging self.* Palo Alto, Calif.: Science Research Associates, 1976.

de Beauvior, S. *The second sex.* New York: Knopf, 1953.

Douglas, A. *The feminization of American society.* New York: Avon, 1978.

Erikson, E. *Childhood and society.* New York: Norton, 1950.

Fabrikant, B. The psychotherapist and the female patient: Perceptions, misperceptions and change. In V. Franks and V. Burtle (Eds.), *Women in therapy.* New York: Brunner/Mazel, 1974.

Forisha, B. *Sex roles and personal awareness.* Morristown, N.J.: General Learning Press, 1978a.

Forisha, B. The role of love, power, and conflict: Socialization for creativity or alienation? Unpublished manuscript 1978b.

Forisha, B. and Goldman, B. (Eds.). *Outsiders on the inside: Women and organizations.* Englewood Cliffs, N.J.: Prentice-Hall (1981).

Freeman, J. The social construction of the second sex. In S. Cox (Ed.) *Female psychology: The emerging self.* Palo Alto, Calif.: Science Research Associates, 1976.

Fromm, E. *Escape from freedom.* New York: Holt, 1941.

Goodman, E. She runs sympathy marathon. *The Ann Arbor News,* August 21, 1979.

Gove, W. The relationship between sex-roles, marital status, and mental illness. *Social Forces,* 1972, 51.

Haan, N. Moral redefinition in families as the critical aspect of the generation gap. *Youth and Society,* 1971, **3**, 259–83.

Haan, N., Smith, M. B. and Block, J. The moral reasoning of young adults: Political-social behavior, family background, and personality correlates. *Journal of Personality and Social Psychology,* 1968, **10**, 183–201.

Hailey, E. F. *A woman of independent means.* New York: Avon, 1978.

Helson, R. Sex differences in creative style. *Journal of Personality,* 1967, **35**, 214–33.

Horney, K. The flight from womanhood. *International Journal of Psycho-Analysis,* 1926, **7**, 324–39. Reprinted in K. Horney, *Feminine Psychology.* New York: Norton, 1967.

Horney, K. The problem of feminine masochism. *The Psychoanalytic Review,* 1935, **22**, 241–257.

Horney, K. *Neurosis and human growth.* New York: Norton, 1950.

Janeway, E. *Between myth and morning: Women awakening.* New York: Delta, 1975.

Kaplan, A. G. Androgyny as a model of mental health for women: From therapy to therapy. In A. G. Kaplan and J. P. Bean, *Beyond sex-role stereotypes: Readings toward a psychology of androgyny.* Boston: Little, Brown, 1976.

Levinson, D. *The season's of a man's life.* New York: Knopf, 1978.

Lerman, H. What happens in feminist therapy? In S. Cox (Ed.) *Female psychology: The emerging self.* Palo Alto, Calif.: Science Research Associates, 1976.

Locke, B. Z. and Gardner, E. A. Psychiatric disorders among the patients of general practitioners and internists. *Public Health Report,* 1969, **84**, 167–73.

Maccoby, E. Women's intellect. In S. M. Farber and R. H. L. Wilson (Eds.), *The potential of women.* New York: McGraw-Hill, 1963.

Marcia, J. E. and Friedman, M. L. Ego identity status in college women. *Journal of Personality,* 1970, **38**, 249–63.

Maslow, A. T. *Motivation and personality* (1954) New York: Harper & Row, 1970.

Menaker, E. The therapy of women in the light of psychoanalytic theory and the emergence of a new view. In V. Franks and V. Burtle (Eds.), *Women in therapy.* New York: Brunner/Mazel, 1974.

Neulinger, J. Perceptions of the optimally integrated person: A redefinition of mental health. *Proceedings from the 76th Annual Convention of the American Psychological Association,* 1968, 554.

Orlofsky, J. Sex-role orientation, identity formation, and self-esteem in college men and women. *Sex-roles,* 1977, **6**, 561–75.

Osmund, H., Franks, V. and Burtle, V. Changing views of women and therapeutic approaches: Some historical considerations. In V. Franks and V. Burtle (Eds.), *Women in therapy.* New York: Brunner/Mazel, 1974.

Perlstein, M. What is a healthy woman? In S. Cox (Ed.), *Female psychology: The emerging self.* Palo Alto, Calif.: Science Research Associates, 1976.

Rice, J. K. and Rice, D. G. Implications of the women's liberation movement for psychotherapy. *American Journal of Psychiatry,* 1973, **130**, 191–96.

Rogers, C. *On becoming a person.* Boston: Houghton, 1961.

Rosen, B. S., Locke, B. Z., Goldberg, I. D. and Babigian, H. Identification of emotional disturbances in patients seen in general medical clinics. *Hospital and Community Psychiatry,* 1972, **23**, 364–70.

Rowe, M. The munitae of sex discrimination. In S. Forisha and B. Goldman (Eds.), *The outsiders on the inside: Women and organizations.* Englewood, N.J.: Prentice-Hall (forthcoming).

Steinman, A. Cultural values, female role expectations and therapeutic goals; Research and interpretation. In V. Franks and V. Burtle (Eds.), *Women in therapy.* New York: Brunner/Mazel, 1974.

Sutheim, S. For witches. *Women: A Journal of Liberation,* 1969.

Terman, L. M. and Oden, M. H. *Genetic studies of genius,* vol. 5. Stanford, Calif.: Stanford University Press, 1959.

Watts, A. *Psychotherapy east and west.* New York: Ballantine, 1974.

Weisstein, N. Psychology constructs the female. In V. Gornick and B. Moran (Eds.), *Woman in sexist society:* *Studies in power and powerlessness.* New York: Basic Books, 1971.

Woolf, V. *A room of one's own* (1929). New York: Harcourt, 1957.

Wolowitz, H. M. Hysterical character and feminine identity. In J. M. Bardwick (Ed.), *Readings on the psychology of women.* New York: Harper & Row, 1972.

# CHAPTER 24

# Fixed Role Therapy

JACK R. ADAMS-WEBBER

*Included in this book are two approaches to psychotherapy based on the theories of George A. Kelly, a man whose work is not as appreciated as I believe it will be in the future. Fixed Role Therapy and Personal Construct Therapy should probably be read in sequence, since they share the same theory.*

*My own love affair with therapeutic role playing is indicated by the fact that I have written three books and a number of articles on the subject. It is my belief that of all the methods of psychotherapy, none is either more logically correct or more therapeutically effective than psychodrama—which is, however, a very difficult process to do correctly. Consequently, I was most pleased to obtain Jack Adams-Webber's account of Kelly's Fixed Role Therapy, which uses psychodrama in an interesting and highly innovative manner. Goethe once said, "If you want a person to change, treat him now as though he were already how you want him to be." As I see it, this statement lies at the heart of Fixed Role Therapy. In the psychotherapy of the future, I am positive this approach will have a strong part.*

Fixed Role Therapy is a form of brief psychotherapy developed by George A. Kelly from the basic principles of his psychology of personal constructs. Essentially, it is an experimental procedure for activating personality change in which the client plays the role of a hypothetical person for a period of several weeks. Kelly (1973) explained that this is not strictly a form of treatment, but rather an investigative project designed to elucidate specific problems in the client's life. The client is the "principal investigator," with the therapist more or less assuming the function of a "research supervisor." During the enactment period, therapist and client meet frequently, usually every other day, to plan specific experiments and to evaluate their outcomes. At the end of the enactment period, the client is invited to appraise the entire experience in whatever terms are most meaningful to him or her.

Other approaches to psychotherapy are derived from Kelly's ideas. Some of these are summarized by this writer (1979) and by Franz Epting (forthcoming). Nonetheless, as Pervin (1975) points out, Fixed Role Therapy is that method of psychotherapy that is "particularly associated with personal construct theory, and it does exemplify some of the principles of the personal construct theory of change" (p. 300).

## HISTORY

The first description of Fixed Role Therapy appeared in *The Psychology of Personal Constructs*, the two-volume work in which Kelly (1955) formulated the general principles of personal construct theory and summarized their applications in the practice of clinical psychology. This is still the best source of information available about the basic procedures. It also includes an illustrative case history.

Kelly (1955) specifically acknowledged the influence of J. L. Moreno upon the development of Fixed Role Therapy. As J. C. J. Bonarius (1970) notes, Moreno's (1934) psychodrama involves the client's reenacting particular episodes from her or his own biography, which can result in both catharsis and new insights into the effects of past experiences upon the client's current life. In Fixed Role Therapy, however, the client enacts the part of an altogether different person, which may afford an opportunity to place some alternative constructions upon one's potentials and life situation.

It is difficult to ascertain what, if any, impact Kelly's introduction of this new method of short-term therapy may have had in terms of actual clinical practice. He himself taught it to many trainees in clinical psychology at Ohio State University (including this writer) between 1950 and 1965, some of whom have taught it in turn to their own students (Bonarius, 1970). Bonarius (1967), a former student of Kelly's, published a brief account of Fixed Role Therapy in a Dutch journal. He followed this with a second paper in the *British Journal of Medical Psychology* (1970), in which he explicated the basic techniques more fully and discussed their underlying rationale in terms of personal construct theory. This paper also included a short case history. In the same year, T. O. Karst (another of Kelly's former students) and L. D. Trexler (a former student of Albert Ellis's) published in the *Journal of Consulting and Clinical Psychology* the results of an experimental comparison between a modified form of Fixed Role Therapy and Ellis's (1958) Rational Emotive Therapy in the treatment of public speaking anxiety. The outcome of their experiment is discussed below. Donald Bannister and Fay Fransella (1971) published another short description of Fixed Role Therapy in the following year.

A comprehensive review of the procedures and the theoretical rationale of this approach

was completed by Kelly shortly before his death in 1967, and was eventually published in 1973. This work is an extremely useful source of basic information for anyone who wishes to become familiar with the details of Fixed Role Therapy.

Skene (1973), a British psychologist who, unlike Bonarius and Karst, had no direct contact with Kelly, reported a case history in the *British Journal of Medical Psychology* in which he described the successful treatment of an 18-year-old male homosexual by means of Fixed Role Therapy. This case is summarized below. Since then no further case histories or experiments based on this technique have appeared in print. Analyses of the available literature have been provided by this author (1979) and by Epting (forthcoming).

## CURRENT STATUS

Kelly's (1955, 1973) own accounts of the theory and technique of Fixed Role Therapy are still the best sources of information about it. Apart from Kelly himself, Bonarius (1967, 1970) has made the greatest contribution to its development. Although, as noted in the preceding section, there have been relatively few relevant case histories (e.g., Skene, 1973) and experiments (e.g., Karst & Trexler, 1970) published so far, Fixed Role Therapy has been discussed widely in textbooks on personality as the method of psychotherapy most closely related to personal construct theory. Other psychotherapeutic techniques based on some of the same theoretical principles, and resembling it in several important respects, have been devised by Bannister and associates (1975), Fransella (1972), and Landfield (1971). Their work has been summarized by this writer (1979) and by Epting (forthcoming).

Fransella (1972), in particular, has developed a method for the treatment of stuttering in which the therapist assists the client in carrying out a series of experiments wherein the client enacts the role of a "fluent speaker." In these experiments, as in Kelly's original Fixed Role Therapy, the client is the principal investigator. Moreover, his or her speaking behavior is the main independent variable, rather than the dependent variable as it is in many conventional methods of speech therapy. The purpose of Fransella's (1972) approach is to give the client an opportunity to learn what to anticipate from others in social situations when he or she enacts the part of a fluent speaker in contrast to that of "stutterer." Her technique resembles somewhat the modified form of Fixed Role Therapy used successfully by Karst and Trexler (1970) in treating public speaking anxiety. She has reported data from a sample of 20 stutterers whom she has treated with her method (Fransella, 1972).

## THEORY

The rationale of Fixed Role Therapy derives directly from Kelly's (1955, 1969, 1970) personal construct theory (summarized by this writer, 1979). This theory is grounded on the "fundamental postulate" that "a person's processes are psychologically channelized by the ways in which he anticipates events" (Kelly, 1955). The basic unit of analysis is the *personal construct*, that is, a bipolar dimension of judgment such as *pleasant/unpleasant* used to organize information about the environment. Kelly assumed that each individual develops a hierarchically organized system of personal constructs, unique in terms of both its structure and content, to interpret and predict events. Thus, within the framework of personal construct theory, people must be understood in terms of the idiosyncratic constructions that they impose on their own experience.

Kelly (1973) pointed out that two specific features of this theory are central to the rationale of Fixed Role Therapy. The first of these is his underlying model of human nature; the client is seen as an incipient scientist with the capacity to represent and anticipate

events, not merely respond to them. Within the context of this model, Kelly conceived of psychotherapy as essentially a program of experimentation in which the client assumes the role of principal investigator and should be fully aware of this fact. The chief responsibility of the psychotherapist from the standpoint of personal construct theory is to assist the client in formulating specific hypotheses, in carrying out relevant experiments to test these hypotheses, and in revising them in the light of the results. As Bannister and Fransella (1971) put it, "in construct theory psychotherapy the model for the relationship between the so-called therapist and the so-called client is somewhat that of research supervisor to research student." Indeed, in his *Autobiography of a theory* Kelly (1969) described himself as having fulfilled pretty much the same functions as both therapist and thesis supervisor throughout his own career as a psychologist.

In short, the function of the therapist, according to Kelly, is to help the client to experiment actively with his or her own constructions of experience, not to represent "reality" to the client. Nonetheless, the therapist must contribute a great deal of what Landfield (1971) terms "methodological construction"; that is, the therapist must "assist the client in the ways of learning, focusing upon personal exploration and experimentation." Kelly (1973) characterized Fixed Role Therapy, in particular, as "an experimental procedure for activating personality change without resorting to applied psychology." That is, he regarded it not so much as a clinical technique but as a form of inquiry designed to elucidate important problems in the client's life. This is clearly consistent with his general assumption that the psychological processes that occur in psychotherapy should be fundamentally similar to those that take place in formal scientific research.

If we bear in mind that the behavior of the experimenter is ultimately the only "independent variable" in any kind of experiment, then Fixed Role Therapy implies a radical form of "behaviorism" in which the client's behavior is the independent variable, not the dependent variable as it is in conventional "behavior therapy" (cf. Skene, 1973). Thus, we can view the client in Fixed Role Therapy as a "scientist" carrying out an open-ended program of research in which he or she continues to pose new questions through his or her own behavior, and interprets the outcomes of these behavioral experiments in terms of his or her own personal constructs.

The second principle of personal construct theory fundamental to Fixed Role Therapy is Kelly's (1955) novel definition of the term "role" as a course of activity carried out in the light of one's own understanding of another person's point of view. This specific conception of role follows logically from Kelly's "sociality corollary," which asserts that "to the extent that one person construes the construction processes of another, he may play a role in a social process involving the other." Thus, according to Kelly, an individual enacts a role only to the extent that his or her behavior is guided by inferences about another's interpretations of events. Kelly (1955) contended that the successful implementation of Fixed Role Therapy requires that both the therapist and client understand the meaning of role in precisely these terms.

Therefore, the "role" enacted by the client should portray explicitly a person who acts in the light of what he or she perceives to be the individual outlooks of particular other people in the client's life situation. Throughout the enactment, the client's attention, as well as that of the therapist, must be focused not only on the behavior of others, but also upon their personal points of view. In short, the client engages in "role relationships" with various important figures in his or her life, perhaps for the first time.

Kelly (1955) presents an excellent description of this kind of role enactment in his history of the case of "Ronald Barratt." There is no attempt on the part of the therapist to directly interpret the client's problems. Instead, Fixed Role Therapy involves the client's undertaking unfamiliar modes of behavior, and progress depends primarily on his developing acute sensitivity to the responses of others, both inside and outside their skins.

## METHODOLOGY

The first step in implementing Fixed Role Therapy is for the client—call her "Joan"—to write a brief character sketch of herself from the perspective of another person who knows her intimately. In eliciting this self-characterization, the therapist instructs her to write a sketch of herself just as if she were the principal character in a play. She is told to write it as it might be written by a friend who knows her very sympathetically, perhaps better than anyone could ever really know her. It should be written in the third person; for example, she might start out by saying "Joan Wilson is . . . ." This specific format was adopted by Kelly (1955) in order to suggest to the client that she should represent her own personality as a coherent whole, rather than to simply catalogue all her faults and virtues.

The purpose of asking clients in Fixed Role Therapy to write self-characterization sketches at the outset is for the therapist to find out how they use their own personal constructs to elaborate their "self-concepts" and structure their behavior in a variety of different situations. The therapist studies the sketch until he or she arrives at a working understanding of the principal axes of references in terms of which the client identifies herself and what the client's own language means to her. It is also important for the therapist to learn how the client typically uses her experience to support her current conceptions of herself, and in what ways she sees herself as developing in the future.

After the therapist has analyzed the client's self-characterization, the "enactment sketch" is prepared. This is a sketch that could have been written by a hypothetical person—let us call her "Nancy"—whose role the client will be asked to play. Kelly (1973) insisted that this enactment sketch depict a role in the personal construct theory sense of the term (defined in the preceding section). That is, "Nancy" should be portrayed as a person who consistently acts in the light of what she perceives to be the outlooks of other people. In short, she concerns herself not only with their behavior and its consequences, but also with their interpretations of events, including her own actions.

In preparing this sketch, the therapist also tries to formulate at least one specific hypothesis to be tested during the enactment period. This hypothesis may either be stated explicitly in the sketch or merely implied. It can also be an alternative to a hypothesis that the client has proposed in her own self-characterization. For example, if the client has represented herself as a "cautious" person, the alternative *from her point of view* may be to play the role of someone who is "assertive." Kelly recommends casting the enactment in terms of a novel dimension—one that never may have occurred to the client before, and that she may find quite difficult to "fit" into the current structure of her personal construct system. Nevertheless, she can explore the implications of this new dimension by playing the part depicted in the enactment sketch. That is, by using the new dimension to structure her own behavior, she can integrate it into her self-concept.

For example, Bonarius (1970) carried out Fixed Role Therapy with a client who construed himself as "free" in the sense that neither he himself nor other people could anticipate what he might do next. Since freedom, from his point of view, implied living on the impulse of the moment, everyone else had to be manipulated into going along with his own whims. The enactment sketch that Bonarius produced for this client portrayed a person whose deepest concern in life was "understanding people." The constructs *listening/persuasion, feeling/discussion,* and *forgiving/compulsive* were also included in the sketch to provide a specific context for elaborating the implications of being an "understanding" person. It was hoped that this client could experiment with the notion of his being "understanding" without reference to the basic issue of "being free" versus "being tied."

The purpose of the enactment is never to eradicate the client's "old" personality, that is, Joan, and to replace it with a "new" one, that is, Nancy. The therapist does not directly criticize or question the integrity of Joan as a personality. Joan is at all times treated with respect. The key to the whole undertaking is that Nancy, by virtue of her contrast to Joan, is clearly a hypothetical rather than a "real" person. Thus the enactment of the part of Nancy is explicitly a test of a hypothesis from the standpoint of both client and therapist.

The personality of Joan, which the client has come to know so well, is also, according to Kelly (1955), only a hypothesis. However, since the client cannot immediately envision any substantial alternatives to her being Joan, she cannot easily grasp the point that her current personality is a hypothetical construction that she herself has created. All of her everyday experiences represent the outcomes of behaving like Joan. Nancy, on the other hand, is so obviously a "made-up" personage that she can be treated as a hypothesis more readily by the client.

Once the enactment sketch is ready, the client is asked to pretend that Joan has gone away on holiday for a few weeks and Nancy has taken her place. The client is given a copy of the Nancy sketch and instructed to read it at least four times a day, especially at night when she goes to bed and again in the morning. She should also read it whenever she has difficulty playing the part. She is told to act like Nancy, talk like her, eat the way she would, and, if possible, even have the dreams she might have. It is agreed that Joan will return after a specific period of time, say two weeks. In the meantime client and therapist do not have to be concerned about her.

Kelly stressed the importance of getting the enactment underway immediately.

Rather than trying to persuade the client that she should act like Nancy, she is treated from the outset as if she actually were Nancy. The therapist expresses surprise or disbelief at any behavior that would be out of character for Nancy. Kelly noted that, although the client may be left completely speechless by this novel experience, her confrontation with a therapist who sees her as Nancy cannot be ignored. She must cope somehow with this situation, and the most obvious ways for her to act are the specific behaviors suggested in the sketch of Nancy.

A successful outcome does not depend on the ease with which the client assumes the prescribed role. On the contrary, Kelly indicated that the client who finds the experience disruptively novel, and whose first expressions in the new part are quite clumsy and inept, may be more deeply affected by the enactment than the skilled actress. This is because the former is likely to invest more of herself in the part.

The client and therapist meet regularly during the enactment period, usually every other day, to plan particular interactions with other persons and to evaluate the outcomes. In these "rehearsals," the therapist usually plays the parts of several figures in the client's life as "supporting roles." There also is a frequent "exchange of parts" between client and therapist. Kelly (1955) viewed this exchange of roles as an essential feature of each rehearsal for two reasons. First, without it, the client might perceive one part as dominant over the other. Second, playing the part of another person forces the client to attempt to reconstruct that person's point of view and thereby enter into a "role relationship" with him or her.

Throughout the entire course of the enactment, the therapist concentrates upon showing the client how specific hypotheses can be used as a basis for structuring interactions between herself and others, and in subsequently interpreting the results. The therapy sessions are planned to include, in succession, rehearsals for at least five different kinds of interpersonal situations, such as: (1) interaction with a supervisor, em-

ployer, or teacher, (2) with peers, (3) with a spouse, lover, or close friend of the opposite sex, (4) with parents or their surrogates, and (5) a philosophical or religious discussion.

The main advantage of beginning with a supervisor or teacher is that relations with such figures, even when they are strained, tend to be fairly simple. That is, they involve relatively few constructs and usually ones that can be readily verbalized. For instance, suppose that the client is a university student. The therapist might suggest that she start out with a brief interaction with one of her instructors. She could engage the instructor in a short discussion after class on some topic relevant to the course. It should be easy for her to concentrate on trying to understand the point of view of the instructor, and she can expect to receive immediate "feedback" on her own attempts to grasp his or her outlook.

In the rehearsal, prior to this interaction, the therapist can assist the client in formulating specific predictions about what the instructor will say and how it will be said. The client herself can assume the instructor's role during an exchange of parts, thereby concretely elaborating her anticipations of how the latter will respond at each stage of the interaction. In the next session the client can report the outcome of this particular experiment, and she and the therapist can go over it together, comparing what actually occurred with the client's original expectations. It will probably help to reconstruct the live interaction, again including an exchange of parts.

After this analysis of the first interaction has been completed, the next one can be planned. Once more the therapist assists the client in predicting what will happen and then in evaluating the outcome during the third session, and so on. It is hoped that, in this brief series of interactions, the client will learn gradually how to experiment more effectively in the context of interpersonal relationships. That is, she may discover how to elicit from others more definite answers to the questions that she poses through her own behavior.

Kelly (1955) indicated that the client is

typically discouraged during the first week or so, and will probably come to a session complaining that she cannot play the part at all. She may be especially unable to think of how to initiate interactions with others in which she can assume the role of Nancy. Kelly warns that it is essential not to become embroiled in a debate with the client about whether she can play the part. Rather the therapist should emphasize that Nancy is only a hypothesis, and should encourage the client to experiment as thoughtfully as possible and observe what happens when a person behaves in a certain way. The therapist should also admit candidly that neither of them really knows what will happen or what sort of person the client will eventually become. This is something that should develop as therapy continues, and if it is successful, long afterward.

After a few weeks, the experimental enactment is terminated and Joan "comes back." She is asked to appraise the entire experience in whatever way makes the most sense to her. Kelly (1973) maintained that the therapist must see to it that the client herself assumes the responsibility for evaluating what has taken place and deciding what she subsequently will choose to undertake. He did suggest, however, that it is probably best for the client to abandon the fixed role of Nancy, no matter how valuable she may feel the enactment of that particular part turned out to be (Kelly, 1955). Her next task is to create, by herself, a new Joan, a process that could take the rest of her life.

## APPLICATIONS

Kelly (1973) did not find that Fixed Role Therapy was applicable to a majority of his own cases. Indeed, he estimated that he employed it with no more than one out of every 15 clients. On the other hand, he did not rule out clients in any specific diagnostic categories as candidates for this form of psychotherapy. He reported having used it successfully with schizophrenics, paranoids, depressives, neurotics, and even mental retardates.

Occasionally Kelly used Fixed Role Therapy when he had less than a month available to see a particular client. He sometimes employed it as a termination procedure following other kinds of psychotherapy. It can be used at the beginning of therapy to test the client's resistance to change. In addition, it can be employed as an adjunct to group therapy, with clients enacting fixed roles during group sessions. Kelly also viewed it as an alternative when other therapeutic approaches proved ineffective.

Kelly (1955) suggested that there is probably less danger of an inexperienced therapist's harming a client in Fixed Role Therapy than in many other types of psychological treatment. Since the entire sequence can be completed in as little as two weeks, there is not enough time for a strongly dependent transference to develop. It can provide extremely defensive clients an opportunity to experiment with therapy without exposing vulnerable areas. It is also, according to Kelly, useful for overcoming intellectualization. Moreover, by emphasizing here-and-now experience, it may help the client to avoid preoccupation with past problems and enhance contact with everyday events.

The most severe critic of Fixed Role Therapy to date has been Carl Rogers (1956). He claims that the client is kept from knowing the purpose of the "play-acting," and, therefore, it "could not be used by any client who had read about it or heard about it, since it is very important that the client regard the new role initially as simply an exercise, and not in any sense as a possible pattern for his personality" (p. 357). It is not clear why Rogers thinks that a client's previous knowledge of the specific objectives of Fixed Role Therapy as formulated by Kelly (1955) would prevent him or her from approaching the enactment as an experiment in every sense of the term. As Kelly pointed out, neither the therapist nor the client can know in advance what will be the outcome, a fact that is true of all scientific inquiry.

In a more positive vein, Bonarius (1970) argues that "only with FRT [Fixed Role Therapy] and behaviour therapy is a realistic falsification possible'' (p. 219). Thus, if after two or three weeks this approach does not produce any positive changes, the client can be referred to an alternative method of treatment without much loss of time or money. Another major advantage noted by Bonarius is that the whole sequence can be planned fully in advance; that is, its duration, number of sessions, and so forth, are determined before it commences. Perhaps the most important feature of Fixed Role Therapy is that it is designed to help the client to cope with problems that may arise in the future and cannot be anticipated specifically by either client or therapist at the beginning of therapy. As Bonarius (1970) puts it, ''FRT is fixated upon neither the past nor the present, but paradoxically provides the patient with a flexible approach to the future'' (p. 218).

Only one relevant study regarding experimental evidence of the efficacy of this technique has been published thus far. Karst and Trexler (1970) demonstrated that a modified form of Fixed Role Therapy was more effective in the treatment of public speaking anxiety than was a version of Rational Emotive Therapy (Ellis, 1958). Both methods of treatment proved more effective than did no treatment at all. A more extensive discussion of the results of this experiment is provided by this writer (1979). Further research along these specific lines is needed before we can begin to evaluate the relative efficiency of Fixed Role Therapy in comparison to other available forms of therapy.

## CASE EXAMPLE

Skene (1973) employed Fixed Role Therapy in the treatment of a 19-year-old Englishman who had been admitted to a psychiatric hospital following his second appearance in court charged with homosexual acts with adolescent boys. He had been detained previously for nine months in a subnormality hospital after his first appearance in court for the same offense. Skene describes this client as an only child, whose mother both overpro-

tected and overindulged him. The results of psychological testing revealed that he was of ''borderline subnormal intelligence'' (full-scale Wechsler Adult Intelligence Scale IQ of 77), as well as ''conventional, defensive and highly submissive to authority.'' The latter interpretation is based on his responses to the Dynamic Personality Inventory (Grygier, 1961). Skene's direct clinical impression was that the client was both exhibitionistic and extroverted, ''but at the same time felt inadequate sexually.''

The client also completed a role construct repertory grid test (Kelly, 1955) prior to treatment, in which he rank-ordered eight photographs of strangers—four women and four men—successively on a sample of his own personal constructs that were elicited from him during a clinical interview. The purpose of this test was to evaluate his general attitudes toward sexual relations. The results, as interpreted by Skene, indicated that:

He had some confusion in his sexual roles. He did not differentiate homosexual from heterosexual feelings and he identified with neither. Homosexuality did not therefore exclude being attracted to the opposite sex. Nonetheless, he saw some differences in the two sexual roles; homosexuality implied being quite manly and happy-go-lucky, but getting one into trouble. Being manly was construed with anxiety. On the other hand, being heterosexual was construed with his being taken advantage of financially. He also put the concept of ''money grubbing'' at his own door, and this too was construed with anxiety. He felt that he experienced no guilt and would not like to change. He would like to have friends who were socially acceptable and liked by his mother. (p. 298)

Skene did not elicit a self-characterization sketch from this client, possibly because of his relatively low level of intellectual functioning. The necessary information concerning the client's self-concept and the system of personal constructs that he used to structure his impressions of his social environment was gleaned from the repertory grid test data summarized above.

In constructing the enactment sketch, there was no attempt to focus directly on the client's "problem behavior," that is, his sexual activities with adolescent boys. Skene specifically created the role of a hypothetical "John Jones," whom he depicted as a "bearded, jolly, very happy-go-lucky chap." "John" was portrayed further as both talkative and a good listener, who is usually casual in conversation and always agrees openly with others. He was described as also interested in current affairs, a good sportsman who organizes games with other patients, and as enjoying dancing.

The client was instructed to enact the role of "John" for six weeks. During this period he met with the therapist 12 times. He also kept a daily diary in which he recorded all of his experiences as "John Jones." He did not, however, play the part of "John" while on weekend leave from the hospital with his parents. No medications were given to him during the enactment period.

Skene informs us that the client experienced very few problems with the part of "John Jones." He participated actively in the functions of the hospital's social center, as well as those of several sports clubs. Also, he learned to dance. The client was able to become friends with several men of about his own age. Furthermore, he started to "go steady" with a woman of approximately his age outside of the hospital. They went out together for several months, with her paying her own way and thus not "taking advantage financially." He claimed that he "demonstrated his affection towards her." Following the enactment, he confided to the therapist that she was married and separated from her husband.

At the end of six weeks, the client was advised that he could discontinue his enactment of the part of "John Jones." He was told also that he could adopt any role he found personally agreeable. Skene reports that the client "continued as happy-go-lucky, interested in sports and entertaining, but apart from this, abandoned the John Jones character." The client described his own experience in Fixed Role Therapy as "just like a play that went off well." Following further psychological testing, he was discharged from the hospital.

A second repertory grid test was administered to him six months later using the same photographs and personal constructs as those employed in the first grid test. Skene directly compared the grid data from before and after treatment in order to determine what significant changes might have taken place in the client's personal construct system during the enactment of the role of "John Jones." He interpreted the results of this comparison in the following terms:

In the grid . . . there is still the association between heterosexuality and homosexuality. In other words, his sexual orientation was still undefined, but the patient wished, and was able, to relate better to the opposite sex and felt less anxious in his current construing. The findings, therefore, indicated that his social anxiety had been alleviated to some extent and he felt more motivated for change. (p. 291)

Skene also reports the results of further testing with the Dynamic Personality Inventory, which revealed that the client had become more outgoing and sociable, more flexible, less conventional, and less submissive to authority. Moreover, Skene indicates that "he adopted sexual roles to a greater extent, although these were basically of a feminine identification (as seen from the Dynamic Personality Inventory)."

A five-month follow-up evaluation showed that the client had found a job, had a circle of male friends of his own age, and had joined a sports club. His girl friend had become reconciled with her husband and had stopped dating him. He said that this had made him feel depressed; however, he was "contemplating courting another girl."

As part of this follow-up assessment, the client completed a third repertory grid test. This time a sample of his own personal associates were used as elements, and a set of personal constructs were elicited directly from the client (cf. Kelly, 1955). The results indicated, according to Skene's analysis, that "he currently construed himself as like people who were attracted to the opposite sex in the usual way."

At the time of this final evaluation, there had been no further reports of homosexual behavior. Skene concludes that "his adjustment might be considered of a more improved heterosexual nature." He also interprets the changes that were detected in the two grid tests following therapy as showing a general increase in social competence, together with less anxiety in relation to heterosexuality. Skene asserts that Fixed Role Therapy produced at least a partial resolution of the client's conflict and promoted the appearance of more heterosexual behavior. He does allow that similar changes might have resulted from Behavior Therapy; however, he feels that an advantage of Fixed Role Therapy over Behavior Therapy "would seem to lie in the fact that the patient himself feels that he is embarking on an adventure and feels that he is in control."

## SUMMARY

Fixed Role Therapy is an experimental procedure for activating personality change in which the client enacts the part of a hypothetical character for a few weeks. Its rationale derives from the basic principles of personal construct theory as formulated by Kelly (1955, 1969, 1970) and summarized by this writer (1979). The two features of this theory that are most important from the standpoint of implementing Fixed Role Therapy are Kelly's model of "person-as-scientist" and his unique definition of the term "role."

Kelly (1955, 1973) conceived of Fixed Role Therapy as essentially an investigative project in which the client serves as "principal investigator" and the therapist more or less fulfills the functions of a "research supervisor." During the enactment, client and therapist meet frequently to plan particular experiments and to evaluate their outcomes.

The purpose of these experiments is to elucidate specific issues in the client's own life. Following the enactment, it is the client who takes responsibility for appraising the entire experience.

The success of this venture depends on both therapist and client understanding the meaning of *role* in terms of personal construct theory, that is, as a course of activity carried out in the light of one's understanding of the points of view of one or more other persons. Throughout the enactment, the attention of the client, as well as that of the therapist, must be focused on the thoughts and feelings of significant figures in the client's life, and not only their behavior. This process can be facilitated by frequent exchanges of roles during "rehearsal" sessions in which the client must reconstruct the points of view of other persons in attempting to anticipate the outcomes of specific interactions with them. It is hoped that during the course of the enactment the client will gradually learn how to experiment more effectively in the context of interpersonal relationships, thereby eliciting more definite answers from others to the questions that he or she poses through his or her own behavior.

In creating the fixed role that the client is to play, the therapist tries to formulate at least one concrete hypothesis to be tested during the enactment. In rehearsal sessions, the therapist concentrates on helping the client discover how this hypothesis can be used as a basis for structuring his or her behavior during social interactions, and in interpreting the results afterward. The key to this undertaking is that the fixed role is so patently hypothetical rather than "real"; the enactment of this role is explicitly a test of a hypothesis from the standpoint of both client and therapist.

After a few weeks the experimental enactment is terminated, and the client is invited to evaluate the experience in whatever ways make the most sense to him or her. The therapist insists that the client assume the responsibility for appraising what has taken place and deciding what to undertake subsequently. Kelly thought that it would probably be best if the client were to abandon the fixed role and begin creating a new personality.

A major advantage of Fixed Role Therapy is that it can be planned fully in advance. Moreover, since it can be completed in a few weeks, if it does not lead to positive change, the client can be referred to an alternative form of treatment without much expense or loss of time. It can also be used as a termination procedure following other kinds of therapies, or when a therapist has less than a month available for seeing a particular client. Perhaps the most important feature of this approach is, as Bonarius (1970) points out, that it is designed to help the client to deal with problems that may arise in the future, and thus cannot be anticipated specifically by either client or therapist at the beginning of therapy.

There have been relatively few studies based on this approach published so far; however, the available evidence is fairly encouraging (see Adams-Webber, 1979; Epting, forthcoming). The best source of information about this tecnique is Kelly's (1955, 1973) own work. Apart from Kelly, Bonarius (1967, 1970) has made the greatest contribution to the development of Fixed Role Therapy, while Karst and Trexler (1970) have devised a successful modification of it for the treatment of public speaking anxiety. Clearly their efforts need to be augmented by further clinical and experimental research.

# REFERENCES

Adams-Webber, J. *Personal construct theory: Concepts and applications*. New York: Wiley, 1979.

Bannister, D. and Fransella, F. *Inquiring man: The theory of personal constructs*. Baltimore, Md.: Penguin, 1971.

Bannister, D., Adams-Webber, J., Penn, W. and Radley, A. Reversing the process of thought disorder: A serial validation experiment. *British Journal of Social and Clinical Psychology*, 1975, **14**, 169–180.

Bonarius, J. C. J. De fixed role therapy van George A. Kelly. *Nederlands Tijdschrift voor de Psychologie*, 1967, **22**, 482–520.

Bonarius, J. C. J. Fixed role therapy: A double paradox. *British Journal of Medical Psychology*, 1970, **43**, 213–219.

Ellis, A. Rational psychotherapy. *Journal of General Psychology*, 1958, **59**, 35–49.

Epting, F. *Personal construct theory psychotherapy*. New York: Wiley (forthcoming).

Fransella, F. *Personal change and reconstruction*. London: Academic Press, 1972.

Grygier, T. G. *The dynamic personality inventory*. London: National Foundation for Educational Research, 1961.

Karst, T. O. and Trexler, L. D. Initial study using fixed role and rational-emotive therapy in treating public speaking anxiety. *Journal of Consulting and Clinical Psychology*, 1970, **34**, 360–366.

Kelly, G. A. *The psychology of personal constructs*. New York: Norton, 1955 (2 vols).

Kelly, G. A. The autobiography of a theory. In B. A. Maher (Ed.), *Clinical psychology and personality: The selected papers of George Kelly*. New York: Wiley, 1969.

Kelly, G. A. A brief introduction to personal construct theory. In D. Bannister (Ed.), *Perspectives in personal construct theory*. London: Academic Press, 1970.

Kelly, G. A. Fixed role therapy. In R. M. Jurjevich (Ed.), *Direct psychotherapy: 28 American originals*. Coral Gables, Fla.: University of Miami Press, 1973.

Landfield, A. W. *Personal construct systems in psychotherapy*. Chicago: Rand McNally, 1971.

Moreno, J. L. *Who shall survive?* New York: Nervous and Mental Disease Publishing Co., 1934.

Pervin, L. A. *Personality: Theory, assessment and research*. New York: Wiley, 1975.

Rogers, C. R. Intellectualized psychotherapy. *Contemporary Psychology*, 1956, **1**, 357–358.

Skene, R. A. Construct shift in the treatment of a case of homosexuality. *British Journal of Medical Psychology*, 1973, **46**, 287–292.

# CHAPTER 25

# *Focusing*

JAMES R. IBERG

*New concepts in psychotherapy arise periodically, as someone transcends usual thinking into a new dimension. The discovery or innovation may be valuable or it may be a kind of bubble that will burst upon fuller investigation. The basic work of Eugene Gendlin, the longtime editor of the journal* Psychotherapy: Theory, Research and Practice, *a former colleague of Carl Rogers, and, incidentally, a fellow student of mine at the University of Chicago, has been on the experiential aspects of psychotherapy. As in the case of Adrian van Kaam, who in this book writes on Transcendence Therapy, he is concerned with within-the-body aspects of psychotherapy and digs deeply into the cognitive aspects of the individual. In the process, it seemed necessary to develop a series of new terms, such as* felt sense, focal completion, reconstitution, *and* parturiency. *It appeared to me, as a student of Dr. Gendlin's thinking, that his conceptualizations were of extreme value—but extremely difficult to communicate. I very much wanted a chapter on Focusing, but was concerned that it should communicate well.*

*In no other chapter was there more consideration of this issue, and no other chapter traveled back and forth more times between the author and me than did this one. Dr. James Iberg was very patient and cooperative in attempting to explain as clearly as possible within the space constraints some essentially new notions that may change psychotherapy in some fundamental ways of thinking and acting. I must warn the typical reader that despite everything, this next chapter will be tough reading—but I believe well worth the effort.*

---

*Focusing* is a special kind of introspection that can resolve problems in which "the unconscious" is not serving the person well in some part of his or her living (see the "Theory" section for a different metaphor for "the unconscious"). Clients and therapists each engage in their own Focusing. Focusing involves holding one's attention quietly, at a very low level of abstraction, to the *felt sense*. Felt sense is the *bodily* sense of the *whole problem*. In Focusing, one doesn't think about the problem or analyze it, but one senses it immediately. One senses *all* of it, in all its complexity, as the whole thing hits one bodily. At the more abstract levels of thinking used in Focusing, one forms verbal descriptions or images of the problem, but one keeps turning back to check their accuracy to the bodily sensed meaning. As one maintains this low level of abstraction, the meaning of the problem is processed so that what is sensed bodily changes. Ultimately, such change in what is sensed bodily restores the felt sense to a state in which it opens up and regains its optimal flowing quality. Once this *nascent state* is restored, insights can be articulated verbally. More basically, however, the person's implicit

---

I wish to thank Eugene Gendlin for his careful reading of the original manuscript and for his many helpful suggestions.

meanings are then capable of changing and adapting in ways necessary to have fulfilling interactions with others. Self-understanding and a capability for cognitive organization are pleasant extra bonuses.

## HISTORY

The concept of Focusing arose out of a confluence of existential philosophy and a long line of research in psychotherapy in the client-centered tradition. Carl Rogers's person-centered method (1951, 1957) minimized interventions by the therapist. Rather than attempting to diagnose or provide expert advice, the Rogerian therapist was trained to communicate understanding of the client's meanings as empathically as possible. This nondirective method represents a therapy in which the therapist's influence on the course of the interaction is minimized and the course of events most "natural" to the client is maximized. Rogers published his view of the process of therapy in *On Becoming a Person* (1961), in which he acknowledged the influence of his colleague Eugene Gendlin on his process conception of psychotherapy. Gendlin soon published his experiential philosophy (1962). He applied his theory to Rogers's data and from them abstracted the introspective procedures characteristic of successful therapeutic outcomes. Focusing is the term he selected for the type of introspective behavior conspicuously in evidence for successful clients and generally absent for unsuccessful clients.

The answers to two questions discriminate *Focusing* from other kinds of inner exploration: (1) *What of the person's thinking, emotions, and experiences is attended to:* and (2) *What kind of attention is given to that?* Gendlin's answer to the first question is "experiencing," which he describes as

concrete experience. . . . the phenomenon I refer to is the *raw,* present ongoing *functioning* (in us) of what is usually called experience. . . . there always is the concretely present flow of feeling.

. . . It is a concrete mass in the sense that it is "there" for us. It is not at all vague in its being there. It may be vague only in that we may not know what it is. (Gendlin, 1962, p. 11)

Examples that suggest the character of experiencing are available from Rogers's (1961) descriptions of the introspection of more successful clients. Successful clients "examine various aspects of . . . experience as they actually feel . . . as they are apprehended through . . . sensory and visceral equipment." They might be "talking about something when wham! [they are] hit by a feeling—not something named or labelled, but an experience of an unknown something which has to be cautiously explored before it can be named at all." For these clients "feelings 'bubble up through', they 'seep through.'" Sometimes experiencing seems at first foreign to the self. Rogers said, "there is surprise and fright, rarely pleasure, at the feelings which 'bubble through'" (Rogers, 1961, pp. 76, 129, 140).

Experiencing is something that is tangibly present to check thoughts and words against. Rogers found evidence of Gendlin's concept of experiencing as a direct referent. He saw clients making a "dawning realization that the referent of these vague cognitions lies within [them], in an organismic event against which [they] can check [their] symbolization and . . . cognitive formulation" (p. 140).

In more recent formulations, Gendlin (1978, 1979) emphasized that experiencing is distinct from body and emotions and the perception of external events. The *felt sense,* the direct referent to which the focuser attends, is the bodily sensed feel of the *whole* of the person's living of a specific concern. All considerations bearing on the concern (bodily symptoms, emotions, role expectations, and habits, relevant past experiences, etc.) can be sensed at once if the person takes a few moments to let form the felt sense of all that. As it forms, the felt sense is a peculiar bodily unease or discomfort. "It" does not seem particularly promising. It seems murky, or fuzzy, or vague. It is distinctly there, at times elusive, but with its own unique quality. This bodily experience, this peculiar "it," can be paid attention to.

In therapy once the felt sense forms, one opens oneself to it and invites it to say more about what is being felt. This addresses the second question: *How does the focuser attend to the felt sense?* Gendlin (1978) says the focuser maintains an attitude of open questioning: "you ask a question, but then you deliberately refrain from trying to answer it through any conscious thinking process." A consistent emphasis in the focusing process is on freshly conceptualizing the personal meanings of experiencing, as opposed to using already existing concepts to categorize those meanings. Rogers (1961) believed his data supported this idea. He reported observing this type of attention in successful clients. He saw them "letting . . . material come into awareness, without any attempt to own it as part of the self, or to relate it to other material held in consciousness" (p. 78). These clients did not do anything to experiencing except to be receptive. Rogers describes them as formulating "self out of experience, instead of trying to impose a formulation of self upon . . . experience" (p. 80). A client's description conveys the kind of attention given to experiencing: "left to themselves the jumbled pieces fall quite naturally into their own places, and a living pattern emerges without any effort at all on your part. . . . the minute *you* tell it what it means, you are at war with yourself!" (p. 114). This represents a special kind of accepting attitude toward experiencing:

One need *not* "accept" what comes in the sense of resigning oneself to it, or trying to think up some way of interpreting it as not so bad. . . . Rather, by letting whatever comes be for a little while, it will change, if it is felt as part of letting oneself feel all, the whole of what comes. Then all considerations which function implicitly and focally shape experiencing will play their role. (Gendlin, 1973, p. 343)

Gendlin and colleagues developed an experiencing scale (Klein, et al., 1970) to assess the degree and quality of the focusing type introspection characteristic of clients in therapy. The researchers initially expected that scores would increase over the course of therapy—that one effect of psychotherapy would be that clients would learn to introspect more effectively. Initial research provided a surprise in this regard, however. Scores on the experiencing scale did indeed predict successful and unsuccessful clients, but in neither group was there significant change on experiencing scores over the course of therapy (Gendlin et al., 1968). Gendlin concluded that therapists and clients were seriously in need of a clearer understanding of Focusing. Focusing was the type of introspection that discriminated failure and success from the beginning of therapy. If this type of introspection is missing, years of therapy could be needlessly wasted. Gendlin has since endeavored to define clearly this specific therapy-success behavior and make it available to therapists, clients, and the general public (Gendlin, 1969, 1978). With a better grasp of Focusing, people should be better able to create productive therapeutic interactions.

## CURRENT STATUS

*Focusing* (Gendlin, 1978) includes a directory of people who may be contacted for focusing training or are therapists knowledgeable in Focusing techniques. Included are people in 22 states, the District of Columbia, and seven foreign countries. Several current empirical studies are reported in the book, and a range of applications of Focusing outside of therapy is discussed.

Gendlin's Chicago office is presently engaged in an effort to coordinate the activities and communication among focusing workers on the national level.

Since Focusing was found to be crucial to long-term outcomes of therapy, this writer (1979) expected that Focusing would have immediately measurable consequences. I predicted that effective Focusing would lead to immediate change in the focuser's manner of experiencing, and that *one* successful focusing session would lead to measurable changes in verbal functioning in a life situation involving the felt sense focused on. An experiment in which this prediction was examined showed statistically significant differences between successful focusers and a control group: people concerned about their job interviews focused before a simulated interview. Successful focusers used a larger variety of types of meaning (cognitions, affects, wants, observations) to express themselves in the interview. This finding supports the hypothesis that Focusing makes immediate differences in the focuser's life, and calls for further investigation of the nature of these differences.

## THEORY

The theory relating to Focusing involves several interrelated terms. In this section I define briefly key terms and then discuss them at more length.

*Experiencing-ImplicitExperiences.* Both of these terms refer to all meaning functioning in an individual at a given moment. Experiencing includes much more meaning implicitly than is explicitly defined (for example, all relevant past experiences). Experiencing includes what has been called the "unconscious" to the extent that it is in any way functioning in the moment (Gendlin, 1962, 1964, 1973, 1979).

*Felt Sense.* This is the bodily feeling quality of the experiencing relevant to a particular situation or person, when it is felt as one whole. If one stops one's normal thinking and doing for a few moments, and asks oneself what is the bodily impact of *the whole meaning* of some particular situation or person in one's life, the felt sense will begin to form. When it forms, it is a subtle, unique, rather peculiar bodily stirring or tenseness that has one's whole complicated reaction in

it. For example, if you stop reading this text and, for a minute or so, quietly pay attention to your bodily sense of all that is going on for you as you read, your felt sense of this moment will form. (Gendlin, 1969, 1973, 1979).*

*Focal Completion.* Experiencing requires certain specific events, behavior, or objects from the person's environment to further the life process. Only certain events will fulfill, or complete, the meanings of experiencing. Hunger cannot be satiated by sexual activity. Interpersonal meanings often have very specific requirements for fulfillment: The other person's words must be just so, or the interaction remains blocked and unsatisfying. What is needed for completion is implied in experiencing: Hunger implies food. The felt sense of an interpersonal interaction implies what is needed from the other person (even though, at any given moment, one may not have identified what that is) (Gendlin, 1973, 1979).

*Carry Forward.* With focal completion, experiencing changes, moving forward to the next, different mesh of implicit meanings. This results in correspondingly different requirements for focal completion of the next moment's experiencing. To say this experientially, the felt sense that forms *after* carrying forward is different from the felt sense *before* carrying forward. The bodily experienced completion of the felt sense defines carrying forward. Without this bodily experience of completion, carrying forward has

*If you do this, you will find that your felt sense includes, implicitly, not only your thoughts and reactions to what you read, but anything else you are reminded of, the other things that you would like to be doing with the time, your feelings about yourself as a reader of such material, and more. These and more contents spring from the felt sense of this moment. The contents are *not* the felt sense—the felt sense is immediately sensible—but are implicit in, and can be explicated from, the felt sense. It often helps the felt sense to form if the focuser refrains from verbal thinking at least until one bodily feeling-quality word is found for the whole of what is involved.

not occurred. Varying degrees of carrying forward short of full focal completion are possible by the right kind of verbal explication of experiencing (Gendlin, 1962, 1964, 1973, 1979).

*Reconstitution*.   In addition to the focal completion of meanings that already were functioning implicitly, carrying forward has another effect. Other implicit experiences that were formerly not functioning regain their functioning. A common example is what happens to all the "little things" one cannot do properly when upset (for example, social courtesies, and behavior expressive of one's higher values for interpersonal relating). When upset, the implicit meanings necessary to perform those things do not function. When carrying forward occurs that is focally completing for what *was* functioning implicitly, those implicit experiences that *were not* functioning implicitly—which are necessary for those little things—begin functioning again (Gendlin, 1964).

### States of Experiencing

1. *Structure bound*. In this state, the implicit experiences necessary for fluid interaction with the environment do not function. The person "projects" the meanings that are functioning implicitly, but the absence of certain normal interactional capacities interferes with the person's ability to interact with the situation in ways that could lead to focal completion (Gendlin, 1964).

2. *Parturient*. Once the structure-bound person lets the felt sense form, focusing on that, he or she enters the parturient state. The meanings of experiencing are still effectively structure bound, but the person has assumed a different relation to them and is in a state in which significant carrying forward can occur. Significant reconstitution has not yet occurred in this state (Iberg, 1979).

3. *Nascent*. When the meanings not functioning in the first two states regain their capacity to function in interaction with

events, the person enters the nascent state. In Focusing this is an "opening up" of the felt sense. The person, as he or she enters the nascent state, feels the lifting of the problem; everything changes as the whole body of implicit meanings shifts and becomes a modifiable constellation of experiences. The person may say, "Ah, I see what is wrong here . . . yes, that's what it is. . . ." The change has occurred at that point, before much has been said about it. Once nascent, the felt sense will permit verbal expression that is deeply meaningful to the person or action that is "authentic" in that it is focally carrying forward (Iberg, 1979).

These terms provide the metaphor of *incomplete experiencing process* in place of the metaphor of the "unconscious." This theoretical change eliminates certain problems that are unfortunate by-products of the unconscious metaphor. The latter suggests that personality change is a matter of "uncovering" certain contents of the mind in the therapy process, implying that those contents (for example, lost memories or id impulses) are "hidden" somewhere in the same form in which they eventually become articulated explicitly. This view goes hand in hand with the concept of "resistance." While it is understood that the patient is not aware of what the analyst interprets as resistance, the patient and therapist are led (by the metaphor) to search for something not actually there at all. When unconscious contents are thought of as just like conscious ones, merely hidden, then it is these finished contents that the patient and the analyst look for within the patient. But this misses a crucial step in the process of identifying problematic contents.

The missing step is what the person finds when looking within, before the contents are knowable in a fully conscious, explicit form. What is found there is the *felt sense*. If the patient or client does not know to let the felt sense form, the contents of the unconscious may never be found, since they do not first appear as fully formed. Therefore, therapy will be retarded.

Since the contents do not first appear fully formed, in what form do they come? At times, emergent contents will be inconsistent with one's self concept and perhaps internally inconsistent with other contents of consciousness. The focuser may notice this and remark, "I have no reason to feel angry, but that's what the feeling is." Or: "She's the person I trust the most, how can I feel suspicious of her?" What is fundamental for effective Focusing is not an analysis of the relationship of emergent contents to existing contents, but a repeated return to the felt sense of which those contents are expressive (Gendlin, 1974).

The initial symbols that fit the felt sense may be primitive, in the sense that they are "childish" or immature when compared with the normal thought processes of the person. As Freud knew when he developed the technique of free association, the emergent material must be able to form *its own* symbolization (utilizing the wealth of extant symbols and experiences that anyone has, drawing analogies, making metaphors). If it must be forced into existing conceptual constraints, such as a therapist's conceptual categories or the client's existing concepts, the emergence will be delayed. Only after the emergence begins with its own just-right symbolization can the material change and become "adult" and consistent with the rest of the client's explicit conscious contents.

However, making unconscious contents conscious is *not* the primary goal. It is old hat that much of what a person does and says is the product of unconscious processes. In focusing theory, we say that the bulk of what determines behavior from inside the person functions only implicitly without explicit contents to represent it. This situation is seen as unalterable: It is not possible to make explicitly conscious all of what functions implicitly (Gendlin, 1962). Therefore, the point of Focusing is not to "expand consciousness."

The reason for Focusing rests on the observation that there are different manners of

functioning of the body of implicit experiences. Some manners of functioning are more optimal than others for living. At times there is a fluid flow of behavior, thought, and feeling in interaction with situations. The meanings and experiences functioning implicitly are capable of modification and subtle adaptation to permit fulfilling (focally completing) interaction with life's situations. The person's conscious and unconscious meanings serve well at such times. This optimal manner of functioning of implicit meanings is what is called the *nascent state* (Iberg, 1979), in which one need not make a special effort to focus because the meanings functioning implicitly are capable of receiving satisfactory focal completion in interaction with events.

For all of us at some times, and for some most of the time, the nascent state is not the state in which we find ourselves. When not nascent, one is in a state of varying degrees of *structure-boundedness* (Gendlin, 1964). When structure bound, implicit experiences do not function smoothly in interaction with situations. One cannot respond appropriately. One has whatever reaction one has, whatever feelings and emotions one has, but these cannot change and modify themselves in interaction with the situation. Hence, one "projects." That is, one acts the static structure that one has in one's reaction, rather than interactively responding to present events. Certain subtleties of implicit experiences are not functioning in this state, so the person cannot effectively interact. In this state, the meanings implicit in experiencing fail to achieve focal completion in action and interaction. In effect, the person cannot get the situation to complete his or her implicit meanings in this state. When in this state Focusing is most appropriate. What is needed is the *reconstitution* of implicit meanings that permit satisfying completion in interaction with situations. Nonfunctioning implicit meanings must be brought back into functioning. The state of implicit meanings must be returned to nascent.

If the problem is that certain implicit meanings are missing, thereby preventing focally completing interactions, how can we restore their capacity to function? Allowing the felt sense to form permits reconstituting completion for meanings that are not completing in the external circumstances of one's life. Although it is not theoretically possible to complete what is not functioning, one can give further completion to what *is* functioning, by allowing the felt sense to form and repeatedly focusing one's attention there, waiting for a few words or an image that precisely describes the crux of what *is* functioning implicitly. This special intrapersonal relationship is *different* from just telling oneself what one is feeling. Implicit experiencing is not so readily available to our scrutiny. Even after the felt sense has formed, some additional time Focusing is usually required before the state-changing words are found.

One must allow for the formation of the felt sense, which takes time. It is not there immediately when you turn your attention inward. Emotions may be there immediately, but the felt sense is not. It only forms after you begin sensing for it. It comes when you wait quietly to let your sense of the whole come to you. Even when it comes, it can be elusive. Once the felt sense forms, the implicit meanings that are functioning can be given further completion symbolically. The first steps of the therapeutic process of Focusing often involve finding a word or phrase or image that is exactly right to capture the quality of the felt sense. Thus what first comes may only be a "handle" (Gendlin, 1978) for the felt sense, not revealing what it is all about, but definitely capturing the bodily felt sense. The felt sense remains mostly closed and vague, still, perhaps, "heavy," or "oddly tense" bodily. This is the *parturient state* (Iberg, 1979). The meanings remain mostly nonfunctional in this state, since they are not modifiable and ready to interact with situations or words. But they are not structure bound in the same way either, since the person is giving receptive attention to the implicit in this state. He or she is no longer projecting, but is, as it were, receiving the projection on his or her own

screen, inviting it to make a really clear and accurate picture or statement of what is implicitly being experienced. Allowing the felt sense to form and accepting emergent material just as it comes is a different manner of experiencing, which already *is* the beginning of change (Gendlin, 1973).

The parturient state is a natural stage of Focusing. This point is often missed, even by experienced therapists, who may become impatient with time spent in the parturient state, as if it were up to one's own will how long it takes being parturient before nascence returns. Such impatience is itself a divergence from the attitude of open questioning necessary for the further completion needed to return to the nascent state. We might say that an impatient focuser has slipped from parturient back to structure bound. If one becomes impatient while Focusing, that impatience is part of the whole and should be allowed in to reform the felt sense.

When the parturient state has been maintained just enough, the whole mesh of implicit meanings shifts in how it sits in the body (Gendlin, 1978). Carrying-forward words can then be found. A deep breath and bodily relaxation often occur at that time. Don (1977) found distinct electroencephalogram patterns in the seconds preceding such shifts. Certain meanings that were not functioning implicitly are reconstituted, regaining their capacity to interact with events. The person returns to the nascent state.* It is just this change that this writer (1979) investigated. I found that the return to the nascent state while Focusing was followed by a more varied expression of self in the related situation. Once nascent, one "knows" what the trouble is. One has not yet found words, but one knows one can. The felt sense is then nascent, not only open to verbalizing but

*If the focuser is unsure about whether the nascent state has been entered, this simple test may help. Can the focuser describe the problem purely in terms of which personal wants or values are being influenced, independent of the particular other persons who happen to be involved? If not, the focuser is not yet nascent, and more Focusing is advised.

open also to actions that would carry it fully forward. If there were no time to tell oneself what it is, because action or interaction was needed instantly, one would move directly into satisfying, focally completing action.

The distinctions between structure bound, parturient, and nascent may seem odd, because these words all apply to what we have only implicitly. If one is structure bound and in a situation, one cannot respond appropriately. One has whatever reaction one has, whatever feelings and emotions one has, but these do not change and adapt to the situation. When such a troubled person stops acting and begins Focusing, allowing the felt sense to form, he or she goes from structure bound to parturient. While still parturient, the implicit is not such that carrying-forward words or actions can come. But this state is one in which one can act more appropriately in situations (if need be) than while structure bound, since the parturient person is watching the felt sense, waiting for nascence to return, and therefore less likely to confuse external events for internal conflicts. The second change that Focusing makes is from parturient to nascent. When nascent, implicit experiences return to the more optimal state of fluid functioning, capable of changing and recombining to permit satisfying and fulfilling interaction with events. The verbal and thoughtful insights that come once the felt sense is nascent are by-products, further results, of this basic change in how experiencing functions. Making formerly unconscious contents conscious is an additional capacity facilitated by the more fundamental change that Focusing makes in the state of experiencing. It is not that the quantity of conscious contents is expanded, but that in the nascent state of experiencing, consciousness is capable of forming new and carrying forward contents.

Focusing Therapy is never really finished. One can improve the ability to focus alone, and one can learn to arrange interactions that help one's Focusing. Therefore one may no longer wish to have a therapist. Life being what it is, however, and people being what

they are, it is unlikely that the need for Focusing ever stops. As situations and persons change, old patterns of behavior no longer fully complete one's changing body of implicit experiences. Focusing makes possible the discovery of new ways to be-in-the-world that more fully complete implicit meanings. Thus persons can benefit by making lifelong use of focusing skills.

## METHODOLOGY

Please examine Table 1. In this section I will discuss primarily the therapist's responsibilities, as I see them. In the "Case Example" section I will illustrate the specific client behaviors outlined in the first column.

One overall responsibility is essentially the same for both the client and therapist: to focus on their own felt sense. For the therapist, this is in the service of facilitating the client's Focusing. For the client, it is entirely to further personal growth.

The importance of the therapist's Focusing should be emphasized. The therapist can optimally perform only when nascent. Only then do all relevant implicit experiences enrich the therapist's understanding of what the client is expressing. Therefore, it is of the utmost importance that the therapist continually check with his or her own felt sense to keep it nascent as much as possible. An example may clarify this.

I was listening to Mark about his difficulties in completing his proposal for his Ph.D. dissertation. Having recently completed my own doctoral work, I initially felt interested and eager to understand his struggles. About fifteen minutes into the session, I noticed feeling tense and worried about not being able to understand Mark as well as I wanted. At that point, I began limiting my responses to reflections of what I was being told, turning more of my attention to my felt sense, which first had the handle "intimidated." While parturient, I noticed that the feeling increased whenever Mark talked about his research, with which he was dissatisfied. I admired the scholarly thoroughness that I interpreted it to have. I com-

**Table 1.   Schematic of Responsibilities**

| For the Client | For the Therapist |
|---|---|
| **Overall**<br>1. Focus inwardly and let a fresh, bodily felt sense form for the whole of each specific problem on which you work.<br>2. Monitor the therapeutic relationship so that it helps you focus. | **Overall**<br>1. Monitor your own felt sense of being with the client to maintain your own nascent state. If you get parturient, limit your behavior to what you can do that will not hamper the client's Focusing.<br>2. Facilitate the client's Focusing. |
| **Specifics**<br>1. Periodically stop talking and let the felt sense form. Say two or three things that describe the felt sense before going on with anecdotes, descriptions of events, thoughts, plans, and so forth.<br>2. Try to maintain a balance so that:<br>　a. You are not swamped and overwhelmed by feeling, but<br>　b. You have something to talk about that is somewhat unknown and vulnerable to discuss.<br>3. Try to take therapist comments as aids to better get in touch with your felt sense. Use them to help you heighten and open your felt sense of what you want to be working on.<br>4. Specifically identify therapist behaviors that interfere with your Focusing or tend to close your felt sense or make it fade away. Ask the therapist to modify these behaviors.<br>5. If you know of something the therapist can do, or does, that would help you focus, describe that to the therapist. | **Specifics**<br>1. Provide plentiful focusing opportunities.<br>　a. Communicate empathy.<br>　b. Stay quiet when the client is Focusing.<br>　c. Respond honestly and briefly to inquiries about what you are thinking. Immediately listen to the impact that has on the client (i.e., return to empathy).<br>2. Teach Focusing.<br>　a. Provide Focusing exercises. (Gendlin, 1969, 1978, 1979)<br>　b. Point out bits of Focusing that you notice the client doing.<br>　c. Offer suggestions for getting the felt sense of the whole.<br>3. Make invitations to focus.<br>　a. Make little invitations that point to the felt sense.<br>　b. Make direct requests that the client stop talking and let the felt sense form. |

pared my approach and felt intimidated by my judgment that his method was more scholarly. Had I not noticed that I needed to focus, my impulse would have been to insist that his method was excellent and that he should not change *that*. But that would have been the start of me arguing with him and asserting *my* authority over *his* experiencing. I would have failed to accept his dissatisfaction with his method. I refrained from that impulse and continued to listen to his perspective. Eventually, it evolved that he was relying too much on his ability to be a "workhorse" to forestall his fear that he would fall short on his incisiveness with the issues. By my staying out of his way, he was able to identify more clearly the cause of his dissatisfaction. He then took on his own challenge to get feedback on his incisiveness, rather than on his ability to work hard. Even though my parturiency had rendered my em-

phatic responses relatively superficial, at least I had not interfered with Mark's Focusing. I was only able to enter Mark's world more fully after I became more nascent. My parturiency had to do with my own evaluation of myself as being less well read than I would like to be. I was confusing that evaluation with my performance as a psychotherapist. After some time Focusing, my bodily feeling of intimidation changed, and I relaxed. At that point, I recognized that evaluation as something meaningful in relation to an article I was working on, and that it applied to that distinctly different situation in my life—but not to doing therapy.

If the therapist becomes structure bound in some way with a client and fails to turn parturient, unfortunate confusion may result about who is feeling what. The likelihood that the therapist is perceived as an authority figure makes this an unfair situation for the client, so the therapist must exercise care to focus and turn parturient when necessary.

Often, a few moments Focusing will bring key words or a phrase to the therapist that catch the crux of the parturiency and return the felt sense to nascent, so that little attention to the client is lost. This should not be a time when the therapist ignores the client. Focusing is not a wordy inward working, since the felt sense can be attended to silently. Therapist Focusing is a being-receptive-to the therapist's full bodily experience of being with the client. If a parturiency is more disturbing and doesn't quickly return to nascence, the therapist may wish to indicate this to the client with some brief statement, such as "I'm feeling grumpy about something and I don't quite know what it is." This represents explicit acknowledgment that something in the therapist requires Focusing, and opens the way for clarifying how the client experiences the interaction. Such interactions often quickly clear up the therapist's parturiency. They may also provide instances of the therapist's Focusing that may be instructive to the client: The therapist can demonstrate how to feel into the unknown parts of experiencing, risking the vulnerability of what might emerge, and trusting his or her experiencing process and the relationship to carry things beyond the parturiency. Occasionally, therapist parturiency persists, and further Focusing, perhaps in consultation with a colleague, is appropriate.

The nascent therapist benefits from taking a few moments to let experiencing enrich empathic responses. Experiencing is the implicit functioning of all meanings available to the therapist to understand the client, not just conceptual meanings. The therapist usually grasps what the client says immediately, but it takes a few moments of Focusing to let the whole felt meaning actually come home to the therapist. If this is done, empathic responses are meaning-rich rather than the outcome of a memory task. Therefore, the therapist generally withholds responses until experiencing gives a bodily sense of

understanding the whole of what the client is experiencing.

Empathy is often all that is required to further the client's Focusing. Thus communicating empathy is extremely important. This therapist task must be accomplished to a high level and is a prerequisite to any other therapist task. If the client's bodily sense of being deeply understood is lost, the therapist must work to restore it by reflections or whatever means he or she has to communicate empathy (see Rogers, 1975; Rosenberg, 1979a). The *client* is the judge of whether or not he or she is being understood. The therapist works to achieve an empathic understanding to the client's satisfaction. Anything the therapist does other than communicate empathic understanding runs the risk of leaving the client feeling misunderstood. Therefore, a therapist engaging in other activities (such as specifics 2 or 3 in Table 1) must be attentive to signals that the client has lost the bodily sense of being understood. A return to straight client-centered listening is a good strategy when this occurs (Gendlin, 1974). At such times, the therapist should be wary of sending messages that have the following structure:

You feel (paraphrase of what the client said), but I (therapist reactions, thoughts, feelings, wants).

Rosenberg's (1979b) advice to restore the client's sense of being understood is to "keep your big 'but' out of there."

When the client is quietly attending to the felt sense, the therapist should wait for the client to begin talking again. Focusing takes quiet time, which the therapist must avoid interrupting.

If the focuser expresses concern about what the therapist is thinking, the therapist should take a few seconds to focus and then say the essence of that which pertains to the interaction. The therapist should then immediately strive to understand what *that* means to the client (Gendlin, 1968). A productive outcome of such an exchange is that hearing the therapist's experiencing throws the whole of the client's feeling into relief *as a felt sense*, distinguishing it from external circumstances. This effect helps the client become more parturient and less structure bound which can, with further Focusing, bring insight regarding how the client typically misperceives certain reactions of others. Achieving this effect depends on the therapist being nascent enough to communicate experiencing in a way which is not critical of the client as a person.

The nascent therapist may, if the client agrees, directly teach Focusing. In some cases the client may wish to attend a focusing training group or read *Focusing* (Gendlin, 1978).

Even with people who, when instructed in Focusing at first cannot do it, some specific parts of Focusing do occur. When they do, the therapist may point out to the person that they just happened, and what these events are. For example, a person might refer to feeling more than he or she can say. The therapist might say, "There, where you feel more than you can say, that is how the felt sense is *bodily*. In Focusing, you just sit quietly and pay attention there for a minute, to see what comes to you." The therapist may notice a felt sense has changed during Focusing. The therapist might say, "That way the whole feel of it changed, so that it really seems different to you now is something which often happens in focusing. When that happens, just stay with the new felt sense of it all."

Suggestions that help the focuser form the sense of the whole are frequently a matter of timing. The client may need to verbally lay out the various aspects of the problem before he or she can get the bodily sense of the whole. For example, one client had been discussing her reactions to the possible end of her primary relationship for fifty minutes. Then the following happened:

T:  How are we doing?

C:  There are so many things to consider, I could talk for hours.

T:  I suggest that you check how all those things feel if you put them all in one big bag. What is the sense of all of that?

C:  (10–15 second silence) Should I be graphic?

T:  Sure.

C:  I feel like throwing up.

T:  Nauseous?

C:  Tense, in here (pointing to her chest).

T:  Just stay with that feeling—let's see what it tells you.

C:  Fear is part of it, and confusion (10-second silence). Fear of being alone. Not just now, but for a long time.

T:  It sounds like having a partner is something you really want, and the thought of not having one leaves you confused and scared of being alone for a long time.

C:  Yeah (crying). But also I get down on myself for having the fear: I should be able to make it alone.

T:  You would really value being able to make it alone?

C:  Yes, but it *would* be lonely (30-second silence). You know, the feeling changed. I got in touch with my confidence that I *can* make it alone if I have to.

The nascent therapist may make little invitations to the client to focus throughout the session. Such invitations are woven into a context of empathy maintained by the therapist, so that each invitation is compatible with the client's flow of expression. The client may speculate about some possible meanings of certain reactions or feelings they have, perhaps culminating with "Maybe that's what it is." The therapist may then say, "But take a minute now, go down and check with your feel of it all. Is that it?" An invitation might be made if the person is talking about some experience but apparently not immediately feeling into it. The therapist could say, "Can you stop and sense right now how that is for you?"

## APPLICATIONS

Focusing methods apply readily to any relationship in which the participants want continuing fulfillment of individual potentials and mutual harmony. Although the therapist and the client are distinct *roles,* an individual need not be limited to one role. We encourage people to learn both roles and to exchange them.

The range of applicability of Focusing can be seen by discussing clients at different levels of ego development (Loevinger & Wessler, 1970). Experienced therapists can likely identify two extreme groups of clients: (1) those who can readily communicate interpersonally and easily make distinctions between their own motives and the experiencing of others; and (2) those for whom there is consistent confusion between their feelings and wants and the behavior and intentions of others. Should we conclude that focusing cannot be learned by clients in the second group?

This would lead to a decision to work only with clients who need therapy the least. It would be tantamount to taking the current level of development as somehow permanent, and, in effect, giving up on attempting to foster growth and change. One of the central thrusts in the development of Focusing theory was just the opposite. Focusing instructions were developed precisely for persons who did not already know how to focus, to teach them this skill necessary for successful therapy. Olsen (1975) found that nonfocusers' experiencing levels did improve with focusing training, although the increases were not fully maintained after the training stopped. Clients at lower levels of ego development may rely more heavily on the therapeutic relationship to help them focus than clients higher on ego development.

Hinterkopf and Brunswick (in press) reported measurable success in teaching elementary versions of both the client and the therapist roles (see Table 1) to "mental patients." Prouty (1976, 1977) applied Gendlin's theoretical conceptions to his work with people labeled "psychotic," "retarded," and "schizophrenic." He found that these people require special responses from the therapist (which he defines) to develop the capacity to form the felt sense.

But is Focusing difficult only for people who are low on level of ego development? In this writer's experience, this is not the case. People at higher levels of ego development also have difficulty focusing, but they have difficulties specific to their level of ego development. I (1979) found that two groups different on ego level (both relatively high) were roughly equal at achieving the nascent state while Focusing. About half the subjects in each group entered the nascent state. A problem specific to people at higher levels of ego development is that they have so much sophisticated conceptual machinery that they can easily spend all their introspective time analyzing the problem without Focusing. They intellectualize it to death, but never stop to sense down into what is felt but not yet known about it all, which is where the desired change can begin. Elegant and comfortably familiar concepts can lure the mind away from the kind of quiet focusing attention to experiencing that so often brings rapid change and relief, once begun. Therefore the therapist, and focusing training, can provide an important service to clients at higher levels of ego development too.

The preceding ego-development discussion engenders a kind of thinking that is *fundamentally different from Focusing.* It takes the reader's attention away from his or her own felt sense and directs it to placing clients into diagnostic categories. While thinking in this way, you are concentrating neither on grasping the meanings of the client's felt sense nor on your own felt sense. Therefore, diagnostic activity interferes with the responsibilities of the focusing therapist (see Table 1).

It is crucial that the therapist not permit diagnostic thinking to overtake his or her mind during therapy to the point where the therapist role is sacrificed. Any diagnostic scheme that categorizes the person across time and situation is inherently at odds with the therapist's task of providing focusing opportunities. Such schemes are designed to reduce the client to a category (see also Rogers, 1975, 1951 on diagnosis). No category can ever capture the whole of the meanings that function in even the most trivial of a person's living activities. But it is *the whole* that must be attended to in a focusing way to bring about change.

If the therapist communicates an investment in putting the client in a category measuring degrees of pathology, he or she may, in effect, gang up with the client's own self-deprecating images. Such images are often a big part of the client's difficulty in maintaining the proper attitude toward the felt sense. This difficulty, coupled with the attribution of expert authority commonly granted to the therapist, is an unfair double whammy that is almost certain to interfere with the client's Focusing. The message is this: *Do your diagnostic thinking at a different time from therapy, and strive to make sure you are not reducing the client to any category when doing therapy.*

The tendency to categorize persons is pervasive and compelling (Mischel, 1979). Suppose you wish to stop, but it keeps happening with a client. Then turn parturient! Let yourself stop talking to yourself about it for a few minutes. Pay attention to the whole situation for you with the particular client. Consider everything that is involved for you, and let yourself feel for the underlying bodily sense of all that. It might at first form as some feeling of "urgency," or some of your own despair, or some kind of enthusiasm. *You* have to let it form. I like to take myself through a focusing exercise in such instances (not while I'm with the client, but when alone or with a colleague) to make sure I stay with Focusing long enough. If you become nascent on one like this, you can expect the next interaction with that client to be richer and fuller.

Focusing can be advantageously integrated into any other therapeutic modality. When so used, it functions like a homing device for the client's growth path. Once the client learns what the felt sense is and how to focus on it, and the therapist can recognize Focusing, little time need be wasted on unproductive procedures. Whatever part of a procedure that does help the client carry experiencing forward can be capitalized upon.

Suppose the therapist is an analyst who offers an interpretation of the patient's motives. If the patient gets in touch with what the interpretation is about and focuses on the felt sense of that, whatever *is* true can come up. The part of the interpretation that misses accurately fitting the patient can be relinquished for another, better interpretation.

All clients, regardless of diagnostic category, and regardless of the orientation of their therapist, can benefit from focusing training and practice. Focusing teaches people how to let the felt sense form and to recognize the resulting bodily experience of change. This empowers them with the ability to evaluate specific therapeutic procedures according to whether the procedures foster that bodily change. Things that do not aid this bodily change can be eliminated, and things that do can be used more often.

In "good-enough" therapy, one should experience more bodily felt change than when one focuses alone. If the bodily experience of change rarely occurs with a particular therapist, even after the client has learned Focusing and the two people have tried to adjust the relationship, I believe the client should seek another therapist.

Focusing enables one to sense one's own as-yet-unclear bodily sense of what is right and wrong for one in life. To evaluate and improve or change one's therapy in accord with this inner source is an experience of relying on one's own organism for guidance. This is a direct learning of a capacity central to developmental growth.

The full realization of improvements made possible in the nascent state occurs outside the therapy hour. This further realization is enhanced if it is possible to go beyond giving therapy and medications. If people and situations can be made available to facilitate finding friends, employment opportunities, and appropriate community resources, therapeutic gains are more likely to be secured.

## CASE EXAMPLE

This section illustrates specific client behaviors outlined in Table 1. The client is a 30-year-old single woman. A central issue for her involves how she handles feelings of vulnerability. In her words:

C:   Somehow being vulnerable is one of the worst things that I can think of being.

T:   Something about being vulnerable that's just—

C:   Awful. It's like the worst thing you can do. There are probably lots of worse things you can do, but that's what seems the worst.

T:   Being vulnerable is one of the worst things you can do?

C:   Yeah. It shows a real lack or something.

T:   It's indicative of a lack in you?

C:   Yeah. (pause) Maybe that I'm not really worth anything, or—

T:   (pause) Something total, real big. That your whole worth would be diminished?

C:   Yeah. It's weird. Like it's probably not that bad a quality, and if you had some other synonym, like ''sensitive,'' or ''delicate,'' or (pause) I can't think of any other words.

T:   There might be a way of looking at that feeling so that it wouldn't have that kind of impact, but mostly it does.

C:   Yeah. Mostly it does. I feel really vulnerable. If people know that, they can take more advantage of you than they usually do.

This client is a delight to work with, in part because she gives me feedback regarding what I do. The following excerpt illustrates what I mean by client behavior number 4 from Table 1: Specifically identify therapist behaviors that interfere with your Focusing or tend to close your felt sense or make it fade away. Ask the therapist to modify these behaviors. In this case the client is making reference to a previous session in which I had asked her to focus when she wasn't ready.

C:   Well, that made me sort of mad, because I was trying to build up, and then by asking me what I was focusing on, I lost track.

T:   That's where I pushed too hard, and you almost felt like giving up on it?

C:   Yeah, but then, when you were finally aware of it, you said, ''Well, let's start over again,'' or something like that. And that was really useful.

T:   Then it was good. And that first thing, was that a place where I was a little too pushy?

C:   Well, it was just that it was irrelevant. I was using it more as a buildup, rather than really wanting to get in touch.

T:   I see. Now I understand a little better what you're saying about a buildup. That's something that I think maybe you do sometimes that I haven't quite recognized.

C:   Yeah. I think I do it a lot. Even talking about my classes. A lot of times it's what I want to talk about, but sometimes it's sort of a way to come in and prepare myself. Sort of an introduction. I mean, it's important, but it's maybe not the most important thing.

T:   But it has another function of working up to what's more important.

C:   It's not really like I'm testing you, because I know you're OK, but it's still sort of ''how am I really feeling, today, and how are you really feeling today? What's going on between us,'' or ''let's use this as a way to find out.''

T:   Both about you, how you are, and about me. As well as the two of us together.

C:   Yeah, yeah. It's the safe topic, or something.

This client also gives feedback illustrating client behavior number 5: If you know of something the therapist can do, or does, that would help you focus, describe that to the therapist.

C: I've been thinking about what it is you do that seems to help me so much. A lot of it, I think, is not putting me into any particular category of "I won't do that," or "that's not the issue." I like it that you are able to take me as I come.

T: I don't have to have you too well defined.

C: Yeah. Or back off and say "therapists don't do this. And I am your therapist, so go away."

T: And *my* role isn't too rigidly defined.

C: Yeah. It's more open.

Another example of the same client behavior refers to the endings of our sessions.

C: It's time to go.

T: Yes, I'd like to stop. Let's just take a minute to see—is this an okay place to stop, or maybe do you want to do one more step of some kind to close it up, or get it so you can come back to it?

C: Yeah. It doesn't feel finished, but I don't think that one more minute would do it either, so it's probably not worth—but one thing I liked two sessions ago was your reluctance to end at a point where I was feeling vulnerable, and your just saying that now makes it a reasonable nonabrupt place to leave it.

T: In terms of the place that you're talking about, it makes a lot of difference if I indicate some reluctance to just drop it?

C: Yeah, rather than "okay, time is up."

T: Because you're feeling vulnerable.

C: So this feels much better, and that's enough.

Less often does this client spontaneously exhibit client behavior number 1: Periodically stop talking and let the felt sense form. Say two or three things that describe the felt sense before going on with anecdotes, descriptions of events, thoughts, plans, and so forth. With my focusing invitations and suggestions, however, she eventually does it.

C: I seem to be more worried about, or more concerned about it, than other people. I don't know why.

T: But you've got it, you can feel it, right?

C: Yeah.

T: Well, just tell me about the feeling quality of it.

C: (long pause) It's just a real *need*.

T: Uh-huh. Can you just sit with that for a minute more? I think that might open up if you do.

C: Oh, I don't know. It probably has to do with my mother or something.

T: Hm. It reminds you of her?

C: Oh, I don't know. Dr. X's big thing was that I had to be a mother to my mother, to get her approval.

T: It doesn't sound like that was very helpful, though.

C: Well, I mean I think it's probably true. I mean I don't think that just localizing it changes it.

T: Right. It doesn't change it. I think you're analyzing it a little prematurely. I think it might be better to just stay with the feel of the need that reminded you of that stuff. Just keep it right over there where you can feel it.

C: Okay. (pause) Well, it's just, part of me is the teacher and part of me is the student, and in (pause) some ways they're probably equal parts, and in a sense to be rejected in the dependent role is like (pause) having my whole being rejected. And the sense that if I ever stop just being the teacher, then I'm no longer going to be accepted.

Risks are attendant to making any kind of suggestion as to what the client should do, such as the above focusing invitations. For example, the therapist may not recognize something the client was feeling at the time of the suggestion. For this reason, client behavior number 2 is important: Try to maintain a balance so that: (a) you are not swamped and overwhelmed by feeling, but (b) you have something to talk about that is somewhat unknown and vulnerable to discuss. The following segment illustrates this kind of balancing.

C: It's sort of like nothing else in my life is any good either.

T: (pause) Uh-huh. The bad impact sort of bleeds into everything else, and colors your sense of yourself in all the different parts of your life.

C: Yeah. I mean nothing is going that (pause) well anyway.

T: There aren't other things that you're really feeling *good* about either.

C: Yeah.

T: Let's see. It might help to try Focusing on the bad feeling. But you might not want to do that. I know you have a mixed reaction to doing that sometimes. Part of you would like to put feelings like that in a closet, and part of you would like to go into them. So I want to check with you and see if you want to try Focusing on that or not.

C: I don't think I do at this point (pause). I have a copy of another letter that I wrote. Would you look at it?

Sometimes the therapist's understanding of the client will not be especially accurate. Such times are when client behavior number 3 is pertinent: Try to take therapist comments as aids to better get in touch with your felt sense. Use them to help you heighten and open your felt sense of what you want to be working on.

C: It makes me feel lousy. I mean it makes me feel defensive and upset, whereas a person who sees himself as accepted has all those groovy feelings a la Rogers. Not feeling accepted gives sort of the other—it does sort of make me want to lash out and feel defensive and hurt and makes it so much harder to communicate.

T: It kind of tightens everything up, and makes you want to strike back?

C: Yeah. I mean it's like I'm fighting against something.

T: Right. What's that? Can you stay with the sense of the fight for a bit? What's the quality of that?

C: Lack of appreciation (long pause). And then I want a validation that I'm not getting.

T: (pause) A certain kind of validation of you as, uh, competent?

C: I think more than competent. Good.

T: Better than competent.

C: Yeah! (pause) I mean, I want a chance to rise, a chance to be in a situation where I can do more and better things.

When the therapist *is* closely understanding the client, behavior number 3 remains appropriate. The client can use good therapist responses to help focus attention inwardly to let the felt sense form. Tracking the changing felt sense is more important in Focusing than the logical sequence of thought. The end of the following segment illustrates C doing this in an instance where her Focusing led to a more nascent state.

C: I haven't had a chance to be anything but bad. Part of me has been so eager to find me bad that I haven't really looked at me for a while.

T: You haven't taken a fresh look?

C: Yeah.

T: I wonder if you could do some of that now?

C: Intellectually, I'd like to do that.

T: Can you ask the feeling? What does the feeling say?

C: (pause) I think it wants to wait for a while.

T: It's got to be very careful about that?

C: Yeah (pause). Also, I don't think it's had any real time to decide, you know, what it really feels, since it's been so busy fighting off the other. It's been in this stance of "keep away from me, keep away from me, I'm not so bad,'' without much beyond being really defensive.

T:   Not much of a positive experience of itself. More it's had to keep fending off this other onslaught. No time to really feel into who it is.

C:   And then that's scary too.

T:   Even that is scary?

C:   Yeah. If it really looks, it will find something out.

T:   It's scary because it doesn't know what it will find out?

C:   (long pause) It's feeling a little bit relieved (pause). Still tense, but—

T:   Just a little bit of easing up.

C:   Yeah. (sigh, and pause) It's good. (pause)

One goal of psychotherapy is change at the level of the whole personality. When successful, the person approaches all situations or subsets of life's situations in a manner systematically different from that prior to the therapy. This client reports change at this level.

I'm more able to take risks and be more vulnerable with you. I feel more comfortable with you than with other people. I could cry with you. I can say more than I expected to be able to say. I can test things out with you, and my risks pay off, which has made me more able to take similar risks with others.

But we now know that change at the overall level only occurs if change is happening *throughout* therapy. This change involves (1) many specific therapy hours that result in nascent states, and (2) many corresponding differences in how the person interacts with situations outside the therapy hour.

When Focusing results in the nascent state, the person takes a different body home. Immediate change occurs in the manner of experiencing in relevant situations. For example, this woman received a letter from a former boyfriend whose marriage had broken up. The letter stirred many feelings, and she felt a need to speak to him. After Focusing, she was able to maintain a distinction when she called him. She could respond caringly without communicating a willingness to relate to him in ways he was suggesting that were no longer right for her.

A more dramatic example of this specific level of change followed a focusing session about her nail biting, which left her in a nascent state. This formerly persistent and disturbing behavior did not occur for the following two weeks. However, as is often the case, the nascent state didn't stay permanently the first time it came. The behavior reappeared along with the former state of experiencing. An overall objective in this area is the permanent elimination of the behavior. But one should expect to have to focus to nascent many times along the way to permanent overall change.

If the nascent state is achieved as the result of therapy sessions, we can be confident that overall change is in progress. On the other hand, if the client never experiences changing to nascent during the course of therapy, overall change is unlikely, and the client should try another therapist.

## SUMMARY

Focusing Psychotherapy's concepts are deeply rooted in research on psychotherapy, and the interaction between concepts and psychotherapeutic experience continues to refine its theory and methods. Rather than placing clients into static diagnostic categories, focusing theory defines the activities relating to personality change.

Although the roles of the client and the therapist are distinct, those who assume the roles are on equal footing as persons. The therapist and the client are expected to become parturient at times, each requiring Focusing to regain nascence and its fuller functioning.

The theory behind Focusing clarifies specifically how to determine whether productive change is occurring. Change is felt bodily, it is not just words. Such bodily change is not something that only happens within the person, separate from living in the world. When experiencing changes, the person in situations is different: He or she can more fully interact with situations immediately. There is no need to wait in confusion for many expensive sessions to find out if change is occurring; the experiential effects of Focusing should be experienced regularly from the beginning of therapy.

Focusing theory is not a theory of persons, it is a theory of how symbols and persons interact during personality change. As such, focusing methods apply to any theory of persons, lending a powerful perspective regarding the experiential impact of the theory on the persons whom the theory purports to characterize.

## REFERENCES

Don, N. S. The transformation of conscious experience and its EEG correlates. *Journal of Altered States of Consciousness,* 1977, **3**, 147–168.

Gendlin, E. T. *Experiencing and the creation of meaning.* New York: Free Press of Glencoe, 1962.

Gendlin, E. T. *Experiencing and the creation of meaning.* New York: Free Press of Glencoe, 1962.

Gendlin, E. T. A theory of personality change. In P. Worchel and D. Byrne (Eds.), *Personality Change.* New York: Wiley, 1964.

Gendlin, E. T. The experiential response. In E. Hammer (Ed.), *Use of interpretation in treatment.* New York: Grune & Stratton, 1968.

Gendlin, E. T. Focusing. *Psychotherapy: Theory, Research, and Practice,* 1969, **6**, 4–15.

Gendlin, E. T. Experiential Psychotherapy. In R. J. Corsini (Ed.), *Current Psychotherapies,* 1st ed. Itasca, Ill.: F. E. Peacock, 1973.

Gendlin, E. T. Client-centered and experiential psychotherapy. In D. A. Wexler and L. N. Rice (Eds.), *Innovations in client-centered therapy.* New York: Wiley, 1974.

Gendlin, E. T. *Focusing.* New York: Everest House, 1978.

Gendlin, E. T. Experiential Psychotherapy. In R. J.

Corsini (Ed.), *Current Psychotherapies,* 2nd ed. Itasca, Ill.: F. E. Peacock, 1979.

Gendlin, E. T., Beebe, J., Cassues, J., Klein, M. and Oberlander, M. Focusing ability in psychotherapy, personality and creativity. *Research in Psychotherapy,* 1968, **3**, 217–241.

Hinterkopf, E. and Brunswick, L. K. Teaching therapeutic skills to mental patients. *Evaluation,* 1977, **4**, 63–64.

Hinterkopf, E. and Brunswick, L. K. Promoting interpersonal interaction among mental patients by teaching them therapeutic skills. *Psychosocial Rehabilitation Journal,* 1979, **3**, 20–26.

Iberg, J. R. The effects of focusing on job interview behavior. Ph.D. dissertation, University of Chicago, 1979.

Klein, M. H., Mathieu, P. L., Kiesler, D. J. and Gendlin, E. T. *The experiencing scale: a research and training manual.* Madison: University of Wisconsin, Bureau of Audio-visual Instruction, 1970 (2 vols.).

Loevinger, J. and Wessler, R. *Measuring ego development,* vols. 1 & 2. San Francisco: Jossey-Bass, 1970.

Mischel, W. On the interface of cognition and personality: Beyond the person-situation debate. *American Psychologist,* 1979, **34**, 740–754.

Olsen, L. E. The use of visual imagery and experiential focusing in psychotherapy. Ph.D. dissertation, University of Chicago, 1975.

Prouty, G. Pre-therapy—a method of treating pre-expressive psychotics and retarded patients. *Psychotherapy: Theory, Research, and Practice,* 1976, **13**, 290–294.

Prouty, G. Protosymbolic method: a phenomenological treatment of schizophrenic hallucinations. *Journal of Mental Imagery,* 1977, **1**, 339–342.

Rogers, C. R. *Client-centered therapy.* Boston: Houghton, 1951.

Rogers, C. R. The necessary and sufficient conditions of therapeutic personality change. *Journal of Consulting Psychology,* 1957, **21**, 95–103.

Rogers, C. R. *On becoming a person.* Boston: Houghton, 1961.

Rogers, C. R. Empathic: An unappreciated way of being. *The Counseling Psychologist,* 1975, **5**, 2–10.

Rogers, C. R. and Dymond, R. *Psychotherapy and personality change.* Chicago: University of Chicago Press, 1954.

Rosenberg, M. B. *From now on.* St. Louis, Mo.: Community Psychological Consultants, 1979a.

Rosenberg, M. B. Personal communication, October 1979b.

# CHAPTER 26

# Functional Psychotherapy

JOSEPH T. HART, RICHARD J. CORRIERE, and WERNER KARLE

*In these introductions I try to be neutral, even though I suppose that clever people can read between the lines and can see my biases. However, being statistically minded, I rated various chapters on a scale of from one to five relative to my consideration of their importance. I shall not make any overt judgments since comparisons are both odious and invidious. But the perceptive reader can guess where I have listed this particular chapter (and a dozen others).*

*Hart, Corriere, and Karle have attempted a total system based on the concept that psychotherapy must not be confined to those who are below par: that the normal and supranormals also need the benefits of psychotherapy. This is the education rather than the sickness model. Moreover, they have established a structure for a complete restructuring of the total personality.*

*This is one of the most ambitious schemas I have run into, and this group of people bear watching, for they may take over the field of psychotherapy. No less seems their aim.*

Functional Psychotherapy and Functional Counseling are labels for the approach developed by these writers and their colleagues during the last 10 years. This approach draws upon the general ideas and methods of early functional psychology and attempts to identify a functional orientation to psychotherapy that is shared by many present-day eclectic and humanistic therapists. This chapter will discuss functional psychology and the functional orientation to therapy in general and our own Functional Psychotherapy in its particulars.

The goal of Functional Psychotherapy is personality change. Clients are helped to feel better and function more effectively by learning new personality skills. This general goal is made meaningful and practical by applying a systematic schedule of individual and group sessions that examine specific personality dynamics in specific life areas. This programmed therapeutic process is facilitated both by helping clients understand and change deficit functioning and through understanding and achieving new levels of positive functioning. Special emphasis is placed upon the psychological fitness model versus the disease, adaptation and psychopathology models. Within the fitness model the focus is not on symptoms or cure but on acquiring the attitudes and skills necessary for psychological health. Psychological fitness emphasizes: (1) the need for personality exercise; (2) the experience of psychological "exercise effects"; and (3) the maintenance of "fitness effects."

## HISTORY

### Precursors

*Functional Psychology.* The founders of functional psychology (William James,

John Dewey, and George Mead, to name the big three) are well-known, and their influence in forming the foundations of general psychology is widely recognized.* In his book *Psychology: The Science of Mental Life* (1962), George Miller says of William James and the other functionalists:

By broadening the definition of psychology, the American functionalists were able to incorporate studies of animals, of children, of the mentally retarded and the insane, and of primitive, preliterate peoples. And they were able to supplement introspection by other methods of collecting data; physiological experiments, mental tests, questionnaires, and descriptions of behavior all became legitimate sources of information in the study of psychological processes. . . . In the U.S. today functional psychology *is* psychology. (p. 66)

Although none of the early functionalists were clinicians and none are usually cited for their contributions to psychotherapy, we will argue that functional psychology is the greatest single unrecognized influence on the attitudes of the majority of today's psychotherapists and counselors. The definition of psychology used by functionalists—the study of mental processes and the behaviors resulting from them—and the inclusive methods applied by them to general psychology are exactly applicable and widely used by therapists of many different theoretical persuasions. Indeed, we believe that in the United States today the functional orientation to psychotherapy *is* psychotherapy.

If we stretch the definition of "therapist" a very long way, we can even speak of William James as a therapist—a therapist who had only one patient, himself. James's psychological and philosophical writings require very little translation to be immediately useful to the clinician. The "stream of consciousness," the significance of choice in

personality change, the acquisition of emotional habits, the use of counterbehaviors to offset negative emotions, the recognition of the role of expression in enhancing and forming feelings, the pragmatic testing of beliefs and ideas are all parts of James's functional psychology and pragmatic philosophy. Not only do these topics form the content and focus of most psychotherapists' endeavors, but they are discussed at a level of discourse that matches the level clinicians most naturally use in everyday psychotherapeutic work.

*Clinical Precursors.*    Three forerunners of the modern functional orientation to psychotherapy are Pierre Janet (1859–1946), Trigant Burrow (1875–1950), and Jessie Julia Taft (1882–1960). Many others could be listed, but these three are of especial importance: Janet because he was a contemporary of the founders of the two other major trends in modern psychotherapy, Freud and Pavlov, and who created his therapy with full knowledge of their work; Burrow because he clearly recognized the need for psychotherapists to develop their own personalities beyond both their individual neuroses and the social neuroses; and Taft because she was the first psychotherapist to deliberately apply the label and ideas of James's, Dewey's, and Mead's functional psychology to psychotherapy.*

## Beginnings

Only *after* a theory is clearly formulated is it possible to look back and recognize intellectual forebears. At the time these writers began our work in 1969, we had no knowledge of the work of Janet or Burrow, and Jessie Taft was just a name to us.

Our work toward the synthesis that would uncover the functional tradition began at the University of California at Irvine in 1969.

---

*See Schultz, 1960, for historical appraisals of functionalism and for discussions of the work of other functional pioneers such as Francis Galton, Charles Darwin, G. S. Hall, and James Angell.

*For more information about these systems of therapy, consult Ellenberger, 1970; Burrow, 1958; and Robinson, 1962.

Working at the Center for Integrative Psychology, we attempted to study therapies and meditation practices psychophysiologically to see if we could identify a relaxed condition common to both therapy and meditation (see Hart, 1970). We studied a number of therapies that claimed to produce major changes in physiological functioning (including Primal Therapy [Karle, Corriere, & Hart, 1973]) and several adjunctive methods used in many therapies (including hypnosis, autogenic training, and other relaxation techniques). Along the way we made basic discoveries about a connection between electroencephalogram brain waves and hypnotic susceptibility (London, Hart, & Leibovitz, 1968) and applied biofeedback techniques to help people who were not susceptible to hypnosis maintain the brainwave pattern (abundant alpha) that would allow them to respond positively to hypnotic suggestions (Engstrom, London, & Hart, 1970). In these scientific investigations we conducted research as participant observers. We measured the physiological effects of the biofeedback technique or therapy technique not only on our subjects but also on ourselves.

## CURRENT STATUS

Our first major step toward what would later become the functional orientation in psychotherapy was the founding of the Center for Feeling Therapy* in Los Angeles in 1971. We continued, in the therapeutic context, the emphasis we had maintained in our research on participant observation by doing therapy on ourselves as well as our clients and by measuring the results of the therapy (psy-

---

*The founders of the Center for Feeling Therapy were: Jerry Binder, Ph.D.; Dominic Cirincione, M.A.; Richard Corriere, Ph.D.; Stephen Gold, Ph.D.; Joseph Hart, Ph.D.; Werner Karle, Ph.D.; and Lee Woldenberg, M.D. These same men later founded the Clinic for Functional Counseling and Psychotherapy and all the related organizations described in the "Current Status" section of this chapter.

chologically, physiologically, and socially) on therapists as well as clients.

The seven founders of the Center for Feeling Therapy brought together a diverse set of backgrounds in psychotherapy. These backgrounds included direct training and therapy experiences with Eugene Gendlin, William Glasser, Arthur Janov, Stanley Keleman, Alexander Lowen, Claudio Naranjo, Fritz Perls, Carl Rogers, and Fred Stoller. We also had extensive academic training in Freudian analysis, Jungian analysis, Reichian analysis, autogenic training, Behavior Therapy, pastoral counseling, social work, psychiatry, and general clinical psychology.

From this smorgasbord of training, experiences, and theories we drew one key theoretical idea and two practical emphases, which were described in our first book about Functional Psychotherapy, *Going Sane* (Hart, Corriere, & Binder, 1975). Our emphasis was on the therapists' responsibility to create and deal with "feeling moments" in every therapy session.

When a person senses that his feeling is incomplete, it is possible to help him move from defending to feeling. Without this sense it would be impossible because defenses would be entirely unconscious. The feeling moment is available to everyone, at least fleetingly. . . . In every feeling moment there is a felt meaning which generates an impulse toward active expression. . . . (Hart, Corriere, & Binder, 1975, pp. 20, 37)

The focus of therapy was defined as recognizing *and* expressing feelings. Feelings were identified as the conscious mediators of personality change.

Two practical emphases were: (1) therapists must continue to get regular individual and group sessions for themselves; and (2) clients can be trained to be co-therapists for one another and, in that way, shift from a reliance on professional help to relying on friends. These two practical emphases were a direct continuation of our research investigations that emphasized participant observation by the experimenters and informed participation by the research subjects. It seemed obvious to us that therapists need therapy for themselves beyond a training analysis and that the people who most benefit from therapy are those who take responsibility for doing it. These practical emphases attracted a good deal of professional and popular attention (see Appelbaum, 1979, and Liddick, 1976).

*Discoveries About Dream Dynamics.*   The next major theoretical advance came from clinical-research investigations of the dreams of our therapists and clients who had been in therapy for several years. We found significant shifts in dream patterns occurring that were indicative of basic shifts in personality functioning. Basically, dreams shifted from a predominance of symbolic, bizarre, and confusing dreams in which the dreamer was anxious, alone, and passive to clear and realistic dreams in which the dreamer was active, expressive, feelingful, and making contact with friends. We described these dream discoveries and the new functional methods for working with dreams in a popular book, *The Dream Makers* (Corriere & Hart, 1977); in a less popular book, *Dreaming and Waking* (Hart, et al., 1979); in a technical book, *The Functional Analysis of Dreams* (Karle, et al., 1980); and in research and clinical articles (see, e.g., Corriere, et al., 1977; Hartshorn, et al., 1977). The central shift we made in working with dreams (experimentally and clinically) was to move from the dream content and interpreting dream symbols to a concentration on the dreamer's functioning—from the question "What does this symbol mean?" to the question "How is this dreamer functioning?"

*The Psychological Fitness Model.* These discoveries about dreams led us to the next major formulation of the functional approach. We came to understand that if typical, normal dreams were often mixed up, bizarre, confusing, and anxiety-laden, it was because they reflected a low level of personality functioning. Once the person, through therapy, learned to use his or her personality more effectively, then dreams changed to a more effective or more psychologically fit level of functioning. We also came to understand that the core personality dynamics that made a difference in whether or not a dream would be functionally effective were also the core personality dynamics for effective functioning in waking.

The psychological fitness model (Corriere & Hart, 1979) also gave us a new understanding of why it is important for therapists to have therapy—not just to deal with negative functioning but to maintain high levels of positive functioning. From the psychological fitness perspective we came to view our role as therapists as much more similar to that of coaches and athletes than physicians or educators.

*New Organizations for Training and Research.*   In 1972 we established a nonprofit, tax-exempt foundation, the Center Foundation, to carry out research and educational programs that would cut across different theoretical biases to bring clinicians and experimenters together. Since 1975 the Center Foundation has sponsored the *Dream Research Newsletter,* a bimonthly publication, which keeps dream researchers throughout the world informed about dream research findings and about research in progress.

In 1977 we founded the Clinic for Functional Counseling and Psychotherapy and the Training Center for Functional Counseling and Psychotherapy in Los Angeles. These organizations supplemented the intensive, long-term, community-based therapy offered at the Center for Feeling Therapy with a shorter-term clinical practice. The Center for Feeling Therapy accepts only 100 or fewer clients per year, but the clinic services more than 1,000 clients yearly. The clinic in Los Angeles employs more than 50 therapists, making it one of the largest private therapy facilities on the West Coast. Affiliated clinics have been opened in Montreal, Munich, and

Boston. Additionally, groups of therapists from Honolulu, Chicago, New York, and San Francisco have been trained through the Training Center. New clinics are planned for these cities, and others, within the next five years.

In 1978 we organized the Fitness Foundation, an educational organization devoted to the promotion of the psychological fitness model in many different contexts (including schools, families, and communities and for many different professional groups). Every summer the Fitness Foundation offers four week-long programs of Psychological Fitness Training to the general public. These programs annually attract more than 1,000 participants. Psychological Fitness Workshops, lasting a day or a weekend, are offered throughout every year by the Training Center for professionals and by the Fitness Foundation for nonprofessionals. The Fitness Foundation also carries out a unique educational program called the Associate Program on Psychological Fitness in which participants are trained and guided in the ideas and practices of psychological fitness by counselors who communicate with them by letter and by telephone. This educational program has been successful in extending Psychological Fitness Training beyond the typical confines of clinical and therapeutic settings (Karle, et al., 1978).

The Center Foundation, the Training Center, and the Fitness Foundation all maintain publication lists of research articles and audiotape listings of lectures, seminars, and therapy sessions.*

## THEORY

In the fitness model we postulate a series of simple working ideas that allow the psychotherapist to practice without referring to quasi-medical concepts for theoretical support.

1.   The personality needs to be exercised.

*The major centers for the programs described are: The Beverly Hills Psychotherapy and Counseling Group and the Montreal Centre for Consultation and Research.

Without exercise personality becomes rigid and dysfunctional.

2.   Fitness cannot be attained or maintained without contact.

3.   To remain in top psychological shape the personality needs to be stressed, just like the cardiorespiratory system. Thus progressive overload in a controlled situation expands the personality's ability to undergo stress and remain functional.

*The Five Personality Dynamics.*   We work with five major personality dynamics: expression, activity, feeling, clarity, and contact. The personality is functional when it has the ability to use these five dynamics in any basic life area. To simplify, we will mention just five basic life areas of work, play, sex, relationships, and sleep and dreams. When viewed as a five-by-five matrix, it becomes quite easy to picture how the personality is functioning by seeing if a person has a mostly positive or mostly negative response to each of the 25 areas of the matrix.

Instead of focusing on what is wrong with a person presenting a problem, we ask instead, "How is he functioning in this particular area?" and then "How is he functioning overall?" When we begin to work with a client, we focus first on his best or strongest area of functioning.

No matter how nonfunctional the best behavior may seem to the outside world, it must be used as the feeling reference point on which all the therapy will hinge. The client then has an emotional reference point to work toward.

## The Cycle of Reintegration or Transformation

This cycle consists of four stages: counteraction, catharsis, proaction, and reintegration.

*The Counteraction Stage.*   The therapist directly and quickly begins counteracting the image that the client presents. The therapist does this by countering the client's meanings, feelings, and behaviors associated with an image that has become dysfunctional.

Counteraction takes place by the therapist instructing the client to increase or decrease his or her use of one of the five personality dynamics, often with reference to a defense or resistance or image. When the counteraction begins to take place, the client experiences stress. A function is being extinguished; during this process the personality is in a state of suspended functioning. We refer to this as *disintegration*. A disintegration experience must occur for a reintegration experience to occur.

**The Cathartic Stage.**    The disintegrative stage often leads to an explosive emotional release, or the cathartic stage. In this stage the client expresses freely the full range of emotions that have been held in by the old personality images. It is sometimes abreactive when the therapist uses this stage to help the client differentiate between the past environment that gave rise to the old level and the new environment that requires new levels of functioning. The major requirement of the cathartic stage is that it must occur within the context of contact or in the feeling moment. Without contact clients often distort what they feel and drain off emotions rather than integrating them.

**The Proactive Stage.**    The client is directed from the cathartic stage toward the reintegration work at the proactive stage. Here the client is helped to develop new behaviors and skills and try them out in the therapeutic environment. At this time the client, who has just undergone a disintegrative crisis, now experiences a new crisis of how to live from new thoughts, new feelings, and new behaviors. It is only through his or her contact with the therapist that a person is willing to try to make this transition. The person does not know the new behavior will be successful. All that he or she knows is that the old behaviors are no longer the ones that are wanted. What is occurring is adult bonding. Clients find themselves once again vulnerable to the environments in which they are being asked to learn new behaviors, but this time, as they are adults, the learning takes place consciously and with consent.

**The Reintegration Stage.**    The first three stages lead to reintegration at a more successful level of integration. What this means is that the client is able to use more of his or her personality in a wider range of activities. The client now feels, thinks, and behaves in new ways, and can acquire new personality images.

What we have presented so far is essentially only the first half of the theory (Karle, Woldenberg, & Hart, 1976). In more recent developments we have been able to recognize that counteraction, catharsis, and proaction become much more powerful when encompassed in a general fitness model.

**The Exercise Effect.**    Counteraction essentially produces an insight effect, catharsis a releaser effect, and proaction a behavioral effect. Many therapies and theories focus on one or more of these effects, but what we have now learned is that all of these effects can easily be subsumed under the functional heading of the exercise effect. The value of each of these types of psychological exercise is multiple. They reassure the client about him- or herself, they solve problems, but, more important, *they exercise the personality.* We suggest that it is the exercising of the personality that makes Functional Therapy, and in fact any therapy, work effectively. The exercise effect, if maintained over time, leads to a fitness effect. The client is not *cured* but has a more functional personality.

## The Cycle of Integration

What we soon discovered after we formulated concepts about the exercise and fitness effects was that equally beneficial results could be attained if we were willing to design an integrative cycle to complement the disintegrative-reintegrative cycle. It was obvious that the most intense disintegrative therapy was inappropriate for the vast majority of clients seeking help.

In fact we found that the positive or integrative exercises were more useful in that they required less time and they could be assimilated more easily. The two cycles make up the complete therapeutic cycle of Functional Therapy.

In the cycle of integration we directly exercise the personality without reference to problems. This process of exercising the personality involves four stages.

*Need Stage.* The therapist helps the client isolate, recognize, and admit a need. Depending on the level of sophistication or level of integration, the need expressed can be as simple as "I need to look at people" or as complicated as "I need to set five-year life goals." In either case the therapist focuses on the process rather than the content. Needs, as viewed in functional theory, are continuous. The process of satisfying needs is the main job of the personality. The personality is the bridge between the biological experience of the need and the outer behaviors required to satisfy that need. We do not postulate hierarchies of needs simply because we are interested in the *process* of need satisfaction rather than the satisfaction of any particular need. We define needs as clearly different from problems. When a client makes the shift from "This is a problem that I have" (the personal application of the medical model) to "This is a need" (in the same way breathing is a need), the client has made room for personality development.

*Choice Stage.* Once the need has been admitted and recognized, then the client is pushed to openly and verbally choose the need. He or she is directed to be self-directed, to respond to his or her needs as reality. In making this choice the client is taking a new philosophical stand from outer-oriented ("The world must be perfect for me to feel good") to inner-oriented ("I can feel good").

*Behavioral Stage.* Once the client has admitted a need and chosen the need as a real value in his or her life, he or she should learn new behavioral skills to fulfill that need. This occurs through the interaction with the therapist, who teaches the client how to behave in new and more functional ways. The teaching springs directly from the need that the client has identified.

*Image Stage.* The movement at each particular stage—need, choice, behavior —leads to a new image. The client is involved in both a discrete process of each stage and the overall process of functioning in a new way. The new image is being developed in the environment created by the therapist-client interaction. The cycle of integration does not deny the operation of resistances and defenses by the client but works with these old behaviors, as they interfere with participation in the cycle.

The purpose of the cycle of integration is to help the client develop more and more images that he or she can functionally use when it is appropriate to do so, bad on the environment that the images fit. This image-building procedure is straightforward and progressive.

*The Substructure of the Cycle of Integration.* Admitting needs, making choices, learning new behaviors, and integrating new images into the personality are all subsumed under the exercise effect. They are all exercises. As the client recognizes what is needed, he or she is increasing the clarity dynamic; in the choice stage he or she is exercising the expression dynamic. In both stages, the client is exercising the contact dynamic through the interaction with the therapist. As the client learns new behaviors, he or she is exercising the activity dynamic. And throughout the entire cycle the client experiences more feelings. It is with feelings that the conscious mediation of behavior change occurs.

The substructure of the cycle of integration is the same as that of the cycle of reintegration. It should be clear that these two processes are interconnected. But, when a client resistantly adheres to a nonfunctional image, the crossover between them must occur only when the disintegrative exercises are clearly called for.

The cycle of reintegration explains how a disordered personality is able to reorder itself by experiencing defenses as limits. This part of the theory is essentially applicable to the limited world of psychotherapy. The second part of the theory, the cycle of integration, defines not only what occurs in the world of psychotherapy but what occurs throughout every adult's life in the real world. It is critical for everyone to be able to develop new images and behaviors based on his or her needs. The theory describes a naturally occurring process in human development and what happens when this development does not occur. When the process does not occur, the personality is trapped in images destined to become nonfunctional as the image does what it was designed to do—satisfy old needs. Images have a limited life span; the personality does not.

## METHODOLOGY

Just as physical fitness programs take a participant through progressive stages of conditioning, stressing, and performance testing, we do the same in Functional Counseling and Psychotherapy. In our training manuals we teach the therapist what areas of personality exercising to cover in step-by-step procedures.

Functional personality theory states that the major cause of personality disorders is a learned mismatching of internal responses to external stimuli. Exercising the personality requires that the therapist gradually teach clients how to match outer expressions to internal sensations. This simple emphasis on teaching expression skills has far-reaching implications. By focusing on expression rather than on empty actions or reactions to behaviors, we emphasize the necessary connection between behavior and experience. It is the absence of this connection, or the mismatching of behavior and experience, that constitutes psychopathology. It is our contention that expression and expressiveness are necessary components of psychotherapeutic change.

## Programs

Essentially we have designed two separate structures* that reflect the intensity of the therapy program the client wishes to undergo. The medium-term Functional Psychotherapy program is basically a 10-month program. This can, of course, be altered to fit the client's needs and desires. The intensive Functional Therapy program (Feeling Therapy) is a longer program and requires a strong psychological commitment to major long-term life changes.

Clients entering the 10-month program are screened initially to determine levels of functioning in different life areas. An informal agreement is then made that the client will go through the whole program or only a limited part of it. It is emphasized to the client that the therapy is definitely part of a well-structured program that allows for individual variation.

## Program Overview

In the Clinic for Functional Counseling and Psychotherapy, each of the first nine months focuses on one of the five personality dynamics or one of the following four life areas: relationships, sex, play, and work. The last month is reserved for a general review. Weekly therapy sessions (individual and group) revolve around the needs of the client, but the therapist always uses a monthly theme as he works with the client's content. For example, if a man complains about the lack of spontaneity in his relationship with his wife during the "Expression" month, the therapist will work dynamically with how the client's personality functions in this area, but he will also emphasize the teaching of expressive skills that can help to not only alleviate the problem but prevent it from recurring.

*A third program, short-term Functional Counseling, is not described here but parallels the program of Functional Psychotherapy. The counselor uses the fitness approach and teaches clients how to make changes in life areas by using the five personality dynamics.

**Table 1. The 10-month program is structured in this way.**

| Month | Weeks | Themes | Session Types (For each of the four weekly sessions) |
|---|---|---|---|
| 1 | 1,2,3,4 | Expression | I, I or G, I, I or G |
| 2 | 1,2,3,4 | Activity | I, I or G, I, I or G |
| 3 | 1,2,3,4 | Clarity | I, I or G, I, I or G |
| 4 | 1,2,3,4 | Contact | I, I or G, I, I or G |
| 5 | 1,2,3,4 | Feeling | I, I or G, I, I or G |
| 6 | 1,2,3,4 | Relationships | I, I or G, I, I or G |
| 7 | 1,2,3,4 | Sex | I, I or G, I, I or G |
| 8 | 1,2,3,4 | Play | I, I or G, I, I or G |
| 9 | 1,2,3,4 | Work | I, I or G, I, I or G |
| 10 | 1,2,3,4 | Review | I, I or G, I, I or G |

[a]I = individual, G = group.

The client is encouraged to participate in peer groups (groups made of clients with approximately equal amounts of therapy experience) by the end of the first month but is not forced to do so. For clients who do not attend all 40 sessions (for whatever reasons), the therapist can tailor the program in any way he sees fit. In this way the client can still get the benefit of covering all or most of the areas included in the 10 months.

Just as the program has a basic structure, so does each session. The therapist is given guidelines for the sessions that suggest a style of greeting the client, briefly visiting the client, eliciting a problem to work with, giving direction to the session, creating specific psychological exercises for the client, and closing the session.

As in the program, the therapist is free to deviate from this session outline whenever this is called for. However, therapists generally try to stay with the specific outline given to them in their program manual, which contains specific descriptions for each of the 40 sessions. Here is a sample from the manual.

Session Sample One (Expression Month, Session One)

I. CHECKLIST
A. Review notes and make sure all details of your client's file are current.
B. Set one simple goal for this session.

II. VISIT
A. Begin by informally visiting with your client. Ask engaging questions like "How do you feel today?" "What was your day like?" Follow up *each* question with either a clear response or another question.
B. Gain impressions of your client.
1. Watch for resistances (vagueness, hostility, evasiveness).
2. Watch for feelings (sadness, excitement, fear).
C. Follow the specifics of your client's comments. Gain a clear picture of your client's thoughts and feelings.
D. Remember that your *main goal* for today is to create a bond between you and your client. You want him to feel *safe and accepted* by you. This is the beginning of a *most important relationship* for your client.

III. PROBLEM/ISSUE PRESENTATION
A. If you do not have a clear area to work with, ask your client "What would you like help with?" or "What would you like to talk about today?"

IV. DIRECTION
A. *Allow your client to talk about his problem.*
When you have established an area to work with, begin your session by teaching your client briefly about the FIVE DYNAMICS.
B. *Positive Approach Talk*
1. Tell your client what he can expect

from this session. Tell him that you will be taking "AWARE-NESS BREAKS" throughout the session. Tell him you will be reeducating him to a new way of seeing and experiencing himself.

2. Inform your client that he will be experiencing discomfort, awkwardness, uneasiness, etc. Tell him there will be times he will feel foolish, silly, inadequate, etc. Teach him that these are all *signs* of his own inward changes and deepening.

V. EXERCISE

A. Talk about your "problem/issue" in your regular voice.
1. Rate your voice from 1 to 5 (1—no expression, 5—intense expression).

B. Now, talk about your "problem/issue" in a voice that is one step *down* from your regular voice.

C. Take an "AWARENESS BREAK."
1. Discuss the changes that happen to your client when he does this. Help him see any *loss* of sensation, movement, general feeling, etc. If he is unaware of any loss, talk about what MAY be happening to him.

D. Now, move one step back up to his "normal" expression level.
1. Be aware that this may be a difficult step up to take from the lower expression level. Be supportive.

E. Take an "AWARENESS BREAK."
1. Discuss the effect a 1-UP step has on the client's sensations, movements, feelings, etc.

F. Now, move your expression level one step above the regular level.
1. If your client has a hard time with this, do it with help. Help him see what to do by showing him yourself. Let him copy you.

G. Take an "AWARENESS BREAK."
1. Discuss the difference in sensation, movements, general feelings, etc.

2. Allow him to talk about how he is and what he notices.
3. Be positive and supportive.

H. Tell your client what you noticed about him. BE SPECIFIC.

VI. CLOSING

A. Ask your client to be more aware of his expression range this week.

B. Ask him to think about what his life would be like *if* he were to EXPAND his expressive range.

Of course, there are cumulative learning and exercise effects as the weeks go by. As the clients learn more and more about the personality dynamics and life areas, the therapist can use this accumulated knowledge and experience in future sessions.

All functional psychotherapy sessions use the fitness approach. Psychological exercise programs are developed in sessions and often extended outside the session so that the client continues to benefit from the exercise effects and achieves a fitness effect.

**Program Overview**

In the structure of the Center for Feeling Therapy, the intensity of the longer-term Functional Therapy called Feeling Therapy and the larger personal commitment it requires are immediately evident. The program begins with two months of almost daily individual and group sessions designed to initiate the major personality changes clients involved in this program are seeking. This is followed by a 12-month period of weekly therapy sessions, which include one intensive, experiential group session and one educational group session. At the end of this period clients decide whether or not they want to graduate into a co-therapy training phase in which they and their peers are trained to educate and counsel each other. They do not learn how to do therapy unless they are qualified to do so. This co-therapy training program lasts another 12 months with an identical weekly session structure. A variety of participatory programs are available at the end of this period, which allows clients to further sophisticate their psychological skills at greatly reduced fees.

Clients cover all life areas and dynamics repeatedly during this period. Many specialized individual sessions and groups are designed to continually stress and exercise the personality in different ways. The therapists' manual for Feeling Therapy is used as a guideline. Of course, the therapist is free to adapt the proposed program to the client's needs, but an attempt is always made to incorporate any changes into the structured string of therapy sessions.

The therapy period that follows the initial two months continually repeats the functional fitness themes at more deeply refined levels. The concentrated learning and exercise effects experienced by clients in this program lead to significant fitness effects within remarkably short periods of time.

## APPLICATIONS

We will describe some of the various areas in which the theory has been put into use in addition to the two programs described in the "Methodology" section. One characteristic of all the applications of functional theory is programming. We use a series of graduated exercises designed to improve personality functioning.

The question that we must direct ourselves to first is "Who can benefit from the use of exercises and the psychological fitness model?" This is most easily answered by understanding the disorder-order theory of personality. The disorder-order theory is not two theories of personality. The personality is always attempting to move from disordered toward ordered functioning. This process is continuous and lifelong. Therefore *everyone* needs to know how to recognize needs, make choices based on those needs, learn new psychological and social skills, and create new images. Just as humankind had to learn to build roads, buildings, and rockets, we are now at a point where we must learn how to

create new and functional images that will allow us to survive in the modern world. Psychological fitness is not just a theory for therapists to use but a theory about how human beings function. When people do not have the ability to create new images that satisfy new needs in response to environmental changes, they are nonfunctional.

Needs are both short-term and long-term. For example, a man's need to develop a profession to support himself and his family is a long-term need. The image necessary to fulfill this need must have a long life span. But at some point even that long-term and nurtured image will become nonfunctional. It will no longer be the dominant image; to remain functional it will have to allow development of other images that satisfy other *needs*. An image is nonfunctional when it no longer satisfies the need it was created for (i.e., the environment in which it arose no longer exists) or if it interferes with the development of other images needed to satisfy emerging needs.

### Associate Program on Psychological Fitness

This is a strictly educational program in which the participant is given a series of graduated personality and life area exercises in an educational format. The purpose of this program is to teach the participant the psychological fitness model. The program requires a letter to or personal phone call with a counselor twice a month. We think that this type of program should be in widespread use in all of psychology. It educates people to the basic ideas of what getting help is about, in a very active but nonthreatening manner.

### Functional Counseling

The major objective of this program is to teach clients the psychological skills they need to overcome problems, while focusing on strengthening their personalities. This is done by taking each client through an agreed number of sessions (5, 10, 20, or 40). Each session lasts from half an hour to an hour. As each step in the program is mastered, the client is taken into a new life area both to strengthen that particular area *and* to achieve a general strengthening of the personality. Early in the sessions, contact with the therapist is not a major requirement. Generally, the counselor depends on the educational power of the program itself. The program focuses on immediate resolution of the presenting problem and uses this focus as the context for exercising the personality.

*Counseling Clients.* Counseling using the psychological fitness model is currently being employed in a variety of settings. It is successful in the typical private clinic, hospital ward, and in outpatient services. It works very well for all age groups, racial and ethnic groups, and educational levels. The fitness model has all the positive parallels with physical fitness. Clients do not ponder their problems. They very quickly understand the theory because of its straightforwardness and its direct application to their lives. They can freely admit weaknesses that cause them trouble because within the model they are able to exercise their personality and get stronger. They see themselves as "getting better and stronger" rather than "getting over an illness."

## Community Training for Professionals

One of the most unusual programs that we have established is the Community Training Program for Professionals. In this program we take a group of professionals who have established or are interested in establishing a joint practice modeled after our practice at the Center for Feeling Therapy. This program consists of a two-month intensive program in conjunction with didactic training in Functional Counseling and Psychotherapy. We send training supervisors every two months to visit the professionals after they return to their home cty; these supervisors help with additional training, business advice, and therapy. The purpose of this training is to develop communities of therapists who give and provide continuous therapy for each other so that the services they provide become increasingly more functional and effective. We are, in effect, establishing therapeutic communities for therapists.

## Cultural Attitudes

We have just recently begun applying the theory of psychological fitness to businesses, schools, religious groups, and to medicine. The practical nature of the theory lends itself to ready applications, and we expect to see the theory applied more widely in the future.

It is of utmost necessity that the general public begin thinking about psychology in new ways. We think that people compound their problems and life difficulties when they apply the medical model to themselves. It is up to psychology to teach doctors, pastors, lawyers, counselors, educators, and other progressive psychological workers to begin using the psychological fitness model of human functioning. When they do, preventive psychology will have taken a long and necessary step forward. If psychology does not make this advance, we will continue to see clients who are needlessly suffering from the psychological effects of internalizing old concepts.

## CASE EXAMPLE

For many clients dreams are extremely useful as a therapeutic vehicle. Their usefulness is twofold: (1) as an index of therapeutic progress and (2) as a mode of working with feelings. In the functional approach dreams are conceptualized as pictures of feelings. The way a person functions emotionally in dreams parallels how he or she functions in waking. The function of dreaming is to provide nightly emotional exercise.

If a person starts from a positive level of functioning, then the dream exercise experiences will stretch the positive sides of his or her personality. If a person starts dreaming from a negative level of functioning, then dreaming provides a rehabilitative form of exercise—moving the personality from negative to neutral functioning or from more negative to less negative functioning. Dream movement is *always* toward more fitness, although that movement may be stalled or reversed when personality limits are reached within a dream sequence.

Here are a few samples from the dreams of one client, M, a male. This client's dreams are discussed in detail in *The Functional Analysis of Dreams* (Karle et al., 1980).

*The first dream:*

I don't remember a whole lot about it, but I woke up dreaming about J [a therapist] who was wearing a bathing suit and we were standing in the street talking to some people and I'm not sure whether there was a little boy there—a little five- or six-year-old boy—and I'm not sure whether I was that boy or not. But the little boy was eating a piece of raw chicken and . . . I don't remember too much about the rest of it except that I think J was saying it was okay for him to do that . . . and my mother said I'd get sick.

The functional perspective suggests a two-step way of working with dreams. First, allow the dreamer to feel how he lives his life at his present symbolic level of feeling. Second, feel what his life *could* be at an expanded, more fit level of functioning. The dreamer is helped to return to the dream and feel how he functions in each dream picture. He is helped to become aware of which feelings were left incomplete, and how this incompletion occurred.

## Working with the Dream

As the dreamer related this dream, he sounded vague—as though discussing a boring film he had seen the night before. The therapist is quite familiar with this client; she knows that the way he dreams, relates his dreams, and lives his life are identical. The session will be directed toward the defenses he uses that keep him from being active in his dream and waking life.

The therapist brings into focus the conflict between his feeling potential, pictured in his dream by J, and his present limits, which are apparent both by the way he relates the dream and in the picture of his mother. He will be helped to feel each picture.

M:   In the dream J seemed really nice and I remember in the dream that I was thinking that the chicken might not be good for him, but J really knew. J was like saying, "No, it's okay."

T:   Did the boy seem like he liked the raw chicken?

M:   Yeah (more excited, more awake). He was really just eating it. Yeah.

M became more expressive as he talked about eating the raw chicken. The therapist noted that M enjoyed the affect associated with the boy. He became enthusiastic, finally admitting liking the chicken, a feeling he omitted when originally reporting the dream.

In his initial dream report he seemed disconnected and confused. In waking, he also often acts confused when he is not. Instead of responding to the impulse of the moment, he separates himself from his feelings and from those around him.

For a client who is overly reasonable, a therapy session must provide more than just another reason for new behaviors. The client must have a reference from his own feeling so that he can choose when and how much to express. He doesn't need reasons or interpretations; he needs to feel and express himself.

T:   If the boy could talk, what would he say back to you in the dream?

M:   (Answers with a shrug of his shoulders) Probably he'd say, "I want the chicken."

T:   Would he just shrug it off like that?

M:   No.

T:   Well, how would he say it?

M:   I want the chicken, I want it. That's all, I want it.

The therapist noted that M was not getting a sense of what he was saying. He was mouthing empty words. She responded immediately.

T:  I don't believe the way you're talking.

M:  That's the way I think a little kid would say it.

T:  Would he hesitate after each word and look up and check it out?

M:  What *I* think of doing is taking it and running.

T:  Do you run away?

M:  Yeah. I do that a lot.

T:  Talk about *that*.

M:  I do that a lot with people. Instead of sticking and talking to people, I'll just stop and skip over things.

T:  Right now, M. You're doing it right now. You're giving me a very concrete explanation. You're hiding behind those words.

At this time the therapist was aware that M was going through the motions of talking to her, that he was being "reasonable" as he generalized about himself. She countered by not allowing him to break contact, forcing him to look and talk right to her.

T:  Look at me.

M:  When I started talking about running away, I started getting sad.

T:  Do you want to hide?

M:  No, I don't. I just do that. You know, the way I'd take it and run and be safe with it so that nobody can take it away from me (crying).

By the end of the session he was able to talk about the dream in a way that was qualitatively different:

M:  That was me coming out by myself (gesturing). I'm not asking permission. J didn't give me the permission in the dream and say it's okay to come out with the chicken. I did it because I wanted to (yelling). Just walked out the way I was. And I was standing there eating it before anybody said it was okay. I was standing there eating it. Munching it. I would feel it dribbling down my face. And that's me. That's me.

T:  Say it strong. Snap it!

M:  That's me! That's me *inside!* I am so alive. I don't want to run away and hide! I don't want to explain anything! I don't have to stop!

The client begins defended and ends connected to the new way he can be. He has seen himself from a new perspective provided by the expansion of his own dream; he has the beginnings of a new personality image.

## Dreams as a Therapeutic Index

A client can choose his defense or choose to express. It is how he or she lives from a psychotherapeutic session that will create change. Functional analysis can become just another interpretation if it doesn't move the person to new modes of functioning outside the therapy session.

We can use dreams to follow therapeutic movement during waking. In the case we have just cited, as M began to change his life, his dreaming changed as well. A week later he reported the following dream:

I was trying to fly. I kept jumping up and down waving my arms. It didn't work. I tried three or four times but would barely get off the ground. I was afraid I'd fall. Then I didn't care if I would fall and just leaned forward. I sort of glided over the ground, just a few feet in the air. My arms were outstretched. It was my way to fly. I never saw anyone fly that way before. I loved the sensation.

He had begun to live from a new reality during the week and was able to exceed reasonable limits in his dream. The feeling of flying was one of power and of powerful sensations in his body. It was distinctly *his way of flying* that meant so much to him. His way of expressing was not acquired in his past or from a present outside source. What was significant was not that he had a power dream, but that he was changing his life. This dream was a clear index of his progress.

In the functional approach we call dreams that show significant shifts in personality dynamics "transformative" or "breakthrough" dreams. They represent a breakthrough from a lower level of personality functioning to a more fit level of functioning. When all personality dynamics are sufficiently energized, there will be a breakthrough from symbolic functioning to realistic functioning and the dream will be satisfying rather than incomplete and confusing.

## SUMMARY

James, Dewey, Janet, Taft, and Burrow shared these core ideas:

1. Feelings are the basic mediators of behavior change and personality change.
2. Feelings must be expressed as well as experienced, to bring about changes, and expressions will modify the feelings.
3. Conflict between affects, cognitions, and behaviors is the crux and source of psychopathology.
4. Removing conflicts requires a positive bio-psychosocial model of how human beings can optimally function.

It is our aim that the modern psychological fitness model of human functioning eventually replace the traditional mental health/mental illness model for both professionals and the general public. We believe that many contemporary therapists who call themselves "eclectic" or who do some form of "humanistic-behavioral-cognitive-analytic" therapy are really practicing within the functional tradition.

Hopefully, as more and more therapists recognize the power and scope of the psychological fitness model and the functional orientation, we can move closer to Jessie Taft's assessment of the value of therapy:

The possibility of providing for the individual in need an artificial growth-producing situation, is, in my opinion, the epoch-making psychological discovery of our era, a discovery that may yet be found to be more momentous for the future of civilization than the unlocking of the forces in the atom. (in Robinson, 1962, p. 175)

## REFERENCES

Appelbaum, S. A. *Out in inner space: A psychoanalyst explores the new therapies*. New York: Doubleday, 1979.

Burrow, T. *A search for man's sanity*. New York: Oxford University Press, 1958.

Corriere, R. and Hart, J. *The dream makers*. New York: Funk & Wagnalls, 1977.

Corriere, R. and Hart, J. *Psychological fitness*. New York: Harcourt, 1979.

Corriere, R., Hart, J., Karle, W., Binder, J., Gold, S. and Woldenberg, L. Toward a new theory of dreaming. *Journal of Clinical Psychology*, 1977, **33**, 807–820.

Ellenberger, H. F. *The discovery of the unconscious*. New York: Basic Books, 1970.

Engstrom, D., London, P. and Hart, J. Hypnotic susceptibility increased by EEG alpha training. *Nature*, 1970, **227**, 1261–1262.

Hart, J. T. Beyond psychotherapy. In J. T. Hart and T. M. Tomlinson (Eds.), *New directions in client-centered therapy*. Boston: Houghton, 1970.

Hart, J., Corriere, R. and Binder, J. *Going sane: An introduction to Feeling Therapy*. New York: Aronson, 1975.

Hart, J., Corriere, R., Karle, W. and Woldenberg, L. *Dreaming and waking: The functional approach to using dreams*. Los Angeles: The Center Foundation Press, 1979.

Hartshorn, K., Corriere, R., Karle, W., Switzer, A., Hart, J., Gold, S. and Binder, J. A reapplication of the process scoring system for dreams. *Journal of Clinical Psychology*, 1977, **33**, 844–848.

Karle, W., Corriere, R. and Hart, J. Psychophysiological changes in abreactive therapy—study I: Primal Therapy. *Psychotherapy: Theory, Research and Practice*, 1973, **10**, 117–121.

Karle, W., Corriere, R., Hart, J. and Woldenberg, L. The functional analysis of dreams: A new theory of dreaming. *Archives of The Behavioral Sciences*, 1980, 55, 1–78.

Karle, W., Switzer, A., Gold, S. and Binder, J. A new model for continuing affective education. *Canadian Journal of University Continuing Education*, 1978, **V** (**1**), 35–39.

Karle, W., Woldenberg, L. and Hart, J. Feeling Therapy: Transformation in psychotherapy. In V. Binder, A. Binder and B. Rimland (Eds.), *Modern therapies*. Englewood Cliffs, N.J.: Prentice-Hall, 1976.

Liddick, B. Going sane around the clock. *Los Angeles Times*, 1976, June 13.

London, P., Hart, J. T. and Leibovitz, M. P. EEG alpha rhythms and hypnotic susceptibility. *Nature,* 1968, **219,** 71–72.

Miller, G. A. *Psychology: The science of mental life.* New York: Harper & Row, 1962.

Robinson, V. (Ed.). *Jessie Taft: A professional biography.* Philadelphia: University of Pennsylvania Press, 1962.

Schultz, D. P. *A history of modern psychology.* New York: Academic Press, 1960.

# CHAPTER 27

# Holistic Education

WILL SCHUTZ

*In my experience, psychotherapists as a group differ from most other people in that they are relatively free. They have, for the most part, achieved the aim of being themselves. And those in this field who have the personal qualities needed to establish new systems of psychotherapy, a pure inner vision of what life should be, tend to test the limits of this freedom and generate a world of their own. Then they attempt to give this message to the world as their most precious gift.*

*I know a number of the chapter authors in this book, and what I have said above is generally true of them: They are in their own private worlds, more or less. And at the head of the list in terms of this vision is Will Schutz, who, as the reader will soon discover, differs from almost everyone else in practically every dimension in his generation of a new world of logic and beauty as seen by his Holistic Education. It was my pleasure to dedicate a book I recently co-edited,* Great Cases in Psychotherapy, *to him.*

*Schutz is in the multimodal mode, and he attempts, as do others such as Shostrom, Hart, Gazda, and Lazarus, to develop the total individual in all possible views. Schutz emphasizes personal responsibility and the importance of choices as much as anyone does. He is an optimist, believing in the strength and goodness of people, that we have the power and capacity for the good and joyful life. The reader is in for a powerful experience in meeting Will Schutz, a truly seminal thinker who pushes back all frontiers.*

Holistic Education is a process occurring between two or more people in which one person, the educator = therapist/teacher/parent/administrator/physician, creates conditions within which the other person or persons, the learner = client/student/child/employee/patient, may choose to learn. The educator's skill is expressed through selection of which conditions to create. The educator is useful to the degree to which the learner chooses to learn. The educator does not educate, does not teach, does not heal anyone. He or she merely creates conditions by talking, by doing, and by being; that is all. Whether learning takes place is determined by the learner.

"Holistic" refers to the assumption that growth is a property of all aspects of a person—physical, social, emotional, intellectual, aesthetic, and spiritual.

For maximum growth of the individual, holism asserts that each of these aspects or properties of the individual must be developed to its fullest, and that all relations among the properties be harmonized. When this is accomplished, the person is an integrated whole, literally, a person of *integrity*.

## HISTORY

Holistic Education developed from the encounter group movement, which, in turn, was influenced by Group psychotherapy, *T-*

groups, group dynamics, psychodrama, gestalt therapy, body methods, and theater games (Schutz, 1973). The encounter format allows new methods and new concepts to be incorporated into the small-group format, thus providing a unique arena for working directly on individual and interpersonal issues simultaneously.

The most recent developments to be assimilated into the encounter format are new body methods, mental imagery techniques, and the concepts of choice and limitlessness. These approaches have helped the encounter group to evolve into Holistic Education (Schutz, 1979a).

As holistic education theory developed, it became clear that the therapeutic technique derived from it must (1) work on all aspects of the person, (2) focus on truth, and (3) emphasize individual responsibility. Individual responsibility is the key concept that led to the extension of the therapeutic method and to the realization that therapy is simply one form of education.

In the holistic education process the person is dealt with at all levels—physical, aesthetic (sensational), intellectual, spiritual, social, and emotional. Activities are designed to exercise and explore these aspects and their integration. The way Holistic Education works is best demonstrated by the first major application of the technique, the graduate program in Holistic Studies at Antioch University West in San Francisco.

## CURRENT STATUS

In January 1979, the first application of Holistic Education was inaugurated at Antioch University West in San Francisco (Schutz, 1979b). A group of 40 students began a 12-week program in Holistic Education. Their schedule reflects the holistic theory:

1. 9:00–10:00 Running (physical activity)
2. 10:00–11:00 Feldenkrais Exercise (aesthetic activity)
3. 11:00–12:00 Meditation (spiritual activity)
4. 12:00–1:30 Lunch
5. 1:30–3:30 Lecture (intellectual activity)
6. 3:30–5:30 Encounter Group (social, emotional activity)

Each activity and the interactions among the activities were approached from the standpoint of personal awareness. Here are some examples of the interactions that occurred in the program.

*Running.* Most people found that running sharpened their awareness and freed them for other activities. In the second week of a subsequent academic quarter, students fasted (water only) for five to nine days while participating in the program. This, too, helped them to be in touch with their bodies and to grow more confident that their bodies were accurate indicators of self-harmony.

*Feldenkrais Exercises.* In these exercises, many people learned how their body movements reflected their total beings. Some people could not do the movements gracefully because they held on to the floor for support too long. They were people who needed security. Others did the movements properly and then could not stop. They were people who went a little too far in their life activities.

*Meditation.* This practice helped many people to shut down their verbalizing and to "hear" other activities of their organism. The defensive use of intellect and the subsequent blocking of being in tune with the self through talking and other activities thus became evident. Learning to stay in touch with one's inner self illuminated the difference between public behavior and private feelings, between the behaviors people do for effect and the behaviors people really feel.

*Lunch.* The lunch hour was an important part of the program. It gave time for assimilation, both of food and of the emotional and intellectual experiences that had occurred earlier in the day. It also provided time for people to be together in smaller, self-selected groups to process their personal material.

*Lecture.*  The effect of emotions on intellect was clarified by the insights, developed during the encounter group (next stage), into the ways in which people listened to the lectures. Those who were anxious about looking bad or believed they had bad memories or felt they could not assimilate scientific material or did not want to hear from an expert an idea that contradicted their own ideas, learned about their blocks to learning.

*Encounter Group.*  This group was the central experience. It provided a "home room" for the myriad experiences the students were having. It was the place where each student explored his or her own being and where each had an opportunity to reflect on and to integrate all activities.

The total program led to a greatly increased experience of the total oneness, the integrity of the organism, to the realization of how truly unified we are and of how essential it is that we view ourselves as a whole if we are to have any opportunity to understand ourselves fully.

## THEORY

### Assumptions

*Holism.*  For maximum growth of an individual, all aspects—physical, intellectual, emotional, aesthetic, social, and spiritual—must be developed to their fullest, and all relationships among these aspects must be harmonized into an integrated whole person.

*Limitlessness.*  Each person is seen as limitless. The only limits people have are limits of belief. If they believe that they are

unlimited, then they may spend their energy learning how to reach their own potential (if they choose to do so).

*Problems.*  Psychological problems result from lies and from incomplete experiences. Holistic Education is aimed at creating conditions within which learners will complete incomplete experiences, become aware of the lies they have told themselves, and choose to know their truth. A common lie is that other people are to blame for the events of one's life.

## Process

*Education.*  Therapy is accomplished through the same educational process as teaching, parenting, healing, curing, and managing. In all these cases, the educator creates conditions—psychological, economic, physical, and political. The learner chooses to respond to those conditions in a certain way—to perceive them, to ignore them, to fight them, to escape them, to subvert them, and so forth. Growth occurs when the learner uses these conditions to grow.

*Change.*  A therapist does not heal or cure a client. Therapists simply create an environment through talk, nonverbal communication, atmosphere, and their own being. The client decides how to perceive the situation and how to make use of it to change. Clients may perceive therapists as domineering, helpful, evaluative, primitive, perverted, supportive, threatening, et cetera. Clients may choose to hear words accurately, understand them, and use them productively, or may choose to distort them, not understand them, and use them destructively.

*Skill.*  Therapists' skill lies in their ability to create conditions that clients choose to use productively. Therapists are "responsible" for creating these conditions. Clients are "responsible" for what they do with these conditions.

## Principles

*Responsibility.* The holistic educator makes clear to clients, from the start of the relationship, the division of responsibility—namely, that clients are responsible for whatever happens to them in the therapy; that they have chosen the therapist freely; that they may leave whenever they wish; that they may follow or not the suggestions of the therapist; that they may arrive late, leave early, go crazy, become ill, get injured, profit enormously, be bored, or whatever they wish. Holistic educators are responsible for whatever they themselves do and whatever they are. They may make agreements with the learner, lay down conditions, terminate the relationship, or do whatever they wish. The holistic educator makes this clear from the outset and throughout the relationship acts in a manner consistent with this concept.

*Truth.* The holistic educator is committed to truth, that is, self-awareness and honesty, and agrees to be totally honest throughout the relationship and committed to maximizing self-awareness. The holistic educator asks the learner to commit to honesty to the utmost degree. This is the fundamental basis of the "contract" in Holistic Education.

## Technique

*Initiative.* The holistic educator takes little initiative in the conduct of a therapy session, especially in the early meetings. After the opening statement regarding responsibility, participation is invited by saying that if anyone in the group wants anything to happen, it is up to him or her to make it happen. The holistic educator then actualizes that statement by waiting for group members to initiate. The beginning activities of the holistic educator are aimed at helping to expose "games," bringing defenses to awareness, and focusing on the learners' willingness and ability to tell the truth and to be aware. After a learner has initiated, the ho-

listic educator typically takes a more active role.

*Methods.* In Holistic Education, all modalities are worked on and any techniques may be used, as appropriate. The body, intellect, feelings, sensations, and spiritual elements are viewed simultaneously and dealt with as an integrated whole. Techniques such as rolfing, imagery, feldenkrais, acupuncture, bioenergetics, psychodrama, running, free association, aikido, t'ai-chi, meditation, or any other methods are available depending on which seem most beneficial at the time.

*Training.* Each person may profit from different experiences at different points in his or her evolution; therefore, the most successful holistic educator has learned a large repertoire of techniques and has accumulated the experience to know the proper time to use each method.

## METHODOLOGY

In Holistic Education all methods are potentially valuable. The question is not "Which methods are best?" but rather "Which methods work best for which people at which point in their evolution?"

From this perspective, virtually all therapies are of value to some people. Rather than attempting to show that other methods are not of value—a risky enterprise considering the sorry state of research on the evaluation of traditional therapy—it is more useful to explore the circumstances under which each technique is valuable.

The methods used in the Antioch experiment with Holistic Education are, of course, not the only ones available. The following are a few methods that are appropriate.

*Physical Activity.* Running, cycling, swimming, handball, racquetball, tennis, skiing, or walking might be included in the program. These activities should all be done with awareness and with a focus on sport as metaphor for the way a person is in life.

*Aesthetic (Sensational) Activity.* These methods might include feldenkrais, rolfing, alexander, hatha yoga, trager mentastics, t'ai-chi, and aikido. These methods also must be done with awareness and with an emphasis on total body harmony and integration.

*Spiritual Exercise.* Meditation, prayer, chanting, and arica spiritual exercises can be included. Any of the various types of these exercises is acceptable; for example, of the many types of meditation—sitting, walking, chaotic, kundalini, or transcendental—any may be employed.

*Intellectual Activity.* Lectures, discussions, reading, and academic course work are used. Any intellectual activity of personal relevance experienced with an awareness of the emotional blocks to learning is beneficial.

*Social Activity.* Encounter, psychodrama, Synanon, and so on, can be employed. Several other useful social activities, such as Dale Carnegie training, Toastmasters, Alcoholics Anonymous, and Recovery, are generally more immediate and are usefully continued into deeper realms. They are often useful as an introduction to social relationships based on truth.

*Emotional Exercise.* Methods including encounter, gestalt, psychodrama, est, bioenergetics, imagery, Fischer-Hoffman, rebirthing, and psychoanalysis might be employed.

This is obviously not an exhaustive list. A recent compendium (Matson, 1977) cites and describes dozens of available methods.

## APPLICATIONS

The tenets of Holistic Education form a social philosophy that directs action in fields be-yond psychotherapy. This philosophy is directly applicable to politics, sports, birthing, law, medicine, education, and many other areas of living. This is true because Holistic Education is based on principles of interaction between people. With appropriate adaptation, the principles apply wherever people interact.

## Principles of Application

The following is the translation of the tenets of Holistic Education, especially limitlessness, truth, choice, and holism, into a basis for application to society.

*Self-Determination.* The aim of any social institution is the creation of social conditions within which individuals find it easiest to determine their own lives. These conditions include removing blocks to and encouraging development of self-determination.

*Freedom.* Permit any action done by an individual that does not impinge on another individual.

*Agreement.* Allow any action between two or more people, performed with awareness by both, that does not impinge upon others.

*Truth.* By eliminating dishonesty, create conditions that make awareness easier.

*Simplicity.* Provide profoundly simple solutions to problems that individuals choose to have dealt with by institutions (e.g., traffic, welfare).

*Choice.* Create conditions within which individuals choose to find it easier to realize that they choose their own lives.

*Options.* Create conditions within which people choose to find it easy to be aware of options.

*Self-Responsibility.* Reward self-responsibility.

*Awareness.*   Reward awareness.

*Transition.*   Provide for a minimum delay in changing social practices to allow the unaware person to become aware and to make a conscious choice.

Obviously, these principles are to be progressively clarified, defined, and measured much more extensively during the course of Holistic Education (see Schutz, 1979a for a start), but even in outline form they provide an adequate basis for many social applications.

The following are some applications of these principles to social phenomena.

## Medicine

In the holistic education approach to medicine, the patient is acknowledged as the sole source of his or her own healing and as the one who has chosen to be ill. (Choosing to be ill is neither an accusation nor an assignment of blame. It is simply a statement of what happened.) Doctors are regarded as teachers who create conditions under which patients choose to heal themselves.

Holistic Education assumes that all illnesses result from out-of-awareness conflicts and are an expression of the total organism, not the expression of just a part. Usual explanations of illness are incomplete, such as "he picked up a bug," "he sat in a draft," "it's something she ate." The patient is seen as the active agent in acquiring the illness or, at least, in choosing not to prevent it.

One of the most dramatic examples of choosing one's illness occurred in the case of Karen Quinlan, the young woman who has been curled up in a comatose, vegetative state for over five years after being taken off life-support equipment following a highly publicized court battle between doctors and her parents.

Her mother reported the "irony" of a poem she found that Karen had written just prior to her illness.

The constant struggle with submission is tiring.

The so-called strength I've gained is just another heavy load.
I wish to curl myself into a fetal rose and rest in the eternal womb a while.

Preferred treatment methods in Holistic Education are those that enhance the organism's own capacities for healing (Glasser, 1976). These methods include fasting (so that the body can detoxify itself), exposure to fresh air and sunshine, feldenkrais exercises, imagery, and a deep understanding of the process of choosing an illness and the self-rewards that accrue from making that choice.

Standard medical practice is recognized as valuable in many instances. Medical research is often useful in discovering the mechanisms, though not the causes, through which illness occurs. Physical diagnosis is helpful for promoting self-awareness. Emergency treatments are still essential, since most people have not mastered the ability to become aware of or to control their own body functions; however, more people are becoming aware of these body functions, and Holistic Education holds that their control is well within human capacities.

## Law

The law is frequently supportive of the lack of self-responsibility:

—Dan White escaped serious punishment for killing two men, including the mayor of San Francisco, partly because of the "Twinkies defense"—he ate a great deal of sugar and sugar leads to violence.

—A man ignites his bed falling asleep with a lit cigarette and sues the tobacco company.

—Bartenders are often held responsible when their customers later get into accidents through drunken driving.

These are instances of almost total disregard of the principle of self-responsibility. They illustrate the notion that the law is often so supportive of our being our brothers' keeper that it neglects to require that we be our own keeper.

The holistic education approach to this issue is exemplified by an experiment in two large cities made by a law agency (Graecen, 1972). In this test first felonies, such as burglaries, were punished through direct interaction between burglar and victim in the presence of a facilitator. This trio was charged by the court to discuss the crime and to agree on a proper punishment. If they agreed the court would accept it.

The results were astonishing. Agreement was reached in 96 percent of the cases. Court costs were reduced 80 percent. And the solutions reached were extremely imaginative. One man, for example, who stole a TV set from an aged woman agreed to mow her lawn and to drive her to the hospital every week for a year, certainly a much more useful solution than incarceration for some period.

## Licensing

Holistic education principles indicate that the current approach to licensing psychologists is on the wrong track. It is now widely acknowledged that licensing psychologists does not protect the public; nor does it guarantee excellence (Hogan, 1979). Licensing procedures are often politicized to maintain the status quo.

The government is not in a good position to decide on technical competence. It *is* in a good position to make certain that people tell the truth. The holistic education approach to licensing would expect truth from therapists and self-responsibility from clients. This may be accomplished through requiring therapists to post publicly, and to make available to prospective clients, full disclosure of all their qualifications—education, experience, and so forth. It is then the responsibility of the client to select a therapist. The government's role is to assure that the therapists' statements are true and to punish lying.

## Health Insurance

The liberal strides toward a national health insurance that would cover everyone in case of illness are well-meaning but not consistent with holistic education principles. Health insurance rewards the sick at the expense of the fit. If we both pay into the plan and I am sickly and you are healthy, then you pay for me.

A holistic education health plan would reward those who take responsibility for their own health and would encourage everyone to take care of his or her own health (Schutz, 1979c). This may be accomplished through government-sponsored fitness centers where everyone is tested and given a regime to follow—exercise, diet, stress reduction—to keep healthy. In a year, everyone would be retested and given a number indicating the percentage of their optimal health they have achieved, based on their original condition.

People as healthy as they could be, probably people who followed the regime, would be given a score of 100. Those who totally neglect themselves would be given a minimum score of 25. *The number received is equal to the percentage of sickness care covered by the insurance.* If you take good care of yourself, your sickness care is fully paid for. If you do not take good care of yourself, you pay a high percentage of your sickness care if you become ill.

This plan involves no coercion, no special favors. It simply rewads treating your body responsibly. Instead of rewarding the ill, as do the present plans, it rewards those who keep themselves healthy.

Suggestions like these follow directly from the holistic education principles. They apply to childrearing, birthing, politics, business, sports, and many other realms. Wherever there are people interacting, the holistic education principles are applicable. The principles of everyday living are consistent with the therapeutic technique.

## CASE EXAMPLE

Cora was a binge drinker. She was 28 years old, married, had an eight-year-old child, and had been binge drinking regularly for seven years. She never touched alcohol between binges, but, at first every six months, then every three months she would go on a bender, drinking beer, wine, vodka, Ny-Quil, vanilla extract, or whatever was available. Cora would drink herself totally out of commission for about five days, sleeping the whole time except for sallies forth to reinforce her drunken state.

When sober she was totally opposite the liquor-soaked, straggly haired, rubber-legged, blankly staring Cora of the binges. She was very attractive, extremely efficient, charming, talented, and extraordinarily reliable. The contrast between the two Coras strained credulity.

She had become the despair of her family. They handled her binges by putting her in the detoxification tank until she dried out, then taking her home and saying little about it.

Cora began working on her drinking problem by going to gestalt and transactional analysis groups, going through psychoanalysis, and by attending an occasional Alcoholics Anonymous (AA) meeting. Through these approaches she acquired insight into the many reasons for her condition:

1. The premature responsibility entailed in having a child at 19.
2. The demands of her very responsible job.
3. Her strained relationship with her mother, who had not spoken to her for five years even though she lived nearby.
4. Her unhappy marriage, which was a model of noncommunication.
5. The stress and guilt of her extramarital affairs.
6. The rejection by a lover on whom she had become very dependent, but who would not leave his wife to be with Cora.
7. The abandonment by her father when she was one and her subsequent fear of abandonment by all men.
8. Her body, which could not assimilate alcohol properly.

With each insight, Cora saw her situation more clearly. Slowly she was uncovering the basis for her trouble. The solutions offered

by the various therapists all made sense: make up with your mother, quit your job, leave your lover, get a divorce, stop drinking. Most of these options were feasible since she was financially comfortable.

She came to see me after considering these solutions and because she was being fired from her job for the second time—for drinking. Clearly, something was not working.

After interacting with her for a while, it became clear that Cora had great insight into her situation and had worked through many of her background circumstances emotionally as well as intellectually. She understood that her last binge had been partly to escape the pressure of her job. She was learning how to take better care of herself.

All of her insights pinpointed the circumstances responsible for her situation: her lover, her husband, her unprepared motherhood, her high-pressure job, her cold mother, her abandoning father, her physiology. The solutions she had entertained, such as quitting her job or getting a divorce, were attempts to alter her environment.

The missing part was Cora taking responsibility for what was happening to her. As we progressed, what became clear to her was:

1. She did not drink because of the pressures of the job. Many nondrinkers have demanding jobs.
2. She did not drink because of her bad marriage. There are many nondrinkers in bad marriages.
3. She did not drink because of her lover's rejection. Many nondrinkers have been rejected.
4. She did not drink because her father left home or because her mother would not talk to her.
5. She did not get drunk because of her physiology.

*Cora drank because Cora chose to drink.*

As soon as she began to accept this idea, which she did very quickly, Cora's whole approach changed. She realized that changing external circumstances, such as quitting a job or leaving a marriage, becomes, at best, temporary relief until a new threatening circumstance arises. She saw that blaming others, such as mother, father, husband, job, must be abandoned. Cora recognized that they did not drive her to drink. They just did whatever they did. *She* chose to drink.

Her attitude toward her alcoholism also changed. No longer did she accept the AA description of herself as an alcoholic, no matter how long she remained dry. Even the solution of abstaining from drinking seemed inadequate. That meant Cora would forever have to expend energy to not take a drink, in the belief that, since she was an alcoholic, one drink would lead her to resume her "addiction."

Cora internalized the idea that she was totally responsible for her condition. She accepted that she had colluded with her parents to elicit the behavior she received from them, that she had chosen her husband, that she had elected to get pregnant at the age of 19, that she had chosen a lover whom she knew would not leave his wife, that she had chosen a hectic job and had decided to interpret her duties as overwhelming. After doing all of that, she had decided to perceive her circumstances as beyond her ability to handle and to drink herself into periodic stupors to get herself out of the situation.

Once she accepted responsibility for her situation, she realized the vital correlate: Cora could *choose* to change.

While she believed she was a victim, she had no power. She could only try to alter or escape from her circumstances. Once she accepted responsibility she was in a position to change herself into a nonbinger. She had the power.

The path that we set out upon was for Cora to take charge of her life. The key to this path is the willingness to be completely truthful. Without truth, growth stutters and often flounders. As a first step, Cora had lunch with her lover and expressed to him all the feelings that she had withheld and found out all the things she wanted to know from him. She left the lunch with many warm feelings

toward him and knowing that she could let go of him.

Next, through one of those synchronicities the universe often provides, Cora's father came to visit for the first time in 12 years. Cora told him exactly how she felt about him now and how she had felt for all of their years together. He responded, as most people do to the deep truth, by being truthful in return. Their visit ended on a warm, loving note with the expectation of a growing, continuing relationship.

After holding back for 7 years, Cora finally told her husband exactly what she was feeling and decided to get a divorce. After some early difficulty, their relationship developed into one of friendship and cooperation around the child.

She also talked honestly to her son, who subsequently has made the adjustment with great ease.

Her relation with her mother remained difficult, and Cora and I felt that there was some unfinished business in that area. We decided that intensive work on clearing out her relations with the parents would be an important step. Cora entered the Quadrinity Process, an intensive 12-week experience that is often effective for people who are ready to deal with their unresolved parental issues. She did extremely well in that program.

It has been quite a while now since Cora's last binge. She feels that her binge drinking is over, not just because of the time she has spent without a binge, but because situations have arisen that were even more pressured than those that formerly led to the benders and she does not even consider the possibility of a drink. Apparently the desire for alcohol has been replaced by the feeling that she can deal with the situation without outside help.

This is what Cora has to say now:

I feel totally different about my binge drinking now than ever before. I am beginning to see who I really am and that I do not need to be stuck in a role of "alcoholic," nor do I need to experience physical withdrawal symptoms. I had totally accepted the AA philosophy that if I took one drink, I was doomed. I felt that something beyond me controlled my life.

I am now clear that *I control my life* and all I need to do is to fearlessly and truthfully pursue what is ME. Through imagery during a severe alcohol withdrawal, I became aware of knowing what my body was doing in order to eliminate the alcohol and that I was not going to die. I saw that I could assist my body to speed up detoxification by working with it rather than fighting against it.

What amazes me most is the knowledge/gut feeling that binge drinking is not a part of ME anymore. I choose not to be a binge drinker not by abstaining, but by knowing that is not who I am. I have changed not because of external threats—job firing, divorce, abandonment—but because I was a fool who saw what a fool I was and who chose to change because I was not that person. I do not fear alcohol anymore! I am regaining daily a greater sense of self-power and testing out my beliefs in my limitless abilities. I feel soft and vulnerable and porous to the universe—my armor is dropping off, and I am truly being reborn in the sense of knowing that I am in charge of myself.

As Cora said, she does not regard herself as an alcoholic. She is someone who *used to* go on benders. When she felt sufficiently sure, and not before, she took a drink in my presence. She remained totally aware of her thoughts, feelings, and total experience while drinking. Next she took a drink alone, also with awareness. She now feels she can drink, if she wishes to, without getting drunk. She does not have to avoid drinking, nor does she have to drink. She is the master of her drinking.

The turning point of the "therapy" was Cora's acceptance of total responsibility for her problem. Once that occurred, her abilities and power were mobilized and she went directly toward mastery. The principles of truth and awareness were followed and a variety of techniques—encounter, gestalt, imagery, Quadrinity—were used as they became appropriate. Cora was regarded as a whole person and her problem understood as a function of her whole being, not just her physiology,

her history, or her present job. The holistic education assumption about Cora is that her drinking is a choice she is making to deal with her total life situation, and that she is fully capable of making the choice to stop drinking.

## SUMMARY

Holistic Education is the name of this method rather than Holistic Therapy, because "therapy" is a misleading word in that it implies that someone "cures" someone else. The therapeutic relationship is regarded as one type of education, just as is parenting, administrating, and doctoring. The basic relationship is educator-learner in the sense that educators do nothing but create conditions, and learners decide how they respond to these conditions.

"Holistic" refers to the assumption that the person is a whole organism—physical, spiritual, emotional, intellectual, aesthetic, and social. This is not just a cliche, but it is an integral, guiding part of the process.

The main principles of Holistic Education are: (1) *limitlessness:* All people are limitless; (2) *truth:* The truth, which includes awareness (self-truth) and honesty (truth to others) is essential for the change to happen. The truth really does make one free; (c) *responsibility:* Everyone chooses everything in his or her life and always has.

All therapeutic techniques are usable within Holistic Education. The educator has a large repertoire and, through experience, uses whichever methods are most appropriate.

The principles of Holistic Education are equally applicable to all phases of human interaction: that is, they form a social philosophy. This philosophy generates social policy in medicine, law, politics, business, sports, birthing, parenting, and daily life.

The theoretical background and applications of Holistic Education is presented at greater length in *Profound Simplicity* (Schutz, 1979a).

# REFERENCES

Feldenkrais, M. *Awareness through movement.* New York: Harper & Row, 1973.

Glasser, R. *The body is the hero.* New York: Random House, 1976.

Graecen, J. "Arbitration, a tool for criminal cases? A proposal for bringing the wisdom of civil settlements into our criminal justice system." Washington D.C.: National Institute of Law Enforcement and Criminal Justice, 1972.

Hoffman, B. *No one is to blame.* Palo Alto, Calif.: Science and Behavior Books, 1979.

Hogan, D. *The Regulation of Psychotherapists (Four volumes).* Cambridge, Mass: Ballinger, 1979.

Huang, A. *Embrace tiger return to mountain.* Moab, Utah: Red People Press, 1977.

Matson, K. *The Psychology Today omnibook of personal development.* New York: Morrow, 1977.

Schutz, W. *Elements of encounter.* Big Sur, Calif.: Joy Press, 1973.

Schutz, W. *Profound simplicity.* New York: Bantam, 1979a.

Schutz, W. Antioch University's experiment with holistic education. *Association for Humanistic Psychology Newsletter,* May 1979b.

Schutz, W. A health-care plan that rewards the fit. *San Francisco Chronicle,* August 1, 1979c.

# CHAPTER 28

# Immediate Therapy

RAYMOND J. CORSINI

*I feel somewhat uncomfortable introducing my own chapter, but I suppose that if I am bold enough to include it, even though no one to my knowledge is using this system, I should be bold enough to say something about it.*

*In my many years of practicing counseling and psychotherapy, I have had hundreds of bright ideas and thousands of various new insights, most of which soon dissipated. I have read probably a thousand articles and books on psychotherapy—and they all impressed me, but in my practice I more or less operate today as I did 25 years ago. I imagine that this is what happens to most of us. As time goes on, we get more set in our ways, and we tend to find comfort in our own procedures. And this is what has happened to me regarding Immediate Therapy: I no longer use it, yet I believe that it is useful in institutional treatment, especially in prisons, where I employed it, as I recall, so successfully. But that is what this book is all about: to show new methods for various individuals and various institutions and settings.*

*What has kept me going through the years in this terrible profession has been the relatively few instances in which I knew that what I had done really made a difference. I feel certain there must be at least two dozen people "out there" formerly in durance vile who are now "normal" as a direct result of Immediate Therapy. And so I suggest that those who work in corrections learn about Immediate Therapy.*

Immediate therapy is based primarily on Heider's (1958) theory of interpersonal relations, Festinger's (1957) theory of "cognitive dissonance" as well as Zeigarnik's theory of incomplete gestalts. Essentially, Immediate Therapy holds that people can make rapid, lasting, ameliorative personality changes under proper conditions. While preparation before Immediate Therapy may take considerable time, nevertheless the therapy itself is of the instant type, occurring with extreme emotionalism on the part of the client. The method of treatment is ordinarily done in a group and the actual procedure is either psychodrama or the behind-the-back technique.

## HISTORY

Throughout history are examples of individuals having made rapid and lasting changes of their personalities (Corsini, 1945). This phenomenon, known as *conversion*, is defined by English and English (1958) as "Radical and relatively rapid change of belief or attitude, especially of religious attitude, with or without corresponding change in character or conduct." The classic example is that of Saul of Taurus who, en route to persecute the Christians, fell from his horse and heard a voice asking him why he was persecuting his people, and as a result had an immediate and lasting change of heart. He changed his name to Paul and became a Christian. In theatricals dramatists often make a central point of a character having a particular attitude that he or she holds on to with great tenacity. The audience, however, knows something that the protagonist does not know. Someone in the drama has this information, but either cannot get it to the protagonist or the protagonist will not permit that person to give him the information. However, when the protagonist learns that information—such as that the condemned person is his own son, or that the vilified individual is actually an ally—then there occurs an immediate change of attitude.

A good many of the "miraculous" cures by the laying on of hands on hysterics are probably nothing more than what I call Immediate Therapy. A person held in high repute by the client informs that person that he or she is now cured of the disability, whereupon that individual announces that this is indeed so. The best-known examples of this in the early history of psychotherapy were the antagonists Johann Joseph Gassner, the exorcist, and Franz Anton Mesmer, the hypnotist, who in the eighteenth century demonstrated all kinds of miraculous immediate cures. Over the centuries many other people have performed such "miracles," and even today a variety of ministers do spiritual healings.

Perhaps the best-known people who performed such rapid psychological cures in our time were J. L. Moreno, who on the psychodrama stage would treat and "cure" patients in a single session, and Frederick C. (Fritz) Perls, who used the "hot seat" technique.

The history of Immediate Therapy dates back to two incidents, both of which occurred in prisons. The first took place about 1945 at Auburn Prison in New York and the second, nine years later, in San Quentin in California. Only after the second one (to be cited below in the "Case Example") did I understand what I had witnessed.

The first case went as follows: An inmate at Auburn Prison requested an interview with me, the prison psychologist. My duties were mostly psychometric in nature. The man who came to see me was about 30 years of age. His statement went approximately as follows:

I used to be skeptical of bug doctors [psychologists and psychiatrists] but now I know I was wrong. Because of you, my whole life has changed. After seeing you I gave up the criminal crowd I had been associating with. I gave up the easy job I had and changed to one in the machine shop. I finished my high school education and passed the Regents' tests, and I am also taking college-level correspondence courses. I have taken a correspondence course in drafting and will work as a draftsman when I get released next week. I have returned to my religion, and I have reunited myself with my family. All on account of you. My parents bless you and pray for you for what you did for me.

I was astounded to hear this paean of praise for me, especially since I was fairly certain I had never met the man before. "Do you have the right person?" I asked. "I don't remember you at all."

"It's you, all right," he replied. "I'll never forget the words you said which so changed my life."

"What were they?" I asked, having thoughts of becoming one of the giants of psychotherapy.

"About a year ago when you tested me you told me I had a high IQ," he replied.

Shocked by the triviality of the reply, I learned upon further questioning that this remark really had had the effect of changing this man's whole life. I did not understand the meaning of this incident and on several occasions I told others this story with the intention of showing the irrationality of some people. Other clients exhibited such rapid changes after hypnosis, but not until the incident to be recounted in the "Case Example" below did I begin to understand what Immediate Therapy was all about.

## CURRENT STATUS

In medicine powerful therapeutics are inherently dangerous and can lead to death. Radical operations, miracle drugs, and the like tend to have serious side effects. No one, except highly qualified people, would dare practice coronary bypass operations or administer powerful drugs. It is my opinion that Immediate Therapy should be restricted only to individuals with proper training in (1) personality theory, (2) psychotherapeutic techniques, and (3) this specific methodology. Due to personal limitations—that is to say, inability to find a proper teaching forum, plus my own personal conservatism in training others—no attempts have been made to propagate this theory or method. On the other hand, in the best interests of science, the findings and the underpinnings as well as the methodology of Immediate Therapy should be known to others in the field of psychotherapy for their consideration and posible utilization.

Essentially, at the present time, I believe I am the only practitioner of Immediate Therapy, and even I use it only rarely and sparingly. However, this technique and the theory itself have been employed by several others, but generally without full understanding. The behind-the-back technique, for example, is being employed by some people who include it in their repertoires in various so-called "encounter" groups.

## THEORY

Essentially the theory of Immediate Therapy goes something like this: The human mind, like the human body, has a built-in tendency to perfection, and will cure itself under proper circumstances. This so-called "growth tendency" or "self-actualization" tendency is implied or made explicit in the writing of many personality theorists, Abraham Maslow (1970) and Kurt Goldstein (1940) most prominently. What this means is that the mind seeks to be free and perfect and well, and that it is the job of the therapist to help nature. The statement made by Ambroise Pare, "I treated him, God cured him," holds. We treat patients, but they cure themselves.

The essence of the theory of Immediate

Therapy is that every individual has the potential for improvement or cure or change in him or her, and it is the function of the therapist to help release this potential. Carl Rogers (1951) made the central point of his theory the capacity of people to cure themselves. And essentially this is what all therapists do: establish conditions under which the patient can cure himself or herself.

*What is psychoanalysis?* A formal method for self-reflection. *What is client-centered therapy?* A means for a person to analyze himself. *What is psychodrama?* A method for allowing oneself to cure oneself. "I treat, God cures" is what all therapists can say.

Physicians know that the body heals slowly, and so they are trained and are biased in the direction of slow, gradual cures. This bias has been translated into their psychological treatment methods and into their theories, with the notion that personality changes slowly and that psychotherapists should operate slowly and carefully. This bias has been accepted by nonphysicians generally and has become a kind of self-fulfilling prophesy. It is well-known that therapists can affect patients in curious ways. Patients of Freudians have Freudian dreams, Jungian patients have Jungian dreams, and Adlerian patients have Adlerian dreams. If a therapist makes the assumption that therapy must last at least a year, then the patient will pick up this concept and will cooperate, albeit unknowingly, with the therapist to make the therapy last that long.

This concept also translates into learning theories, which fall into two groups. One is that personality learning is of the gradual, incremental type, just as in learning how to ski or speak a foreign language. The second kind of learning is of the saltatory (from *saltatorius,* which is Latin for "leap") type, and is sudden and immediate, as for example when one learns the point of a joke. Most therapists see psychotherapy as learning of the first type, incremental, and so they operate in this manner—as though this were the right, the correct, and the only way. Other therapists, such as Moreno, Perls, and Albert Ellis, start off with a bang with practically instant diagnosis and correction, having no use for long, drawn-out therapeutic processes.

Naturally, psychotherapists who have been imbued with ideas that stem from an analogy to physiotherapy, or from the incremental theory of learning and unlearning, will consider those who use Immediate Therapy as doing superficial therapy, since deep therapy must be long-lasting. Nonsense!

Good therapy need not be interminable. Quick therapy is better than drawn-out therapy. The elegant way to do therapy is to do it quickly, simply, cheaply. Consider the concept of resistance, the single major enemy of all therapists. As was realized by Sigmund Freud, and reaffirmed by all therapists since, practically every patient who comes for therapy shows resistance, and the cleverer the patient, the more the resistance. Therapy essentially becomes a power contest in which the therapist says, "Get cured" and the patient says, "No!"

The main intent of Immediate Therapy is to avoid this power contest and to achieve therapy through singleminded cunning, guile, stealth, and forceful action. These pejorative terms are deliberately selected, since the therapist must "betray" his patient by hurting him deeply, suddenly, unexpectedly—for his own good.

The following analogies help explicate the theory behind Immediate Therapy.

*The Balloon Analogy.* Let us imagine the total personality, the psyche, as a helium-filled balloon that wants to soar to its proper destined height of appropriate adjustment. The balloon, however, is weighted down by a heavy rope. Were the rope to be released, the balloon would go up to 1,000 feet; but the balloon is now only 25 feet from the ground. The rope is 25 feet in length and so the bottom of the rope just touches the ground. Working in conventional ways, to release the balloon we pull the rope down a bit at a time, and this takes a long time. Were we able to get on a ladder, we could cut the top of the rope in one clip. This is what Immediate Therapy is all about: to cut that rope immediately at the very top, so that the balloon immediately soars to its proper level.

*The Log-Jam Analogy.* A second analogy has to do with a log jam. Imagine a thousand logs have been cut down in a forest and are being floated down the river. Imagine that a single log manages to get caught between some rocks and that this single log now generates a log jam. When the lumberjacks discover the problem, they approach it from the back, as it were, going to the very last log, carrying it past the other logs and over the crucial log; then getting another log, and so on. Eventually, they finally get to the key log and remove it from its jammed position. In contrast, in Immediate Therapy, we find the key log and we blow it out of place; then all the logs come down the stream.

*The Splinter Analogy.* One further analogy is needed to complete the theory: Imagine that a person has a splinter in his hand, and that another person is to take the splinter out. Let us assume that the one who is to serve as the "surgeon" is blind and does not know where the splinter is. The blind surgeon now begins to probe but can only tell where the splinter is in terms of the pain he causes the patient. The patient "knows" where the splinter is, but the surgeon can only know when the patient cries out. Immediate Therapy's view is that the patient is his own therapist and knows where the treatment is needed, but he enters into a power contest with the therapist because he fears the hurt necessary for therapy.

Immediate Therapy can be explained in this way: Over time a person comes to have a rather set series of concepts and ideas about self and others. Alfred Adler (1960) referred to this personal set of concepts as private logic and private intelligence. The combination of these ideas, of which some are incorrect, leads to maladjustment. In Immediate Therapy matters are arranged so that there will be a confrontation between the person's concepts and reality. The resulting contrast leads to a situation of "cognitive dissonance" (Festinger, 1957) that upsets the person's pattern, or gestalt, of thinking; leads to confusion and disruption, which is shown by dissonant feelings and external evidence of tension; and then moves inevitably to a new restructuring of thinking due to tension resulting from the disturbed gestalt, as explained by Zeigarnik (1927) and called "unfinished business" by Holt (1959).

## METHODOLOGY

The first step in the methodology of Immediate Therapy calls for the patient to be "prepared" or "set up" to receive the treatment. A sensitive and competent therapist generally knows when and where to operate. The next step is to have a one-time confrontation, so orchestrated as to achieve maximum results in minimum time. This confrontation must be of such intensity as to transcend the individual, to send him or her into an emotional state so that he or she will lose control. The third step, crucial for Immediate Therapy, is to stop everything immediately when the individual gets to an unbearable moment, and to cast that individual out of the group to work out the problem on his or her own.

The three steps of Immediate Therapy are warmup → confrontation → expulsion.

*Warmup.*    This step calls for gaining the client's confidence, leading him to the point where he will want to participate in the therapeutic procedure. Since Immediate Therapy almost always occurs in group therapy, the most obvious way to achieve this confidence is for the patient to see others benefiting from this treatment. So if client D sees A, then B, then C, participating and getting benefit, this observation will tend to give him confidence that when his turn comes, he too will benefit. It also calls for the therapist to be determined, patient, wise, and courageous, since Immediate Therapy is extremely exhausting and fatiguing emotionally. The

length of time for the warmup varies. In the case cited earlier, the client who heard the words "You have a high IQ" was already "warmed up" (ready to change); otherwise the words would have had no meaning for him.

*Confrontation.*    This is the moment of therapy in which the therapist orchestrates the treatment in such a manner as to achieve the desired results of "blowing up the log jam"—getting to the heart of the matter.

*Expulsion.*    The last step is simple: During the moment of most extreme excitement, when the patient has been driven to the edge of anguish, screaming in agony, the group expels—immediately and in silence—the patient, who now must reassemble himself.

One technique frequently used in Immediate Therapy is psychodrama. I shall not attempt to describe this process, since there are several books on the subject (see Corsini, 1965; Moreno, 1946; etc.). The procedure sometimes used is the behind-the-back technique (Corsini, 1953, 1968, 1973), which I will now describe.

1. Group meets in a circle and members agree to volunteer in a predetermined sequence. Should B not take his turn, then C must take his place.

2. The client has this assignment: "Tell everything about yourself." Each client will usually be given one-half hour to do this.

3. Everyone plans what to say when his turn comes, which may be from one week to several weeks ahead.

4. At the treatment session, the person who was the subject the week before tells the group what the session meant to him or her.

5. Then the current subject speaks for a half hour (or whatever time is established), telling the others *everything* about him- or herself.

6. When the statement is finished, the protagonist "leaves" the room symbolically, by going to the outside of the group and facing outward. The rest of the group discusses him "behind-his-back," while he listens but does not look.

7. Meantime the director keeps notes of what was said by the group. When the client comes back into the group, the director reads from the notes and informs the client of what was said. (The fiction is that the patient was actually out of the room.) The purpose of this is to repeat the highlights.

8. The protagonist is asked to comment or defend him- or herself. He or she sits in the center of the circle.

9. Now the therapist and the group members ask questions, make comments, and proceed deliberately to upset the client, with the client defending him- or herself.

10. If the technique is to succeed, the client, goaded by the questions and comments, will get upset, and this degree of upset is carefully noted by the therapist. If the client gets terribly upset, the group must fall silent at a quick clap of the therapist's hands and the client is "pointed out of the room" by the therapist. Not until he or she leaves does the group continue with further business.

11. When the client returns at the next session, he or she is asked to recapitulate what happened to him or her after being sent out of the group. Whenever the therapy is successful, statements such as the following are heard: "I left the group in a daze"; "I was terribly upset"; "I don't know how I got home"; "I walked the streets for hours"; "I couldn't sleep"; "I didn't have any appetite"; "My head went round and round for hours."

*Follow-up.* After the client comes back next session and gives his or her report, the general question is: "Did you learn anything?" Generally, the client begins with such statements as, "I really never believed . . ." or "I suddenly realized . . ." and then typically has some explanation of the origins of his or her behavior pathology. The therapy is completed! After listening, the next client presents him- or herself and the group goes through the same process again.

Perhaps the most important part of the methodology is the respect paid to all members of the group by the therapist, who takes them on as full partners and who also operates as a full partner in the enterprise. The therapist is merciless in his analysis, and must speak fully from his heart, thereby encouraging all others to be equally honest and forceful.

## APPLICATIONS

Immediate Therapy is especially designed for those individuals who are resistant to therapy, who are smart and highly likely to use ingenious methods to avoid the benefits of therapy. While it can work well with those who are innocent and willing to go along, Immediate Therapy is especially useful with those complex, complicated characters who ordinarily will make their therapy interminable and who delight in defeating the therapist. Therapists and patients are in a power struggle; the patient who wants therapy, who pays for it, who takes time out to pursue it, nevertheless is bound generally to do whatever he or she can to defeat the therapist—and not change. Resistance is the means used to win the game. The cleverer the person, the cleverer the form of resistance. Immediate Therapy is directed to destroy resistance.

The following summaries of some individual cases will serve to explicate the kinds of problems that can be solved through Immediate Therapy.

1. A black prisoner, in solitary confinement for refusing an assignment, stated that he would rather serve the rest of his

life in solitary than take on a mopping job, which he considered beneath him and which he felt was intended to make him feel violated. As a result of a behind-the-back treatment, he changed his mind and admitted that he was prejudiced against whites and that he provoked them into mistreating him so that he could get even with them.

2. A man learned that he had abused a child sexually in front of witnesses in order to go to prison to atone for his desire for his father's death (Corsini, 1951b).

3. A man stated he wished to kill his brother, who he felt had mistreated him; however, as a result of psychodrama, he realized that he loved his brother and did not want to harm him any more.

4. A man who had committed a number of senseless crimes involving bad checks discovered, following a behind-the-back session, that his secret hatred of his father was the cause of his actions; he desired that his father be disgraced.

5. An alcoholic woman with anorexia nervosa, who weighed less than 70 pounds, was "killed" in role playing and had a talk with "God." During the talk she was led to understand that her great "sin" of marrying a Catholic priest would be forgiven.

6. A completely reckless psychopathic youth was "killed" in a psychodrama demonstration and "buried" amid weeping "relatives." He changed his personality immediately, to the surprise of all who knew him.

Every one of these individuals was essentially a hard-core person, resistant to psychotherapy, and was "blasted" into a confrontation-type encounter. They were all put into a situation as described by Zeigarnik (1965) in which their tight gestalt of concepts was shattered by the logic of the situation and of the opinions of the group members. This generated unbearable tension, which could only be resolved by a complete personality restructuring, that is to say, by new conceptions of their fundamental views of self and others.

The behind-the-back technique has been employed with hospitalized paranoids, with criminals, with ordinary neurotics, with fighting husbands and wives. If employed properly—that is, if the therapist is able to generate the unbearable tension that is the essence of Immediate Therapy—then rapid changes occur. Essentially, the ideal client for this kind of therapy should be strong, opinionated, and certain of self. This system's intent is to take such people and shake them up so that they now have to deal with the cognitive dissonance between their original opinions and beliefs and strong evidence of the incorrectness of their position.

To give an analogy: Suppose that one believes (and some still do) that the earth is flat, not round. Suppose that all contrary evidence is discounted as propaganda. Now, suppose that person goes up in a spaceship. The earth gradually recedes until it can be seen that it really is round. We now have a conflict within the person, between the old beliefs and the new vision. This is exactly the situation in Immediate Therapy. Evidence is put in front of the client that contradicts past concepts. The resulting internal upheaval is due to the incompatability of the two notions: When therapy occurs, truth wins out.

## CASE EXAMPLE

Frank was an inmate at San Quentin, serving a sentence for a series of crimes of the same type. He would meet a woman, woo her, marry her, then steal her money, car, and so forth, and run away, and then search for another victim. A heavyset person with a sneering expression, Frank was nominated to attend this writer's therapy group by another inmate. I had a short talk with Frank about the group, which featured psychodrama (see Corsini, 1957, pp. 198–217), and accepted him, though I was not impressed with him or his attitude. I explained that he should attend at least three group sessions before deciding whether to remain. He accepted these terms.

In the group, he was more or less a spectator. Psychodrama was the main instrument of treatment, but he did not volunteer to participate as a subject. According to our pattern, every eighth session was a breather, a relaxer, run nondirectively, and at one of these sessions the discussion got onto Frank and his nonparticipation. Other group members questioned Frank's motive for joining the group and his lack of involvement. He then agreed to participate at the next regular session. However, the next week when I gave him the floor, he stated that he had nothing to say and had no intent to role play.

This was an impasse. I then suggested that he tell the group "everything about yourself" and that we would listen to him for 15 minutes in silence. He agreed to this, and a summary of his statements went as follows:

My father was Jewish and my mother was Italian. My mother told me never to trust anyone, because people will take advantage of you. My father used to tell me the story of the Jewish man who wanted to teach his son about business. He got the son to climb on a table and then on a chair and asked the son to jump and that he would catch him. When the son jumped, the father moved aside and the child fell. The father then told his son that he had shown him the secret of success in business: "Never trust anyone."

Well, throughout my life I have been screwed by others. Once on a train ride, there was a mother with a child. The child was crying. It was hungry. The mother told me she had no money to buy it food. The kid kept crying and bothered me. So I offered to buy the kid a container of milk, and gave the mother fifty cents. Then she came over and sat by me. We talked and she told me her troubles. Then I fell asleep. When I woke up she and the kid were gone and so was my wallet. See, I was a nice guy, bought the kid milk, befriended the mother and what happened? She stole my money.

That's how life has been. Everyone is out to get you. You got to look out for yourself. . . .

Frank went on and on with his account. Some background information and details of my previous interactions with him will help clarify my attitude toward him at the time he was telling his story.

In the first week of membership in the group he had asked me to violate one of the rules of the prison. He asked me to "kite" (mail out) a letter to his "wife." Ordinarily, I did not care to know what a person's crime was, curious, I checked his records and discovered that this "wife" was one of several women he had married bigamously and who had filed charges against him in another state. In the files was a piteous letter from her, intercepted by the censor, asking him why he had stolen her money and ruined her life.

One time while I was walking in the prison yard, he called me over. When I came over, he waved several of his buddies toward us. Surrounded by them, he faced me, pulled out from under his jacket a two-pound brick of cheese, stolen from the kitchen where he worked, and told the others, "See, he's my therapist. He can't tell them that I did this." Angry with this mistreatment of me, I broke through the circle and went on to my office.

Frank eventually finished his story, and there was silence. I then asked Frank to go outside the circle, to sit with his back to me, and to listen to what we would say. I asked the other members to come closer to each other so that we formed a tight circle.

"Now, men," I said, "we have all heard Frank. Now, what I want to ask you is this: will each of you give your opinion of Frank, your overall impression—in the group and in the institution. Jim, will you start?"

Jim replied: "I have nothing to say."

"Pete?"

"Sorry, I have nothing to say either."

"Danny?"

"Me neither. . . ."

I looked around the group. They were all tight-mouthed, their features firmly set. I could tell none would speak up unless I was able to convince them.

"Let me tell you something, every one of you. We are not fooling around. I can see you fellows don't like Frank. I don't like him either. But he is a member of our group. He has attended seven or eight sessions. He has not participated much. I don't like his attitude here, but it is our duty to try to help him. And the way you can help him, me, yourself, the other members of the group, and even society, is to tell the truth, exactly how you feel about Frank. What do you say, Jim?''

Jim looked me in the eye, took a deep breath, and began. ''He is a shit. A bastard like him doesn't deserve to live. . . .''

When he finished, Pete began. ''I feel ashamed that I belong to the human race if a scum like Frank is one too. Why, that son-of-a-bitch hesitates about buying a hungry baby some milk . . .'' and on he went.

''Danny?''

''I wanted to quit this group when Frank came in. People say that no one is all bad. They never met Frank. I know him well. He is the laziest, crookedest, meanest bastard in the world. It's guys like him that make it hard for others. . . .''

When it came my turn, I said nothing about his crimes, the letter from one of his ''wives,'' his asking me to kite the letter, or the incident in the yard but I said something like this:

''I dislike the man. I think he is cunning, sneaky, vicious. But I don't know enough about him to understand what made him the way he is. I am sorry he is in the group, but he is in, and I am happy we are having this discussion.''

We continued until we had all finished, and then I called Frank and asked him to comment on the comments. He entered the group, remained standing, and his remarks went something as follows:

''I heard what you bastards said. As far as I am concerned you are a bunch of ————-suckers, all of you. You are all full of shit. This is what I think of you. . . .'' He then cleared his throat, spit on the floor, turned around and left the room.

I thought that was the end of Frank. I was happy to see him go, and so were the others. He was just no good; no damned good. . . .

About three months later I got a note from Frank asking me for an interview. I threw it into the wastebasket. I just didn't want anything to do with him. However, as I pondered the situation, I had a kind of personal confrontation. Here I was, a prison psychologist, supposed to be ''rehabilitating'' persons and refusing a man an interview. Ashamed of myself, I made arrangements for Frank to see me the next day, not knowing what to expect.

When he arrived, my attitude was cold and hard. ''What can I do for you?''

''Why did you kick me out of your group?''

''I didn't kick you out. You got up, told us what you thought of us, spit on the floor, and that's the last I saw of you.''

''Why did you and the rest say all those terrible things about me?''

''We only said what we believed.''

''Well, they are all untrue. I am a nice guy.''

''Is that what you really think?'' The concept of Frank being a nice guy was so monstrous that I was 'shaken' by the very idea.

''Sure, everyone is against me. I don't deserve what they said.''

''Why do you think they said it?''

''Did you put them up to it?''

''Do you believe that?''

''No.''

''Well, what do you want?''

''Christ, I haven't been able to sleep well since that day. I can't get over what they said. All of them. What they think of me.''

''I am sure everyone said just what they thought about you.''

''Well, then I need help to change. I came here to ask you to let me back in the group.''

''No way. You left. You are out. That's final.''

''Then, see me personally. Give me individual treatment. I need help.''

''No way. Frank, I want to tell you I can't work with you because I don't like you. You know what you did, tried to get me to kite a letter. Remember that incident in the yard with the cheese? Besides which, I want to tell you that I have contempt for you because of your record. I have more respect for murderers than a man who did what you did. So I would be the last one for you to have therapy with."

"You are supposed to rehabilitate me. What the hell is all this about rehabilitation?"

"Look, there are others in the psych department: psychiatrists, psychologists, social workers. Ask one of them."

"I want you."

"And I don't want you."

We looked at each other in silence. Finally a thought came to me. Some time before, the male nurse in the prison psychiatric hospital unit in which I worked reported that he could not find attendants for the geriatric ward, and asked us to search for possible attendants. No one would want to work with these old, senile convicts. For the most part they were just waiting to die. Working in the B ward was the least desirable job in the institution. "Frank, I'll make a deal with you."

"What's that?"

"They need attendants in the old men's ward in the hospital. You volunteer for a job there, you stick with it six months, and you never talk to me. If you keep the job six months, then I'll see you for therapy."

To my surprise, he agreed.

The next day the chief nurse came to see me. "How did you do it, Corsini?" he asked. "This fellow Frank volunteered to work in B ward."

"Bill, do me a favor. Keep an eye on Frank and let me know from time to time how he is doing."

Periodically, Bill would inform me of Frank. The first week, Frank kept vomiting, showing great distaste for having to clean these old men who urinated and defecated in their beds. He had trouble feeding them or dealing with them. "If he finishes the first week," Bill told me, "I'll be surprised."

But Frank stuck it out, and Bill's reports were enthusiastic as time went on. "He's very devoted." "He turns the men over very carefully." "He is there when they want him." "He is very gentle with them." "He's my best man." "I saw him crying as one of

them died." "He's reading nursing books." "The other attendants look up to him." "The old men brighten up when he shows up." "He's really devoted." "He stayed all night with a dying man, holding his hand."

I wondered about this magical transformation. When I would pass Frank in the hallways, he would pay no attention to me. He was losing weight, and from an estimated 200 pounds, he now probably weighed about 150. His appearance and his expression were different. I noted that the other inmates respected him. One or two of the men of my therapy group referred to the change they had noted in him.

Six months to the day after that interview, Frank showed up, waiting in a chair outside my room. I motioned him in.

"Well, I am ready for my therapy."

I shook his hand. "Frank, you have had it. You don't need any more therapy."

"I think you're right."

"What happened? What made the change?"

"It was that behind-the-back session. It bugged me. I couldn't believe that everyone in the group really hated me like they said they did. The difference between what I thought of myself and what they—and you—thought was too much. When I left the group I was very angry with all of you. I figured you all plotted against me. But then I figured that couldn't be. Then I had to face the fact that you all really believed what you said; each of you had independently come to the conclusion I was no good. This contradicted what my mother and father told me. It contradicted what I thought of myself. And then I began to think that maybe you guys were right, that maybe I was a bastard. Now, that really took a lot of time to believe. I was terribly upset for a whole week, and finally I came to the conclusion, hell, look what I did to those women. They really didn't deserve it. So I agreed with you all. So I decided that I'd change. But it still bothered me that you and the other guys had that bad opinion of me. I hated you and I didn't want to have anything to do with any of you. I stuck by myself, but that bothered me. I wanted you to like me. That's why finally I came to see you. And when you refused to see me I could understand why. And when you offered to see me in therapy if I would become an attendant I jumped at the chance to prove to you that I was Okay. Boy—that was some shithouse you sent me to. I thought I'd puke my brains out the first week. God—I was always afraid of death. Those old, dying men. But I stuck it out, and now I love my work. I'm going to become a nurse. I'm studying books. I've found my vocation. I really want to thank you.''

"Anything you want from me?''

"Nothing.''

"How about a letter or something telling about your rehabilitation? Maybe the other state will go easy on you.'' (I still had my reservations about Frank.)

"Nothing. I'll take my medicine. I'm going to the parole board here and then I have to face the jury in the other state. No, I'll take life as it comes.''

Frank was in the institution for another three to four months, during which time we met informally several times. There was no doubt in my mind that he had experienced a 180-degree change. This change was confirmed by all other prisoners who had dealings with him; Frank had changed—for the better.

## SUMMARY

Immediate Therapy is not a system of psychotherapy in the same sense as, for example, psychoanalysis or reality therapy, which have a more or less complete system of conceptualizations about personality growth and development. It is instead a psychotherapeutic system that could well be fitted into other personality theories. I myself am a follower of Alfred Adler's individual psychology theory, and at various times I use a variety of techniques, such as nondirective interviewing, free association, group therapy, family counseling, and so forth. One of these techniques is Immediate Therapy—an attempt to break through a person's defenses by a swift, powerful, coordinated attack.

In my opinion, some forms of therapy are based on the fallacious notion, rooted in physical medicine, that psychotherapy, to be effective, has to be "deep" and "long-lasting." This is just not so. Good, significant, meaningful therapy can be short. Long-lasting, permanent changes can occur quickly. Traditional methods of operation can be counterproductive. The work of Moreno, Perls, Ellis, as well as many others, including those who use hypnosis and a variety of encounter techniques, indicate that "Immediate Therapy" is a valid means of treatment.

## REFERENCES

Adler, A. *What life should mean to you.* New York: Capricorn Books, 1960. (Originally published 1931.)

Corsini, R. J. Criminal conversion. *Journal of Criminal Psychopathology,* 1945, **7**, 139–146.

Corsini, R. J. The method of psychodrama in prison. *Group Psychotherapy,* 1951a, **3**, 321–326.

Corsini, R. J. Psychodramatic treatment of a pedophile. *Group Psychotherapy,* 1951b, **4**, 166–171.

Corsini, R. J. Immediate therapy. *Group Psychotherapy,* 1952, **4**, 322–330.

Corsini, R. J. The behind-the-back technique in group therapy. *Group Psychotherapy,* 1953, **6**, 102–109.

Corsini, R. J. Criminal and correctional psychology. In F. L. Marcuse (Ed.), *Areas of psychology.* New York: Harper, 1954a.

Corsini, R. J. Group psychotherapy with a hostile group. *Group Psychotherapy,* 1954b, **9**, 184–185.

Corsini, R. J. *Methods of group psychotherapy.* New York: McGraw-Hill, 1957.

Corsini, R. J. Group psychotherapy in correctional rehabilitation. *British Journal of Delinquency,* 1964, **15**, 272–278.

Corsini, R. J. *Roleplaying in psychotherapy.* Chicago: Aldine, 1965.

Corsini, R. J. Immediate therapy in groups. In G. M. Gazda, *Innovations to group psychotherapy.* Evanston, Ill.: Charles C Thomas, 1968.

Corsini, R. J. The behind-the-back encounter. In L. Wolberg and E. K. Schwartz (Eds.), *Group psychotherapy, 1973.* New York: Intercontinental Medical Books, 1973.

Ellis, A. *Reason and emotion in psychotherapy.* New York: Lyle Stuart, 1962.

English, H. B. and English, A. C. *A comprehensive dictionary of psychological and psychoanalytic terms.* New York: Longman, Green, 1958.

Festinger, L. A. *A theory of cognitive dissonance.* Evanston, Ill.: Row, Peterson, 1957.

Goldstein, K. *Human nature in the light of psychopathology.* Cambridge, Mass.: Harvard University Press, 1940.

Greenwald, H. *Direct decision therapy.* San Diego: EDITS, 1975.

Heider, F. *The psychology of interpersonal relations.* New York: Wiley, 1958.

Holt, R. R. Discussion of "Further observations of the Potzl phenomenon: A study of day residues" by Charles Fisher. *Psychoanalytic Quarterly,* 1959, **28**, 442.

Maslow, A. H. *Motivation and personality,* 2nd ed. New York: Harper & Row, 1970.

Moreno, J. L. *Psychodrama* (Vol. 1). New York: Beacon House, 1946.

Perls, F. *Ego, hunger, and aggression.* New York: Random House, 1969.

Rogers, C. R. *Client-centered therapy.* Boston: Houghton Mifflin, 1951.

Schutz, W. *Joy.* New York: Grove, 1971.

Zeigarnik, B. V. Uber das behalten von erledigten und unerbedigten handlungen. *Psychologische Forschong,* 1927, **9**, 1–85.

Zeigarnik, B. V. The task of psychopathology. In *Problems of experimental psychopathology.* Moscow: Gos. Nauch. Issled. In-t. Psikhiatrii, 1965.

# CHAPTER 29

# *Impasse/Priority Therapy*

NIRA KEFIR

*I was present in 1971 at a workshop given in Jerusalem on Adlerian Therapy when Nira Kefir introduced her highly original ideas about priorities and impasses. Interestingly enough, Kefir's views have generally been incorporated into Alfred Adler's system of individual psychology, which is a great compliment since very little that is new has been accepted as part of the theory since its founder's death in 1937. Kefir has therefore made a substantial contribution to personality theory.*

*And now she has further developed her concepts into a total therapeutic approach, innovative and unusual in many ways, not the least being the length of the therapy—it generally lasts for two years. The reader is in for a real treat and an absolutely unique conception of what psychotherapy is all about.*

Impasse/Priority Therapy (IPT) is a four-part therapeutic structure developed with the primary goal of leading individuals from a minus to a plus position. A minus position is defined as one in which an individual has a distorted view of the human social environment, perceives others as threatening, and, consequently, is paralyzed in moving in life. Situations of the minus type are those in which the human encounter is seen as a threat—a hindering force.

In line with Alfred Adler's holistic personality model, every person is seen as a creative, self-determining, "becoming" being who moves toward fictional goals within a phenomenal social field. The minus situation is normally an impetus to growth and the feeling of significance, but it can lead to impasses and a reduction of behavioral repertoires—even to "illnesses"—owing to a distorted social learning process developed in early childhood.

IPT involves a repetition of the child's socialization process as well as training in social interest, advancing clients to a higher state of being, in which they are open-ended, active, and always oriented to other people.

IPT is designed as four stage-process including: (1) meeting individually with a therapist for diagnosis and a treatment plan, (2) participating in an intensive marathon, (3) being in an extended workshop program, and (4) studying human relations.

## HISTORY

An unattributed saying is that when a person says "I think" he is probably lying, or at least uttering a half truth, because our thoughts are an accumulation of previous thoughts, our reaction to them, and our associations connected with the actions of other people. The finished thought that accompanies the "I think" encompasses all these previous thoughts. That is why the concept of priorities and Impasse/Priority Therapy—which is, as far as I can determine, my own creation—evolved through a process of filtering and absorbing the ideas of other people, beginning in childhood with what was learned in the family. I also incorporated the ideas of Hillel, Alfred Adler, Rudolf Dreikurs, Jean-Paul Sartre, Viktor Frankl, and many others. Hillel's basic thought, "Love thy neighbor as thyself," is the essence of the Torah he proclaimed. This idea, similar to Adler's concept of "social interest," places supreme value on social relationships. I regard the purpose of the therapeutic process as mainly one of helping individuals find their place among other human beings, helping them to enlarge their social interest and to develop a personal significance in connection with others.

In my training with Rudolf Dreikurs I learned and accepted Alfred Adler's individual psychology as a socioteleological system that emphasize looking at the individual holistically within the present social field. What is important is not so much what happened in the past but rather where one is now heading. The individual's life style, the apperceptive ways one looks at oneself and the external world, and how one moves behaviorally through life toward an idealized goal of superiority (the "plus") is believed to be formed by the age of four to six years.

After working for several years with the basic Adleian tool of the life style, I found that uncovering it does not show the therapist or the client the individual's mode of behaviors but only one's perception of the self, one's outlook on life and the way in which other people are perceived. This realization led to my formulation of the concepts of "impasse" and "priorities," both of which are regarded as being created by each individual in the preconceptual stage of development; that is, they are created both prior to and coincident with the establishment of the life style. The concepts of impasse and priorities appear to indicate the different conditions under which an individual feels a sense of belonging and, consequently, feels significant. The ideosyncratic condition(s) under which each person sets to find the sense of belonging leads to the establishment of a preferred mode of behaving—of moving on

the social map. Four basic categories of impasse/priority have been postulated and will be elaborated on below.

The development of the IP theory also coincided with certain professional developments in Israel. Following the Yom Kippur War (1973), therapists came to realize that people suffering from shell shock are best treated in a group rather than in the traditional one-to-one setting. The traumatic events that trigger shell-shock symptoms are social ones. When a soldier is traumatized by seeing his closest friend killed, he tends to feel unbearably guilty because he alone was spared. Since the trauma is a socially connected event, then theoretically the therapy, a remedial experience that reprocesses the traumatic event, should likewise be done in a social, that is, group, setting.

The impasse as described in IP theory also results from a social shock arising from relationships with others. Consequently, in IPT are incorporated social therapeutic techniques, specifically an intensive marathon and workshops that involve working closely with other people, thus providing a remedial experience where the patient can *relearn* and *unlearn* inappropriate interpersonal relationships. The workshops and the intensive marathon are designed to be "guided self work" that instills the concept of "the other(s)" into the life of the patient.

IP theory has enabled clinical staff to develop techniques for diagnosing, confronting, and treating in an efficient and reliable manner.

## CURRENT STATUS

The concept of priorities was first enunciated in 1971 at the International Adlerian Summer School session held in Israel. It aroused much interest and was subsequently introduced at meetings in the United States and in Europe by myself and colleagues from other countries. A theoretical paper on the concept was first published in 1974 (Kefir & Corsini, 1974). Jacqueline Brown adopted the priorities concept and independently developed it into an action-oriented diagnostic process (Brown, 1976). John M. Sutton (1976) tested the validity of the priorities concept with 385 college students with encouraging results. Donald E. Ward (1979) wrote an analytical review of the concept in which he said:

Priorities constitute a cognitive framework which can help the client feel a strong sense of mastery and ability to handle him or herself. . . . the personality priority assessment strategy allows a person to retain the "who" of what he or she is [i.e., the priority] but encourages [its] use in more useful, social-interest directed ways. (pp. 14–15)

Impasse/Priority Therapy is actively practiced in Israel, principally at the Alfred Adler Institute of Tel Aviv. Since 1978 many therapeutic and educational institutions in Israel have referred people to the workshops at the institute. Today a skilled team of leaders carry on the work. The IPT intensive marathon was introduced for the first time outside of Israel during the summer of 1979 in Washington, D.C. There the purpose was essentially didactic, to show professionals the kind of work we are doing.

As yet a systematic inquiry has not been done to measure the effectiveness of the therapeutic method of IPT, and this chapter is one of the first attempts at describing the system. The psychologists and social workers now using this approach periodically assess their experience and refine the workshop and marathon techniques. The general impression is that IPT is a promising innovation in psychotherapy, which we at the institute believe could be effectively used throughout the world.

## THEORY

It might seem pretentious to propose yet another concept aimed at changing people's behavior, not only because of the French proverb *Plus ça change, plus c'est la même chose,* but because, in a world of accelerating

change, the attempt to define the concept *change* becomes ever more elusive. Change in our present era might actually act to preserve existing values in a changing world. Yet people feel compelled to find a better way of living, whether for immediate benefit or in order to find a meaning and purpose in their lives.

This model of psychotherapy holds as a basic underlying concept that people are in constant motion; that change is inevitable; that, as Heraclitus said, it is not possible to step into the same river twice. Motion in life is always directed toward an ideal, a goal. Changes in our relationships are likewise directed toward attainment of those goals in terms of our idealized conceptions of self, of others, and of the final result.

A therapist who operates on the premises of Adlerian theory assumes the position of leader in the therapeutic process. The therapist's role aims at enlarging the individual's social interest, helping him or her to overcome feelings of inferiority, helping the individual modify his or her goals, as well as training the client toward greater contribution within interpersonal relationships. The therapeutic process is thus essentially an educative one that results in a tangible movement forward for the individual.

Psychotherapy as directed movement involves a reprocessing of the childhood pattern of development, and especially its social aspect. Socialization is a process, beginning in childhood, of finding one's place in society, of feeling a sense of belonging and of contributing, which occurs simultaneously with the individual's constant forward movement in life. The flow of life thus involves a developing sequence of circles of belonging with widening possibilities of contribution and new goals.

### Circles of Belonging

Every new human being becomes the center of a new world, the center of a human circle. The infant forms a first human relationship with the person who takes care of him or her, generally the mother. However, the infant's efforts and creativity in the development of this relationship must be stressed. He or she is definitely not simply a receptive object of the mother's ministrations, but is an active participant in the transaction. As a creative being, the child's development is directed from the interior to the exterior, to the world of other objects. Generally, psychologists have ascribed variable personality development to the environment of the child. They focus on the attitudes of others toward the child, the projection of their personal needs in the relationship with the child, and their responses to the child's existence and behavior. In contrast, and taking the existential viewpoint, IP therapists regard the life movement of all people, including the newborn, as directed from the inside to the outside, as a reaching out from a relatively secure and comfortable existence to an unknown condition. This risk taking in reaching to the external world is the heart of the development process, the motivation for advancement.

The relationship with the mother is the first ring in the development of the child's circle of belonging. The child's social development proceeds through a sequence of widening concentric circles, which can be pictured as a radius projected outward from the nuclear center to encompass the enlarging circles of belonging that develop in life. As illustrated

in Figure 1, the first circle is likely to be the mother. The second circle includes other members of the nuclear family; subsequent circles represent the widening social experiences of the individual, which are unique to each child. When such a diagram is created for an individual, every social framework is not included, but only those where the individual feels belonging by contributing to and receiving meaningful feedback. Social frameworks that are not a meaningful part of the individual's existence are not included.

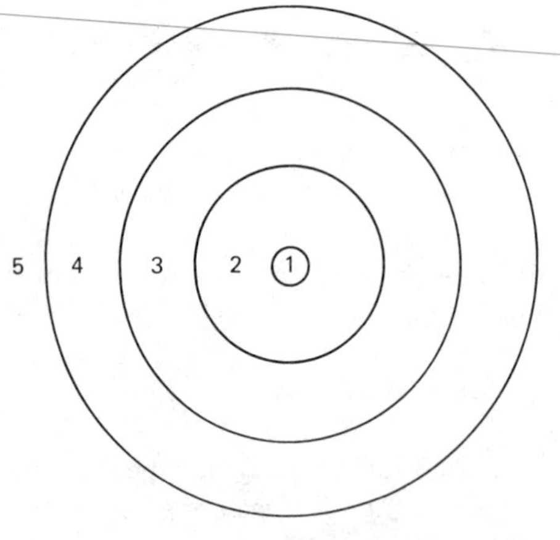

## Contribution

Contribution, a concept related to social interest, is central to IPT. During the socialization process, the individual acquires skills, such as being able to speak up and address people, to find assistance, to inspire affection and appreciation, to relate the body to various configurations of space, to listen and use feedback, and so on. These skills become part of the individual's behavior repertoire, but for some people these skills are underdeveloped or missing. IP therapists attempt to give individuals new social skills and associated attitudes so that they can contribute more meaningfully and thereby enlarge their feeling of significance. Where there is a severe limitation in the development of the social repetoire, there we find impasses.

## Impasses

The impasse concept developed from a determined search for the precursors of the life style. IP therapists came to understand that the child's self-determination process and adoption of a life-style pattern was not only a process of selective choice but also a process of wary elimination. Every positive decision is also a decision to avoid and negate alternatives. When a person decides to go to the movies, he also decides not to stay home or to read or to be with friends. In other words, any decision reflects a process of elimination. In childhood the process of elimination is not a random matter but often

Figure 1  Circles of belonging: How they might be for a particular person. (1) Mother. (2) Family. (3) Social group. (4) Professional group. (5) Political party.

arises from a negative or traumatic social experience.

Human life involves a process of searching how to be significant. This process begins at birth—with mere survival—since survival is a condition of life. To survive, the child first learns what must be avoided—which is a negative learning. Negative learning can be divided into two forms: (1) *physical negative learning*—the avoidance of fire, water, falling, and so on; and (2) *social negative learning*—the avoidance of ridicule, stress, mistakes, self-depreciation, and so forth. This learning becomes rigidly fixed in the early years of life and serves as a reminder of what is dangrous, both physically and psychologically. This learning is based upon the child's biased perception of self and the world. This may explain why a child disregards many influences of the social environment once the life style is formed, especially if those influences do not fit his or her apperceptive schema. If social experiences remain equally influential throughout life, then one's life style would change with varying influences. However, once the life style is formed, the basic personality appears to remain fixed; despite a myriad of later social influences, it does not change to any significant degree. Negative learning probably precedes positive learning in the creation of the personality, and leads to the development of physical and social avoidance strategies. Just as the child learns to avoid fire or being burned, falling, and so forth, he or she develops a similar avoidance strategy toward social situations where he or she feels nonsignificant. The child's behavior then becomes focused on conduct and actions that assure a feeling of significance.

An impasse is viewed as a nexus or a complex of feared social behavior that the person always avoids. The term "always" is used deliberately because I am convinced that a persona always operates in terms of impasses, avoiding them like a burned cat avoids a flame.

The traumatic experience that produced the impasse was always a social one and so leads to an avoidance strategy in the social living of the individual. *Impasse* implies the end of the road, a roadblock, from which one cannot advance further. And, as a driver avoids roads marked "dead end," so in life also a person stops moving in a certain direction when he or she psychologically reads "dead end."

Some other psychological theories include a concept of impasse or deadlock. Psychoanalysis traces deadlocks to the unconscious formation of intrapsychic conflicts. In Primal Therapy, the impasse is traced to shock experiences that took place in infancy or early childhood, and its therapy is directed to releasing the person from this shock through abreaction techniques. Gestalt herapy deals with present deadlocks in a concrete and holistic manner; here the individual works on the deadlock himself but it is carried out in a group setting. Forms of therapy such as Encounter, Rebirthing, and Creative Aggression all deal with breaking down of deadlocks by means of support, release of aggression, or relearning. What distinguishes the IP approach to deadlock or impasse is its strong emphasis on the social setting and relations that initiate the impasse and are involved in its resolution.

Even though the original traumatic events may have been diverse and may have occurred at different times during the child's early development, they tend to fall into four generalized categories, which are called the four basic impasses. They are: (1) appearing *ridiculous;* (2) being *insignificant;* (3) being *rejected;* and (4) avoiding *stress.*

*Ridicule.*   A person who has this impasse is afraid of being in a situation in which he or she is not in control, where he or she might behave in a socially unsuccessful manner, or might seem not to understand the rules of the environment. A person blocked by ridicule sees others as scornful and hostile.

*Meaninglessness.*   A person with this block is afraid of being insignificant, having no influence on the environment, having no value, no possibility of proving himself, being unimportant.

*Rejection.*    Persons with this impasse fear rejection—being unwanted, unappreciated, disregarded, overlooked, unloved. Therefore, they believe themselves incapable of living alone and think that others provide justification for their existence.

*Stress.*    People with this impasse fear for their very existence. They feel a lack of energy, lack of breath, when confronting an anticipated stress. To them, others seem to be constantly confronting them, which heightens their feeling of threat to their existence. Even routine tasks are viewed as stressful—and something to be avoided.

These impasse situations appear as existential dangers, as though one were entering a dark tunnel with no exits. Dread of confronting these impasses is inflated beyond proportion. Through repetitive experiences, first within the family and then later in larger and larger circles (see Figure 1), we begin to form a strategy of living, dominated by our desire to avoid those situations that could bring forth the impasses we dread. As a consequence, one's choices in life are restricted and one is operating minimally, always in fear of the impasses. The paralyzing fear and limited choices therefore restrict possibilities for living fully, for contributing and finding meaning and happiness in life.

## Priorities—The Existential Precondition

Avoidance strategy, the movement away from expected social danger, is the first stage in the development of the life style. The young child either overcomes the basic fear that the social trauma/impasse generates or the fear becomes intensified, leading to an avoidance strategy. At this point one of the most important decisions in life is made: whether movement in life will be mainly toward goals or away from dangers.

Both are movement strategies, since all life is movement. But there is a difference between when we move toward something or away from something. When we move toward something, there is a sense of positive

direction; when we avoid, out of fear, there is no direction, only chaotic flight. Priorities arise out of our creative power to organize chaos. Priorities clear a pathway for organizing human relations. As the choice of the priority arises from the impasse, the best way to discover each priority is to trace it back to the impasse. Priorities are there not because they are preferred behavior, but because they are seen as the *only* way to significant social survival.

Four priority dynamic patterns have been identified. They are:

*The Controller.*    Being a controller is a guarantee against being ridiculed. This means that the person must not be laughed at, must not appear ridiculous, and must be in complete control of the current situation so that he or she will not suffer any embarrassment. Such people are socially sensitive and are greatly concerned with proprieties.

*The Pleaser.*    Pleasers must avoid rejection. To do so, they seek constant acceptance and approval. They will do anything to achieve approbation since they dread being disliked or found unimportant. The pleaser is agreeable only as long as approval is given.

*The Morally Superior.*    Such persons avoid anonymity. They obtain significance and influence on people by high achievement, leadership, martyrdom, or in any fashion that makes them feel that they are "superior" persons.

*The Avoider.*    Avoiders are reactors; they use delay and specialize in unfinished business, unresolved problems, and unmade decisions—avoiding anything that implies *stress.* In avoiders, unlike in the other dynamic patterns of behavior, the chaotic flight generated by the social impasse was never organized in a behavioral or temporal sense. Avoiders see their lives as always in a temporary state.

Each priority gives us different ways of being

significant. In each priority one can be more active or passive, more cooperative and contributing, more useful and useless—there is a whole range of possible expressions. For example, one might ask, "How does an avoider gain significance?" The logic behind this behavior might be: "I am significant when I am secure, and I am only secure when I am left alone." This is a passive way of life as an onlooker. Noninvolvement, watching others, becomes a way of being on top of the situation. With moral superiority, significance can be achieved by contribution, but one can also feel superior in a negative way by being a victim.

To become fully aware of ourselves, we have to learn: (1) what our priority and condition for feeling significant is; (2) what our avoidance strategy is based on—in other words, what the impasse was; and (3) how we can find alternative ways to gain significance using a larger repertoire.

### Structured Stages of Therapy

Psychotherapy is not generally studied in universities; rather it is usually learned during unstructured transactions between supervisors and trainees. Psychotherapy is undoubtedly a creative art. Yet unlike Leonard da Vinci's apprentices, who spent some of their best years in study, we allow novices only a brief glimpse into the holy of holies—the therapy room—because most of us have difficulties describing what actually takes place there. In constructing a therapeutic setting, I have tried to turn a mysterious process into a teachable one that is not overaffected by the charismatic personality of the therapist.

In Impasse/Priority Therapy, the emphasis is placed on work caried out by the client under the guidance of the therapist. This involves a reprocessing of the patient's socialization, with the goal being to encourage movement forward in conjunction with an activation of social interest. The different stages of therapy designed to reach this goal are part of the resocialization process.

The first stage is a *diagnosis* and *structuring;* a one-to-one relationship between client and therapist that mirrors the first circle of belonging. The second stage, the *marathon,* is similar to the social setting of the family. The third stage, the *workshop,* represents the larger social sphere (school, work, community). The fourth stage, *study,* represents independent functioning in the social world. This four-part therapeutic structure is designed to guide the individual from awareness to breaking through the impasse, a process that takes place during the first two stages. Thereafter, the workshop stage encourages the acquisition and practice of broader social skills, which are further developed in the fourth stage. One can view these four stages as a process of learning, unlearning, relearning, and reinforcing goals.

## METHODOLOGY

In some places psychotherapy has acquired a negative stereotype. In Israel the client's encounter with therapists prior to the intake interview generally involves a series of bureaucratic procedures—coming to an office, registering, paying in advance, and then waiting up to six weeks for the first interview to take place. No wonder the client has a low level of expectation at this point and is totally unaware that he or she is about to enter an unforseeable experience.

The creativity of the therapist in IPT is of crucial importance, especially during the intake interview and in the first stages of the therapeutic relations. In this field there is no greater danger than routine. The therapist needs to be original, thinking constantly in terms of new ideas and forms; he or she must always be sure of being understood. Regarding creativity, solo private practice is not a satisfactory therapeutic approach because it lacks the feedback and contributing ideas of a team. The one-to-one pattern similar to parent/child, teacher/pupil, sinner/confessor common to private practice work is too limiting for IPT.

## The Intake Interview and Individual Therapy

The intake interview is conducted by a senior therapist in conjunction with another member of the staff. The interview is a diagnostic one in which we discuss problems, bring them into focus, and arrive at a common goal. The goal is a guideline by which to assess the client's advance in therapy. A typical question explored is: "If you could change your life by pressing a button, what would it be like?" This question is particularly useful when people come in with a generalized problem or condition. In such cases, we tell the client to come back with a more concrete idea of what is wanted. For example, the general complaint of "depression" is insufficient as a reference point for therapy. We have to focus and find a common desired goal from which to proceed.

We approach the intake interview in an antibureaucratic way. We do not focus on the collection of many personal details or facts, but rather concentrate on the therapeutic contract and the setting of goals. Here creativity and flexibility are essential. To illustrate: N, a man of 38, came to the first interview well supplied with information about himself. A student in a rabbinical academy, he was well read in psychological literature and identified himself as a schizophrenic. He felt therapy offered no chance for him, but because he had found Adler's theory plausible he was willing to give it a try. His manner was both arrogant and engaging. He was clearly testing us; and, indeed, he succeeded—so much so that it was very tempting for the therapist to roll up sleeves and plunge into an intellectual power conflict, which sometimes is taken for therapy. It was clear that there was no common goal. Paradoxically, we asked N to prepare a paper on schizophrenia, comparing at least three theories, and for him to try to establish which theory was most applicable to him. We promised that after examining his work, we would present it to the staff. In this way we hoped to gain his commitment and cooperation. And it worked.

*Individual Therapy.* The first stage of the IPT process generally involves 15 to 20 individual sessions that continue at the same time as participation in the marathon or workshop stages. During this stage the client learns about his or her life style, early deadlocks or impasses, existential preconditions or priorities, and the way he or she moves on the social map. This is the only stage that deals with interpretation and self-awareness through exploratory exercises and homework. Members of the client's family—the family of origin or one the client has built; in the absence of either, a close personal friend—are invited to participate. The purpose of including significant others is to get a three-dimensional insight into the client's position in the family constellation, and, at the same time, to check the credibility of the client's self-image with others. From this point the client moves on to the next stage.

*The Marathon.* The marathon is structured as an intensive group experience that runs for five consecutive days, eight hours each day. About 20 participants have an opportunity to work on the various concepts introduced each day. These personal observations are discussed and actively experienced in the group setting. A variety of learning techniques are utilized that expose the participants to the concepts in an intensive way through lectures, guidance, short therapy, and help from the group. The marathon is designed to be a self-growth process, in which clients are aided by the help from and support of other group members.

The marathon is designed to provide the time, concentration, and guidance for the individual participants to move from *awareness,* a passive state, to *connections*—energized, gestaltic moments. In the marathon, awareness becomes integrated into a holistic, encompassing focus for action.

To distinguish *connection* (bonding) from *awareness* (insight), it is useful to use the example of orgasm. The literature on sexual techniques explains well what takes place within ourselves during sexual intercourse, and also guides us, via positions and operations, to learn how we can attain the longed-for result. However, even if we follow instructions to the letter, an orgasm is not guaranteed, because the orgasm is an authentic occurrence involving all our mental and physical being. An orgasm takes place in the brain and can even occur without physical stimulation. Paradoxically, orgasm appears to occur at a peak point of self-control and concentration and at the same time calls for loss of control and abandonment. In this paradoxical condition the authentic orgasm is experienced.

Similar to the orgasm, connection occurs on a different level from awareness. A combination of physical and mental states is necessary for a connection to take place. Like the orgasm, the moment of connection is brief, fleeting, and cannot be sustained. Another similarity between the two phenomena is the difficulty of describing either experience in words. By their nature, they are personal phenomena whose meaning exists solely for the self. And, notwithstanding all the help of others, the individual experiences them alone.

Individual therapy supplies the patient with good insights, and he learns much about himself by clarifying experiences that had previously been unclear. However, movement forward (energized action) cannot take place without "orgasmic" connections.

Connections may occur in therapy only if the following conditions exist: (1) an intensive social setting; (2) a specific system of stimuli combining mental and physical activities that lead to intense concentration and release; and (3) hard work. At the moment of connection one feels energy flowing out from one's center to the world. It is a metamorphic experience.

The concentrated group work of the five marathon days forms the link in a chain that enables the individual to make connections. Following the first stage of individual therapy, where the main objectives are to form a therapeutic contract and to provide insight, awareness, and clarification of goals, the marathon fosters a breakthrough of impasses, thus opening up new possibilities for growth.

The techniques used in the marathon are varied and specifically designed to aid the participants in reexperiencing the basic social impasses, to "survive" them, and to discover new strengths and energy. Screaming, fantasizing, relaxation versus physical exertion, breaking into a closed circle, physical closeness, singing, dancing, and so forth, are characteristic activities. Other activities include elaboration of the life style and the priorities, or existential preconditions, both through personal writing and group experiences. All of these activities serve mainly as catalysts for making connections.

In the marathon, as in the sexual act, there are those who "come quickly"; that is, for some the climactic connection happens on the second or third day. However, unlike the sexual act, those who come quickly remain with the group and supply others with the new energy discovered within them. Others "come" slowly, or on the last day, and sometimes only later, at home, does the longed-for connection take place.

*Workshop.*    The workshop stage of therapy takes place over the course of a year. Usually the client starts to participate in a workshop shortly after completing the marathon.

The workshop approach evolved as a fruitful alternative to classical group therapy. The institute staff in Israel has worked with group methods since its inception in 1963, and has found there are definite limitations to group therapy as generally practiced. These limitations include: (1) the burned-out therapist phenomenon; (2) the problems posed by passive members and the efforts spent trying to activate them; (3) the difficulty of determining when to end a group; (4) the dependency and pressure on the therapist as the leader, teacher, and authority figure; (5) the inadequacy of verbal communication (typical of classical groups) to meet the needs of certain participants; and (6) the fact that classical group methods, while adequate for providing feedback to individuals, are not a good tool for helping them move forward within and without the group. As a consequence, the staff at the Alfred Adler Institute of Tel Aviv developed a new group work model, the workshops, that stimulate clients to activate and actualize their advancement better.

Six kinds of workshops were developed to fit the needs of the client population. There are workshops for (1) married couples, (2) young adults, age 20 to 30, (3) midlife adults, age 30 to 50, (4) elderly people, age 50 to 70, (5) teenagers, age 15 to 18, and (6) families. Each workshop involves between 20 and 30 participants and includes both men and women. A team of two staff members conducts each workshop, which runs for between eight and nine months with a total of 40 weekly sessions.

Every other week all workshop members attend a five-hour session. On alternate weeks, from the second meeting on, workshop members are divided into "home groups" of six to eight people. Thus, all participants meet together for 20 sessions; for the other 20 sessions they meet in small groups in private homes on a rotating basis and work in leaderless fashion discussing topics brought up in the large workshop meetings.

The workshop approach is designed to enable people to learn in their own way. There are basically three ways in which people learn: (1) rational or cognitive, (2) experiential-emotional, and (3) passive observer. Every large assembly workshop is designed to foster all three forms of learning. A topic that needs thinking, interpretation, teleological reasoning, and so forth, is presented, and part of the evening is designed for experiencing through active, physical movement —body image work, fantasizing, creative drama, art therapy, and so on. Last, part of each large session is set aside for demonstrations where participants can learn by observing other people who are the focus of attention. Such demonstrations are likely to include an exposition of a life style, work with early recollections or family constellation, or focusing on a married couple or family. Thus, in the course of the five-hour session, all participants can find a meaningful way to learn.

Skill building and the social framework is another important aspect of the workshop's therapeutic endeavor. Over the course of the year, the participants become mutually responsible and help each other in meeting certain life challenges. They provide the support and encouragement for the individual to carry out a change in his or her life patterns.

The home groups contribute much in this respect. The rotational scheme of meeting in homes means that everyone, without exception, must serve as a host to the others and provide a basic refreshment (simple coffee and biscuits with minimal time involvement). This process enhances the development of social skills for young people and those who feel socially inadequate. It emphasizes the social equality of all members, and provides an opportunity for them to observe the host member in a home setting. Through feedback and support, the group exerts a strong influence on the others. Through sharing and mutual help, the individuals experience the rewarding sense of contribution and the concrete meaning of social interest.

The feeling of belonging generated encourages group members meet the challenges in other aspects of their lives. The groups provide an antidote to the alienation and loneliness of contemporary society by creating a feeling of family in the best sense, beyond the petty competition and rivalry that infects so many real families. In sum, the home groups have become a remarkable meeting point from which all sorts of things emerge for the participants despite their wide-ranging backgrounds and interests. The home groups are the most influential part of the program, but most participants feel this could only take place as an outgrowth of the larger workshop framework.

*Advanced Study and Community Work.* By the time the clients have completed the three stages of individual therapy, the marathon, and the workshop, they are ready for advanced study. In the prior stages they were focused mostly on themselves. Now they need a larger conceptual framework in which to relate and practice what they have learned on the world at large. At this level, it is strongly recommended that clients—who are now referred to as "students"—enroll in courses in social studies and human relations provided by the Adler Institute and other institutions. Such courses open the way for them to become involved in community work and thus actively contribute to others. Some students have volunteered to answer telephones for "hotline" mental first aid programs, while others have worked with underachieving children in volunteer programs, and so forth.

## APPLICATIONS

It is necessary to see Impasse/Priority Therapy in its larger context as a functional unit of the Adler Institute, which is primarily oriented toward improving human relations for the individual, the family, social organizations, and the community at large. This ties in to the concept of the circles of belonging described earlier, and to the basic Adlerian belief that individual growth is a movement toward increased contribution or social interest. The institute is designed to foster the realization of these goals whether through IPT for individuals and small groups or various other educational programs and community services.

## CASE EXAMPLE

M was 26 when she entered therapy. She was on probation and referred for therapy by her parents under pressure from the court. Her transgression: She had been caught in an apartment where police uncovered a brothel, drug dealing, and orgies. A firstborn daughter, M had a sister three years younger. Her parents had survived the Holocaust and met and married on a refugee ship that brought them to Israel in 1948.

My first impression upon meeting M was that she was an attractive and provocative

person who possessed an uncommon intuitive sensitivity to people, odors, feelings, and nature. She was imaginative, audacious, and daring with a rich, internal world. Her vocabulary, however, was poor and strongly infused with street slang. She had a considerable capacity for creating contact with almost anybody.

## Intake Interview

M appeared at the therapist's office at the appointed day and hour. She came into the office barefoot, having walked miles on the blazing roads from her house. The soles of her feet looked like those of the Bedouins who are accustomed all their life to walk barefoot on the sands and rocks of the desert. She was wearing a bright, transparent, light cotton dress with nothing underneath, and her large breasts were almost uncovered. An enormous mass of blond hair curled almost down to her hips. She had no purse or any other article of dress. Our opening dialogue went as follows:

M:  You gonna be my therapist?

T:  No.

M:  Why, don't you deal with whores?

T:  No.

M:  Junkies?

T:  No.

M:  Tough asthmatic cases?

T:  No.

M:  So who do you deal with in this office anyway?

T:  With children who don't like to do their homework (laughter).

M:  Last night I made it with five men. Don't that blow your mind?

T:  No.

M:  For a therapist, your vocabulary is quite poor. (Laughter; both are still standing. Long silence, watching each other.)

M:  I didn't make it with them—they raped me. They were five marketstand owners, regular clients of mine. They all came up together, but when I wanted to split, they raped me. In the end, they left some dough anyway. (Her expression was unemotional with a penetrating gaze that didn't fit the silly smile on her face.) Wanna hear the details? (Provocatively.)

T:  I don't think so.

M:  Maybe we'll sit down already?

T:  Sure.

M:  When we are standing, we look like two suspects waiting in the corridor of the Hall of Justice. You ever been there?

T:  Yes, but I didn't wait. I was in the judge's chamber.

M:  How long will my therapy take?

T:  I haven't decided to accept you yet.

M:  If you're thinking of putting me through tests, forget it—I always fail. In all tests I've taken in my life, I have failed.

T:  In what didn't you fail? (Both sitting down.)

M:  You tell me.

T:  In impressing people. (Laughter.)

## Summarized History from the Probation Report

M was born in 1948 and suffered from severe asthma during her childhood. At school she was considered almost retarded and did not form any contacts with teachers or students. As the eldest daughter whose parents had survived the Holocaust, she had been overprotected to the point of suffocation, while at the same time she was severely punished by her mother for her disobedience, low achievement, escapes, wandering the streets, and so forth. She had always been close to her father, but as the weak person in the family, he felt obliged to be loyal to his wife, and thus "betrayed" M in her most difficult moments. There was no meaningful relationship with her sister.

M's beauty, height, and wit were impressive, and she irritated others because of her indifference toward the world and achievement. At the age of 14, she was sent to a

kibbutz from which she absconded after a year and returned home. Following months of idleness, she met Y by chance, and he induced her to work the streets as a prostitute. At 16 she left home and has had very little contact with her parents since. After a brief period working as a model, she left Israel for Germany and worked as a hooker in Hamburg for three years. There she was abused by Y, whom she loved. She was arrested and spent two weeks in the Hamburg city jail, which she passed in continuous fantasizing. She imagined being in Auschwitz where her mother had been incarcerated. Her release from jail, expulsion from Germany, and return to Israel are remembered as if seen through a screen. When she returned to Israel three years ago, she resumed working as a call girl. Y disappeared from her life; he went to work at sea, smuggling. She, meanwhile, made a lot of money, got involved with drugs, and her asthmatic condition worsened.

## Stages of Therapy

Individual therapy with M, the first stage, extended for six months. In spite of her using a variety of symptoms her repertoire of skills for life were very limited. During this stage, we elaborated upon her impasses and priorities. Her social repertoire had become so small because all alternatives had been eliminated or become impossible for her. It was impossible for her to deal with people because any slight feeling of rejection was alarming to her. She also had to be on top of every situation, in complete control. That limited her mostly to one-to-one relations and, further, to relate only to others whom she could dominate. Such persons were typically social misfits, drug addicts, or frustrated artists and others who depended on her economically and for ego support.

That helps to explain her sense of persecution. She felt persecuted by herself, by her crazy fears, and by her own power of destruction. She also suffered from the impasse of avoidance of stress, because she had not had any successful experiences in coping with life tasks. Thus she couldn't dare to take a job or even to do something about her asthma. Apart from our meetings, she was always late for anything she did, wore no watch, and had no daily schedule. The idea of planning was not in her repertoire, because planning itself was stressful. But the strongest impasse for M, however, was not to be insignificant, and her number-one priority became striving for moral superiority. Even her imbecilic behavior enabled her to gain significance because of its shocking effect on others. The biggest issue for her was over-ambition within, which was combined with the desire to be perfect in all the priorities, which in turn only reinforced and strengthened the impasses.

As part of M's individual therapy stage, different members and then her entire family participated in order to start a new, accepting relationship that gave her a feeling of belonging in the first circle of belonging. Then she was ready to move beyond one-to-one relationships and from awareness to connections.

Her main benefit from participating in the marathon was that she engaged in intensive group work in which she worked only for herself, neither attempting to excell or be different in any way. She thus discovered a sense of belonging by merely participating as all the others did. All her bizarre behavior, which usually brought her attention, was permitted but ignored. She came as close as possible to her impasse, and there made the most important connection of all. She discovered that she was always significant to herself, that she provided her own significance and no longer needed to depend on others to be significant.

During the workshop stage, M moved from attention getting to leadership, undertaking responsibility in the process. Through other people she learned about life tasks and how they are met by others. She also learned firsthand the roles of both the helper and the helped. She developed skills such as expressing herself in a group setting, listening, being passive, and not quitting when she felt like

it. She also learned for the first time in her life the "we" feeling in a setting that permitted her to stay "I." During this period she was encouraged by the group members to start a business, which she later did. For her, the most important experience of the workshop was just being with people and feeling at ease with them. Although prostitution was never a major issue between us, symbolically she stopped this work as she prepared to host the home group for the first time.

**Fourth Stage**

By the end of the workshop, one and a half years had passed since M started therapy. She was ready to move and to learn. She was hungry to be significant in the real world, and thus she enrolled in the Open University to study Judaism and Jewish history (symbolizing her desire for belonging and roots). At the same time, she began her own fashion boutique. To this day, some two years later, she sees her therapist occasionally. She now owns three boutiques, does her own designing, employs 15 people including two former workshop members, and, after a long period of exclusively platonic social relations, is preparing, at age 30, for a mature love relationship. As busy and as self-actualizing a person as she has become, she revealed not long ago that the only thing she truly wants is to change her childhood memories.

**SUMMARY**

In Impasse/Priority Therapy, movement forward, from a minus to a plus situation, is regarded as an integral part of therapy. Meaningful interpersonal movement is considered the criterion for mental health. Disturbances in the flow of life are seen as stemming from early deadlocks, or impasses, due to failures in social learning. The impasses we acquire early in the socialization process are always one or more of the following:

1. I cannot move while I am ridiculous.
2. I cannot move while threatened with being insignificant.
3. I cannot move while I am in danger of being rejected.
4. I cannot move while under pressure.

After the formation of one or more of these impasses, the life style crystallizes, incorporating the individual's idiosyncratic view of the self, the world, and his or her position in the world. Because the life style emerges after the impasses have been created, it is derivative of the prior deduction and the elimination of alternatives. Through the life style, for instance, especially as it is mirrored in childhood recollections, we can determine the strategic priorities the individual has chosen because we can see which directions of movement are considered "impossible." In the life style we can discern four personality priorities: (1) *control,* (2) *moral superiority,* (3) *pleasing,* and (4) *avoidance.* These are not preferred behaviors, they are "musts." Only permanent control of the situation precludes the danger of seeming ridiculous; only superiority guarantees against being insignificant; only pleasing averts rejection; and only avoidance prevents pressure and stress.

The diagnostic process in IPT clarifies the individual's movement on the map of life that is always populated by other people. How does the individual move among them? What is the direction of the movement? What is seen as an obstacle? By what direction is this obstacle evaded? Therapy, then, deals with these issues in a connected approach through: (1) priorities evaluation (individual consultation and family therapy); (2) experiencing deadlocks or impasses (the marathon); (3) enlarging the social repertoire (the workshop); and (4) activating social interest (studies, community work).

The impasse/priorities therapeutic program has four parts, some of which may overlap with others: (1) individual sessions for diagnosis and planning of the program; (2) an intensive marathon that runs for eight hours a day for five consecutive days; (3) a workshop that meets weekly, for eight to nine months, consisting of one group session of about 20 people or one home session of about six to eight people; and finally, an open-ended self-development program intended to help people to help others.

IP philosophy is consonant with Alfred Adler's idealism in stressing social interest and with the ideas of Hillel, who said, "If I am not for myself, who will be? But if I am only for myself, what am I?"

To contribute, to learn, to move forward, to feel the need to move others along with us—IP therapists are doing just what the moon is doing, illuminating the world.

## REFERENCES

Adler, A. *The individual psychology of Alfred Adler,* ed. H. L. Ansbacher and R. Ansbacher. New York: Basic Books, 1956.

Adler, A. *Superiority and social interest,* ed. H. L. Ansbacher and R. Ansbacher. Evanston, Ill.: Northwestern University Press, 1964.

Adler, A. *Study of organ inferiority and its psychical compensation.* New York: Johnson Reprint Corp., 1972. (Originally published 1917.)

Brown, J. F. *Practical applications of the personality priorities,* 2nd ed. Clinton, Md.: B & F Associates, 1976.

Buber, M. *I and thou.* New York: Scribners, 1958.

Dreikurs, R. *Group psychotherapy and group approaches: Collected papers.* Chicago: Alfred Adler Institute, 1960.

Dreikurs, R. *Psychodynamics, psychotherapy and counseling: Collected papers.* Chicago: Alfred Adler Institute, 1967.

Dreikurs, R. Private logic. In H. H. Mosak (Ed.), *Alfred Adler: His influence on psychology today.* Park Ridge, N.J.: Noyes Press, 1973.

Frankl, V. *Doctor and the soul.* New York: Knopf, 1965.

Frankl, V. *Psychotherapy and existentialism.* New York: Simon & Schuster, 1968.

Janov, A. *The primal scream.* New York: Dell, 1970.

Kefir, N. Priorities—a different approach to life style and neurosis. Paper presented at ICASSI, Tel Aviv, Israel, 1971.

Kefir, N. and Corsini, R. J. Dispositional sets: A contribution to typology. *Journal of Individual Psychology,* 1974, **30 (2)**, 163–178.

Perls, F. *Gestalt therapy verbatim,* ed. J. O. Stevens. Toronto: Bantam Books, 1969.

Perls, F. S., Hefferline, R. and Goodman, P. *Gestalt therapy: Excitement and growth in the human personality.* New York: Delta, 1951.

Pew, W. L. The number one priority. *International Association of Individual Psychology Monograph* (Munich, Germany), August 1, 1976.

Sartre, J.-P. *Being and nothingness.* New York: Philosophical Library, 1956.

Sutton, J. M. *A validity study of Kefir's priorities: A theory of maladaptive behavior and psychotherapy.* Ed.D. thesis, University of Maine at Orno, 1976.

Ward, D. E. Implications of personality priority assessment for the counseling process. *Individual Psychologist,* 1979, **16(2)**, 12–16.

# CHAPTER 30

## Integrative Therapy

WALTER J. URBAN

*Although Walter J. Urban is a research psychoanalyst, which immediately brings to mind someone tied to the couch technique of Sigmund Freud, his method of Integrative Therapy is exactly the opposite.*

*As I understand Integrative Therapy, it enables the therapist to employ various procedures in order to achieve goals for the patient. The art of the process is to integrate these procedures smoothly.*

*The method of Integrative Therapy can be likened to the method of a swimmer who wants to reach land. He or she will use, at different times and as conditions necessitate, the breast stroke, the crawl stroke, the side stroke, and the backstroke. Yet each time he or she changes strokes, the one main aim remains—to get to shore.*

*While some therapists might hold a contrary point of view—that one should keep consistently to one process, which can accomplish everything, and that too many changes will confuse clients, there are in between ways of operating: to have a few methods that one employs differentially. In my own experience, in about 90 percent of my interactions I employ the simple interview; sometimes I use some role playing; and sometimes I use some unusual techniques and will even at times invent my own. This freedom is what Integrative Therapy is all about.*

Integrative Therapy is a theory, technique, and clinical method developed by this writer, a research psychoanalyst, in the 1970s. It involves using a combination of techniques from different therapeutic modalities based on the therapist's judgment of which particular technique will provide the greatest benefit for the client at a given moment. The integrative therapist works toward freeing natural energy and creativity and enhancing the capacity for love, work, and knowledge. Energy is drained when painful experiences are buried. The reliving and working through of old wounds combined with appropriate adult ego integrative processes releases energy.

The body is one's most precious possession. An internal and external balance with oneself and the world determine the pleasure, peace, freedom, openness, and responsibility that occurs in life on a daily basis. The mature personality is motivated toward and practices daily self-care. Integrative Therapy is a continually developing approach to human growth, encouraging the creative development of both client and therapist.

## HISTORY

### Precursors

Human beings are a whole and part of a greater whole—the family, the society, and the universe. A holistic approach to therapy is in keeping with the essence of humanity.

A desire to understand the body and mind goes back to the origins of humanity itself, and can be seen throughout history. The Greek and Roman philosophers advised "Know thyself." Separation of the body and mind was of the human being's own thinking, and the reintegration of the body and mind as seen in psychosomatics is also the human being's thinking. Simply put, to understand the self, man had taken himself apart and then put himself back together.

The following is a brief summary and review of some concepts of major theorists from which Integrative Therapy emerged.

Sigmund Freud (1953) stressed the role of the unconscious and dynamic forces. He developed the concepts of free association, transference, and resistance. Alfred Adler (1958) suggested a holistic approach, and said that man could be understood only as a whole and was an indivisible unity. Carl Jung (1954) posited an instinct toward individuation and the existence of autonomous forces that push us to achieve wholeness. Wilhelm Reich (1949) believed that the body must be the primary area of focus and that the musculature of the body stores energies. When energy becomes bound in muscular contraction and armoring occurs, the natural functions of the body are blocked. Relieving this situation releases repressed emotions. Fritz Perls (1951) focused on what is and the here-and-now. Awareness is of vital importance; each moment the new changes, and thus awareness is always changing. Alexander Lowen (1975) focused on the body. The body reflects one's basic attitude toward life, seen in posture, carriage, and general movement. Arthur Janov (1970) focused on the pain that results from unmet needs. When pain is out of awareness, one's basic need becomes buried and a split occurs. Eric Berne (1961) stressed stimulus hunger, ego states, transactions, games, and life scripts. He saw the "stroke" as a fundamental unit of social intercourse. A deficit in stroking leads to psychopathology. Albert Ellis (1979) declared that a person's negative emotional reactions do not result directly from events but from beliefs about events. B. F. Skinner

(1974) claimed that neurosis is caused by learning unadaptive behavior and that the goal of therapy is to modify the unadaptive stimulus-response connections.

William Glasser, Carl Rogers, Randolph Stone, Jacob Moreno, Ida Rolf, Abraham Maslow, Harry Stack Sullivan, Melanie Klein, Margaret Mahler, Heinz Hartman, Edith Jacobson, Moshe Feldenkrais, among others, have also contributed to the foundation of Integrative Therapy.

The basic concepts of catharsis, abreaction, unconscious, awareness, ongoing diagnoses, energy systems, the here-and-now, transference, resistance, ego states, and so forth, are all important in Integrative Therapy.

## Beginnings

Integrative Therapy is the outgrowth of this writer's 25 years of professional experience, thinking, and empirical approach. My postgraduate training as a psychoanalyst was at the National Psychological Association for Psychoanalysis. I also trained at the Family Institute and the Postgraduate Center for Mental Health. After 12 years of didactic Freudian psychoanalysis and the rigidities of psychoanalytic theory and training, I felt it was necessary to regain an open-minded and flexible approach. My curiosity led me to experience various therapies such as gestalt, primal, bioenergetics, transactional analysis, polarity therapy, acupressure, Shiatsu, Esalen massage, and so forth, as well as to attend various training seminars and workshops. With psychoanalsis as my foundation, I gradually began to introduce different techniques in my therapeutic work. Techniques were incorporated one at a time, until a sense of ease, comfort, and confidence developed.

I was careful not to disturb ongoing therapy or to contaminate transference. At first there was some negative reaction from clients who were used to a traditional approach. However, eventually a mutually agreed upon experimentation of new modalities took place. The modalities were found to be helpful and expedient, and as a result, both therapist and clients grew. Meanwhile, I began to develop the theoretical framework for Integrative Therapy. Different modalities were successfully integrated into therapy sessions when it made clinical sense.

## CURRENT STATUS

Integrative Therapy is a relatively new approach. I have been perfecting it gradually since 1969. I am not aware that anyone else currently uses the theory and techniques of Integrative Therapy as outlined in this chapter as well as in *Integrative Therapy: Foundation for Holistic and Self Healing* (1978). In 1978 I held the first training seminar in Integrative Therapy for a small group of psychotherapists in Los Angeles.

Various psychotherapists have discussed theories and procedures that closely relate to Integrative Therapy. Frederick Thorne (1973) used Eclectic Psychotherapy, which involves the selective application of basic scientific methods using the most valid current knowledge available for specific clinical situations according to indications and contraindications. Advocacy of his eclecticism was based on a broad spectrum of experience, a wide sample of cases, and clinical methods.

The psychotherapy curriculum in graduate schools of psychology has gradually broadened, and courses currently include a wide range of therapeutic modalities. In recent years holistic health centers have sprung up throughout the country, and some growth centers have changed their orientation to become holistic health centers. New publications, such as *The Journal of Holistic Health,* have begun.

Annual conferences and training institutes have offered workshops in which various therapies have been combined. For example, Ilana Rubenfeld has given workshops in Gestalt Therapy, Alexander technique, and the Feldenkrais exercises; she calls her work Gestalt Synergy. Michael Conant has combined the bioenergetic and gestalt approaches. Other practitioners have integrated various modalities, such as employing Primal Therapy in a psychoanalytic session. These syntheses of techniques point to the emergence of what is coming; namely, the integration of all therapeutic modalities.

A full survey of the current status of Integrative Therapy or what might be considered its underpinnings, is a task beyond the scope of this chapter.

## THEORY

### Personality

Integrative Therapy utilizes and includes all reasonable and major theories of personality development. Its theoretical foundation is based on viewing the whole person as a physical, psychological, and spiritual being. Any theory of personality as a purely psychological phenomenon is highly limited. A sound theory of personality needs to describe humans as they really are rather than being limited to a reductionistic viewpoint.

Integrative Therapy does not have its own theory of personality. It draws upon the work of many theorists. Each major theory of personality or therapy offers valuable conceptual information for understanding human development. Integrative Therapy focuses on those aspects of theory that appear sound, useful, practical, and generally of value as building blocks for an inclusive theory. Integrative theory is open-ended. Thus the theory may grow and become rich in accordance with practitioner's motivations and capacities.

### Energy

We are all born with a vital energy life force, the core of our being; this is of primary concern in Integrative Therapy and theory. Energy is the essence of our existence. From the moment of conception, the vital energy of the organism reacts to itself and to its immediate and universal environment. For example, a multitude of interactions take place between the just-born infant and the doctor, the nurses, the mother, the father, and the physical environment.

As these interactions take place, the person's natural vital energy is affected. Its flow may be facilitated or thwarted to various degrees. When natural energy is thwarted, a reaction occurs. The type of that reaction depends upon the context and circumstances in which the thwarting took place. Some thwartings may result in the inhibition of natural feelings or emotions. A child desiring to be loved who is repeatedly pushed aside by a busy, anxious, or angry parent may become inhibited or blocked. The block may develop into a psychological reaction, a physiological reaction, or a combination of the two.

When a person recaptures his or her natural vital energies, which is a primary goal of Integrative Therapy, self-concept becomes modified. One becomes more self-accepting. As energy increases, the person tends to become more outgoing and occupies a greater space and feels greater freedom in the world. When energy is released, the person develops a better body image and experiences more vitality. A clearer identity develops. In general, all these changes contribute to an overall enhanced self-concept.

As a person is freed from depression and negative feelings, a new sense of meaningfulness and enthusiasm for life develops. Energy now is more available for intimacy and contact. One experiences a good sense of being connected to oneself and to the world.

Behavior changes when the vital life energies are free and are manifested in increased meaningful action, increased sense of responsibility for oneself, a new capacity for decisiveness, and general behavior of a healthier nature. Constructive action patterns replace destructive ones.

## Theory of a Therapy Session

The following are the general guidelines for integrative therapy sessions. These steps do not necessarily take place in every session.

*Basic Relationship—Rapport.* Rapport is especially important in initial sessions as well as throughout therapy. Rapport occurs when there is equality between therapist and client. The therapist has expertise and ideally is free-flowing—loose and natural with latent focusing capacity. The therapist accepts and supports the client's resources and helps create an optimal atmosphere for therapy. The therapist's attitude regarding equality is shown by his or her behavior. For example, the therapist does not sit behind a desk, but sits in a chair similar to the client's chair. When the client uses a mattress for body or regressive work, the therapist may sit on the floor near the client. The therapist does not maintain a special image when working as a therapist, but is natural and genuine at all times.

*Observing, Listening, and/or Eliciting.*
From the moment the client presents himself he is communicating verbally or nonverbally. The therapist elicits and/or facilitates communication. The therapist "tunes into" the client's feelings and/or thoughts of the moment. Given sufficient time to make an evaluation of the status of the moment within the context of what is already known about the client, the therapist can begin to interact purposefully.

*Selecting the Focus.* The therapist's interventions are based upon the clinical judgment of the moment. The therapist's strategy is based upon the client's productions. At one moment being supportive may be more important than probing, reflecting, interpreting, confronting, or eliciting. Selecting a focus informs the client about what is important to the therapist. However, that focus may not be important to the client. If the therapist senses this, then mutual agreement about the focus may be established by discussion or explanation. Selecting a focus without maintaining an adequate agreement reduces the therapeutic effect.

*Deepening the Focus.* Both client and therapist contribute to deepening the focus.

In the beginning, the therapist's questions and/or statements may be helpful. As the client becomes more used to and accepting of therapy, he may spontaneously focus. The client's becoming aware of overt feelings or latent feelings also often deepens the focus. To keep deepening focus, the therapist uses verbal and nonverbal cues given by the client, as well as his own internal reactions. The eyes and face are especially revealing of cues. Gradually, the deeper focusing gets, the more expressive the client becomes, and the therapist becomes the active listener.

***Selecting the Modality.*** Once the client is expressively involved and the ball is rolling, the therapist decides which therapeutic modality would be most helpful. Would a gestalt technique, such as using the empty chair and pretending to talk to the client's mother, be most helpful? Would lying on the mattress and using regressive techniques be most helpful? Would a cognitive approach of understanding ego states (parent, child, and adult) be most helpful? The integrative therapist reflects on the therapeutic modalities in his repertoire and decides which one would be most helpful at the moment. Once the modality is selected, it is used for a sufficient time so that both client and therapist have a chance to "test" it.

***Evaluating the Modality.*** To evaluate the therapeutic modality selection, the therapist must allow sufficient time and have patience with the client and the process. Criteria for the evaluation may vary even though the same therapeutic modality is used. *Is the client really involved in what is happening?* A good sense of connectedness to the process is one evaluation criterion. Connectedness may be evidenced by a flowing activity, whether cognitive or emotional. Emotional meaningfulness and experiencing a feeling is important. Bodily sensations, such as a lump in the throat, constriction in the chest, a knot in the stomach, and so forth, are also indications of movement and of connectedness to the process. When there is a sense of flow of ideas, and/or emotional experi-

ence, and/or bodily sensations, then the modality is effective. However, sometimes the therapist must be aware of the resistive and/or defensive aspects that may be taking place. If the process does not "take"—that is, if the therapist experiences the client as not connecting to himself and to the process—then the therapist may decide that this modality is not useful at this time.

***Checking the Time Frame.*** Since therapy sessions usually run for a specified time, the therapist must be aware of how much time has been spent evaluating the chosen modality. The therapist may decide after two or three minutes that the therapeutic modality has fallen flat and that it serves no purpose to continue. On the other hand, the therapist may sense that the client is on the verge of something therapeutically useful. This is a matter of clinical judgment. The amount of time spent on any modality is an important consideration, since time is limited. Obviously, if the client is deeply involved and the modality is working, it is worthwhile to continue.

***Continuing the Work and Evaluating the Contact Level of the Client with Self and/or Therapist.*** When the therapist decides the client is sufficiently connected to himself in a therapeutically meaningful way, or connected in a therapeutically significant interaction with the therapist, then continuation of work in that modality is indicated. On the other hand, if the therapist decides that there are no significantly meaningful occurrences taking place in a given period of time, he may decide either to continue that modality for a further test period, if the cues are sufficient to warrant doing so, or to terminate it.

***Transition to a New Modality.*** The therapist should have a positive attitude about any therapeutic modality's lack of productivity. The idea of the client's having failed is therapeutically negative. Rather, it should be recognized that at this time this approach is not the best one. This attitude may be conveyed verbally or nonverbally. The manner, style, and spirit with which this is done is of the utmost importance. Often no discussion is even necessary. The therapist simply moves in a casual, easy manner and introduces a new modality so smoothly that the transition is barely noticed by the client. If done with sufficient skill, the transition may not be noted as a disruption but rather as a natural, easy turn of events. If done properly, it is experienced as a continuous process, just like turning the page of a book is accepted as a normal procedure by the reader.

*Regressive Work.* Regressive work in the service of the ego is often a significant part of a good integrative therapy session. The concept of reexperiencing and reliving buried feelings is important. Some sessions give indications that regressive work needs to be done. When the client overreacts to a particular situation, the chances are that the situation has triggered off old buried feelings. Using regressive techniques to get in touch with buried feelings in the old situation may be indicated.

*Client Active and Primed When Necessary.* It is a positive indication when the client becomes actively and responsively involved in the therapeutic process. Such activity and initiative is natural once defenses and/or blocks are reduced. However, it must be remembered that silent times may be pregnant with inner activity. If the therapist decides that the client is not sufficiently involved, he has to prime the client to keep the process rolling. This may be done by the therapist's asking the client a question, making a statement, or giving the client a particular look.

*Catharsis, Cognition, and Dynamics.*
Each good integrative therapy session contains emotional catharsis, clear cognition, and an understanding of dynamics. The positive effects of emotional catharsis are well discussed in the literature and need no elaboration here. The processes of reasoning, understanding, evaluating, and other mental

functions are a necessary part of a good session. The adult ego needs to synthesize the meaningfulness of what has happened. The therapist needs to understand the dynamics involved to connect things in a meaningful way. When the therapist has made the connections, they can be conveyed to the client. However, there are times when the client is able to make the connections for himself.

*Summary, Conclusion, and Work to Be Done.* It is often helpful to summarize the session. The therapist may do this in two or three short, clear sentences, or the client may be encouraged to do this. For example, the statement "You hated your mother and were afraid to tell her" may serve both as a summary and conclusion to a session. The client should have a continual understanding of future work to be done. Very often one therapy session leads to the next, and the continuity of the therapy experience is stressed by the therapist. For example, the therapist might end a session with "Let's find out why you were afraid." However, each therapy session does not necessarily have to have a summary, conclusion, and a statement about future work to be done; it is up to the therapist.

*Reestablishing Rapport.* At the end of every therapy session, it is helpful to reestablish rapport and simultaneously check out where the client is and how he or she has experienced the session. The rapport and ego alliance take place through a brief contact only at this time. It is important for the therapist to convey a continued warm, friendly, supportive attitude. Rapport may be reestablished through a simple statement.

## METHODOLOGY

### The Use of Techniques

The integrative therapist proceeds with his own personal therapeutic style during the initial contact and interview. As the treatment proper continues, the therapist, perceptive and sensitive to the client's reactions, gradually introduces a variety of techniques and information. For example, a client may find it is "silly" to talk to an empty chair, pretending that his mother is sitting there. The therapist accepts the client's reaction and decides whether to explore the reaction or to drop the particular technique. Such decisions are based on an overall assessment of the client, the client's needs, and the therapist's goals. But the option must be selected on the basis of whether it is more important to explore the resistance (i.e., "feeling silly"), to stay with the original focus (i.e., mother), or to use the resistance to explore issues of control. The therapist must decide immediately what he is after.

If the therapist chooses to drop the technique, he may say, "It's okay," he may suggest that the client can try it another time, or he may try to explain the purpose and value of the technique.

When a resistant client is encouraged to try a technique, the therapist must administer the right amount of suggestion. The client's reaction to authority may be observed, adding to the information that the therapist has about the client.

Initially in Integrative Therapy relatively few techniques are used, so that the client has a chance to develop a sense of security about therapy itself. Repetition of techniques help fulfill client expectations. As security grows, the client becomes more willing to try new techniques.

Introducing a new technique requires a clinical sense of timing so that the client will recognize that the technique will yield productive results. As therapy progresses, techniques may become more experimental. If there is no therapeutic yield, the technique should be dropped without causing significant negative conditioning.

As a technique is successfully established and integrated in treatment, another can be introduced. If each new one is successfully used before the therapist moves on to another, the client experiences the techniques as tools of therapy rather than as a "bag of tricks" that the therapist is trying out until he finds one that works.

Autonomy in therapy increases when the client begins to have urges to use certain techniques. As the therapist becomes aware of the client's growing autonomy and willingness to experiment, the therapist must monitor and evaluate the client's options, so that the therapy continues and progresses, rather than becoming diffused and unfocused.

When the usefulness of a particular technique has been evaluated, the therapist returns to the original subject matter of the interview. The client thus sees techniques in terms of their having specific usefulness rather than simply as varieties of procedures. When a technique or a set of techniques overtakes the whole therapy, we are really back into a single therapeutic modality with its limits and rigidities. The therapist educates the client about this view of techniques by closure after using one or more new techniques. The client now has the opportunity to integrate the experience whenever regression has occurred during the use of a particular technique.

**Transition**

Transition into a particular therapeutic technique can occur in many ways. The artfulness with which the transition is prepared and carried out can produce expression of creative therapeutic skills and continuous flow of the client. Elements interweave and flow together into an experience of mutual desire and communication. If the therapist is creative, he or she can gradually lead the client into needed experiences. The client must get in touch with deep inner feelings to achieve the relief, security, and gratification that is sought.

The transition period in Integrative Therapy differs from the usual therapy where only one modality is followed. The integrative therapist hopes to find the client on new territory that may be particularly helpful and may lead to emotional experiences. The therapist experiences a sense of accomplishment when the transition is successfully made.

The excitement generated by these discoveries has an energy that may affect the client so that he is in a better position to continue the work to be done; the therapist's excitement and enthusiasm are contagious.

The transition period begins when the therapist decides to change the natural direction of the client's productions. This decision is made while the client continues along his pathway. The therapist begins to function on two tracks simultaneously: He continues to listen to the client while at the same time developing his strategy. The sensitive client may pick up the loss of the therapist's full concentration; he may develop two lines himself, or he may report the experience to the therapist, in which case the therapist should respond with complete honesty. The therapist's strategy must be formulated quickly and effectively, so that his intervention does not lag too far behind the client.

The therapist makes his decision from cues picked up from the client's flow. Learning to read such cues is part of the therapeutic art. The therapist looks both to the client and to his own inner process. When the therapist makes his decision, he must move quickly or the moment for the deepening process will be lost. Moving in at the right moment facilitates therapeutic effectiveness. The therapist's combination of relaxation and hovering alertness allows him to make his move when the timing is right. This capacity grows with experience and good self-supervision.

The goal of the moment, the decision of the moment, and the action of the moment contribute to the excitement. The immediacy of the action and the need to move quickly further challenge the integrative therapist.

## Triggering the Flow and Promoting Regression

One purpose of the cathartic experience is to release energy bound up in buried feelings. To release energy, the client must reexperience feelings. As he does so, defensive and protective patterns are revealed. As each specific defense is understood, the therapist facilitates the client in understanding and overcoming defenses. Attempts to uncover these feelings is always productive, since the process of triggering the flow yields more information for the therapist.

During sessions the therapist observes how the client's body reacts. As the therapist notes reactions in different parts of the client's body, he may choose them as focal points and change therapeutic modalities. For example, tension may develop in a client's feet and they may begin to move. The therapist may check if the client is aware of the movement, and then direct the client's attention to his feet and use the gestalt technique of giving the feet a voice; or he may use a polarity therapy method and work directly with the feet and toes, and so forth. Alternatively, the therapist may decide not to change focal points even though cues are present; however, this decision is based upon the goal of the moment.

Let us examine one method for triggering the flow of the client's energy.

First the client is asked to lie down on a mattress and close his eyes. On the surface, this appears to be a simple request; however, many hidden issues are involved. When the client closes his eyes, he can no longer see the therapist, so in effect he experiences the therapist differently. Lying down may promote relaxation and recapitulate regressive experiences. The client may become more involved with his internal world rather than with any external focus. There is a helplessness associated with this position that repeats early child-parent relationships. The whole body of the client is now consciously involved in the process. The request to lie down carried an implicit suggestion to *let go*. The therapist can observe the client's entire body and may become more conscious of it. The observing ego of the client is stimulated when he lies down and closes his eyes. Finally, the therapeutic alliance is reaffirmed in this act in which the client follows the suggestion of the therapist, hoping to achieve some benefit.

Then the client is asked to become aware of his breath. He is instructed to breathe in through his nose and out through his mouth. This introduces an awareness of part of his body. The suggestibility level is increased as the client proceeds to accept and act upon suggestions (lie down; close your eyes; be aware of your breath; breathe in through your nose; breathe out through your mouth). As conscious breathing continues, the breath often deepens, and the flow of oxygen is increased and affects the body accordingly. Air is a vital life force, and the breath of life helps the client to connect to himself, receive increased vital supplies, and reconnect to the world. Breathing now takes place on a more conscious level, and the client becomes more aware of a voluntary controlling process.

After the client takes several breaths, he is asked to become aware of his body. Confirmation of his existence takes place during this process by greater awareness of sensations and feelings. If the client reports what he is experiencing, he may describe a series of changing sensations. For example, a pressure on the chest may change to a band around the entire chest and then may change to a pain in the eyes. This may further change to pressure on the temples, and then into a headache and tension in the neck. Following these changes of bodily sensation can provide valuable information to the therapist.

As body awareness and sensation develop, the client is asked to make a sound appropriate to what he is experiencing. If the client is unable to do this, the therapist may make a sound he thinks reflects the client's state. The therapist may say *oh, ah, eee, uh,* or may whimper, and so forth. The therapist thus is modeling behavior for the client and giving permission to communicate in an archaic way. This facilitates a regressive process. The therapist may ask the client to repeat the sound several times until he senses the client is beginning to connect to the sound. This introduces vocalization of the body experience. If a particular sound does not take hold, the client is encouraged to try another. The client must be given a certain amount of leeway so that he can connect to himself. The therapist must decide when to intervene and when to back off. When the sound begins to connect, the therapist must allow the connection to take place without interruption.

The client is encouraged to stay with the sound. The repetition may become his own expression rather than a response to the therapist's suggestion, as in the previous step. When this occurs, the client is beginning to let go and get into the sound. The therapist must be careful not to interrupt this process.

When the sound production appears to have taken hold, the therapist should encourage the client to *let go* into the sound. The therapist repeats the suggestion of letting go several times. This is done in a sensitive and gradual way, to maintain contact with the client without disturbing his inner flow.

Then the client is instructed to follow the flow wherever the sound leads him—to more sounds, a different sound, words, silence, bodily sensations, feelings, or thoughts. If silence occurs, the therapist is patient and allows sufficient time to pass before saying anything. Often the client emerges from the silence on his own.

At this point, the client is encouraged to take his time and be with himself, where he really is. The therapist thus reflects his patience and his genuine care about the intimate state of the client. Encouraging the client to take his time helps the client experience the therapist's availability, understanding, and encouragement. This may become an important communication to the client that facilitates the trust needed to *let go.*

Once the client lets go and the flow process starts on a verbal and/or nonverbal level, the therapist steps back and lets the client do the work. The therapist may experience himself through a sense of his presence, rather than being actively involved. This is an important time for the client, who now begins to get fully and deeply in touch with himself. The client may be reliving the more recent past or some early life experiences, during which he may have turned off basic needs, such as the need for love, warmth, and closeness. He may be reliving painful or hurtful feelings connected to fear, anger, frustration, aloneness, sadness, or helplessness.

When these needs and pains were originally turned off and put away, the free-flowing energy that was a connection between self and the world became disconnected. This disconnectedness then caused a splitting effect in the personality, and a sense of an unreal self began to develop.

As the client continues to work and experience his flow, he may cry, talk, make various sounds, scream, become frozen, numb, or still, tremble, move, become silent, or withdraw.

As this flow continues, the therapist may become an active guide. When and how to guide depends on many criteria, and the therapist uses his understanding, compassion, empathy, intuition, courage, and prior experience. At such times the therapist may ask himself the following:

*Has the flow run its course?*

*Is the client becoming defensive?*

*Does the client need to finish a particular piece of work that he is avoiding?*

*Am I getting uncomfortable?*

*Would the client benefit from an intervention? How? Which?*

*Do I need to study this client in greater depth?*

*Am I overidentifying with the client?*

*Am I intervening because of needs of my own?*

The therapist may guide when he decides it is necessary, using various therapeutic tools from different modalities. When unable to follow the flow or unclear about some communication, the therapist must ask appropriate questions. However, there may be times when the therapist decides to by-pass an unclear moment so as not to interrupt. He may come back to this at a later point in the session.

The therapist accepts the client's blocks.

As the flow continues, blocks, impasses, or sticking points may develop. When it is clear that the client is unable to go on, the therapist needs to accept these points. If the therapist sees these points as valuable, he communicates this to the client. He may explain the general meaning of blocks as old methods developed to cope with particular experiences. The therapist now has the opportunity for further study and analysis of the client's defenses. If this point of view is taken, the therapist can convey positive feelings to the client.

Finally, the therapist encourages the client to fully experience blocks. The therapist's combination of patience and reassurance helps the client accept where he is at the moment, rather than forcing him to make demands on himself. Experiencing blocked parts helps him to understand the nature of less obvious defenses. By working through these defenses rather than bypassing them, the therapist promotes a real reconstruction rather than a readaptation. After blocks are experienced and accepted, and are seen as an integral part of the flow by both therapist and client, the process continues.

In the early stages of therapy, the client may not understand blocks as part of flow. The therapist's language must give the client the feeling of being understood as he is. The therapist may say, "Go back to it," "Try again," or "Let yourself go" at the outset, whereas later on he may say, "Continue" or "What are you experiencing now?" or "It's okay, go on" or he may say nothing at all.

After the flow ends or is cut off by the therapist, the therapist helps the client understand and integrate his adult ego state. The therapist sets his priorities in relation to the time remaining. He must set forth the work that needs to be done in the future, and he asks the client to do the same, so that a mutual agreement can be made. The therapeutic alliance is reaffirmed and the preparation for more work is made. The therapist checks with the client as to his current state, makes his own independent assessment, and

proceeds to do whatever he sees fit therapeutically. The session is wrapped up; but,
if the client is being seen frequently enough,
certain ends may be left hanging for the client
to cope with.

## APPLICATIONS

Since Integrative Therapy draws upon all the
psychotherapies and has a flexible, creative
approach that is particularly sensitive to the
needs of the client, it is an extremely practical
therapy. Integrative Therapy has been especially helpful to clients who had had unsuccessful prior therapy, since it offers an
enthusiastic and fresh approach. Integrative
Therapy has been particularly helpful to psychotherapists as clients themselves who have
reached professional and personal maturity,
yet who have not fully resolved certain problem areas or who are dissatisfied with their
level of self-care or life style. Locating well-
defended or hidden areas that create energy
blocks is what Integrative Therapy can do
well.

Integrative Therapy has been helpful to
people suffering from psychosomatic problems, as it has a body-mind orientation. It
has been successful in treating people with
migraine, high blood pressure, ulcers, men-
strual pain, dizziness, vertigo, and so forth,
even after other methods, both psychotherapeutic and medical, have failed. It may be
considered to be the prime trouble-shooter
and problem-solver therapy because of the
array of techniques available.

Integrative Therapy is of particular value
for people who feel hopeless and futile. It
is of interest to those in the creative arts,
because it frees more energy for the creative
process. It helps a creative person enhance
performance while freeing him or her from
the compulsive drive components, so that
conscious choice is allowed.

High-powered and successful people who
suffer from stress are also helped by Integrative Therapy. Some of the techniques used
in getting a person in touch with his natural

flow facilitate a releaase of pent-up emotions
in a rather short time. This release capacity
varies according to the strength of the defenses.

Integrative Therapy is suited to people
oriented toward self-care and prevention of
disease, because the types of modalities it
incorporates is ever expanding. Each practitioner gradually expands his knowledge by
adding new modalities to his repertoire. The
integrative therapist's interests and desires
are directed toward growth.

The limitations of Integrative Therapy are
not yet clearly established. Due to its newness, neither a sufficient amount of time nor
a sufficient variety of populations have been
treated to establish clear limitations.

## CASE EXAMPLE

The following is a brief synopsis of a case
in which Integrative Therapy was successfully used. Due to space limitations, only a
minimum amount of material is presented.

Tony, a 32-year-old man, employed by a
large chemical company, had recently been
divorced. His relationship with his wife had
been unsatisfactory as it lacked warmth,
love, and communication. Tony was frozen
sexually and emotionally. He suffered from
inferiority feelings, low self-esteem, guilt,
depression, and a deep sense of worthlessness. He experienced himself as being very
mechanical and had no pleasure in life. He
often complained of feeling lethargic and
heavy. He had had high blood pressure for
the past 10 years. He felt that his life was
drudgery and was fearful of living alone. He
had difficulty meeting women and preferred
masturbation to sex involving another person. He feared being open and anticipated
being hurt and left by women, so he kept his
distance with people.

His mother beat him frequently when he
was a boy. She would become hysterical with
rage and at times would attack and kick him
while he was in bed. His father worked very
long hours, seven days a week in his own

business, and would come home late in the evening. Further, his father was impassive to his mother's beatings and offered no help.

During the course of therapy Tony got in touch with his murderous rage toward his mother and recognized his painful longings to be loved by her. He finally reconnected to his own early loving feelings and regained a sense of openness. He was able to recognize how he displaced his ambivalent feelings of love and hate toward his mother onto his new girl friend. As he reexperienced the rage toward his mother, his depression and high blood pressure reduced. He became more assertive, returned to school and completed a master's degree, and received several promotions on his job. He has become able to feel emotions and has been living with a woman he plans to marry.

The following material is from a session in which Tony started by complaining about the difficulty he was having with overeating and drinking. He discussed some of his fears and his thoughts of anger, and that perhaps he was angry at his mother. However, his current feelings were those of depression, weakness, and lethargy. At the outset of the session, I introduced some techniques that changed his depressed, weak feeling very quickly, and a great deal of material emerged.

At first I suggested that he do a polarity wood-chopper exercise, which consists of standing with one's feet spread apart a little more than shoulder distance, clasping hands together with the arms stretched out over the head, bending backward, then leaning forward, bending the back and swinging the arms, as if chopping, between the legs.

After he did this about 10 times, he began crying. As he began crying, I suggested that he lie on the mattress. He had difficulty really getting a release, so I used the bioenergetic technique of pressing into the musculature around the cheekbones. As I did this, he began to feel more of a release in his body and his feet began twitching. Then his toes began twitching and the energy seemed to be moving down toward his toes. At this point, I

continued with another technique from polarity therapy, which involves stretching the toes and hearing the cracking noise in the joints, similar to cracking the knuckles. This seemed to give him a complete release, and then he began sobbing. As he sobbed, he began to turn away and hide. He covered his head with his hands and said he felt a blackness, as if he were in the womb, secure and protected. He had suddenly regressed. He took the pillow that was under his head and said, "I can hide under that pillow forever."*

T: When I did that, it was like burrowing into a dark hole, feeling safe, and back in the womb. It's a crazy world. There are killings. I feel threatened by everything in the outside world. I want to drink now. People frighten me. Harm is being done to me. Something is out there waiting to get me. I feel like crying.

At this point Tony became silent. After waiting a few minutes, I suggested that he go on.

T: Something or somebody will kill me. I'll be destroyed, hurt, punished, for doing wrong, or for not doing right.
U: What do you mean by "doing wrong"? What comes to your mind about doing wrong?
T: Sex. I'm impure and evil. Sex is wrong. Sexual thoughts and fantasies are wrong.
U: Where did you get those messages?
T: From my religion, my mother. Sex and masturbation are evil. Sex is dirty. Sex is wrong. It's evil, smelly, disgusting, revolting, smelly, ugly, I don't want to touch it, lick it, smell it, be close to it.
U: What's the *it?*
T: The vagina. It's ugly, smelly, slimy. I want to grab it, twist it, squeeze it and bite it, and put my finger up and rip it. Have a big prick so I can fill it and burst it and rip

*In the following dialogue, *T* refers to Tony, *U*, to Walter J. Urban.

it and be bigger than it. I put my penis inside and the vagina is bigger. I want a big prick so I have inches left over on the outside. I don't enjoy sex because I feel small, less than. It's bigger than me. No matter how big my erection I still can't fill it, gorge it. It's bigger than me.

At this point, I let the flow continue; I was silent but actively listening.

T: I feel hungry now. I'd love to stuff my face now.

U: Why now?

T: I enjoy it. I'd be overpowering the food. I overpower the food. I swallow it all, eat it all, consume and chew everything. I consume a lot. There is something in consuming a lot of food which fills me up and makes me feel big and bloated. I get angry at putting on weight. It has to be a lot. I've got to have Alice's food too. All the food. I've got to finish it, stuff it in, finish it all. I've got to conquer the food, consume it, I've won. I want to chew, like steak, pizza, bread, to get my teeth into it and feel something. Other times I just shovel it in. Drinking is to put something in my mouth and swallow. I have to eat quickly, I have to eat fast. To stuff it in. I have to finish it even though I don't want it. I have to finish it all. Even if it's soggy french fries. I feel it's very difficult to leave food on the plate. I look for the biggest portion and have more than anybody else. I want the biggest slice of pizza. When she finishes, I nibble her bones and pick up the last piece of meat. (He opens his eyes.) I do want to stop eating.

U: What is the meaning of your eating as you see it now?

T: Anger. I love filling myself up. Food from mother. I've got to have a large amount. Five pork chops, not three or four. Frankfurters. (Here we can clearly see his oral destructiveness.) I want to conquer. Love crunches. I love crunching and chewing.

U: Here you feel your power. Jaw clenching is your power. Your biting power.

T: I nibble on Alice; that gives me strength. I order the biggest hamburger after group (the group therapy sessions), the most. I enjoy tearing away food from the bones, when I eat spareribs.

I comment on his wish for destroying, having power, and conquering.

T: I'm handling anger in an infantile way. Lately I could eat all day long. I've got to have more than anybody else.

U: Why?

T: I always want more. A second helping. As a kid, I rushed through the first helping to get the second. I barely tasted the first helping, but I wanted to get more. If food is love to me, I didn't get love, so I finish Alice's food. I'm disappointed when she doesn't leave me food on her plate.

We discussed his recognition of the use of the food to deal with his need for love and for a release of his anger. He said, "When I get the urge to stuff, I'll have to get into my adult." I urged him to be aware of the meaning of the eating, and that it was important for him to be able to develop his capacity to cope from his adult ego state. What was necessary now was for him to make the decision to do it. He agreed by saying, "Yes, this is something I am going to develop now," meaning to increase his capacity to tolerate the urge to stuff himself and not act on it.

In this session, polarity techniques, bioenergetic techniques, free association, regression, ego psychology, and decision-making techniques were used.

## SUMMARY

Integrative Therapy is an open-ended theoretical and clinical approach. It provides a sense of freedom for both client and therapist. It is alive, dynamic, fresh, stimulating, creative, and challenging. Designed for and capable of meeting unique individual needs, it gives new hope and offers a short-term approach to many.

Through the understanding and use of Integrative Therapy, the foundations for holistic healing can be formulated. As the integrative therapist adds new therapeutic modalities to his original studies, he develops a sense of the interrelationships between procedures. Gradually he expands his repertoire until around the basic core a new entity begins to form, with a life and energy systems of its own. The curiosity and challenge that emerges because of the interplay of forces fosters the seeking of more and more information. Each piece of new information that comes from a therapeutic modality or a related field is now no longer seen in isolation, but rather as an element with a direct and meaningful relationship to the dynamic core. A certain inner frame of reference is established that fosters the acquisition of further new information. The core acts as a magnet.

The connection with new information is experienced as a "clicking-in" with the dynamic core, rather than as a piece of information from another modality that one is trying to relate to the original modality. The connection is an energetic one, and the integrative therapist experiences it as a new and necessary piece of the whole core. As each new piece connects, the whole dynamic core grows and increases its capacity to attract more pieces. It is as though the core becomes a larger and larger magnet with the integration of each new piece.

Or each new piece of information is like a new brush stroke on a canvas. The old dynamic balance is affected and loses its full potency, but the change that takes place facilitates a new and even greater potency. Thus the whole core reconstitutes and reorganizes itself, forming a new whole. In this holistic core reorganization, each element is truly integrated rather than being tacked on.

This concept is the true foundation for holistic healing. The umbrella concept—that is, the gathering of various professionals under a single umbrella—used in holistic healing centers is an excellent beginning. However, a more solid and meaningful foundation can be found in the core reorganization that takes place in Integrative Therapy.

Integrative Therapy is in its infancy and is growing steadily. Therapists are recognizing the limitations of their particular training and are opening up to an integrated approach. As this occurs, professional cooperation increases, and ultimately the client benefits and becomes more informed and responsible for his or her own well-being.

## REFERENCES

Adler, A. *What life should mean to you.* New York: Capricorn Books, 1958.

Berne, E. *Transactional analysis in psychotherapy.* New York: Ballantine, 1961.

Ellis, A. Rational-emotive therapy. In R. J. Corsini (Ed.), *Current psychotherapies.* Itasca, Ill: F. E. Peacock, 1979.

Freud, S. *Collected Papers,* vols. 1–5, ed. E. Jones. London: Hogarth Press, 1953.

Janov, A. *The primal scream.* New York: Dell, 1970.

Jung, C. *The practice of psychotherapy.* Princeton, N.J.: Princeton University Press, 1954.

Lowen, A. *Bioenergetics.* New York: Penguin, 1975.

Perls, F., Hefferline, R., and Goodman, P. *Gestalt therapy: Excitement and growth in the human personality.* New York: Delta, 1951.

Reich, W. *Character-analysis,* trans. T. Wolfe. New York: Orgone Institute Press, 1949.

Skinner, B. F. *About behaviorism.* New York: Knopf, 1974.

Thorne, F. E. Eclectic Psychotherapy. In R. J. Corsini (Ed.), *Current psychotherapies.* Itasca, Ill.: F. E. Peacock, 1973.

Urban, W. *Integrative therapy: Foundations for holistic and self healing.* Los Angeles: The Guild of Tutors Press, 1978.

# CHAPTER 31

# *Integrity Groups*

ANTHONY J. VATTANO

*The creators of the therapies described in this book are a group of remarkable people—highly inventive, strongly motivated to change the world, having the capacity to see clearly where others cannot see at all—they are people who have the ability to restructure reality. But possibly none is more of an intellectual rebel than O. Hobart Mowrer, who has attempted a kind of Copernican revolution in the field. His primary view is that neurosis is the result of secret violations of commitments and contracts, what some people call "sin."*

*I know Hobart, as he is generally called, quite well, although I have met him only a few times. A man totally devoid of artifice, he is similar to Albert Ellis and Carl Rogers, two of my favorite humans in our profession. Mowrer, who has made important contributions to learning and personality theory, has attempted to generate a Utopia, and he should be considered, I believe, a religious leader.*

*Anthony Vattano's account of Integrity Groups should be read carefully since it is essentially a complex moral tract. The time has come for us all to realize again that morality has a central importance in human affairs.*

Integrity Groups (IG)* are mutual-aid or self-help groups that assist people in dealing with problems of alienation and identity. They provide a uniquely structured opportunity for individuals to examine and disclose their thoughts, feelings, and actions with a group of concerned others. The focus for exploration and discussion is on the group members' practice of honesty, responsibility, and involvement, since it is hypothesized that these are significant factors in achieving and maintaining one's personal integrity and sense of community with others.

These groups were developed by O. Hobart Mowrer in the 1950s following his re-

conceptualization of the causes and treatment of so-called "neuroses." The hypotheses of Sigmund Freud and Joseph Wolpe that related these disorders respectively to an overstrict conscience or false fears were replaced by an alternative view. The central concept of IG is that people become alienated from themselves and others when they have not been honest, responsible, and involved with the significant people in their lives. Integrity Groups provide a community-based support system for helping individuals examine and modify their behavior in other social contexts. The IG procedures that guide this support system enable people to change their actions, thoughts, and feelings in such a manner as to enhance their sense of identity (Mowrer & Vattano, 1976).

The objectives of IG are accomplished by means of a group social learning approach

---

*In 1969 Mowrer changed the name of his approach from "Integrity Therapy" to "Integrity Groups." This was done to reflect the fact that the groups emphasize mutual-aid or self-help endeavors rather than professionally directed therapeutic activities.

that has the following features: a distinctive group structure; group intake, with modeling procedures demonstrated by experienced members; specific goals that focus on each member's responsibility for personal behavior change; contractual agreement to embrace the core values of honesty, responsibility, and involvement; a commitment to move beyond self-disclosure by translating words into deeds; leadership shared by the participants; and group support and reinforcement for individual behavior change. The combination of self-responsibility and mutual support is expressed in the IG motto: "You alone can do it, but you can't do it alone" (Mowrer, 1971).

## HISTORY

### Precursors

The origins of Integrity Groups are found in the self-help or mutual-aid groups that have been part of human experience since the beginnings of tribal and social life. In these groups the healing power of discussing one's misbehavior with friends and relatives was known throughout the ages, and to people in all parts of the world (McNiell, 1951; Mowrer et al., 1975; Mowrer, 1976). Both the Old and New Testament contain accounts of individuals experiencing troubled emotions after engaging in deviant behavior. Prior to the development of the institutional church, early Christianity was essentially a small-group movement. The members engaged in a close form of fellowship, with mutual openness, the making of amends, and concern for one another. There was an emphasis on public admission of wrongdoing, restitution, and the rehabilitation brought about by these practices. The growth of this movement was in no small way due to the psychological peace of mind and feeling of support that these groups engendered in their members.

More recently, outside of the church, Alcoholics Anonymous (AA) pioneered the use

of openness, personal responsibility, and fellowship to assist people with their drinking problems. AA has demonstrated how structured procedures, a defined value system, and group support can foster individual behavior change. Much of AA's success is due to the belief that one can help him- or herself by assisting others who share the same problem. AA has served as a model for Integrity Groups and for many of the other clinical self-help groups that are being developed.

### Beginnings

To understand how Integrity Groups evolved, it is necessary to consider some important events in Mowrer's personal and professional life. Mowrer's special understanding of the abovementioned historical developments and their implications for present-day mental health came about through his own intimate experiences with psychopathology. He was born on a modestly prosperous farm near Unionville, Missouri, in 1907. His early years in the country and later in town were characterized by a love of nature and a penchant for learning that limited his social interaction and his involvement in household chores. He experienced a good measure of affection and support from his parents, his brother and sister, and the many relatives living nearby. This idyllic childhood was shattered when he was 13 by the unexpected death of his father. That event was closely followed by the loss of his family home, separation from his mother and siblings, and the stress of beginning high school while rooming in a rundown boarding house.

Mowrer's high school career was marred by periodic episodes of anxiety and a variety of depressive symptoms, including feelings of depersonalization. Mental health resources were in short supply at that time and place. The young student was seen by several practitioners, who attempted to treat him by means of diet, bed rest, chiropractic treatments, and a tonsillectomy (Mowrer, 1966a). He also joined the church and attempted to obtain help through prayer.

When neither medicine nor theology cured him of his recurrent anxiety and depression, Mowrer resolved to enter college and study psychology in the hope of finding a solution. This pursuit embarked him on a journey that resulted in his signal contributions to psychology and the development of Integrity Groups. Along the way he was to be hospitalized for depression in 1953 and 1971.

After graduating from the University of Missouri, Mowrer entered Johns Hopkins University in 1929 for graduate work in psychology. He also started psychoanalysis in the continued effort to find relief from his emotional difficulties. Following graduation, his reputation as a researcher on learning and personality enabled him to obtain teaching and research positions at Northwestern University, Princeton, Yale's Institute of Human Relations, and Harvard's Graduate School of Education.

Despite his academic success, Mowrer continued to experience periods of anxiety and depression. His work with three different psychoanalysts did not prove helpful. Eventually, his long-time association with Freudian theory and therapy convinced him that Freud's views of neurosis were in error. This impression was further strengthened when Mowrer attended several of Harry Stack Sullivan's seminars at the Washington School of Psychiatry. There he heard Sullivan describe neurosis as a manifestation of *interpersonal disturbances* and the fear of having one's personal pretenses revealed to oneself and to others.

In 1948 Mowrer was appointed a research professor of psychology at the University of Illinois. From the middle 1940s to the early 1960s, he pursued his systematic work on an alternative to Freud's view of neurosis. In this connection, Mowrer studied the practices of the early church. He also worked with some of the leading religious and moral scholars in the United States and abroad (Mowrer, 1967).

In 1961 the Eli Lilly Foundation established a fellowship program at the University of Illinois under Mowrer's direction. This program supported his collaboration with Protestant, Jewish, and Catholic educators to explore the mental health contributions of psychology and religion. Some of Mowrer's fellow psychologists across the country took a dim view of one of their most prodigious researchers fraternizing with members of the clergy. They also did not appreciate his work, which resulted in such articles as " 'Sin,' the Lesser of Two Evils" (Mowrer, 1960). Several even erroneously believed he had been converted to Catholicism. It is interesting to note that while Mowrer's use of theistic terms, such as "confession" and "sin," stirred up controversy, his later employment of their secular counterparts, "self-disclosure" and "breaking commitments and contracts," became quite acceptable to most mental health professionals.

Mowrer's exploration of the church's potential contributions to the current problems of mental health led to disappointment. He discovered that many of the healing practices of the early church, such as openness and fellowship in small groups, had been abandoned. Furthermore, a large number of the clergy had embraced Freudian psychology. Thus, after exploring psychiatry and religion, Mowrer (1961) concluded that neither discipline was dealing effectively with the problems of emotional disturbance. Nevertheless, he maintained his interest in the nontheistic practices of "religion" in the literal sense of that word, that is, *reconnection*. The practices center on the healing power of self-disclosure to others, individual responsibility for behavior change, and the support found in the small-fellowship group. Mowrer noted that these elements were also presently found in Alcoholics Anonymous, and AA had proven successful with problem drinkers whereas professional approaches had not. Along with others, he began to wonder if AA's procedures could be employed to help other types of troubled people.

While Mowrer was exploring new ways to conceptualize emotional problems and their treatment, students and others sought his help. As he worked with these people,

Mowrer focused on the details of their interpersonal relations. He discovered that many individuals were concerned about instances of dishonesty and failure to remain open in their transactions with others. However, apprehension and guilt made it difficult for them to discuss their deceptive practices. In an effort to help his clients trust him and give up their evasion and denial, Mowrer hit upon the idea of modeling. He would in effect "go first" and relate examples of guilt-producing behavior from his own life. The persons who consulted him responded favorably to this procedure and to his suggestion that they move beyond discussing their deviant behavior with him. They agreed to disclose the same material to the people who had been hurt by their deception and also resolved to make restitution. Some clients were surprised at Mowrer's "homework assignments," since they expected that "treatment" would occur in the office. Occasionally, secretive, guilt-ridden persons would resist Mowrer's best efforts to help them disclose their misdeeds to their significant others. However, he found that such people were willing to have a joint session with another individual in Morwer's caseload. In these sessions, clients freely discussed their guilt-producing behavior. From this beginning, Mowrer moved to the establishment of groups—Integrity Groups—composed of eight to ten persons. He also increased the time for each session to three hours and centered the group's focus on the three cardinal principles of honesty, responsibility, and mutual involvement (Mowrer & Vattano, 1976, pp. 421–424).

## CURRENT STATUS

Integrity Groups began and continue as lay mutual-help organizations (Gartner & Riessman, 1977; Lieberman & Borman, 1979). They are part of the general small-groups movement and are a useful community mental health resource. The first "IG Community" of several groups was established by

Mowrer in the cities of Urbana-Champaign, Illinois, in the middle 1960s. At first Mowrer and his wife, Dr. Willie Mae Mowrer, a former classmate at Johns Hopkins, operated these groups in their house. Later, the current practice evolved of meeting in members' homes on a rotating basis or in the meeting rooms of churches or other community buildings. Mowrer also organized Integrity Groups at the Galesburg State Research Hospital with the assistance of the clergymen who attended the Lilly Foundation program. These clergymen later returned to their home communities across the nation and began a number of Integrity Groups. The largest IG community has been developed by Dr. John Drakeford (1967) at the Southwestern Baptist Theological Seminary in Fort Worth, Texas.

In 1969 the Mowrers started teaching a seminar and practicum in IG for graduate students in psychology, social work, child development, and education at the University of Illinois. This writer and several other faculty members have been associated with them each semester over the past nine years. Since the course began, approximately 400 students have learned how to facilitate Integrity Groups. Following graduation, they have settled in different parts of the country and abroad. Many have taken jobs in community mental health or in academic settings where they continue to group and train others in the IG process (Bixenstine, 1970; Madison, 1972).

A number of publications* are available that describe the theory underlying Integrity Groups and its operations. Some of these publications have been translated into other languages.

Mowrer's views on psychopathology are summarized and IG theory and practice are described in a "manual" entitled *Integrity Groups: The Loss and Recovery of Community* (Mowrer et al., 1975). This text describes the history and operation of Integrity

---

*See Mowrer, 1961, 1964, 1966a,b, 1968, 1972, 1973, 1979; Mowrer & Vattano, 1976; Johnson, Dokecki, & Mowrer, 1972.

Groups in considerable detail. It provides students and others with the information they need to organize and operate these groups.

As with most self-help or mutual-aid groups, there is not a great deal of systematic research available on IG. However, graduate students and psychologists have investigated Mowrer's approach to dysfunctional behavior and have generally corroborated his views (Vogel, 1976; Kaye, 1973; Jessop, 1971; Rolls, 1968; Peterson, 1967). Mowrer (1968) has summarized the research evidence for his work on the nature of psychopathology.

## THEORY

Many individuals have had experience with one or more natural groups where they could talk about their daily problems in living and receive counsel and support. In so doing, they became socialized and personally involved with others. If all went well, they also learned the important characteristics of honesty, responsibility, and trust. Such experiences facilitated the harmonious development of thoughts, feelings, and behavior. The mutual sharing that occurred in these interactions gave people the knowledge and skill needed to deal with life's problems.

These natural groups furnished their members with valuable interpersonal experiences. They also provided them with an important social support system for coping with the joys and sorrows of everyday existence. However, not everyone is fortunate enough to have had such experiences or to have support systems available when they are needed. This has been particularly true since the industrial revolution began to produce drastic changes in the culture and institutions of society. Technological advances in the United States and elsewhere have increased the material standard of living for many people at the expense of the support systems that traditionally helped individuals develop a sense of personal integrity and identity. Many of our basic institutions have been affected by

these developments, especially the family, the community, the neighborhood school, and organized religion (Mowrer, 1972). In addition, the mobility and transient human relationships characteristic of modern-day society provide little opportunity for the development of trust, intimacy, and involvement with significant others (Keyes, 1973; Sarason, 1974). These societal changes have been associated with a media-fed emphasis on the pursuit of happiness and personal fulfillment through material possessions. It becomes increasingly apparent that the present culture of rising expectations is incompatible with our diminishing economic and natural resources. This situation has caused some observers to refer to our era as the "age of anxiety."

Many of us have encountered individuals who are struggling with the consequences of these developments, particularly the discrepancy between desires and reality. In attempting to meet their needs, people often blame others and engage in behavior that violates their personal values and their interpersonal commitments or contracts. Such behavior has a negative effect on a person's thoughts, feelings, and actions. He or she may experience a variety of symptoms, such as anxiety, guilt, and alienation. These symptoms lead to a breakdown in personal integrity and result in the condition Mowrer and others call an identity crisis.

Following Freud, the traditional view of psychopathology is that the crux of neurosis is an emotional problem caused by people's reactions to the unrealistically stringent moral standards imposed by the significant others in their lives (parents, teachers, associates, etc). Some people have been taught the rules and standards of society so well that they are, in effect, "oversocialized." From this perspective, it is the behavior of others that is responsible for their "inappropriate" emotions. These emotions in turn lead to symptoms of neurotic behavior, such as anxiety, guilt, and alienation. The therapeutic task in this model is to alleviate the symptoms by assisting the individual in undoing the effects of the presumed oversocialization. This is accomplished through helping him or her "understand" that it is wrong to feel responsible for emotions. (See Figure 1.)

Mowrer's alternative view is that the essence of psychopathology is primarily behavioral rather than emotional. The major difficulty lies in the individual's violation of the norms of his or her own reference group. This includes breaking commitments and contracts with the significant people in his or her life. The problem is one of being "undersocialized" in one's behavior with others. The practice of deception with oneself and others results in *appropriate* emotional discomfort and symptoms of anxiety, guilt, and alienation. These symptoms produce an erosion in personal integrity and a crisis in identity. Since the disorder, or "osis," is in the individual's interpersonal relationships rather than neurons, the term "sociosis" comes closer to describing this condition than the more common term "neurosis" (see Figure 1).

Mowrer recognizes that our behavior is influenced by the actions of others as well as by the social events in our environment. However, he holds that we are not totally controlled by such forces. We can learn to keep our commitments and contracts by engaging in self-management and can thereby influence people and the environment through our own actions. The most direct way to do this is not through supportive "therapy" or the achievement of insight, but by participating in open and honest transactions with a group of similarly engaged people who will assist us in changing our behavior. The beneficial effects to the individual of such transparent interactions have been documented by Sidney Jourard (1971).

After practicing honest, responsible, and involved behavior with the support of the group, individuals transfer this activity to other people in the natural environment. These people ordinarily respond to such positive actions in a favorable manner, thus reinforcing their continued occurrence. If difficulties in such transfer arise, the group serves as a back-up social support system providing feedback, clarification of problems, and a place to test out alternative responses. Taking affirmative action to change one's behavior alleviates guilt, anxiety, and alienation. This leads to positive changes in thoughts, feelings, and actions. As these are brought into harmony, the crisis in identity diminishes. The individual is then ready to experience a renewed sense of personal integrity in community with others.

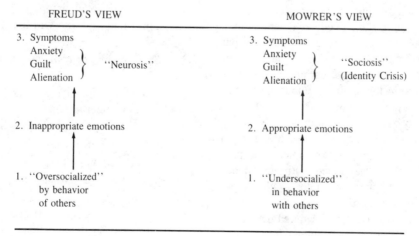

Figure 1. Schematic representation of Freud and Mowrer's views of psychopathology. (Source: Mowrer, 1966a.)

## METHODOLOGY

There are two types of Integrity Groups: those that operate in the community (nonacademic) and those that operate in academic groups. The community groups are primarily composed of people from all segments of the population who participate because of a variety of painful experiences in their interpersonal life. Academic groups consist of students in the different mental health professions who wish to study the operation of Integrity Groups as part of their education. However, over the years it has been noted that the concerns and interests of the two groups overlap to a considerable extent. Along with their "treatment," community group members also receive "training" in IG theory and practice; and all learn how to establish and facilitate the operation of new groups. While students are primarily interested in learning the principles and operations of IG, they also learn to practice honesty, responsibility, and involvement in their practicum group. In so doing, they open up important areas of their life for examination. Most report that their IG experience provides them with "treatment" as well as "training."

The community (nonacademic) and academic groups employ the same practices and procedures in their operations. However, community group members are admitted through an intake procedure. Potential members submit a letter of application and participate in an intake interview. The interview is with a committee of current IG members, who inform the applicant about the IG process and requirements, discuss how they are currently working in their group, and explore the applicant's interest and potential for benefiting from such an experience. The practicum groups associated with the student seminars of necessity employ academic procedures for admitting members.

The most current and detailed description of IG methodology is contained in the "manual" *Integrity Groups: The Loss and Recovery of Community* (1975). The following material is taken from this manual with minor changes.

New IG members are expected to commit themselves to the principles of honesty, responsibility, and involvement. However, it is only as individuals disclose painful information about themselves and give others feedback about how they are "coming across" that these principles become meaningful. In the process, group members engage in self-disclosure, confrontation, and emotional support. They examine their behavior in relation to the three principles by asking: (1) How truthful am I with myself and others? (2) To what extent do I carry out my accepted responsibilities (commitments)? (3) How much love and concern do I express for my significant others?

### Behavioral Guidelines

In exploring these questions, group members follow a series of 10 behavioral guidelines that have evolved over the years. In the interest of space, these guidelines will merely be listed here. The reader is referred elsewhere for specific details (Mowrer et al., 1975; Mowrer & Vattano, 1976). The "won'ts" in the guidelines relate to behavior both in and outside of the Integrity Groups. The first word "I" is understood.

1. Won't interrupt, but will listen to others.
2. Won't blame, or complain about other people.
3. Won't "act-off" negative feelings, but will talk about them.
4. Won't subgroup, but will participate in the group as a whole.
5. Won't "yes . . . but!" I will simply say, "I did it, and I will not do it again."
6. Won't "talk back or argue." When corrected, I will say "thank you."
7. Won't mind-read or expect others to do so.

8.  Won't cheat. I will keep or renegotiate agreements.

9.  Won't double-talk or lie, but I will "say it like it is."

10. Won't tit-for-tat when challenged by another.


## Ground Rules

In addition to the 10 guidelines, the following ground rules govern the operation of Integrity Groups. (Details may be found in the sources listed above for the behavioral guidelines.)

1.  IG meetings last for three or three and one-half hours.

2.  Groups meet once each week, but extra or "extended" time meetings may be called if necessary.

3.  Members will be responsible to inform the group if they are unable to attend a meeting.

4.  If a person is late to a meeting, he or she should give an explanation.

5.  Meetings are chaired on a weekly rotating basis. The chairperson may be flexible, but ordinarily will begin with a "go-round," asking each member "where he or she is" and whether he or she wants time to talk.

6.  Members are free to use any language or sounds they wish (yelling, crying, etc.) during a meeting.

7.  A member may be expelled from a group for any act of physical violence.

8.  If necessary, a member may ask to attend another person's group for the purpose of challenging or giving feedback to that person.

9.  A person who "walks out" during a "run" (i.e., during active interchange about his or her problem or feeling) automatically "resigns" from the group. He or she must apply for readmission.

10. A person may quit, or "split," from a group. However, it is recommended that the intention to leave be discussed with the group.

11. It is desirable to end IG sessions with general "feedback." This consists of "going round," with each person giving an overall reaction to the session and to the behavior of others and themselves.

Despite what may seem like a considerable amount of structure, the guidelines and ground rules permit a large measure of individual choice, freedom, and flexibility in the operation of Integrity Groups. Experience has demonstrated their usefulness in facilitating effective group interaction.


## How Integrity Groups Change Individual Behavior

Integrity Groups contain all of the "curative factors" that were first described by Corsini and Rosenberg (1955) and later elaborated by Yalom (1975) to account for the changes that occur in professionally directed group psychotherapy. These factors are: (1) instillation of hope; (2) universality; (3) imparting of information; (4) altruism; (5) the corrective recapitulation of the primary family group; (6) development of socializing techniques; (7) imitative behavior; (8) interpersonal learning; (9) group cohesiveness; (10) catharsis; and (11) existential factors.

However, the mutual-aid or self-help orientation of IG, with its particular constellation of structure, goals, and leadership, modifies the operation of these factors. They are also affected by the specific behavioral components in IG. These are apparent in the specification of discrete aspects of behavior, the use of commitments, and reinforcement for behavior change.

As group members practice introspection, self-disclosure, and feedback, they become aware of specific aspects of their behavior that are personally and interpersonally dysfunctional. This awareness permits them to decide whether they want to engage in the difficult process of modifying their behavior. When an individual indicates the areas he or she wants to work on, the group helps him or her pinpoint specific experiences in or outside the group where new ways of behaving can be tested. After group members have carefully considered the behavior changes they wish to make, they are expected to give a verbal or written commitment of their specific intention to carry out some action. These pledges are taken very seriously in IG. Once a commitment is made, there is a strong expectation that it will be honored. Commitments that are kept are always reinforced by verbal praise and support. Group members may also provide a physical embrace for a job well done. Broken commitments call for careful examination. If the results indicate irresponsible behavior, confrontation and group reprimand may follow.

IG members have been able to initiate and sustain difficult behavior change through the use of commitments. The external support and reinforcement from the group has been instrumental in developing internal "self-control." As people modify their behavior in the natural environment outside the group, they receive additional reinforcement from their significant others. Alienation is diminished, and a sense of community is enhanced.

## APPLICATIONS

The major concern of Integrity Groups is to help people combat alienation through recovery of personal integrity and identity. The theoretical views related to alienation have already been discussed. However, there are a number of biopsychosocial events that may be associated with this condition. These include intrapersonal, interpersonal, and environmental concerns.

Integrity Groups were specifically designed to help troubled individuals cope with anxiety, guilt, and alienation in their struggle for a sense of identity. These symptoms are experienced by a considerable number of people irrespective of age, race, sex, and social class. Integrity Groups have been employed to help students, adults, and the elderly change their thoughts, feelings, and actions. The level of psychosocial integration in IG members has ranged from mild anxiety to frank psychotic symptoms. While the latter are best helped by means of other strategies, such as medication, IG has served as an important social support system for the acute or chronic mentally ill who are attempting to reestablish themselves in the community. Integrity Groups have been less successful with the severe character problems of the so-called sociopath or antisocial personality. However, they have been of assistance to persons suffering from other kinds of character disorders, depression, and reactions to physical illness. This is particularly true in those cases where self-disclosure, confrontation, feedback, social reinforcement, and support are indicated.

Interpersonal problems that have been helped by IG are: marital and sexual conflict, parent-child relations, difficulties with co-workers, and troublesome social relations. There is a standing rule in IG that any "significant other" with whom one needs to work out interpersonal difficulties may join the group at any time, if this will not unduly affect group size. Ongoing groups have been composed entirely of marital couples. However, in marital conflict it may not always be indicated for a couple to be in the same group continuously or in a group composed solely of other couples. In the student groups, additional concerns have centered on academic responsibilities, emancipation from parents, men-women relations, and conflicts between roommates.

While the major thrust of Integrity Groups is directed toward individual behavior change, these groups also help their members by intervening in the social environment. This is done, for example, by encouraging a member to invite a significant person from his or her environment into the group where both people can work out their transactions in the here and now. At times individual group members will accompany a troubled member outside of the group and help him or her interact more effectively with a person or agency in the natural environment.

In the "History" section it was explained how Integrity Groups developed partly in response to significant changes in our social environment. Many of the societal changes have proven to be a mixed blessing for those who have achieved greater economic security at the expense of emotional insecurity. Through the experiences and struggles of individual group members, we come to learn the aversive nature of our "natural" environment and identify targets for social change. For example, before she could get in touch with her own feelings and true identity, a former airline stewardess in one of our groups had to unlearn all of the artificial behavior (including inappropriate smiling) that her employers had reinforced her for manifesting. Another example of a dysfunctional environment was seen in an Integrity Group composed of medical students. The group was the only place where the future doctors could relate to each other without intense competition, evasion, and defensive behavior. The caring and sharing that developed in this group provided these students a major source of support in dealing with the stress of medical school. These experiences raise questions about environmental arrangements that distort identity and prevent the development of a sense of community with one's peers.

It is difficult for an Integrity Group to act as an advocate for its members with institutions such as airline companies or medical schools. However, Integrity Groups belong to a larger constituency of mutual-aid or self-help groups whose impact on the social environment is being increasingly felt in this country and abroad. Perhaps in the not too distant future Integrity Groups will be as active in bringing about change in the environ-

mental dimension as they are in the other areas discussed here.

## CASE EXAMPLE

Joe and Jean were a married couple, both 24 years old. They had referred themselves to the community Integrity Group and indicated that they needed help in achieving better "communication" in their marriage. They were an attractive couple. Joe was an accountant for a large firm and gave the impression of being an ambitious, hard-working man. Jean was two months pregnant with their first child. She had recently quit her job as a secretary in a local bank.

During the first group session, both people discussed their relationship in somewhat neutral terms. Some members commented that Jean appeared particularly tense. In the second session, Jean came in red-eyed and tearful. During the go-round at the beginning of the session, she said she and Joe needed time to run something important. The chairman suggested that they bring up their concern first. Jean began crying, and Joe looked pale and upset. Jean said that she had recently discovered that Joe was having an affair. She felt completely devastated by his cheating, particularly since she was pregnant. She was angry and depressed and said she was frantically checking up on all of Joe's actions.

Group members asked Joe for his comments. He reluctantly admitted that he had become friendly with one of his co-workers and that he had slept with her on one occasion. He tried to hide the affair from Jean because she had always been jealous of him, even though she had slept with another man when they were engaged. Joe had promised Jean that he would not have further outside sexual affairs, but he wanted to "grow emotionally" by having close friendships with other women. He resented Jean's mounting suspicions and her constant checking up on him. Jean sobbed that her suspicions were well founded. She could not trust him. She felt vulnerable because of her pregnancy. Thus the couple had reached a standoff in their involvement with one another. Communication had broken down in their relationship outside of the group. Joe and Jean received confrontation and support from different members of the group. Even though they felt uncomfortable with one another, it was suggested that they face each other and hold hands while they discussed their painful feelings.

After considerable exploration and expression of emotion, Joe said that he had acted irresponsibly by cheating on his wife. Jean was informed that she was being irresponsible in not being willing to trust him when he had given her his word to be faithful. Before the session ended, group members encouraged the couple to make a joint commitment. Joe would agree not to have sexual relations with anyone else, and Jean would stop mistrusting him and checking up on his whereabouts. Both people felt uncertain of the other's ability to uphold the commitment, but they agreed to go along with the suggestion of the group members. It was understood that both people would feel free to ask for a "special" group session, or phone one of the group if they needed help before the regular weekly meetings.

During the subsequent sessions, Joe and Jean had periods of pain and doubt about each other, but they worked on their commitments with the continued monitoring and support of the group. With further exploration of their feelings and behavior, it became apparent that the prospect of impending parenthood had reawakened old conflicts over Joe's need for independence and Jean's control of his behavior. During their runs over a period of several weeks, they were able to communicate their concerns to each other directly with the interested exploration and support of the group.

By the end of three months, Jean and Joe were still keeping their commitments. They had learned to talk over their feelings both in and outside of the group. As Jean began to trust Joe and communicate with him in a

more meaningful way, he had less need to seek companionship outside of the marriage. One year after the couple left the group, they visited one of the group resource people. They were both enjoying their role as parents of a baby girl. Joe had been promoted, and Jean was looking forward to returning to work when the baby grew older. Both people commented that their IG experience had helped them to be more honest and involved with each other and this had helped to strengthen their marriage.

## SUMMARY

Technological progress has produced a society characterized by a general absence of community. The report of the President's Commission on Mental Health (1978) revealed that as many as 25 percent of the population may suffer from depression, anxiety, and other types of emotional disorder. Many individuals today are alienated, isolated, lonely, and in need of help. There has recently been a reemergence of mutual-aid or self-help groups that assist people in coping with a wide array of human concerns.

Integrity Groups are part of this movement. They are designed to aid those who are troubled by alienation and the lack of identity. Integrity Groups help individuals move into community with others by encouraging the practice of honesty, responsibility, and involvement. These groups are highly democratic, and they do not charge a fee. While providing help, they also furnish their members with training that equips them to organize additional groups in the community. The social learning approach employed in IG has a strong behavioral emphasis. However, these groups are equally concerned with the thoughts and feelings of their members. The distinctive aspects of IG are its unique group structure, shared leadership, and specific goals.

Integrity Groups provide an ideal support system for delivering community mental health services. The cost is minimal since there are no salaries to pay or buildings to rent. Two or more experienced ''resource people'' can start a group with seven or eight other individuals who will in turn ''seed'' additional groups. This ''pyramid training'' model (Jones, Fremouw, & Carples, 1977) provides an effective way of supplementing other kinds of community mental health services over a wide geographic area.

Some individuals believe that professional involvement is incompatible with the aims of self-help groups. Therefore, it is significant that Integrity Groups were developed by Mowrer, who is a professional psychologist. The IG experience has shown that professionals and community people have much to learn from each other. It has also demonstrated that professionals can make important contributions to a self-help group without co-opting or controlling its members. Professionals may operate as organizers or facilitators of new groups, particularly in the beginning stages. They also are in the best position to do needed research on the problems the group is dealing with and the effectiveness of the group's methods and procedures. Professionals can also conceptualize the self-help group's experiences and provide the feedback and theory building necessary for further development (Vattano, 1972).

A final word about Mowrer's search for the causes and treatment of emotional difficulties. Despite two hospitalizations for depression, his personal and professional life has been rewarding and productive. Mowrer has concluded that his depressions were most likely the result of several circumstances. Most important were the deception and alienation of his early years and the combination of constitutional predisposition, nutritional factors, and personal loss. As for the present, Mowrer continues to teach, write, and enjoy life. These activities are associated with his ongoing practice of honesty, responsibility, and involvement with others. Mowrer's search ended with his discovery that ''You alone can do it, but you can't do it alone.''

## REFERENCES

Bixenstine, V. E. Community house and its groups: A new approach to community mental health (mimeographed). Kent, Ohio: Department of Psychology, Kent State University, 1970.

Corsini, R. and Rosenberg, B. Mechanisms of group psychotherapy: Processes and dynamics. *Journal of Abnormal Social Psychology*, 1955, **51**, 405–411.

Drakeford, J. *Integrity therapy*. Nashville, Tenn.: Broadman Press, 1967.

Gartner, A. and Riessman, F. *Self-help in the human services*. San Francisco, Calif.: Jossey-Bass, 1977.

Jessop, N. A semantic differential analysis of integrity groups. Ph.D. dissertation. University of Illinois, 1971.

Johnson, R. C., Dokecki, P. and Mowrer, O. H. (Eds.). *Conscience, contract and social reality*. New York: Holt, Rinehart, Winston, 1972.

Jones, F., Fremouw, W. and Carples, S. Pyramid training of elementary school teachers to use a classroom management ''skill package.'' *Journal of Applied Behavior Analysis*, 1977, **10**, 239–253.

Jourard, S. *The transparent self: Self-disclosure and well-being*. New York: Van Nostrand, 1971.

Kaye, B. An inventory for evaluating Integrity Groups (mimeographed). Champaign-Urbana, Ill.: University of Illinois, 1973.

Keyes, R. *We, the lonely people: Searching for community*. New York: Harper & Row, 1973.

Lieberman, M. and Borman, L. *Self-help groups for coping with crises: Origins, membership, processes, and impact*. San Francisco: Jossey-Bass, 1979.

McNiell, J. *A history of the cure of souls*. New York: Harper & Row, 1951.

Madison, P. Have grouped, will travel. *Psychotherapy: Theory, Research and Practice*, 1972, **9**, 324–327.

Mowrer, O. H. ''Sin,'' the lesser of two evils. *Contemporary Psychology*, 1960, **15**, 301–304.

Mowrer, O. H. *The crisis in psychiatry and religion*. Princeton, N.J.: Van Nostrand, 1961.

Mowrer, O. H. *The new group therapy*. Princeton, N.J.: Van Nostrand Reinhold, 1964.

Mowrer, O. H. Abnormal reactions or actions? An autobiographical answer. In J. A. Vernon (Ed.), *Introduction to psychology: A self-selection textbook*. Dubuque, Iowa: William C. Brown, 1966a.

Mowrer, O. H. Integrity therapy: A self-help approach. *Psychotherapy: Theory, Research and Practice*, 1966b, **3**, 114–119.

Mowrer, O. H. (Ed.). *Morality and mental health—a book of readings*. Chicago: Rand McNally, 1967.

Mowrer, O. H. New evidence concerning the nature of psychopathology. In M. Feldman (Ed.), *Studies in psy-*

*chotherapy and behavior change*. Buffalo, N.Y.: University of Buffalo Press, 1968.

Mowrer, O. H. Peer groups and medication: The best "therapy" for professionals and laymen alike. *Psychotherapy: Theory, Research and Practice*, 1971, **8**, 44–54.

Mowrer, O. H. Integrity groups: Principles and procedures. *The Counseling Psychologist*, 1972, **3**, 7–32.

Mowrer, O. H. Autobiography. In G. Lindzey (Ed.), *The history of psychology in autobiography*, vol. 6. Englewood Cliffs, N.J.: Prentice-Hall, 1973.

Mowrer, O. H. Therapeutic groups and communities in retrospect and prospect. *Proceedings of the First World Conference on Therapeutic Communities* (Norrköping, Sweden). Montreal: Portage Press, 1976.

Mowrer, O. H. Is much psychotherapy still misdirected or misapplied? *Canadian Counsellor*, 1979, **13**, 120–126.

Mowrer, O. H. and Vattano, A. J. Integrity groups: A context for growth in honesty, responsibility, and involvement. *Journal of Applied Behavioral Science*, 1976, **12**, 419–431.

Mowrer, O. H., Vattano, A. J., Baxley, G. and Mowrer, M. *Integrity groups: The loss and recovery of community*. Urbana, Ill.: Integrity Groups, 1975.

Peterson, D. The insecure child: Oversocialized or under-socialized? In O. H. Mowrer (Ed.), *Morality and mental health*. Chicago: Rand McNally, 1967.

*Report to the President from the President's Commission on Mental Health*, vol. 1. Washington, D.C.: U.S. Government Printing Office, 1978.

Rolls, L. J. The interrelation between guilt and anxiety in the Freudian and Mowrerian hypotheses. Ph.D. dissertation. University of Ottawa, 1968.

Sarason, S. *The psychological sense of community: Prospects for a community psychology*. San Francisco: Jossey-Bass, 1974.

Vattano, A. J. Power to the people: Self-help groups. *Social Work*, 1972, **17**, 7–15.

Vogel, P. The development of a social integration measure (SIM) for the study of small-group process. Ph.D. dissertation. University of Illinois, 1976.

Yalom, I. *The Theory and practice of Group Psychotherapy*, rev. ed. New York: Basic Books, 1975.

## CHAPTER 32

# Interpersonal Process Recall

NORMAN I. KAGAN and RICHARD McQUELLON

*In a famous couplet Robert Burns wrote:*

O wad some Power the giftie gie us
To see oursels as ithers see us!

*Generally, in the psychotherapeutic setting electronic recording devices have two major purposes: either reproduction of the therapy situation for training purposes or reproduction for the same purpose mentioned by Robert Burns—to see ourselves as others see us. In some police departments audiovisual recordings are made of drunks so that when sober they can see how they looked, acted, and spoke when they were intoxicated.*

*In the next chapter, Norman Kagan and Richard McQuellon discuss the use of audiovisual devices in ways that are unusual both in terms of purpose (greater insight through introspection) and process (having a neutral inquirer dealing with the repeat process). Another important aspect of this chapter is the story of how the therapy developed, which is the same as for a scientific experiment. This method is contrary to almost all of the other systems in this book, which are generally brilliant insights that developed from creative thinking and were then tested in the field.*

*In my judgment IPR represents a powerful technique with great promise, and it may be the technical solution to what I consider a major problem of psychotherapy—the economic aspect, or how to provide the most therapy for the least money.*

Interpersonal Process Recall (IPR) consists of specific techniques for examining interpersonal behavior. The heart of the method is the recalling of thoughts, feelings, intentions, and images that occur during an interaction through immediate videotape playback of the participants and by open-ended questioning by a third party called an inquirer. An inquirer helps subjects examine reactions that occurred during the videotaped session by means of noninterpretive in-depth probing, from a relatively neutral frame of reference.

## HISTORY

### Precursors

The key elements in the Interpersonal Process Recall method—that is, the use of immediate videotape playback and a trained inquirer—have philosophical as well as technological precursors. The inquirer role and function has its roots in the Socratic method in which questions were posed as a way of stimulating learning. In IPR the learning occurs in the context of the client-counselor relationship relived through videotape playback. The crucial difference between the Socratic method and the inquirer role is that the inquirer does *not* have a predetermined goal or answer in mind. The inquirer's primary function is to pose questions and facilitate client self-exploration about the videotaped session.

Efforts at self-exploration and understanding have been with us in one form or another for centuries, long before Socrates uttered his famous dictum "know thyself." The scientific study of mental processes began in the laboratories of the early psychological experimentalists who attempted to understand the human mind through introspection, which was seen as a skill requiring training and practice. People were trained to report what was going on in their minds. Wilhelm Wundt and other introspectionists observed that many things were forgotten when subjects were asked to recall specific events. The advent of audio and video recording permits psychologists to once again use a form of introspection as a refined experimental procedure. IPR employs videotape and an inquirer as aides to recalling specific reactions during an interaction. These techniques stimulate considerably more introspective analysis than can be achieved by memory alone.

Bernard Covner (1942, 1944) reported the use of self-confrontation techniques in counseling practice and research, and Carl Rogers (1942) used audio recordings in research and teaching, but Herbert Freed (1948) appears to have been the first therapist to report the use of audio recordings as a central component of the therapy process as a means to initiate self-confrontation, which he claimed was particularly helpful with children and in the treatment of character disorders. Today it would be difficult to find a therapist who has not used some form of recording technology either in training or in treatment.

Closed-circuit television was used as early as 1953 in a mental hospital so that ongoing group psychotherapy sessions could be viewed by other patients (Tucker, et al., 1957). It was reported that patients improved

with this brief exposure. Moore, Chernell, and West (1965), who conducted the first controlled experiment with video procedures, reported improvement in psychotic patients. Others have also reported positive effects from using television in therapy (Walz & Johnston, 1963). Recent developments include more systematic, structured applications of the new video recording technology. A number of such applications are described by Berger (1978). The IPR method is one such approach.

A technique similar to IPR was used by Bloom (1954), who used audio tape recordings to stimulate recall of students in classroom interactions. Tapes were replayed to students and stopped at what appeared to the investigator to be significant points. The subject was asked to recall what thoughts were occurring at that time. Students reported their experiences and thoughts in remarkable detail. In studying self-confrontation, Gerhard Nielsen (1964) used films to stimulate recall and found that subjects could engage in self-confrontation, but also could recall many of the feelings they had at specific points even though there was a time delay because the film had to be developed.

## Beginnings

The Interpersonal Process Recall method was developed by Kagan and associates (1963, 1967, 1969) following Kagan's observation in 1961 that viewing a videotape playback with the help of a probing, nonevaluative inquirer who allowed the viewer full responsibility for determining when the tape would be stopped provided a powerful stimulus for self-examination and change. This serendipitous discovery occurred when distinguished psychologists were invited to lecture at Michigan State University. Their lectures were videotaped and subsequently viewed by them, curious about themselves as well as the new video recording technology. The psychologists often stopped the tape to react to their own images. They were politely questioned by Kagan (assistant professors question distinguished psychologists politely); the visitors were intrigued by the process, could recall covert processes in remarkable detail, and noted that they were learning important facts about themselves. This led to a series of research projects using the recall of interpersonal processes via videotape playback as an aid to introspection.

Initially, the focus was on training of counselors by applying the IPR technique to supervisory sessions. Numerous applications of IPR proved it a useful method by which mental health workers, teachers, physicians, and a myriad of other professional and paraprofessional caregivers could improve their ability to interview, communicate with, or help other people. A logical next step was to investigate its potential for accelerating client growth in therapy, since in many graduate school training programs the supervisor-supervisee relationship is analogous to the counselor-counselee relationship (Doehrman, 1976; Mueller & Kell, 1972). It may have been logical to proceed in this direction, but it certainly was not without difficulty.

A research group* began by developing specific outcome measures. They operationalized specific criteria of client growth—the so-called *Characteristics of Client Growth Scales*—and proceeded to conduct a series of studies. From this early research there were indications that the application of a structured approach to the examination of the videotape accelerated movement in therapy (Kagan, Krathwohl, & Miller, 1963; Resnikoff, Kagan, & Schauble, 1970). Initially intensive case studies were conducted and then followed by research with a larger sample of counselors and clients (Kagan, et al., 1967).

These initial observations led to further research comparing traditional counseling with traditional counseling plus IPR techniques. While the results of this research are not conclusive, some studies have found significant evidence that IPR accelerates client improvement under certain conditions.

## CURRENT STATUS

The IPR method is currently being applied in a variety of settings. When applied in a training setting, the counselor/trainee is in some sense viewed as a client. The focus is not on problem resolution of psychopathology but rather on interpersonal behavior and its consequences. The model focuses on counselor as client in the sense that self-exploration of interpersonal behavior and understanding underlying processes are the goal of both training and treatment.

Reliable replication of the IPR model by others has been a primary concern to us. The inquirer role, so basic to the client recall process, is very difficult to communicate in writing. This concern has led us to experiment with "packaging" the entire model to simplify the instructor's task and to make the IPR model reliably replicable without the need for "outside" consultants. The first attempt was a black-and-white film and videotape series containing illustrations, instructions, demonstrations, and didactic presentations aimed primarily at mental health workers. The package was used by more than 40 universities, schools, and social agencies, most of which reported satisfactory experiences. A controlled evaluation at New York University (Boltuch, 1975) indicated that counseling students taught by instructors using the package made significantly greater gains than a control group receiving an equivalent amount of other curriculum offerings. The film series, known as *Influencing Human Interaction*, was revised and expanded so that it now consists of color films or color videotapes (Kagan, 1975a) and contains illustrations from medicine, teaching, and family therapy as well as counseling. The new series also contains scenes designed to stimulate discussions on sexism and racism. An instructor's manual and student handouts were also prepared. The new program, like the

---

*During the first four years David R. Krathwohl and William Farquhar were co-researchers with Kagan.

original one, can be implemented with a minimum of instructor preparation and is currently in use in medical, pharmacy, and law schools, hospitals, secondary schools, agencies, and prison personnel programs in the United States, Canada, England, Australia, Sweden, Denmark, Norway, Germany, Puerto Rico, Israel, and elsewhere. At Michigan State University it is an integral part of several graduate programs, including medical education.

The revised IPR model consists of a number of modules that have specific applicability to the settings mentioned earlier. The model includes seven basic units. The first, titled *Elements of Effective Communication,* presents four verbal response modes—exploratory, listening, affective, and honest labeling responses. The second unit, *Affect Simulation,* makes use of stimulus films or videotapes consisting of brief vignettes depicting people communicating "difficult-to-deal-with" messages directly to the viewer. The vignettes might be thought of as depicting "the worst possible things" that might underlie fear or excess cautiousness in the neophyte. The vignettes are usually perceived as stressful for the viewer. They are designed to stimulate thoughts, feelings, and reactions, and to help the viewer increase sensitivity to his or her own reactions and overcome fears of involvement with clients. The third component in the IPR model, *Interviewer Recall,* introduces the inquirer role and the recall process. First the trainee conducts an interview. The client (a fellow trainee or paid actor who simulates a genuine concern) then leaves the room and the "recall" session follows immediately. The trainee is encouraged to report reactions to the interview while reviewing the videotape. The trainee is given control of the recorder and is asked to stop the playback whenever any thoughts or feelings are recalled. The purpose of this unit is to help trainees learn to study themselves in action by making explicit important information they perceived but did not act on. The fourth unit is entitled *In-Depth Study of the Inquirer Role.* The inquirer's function is to conduct the recall ses-

sion. This is the heart of the IPR process, because the ability and willingness of a person to recall interpersonal process events depends largely on a skilled inquirer. The role is clearly defined and teachable. The fifth unit, like the third, focuses on the recall process again, but in this instance on the *Client's Recall.* This experience is designed to help the counselor learn about client dynamics directly from the client. The client's recall is the basis for learning about client needs and wants. The sixth unit brings the trainee and client together for a *Mutual Recall Session* where either participant stops the video playback to comment about reactions during the previous interview. The inquirer encourages each to talk about unexpressed thoughts, feelings, and intentions in each other's presence. The purpose of mutual recall is to help trainees learn to be able to turn the implicit process of an interaction into explicit content, to talk about the here-and-now in interaction whenever such dialogue might be of use. The final IPR unit provides a *Theory Discussion* and is designed to give the trainee a cognitive framework to make some "sense" of the largely experiential program.

Although the IPR model was originally intended as a training device, its use has not been confined to this area. One of the more exciting areas for development lies in its potential for accelerating client growth in therapy. Research on applications in this area has produced conflicting but promising results (Tomory, 1979).

## THEORY

Constructs from a variety of theorists, both analytic (Horney, 1950; Sullivan, 1953) and behavioral (Lazarus, 1971), can be used to explain why Interpersonal Process Recall is effective in fostering growth and behavior change.

### Basic Assumptions and Interpersonal Manifestations

Two basic dynamics have been observed or

inferred from the application of the IPR method. First, people need each other, not only for physical survival but for an optimum level of interpersonal stimulation. People are potentially the most complete source of joy for each other—more interesting, stimulating, and satisfying than any other single source of satisfaction in the environment. The second basic dynamic is that people learn to fear each other. Just as relationships can provide a potent source of satisfaction, so they can also be a source of intense pain.

The fears we have of each other cluster into one of the following four categories:

1. *You will hurt me:* If we develop an intimate relationship, you will do something that will cause me pain.
2. *I will hurt you:* In like manner I could hurt you.
3. *You will engulf me:* If we relate intimately, you will somehow overwhelm me, negate who I am. My sense of self will be engulfed in who you are.
4. *I will engulf you:* In a similar manner I could engulf you.

These fears develop early in life and are the product of being a "small person in a big person's world." Vague feelings of fear and helplessness are the natural result of lengthy childhood dependence, and such feelings may persist throughout life. IPR therapists think this is the reason why so many of the intense feelings described by clients in recall sessions appear infantile—living vestiges of early fears. Such feelings are usually unlabeled, unstated, and thus inaccessible to the logic of language.

These basically opposed states, the need for people and the fear of people, evince themselves in many interpersonal behaviors. Each attitude is reflected in interpersonal behavior designed to avoid the feared consequences of intimate human interaction. One manifestation can be seen in the approach–avoidance behavior that seems to characterize most human interactions. People appear to both approach and retreat from

direct, simple intimacy with others in a cyclical fashion—intimacy followed by relative isolation, followed by new bids for intimacy. This process appears to establish a specific range of "safe" interpersonal distance unique for each individual. An established psychological distance allows for some level of intimacy along with a feeling of safety from the potential risks that accompany close relationships. The attempt at establishing a safe interpersonal contact range may be seen as an effort to find a balance between the pain of boredom and sensory deprivation when contact is too distant and the experience of anxiety when it is too close. The stronger the fear, the more likely the person will be to avoid intimate relationships. Conversely, if people are not frightened of each other, they will be more able to achieve sustained, intimate contact. This genuine intimate contact with another also then allows for periods of aloneness without panic. Maslow (1968) suggested that more fully functioning people are capable of gratifying periods of being alone possibly because of their ability for deep levels of intimate relating. It is as if knowing that the potential for intimacy is available frees one to experience aloneness without fear.

As people interact they sense each other on many levels, but they label or acknowledge only a very limited range of what they send or perceive. This is a part of all human interactions and serves to reduce the level of genuine intimacy.

The fears people have of each other usually become translated into an interpersonal mythology and expectations—a "slogan" that enables one to avoid frightening interpersonal nightmares, such as "People have always perceived me in certain ways and ultimately react to me accordingly, and they always will." These anticipated reactions by others then foster a self-fulfilling prophecy in which people make their nightmares happen.

Interpersonal closeness or distance is a subjective event not easily observed. Such events have behavioral consequences that can be organized in a two-stage model. The first stage consists of typical response modes in the immediacy of interaction, the way a person acts in daily encounters. The second stage is characterized by a long-term interpersonal posture. The recurrent use of specific interpersonal behavior (Stage 1) leads to the development of a pattern of interaction (Stage 2). Some of these observations closely parallel those of Karen Horney (1950).

The basic interpersonal response modes in Stage 1 are characterized by three behaviors—attacking, withdrawing, and conforming. As one perceives other people impinging, one can attack or strike out. On the most extreme end of the aggression continuum the word attack is appropriate, for the behavior that occurs is a vicious, angry striking out. On the other end of the aggression continuum, one might think of simple assertiveness. This continuum is referred to as ''attack.'' Some people operate almost exclusively on an attacking response mode.

A second basic social response mode is withdrawal. On the most extreme end there is complete ''withdrawal'' and on the other end the ability to back out graciously. Some people rely almost exclusively on a withdrawal modality.

The third basic mode is conformance. At one extreme end is the pure conformist, the chameleon. A less negative extreme position would be the ability to be agreeable.

Some people who attack achieve a life style not of engagement and stimulating direct involvement, but rather of withdrawal. The person may attack not to engage people, but as a way of ultimately withdrawing. The attacking posture may achieve a long-term posture of withdrawal.

Another pattern is attack with conformity as a long-term achieved status. People strike out so that they can maintain an unchallenged loyalty to a set of beliefs or a family. Such basic conformists as the television character Archie Bunker fit that description. An attacking interpersonal style then may be developed to conform or to withdraw from involvement.

Withdrawal can also be a way of achieving a long-term attack or hostile posture. The classic passive-aggressive personality type develops a long-term posture of attack through passive withdrawal.

Withdrawal can also be a way to conform, to maintain a belief system, a loyalty, a set of interpersonal relations unchallenged. Here we find people who will go limp interpersonally, withdrawing to protect themselves from change. It is very hard to have an impact on such people.

Conforming can serve a long-term posture of attack. This can be seen in the pseudo-conformist who strikes out when backs are turned. The hostile social manipulator is of this type.

Finally, a conforming reaction can be a vehicle for ultimate withdrawal and avoidance of human interaction. One can conform to maintain distance and safety, but often boredom and loneliness result.

More fully functioning people appear to be those who have a wide repertoire of behavioral patterns—who can be assertive but are not driven to be, who can back down as well as conform.

## IPR Applied in Psychotherapy

The potential effectiveness of IPR with clients in treatment can be understood from a relationship theory of counseling in which the client-counselor relationship is the critical variable in client growth. This perspective, first described by Carl Rogers (1957) and later by Patterson (1974), views the client as a positive force in the resolution of his conflicts. The client is capable of achieving insight leading to more appropriate behavior. The client has learned an interactional style, a way of coping and behaving, that will be demonstrated in the counseling session. The maladaptive interpersonal behavior that brings the client to treatment will be manifested with the counselor, usually in the intra- and interpersonal behaviors and perceptions previously described. It becomes the task of the counselor to help the client explore this interactional behavior.

A client's response to anxiety in the counseling situation is assumed to trigger the same defenses and interpersonal patterns characteristic of client interactions outside of the counseling session. Kell and Mueller (1966) and Kell and Burow (1970) have described a theory of counseling based on this idea. They suggest that while the client wants to change, there are no alternatives to the maladaptive coping behaviors that have become so familiar. These behaviors are mobilized in the counseling situation because the prospect of change is threatening and anxiety provoking. Since anxiety can hinder the client's efforts at change, it is crucial that the counselor reduce nonproductive anxiety and create a therapeutic atmosphere.

If one considers the counseling session as an emotional experience characterized by frequent high levels of anxiety, then the value of IPR for accelerating the counseling process becomes evident. Anxiety interferes with the perceptions of client and counselor and often acts as a hindrance to therapy. The "acknowledged" content usually does not include the most pressing client issues because of high levels of anxiety. The IPR method serves to create an environment characterized by reduced anxiety levels. This is achieved by viewing interactional behavior immediately after it has occurred so that the accompanying thoughts and feelings can be recalled in depth. Videotaped interaction is less threatening than actual interchange since both participants know they survived the encounter, a fact not known in an ongoing interaction. A second source of safety is the nonjudgmental inquirer.

The basic IPR process has two central therapeutic features: (1) videotape technology, which provides an immediate re-creation of the previously experienced interaction, and (2) the use of stimulated recall methodology to facilitate the client's ability to introspect, a necessary skill if therapy is to proceed successfully. The recall process and inquirer role in the IPR model provide structure and a rich theoretical foundation for accelerating client growth in therapy.

***The Recall Process.*** The IPR format consists of the client and inquirer viewing the videotape replay of a portion of the counseling session without the counselor present. The client stops the playback at any point where thoughts or feelings were stimulated but not discussed fully. In such sessions clients usually begin to recognize ways in which their relationship with the counselor parallels their relationships with significant others. In "mutual recall" both client and counselor tell each other and the inquirer of their covert processes in the recorded session, and behavioral rehearsal of immediate intimate exchange can also occur with client and counselor given practice at talking about their relationship. Both then become more like participant-observers of their own interaction—stepping back from the immediacy of their interaction and replaying the "videotape in their head." In this manner they learn to discuss what happened in the session. This also happens in real life with a significant other when a recall session is held between the client and a friend, spouse, or some significant other with the counselor functioning as inquirer. In each format the inquirer is to pose questions in a gentle, probing fashion.

Therapy is an emergent process, developing as the client becomes increasingly aware of interpersonal processes through recall. Engaging in the recall process enables clients to label (in spoken language) their perceptions and expectations. This often invokes the logic of language onto emotional experiences that ordinarily are unreported and unrecognized. This amounts to finding words for what had been prelanguage feelings, learning about oneself in language. The labeling process may literally be informing one part of the brain about the content of another (Sagan, 1977).

Tomory (1979) has suggested further reasons to justify client recall in psychotherapy. First, the videotape recall provides the client with a "neutral" source of feedback. The client is not being told *about* his or her behavior. The client views it in relation to the counselor. The videotape is objective and valid in providing feedback. Second, with the help of the inquirer, the client is free to explore in depth the covert processes underlying the interactional behavior. Since the feedback is neutral, clients are free to accept or reject it without challenge. Given accurate feedback and nonthreatening environment, clients are less likely to deny or rationalize and can take responsibility for their behavior. The playback allows clients to examine the client-counselor relationship from a relatively safe vantage point (the immediate outcome of the interactional sequence is known since it has already occurred). Lowered levels of client anxiety provide favorable conditions for emotional, cognitive, and behavioral relearning. Third, clients may learn that they invest a lot of energy in the client-counselor relationship even when discussing third-party concerns that lie outside the dyadic counselor relationship. The client can literally "see" how he or she relates to his or her presenting problem. Fourth, in client-recall, the client can explore interpersonal patterns without relating directly with the therapist.

*The Inquiry.* The effectiveness of the recall process largely depends on the inquirer. The inquirer's function is to facilitate stimulated recall and self-analysis. The inquirer helps clients direct their energy into self-analysis as the videotape is reviewed. (It is not unusual for clients and counselors to incorporate inquirer questions into their repertoire and then to function as their own inquirers.) Clients are discouraged from talking with the inquirer at length about external relationships or material not discussed on the videotape. The focus during the inquiry is on examining the recorded interactional behavior and avoiding a therapeutic relationship with the inquirer. The task is to "debrief" the videotape, with the client serving as authority on the meaning of the interaction and the inquirer as expert in asking questions. It is assumed that as clients reflect on their behavior and the concomitant, covert thought processes, they will begin to discover the antecedents and consequences of specific interpersonal behaviors.

A social-psychological perspective provides an alternate explanation for the effectiveness of the inquiry. A powerful influence in facilitating the therapy is the manner in which the inquirer handles the recall session and, by implication, defines a theory of human interaction for the client. From this perspective, the defining of the situation, as described by McHugh (1968), is the key to the power of the inquirer role. In any social encounter the people involved have the task of organizing meaning in social interaction, thus producing a highly unique definition of the situation. This definition stems from the question Goffman (1974) suggests all people pose when engaged in face-to-face encounter: "What is it that's going on here?" The inquirer defines the therapy session as a situation in which the client will discover and express heretofore hidden aspects of interpersonal behavior. The inquirer helps the client find an answer to "What is it that's going on here?" This is done in several ways. First, a series of specific instructions is presented to the client, suggesting that there is a universal human phenomena in which many possible interactional responses are censored for a variety of adaptive purposes, but this censoring may be maladaptive. An expectation is thus set for discovering "censored" items. The client is expected to see and explore things glossed over in the session. Second, the posing of probing questions by a nonjudgmental inquirer helps the client self-explore in a nonthreatening relationship. The inquirer is neutral but curious about the meaning of the client's behavior. The questions the inquirer asks stimulate the client to ask "What were my implicit thoughts, feelings, beliefs, attitudes that occurred with my counselor?" The inquirer defines the recall session to create the expectation of exciting self-discovery.

These discoveries, along with curiosity about self, are integrated into the therapeutic relationship where the counselor facilitates client change by addressing interactional themes characteristic of the client. The parallel process of client-counselor and client-other interaction can then be elucidated.

## METHODOLOGY

The first step in employing Interpersonal Process Recall is to assure adequate videotape facilities. The equipment is located in one room where both the counseling and recall session are held.

Before the taping process begins, the rationale for IPR and the use of video equipment is explained. The client is free to voice any reservation about the procedure and, as in any form of counseling, choose not to engage in the procedure. If the process is accepted, the client and counselor tape a session, which can be as brief as 10 minutes or the traditional 50 minutes. If the IPR format is to be "client recall," the counselor leaves the room after the taping and the inquirer takes his or her place.

The inquirer then instructs the client on the purpose of the recall process. The following assumptions taken from Kagan and associates (1967) are made explicit to the client before recall is begun:

1. We know that the mind works faster than the voice.
2. As we talk with people, we think of things which are quite different from the things we are talking about. Everyone does this and there is no reason to feel embarrassed or to hesitate to "own up to it" when it does occur.
3. We know that as we talk to people, there are times when we like what they say and there are times when we are annoyed with what they say. There are times when we think they really understand us and there are times when we feel they have missed the point of what we are saying or really don't understand what we were feeling, of how strongly we were feeling something.
4. There are also times when we are concerned about what the other person is thinking about us. Sometimes we want the other person to think about us in ways which he may not be.

5. If we ask you at this moment just when you felt the counselor understood or didn't understand your feelings, or when you felt you were making a certain kind of impression on him, or when you were trying to say something and it came out quite differently from the way you wanted it to, it would probably be very difficult for you to remember. With this T.V. playback immediately after your interview, you will find it possible to recall these thoughts and feelings in detail. Stop and start the playback by means of the switch as often as you remember your thoughts and feelings. The recorder is on remote control so that you are not troubling anyone no matter how often you stop and start the playback. As you remember thoughts and feelings, stop the tape and tell me what they were. (p. 13)

Clients differ widely in their ability to engage in this process, requiring more or less encouragement by the inquirer. The inquirer avoids counseling or interpreting. Recall sessions last approximately 40 minutes and, depending on the client, only 10 to 15 minutes of the interview may be covered. Exploratory, brief, open-ended questions about thoughts and feelings are posed.

A number of general areas often prove fruitful for inquiry. When the client stops the tape to make observations about a theme, the experienced inquirer pursues that theme and then introduces other areas. For example, questions that stimulate affective themes include: Were you aware of any feelings? What did you decide to do with that feeling? How did you decide not to express that feeling? To encourage cognitive examination an inquirer might ask: What were you thinking at that time? What was going through your mind when you said that? What thoughts were you having about the other person? Did you want to say anything else at that time? Further exploration can be encouraged in the area of physiological and other nonverbal behaviors—body sensations, images, and expectations—by asking questions such as: Do you recall how your body was feeling at that time? Were you having any fantasies or images at that moment? What did you want your counselor to tell you? Were you expecting anything from your counselor at that point? Also, questions might lead into other associations or help to check out unstated agendas: Did your counselor remind you of anyone else in your life? (If the answer is yes, then ask: What effect did that have on you?) What reaction did you have toward your counselor's statements? What would you have liked to have said at that point? Was there anything you felt like doing at that time?

One area to explore is the client's perception of the counselor's view of him or her, which strongly influences the interaction during the session. Inquirer probes include: What do you think your counselor was feeling about you? What message do you think he was trying to communicate to you? How were you being seen at that point? How did you want to be seen? How did you not want to be seen? How do you think he felt about discussing this problem?

Clients vary in their ability and/or willingness to explore particular areas. For example, if the counselor is observing the recall process, the client may be somewhat less willing to reveal perception of the counselor.

Inquirer leads (Kagan & Burke, 1976) can be used in a variety of areas in order to encourage active client involvement during the inquiry. This involvement centers around (1) the origin and development of the client's thoughts and feelings as experienced during the interview; (2) the way the client sees him- or herself in terms of likes, dislikes, fears, fantasies, and so forth, about self; (3) the way the client would like to be seen by the counselor; and (4) the way the client believes the counselor actually does perceive him or her. We have found that inquirer questions can facilitate self-exploration and increased awareness and involvement if they encourage a self-questioning rather than a self-explanatory attitude. We do not want clients to attempt to explain *why* they behave the way they do; rather we want the client to fully explore the *what* and *how* of his or her interpersonal behavior. Consequently, "why" questions are avoided in the recall session.

This is not to suggest that client motivation and historical antecedents are not important, but rather that the recall session is designed to focus more on the "what" of behavior. The therapeutic relationship is the place for the client to further explore the reasons of idiosyncratic behavior.

## APPLICATIONS

Interpersonal Process Recall has been researched extensively as a training device and to a lesser extent as a method for psychotherapy. In both applications the emphasis is on self-study through observation and discussion of interpersonal behavior and exploration of concomitant covert processes. It is postulated that knowledge about one's own interpersonal behavior is invaluable in learning to be an effective therapist. Relationship conflicts emerge between client and counselor that parallel (Doehrman, 1976) those that develop between counselor and supervisor (Mueller & Kell, 1972). The relationship dynamics in the client-counselor relationship reflect, to some degree, the presenting problem for which the client is seeking therapy. Thus a counselor in training is viewed much as a client is viewed, although there is an obvious difference—the counselor uses self-study to become an effective therapist, whereas the client usually seeks resolution of personal problems. The reasons that counselors and clients use IPR are different but the processes are similar. In many ways the dynamics of supervision are analogous to those seen in psychotherapy (Chiles & McQuellon, 1978). The research based on IPR in counselor training and other areas is available elsewhere (Kagan, 1975b).

IPR as a method for accelerating client progress in counseling and psychotherapy has been reported in several controlled experimental research studies (Hartson & Kunce, 1973; Hurley, 1967; Schauble, 1970; Tomory, 1979; VanNoord, 1973) and in case studies (Kagan, Krathwohl, & Miller, 1963; Kagan, et al., 1967; Resnikoff, Kagan, & Schauble, 1970).

Hurley (1967) conducted one of the first studies using IPR recall in small counseling groups. A single recall session was introduced during the fifth session of a 10-session group. The IPR intervention did not result in a statistically significant advantage on measures of self-disclosure when compared with two control groups, but it did alter the style of group interactions in a positive direction as reported by group leaders and supported by analysis of pre- and postsession tape recordings. It was concluded that more IPR treatments might have increased self-disclosing behavior, the main criterion measure used.

Affect simulation through filmed stimulus vignettes was incorporated into the IPR model to facilitate the client's discussion of reactions to highly emotional interpersonal situations, to discover individual client stereotypes in interpersonal behavior, and to uncover conflict areas (Danish & Kagan, 1969; Kagan & Schauble, 1969). The vignettes depicted mild to intense degrees of affect in the areas of hostility, fear of hostility, affection, and fear of affection. These brief filmed vignettes were used in a variety of formats. In one format vignettes were shown to clients while they were being videotaped. This was followed by a recall session. The vignettes were also used without videotape and recall. It was found that the vignettes were particularly helpful in the initial stages of counseling. This finding influenced later researchers to apply IPR methodology with clients in a developmental manner from least to most threatening experiences.

Schauble (1970) compared traditional counseling with IPR techniques using two advanced doctoral candidate intern therapists and 12 female counseling center clients. Both treatments consisted of six sessions. The IPR treatment group followed a structured sequence proceeding from least to most threatening experiences. This approach stemmed from an earlier pilot study suggesting a series of developmental tasks facing the client during the counseling or therapy process. The theory underlying this developmental approach was: (1) Clients first needed to learn

how to talk about feelings and explore them in a safe environment (videotape recall or stimulus films). Under these conditions, that is, without debilitating anxiety, emotionally stressful interpersonal situations could be examined for maximum learning. (2) Clients needed to begin to identify the behavior patterns and feelings experienced during the counseling session but had to do this in the relative safety of an objective third person—the inquirer (client recall). (3) Finally, clients needed to learn to be able to discuss their behavior and feelings as they occur, that is, to deal with the "here-and-now" of the counseling relationship (mutual recall). Significant between-group differences favoring the IPR group emerged on most of the five dependent variables employed as pre- and postmeasures. Client feelings about coming to the session and client feelings about progress made in the session as measured by the *Therapy Session Report* (Orlinsky & Howard, 1966) favored the IPR treatment group.

VanNoord (1973) conducted a similar investigation using a highly structured sequencing of the IPR model, employing 12 therapists, each seeing only one client (half were in the IPR treatment group and half in the control group) and adopting a posttest only design. He made several other modifications, most notably adopting different criterion measures. The sequencing of the IPR model proceeded in the following manner: (1) session 1—*traditional;* (2) session 2—*stimulus films;* (3) session 3—*video recall of stimulus films;* (4) sessions 4 and 5—*client recall with counselor observation through a one-way mirror;* (5) session 6—*mutual recall.* No significant differences were observed between groups on the objective measures, although subjective comments by clients suggested that IPR techniques were beneficial in self-exploration and in exploration of the client-counselor relationship.

Tomory (1979) attempted to build on the Schauble and VanNoord researches in evaluating the potential of IPR in accelerating client growth. He noted that both Schauble and VanNoord reported a frequent therapist criticism of the rigid structure in the IPR treatment groups. The therapists did not view this as helpful because it did not allow for individual client differences in terms of growth rate and needs. Tomory introduced flexibility into the research design by allowing therapists to apply five IPR techniques (stimulus films, video recall of stimulus films, client recall, mutual recall, and "significant other" recall) whenever they deemed it appropriate. He increased the number of subjects to 50 and allowed for variability in the number of treatment sessions. Unfortunately, the therapists received only five hours of training in the IPR methods. The therapists in the IPR treatment group were required then to use the techniques in (1) 50 percent of the first 10 sessions and (2) at least every other session or in two consecutive sessions followed by two traditional sessions. Like VanNoord, Tomory found no significant differences between the traditional counseling group and the traditional counseling in addition to IPR treatment on the objective measures used, but clients' statements on the use of the videotape feedback were overwhelmingly positive. Therapists without exception stated that IPR videotape and stimulus film intervention techniques were helpful with their clients.

In a study assessing the effectiveness of IPR in accelerating group psychotherapy, Hartson and Kunce (1973) used a combination of stimulus films, dyadic recall, and group recall techniques. In six sessions IPR treatment clients demonstrated significantly higher changes in self-disclosure and readiness for group behavior and participated in more therapeutic interchanges than clients in traditional T-groups. The T-group clients did, however, show significantly higher satisfaction scores. A differential treatment effect was reported with the two sample groups observed: IPR self-confrontation methods were helpful to low self-esteem, socially inactive (counseling center) subjects on whom the direct confrontation methods of the T-group had an adverse effect. No treatment differences were observed between high self-esteem, socially active (YMCA) subjects.

The authors suggested that further research should focus on the appropriateness of specific IPR techniques according to client needs and personalities.

Additional applications of the IPR model in controlled experimental studies have investigated the effects of varying the frequency of videotape feedback during short-term counseling (Grana, 1977) and have examined the ability of clients to accurately recall feelings of comfort and discomfort while watching a videotape of a previous session (Katz & Resnikoff, 1977). Kingdon (1975) explored the cost/benefit of IPR application in terms of the inhibitory effect of using videotape on client self-exploration (cost) and client satisfaction, increased counselor empathy ratings, and increased supervisor ratings. Rather than inhibiting self-exploration, she found that IPR served to positively influence depth of client exploration.

Intensive case studies have been reported with a 30-year-old female who suffered from periods of depression and a rigid, nonsexual relationship with her husband (Kagan, Krathwohl, & Miller, 1963); a 21-year-old male who had problems with dependency, social inadequacy, and sexual uncertainty (Woody et al., 1965); and with more severely disturbed clients (Resnikoff, Kagan, & Schauble, 1970). In these studies and others, IPR methods have been used in a variety of ways, with variations in the structure and technique applied.

Other applications could be developed. The entire IPR training course could be given to groups of clients as an adjunct to therapy not only to facilitate their work in therapy but also to improve their communication skills. The IPR model could be used directly to influence clients' relationships with significant others by videotaping couples or families and having the therapist then serve as the inquirer (Kagan, 1975a). In the IPR counselor training program the counselor and inquirer review a tape without the client during the first recall experience. The focus is on therapist recall. The therapist is encouraged to label impressions and strategies as well as aspirations, frustrations, satisfactions, and anxieties evoked by the interaction with the client. In accelerated therapy applications, this possibly critical aspect is usually omitted by therapists, who "prescribe" only client recalls. Perhaps therapist recall alone should be included as part of the use of the process in psychotherapy.

## CASE EXAMPLE*

### Background

The client (referred to as George) was a very bright and well read 18-year-old college-bound high school senior. His immediate family consisted of his mother and two younger sisters, one an illegitimate child. When George was only two years old his father had died of natural causes. His mother had remarried and divorced twice; she was hospitalized with emotional problems following her second and third marriages and used alcohol excessively. She had wanted a girl and clearly communicated a rejecting attitude toward George. George lived with a number of relatives who often beat him and considered him a burden until the age of 14, when he entered an agency. When he began therapy he was still residing in the agency setting.

### Problem

George was diagnosed as suffering from mild to acute psychotic reactions. He had trouble with authority figures, a fear of people generally, and his behavior with women was highly sexualized and acting-out. At the age of 14 he had begun drinking heavily and eventually became an alcoholic. Shortly before he entered therapy, he made his second suicide attempt.

*Originally reported by Resnikoff, A., Kagan, N. and Schauble, P. G. Acceleration of psychotherapy through stimulated videotape recall. *American Journal of Psychotherapy*, 1970, **24 (1)**, 102–111.

### Treatment

The client was seen twice a week for hour-long interviews by a clinical psychologist who planned an intensive 20-week insight-oriented treatment regimen. The initial two sessions were filled with many painful childhood and adolescent memories in addition to repeated questions regarding his sanity, capacity to love, and his worthiness to receive love. The third interview was focused on the first of a series of dreams reported by George. These proved to be helpful in sorting out his mixed feelings toward his mother and discovering that his angry thoughts and feelings were not, of themselves, destructive. The themes uncovered in the four interviews were examined more fully in sessions 5 through 8. George began to see the origin of his generalized fear of people in his earlier mistreatment at the hands of his relatives. Sessions 9 through 11 consisted of client attempts to connect his intense feelings with his recognition of anger and, at length, love. He became increasingly aware of his confusion concerning sexual intercourse and also of ambivalent feelings toward his therapist. When George's affect became noticeably depressed in the eleventh interview, it was decided to employ an IPR intervention in order to more clearly understand the dynamics underlying the depression.

*Twelfth Interview—IPR Session.* To keep the entire session one hour in length the therapist conducted a 20-minute interview followed by a 40-minute recall session. George was not aware of the method when the session began, but was informed of the procedure in general and introduced to the inquirer following the 20-minute interview. During the recall only nine minutes of video material stimulated all of the 40 minutes of client recall.

The client seemed mildly depressed during the interview session with the therapist. He told of a visit by his mother, who had given him a cigarette case and made reference to his sister. He also noted that his plans for summer vacation were unclear.

During the recall session the client communicated freely with the inquirer. There was a marked difference in George's participation during the recall when compared with the 20-minute therapeutic session. He spoke with added clarity and rapidity of speech and he stopped the videotape playback often—a characteristic of productive recall sessions. George was both surprised and pleased at what he was learning about himself. It became clear during the recall that his imagery had been very rich but not entirely revealed to the therapist and that he had worked through much of the material covered in earlier interviews without reporting such gains to his therapist. Also, George's commitment to his therapist and their relationship was much stronger than he had been willing and/or able to admit and stronger than the therapist had realized.

One of the client's intense reactions to the recall session was anger at the point in the tape where he spoke about his grandfather's not caring for his father following a brain tumor operation. This theme had been addressed during the interview with the therapist, but little affect had been demonstrated. The intensity of anger associated with this recollection was much more clearly demonstrated during the recall session. Several other associations were prompted including thoughts and feelings about his mother and sisters.

An apparently important discovery was made when George described that he had avoided revealing his "real" thoughts to his therapist. The recall session seemed to help George expand on his feelings toward his family and begin to understand the nature of his irrational feelings toward people and his ambivalent feeling toward women. Subsequent therapy sessions were rich in associations and more spontaneous. This change resulted from the therapist's new approach to inducing associations.

The recall data (the therapist had reviewed the recall session with the inquirer) helped the therapist to better understand George's ideational systems and to modify his approach to include, for instance, asking that George focus on the images he "saw" when discussing problem areas. This single statement stimulated a flow of material relevant to his dynamics and concerns. George's avoidance behavior, that is, discussion of authors and their works, began to disappear in favor of the issues that presented difficulties for him.

This single exposure to an IPR session served to help George move through a therapeutic impasse by opening up areas that had not been addressed in the therapy session. George demonstrated different behavior in therapy following the IPR treatment, perhaps as a result of that session. He began to own up to his own discomfort, make a commitment to change, differentiate his thoughts, feelings, and visual imagery, and finally behave differently.

## SUMMARY

Interpersonal Process Recall is a method of influencing and improving human interaction using stimulated recall and learning-by-discovery. When applied in training or in counseling/psychotherapy, audio/videotape is used for stimulated recall so that the original experience of the client-counselor interaction may be viewed and relived. The core of the IPR process lies in the immediate replay of the counseling session and the skills of an "inquirer" in helping participants relate their recalled thoughts and feelings. Filmed vignettes are also used to help clients identify their worst "interpersonal nightmares."

The method relies on both analytic and behavioral constructs and does not evolve from any specific personality theory. The basic assumptions of IPR center around the conflict of (1) a universal need for interpersonal stimulation and (2) the learned fear of intimate relationships. These opposing needs motivate interpersonal behaviors that can be categorized into a typology of attacking, withdrawing, and conforming behavior. These interpersonal behaviors may function to create certain long-term consequences or interpersonal "postures." Six basic typologies are postulated including: (1) *attack to withdraw;* (2) *attack to conform;* (3) *withdraw to attack;* (4) *withdraw to conform;* (5) *conform to attack;* and finally (6) *conform to withdraw.*

Behavior in the counseling situation is assumed to reflect the interpersonal patterns characteristic of client interactions in other settings. Thus the study of client-counselor interaction becomes a major focus of counseling to help the client learn about interpersonal behavior elsewhere.

The inquirer role consists of helping the client engage in the recall process and become an active participant in self-analysis and learning. Through the recall process clients come to know their interactional processes with the counselor and to try out new behaviors within the client-counselor relationship. The inquirer role functions to increase client awareness of such vaguely perceived ideas about interpersonal behavior by encouraging the client to verbalize his or her perceptions. Through the recall process clients come to know their fears of others and their "less adaptive" behaviors. If observation and analysis of one's own interpersonal behavior, mental processes, and emotional states is a necessary condition for behavior change, then the value of IPR in counseling and psychotherapy becomes evident.

# REFERENCES

Berger, M. A. *Videotape techniques in psychiatric training and treatment,* rev. ed. New York: Brunner/Mazel, 1978.

Bloom, B. S. The thought processes of students in discussion. In S. French (Ed.), *Accent on teaching.* New York: Harper, 1954.

Boltuch, B. S. The effects of a pre-practicum skill training program, *Influencing Human Interaction,* on developing counselor effectiveness in a master's level practicum. Ph.D. dissertation. New York University, 1975.

Chiles, R. and McQuellon, R. A growth model of supervision: Training the beginning psychotherapist in the community mental health center. *North Carolina Journal of Mental Health,* 1978, **8 (9)**, 35–40.

Covner, B. J. The use of phonographic recordings in counseling practice and research. *Journal of Counseling Psychology,* 1942, **6**, 105–113.

Covner, B. J. Written reports of interviews. *Journal of Applied Psychology,* 1944, **28**, 89–98.

Danish, S. J. and Kagan, N. Emotional simulation in counseling and psychotherapy. *Psychotherapy: Theory, Research and Practice,* 1969, **6 (4)**, 261–263.

Doehrman, M. Parallel processes in supervisor and psychotherapy. *Bulletin of the Menninger Clinic,* 1976, **40 (1)**, 3–104.

Freed, H. On various uses of the recorded interview in psychotherapy. *Psychiatric Quarterly,* 1948, **22**, 685–695.

Goffman, E. *Frame analysis: An essay on the organization of experience.* Cambridge, Mass.: Harvard University Press, 1974.

Grana, R. K. Videotape feedback: Frequency of usage and its value as a counseling technique. Ph.D. dissertation. University of Akron, 1977.

Hartson, D. J. and Kunce, J. T. Videotape replay and recall in group work. *Journal of Counseling Psychology,* 1973, **20**, 437–441.

Horney, K. *Neurosis and human growth.* New York: Norton, 1950.

Hurley, S. Self disclosure in counseling groups as influenced by structural confrontation and interpresonal process recall. Ph.D. dissertation. Michigan State University, 1967.

Kagan, N. Influencing human interaction (filmed training series). Mason, Mich.: Mason Media, 1975a.

Kagan, N. Influencing human interaction: Eleven years with IPR. *The Canadian Counselor,* 1975b, **9**, 74–97.

Kagan, N. and Burke, J. B. *Influencing human interaction using interpersonal process recall (IPR): A student manual.* East Lansing.: Mich.: Michigan State University Press, 1976.

Kagan, N., Krathwohl, D. and Miller, R. Stimulated recall in therapy using videotape. *Journal of Counseling Psychology,* 1963, **10**, 237–243.

Kagan, N., and Schauble, P. G. Affect simulation in interpersonal process recall. *Journal of Counseling Psychology,* 1969, **16**, 309–313.

Kagan, N., et al. *Studies in human interaction: Interpersonal process recall stimulated by videotape* (Research Report 20). East Lansing, Mich.: Educational Publication Services, 1967.

Katz, D. and Resnikoff, A. Televised self-confrontation and recalled affect: A new look at videotape recall. *Journal of Counseling Psychology,* 1977, **24**, 150–152.

Kell, B. L. and Burow, J. M. *Developmental counseling and therapy.* Boston: Houghton, 1970.

Kell, B. L. and Mueller, W. J. *Impact and change: A*

*study of counseling relationships.* New York: Appleton, 1966.

Kingdon, M. A. A cost/benefit analysis of the interpersonal process recall technique. *Journal of Counseling Psychology,* 1975, **22,** 353–357.

Lazarus, A. A. *Behavior therapy and beyond.* New York: McGraw-Hill, 1971.

McHugh, P. *Defining the situation: The organization of meaning in social interaction.* Indianapolis: Bobbs-Merrill, 1968.

Maslow, A. H. *Toward a psychology of being,* 2nd ed. New York: Van Nostrand, 1968.

Moore, F. J., Chernell, E. and West, J. M. Television as a therapeutic tool. *Archives of General Psychiatry,* 1965, **12,** 217–220.

Mueller, W. J. and Kell, B. L. *Coping with conflict: Supervising counselors and psychotherapists.* Englewood Cliffs, N.J.: Prentice-Hall, 1972.

Nielson, G. *Studies in self-confrontation.* Copenhagen: Munksgaard, 1964.

Orlinsky, D. E. and Howard, K. I. The therapy session report. Chicago: Psychotherapy Session Project, 1966.

Patterson, C. H. *Relationship counseling and psychotherapy.* New York: Harper & Row, 1974.

Resnikoff, A., Kagan, N. and Schauble, P. G. Acceleration of psychotherapy through stimulated videotape recall. *American Journal of Psychotherapy,* 1970, **24 (1),** 102–111.

Rogers, C. R. The use of electrically-recorded interviews in improving psychotherapeutic techniques. *American Journal of Orthopsychiatry,* 1942, **12,** 429–434.

Rogers, C. R. The necessary and sufficient conditions of therapeutic personality change. *Journal of Consulting Psychology,* 1957, **21,** 95–103.

Sagan, C. *The dragons of Eden: Speculations on the evolution of human intelligence.* New York: Random House, 1977.

Schauble, P. G. The acceleration of client progress in counseling and psychotherapy through interpersonal process recall (IPR). Ph.D. disseration. Michigan State University, 1970.

Sullivan, H. S. *Interpersonal theory of psychiatry.* New York: Norton, 1953.

Tomory, R. E. The acceleration and continuation of client growth in counseling and psychotherapy: A comparison of interpersonal process recall (IPR) with traditional counseling methods. Ph.D. dissertation. Michigan State University, 1979.

Tucker, H., Lewis, R. B., martin, G. L. and Over, C. H. Television therapy: Effectiveness of closed circuit TV for therapy and treatment of the mentally ill. *Archives of Neurology and Psychiatry,* 1957, **77,** 57–69.

VanNoord, R. Stimulated recall with videotape and simulation in counseling and psychotherapy: A comparison of effects of two methodologies with undergraduate student clients. Ph.D. dissertation. Michigan State University, 1973.

Walz, G. R. and Johnston, J. A. Counselors look at themselves on videotape. *Journal of Counseling Psychology,* 1963, **10 (3),** 232–236.

Woody, R. W., Kagan, N., Krathwohl, D. R. and Farquhar, W. W. Stimulated recall in psychotherapy using hypnosis and videotape. *American Journal of Clinical Hypnosis,* 1965, **7,** 234–241.

# CHAPTER 33

# *Mainstreaming*

WERNER M. MENDEL and SOPHIE GOREN

*I am grateful to my friend Dr. Arnold D. Schwartz for directing me to Werner Mendel and to Mainstreaming, the subject of the next chapter. We all are well aware of the social movement away from the huge state institutions for the mentally ill, who are now being returned to society.*

*But such people need special assistance; they often face negative attitudes from the community; they often just do not have the practical skills for getting along in the community. And they do not know how to deal with these negative attitudes or with the necessary obligations of social living. How can such people be helped to make adjustment to society and to themselves? How can we counteract the harm that has been done to them by their families and the institutions they have been in?*

*The solution offered here is sensible, bold, imaginative, and practical, and represents a new social way of looking at and dealing with a new class of humans, those formerly and presently incapacitated people who are put back into society. Mainstreaming is a most important humanistic project, and one that I suspect will gain momentum in the years to come.*

*Mainstreaming is a unique concept and quite different in its character and approach from almost all other systems in this book. It has close ties with Direct Psychoanalysis and Multiple Impact Training, which should be read in conjunction with this chapter.*

Mainstreaming is the technique of using the normal support resources available to all citizens, outside of the mental health network, as a means of helping the chronically and severely mentally ill patient to live and function in the community. Ordinary people in a normal environment and everyday life activity in the real world are the matrix for this treatment program. Mainstreaming provides special services to help the patient to learn to use usual community resources as a means of support. Imbedded in the community, such chronic patients show relief of symptoms and a minimizing of discomfort, distress, and dysfunction.

## HISTORY

At the close of the 1970s, the chronically ill psychiatric patient remains a major treatment problem. Over the past 30 years there have been changes in treatment approaches for such patients (Mendel, 1968). These changes have moved the patient out of the hospital and provided medication for suppression of target symptoms. Various attempts at community support have been developed, but all rely heavily on supporting services provided by a mental health network (Erickson, 1975). These support services are delivered as partial hospitalization, day treatment, outpatient clinics, rehabilitation workshops, and community mental health centers. All of these services require special funding, highly skilled and expensive mental health personnel, massive financial support by various branches of government, and a huge overhead of coordinating and regulating agencies representing the federal, state, county, and local government. This community mental health approach, if properly staffed, funded, and carried out, seems to be beyond the financial means of society and has recently been limited by the spreading taxpayer revolt. To discharge chronically ill resourceless patients into the community has not worked. The response of the community generally has been characterized by hostility and rejection, and the patient has suffered and lived in circumstances that are unacceptable both to him and to society. Returning the patient to the hospital is no longer an acceptable alternative for all the reasons that the state hospitals have been dismantled.

Out of this perspective the technique of Mainstreaming was developed. Over the past 25 years the writers have worked with the chronically impaired, severely disorganized, psychiatrically ill patients (Mendel, 1975). In the attempts to provide a supporting network through mental health services, it has been noticed that patients often used informal support in the community that had not been taken into account by the therapists. A neighbor, a church group, a grocery clerk, a bus driver, a telephone operator, a school crossing guard, even an automatic telephone service giving a prayer for a day or the time of day provided important means of support.

These ordinary community services are often not used by patients because the severely impaired psychiatric person ordinarily lacks the skills to use them. With some special assistance and training, the patients can learn to get support from such common resources in the community, which are also used by ordinary citizens. The development of such skills is the purpose of the mainstreaming technique.

## CURRENT STATUS

The Mainstreaming program started in 1968, specifically for the treatment of patients with schizophrenia. (Schizophrenia is used as the model illness for the chronic, severely ill psychiatric patient [Mendel & Allen, 1977]). However, the technique and program is useful for all people who have chronically impairing psychiatric difficulties that cannot be resolved by definitive treatment. More than 50 severely and chronically ill patients have thus far participated. Even though all these patients spent most of their time in hospitals prior to Mainstreaming, during the program the longest hospital stay was for 10 days and hospitalization was prescribed in only 4 out of 50 cases at any time. Hospitalization was rarely indicated because the major function of the hospital could be better carried out and less expensively provided, and fewer side effects were created, when resources in the community were mobilized for the patient. The mainstreaming program provides the catalytic agent essential for the chronic patient to be able to use ordinary community resources. The decreased need for hospitalization is of benefit to patients; it avoids the complications of excessive dependency gratification, prevents reifying the patient's failure in life, and averts further removal from contact with the real world.

Over the past three years the mainstreaming technique has been refined and formalized. However, at the present time lack of funding for mainstreaming services is a serious problem. Since such services do not fall into the usual model of psychotherapy—counseling, psychiatric treatment, or hospitalization—insurance companies, health plans, and government agencies do not provide payment through customary reimbursement channels. This shortsighted policy has continued, even though Mainstreaming can be demonstrated to be more cost effective in reaching specific treatment goals than either prolonged hospitalization or the usual revolving-door arrangement between the hospital and community mental health systems. Mainstreaming moves the patient toward partial independence and away from professional care; in effect the program refers the patient to "life." Goal-attainment scaling and critical-incident cost accounting can be used to demonstrate that Mainstreaming is less expensive than other approaches to supportive care. However, at the present time all funds for Mainstreaming come either from the patient and his family (private resources) or from specially funded programs supported by various government agencies as demonstration projects.

## THEORY

The theory of Mainstreaming rests on three observations:

First, it is recognized that the normal population uses both formal and informal resources in the community as a means of support. These resources are generally free and are in no way identified with the mental health network. Were they to have the skills to use them, these same resources are available to the chronically mentally ill members of society. Most chronically ill psychiatric patients do not have these skills; they require training and assistance to develop the necessary skills to use these resources.

The use of support resources in the community that are not related to the mental health system has many advantages. Since these resources do not involve professional services, they are much less expensive. Since they do not group patients together, each patient can be surrounded by a normal group of people. This helps the patient avoid some of the stigmata of being mentally ill that follow him throughout life as long as he is associated with the mental health establishment.

These support resources include groups with cultural, political, religious, community action, and educational interests. A wide

spectrum of these groups is available, providing a great possibility of connection for the patient. The patient's ability to use that support resource and to function within the group does not depend on his identifying himself as mentally ill or as a patient, but rather depends on his social and interpersonal skills, skills he can learn from the team members who function as social preceptors in the mainstreaming program.

Second, it has been noted that severely chronically ill psychiatric patients change their behavior, thinking, and feeling by modeling themselves after other people in their immediate environment who are available as concrete examples of how to be in the world (Bellack, 1976). If these patients spend their time in the mental health network, be it in the hospital or in the community mental health system, they are in contact with other patients and therefore identify with "sick" models.

In providing supportive care within the mental health network to chronically ill schizophrenic patients, we have been concerned with the problems created by grouping severely ill patients with each other. Such grouping insures that each patient has major interpersonal contacts with other severely ill and disturbed psychiatric patients in a "sick"-oriented environment. Even when the patient gets a great deal of attention—by seeing a therapist daily or by participating in group or milieu programs—this represents only a small portion of his 168-hour week. The major part of the week is spent with other psychiatric patients. Mental hospitals and community mental health systems, therefore, tend to teach patients how to be sick rather than how to be well.

By participating in Mainstreaming, psychotic patients improve clinically, not only as a result of medication and psychotherapy, but also because they learn how to be normal and to become "as if" persons. They do this by learning from others how to feel, think, and behave. They model themselves after the people around them. One crucial function of treatment is providing the severely ill patient a "healthy" role model. We must show how normal people respond to anxiety in ways other than going crazy. We must demonstrate behaviorally that normal people respond to anger in socially acceptable ways. We can teach our patients how to respond to fear and loneliness in ways other than cutting wrists or overdosing on medication (Serban, 1975).

Mainstreaming pays a great deal of attention to the role models provided during the entire 168 hours per week that the patient spends in the world. The severely ill psychiatric patient has the usual life problems of normal people. The difference is that he or she has a severely impaired ability to respond to life's usual crises. Social remission is achieved when the patient has learned to manage anxiety, to develop interpersonal skills, and to live as an "as if" person. The major task of the mainstreaming program is to teach more adaptive ways to deal with life's problems by providing health role models.

Third, it has been recognized that the medical model of intervention, which in its ideal form includes diagnosis, treatment, cure, and the abolition of the defect, is not applicable in the care of the chronic psychiatrically ill person. The rehabilitation model, which accepts a stable defect caused by illness but then focuses on minimizing the disability caused by the defect, seems more appropriate for the chronic psychiatric patient. This model of intervention develops techniques that allow for limited goals while maximizing the patient's function and satisfaction in life.

There is great advantage in the rehabilitation model for this patient population. They, for the most part, have defects that we cannot correct with our present knowledge of biological, psychological, and social processes and interventions. Working with limited goals is difficult for the patient, the community, and the treatment staff. The rehabilitation model provides the potential for success both to the patient and to the treatment staff. Within this model a much wider spectrum of goals is available, since for each individual patient there are infinite gradations of improved function in a multitude of areas. The experience of success is absolutely essential. These patients do not tolerate failure well since most of them have failed much of their lives.

In the medical model treatment staff burns out quickly in dealing with chronic patients. They are constantly faced with their impotence, helplessness, and uselessness in treating these patients. However, in the rehabilitation model the staff can adopt more realistic goals for specific patients. They can measure and experience improvement in function and satisfaction in the patient's life.

## METHODOLOGY

When a patient is referred to the mainstreaming program, first the diagnosis is confirmed. Psychiatric evaluation includes a detailed history, psychometrics, and a present state examination. After the diagnosis of schizophrenia is confirmed, the chronicity of the illness demonstrated, and the stability of the defect clearly established, the treatment history is then reviewed in detail. Usually the people referred to the program have been ill at least 10 years, have been treated with a wide variety of approaches including the use of medication, electroconvulsive treatments, extensive hospitalization, and extensive individual and group psychotherapeutic interventions. Usually the patients have also had major dietary treatment and special fad approaches. As a group they would be described as poor prognosis and process schizophrenic patients.

Once the patient is accepted for treatment in the mainstreaming program, he or she must consent to live in the community and to participate with a mainstreaming team. Acquiring this consent usually poses no difficulty, because the program is certainly more desirable than the usual hospital situation and is the least restrictive environment offered to the patient.

The patient is assigned to a team consisting

of a team leader, who is usually a graduate certified rehabilitation counselor or a social worker, and three or four team members called rehabilitation technicians who serve as social preceptors. These team members are generally graduate students at various local colleges engaged in studies of the helping professions. Team members are chosen to represent the dominant culture to which the patient must adjust. The ideal member would be one who resembles the patient in family background, level of vocational expectations, and social class values. He or she should have achieved some degree of self-sufficiency and have demonstrated the ability to support him- or herself emotionally, intellectually, and economically. The team member should be similar to the person the patient was becoming when he became ill. It is not possible to have as team members only persons who exhibit all of these ideal characteristics. However, three or four team members together can represent these qualities.

Two general approaches to helping people are taught in the graduate programs from which interested and talented students are chosen. The training offered in graduate programs in psychology and social work emphasizes self-awareness and self-understanding so that the person being helped can understand his motives for his behavior and can choose to change his behavior to better meet his needs. Team members trained in this manner seem to be more effective for neurotic patients than for the chronic mentally ill. The second approach—taught in the disciplines of nursing; rehabilitation; and occupational, recreational, and activity therapy—emphasizes the evaluation and modification of maladaptive behavior to conform better with current social standards. The student who has had training in these programs is well able to evaluate behavior and finds it easy to work with chronic psychiatric patients. The patients respond better to an activity-oriented here-and-now approach. Therefore, most team members are drawn from these programs.

Graduate students are generally excellent team members because the program offers them valuable professional experience; however, other individuals without such training have also become successful team members as long as they meet the basic requirement of wanting to help people and are willing to do so in direct, practical ways.

The size of the team depends on how many services the patient needs. If the patient is just leaving the hospital and is very frightened by the thought of living alone in the community, he may require a great deal of service for the first few days while becoming imbedded in the community resources. However, soon the typical patient will require only a few hours' help every day in finding a job and attaching himself to various community resources.

Members of both sexes are included in each team, except in occasional cases where the patient might feel threatened by the opposite sex. The inclusion of both sexes on the team gives the patient the opportunity to identify with members of his own sex and to practice social skills with both.

The primary function of the mainstreaming team is to provide immediate and helpful feedback and emotional support to the patient and to act as role models and social preceptors. Team members teach the patient by modeling and direct instruction on how to behave in the community and how to attach to the social support systems available. The chronic mentally ill patient has great difficulty with interpersonal relationships and therefore frequently is quite socially isolated. He has often spent years in hospitals, board and care homes, and day-care programs. His social skills are clumsy and his social behavior tends to be regressed and idiosyncratic. The team provides a customized social circle where undesirable behaviors can be selectively ignored or pointed out as maladaptive and more mature behavior can be explained, modeled, and reinforced. The team gives realistic, immediate feedback whenever possible so that the patient can gain an understanding of society's reaction to him.

Team members react to the patient's attitudes, values, and behavior much as the ordinary person in the community would. Bizarre, idiosyncratic behavior is experienced by the team members as sharply different from the norm and is pointed out by them to the patient as unacceptable or uncomfortable to others. This feedback, however, must always be given to the patient with sensitivity and kindness so that he or she can modify maladaptive behavior to more acceptable conduct without further impairment of the already severely damaged self-esteem. Some patients who are unaware of the effect of their behavior on others often experience rejection without ever knowing why. When a team member can point out such behavior as seeming rudeness and the effect it causes in the other person, such as withdrawal or the wish to retaliate, then the patient can learn to modify his or her behavior. From the beginning in the mainstreaming program team members offer support, encouragement, and positive reinforcement to the patient. After a time, the patient begins to trust that he will be supported. He may choose his team members as a special circle of confidants.

The team provides role models for the development of the patient's coping skills and problem-solving abilities. As the patient engages in the various activities, a team member demonstrates appropriateness in manner, proper interchange with persons in the community, and useful coping devices to manage the common problems in living. Team members of the same sex provide an opportunity for the patient to strengthen his sexual identity by adopting an appropriate role.

All of the patients in the program live by themselves, in an apartment in the community. At the beginning of the program the patient may still be living with his or her family, but one goal is to have the patient move toward independent living as quickly as possible. For many patients this requires a great deal of training in the ordinary, everyday skills of caring for self, meal planning and preparation, grooming, managing money, and shopping.

Countertransference problems for team members are many, since providing support to the chronic patient is a difficult task (Mendel, 1979). The mainstreaming program takes several years to complete. Because progress is slow, team members have a tendency to either burn out or to become overinvolved with the patients. These patients exhibit behavior that has developed over many years of illness, has been learned from other psychiatric patients in hospitals, or is the result of their family's accommodation to idiosyncratic and bizarre behavior patterns. Maladaptive behavior that has not been modified by the usual social contacts is overlearned, and it requires patience, consistency, and firmness on the part of team members to change it. The work can be stressful, exhausting, discouraging, frustrating, and irritating. Frightened, severely impaired patients require dependable, sustained supporting relationships. This is demanding and difficult for the team members. There is a tendency to slide from the therapeutic rehabilitative position to one of parentlike scolding, correcting, and nagging, which is antitherapeutic. The team member must not react to frustrations and irritations in a spontaneous and thoughtless way, but must always run the response through a therapeutic filter, asking whether his or her response or confrontation is helpful in accomplishing the therapeutic goal with this patient at this time. Yet team members must be allowed the opportunity to share their negative feelings in some way to guard their own well-being and effectiveness as helpers. All of this is accomplished by providing ongoing training and support to the team members. The team leader's role is to provide such support and to organize the in-service training. The primary therapist in charge of the case and who meets with the patient, team, and team leader usually once every two weeks must deal with these countertransference problems by giving support, instruction, and by setting appropriate goals. At these biweekly meetings both short- and long-term goals are set and goal attainment is evaluated. In setting goals the therapist must keep in mind the need of the patient for success, as well as the needs of the team members for structure, support, and encouragement. Goals must be set in such a way that they are not beyond the emotional means of the patient, yet they must not be so low that they tend to hold the patient back. One of the great difficulties for the therapist is determining the fine line between expecting too much or too little. The therapist should not forget that patients change constantly and that any particular patient is not the same as he was two weeks previously. The problem of both underestimating and overestimating a patient's abilities is a constant issue even for the experienced therapist.

The ultimate goal for each patient is maximizing pleasure and function within his limitations and minimizing pain and dysfunction. The expected outcomes include independent living, involvement in the social network, and competitive employment in an appropriate and satisfying job. The task of goal planning is to evaluate the patient in relation to these long-term goals and to set intermediate (two-week) goals in the time frame in which they can be accomplished.

An early task is that of acquainting the team members with the patient and of engaging the patient in the activity of finding an apartment. This is usually accomplished in the first 15 days. Subsequently, the team will help the patient to get acquainted with necessary services, such as grocery stores, banks, and libraries, in his or her immediate community. During the early phase of the program, the emphasis is on building a working relationship between the patient and the team in the context of activities that may include marketing, taking walks, riding a bicycle, touring a museum, or opening and managing a bank account. Patients are often fearful and reluctant to participate in activities that involve a change from their customary patient role. The team members' attitude should be one of encouragement and firmness, with specific instruction if necessary.

Team meetings are used to guide the direction and timing of the effort and to decide whether the patient is to be urged gently forward to new involvements and activities or to be allowed to slip back to a more familiar ground. The patient must be constantly evaluated for the ability to tolerate increased anxiety and for potential for disorganization. The team must be sensitive to the patient's tolerance of stress and must learn to recognize the patient's level of discomfort. When members of the family are available and supportive, they are invited to participate in the program as much as possible and as appropriate for the age and status of the patient. If family members do participate, they frequently require support and instruction to help them modify prior unsatisfactory relationship patterns.

As mentioned, one important function of team members is to help the patient become imbedded in the community. Team members make contact with potential employers, recreational and educational resources, and special interest groups. Since prior discussion with members of these groups on behalf of the mainstreaming patient may produce an undesirable prejudicial set, this is a most delicate task. Frequently team members will need to accompany the patient as he first participates in some of these activities. In some instances their presence may appear quite appropriate, as when a patient goes with a friend to a club or class activity. However, in work and other situations, the presence of what appears to be a chaperon will be questioned, and some explanation may be necessary. Individual team members need a great deal of creativity, which comes from experience, in dealing with this particular problem.

## APPLICATIONS

Mainstreaming is particularly suitable as a technique of supportive care for schizophrenic patients who live in the community. Schizophrenia is a psychobiological illness characterized by a cluster of three simultaneously occurring basic defects. These are

(1) ineffective and expensive anxiety management, (2) clumsy and disastrous interpersonal misadventures, and (3) failing historicity. All psychotic symptoms can be understood either as consequences or attempted restitution secondary to these three basic defects. The illness usually begins in late adolescence, is characterized by periods of exacerbation and remission, and is chronic in nature (Mendel, 1976).

Supportive care minimizes the disruption and disorganization caused by intermittent exacerbations and minimizes the symptoms caused by the three nuclear defects. By providing ongoing support, the schizophrenic patient can minimize dysfunction and maximize the difference between his defect and disability.

Mainstreaming is also of value in treating other chronic conditions that require ongoing support. As a technique of supportive care, Mainstreaming is suitable for any patient who lives in the community and suffers from an incurable illness that requires lifelong care. Mainstreaming aims to convert the chronic psychiatric patient who relies on services provided by the mental health network to a person who lives in the community and uses the ordinary support services available to all citizens. A good outcome is to have the person function as an interesting and lovable eccentric without his having to make a career of patienthood.

Mainstreaming is not a suitable system of treatment for patients who require definitive care for conditions that can be cured, resolved, or are self-limited. These patients mainstream themselves once the illness is terminated. They do not require long-term supportive care.

## CASE EXAMPLE

Susan is a 31-year-old single Caucasian female, the youngest of two children. Her sister, who is two years her senior, is a successful attorney, living 4,000 miles away. Her father was a well-known attorney, hardworking and successful, who died about 10 years ago of a sudden heart attack. Her mother, now 64, has devoted the past 11 years of her life entirely to the care of Susan.

In 1965 Susan was graduated from high school at age 17. She had an excellent academic record and was accepted at three major universities. She entered a university but during the first semester took LSD and experienced severe side effects. She withdrew from school after two months.

In January 1966 Susan entered another university. During her second semester she was recommended for a scholarship by her art professor. When she did not receive the scholarship, she considered herself a failure. She compared herself unfavorably to her sister, who has always been successful. The patient's disorganization increased and her dormitory friends referred her to a psychiatrist. Susan's parents met with the psychiatrist, who told them that the patient was "hanging on by a thread." Subsequently Susan and her parents met regularly with a psychologist.

Susan dropped out of the university before completing the semester. She moved to a small apartment in a poor area of town. She took a job as a file clerk in an automobile insurance company (her father knew the president of the company and obtained the job for her). She walked off the job a short time later and has not worked since.

She became hostile, wandered away from home many hours each day, and smoked marijuana with other young people. On the evening of Susan's twentieth birthday, after a luncheon party in the family home attended by a number of her dormitory friends, she overdosed with sleeping pills. She was hospitalized in the psychiatric ward of a local hospital. Four months later her father suddenly died of a heart attack. While on a pass home from the hospital, Susan searched out some pills and took them back to the hospital and overdosed there. She remained in the hospital for one and one-half years. Then her mother decided that more had to be done for her daughter, and they visited five psychiatric hospitals in the East. She then arranged for two independent psychiatric evaluations of her daughter. Both evaluations concluded that the patient needed further hospitalization.

Susan was then transferred to a large private hospital in the East where she remained for one and one-half years without change. In fact she learned even more bizarre behaviors, identifying with other patients on the ward and learning how to be crazy. In addition, those patients who had been on pass brought in drugs, and she learned how to get high by drinking coffee loaded with nutmeg.

As the hospital stay was not improving Susan's condition, her mother was told by a treating psychiatrist to place her in a long-term state hospital. Susan and her mother returned to California, where another psychiatrist was consulted. He suggested that Susan should go to a foster home, since he felt it might be traumatic for the patient to go home. The mother agreed to this plan, believing Susan might do better with foster parents. In addition she hired a woman who had been acting as a therapeutic companion to patients to be with Susan.

While in the foster home, Susan was given responsibility for taking her own medications; she swallowed the entire prescription, 100 tablets, and was found unconscious, her face covered with vomitus. She developed aspiration pneumonia and was placed in the intensive care unit of a local hospital. On her medical recovery Susan moved back to her mother's home.

The mother, who had taken workshops at the Los Angeles Institute of Reality Therapy, engaged one of the staff psychiatrists to treat her daughter. Another year went by without change. During this year a psychiatric social worker was also engaged to assist with the treatment of Susan, but there was no improvement.

A new psychiatrist, the medical director of the local day hospital, was consulted. After a year of treatment, Susan entered the day hospital program. Even though the structure of the program was excellent, she was not able to function in the facility due to her fears and paranoia, which had become her way of life.

After two years in day care, Susan moved to a board-and-care home. During a year's stay there, no improvement was noted. Susan was placed in another foster home recommended by the previous social worker. A new psychiatrist was engaged. Family meetings were held including the foster parents and the patient. The foster parents and the two young children in the home were a fine family, but the foster mother was home very little and Susan was left alone most of the day. After a nine-month stay, no improvement was noted. The patient was not willing to stay any longer—she threatened suicide several times, and she was allowed to return to her mother's home again.

Another psychiatrist, the medical director of a private psychiatric hospital, was consulted. He made a house call, saw the patient, and had her involuntarily hospitalized. There she was given lithium, without therapeutic response. All medications were discontinued at once and the patient suffered severe withdrawal. She stayed in bed, cried much of the time, and begged to go home. After three months the psychiatrist said that Susan might as well go home.

Susan became very agitated and violent at home and was again hospitalized. This time she was placed in the local county hospital and treated with propranolol for a six-week period. Upon leaving the hospital, she returned to live with her mother but also began Mainstreaming. A team was developed consisting of four female team members who visited with her every day for three or four hours and took her to various activities, including cooking and sewing classes at the local high school, bicycle riding, and visits to the museums. At the biweekly team meetings the mother, therapist, team leader, and team members met. The patient attended two team meetings, but she could not stand the discomfort of being discussed and chose not to attend future meetings. Each two weeks the patient was evaluated, and new goals were set.

In the course of the last seven months the patient has moved out of her parental home into an apartment to live independently. Unfortunately, soon after she moved out the first time, her apartment building was sold to be converted to an office building. At that time the patient developed considerable exacerbation of her symptoms, became frightened, developed fantasies of being raped and followed, and decided that she had to return home. After an uncomfortable two months of living at home, she moved into another apartment. This time she became imbedded in the community in which she lived. She learned to cook her own meals, clean her own apartment, and live her own life. She continued with some classes and activities and now works as a volunteer clerk in a senior citizen center three days per week. Each time she goes to work, one of her team members goes with her and helps her in the work. She has changed her image from being a patient to being a working young woman. She has a work wardrobe and work ethic. It is planned that within the next few months she will move on to competitive employment in the facility in which she now volunteers. She manages her own money ($7 per day allowance), which is given to her three days at a time. She frequently spends this money foolishly and then finds that she has nothing to eat in the house for a couple of days. However, her freezer is well stocked with supplies provided by her mother. Her visits home are now limited to one afternoon and evening every two weeks, including a dinner at home with her mother. She has telephone contact with her mother once every two days and the relationship has generally improved. She no longer feels like a little girl under the control of her mother, and her mother no longer feels so responsible for the behavior of her daughter. Approximately six months ago an attempt was made to introduce a male member into the team. The patient found this impossible to tolerate. She became increasingly anxious, showed marked exacerbation of symptoms, and it was necessary to back off from that plan. At this time she is again talking about wanting a male member on the team, although she wonders how she will handle that relationship without making it either sexual or inappropriate.

At this point, approximately 11 years after the beginning of her illness and at age 31, the patient has had the best and longest period of good adjustment. She lives independently, appears generally appropriate, takes small doses of antipsychotic medication, and works at a volunteer job in the community. She spends her time with healthy companions—the team members who make up her social circle. The major emphasis of the team members is to shape her behavior and her appearance so that she has now learned to appear, behave, and think in a much more healthy way. The therapeutic thrust is to constantly say to her in our behavior and verbalization "Let us show you what to do about your fear and your loneliness and your anger other than going crazy or cutting your wrists or being inappropriate." The patient also sees the therapist once a week for both the management of her medication and for psychotherapeutic reinforcement of the supporting position and the normalizing attitude.

## SUMMARY

Mainstreaming is a technique of supportive care for chronically and severely ill psychiatric patients carried out in the community. It is an alternative to both hospitalization and the usual community mental health system. This approach allows for severely impaired patients who live with schizophrenia or other chronic psychiatric illness who otherwise could not be maintained out of the hospital to function in the community. Mainstreaming allows the patient to use the usual and normal support systems available to the average citizen in the community that are outside of the mental health network. The interventions are structured within the rehabilitation model. The mainstreaming technique makes it possible for severely ill psychiatric patients to use healthy people as role models and social preceptors. Even at the beginning of treatment Mainstreaming is less expensive than the usual mental health services in the community. The final goal for each patient is to obtain as much support as necessary from the usual community resources that are free of charge. Mainstreaming takes individuals who are unable to live in the community because they are sick and disorganized, and helps them to develop techniques to enter the "normal" world. Patients who have been mainstreamed can often live independently, support themselves, and take a more useful position in society than patienthood would offer.

## REFERENCES

Bellack, A. S. Generalization effects of social skills training in chronic schizophrenics: An experimental analysis. *Behavior Research & Therapy*, 1976, **14**, 391–398.

Erickson, R. C. Outcome studies in mental hospitals: A review. *Psychological Bulletin*, 1975, **82**, 519–540.

Mendel, W. M. On the abolition of the psychiatric hospital. In L. M. Roberts, N. S. Greenfield, & M. H. Miller (Eds.), *Comprehensive mental health*. Madison, Wisc.: University of Wisconsin Press, 1968.

Mendel, W. M. *Supportive care: Theory and technique*. Los Angeles, Calif.: Mara Books, 1975.

Mendel, W. M. *Schizophrenia: The experience and its treatment*. San Francisco, Calif.: Jossey-Bass, 1976.

Mendel, W. M. Staff burn-out: Diagnosis, treatment, and prevention. *New Directions for Mental Health Services*, 1979, **2**, 75–83.

Mendel, W. M. and Allen, R. E. Treating the chronic patient. In J. H. Masserman (Ed.), *Current psychiatric therapies*, vol. 17. New York, N.Y.: Grune & Stratton, 1977.

Mendel, W. M. and Allen, C. Rehabilitation model in psychiatry. In *Conference Proceedings, Adult psychiatric day treatment: 2d multi-disciplinary national forum*. Minneapolis, Minn.: University of Minnesota Press, 1978.

Serban, G. Stress in schizophrenics and normals. *British Journal of Psychiatry*, 1975, **126**, 397–407.

# CHAPTER 34

# *Meditation*

ROGER N. WALSH

*It would be a kind of cosmic joke if the key to understanding the self and curing malad-justment were to be under our nose, and to have been there for some 3,000 years. This is the implication of the next chapter by Roger Walsh.*

*Meditation, a recent import from Asia, has become quite fashionable and popular in a variety of guises; and in this book, a number of the systems, including Autogenic Training, some of the Body Therapies, Comprehensive Relaxation, and Covert Conditioning, just to mention a few, contain elements compatible with classical meditation. Even though people brought up in Western philosophical traditions, where an outward, interactional approach rather than an inward, autochthonous approach is emphasized, seem strongly resistant to Meditation, there seems to be not only growing interest in Meditation, but also some laboratory evidence that the process can produce measurable physiological changes.*

*I found this chapter quite exciting. In discussing his own experience Dr. Walsh makes the challenge of Meditation real, and in this chapter the reader will be given an opportunity to experience Meditation for himself or herself. Would it not be amazing if eventually Meditation becomes the ideal therapeutic system: cheap, simple, and effective? We looked so long and so hard, and people have been doing it for three millenia. It could be. . . .*

It is the mind that maketh good or ill
That maketh wretch or happy, rich or poor.
                                        Edmund Spenser

The term "Meditation" refers to a family of practices that train attention in order to heighten awareness and bring mental processes under voluntary control. Their ultimate aim is the development of the deepest insight into the nature of mental processes, consciousness, identity, and reality, and the development of optimal states of psychological well-being and consciousness.

## HISTORY

Specific meditation practices have evolved across the centuries, reflecting the insights, proclivities, and cultures of its practitioners. For example, the basic practices taught by the Buddha some 2,500 years ago have been largely maintained in their original form in Southeast Asia, elaborated into a complex family of practices emphasizing visual imagery in Tibet, and merged with Taoism and other disciplines to form Zen in Japan.

The last two decades have seen an explosion of interest in Meditation in the West. Until then there was only scattered episodic interest punctuating general skepticism and disbelief. Several factors seem to have facilitated this shift. These include the human potential movement, the diminution of the materialistic dream and a search within for the satisfaction that was not found outside, a growing interest in nonwestern cultures and philosophies, and research into the nature of altered states of consciousness.

From the research on altered states came the recent and startling recognition that portions of some of the world's great religions can be viewed as state-specific technologies for the induction of higher states of consciousness. At the esoteric core of these disciplines, as opposed to the articles of dogma to which the masses adhere, lie precisely delineated practices aimed at training awareness and mental processes. One of the most widespread and central of these practices is Meditation, which is often regarded as a cornerstone of advanced work in these disciplines.

These recognitions led to the awareness that self-actualization was not the summit of psychological well-being. Rather it began to be recognized that there lay realms and states of consciousness beyond those encompassed by traditional Western psychological models and that some of these states held radically different and larger potentials than those we had formerly acknowledged.

## CURRENT STATUS

Meditation is probably the most widespread and popular of the ''innovative psychotherapies,'' having been learned by several million people in the United States and probably some 50 million worldwide at a conservative guess. Its status in the East remains much as it has for centuries; namely, it is a widely practiced discipline that is regarded as a central practice for any people wishing to explore or develop themselves to the highest psychological or religious levels.

In the West a relatively small percentage of people also practice it with this perspective. However, a much larger population uses it for its short-term benefits as as relaxation, stress management, self-confidence, and a generally heightened sense of psychological well-being.

Behavioral scientists and mental health practitioners have also become interested, seeing Meditation as a tool with potential both for facilitating the therapist's effectiveness and as a self-regulation strategy useful for a variety of clinical disorders. A sizable body of research provides evidence of its clinical effectiveness and lends support to some of the claims made by practitioners across the centuries. This research literature is rapidly expanding, and more than half of it has been published within the last five years. For reviews see Shapiro and Giber (1978), Walsh (1979), Shapiro (1980), Shapiro and Walsh (1980), and Walsh and Vaughan (1980a).

For those who wish to learn to meditate there are several helpful books. Those beginners may find helpful include Goldstein (1976), Ram Dass (1978) and Levine (1979). However, books by themselves are rarely sufficient, and it is extremely helpful to have the support and guidance of a teacher and fellow meditators. Meditation teachers and centers can often be found by a perusal of the phone book, particularly for the more popular varieties such as Transcendental Meditation or Zen. A useful reference book listing centers and teachers is contained in the appendix of the book by Ram Das (1978).

## THEORY

Meditation stems from and leads to a view of human nature, mind, psychology, and consciousness that differs markedly in some ways from our traditional Western psychological perspectives. In this section we will first examine the nature of the meditation model, then compare the traditional Western view with it, and finally examine the mechanisms that may be involved in producing the effects of Meditation.

### The Meditation Model of Consciousness

Our traditional psychological and psychiatric models posit a limited number of states of consciousness, and our usual waking state is assumed to be optimal. Some other states may be functionally useful—for example, sleep and dreaming—but most are viewed as degenerate and dysfunctional in one way or another—consider delirium, psychosis, or intoxication. No consideration is given to the possibility that states may exist that are even more functional than our usual waking one.

On the other hand, most meditation theories view our state as suboptimal. The mind is seen as largely outside voluntary control and continuously creating a largely unrecognized stream of thoughts, emotions, images, fantasies, and associations. These are held to distort our awareness, perceptual processes, and sense of identity to an unrecognized degree. This distortion is described in various traditions as *"maya," "samsara,"* or "illusion" (Goldstein, 1976; Goleman, 1977). The term "illusion" has often been mistaken to mean that the world does not exist. However, it actually refers to the concept that our perception is distorted to an unrecognized degree and hence is rendered illusory. From this perspective we might argue that all human problems originate from the unrecognized inability to differentiate mind-produced fantasies and distortions from objective sensory data. For example, how rarely do we directly recognize and experience that we are the active creators of our perception and that the unpleasantness, provocation, attraction, aversiveness, beauty, ugliness, and so on, that we think we see in the world are actually creations of our own mind? According to Ram Dass (1975): "We are all prisoners of our own mind. This recognition is the first step on the journey of awakening."

Fortunately, these claims about the nature of our usual state of consciousness, our lack of awareness, the unrecognized involuntary nature of much of our mental processes, and the distortions to which they are subject are readily open to personal testing. Anyone willing to undertake a period of intensive training in observation of his or her own mental processes—such as in an insight meditation retreat of one or two weeks' duration—will become painfully aware of this fact. Indeed, one of the major dictums of all the meditative traditions is that these phenomena should be experienced and known directly by the individual rather than by what others say about them. Many a behavioral scientist and therapist who has heard of these things has been grudgingly shocked into acknowledging their potency only after personally experiencing them (Walsh, 1977, 1978; Ram Dass, 1978; Shapiro, 1978, 1980).

Trained meditative observation reveals that our usual consciousness is filled with a continual flux of subliminal thoughts, internal dialogue, and fantasies. In becoming lost in and identified with this mental content, awareness is reduced and distorted, resulting in an unappreciated trance state. Thus from the meditative perspective our usual state of consciousness is seen as a state of hypnosis. As in any hypnotic state, there need not be a recognition of the trance or its attendant constriction of awareness, or a memory of the sense of identity prior to hypnosis. Those thoughts with which we have identified create our state of consciousness, identity, and reality (Walsh & Vaughan, 1980a,b). In the words of the Buddha: "We are what we think./All that we are arises with our thoughts./With our thoughts we make the world" (Byrom, 1976).

From this perspective the ego appears to represent the constellation of thoughts with which we usually identify and comes into existence as soon as awareness identifies unconsciously with thought. Indeed, deep meditative observation reveals that what we take to be our continuous abiding ego, or "self," turns out to be a rapid flux of individual thoughts that, because of our usual limitations of awareness, is perceived as solid and continuous. This is analogous to the experience of continuity and motion that our perception of the individual frames of a movie provides.

Since they view the usual state as suboptimal, the meditative traditions obviously hold that more optimal states exist. Indeed they suggest that a large spectrum of altered states of consciousness exist, that some are potentially useful, and that a few are true "higher" states. The term "higher" indicates that a state possesses all the capacities and potentials of the usual states plus some additional ones (Tart, 1975).

These higher states are seen as realizable through mental training, with Meditation being one particular type of such training. Higher states are seen not as something created *de novo* but rather as preexisting within the deeper layers of the psyche, though commonly covered and rendered imperceptible by the usual mental activity and distortions. Thus growth is seen as a recognition and realization of these states through the unlearning and reduction of unskillful and distorting mental habits and processes so that preexisting capacities and states can be revealed.

At the summit of mental development lie those states of consciousness that are the goal of advanced Meditation, known variously as *enlightenment* or *liberation* (Walsh & Shapiro, 1980). These are states in which awareness is said to no longer identify exclusively with anything. Without exclusive identification the me/not me dichotomy is transcended and the individual thus perceives him- or herself as both no thing *and* every thing. That is, such people experience themselves as both pure awareness (no thing) and the entire universe (every thing). All defenses drop away, since when experiencing oneself as no thing there is nothing to defend; when experiencing oneself as every thing there is nothing to defend against. This experience of unconditioned or pure awareness is apparently very blissful. It is described in the Hindu tradition as comprised of "sat-chit-ananda": awareness, being, and bliss.

To those with no experience of these states, such descriptions sound paradoxical if not bizarre. However, there is a remarkable similarity in such descriptions across cultures and centuries by those who have taken these practices to their limits. So consistent are descriptions of these states of consciousness

and the world view that originates from them that they have comprised the basis of what has been called "the perennial philosophy," a description of consciousness and reality that can be found at the core of all the great meditative and yogic traditions (Wilber, 1977, 1980).

## Comparing the Meditative and Western Psychological Models

When the traditional Western psychological and the meditative models are compared, what Thomas Kuhn (1970) has called a "paradigm clash" necessarily ensues. What happens when the claims of the consciousness disciplines are examined from within the Western framework?

First, all claims for the existence of true higher states will be automatically dismissed, since the usual state is believed to be optimal and there is thus no place in the Western model for anything better. Not only will they be dismissed but because many of the experiences accompanying these states are unknown in the Western model, they are likely to be viewed as pathological. Thus, for example, the experiences known as *satori* or *kensho,* intense but short-lived enlightenment experiences, include a sense of unity or oneness with the rest of the universe. However, since our traditional Western model recognizes such experiences only when they occur in extreme psychosis, they are likely to be pathologized. Without an awareness of paradigmatic assumptions, it becomes easy to dismiss such phenomena as nonsensical or even pathological, a mistake that has been made even by some of the most outstanding Western mental health professionals (Deikman, 1977; Krippner & Brown, 1979). Thus, for example, Freud (1962) dismissed oceanic experience as infantile helplessness, Alexander (1931) interpreted Meditation as self-induced catatonia, while the Group for the Advancement of Psychiatry (1976) viewed mystics as borderline psychotics.

When we reverse viewpoints and examine

the Western model from the perspective of the meditative model, even more startling conclusions arise. The meditative model is inherently broader than the traditional Western perspective, since the former encompasses a wider range of states of consciousness, including all those recognized by the latter. Indeed the Western model can be viewed as a specific subset of the meditative one.

Thus the Western model has a position vis-à-vis the meditative model analogous to the Newtonian model vis-à-vis an Einsteinian model in physics. The Newtonian model applies appropriately to objects moving at relatively low velocities but no longer fits when applied to high-velocity objects. The Einsteinian model, on the other hand, encompasses both low and high speeds; from this broader perspective the Newtonian model, and its inherent limitations, are perfectly logical and understandable (employing Einsteinian and not Newtonian logic, of course). However, the reverse does not hold, for Einsteinian logic and phenomena are not comprehensible from within a Newtonian framework. To try to examine the larger model from the perspective of the smaller is inappropriate and necessarily productive of false conclusions since what lies outside the range of the smaller model must necessarily be misinterpreted by it (Walsh, 1980; Walsh & Vaughan, 1980a).

Viewing our usual state of consciousness from this expanded model results in some extraordinary implications. Our traditional model defines psychosis as a state of consciousness in which reality is misperceived or distorted without recognition of that misperception. From one perspective of the meditative model our usual state fits this definition since it is suboptimal, provides a distorted perception of reality, and fails to recognize that distortion! From this perspective, our usual state is seen as a hypnotically constricted trance. Like individuals who live their lives in a smog-filled city and only recognize the extent of the pollution and limited visibility when they climb into the surrounding mountains, most of us live our lives unaware of our restricted awareness.

## Possible Mechanisms Involved in the Production of Meditation Effects

In all likelihood a large number of mechanisms are involved in producing the effects of Meditation. In this section we will first examine possible mechanisms proposed by Western psychology and neurophysiology and then discuss a nonwestern model from Buddhist psychology.

From one perspective Meditation can be viewed as a progressive heightening of awareness of, and disidentification from, mental content. In practices such as Insight Meditation, where the student is trained to observe and identify all mental content and processes rapidly and precisely, this is particularly clear (Goldstein, 1976; Goleman, 1977). This is a slow process in which a gradual refinement of perception results in a peeling away of awareness from successively more subtle layers of identification. Thoughts with which one formerly identified become recognized as just thoughts.

For example, if the thought "I'm scared" arises and is seen to be just a thought, then it exerts little influence. However, if the individual identifies with that thought, then the experiential reality is that he or she is scared. This identification sets in train a self-fulfilling, self-prophetic process in which experience and psychological processes appear to validate the reality of that which was identified with. This thought "I'm scared" is now not something that can be seen, rather it is that from which everything else is seen and interpreted. Awareness, which could be transcendent and positionless, has now been constricted to viewing the world from a single self-validating perspective.

However, "there is nothing more difficult than to become critically aware of the presuppositions of one's own thought. . . . Every thought can be scrutinized directly except the thought by which we scrutinize"

(Schumacher, 1977). With the heightened awareness a trained mind can bring to bear, the individual thought may now be recognized again; in recognizing it as only a thought, the individual goes from thinking that he or she is a scared person to the experience of being aware of the thought. This may be seen as *dehypnosis* (Walsh, 1979).

A number of other mechanisms are clearly also involved. Suggested psychological mechanisms include relaxation, global desensitization to formerly stressful stimuli, habituation, expectation, deautomatization, counterconditioning, and a variety of cognitive mediating factors. At the physiological level suggested mechanisms include reduced metabolism and arousal, hemispheric lateralization (a shift in the relative activity of the two cerebral hemispheres), brain-wave resonance and coherence, and a shift in the balance between the activating and quieting components of the autonomic nervous system (Shapiro & Giber, 1978; Walsh, 1979; Shapiro, 1980; Shapiro & Walsh, 1980; Walsh & Vaughan, 1980a).

Another way in which meditative mechanisms can be viewed is in terms of Charles Tart's (1975) systems model of consciousness. Tart views consciousness as a complex, dynamic system constructed from various components such as thought, emotion, attention, identity, arousal, and so forth. Different types of Meditation can be viewed as cultivating specific components. While Insight Meditation specifically trains attention, other types work with, for example, emotion or the sense of identity. Some practices use specific strategies that we would now recognize as counterconditioning and classical conditioning to cultivate love. When this or any other component of consciousness is cultivated to a sufficient degree, it may result in significant shifts in the state of consciousness. Although different practices employ different starting points, it is interesting to note that they all aim for a final common state—enlightenment.

Several nonwestern psychologies also contain models that attempt to explain how meditative effects are produced. One Buddhist psychological model based on "mental factors" is particularly useful in making comparisons with Western psychotherapeutic practices.

Mental factors are qualities or states of mind said to determine the relationship between consciousness and the object of consciousness (the sensory stimulus of which consciousness is aware). Thus, for example, the mental factor of aversion describes a state in which consciousness tends to withdraw from or avoid a particular stimulus. Buddhist psychology describes some 50-odd mental factors; of these, the seven so-called "factors of enlightenment" will be examined here. These are seven qualities that are deliberately cultivated by Buddhist meditators, since it is held that when they are cultivated and balanced one with another they result in an optimal relationship of awareness to each moment of experience (Goldstein, 1976; Walsh, 1978; Kornfield, 1979; Walsh & Shapiro, 1980).

The first of these qualities is *mindfulness*, which is the quality of being aware of the nature of the object of consciousness. Thus, for example, a fantasy is recognized as such, rather than the individual becoming lost in it without recognizing that it is merely a fantasy.

The remaining six mental factors are divided into two groups of three that should be balanced for optimum psychological well-being. The first group are essentially energizing or arousing factors and comprise *energy, investigation,* and *rapture.* These are balanced by three calming factors of *concentration, tranquility,* and *equanimity.* The energy factor refers to the arousal level, which should be balanced between the extremes of agitation and torpor. Investigation refers to the active exploration of the moment-to-moment experience and state of mind, while rapture refers to a positive sense of joy and intense interest in the moment-to-moment experience. The calming factors involve concentration, which is the ability to maintain attention on a specific object; tranquility, which is calm and freedom from anxiety and agitation; and equanimity, the capacity to experience any sensation without disturbing the mental state.

Western therapists of all persuasions have tended to emphasize the active factors of energy and investigation in psychological exploration. What has not been appreciated is that perceptual and intuitive sensitivity and insight are limited without a complementary development of concentration, tranquility, and equanimity. On the other hand, Eastern traditions have sometimes overemphasized these factors so that the individuals may develop intense concentration and calm without a balanced complementary cultivation of investigation and energetic observation. Such practices lead to euphoric experiences but relatively little deep wisdom or permanent liberation from mental conditioning. Rather, optimal effects are held to occur when all seven factors are cultivated in a balanced, mutually facilitating manner.

## METHODOLOGY

While the general principles and methods of practice are the same, the intensity and degree of commitment required for a person wishing to use Meditation for intensive exploration and growth is far greater than that of the person who wishes to employ it merely as a self-regulation strategy for a limited psychological or somatic disturbance. The major part of this section will deal with intense practice since this also encompasses the lesser demands of using Meditation as a clinical self-regulation strategy.

For an individual committed to the deepest and most thoroughgoing self-transformation, Meditation is best viewed as but one component of a shift in attitudes, thought, speech, and behavior aimed at the deepest possible transformation of mind, awareness, identity, life style, and relationship to the world. Any meditator soon recognizes that

while behavior originates from the mind, all behavior also leaves its imprint on the mind and conditions and imprints the state in which it was performed. Training in Meditation is therefore usually accompanied by preliminary and concomitant shifts in life style designed to enhance positive mental states and reduce negative ones.

Thus, for example, the meditator is advised to be strictly ethical in all behavior. Buddhist psychology recommends at a minimum refraining from lying, stealing, sexual misconduct, killing, and the consumption of mind-clouding intoxicants. Traditionally this is said to lead to what is called "purification" in which unskillful and counterproductive motives and behavior are gradually winnowed away.

This ethicality is not to be confused with externally imposed or sanctioned moralism that adopts a judgmental right/wrong, good/bad perspective on behavior. Rather, no meditator can long remain unaware that unethical behavior is motivated by emotions and states such as greed, anger, and aversion, that unethical behavior enhances these states, and that they in turn disrupt the mind, leaving it agitated, guilty, and trapped still more deeply in painful conditioning.

Other useful practices include the cultivation of generosity and service to others as ways of reducing egotistical self-centeredness and desire. The meditator may wish to be selective in friendship since people without such motives may not provide a supportive environment for these initially difficult practices.

Practitioners may also be drawn to a life of what has been termed "voluntary simplicity" (Elgin, 1980). With deepening practice meditators recognize the disrupting effects of greed and attachment. At the same time, they find themselves better able to generate a sense of well-being and the positive emotions for which they were formerly dependent upon external possessions and stimuli, and they may thus experience less need to own the latest and biggest car, boat, or color television. Rather, greater pleasure is found in a deepening sensitivity to the moment-to-moment flow of experience and each moment, no matter what one is doing, becomes a source of rich and multifaceted stimulation.

For most people Meditation is a slow cumulative process; people should not commence it unless they are prepared to commit themselves to daily practice for a minimum of about a month. Practice may be begun with either short daily sessions of 20 minutes or half an hour once or twice a day, or for individuals who wish to jump in, with a retreat in which one engages in more or less continuous meditation for a period of days or weeks. The latter is more difficult in that initial intensive practice can often be quite arduous, but it is also more rewarding; even several days of intensive, continuous practice will be sufficient to produce a range of experiences and insights beyond the ken of normal daily life. While it is possible to make some progress unaided, any deep practice is greatly facilitated by a good teacher or guide with considerable personal experience of the discipline.

Meditation practices can be subdivided into two main categories: concentration and awareness practices. Concentration meditations aim especially at developing the ability of the mind to focus attention imperturbably on specific objects such as the breath, an emotion, or mental factor. Awareness meditations, on the other hand, aim at examining the nature of mind, consciousness, and the ongoing flux of moment-to-moment experience. Meditations such as Transcendal Meditation, which focus on a repetitive internally generated sound or thought, can be seen as concentration practices; Zen or Insight Meditations, which ultimately aim to open the individual to an awareness of whatever passes through the field of awareness, can be seen as awareness trainings.

In Concentration Meditation, the individual attempts to fix attention on a specific stimulus, such as the breath. However, attention remains fixed for a remarkably short period and the individual soon finds him- or herself lost in fantasy, inner dialogue, or unconscious reverie of some type. As soon as this is realized, attention is brought back to the breath and maintained there until lost again. This rapidly results in a startling and disconcerting recognition: namely that the degree of awareness and control over attentional processes is far less than we usually recognize. Most beginning meditators are astonished to recognize just how much of their life and mental processes are on unconscious automatic pilot.

Since the power and extent of this automaticity is so difficult to convey to someone without personal experience of it, it is worthwhile for any nonmeditator to try the following exercise.

Set an alarm for a minimum of 10 minutes. Then take a comfortable seat, close your eyes, and turn your attention to the sensations of breathing in your abdomen. Try to stay with the sensations continuously as the abdominal wall rises and falls and focus your attention as carefully, precisely, and microscopically on the sensations that arise and pass away each instant. Do not let your attention wander for a moment. If thoughts and feelings arise, just let them be there, and continue to focus your awareness on the sensations of the breath.

While you continue to pay close attention to the sensations, start counting the breaths from 10 down to one and after you reach one go back to 10 again. However, if you lose count or if the mind wanders from the sensations of the breath, even for an instant, then go back to 10 and start again. If you get lost in fantasy or distracted by internal or external stimuli, just recognize what has happened and gently bring the mind back to the breath and start counting again. Continue this process until the alarm tells you to stop; then estimate how much of the time you were actually fully aware of the experience of breathing.

Most people will find that only a very small percentage of their time was spent fully aware of the sensations of the breath. With continued practice and longer durations, you would find that this awareness was even less than you initially thought since much of the time spent lost in fantasy is not initially recognized. However, this brief exercise should be sufficient to give a slight flavor of the problem.

With prolonged practice, concentration gradually improves and meditators are able to maintain their focus for progressively longer periods. As they do so, a number of concomitant experiences occur such as calm, equanimity, a sense of lightness and well-being, and ultimately a range of altered states (Brown, 1977).

Although the practice of concentration can be useful and pleasurable, some traditions view it more as a facilitator of Awareness Meditation than as an end in itself. Insight or awareness practices also aim at directing attention but allow it to shift to focus electively on whatever is predominant within the field of awareness. Thus, the individual practicing Insight Meditation might begin by focusing attention on the breath; as other stimuli such as thoughts, sensations, or emotions become predominant, attention is allowed to focus on and examine each of them in succession.

In doing this the first level of insights that develop are what might be called psychodynamic. That is, the individual recognizes patterns of thought and behavior such as might be recognized in traditional psychotherapy. However, as the practice deepens, the significantly enhanced capacities of concentration, calm, and equanimity allow deep insights into the nature of psychological processes. This level of insight brings an illumination of how the mind is constructed. One begins to see, for example, the way a single thought may arise into awareness and modify all perception. The arising of desire may be seen to modify perception and result in the production of a state and motivational system aimed at not only obtaining, but clutching to and resisting detachment from, the object of the desire. Simultaneously, associations and fears concerning the possible loss of the object may be observed. One begins to gain

insight into the fundamental nature of processes such as motivation, perception, and ego. Everything in the mind is seen to be in constant change, and the illusion that there abides deep within the psyche a permanent unchanging ego or self is seen to be an illusory construction of perceptual insensitivity. With this recognition there occurs a letting go of egocentric motivation and an enhanced identification with others and the universe at large.

The range of experiences is extraordinarily large and intense, far beyond anything experienced in daily life, and suggests that almost any experience may occur in Meditation as a result of greater openness and sensitivity (Kornfield, 1979). Indeed, more experienced meditators state that what tends to emerge as one continues to have more and deeper experiences is an underlying calm and nonreactive equanimity so that this greater range of experiences can be observed and allowed without disturbance, defensiveness, or interference. More and more the individual identifies him- or herself with the calm observer or witness of these experiences rather than with the experiences per se (Goldstein, 1976; Ram Dass, 1978).

Many meditators, including behavioral scientists, have reported that as they continued to meditate there has been a deepening of their intellectual understanding of the statements of more advanced practitioners. It therefore appears that intellectual understanding in this area demands an experiential basis and that what was incomprehensible at one stage may subsequently become more understandable once the individual has experienced some of the meditative process.

Occasionally some of the experiences that occur may be disturbing—for example, anxiety, tension, anger, perceptual changes in sense of self and reality (Lazarus, 1976; Kennedy, 1976; Kornfield, 1979; Walsh & Roche, 1979). These may sometimes be quite intense but generally are short-lived and remit spontaneously. In many cases they seem to represent a greater sensitivity to, and emergence of, previously repressed psychological memories and conflicts. Thus the initial discomfort of experiencing them may be a necessary price for processing and discharging them.

## APPLICATIONS

The applications of Meditation can perhaps be best considered in terms of the levels and degrees of psychological intervention that are available. One useful division views such interventions in terms of three levels: therapeutic, existential, and soteriological (Wilber, 1977). The therapeutic level is essentially aimed at reducing overt pathology, whie the existential aims at confronting the givens of existence such as responsibility, finitude, death, and so forth. The soteriological level is aimed at liberation or enlightenment and, as such, has been little recognized in traditional Western models. ''We have on the psychology of liberation—nothing'' (Gordon Allport in Smith, 1976).

At the therapeutic level a considerable body of research data is available to suggest that Meditation may have a wide range of application for both psychological and somatic, particularly psychosomatic, disorders. The general picture that is emerging suggests that Meditation may enhance psychological well-being and perceptual sensitivity (for extensive reviews see Shapiro & Giber, 1978; Shapiro, 1980; Shapiro & Walsh, 1980).

Many studies have reported that Meditation reduces anxiety, either for nonspecific anxiety and anxiety neurosis (Girodo, 1974; Shapiro, 1976), or for specific phobias, such as of enclosed spaces, examinations, being alone, or of heart attack (Boudreau, 1972; French & Tupin, 1974). Clinical research has indicated that drug and alcohol use may be reduced (Shafii et al., 1975; Lazar, 1975; Benson, 1961; Benson, et al., 1972; Shapiro & Zifferblatt, 1975; Marlatt, et al., 1980), while hospitalized psychiatric patients with a variety of disorders may benefit from daily

Transcendental Meditation (Glueck & Stroebel, 1978).

There have also been reports of psychosomatic benefits. Meditation has been employed successfully for rehabilitation after myocardial infarct (Tulpule, 1971), to treat bronchial asthma and insomnia (Honsberger & Woolfolk, 1976), and to reduce high blood pressure (Daley et al., 1969; Benson & Wallace, 1972; Patel, 1975; Stone & DeLeo, 1976).

Positive effects have also been noted in healthy nonclinical populations. A number of studies have suggested that meditators change more than controls in the direction of enhanced confidence, self-esteem, sense of self-control, empathy, and self-actualization (Lesh, 1970; Nidich, Seeman, & Dreshin, 1973; Hjelle, 1974).

In summary, experimental evidence clearly indicates that Meditation may have considerable therapeutic potential. However, few definitive claims can be made and many points remain unclear. For example, many studies have been flawed by such methodological problems as the lack of adequate control groups, uncertain expectation and placebo effects, and dubious measurement procedures. Furthermore, several recent studies have suggested that Meditation may not necessarily be more effective for clinical disorders than are other self-regulation strategies such as relaxation training and self-hypnosis (Kirsch & Henry, 1979; Marlatt et al., 1980). On the other hand, in several studies subjects have reported meditation experiences to be more meaningful, pleasurable, and relaxing than those of other strategies, even where objective measures did not separate them. Patients who are most likely to benefit from Meditation are probably those who are not severely disturbed and who perceive themselves as possessing an internal locus of control.

Experimental measures also indicate greater perceptual sensitivity. Sensory thresholds, the lowest levels at which a stimulus can be detected, are lowered (Davidson et al., 1976), while the capacity for empathy

(Lesh, 1970; Leung, 1973) and field independence (Linden, 1973; Pelleteir, 1974) are increased. Thus both phenomenological and objective studies agree with classical literature that Meditation enhances perceptual sensitivity.

Meditation may also be useful for therapists. A number of subjective reports and two experimental papers (Lesh, 1970; Leung, 1973) suggest that Meditation may enhance empathic sensitivity and accuracy. The deep insights into the workings of one's own mind that Meditation provides also seem to allow for insight into, and compassion toward, the painful mental patterns that clients bring to therapy. As in many traditional Western psychotherapies, it is recognized that the meditator's own self-insight and wisdom are the limiting factors for successful help to others. Therefore, the meditator is urged to continually deepen his or her own practice as the most effective way of benefiting others.

Finally Meditation is available as a tool for those who wish to plumb the depths of their own being. Here it can be used to explore the nature of mind, identity, and consciousness, to grapple with the deepest questions of existence that any human being can confront, and to seek to ultimately transcend them all in a radical transformation of consciousness and the seeker.

For such a person Meditation provides an invaluable tool that can be used from the beginning to the very end of the quest. Such a path is not for the fainthearted, since the individual must be willing to confront any and every experience that the mind can create, and that range is vast indeed.

Although the deepest insights may occur at any moment, such a practice is usually to be reckoned in years rather than hours or even months. As Ramana Maharshi, one of the most respected Hindu teachers in the last century, noted: "Mind control is not your birthright. Those who have succeeded owe their liberation to perseverance" (Kornfield, 1977). This recognition prompted Medard Boss (1963), one of the earliest Western psychiatrists to examine meditative practices

firsthand, to comment that compared with the intensity of yogic self-exploration "even the best western training analysis is not much more than an introductory course."

Coming to full voluntary control of one's own mind has been called the art of arts and science of sciences. While this has a hyperbolic ring to it, few people who have tried it would probably disagree.

Of course one does not have to commit oneself totally to this path. All of us can explore it as little or as much as we wish and can expect proportionate benefits. Nowhere is the old maxim about getting out of something what you put into it truer than in meditation. Although initially often quite difficult, the practice is both self-reinforcing and self-fulfilling, and the progressive experiences of deepening calm, equanimity, understanding, and compassion may draw one gently and pleasurably into deeper and deeper exploration.

The thought manifests as the word, the word manifests as the deed.
The deed develops into habit, and the habit hardens into character.
So watch the thought and its ways with care
And let it spring from love born out of respect for all beings.
For all beings are One.

                                                          Anonymous

## CASE EXAMPLE

As an example of a successful outcome, I am presenting a condensation of papers describing my own meditative experiences (Walsh, 1977, 1978). Some readers may suspect that I am biased in presenting this particular case and describing it as successful. They are, of course, correct!

However, for obvious reasons I have better insight into these experiences than I do those of most other people. In addition, the practice was undertaken out of curiosity and for personal growth rather than to deal with any specific clinical problem and was pursued

more intensively and further than most westerners do. Such a report by a fellow mental
health professional may be of personal interest to readers of this volume who are considering the possibility of trying Meditation
for themselves. For those readers who wish
to see a detailed case study of Meditation
employed for a specific clinical disorder, an
excellent account is available in Shapiro
(1980).

Because parts of this account describe experiences that occurred during very intensive
continuous Meditation in retreats, many of
the experiences are far more intense and difficult than those usually encountered by people practicing for brief daily periods.

This is an account of my subjective experiences of some two years of Vipassana,
or Insight Meditation. During the first year
this practice took an average of one hour per
day; during the second this was increased to
about two hours, as well as some six weeks
of intensive meditation retreats, usually of
two week's duration. During these retreats
about 18 to 20 hours per day were spent in
continuous walking and sitting Meditation
performed in total silence and without eye
contact, reading, or writing. While this
amount of practice may be vastly less than
that of more experienced practitioners, it has
certainly proved sufficient to elicit a range
of experiences beyond the ken of day-to-day
nonmeditative living.

I began Meditation with one-half hour each
day. During the first three to six months,
there were few times during which I could
honestly say with complete certainty that I
was definitely experiencing benefits from it.
Except for the painfully obvious stiff back
and sore knees, the psychological effects
other than occasional relaxation were so subtle and ephemeral that I could never be sure
that they were more than a figment of my
wishes and expectations. The nature of Meditation seems to be, especially at first, a slow
but cumulative process, a fact that may be
useful for beginners to know.

However, with continued perseverance,
subtle effects just at the limit of my percep-

tual threshold did begin to become apparent.
I had expected the eruption into awareness
of powerful, concrete experiences that, while
perhaps not flashes of lightening and pealing
of bells, would at least be of sufficient intensity to make it very clear that I had "gotten
it," whatever "it" was. What "it" actually
turned out to be was not the appearance of
formerly nonexistent mental phenomena but
rather a gradual, incremental increase in perceptual sensitivity to the formerly subliminal
portions of my own inner stream of consciousness.

"When one sits down with eyes closed to
silence the mind, one is at first submerged
by a torrent of thoughts—they crop up every-
where like frightened, nay, aggressive rats"
(Satprem, 1968, p. 33). The more sensitive
I became, the more I was forced to recognize
that what I had formerly believed to be my
rational mind preoccupied with cognition,
planning, problem solving, and so forth, actually comprised a frantic torrent of forceful,
demanding, loud, and often unrelated
thoughts and fantasies that filled an unbelievable proportion of consciousness even
during purposive behavior. The incredible
proportion of consciousness that this fantasy
world occupied, my powerlessness to remove
it for more than a few seconds, and my former state of mindlessness or ignorance of its
existence staggered me. Interestingly this
"mindlessness" seemed much more intense
and difficult to deal with than in psychotherapy (Walsh, 1976), where the depth and
sensitivity of inner awareness seemed less,
and where the therapist provided a perceptual
focus and was available to pull me back if
I started to get lost in fantasy.

The subtlety, complexity, infinite range
and number, and entrapping power of the
fantasies that the mind creates seems impossible to comprehend, to differentiate from
reality while in them, and even more so to
describe to one who has not experienced
them. Layer upon layer of imagery and qua-
silogic open up at any point to which attention is directed. Indeed it gradually becomes
apparent that it is impossible to question and

reason one's way out of this all-encompassing fantasy since the very process of questioning, thinking, and seeking only creates
further fantasy.

The power and pervasiveness of these inner dialogues and fantasies left me amazed
that we could be so unaware of them during
our normal waking life; they reminded me
of the Eastern concept of *maya,* all-consum-
ing illusion.

### The First Meditation Retreat

The first meditation retreat, begun about one
year after commencing sitting, was a very
painful and difficult two-week affair. A
marked hypersensitivity to all stimuli, both
internal and external, rapidly developed, resulting in intense arousal, agitation, discomfort, and multiple chronic muscle contractions, especially around the shoulders.

One of my most amazing rediscoveries
during this first retreat was the incredible
proportion of time, well over 90 percent,
which I spend lost in fantasy. Most of these
fantasies were of the ego self-aggrandizing
type, so that when eventually I realized I was
in them, it proved quite a struggle to decide
to give them up and return to the breath, but
with practice this decision became slightly
easier, faster, and more automatic. This by
no means happened quickly, in fact, in the
first four or five days the proportion of time
spent in fantasy actually increased as the
Meditation deepened. During this period
each time I sat and closed my eyes I would
be immediately swept away by vivid hallucinations, losing all contact with where I was
or what I was doing until after an unknown
period of time a thought would creep in such
as, "Am I really swimming, lying on the
beach?" and so forth. Then I would either
get lost back into the fantasy or another
thought would come: "Wait a moment, I
thought I was meditating." If the latter, then
I would be left with the difficult problem of
trying to ground myself, that is, to differentiate between stimulus-produced percepts

("reality") and entirely endogenous ones
("hallucinations"). The only way this
seemed possible was to try finding the breath,
and so I would begin frantically searching
around in this hypnagogic universe for the
sensations of the breath. Such as the power
of the hallucinations that sometimes I would
be literally unable to find it and would fall
back into the fantasy. If successful, I would
recognize it and be reassured that I was in
fact meditating. Then in the next moment I
would be lost again in yet another fantasy.
The clarity, power, persuasiveness, and continuity of these hallucinations is difficult to
express adequately. However, the effect of
living through three days during which time
to close my eyes meant to lose contact almost
immediately with ordinary reality was extraordinarily draining, to say the least. Interestingly enough, while this experience was
uncomfortable and quite beyond my control,
it was not particularly frightening; if anything, the opposite. For many years I had
feared losing control if I let down defenses
and voyaged too far along the road of self-
investigation and discovery. This appears to
be a common fear in most growth traditions
and seems to serve a major defensive function. Having experienced this once-feared
outcome, it now no longer seems so terrifying. Of course, the paradox is that what
we usually call control is actually exactly the
opposite, a lack of ability to let go of defenses.

While a good 90 percent or more of this
first retreat was taken up with mindless fantasy and agitation, there did occur during the
second week occasional short-lived periods
of intense peace and tranquility. These were
so satisfying that, while I would not be willing to sign up for a lifetime in a monastery,
I could begin to comprehend the possibility
of the truth of the Buddhist saying that
"peace is the highest form of happiness."
Affective lability was also extreme. There
were not infrequently sudden apparently un-
precipitated wide mood swings to completely
polar emotions. Shorn of all my props and

distractions, it became clear that I had little more than the faintest inkling of self-control over either thoughts or feelings and that my mind had a mind of its own.

This recognition is commonly described as one of the earliest, strongest, and most surprising insights that confronts people who begin intensive meditation practice; they are always amazed that they had not recognized it previously (Goldstein, 1976).

## Attachments and Needs

It soon became apparent that the type of material that forceably erupted into awareness and disrupted concentration was most often material—ideas, fantasies, thoughts, and so on—to which I was attached (addicted) and around which there was considerable affective charge. There was a definite sense that attachments reduced the flexibility and power of the mind, since whenever I was preoccupied with a stimulus to which I was attached, I had difficulty in withdrawing my attention from it to observe other stimuli that passed through awareness.

Paradoxically, it seems that a need or attachment to be rid of a certain experience or state may lead to its perpetuation. The clearest example of this has been with anxiety. I suddenly began to experience mild anxiety attacks of unknown origin that, curiously enough, seemed to occur most often when I was feeling really good and in the presence of a particular person whom I loved. At such times I would try all my various psychological gymnastics to eradicate it since I did not want to feel anxious. However, these episodes continued for some five months in spite of or, as it actually turned out, because of, my resistance to them. During this time my meditation practice deepened, and I was able to examine more and more of the process during Meditation. What I discovered was that I had considerable fear of fear; my mind therefore surveyed in a radarlike fashion all endogenous and exogenous stimuli for their fear-evoking potential and all reactions for any fear component. There was a continuous mental scanning process preset in an exquisitely sensitive fashion for the detection of anything resembling fear. Consequently there were a considerable number of false positives, that is, nonfearful stimuli and reactions that were interpreted as being fearful or potentially fear provoking. Since the reactions to the false positives themselves comprised fear and fear components, there was of course an immediate chain reaction set up with one fear response acting as the stimulus for the next. It thus became very clear that my fear of, and resistance to, fear was exactly what was perpetuating it.

This insight and the further application of meditative awareness to the process certainly reduced but did not eradicate these episodes entirely. Paradoxically, they still tended to recur when I felt very calm and peaceful. It was not until the middle of the next meditation retreat that the reasons for this became clear. After the first few days of pain and agitation, I began to feel more and more peaceful. There came a sitting in which I could feel my Meditation deepen perceptibly and the restless mental scanning slow more and more. Then as the process continued to deepen and slow, I was literally jolted by a flash of agitation and anxiety accompanying this thought: "But what do I do now if there's no more anxiety to look for?" It was apparent that if I continued to quieten, there would be neither anxiety to scan for nor a scanning process itself, and my need to get rid of anxiety demanded that I have a continuous scanning mechanism, and the presence of the mechanism in turn created the presence of anxiety. My "but what do I do now?" fear had very effectively removed the possibility of the dissipation of both, and its occurrence at a time when I was feeling most peaceful, relaxed, and safe of course explained why I had been subject to these anxiety episodes at the apparently paradoxical times when I felt best. It appears that within the mind, if you need to be rid of certain experiences, then not only are you likely to experience a number of false positives but you may also need to have them around continuously so you can keep getting rid of them. Thus within the province of the mind, what you resist is what you get.

## Perception

With continued practice the speed, power, loudness, and continuity of thoughts and fantasies began to slowly diminish, leaving subtle sensations of greater peace and quiet. After a period of about four or five months there occurred episodes in which I would open my eyes at the end of Meditation and look at the outside world without the presence of concomitant internal dialogue. This state would be rapidly terminated by a rising sense of anxiety and anomie accompanied by the thought "I don't know what anything means." Thus I could be looking at something completely familiar, such as a tree, a building, or the sky, and yet without an accompanying internal dialogue to label and categorize it, it seemed totally strange and devoid of meaning. It seems that what made something familiar and hence secure was not simply its recognition, but the actual cognitive process of matching, categorizing, and labeling it. Once this was done, then more attention and reactivity was focused on the label and labeling process rather than on the stimulus itself. Thus the initial fantasy and thought-free periods may feel both strange and distinctly unpleasant; we are at first punished by their unfamiliarity. We have created an unseen prison for ourselves whose bars are comprised of thoughts and fantasies of which we remain largely unaware unless we undertake intensive perceptual training. Moreover, if they are removed we may be frightened by the unfamiliarity of the experience and rapidly reinstate them. "We uphold the world with our internal dialogue" (Castaneda, 1974).

Presumably this labeling process must modify our perception in many ways, including reducing our ability to experience each stimulus fully, richly, and newly, by reducing its multidimensional nature into a lesser dimensional cognitive labeling framework. This must necessarily derive from the past, be less tolerant of ambiguity, less here now, and perpetuative of a sense of sameness and continuity to the world. This process may represent the phenomenological and cognitive mediational basis of Deikman's (1966) concept of automatization and Don Juan's "maintaining the world as we know it" (Castaneda, 1971, 1974).

Interestingly, the extent of reaction to the stimulus itself as opposed to the label seems to be a direct function of the degree of mindfulness or meditative awareness. If I am mindful, then I tend to be focused on the primary sensations themselves, to label less, and to react to these labels less. For example, there was a period of about six weeks during which I felt mildly depressed. I was not incapacitated but was uncomfortable, dysphoric, and confused about what was happening to me throughout most of the waking day. However, during daily Meditation this experience and its affective quality changed markedly. The experience then felt somewhat like being on sensory overload, with many vague ill-defined somatic sensations and a large number of rapidly appearing and disappearing unclear visual images. However, to my surprise, nowhere could I find stimuli that were actually painful. Rather there was just a large input of vague stimuli of uncertain significance and meaning. I would therefore emerge from each sitting with the recognition that I was actually not experiencing any pain and was feeling considerably better. This is analogous to Tarthang Tulku's (1974) statement that "The more you go into the disturbance—when you really get there—the emotional characteristics no longer exist."

However, within a very short time I would lapse once more into my habitual nonmindful state. When I next became mindful once again I would find that I had been automatically labeling the stimulus complex as depression and then reacting to this label with thoughts and feelings such as "I'm depressed. I feel awful, what have I done to deserve this?'' A couple of moments of relaxed mindfulness would be sufficient to switch the focus back to the primary sensations and the recognition once again that I was actually not experiencing discomfort. This process repeated itself endlessly during each day. This effect of mindfulness or phenomenology and reactivity should lend itself to experimental neurophysiological investigation. It is also an interesting example of one difference in the therapeutic processes of Meditation and traditional Western therapies. Where the latter attempt to change the content of experience, Meditation is also interested in changing the perceptual-cognitive processes by which the mind produces such experiences.

## Perceptual Sensitivity

One of the most fundamental changes has been an increase in perceptual sensitivity, which seems to include both absolute and discrimination thresholds. Examples of this include both a more subtle awareness of previously known precepts and a novel identification of previously unrecognized phenomena.

Sensitivity and clarity frequently seem enhanced following a meditation sitting or retreat. Thus, for example, at these times it seems that I can discriminate visual forms and outlines more clearly. It also feels as though empathy is significantly increased and that I am more aware of other people's subtle behaviors, vocal intonations, and so forth, as well as my own affective responses to them. The experience feels like having a faint but discernible veil removed from my eyes, a veil comprised of hundreds of subtle thoughts and feelings. Each one of these thoughts and feelings seems to act as a competing stimulus, or "noise," that thus reduces sensitivity to any one object. Thus, after Meditation any specific stimulus appears stronger and clearer, presumably because the signal/noise ratio is increased. These observations provide a phenomeno-

logical basis and possible perceptual mechanism to explain the findings that meditators in general tend to exhibit heightened perceptual sensitivity and empathy.

One unexpected demonstration of greater sensitivity has been the occurrence of the synesthetic perception of thoughts. Synesthesia, or cross-modality perception, is the phenomenon in which stimulation of one sensory modality is perceived in other modalities, as, for example, when sound is seen and felt as well as heard (Marks, 1975). Following the enhanced perceptual sensitivity that occurred during my prior psychotherapy, I began to experience this phenomenon not infrequently, suggesting that it may well occur within all of us though usually below our thresholds (Walsh, 1976). Now during moments of greater meditative sensitivity I have begun to experience this cross-modality perception with purely mental stimuli—with thoughts, for example. Thus, I may initially experience a thought as a feeling and subsequently become aware of a visual image before finally recognizing the more familiar cognitive information components.

Another novel type of perception seems to have occurred with continued practice; I have gradually found myself able to recognize increasingly subtle mental phenomena when I am not meditating but rather am involved in my daily activity. This has resulted in an increased recognition of affects, motivations, and subtle defensive maneuvers and manipulations. Indeed these latter recognitions now seem to constitute the sensitivity-limiting factor, since the discomfort that attends their more frequent perception is often sufficient to result in a defensive contraction of awareness.

## Trust and Surrender

These experiences have led to a greater understanding of and willingness to surrender to the meditative process. In the West, surrender has connotations of succumbing or being overwhelmed, but with increasing experience I have begun to surrender to the process in the sense of trusting, following, and allowing it to unfold without attempting to change, coerce, or manipulate it and without necessarily requiring prior understanding of what I may be about to go through or predicting the outcome. Thus, for example, one of my major fears has been the threat of losing certain psychological and intellectual abilities—for example, of losing intellectual skills, scientific capacities, and control. This seems reminiscent of Fadiman's (1977) statement that one of the major barriers to moving on to the next level is the fear of losing what we have.

Although I must emphasize that this surrender is far from complete for me, I have come a long way. The experiences that have contributed to this surrender are as follows. First of all, to the best of my knowledge the feared catastrophies have not eventuated. My intellectual and scientific skills seem to have remained intact. In addition, Meditation seems to have provided a range of experiences, insights, and developments formerly totally unknown to me. Thus, to expect, demand, and limit learning to extensions of that which is already known can prove a major limitation. As both Bugental (1965) and Rajneesh (1975) indicate, growth is always a voyage into the unknown.

Furthermore, it now seems clear that allowing experiences to be as they are and experiencing them without forcibly trying to change them is effective. This is especially true when it is recognized that any experience can be used for growth even to the point of perceiving the experience as necessary and perfect for the process. Indeed, recognizing the perfection and functionality of each experience appears to be a highly productive perspective for several reasons. First, it reduces the deleterious agitation, resistance, and eruption of defenses and manipulations that occur secondary to judgment and negative perspectives. Second, contrary to my previous beliefs, acceptance and a nonjudgmental attitude toward an experience or situation do not necessarily remove either the motivation or capacity to deal with it in the most effective manner. (My prior beliefs were that I *needed* my judgments, aversions, and negative reactions in order to power my motivation to modify the situations and stimuli eliciting them.) It should be noted here that the experience of perfection is just that, an experience. This may say more about the psychological state of the individual perceiving it than about the stimulus per se and may not necessarily in any way vitiate the perceiver's perception of the need to modify it. Finally, there has been the recognition that the great meditation teachers really knew what they were talking about. Time and time again I have read descriptions, explanations, and predictions about Meditation, the normal psychological state, the states that arise with more and more Meditation, latent capacities, and so forth, and have scoffed and argued against them, feeling that they were just so removed from my experiences and beliefs that they could not possibly be true. However, I have now had a variety of experiences that I formerly would have believed to be impossible and have gained the experiential background with which to understand more of what is being taught. I now have to acknowledge that these people know vastly more than I do and that it is certainly worth my while to pay careful attention to their suggestions. Thus experiential knowledge may be a major limiting factor for intellectual understanding of psychological processes and consciousness; even highly intellectually sophisticated nonpractitioners may not fully understand such phenomena.

## SUMMARY

Meditation is a 3,000-year-old "innovative psychotherapy," which across centuries and cultures has been held to be capable of leading to the summa of human psychological development. Its recent discovery by the West has meant that millions of Westerners have joined tens of millions of nonwesterners in this practice. However, in the West its most popular application has been for relaxation and stress management rather than for the deeper psychological insight and altered states of consciousness for which it is most frequently used in the East.

Empirical research has clearly demonstrated significant psychological, physiological, and chemical effects of Meditation. It has also been clearly demonstrated to be an effective treatment for a variety of psychological and psychosomatic disorders, although it remains less clear whether it is more effective for these purposes than are other self-regulation strategies, such as relaxation training and self-hypnosis. Occasional studies report significant and unique psychophysiological effects in advanced practitioners, but in general the effects that meditation was originally designed to induce, such as subtle shifts in perception and consciousness, remain largely untested by Western empirical approaches.

This is regretable in that Meditation challenges some of the most fundamental assumptions and paradigms of Western behavioral sciences. For example, its claim that our usual state of consciousness is suboptimal and that our usual perception is clouded and distorted to an unrecognized degree runs counter to our basic assumptions that our usual state is best. Similarly, Meditation suggests the existence of true higher states of consciousness and claims that these are realizable through training. In the West, since we regard the usual state as best, there is no space for anything better. These claims are so fundamentally divergent from our usual assumptions that until recently they were dismissed as nonsensical. However, it is clear that we can no longer afford to dismiss such statements so casually. A growing network of concepts and data points to their possible validity and has already begun to shift our own assumptive framework.

Meditation may offer several advantages over many clinical interventions and self-regulation strategies. First of all, it is certainly cheap. The practitioner is independent of location and instruments and can practice as much or as little as desired. As a self-therapy

or self-regulation strategy there is very little difficulty with dependency. In fact, there is relatively little need for professional time and energy once the basic practice has been established. It has a wide range of application, being useful for certain clinical difficulties as well as for psychological growth at all levels. Casualties are rare, and both clients and therapists may find it beneficial. It can be used as a useful adjunct to more traditional therapies and, last but not least, it is often very enjoyable.

These are unusual claims: a cheap, widely applicable, relatively harmless, enjoyable self-regulation strategy, useful for both clinical difficulties and the heights of psychological well-being! Are these claims valid? All meditation traditions would agree that the ultimate test is to try it for oneself. In the words of an ancient Tibetan sage: "To see if this be true, look within your own mind."

## REFERENCES

Alexander, F. Buddhistic training as an artificial catatonia (the biological meaning of psychic occurences). *Psychoanalytic Review*, 1931, **18**, 129–145.

Boss, M. *A psychiatrist discovers India*. New York: Basic Books, 1963.

Bugental, J. F. T. *The Search for authenticity: An existential analytic approach to psychotherapy*. New York: Holt, 1965.

Byrom, T. *The dhammapada: The sayings of the Buddha*. New York: Vintage, 1976.

Castaneda, C. *Tales of power*. New York: Simon & Schuster, 1974.

Deikman, A. Deautomatization and the mystic experience. *Psychiatry*, 1966, **29**, 324–338.

Deikman, A. Comments on the GAP report on mysticism. *Journal of Nervous and Mental Disease*, 1977, **165**, 213–217.

Elgin, D. *Voluntary simplicity*. New York: 1980.

Fadiman, J. Talk given at Frontiers of Transpersonal Psychology meeting, San Francisco, February 1977.

Freud, S. *Civilization and its discontents*. New York: Norton, 1962.

Goldstein, J. *The experience of insight*. Santa Cruz, Calif.: Unity Press, 1976.

Goleman, D. *The varieties of the meditative experience*. New York: Dutton, 1977.

Group for the Advancement of Psychiatry. *Mysticism: Spiritual quest or psychic disorder?* New York: Group for the Advancement of Psychiatry, 1976.

Kornfield, J. *Living Buddhist masters.* Santa Cruz, Calif.: Unity Press, 1977.

Kornfield, J. Intensive insight meditation: A phenomenological study. *Journal of Transpersonal Psychology,* 1979, **11,** 41–58.

Krippner, S. and Brown, D. Altered states of consciousness and mystical-religious experiences. *Journal of the Academy of Religion Psych. Research,* 1979, **2,** 93–110.

Kuhn, T. S. *The structure of scientific revolutions,* 2nd ed. Chicago: University of Chicago Press, 1970.

Levine, S. *A gradual awakening.* New York: Anchor, 1979.

Marks, L. E. On colored-hearing synesthesia: Cross modal translations of sensory dimensions. *Psychological Bulletin,* 1975, **82,** 303–331.

Nidich, S., Seeman, W. and Dreshin, T. Influence of transcendental meditation: A replication. *Journal of Counsel. Psychol.,* 1973, **20,** 565–566.

Rajneesh, B. S. *The way of the white cloud.* Poona, India: Rajneesh Center, 1975.

Ram Dass. *The only dance there is.* New York: Doubleday, 1975.

Ram Dass. *Journey of awakening: A meditator's guidebook.* New York: Doubleday, 1978.

Satprem. *Sri Aurobindo, or the adventure of consciousness.* New York: Harper & Row, 1968.

Schumacher, E. F. *A guide for the perplexed.* New York: Harper & Row, 1977.

Shapiro, D. *Precision nirvana: An owner's manual for the care and maintenance of the mind.* Englewood Cliffs, N.J.: Prentice-Hall, 1978.

Shapiro, D. *Meditation: Self regulation strategy and altered states of consciousness.* New York: Aldine, 1980.

Shapiro, D. and Giber, D. Meditation: Self control strategy and altered states of consciousness. *Archives of General Psychiatry,* 1978. **35,** 294–302.

Shapiro, D. and Walsh, R. (Eds.). *The science of meditation: Theory, research, and practice.* New York: Aldine, 1980.

Tart, C. *States of consciousness.* New York: Dutton, 1975.

Tarthang Tulku. On thoughts. *Crystal Mirror,* 1974, **3,** 7–20.

Tulpule, T. E. Yogic exercises in the management of ischaemic heart disease. *Indian Heart Journal,* 1971, **23,** 259–264.

Walsh, R. N. Reflections on psychotherapy. *Journal of Transpersonal Psychology,* 1976, **8,** 100–111.

Walsh, R. Initial meditative experiences: I. *Journal of Transpersonal Psychology,* 1977, **9,** 151–192.

Walsh, R. Initial meditative experiences: II. *Journal of Transpersonal Psychology,* 1978, **10,** 2–28.

Walsh, R. Meditation research: An introduction and review. *Journal of Transpersonal Psychology,* 1979, **11,** ???

Walsh, R. The consciousness disciplines and the behavioral sciences. *Journal of American Psychiatry,* 1980 (in Press).

Walsh, R. and Roche, L. Precipitation of acute psychotic episodes by intensive meditation in individuals with a history of schizophrenia. *American Journal of Psychiatry,* 1979, **136,** 1085–1086.

Walsh, R. and Shapiro, D. (Eds.). *Beyond health and normality: Explorations of extreme psychological well-being.* New York: Van Nostrand, 1980.

Walsh, R. and Vaughan, F. (Eds.). *Beyond ego: Transpersonal dimensions in psychology.* Los Angeles: J.P. Tarcher, 1980a.

Walsh, R. and Vaughan, F. Beyond the ego: Towards transpersonal models of the person and psychotherapy. *Journal of Humanist. Psychol.,* 1980b (in Press).

Wilber, K. *The Spectrum of Consciousness.* Wheaton, Ill.: Theosophical Publishing House, 1977.

Wilber, K. *The Atman Project.* Wheaton, Ill.: Quest, 1980.

# CHAPTER 35

# *Morita Psychotherapy*

DAVID K. REYNOLDS*

*I was quite fortunate in being able to persuade David K. Reynolds to write this chapter on Morita Therapy as well as the one on Naikan. I was very eager to get some Asian systems in this book, and through the efforts of my friend Dr. Paul B. Pedersen I eventually was able to persuade Dr. Reynolds to contribute the two chapters.*

*Morita is quite similar to an almost completely forgotten rest treatment approach to the treatment of neurotic conditions, originally developed by Dr. S. Wier Mitchell, a psychiatrist who died in 1914. From one point of view both systems involve regression to infancy. From another point of view Morita is a stern injunction that people should do their duty and accept their feelings.*

*In the next chapter, the perceptive reader will learn that many apparently complicated systems essentially are based on simple injunctions about life, such as "Do your duty" or "Suffer without complaining." Here is a simple, novel, and workable system applicable to any society.*

Morita Psychotherapy is a Buddhist-based treatment for neurosis developed in Japan by Shoma Morita, a psychiatrist, around the turn of this century. Through verbal instruction and guided activity the therapy aims at teaching the patient to accept his or her symptoms as part of everyday reality. The patient learns to live a constructive life in spite of feelings of shyness, anxiety, tension, and fears.

## HISTORY

The first paper on Morita Therapy appeared in 1917. It outlined a treatment method developed during the previous 15 years by a Japanese psychiatrist named Morita. A graduate of Tokyo University and chairman of the department of psychiatry and neurology at Jikei University School of Medicine, Morita was influenced by both Eastern and West-

ern treatment modalities. His method grew out of his personal experience as a self-cured neurotic, his practical experience treating Japanese patients, and his familiarity with contemporary Western modes of treatment.

As a young man Morita suffered from a variety of neurotic complaints, including inability to concentrate, death anxiety, palpitations, and gastrointestinal complaints. The more he struggled with himself in an attempt to overcome these problems, the deeper he found himself enmeshed in them. Only after "giving up" on the struggle and focusing on the tasks at hand did his symptoms recede. Morita began applying the same approach to his patients, generally treating them in his home so that they could see the working out of his thought in everyday life.

Specific techniques were borrowed from S. Wier Mitchell's system of absolute bed rest and Paul Dubois's method of regulated living, but these external forms were put to different uses. For example, Wier Mitchell

*Case material by Radmila Moacamin

**489**

saw neurosis as a physiological exhaustion of the nervous system that required long-term bed rest for recuperation. Morita used the bed-rest method, but he, like Freud, perceived the essentially psychological nature of neurosis and so employed bed rest in order to affect the mental state of his patients.

Following Morita's death in 1938, students and former patients carried on the treatment method within an inpatient setting. After World War II outpatient treatment became increasingly popular among Morita therapists, although Moritist hospitals have not yet disappeared from the scene. In the late 1960s a nationwide Moritist mental health organization emerged with chapters in all the major cities of Japan. Called Seikatsu no Hakkenkai (literally "The Discovery of Life Organization"), this movement is now the most powerful force for uniting practitioners, developing theory, and training new therapists.

Historically, Morita Therapy has moved from a narrow inpatient focus to encompass outpatient therapy, group therapy, public education, and recently, therapy by correspondence and cassette tapes. Similarly, the power base has moved from Jikei University to several Japanese universities (Kyushu, Okayama, and Hamamatsu) and finally, out of the university system altogether into the public organization mentioned above. Correspondingly, the initial core of psychiatrists (e.g., Nomura, Noda, Kora, and Suzuki) has been augmented by communications professionals, psychologists, physicians in other specialties, and laypersons who have had personal experience with Morita's methods (Morita & Mizutani, 1956).

Similar trends may be seen in the broadened definitions of which sorts of patients may be appropriately treated by this therapy (see "Applications" section). Furthermore, widening theoretical perspectives have gradually permitted other therapies (such as chemotherapy, hypnosis, Behavior Therapy, and autogenic training) to be used in conjunction with this method (Yokoyama, 1968; Ohara & Reynolds, 1968).

In sum, Morita Therapy has been able to maintain a core theory and practice while adapting to the extreme sociocultural changes in Japan over the past 60 years. It was introduced in the United States in the late 1940s. Classical Freudians did not accept it because it refused to deal directly with the unconscious (Jacobsen & Berenberg, 1952), but it received a more sympathetic reception among neo-Freudians such as Karen Horney (Kondo, 1953). Formal training of American psychiatrists, psychologists, and social workers in Morita Therapy began in the early 1970s at the University of Southern California School of Medicine (Reynolds, 1976). Although English-language articles on the subject have existed for 30 years, the first book in English on Morita Psychotherapy appeared in 1976 (Reynolds, 1976).

## CURRENT STATUS

Morita Therapy is currently being practiced on an inpatient basis in some 33 hospitals and clinics in Japan. In addition, therapists at these facilities treat *outpatients* with the method, as do physicians at several university outpatient clinics (among them Jikei University, Hamamatsu University, and Okayama University). The national Seikatsu no Hakkenkai organization has a membership of over 3,000. The central office of Hakkenkai is in Tokyo. Fifty-two local chapters meet monthly throughout Japan with supplemental retreats and training courses offered widely.

There is a vast literature on the subject in Japanese. A number of scholarly and popular books dealing with Morita Therapy appear each year. The Hakkenkai organization publishes a monthly magazine, and several Moritist hospitals also put out magazines for patients and former patients.

The impact of Morita's ideas on psychotherapy in Japan cannot be accurately assessed by the number of psychotherapists who call themselves Morita therapists. Just as Freud's ideas have permeated the psychotherapeutic establishment in the West, providing a reference point for agreement or dissent, so Morita's ideas have provided a benchmark for practice in Japan even though the number of trained Morita therapists probably is less than 100.

In the United States nearly 100 psychiatrists, clinical psychologists, and social workers have received some formal training in Morita Therapy. Only a handful of practitioners have had direct supervision, however. Until 1979 training was centered at the University of Southern California School of Medicine. Currently, there are Morita therapists practicing on an outpatient basis in the Los Angeles, San Francisco, and Houston areas. Because there is no formal organization of Moritists in the United States and no systematic correspondence among them, it is possible that the method is being practiced elsewhere in this country as well.

## THEORY

The flow of awareness and attention is the basis of understanding neurosis and psychotherapy, because that flow is all that any of us knows. The stream of consciousness normally flows from topic to topic in concert with the requirements of the situations in which we find ourselves. Each moment brings ongoing or fresh ''tasks'' that require our attention and appropriate response. These ''tasks'' may be weeding a garden, following a conversation, daydreaming, writing an article, planning a vacation, answering a telephone, and the like. The awareness of a mature individual recognizes these tasks and loses itself in them. The healthy person finds himself immersed in constructive activity (including the constructive behaviors of napping, recreation, and so forth).

The flow of awareness in the neurotic person is blocked and turned inward, away from the circumstances in which he finds himself. The neurotic person is characteristically *self*-centered in the sense that he is attending to internal events—shyness, fear, sadness, feelings of abandonment or inferiority—rather

than to the environment. He may be living in a world of unreality; not the unreality of the psychotic world, but the unreality of ''I wish,'' ''if only she had,'' ''I shouldn't have,'' ''what if,'' and so forth (Reynolds, 1980). Again, attention has drifted from what *is* to what could happen or what did not happen. The beginning of realistic change comes with acceptance of what is. Acceptance of reality is not passive, it is the only first step for active intervention in the world. The neurotic person, however, faces not reality but perfectionistic ideals, abstract possibilities, and his own feeling states.

Thus far, the argument has been written as if there were neurotic and healthy *persons*. To be more precise, there are neurotic and healthy periods of time for all of us. We all experience moments of blocking and freezing of our thoughts. We all have periods of dysfunctional self-consciousness. The internal struggle to make oneself *want* to get out of bed on a cold morning or the effort involved in *trying* to create inspiration as one sits before the typewriter are examples of neurotic moments. The discomfort as conversation dwindles over dinner with a new acquaintance or the spiral into passive misery as one sits at home alone trying to decide what to do that evening are further examples of the turning inward of attention away from awareness of and commitment to the requirements of the situation. In essence, the neurotic person has more neurotic moments and blocks over a wider variety of situations than the healthy person, but qualitatively his experience is not unlike that of the normal person.

The normal person feels a range of emotions, as does his neurotic counterpart, but he does not allow the emotions to interfere with his doing what he perceives needs to be done in most situations. Moritists make a clear distinction between feelings, moods, and thoughts on the one hand, and behaviors on the other. Feelings are not controllable directly by one's will. They arise from nothingness, as do thoughts, and they pass away in time unless they are restimulated behaviorally. Put more concretely, there are times when we believe we can pinpoint the source of a feeling or mood, but it is likely that similar circumstances may have provoked a different emotion in the past, and often we cannot find an apparent origin for a mood. So Moritists take feelings as "givens" in a way no Freudian would find acceptable. Similarly, thoughts seem to bubble to the surface of our minds and pass away to be replaced by other thoughts. One begins an utterance without knowing precisely how the sentence is to end, yet word follows word, appearing from chaos. If we have no direct control over such internal events, we have no responsibility for them (i.e., *all* feelings are acceptable), and our best strategy for dealing with terror, panic, depression, joy, lack of confidence, timidity, and the like is to accept them as part of the reality of the moment in which they appear. Thus, the Moritist gives "permission" to the patient to feel as he feels. What else can he do? There is no need to struggle with this side of the self.

In contrast, *behavior* is controllable at all times despite what one is feeling. This position holds that one is morally, socially, and personally responsible for what one *does,* regardless of whatever feelings are present. Neither Americans nor Japanese customarily make clear conceptual distinctions between feelings and behaviors. And often when distinctions are made, feelings are cited as excuses for acts that are harmful to the self or to others. Such statements have no meaning within the Moritist system. When one has the experiential sense (not a mere intellectual understanding) based on practice of the principle that behavior is controllable despite one's emotional state (read: despite the presence of symptoms) a new condition of freedom occurs. One is free to feel the depths of anger at an impolite bus driver, love for a charming student, fright at a horror film, because one knows that one's *behavior* is under control and will not produce some act that will cause embarrassment or other trouble. A basic trust in one's ability to behave appropriately in each moment grows out of a history of behaving appropriately, not before.

This trust exemplifies the principle that links feelings and behavior in Moritist theory. The principle is that behavior indirectly influences feeling. By behaving in a loving, caring way toward some person or animal or plant, the feelings of love and concern begin to emerge. Confidence in behavior control comes after repeated experiences of controlling behavior, not before. The client works out his or her own cure in Morita Therapy.

In a sense, one can say that when the patient is not attending to depressed or anxious feelings, he is not depressed or anxious. Most of life is not experienced as happy or sad or pleasant or lonely. We spend most of our existence attending to the moment's task without any awareness of our feeling states at all. Such a condition is normal.

It is important to emphasize that Morita therapists do not propose that patients should attempt to ignore or deny their feelings. Emotions are to be recognized and accepted as they are when they appear in awareness. Then the patient is to go about doing what needs to be done regardless of the feelings. He is to build his life on behavior that is directly controllable by his will.

There is a third principle to be added to acceptance of feelings and control of behavior; it is recognition of purpose. This principle is the formal expression of the attention to what needs to be done in any given situation. Feelings may provide information about what needs to be done, and recognition of the situational requirements guides one's behavior. The three principles are linked in this way but remain conceptually separate.

Finally, Moritist theory offers some broad explanation for why some people become neurotic. This explanation applies particularly to one type of neurosis common in Japan called *shinkeishitsu* (see "Applications" section) but may have broader application, as well. Briefly put, the neurotic person is considered to have a surplus of the need to actualize the self, to succeed in life. This excess may have roots in genetic disposition and in childrearing practices. In any case, the neurotic person perceives that what he wishes to do and be is in conflict with his actual limitations (much as Karen Horney's neurotic struggles between his ideal self and real self). He becomes obsessed with the limitations of the self rather than the potentials of the situation.

Just as Freud used hysteria as a model for the development of his theory of neurosis, so Morita used obsession as the model for his theory. All neurosis is a kind of obsession with the self. Moritist theory holds that when this strong need to achieve and excel is properly channeled so that attention is directed away from the self to the accomplishment of each moment's tasks, the neurotic person has the potential of becoming not merely a normal human being but a superior one.

## METHODOLOGY

Morita therapists are explicitly directive. They are teachers, experienced guides who, for the most part, have surmounted their own self-imposed limitations through this method (Reynolds & Yamamoto, 1973). Although the therapist offers authoritative advice, he does express genuine interest in the patient. Avoiding a cold, authoritarian approach, he seeks to establish rapport knowing that a positive relationship will facilitate the therapy process. Nevertheless, the therapist cannot directly control his own feelings of likes or dislikes for certain patients. Much less can he control the patient's feelings for him. So he goes on with instruction in the Moritist lifeway whatever the relationship. The therapist, like the patient, must know his behavioral purpose and cling to it.

Inpatient treatment by Morita Therapy is not practiced in the United States, and it appears to be on the decline in Japan. It is time-consuming (lasting several months or longer in recent times), relatively expensive, and necessary only for severely disturbed neurotics who cannot work or study under normal circumstances.

A detailed description of inpatient treatment may be found in *Morita Psychotherapy* (Reynolds, 1976). Briefly, its chief characteristics include absolute isolated bed rest and guided work therapy. Absolute isolated bed rest involves a week of bed rest with no reading, writing, television, or other diversions. Only three meals a day and the carrying out of necessary bodily functions are permitted. The patient must lie alone with his own thoughts and feelings. There is no escape from the task of coming to terms with the self. He must accept himself with all his limitations. He observes the capriciousness and the natural decline of his own feelings. And he realizes that isolation and extended inactivity are unnatural and unpleasant. At the end of a week he is quite bored and eager to involve himself in work, that is, in the losing of himself in various tasks. Other inpatient treatment techniques are similar to those used in the outpatient setting (Kora, 1965).

Outpatient treatment as practiced in Japan and the United States has a broader appeal and is more economical for patient and for practitioner. Treatment begins with the therapist listening to the patient's account of the troubling symptoms. It proceeds in an instructional mode with the therapist explaining the principles of the natural decline of feelings unless they are restimulated, the controllability of behavior despite one's emotional state, and so forth. Examples, demonstrations, and illustrations are taken from everyday life to insure that the patient understands intellectually what he is to do.

The patient may then be required to keep a diary. The diary format may vary somewhat, but the one in common use in the United States involves dividing a sheet of paper in half lengthwise and writing on one side of the page what was done at a particular time. Opposite that entry the patient writes what he felt and thought at that time. At least a page a day is written. The diary is brought to the weekly therapy sessions for the therapist's inspection and comment. Through diary guidance the patient gains the ability to analyze his daily life into the categories of controllable and uncontrollable aspects. Furthermore, he begins to see that much of what we do is done because there is something that must be done, not because the activity and our feelings or desires to do the activity necessarily correspond. The patient perceives the fluctuation of his unstable feeling states and the possibility of steady behavior in spite of that fluctuation. The diary becomes a permanent record of what he was able to do in spite of his fears or tension or other misery.

In similar fashion the patient may be asked to describe in detail the events of the recent past. Neurotic persons tend to describe their world in global generalities and broad abstractions—"All this week I felt terrible," "No one cares about me at all," "Yesterday I didn't do anything." The therapist forces the patient to examine minute details of the morning of the therapy session, for example. Questions might include: What side of bed did you get up on? Did you put on slippers? Which hand did you use to throw off the covers? In what order did you wash your body in the shower? and so forth. Knowing that he will be quizzed by the therapist, the patient begins to observe his everyday behavior and surroundings. He is being brought out of focus on himself into "reality." He may realize that while he showered and brushed his teeth he was not noticing whether he felt good or bad. He may begin to recognize the waves of feeling, the variation in what seemed an overwhelming constancy before.

Readings may be assigned or specific tasks. In lieu of a fee I may ask some of my patients to bring me something they have made while feeling depressed or tense or lonely. Thus they get the experience of constructive activity and fulfillment of a social debt while feeling bad.

The principles of Morita Therapy, as stated above, are neither complex nor many in number. Therapy sessions focus on the application of these understandings and suggestions for living to the patient's daily life. The applications, of course, are numberless. But after a few months of therapy(and even sooner for some) the patient has a pretty good idea of what the therapist will say in a given situation. In other words, the patient perceives what needs to be done in given life situations. Only the patient can do what is necessary. The result of the repetitions in therapy is that there is a gradual decline in the need to meet. Interest can be sustained somewhat longer by role reversals in which the therapist asks the patient what he would suggest to a patient who came in with this or that complaint.

When the patient responds to each life situation with the cognitive process "What needs to be done now?" "Hmmm, now I'm feeling anxious (sad, excited, pleased, terrified). That's interesting. What needs to be done now?" and then goes about doing what needs to be done, he is no longer in need of further work on Morita Therapy. Long before this ideal state is reached a natural termination of therapy will occur. The patient will have realized that there is nothing further to learn from the teacher/therapist. The patient's own effort in applying the principles will result in further progress.

## APPLICATIONS

The Japanese patients for whom Morita Therapy was devised were said to be suffering from *shinkeishitsu* neuroses. *Shinkeishitsu* neuroses are characterized by a strong desire to get rid of symptoms and by perfectionism, idealism, and extreme self-centeredness (Kora & Ohara, 1973). These neurotics are usually brighter than normal with better than average school histories. Initial difficulties in living generally occur during the junior or senior high school and usually worsen until treatment despite the patient's strong efforts to control the symptoms. *Shinkeishitsu* neuroses are of three subtypes: obsessions and phobias, anxiety neuroses, and neurasthenia. The most common symptom complex treated in Moritist hospitals and clinics involves a sort of social phobia called *taijin kyofusho*. This social phobia begins in adolescence and takes the form of sensitivity to what others are thinking about oneself, concern with where to look when conversing, worries about blushing, trembling, and general discomfort around social superiors and persons of the opposite sex. This extreme shyness may make difficult such activities as riding in buses or trains, shopping, attending classes, going to work, and dating. Such patients in Japan and in the United States respond most satisfactorily to Morita's style of treatment.

Perhaps two-thirds of the patients treated in Moritist clinics and hospitals are in their teens and twenties. The remaining one-third are mostly middle-aged. The clients suffer from a variety of neurotic complaints not unlike those found in most clinics in the United States.

Psychotics and depressives are treated with medication and Morita Therapy. Customarily, sociopaths, children, addicts, and mentally retarded persons are not treated by this method. The clients, however, need not be highly verbal, and neither a high level of formal education nor cultural sophistication in the client is necessary.

In the United States a variety of neurotics and mild schizophrenics have been effectively treated, the latter with concomittant psychopharmacological intervention. At the University of California at Los Angeles, Andrew Kumasaka, a psychiatry resident, and Millie Warwick, a nurse, have begun to apply Morita's ideas to treatment of the long-term physically ill patient and patients in chronic pain. Dr. Karem Monsour and his staff of the Student Counseling Services at the Claremont Colleges have focused on adolescent study problems. Radmila Moacanin, a psychiatric social worker at the Los Angeles County General Hospital-U.S.C. Adult Psychiatric Outpatient Clinic, has used Morita Therapy as a primary and adjunct treatment form in her practice.

It might be noted that commitment to a Buddhist belief system is not required of the patient. Suitably translated, "accepting reality as it is" can be taken to mean "accepting God's will as it is." A doctoral dissertation by Brian Ogawa (1979) at the San Francisco Theological Seminary examines the implications of Moritist thought for pastoral counseling and Christian clients.

The highly motivated client is likely to do well in most therapies; Morita Therapy is no exception. Particularly because the burden of living out the instructions lies with the patient, those with high secondary gain from their symptoms are unlikely to continue with a therapist who uses a Moritist approach.

## CASE EXAMPLE

A question has been raised by Jacobsen and Berenberg (1952), Levy (1965), Kumasaka (1965), and others concerning the effectiveness of Morita Therapy outside the Japanese cultural milieu. The issue can perhaps best be considered a testable hypothesis. Rather than reject Moritist methods on a priori grounds, we have begun treating Western patients and evaluating results. This section describes the therapy course of the first patient treated by Morita Therapy at the University of Southern California Adult Psychiatric Outpatient Clinic. Radmila Moacanin, M.A., M.S.S. was the therapist with consultation by the author. More detailed case-history material appeared in Japanese in Reynolds and Moacanin, 1977.

Certainly, a single successfully treated case does not demonstrate the effectiveness of a therapy. This case is presented to provide an illustration of one way of adapting an Eastern therapy to the treatment of a Western patient. It is organized in Moritist style, with progress notes along with commentary—a blend of concrete example and interpretation—just as everyday reality is encountered in a blend of what is and what we attend to. The commentary is in brackets.

### Presenting Complaints

Mr. W was a 31-year-old Caucasian, Catholic, married man, father of a three-year-old son. He was a college graduate and was employed as a clerk in a government office. He had been seen in the psychiatric outpatient clinic by several different therapists both individually and in groups for seven years. He terminated treatment about a year previously, but returned at this time seeking further treatment for anxiety and depression subsequent to eviction from the apartment where his family lived and his wife's threat to leave him. Other complaints included dissatisfaction with his job (which he perceived to be insignificant, routine, and much below his abilities), lack of friends, and financial problems. Mr. W felt overwhelmed by these life circumstances.

*October 28*

Since the initial interview on October 21, the housing problem has been resolved. Mr. W found another apartment. [Actively seeking an apartment, in spite of his overwhelming feelings of despair, has paid off for him.]

His wife has returned to him. Now his main desires are for further education and training. He is convinced that he will "fall apart" if he continues in his present job.

*November 4*

Mr. W quit his job and is now exploring the possibility of enrolling in a training program. In the meantime his wife has started working and has agreed to support the family until he gets on his feet. We discussed goals in therapy and the need to focus on his behavior rather than wander in many different directions allowing his feelings to control and overwhelm him. [A key feature of Morita Therapy is acceptance of one's feelings as they are—not denying or suppressing or trying to ignore them—yet acting with consistency, responsibility, and productivity regardless of the feelings.] Morita Therapy was explained to him briefly.

*November 10*

Mr. W went to the Department of Vocational Rehabilitation and discussed with a counselor the possibility of enrolling in a training program. He is already more focused on the goal he wishes to pursue and realizes that one of the major problems all his life has been "I

am general about everything and unwilling to commit myself to anything." He now accepts the need for some discipline in his daily activities. [The neurotic person tends to "overthink and underact." He plans, speculates, evaluates, wishes life were otherwise, daydreams, and focuses on inner conflicts and processes to the degree that he fails to behave appropriately in the situation in which he finds himself this very moment.] Further explanations about Morita Therapy and its methods were given to him, and he was asked to keep a daily diary. On one-half of each page of the diary he was directed to write what he felt and thought; on the other half of the page, what he did, what he accomplished. [This clear dichotomy between feelings, moods, fantasies, and thoughts on the one hand and behavior on the other hand is fundamental to Morita Therapy.] Patient stated that the assignment made sense to him.

*November 17*

Mr. W brought his diary and reported it has been helpful to him. He accomplishes more work now. At this time he works as a night watchman. He is alone and afraid on the job. It entails some realistic risks to his life, but nevertheless he goes to work. He wants to build a better work record than the one he has had in the past. He is also exploring further possibilities with the Department of Vocational Rehabilitation.

Mr. W's new job is not significantly different from his last one in terms of the interests and stimulation that it offers him. The difference is that he is more accepting of it now.

*November 25*

Patient reads entries from his diary and states he understands Morita Therapy better. He intuitively feels this is a logical and simple way of working with his life, but also a very difficult one. [Gains in therapy follow from the patient's effort. The goal is a sort of character development. The successes are his, earned through his moment-by-moment struggles.] The diary organizes his thinking, and after completing the necessary daily chores he feels a burden off his shoulders. [How much of our energy is wasted rescheduling, avoiding, putting off chores that could be done now and then forgotten.] He already feels better, although he does not know why.

[It is not important to have elaborate intellectual/theoretical understanding why these principles are effective. To put them into practice brings experiential understanding. Again, we cut through the neurotic's tendencies for mental wheelspinning with direct, straightforward action.] At this point, as after similar statements, the patient is reminded that feeling better is not the goal of therapy, but rather the aim is a vigilant adherence to his immediate tasks. [The beginning patient may be attracted to this therapy when he discovers that his misery goes unnoticed as he involves himself (loses himself) in his activity. He also learns that negative feelings diminish over time unless they are restimulated. But so do positive feelings. Life need not be constructed on the unpredictable fluctuating base of emotions. Successful behavior patterns are likely to bring overall satisfaction, but satisfaction or not, each moment requires our full attention and appropriate behavior.]

Several times this past week Mr. W did not want to go to work, but he did go anyway. On his days off he had an urge to go to a bar in the evening, but instead he stayed home knowing that he needed the rest in order to be able to go to work the following evening.

## December 1

Mr. W has been accepted into a vocational school. During this session he comes to the recognition that the only time he is "happy" is when he is not worried about his past or his future. He is instructed to focus on the present moment without lingering in the past or daydreaming about the future. [Of course, some evaluation of past actions and some future planning are necessary tasks of life.

It is the excessive rumination that debilitates and paralyzes the neurotic person.]

## December 10

Patient has been anxious and depressed this past week after he met with a friend and the two reminisced about old times in their native home. [Feelings, moods will fluctuate. When he is anxious, he is anxious. That is reality. But when he knows by experience that his behavior is under control regardless of his anxiety, he is free to feel that anxiety fully, even to treasure it.] Patient's attention was redirected to his present life situation. He expressed satisfaction with the prospect of starting school the following week and with the progress he has already made in therapy. He has started working on a second job part time.

## January 5

Mr. W likes his school, wants to complete it, and then give something of himself to others. [Note the emerging social consciousness. Neurotic persons tend to be self-centered. Most Western therapies focus even further attention on the self. This spontaneous budding of selflessness in Mr. W is a consequence of the new outer-direction of his awareness.] He perceives as "illusion" his constant desire for something other than what he already has, such as another woman, a close male friend, and another country. He believes his marriage is working out at this time.

## January 13

Mr. W has been depressed this past week, but kept on with his tasks, went to school regularly, and drove his wife to and from work. At times he feels he is not advancing, but nevertheless he keeps up.

Today Mr. W wants to know more about Morita Therapy, particularly how it is like and unlike Behavior Therapy. He recognizes deep urges in himself for a fuller life, which he realizes were there even before therapy.

[This desire to live fully, the drive for self-actualization (called *sei no yokubo* by Morita therapists) provides the momentum for cure but also for neurosis. In the past, this energy source has been misdirected; during therapy it is refocused on productive living.]

In response to his observation that Morita Therapy somewhat resembles Behavior Modification Therapy, it was stressed that our goal is not to mold him to produce any particular behavior but to make him a freer individual. At the same time the therapist pointed out the necessity of learning and adhering to discipline—which he himself has identified as lacking in his life so far—in order to reach and maintain that freedom. [The *environment* holds "responsibility" for what we do, according to Behavior Therapy. And changing the reinforcers of the environment produces cure (i.e., symptom reduction) as well. Morita's method holds *the patient* responsible for his or her behavior. And the goal is not the symptom reduction but symptom transcendence through acceptance of feelings and self-control of behavior.]

Through his diary Mr. W has learned that his main conflict revolves around his sexual identity. [Patients often try to simplify their problems into a single complaint. "If only I had been born to other parents." Or, in this case, "if only I were more masculine. . . ."] He feels incapable of resolving that problem, yet he has been attentive to his wife and has not failed to satisfy her needs. The therapist pointed out that despite some conflicting emotions, Mr. W has been attending to his duties as husband. The patient also reports that although he often feels "bad" while in school, he pursues his classes. He sees a similarity between the required discipline in school and in therapy.

### February 10

The past week Mr. W felt good, happy, very happy, depressed, anxious, fatigued, and so forth, but pursued his work and concentrated on his daily tasks. Occasionally he suffers mild anxiety attacks in class, but keeps on with the work. He asked what he should do in such instances. He is urged to continue the work he is engaged in at that moment. He again discusses the need to make some judgment at times when faced with two or more simultaneous conflicting demands for action. He is now more confident about making his own decisions at such times, implementing his decisions, and assuming responsibility for them.

### February 24

We continue to work on the recognition that despite fluctuation of his feelings—within one single day and from moment to moment—he can maintain constancy in his actions. Mr. W can see this very well as he goes over his daily diary. He further recognizes that often when he does not feel good but keeps on with his tasks, the feeling changes. He has been able to take the pressures at school although many of his fellow students quit. [He is building a history of perserverance and success. Confidence *follows* accomplishment more often than it precedes it.]

Mr. W is eager to spend more time with his son and participate more actively in the child's upbringing. He decides to make it his task to do so. After each session the patient reviews what we have discussed.

### March 2

Mr. W is having trouble concentrating on his reading assignments. When intruding thoughts of possible failure appear, he is to keep on scanning the page, keep on repeating the definitions to be learned so as not to divert his attention to useless worries over his future. [Intrusive or wandering thoughts are problems for all of us. To try to get rid of them is to focus even more attention on them. They are to be accepted while we continue to go about what we are doing. Eventually, a word of phrase from the text will "catch" his attention and he will be "lost" again in his studying.]

## March 9

Mr. W's grades at school have gone up, and he has been able to study well. Once again he realizes that "this therapy works."

## March 16

Mr. W did well on his examinations. He reports that when he does what needs to be done and pursues the required actions, his feelings spontaneously change so that he becomes less lonely and depressed. Loneliness never fades away completely, but he now accepts the fact that he may never be able to conquer it. He discovered that when focusing his thinking on one task at a time, he is more likely to be successful. For example, when he studies anatomy, he now thinks of anatomy only, and not how he is going to pay his rent. Then when he passes his examination he feels relieved and may even no longer worry about the rent. Furthermore, he has learned to handle previously distasteful tasks. For instance, although cleaning up an incontinent patient used to make him vomit, he now performs his job without being bothered by it. He believes that if he had not learned to focus on and accept whatever the demands of the tasks, he would not have been able to continue his studies.

## April 6

Today Mr. W says he is "in good shape." He finds himself more efficient the more he is bombarded with problems. He has learned to "get into the rhythm of things" and accomplish one task after another. His wife may be pregnant, and he is accepting this possibility without worrying unnecessarily about their meager financial resources.

## May 17

Mr. W and his wife will leave for Europe in two days. He considers this trip to be a va-

cation, but, moreover, an educational experience. Reviewing his gains in therapy, he states that even though he did not complete his vocational school at this time, he learned a more important lesson in life. He learned "to take every day as a new birth." He has surmounted his difficulties and revulsion about certain nursing chores, and he is now able to do anything that is required of him.

We reviewed his progress in other problem areas that he presented at the onset of therapy. The relationship with his wife has significantly improved. He now has a skill in a field that gives him genuine satisfaction, a field in which he can always obtain employment. Consequently, he no longer has financial worries. He no longer has the feeling of lacking control over his life. Mr. W now realizes that he does not need to stop and be overwhelmed by an event, but, as he proceeds, the event assumes smaller proportions and often resolves itself. He gave as an example a recent incident in which he got a $25 traffic ticket on his way to work. His first impulse was not to go to work, for in one day he would not make enough money to pay the ticket. Nevertheless, he did go to work, and as he kept working his preoccupation with the ticket lessened and the problem diminished. Mr. W also remarked that until recently he had many "dualities" in himself that kept him from going ahead. He feels that now he has resolved those dualities.

## Summary of Case History

The patient maintained a daily diary. He read his diary entries aloud at each therapy session. His diary was a key instrument of therapeutic work between sessions and became the focus of our discussion during each session. Occasionally Mr. W would dwell on the past or would question the Moritist method, finding it confining, restricting, demanding of excessive discipline, and apparently irrelevant to the more creative aspects of life. His anxieties, worries, and questions were acknowledged with empathy, but his attention was firmly redirected to his current tasks. There was neither avoidance of feelings nor focus on them, no psychodynamic analysing or interpreting as they arose in the therapy sessions or in his diary. By directing his energies to specific tasks, the waste and diversion of energy on fruitless emotional and mental activities was minimized. Without undue worry about future problems, regrets over past failures, or avoidance of present tasks, the patient became able to use his energies to more fully involve himself in life. A meaningful occupation, satisfying relationships with his wife, son, and mother, and a broadened social awareness have resulted.

Mr. W was repeatedly reminded by the therapist and by his daily living of the fluctuations in feelings from day to day and moment to moment (as were clearly reflected in his diary) despite a constancy and regularity in his actions. The inevitable ups and downs of his emotions, from depression and acute anxiety to peacefulness to exhilaration to feelings of harmony, did not necessarily deter him from his pursuit of daily tasks. He was thus gradually but steadily building up positive and constructive behavior patterns. Deep urges from an unknown source within himself directed him toward a meaningful life for himself, and a usefulness to society. (We must recognize the possibility that we have no real grasp of the source of our impulses and feelings, accept them, and get on with using them. In this manner we transcend them.) By focusing on specific daily activities his personality could unfold spontaneously, unhindered by useless habits and obsessive destructive thought patterns.

The diary fostered a sort of meditative process by which Mr. W developed an increased capacity for observation of his feelings and thoughts from moment to moment in a neutral way.

The patient's trust in the therapist was a critical element in his willingness to undergo Morita Therapy and give it an experiential try in his daily life. Yet once the unique insights and strategies for dealing with feelings and behavior are mastered by a patient, they can be maintained and strengthened after therapy has been formally terminated.

## SUMMARY

Through application of three principles—*recognize purpose, accept feelings,* and *control behavior*—the client in Morita Therapy seeks to build his or her character rather than merely reduce symptoms. In fact, from the Moritist perspective, symptoms such as anxiety and lack of confidence are not considered accretions to be removed as a surgeon would excise a tumor. Rather such feelings and attitudes are part of the reality that exists for a patient; they are elements in the flow of his awareness. Neither good nor bad, they simply are.

In practice, symptom complaints *are* reduced (Suzuki & Suzuki, 1977), but that is merely a side effect. What is important is the growing ability of the patient to live responsibly and constructively whether symptoms are present or not. The normal person has anxiety too. However, the normal person is *not* "trapped" by his anxiety; he is not boxed into a corner of excessive self-focus and passive dependency by his feelings.

The therapist cannot make a patient feel better. He cannot control his own feelings, much less those of his client. The Morita therapist only offers what he has experienced himself. And when success comes to the patient, it is the result of the patient's putting what he has learned into practice. That effort is the solid behavioral basis for a lasting sense of self-worth.

## REFERENCES

Jacobsen, A. and Berenberg, A. N. Japanese psychiatry and psychotherapy. *American Journal of Psychiatry,* 1952, **109,** 321–329.

Kondo, A. Morita therapy: A Japanese therapy for neurosis. *American Journal of Psychoanalysis,* 1953, **13,** 31–37.

Kora, T. Morita therapy. *International Journal of Psychiatry,* 1965, **1** (4), 611–640.

Kora, T. and Ohara, K. Morita therapy. *Psychology Today*, 1973, **6** (10), 63–68.

Kumasaka, Y. Discussion. *International Journal of Psychiatry*, 1965, **1** (4), 641–642.

Levy, J. Discussion. *International Journal of Psychiatry*, 1965, **1** (4), 642–643.

Morita, S. and Mizutani, K. *Sei no Yokubo (The Desire to Live Fully)*. Tokyo: Hakuyōsha, 1956.

Ogawa, B. K. *Morita psychotherapy and Christianity*. Ph.D. dissertation. San Francisco Theological Seminary, 1979.

Ohara, K. and Reynolds, D. K. Changing methods in Morita psychotherapy. *International Journal of Social Psychiatry*, 1968, **14 (4),** 305–310.

Reynolds, D. K. *Morita psychotherapy*. Berkeley, Calif.: University of California Press, 1976.

Reynolds, D. K. *The quiet therapies*. Honolulu: University Press of Hawaii, 1980.

Reynolds, D. K. and Moacanin, R. Eastern therapy: Western patient. *Japanese Journal of Psychotherapy Research*, 1977, *3* (2), 65–74. (In Japanese.)

Reynolds, D. K. and Yamamoto, J. Morita psychotherapy in Japan. *Current Psychiatric Therapies*, 1973, **13,** 219–227.

Suzuki, T. Morita rhyōhō no tachiba kara (From the standpoint of Morita therapy). *Seishin Igaku*, 1967, **9** (7), 11–19.

Suzuki, T. and Suzuki, R. A follow-up of neurotics treated by Morita therapy. VI World Congress of Psychiatry, Honolulu, 1977.

Yokoyama, K. Morita therapy and seiza. *Psychologia*, 1968, **11** (3–4), 179–184.

# CHAPTER 36

## *Multimodal Therapy*

ARNOLD A. LAZARUS, CHARLES B. KREITZBERG, and VALERIE J. SASSERATH

*When I do marriage counseling and listen first, say, to the wife, I sympathize with her and realize that she is correct in her views. Then when I interview the husband and hear his position, I sympathize with him and see his views. Thus I put myself squarely on the fence and, to mix metaphors, find myself standing firmly in midair. Certainly those readers who have been taking my prefatory comments seriously may be wondering at my general excitement about each of the various systems. The answer is that each does excite me. I think all systems in this book (well, practically all) are valuable and meaningful.*

*But on to this chapter. My opinion of it is indicated that I had duplicates made of it and sent these to various authors of other chapters who requested the assistance of a good sample chapter. I also used this next chapter to show authors what a well-written chapter should be like.*

*I believe that eventually all systems will merge and that therapists will be trained simultaneously in one eclectic theory and many procedures, much as allopathic medicine does now. Lazarus's approach is eclectic, and may be a serious contender for a final breakthrough system acceptable to all. This chapter on Multimodal Therapy is a model of a well-prepared and well-conceptualized total approach to psychotherapy.*

Multimodal Therapy is a comprehensive psychotherapeutic approach covering seven interactive modalities—behavior, affect, sensation, imagery, cognition, interpersonal relationships, and biological factors. Rather than trying to fit a client's problems into the framework of a preconceived theory, the multimodal approach takes into account the uniqueness of each individual and tailors treatment to the broad range of personal needs and situations.

In the multimodal approach, therapy is viewed as an educational process in which the client learns adaptive response patterns to replace maladaptive ones, both to ongoing problems and potential life stresses. The goal of Multimodal Therapy is rapid and durable change. Problem assessment and the development of an intervention plan is guided by

significant deficits and excesses across the client's BASIC ID (behavior, affect, sensation, imagery, cognition, interpersonal relationships, and drugs/biological factors). This approach insures systematic and comprehensive coverage of diverse interactive problems.

The term "drugs" is used generically to represent the *biological* modality, for the acronym BASIC ID is more compelling than BASIC IB. Besides, when dealing with biological factors (which includes nutrition, hygiene, exercise, and somatic concerns) medication (psychotropic drugs) is often at the forefront in the treatment of several conditions.

In essence, Multimodal Therapy is the thorough and systematic assessment of the BASIC ID, and methodically covers the treatment of excesses and deficits that arise within each of these seven modalities.

## HISTORY

Multimodal Therapy was developed by Lazarus (1973, 1976, 1981) as a result of his recognition that existing therapeutic systems are ineffective in producing both rapid and durable change. Noting that Insight Therapy and "cognitive restructuring" were often insufficient to effect behavioral change, Lazarus (1958) enthusiastically embraced a behavior therapy viewpoint and developed a number of techniques to facilitate behavioral change (Lazarus, 1961, 1963; Wolpe & Lazarus, 1966).

Follow-up investigations of individuals treated by behavioral techniques suggested that, while behavioral interventions readily produced behavior change, this change was often not durable (Lazarus, 1971). Confronted by subsequent life stress, many clients reestablished previous maladaptive behaviors or developed new but suboptimal patterns of coping. Accordingly, Lazarus began experimenting with a broader range of techniques than those employed in Behavior Therapy, including the numerous cognitive interventions developed by Albert Ellis (1962) and a variety of imagery techniques (Lazarus, 1978).

As a result of his experimentation, Lazarus concluded that while behavioral techniques tend to produce rapid but nondurable change, and verbal techniques alone are generally inadequate to produce behavioral change, a judicious combination of behavioral and verbal (cognitive) techniques can be effective in producing change that is both rapid and durable. In particular, behavioral techniques can reduce undesired response patterns and facilitate the acquisition of prosocial habits. Verbal techniques are employed to alter the individual's patterns of self-reinforcement and to anticipate and instill coping strategies to deal with future life stresses. Lazarus presented some of these ideas in his book *Behavior Therapy and Beyond* (1971).

Having discovered the synergistic properties of verbal and behavioral methods, Lazarus sought to develop techniques that would lend a more efficient structure to the therapy process. The approach he developed has served as the foundation for Multimodal Therapy (Lazarus, 1973), and is based on the observation that we are beings that move, feel, sense, imagine, think, and relate to one another—all of which rests on a biological substrate.

Outcome and follow-up studies (Lazarus, 1976) revealed that durable change (according to three-year follow-ups) depends on the thoroughness with which problems in each of these modalities are assessed and then remedied. Before turning to a discussion of significant theoretical underpinnings, some examples of typical problems that fall into each of the seven modalities may clarify what has been said thus far.

| Behavior | Excesses: | Overeating, compulsive handwashing, temper tantrums, enuresis. |
|---|---|---|
| | Deficits: | Insomnia, anorexia, unassertiveness, avoidance behaviors. |
| Affect | Excesses: | Anxiety, depression, anger, guilt. |
| | Deficits: | Flat affect, inability to feel anger. |
| Sensation | Excesses: | Pain, dizziness, "butterflies" in stomach, tachycardia, hot flushes. |
| | Deficits: | Lack of sexual pleasure, lack of energy or appetite, numbness. |

| Imagery | Excesses: | Hallucinations, obsessive and intrusive mental pictures, fearful and depressive images. |
| | Deficits: | Inability to picture positive events. |
| Cognition | Excesses: | Paranoid ideation, catastrophic thinking, overgeneralizing, "shoulds" and "musts." |
| | Deficits: | Inability to concentrate, low intelligence, lack of ability to see connections between thoughts and feelings. |
| Interpersonal | Excesses: | Manipulative, argumentative, promiscuous, demanding. |
| | Deficits: | Isolated, withdrawn, timid, shy. |
| (Biological factors) Drugs | Excesses: | Medical problems, substance abuse. |
| | Deficits: | Poor nutrition, lack of fitness, refusal to take essential medication. |

## CURRENT STATUS

While Multimodal Therapy as distinct from broad-spectrum or cognitive Behavior Therapy is relatively new (Lazarus, 1973), a considerable number of individuals have been using the BASIC ID in their assessment and therapy. The first book on multimodal procedures had 11 contributors (Lazarus, 1976). Other publications using the BASIC ID in a formal and systematic manner are fairly wide-ranging and include the treatment of agoraphobia (Popler, 1977), career education (Gerler, 1977), behavioral medicine (Richard, 1978), mental hospital treatment (Brunell, 1978), children's problems (Keat, 1979), and even community disasters (Sank, 1979). The entire issue of *Elementary School Guidance and Counseling*, volume 13, 1978, was devoted to multimodal approaches.

Training in Multimodal Therapy is a formal aspect of the Ph.D. and Psy. D. programs at Rutgers University, New Jersey, and a number of former students now teach Multimodal Therapy at various universities and centers throughout the United States. Training seminars are also provided by the staff members of several Multimodal Therapy Institutes, located in Kingston, New Jersey; New York City; Philadelphia; Virginia Beach; and Cleveland, Ohio.

A number of doctoral dissertations are in preparation, each of which tests specific and significant aspects of the approach. One of our colleagues, John J. Shannon of Seton Hall University in New Jersey, is conducting systematic research on multimodal methods, with special emphasis on the treatment of agoraphobia.

## THEORY

Multimodal Therapy employs an educational, social-learning, cognitive, and a communications or systems model to account for the acquisition of maladaptive response patterns and therapeutic change. However, multimodal therapists also recognize that the current state of psychological knowledge does not permit the development of an accurate theory of human functioning. Accordingly, theory in Multimodal Therapy concentrates largely on determining *what* interventions are effective rather than explaining *why* they are effective.

To claim that "*what* questions" are the most important is to say that multimodal therapists are empiricists; we believe that explanatory theory must be parsimoniously induced from an observational basis. The history of science reveals many false paths followed by thinkers who failed to follow this basic principle. For example, it was once widely believed that the process of combustion resulted from a loss of a mysterious "fluid" called phlogiston. Acceptance of that unproved explanatory postulate impeded the progress of physical science. Similarly, mental dysfunction was once attributed to imbalance of basic fluids or "humours," a specious explanation that led to the design of inappropriate interventions.

The emphasis on "*what* questions" has proven useful in medicine. No one yet knows why the phenothiazines are effective in treating schizophrenia, but the use of these compounds has relieved the suffering of thousands of individuals. The principle of "technical eclecticism" (Lazarus, 1967) permits the multimodal therapist to develop a wide range of interventions. A technical eclectic adopts techniques on the basis of their demonstrated effectiveness without necessarily subscribing to the theoretical explanations their originators propound. For example, systematic desensitization has proven useful in dealing with certain phobic responses; however, Wolpe's (1958) explanation in terms of reciprocal inhibition has been subjected to theoretical criticism (e.g., Wilson & Davison, 1971; Davison & Wilson, 1973). Multimodal therapists employ desensitization when appropriate without necessarily accepting the reciprocal inhibition paradigm.

## Social Learning Perspective

Within the context of theoretical parsimony, Multimodal Therapy employs a broad social learning perspective to account for personality development and change (Bandura, 1969, 1977). Multimodal Therapy conceptualizes personality as a process constantly developing during the individual's life span. At the time of conception, the individual is endowed with biological (genetic) potentials that, in part, determine the course of subsequent development. Environmental factors play a major role in influencing the individual's growth processes. As important as biological and environmental factors is the role of the individual. Individuals selectively attend to, process, and manipulate the environment, and in so doing affect themselves. Because individuals are actively processing

at all times, they are in a constant state of development. This self-constructivist view is an aspect of Multimodal Therapy that distinguishes it from the passive deterministic philosophy espoused by behaviorism, which assumes that human behavior is subject to causal determination no less than billiard balls or falling bodies (Wolpe, 1973).

Reinforcement, a fundamental principle, is interpreted in terms of the individual's world view. The reinforcement value of events depends upon the individual's interpretation of them as well as inherent properties within the events themselves. Such processes as identification, concept formation, modeling, vicarious reinforcement, and hypothesis generation and testing are key factors in the development of personality.

Multimodal therapists avoid the use of general labels in favor of more precise descriptions. Accordingly, trait descriptions are rarely employed. For example, rather than describing an individual as "anxious," the multimodal therapist will specify the situations in which an individual tends to experience anxiety and will describe the situation-specific reactions in terms of the BASIC ID structure. This process helps clarify the problem both to therapist and client, suggests specific interventions, and avoids the overgeneralizations encouraged by nonspecific labels.

## The BASIC ID

A major premise of the multimodal approach is that human problems and the factors that cause and maintain them are multidimensional, and that it is essential to cover these different but interrelated dimensions for long-lasting change to accrue. Therapy that does not take into account the many dimensions of human functioning is almost bound to have short-lived efficacy because individuals may fail to acquire a sufficiently broad range of coping skills to permit them to deal effectively with life's broad range of demands. In addition, although the many aspects of human functioning are deeply intertwined, specific and discrete interventions are needed to insure that a change in one part of the system will have positive effects on the rest of the system. In other words, the more comprehensive the assessment and treatment, the more compelling and long-lasting the change.

To reiterate, BASIC ID is an acronym that stands for behavior, affect, sensation, imagery, cognition, interpersonal relationships, and drugs/biological factors. These seven modalities provide a structure within which assessment and intervention are conducted. By carefully exploring each modality, the therapist obtains a systematic and comprehensive picture of the client's problems. By developing an intervention plan that involves multiple modalities, the therapist increases the likelihood of durable change. Moreover, the process of employing the BASIC ID as a conceptual structure encourages precise, holistic thinking that fosters creative therapy.

### Integrating the Modalities

We have stressed the importance of a comprehensive structure in therapeutic assessment and intervention that considers the multidimensional nature of human functioning. Equally important are the integrative mech-anisms that relate the modalities in problem assessment and treatment. These integrative mechanisms are the systems of the BASIC ID, and they make the structure of the BASIC ID a cohesive one in which the modalities of human functioning, rather than seeming artificially compartmentalized, are treated as interactive components in a constant state of flux.

A clearer understanding of the relationships among modalities of the BASIC ID may be gained by organizing the seven modalities into a hierarchical system in which the drug modality represents the biological substrate of human functioning (bottom of the hierarchy) and the interpersonal modality represents the structure that is the culmination of the interplay of the other modalities (top of hierarchy). This hierarchy of modalities of human functioning is represented in Figure 1.

The basis of all human functioning is ultimately biological; hence, biology is placed at the base of the hierarchy. Sensation is most closely related to biology since it is physically experienced. Affect is linked to sensation but also includes cognitive, imaginal, and expressive components. The next level of the hierarchy includes the cognitive and imagery modalities that are internal processes

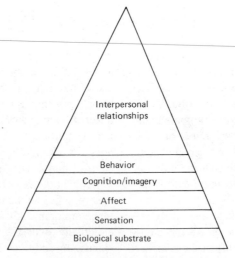

Figure 1  Hierarchy of the BASIC ID.

but may also be considered behaviors on a covert level. The behavior modality is influenced by the five modalities preceding it in the hierarchy. Finally, the interpersonal relationships modality is a special case of behavior that involves more than one person. This modality is placed at the top of the hierarchy since it is influenced by the other six modalities and because it represents the least internalized and most outwardly focused aspect of human functioning in the BASIC ID.

## The Educational Model

In the multimodal approach, as in other learning-based approaches, therapy is viewed as an educational process in which the therapist works with clients to facilitate the learning and maintenance of adaptive modes of responding. The rationale underlying the educational approach to psychotherapy is that since individuals "acquire their deviant behaviors in the same way they learn adaptive or prosocial responses (i.e., by observation, imitation, information, and various forms of association and conditioning) . . . psychotherapy is essentially a process of social learning and relearning" (Lazarus, 1971, p. 15). Multimodal therapists view themselves as teachers providing an education in living.

The educational model differs from most medical models in that it does not regard individuals in therapy as patients who are emotionally ill but as clients who are seeking consultation about problems in some aspects of living. Within the multimodal approach, it is recognized that biological factors contribute to psychological functioning and that it is important to distinguish medical from psychological problems; however, biological processes rarely become the sole focus but are usually examined in the context of the six other modes of functioning.

## Facilitation of Transfer and Generalization

Implicit in the educational model is concern with the transfer (or generalization) of learn-

ing from the consulting room to *in vivo* situations. Of particular importance is the generalization from cognitive understanding to behavioral change, and the generalization of adaptive response patterns to a variety of novel situations. Transfer from the therapy situation to life situations is a form of stimulus generalization in that the client employs previously learned responses in a new stimulus situation. Transfer from cognitive or imagery modalities to behavior is a form of response generalization in that the client generalizes from previous learning to produce new responses.

The multimodal therapist facilitates transfer through the liberal use of *in vivo* homework assignments that encourage the client to rehearse overt responses and to employ these responses in significant real-life situations. The amount and type of practice is carefully tailored to the individual. The therapist evaluates the level of risk-taking and the various difficulties involved in each assignment by closely evaluating the client's frame of reference. Optimal homework assignments involve moderate risk, fairly high probability of success, and the potential for generalization.

There is a proverb that says "to give a person a fish is to feed him or her for a day, but to teach a person to fish is to feed him or her for life." Multimodal therapists are concerned with teaching clients skills that will enable them to cope with present and future life stresses in an adaptive manner. This is accomplished by teaching techniques and strategies that the client can generalize to novel situations, as well as by concentrating on specific problem-oriented coping responses.

## METHODOLOGY

Multimodal Therapy is a flexible approach that allows for individual differences among therapists and clients. Generally, Multimodal Therapy is organized around four processes:

1. *Assessment* of problems according to the BASIC ID framework.
2. *Development* of an individually tailored intervention plan based on each problem across the BASIC ID (modality profile).
3. *Implementation* of the intervention plan as a cooperative client/therapist enterprise.
4. *Refinement* of the intervention plan (and of the modality profile) through ongoing evaluation and feedback.

All four processes are employed during the course of therapy, but the emphasis given to each varies. Early in therapy, the therapist concentrates on assessment and the development of an intervention plan. As therapy progresses, the intervention process receives increasing emphasis. Feedback and refinement are ongoing processes during the course of therapy.

**Assessment**

The first step in Multimodal Therapy is the development of a clear statement of the presenting problems. Few clients enter the consulting room with their problems sufficiently well defined to permit immediate implementation of an intervention program. The therapist employs the BASIC ID in a systematic (but not mechanical) fashion to obtain a comprehensive picture of the presenting problems.

For example, Jane B, a 28-year-old woman, came for therapy complaining of "an unfulfilled life." A multimodal assessment revealed that her vaguely stated problem was comprised of a constellation of specific symptoms. The assessment profile shown below was developed during the two initial sessions.

By specifying the problems in terms of the BASIC ID structure, the therapist develops a systematic and comprehensive assessment that facilitates the design of a thorough intervention plan. The modality profile also helps the client conceptualize problems in specific terms. Often this is the first time that clients verbalize and reflect upon the precise nature of their problems; the process facilitates therapist/client communication and often proves to be reassuring. Within each mode of the BASIC ID, the therapist concentrates on two main categories: (1) maladaptive responses that are targets for reduc-

| | |
|---|---|
| Behavior | Does not assert herself; compulsive eating, especially following unexpressed anger at her mother; constantly "on the go" but engages in nonproductive activities. |
| Affect | Primarily guilt and depression; anger often not expressed but occasionally explodes with rage; low self-esteem and feelings of inferiority. |
| Sensations | Tension headaches; often feels "out of sorts"; dizziness. |
| Images | Negative self-images abound; has few future-oriented images of how she would like to be. |
| Cognitions | Many irrational beliefs; among the most salient appear to be: "I am responsible for my parents' unhappy marriage" (unreasonable, childlike, self-blame), "It would be selfish of me to consider myself or my feelings at any time; I can only live for others." |
| Interpersonal | Married for two years without any sexual contact (marriage was annulled); now living with parents (shares bedroom with mother) in a highly tense family environment. |
| Drugs (biological factors) | About 120 lbs. overweight; fainting spells (medical examinations reveal no cause); no exercise. |

tion or elimination, and (2) response deficits that need to be increased or augmented.

Even a mechanistic application of the BASIC ID can be extremely useful in systematizing and structuring assessment. The process of constructing a modality profile facilitates the therapist's conceptualization of the problems and points to specific intervention strategies. Thus, in the case of Jane B's "unfulfilled life," even a cursory inspection of the modality profile reveals an interactive range of problem areas that call for immediate change. During the course of therapy, the functional value and the interactions between discrete problems usually become more apparent and facilitate the treatment process.

## Development of an Intervention Plan

The multimodal therapist employs the modality profile to develop an intervention plan. In selecting specific interventions, the therapist draws on a well-stocked inventory of techniques. Multimodal therapists are constantly searching for new techniques and endeavor to remain aware of current clinical practices. Techniques derived from a cognitive social learning perspective are the most readily considered; other promising methods are also incorporated without the dogma that often surrounds them.

Although the principle of technical eclecticism admits any psychotherapeutic technique of potential value, most multimodal therapists employ a common core of intervention strategies. The most frequently employed techniques are:

1. Cognitive techniques—restructuring of beliefs and value systems, altering decision-making and problem-solving patterns. Bibliotherapy is often employed.
2. *In vivo* techniques—homework, risk-taking, and shame-attacking exercises, assertiveness assignments.
3. Exploration and modification of interpersonal systems (couples and family therapy are an integral aspect of the interpersonal modality).
4. Relaxation, meditation, and biofeedback.
5. Imagery techniques—the emphasis is generally on future-oriented coping images.
6. Other techniques, including: desensitization, flooding, participant modeling, behavior rehearsal.

As an example of a typical multimodal intervention strategy, consider the plan developed for Jane B.

The intervention plan for Jane B incorporates a number of characteristics typical of Multimodal Therapy. First, interventions cover all modalities in accordance with the hypothesis that multimodal intervention is required for effective and long-lived change.

| Modality | Problem | Proposed Intervention |
|----------|---------|-----------------------|
| Behavior | Lack of assertiveness | Assertion training, preferably in a group with a female leader. |
| | Compulsive eating | Attend self-help group; monitor food intake as a first step in developing an individualized modification program; work toward employing more appropriate coping behaviors for dealing with anger at her mother. |
| Affect | Guilt and depression; rage attacks | Assertion training (see Behavior) should facilitate more appropriate expression of feelings; exercises to foster development of positive future-oriented goals and images (see Imagery). |

| Modality | Problem | Proposed Intervention |
| --- | --- | --- |
| Sensation | Tension symptoms | Relaxation training; assertion training may also help (see Behavior); sensate exercises to help client acquire positive pleasure-seeking behaviors (warm baths, lying on beach, massage). |
| Images | Deficit in positive future-oriented images | Homework assignments to visit apartments and houses for rent and engage in imagery exercises to furnish and decorate them; look through want ads in newspapers and imagine herself in various jobs. (The purpose of these exercises is to help elaborate a series of positive images of herself six months and one year in the future. She also used images of herself losing weight and fitting into smaller sized clothes to help her weight-loss program.) |
| Cognitions | Irrational beliefs | Dispute validity of irrational beliefs; bibliotherapy: *I Can If I Want To* (Lazarus & Fay, 1975), *Your Perfect Right* (Alberti & Emmons, 1978). |
| Interpersonal | Family tension | Work toward getting her own apartment which should relieve much family stress; permit Jane to control her own food intake; provide her with much-needed privacy; possibly schedule some family therapy sessions. |
| | Sexual inexperience | Weight reduction will increase her opportunities for sexual relationships. Feelings of anxiety and guilt will be explored and congnitive restructuring initiated; possible bibliotherapy: *Becoming Orgasmic* (Heiman, LoPiccolo, & LoPiccolo, 1976). Sensate exercises should help in development of sexual expression. |
| Drugs | Overweight | Diet program (see Behavior); mild exercise with medical approval. |

Second, individual therapy was supplemented with an assertion-training group, a weight-control program, and the possibility of family therapy. By involving Jane in these groups, the therapist hoped to facilitate her gains and to provide opportunities for productive social interaction. Third, the plan included bibliotherapy to provide a rationale and reinforcement for the assertion training *(Your Perfect Right)*, to facilitate identification of irrational beliefs *(I Can If I Want To)*, and to provide some basic sexual information *(Becoming Orgasmic)*. Fourth, the therapist suggested imagery exercises to help the client set realistic and appropriate goals and to help her evaluate proposed activities in terms of their contribution to her goals. Fifth, the plan considered both self-reinforcement (cognitive restructuring and sensate exercises) and dealt with environmental stress (by encouraging Jane to take her own apartment). The modality profile serves as a "blueprint" for therapist and client to monitor progress, to look for stumbling blocks, and to provide meaningful and precise treatment goals.

### Implementation and Refinement

The implementation of treatment plans is carried out in stages. The therapist and client both participate in the decision as to how the plan is implemented. The focus of the initial therapy sessions is largely on assessment and the development of a plan, although intervention is almost always introduced in the first session(often in the form of a homework assignment).

In later sessions, interventions become the primary focus of therapy. Successful interventions are elaborated, unsuccessful interventions are eliminated, and an attempt is made to determine and alter the factors that inhibit progress. The multimodal therapist usually deals with "resistance" by identifying and attacking various secondary gains. We have found that problems of noncompliance also stem from the therapist's failure to recognize the client's "response proclivities." For example, if a client responds predominantly in sensory/cognitive/affective modes, a homework assignment to practice *imagery* exercises or to carry out *behavioral* tasks may meet with "resistance," whereas sensory, cognitive, and affective assignments would be completed with alacrity. In some cases the therapist's initial plan is carried through with only minor changes; in others, both the problem statements and the intervention strategies change radically over the course of therapy.

**Terminating Therapy**

As the client progresses, the therapist places increasing emphasis on consolidating change and helping the client prepare for anticipated life stresses or to minimize "future shock" (Lazarus, 1978). For most clients, the course of therapy is between six and 12 months. Sampling the last 50 clients, we found the mean number of sessions to be 41.25 with a range of 5 to 150 therapy hours.

**APPLICATIONS**

Regardless of one's theoretical orientation, most therapists undoubtedly do best with clients who are intelligent, cooperative, and genuinely motivated to change. Furthermore, we all usually enjoy working with clients whose excesses and deficits across the BASIC ID are not especially rigid, encrusted, or pervasive. In examining our own treatment

failures, we can claim no special or consistent successes with floridly psychotic individuals, sociopathic personalities, repeated substance abusers, and vegetatively depressed persons. However, it should be underscored that even these recalcitrant categories of disturbance have yielded to Multimodal Therapy when the mesh and artistry between client and therapist was such that thorough coverage of the BASIC ID was accomplished. Science has told us *what* to do, but not necessarily *how* to implement what needs to be done. The "how to" category rests heavily on each individual therapist's sensitivity, wisdom, and talent.

In discussions with our colleagues who practice Multimodal Therapy, we all seem to be especially pleased and gratified by our outcomes and follow-ups with the following problem areas: marriage and family problems; sexual difficulties; childhood disorders; inadequate social skills; smoking; fears and phobias; anxiety states; obesity; psychosomatic complaints; and depression. We also have achieved a fair measure of success with agoraphobics who had failed to respond to other treatment approaches, and we can claim some impressive results with certain obsessive-compulsive problems.

In terms of some overall statistics, over the past seven years we have consistently found that we achieve our treatment goals with more than 75 percent of the people who consult us. Follow-ups reveal less than a 5 percent relapse rate.

**CASE EXAMPLE**

Mr. and Mrs. A were contemplating divorce. He explained: "We love each other and would like to remain married, but we can't get along." They were an attractive couple in their mid-twenties who had been married for two years. The wife stressed that they were often "at war" with each other. She added that she felt "very unhappy" but also feared losing her husband. He complained that she was inclined to nag and criticize him, and he felt that if his wife would stop her verbal attacks and demands, the two of them would be able to achieve a stable and happy relationship. She countered with the allegation that he "forced" her to carp at him.

According to the husband, a previous therapist whom he consulted alone viewed the problem as a product of Mr. A's inconsistent behavior. He had pointed out that when faced by Mrs. A's carping criticisms, Mr. A sometimes withdrew, sometimes defended himself, and sometimes counterattacked. The therapist explained that inconsistent behaviors merely serve to reinforce the very responses one might wish to extinguish. In order to stop reinforcing his wife's outbursts, he was advised to be consistent—always to ignore her complaints and to respond positively only when she was behaving pleasantly. Mr. A did his best to follow these instructions, but instead of solving the couple's problems, it only aggravated their mutual strife.

After the initial interview with the couple, I* met with each of them individually for a single assessment interview and then drew up the following modality profiles:

A perusal of the modality profile indicates that Mr. A, a reserved, emotionally constricted, and achievement-oriented man, is married to a rather passive-aggressive, dependent, anxious woman. They seem to have little in the way of common interests and shared activities, and a lot of parallel (rather than convergent) areas prevail in their marriage. It is easy to see how Mrs. A readily misperceives her husband's reserve and uncommunicative habits as a personal affront, how she views his aloof attitude as a personal shortcoming, and ends up fearing that she is unloved and unwanted. In searching for reassurance, she unwisely resorts to criticisms and demands, which not only fail to evoke the hoped-for reassurance but create even greater emotional distance within the marriage.

Clearly, the modality profiles call for several significant intraindividual and interpersonal changes. Perhaps the worst advice would be for Mr. A to ignore his wife's complaints. The woman felt ignored much of the time, and by being further ignored when

| Modality | Husband | Wife |
|---|---|---|
| Behavior | Reserved, unexpressive. Preoccupied with work. Plays tournament bridge. Goes to pottery classes. | Critical, demanding. Does important committee work. Reads a lot. |
| Affect | Unexpressive, somewhat moody, does get angry. | Depressed, angry, rather anxious. |
| Sensation | Prone to gastric upsets. Some lower back pain. Enjoys tennis and swimming. | Tension headaches. Strong sense of aesthetic appreciation. |
| Imagery | A predominance of "success" and "failure" images, especially in business. | Pictures herself being lonely and abandoned. |
| Cognition | Work ethic values plus stereotyped ideas about "masculinity." | "I am helpless and need to be taken care of." |
| Interpersonal | Somewhat introverted. Enjoys no close friends. Somewhat over-competitive. | Dependent on her husband, but socially successful with women friends. |
| Drugs | Takes various medications for stomach problems and backache. | Drinks too much coffee. Smokes heavily. |

*In this case example, A. A. Lazarus was the therapist.

seeking reassurance (albeit incorrectly and immaturely), her feelings of inadequacy and her fears of rejection would only intensify.

My first therapeutic intervention was to share the modality profiles with the couple. They were in basic agreement with my impressions and were able to add additional items across their respective BASIC ID categories that amplified my cursory analysis. We discussed their personal ''hangups'' and the ways in which these individual problems impacted on the relationship. Two specific recommendations arose out of the discussion.

1.  They were to find some activity that they could pursue together. (At first Mrs. A suggested that she would take up tennis and learn to play bridge, but the potential competitive overtones led us to find a new activity for the two of them. Horseback riding and photography were finally selected.)
2.  Mr. A was advised to respond to his wife's complaints and criticisms by reassuring her that he loved her and had no wish to reject or abandon her.

The second tactic, according to strict operant formulations, would most likely exacerbate the problem since the husband would be dispensing positive reinforcement for her complaints, in which case they should increase in frequency. But the ''reassurance tactic'' resulted in a dramatic decrease of nagging and complaining from Mrs. A. As she later explained: ''I didn't realize that I would start up a fight whenever I felt [my husband] slipping away from me. . . . At least I got a reaction out of him, even though it wasn't the kind of reaction I wanted to get.''

Further attention was devoted to fostering various activities that the couple could pursue together rather than separately. Their general lack of mutual assertiveness and expressiveness was also dealt with. Several sessions were devoted to the correction of Mr. A's stereotyped thinking and Mrs. A's proclivity to assume the ''helpless female role.'' They each derived considerable benefit from Med-

itation and relaxation training—Mr. A's gastrointestinal problems improved and Mrs. A's tension headaches cleared up.

Throughout the course of therapy (which covered a total of 23 sessions over a period of seven months), we kept referring to the modality profiles, which served as a ''blueprint'' or ''compass.'' We reached consensus on the fact that Mr. A was far less reserved, no longer unexpressive, much less prone to moodiness or outbursts of anger, no longer troubled by frequent gastric upsets, less concerned about the ''tough, hard-working male image,'' and more concerned with displays of empathy and sensitivity and the cultivation of genuine friendships. Mrs. A was far less critical and demanding, no longer depressed, less angry and anxious, far more self-sufficient and optimistic, and entirely free from tension headaches. The results have been maintained for more than three years to date.

## SUMMARY

Multimodal Therapy is a comprehensive, systematic, and holistic approach to psychotherapy that seeks to effect durable change in an efficient and humane way. Although Multimodal Therapy shares common goals with other forms of therapy, it differs from them in important ways.

Multimodal Therapy does not employ the explanatory constructs of psychoanalysis but rests on more parsimonious and empirically testable theories of personality and behavior. It is broader in scope than Behavior Therapy with which it shares a number of intervention techniques. It is more active-directive than client-centered therapy, and more systematic than rational-emotive therapy.

Multimodal Therapy is an open system. The principle of technical eclecticism encourages the constant introduction of new techniques and refinement or elimination of existing ones. Multimodal therapists subscibe to no dogma other than the principles of theoretical parsimony and therapeutic effectiveness.

In summary, Multimodal Therapy is characterized by the following statements:

1. It employs an educational rather than medical, disease-oriented model to account for the acquisition and elimination of maladaptive responses.
2. Assessments and interventions are structured around seven modalities summarized by the acronym BASIC ID (*be*havior, *a*ffect, *s*ensation, *i*magery, *c*ognition, *i*nterpersonal relationships, and *d*rugs/biological factors).
3. A wide range of intervention strategies is employed through the principle of technical eclecticism.
4. Considerable attention is focused on teaching the client strategies to cope with both present and anticipated life stress.
5. The therapist assumes the role of mentor in a consultant/client relationship.
6. Liberal use of homework and *in vivo* exercises is employed to increase therapeutic efficiency and to facilitate generalization of therapeutic gains.

# REFERENCES

Alberti, R. E. and Emmons, M. L. *Your perfect right: A guide to assertive behavior*. San Luis Obispo, Calif.: Impact Press, 1978.

Bandura, A. *Principles of behavior modification*. New York: Holt, 1969.

Bandura, A. *Social learning theory*. Englewood Cliffs, N.J.: Prentice-Hall, 1977.

Brunell, L. F. A multimodal treatment model for a mental hospital: Designing specific treatments for specific problems. *Professional Psychology*, November 1978, 570–578.

Davison, G. C. and Wilson, G. T. Processes of fear reduction in systematic desensitization: Cognitive and social reinforcement factors in humans. *Behavior Therapy*, 1973, **4**, 1–21.

Ellis, A. *Reason and emotion in psychotherapy*. New York: Lyle Stuart, 1962.

Gerler, E. R. The "BASIC ID" in career education. *The Vocational Guidance Quarterly*, 1977, **5**, 238–244.

Heiman, J., LoPiccolo, L. and LoPiccolo, J. *Becoming orgasmic: A sexual growth program for women*. Englewood Cliffs, N.J.: Prentice-Hall, 1976.

Keat, D. B. *Multimodal therapy with children*. New York: Pergamon, 1979.

Lazarus, A. A. New methods in psychotherapy: A case study. *South African Medical Journal*, 1958, **32**, 660–664.

Lazarus, A. A. Group therapy of phobic disorders by systematic desensitization. *Journal of Abnormal and Social Psychology*, 1961, **63**, 505–510.

Lazarus, A. A. The results of behaviour therapy in 126 cases of severe neurosis. *Behaviour Research and Therapy*, 1963, **1**, 69–79.

Lazarus, A. A. In support of technical eclecticism. *Psychological Reports*, 1967, **21**, 415–416.

Lazarus, A. A. *Behavior therapy and beyond*. New York: McGraw-Hill, 1971.

Lazarus, A. A. Multimodal behavior therapy: Treating the "BASIC ID." *Journal of Nervous and Mental Disease*, 1973, **156**, 404–411.

Lazarus, A. A. *Multimodal behavior therapy*. New York: Springer, 1976.

Lazarus, A. A. *In the mind's eye*. New York: Rawson Associates, 1978.

Lazarus, A. A. *The practice of multimodal therapy: Systematic, comprehensive, and effective, psychotherapy*. New York: McGraw-Hill, 1981.

Lazarus, A. A. and Fay, A. *I can if I want to*. New York: Morrow, 1975.

Popler, K. Agoraphobia: Indications for the application of the multimodal behavioral conceptualization. *Journal of Nervous and Mental Disease*, 1977, **164**, 97–101.

Richard, J. T. Multimodal therapy: An integrating model for behavioral medicine. *Psychological Reports*, 1978, **42**, 635–639.

Sank, L. I. Community disasters: Primary prevention and treatment in a health maintenance organization. *American Psychologist*, 1979, **34**, 334–338.

Wilson, G. T. and Davison, G. C. Processes of fear reduction in systematic desensitization: Animal studies. *Psychology Bulletin*, 1971, **76**, 1–14.

Wolpe, J. *Psychotherapy by reciprocal inhibition*. Stanford, Calif.: Stanford University Press, 1958.

Wolpe, J. *The practice of behavior therapy*, 2nd ed. New York: Pergamon, 1973.

Wolpe, J. and Lazarus, A. A. *Behavior therapy techniques*. New York: Pergamon, 1966.

# CHAPTER 37

# *Multiple Family Therapy*

JOHN W. RAASOCH

*Many years ago I searched for the origins of group psychotherapy and found that about a dozen people had discovered or developed it in about the same decade, all quite independent of each other. The same is true of Multiple Family Therapy, which in this next chapter is credited to H. Peter Laqueur. I was trained in it by Dr. Rudolf Dreikurs in about 1950, and he in turn had been trained by Alfred Adler about 1920. When I first moved to Hawaii I discovered that a form of this kind of Multiple Family Therapy, with the additional innovation that there were also multiple therapists, was being done by Dr. Daniel Fullmer. I suppose that it is either a case of great minds going in the same directions or perhaps, even more likely, that procedures such as Multiple Family Therapy, as well as group psychotherapy, are a function of the cultural Zeitgeist—an idea whose time has come.*

*This chapter by John Raasoch gives a clear indication of a most useful and practical method of family counseling and psychotherapy. It seems to be a more complex version of what occurs in primitive cultures when the extended family group meets in council for the purposes of settling disputes, making decisions, and the like. In my judgment MFT is an important technique, with many economic and social values, and bears further investigation and replication.*

Multiple Family Therapy (MFT) is a combination of individual family therapy and group therapy. In MFT three to five families are seen simultaneously.

There are two basic models of MFT. The first model entails doing family therapy for one family while the other families observe. One family is on the "hot seat" each week. The second model involves maximizing group interaction and group process. Here each family's concerns are addressed at each session. The second model will be described here.

## HISTORY

H. Peter Laqueur is usually cited as the pioneer of Multiple Family Therapy because of his work at Creedmore State Hospital in New York. His first publication regarding MFT appeared in the *Journal of Neuropsychiatry* (1962). However, Detre, Kessler, and Sayers (1961) as well as Hes and Handler (1961) described meetings of patients and families occurring earlier.

Laqueur fondly recalled those early Sunday afternoons at Creedmore in an auditorium with 50 patients and families together for both an educative program and patient government. After achieving many successes even from that chaotic interaction, he followed the suggestion of a family therapist friend and began seeing 10 groups of five families each. When Laqueur realized that these groups fared better and had decreased readmission rates, MFT as a legitimate therapy was born.

MFT was later refined as a therapy when the Laqueurs moved permanently to their summer home in Vermont. Even rugged, private, backwoods Vermonters would brave two hours of traveling through ice and snow to attend these highly valued MFT groups. Initiating group therapy, especially in Vermont, was difficult. Asking three to five families to "go public" for MFT was an almost insurmountable task. When the MFT group was finally formed, it was a tedious process to build trust and encourage sharing of meaningful information. Techniques and exercises to accelerate this process have been published elsewhere (Laqueur, 1976). These exercises include all the mothers coming to the center of the room to discuss with each other what kind of spouses and parents they are. The fathers then follow the same procedure. Other subgroups identified by the therapist, such as "good kids" and "bad kids," also meet separately to identify their similarities. This process facilitates early cohesiveness and identification with subgroups.

The method of training therapists has also been modified over the years. The early process of training MFT therapists required at least five steps, each usually lasting for about six months. The progression of training steps was from silent observer, to operator of the video camera, to active observer, to co-therapist, to therapist. Innovative techniques to accelerate this learning process, such as simulating MFT in workshops for professionals, have been developed (Raasoch & Laqueur, 1979).

## CURRENT STATUS

Multiple Family Therapy has grown by leaps and bounds and is currently in practice throughout the world. MFT-type meetings with families now occur in schools, prisons, and nursing homes as well as in traditional psychiatric hospitals and outpatient clinics. The MFT method is applicable to mental health centers with long waiting lists and is useful to the many different specialty populations that a mental health center serves.

It is interesting to compare and contrast MFT with different models of family education. Most traditional models of family education teach parents about parent-child communication in a structured, intellectual manner without children present. In MFT, parents learn informally along with their children by modeling and example. Out of the knowledge gained from MFT, it has been recommended that children be present when courses are taught to parents on how to communicate more openly with their children (Raasoch & McCollester, 1977).

An excellent review of the literature of MFT was done by A. H. Strelnick (1977).

## THEORY

Multiple Family Therapy theory borrows from systems, family, and group theory. MFT takes exception with the often cited eight to ten client maximum thought to be desirable for functional group therapy (Yalom, 1970). Even though MFT has been referred to as crowd control or a three-ring circus, it can be organized. Meeting with 20 individuals from four families is not the same as meeting with 20 unrelated individuals. In MFT the therapist can divide a large group into subsets. The therapist is then essentially dealing with four or five entities at a single moment. The situation then becomes almost analagous to doing group therapy with four to five clients. These subgroups, however, are constantly changing. For the first 10 minutes of a session one may be dealing with the Browns, the Smiths, and the Joneses, and then switch to the mothers, fathers, problematic kids, and "good kids." By the end of the session there may be groups of angry screamers, quiet stompers, and passive observers. With such a large group the therapist needs to encourage identification with subgroups among clients by pointing out similarities among members. Frequently the therapist needs to physically maneuver clients into various groupings.

Objectivity is another major asset of MFT. Family members can be much more objective in viewing another family's dynamics than their own. It is common for Mr. Brown to comment on Mr. Smith's interaction with his family and then reflect on his own family; for example, "George, you're really lecturing Johnny. Hmmm. . . . Maybe I do the same to my son."

Support among clients is probably the greatest benefit of MFT. A great deal of support can occur between families in a well-functioning MFT group. A family's crisis does not have to become a crisis for the therapist when the other families empathize and help solve the problem. If the therapist has modeled helpful behavior in past sessions without rescuing, he frequently needs to only direct traffic while the other families do the "therapy."

Modeling is another benefit provided by MFT, especially with co-therapy teams. The ideal is to have a harmonious male-female co-therapy dyad that models openness and sharing of decision making. MFT can be an open modality for sharing therapeutic techniques with the entire group. When MFT groups are used for training professionals, a supervisor may confront a learning therapist in the midst of an MFT session and ask him to justify to everyone what he is trying to accomplish. Maximizing openness of techniques in front of clients facilitates the process of their becoming cotherapists.

Co-therapy by clients is another achievable goal. Many families with "seniority" in the group have returned for several sessions after their logical termination to help engage new families in an MFT group. Long before logical termination, certain families or members are far advanced in specific areas and can be referred to as models—there may be bedtime-setting experts, relating-to-adolescents experts, or the experts at bringing up parents.

In various stages of MFT, competition can be encouraged. Competition is a positive factor when clients and families compete to see who gets better faster. Competition to become a good example and/or a co-therapist is also desirable.

In this day of fragmented families, it is striking how well MFT is suited to deal with absent members. The anger toward an alcoholic father who has practically deserted the family can be worked through with another father in the group. In individual family therapy these resentments may come out much slower and take longer to work through.

## METHODOLOGY

Beginning any group takes a lot of a therapist's energy, and Multiple Family Therapy is no exception. To begin MFT requires a directive salesman who is totally sold on the value of his service. The enthusiastic salesman also needs endurance, since many families who are screened may reject the idea of MFT as totally absurd before three to five families willing to participate are found. Dropout rates are at least as high as for other group therapy modalities (Yalom, 1970).

Not being directive enough in the early sessions is an easy trap to fall into. Lack of direction leads to individuals and families feeling neglected in such a large group. It also allows aggressive or crisis-prone clients to dominate.

Families feel very uncomfortable being "exposed" to other families, and the therapist has to demonstrate his abilities and the benefits of MFT very early in the sessions. In spite of these efforts, it is not uncommon for it to take a year or two for members of an MFT group to engage themselves in the therapeutic process and for the group to become well established.

The ideal process of an MFT session includes six stages. The first stage is to *gauge the affect*, that is, obtain the feeling tone of each member of the group, including general information of most recent events in the family.

The next stage is to *develop a common theme*. It is important to find and label a theme common to all or most of the families. When a more specific discussion involves a particular family, the other families can then relate their own problems to the discussion. If three families each presented with a crisis—such as a suicidal mother, a son arrested for drug charges, a grandmother moving out of the family home—the common theme could be defined as a power struggle. Given the many diversities of content that can be presented, it is most important to reduce issues to the most basic, feeling levels.

The third stage is to *find a relevant exercise*. The goal is to utilize a nonverbal exercise to break through much of the verbal preoccupation with minute details and deal instead with the gut-level responses. To deal with the power struggles cited above, a sculptured "back-to-back" exercise can be utilized effectively. The two clients involved are asked to stand in the center of the room with their backs together, arms folded across their chests. They are instructed to solve their problems *without* words: "Show us action, not talk." If one of them chooses to walk away from the conflict, the therapist states that that is one alternative. The therapist then yanks the client back into the center of the room and instructs him to find *another* alternative. Sculpturing is a visual representation of family dynamics first developed by Duhl, Duhl, and Kantor (1973).

Stage four is a decision to *intensify or diffuse the process*. Since there are so many ages in families, it is important to maintain a level of intensity that keeps everyone's interest. Nonverbal techniques, such as family sculpturing, can hold children's interest, while they intensify the tone for adults and force them to function on a more primary process level. Depending on the timing, the therapist can either intensify or diffuse the session by having group and family members talk about themselves as colors or animals. A father's intense anger can be diffused by comparing him to a grizzly bear with subsequent discussion of the bear's positive attributes.

Stage five, *winding down,* and stage six, *leaving with positive feelings,* frequently run together. If, somehow, someone in each family does not leave with a positive feeling, the MFT group likely will not survive. With entire families coming each week, it is difficult to keep everyone engaged. Many conflicts in schedules arise and frequently someone

ends up pleading not to come back. It is valuable to give the clients a chance to catch their breath and leave on a friendly social note with the others. Summing up, providing some resolution, and assigning homework tasks are helpful.

The essential ingredient in the above stages is the directiveness of the therapist. MFT is unique because of the large numbers of clients dealt with at one time, which necessitates that the therapist adopt the role of a ringmaster. The therapist may gradually evolve a laissez-faire stance as the group becomes cohesive, but initially an enthusiastic optimist must take charge. An earlier reference was made to the therapist *yanking* a client back to the center of the room. This is not an overstatement when it comes to nonverbal exercises. If the exercise is to have any chance of success, it must be spontaneous. The therapist cannot take no for an answer; he has to feel confident that the client will stand up. This is analogous to admitting ambivalent schizophrenics to the hospital. Young psychiatric residents may spend hours in the emergency room trying to talk future inpatients out of their ambivalence. However, the resident soon learns to elicit family support. He also learns that gentle, firm, constant pressure on the patient's back will succeed in getting the patient to the elevator.

Another analogy is that of an aggressive coach pacing the sidelines and yanking players off the bench to enter the game. The time of inserting someone into the action is crucial and, like the coach, the MFT therapist must know his players' strengths and vulnerabilities very well.

## APPLICATIONS

Multiple Family Therapy works for almost every diagnostic category and level of psychopathology. The benefits of MFT include simultaneous training of many professionals and reduced boredom of therapists. It can also be justified on economic considerations. Even more so than in traditional Group Therapy, the professional can see large numbers of clients with a minimal expenditure of time.

MFT can even be justified for clinical needs. Chronic schizophrenics and their families can be boring after a few years and, if seeing groups of these families stimulates the interest of a therapist, certainly the quality of clinical treatment will improve.

In discussing applications of MFT the needs of two groups of people should be considered—the professionals and the clients. The professional category includes third-party payers to whom the economic benefits of MFT are obvious.

Training therapists is quite applicable to MFT. Many observers can watch and participate in meaningful ways, such as behind a video camera. It also presents an opportunity for a trainee to observe several families' dynamics in one session. Much more time would have to be spent in order to see those same families individually. Medical students especially find MFT useful in providing maximum exposure to families in a limited time period.

Clinical indications for MFT are not as obvious. Two questions arise: What can a client do for the group? and What can the group do for a client? The group needs diversity—socioeconomic diversity, for example. If five corporate lawyers and their families meet together they inevitably discuss corporate law. Families of a college professor, a welfare mother, and an old New England farmer will comprise a far superior group, since the fact that they have so little in common forces them to deal with the common denominator of basic family conflicts. In a specific MFT group it may be preferable to have families whose children's ages are similar; for example, families with adolescents or families with preschoolers. Laqueur, however, preferred to have the most diverse ages possible.

Most family problems are included when considering indications for clients to benefit from MFT. Because of the enormous group support, MFT is especially helpful for adolescents separating from their families. This is clearly effective when an older adolescent has resolved this conflict and can serve as a role model.

MFT groups can also help parents recognize when they are scapegoating their children for marital conflicts. Single parents can receive the support they so desperately need to make it on their own, which helps prevent them from immediately turning to the first available spouse. MFT has also risen to the occasion to help an ''untreatable'' individual or family so labeled by the referral source. Seeing an individual in the context of his family and, particularly, in a group of families facilitates work.

Before a family can benefit from MFT, it must be convinced to ''go public,'' which is no small task. Because of this difficulty, sometimes the only criteria left for a family to pass the screening process is its willingness to be exposed in front of other families.

A relative contraindication for inclusion in the group would be the acutely psychotic individual, as Guttman (1973) mentioned. However, the present MFT group composition would be an important factor to consider since a supportive, well-functioning group could probably handle this individual with a very nonthreatening, slow-pace approach.

Other categories that signal the need for caution because of possible detrimental effects to the client include the extremely subassertive individual and the passive schizophrenic. As published previously (Raasoch & Laqueur, 1979) these clients may be double bound by feeling abandoned yet unable to mention it.

## CASE EXAMPLE

The following example represents a composite of several MFT groups; specifics have been changed to protect confidentiality. The MFT group consists of the following families.

### The Red-Blue Family (Blended Family)

| | |
|---|---|
| Mr. Red: | Father, lawyer, age 47, previously married, nearly constantly angry. |
| Red Jr.: | Son, age 17, product of father's first marriage, |

in conflict with father because he does not want to be a lawyer.

| | |
|---|---|
| Mrs. Blue: | Mother, salesclerk, age 38, previously married, usually depressed. |
| Bluette: | Daughter of Mrs. Blue's first marriage, age 17, usually bubbly. |

(Two other daughters of Mrs. Blue, ages 23 and 21, live out of the home and are nondescript. They attended sessions 3 and 4 respectively.)

## The White Family (Single Parent)

| | |
|---|---|
| Mrs. White: | Mother, schoolteacher, divorced, age 37, usually righteous. |
| Black: | Son, age 19, always in trouble. |
| Gray: | Daughter, age 16, not as much trouble. |

## The Green Family (Single Parent)

| | |
|---|---|
| Mrs. Green: | Welfare mother, age 30, eighth-grade education, constantly worried about money. |
| Greener: | Son, age 12, always "better" than Greens. |
| Greens: | Daughter, age 11, vegetarian. |
| Greenie: | Infant daughter, age 9 months. |

## The Burgundy Family

| | |
|---|---|
| Mr. Burgundy: | Father, machinist, age 56, alcoholic. |
| Mrs. Burgundy: | Mother, age 55, a happy homemaker. |
| Burgy: | Daughter, age 23, unmarried, tomboy, still living at home. |
| Burnt-Out: | Daughter, age 17, schizophrenic. |

| | |
|---|---|
| Bundy: | Daughter, age 7, always fighting with siblings and peers. |

## Summary of First Four MFT Sessions

*Session 1.* The Red-Blue, White, and Burgundy families, along with a fourth family X, were introduced to each other. Mothers, fathers, "good kids," and "bad kids" all came to the center of the room sequentially and were encouraged to identify with each other. Parents became polarized with the group of "bad kids" when the therapist redefined "bad kids" as having more fun. When the Burgundy family was sculptured, this polarization was slightly diffused. (See Figure 1a.)

*Session 2.* Only the Red-Blue, White, and Burgundy families returned, while family X was absent. The group was very slow starting but by the end of the session some early cohesiveness was beginning to build. (See Figure 1b.)

*Session 3.* The Green family was added to the Red-Blue, White, and Burgundy families, and family X returned. Family X was very negative about MFT, which made it difficult to convince the Greens that this was a workable treatment modality. Family X never returned. (See Figure 1c.)

*Session 4.* The Green family returned with the Red-Blues, Whites, and Burgundys. The four families began functioning as a group. After the Green family was sculptured, they were well integrated into the group. (See Figure 1d.)

In figure 1, showing sessions 1 to 4, the shift from families sitting together to dispersing throughout the group can be noted. This shift of seating attests to the alliances that are formed between mutually supportive clients. When a new family (the Greens) is added in session 3, they cling together for security. By session 4, however, they are already beginninng to disperse throughout

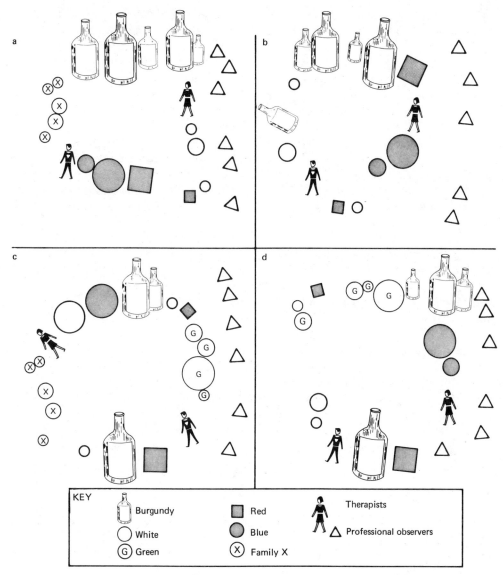

Figure 1   Sessions 1 to 4.

the group. By session 4 alliances are established between fathers, mothers, and "bad kids."

## Session 10—All Four Families Present

Mr. Burgundy announced his third consecutive week of sobriety and was very active throughout the session, emerging as the first client co-therapist.

Red Jr. presented a huge fight with his father, which resulted in his decision to go and live with his biological mother. He also accused his stepmother, Mrs. Blue, of having an affair. At that point Greens broke into tears over not having seen her divorced father for three years and even Black was able to relate what a hassle a divorce was for a son. At this point, one of the therapists crossed the room to Greens, asked Mrs. Blue to watch Greenie, and encouraged Greens to physically join Red Jr. and Black (See Figure 2.)

Mr. Burgundy pointed out how Mr. Red and Mrs. Blue must not allow Red Jr. to continually threaten to return to his mother and play on their guilt. Red Jr. admitted that he really did *not* want to return to his mother because she was an alcoholic like Mr. Burgundy. He then described in detail how totally obnoxious a drunk parent can be. Talking about divorce and separation led Black to a very emotional resolution that his parents would never reunite.

The session ended on a light note when Greenie, the ninemonth-old, poured soda into Mrs. Blue's pocketbook. (Figure 2.)

### Session 20—Red-Blue, Green, and Burgundy Families Present

This session began with a long intellectual discussion between Mr. Red and Mr. Burgundy. Mr. Burgundy's plant was about to unionize and Mr. Red was expounding on all the legal ramifications of unions. On a hunch, one of the therapists sat Mrs. Blue on the floor in the center of the room, po-

sitioning her head down. Within seconds she began to cry intensely, whereupon Mr. Red began swearing at Mr. Burgundy. Then Mrs. Blue rose to her feet, threw her glasses across the room, and stormed out the door, slamming it behind her. Red Jr. ran out after his stepmother. When the two did not return to the group, Mrs. Green left the room and eventually convinced Mrs. Blue to return. In the ensuing discussion a pattern was identified between Mr. Red and Mrs. Blue. Every time Mrs. Blue got depressed Mr. Red became extremely angry and Red Jr. always ended up in the middle.

During the discussion that followed, Mrs. Burgundy was able to confront Mrs. Green with the observation that her interaction with her 12-year-old, Greener, was very similar to Mr. Red's interaction with Red Jr. The therapists were able to use Mrs. Burgundy's style of very openly relating to adolescents as an example of listening to and truly respecting them. (See Figure 3.)

### Session 40—All Four Familes Present

This session had been previously set as the termination date for the Red-Blue family.

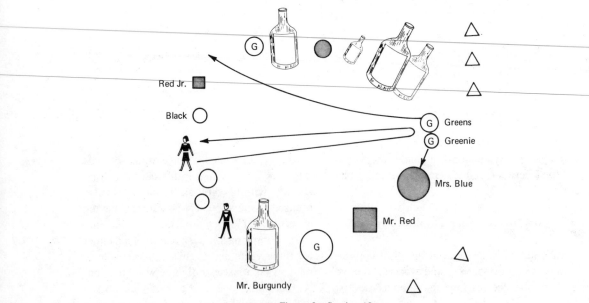

Figure 2   Session 10.

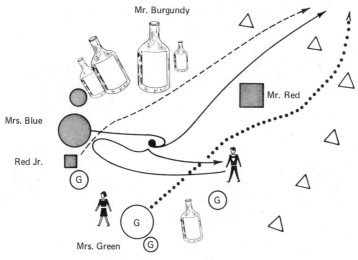

Figure 3    Session 20.

The Red-Blue family was sculptured—first, the way they had presented almost a year earlier and then their present status. (See Figure 4.)

The progress and shifts of this family were very dramatic and obvious to everyone. The Red and the Blue families were finally integrated and a new family—Purple—emerged. The Greens were also discussing termination, and a tentative termination data was set two months away. The families were updated about the screening process for new families for the group.

Throughout most of the session the younger children—Greener, Greens, and Bundy—had been drawing and seemed fairly distant from the group process. Near the end, when asked if they wanted to give their drawings to anyone, they unanimously chose Burnt-Out as the recipient. Burnt-Out had been almost catatonic recently and was clearly moved when she was awarded the drawings. She then volunteered that it was her birthday. It was interesting to note that all of the drawings were of cats and that Burnt-Out's T-shirt had a picture of a tiger on it.

## SUMMARY

MFT utilizes the best of both worlds, combining the excitement and advantages of group and family therapy. This modality represents much more than merely a large group of 20 individuals. Each member is already a member of a family in the group, and the co-therapists continually look for innovative was to help the clients see themselves as part of other subgroups. Through these subgroups and the natural caring that is fostered in this process, a tremendous amount of support emerges for troubled individuals.

Objectivity is another advantage of having several families present. Seeing one family alone, a single professional can easily get caught up in that family's psychopathology. In MFT more than one professional is usually present and the rest of the group provides valuable input. In fact, other family members are encouraged to become "co-therapists."

The rich supply of family dynamics and psychopathology makes MFT a very efficient modality for training professionals. Innovative ways to learn MFT process are also available such as workshops for professionals

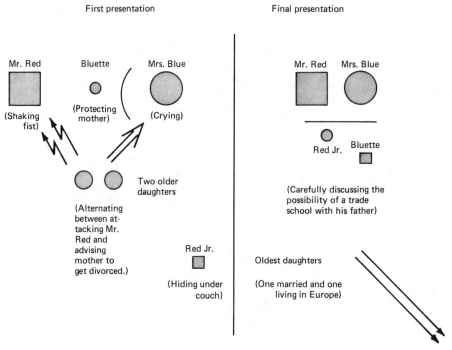

Figure 4   Session 40.

that simulate MFT groups (Raasoch & Laqueur 1979).

Whether in a workshop or an actual MFT
group, a very directive salesman-type therapist is needed. The MFT therapist must be
confident and comfortable with moving people physically about. This person is frequently "on stage" and is a continual model
for the group. The "performance" part
—utilizing nonverbal exercises with spacial
imagery—is needed to maintain interest.

## REFERENCES

Detre, T., Kessler, D. and Sayers, J. A socio-adaptive
approach to treatment of acutely disturbed psychiatric
in-patients. *Proceedings of the Third World Congress
in Psychiatry*, 1961, **1**, 501–506.

Duhl, F., Duhl, B. and Kantor, D. Learning, space and
action in family therapy: A primer of sculpture. In D.
Block (Ed.), *Techniques of family psychotherapy*. New
York: Grune & Stratton, 1973.

Guttman, H. A. A contraindication for family therapy.
*Archives of General Psychiatry*, 1973, **29**, 352–355.

Hes, J. and Handler, S. Multidimensional group psychotherapy. *Archives of General Psychiatry*, 1961, **5**,
92–97.

Laquewr, H. P. Multiple family therapy. In P. J. Guerin,
Jr. (Ed.), *Family therapy theory and practice*. New
York: Gardner Press, 1976.

Laqueur, H. P. Multiple family therapy. In P. J. Guerin,
Jr. (Ed.), *Family therapy theory and practice*. New
York: Gardner Press, 1976.

Raasoch, J. and Laqueur, H. P. Learning multiple family therapy through simulated workshops. *Family Process*, 1979, **18**, 95–98.

Raasoch, J. and McCollester, G. Multiple family therapy or edcation. Workshop presented for The American
Association of Psychiatric Services for Children, Washington, D.C., 1977.

Strelnick, A. H. Multiple family group therapy: A review of the literature. *Family Process*, 1977, **16**,
307–35.

Yalom, I.D. *The theory and practice of group psychotherapy*. New York: Basic Books, 1970.

# CHAPTER 38

# *Multiple Impact Training*

GEORGE M. GAZDA

*Two patients, while in a doctor's waiting room, started to talk. They learned that even though they had very different symptoms, their doctor had prescribed for them the very same regimen of fresh air, good food, and rest. When the doctor came out, they attacked him as a quack.*

*George Gazda's general position is that all people with psychological problems can probably be helped by the equivalent of fresh air, good food, and rest—that is, by learning important social skills, the lack of which may have been the underlying cause of the maladjustment symptoms that they have been demonstrating. In short, one form of psychotherapy may simply be training the client to be more competent in meeting life.*

*In the next chapter, Dr. Gazda zeros in on individuals' deficits, operating in the common-sense and well-tried process of first diagnosing deficiencies, then prescribing a course of treatment relating to the deficiencies, and, finally, reevaluating the individual. This broad, sensible approach is quite similar to what is done in industrial training and in medical monitoring of treatment.*

*I can see this model becoming a standard procedure for any institution that aims to correct or improve people, whether it be a school, a mental hospital, or a prison. This approach should in no way contradict the usual communication type of psychotherapy, but could be the broad, umbrellalike method to cover all ameliorative efforts of any institution.*

Multiple Impact Training (MIT) is therapy but not in the traditional sense, since it is based on an educational rather than a medical model. As the name implies, its impact is multiple, not only in terms of various therapy modalities but, more important, in teaching/training life skills.

Persons who seek therapy rarely suffer from a single life-skill deficit; however, some life-skill deficits are more important than others for effective social functioning. For example, poor interpersonal relationships may be more crucial to a person's effective functioning in life than poor decision-making abilities. In working with clients in a variety of locations, I have noted that practically everyone is in need of counteracting some life-skill deficit.

MIT therapists recognize that a variety of skills are needed to succeed in life. These skills are defined within the psychosocial, physical-sexual, vocational, cognitive, moral, ego, and emotional areas of human development. Many so-called "mental problems" will be alleviated or resolved if people learn such skills. MIT is concerned with training/teaching such skills as an essential part of any comprehensive psychotherapy/counseling process.

I wish to acknowledge the contribution of the case example by Mildred Powell, R.N.

## HISTORY

Multiple Impact Training was first named in 1978; however, the concept was first presented in this writer's book *Group Counseling: A Developmental Approach* (1971). Only two major human developmental areas were included in this publication: the *psychosocial stages of development* of Havighurst (1953, 1972) and Erik Erikson (1963) and the *vocational stages* of Super (Super, 1963; Super et al., 1957). In the second edition of this publication (1978), the *physical-sexual stages* of Gesell (Gesell, Ilg, & Ames, 1956; Gesell et al., 1946), the *cognitive stages* of Jean Piaget (Flavell, 1963; Wadsworth, 1971), and the *moral stages* of Kohlberg (Kohlberg, 1973; Kohlberg & Turiel, 1971) were included. Since then two more areas seem worthy of inclusion: the *ego stages* of development of Loevinger (1976) and the *emotional stages* of Dupont (1978). (At the time of this writing, the ego and emotional stages of development have not been fully incorporated into MIT.)

The basic human development areas are considered major intervention domains for individual and group counselors. Figure 1 illustrates how the impact is conceptualized currently.

In 1964 MacGregor and associates wrote a book entitled *Multiple Impact Therapy with Families*. Although the title of this therapy is similar to Multiple Impact Training, in fact the treatment process is quite different. MacGregor and associates described the treatment of families through the use of multiple therapists (a team) who typically met with a given family over the course of two days with follow-up after six months. Family members were interviewed individually and together by one or several therapists. The basic team consisted of a psychologist, psychiatrist, and social worker.

The thrust of the Multiple Impact Therapy can be summarized in the following quotation:

In the final family-team conference, the work of the two days of MIT was reviewed in terms of its applicability to the practical situation to which the family would return. By this time the relevant recurring patterns of troublesome family interaction tended to be clear to various family members. The family was urged to be vigilant to the recurrence of these troublesome patterns and to view them as warning signals—signals that should set the family to work to devise a sound solution to a crisis. The work of the two days was looked at in terms of the practical situation to which they must return. (MacGregor, et al., 1964, p. 70)

There is also a similarity between Multimodal Behavior Therapy (MBT) of Lazarus (1975) and the Multiple Impact Training model. Lazarus defined Multimodal Behavior Therapy as "a systematic problem-solving process that examines and, if necessary, endeavors to remedy maladaptive responses across six separate but inter-related modalities—behavior, affect, sensation, imagery, cognition, and interpersonal relationships" (p. 150).

There are, however, several basic differences between Multiple Impact Training and Multimodal Behavior Therapy, the central difference being the conceptualization of the human dimensions subject to deterioration or ineffective functioning and consequently needing improvement. In certain areas, however, the two systems overlap. For example, Lazarus's *interpersonal relationships* are similar to the life skill of *interpersonal communications*.

Another major difference is in Lazarus's emphasis on locating deficits versus the MIT emphasis on locating areas of strength as well as areas of weakness. However, insofar as Multimodal Behavior Therapy emphasizes an educational approach to solving problems versus the medical "treatment" model, the MIT and MBT models are quite similar.

MIT and MBT are alike in their assumption that individuals experiencing psychological/emotional problems suffer from multiple deficits that require multiple intervention strategies. Lazarus (1975) stated his position on this issue as follows: *"The multimodal behavior therapy approach stresses the fact that patients are usually troubled by a multitude of specific problems that should be*

The whole person

Cognitive
Problem solving skills,
Applied learning skills, etc.

Psychosocial
Interpersonal communication skills,
Group relationship skills, etc.

Physical-sexual
Family relationship skills,
Physical fitness/health main-
tenance skills, etc.

Problem-area

Vocational
Career development skills,
Consumer resources skills, etc.

Moral
Identification of personal
values,
Self-evaluation skills, etc.

Figure 1   Basic developmental modalities and illustrative life skills.

dealt with by a similar multitude of specific treatments'' (p. 165).

Insofar as Ellis's Rational-Emotive Therapy (1975) uses an educational rather than a medical or psychodynamic model, it too has components that are similar to MIT. Ellis contends that rational-emotive therapists use group processes as the method of choice, and in that regard RET is similar to MIT.

## CURRENT STATUS

The multiple impact training model has been under constant development since it was de-

scribed in *Group Counseling: A Developmental Approach* (Gazda, 1971).

The setting in which this model has been developed most completely (though it is still not complete) is the psychiatric division of the Veterans Administration Medical Center in Augusta, Georgia. This writer has served as a consultant to this center since 1972.

A psychiatric hospital such as a Veterans Administration hospital provides an ideal setting for MIT. Any other setting where there are numerous professionals in the "helping" professions with a great variety of interests and skills would be equally suitable.

Since so many different life-skills areas are involved, "helping" professionals involved in MIT have the opportunity to choose one or more areas in which to specialize and therefore do not have to be everything to everybody. The system thus permits maximum skill development in the life-skills areas of interest to the staff members. For example, certain staff members are interested in marriage and family counseling and teaching parenting skills. They can develop a model for teaching "family relationship" skills for those patients who need to develop such skills. Since the chaplains are already doing spiritual counseling, they are usually interested in developing a model dealing with "purpose/meaning in life" (identification of personal values).

Because of the several life-skills deficits generally found in psychiatric patients, the staff must develop many areas of expertise; however, because of the interdisciplinary nature of the staff, there is much expertise available for utilization in the typical clinic or mental health center. With proper encouragement and management, a built-in team approach to the delivery of psychiatric care is possible through MIT. One of the positive side effects is the staff's increased feeling of self-worth, their greater cooperation, and their higher morale as a result of working together in a common project, each utilizing his or her best skills.

## THEORY

Multiple Impact Training had its origin in a developmental conceptualization of human growth and development (Gazda, 1971, 1978). The assumptions that underlie MIT are essentially the same as those of developmental psychology/education (Gazda, 1977).

Several primary assumptions are at the heart of MIT:

1. There exist definite states through which all persons must develop if they are to be able to function in society (see Erikson, 1963).

2. There are specifiable stages through which all persons must progress in *all the basic areas of human development if they are to function effectively.*

3. There are certain age ranges in which certain life skills are most easily or optimally learned. Havighurst (1953) puts it this way:

A developmental task is a task which arises at or about a certain period in the life of the individual, successful achievement of which leads to his happiness and to success with later tasks, while failure leads to unhappiness in the individual, disapproval by society, and difficulty with later tasks. (p. 2)

4. The capacity for learning is inherited, but the degree to which a person is able to achieve his or her maximum potential is the result of his or her environment or life experiences.

5. Neuroses and functional psychoses are the result of failures in the development of life skills.

6. Basic life skills can be identified within the several areas of human development.

7. Life skills can be taught. Neuroses and functional psychoses can be most effectively and efficiently overcome through the direct teaching/training of clients/patients in the life-skill area deficits.

The theory underpinning MIT is based primarily on education/reeducation rather than treatment, à la the medical model. Teaching/training in life skills is based on the assumption that they can be taught in much the same fashion as the 3 R's are taught in schools. Different life-skill areas will require different educational models for most effective and efficient learning. For example, developing physical fitness/health maintenance skills includes more direct physical action or practice than, say, discovering one's purpose or values in life.

The assumption is made that one's self-concept, emotional status, and behavior are modified through learning and perfecting basic life skills. The more mastery one has over his or her life skills, the more capable he or she will be in meeting and solving life's daily problems. The more often one is able to meet and solve daily problems, the better will be his or her self-concept, emotional state, and behavior. Persons who gain mastery in the basic life-skill areas will be able to use these skills in creative ways to solve complex problems. They will thus gain security and happiness because they have achieved at least some control over their environment through their increased capacity to cope.

## METHODOLOGY

Multiple Impact Training, as the name implies, is based on the assumption that most clients or patients seeking help for psychological or emotional problems have deficits in "multiple" life-skill areas. Determining these deficit life-skill areas can be done through individual, group, or combinations of individual and group approaches.

The model of MIT methodology to be outlined herein is currently in operation at a Veterans Administration hospital. The process begins with a referral by the client's primary therapist to an "interdisciplinary screening group." This group may be led by any staff member or members from the several departments of the hospital. At any one time it may be led by a psychologist and a nurse, or a nurse and a social worker, or a chaplain and a nurse, and so forth. Although usually there are at least two professionals leading these groups, this is not a requirement.

These interdisciplinary screening groups function in a manner similar to the traditional open-ended interview therapy groups. They meet two or three times a week and the leaders attempt to diagnose the patient's life-skill deficits within three sessions. In addition to these interviews, the staff, of course, uses other available opportunities and data such as individual patient interviews, examination of the patient's social and medical history, ward observation by staff, interviews with the patient's family, and the like.

Life-skill teaching/training groups are then made available for the areas where the majority of patients have skill deficits. In the Augusta Veterans Administration Medical Center, the most frequent areas of life-skill deficits are interpersonal communications, physical fitness, meaning/purpose in life, decision making/problem solving, use of community resources, vocational choice, and parenting and family/marital relationships. A patient is encouraged to choose as many of these life-skills groups as he or she wishes to attend, but when the patient has more deficits than he or she has time for group attendance, the patient ranks the groups according to preference and then attends the two or three of highest priority. When it appears that a patient will be in the hospital for several months, he or she is encouraged to attend certain groups as prerequisite to others to follow. For example, the "purpose-in-life" group is a good prerequisite for the vocational choice group because once the patient achieves some purpose in life, he or she is more highly motivated to explore a vocation.

An open-ended traditional therapy group is always available for those patients who need the opportunity to continue exploration of self along with life-skill training groups. This group also helps patients integrate the skills from their training groups as well as isolate new areas of strengths and deficits.

In this particular setting the patient's primary therapist is responsible for monitoring the patient's progress and for recommending the patient's release. Ward-team staffing of patients, along with a written progress chart, provide the interdisciplinary treatment group with opportunities to exchange information about the patient's progress and to make recommendations regarding life-skill group placements.

It should be obvious by now that MIT is basically a multigroup treatment/training model. Since life-skills training is most effectively and efficiently done in the small group of eight to ten members, group instructional methods are most commonly employed. However, all life-skills groups are designed to include a combination of didactic and experiential (action) teaching/training methods. All groups heavily emphasize the practice of the life skills in the small group setting.

## APPLICATIONS

Multiple Impact Training was developed in a Veterans Administration psychiatric hospital and even difficult psychiatric patients have been found to be suitable clientele. Obviously, patients who are acutely psychotic and unable to attend meetings and to communicate would be excluded from MIT. These might include the hebrephrenic, paranoid, and catatonic schizophrenic types and manic-depressives in the manic stage. Any patient who could not control him- or herself or was otherwise disruptive would be excluded from the group training. However, some of these patients could still be assisted by MIT through individual training or instruction.

Since MIT is essentially an all-inclusive treatment model, virtually all individuals suffering from any of the life-skills deficits would be suitable clientele. Let us, for example, consider the application to persons suffering from substance abuse, say alcoholism. It is quite likely that the person classified as an alcoholic is lacking in some of the basic life skills. It is quite apparent that virtually all alcoholics have deficits in the area of physical fitness and need a physical fitness/health maintenance program. Many alcoholics are without a purpose in life and can benefit from a group that focuses on this issue. Still another area of deficit for the alcoholic is interpersonal communications. Most substance abusers can benefit from direct training in interpersonal communication, including assertiveness training. Some very anxious alcoholics can benefit from relaxation training/therapy. Others with marital problems need family relationship training (marital therapy).

Multiple Impact Training is especially suitable in institutional settings where there are a variety of trained professionals with differing interests and life-skill training expertise. For example, a university counseling or mental health center would usually have psychologists, psychiatrists, social workers, and nurses on staff. Some of the personnel might be counseling psychologists who could help students with life-skill deficits in career choice or vocational development. Some of the staff might be experts in interpersonal communication training. Still others will need to be able to teach/lead purpose-in-life groups. There will be students with physical fitness/health maintenance deficits who will need instruction in nutrition, diet, and so forth. In other words, college and university students represent a broad spectrum of the population with life-skill deficits in all areas and in varying degrees.

Community mental health clinics are similar to college and university mental health centers, but generally their clientele are more seriously lacking in life skills. The professional staffs of community mental health clinics are generally interdisciplinary in training and therefore have the potential to develop expertise in all the life-skills areas. Insofar as the staff generally functions from a medical model, reorientation in philosophy may be necessary. That is, the concept of "mental illness" will need to be changed to "life-skills deficits" for which teaching/ training is the preferred treatment. Assuming that the "balanced services" community mental health model (equal emphasis on prevention and rehabilitation) of the Carter administration will prevail, MIT becomes an ideal model for the delivery of community mental health services.

MIT, with its emphasis on "training" rather than "therapy," is also an ideal model for use in elementary and secondary schools because it is an educational and preventive model. Prevention of psychological/emotional problems can best be achieved through a comprehensive life-skills curriculum in the schools. Operating from the MIT model, counselors, school psychologists, school social workers, school nurses, special education personnel, and so forth, would all be involved in teaching life skills.

All students would be taught effective life-skills models for interpersonal communication, decision making/problem solving, physical fitness/health maintenance, emotional awareness, conflict resolution, group skills, family relationship skills, self-evaluation skills, principles of applied learning, organizational/institutional functioning, and so on. The life skills hold a striking resemblance to the seven cardinal principles of secondary education, which can be summarized as follows: (a) health, (b) command of fundamental process, (c) worthy home membership, (d) a vocation, (e) good citizenship, (f) worthy use of leisure time, and (g) ethical character. Shane (1977) contends that the seven cardinal principles "have retained their usefulness and their importance even after the passage of nearly 60 years." The National Assessment of Educational Progress (1975), a division of the Commission on Education of the States, cited (ironically) *seven* areas that were recommended by a planning committee as *basic skills*. The seven skill areas were the following: (a) consumer, (b) health maintenance, (c) interpersonal, (d) citizenship, (e) family relationship, (f) community resource utilization, and (g) career and occupational development.

Because MIT is an educational model and because it is most effectively and efficiently applied in the small group setting, it is especially appropriate for use in institutional settings where there exists a variety of trained professionals with a variety of interests and expertise. It would be least suitable for private practitioners unless they were a part of a larger practice with referral possibilities to other professionals who specialize in three

or four areas of life-skills training. For those private practitioners who would be willing to work as part of a large team, MIT can be a valuable therapeutic modality.

## CASE EXAMPLE*

This is the first psychiatric admission (5/11/79) for a 51-year-old white male diagnosed as a passive-aggressive personality with depression. Mr. Banks* has hypertension, arthritis, and is obese. On admission this patient was red-faced, unkempt, weighed 310 pounds, and had a blood pressure (B/P) 168/110. He was very shy, unable to make eye contact, and spoke in a low monotone. Mr. Banks stated that he lost his temper easily, had been explosive at times, had crying spells, felt tired all the time, and had been socially withdrawing for the past six months. The patient also related that his wife failed to have sexual relations with him because he was fat, sloppy, and fearful that she would get pregnant. Although Mr. Banks worked, he had no social outlets.

Mr. Banks's treatment plan included a mild antidepressant, 1,200 calorie diet, antihypertensive drug, and group therapy. He had Interpersonal Communications Skill Training, Assertiveness Training, Reality-Oriented Problem Solving, Relaxation Therapy, Diet Therapy (Physical Fitness/Health Maintenance), Occupational Therapy, and Corrective Therapy (see Table 1).

On discharge on July 31, 1979, Mr. Banks weighed 291 pounds, had a lowered B/P of 128/80, had a vasectomy, had initiated marital counseling, and was active and neat in appearance. During his course of hospitalization the patient was able to learn how to initiate conversation with others and was able to assert himself as chairman of ward government. He signed a nursing referral to be

*The case used here is fictitious to protect identity of the patient. Mildred Powell, R.N., of the Augusta, Georgia, Veteran's Medical Center, developed this case.

**Table 1.  Mr. Banks's Treatment Program**

| | Group Therapy | Relaxation Therapy | Physical fitness Health Maintenance | Assertiveness Training | Occupational Therapy | Corrective Therapy | Problem solving | Interpersonal Communications Skill Training |
|---|---|---|---|---|---|---|---|---|
| Psychosocial | X | | | X | | | | X |
| Vocational | | | | | X | | | |
| Physical-sexual | | X | X | | | X | | |
| Moral | | | | | | | | |
| Cognitive | | | | | | | X | |

**Table 2.  Patient Progress Report[a]**

| Client: Ed Banks | | | | Counselor: John Herman | |
|---|---|---|---|---|---|
| Dates: | 5/11[b] | 5/25 | 6/9 | 7/23 | 7/31 |
| Area of Development | | | | | |
| Psychosocial | D | D | C | B | B |
| Vocational | C | C | B | A | A |
| Physical-sexual | C | C | B | A | A |
| Cognitive | C | C | B | B | B |
| Moral | B | B | B | B | B |

[a]Typical rating scale, based on Multiple Impact Training. Numbers refer to dates of evaluation: 5/11 represents initial evaluation of the client/patient; 5/25 represents first evaluation, and so on. (Time periods may vary, but we recommend twice-a-month evaluations).
[b]D—gross deficit; C—deficit; B—average; A—good,

followed up in his community, and he plans to attend the local mental hygiene clinic. Mr. Banks will return to his carpenter's job (see Table 2 for Mr. Banks's progress report).

## SUMMARY

Several features make Multiple Impact Training a unique model. First, MIT is a potent form of treatment/training because the recipient is learning simultaneously new skills in several areas of functioning. Second, MIT is an educational model that teaches life skills and therefore should endure or result in fewer relapses for the recipient. Third, since MIT is an educational model, there is much less stigma attached to it. Fourth, participants are *actively* involved in learning or perfecting life skills and therefore are likely to feel more ownership of the process. Fifth, MIT is appropriate both in prevention and remediation of mental health problems. The basic as-

sumption of MIT is that the so-called functional neuroses and psychoses are the result of deficits in life skills, that life skills can be learned, and that the most effective and efficient way for life skills to be learned is to teach them directly.

The paradox of MIT is that its real strength lies in its conceptualization as an educational model. Yet since the majority of "helping professionals" in the mental health domain still accept the medical treatment model, MIT can be expected to meet with much resistance.

## REFERENCES

Dupont, H. Meeting the emotional-social needs of students in a mainstreamed environment. *Counseling and Human Development*, 1978, **10**, 1–12.

Ellis, A. Rational-emotive group therapy. In G. M. Gazda (Ed.), *Basic approaches to group psychotherapy and group counseling*. Springfield, Ill.: Charles C Thomas, 1975.

Erikson, E. H. *Childhood and society,* 2nd ed. New York: Norton, 1963.

Flavell, J. H. *The development psychology of Jean Piaget.* Princeton, N.J.: Van Nostrand, 1963.

Gazda, G. M. *Group counseling: A developmental approach.* Boston: Allyn & Bacon, 1971.

Gazda, G. M. Developmental Education: A conceptual framework for a comprehensive counselling and guidance program. *Canadian Counsellor,* 1977, **12,** 36–40.

Gazda, G. M. *Group counseling: A developmental approach,* 2nd ed. Boston: Allyn & Bacon, 1978.

Gesell, A., Ilg, F. L. and Ames, L. B. *Youth: The years from ten to sixteen.* New York: Harper, 1956.

Gesell, A., et al. *The child from five to ten.* New York: Harper, 1946.

Havighurst, R. J. *Developmental tasks and education,* 2nd ed. New York: McKay, 1953.

Havighurst, R. J. *Human development and education,* 3rd ed. New York: McKay, 1972.

Kohlberg, L. Continuities and discontinuities in childhood and adult moral development revisited. In P. B. Baltes and K. W. Schaie (Eds.), *Lifespan developmental psychology: Personality and socialization.* New York: Academic Press, 1973.

Kohlberg, L. and Turiel, P. Moral development and moral education. In G. Lesser (Ed.) *Psychology and educational practice.* Chicago: Scott Foresman, 1971.

Lazarus, A.A. Multimodal behavior therapy in groups. In G. M. Gazda (Ed.), *Basic approaches to group psychotherapy and group counseling.* Springfield, Ill.: Charles C Thomas, 1975.

Loevinger, J. *Ego development.* San Francisco: Jossey-Bass, 1976.

MacGregor, R. T., Ritchie, A. M., Serrano, A. C., Schuster, F. P., Jr., McDonald, E. C., Jr. and Goolishian, H. A. *Multiple impact therapy with families.* New York: McGraw-Hill, 1964.

National Assessment of Educational Progress. *Draft of basic skills objectives.* Denver, Colo.: National Assessment of Educational Progress (division of the Commission on the Education of the States) August 1975.

Shane, H. G. *Curriculum change toward the 21st century.* Washington, D.C.: National Education Association, 1977.

Super, D. E. Vocational development in adolescence and early adulthood: Tasks and behaviors. In D. E. Super, *Career development: Self-concept theory.* New York: College Entrance Examination Board, 1963.

Super, D. E., Crites, J., Hummel, R., Moser, H., Overstreet, C. B. and Warnath, C. *Vocational development: A framework for research.* Monograph No. 1, New York: Teachers College Press, 1957.

Wadsword, B. J. *Piaget's theory of cognitive development.* New York: McKay, 1971.

# CHAPTER 39

# *Mutual Need Therapy*

JESSE LAIR

*This next chapter is one of the most "religious" in this book, and joins a number of other chapters, such as Natural High Therapy, Holistic Education, Integrity Groups, Naikan, and Transcendence Therapy, which explicitly stress transpersonal concepts and moralistic ideas.*

*Jesse Lair did something quite simple and straightforward in developing Mutual Need Therapy. He knew that a number of self-help groups, such as Alcoholics Anonymous, were quite successful in dealing with special problem groups such as alcoholics, drug addicts, and gamblers. He investigated these groups to see what they had in common. What he found in these so-called "12-step groups" he applied to his own system; thus his may be called a synthetic approach.*

*In this system the therapist is not playing the role of "doctor" or even "leader" but rather co-participant. I believe this is a position we must consider carefully—it has revolutionary implications for psychotherapy.*

*The concepts in this chapter are important enough to call for close examination and possibly for rethinking all of psychotherapy, since what Lair seems to say is that all of us—all—are on the wrong track. Where is psychotherapy going—and where should it be going? This chapter challenges almost every psychotherapeutic position ever taken—and so it calls for unhurried examination.*

Mutual Need Therapy (MNT) refers to any of the so-called 12-step self-help groups, such as Alcoholics Anonymous, Gamblers Anonymous, Overeaters Anonymous, and Emotions Anonymous. This form of therapy is seen as a process of seeking and maintaining relationships with people who will accept us just as we are, for what we are, and in dealing with others on a similar basis—with each simultaneously benefiting.

In MNT relationships the people involved have a new set of experiences that causes them to undergo fundamental changes in their attitudes toward themselves, the world, and the people in their world. Whereas before people received pain from other human relationships, now they experience acceptance, joy, and pleasure.

When people examine their present relationships, they usually find that few of them are based on mutual joy; ordinarily most are based on trying to get something from the other or trying to dominate the other. Mutual Need Therapy attempts to translate the principles of various 12-step programs into a system of general value for improving the total individual's spiritual, intellectual, and behavioral experience.

## HISTORY

Over the past 15 years, this writer has conducted an in-depth study of Alcoholics Anonymous (AA) and similar groups whose success at treating was an interesting puzzle. My

534

question was: Why did AA succeed in helping even skid-row alcoholics recover where conventional psychiatry and religion had failed? Were there principles in the AA 12-step program that could be used by people without the specific compulsion of alcohol, food, or gambling?

Mutual Need Therapy is an attempt to employ the dynamics of the 12-step treatment program for nonaddicts. The 12 steps as used in Alcoholics Anonymous are:

We—

1. Admitted we were powerless over alcohol; that our lives had become unmanageable.

2. Came to believe that a Power greater than ourselves could restore us to sanity.

3. Made a decision to turn our will and our lives over to the care of God as we understood Him.

4. Made a searching and fearless moral inventory of ourselves.

5. Admitted to God, to ourselves, and to another human being the exact nature of our wrongs.

6. Were entirely ready to have God remove all these defects of character.

7. Humbly asked Him to remove our shortcomings.

8. Made a list of all persons we had harmed, and became willing to make amends to them all.

9. Made direct amends to such people wherever possible, except when to do so would injure them or others.

10. Continued to take personal inventory, and when we were wrong promptly admitted it.

11. Sought through prayer and meditation to improve our conscious contract with God as we understood Him, praying only for knowledge of His will for us and the power to carry that out.

12. Having had a spiritual awakening as the result of these steps, tried to carry this message to alcoholics, and to practice these principles in all our affairs.

(Alcoholics Anonymous 1976)

Two aspects of the AA program attract the attention of outside observers almost immediately. One is the emphasis on the "spiritual." The other is the notion that a person never completely recovers from addictions.

One psychologist who observed people in AA concluded that, in their emphasis on spiritual matters, they were like a "fundamentalist religion." A fundamentalist religion is typically one with a complete dependence on a literal interpretation of the Bible. I find AA's spiritual emphasis to be quite the opposite. AA members are asked to accept that there is some "power" outside themselves they can believe in, a "higher power." Most alcoholics have a problem, especially at first, with the word "God" or any higher power, but they nevertheless manage to stop drinking with the support of the group and the principles of the AA program.

A statement by Carl Jung to one of his patients led to the founding of Alcoholics Anonymous. Roland H, a man with an alcohol problem, had gone to Jung for treatment in 1930. After a year of treatment he felt he was cured, but soon after he started drinking again. When he returned to Switzerland, Jung told him that he did not feel any further medical or psychiatric treatment would be beneficial. When Roland asked if there was any hope, Jung told him a spiritual or religious experience—a genuine conversion—might reorder his personality. Roland then joined the Oxford Movement, which emphasized self-survey, confession, restitution, the giving of oneself in service of others, meditation, and prayer. In those surroundings Roland had a conversion experience that released him from his compulsion to drink.

Roland H told Edwin T, who then also was able to have a spiritual experience, and Edwin T told his friend Bill W, a hopeless alcoholic. A little later Bill W was hospitalized for his alcoholism and accidentally saw on his chart that his family doctor had written there was no hope for him: a mental hospital or death were his only alternatives.

Bill W. knelt by his bed and cried out in despair, "If there be a God, will he show himself." He immediately had an illumination of enormous impact and dimension and he was released from the alcoholic obsession. He was a free man and went on to co-found AA.(Anonymous,Grapevine,1968)

Bill W wrote to Carl Jung in 1961, telling the crucial part that Jung's conversation with Roland H had played in the formation of AA. Jung wrote back to Bill W; the letter reads as follows:

Dear Mr. W.:

Your letter has been very welcome, indeed.

I had no news from Roland H. any more and often wondered what has been his fate. Our conversation which he has adequately reported to you had an aspect of which he did not know. The reason that I could not tell him everything was that those days I had to be exceedingly careful of what I said. I had found out that I was misunderstood in every possible way. Thus, I was very careful when I talked to Roland H. But what I really thought about, was the result of many experiences with men of his kind.

His craving for alcohol was the equivalent, on a low level, of spiritual thirst of our being for wholeness, expressed in medieval language: The Union with God.* How could one formulate such an insight in a language that is not misunderstood in our days?

The only right and legitimate way to such an experience is, that it happens to you in reality and it can only happen to you when you walk on a path which leads you to higher understanding. You might be led to that goal by an act of grace or through a personal and honest contact with friends, or through a higher education of the mind beyond the confines of mere rationalism. I see from your letter that Roland H. has chosen the second way, which was, under the circumstances, obviously the best one.

I am strongly convinced that the evil principle prevailing in this world leads the unrecognized spiritual need into perdition, if it is not counter-

---

*"As the hart panteth after the water brooks, so panteth my soul after thee, O God:" (Psalm 42: 1).

---

acted either by real religious insight or by the protective wall of human community. An ordinary man, not protected by an action from above and isolated in society, cannot resist the power of evil, which is called very aptly the Devil. But the use of such words arouses so many mistakes that one can only keep aloof from them as much as possible.

These are the reasons why I could not give a full and sufficient explanation to Roland H. But I am risking it with you because I conclude from your very decent and honest letter that you have acquired a point of view above the misleading platitudes one usually hears about alcoholism.

You see, "alcohol" in Latin is "spiritus" and you use the same word for the highest religious experiences as well as for the most depraving poison. The helpful formula therefore is: *Spiritus contra Spiritum.*

I remain,

Yours Sincerely,

C.C. Jung

## CURRENT STATUS

The more I studied the AA program, the more I realized it was peer-group therapy. It emphasized each person's personal recovery, but as each person worked on his own recovery, this helped other people. I noted that the principles of AA were practiced not just in the meetings but outside of them as well. Many of these principles were operating in the therapy I was doing with my students incidental to my teaching educational psychology.

In November 1972, I called a meeting of psychologists on campus who were working with students in some therapeutic way. Out of that meeting came a small discussion group consisting of faculty members of Montana State University, Frank Seitz, Richard Horswill, and myself. We met every other week for about six months.

We talked about what we were doing with students. Part of the time we looked at Mutual Need Therapy as it applied to our counseling. Questions we asked ourselves included: Did we as therapists get any personal gain from our counseling? What were our needs in the therapy process? How did we meet those needs? Did we admit to our needs to the clients we were counseling?

As we discussed such questions the concepts of the mutual need therapy process became clearer. In 1973 I conducted an evening class for teachers in the Bozeman, Montana, school system, where I stated the theory and explained the true practice of MNT as well as I could. The teachers questioned me and each other on how to apply such a theory to their teaching and their lives.

The tape recordings of this class were the basis for my book, *I ain't well, but I sure am better—mutual need therapy* (1975). The work I continued to do in order to facilitate my own growth resulted in the next book, *Ain't I a wonder and ain't you a wonder, too?* (1977).

The principles of Mutual Need Therapy are at the heart of *Sex—if I didn't laugh, I'd cry* (Lair, 1979), and they will figure strongly in a book I have just finished called *I don't know where I'm going, but I sure ain't lost.* (Lair, 1981)

Another application of Mutual Need Therapy is in the "schools" of Bozeman, Montana. The first was held for one week in July 1977. This led to a semiannual "School of Life" held in Phoenix, Arizona for one week in mid-January and in Bozeman in mid-July. Students come from all over the United States. There are no formal academic requirements. The experience students have of being valued as they are—of Mutual Need Therapy—gives them an opportunity to reorganize their attitudes toward themselves and the world.

Mutual Need Therapy is simply an idea meant to help people better understand the therapeutic process seen in the Alcoholics Anonymous and other 12-step programs. Hopefully, this process can then be applied to the broader context of people solving their own emotional problems.

## THEORY

An individual's emotional growth can be divided into two parts: (1) parts that develop fairly normally and do not give many or se-

vere problems in living and (2) parts characterized by "problems."

During both these parts of a person's emotional life, some degree of emotional growth goes on. Mutual Need Therapy attempts to understand this growth—what promotes it and what retards it—so that a person can better foster his or her own emotional growth.

Mutual Need Therapy sees the person as physical, mental, and spiritual. An imbalance in one of the three areas leads to what we call "sickness." But because of the interrelationships, seldom is just one of the three parts "sick." For example, physical "accidents" have an emotional component meeting some need of the individual, as in the case of accident-prone person. A seemingly simple infectious disease is very likely a temporary breakdown in the body's immunological system as a result of the individual's reaction to some external stress.

Breaking the whole person down into three parts for the sake of the analysis gives us a body, a mind, and a spirit. The body is the physical form. The mind is the part that gathers information and solves problems. The spiritual part is our relationship to the world and experiences whatever harmony or lawfulness (or lack of it) we see around us.

In the spiritual part are our attitudes toward life, people, and the world. These attitudes came about through our experiences with the world and the people in it. From all our past experiences we come to have certain fundamental viewpoints as to what we want to happen to us and expectations of what is going to happen to us. This attitude structure is the source of most of our feelings. If we expect the world to respond to us in a certain way and it does not, we get angry. If we get the response we wish, we experience comfort.

Most difficulties of body, mind, and spirit come from a maladaptive development of the spiritual-emotional side. As a result of our early experiences, we made generalizations about the world that would hurt us later. Perhaps we did not experience the love and affection we needed; we may have concluded that something was wrong with us and that we would have to accomplish something to get love. Or we didn't realize that we did not get love because the people around us had their own problems and were limited in their ability to give love. But due to the self-centeredness of the childish mind, we saw ourselves as the only part of life that had an effect on things around us.

Mutual Need Therapy is a process of creating new experiences where we can see that we are loved for being what we are rather than for what we do or what we have. Mutual Need Therapy is finding situations where we can be loved for being just as we are. Experiencing that we are lovable just as we are helps us throw away old attitudes and helps develop a new set of attitudes; instead of expecting pain from life, we now expect love and joy.

Such fundamental changes in attitude will give rise to a totally different set of emotions. Expectation of pleasure from life changes our whole body chemistry from preparing to fight or flee to preparing to accept love and pleasure. Relief from the anxiety for our safety and well-being lets our mind function more freely and creatively. So the whole person with these new attitudes is enriched in all three areas of body, mind, and spirit.

Mutual Need Therapy is a formal process of seeking out relationships with people who we value as they are and who value us as we are. In these relationships we see ourselves in action in a way we never before experienced. And we see ourselves in a way we had never imagined we were. These relationships start the healing process, which continues as we deepen our present relationships and add new ones.

Our earlier relationships often had some mutual need relationships among them. But usually most were with people we wanted something from. The other person in the relationship also wanted something from us, or he or she would not have been in the relationship either. This is not a true mutual need relationship because we were not being valued as what we were deep inside; instead we were valued for some surface reason, such as what we looked like, what we could do, or what use we could be to someone. Essentially, these are exploitative relationships.

People have to hurt badly before they are willing to give up old ways and old relationships. When this finally happens, sometimes they are ready to consider giving themselves up completely to finding new relationships that will work better for them. In the 12-step program setting, such new relationships are first experienced in groups. As the person's ability to develop constructive relationships grows, more and more good relationships form outside the groups.

The result is that the person experiences himself or herself a person worthy of love and respect and comes to give up old self-negating attitudes. Each person is now ready to look at new, more positive attitudes about the world and his or her place in it. This process can be called spiritual. Then the person has what Jung referred to in his letter as a spiritual experience, a fundamental reorganization of the personality.

In this understanding, anything that changes the personality is seen as spiritual because it affects the person's relationship with him- or herself and the people around the person. These spiritual experiences are very seldom the dramatic kind that Bill W had. In most cases they are small insights that make us different people and let us experience more harmony with life and others just as we are. These small accretions add up to a very large experience.

## METHODOLOGY

Mutual Need Therapy is a way of structuring the relationship between the therapist and the client. The therapist's emphasis is focused on what the client is doing for the therapist. It is solely up to the client to say what the therapist is doing for the client.

Emphasis is on the experiencing of that relationship by both parties. Because in a mutual need relationship, the highest possible good feeling must exist between the two people, the role of the therapist is often sharply limited. Usually therapists cannot relate well to each and every person who comes to them. In Mutual Need Therapy their role is to show their love, concern, and belief in a person by admitting to the limitations of the relationship that exists between them and guiding the client to the most productive relationships. Except for cases where there is a good fit between the therapist and the client, the therapist is more of a teacher who helps the person see the good and poor relationships in life and the reasons for them. In doing this, the therapist is practicing a mutual need relationship in terms of their fit or mutuality for each other.

The therapist, in such a case, admits feelings in the relationship. He or she might say, "You're a good person and deserve the very best relationships. I don't feel you and I are perfectly suited to each other. I'm not just exactly your cup of tea and you're not exactly mine." In that honesty there is a great valuing of the other person and a modeling of a good relationship, especially compared to maintaining a fiction of really liking a person when the opposite is more nearly true.

While clients are in treatment, they are encouraged to find mutual need relationships so they can experience the positive benefits they can give. The client is encouraged to take over the process of directing relationships as quickly as possible. Twelve-step groups such as Al-anon, AA, Emotions Anonymous, and Overeaters Anonymous, or other types of growth groups are recommended so the client can make a quick start in forming new, different, and better relationships.

Another role of the therapist in Mutual Need Therapy is to direct clients' attention to their attitudes toward themselves and their world and to understanding the experiences that formed those attitudes. These attitudes, clients' expectations of the world, are the spiritual side. As clients are made more aware of their expectations and the experiences that formed them, they can better understand their need for positive experiences of themselves as individuals and the consequences for them so they can change to a more positive set of attitudes.

Mutual Need Therapy in groups has important implications for the therapist. Here the therapist acts chiefly as a participant meeting his own needs and working on his own problems. It is always a powerful temptation to teach others or help others. The lesson of the 12-step programs is that the most powerful way we can help others is through helping ourselves.

## APPLICATIONS

Mutual Need Therapy has been and will continue to be used in the peer groups of Alcoholics Anonymous, Al-anon for the relatives of the alcoholic, Overeaters Anonymous, Emotions Anonymous, and Gamblers Anonymous. There are chapters of these organizations in almost every city and town in the United States and in many foreign countries. In a major city there are typically hundreds of 12-step groups available.

These groups offer a major resource to therapists. The therapist can work with the client individually at the same time as the client works in the groups. The groups can also provide a lifetime follow-up program for clients after individual therapy is no longer required.

The character disorders, especially alcoholism, overweight, and gambling, have often been most difficult to treat with conventional therapies. With these types of problems, MNT can offer the most aid.

Another application is with individual clients. Much psychiatric training is focused on the therapist keeping emotional and physical distance from the client. MNT offers an alternative that is pretty much on the other end of the spectrum: The therapist participates as an equal partner in the therapeutic process with the emphasis solely on the improvement of the therapist's functioning. By broadening the spectrum of strategies available, the therapist would have more flexibility in meeting the needs of individual patients as well as meeting his or her own needs as a therapist.

MNT is of limited use with psychotics. They are usually so disruptive and disoriented in groups that they receive little benefit, and the group's functioning is impaired somewhat as the psychotic tries to fit into the group. Except in the special cases where the psychotic's problem is mild enough to let him or her fit in with the group and gain from it, psychotics usually drop out of the group after a few meetings.

MNT might be useful in research on the effectiveness of therapy. In the typical controlled studies on the effects of psychological treatment, people presenting themselves for treatment are treated or put in a control group. When a person finally gets to the point where he or she sees the need for professional help, the client is likely to seek help from a person or persons with whom some mutuality is felt. If this is the case, then the psychologist becomes just one of two, three, or even more mutual relationships. What the studies show, then, is simply the result of adding a professional on top of two or three other relationships. When we look at the research in this way, we can see how nearly impossible it might be to separate out the effects of the professional. Additionally, if the degree of mutuality is a big key to the therapy, then the professional has an extra handicap because now the mutuality is limited by the presence of an "outsider." Research on the number and extent of mutual need relationships operating in studies of therapies' effectiveness might be beneficial.

## CASE EXAMPLE

Jean M was a white female, 26 years old, when she came to her first MNT group meeting. She was married to an engineering graduate who was working as a carpenter so he could continue to live in the town where he went to school. His home was in another part of the state where his parents were farmers.

Jean had left her home state to go away to school. While there she had lived with one boyfriend for a while before she met and married her husband. She had left home because she had not been able to get along with her parents, especially her father, with whom she fought at practically every contact. She had two sisters, one younger and one older.

Jean's first contact with a 12-step group was with Overeater's Anonymous (OA). Although she was slim she said she had an eating problem. After a few meetings, the small OA group broke up. Some of the members were also in Emotions Anonymous, another 12-step group, so Jean switched to that group.

When she first came to meetings the group ranged from 4 to 20 people. Jean would come with her knitting or with a book, getting there early enough to secure an overstuffed chair she was used to sitting in. She would curl up in the chair and read, knit, or sew until the meeting started. At the opening of the meeting where the members of the group would stand, hold hands, and say the Serenity prayer,* Jean would stand and hold hands but would be silent.

After the meeting started Jean would curl back up and usually shut her eyes as if she was sleeping. When the leader of the meeting for the evening discussed one of the steps and go around the circle giving people an opportunity to talk, Jean would usually choose to pass (not to talk) or would speak briefly of some personal difficulty with her husband, neighbor, parents, or herself.

This behavior continued for a year and then, in a moderated form, Jean started to participate more in the group for another year. Earlier she had been so little a part of the group and had participated so little that other group members were somewhat un-

---

*God Grant me the serenity to accept the things I cannot change, the courage to change the things I can, and the wisdom to know the difference.

comfortable with her and speculated among themselves as to the reason she came to meetings.

In the second year of once- or twice-a-week meetings of about two hours, Jean began to participate more by sometimes paying closer attention to what people said and watching them as they talked instead of having her eyes closed. She began to identify with what one member of the group would say, a woman in her late forties. Eventually Jean began to tell her own story of her personal difficulties and some of the problems in her family and her marriage.

One night a member told of his eating compulsion. He was a man about 32 and about 30 pounds overweight. As he told of eating binges in the evenings in which he gorged himself because of his feelings of unease, Jean confided to him and the other two people that she had an eating problem also. This was the first time she had admitted such a personal problem to the group.

That week she contacted the older woman with whom she identified and spoke out to her about her eating problem. Jean would go on eating binges one to four times a day and then throw up to avoid gaining weight. She had been extremely fat in high school, but her grandmother had put her on a diet that got her weight down to normal. As she began to lose control over her eating shortly after her weight was down, she turned to vomiting to avoid gaining weight again.

Jean's vomiting was such a constant pattern that a new septic tank had to be pumped out after a year because of all the food she had vomited up.

This particular experience was the first her husband knew of her eating problem. They didn't discuss her problem because neither of them were prepared to. But this experience made her seek counseling, which hadn't helped because she was unwilling to admit to the counselor the exact nature and consequences of her problem.

After this disclosure, Jean began identifying herself as a food-aholic as well as someone with emotional problems. In a sub-

sequent group meeting Jean told of a backpacking trip she and her husband had once taken. She had gotten up during the first night and eaten all the food for the three-day trip so they had to come home the next day. She loved to go backpacking, but her urge to eat overcame her. She told how angry her husband was with her for what she had done.

In the third year in this group Jean began to disclose more and more of her relationships with her parents, two sets of grandparents, and her sisters. The pattern that emerged was one of constant fighting in the family with parents and grandparents.

Jean began to come to the meetings without a book or knitting, and she took an active part before and after meetings. She began to form some relationships with people in the meetings, some of which she began to maintain outside the meetings. She began to confide in one couple in their late forties about personal things she did not talk about at the meetings. In addition, she began to take more and more initiative in helping run meetings and helping with the affairs of the organization.

In the first two years of attending meetings, Jean avoided anything but a minimal telephone contact with her parents, who lived a thousand miles away. They had come to visit before she started attending meetings, but it had been a week-long fight.

After the second year of membership Jean was talking to both her parents on the phone. If her father said something that before would have angered Jean and started her fighting, now she just let it go by. Learning this, her mother asked her what was wrong with her.

In the middle of her third year, Jean and her husband went to visit her parents and there was almost none of the old fighting and Jean rising to the bait. Her parents didn't remark at the change in her but her grandparents did and expressed their happiness at what happened.

In her fourth year in EA Jean began to be radiantly happy. She had a new driver's license picture made that showed a smiling young woman with a loose, flowing hairdo.

The old picture from four years earlier showed a woman with a tight, pinched, angry face with her hair pulled back in a severe hairdo. She carried the two pictures around in her purse to show to friends.

Jean reports a drastic improvement in her whole life. Her relationships with her husband, friends, neighbors, and most of her family members has changed from angry confrontations to happy exchanges. Only her parents continue to give her some problems, but now she handles them without all the old anger. She discovered that her mother is an alcoholic. This plus her father's withdrawal makes visiting home hard on her and makes her life harder for a month or two after she visits home.

Jean realized she was somewhat frigid sexually with her husband. When they decided to have a baby about three years ago, she found she could not get pregnant. She began to believe that her emotional state was a cause of her irregular periods and not being able to get pregnant. About a year ago Jean conceived but had a miscarriage. She believes her body is slowly coming to have more balance and evenness. Her periods are much more regular, and at the time of this writing she has been pregnant for two months and feels sure she will carry the baby full term.

The transformation of Jean M is so noticeable that she is constantly being asked by friends and relatives what happened to her. So far she has only been able to tell a few of them that she is in Emotions Anonymous; she just recently told her parents.

Jean has recently become more aware of the deep anger in her that is and has been so much a part of her whole life that she was not able to see before. She is also seeing the deep anger in her husband. She is accepting the anger in both of them and working on reducing her own anger.

Jean is now contributing substantially to the work of helping with the meetings and in reaching out to the people who come to meet her own needs.

She feels that the group has contributed so much to her life that she is looking forward to deeper and deeper realizations about herself and deeper and deeper experiences of a better life for herself.

## SUMMARY

MNT is a therapy system that attempts to put into theory what happens in the 12-step groups of Alcoholics Anonymous, Al-anon, Overeaters Anonymous, Emotions Anonymous, and Gamblers Anonymous.

One of the characteristics of the therapy in the 12-step programs that seems very different from most conventional therapies is the emphasis on God as each person understands him. Closer examination shows that God in that context is very different from the God used in the religious context. In MNT God is used in a spiritual sense and in the very broadest meaning of spiritual, which is simply a belief in some—any—power outside ourselves. The belief of psychologists in the lawfulness of his or her data is a belief in a power outside themselves.

The main implication of the therapy system is that it presents therapy as a process between equal partners who are each working exclusively on getting well or better themselves. Any help that is given to others is simply a by-product, a side effect, of the person openly and honestly working on him- or herself. This viewpoint can give a therapist a different or broader perspective on the therapeutic process.

The success of the 12-step programs at treating alcoholism, drug addiction, and other problems that have been difficult to treat with conventional therapies suggests to this writer that psychologists must study these programs to see what can be learned from them to improve existing therapies. It is also valuable for therapists to understand the psychological principles operating in these programs so the appropriate clients can be referred to a suitable program where indicated.

# REFERENCES

*Alcoholics anonymous*. New York: Alcoholics Anonymous World Services, 1976.

*Alcoholics anonymous comes of age*. New York: Alcoholics Anonymous World Services, 1974.

Anonymous, The Carl Jung/Bill W. letters. *Grapevine*, January 1968, p. 17.

Casriel, D. *A scream away from happiness*. New York: Grosset & Dunlap, 1972.

W. W. Co-founder, The society of alcoholics anonymous. *American Journal of Psychology*, 1949, **106**, 370–375.

Lair, J. *I ain't much baby—but I'm all I got*. New York: Doubleday, 1972.

Lair, J. *I ain't well—but I sure am better—mutual need therapy*. New York: Doubleday, 1975.

Lair, J. *Ain't I a wonder and ain't you a wonder, too?* New York: Doubleday, 1977.

Lair, J. *Sex—if I didn't laugh, I'd cry*. New York: Doubleday, 1979.

Lair, J. *I don't know where I'm going . . . but I sure ain't lost*. New York: Doubleday, 1981.

Lair, J. and Lair, J. C. *Hey, God what should I do now?* New York: Doubleday, 1973.

Tournier, P. Relationships—the third dimension of medicine. *Contact* (Christian Medical Commission, World Council of Churches, Geneva, Switzerland), 1978, **47**, 1–8.

*Twelve steps and twelve traditions*. New York: Alcoholics Anonymous World Services, the AA Grapevine, 1952.

# CHAPTER 40

# *Naikan Psychotherapy*

*Naikan Therapy reminds me very much of the Catholic Church's viewpoint about sin, as it was explained to me some 50 years ago when I went to a parochial school. It is a moralistic, philosophical point of view, and this position is very similar to O. Hobart Mowrer's theory, which is summarized in the chapter on Integrity Groups by Anthony Vattano. In traditional Catholic practice, before one goes to sleep one is supposed to go over the day's events, meditate on what one did that was right and what was wrong, to feel truly sorry for one's mistakes and grateful for what one has received, to pray for guidance and understanding and the strength to live the good life—and to consider making reparations for any wrong one has done. Generally, this is known in Catholic thinking as examination of the conscience.*

*As I read it, this essentially is the message of Naikan Therapy. Note that in this Asian process the therapist plays a genuinely nondirective role. The therapy is a true self-therapy of the kind that Sigmund Freud did, that Karen Horney wrote about, and that Theodore Reik said was the best of all modes of psychotherapy. This chapter has many important implications for the future of psychotherapy and should not be considered an alien system; rather it calls for very close examination. David Reynolds presents a most persuasive point of view relative to an innovative approach to psychotherapy.*

Naikan Psychotherapy is a meditative treatment form developed in Japan from Jodo Shinshu Buddhism by Isshin Yashimoto, a lay priest and former businessman. Through guided self-reflection on his past, the Naikan client comes to realize how much others have done for him, how little he has returned to them, and how much trouble and worry he has caused the significant others in his life. The therapy explicitly aims at producing an existential guilt and, simultaneously, a sense of having been loved and cared for in spite of one's own inadequacies. These preparatory realizations produce a desire for self-sacrifice in the service of others in order to begin to right the social balance. In the pro-

cess, excessive self-concern diminishes and symptom focus is relieved.

## HISTORY

Naikan Therapy grew out of *mishirabe*, the religious practice of a subsect of Jodo Shinshu Buddhist priests. In order to achieve enlightenment these priests would enter caves or other isolated settings to meditate for long periods of time on the expression of the Buddha's love in their lives. Going without food, water, and sleep, they sought to abandon the comforts of life in the effort to gain spiritual insight. After some initial failures, Isshin

544

Yoshimoto gained *satori* ("enlightenment") by this means. He decided to adapt the *mishirabe* practice for the lay person as a character-development technique. Yoshimoto added structure to the meditative process by developing the three themes of (1) what was received from others, (2) what was returned to them, and (3) what troubles were caused them. He removed the ascetic elements of fasting and sleeplessness. Finally, he simplified the isolation restriction and devised a process of frequent checks on the progress of the client's self-reflection.

In the early 1950s, having become wealthy in the synthetic fabric business, Yoshimoto turned over to others the running of his commercial enterprise and devoted himself entirely to Naikan Therapy. Naikan's first successes came within the Japanese prison system. Naikan was used in the rehabilitation program for sociopaths and addicts in juvenile reform centers and prisons for adult offenders (Kitsuse, 1965). Recidivism rates for prisoners who had done Naikan were significantly lower than for those who did not, and the treatment flourished for a while before political pressures severely restricted its use in the country's penal institutions.

Meanwhile the number of private clients treated at the Nara Naikan Center were increasing to upward of 30 per week. These clients came for treatment because of family problems, difficulties at work, unhappy love relationships, psychophysiological complaints, and a wide variety of neurotic symptoms. Others wanted to strengthen their character or find a practical method for developing their spiritual self.

In the mid 1970s other Naikan centers opened, and by 1979 more than 15 private Naikan settings were in operation. Some catered to devout believers in Shinshu Buddhism or other religions; some were psychiatric facilities with strong programs of rehabilitation for alcoholics; others used Naikan with hypnosis (Ishida, 1969), autogenic training, and other meditative techniques (Reynolds, n.d.).

Since the 1960s two other areas in which Naikan has operated are the business world and the school system. One facility in Tokyo provides special services for businessmen. Many companies in Japan send their employees, particularly new ones, to special programs for character training (Rohlen, 1976). Some companies (including hospitals) utilize Naikan as part of these *seishin kyoiku* training programs, paying their employees' fees and travel expenses. In schools individual teachers have encouraged Naikan practice both in the classroom and on sports teams. However, Naikan's resemblance to religious practice and the lack of apparent immediate relevance to success in college entrance examinations prevents this method from gaining wide popularity in the public educational institutions of Japan.

Very few westerners have undergone a week of intensive Naikan in Japan, although perhaps 10 researchers and clinicians have visited the Nara Center for brief periods of observation. Even fewer neurotics have been treated by Naikan in the West. The therapy remains essentially untried in the United States. However, recent innovations in technique make Naikan a more likely candidate for serious trial in the West.

The literature on Naikan in Japanese is not as extensive as that of Morita Psychotherapy. Much case history material exists, however, and verbatim audio tapes and transcriptions of Naikan interviews are readily available. Within the past few years a concerted effort has been made to broaden the scope of Naikan and to make it more respectable in academic psychology and medical circles (Murase & Johnson, 1973). Careful scientific study has begun and a national organization of therapists, researchers, and former clients was founded in 1978. Annual meetings attracted some 150 members from Hokkaido in the north of Japan to Kagoshima in the south. The heart of Naikan influence remains in the history-rich Kansai area of central Japan.

Few works dealing with Naikan have appeared in English (see references). The first book-length manuscript on the subject in English has been submitted for publication (Reynolds, n.d.), and translations into English of Japanese volumes are in progress.

## CURRENT STATUS

Some 2,000 clients undergo intensive Naikan Therapy each year. Some of them continue to do daily Naikan at home, but a sizable number return to do intensive Naikan a second or third time.

Recently Naikan has been used with increasing frequency in the Japanese prison system and particularly in juvenile rehabilitation centers because of its strong impact within a short period of time. The trend in Japan, as in the United States, is toward shorter sentencing for most criminal offenses. Reports of cure and improvement rates of 60 percent over a two-year follow-up period have drawn much interest toward this method as a treatment form for alcoholism. Several psychiatric hospitals regularly use it in conjunction with broader rehabilitation programs.

The heart of Naikan in Japan remains at the Naikan Kenshu Jo, the Naikan Training Center in Nara, Japan, where Yoshimoto practices. Though a national organization exists with a business office in Tokyo and members throughout Japan, the organization functions primarily to coordinate the annual meeting, encourage research, and distribute *Naikan* magazine.

Physicians, psychologists, priests, educators, nurses, and lay people practice Naikan. Training to become a Naikan therapist involves undergoing a week of intensive Naikan at one of the Japanese centers, preferably the one in Nara. During this week the potential therapist is given the opportunity to accompany the attending therapist on his rounds of the Naikansha clients and then to make the rounds on his own. The cost of interpreter, room, board, and therapy experience for the week would be about $250. At present this writer is the only American therapist qualified to practice Naikan.

## THEORY

Naikan holds that from early childhood we learn to use other people to our own ends. In myriad ways each day we take from others without adequately appreciating or reciprocating their contributions to our lives (Murase, 1974). We ignore or rationalize this selfishness because we fear the guilt and self-blame that comes as a natural consequence of taking a straight look at ourselves. Maintaining a positive self-image through this process of distortion requires energy and a sort of twisted perspective on living. The Naikan technique is designed to force the client to take a cold, hard look at himself for perhaps the first time in his life. He is instructed to prosecute himself as an attorney would in court (Takeuchi, 1965). The result of this seemingly harsh tactic, however, is rather surprising. Along with the tears of sorrow and repentance come a recognition that we have been loved and cared for by others in spite of our taking them for granted, hurting them, using them. An existential relief follows from squarely facing one's self at one's worst. The myth of individualism and the self-made person is exploded (Reynolds, 1977). And the natural consequence of this cathartic realization is intense gratitude and the desire to try to begin righting one's social balance by offering oneself in the service of others.

The initial model for the giving significant other is the human mother. Whatever faults our mother (or mother surrogate) may have had, it was her effort that brought about our birth and kept us alive during the helpless dependent years when we were unable and/or uninterested in returning her services in equal measure. One begins Naikan reflection on the topic of one's mother.

To the Western theoretician this approach may seem rigid and antitherapeutic at first glance. We all know persons whose mothers seem at least to share large responsibility for psychologically deforming their offspring. It would appear almost obscene to suggest an attitude of gratitude and guilt toward such mothers. Yet on another level, the Naikan therapist is not seeking to change or evaluate critically *the mother* at all. Whatever evil she inflicted on the client, a careful reflection on the past will turn up positive, nuturant behavior as well. If not, the client would probably not be alive. At any rate, the focus is not on the mother herself but on what the client did (or did not) do for her and to her. Whatever may have been her faults in the relationship, it is certain that the client was less than a perfect child. And it is the *client* who is to grow by reexamining his harsh evaluations of others and appreciating and serving them. The client is not told that he *must* find his mother to have been an *ideal* person. Rather he is to seriously consider those things she did for him, those things he returned to her, and the troubles he caused her. In most cases, the result of such a review of the past is a new recognition of the detailed ways in which, as the Japanese put it, "one was caused to be lived."

Viewing the therapeutic process from a broader perspective, it is clear that our current behaviors are influenced by what occurred in our past. It is also obvious that the past cannot be changed. It is frozen, unalterable. However, if we can come to restructure our perception of the past, its influence upon us may be altered. Restructuring our view of the past is precisely what Naikan is about.

Perhaps the theoretical perspective in the West that most closely fits that of Naikan is O. H. Mowrer's. Simply put, Mowrer (1964) argues that the sources of neurotic symptoms are our misdeeds and our attempts to conceal those misdeeds from significant others in our lives. He places the locus of responsibility for neurosis not on the environment, not on childbearing, not on some abstract "society," but on the neurotic individual himself. I am reminded of the problems I had in Japan during my first period of fieldwork there. My

ability with the Japanese language was very poor at that time. Yet I attempted to conceal my inadequate language preparation by nodding and acting as if I understood even when there were gaps in my vocabulary, when I wasn't following the conversation. As a result of this effort to hide my limitations, it was necessary to keep conversations brief and to remember whom to avoid. Long conversations or repeated conversations with a person increased the likelihood of discovery of my secret, my lie. Social relationships became unsatisfying, even burdensome. When I was finally able to admit my inadequacy to others, to ask for repetitions and slower rates of speech, the unnecessary tensions that had been added to these interactions disappeared.

Mowrer indicates that the appropriate therapy for the neurotic who is attempting to conceal his weakness and "badness" from others is to confess his deviousness to them and to attempt to make restitution for his wrongs. Effectiveness aside, that is surely a difficult solution to the problem. It is easier to sit quietly in the therapist's office in an attempt to convince oneself that what one is doing is all right as it is. Yet Mowrer's solution is character building, in a way, and character development is precisely the tack that Japanese therapists in general and Naikan in particular take in treating neurosis.

As we shall see, the *Naikansha* confesses his social omissions and misdeeds to the therapist, then to a group of his peers, then to the significant others in his daily life outside the therapy setting. Finally, he attempts to repay those in his social world out of the feelings of gratitude and obligation that have welled up from within.

## METHODOLOGY

The practice of Naikan is simple and readily described. In essence, it requires the *Naikansha* (client) to reflect on his past and report those reflections to his therapist, or *sensei*. The settings and styles vary somewhat, but the process is likely to go somewhat as follows.

The Naikan client may have read in the newspaper about Naikan; he may know someone who has done Naikan; or he may have been sent by his school principal, boss, or doctor. On arrival at the Naikan Center, he talks briefly with the therapist about his reasons for coming, then he listens to a short orientation tape. Within 30 minutes after his arrival he is doing Naikan seated behind a folding screen in the corner of a room (or facing the wall). He sits in any position that is comfortable on the pillows provided for him. He is not to lie down for fear of drifting off to sleep.

His initial assignment is to reflect upon how he behaved and felt toward his mother through the first years of grammar school. He is to consider what she did for him (20 percent of his meditation time), what he returned to her (20 percent), and what troubles and worries he caused her (60 percent). The aim is to recall in vivid detail specific events and acts during that period. Within an hour or two the therapist comes, bows before the screen, opens it, bows again, and asks the *Naikansha* what he has been reflecting on. The client then "confesses" within the structured format of what was given, what was returned, and troubles caused. He is then told to continue recalling his past self in relation to his mother up through the sixth grade. If he has no questions, the interview is ended with bows and he is left to continue with his memories.

During each interview the therapist simply listens humbly and gratefully to the outpouring from the client. The therapist then assigns the next topic, answers questions, and perhaps offers a word of encouragement, such as "Reflect deeply, please."

Usually assignments proceed in three-year steps up to the present (five- or ten-year steps may be used for elderly clients). Then the topic for reflection may change to the father. Again, the time periods begin with early school years and work up to the present. The pattern is repeated for mother, father, sib-

lings, aunts, uncles, teachers, bosses, schoolmates, workmates, husband, wife, children, and other significant persons in the *Naikansha*'s life. Special topics such as lying, stealing, breaking school rules, gambling, and drinking may also be assigned. Time frames may be adjusted to fit the topic or to focus in on yearly or even monthly steps in the recent past.

The interviews may be taperecorded. With permission from the clients, the best tapes are reproduced and sold to clients with similar problems. Several times during the day, sample tapes are broadcast over a loudspeaker system. They provide models of proper Naikan and an education in the Naikan way of thinking.

The first few days are the most difficult ones. Inability to remember, muscle cramps, and boredom are common. But once the client gets into deep Naikan, the therapist, rather than assigning the subsequent topic, may ask the client who he wants to reflect on during the next time period. The Naikan reflection lasts from 5 A.M. until 9 P.M. for a week. In most settings clients arrive Sunday afternoon and leave the following Sunday morning.

At the Naikan Center the day is broken up by three meals, a bath, toilet functions, and a brief cleanup period each morning. The client eats his meals behind his screen. He is assigned a 10-minute bath period. He is told not to do Naikan while bathing but to bathe while doing Naikan. The same advice applies to eating and even urinating. Outside of the interview exchange, he is to remain silent.

Twice during the week, once on Monday and once on the final Sunday, group meetings are announced. The *Naikansha* assemble to hear the therapist's lecture and to ask questions. On the last day those who wish to are encouraged to talk about their experience before the whole group. This meeting is recorded, and the tape is duplicated for those who wish to purchase it.

Some clients maintain contact with their therapists through correspondence after discharge. Recently the national magazine and ex-client groups provide the opportunity for periodic reinvolvement with the people and ideas of Naikan. Discharged clients are encouraged to do Naikan reflection for at least one half hour twice daily. In the morning they are to reflect in sequence as they did during intensive Naikan. In the evenings they are to reflect on the events of that day—what they received, returned, and what troubles they caused others. Follow-up studies indicate that only a few continue with *nichijo,* or everyday Naikan. Fewer still report their reflections to a therapist by postcard.

## APPLICATIONS

Naikan has been applied to a broad spectrum of clients. Psychosomatic problems, interpersonal difficulties, neuroses, addictions (including alcoholism), and criminal behavior problems have responded well to this treatment. Normal persons seeking character development or spiritual insight have also found Naikan useful.

Psychoses, senility and other organic brain syndromes, physical disorders, and many neurological conditions are not appropriate for Naikan treatment. Some practitioners, however, claim individual cures for clients previously diagnosed as suffering from schizophrenia, senile dementia, depression, and Parkinson's disease.

In practice, the number of dropouts during a week of Naikan varies from almost none to one-third, depending on the setting. Some settings have large percentages of clients who have been sent by school or legal authorities or by their employers or families. Such clients are not motivated to exert themselves in effortful Naikan, though some, in fact, do complete the week successfully. As yet there are no good predictive scales for determining who would benefit from Naikan.

Subjective ratings of Naikan depth maintained over a number of years at Nara indicate that the best clients tend to be middle-aged persons of both sexes.

Elderly persons present special difficulties in terms of memory deficits. On the other hand, adolescents may have motivational deficits. The youngest *Naikansha* was six years old at the time, but twelve or thirteen years seems to be an appropriate lower age limit.

Recent innovations have expanded the applicability of Naikan somewhat. A week of intensive Naikan is impracticable for some who might benefit from this form of self-reflection. A Naikan diary maintained at home covering recollections for an hour or more each day and brought to the therapist's office for weekly comment is one new possibility. Another involves the use of correspondence or audio tapes covering Naikan meditation at home. Since Naikan as practiced today is already an adaptation of another process *(mishirabe),* there is no substantial opposition to other innovative techniques provided that the fundamental self-reflection on the three themes is followed by some sort of confession to a caring other.

Naikan has been used in conjunction with hypnotherapy, autogenic training, various other forms of meditation, and psychoanalysis. It has been used to educate and motivate prisoners and alcoholics in programs of rehabilitation.

## CASE EXAMPLE

This client, Mrs. O, is a middle-aged woman, a housewife and innkeeper. Her husband is the owner of a *ryokan* (a Japanese inn) and head of a construction company. Her complaints were as follows:

Every day my head was heavy; I couldn't do my work well. I kept going over and over things in my mind. I couldn't express myself well to others. I walked around with a depressed-looking face and caused a lot of trouble for my family. Someone told me to go to Nara for Naikan, that there was someone in Nara who could help depressed people. I didn't really know anything about Naikan, hadn't heard anything about it, hadn't read a word about it, but why not try? I thought.

The depression had begun about five years earlier, occurring a few times a year for a week or two each time, but it became a severe problem about six months prior to Mrs. O's admission to the Nara Naikan Center. More specifically, the symptoms involved a sudden dislike of work, a dissatisfaction with life. She would simply go to bed and stay there, getting up only when she felt like it. Her husband was an easygoing fellow; he never scolded her for her actions, though he couldn't have been pleased with this sort of behavior. She had no particular pains, but she felt tired and unwilling to do housework.

Mrs. O's Naikan reflection began with the assignment of considering herself in relation to her husband on a month-by-month basis from six months earlier. We pick up the transcription of her Naikan interviews about midway through the week. Yoshimoto Sensei is the interviewer.

Y: What did you reflect upon for the month of August?

O: My husband calls the family together each year in August for a family trip. All the children and grandchildren come. We all go somewhere together. There's nothing so wonderful as that, but I always put on a grumbling face. "Well, since everyone is here I suppose I'll go too," I'd say and go along with them.

Y: What did you receive from your husband, what did you return to him, and what troubles did you cause him?

O: That he took me along on the trip was something I received from him.

Y: And what did you return to him?

O: Well, the family asked me to make rice-balls for everyone, and though I didn't feel like it, there was no way out of doing it. But I made them too salty.

Y: What trouble did you cause him?

O: Even though it was a pleasant trip, an enviable trip, I never showed any happiness, never spoke a word of gratitude. The crowd of grandchildren never called for me, and I never minded at all. I don't like children, I told them. They all liked Grandpa. When my daughter asked them who they liked best, they all said they loved Grandpa. When they said they didn't like me, my daughter asked them if it was nice to talk like that with me standing right there. Well, they said, she's just average. Whenever I went shopping I never got anything for the grandchildren. Now I've been reflecting on why I never bought anything for them.

Y: How have the first few days of Naikan been for you?

O: The first few days I really didn't know the meaning of Naikan. What shall I say? The first few days I simply sat and wasted time. At night I couldn't sleep. Then on the fifth evening I got to thinking. What are you doing here? I've been hearing the tapes of other Naikansha. By the third or fourth day they all seemed to be able to do Naikan, giving proper replies to the sensei. What's the matter with me? I wondered. I must be some sort of idiot. I was terribly sad. What should I do? Even during the war years we had plenty of rice, traded rice for medicine. We didn't lack anything. Maybe if I gave something up. Tomorrow I'll do without breakfast, I thought. So even though Mrs. Yoshimoto's meals are outstanding, I did without breakfast. Also instead of shifting my sitting position and standing once in a while, I sat all morning in formal position with my legs tucked under me. I think that's when I began to do Naikan.

Y: You went without lunch and dinner yesterday also, didn't you? Didn't you feel hungry?

O: Not a bit. Before, even when I ate a lot, my stomach rumbled, but not now. And I'm not in the slightest bit bored. Whether I have two or three days left I want to use them wholeheartedly, without eating.

Y: Fasting isn't an essential part of Naikan, but it is true that when one is really involved in self-reflection and forgets to eat, one's appetite doesn't seem to give much trouble.

O: That's certainly true. I'm not a bit hungry.

Y:   Now please continue reflecting on your husband. Time is getting short, so bear down.

O:   I shall. Thank you.


Y:   What have you been reflecting upon this time?

O:   I've been reflecting upon myself in relation to my husband in the month of September, what I received from him, returned to him, and the trouble I caused him. (Her voice has become soft and seems to come from far away.) At that time my blood pressure rose. I went to bed and I began to have stomach trouble. My husband assisted me in getting to the bathroom. He held me up and did other kind things for me. He even cleaned me off. As I did Naikan I realized what a special thing he did for me.

Y:   Now you feel gratitude. What about at that time?

O:   Then I didn't think a thing about it, only that it was part of being a husband. My children told me how fortunate I was to have a husband like that. He is a good provider, manly, and kind. They told me I should be thankful to have one like him.

Y:   When they said that what did you think?

O:   I just thought that this was natural, he was merely the way he should be. He was my husband; after all, when I'm sick he should take care of me.

Y:   How do you feel about him now?

O:   I realize how selfish I've been. I feel sorry and apologetic. (She cries.)

Y:   What did you return to him in September?

O:   Nothing in particular.

Y:   What trouble did you cause him?

O:   I always slept when I felt like it and got up when it suited me. I didn't do anything for him that a wife should do.

Y:   If you were your husband in such circumstances, what would you have done?

O:   I'd become sad.

Y:   If you saw your daughter-in-law doing as you've been doing, what would you do?

O:   I'd warn her. You can't do such things. Behave more properly.

Y:   How did your husband react?

O:   He always stayed the same. Perhaps he had given up on me. He laughed around the house, as usual. And he continued to treat me with kindness.


Y:   What have you been reflecting on during this period?

O:   December, what I received from, returned to, and the troubles I caused my husband. December is a very busy time for us at work. My husband's head is filled with thoughts about bills and the like. The year-end bonuses for employees at the inn were all prepared by him. I'm really grateful for that. As for what I returned to him, on December first I had responsibility for preparing the meal for a big celebration. About the trouble I caused him, on the day of the celebration I did what I had to do, but I grumbled and only appeared before the guests when I absolutely had to. As I think back over the day, I only said unpleasant things and presented a troubled face to the guests. Later that month when my daughter came home suddenly I treated her as if I didn't know her. That's the only time I've ever seen my husband cry. Whatever she said I felt nothing. She even told me that I wasn't much of a mother. To think that my husband had to raise the children practically alone. (She cries.)

Y:   Next time, will you reflect on January?

O:   Yes, thank you.

Y:   Please reflect deeply. Do you have any questions?

O:   I had a question but I seem to have forgotten it.

Y:   Such a question isn't worth worrying about; please continue with your Naikan.

O:   Thank you.


Y:   You haven't been eating. How do you feel?

O:   Not a bit hungry.

Y:   How many meals have you skipped now?

O:   Five.

Y:   Have you done such a thing before?

O:   Never.

Y:   At home do you eat a lot?

O:   When I'm sick I don't have much of an appetite, but otherwise I eat a lot, always three meals a day. People tell me I'll get fat.

Y:   What is the greatest number of meals you have skipped before?

O:   One meal, when I was depressed.

Y:   Now if you were to return home and someone asked you about your depression, what would you reply?

O:   I am completely cured. (Her voice is bright with enthusiasm.) Naikan is marvelous! I plan to tell everyone and encourage them to try Naikan too.

Y:   Do you have any questions?

O:   Three years ago I saw a couple that really impressed me. The husband's face was bright and the wife seemed to be taking good care of him. She respected him and showed him so. I want to be like that, I thought. But I couldn't put that hope into effect, unfortunately.

Y:   Did you want to ask me something about that?

O:   Oh yes, when I thought of that event three years ago I thought also of your face. Your wife shows you the same supporting respect I saw back then. Comparing myself with them, I realized how lax I've been.

Y:   Well, tomorrow you leave here, don't you? Use every second as if your life depended upon it.

O:   Yes, thank you.

About two weeks after she returned home, Mrs. O telephoned the center. She was doing exceptionally well, working hard. Her husband was pleased with the change, and her friends were talking of coming for Naikan too. She said that she was not continuing to sit in formal Naikan, but each day she thought about the three themes as she worked. Her work had become interesting again. Her children remarked on the complete change in their mother. "I really understand how bad I've been," she said. She expressed her gratitude again and again, and promised to call Mr. Yoshimoto periodically to report on her progress. At that time she also made a reservation to return for another week of Naikan in the early summer, accompanied by her daughter.

## SUMMARY

A week of intensive Naikan is, for many clients, an impactful life-altering experience. A new perspective on life is obtained. One feels guilty but grateful, one feels unworthy but loved in spite of the unworthiness. Ordinary feelings of guilt and inferiority are trivial in comparison with the existential blows to one's self-image received in Naikan. So a new benchmark is created, a new standard for self-assessment is formed. Evaluation of one's day shifts from "Why did this have to happen and did I get my share?" (with the implication that *I* deserve better) to "How grateful I am for whatever happened today, and what did I do for those around me?" On one level it is certainly unreasonable to be grateful for unnecessary delays, missed telephone calls, or an engine breakdown. But on another level gratitude is not unreasonable at all. Moreover, after learning Naikan clients exhibit a shift from the mode of passive recipient of "the slings and arrows of outrageous fortune" to the actor in others' behalf, a shift from self-centeredness to other-centeredness. That shift, for some, is the marker for the change from childishness to maturity. Furthermore, it may signal a movement from misery to joy.

## REFERENCES

Ishida, R. Naikan analysis. *Psychologia*, 1969, **12**, 81–92.

Kitsuse, J. I. Moral treatment and reformation of inmates in Japanese prisons. *Psychologia*, 1965, **8,** 9–23.

Mowrer, O. H. *The new group therapy*. Princeton, N.J.: Van Nostrand, 1964.

Murase, T. Naikan therapy. In Lebra, T. and Lebra, W. (Eds.), *Japanese culture and behavior*. Honolulu: University Press of Hawaii, 1974.

Murase, T. and Johnson, F. Naikan, Morita and western psychotherapy: A comparison. Paper presented at the American Psychiatric Association Meetings, Honolulu, 1973.

Reynolds, D. K. Naikan therapy—an experiential view. *International Journal of Social Psychiatry*, 1977, **23** **(4),** 252–264.

Reynolds, D. K. *The quiet therapies*. Honolulu: University Press of Hawaii, 1980.

Reynolds, D. K. *Naikan therapy: Meditation for self development in Japan*. Submitted for publication (n.d.).

Rohlen, T. *For Harmony and Strength*. Berkeley: University of California Press, 1976.

Takeuchi, K. On "Naikan." *Psychologia*, 1965, **8,** 2–8.

# CHAPTER 41

# *Natural High Therapy*

WALTER E. O'CONNELL

*Psychotherapy, as practiced and as innovated, undoubtedly reveals the personality of the practitioner/theoretician, and the next account should introduce you to a unique personality of our times, equivalent in many ways (including style of writing) to our mutual hero, Dr. J. L. Moreno.*

*Undoubtedly, Buzz O'Connell has something very important to say. Heavily influenced by both Alfred Adler and Carl Jung, O'Connell has developed something new, much closer to Adler in terms of common sense, with strong elements of Jung's mysticism but interlaced with Moreno's expansiveness. This chapter and O'Connell's other writings should intrigue individuals who are of a particular complex cast of mind, say those who appreciate the writings of Trigant Burrow. In any event, what follows, though perhaps difficult to understand, is well worth careful reading. I would equate O'Connell in many ways, including importance, to Egon Brunswik, another seminal thinker. Read the next chapter very slowly and very carefully.*

Natural High (NH) Therapy is an optimistic, action-oriented approach to living in the here-and-now that stresses the response-ability of each person for the creation of one's own state of self-actualization. This theory and therapy focuses directly upon the sense of humor, in all its ramifications, as the essential criterion of the actualization process. A sense of humor is the end result of self-training for the expansion of one's sense of worth and feelings of universal belonging, plus the development of an appreciation for the basic paradoxes of the human condition. Techniques of inner and outer change, both individual and group, are used in NH Therapy to encourage persons to become active agents in the game-of-games, one's actualization through training and practice of self-esteem (SE) and social interest (SI).

Level 1, *machinations of inner ego constrictions*, is the cornerstone of the whole actualization approach. Level 2, *encourage-*ment, gives the ideal movements of active social interest. *The transpersonal dimension,* level 3, has as its goal further enhancement of SE and SI by transcending ego-addictions and experiencing the timeless eternal self. The super-natural high is similar to the natural high in feelings of unconditional worth and basic similarity and belonging. Moreover, this numinous state is produced under "marketplace" situations of severe stress and is the affective counterpart of the cognitive-perceptual sense of humor.

## HISTORY

### Precursors

The salient influence upon NH creation has been the individual psychology of Alfred Adler (Ansbacher & Ansbacher, 1956, 1964), especially as concretized and modeled by Rudolf Dreikurs (1971). The Palo Alto Group, which systematically studied the movements of communication, added greatly to the particulars of level 2, the dyadic-interactional. From their work on the pathologies of communication, the importance of self-disclosure and feedback first became evident. Haley (1963) formulated what has been standard practice for therapeutic interactions of natural high therapists. Symptoms are encouraged; resistance is depicted as expected cooperation; and the therapeutic figure embodies a resolution of opposites, as a gently benevolent person who moves the patient into painful situations. Natural High Therapy received much of its didactic-experiential theme from the National Training Lab (NTL) orientation, especially that of the Bethel group. The psychodramatic techniques of J. L. Moreno, together with his oft-maligned nebulous psychospiritual outlook, made a pronounced contribution to natural high growth (O'Connell, 1976c). The school of analytical psychology of C. G. Jung (1961) has given tremendous support to the theory and practice of level 3, the transcendental humanistic facet of the natural high theory (O'Connell, 1978a). Ram Dass, the former Dr. Richard Alpert of psychedelic fame, has stimulated level 3 development by his use of Meditation to develop the quiet, expansive space-between-thoughts (Ram Dass & Levine, 1977).

## Beginnings

Four life-style foibles of this writer, buoyed with social interest, have stimulated theoretical biases. The first foible is a concern for the person, especially for the discovery and implementation of the secrets of joyous, socially responsible existence. The second foible is a persistent penchant for synthesizing persons, ideas, and techniques into practical, simple (yet seldom easy) alternatives. A thorough distrust of institutional ways—in schools, homes and professions—has certainly been most pronounced. And the final foible is a wariness of institutional subtleties

for constriction of personal self-esteem and social interest. All these have given birth to Natural High theory and Therapy, a psychospiritual avenue to actualization. Perhaps the most important stimulus for the creation of NH Therapy is my lifelong need to control, honed, by decades of frustration, into the deep and wide belief that only one's self-esteem and social interest are amenable to absolute personal control.

Research by this writer on the sense of humor followed a lifelong curiosity on the "hows" and "whys" of humor—rather than hostility—among the significant figures of childhood. My research and clinical studies were viewed as professional oddities until the recent surge of interest in studying actualizing rather than pathologizing attitudes (O'Connell, 1975, 1976b, 1977, 1979b). Humor was desperately in need of theory building and inferences based upon observed behavior from lived lives, instead of abstract armchair speculation.

Psychodrama was a forerunner of Natural High Therapy. For seven years I employed it at the Waco Veterans Administration Hospital as a treatment method of choice for chronic schizophrenics, as a training device for personnel, as a diagnostic methodology for interpersonal competence, and as a data-gathering therapy for theory building (O'Connell, 1978b). When I transferred to the Houston Veterans Administration Medical Center in 1966, I was introduced to the techniques of the patients' interactional training lab (O'Connell, 1975). As the hospital's research psychologist, operating from a ward oriented toward the methodology of Kurt Lewin, there was ample opportunity to integrate the views of Adler and Moreno with those of the National Training Lab's (NTL) instrumented, trainer-led and development groups (T- and D-groups).

Following training at the Bethel NTL Center, I felt that the instrumented group approach worked well for those already close to actualization, but failed to deal adequately with the constriction of the average ego-addicted individual. Cooperation-as-equals could become a fact only after an awareness and appreciation of ego-induced mistakes and foibles, within an optimistic theory of change.

To this writer, much valuable time seemed to be wasted in Action Therapy hoping to have patients discover, completely by themselves, the movements of actualization. Also about that time the particular question on my mind was simply a reiteration of what numerous members of psychodrama groups had broached: "How about showing us the right way?" So in 1971 I launched the first Adlerian encouragement labs, an admixture of Adler-Dreikurs-Lewin-Moreno perspectives.

In 1976 I began Natural High Therapy in earnest, both as a treatment and research method for outpatient addicts and as a way of interacting and program problem solving for the clinic staff (O'Connell, 1976a; O'Connell, Bright, & Grossman, 1978).

## CURRENT STATUS

This writer has taught courses and organized workshops throughout the United States. In 1977 I taught in Holland with the International Committee for Adlerian Summer Schools and Institutes (ICASSI). I am on the faculty of the University of St. Thomas, Baylor College of Medicine, the University of Houston, and the C. G. Jung Educational Center. With two former students, Pattye Kennedy and Dayton Salisbury, I founded the Institute for Creative Community Living at the University of St. Thomas. In 1970 I was instrumental in organizing the Texas Society of Adlerian Psychology and a family education center in Houston. Two Adlerian priests, Fathers Maurice Ouellet and Dayton Salisbury, later succeeded me in directing the center.

Death and Transformation Labs have contributed in some measure to the hospice movement in Houston. When institutions become sufficiently instrumental in assisting persons to grieve and die with dignity, such workshops provide the setting for personal bereavement and the training for staff development.

Action Therapy, psychodrama workshops, and natural high labs are also available through the auspices of the Jung Center and other Texas growth centers. All labs are similar in their use of group exercises, active imagination, instrumented procedures, and psychodramatic settings (O'Connell and Bright, 1977).

In the Houston area television viewers received initial exposure to Natural High Therapy during my dozen one-hour interviews on the local *Spotlight* television show during the 1970s. Almost 100 persons have continued their self-education by volunteering to participate as auxiliaries, along with Veterans Administration trainees, in my ongoing groups. I have written over 200 publications, some available from the C. G. Jung Educational Center in Houston, Texas, and from the Alfred Adler Institute in Chicago, Illinois. My books include: *The Odyssey of a Psychologist* (1971), *Action Therapy and Adlerian Theory* (1975), *Psychotherapy: Theoretical and Technical Readings* (1976c), *Natural High Primer* (1977, with M. Bright), *Super-Natural Highs* (1979), and *The Natural High: The Humorous Pilgrimage From Ego to Self-Identity* (1980).

## THEORY

In Natural High (NH) theory, all life is dyadic: To live is to be able to focus the attention on only one object at any given time. Every interaction at the human dimension involves behavioral movement (or lack of it), perceived by an imperfect perceiver. The perceiver infers meaning, mainly unconsciously, and is always responsible for creating the subjective evaluations that define this meaning. Therefore in every human event, there is the contributor (who cannot not communicate) and the perceiver (who is responsible for generating meaning). In lived life, these actions and reactions go on rapidly and interminably. While each dyadic player in NH is responsible for the interaction, no one is to blame. Each acts and perceives according to the state of self-actualization (amount of self-esteem and degree of social interest). Persons have absolute control over only these two variables: self-esteem (SE) and social interest (SI). Only those who realize this basic NH premise have this control.

A completely actualized person (level 3) feels "as if" he or she is a wonder-full person, regardless of the environment, but has no urge to prove it to anyone (high self-esteem). The actualizer likewise feels belonging in life and experiences overriding similarities with living beings across time and space (wide social interest). Another necessary condition is to have mastered (to understanding, not perfection) the dyadic movements of encouragement (level 2). By loving the mysteries of life (the paradoxes) and being able to make quick perceptual swings between the poles of paradoxes, the actualizer qualifies as a humorist (level 3). NH sees life as a serious, but not grave, game. To become competent in a game means to accept imperfection. Practice is an essential element in games. A worthy opponent (in NH, a discouraged person) is a necessary ingredient for skill development. En route to game competency, one must learn his or her mistakes, mainly from observations and feedback from self and others. To excel, not simply to win over others, some athletes practice mistakes, share, and celebrate them. When one fights mistakes, or hypnotizes the psyche into discouragement, symptoms of mental dis-ease persist.

This narrowing of what one must think, feel, and do and how one must behave toward others was the start of ego identity. The constrictions can be outgrown only through self-actualization. One needs an ego identity. It is necessary to experience its limitations and pitfalls humorously before going to the inner voyage to experience self-identity (level 3). An ego identity compels attachments to roles, goals, and controls. It motivates the search for differences and separateness, for the *unique* identity. The basic fear of catastrophies, centered in the loss of the ego (as in death and insanity), is the prime panic rumbling beneath ego-identity consciousness. The difficulties of solitary self-help are immense because one of the rules of any ego identity is that one must never be aware of the operation of the grave game.

The "sinister circle" proceeds in this manner: unconscious invidious comparisons constricting SE and SI, followed by cognitive demandments. The latter are readily accessible to consciousness, given the help of a gentle-strong guide who is friendly, firm, and active. Since demandments (Table 1) are not usually satisfied unconditionally beyond infancy, frustrations of hidden arbitrary "musturbatory" (Ellis, 1974) wishes are assured.

**Table 1.   The Twelve Demandments[a]**

1.  I MUST be loved and approved of by everyone for everything at all times.
2.  I MUST be thoroughly competent, adequate and achieving in *all* possible respects.
3.  Some people *are* bad, wicked, or vile and MUST be punished.
4.  Things MUST go the way I very much want them to or it would be *awful, catastrophic*, or *terrible!* (awfulizing . . . terriblizing)
5.  Unhappiness is externally caused so I MUST control things and others.
6.  One MUST remain upset or worried if faced with a dangerous or fearsome reality.
7.  I MUST avoid responsibilities and difficulties rather than face them.
8.  I MUST have a *right* to be dependent and people MUST be happy to take care of me.
9.  My early childhood experiences MUST continue to *control* me and determine my emotions and behavior!
10. I MUST become upset over my and other people's problems or behavior.
11. There MUST be *one* right, precise, and *perfect* solution and it would be *terrible* or *catastrophic* if this perfect solution is not found. (catastrophizing . . .)
12. The world MUST be fair and justice (or mercy) *MUST* triumph.

[a]Adapted from list of common irrational ideas, Ellis (1974). Reprinted with permission from O'Connell and Bright (1977).

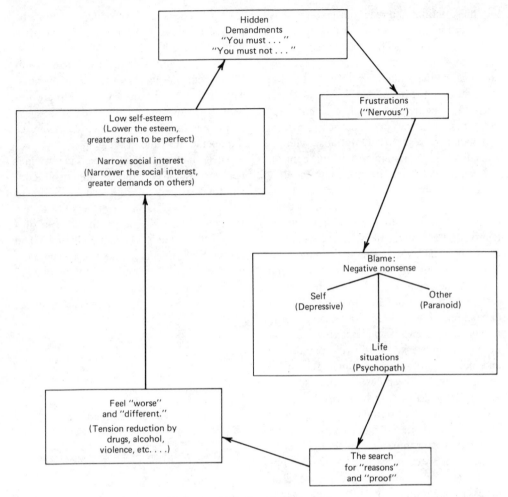

Figure A:   EGO Constricting Activities

Frustration needs no definition. Everyone has experienced the ego tensions from frustration. From this point interpretations in NH Therapy proceed back to a focus on the internalized sentences of demandments or forward on the circle to "blame," the gist of negative nonsense. Blame of self can lead to depression. Centering the onus on others culminates in our ever-popular paranoid stances. Taking it out on life is seen in psychopathic games. In this sense, blame is a social plague, and serves no useful purpose except to provide actualizers with intense adversaries. Once blame becomes certain, through inner training, one can find or provoke the proof to maintain the blame object. Creating blame is the opposite of the scientific attitude according to which one tests the null hypothesis of no relationship. In constricting, one assumes the necessity and certainty of the blame, and finds the proof one is looking for. What in descriptive psychiatry is viewed as sickness is regarded as creative (but not actualizing) behavior in NH. After the proof comes the tensions of misery, which are temporarily diminished through drugs, alcohol, promiscuity, and more open forms of violence.

Another basic idea of NH is that one cannot encourage or discourage another. One dyadic partner merely "behaves," even though the hidden motives may be for attention, power, revenge, or display of disabilities (Dreikurs, 1971). Each person is responsible for his or her own perceptual judgment, but the weak (low SE and narrow SI) do not know and/or believe this premise.

Natural high theory differentiates between three concepts often lumped together to the detriment of dynamic understanding. Common usage to the contrary, *power, ego esteem,* and *self-esteem* are not synonymous. Everyone needs and gets power wherever human interaction takes place. Power or influence is therefore communicated or subtly negotiated with every social transaction. To be utterly powerless in human interactions is impossible. When people are called "powerless," the implication is that they are lacking positive influence to the point of being highly creative, with extreme nuisance value (O'Connell, 1975).

Any quest for external signs and symbols of personal and social power is, at best, an overcompensation for undeveloped strength. Those with actualizing attitudes and a loving community (level 2) are not addicted to power. Strong (SE and SI) persons do get positive power, but without clinging and grasping greedily for attachments.

Ego esteem has similar affective qualities as self-esteem; therefore, one can experience natural highs by receiving signs and symbols of success from the environment. In such instances, though, the psyche is not centered and runs the risk of being addicted to external sources for proof of worth and belonging. Hence the declaration in NH that such circumstances of proof are ego addictions, a risky search for ego esteem outside of the self. The ego addict, lacking the energies of self-identity, needs to "score" on others. Without the external fix, the withdrawal symptoms of anxiety and other psychic pain follows immediately. The pattern is that of attachment to roles, goals, and controls that need subjective proof of the support of significant others (or in extreme cases, assurance from all others, at all times). Self-esteem is a giant's step beyond the ego-imposed limitations of the externalizer. A person cannot shortcut this journey from ego

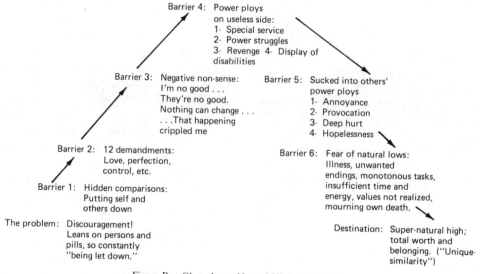

Figure B:   Obstacles to Natural High Actualization

to self any more than levels 1 and 2 can be circumvented for instant SE and SI at level 3, the dimension of self-generated SE and SI.

It is axiomatic to NH that any psychospiritual pilgrim will be prevented from venturing into levels 2 and 3 for long, without discouragement, by the ego-induced monsters of hyperdependency, competition, and ignorance of the effects of human transactions. Such creative discouragement is not to be shocked, cut, or chemically drowned out of commission. All resistance is "grist for the mill" for the NH therapist. Through alternative perceptions, the patient is shown the tremendous creativity and power, perhaps for the first time, hidden beneath constrictions and symptom formation.

Level 3 is an introduction to the deep self, the object of curiosity and contentment for generations of mystics, including C. G. Jung. Personkind needs a certain support, beyond the ego, to justify the monotonous struggles toward actualization in a discouragenic world. Yet the ego (level 1) and other (level 2) dimensions cannot be ignored in favor of a hyperdependent, helpless, and hopeless stance toward an utterly externalized God, as in institutionalized religiosity. Ego actualization and encouragenic movements toward others precede the spiritual dimension in time; hence, the re-solution of opposites in the term "psychospiritual," with the psychic (level 1) first. Later comes the attention on the experiencing of the deep self and connections with the universe, a facet now becoming popular through Meditation and contemplation (level 3). When level 3 becomes paramount, there is no diminution of the attention on the preceding psychosocial levels, 1 and 2. They are equally important for the continuation of the actualization process, which is never a static state or encapsulated entity.

We never completely overcome our early constrictions. There is no quick, easy, pain-free authentic human existence. NH is simple; but it is not easy or painless. If there were packaged actualizations for over-the-counter bartering (the implicit goal of the chemically addicted), humans would have no use for humor and little need for self-disclosing, feedback-rendering, support groups. These groups can tell us gently and firmly our mistakes when we "con-strict" ourselves into narrow ego traps. They offer psychic nurturance and growth. Yet again paradoxically or ironically, we are responsible for creating and maintaining such groups through our own loving of ego, others, and self, put into inner and outer action.

With the sense of humor, we watch with awe the invidious comparisons, demandments, and negative nonsenses (level 1) develop, from the space-between-thoughts, the disinterested seat of the timeless, universally connected self (level 3). Through Meditation, contemplation, and concentration, persons learn not to collapse before moods. NH people do not solidify discouragements by inner struggles against its constrictions, as the neurotic does, so becoming inseparable from his symptoms.

The humorous attitude evolves from an acceptance of the necessity of an experiential understanding of the movements of the three levels of natural high theory and practice. With an increase of self-worth and belonging comes a willingness to share and celebrate the mistakes of here-and-now ego constrictions. Well-practiced Meditation contributes to an enlivening distancing from chronic ego attachments to demandments and negative nonsense. Such a "witnessing" of mistakes, then letting the "musturbations" and negative certainties flow on, is not even slightly akin to the pathological depersonalization and derealization emanating from inadequate SE and SI. It is rather a curious disinterested inner-watching that does not degenerate into catastrophizing or fighting untoward ego reactions of any person. Reactive resentments and strenuous struggles of resistance frequently stabilize into symptoms and become part of one's search for power on the useless side of life. A premise of natural high theory is that early constrictions are always potential stress reactions. Humor, coming after SE and SI expansion and an appreciation for life's paradoxes, gives a distancing perspective, a "God's-eye view," that nips constrictions in the bud. Humor is the chief coping capacity. Beyond being in the service of the ego addictions, humor is a perspective in the service of the self, the royal road toward actualization.

## METHODOLOGY

### Private Patients

All private patients are told that individual psychotherapy would be appropriate initially to work out individual expectations and demands and to receive individual instructions in the practice of natural high actualization. Early in therapy, homework is introduced, suggesting (but not demanding) that the client focus on habitual inner reactions that prevent or enlarge on opportunities for expansion of feelings of self-worth and belonging. Since all persons operate by cognitive maps of the world, even if they cannot read their own, NH therapists are ever concerned about making the inner creative process conscious and acceptable. Beyond this awareness, there is the ever-active effort to specify steps to the client for self-training in actualization in a discouragenic world.

Group Psychotherapy follows after a few individual sessions. As they enter Group Psychotherapy, the patients/students/clients are given the option of discontinuing individual psychotherapy or selecting a schedule less frequent than once a week. It is in Group Therapy that patients practice the steps of level 2 encouragement, especially the search for similarities. Members routinely rehearse self-disclosing present, past, and perhaps even future constrictions. They give feedback to other members about reactive feelings and ask for feedback from peers. Group Therapy, and occasionally psychodrama, of-

fers an opportunity to share projections and be able to reach cooperation-as-equals through honest, open communications. The therapist is an integral part of this disclosure-and-feedback system, modeling attempts at actualization, giving and receiving feedback, and reinforcing encouragenesis, whenever it appears ("Thanks, that effort helped me . . .").

All the steps of level 2 (encouragement) were formed to provide a behavioral prescription for the accepting atmosphere. Level 2 is attuned to the regressive urge of constrictive identity seeking through shades of psychic isolation and worthlessness (level 1). Level 2 is not verbal pablum, but requires strength (adequate self-esteem and social interest) to risk courageous self-disclosure and feedback.

The therapist will give the patient structured movement of "what to do," not insisting, in a senseless power struggle, that this student will ever perform this dyadic dance. Rather the tutor will *anticipate* what the neophyte will do to avoid these courageous (active SI) acts. With this anticipation is admiration, expressed by the body as well as the words, for the well-practiced creativity of cooperation-as-*unequals*.

In general, those pilgrims who are spoilsports on level 2 are likewise on level 3. Similar dynamics operate. Without the psychic energy of abundant SE and SI, the unactualized will not accept the challenges, homework, and persistent practice of the dyadic and transpersonal dimensions of NH. Anyone ego-trapped into diminishment (of SE and SI) and into nonconscious, reactive one-upmanship (or "pride") will not approach the practice of movements for psychic increase with equanimity. The diminishment process, on the other hand, is in the service of hyperdependency, competition, and ignorance of psychic connectivity, all assumed to be part of the quest for ego identity ("who you must be . . . or not be") and subsequent reactions to this basic condition.

On the other hand, those beings who are

motivated to leave the fixations of childhood identifications and experience the possibilities of self-generated alternative perceptions can practice steps of level 2 as well as share and ultimately celebrate life-style constrictions. As continuous practice is part of any serious game, level 2 behaviors can be put into action either overtly or covertly. Using level 3 techniques of contemplation and concentration, the NH student focuses his mind (or attention) on symbols or signs of encouragenic level 2 (or level 3) movements. With contemplation, the mind is blanked by one-pointing (e.g., attention on nostrils, feeling the inhalations and exhalations). Concentration, the opposite of free association, keeps the attention on thoughts of the action in question. As with any focusing of the mind, inner resistance to the task is not catastrophized or otherwise fought. The attention gently but firmly goes back to the task at hand. At the completion, the student learns to stroke the self for effort, never for perfection (which simply cannot be attained).

## Workshops and Labs

In encouragement labs, lectures on the topics precede any practice. Participants are then paired and the partners interview each other in turn. For encouragement labs, the question for each interviewer to consider might be "How do you prefer to be encouraged by others?" In a death and transformation workshop with a similar introductory format, the theme for the dyadic interview could be "What do you want to get out of this workshop, and what are you willing to contribute?" "What do you do to prevent natural highs?" is a suitable question for natural high lab interviews. While doing the interviewing, the participants are getting practice on the 12 steps of encouragement: (1) stop, look, and listen; (2) paraphrasing and guessing; (3) searching for similarities; and (4) attempting encouragenic body language. After an allotted period of time, each interviewer self-discloses (step 5) the image formed of the interviewee. The latter then gives non-

judgmental feedback (step 6) on the perceived correctness of the interviewer's task. Dyads are then combined into groups of eight, each member in turning self-disclosing to the group the similarities (step 4) discovered with the partner.

A number of group exercises are distributed, in instrumented group format, for participants to learn the content of encouragement and experience in putting it into practice. A number of self and group rating scales are also available for the process of feedback and self-disclosure. Group exercises are constructed for participants to make rankings of endings and then work together in the stress of trying to arrive at consensus.

One of this writer's favorite procedures is to roleplay with all groups, singly before combined groups. I play a discouraged person of any age, sex, diagnostic category, or presenting problem desired, with members of each group playing encouragenic persons. Afterward they self-disclose their reactions to the problem. Others in the lab share their similar experiences and give feedback about behavior noted. Playing the discouraged person illustrates behaviors not to be engaged in: goals on the useless side of life (step 12). Participants realize, through this type of exercise, how easy it is to reinforce negative goals (step 12). Other behaviors of encouragement include (step 7) acknowledging skills of the other, even when they frustrate our ego drives; telling others how they have encouraged and could do so more (steps 8, 9, and 10); and guesses as to how we encouraged others and could do so even more (step 11).

Close to 5,000 persons have participated in death and transformation labs as they progressed in content and aim from a limited focus on terminality of patients to didactic-experiential means of self-actualization (O'Connell and Bright, 1977). This writer directs an average of six death and transformation labs annually, working whenever possible with music and art therapists. Ideally the lab is a weekend workshop, the participants living together in a retreat setting. As far as is known, there have been no psychological casualties from these labs, despite many grim professional warnings that the death experiences would provoke masochistic, suicidal, and depressive attacks. I believe that the success of the workshops, in which almost all participants have emotional experiences, is due mainly to three factors. First and foremost, the lab structure is one in which crying is expected and regarded as positive involvement. No one is labeled negatively or pampered for crying. Moreover participants are told many times that they do not have to participate and no one should have the effrontery to categorize nonparticipation as "sick." Because, or in spite of, these instructions, very few people ever decline to participate. A second factor is my insistence that groups learn to be open, sharing, and authentic (level 2) before death and dying exercises commence. In this manner, participants, for the most part, have a ready-made support group before facing the issue of the death of significant persons. An essential part of the workshops involves guided imagery of one's own death; psychodramatic involvement in playing one's most significant survivor; and dialoguing with death and with dead persons with whom there is unfinished business. A third vital safeguard is the focus on humor after the emotionally charged experiences, guided imagery, and psychodramatic techniques. Art and music exercises are used to give the participants a sense of competence and purposiveness in facing the certainty of death for all bodies and egos. In humordrama, after empathy is developed for the plight of others, doubles are employed in the psychodramas to stimulate alternative humorous responses to one's death sentence.

## Institutional Patients

In seven years at an outpatient drug clinic, this writer never witnessed a discussion, instigated by anyone else, concerned with treatment as a *dyadic* responsibility. In contrast, NH treatment is a serious game in which healers try to contribute behaviors that will assist the client in expanding self-esteem and social interest, and to guess, often aloud, at how the other will resist encouragenic efforts. No negative judgments are made of the patient. In fact he or she is regarded as creative, not sick, in efforts to resist. In institutions concentration upon *dyadic* responsibility is an unpardonable sin. I believe that this one observation—whether staff and patients are allowed to focus upon how each person contributes to discouragement of others—is the prime interaction that separates institutional from instrumental settings. The constant dyadic quality of the interactional human system is totally ignored, suppressed, or repressed by the institutional mind.

Natural High Therapy for addiction has entered another stage, one that the addicts appreciate and practice much more. They learn to meditate and clear the mind of ego noise in groups. At the same time they start to treat themselves gently, perhaps for the first time. When the mind wanders, they bring the mind (the focus of attention) back to breath counting (feeling the breath at the top of the nostrils). When patients can one-point (do one thing at a time, with relaxed alertness), they are ready to concentrate and contemplate. Starting with five-minute periods per day, they concentrate or focus fully on a segment of natural high theory (e.g., self-esteem, social interest). Then may come contemplation, letting the symbols unfold without diagnosing, judging, or interpreting. Even if the mind wanders, the addict's reactions or even the contents of the wanderings are a projective test of where one is on the actualization pilgrimage. Any patient may focus on the elements of encouragement and practice (e.g., step 4), looking for similarities with others. Even more important is familarity and acceptance of the "space between thoughts" that may have commonality with the Jungian self, spirit, or soul, and with right-brain speculation (Watzlawick, 1978). Whenever patients feel level 1 ego constrictions taking place, they can one-point, clear the mind, and so avoid the aftermath of ego-induced frustrations, the chemical fix.

## APPLICATIONS

Natural High Therapy applies to all categories of persons; the focus is on a wide base of inner and outer behaviors, from psychopathology to psychospiritual self-actualization. Natural high theory and techniques have been used in individual and group psychotherapy and counseling, didactic-experiential workshops, and in teaching through lectures and television presentations. The limiting boundaries are, as in any learning situation, intelligence and motivation. The emphasis on identifying feelings and movements in the here-and-now, rather than on remote abstractions, lowers the parameters of NH applicability, when compared with orthodox verbal "talking-about" psychotherapies. Age and diagnostic categories are therefore less limiting factors in NH Therapy.

Natural High Therapy began as a therapy for hospitalized psychotics and continued as treatment for hospitalized alcoholics and drug addicts. Currently this writer works with outpatient drug addicts, but the same NH approach is used with individuals, families, and groups in private practice. Although I do not work with children and adolescents outside of the family context, some expressive therapists (art, music, dancing) specialize in their natural high practices with young persons.

An outstanding feature of NH is the democratization of the therapy situation. The same concepts and constrictions apply to everyone. However, with children, as a rule, life-style certainties are not so well-practiced over time, so environmental factors carry more weight. This egalitarian atmosphere does not imply sameness. Both therapist and patient are born, exist, and die differently. They have their own lived skills and experience dissimilarities. But similarities in needs, hopes, fears, and constrictions are accepted and often shared in NH learning. Hopefully the natural high therapist personally practices and actualizes the steps of levels 2 and 3 and has past and present experience and awareness of level 1 constrictions.

The therapist must be the more learned intellectually and behaviorally on the natural high dimension; otherwise there is no need for the learning relationship to exist. Yet this superiority in one facet of life never implies superiority of individuals.

According to natural high theory, there are no unmotivated persons. Children and patients typically classified as unmotivated are often so highly motivated to be perfect that they will avoid interactions so as not to risk failure of power and esteem (displays of disability). Undoubtedly many such persons are more powerful than the therapist in resisting influence. The therapist does not use this supposition to discourage self or patient. Perhaps at other times, with different supports and perceptions, the patient may change. But even without change, the worth of the person in the ultimate scheme of things is not questioned. Therefore, the natural high therapist maintains contact, but does not get involved with power struggles, revenge, or other hyperdependent dyads with the discouraged others. Looking to the therapist's own self- (and other-) encouragenesis makes the therapist perceive the world as a vibrant interacting system in which the tutor is responsible for his own resolution of paradoxes, as well as for actively pursuing here-and-now dynamic interpretations. In all relationships the natural high therapist, within and without of the therapy game room, may have certain superior skills, but is no molder of uniquely superior persons.

Since the actualization process applies to all, so does Natural High Therapy and training. Incorporating Adlerian psychology and instrumental religious actions, NH brings schools, homes, and churches into the same serious game as clinics, hospitals, and the rest of the moving, developing community.

## CASE EXAMPLE

A typical case is that of Frank, a 45-year-old white single male. A former minister, now a counselor in a state alcoholic rehabilitation project, Frank came to therapy with the presenting symptoms or "calling cards" of chronic ennui and depression. He discovered this writer and Natural High watching a local television talk show, coming as a self-referral.

The contract session, for which there is no payment, was to further understanding of the expectations of both participants for an optimal relationship. Goals were articulated and the psychological pitfalls postulated (e.g., identifying possible expectations that, when unvoiced, might become pathological demands). The client was then told to call back if he decided he wanted to "work-play" with the therapist. Frank made the commitment.

At his next session, Frank was interviewed for his family constellation, early recollections, and dreams. He was also given ongoing homework (or "homeplay") assignments as per his agreement during the contract session. The tutoring sessions of individual psychotherapy were not to be used for the teaching of the abstract "psychomaps" of levels 1, 2, and 3. They were rather for helping the client/student to get his own bearings (mistakes, purposes) on his natural high pilgrimage. Questions could be asked and answered, but the natural high therapist was not there for generalized lectures. Frank, well aware of this interactional structure, on his own volition enrolled for a weekend death and transformation lab and a course also taught by this writer on the sense of humor at a local university.

Individual tutoring discussions on level 1 began with the client's frustration and then followed the "sinister circle" of constriction; to gather information for both therapist and patient; and to watch defensive reactions and discuss them disinterestedly with the patient/pilgrim. Frank experienced frustrations as "unbearable tensions and shakings." The immediate blame-object was himself (depression): "no good shit . . . damned monkey . . . failure, failure." He could find proof for discouragement anywhere. "I can't express anything out in the open . . . either want to run and cry or start to insult others."

The unpardonable sin, the ultimate irreversible stigmata, was: "I've always been a sissy and queer." Frank rated his demandments from zero to four. Later in therapy, between sessions, he recorded in his journal, without blame and punishment, the instances of demandments. Automatic-appearing invidious comparisons appeared in most human male contacts; females were simply not interesting.

As I anticipated and acknowledged, I was soon cast in the father-figure role. Frank then became silent, nervous, and discouraged about his progress, wanting to stay away after the third session. From the earlier testing, I expected this occurrence. I readily but tentatively gave a genetic interpretation, prefaced by "spitting in the soup" (O'Connell, 1975). "I would like to give you my guess as to how you're constricting yourself and why right now. But if I do, I think you might get yourself more angry and depressed and use your feelings as an excuse to drop out of therapy, as you have in the past. What's your reaction to what I've told you?"

Frank could readily make the perceptual connection between past and present behaviors and did start to express himself more honestly with me. At this point, the time seemed ripe to talk of "how" and "why" miscasting, defining, validating, and invalidating by parental persons and peers are allowed to determine present constrictions. I self-disclosed how my former constrictions were my ego-induced efforts at maintaining early dependencies. Frank reported he felt less isolated. He then related homosexual experiences at the age of five to nine with his oldest stepbrother, his father's favorite. Frank was seen by his nuclear family, he believed, as "no good shit . . . damned monkey . . . failure, failure," especially by his father and three stepbrothers. Frank was the youngest child with two pampering sisters and a pampering mother, all three reinforcing his avoidance and ineffectuality in relating to males.

After six sessions Frank was beginning to understand intellectually the natural high theory and his part emotionally in becoming an active agent in creating constrictions. Three more sessions of role playing with the therapist followed. Frank did empty-chair assignments with significant members of his family, experiencing both "as it was" and "how I want it to be now." Although he could express anger and later forgiveness even with the oldest stepbrother, he balked at playing the father in the empty-chair technique. "I'm simply too scared and my mind is blank." I played father, as I saw him through the patient's eyes. Frank moved through 20 minutes of tears, followed by 15 minutes of loud, intense anger. Before the close of that session, Frank was able to finally make his peaceful farewell with the father who had died two years earlier. Frank had not attended the funeral, having given "poor health" as his excuse. Depression had followed and he quit his parish work three months later.

I reframed Frank's faith in "early psychic traumata" and "probable libidinal defects" as the cause of his homosexuality into here-and-now life-style constrictions. It was especially important for me to focus Frank on how he constricted himself, by his learned internalized sentences, just before his unwanted homoerotic fantasies. He then became his mother's and sisters' helpless, hopeless little boy, searching for an ideal male to transform him magically into one of his father's manly sons. Even his dreams followed the same pattern: passively incorporating the magic semen of a male who was competent, assertive, and had a profusion of hair on the head and more on the body. (Frank saw himself as ridiculed by his whole family for being a bald monkey, a small manicky creature with grossly misplaced hair). The passive sexual fantasies were often followed by raping the male ideal in both orifices. In actuality Frank reported that he acted out only two passive homosexual encounters with strangers in adult life. He masturbated over the active fantasies, more to reduce tension over inhibited hostility than

the sexual content per se. Frank could understand all this content in the frame of his ego-identity problems: his current ideals and family-induced constrictions.

He practiced haltingly the steps of level 2, giving feedback and self-disclosure assertively yet gently and appropriately to both males and females. In early therapy sessions, I pointed Frank toward expressing hidden feelings of frustration about the discouragenic acts of others. After acknowledgment of and awkward practice in the expression of negative emotions in therapy, Frank was ready to think and perceive dialectically. In other words, he considered that he saw according to his level of self-esteem and social interest processing. As he actualized, Frank could harbor and share positive emotions. Untoward behaviors of others now became simply reflections of *their* constrictions. Frank then noted that he was either stimulating and/or noticing more the positive respect from others. And above all, the rejections of others became "gifts" from them, a chance to give an encouragenic volley to their provoking serves. Frank was now looking at his life at times from the humorous God's-eye view, becoming a useful player in the game-of-games. The same behavior that stimulated angry frustrations was now evaluated more dispassionately, from the perspective of an evolving interactional system in which he played an important part.

The time was then ripe to place Frank into my group of three males and four females, who were well schooled and pacticed on their own constrictions and the theory and techniques of actualization. Frank was able, in 20 sessions, to put in his own words the personal details of his aforementioned dynamics. Early in group sessions, he voiced feelings about perceived pampering by the females and rejection by the males. He self-disclosed his generalized tendencies to compete with males unsuccessfully and seek nurturing females when defeated. After the sixth session, Frank started to share humor. He caught the ridiculous way he diminished himself and foolishly recoiled in passive anger. The group stroked him for his courage in taking this risk of self-disclosure and thereby helping them to share similar reactions.

The last ego-obstacle noted in many incipient actualizers is the fear, in fantasy and dreams, that a catastrophe would overwhelm them, and possibly the world, if they performed well or succeeded. Frank felt it too. To diminish this fear, Frank went beyond his continued sharing with group and put extra hours into creating a ritual of meditation, contemplation, and concentration. At this time he returned for two individual sessions to learn techniques of level 3 for self-expansion of worth and belonging.

At present Frank has been married for over two years in his native Montana. He considers himself quite successful in parish work and counseling. He continues to correspond intermittently with me, sharing novel ways in which he handles with humor any recurrence of his time-honored constrictions. The main-tent for Frank's life is now with others; constrictions are merely an interesting sideshow of his former existence. (For another case study, with a female client, see O'Connell, 1979a.)

## SUMMARY

Natural High is a broad, holistic therapy, not a minitheory of narrow concepts and techniques. It transcends pop psychology's promise of instant ecstasy in its emphasis on continuous practice within the serious (but not grave) game model. NH is the only therapy that has at its core a well-formulated focus on the sense of humor as a criterion of actualization. Traditional psychopathology finds its place in the ego constrictions and subsequent ego defenses of level 1.

The therapist himself is responsible for his own actualization as well as communication of encouragement (and the knowledgeable awareness of the ''hows'' and ''whys'' of discouragement). The active, encouragenic, therapist/tutor is the key element of the change process; therefore, the state of actualization is not totally ignored in NH, as it is in contemporary professionalization and institutionalization. NH stands apart from dualisms of persons and professions, centering on overcoming ego-identity defects and the attachments to tentative ego esteem. The process of creating unconditional self-esteem and universal belonging is regarded as paramount for all persons and the most pertinent goal of all human activities. NH is therefore seen as the treatment (or education) of choice, the overt manifestation of the ideals of the perennial philosophy and democracy-in-action. The premises and techniques of all humanistic depth psychologies are incorporated within NH. NH goes beyond conventional therapies in not separating experiential education from the tasks of psychology, psychiatry, education, and religion. NH has a strong Adlerian base, but goes beyond the Adlerian social dimension to symbolic transpersonal catalysts of self-esteem and social interest expansion. NH spells out the steps of encouragement, as well as concretizing and systematizing the nuances of diminishment. The tragic side of life so neglected in Adlerian psychology, as well as by other therapies, is embraced by NH in the appreciation of the presence of natural low states and constricted others, so vital to one's own practice of self-realization.

NH represents a continuation of Jung's emphasis on the inner dialogue between ego and archetypes (behavioral potentials) of the collective unconscious. NH stresses the signs and developmental steps of this strong or actualized ego, a prerequisite to accepting (and not diagnosing, judging, or interpreting) the expansive energies of the collective unconscious. It carries on, through its transcendental courage, Jung's later concern with the human partnership in transforming the divine or cosmic shadow. NH is not phobic about the mystical thrusts (e.g., Teilhard de Chardin) that drastically elevate both the human worth potential and our innate universal belonging. The avoidance of false dichotomies fructifies the latent positive relationship between actualizing psychologies and instrumental humanistic religions. The bedrock of NH is each person's awareness of ego constrictions (level 1) and social obligations (level 2) *before* and basic to transpersonal explorations (level 3). Present cognitive and behavioral deficiencies of both the unactualized ego and institutionalized social settings cannot be circumvented by demands for an instant magical-egotistical euphoria.

## REFERENCES

Ansbacher, H. and Ansbacher, R. (Eds.). *The individual psychology of Alfred Adler.* New York: Basic Books, 1956.

Ansbacher, H. and Ansbacher, R. (Eds.). *Superiority and social interest: A collection of later writings.* Evanston, Ill.: Northwestern University Press, 1964.

Dreikurs, R. *Social equality: The challenge of today.* Chicago: Regnery, 1971.

Ellis, A. *Humanistic psychotherapy: The rational-emotive approach.* New York: McGraw-Hill, 1974.

Haley, J. *The strategies of psychotherapy.* New York: Grune & Stratton, 1963.

Jung, C. *Memories, dreams, reflections.* New York: Random House, 1961.

O'Connell, W. *The odyssey of a psychologist.* New York: MSS Information Corporation, 1974.

O'Connell, W. *Action therapy and Adlerian theory.* Chicago: Alfred Adler Institute, 1975.

O'Connell, W. The "Friends of Adler" Phenomenon. *Journal of Individual Psychology,* 1976a, **32,** 5–18.

O'Connell, W. Freudian humour: The eupsychia of everyday life. In A. Chapman and H. Foot (Eds.), *Humour and laughter: Theory, research, and applications.* London: Wiley, 1976b.

O'Connell, W. (Ed.). *Psychotherapy: Theoretical and technical readings.* New York: MSS Information Corporation, 1976c.

O'Connell, W. The sense of humor: Actualizer of persons and theories. In A. Chapman and H. Foot (Eds.), *It's a funny thing, humour.* London: Pergamon, 1977.

O'Connell, W. A re-solution of Adlerian-Jungian opposites. *Journal of Individual Psychology,* 1978a, **34,** 170–181.

O'Connell, W. Action therapy. *The Individual Psychologist,* 1978b, **15,** 4–11.

O'Connell, W. The demystification of Sister Saint Nobody. *Journal of Individual Psychology,* 1979a, **35,** 79–94.

O'Connell, W. *Super-natural highs.* Chicago: North American Graphics, 1979b.

O'Connell, W. *The natural high: The humorous pilgrimage from ego to self-identity,* to be published in 1981.

O'Connell, W. and Bright, M. *Natural high primer.* Houston: Natural High Associates, 1977.

O'Connell, W., Bright, M. and Grossman, S. Negative nonsense and drug addiction. *Rational Living,* 1978, **13,** 19–24.

Ram Dass, B. and Levine, S. *Grist for the mill.* Santa Cruz, Calif.: Unity, 1977.

Watzlawick, P. *The language of change: Elements of therapeutic communication.* New York: Basic Books, 1978.

# CHAPTER 42

# *The New Identity Process*

DANIEL M. CASRIEL, M.D.

*Throughout the centuries there have been voluntary institutions, such as monasteries, and involuntary institutions, such as prisons, dedicated to reforming individuals, changing them in a direction desired either by the person himself or herself or by others. Perhaps the oldest and best known of these was at Epidaurus in Greece, a healing center that existed as such for over 1,000 years.*

*In recent years, a somewhat different type of treatment center has developed, based more on psychological rationales than on the physiological ones of the watering spas. Examples range from the meditational ashrams of the Orient, to diet-oriented "fat farms" for the wealthy and bored, to Synanon, an organization that has itself spawned a wide variety of other treatment modalities—Daytop Village and Habilitat, for example.*

*Daniel Casriel, the author of this chapter, was conventionally trained in psychodynamics and psychiatry. After visiting Synanon, he changed his thinking and his life. Eventually he developed the concepts of Synanon into this own system, first called Scream Therapy and now New Identity Process, which is similar in many respects to several other approaches in this volume, especially Integrity Groups and Reevaluation Counseling. As the reader will soon find out, the entire process is well conceived, theoretically consistent, and from all indications is being accepted and is developing at a rapid rate.*

The New Identity Process (NIP), also known somewhat less precisely as Scream Therapy, is a comprehensive therapeutic system for reeducating a person's emotional, thinking, and behavioral responses, especially those that have to do with giving and getting love.

The tools of NIP are bonding—physical closeness with emotional openness; screaming for discharging historic emotion and preparing the person to incorporate fresh messages; confrontation of behavior; and new information about the ABC's—affect, behavior, and cognition.

The aim of the process is not simply adjustment—cognitive absence of painful emotion—but happiness—cognitive awareness of a preponderance of pleasure. A happy person is autonomous, successful, fallible, able to put things in perspective, and capable of giving and receiving love, expressing needs, and getting those needs filled in a responsible way.

NIP is effective with all degrees of neurotic and character-disordered personalities, including the delinquent, the addict, and the alcoholic. It is also effective in treating the so-called borderline schizophrenic, provided the disorder is not organic in origin.

## HISTORY

The main ingredients that went into the development of the system were: (1) training in Adaptational Psychodynamics; (2) work with drug users and exposure to Synanon in

---

Manuscript edited by Jacqui Bishop.

1962; and (3) work with Synanon techniques at Daytop and with private patients.

*Adaptational Psychodynamics.* After graduating from the Cincinnati College of Medicine in 1949, this writer attended the Columbia Psychoanalytic Institute for Training and Research, at that time directed by founders Sandor Rado and Abram Kardiner, who formulated Adaptational Psychodynamics. Their theory advanced Freudian tenets by attributing pathology not to instinct alone, but also to the conditioning the individual is subjected to in infancy and childhood by those responsible for meeting his or her needs. Later, spurred by 18 months of exposure to a different culture on Okinawa, I contacted Kardiner, who was well-known for his anthropological approach to the human personality. I was an analysand of Kardiner's for over seven years, and through that experience became convinced that no inborn human feature was without purpose.

*The Synanon Experience.* Shortly after opening my private practice in 1953, I began working with various government and judicial bodies to apply psychoanalytic techniques to rehabilitating young drug addicts, most of whom were severely character-disordered personalities. I found, as had so many of my colleagues, that the transference integral to successful analysis simply did not develop with addicts, and the program failed. I concluded that there were only two ways to deal with drug addicts: maintain them on their habit or lock them up.

My attitude changed drastically in 1962, as a result of exposure to Synanon, a California drug and alcohol rehabilitation community consisting at that time of about a hundred people. The visit, part of a nationwide survey of drug treatment facilities for the National Institute of Mental Health, was to change radically my approach not only to drug addiction, but to the entire field of applied psychiatry.

Apart from tremendous productive phys-ical activity and a rigidly authoritarian structure, the two ingredients I saw as most critical at Synanon were: (1) people expressing genuine love and concern overtly; and (2) the focus on behavior through highly charged emotional confrontation in groups, known widely today as Synanon games. Their belief was that when one changes one's objectionable behavior *first*—that is, stops taking dope *first*—only then can inner change take place. And addicts *were* changing into productive, responsible, loving human beings.

*My Work with Synanon Techniques.* Fired with excitement by the possibilities Synanon had suggested, and by the love and insights I had experienced during the confrontation groups I'd participated in, I returned to New York and over the next two years co-founded Daytop Lodge; a Synanon center in Westport, Connecticut; and Daytop Village in New York, which became a model for scores of government-sponsored therapeutic communities that sprang up worldwide over the next 15 years.

I was equally intrigued by the potential that the Synanon type of group might hold for speeding treatment of my more recalcitrant neurotic patients. Using some Synanon-trained people as catalysts, I first introduced the technique in 1963 to a group of eight patients from my private practice. The technique was astoundingly successful, producing breakthroughs that dramatically speeded progress in individual analytic sessions. Soon people were coming asking for group treatment only. At first, I was hesitant, but gradually, as I became more comfortable with the group process and the safety it provided, I dropped the requirement for individual sessions.

Within six years it was necessary to move three times to accommodate the flow of patients. In 1970 I left Daytop to begin my own residential program for middle- and upper-class addicts. By that year almost 600 patients were participating in groups each week.

In the 10 years since then, NIP has evolved considerably. The highly charged emotional group is ''an emotional microscope'' through which we can see clearly and map for the first time the geography of emotions. The process today has shifted emphasis more toward bonding and toward what we experience as love. ''People are starving, and love is the only thing that will feed them.''

## CURRENT STATUS

As of this writing, the headquarters for NIP treatment and training is in a brownstone building in New York City. There, around the clock, seven days a week, five programs are offered tailored to meet individual needs. These include:

1. AREBA (Accelerated reducation of emotions, behavior, and attitudes), a residential treatment program that rehabilitates young addicts. The term of residence in the three-phase program ranges from 12 to 24 months, with an average of 15 months. Of those who complete the program, over 90 percent are cured—drug-free, socially functioning, and educationally or vocationally employed.

2. Intensives, a residential program for nonaddicts that consists of three groups a day, six or seven days a week.

3. Outpatient group therapy sessions, which often include residential patients.

4. Individual therapy to deal with special problems or with people who for one reason or another are not available for group work.

5. Various training programs for individuals wanting certification as NIP group leaders, including one-year training internships and less concentrated programs for practicing therapists.

In addition I travel for about four months a year in Europe and another two to three

months a year in the United States, giving workshops and training therapists.

As of 1980, there will be seven national societies of the New Identity Process in the United States, Sweden, Switzerland, Germany, Holland, France, and Venezuela. An estimated 15,000 people a week are experiencing the process or a modification of it.

The process is explained in more detail in *A Scream Away From Happiness* (Casriel, 1972) and an upcoming volume, tentatively titled *The Huggers*, (Casriel, forthcoming).

## THEORY

In evolving New Identity Process theory, I have blended humanistic, neo-Freudian, and behaviorist thinking with insights arising out of my own experience and observation. The theory can be summarized as follows.

1. *The origin of pathology:* A human being is born with intrinsic value and entitlements. Pathology originates from early conditioning that opposes these basic entitlements by making the process of getting one's needs met painful. On the basis of early conditioning, a person makes decisions regarding the pleasure and pain of getting biological needs met; these decisions constitute the central dynamic of his or her disorder and are what distinguish one category of disorder from another.

2. *The locus of pathological patterns:* The individual acts out these early decisions in relation to bonding, the one biological need for which, even as an adult, he or she must continue looking to others to satisfy.

3. *The keys to change:* To change destructive patterns, we must rectify the current vast ignorance regarding the dynamics and biology of emotion, and apply new understanding of how thinking, feeling, and behavior interrelate and perpetuate pathological patterns.

## The Origin of Pathology

In the NIP system, people are born good, having value simply for being alive. As such, they are each entitled to (1) exist as separate beings with an identity of their own, (2) have physical and emotional needs and get them met, (3) be happy, and (4) be imperfect. Pathology originates during our dependent years with conditioning that subverts these basic entitlements by suggesting that we have to earn them or be something we are not in order to have them. This subversion is painful.

All animal behavior is motivated by the pursuit of pleasure and avoidance of pain. Feeling entitled is pleasurable; feeling unentitled is painful. We learn to feel entitled in infancy and early childhood when our caretakers meet our biological needs (physical, mental, and emotional) in a caring, loving way with a minimum of pain. We learn to feel unentitled when we do not get that loving care, when we have to beg; or wait interminably; or manipulate; or do without, with too little, or with too much.

Faced with this dilemma, we eventually make two major decisions, one about dealing with pleasure, the other about dealing with pain. Because the decisions relate to dependency needs, it is only to be expected that as adults we act out our pathology in those areas in which we still feel dependent on others, in personal relationships.

*Acceptors and Rejectors.* How we decide to deal with pleasure puts us in one of two categories: *acceptor* or *rejector*.

In the acceptor's experience the pleasure of getting needs met exceeds the pain, and they decide "I have to get my needs met no matter what." Later on they accept human relationships even at the price of pain, humiliation, and loss of freedom and identity.

Rejectors experience the pain as greater than the pleasure and say, "To hell with it. I'll suck my own thumb and do it myself, as much as I can." Later on they reject human relationships no matter what price they

have to pay in pain, deprivation, and isolation.

*Neurotics and Character Disorders.* The decision about how to deal with pain is what differentiates neurosis from character disorder.

Neurotics are aware of their pain, but are afraid to express it, and they utilize elaborate defense mechanisms to keep from doing so, especially if there is associated anger. They say something like, "If I let out my pain, I'll never stop," or "Someone (everyone) will reject me, I won't get my needs met, and then I'll die."

By contrast, character-disordered personalities say, "The pain's too great, I won't feel it." They don't opt for "fight or flight," they "freeze," simply detaching from the pain, and keeping it at bay by acting out in ways destructive to self and others. Most addicts—from alcoholics to workaholics—are "on" their habit to blot out pain they don't even know they have.

## The Locus of Disordered Patterning: The Continuing Need for Bonding

As we become self-sufficient in meeting our own needs for proper temperature, food, water, and so forth, the attitudes and feelings that were originally conditioned around those needs are uncoupled from them, but reattach themselves to those other needs for which the individual must still depend on others. Ultimately there is only one such need, and that is the need for bonding.

Bonding is physical closeness combined with emotional openness. One without the other does not meet the need. Bonding is not sex, because sex without emotional openness does not meet the need.

From the moment we are born to the moment we die, bonding is essential to human health. This is especially true, of course, in infancy. James W. Prescott, a developmental neuropsychologist with the National Institute of Child Health and Human Development in Washington, D.C., is conducting studies whose results suggest that early lack of bonding actually produces brain damage. Specifically, its lack retards or distorts development of the dendrites—nerve-cell branches in the neuronal systems that control affection and violence. Prescott suggests that the inability to experience affection and to control violence will be at levels inversely proportionate to levels of infant affection because of this impaired nerve-cell development. Other recent studies in California and Illinois comparing brain-cell branch development in monkeys reared in colonies or in isolation show similar impairment in isolation-reared animals. Bonding is not precious as diamonds are precious. Bonding is essential, as water is.

Filling one's need for bonding gives rise to pleasure. Failing to fill it creates pain, just as not getting enough food creates hunger, which is painful. The greater the need or desire for bonding, and the higher the quality and quantity of its fulfillment, the more we experience it as love. Without bonding, we don't feel lovable, good enough, or entitled, and we remain "weary, leery, teary, or phobic of emotional intimacy." We lack concentration or wrestle with obsession, our perception narrows, and we feel empty. With sufficient bonding, we feel lovable, potent, loving, and right: Whatever life throws at us, we can cope.

In Western culture, in both the United States and Europe, deprivation of bonding is almost universal. Infantile physical contact varies between 5 and 25 percent of the time, compared with 70 percent of the time for the Kung bushmen, whose tribal living style approximates that which formed the basis for millions of years of human evolution. The pain that results from this deprivation underlies the vast majority of emotional disorders. The solution isn't pills. Hungry people show symptoms of the biological need for food; they're not sick. We don't prescribe a pill for deadening their feeling of hunger. We feed them to fill their biological need, and the hunger disappears. So it is with the need for bonding.

## The Keys to Change

In NIP a person is seen as triangular; a free interplay of thoughts, emotions, and behaviors clustered around a biological organism that is in the process of taking in fuel, converting it to energy, and discharging that energy in various ways. In the healthy human, thinking and emotion help organize perception and experience and guide behavior to maximize sensations of pleasure and minimize sensations of pain.

***The Logic of Emotions.*** All affect is a response to pain, danger (the anticipation of pain), pleasure, or desire (the anticipation of pleasure). Emotions arise in response to intense thoughts related to pleasure or pain, to sensations (including biological processes), and nothing else. There are five basic emotions: pain, pleasure, fear, anger, and love.

Although the five emotions are experienced locally in the body (pain in the abdomen, pleasure in the pelvis, fear in the throat, anger in the chest, and love in the heart), they are biochemically a full-body reaction called for by the autonomic nervous system from the glandular system. The autonomic nervous system consists of two parts—the sympathetic and the parasympathetic systems. The combined action of all these systems prepares us physically and psychologically to cope with stimuli of all kinds: Our sense of physical readiness increases confidence while our emotions release energy to power effective action. Clearly, emotions evolved as a crucial part of our survival system.

If pain or danger is the original stimulus, then, neurophysiologists tell us, the sympathetic nervous system is activated to help the body mobilize to *flee* or *fight*. The body's metabolism is increased, sugar floods into the bloodstream for quick energy, blood carrying oxygen and glucose goes to the skeletal muscles for great strength and speed in running or hitting. The body assumes a slightly crouched, self-protective stance. A third option, taken when escape is impossible and fighting dangerous or pointless, is to "*freeze*"—mentally and/or physically to withdraw or detach from others and from one's own body, to immobilize one's body and thus one's emotions. More research is needed to determine the biological operation of the withdrawal or freeze response.

It is natural to hypothesize that a stimulus of pleasure or desire activates the parasympathetic system to prepare the body for taking in pleasure and love. This is a logical extension of what neurophysiologists already tell us: that the parasympathetic is a anabolic agency that assists in taking in and storing energy and repairing the body systems. The body's processes are reversed—blood flows from the extremities, the heart slows, as does the metabolism. The body assumes an open stance, shoulders back and pelvis forward, as in a yawn.

What we experience as psychological preparation is a biochemical change effected throughout the body by the glandular system, sometimes referred to as the third nervous system, which can be equated to emotion itself. Certainly it is experienced as emotion.

Further proof of the biochemical/glandular nature of emotion is emerging from research, which is beginning to discover a whole chemistry of emotions: adrenaline for fear; noradrenalins for anger; steroids and fatty acids for pleasure.

Research has also found evidence suggesting that general body preparedness to cope with stress is indicated by the level of eosinophiles in the blood. An alcoholic craving a drink has an eosinophile level of practically nil. After taking a drink—his or her way of coping with stress—the alcoholic feels much better and his or her eosinophile level has risen to between 80 and 100 per cubic millimeter. Blood samples taken before and after screaming show similar changes, more than a 15-fold increase, from 5 per cubic millimeters to between 80 and 100 per cubic millimeter. With an increased eosinophile level, of course, people feel much better, far more prepared to cope.

It is critical to psychological and physical health to be able to mobilize emotions quickly and utilize the energy they provide; otherwise our sense of being able to take in strong pleasure or defend against pain is crippled, and we feel insecure, frightened, tense, unready to face life's tests. When we do feel prepared, we feel better, even if the emotions involved are "negative." Fully expressed, anger can be experienced as potency, fear as excitement, pain as bearable or releasing, and pleasure and love as nourishing.

The blocks to achieving the sense of psychological preparedness lie less in the emotions themselves than in the ways in which specific emotions are associated with decisions and attitudes about emotions, entitlement, survival, and identity.

***Attitudes and How They Relate to Emotions.*** The word "attitude" refers to thought, but as we treat issues closer to the core of a person's identity, the lines between thought and feeling and between one feeling and another become increasingly difficult to draw. This is because such attitudes involve deep-level, preverbal programming, incorporated before the person has developed the skill to discriminate between thought and feeling. There is evidence to suggest that decisions arising from this early conditioning are lodged in an emotional memory in the cortical level on the nondominant side of the brain. If so, these attitudes are unlikely to be accessible for treatment through rational, verbal methods: instead, the therapeutic course must be navigated through emotional seas.

Take the attitude "People can't be trusted." It is often programmed into the person within the first year of life and relates to survival—life and death. Associated with the attitude are repressed emotions of fear, pain, and anger. Until those associated feelings are discharged, there will always be an underlying sense of mistrust, which the person will continually seek to reinforce by the way he or she interacts with the environment. No treatment will quite hold when the heat is on. It's as if the negative attitude were a string of words cut out of cloth and nailed to the personality by deep spikes of negative emotion. Not until the spikes are removed will the negative attitude be released for deep, lasting change that is strong enough to persist through deep crisis, to permit the risk of openness with others.

Before the emotional spikes can be pulled out, a person must overcome attitudes preventing the expression of specific emotions. A most common one is that one or more emotions is "good" or "bad." This attitude can be learned very early; for example, when a baby cries in anger because he isn't getting picked up or fed, and the overworked mother repeatedly responds with disapproval, anger, and rough handling, the baby, responding with fear to her anger, quickly learns that being angry is dangerous. To avoid the danger, the child concludes that whenever he is angry, he is "bad" and liable to be punished; thus he learns to repress his anger.

Such attitudes are numerous. Table 1 lists some other common ones.

A special note about love: Our society has distorted, even perverted, the concept of love. So powerful have these attitudes been that it has been necessary to redefine the word "love" in NIP. Eventually each of us comes to our own understanding—love is a personal matter—but in NIP, love is defined as just a feeling—no more, no less—not something one can promise, recall, or sustain, not a commitment or a relationship, just a feeling for now. It is this kind of thinking that enables many people to accept that it is possible to feel love for someone across the room whose name we don't even know, and whom we'll quite likely never see again.

**Table 1.    Emotions and the Attitudes They Inspire**

| Emotion | Attitude About Expressing the Emotion |
|---------|----------------------------------------|
| Anger | I will go crazy, destroy others, be destroyed, be a bad person. |
| Fear | I'll be helpless, crazy, unable to defend myself, unmanly, bad. |
| Pain | I'll die, fall apart, hurt forever, disappear, go crazy, be ugly. |
| Pleasure | I'll be bad, childish, irresponsible; someone will be angry, punish me; I'll have to pay it back. |
| Love | I'll be trapped, hurt, abandoned, scorned, obligated, resented by others, responsible for the loved one (completely). |

***Behavior.***    NIP focuses considerable attention on behavior. We live in a character-disordered society, very few patients come in without some degree of character disorder, and behavior is the character-disordered personality's primary insulation against having to grapple with feelings. Stripping the person of that insulation is the fastest way to get him or her to deal with emotions.

Demanding that a character-disordered person stop acting out is also the best way to test motivation. Because the person is unaware of his pain, his motivation to change is practically nil. Only when he encounters unavoidable pain is he likely to show up for treatment, and even then, he tends to stay only as long as the pain lasts. He's woven an elaborate and often brilliant web of behaviors and ideas about the world and people to defend himself from having to change; he gives up that protective web only as a last resort and will take it up again at the least indication that it might work again, even temporarily. His fear of emotional pain is so great that often the faintest taste of it will reactivate his decision to act out rather than to feel.

Knowing this, AREBA staff and participants don't use kid gloves with character-disordered newcomers. When a young addict comes in off the street, they don't ask, "What painful feelings brought you here?" They ask, "Who's on your tail?" and they don't accept the person into the program until they've heard a cry for help as genuine on an emotional level.

Behavior is important in treating neurotics too, but on a more subtle level, and primarily at a later phase in treatment. With neurotics NIP focuses on signaling, bringing the language of the body into line with the new attitudes and feelings the person has been acquiring.

*What is the person's level of maturity in each functional area?* The functional areas include (1) social, sexual, and personal relationships, and (2) vocational and educational pursuits.

The four basic levels of personality maturation are:

| | Infant | Child | Adolescent | Adult |
|---|---|---|---|---|
| Attitude | Helpless Unreal | Dependent Dishonest | Defiant Dishonest | Self-reliant Honest |
| Transference | Worship Magical Wish, Deity | Seductive, timid Manipulative | Resentful Provocative | Objective Confrontation |
| Emotion | Panic | Insecure, Fearful | Angry Controlled | Appropriate |
| Behavior | Impotent | Helpless Irresponsible | Aggressive Irresponsible | Responsible |

## METHODOLOGY

When a person first arrives at the Casriel Institute, he or she goes through an intake interview and an introductory group before being allowed to participate freely in the general programs. During this time, the therapist begins to check off answers to the following questions. They provide a description of pathology that is not symptomatic (e.g., anxiety reaction or depressive reaction) but dynamic.

*Is the person emotionally open or closed?* Emotionally open means one expresses feeling. Pseudo-open refers to the hysteric, who is not in touch with real emotion. Emotionally closed means someone who has no experience with emotions or feelings. Pseudo-closed refers to a person who never expresses feelings, doesn't know he has them, but when uncorked, his feelings tumble out in full resonant emotional communication.

*Is the person a rejector or an acceptor?* Pseudo-rejector or pseudo-acceptor (acting "as if" but relenting eventually) or other possibilities.

*What are the person's primary and secondary behavioral defenses against pain* (flight, anger, withdrawal, or control) and what attitudes are attached to those behaviors?

*Is the person functioning up to potential vocationally and socially?* Is he taking advantage of the best options available to him?

*Is the person able to deal effectively with all emotions from self and others* (accepting and expressing anger, love, fear, pain, and pleasure)?

With the answers to these questions, a NIP therapist can understand symptoms dynamically. For example:

Sadist  
Attitude: A love object is dangerous  
Feeling: Anger  
Behavior: Neutralizes the power of the love object until he or she feels safe.

Masochist  
Attitude: I don't deserve pleasure  
Feeling: Guilt, fear  
Behavior: Punishes self to pay/atone for having pleasure

| Anal-Obsessive | Attitude: | I can't be separate from Mommy |
| | Feeling: | Fear, anger, guilt, depression |
| | Behavior: | Acts only *for* or *against* authority, never for self. |

Once a person is accepted for therapy, the basic sequence of treatment is as follows.

***Introduction to NIP.*** Routinely, the therapist shows a videotape of an NIP process in progress, which includes some basic information on the logic of emotions and the need for bonding, the difference between emotional memory and intellectual memory, and the purpose of the process—to discharge and reeducate emotions as a mandatory step in changing the quality of one's life.

Patients are also introduced to the institute's rules: (a) no violence; (b) no drugs or alcohol; (c) no sexual intercourse on the premises. In group meetings there are three other rules: (d) no smoking; (e) no dishonesty; and (f) no storytelling— the focus must be on feeling, not on facts.

***A Positive Experience of Bonding.*** Since bonding must take place in the context of emotional openness, the first step is to help a new patient get to his or her feelings. This takes place in "emotional" groups.

Generally, a group begins with a "go-around," in which each person shares how he or she is feeling at the moment, and what he or she wants to work on. If there are feelings at the surface, the therapist will deal with them briefly; otherwise the entire group reports, and more extended work takes place later.

Often a person's first feeling is fear about being in group. Let's take Mandy: The therapist has her make eye contact with each person in turn and say, "I'm afraid." The fear seems acute, so the therapist urges her to say it louder and louder until finally she is screaming out the fear full measure. Jane rises and goes to hold her, providing warmth and support. After a minute or so, it is clear that Mandy is less withdrawn and feels better. She says so, states her reasons for being in the group—she is depressed because her

fiance has left her—and the "go-round" continues.

After the "go-round", when a few people have worked, the therapist comes back to Mandy and says, "Look at each person, and say 'I hurt.'" Mandy obediently goes around, tears streaming, crying pitifully. "Now imagine your fiancé on the mat and tell him 'You *hurt* me!'" Mandy begins to say, "You hurt me," and within just a few repetitions, her body comes out of its collapsed attitude, her voice takes on strength, and she begins screaming in rage from deep in her belly, "You *hurt* me, you *bastard!*" She continues screaming for a few minutes, and then turns around and says with her eyes snapping, "I'm *angry!* I think I could kill him." She suddenly looks guilty and draws her arms in. "It's not Okay to do it, but it's sure Okay to feel that way," says the therapist. "Go around and tell everybody, 'My anger is not bad.'" Mandy does so, looking less guilty as she gets nods of agreement and support from the group. "Now pick someone and go in the other room to get some more of that anger out and take in some pleasure."

Therapists have different styles of working. Some do all their work in one room; Mandy's current therapist uses two: One room, lined with mats, is exclusively for emotional work (working through feelings while bonding with someone), the other is for attitudinal work. Mandy chooses Jane, and they go to work. Mandy continues screaming while Jane holds her, providing support and encouragement, sharing her own experience and—most of all—just being there, a warm teddy bear to hold on to. Little by little Mandy will learn that anger and pain don't have to be total. One can take in pleasure while going through the pain. She is now being taught specific techniques for doing just that—for example, breathing through her mouth instead of clenching her jaw.

When the overload of emotion has diminished somewhat, Mandy and Jane return to the group for attitudinal work.

### Reprogramming Attitudes Through Screaming.
This is where the real work of change, lasting change, begins. It is nothing less than the reclamation of basic entitlements—to exist, need, be happy, make mistakes, feel, think clearly, love and be loved, be successful, powerful, weak—to be, in short, what we are.

Basically, the therapist takes attitudes that were uncovered through the emotional work and suggests corrective messages for the individual to work with. The mechanism of screaming is used to reprogram—for what sometimes seems an endless period of time, but in reality is not.

In Mandy's case, much of the anger covers fear that if her fiancé doesn't love her, it proves she isn't lovable, and she won't be able to get her needs filled. So the therapist concentrates on messages that assert Mandy's worth and her need to be loved. First she goes around the circle, saying, "I'm Mandy and I have value." Her voice is toneless, even at volume. "Tell your father. Tell him 'I'm Mandy and I'm *important!*'" the therapist says. Mandy appears to wilt before our eyes. "He wouldn't hear. He thinks I'm a foolish child, and stupid," she quavers. Jane lets out a roar of anger, and another and another. "Don't let him do that to you!" she howls at Mandy. "Stand up and tell the bastard off. Fight for yourself!" Mandy shifts uncomfortably. "What's the point? He wouldn't care." "*You* care!" yells Rick from across the room. "You're doing just what *I* do. *Stop it!* Care for yourself!" "You can do it, Mandy," urges Jane. "Stand up and tell him, like this." Jane stands up, throws her head and shoulders back, and says over and over, full volume, "*Listen* to me, I'm Mandy and I'm *important!*" Mandy watches, her mouth open. She glances at the therapist, who nods a go-ahead. She gets up and, in a fair imitation of Jane, begins to assert herself. As she taps into her anger, her voice strengthens. Jane draws back, cheering her

on. Mandy goes around the group three times. By the time she stops, she is flushed and vital looking. Group members are grinning in delight.

This marks the first of many times that Mandy will need to exercise her feelings of self-love. So long dormant, they must be nourished through a new emotional-attitudinal conduit, which can be etched in only by repeated reinforcement.

Hal provides another case in point, the difficulty of accepting one's need for others. A textbook character-disordered personality, Hal chose orthopedic surgery as his first addiction, barbiturates as his second, and came for treatment only after having sacrificed his marriage, children, professional partners, and personal health on the altar of "service to humanity." It has taken cancer to take him out of the operating theater and put him in touch with his pain. He is bewildered and angry, terrified of a life without his work, and in dread of a lonely death.

Even under such pressure, it takes a week of "Intensive" before he can bring himself to admit aloud that he needs anything emotionally. Even then, it is an intellectual conclusion reached during an individual session. Nevertheless, it is enough: He accepts intellectually that getting in touch with his need and his basic entitlement to need is a requisite for getting well. Even though he doesn't feel the need, he commits to doing the necessary work. And work it is.

He spends many hours lying on the mats repeating, "I need," "I need to be loved," and "Love me." And the feelings come up. First the ritual anger, then fear, and finally, after three days, the first cries of anguish for years of deprivation.

Each time a new set of feelings come up and out, Hal moves back to the attitudinal group to report on and deal with the attitudes around needing. He is given new attitude statements, such as "I'm not weak when I need"; "If I show you my need, you won't hurt me"; "I'm not bad when I need"; "I'm a man, and I need."

Two weeks later, one can hear a new note in Hal's voice. At last he begins to be able to say "I need," not as a confession of weakness or an indictment of caretakers, but as a statement of fact and rightness, and an invitation to share. He is beginning to accept that his need can be a pleasure for someone else to fill.

***Confrontation of Behavior.***   The stated purpose of a confrontation group is to increase intimacy through honest expression of feeling and thoughts. Originally patterned after the Synanon model, the NIP confrontation group has some added features.

The formula is: (1) get out the feeling that keeps you from getting close to the other person; (2) say what the feeling is about; and (3) say what you want from the other person. This last component is critical and is what keeps a confrontation from becoming a shooting match, and a group from turning into a firing squad, as often happened at Synanon.

The benefit of confrontation is to the confront**er**, not the confront**ed**. Each person is expected to deal honestly and openly with his or her feelings, and that means expressing them full measure, by screaming.

In fact, there are many benefits of honest confrontation. What typically happens is that the behavior that A objects to in B is what A him- or herself does, and this becomes evident to A as the process proceeds. People learn that honesty on a feeling level doesn't kill anyone, that no one bleeds. In fact, it is common to have the confronters end up in one another's arms. For this reason many married couples having trouble come in to work out their difficulties within the protection of the group. And they learn that no matter how unlovely their feelings and attitudes may be by social norms, honest expression is ultimately preferable to a coverup.

## APPLICATIONS

New Identity Process is best suited for neurotics and character-disordered persons of all degrees. In order of their frequency and importance, the most common problems dealt

with at the Casriel Institute are (1) the inability to accept love, (2) the inability to express anger, (3) the inability to accept anger, and (4) the inability to give love.

*The inability to accept love* is primary for the rejectors, who have found that pain exceeds pleasure in intimate relationships. The key phrase here is "Am I lovable?" As the person hears and begins to take in answers in the affirmative, he or she experiences first a sense of wonder and then tremendous pain for all the years of deprivation. When the person has shared this pain, and only after, someone who has avoided love can begin to accept it.

This exercise is also helpful for acceptors, who feel entitled to love, but not fully so, or only for a price.

*The inability to express anger* is primarily an acceptor's problem. Acceptors have repressed their anger as part of the price they believe they have to pay for love. They need anger exercises to help them assert the strength of their personalities.

For rejectors, anger exercises help when expressed at the deepest level, called the Identity level. The statement to elicit is "I've been hurt. It wasn't fair. I'm angry, and I'm not going to allow that to happen again."

Some people cannot separate the expression of anger from physical aggression, or from rejection; they suffer from *the inability to accept anger.* In confrontation, however, within a safe structure, they can learn that they can accept anger without being wrong and without getting hurt, be wrong without being guilty, and make mistakes without being bad or stupid.

*The inability to give love* afflicts some people who fear that if they love someone, they then become responsible for that person. Others feel so inadequate that they think their love has no value. It is when the fear, pain, and anger are expressed fully that a person can understand and begin to let him- or herself feel love for others.

NIP is also ideal for people who defend themselves by intellectualizing—the kind of people who can spend years increasing their understanding and never change. In NIP, achieving a new level of happiness—good feelings—is the jackpot. Understanding, as always, is the booby prize.

## CASE EXAMPLE

Henry, only son of a physician, was youngest of three children. His father was a self-made man, son of a Roumanian family; his mother, of German stock, was a housewife. Until age five, Henry was a quiet child, and very bright; he read from the age of three and a half, and later posted an IQ of 148.

As soon as he went to school, Henry became hyperactive, partly because he was so bored, he recalls; but owing to his inability to fit in, he concluded that he was stupid. He was also accident-prone, constantly requiring stitches and bandages from his doctor father. "It was the only time he paid any attention to me," he says.

Starting at age eight, he began to get into trouble—trespassing, vandalism, shoplifting. At the age of 11, he was thrown out of sixth grade for screaming at a teacher. Then, in the summer between sixth and seventh grade, his family moved to another town, and Henry, feeling stupid, out-of-step, accident-prone, and lonely, lost what peer support he had had. Always a voracious reader, Henry began to withdraw even further into books.

At his new school, Henry began tripping on LSD, amphetamines, barbiturates—anything he could get his hands on. He stole sleeping pills from his mother and swigged whiskey on the sly. He devoured food as rapidly as he consumed books and drugs, and gained weight rapidly.

By ninth grade, Henry was high practically all the time, mostly on LSD and barbiturates. Then he began to experiment. He shot "speed" (benzedrine) for the first time, and a little later began to deal in "speed" and marijuana. Before the year was out he'd shot heroin for the first time. By the end of tenth grade, he was shooting heroin every day and

traveling to Harlem to buy and deal. "I hated going up there, and to the Bowery, and all those places. I knew how my life was going—it was going to be bad, and I always figured when it got bad enough I'd kill myself."

All the while, Henry was still reading, developing a philosophy that was negative enough to justify his eventual suicide.

At the age of 16 he did make an effort of sorts to kick heroin. "It was messing up my life, my friends were mad at me." He attended some group therapy sessions for about four months, but there was no change. "I never met a shrink I couldn't corner in those days," says Henry.

It was a rough year. He had sex with a girl for the first time and experienced it as "weird," so became terrified he was homosexual. Also, for the first time, he lost a friend who overdosed on heroin; another friend was sent to prison on a manslaughter charge.

Where were Henry's parents during all this? Oblivious, for the most part: No one had arrested Henry because his father was a doctor, and until the next year he did well enough in school.

Then, in eleventh grade, at the age of 17, he quit high school and withdrew almost totally from everyone. At that time he also stopped eating and became anorectic. He was taking four fixes a day, and he had contracted hepatitis. His parents, finally worried, sent him to a psychiatrist, but he cornered him easily and quit.

In June of 1972, one of Henry's sisters, a straight-A-student at college, became worried when she began receiving odd letters from him. She went to see him. She found him anorectic, delusional, suicidal, depressed, and immovable. He weighed 95 pounds. He no longer cared what happened to him. She persuaded her parents to send him to the Yale Psychiatric Institute. There he managed to create such chaos in the wards and groups that at the end of August, they "threw him out." He remembers feeling so tired—sick of the world, people, himself.

It was then that he heard of the AREBA program for drug addicts. He could have gone back to his old life, but he was weary—it was just too exhausting to think about going back to the rat race and the pressure of getting drugs, going down to Harlem, feeling so wasted. And the pain didn't really disappear. There was always time, especially just before getting a fix, when the pain and hatred would become overwhelming.

In this state of mind and body, Henry arrived at the Institute. Once in residence, however, it was another story. He became panicky. It was like going to another planet. "You don't know anything," he was told, "except how to shoot dope. So listen, and do what you're told." He saw people being reprimanded openly on behavior—"pulled up." He saw people screaming at one another. He saw people caring and being physically close. He heard people accepting both the reprimands and the love and making changes.

He focused all his wits on convincing the staff he couldn't be pressured. "For four months I never opened my mouth in group. I feigned illness constantly, and I looked sick enough to get away with it. I spent most of my time reading."

Then one day, Alan, a resident staff member, came in while Henry was reading in bed—he'd convinced them he was too sick to work that day—but was invited to write up a complete list of what was wrong with AREBA. Everything. Recalls Henry:

I had a ball. I've always been pretty sharp about where people are, and what kind of games they're playing, and I'd done a lot of watching and listening. I didn't leave anybody out. From that point on, they knew I wasn't crazy the way I'd made out I was.

Not that I didn't need help. I had plenty of problems: I related to myself at the time as asexual. And I was anorectic, but they hadn't yet picked that up yet. Male anorexics are incredibly rare, and it was natural to attribute my thinness to heroin. Also, I'd learned in the hospital to eat and then throw up later when no one was watching.

It was Dan (Casriel) who caught on finally. It was my way of rejecting of my own unmet needs for love, and it contributed to my inability to take in pleasure.

But it was from that point that I began to turn around attitudinally. I stopped acting out negatively and I began to work emotionally in groups.

The first issues Henry worked on concerned the hostility he felt toward anyone who cared for him. It was, he found, because they represented a barrier to his eventual suicide. He worked actively with both fear and anger, but wasn't able to accept or express his pain.

After being given socializing privileges eight months after arriving, Henry began to run into problems. He had done no work to that time on his sexual identity problems, but they came to torment him. He would go out with the assignment to date girls and be rejected time after time. Then he would come back to the Institute and throw up. It was through this that he first got in touch with his pain, and began working through the historical pain of his mother and father's indifference to him. As he worked, he started gaining weight and stopped throwing up regularly. He had an unhealthy addiction to sugar and coffee, though, and he was not dealing with his fears of homosexuality, or with his pain over problems of impotence and rejection.

In June Henry was promoted to Second Phase, which means living at the institute, attending a group each day, but working and socializing outside. He took a job in a small retail store and was seduced by the 29-year-old manager. He wasn't conscious of being able to take in pleasure, but he adored her. When she dumped and fired him 10 weeks later, he left AREBA, became severely anorectic, and returned to his old neighborhood to buy some heroin. One day later he was back: He had run into some friends, and they looked like old, old men. He couldn't go back to that.

He was returned to First Phase for a month, and assigned to working in Intensive emotional groups. Most of that time Henry spent working on the mats, learning to take in pleasure and expressing his hostility toward his mother and the pain of rejection by his father. He was also required to eat with a staff member, because he was still partially anorectic and weighed only 105 pounds.

After a month, he was returned to Second-Phase status, and he took another job, this time with an uncle in a retail store. At the institute, he continued going to groups, and he held a position as house "guru," responsible for individual sessions with First Phasers. This was consistent with the theory that if one "acts as if" one were already well, one will eventually think as if and feel as if.

By Christmas of 1973, a little over a year after his arrival, he weighed 130 pounds, and although he was doing well enough, he felt stalled. He still had trouble getting dates, and he was watching friends in AREBA pass him by. That hurt. Then in January his uncle attempted suicide and closed the store, thus cutting off the one family tie he enjoyed. At the same time, the fiancé of one of his sisters died, and as his family gathered around her for support, he experienced tremendous anger and jealousy that a girl was able to get support but that he was not.

His next job was clerking in a bookstore. In four months, he rose to become a buyer and then assistant manager. However, he was still somewhat anorectic and still had trouble taking in pleasure. But he had finally begun to open up the issue of his sexual fears.

Shortly after starting at the bookstore, he started taking courses at Long Island University. In June he moved out into his own apartment for the third phase of AREBA, during which time one continues to hold responsibilities in the AREBA structure while living, working, and socializing outside.

To graduate from the AREBA program, a person must (1) be clean—free of drugs and alcohol; (2) have a solid relationship with a person of the opposite sex; and (3) be either vocationally or educationally occupied. By June of 1974, Henry qualified. He had a nice relationship going that included a sexual relationship; he had become night manager of

the bookstore; and he was maintaining straight A's with a full courseload at LIU. His schedule was too heavy to maintain, so he dropped out of the AREBA program, but continued with individual therapy twice weekly at the Institute. The focus of that individual work was mainly on enlarging his self-image. During the ensuing year, he gradually became more comfortable with his sexuality and brought his anorexia under control.

After two years at Long Island University, Henry transferred to Antioch. There, for the first time, he felt truly challenged intellectually. He recalls: "I had a field day. I became very political. There wasn't a rally I didn't attend. I also began doing more creative work—writing, drawing, and photography, and I developed a relationship with a wonderful girl."

Henry graduated from Antioch in 1978, at the age of 24, with a double major in psychology and communications and almost a year's worth of extra credits. Today, a year later, Henry is living in New York, working part time as a freelance photographer and also parttime as a Second Phase adviser on the AREBA staff. He is anticipating a full and varied life, possibly but not necessarily including further work with addicts. He is still seeing his girl from LIU and feeling good about his sexuality. He weighs 145 pounds.

## SUMMARY

Many people mistakenly confuse the New Identity Process with Primal Therapy. Apart from the fact that they both use screaming to discharge excess emotion, they are very different.

Janov's process focuses primarily on pain, regressing to early experiences repeatedly until the historic emotions are exhausted. The theory is that when the old emotions are exhausted, the personality will then be able to right itself. Primal Therapy uses isolation and other forms of stress, and deals minimally with cognition and behavior.

NIP, by contrast, focuses on pleasure in the here-and-now, and deals with negative emotions only when they block a person's ability to take in pleasure and love. Screaming is used not only for ventilation, but to prepare the body to take in new messages. Cognition and behavior are dealt with as extensively as affect. NIP is primarily reconstructive in focus.

Perhaps the most critical difference between Primal and NIP Therapy is that NIP is a group process. It's hard to improve on a statement made by Richard Beauvais, a member of Casriel's group in 1964:

We are here because there is no refuge, finally, from ourselves.
Until a man confronts himself in the eyes and hearts of his fellows, he is running.
Until he suffers them to share his secret, he has no safety from it.
Afraid to be known, he can know neither himself nor any other—he will be alone.
Where else but in our common grounds can we find such a mirror?
Here, together, a man can at last appear clearly to himself,
   not as the giant of his dreams
   nor the dwarf of his fears,
   but as a man—part of a whole with his share in its purpose.

In this ground we can each take root and grow not alone any more as in death,
but alive, a man among men.

We live in a character-disordered society; that is, a society that has decided not to feel its pain, and that acts out in ways destructive to self and others. Much of our behavioral insulation is socially useful, but because it sustains our estrangement from our feeling selves, it is pathological.

It is therefore destructive, to individuals, to society, and, ultimately, because of the power wielded by Western nations, to the world. How can we appreciate the suffering of others when we are so cut off from our own feelings, our own pain?

## REFERENCES

Casriel, D.H. *So fair a house: The story of Synanon.* Englewood Cliffs, N.J.: Prentice-Hall, 1963.

Casriel, D.H. *A scream away from happiness.* New York: Grosset & Dunlap, 1972.

Casriel, D.H. and Amen G. *Daytop: Three addicts and their cure.* New York: Hill and Wang, 1971.

Casriel, D.H. *The huggers.* (forthcoming).

# CHAPTER 43

# *Nondirective Psychoanalysis*

I.H. PAUL

*I view the field of psychotherapy as a kind of vast struggle, with proponents of the various theories and systems contending in a life-and-death battle for supremacy. These days, as the reader can see, there are many psychotherapeutic contenders for supremacy—at least 300. Even though there are probably as many roads to mental health and enhancement of self as there are roads to salvation, I believe that, in theory, differences among systems of psychotherapy cannot always be tolerated. While individual practitioners can get along despite theoretical and philosophic differences, in the long run some system must take over and all others must become subordinate. Look what has happened to DuBois's Medical Moralizations, Weir Mitchell's rest treatment and Burrows's Phyloanalysis—they are all systems that have fallen into desuetude.*

*The final emergent system will probably manage, in a resolution of differences, to combine what are currently considered incompatible elements. I. H. Paul's Nondirective Psychoanalysis is an example of the direction I think eclectic psychotherapy will take. Eventually, the brilliant insights of the great pioneers and the many others working in this maddening field of psychotherapy will be gathered together in a system that will be universally accepted. It may take centuries—but I believe it is only a matter of time until we have an allopathic psychotherapy. Nondirective Psychoanalysis may be the final answer.*

Nondirective Psychoanalysis is a blending of traditional psychoanalysis and Client-Centered Therapy. It is both interpretive and nondirective. Its format is one to one, its mode is mainly verbal, and its central process is inquiry focusing primarily on the patient's intrapsychic (phenomenal and mental) realm. To sustain a thoroughgoing nondirectiveness, the therapist maintains a stringent neutrality and impersonality, and relies chiefly on the interpretive mode of intervention to supervise the therapeutic process. This, along with its reliance on the principal conceptions of psychoanalysis's clinical theory (resistance, regression, transference, and catharsis), qualifies the method as psychoana-

lytic. It qualifies as nondirective insofar as the patient is given a maximum feasible role in determining the form and content of the sessions, and the therapist strives for a non-authoritarian and unique role definition, which entails regard for the patient's individuality and autonomy, as well as self-healing and actualizing potentials, characteristic of nondirective Client-Centered Therapy. Accordingly, this form of therapy can be construed both as Client-Centered Therapy with interpretations and/or as psychoanalysis stripped of directives.

In published writings this writer (1973, 1975, 1979) has chosen to designate the method informally as "psychotherapy." For the purposes of this book, however, it will be given the descriptive title "Nondirective Psychoanalysis."

## HISTORY

The evolution and vicissitudes of psychodynamic psychotherapy are Nondirective Psychoanalysis's heritage. More specifically, it shares the same history as psychoanalysis and Client-Centered Therapy.

Insofar as the analyst's principal mode of intervention is interpretation, and fundamental attitude one of neutrality, psychoanalysis is inherently a nondirective form of therapy. However, following Freud, analysts (such as Menninger [1958] and Brenner [1976], to cite only two) have felt that a set of directives and task requirements was necessary to establish and sustain the "analytic process." There was never unanimity on the composition of the set, and some influential analysts (e.g., Fenichel [1941], Singer [1965], and Langs [1974]), out of a conviction that certain directives and task requirements were unnecessary on balance, have advocated flexibility in regard to them. The requirement of daily sessions and the use of the couch, the instructions to free-associate and to report dreams, and the several abstinence proscriptions have variously been modified and softened. To cite an extreme instance, Hellmuth Kaiser (1965) evolved out of psychoanalysis a method that is radically nondirective, in that the only requirement of patients is to appear for sessions. There is no requirement as to what they talk about, and the analyst is limited to interpretations of their defenses against the awareness of feelings, impulses, and motives. Kaiser formulated the analyst's task in a way that placed the greatest emphasis on promoting in patients a sense of responsibility for their thoughts and actions. Similarly, many therapists in the Rogerian tradition have loosened its restrictions on interpreting and moved in a psychoanalytic direction. Levy (1963) and Bone (1968), for

example, have argued that the differences between psychoanalytic and client-centered procedures have been overstated and misconstrued, and the two methods have had more in common than was generally recognized. Are interpretations necessarily judgmental? Do they necessarily violate the patient's rate of exploration? Do they "create" resistances and transferences? These are the crucial questions. And Rosalea Schonbar (1968), for one, has concluded that they do not. She describes how she introduced the interpretive mode into the structure of Client-Centered Therapy, and concluded that the act of interpreting does not require any significant change in the basic attitudinal aspects of that therapy—which, she contends, are basic to becoming an effective therapist of any kind.

The specific history of Nondirective Psychoanalysis is twofold: my training first in Client-Centered Therapy and then in psychoanalysis, and my subsequent experience teaching therapists. My training determined its structure and orientation; my teaching experiences are largely responsible for its emphasis on technique. In addition to clinical practice, the method evolved out of pedagogical considerations and experiences, out of the need to articulate explicit and concrete principles and guidelines that could be acquired by appropriate study and training, and that did not rely too heavily on certain kinds of predispositional personality traits and talents. Consequently, conducting psychotherapy came to be regarded as a craft with objective and specifiable technical requirements, minimally dependent on unlearnable traits. A method had to be fashioned that was craft-oriented, that required an exact technique, and whose constraints allowed relatively little latitude with respect to a therapist's personal characteristics.

During the course of 10 years of teaching psychotherapy, my method grew increasingly rigorous and parsimonious. For instance, the interviewing mode—interrogating and probing—was entirely abandoned; the use of confronting and diagnostic interpretations was sharply curtailed; and the distinctive role definition of the therapist was kept consistent throughout the entire therapy. The reasons for these developments are several, but one is paramount: Clinical experience strongly suggested that therapeutic efficacy was correlated with technical purity and rigor. At any rate, the method that evolved—Nondirective Psychoanalysis— requires study, work, and practice; and the main natural talents the therapist needs are sensitivity, empathy, and clarity. The ability to understand, and to communicate understanding, accounts for the bulk of the variance; and that ability is largely a function of comprehending the special dynamics of the method itself. The technical precepts and principles of Nondirective Psychoanalysis rest upon these specific dynamics.

## CURRENT STATUS

Within the broad category of psychoanalytically oriented psychotherapy, but also under the rubric of existential and humanistic therapy, psychotherapy that is both nondirective and psychoanalytic is widely practiced and taught. Nondirective Psychoanalysis is a particular form of that therapy, practiced and taught at the clinical psychology program of the City University of New York's graduate school at City College.

I have described and explained the method in two books and a paper. *Letters to Simon: On the Conduct of Psychotherapy* (1973) is an informal treatise, written in the form of letters to a hypothetical student that discuss and exemplify a wide range of issues pertinent to its theory and practice. "Psychotherapy as a Unique and Unambiguous Event" (1975) is an elucidation of the method's basic orientation and principal conceptions, organized around a paradigmatic clinical situation explored in concrete detail. *The Form and Technique of Psychotherapy* (1979) is a comprehensive explication and

discussion of the method's main technical precepts and principles, as well as theoretical rationales. The book examines in detail the interventional modes of psychotherapy, the problem of timing, the structure and formulation of interpretations, and the nature and limits of neutrality, impersonality, and consistency.

## THEORY

Nondirective Psychoanalysis does not rest on any single theory of behavior and personality. Because it is a relatively pragmatic method, based largely on procedures and principles that have proven useful in clinical practice, it is compatible with a variety of quite different and even nonpsychoanalytic theories, and draws on a wide range of conceptions pertaining to the structure, functioning, development, and change of personality and behavior.

A theory of unconscious mentation, for instance, is useful but not indispensable. Perhaps its chief utility is in helping insure that our interpretations remain sufficiently nondiagnostic and nonconfronting. For when we accept the hypothesis that an effective interpretation addresses preconscious derivatives of unconscious mentation, and that its ideal function is to facilitate the emergence of unconscious ideas, memories, and fantasies (i.e., to help patients discover what is in their mind), then we have a practical guideline for ways to formulate and structure, as well as time, our interpretations. The same can be said for the concept of defense; the effective interpretation aims to make contact with a kind of barrier (a threshold, a countercathexis, or a defense) and, in one way or another, weakens it to permit not only the uncovering of unconscious contents but also their reorganization. Another theory that is clinically useful centers around the conception of "ego"; for when it is construed as the personality's executive agency, under pressure from competing and conflicting forces, then our interpretations will take account of ego's intrinsic and often conflicting interests by speaking to its "synthetic function" (Hartmann, 1958).

The psychodynamic point of view, on the other hand, is probably quite indispensable; but it can be limited to the proposition that behavior and experience are both purposeful and goal-directed. Every psychological act is presumed to be either instrumental or consummatory with respect to purposes and goals; all behavior is based on needs, drives, wishes, fantasies, and the like. To be sure, the dynamic point of view can be a more complicated motivational theory; it can construe behavior to be the result of a hierarchy of forces acting in concert and in conflict, and additionally make the assumption that no behavior is the result of a single drive or purpose—there are always two or more at work. When these forces act together, the behavior is conceptualized as overdetermined or multiply functioned (Waelder, 1936); when they act in dissonance, it is conceptualized as conflict. Maladaptive behavior can be understood as the result of conflict, enhanced and magnified and sustained by overdetermination.

While the practice of Nondirective Psychoanalysis does not require or imply a particular psychological theory, it does rely heavily on a particular theory of psychotherapy, as well as on conceptions about the processes that inhere in therapy. Its basic premise is that psychotherapy can be a unique situation, and that, as psychotherapists, we can define ourselves in a distinctive way. Its basic thesis is that psychotherapy can be relatively unstructured without being concomitantly ambiguous; and our nondirectiveness and neutrality do not prevent us from being active and effective.

The short-term or proximate goal is for the patient to have a distinctive psychological experience, an experience that is designated as the *therapeutic process*. The therapeutic process is defined as the core event of Nondirective Psychoanalysis. It is conceptualized as an intrapsychic and mental process, as distinct from interpersonal and behavioral;

it is presumed to be based on the act of discovering, as distinct from learning; and it shares many of the theoretical features of psychoanalysis's "relative ego-autonomy" (Rapaport, 1967). In empirical terms, the therapeutic process refers to patients' work, as well as their subjective experience, when they express, examine, and explore their inner and outer realities; when they strive to articulate and to understand their behavior, their self, and their mind. It entails the acts of reflecting and introspecting, reminiscing and recollecting, and reorganizing and reconstructing; it implies a major focus on the inner reality of affects and impulses; of needs and expectations; of attitudes, beliefs, and values; of habits, defenses, and fantasies. And a special emphasis is placed on the experiencing of individuality and autonomy, as well as sense of volition. Finally, it is a process that comes down to the complementary acts of "understanding" and of "being understood."

In short, the therapeutic process is an activity of self-inquiry that strives to articulate, to comprehend, and to discover. This is a broader conception than psychoanalysis's "analytic process"; it does not mandate genetic reconstructions, nor does it necessarily require the resolution of experiences and behaviors into component parts and determinants. It relies on the exercising of choice and decision, not on the more passive free-association mode. It shares with the "analytic process" (as well as with corresponding conceptions of Existential Therapy, Humanistic Therapy, and others) the conviction that the actuality of the patient as an individual with volition and responsibility, as an agent active in the direction of his or her life, must be the principal subject of discovery that lays the groundwork and provides the framework for the crucial process of therapy. The patient's essential autonomy is the paramount subject for discovery, and serves as the main context for self-inquiry.

The technical precepts and principles that guide us, as therapists, are fundamentally and intimately linked to the goal of facilitating and optimizing the therapeutic process. Insofar as this process is viewed as the core event of Nondirective Psychoanalysis—and the event that effectuates the long-range alterations and reorganizations that are the goals of the therapy—we as therapists have to protect its integrity by behaving in ways to promote and sustain its full development; and we must strive to avoid behaving in ways that prevent, impede, or interfere with it.

Accordingly—and to the limits of feasibility and good clinical practice—nondirective therapists refrain from directing the patient in any way; we do not interview or counsel; we do not judge or criticize; we provide no reinforcements in the forms of rewards, punishments, and incentives of any kind; and we do not share our personal feelings, attitudes, beliefs, and opinions. Instead, though we are as caring and as tactful as possible, we maintain a position of neutrality and impersonality; we observe without much participation beyond empathy, along with a degree of warmth and enthusiasm; and we bend ourselves entirely to the purpose of understanding the patient, relying principally on the instrumentality of interpretation to share that understanding.

Offering interpretations is our way of "participating" in the therapeutic process. This formulation, however, is potentially misleading, insofar as it portrays therapists as providing understanding or information about patients' inner and outer reality, and doing it for their sake; or it may imply that therapists help patients make discoveries by making interpretations to maximize the occurrence of such discoveries. Instead of that congenial formulation a more awkward one is preferable: Interpreting is the nondirective therapist's way of "supervising" the therapeutic process. This formulation emphasizes that the main purpose in offering interpretations is to promote the ongoing process itself. And since the process is conceptualized as intrapsychic and as entailing autonomous action on the part of patients, and since the overriding goal is for them to be active (actively strive for understanding, actively ex-

ercise and strengthen their synthetic function, and thereby maximize their control and freedom), it follows that the therapist's chief goal is not to impart information, not to give understanding and insight; instead, it is to provide the optimal conditions for patients to examine themselves openly and freely, and to experience themselves as fully and as authentically as they can. Accordingly, it is dissonant with the aims and spirit of Nondirective Psychoanalysis for roles to be divided in such a way that the patient provides the facts and therapists the meanings. And it is also somewhat dissonant to conceive of therapists as participating as a kind of partner in the uncovering and explaining process. Our function as therapists is chiefly to promote the work of therapy itself, and our promise to speak when we have "something useful to say" (see "Methodology" section) really means "useful for the therapeutic process."

Nondirective Psychoanalysis requires a full faith in the therapeutic efficacy of patients' choosing freely what they will talk about during the sessions. As therapists we must hold in abeyance all convictions about the differential fruitfulness of topics (childhood memories, traumatic experiences, interpersonal relations, fantasies and dreams, etc.). We have to be prepared to work not only from the surface of the patient's consciousness but also from the matrix of the patient's decisional and volitional processes. And we must try to keep from using the interpretive mode in a directive way. Whether this is altogether possible is a theoretical question, but it can be examined at the empirical level.

An interpretation, broadly defined, is any attempt to articulate thoughts, wishes, intentions, and feelings—a remark that addresses what is in (and on) the patient's mind, even if the remark doesn't seek to explain why, and even if there is no reason to believe it was obscure or disguised or preconscious. At the very least, an interpretation implies the directive "Am I correctly understanding you?"; at the most, it implies the directive

"Pay attention to this!" But when it resonates with the patient's focus of attention, when it addresses what the patient is addressing, even the latter directive becomes inconsequential. Therapists' central timing criterion requires that an interpretation be offered only when its attention-deflecting properties are at a practical minimum, only when it doesn't impose a fresh idea or deflect attention. The effective interpretation explains only when the patient is interested in having something explained, and it tries to explain in ways that are consonant with the patient's mode of explaining and understanding. Furthermore, it is formulated in a way that corresponds directly to the patient's thinking and experience, and does not draw upon theoretical or nomothetic considerations. It is not diagnostic in form, or is it confronting in nature. Its directive properties can, accordingly, be held to a minimum.

A nondirective psychoanalytic session cannot be construed as an interview, because the interviewing mode is stringently avoided. This means therapists keep from asking questions and probing for feelings, and neither do we confront ("hold up the mirror"). The interviewing mode tends to define us as diagnosticians, troubleshooters; and the same can be true for the confronting mode, which, in addition, defines us as alert observers. Both modes tend to put patients into a passive and objective position. By contrast, the interpretive mode defines us as observers who try to understand and empathize, whose aim is not so much to uncover problems as to apprehend and comprehend them; and insofar as our interpretations embody the act of sharing rather than giving, we allow patients to take a more active and subjective position. To the extent that well-formulated and well-timed interpretations are shared discoveries rather than of one-sided observations, they run less of a risk of defining us as the controlling one, and they maximize a patient's short-term freedom and long-range autonomy.

There are, however, circumstances in which certain directives can support the therapeutic process without impairing it. One relates to unclarity or ambiguity of communication, another to silence. To ask, "What are you thinking?" when a patient falls silent may sometimes be necessary, and an argument can be made for its distinctiveness as a directive. This is especially true for the clarification question ("What do you mean when you say . . . ?), which has a special position in respect to the therapeutic process. Such directives can be fully consonant with the principles of Nondirective Psychoanalysis; their use—along with other noninterpretive modes of intervention that are commonly used in therapy—depends on context and clinical judgment.

## METHODOLOGY

To divide a course of psychotherapy into three stages—the beginning, the middle, and the ending—is more than a didactic tradition; the stages can be a vital aspect of the therapy's dynamics, having significant ramifications for procedure and technique. Though our aim as nondirective therapists is to participate chiefly by offering interpretations, therapy has to be carefully conducted through its developmental stages and their vicissitudes, and we have to be sensitive to a variety of possibilities and exigencies (impasses and crises, for example). It is useful to bear in mind that not everything that transpires in therapy is grist for the interpretive mill; there are issues that need to be dealt with directly. (Being nondirective does not mean being indirect.)

These issues include matters of "business," which can be broadly defined to include the structure and format of the therapy, the schedule and fee, as well as the nature and limits of our expectations and requirements. If, for instance, a patient wants the therapist to take an active role in the sessions, say, by asking leading questions, it can be a mistake to respond with an interpretation seeking to explain the wish. (For one thing, the patient may not be interested in having the wish explained.) But it is entirely consonant with the method's orientation to respond by saying that nondirective therapists prefer not to make such a modification, and to explain the rationale—provided, of course, we choose not to comply with the wish and introduce the modification.

Moreover, Nondirective Psychoanalysis entails no proscription of "manipulation." Any action on the therapist's part, or modification in the procedure, that a patient requires or requests has to be weighed against the state of the therapeutic process. If the patient needs it for the process to work best, then that counts as a salient criterion. Any action or modification is weighed against this further criterion: Will it interfere with the therapist's ability to listen and remain sufficiently neutral, so that he or she can supervise the therapeutic process in a satisfactory way? This can be a function of our flexibility, among other things, and can also depend on the developmental stage of the therapy—what has gone before, and where the therapy stands. It can make a significant difference whether we introduce a modification into a therapy that has only recently begun or into one that is well into its middle stage.

The beginning stage is mainly concerned with defining and clarifying the structure and format of the therapy. The therapists' principal task is to inaugurate and facilitate the therapeutic process. In practice, we have to establish the nature and limits of our nondirectiveness, our neutrality and impersonality, and also our caring; and we have to introduce the patient to the method in a way that minimizes ambiguity even as it maximizes unstructuredness. Consequently, it may be quite unavoidable to give an instruction; but the instruction can be formulated carefully so as to keep its directive properties to a minimum. A succinct formulation, which notifies more than instructs, which conveys the essence of Nondirective Psychoanalysis's format and orientation and provides patients with the widest, most feasible latitude to begin the way they want and deem

appropriate, is worded as follows: *"You can talk about the things you want to talk about. It's up to you. I will listen and try to understand. When I have something useful to say I will say it."* This *basic instruction* informs patients that they are free to speak as openly and self-directedly as they want. It does not request them to share their thoughts or express their feelings, and neither does it suggest they tell about themselves. They can do these things if they choose to and want to.

In addition to issues and problems that commonly accompany the basic instruction and pertain to the method's structure and requirements, the beginning stage is often marked by themes that center around the meanings and implications of being in therapy. There is the frequently encountered fantasy of a passive cure ("Once you have all the facts you will proceed to straighten me out"); there is the conviction that being in therapy is something to be ashamed of, it's a kind of defeat ("I can't do it myself, after all"); there is the expectation of being shocked and hurt, of hearing things that will confirm their most dreaded judgments of themselves, that they are insane or abnormal; and there is the fear that therapy will make them worse off in certain ways. These themes—together with the issue of trust ("Can I really count on you?") and the exposition of presenting problems, life history, significant experiences, current functioning, and the like—are the earmarks of the beginning stage.

In the middle stage—similar to the development section of a sonata—the exposition and themes of the beginning are subjected to repetition, articulation, variation, and development. This is when the major reorganizations and transformations occur, as well as the major discoveries and insights, the major transferences, and the major impasses. This is when the main struggle for and against change takes place. The beginning is often marked by optimism and enthusiasm; the middle, by contrast, is often marked by despair and resistance, because now the patient's basic unwillingness to change becomes manifest and powerful, and pits its strength against the forces of change and development. It is now that long-entrenched patterns of behavior can be weakened and altered; and the transferences reaches their full intensity and exerts their full force. Therefore, during the middle stage the therapist's technical skill and resourcefulness is usually put to its severest test, for here the art and craft of making effective use of the interpretive mode becomes paramount.

The criteria for well-formulated and well-timed interpretations may change as therapy develops. During the beginning some useful functions can be served by interpretations that become quite unnecessary during later stages. For instance, patients have to learn at first how therapists participate—how we listen both empathically and dispassionately, how we formulate understanding without judging and criticizing—and we may choose to offer interpretations with that goal alone in mind. Furthermore, it is not uncommon (especially early in therapy) for interpretations to be taken as directives and as criticisms, and for patients to react as if they'd been evaluated. Those unintended and unwanted side effects cannot be entirely avoided, but we can take active measures to undo them, both by keeping patients informed of our neutral intentions and by interpreting their reaction. Nevertheless, it is an aspect of good technique not only to listen for a patient's reaction to each interpretation but also to avoid interpretations that carry too strong an implication of evaluation and direction. Two kinds of interpretations are particularly vulnerable to such implications (especially during the beginning): diagnostic and confronting ones. Therefore, such interpretations should be reserved for the later stages, and only used even then when unavoidable. They are difficult to avoid when defense and resistance are the subjects; for it can be difficult, and sometimes not entirely possible, to make sound and responsible interpretations of defense and resistance without being diagnostic and confronting.

Another technical guideline centers around

clinical tact: nondirective therapists avoid shocking the patient or generating intense emotions that may elicit defensive measures. Clinical tact cannot be described and characterized in a simple way—it is best illustrated and exemplified—but it plays an important part in Nondirective Psychoanalysis and contributes importantly to its uniqueness. Patients must enter each session free from the apprehension that they are in for rude shocks and intense emotions at our hands; whatever shocks and emotions occur will be of their own doing. Considerations of tact—as well as of effectiveness—can be served when our interpretations are succinct but not curt, and when they are offered in a gradual or stepwise fashion. It is often possible to divide an interpretation into parts that gradually zero in on the issue and allow the patient to participate in its final formulation. (This is quite different from cryptic or allusive interpretations, which are generally ineffective.)

The ending is usually the most problematic and ambiguous of the three stages. Because of its manifold meanings and implications, and because it brings to the forefront the issue of separation, the problem of termination is commonly the main theme. The potential ambiguity centers around two questions: Does Nondirective Psychoanalysis have a natural kind of conclusion? and, What marks the "cure"?

We can accept the proposition—at least, as a strong and useful working hypothesis—that Nondirective Psychoanalysis has a natural developmental course that is relatively independent of "cure," or of change in personality and behavior, or of amelioration of symptoms and problems. Another way of putting it is that the therapeutic process, similar to an organic process, is characterized by naturally occurring stages of maturation. Accordingly, the ending, like the beginning and the middle, is the result of processes indigenous to the therapy itself; and it has defining characteristics.

The ending stage is often as distinctive as the beginning. This is particularly the case when it is substantially taken up with the issue of separation, but it can be distinctive in other ways as well—as, for example, when patients turn their efforts to consolidating the gains they experienced from therapy, when they turn their attention to the future, and the like. Sometimes the transition to the ending can be marked by impasse, sometimes by a burst of intense therapeutic work, sometimes by the appearance of an altogether fresh theme, and sometimes by a regression or the reappearance of an old symptom. And the ending is often strongly resisted—mainly because of its association with termination.

The ending presents therapists with a variety of methodological problems and pitfalls, and it can test our rigor and consistency. Our principal task is to insure that the decision to terminate is substantially the patient's and not ours. Just as the patient took an active role in initiating the therapy, so must the patient take an active role in ending it; optimally, the decision should not be imposed. It is quite typical of patients to experience termination as our decision: and we must try to be in the position to say to them, "It was my interpretation, yes, my formulation; but it was based directly on your experience of therapy; it was based on your thoughts and feelings."

We must also be convinced that termination is an integral part of the process, and that no course of Nondirective Psychoanalysis can be considered complete before it has amply dealt with the conflicts and fantasies associated with it—most notably, of course, the issue of separation. Moreover, since it is central to relative ego autonomy, separation is central to the fundamental dynamics of Nondirective Psychoanalysis. To be autonomous and free is to have come to terms with separation. Nevertheless, just as autonomy is relative, so is separation; and termination can be regarded as a kind of trial period. Just as the beginning of the beginning stage can be viewed as a period of trial, so the ending of the ending can be viewed as not irrevocable.

## APPLICATIONS

When we face the task of determining whether a patient is suitable for Nondirective Psychoanalysis, and vice versa, we must rely on clinical judgment along with a grasp of the nature and requirements of the therapeutic process. To begin with, however, the patient has to choose the therapy; to a significant and substantial extent, the kind of experience it offers has to be "wanted." Therefore, the patient must be capable of comprehending the nature of the method and of fulfilling its requirements; and having understood what the methods entails, the patient has to be in a position to exercise choice.

The patient has to be capable of self-inquiry, of reflection and introspection; this rests on the ability to distinguish inner from outer reality, to locate events in the inner realm, and to attribute causality and responsibility to self events. Therefore, a certain amount of reality testing and psychological-mindedness is requisite. Also, a degree of frustration tolerance is necessary; the patient must tolerate the therapist's neutrality and impersonality, which can frustrate the most basic of human needs (for support, for nurturance, dependency, love, and the like).

An important consideration is time and the urgency of the patient's problems. Since a course of Nondirective Psychoanalysis lasts several years (generally, a period of two to four years), and since its beneficial effects may not occur until late in the therapy—and, indeed, may occur only after therapy has been completed—the presenting problems have to be the sort that do not require immediate resolution. Therefore, an estimation of how seriously debilitating they are must enter into our consideration. Finally, a felt need for change is an important requisite. The patient has to want change, and see the benefit of changing: if the problem is located in outer reality, and the patient feels no sense of responsibility for it, then Nondirective Psychoanalysis may not be appropriate.

Do these requirements and criteria lead to

the conclusion that a "normal" adult is our only suitable patient? Do they so sharply restrict the range of appropriate patients to only a few? Have we ruled out children, psychotics, and all but a narrow range of neurotics and character disorders? Have we excluded people with serious symptoms and problems? The answer is yes only if we construe the requirements and criteria too stringently, and if we construe Nondirective Psychoanalysis as an inflexible and unmodifiable method. To be sure, its requirements are unfeasible or impractical for some patients, and for others the method could prove detrimental. A patient suffering an acute depression, for example, can hardly be expected to tolerate most of the requirements, much less benefit from them; similarly, neither can a patient in an acute state of crisis. Patients who show serious impairment of reality testing, who are psychotic or perhaps even borderline psychotic, are generally not suitable. Moreover, there are patients whose chief need is for medication, or for reconditioning, or for an authentic interpersonal encounter, or Group Therapy. A patient who seeks a method that can most directly remove a symptom is best advised not to enter Nondirective Psychoanalysis.

But Nondirective Psychoanalysis is not a rigid system governed by rules. The method's precepts and principles are, at most, ideal standards toward which we strive but can never hope to achieve perfectly; and modifications of one sort or another are generally possible and necessary. Moreover, each of its requirements and criteria has to be measured and weighed; such qualifiers as "a degree of," "a certain amount," and "to a significant and substantial extent," are crucial; and they can only be based on clinical judgment. Furthermore, a person can have sufficient motivation, sufficient reality testing and psychological-mindedness, sufficient frustration tolerance, and the rest, and still suffer from a wide range of psychological problems, including anxiety, depression, inhibitions, symptoms, and the like. Finally,

it bears mentioning that an experience of Nondirective Psychoanalysis can be beneficial to someone who is quite "normal."

At the outset of Nondirective Psychoanalysis the therapist's task is to determine whether the patient is suitable for the method and whether modifications may have to be made; therefore, we have to evaluate and assess. Circumstances may call for a series of diagnostic interviews, which can readily be defined for the patient as antecedent to therapy itself. Under certain circumstances we can expect to secure an adequate assessment without the instrumentality of an interview, and instead rely on the initial sessions of the therapy. It is often possible to glean sufficient diagnostic evidence to judge whether any major modifications need to be made, or whether the patient needs an altogether different form of therapy or treatment. We can accept the working hypothesis that Nondirective Psychoanalysis will be the appropriate and suitable treatment, and then use the opening sessions to confirm or reject that hypothesis. The advantage of beginning this way is not only that it is economical; rather, it lies in the fact that every transaction in the therapy—starting from the beginning of the beginning stage—can have significant implications for the course it takes; each detail contributes something to the distinctiveness and uniqueness of the therapy, and details can have a cumulative significance.

To be sure, each patient has to learn whether this is the right therapy for him or her, and also whether the therapist is the proper one. Therefore, the way the therapy will proceed—its structure and form, its conditions and limits, as well as its probable duration—have to be explained and discussed. This can be construed as "business" and treated as such. Similarly, the therapist's professional credentials and experience must be discussed. Though we strive to maintain a stringent impersonality, we must detail what is directly germane to our ability to conduct therapy for this particular patient. Additionally, the crucial questions "Is this the right treatment for me?'' and ''Are you the right therapist?'' can best be answered by defining the beginning sessions as a trial period.

Whether or not a trial period has been explicitly defined, it is important that we make an effort during the beginning to show patients the full range of our approach and technique. This is true for two reasons: First, we want to be able to judge the quality and nature of their work, to learn whether they are suitable for our method and whether modifications will have to be introduced; second, we want to make these sessions a fair sample of the therapy so that they can best judge for themselves whether it suits them, whether they want it. Nondirective Psychoanalysis requires that patients never be in a passive and submissive position vis-à-vis the therapist, and this has to extend to the decision to enter therapy itself. It is vital that the patient freely choose and actively decide; this places a substantial constraint on our willingness to advise and persuade, or even to advocate and suggest. But even this requirement can be softened—to a degree.

## CASE EXAMPLE

The patient was referred by a consultant who had described two options for him. One was a behavioral therapy that would focus on his symptoms—a recurring state of mild but disruptive anxiety and an intermittent but recently more frequent sexual impotency. The patient preferred the second option, a traditional psychoanalytic therapy, and after learning that it would take about six months to see whether the method was helpful, decided to give it a trial. When he called me to arrange an appointment (after I'd heard from the consultant) he offered this contract: If at the end of six months there was no substantial amelioration of his symptoms, he would switch to a behavioral therapy.

The initial session began with his standing in the middle of my office, staring at the couch a few seconds, then asking, ''Where do you want me to sit?''—even though there were only two seats, and I was already sitting down in one. His next remark was ''What do you want me to tell you?'' When I responded with the basic instruction, he looked puzzled. ''So I guess you want me to tell you about myself,'' he said; and without giving me a chance to respond (i.e., to clarify the first part of the basic instruction), he proceeded to give a full, orderly, and systematic account of his *vita* (omitting only to tell me his age). In a subsequent session he ''confessed'' to having carefully rehearsed the narrative because he was sure I was going to ask for it, and it was ''the right thing to do.''

He was a short, somewhat overweight man, who appeared to be about 30; rather stiff and awkward, he spoke quickly and fluently, often with a breathless intensity, and took a down-to-earth, businesslike attitude toward therapy. He told of never having been in psychotherapy, because he was convinced that he could handle his own problems. He spoke of being independent and self-reliant, active and ambitious. He described himself as a bachelor. currently ''seriously involved'' with a woman who wanted to marry him, but given his sexual problem he felt it would be unfair to her. A pianist and composer by profession, he said he was satisfied with his career, and the only problem was that his anxiety sometimes impaired his ability to practice. He had two older brothers who lived away from the city, which left him to carry the burden of caring for his mother who was needy and often sick. When he was 12 his father had died of cardiovascular disease.

At the outset of the second session he asked for the ''rules.'' (Didn't I expect him to tell about his childhood? Wasn't he supposed to free-associate, to lie on the couch?) When I reiterated the basic instruction and spelled out the extent of my intention to be nondirective, he seemed skeptical and uncomfortable. Nevertheless, in a way that was to be characteristic, he quickly dismissed his feelings and went ahead with a narrative. It didn't take many sessions till it became clear that he needed to avoid decisions and had a number of externalizing strategies to keep from feeling in active control of his life. The main one was to set things up so that others, or the objective situation, would dictate requirements; then he could respond passively and submissively. He habitually returned to the question of whether an action was right or wrong, good or bad, which then became the basis for action and served his need to keep from acting on impulse and wish. Consequently, since my way of doing therapy must be "right" (the consultant had told him I was the "right" therapist for him), he would be "good" and do it. During the beginning stage he regained a memory of early childhood in which his father repeatedly admonished him to be a "good boy." He also acknowledged a sense of shame at being in therapy; as if it were a mark of weakness, as if it meant he was a "bad boy." And "I am a bad boy" was a major theme of the therapy and a central feature of his self-image.

Throughout the course of therapy, with only a few significant exceptions, the sessions consisted of a coherent narrative on a single topic (one devoted to his relationship with his mother, another to his girl friend, one to his career, another his sociopolitical views), each carefully composed to fit the 50 minutes. When he estimated the time wrong and was left with some "free time," he experienced discomfort. So seamless was his talk that I had to interrupt in order to make a remark.

He came to recognize that he was intent on avoiding spontaneous thoughts and memories, as well as keeping me from speaking. One reason was a worry lest I say something wrong (and "dumb"), and then he'd feel disappointed in me—and it was vitally important that he never experience any disappointment at my hands, which had significant transferential ramifications in respect to his father. Another was a worry lest I say something that would hurt him—mainly by confirming his worst fears about himself: that he

was "a bad boy." He also grew obsessively concerned over whether he was curing himself in the therapy or whether I was going to do it to him; a passive-submissive fantasy emerged, in which he saw me as the good mother who could save him from death, unlike his bad mother who couldn't save his father. He acknowledged having had, from the outset, the conviction that I was waiting for the propitious moment to give him a thoroughgoing diagnostic evaluation (the "cure"). And he also discovered that his punctuality and diligence in attending sessions and paying his bill on time was meant to forestall my indictment of him as bad. The fact that he rarely fell silent, and felt uncomfortable whenever he did, led to the discovery that silence had several meanings, among which was an important identification with the dead father (who frequently had been morosely silent, while his mother was an incessant talker). And keeping me silent had important transference implications, some of which emerged during the ending and were associated with fantasies of my death.

Two transference reactions ushered in the middle stage. One was a growing sense of curiosity about me. He'd been told by the consultant that I was knowlegable about music; during accounts of his professional experiences he would sometimes speak of technically obscure musical matters in order to see whether I'd ask for clarification. This furtive interest in my music experience led to an equally furtive interest he recollected having had in his father's "business"; not only did the father never talk about his work, he never allowed himself to be seen naked.

The second transference reaction centered on the issue of caring, and occurred first around my remembering what he'd told me. A few remarks of mine early in therapy had impressed him because they indicated that I remembered the details of his narrative, and this made him uncomfortable. It meant I was paying too close attention, I cared too much—and perhaps for "bad" reasons, one of which raised the issue of voyeurism, something he "confessed" to and was deeply ashamed of. This turned out to be one reason for the remarkable fact that he never spoke about sex in anything but the most general terms. ("I couldn't perform" was the extent of his depiction of an unsuccessful attempt at intercourse.) Despite the fact that after about three months of therapy he enjoyed an almost total remission of his impotency—and it was, after all, a main reason he sought therapy—he scrupulously avoided the subject of sex. ("I performed very well last night," and that was that.) He did, however, explore the reasons for his avoidance; he came to understand that he regarded sex as shameful and secret, and that he had long had exhibitionistic fantasies of a forbidden nature. But he couldn't shake off the conviction that I would be disgusted and repelled, as well as fascinated and aroused, were I to hear the details.

My ability to remember had several significant consequences. It became characteristic of him, each time he mentioned someone, to remind me exactly who it was; this reached caricature proportions one session when he caught himself reminding me who his girl friend was—and he'd been speaking about her a great deal. He then recognized both a need to keep me at a safe distance and to avoid testing my memory for fear that I would fail the test, and then he'd feel outraged and disappointed. But my memory did fail me once when I forgot about a pending cancellation that he required. After first trying in vain to take all the blame, he experienced a deep and out-of-proportion discomfort at the possibility that I had simply forgotten. This turned out to have important transference implications, and brought to the foreground his inability to recollect, or to experience even retrospectively, any anger and disappointment toward his father. He discovered how his image of his father was idealized and unrealistic—just as his image of me was—and accepted the likelihood that anger and disappointment had figured importantly in his feelings as a child. But it was only later in therapy that he came to experience any of these feelings in a full and

genuine way; it was when he faced termination, and the fantasy that if I were perfect I wouldn't abandon him, that he reintegrated the fantasy he'd had that if his father had been perfect (and he himself had been a "good boy"), he would not have died.

The middle stage of therapy was ushered in by an impasse ("I've told you everything there is to know—what now?"); and though he acknowledged that he hadn't been feeling in control of the therapy but was only doing the "right thing," he wanted me to take directive control of the sessions. After several sessions were devoted to exploring how he avoided a sense of control in his everyday life by externalizing responsibility and structuring things according to his value system, he became preoccupied over whether he should lie on the couch, and tried in a variety of ways to get me to give him that directive. ("Tell me, at least, whether in your professional opinion it might be helpful!") Finally, with a remark to the effect that he was feeling tired that day, he took the couch—and delivered an especially well-composed narrative on the politics of the music profession.

During the middle stage the six-month trial period passed by virtually unnoticed. By this time he was feeling a substantial dependency on the therapy, which continued as a major theme until the ending. His sexual problem had abated, but he continued to experience episodes of anxiety. He noticed that the anxiety tended to occur when he was alone and working, especially when at the piano; and he discovered that it was related both to a feeling of being trapped as well as to a temptation to masturbate. (He had a long history of masturbating, which he alluded to but never explored; and he gave up the habit early in the therapy, but it made a brief reappearance during the ending as part of an attempt to forestall termination and evoke disappointment.) He also explored the possibility that his anxiety was associated with feelings in relation to caring for his mother, together with fantasies about taking his father's place. Nevertheless, he continued to feel impotent against the anxiety, and tried to get me to endorse his decision to give up on it and simply learn to live with it. This was part of a larger resistance against any major changes in his personality, and it was formulated in these terms: "The stubborn and disappointed child [in me]—the bad boy—is dead set against changing."

A critical incident occurred during the middle. His mother fell ill and required an operation. When, on the day following the operation, I did not ask him how it went, he reacted with the outraged feeling that I didn't care. For the first time in therapy he experienced feelings of anger toward me, and it was an anger he dimly recalled having had when he was a child. A major discovery then emerged: a fantasy that his mother hadn't sufficiently cared for his father, that she hadn't taken adequate care of him, and therefore he died. What also emerged was the recognition that his own overweening emphasis on independence was based on the conviction that he had to take care of himself because his mother would not. And this theme was soon elaborated by the discovery of an older fantasy: His mother had wanted him to be a girl (and he, alas, was a "bad boy"!); therefore she didn't care for him the way she cared for his brothers. This discovery had profound ramifications in respect to his self-image, and led him to pursue a variety of formulations (about his identity and his defenses) that were based on the wish to be a girl. It was during this period of therapy that he burst out with "This therapy really works!" And for the first time the therapeutic process was characterized by some spontaneity and enthusiasm.

The ending stage (late in the second year of therapy) was heralded by the theme of his imminent death, which took the form of a fantasy-cum-conviction that he was destined to die like his father. This theme was evoked by a vivid dream. The patient rarely told his dreams, and didn't believe they had much significance; this one, however, provoked strong feelings and preoccupied him for several sessions. It involved a funeral ceremony, ostensibly his father's, but the coffin was empty. At first he resisted the suggestion that the funeral in the dream was his own, and he rejected the idea that it had implications for the therapy and meant he was entering the ending stage. Only when I pointed out that the stage didn't have to be brief and precipitous, and also that it could be construed as a trial period, did he accept the fact that he was facing the issue of separation. Most significantly, however, he now faced the problem of mourning, and made the discovery that he had never adequately mourned his father's death. This, in turn, led him to explore the ways in which his habits and traits could be construed as a form of mourning, and also as attempts to avoid the work of mourning.

The ending was taken up mainly by recapitulation. He made a number of attempts to get me to relax my neutrality and impersonality, and tried to induce diagnostic interpretations as well as advice. A brief exacerbation of anxiety occurred, and he experienced a temporary and mild phobia of being in enclosed spaces by himself. But the major event was his decision to move in with his girl friend and set a marriage date. A few weeks before termination (after two and a half years of therapy) he proudly announced that they were expecting a baby.

## SUMMARY

Nondirective Psychoanalysis is designed to provide a unique and distinctive kind of therapeutic experience, based principally on free self-inquiry. Its format and orientation stem largely from the premise that psychotherapy is potentially a distinctive and unique event, different from virtually all socially familiar interpersonal and professional paradigms; and psychotherapists can articulate a unique and distinctive role definition, one that doesn't borrow from other professionals who provide human services in our society. A therapist can work in ways that differ significantly from the ways a physician, a social worker, a teacher, an engineer, or a priest works; a therapist can work, and relate to patients, in ways that are uniquely those of a "psychotherapist."

Two fundamental theses underlie the method. The first is that psychotherapy can be relatively unstructured without being concomitantly ambiguous. The second is that a therapist can be nondirective and neutral and, nevertheless, function actively and effectively. In fact, the method rests on the conviction that the efficacy of an average-expectable course of psychotherapy can be profoundly enhanced when a therapist remains as nondirective and as neutral as it is feasible to be, giving the patient little, if any, guidance and counseling, as well as little, if any, evaluation and reinforcement. It is then that the therapist can participate actively in the vital processes of therapy and thereby promote its effectiveness.

## REFERENCES

Bone, H. Two proposed alternatives to psychoanalytic interpretation. In E. F. Hammer (Ed.), *Use of interpretation in treatment*. New York: Grune & Stratton, 1968.

Brenner, C. *Psychoanalytic technique and psychic conflict*. New York: International Universities Press, 1976.

Fenichel, O. *Problems of psychoanalytic technique*. New York: Psychoanalytic Quarterly, 1941.

Hartmann, H. *Ego psychology and the problem of adaptation*. New York: International Universities Press, 1958.

Kaiser, H. *Effective psychotherapy*. New York: Free Press, 1965.

Langs, R. *The technique of psychoanalytic psychotherapy*. New York: Aronson, 1974.

Levy, L. *Psychological interpretation*. New York: Holt, 1963.

Menninger, K. *Theory of psychoanalytic technique*. New York: Basic Books, 1958.

Paul, I. H. *Letters to Simon: On the conduct of psychotherapy*. New York: International Universities Press, 1973.

Paul, I. H. Psychotherapy as a unique and unambiguous event. *Contemporary Psychoanalysis*, 1975, **12**, 21–57.

Paul, I. H. *The form and technique of psychotherapy*. Chicago: University of Chicago Press, 1979.

Rapaport, D. The theory of ego autonomy: A generalization. In M. M. Gill (Ed.), *Collected papers*. New York: Basic Books, 1967.

Schonbar, R. Confessions of an ex-nondirectivist. In E. F. Hammer (Ed.), *Use of interpretation in treatment*. New York: Grune & Stratton, 1968.

Singer, E. *Key concepts in psychotherapy*. New York: Random House, 1965.

Waelder, R. The principle of multiple function: Observations on overdetermination. *Psychoanalytic Quarterly*, 1936, **5**, 45–62.

# CHAPTER 44

# *Orgone Therapy*

ELSWORTH F. BAKER and ARTHUR NELSON

*One of the most fascinating individuals in the history of psychotherapy is Dr. Wilhelm Reich. Conventionally, he is considered a genius during his early years as an orthodox analyst and a madman in his later years, when he developed his own system of psychotherapeutics.*

*I believe quite a few of my psychological confreres are misinformed about Reich's ideas and procedures, and I am most pleased to be able to present to a wide audience a balanced account of Reich's theory of the orgone and orgone therapy. As many readers probably know, a good many derivatives have emerged from Reich's work. Whether they are advances or not over Reich's original concepts I have no way of knowing, but I feel that in providing readers reliable information about orgone therapy, I am contributing significantly to the field.*

*A number of the newer methods that employ a wide variety of techniques in a kind of helter-skelter manner frequently use some of the body procedures and concepts originated by Reich, usually without attribution. It is my guess that the final therapy of the future will contain elements of Reich's orgone theory; the reader is fortunate to be able to get the story straight from Elsworth Baker and Arthur Nelson.*

Orgone therapy is based on the work of Wilhelm Reich. It involves a concept of health based on the functioning of biological energy ("orgone" as Reich called it, from "organism" and "orgasm") in the body. When this energy flows freely and fully in the body, a condition of health exists. When this energy is blocked, psychopathology and, at times, even functional physical pathology can develop. Orgone therapy per se involves the methodology Reich evolved to bring the patient to a state of health by removing obstacles to the free flow of energy in the organism.

## HISTORY

Reich became interested in psychoanalysis as a medical student and was given the unusual privilege of joining the Vienna Psychoanalytic Society in 1920 while still an undergraduate. He rose quickly to importance and became director of the Vienna Seminar for Psychoanalytic Therapy in 1927. Reich became interested in the outcome of analysis; he especially sought the basis for unsatisfactory results. He found that those patients who were successful had all developed a satisfactory genital life, whereas those who failed had not. Reich began to ponder what constituted a satisfactory sexual life. Sexual activity per se did not guarantee this, even when the man ejaculated and the woman climaxed. He found that a specific type of capacity for sexual gratification was necessary—Reich called this "orgastic potency." It occurred when, through successful therapy, all holding and resistance dissolved.

The orgasm of patients who had achieved orgastic potency showed characteristics far different from those of neurotic individuals. Orgasms of such patients had to be triggered by genital union (in the female, the vagina rather than the clitoris was involved); orgasms from stimulation of pregenital zones did not produce the same effect. Orgasm was far more than a local climax—rather it involved total bodily convulsions of an involuntary nature, that is, involuntary contraction and expansion of the total plasmatic system. There was also complete cessation of psychic activity—there were no conscious fantasies whatsoever, but rather a blurring of consciousness at the moment of acme.

In his book *Character Analysis* (1971), Reich coined the term "character armor" to denote the individual's chronic (defensive) mode of reaction, which has its origins in childhood—the chronic alterations of the ego that it evolves to protect itself from external and internal dangers. As a result, the individual develops characteristic defensive modes of behavior, manifested in the *manner* rather than the *content*—the *how* rather than the *what*. It is these traits—for example, compliance, mistrust, arrogance, and so forth—that function as resistance in analysis. This intuition led Reich to develop his technique of character analysis. The entire neurotic character becomes manifest in treatment as a condensed rigid and inflexible defense mechanism. With successful analysis of these character traits, Reich often elicited strong emotions that he encouraged the patient to express. He noticed, too, that with the thorough release of affect, often locked up since childhood, there occurred changes—at times profound—in bodily attitudes, expressions, posture, and tonus. He became aware and convinced that concomitant with the psychic character armor, there is a somatic muscular armor.

As Raknes (1970), one of Reich's proponents, noted:

It soon became clear to Reich that the muscular armor, which consists of spasms, cramps, and tensions, is nothing but the bodily expression of the repressed emotions and ideas, and the somatic anchoring of the neuroses. In psychoanalytic circles the question had often been raised as to where the repressed ideas and emotions were located, and the answer was as a rule that they were in the unconscious. Now Reich showed that they were bound as well in the muscular armor, in the spasms, holdings and tensions of which the individual had no consciousness or understanding.

This discovery led to another innovation in psychotherapeutic technique, namely attacking the neurosis from the bodily side, partly by calling the patient's attention to the chronic tensions, partly by making him feel them by direct manipulation. By thus loosening up the holdings and tensions, one could bring into consciousness emotions and memories which had hitherto been completely repressed. (pp. 20–21)

The somatic armor, with its psychic concomitants, binds energy. It interferes with the free flow of energy through the organism. Undischarged energy continues to build up, to produce stasis, and eventually to overflow in the form of symptoms. The goal of therapy is to overcome this stasis by breaking down the armor, reestablishing the free flow of energy, and attaining orgastic potency.

## CURRENT STATUS

The educational and training aspects of Orgone Therapy are administered by the American College of Orgonomy in New York City. (This is not a school, but an organization analagous to the American College of Physicians.) It is an organization of dedicated physicians and others who have the proper qualifications and have contributed significantly to the advancement of orgonomy.

Standards for training of orgone therapists are high—an M.D. degree, together with a medical internship plus residency training in either psychiatry or internal medicine. Members of the college give technical seminars and supervise therapists/trainees, as well as administer the necessary personal therapy. There are usually several trainees at any given time. The duration of training is dependent mainly on the degree of character restructuring required so that objectivity in treatment of others is insured. The average training period takes a minimum of three years. At present qualified candidates possessing the Ph.D. degree are being trained for competency in orgonomic counseling.

The college also publishes the *Journal of Orgonomy,* a semiannual containing up-to-date clinical and theoretical articles on Orgone Therapy, orgone physics, biosocial problems, and related topics of interest. This journal is now in its thirteenth year.

A thorough exposition of Orgone Therapy is given in Baker's *Man in the Trap* (1967) and in a two-part article in the *Journal of Orgonomy* (Baker, 1978). For the historical and theoretical development of Orgone Therapy, the reader is referred to Reich's books, *The Function of the Orgasm* (1970) and *Character Analysis* (1971). An overview of the many aspects and ramifications of Reich's work can be found in a book by Raknes, *Wilhelm Reich and Orgonomy* (1970).

An ongoing course on the work of Wilhelm Reich for the layman or other professionals is given at New York University School of Continuing Education. The fall semester focuses on scientific orgonomy, the spring semester, on social orgonomy.

## THEORY

Reich's work was based on psychoanalytic precursors that are still considered valid in orgonomy. One, of major importance, is human psychosexual development, which is paired with the vicissitudes of the libido. The ego evolves through various developmental stages, culminating in the Oedipus complex, whose successful resolution leads to the establishment of genital primacy and a state of emotional health. Fixations, or regressions to pregenital stages and/or difficulties in resolving the Oedipal conflict, result in emotional disturbance. This involves binding energy, which makes less energy available for autonomous adult functioning. To Freud, "psychic energy" was a metaphor. To Reich, it had a physical, objective existence, which he was able to demonstrate experimentally, and which he called "orgone."

Individual charcter development is, then, dependent on the degree of fixation, or armoring, at any particular erogenous zone where the major part of the energy is concentrated. Therefore it is evident that symptoms characteristic of these levels are present whenever there is an increase in energy concentration or block at that level. Blocking or armoring may occur at any zone and implies that the individual has been able to develop beyond that zone, but has not been able to give up that zone completely. Resultant symptoms color the personality and, most important, interfere with complete genital discharge, thus with emotional health. There are two types of blocks: repressed and unsatisfied. The latter is felt constantly as a need, as, for example, the overeating or over-talking of the oral unsatisfied block. The former results in a need to defend against any expression at all from the blocked zone, as manifested, for example, in a lack of interest in food, or in laconic speech.

Blocking is functionally identical with muscular armoring; an oral block, for example, will be manifested by spasm in the muscles of the head and face, such as the submentalis, masseters, and so forth. Character types (see Baker, 1967, and Reich, 1971) are determined by the particular constellation of blocks of the erogenous zones. Blocking in nonerogenous segments determines rigidity of the character type. In orgonomy four major erogenous zones are recognized: ocular, oral, anal, and genital. The ocular zone is a major addition to accepted analytic theory; orgone therapists feel that its blocking accounts for such major pathology as paranoia and schizophrenia. In healthy development each stage fulfills its temporal function, is not blocked, and the individual develops through to genital primacy.

The vast majority of people reach an early genital stage of development (phallic narcissistic, or hysteric), but earlier pregenital blocking may result in regression to a previous libidinal stage. In the case of a phallic with a dominant oral repressed block, for example, the phallic type of functioning is largely given up and behavior is predominantly of an oral type—depression, for example.

Therapy functions to reverse the armoring process. The armor is removed by evoking and discharging repressed emotions in an orderly and consistent fashion. For it is the movement of energy in the body that is felt as emotion; in the muscles as rage, for example; in the skin as pleasure; or inwardly, as anxiety. When armoring is removed, and natural sexuality is reached, one sees a unique physiological event that is an objective criterion of therapeutic success. There occurs a spontaneous tilting forward of the pelvis at the end of complete respiratory expiration, together with a coming forward of the shoulders. This is what Reich called the "orgasm reflex." It signifies that the patient is orgastically potent, has the ability to discharge all excess energy that is normally built up in living, and now has a healthy sex economy. Such an organism can no longer maintain a neurosis, since neuroses exist only on the basis of energy (libido) stasis. The function of the orgasm, then, is to regulate the energy economy of the organims.

As the patient achieves orgastic potency, he or she undergoes fundamental changes. Symptoms are lost. His or her body becomes relaxed, as opposed to previous rigidities caused by muscular contractions holding repressed feelings. This is seen often in a softening of the face, with more expressiveness. The eyes are bright and there is a buoyancy in the whole organism, coupled with a general feeling of "well-being." Many fundamental attitudes change spontaneously.

## METHODOLOGY

There are three avenues of approach in the practice of Orgone Therapy—breathing, directly attacking the spastic muscles, and maintaining the patient's cooperation. The priority of each depends upon the individual case, although all three are often necessary tools in every case.

First let us consider breathing, which has several functions. Clinically, the first somatic blocking (or defense) observed in infants is that of the breathing mechanism. The breath is held, and this reduces both anxiety and feeling in general. This breathing inhibition becomes chronic, and the adult is usually seen on the couch with his or her chest in a chronic inspiratory position with little excursion on respiration.

In therapy the patient is asked to breathe as fully and deeply as he or she comfortably can, concentrating on chest movement. This reverses the patient's historical inhibition of breathing. This maneuver often of itself produces considerable emotional release, especially of anger or crying. It helps to reveal and overcome severe blocking in other parts of the organism.

Breathing "charges" the organism energetically. This is often manifested by tingling and streaming sensations felt in the body. The increased charge exerts an inner push on blocks. In analytic terms, deep and full breathing facilitates loosening of repression.

The second avenue of approach consists of directly attacking the spastic muscles to free the contraction. The contraction of the skeletal muscles can be worked on directly, that of the muscles of the organs and tissues only indirectly. To mobilize the skeletal muscles, one must first increase the contraction to a point that cannot be maintained. This is done by direct pressure on the muscle with the thumb or by otherwise irritating it. Best results are obtained by pressure near the insertion of the muscle, which is the most sensitive area. Of course, the muscle will only contract again unless the emotion (or idea) that is being held back is released and expressed. Where muscles cannot be reached by the hands, other methods must be used, such as gagging to open throat muscles or mobilizing the eyes by having the patient follow a moving penlight with his or her eyes.

Third, orgone therapists work to maintain the cooperation of the patient (using character-analytic methods). This is accomplished by bringing the patient's resistances to therapy and the therapist into the open and overcoming them. This is extremely important because the patient will in every way endeavor to maintain his or her immobility, trying desperately not to reveal the self. Behind this is an intense fear of expansion and movement. The patient always begins therapy with distrust and suspicion. This resistance is emotional and cannot remain hidden indefinitely. It must be recognized and brought to the surface. Every defense begins with a negative transference. The patient must discuss this freely. A lack of negative transference is due to its being blocked by the therapist's attitude—being consistently friendly or otherwise preventing the patient from expressing hostile feelings toward the therapist. One must point out the patient's attitudes to him or her repeatedly or mimic his or her behavior. It is necessary to be consistent. The armor protects against stimuli from without and from within. Therapy upsets this equilibrium, which is what the patient resists. The resistance is always attacked from the ego side. The patient understands it better and thus the negative transference is dissolved. We are not concerned with what the patient wards off, but that he or she does ward off and how. Finally, *what* is warded off comes out.

Dissolving the armor renders the patient helpless. His potency breaks down from castration anxiety, and he feels his whole character as sick, not just his symptoms. If potency does not break down, therapy has not touched him.

Anxiety is the basis for all repression and is behind all contractions. The patient is always trying to control anxiety, and cure is effected by forcing him or her to face this anxiety and express forbidden feelings. The most important emotion to elicit is rage, and, until this is released, the patient cannot experience the softer feelings of love and longing. It must be released from every segment.

Through reactions of the body during the process of dissolving the armor, Reich discovered that the body was functionally divided into seven muscular segments, each of which reacts as a unit and is to a certain degree independent of the other segments. The seven segments are the ocular, oral, cervical, thoracic, diaphragmatic, abdominal, and pelvic. One works from the head down, removing the layers of armoring from the superficial to the deep. Any one segment may fail to respond completely until further segments are freed. With each release of a segment, armoring in earlier segments may recur and require further attention because the organism is not used to movement and tries to return to its former immobility. It must gradually become accustomed to free mobility. Treatment requires that the patient lie on the couch with only minimal clothing on, so that the therapist can adequately observe and treat the condition the patient has presented. The patient must understand this.

After working through the three areas of approach, therapists are now prepared to start dissolving the armor in the various segments individually. The chest is usually chosen first. Breathing is the most important aspect of therapy. It raises the energy level and promotes movement of energy. If the chest is not too tightly held, breathing is not too difficult an assignment. If the chest is held high in inspiration and does not move, it is heavily armored; here the therapist steps in and works manually on the muscles of the chest, particularly the intercostals and spinals. The latter cause holding back, "I won't," and spite. The pectorals and trapezii are also loosened. Pressure is exerted on the chest as the patient breathes out. In all cases, the patient is given a chance to breathe for some time before any active attack is made on the armor.

The chest holds rage, bitter sobbing, and longing. When it is freed, there is a feeling of lightness and buoyancy. Rage may be elicited by hitting, choking, twisting, and scratching. We encourage the patient to give in completely by wildly letting go. The chest cannot be rendered completely free until the first three segments are freed, and residuals come out only when one has reached the pelvis. After a moderate loosening of the chest, so the patient can at least breathe adequately, we proceed with the segments in order from above down.

Armoring in the ocular segment is shown by a stiff or immobile forehead. It may appear flat. The patient cannot open his eyes wide, and they may appear dull, vacant, anxious, sad, or defiant. Eye motility is markedly decreased. Schizophrenics appear to be staring into the distance, and the eyes have an empty look. Those few patients whose eyes are free have a trusting look.

The patient is asked to move the forehead; sometimes it may be necessary to start the process by manually moving it. Then the patient is instructed to roll the eyes, focusing on the walls, and open and squeeze them while breathing. The therapist has the patient follow a moving light or a finger with the eyes. One tries to get the eyes wide open. Here again it may be necessary to open them wide with the fingers. We try to elicit emotional expression in the eyes: anger, sorrow, anxiety—the last while screaming with the eyes open. Suspicion is elicited by having the patient look out of the corner of the eyes. Last, flirting, smiling, or longing are elicited by having the patient open his or her eyes wide while breathing out and smiling.

When the eyes are free, one will notice movements and an increase in tension in the lips and jaw. It is now time to proceed to the second, or oral, segment. This is an extremely important segment, for only the oral and genital segments can initiate the orgastic convulsion. They are the only major erogenous zones that provide actual contact and fusion with another organism. The oral zone provides means for the intake of food, fluid, and air, and for vocal communication, emotional expression, and erotic contact. If functioning is inhibited by repression, satisfaction is lost in all these important functions, and the joy of living is replaced by the misery of merely trying to survive and, eventually, by depression. For the rest of his or her life, the unsatisfied individual will try to make up this need through overeating, drinking, talking, and emotional vacillation.

Full expression of the oral segment depends on free mobility of the ocular, or first, segment and sometimes on loosening the lower segments. The jaw usually is tight with clenched teeth, although it may be unnaturally loose. The chin may sag or be drawn, flat, pale, and lifeless. It may be pushed forward in defiance or pride, causing a tightening of the floor of the mouth, which holds back crying. The therapist gently pushes the jaw backward and has the patient breathe, and try to let the jaw be loose. This may bring out crying.

The patient may speak little or talk constantly under pressure. One may observe contempt, a sarcastic smile, or a silly grin. The mouth may be sad or even cruel. The oral segment holds back angry biting, yelling, crying, sucking, and grimacing. The patient almost always needs to bite and is allowed to, on a suitable object such as a towel. When work is done on the submental muscles, or when the patient gags, crying may be brought out. Sometimes screaming does this. If not, the patient may be asked to imitate crying. Suppression of crying is frequently associated with nausea due to tension of the muscles in the floor of the mouth.

The cervical segment mainly holds back anger and crying. The neck is stiff, the muscles are tense, and the neck may balloon in breathing. Anger and crying may be literally swallowed down without the patient's being aware of it. Cervical blocking also gives rise to voice changes, a whining, thin voice, or harsh breathing and coughing.

The gag reflex is important in loosening the throat, but work may have to be done directly on the sternocleidomastoids and deep muscles of the neck, while having the patient scream repeatedly.

The diaphragmatic segment is one of the most difficult to deal with. When this is met, you may be sure you are in for a hard time. This block contains murderous rage. It may be recognized by lordosis and paradoxical respiration. Breathing out is difficult. The therapist repeatedly elicits the gag reflex without interrupting breathing. The patient is encouraged to express rage and to risk feelings of wanting to murder. The first four segments must be free before the diaphragm can be loosened. When this segment is opening, vomiting occurs. Then wavelike movements appear in the upper body, accompanied by a feeling of giving.

The sixth, or abdominal, segment usually causes little difficulty if the upper segments are free.

The pelvis, the seventh segment, is always freed last. If it is opened earlier, the individual cannot handle the sexual impulse, and either confusion and disintegration follow or else earlier problems such as sadistic impulses are carried into the sexual life.

The pelvis contains anxiety and rage. The latter is either anal and crushing, or phallic and piercing. The patient is asked to kick or stamp to discharge the anal rage and to strike with the pelvis to let out the phallic rage. Until anger is released, pleasure in the pelvis is impossible. The various spasms must be released. Spasm in the floor of the pelvis is released by having the patient repeatedly relax and contract the anal and vaginal sphincters. When this is accomplished, the pelvis moves forward spontaneously at the end of each complete expiration. This is the orgasm reflex. The organism is now capable of complete surrender, a capacity that gradually increases during the year or two following the completion of therapy.

## APPLICATION

The first step in treatment is the selection of patients. Except for young children and infants, it is advisable to accept only those who request therapy themselves, not those who come because a husband, wife, parent, or friend pushes them to have therapy. It is difficult enough when the patient earnestly desires help—impossible when it is forced on him or her. One should never accept a patient one does not like. Therapy is too difficult to deal objectively with someone you do not like, and it is not fair to either the therapist or the patient. Also, it is advisable to take those one understands the best and can work with the most easily.

The second consideration is whether the candidate is ready for therapy. This may not be determined immediately but should be watched for very carefully. The situation is suspect if the patient cannot grasp what is required of him or her and therapy seems alien and not comprehensible. Those who grasp it immediately and understand what you are trying to do are usually good candidates. Unusual reaction such as blanking out, irrational reactions, turning blue or gray, shock, or extreme weakness make one wary and call for extreme caution. A tendency to develop serious physical symptoms as therapy continues is reason enough to discontinue treatment.

Prior to any therapy, it is essential to obtain both an adequate history and a physical examination. The history itself is relatively meaningless. What is important is the patient's reaction to the events that are anchored physiologically in the character structure. These are the things that therapy stirs up. It is important to estimate the "stuff the patient is made of." Has he or she accomplished a great deal against all odds, or has the patient succumbed to the least frustration? Has he or she been able to socialize, or has contact with people been avoided? Has he or she made a good adjustment to the opposite sex or not? Is the patient willing to make a real effort to get better, or does he or she want it made easy?

Obstacles to success are age, rigidity, severe orthodoxy (religious and/or political), and environment. The last factor may present real circumstances over which the therapist has no control. For example, a woman who has many young children may be married to an impotent man whom she cannot leave for security reasons.

Any physical disease is a complication to therapy and should be corrected if possible. The somatic biopathies—that is, those physical illnesses due primarily to emotional repression—make therapy that much more difficult. In our experience, cancer cases, including those surgically treated with no recurrence even after years, are not candidates for this therapy.

These caveats aside, most psychiatric conditions are amenable to Orgone Therapy, especially the neuroses and schizophrenia.

However, not all cases can be treated; some can only be made worse. It is important to recognize and screen out the individuals who cannot tolerate expansion and movement, react badly to every advance in therapy, or break down into serious somatic illness.

Orgonomic technique is less dependent on verbal communication from the patient than other therapeutic procedures, and therefore can be frequently very effective in attacking pathologic structure not reached by other modalities. It is in part a body-oriented technique, but it also entails consistent character analysis of the patient's resistance. The technique is deceptively simple, but Orgone Therapy is not simply a matter of "working on" muscle spasms or producing dramatic emotional outbursts. One must be able to make an accurate diagnosis, understand character structure and underlying character dynamics, to know when and how to consistently and logically apply orgonomic techniques. In addition, a knowledge of physiology and anatomy is necessary, in order to deal safely with chronic muscular

spasm, untoward physical responses, and any biopathic (psychosomatic) conditions. Proper training, experience, and background, therefore, are a necessity—or disaster may ensue. This is especially so because of the profound emotional and physical depths that can be plumbed. The possibility of suicide, psychoses, or serious physical illness as a result of mismanagement is very real. As Reich stated, Orgone Therapy is "no more and no less than bio-psychiatric surgery and can only be done securely by well skilled and well trained hands and structures. . . ."

Many "body" and other cathartic therapies have borrowed from or are derived from the work of Reich. Bioenergetics is one of the few therapies that acknowledges its origins from Reich. Bioenergetics utilizes the concepts of muscular armor and movement of energy. Many of the therapeutic techniques are similar.*

## CASE EXAMPLE

The following case,† conducted by Charles Konia, M.D., of Easton, Pennsylvania, represents a clear, uncomplicated picture of Orgone Therapy.

### Anamnesis

The patient was a 25-year-old single white school teacher who came to therapy because she wanted to settle down and stop running from herself. The aspect of her behavior that she found most disturbing was her relationships with men. She had a history of repeated unsatisfying, short-lived sexual experiences.

---

*Bioenergetics has, however, dropped the cornerstone of therapy—the orgasm theory and the goal of orgastic potency. Possibly this is a result of a fatal altering of Reich's theory and technique by removing the pelvic armoring prematurely—thereby insuring that orgastic potency will rarely be achieved.

†Excerpted with permission from Konia, C. Orgone therapy: A case history. *Psychotherapy: Theory, Research and Practice*, 1975, **12(2)**, 192–197.

In general she chose men who treated her abusively, often to the point of physical punishment. She was entirely unable to protect or extricate herself from these situations, which invariably ended with her being jilted. . . . When I first saw her she was about 25 pounds overweight. Typically she ate when depressed or anxious, following a disappointing love affair. She was unable to be alone for any length of time, requiring the constant reassurance of someone near. She was frigid and was able to have only minimal genital sensations through oral genital foreplay. This was often accompanied by masochistic fantasies of being forced to submit sexually, or imagining that she herself had a penis.

## Past History

The patient was an only child. Her memories of her father are few; however, there were two distinct screen memories that she recalled. The first was of being chased under her bed by her father after she cut her mother's dresses with a pair of scissors and then not being punished by him; this left her with a definite feeling of sexual excitement. The second occurred just prior to his death, when she was eight. At that time she had inadvertently seen him naked, and she interpreted his death as a punishment. Immediately following his death she began overeating to the point of becoming obese. In addition, she became spiteful toward her mother until she was totally out of her control and had to be restrained by a maternal uncle. She related this behavior to being angry with her mother for not remarrying and bringing another father into the home. At the same time, her behavior produced a fear that her mother would also leave her, and she turned into a "good little girl."

## Biophysical Examination

The patient tended to be soft-spoken and seductive. When frightened, her facial expression became indifferent or calm. She was of average height and heavily built. Aside from her obesity, which was mainly centered in her legs, thighs, and abdomen, the most prominent feature was her mouth, which seemed to be stuck with a tremendous emotional charge behind it. The expression varied between a smirk, disgust, indifference, or boredom, depending on her mood. Her face appeared tense and bloated. Her eyes were frightened and slightly bulging, but were lively and expressive.

## Treatment

*The Ocular and Oral Segments.* I began by focusing on her indifferent facial expression, which I felt concealed her most superficial layer of rage. She admitted that behind her indifference she was afraid of showing her anger and felt that she would get "kicked in the face" if she ever revealed her true feelings. At the same time I worked on her facial tension by having her make faces. This made her frightened, and she recalled her inability to express her anger toward her mother's helplessness and lack of understanding. When she behaved spitefully, her mother's favorite phrase was "What did I ever do to deserve you?" This made the patient feel frustrated and worthless, but she invariably got even with her mother by becoming even more spiteful.

Gradually when her face lost some of its bloated appearance and looked somewhat more expressive, her distrust of men began surfacing. She admitted not knowing how to be herself with someone who was not as bad off and "crazy" as she was. She was afraid that any other kind of man would find out what she was really like and have nothing to do with her. Therefore the surest way to avoid rejection was to submit sexually and become a "receptacle."

Discussion of this material was soon followed by a sneer, and she was able to express a few brief angry shouts. However, her anger soon became stuck in her chest and she became dyspneic. I prodded her trapezius muscle to mobilize this anger, and that produced more angry faces and shouting. She was greatly pleased with this outburst but immediately became frightened and had the urgent feeling of having to do something more. I interpreted this as a fear of incurring my disapproval by not being a good patient, and related it to pleasing men out of fear. She left with a serious look on her face. In the following sessions she entered feeling angry with me for what I had said last time, but knew that I was correct. As she became somewhat more trusting, she stated that I was the only man that she didn't have to please. I took this declaration with a grain of salt, since I knew that she was still unable to show emotions, especially anger, fully in her eyes. I therefore went back to mobilizing her eyes by having her roll them and express fear. Gradually they became less proptotic. Then with pressure on the masseters, she was able to show anger in her eyes while shouting "Stop it!" She looked as if she could stab me. This was the strongest anger that she had expressed, and following this her face appeared more open. She began asserting herself in her daily life.

When she began to enjoy making angry faces, and became somewhat contactless with herself, I knew that a layer had been worked through and waited to see what would happen next. I didn't have to wait long. In the next session she had a lost look in her eyes, and reported that her weight had been steadily increasing. Her distrust became intensified. Expressing rage in her face beyond a certain threshold produced a great deal of fear; she turned her head away so that I would not see her angry looks. I again mobilized her terror by having her look startled with her eyes. This produced the strongest fear she had ever known. She cried and felt afraid of being alone. When I saw her in the next session her face had regained that typical swollen, bloated appearance that she had when I first saw her, and she reported that she had eaten voraciously all week. She looked intermittently confused, lonely, frightened, and angry. During the session I kept after her tendency to please me, and

related it to her fear of being abandoned, pointing out that any display of anger means desertion. Mobilizing fear from her eyes at this time was fairly easy. Rolling her eyes, she would scream in panic for entire sessions at a time. This was often accompanied by crying and an expression of sadness in the lower part of her face. Intensification of her fear made it necessary for her to block off her deeper emotions from her throat. Squeezing a towel (which often helps relieve a spastic throat) partially helped to mobilize the throat block, but then her tongue interfered.

At this time, in spite of her fears, she terminated an unsatisfying relationship with a boyfriend. She began to assert herself with men, and to feel that she had some rights in a relationship. In therapy she became somewhat brazen and decided she was not going to please me by showing feelings, unless she genuinely felt them.

At this time I attempted mobilization of her oral rage, by pressure on the masseters, but this proved to be premature. She became distrustful again, and looked at me as if I were going to leave her. I therefore went back to her eyes and had her express more fear alternating with anger. This brought out murderous thoughts and feelings directed at me, but this made her feel guilty. As she became able to tolerate her fear, her throat spontaneously became mobilized and she began making deep frightened sounds. At this time her fear was so intense that she had to touch me to convince herself that I was still in the room. She recalled that her mother could not tolerate any display of anger, and felt at those times as if she were actually going crazy.

Now her deep oral rage, in the form of biting became accessible. She growled, moved her jaw with a biting motion, and felt like killing. This was the strongest anger that she had felt thus far. It took the form of a blinding rage toward her mother for being so controlling and hypocritical, and this was followed by quivering of her lips for the first time.

*The Abdominal Segment.*   In the next session she reported the following dream: Her father is sick, and her mother is preventing her from seeing him. She recalled that at the time of her father's death she was never told that her father had died, only that he was sick and went away. This made it possible for her to deny the reality of his death and years afterward she still searched for him. At this time, mobilizing fear from her eyes brought out her deep fear of abandonment. She felt terror and wanted to scream out "Daddy don't leave me," but could not. This gave in to deep sobbing. She began feeling her mourning over her father's death.

In her daily life she began to tolerate being alone for longer periods of time, and in therapy she came in touch with the intense rage in her abdomen (where most of her fat was centered). This rage, in turn, intensified fears of abandonment. She became "scared stiff" and screamed out in panic. This alternated with more abdominal rage, which finally ended in strong abdominal cramps. She recalled the time just prior to her father's death, when she had accidentally seen him naked. She felt somehow responsible for his death since this image was frightening and prohibited. It was immediately after his death that she began to overeat.

Deeper mobilization of her fear of abandonment produced dyspnea accompanied by a fear of dying, and she began to quiver in her arms and chest. She identified this fear as a punishment for having killed her father. Then followed very strong rage toward me which she also felt down to her abdomen. She looked hatefully at me and shouted "I hate you!" She compared me to her father and stated that she loved me, but that I didn't love her, and would leave her just as her father had done. This outburst was followed, during the next week, by a moderate amount of weight loss from her abdominal area. This weight loss intensified her terror, and strong, frightened shouting poured out of her for long periods of time. This resulted in sensations in her pelvis and thighs, although her genital was bypassed.

Then followed deep sadness at her father's death. She felt a deep longing for him, accompanied by an emptiness in her stomach, and described having fantasies of her father being in her abdomen. She felt strong reluctance to face her sadness since this made her feel vulnerable. She also began having genital sensations for the first time in her life, but was afraid to tell me, for fear of being discharged as cured. I reassured her that this was not the case, and that she was only beginning to have genital feelings. There was still a lot of work to be done.

As she began to trust me more, the spasm in her lower abdomen gradually began to yield and she began experiencing an almost unbearable longing for her father. She cried out uncontrollably, "Daddy, why did you leave me, why did you have to die?" Further expression of this longing from her lower abdomen produced strong anxiety in her perineum. At this time she developed a fear of getting appendicitis and dying. She felt this would be a punishment for having sexual feelings for her father. The longing for her father gradually developed into fantasies of swallowing him both through her vagina and orally.

***End Stage: The Pelvic Segment.***   I then gently massaged her jaw. This produced very strong biting from her mouth, accompanied by squeezing of her pelvic floor. She expressed a very strong rage in her pelvis and thighs, as if she were biting with her vagina. Following this she felt intense genital longing, and felt that her vagina wanted to be filled with a penis. During the session breathing produced a pelvic retraction on expiration (preorgastic sensations).

In the following session jaw mobilization resulted in very powerful clonisms, which terrified her. I knew that once her jaw finally gave, she would quickly develop the orgasm reflex provided that she did not clamp down in another segment. I was not wrong. Within

a few minutes the reflex appeared. This at
first terrified her, and she cried out of fear.
But then very strong surges of sexual excitement overcame her, and she cried "I can
feel! It's wonderful!" Her jaw looked open,
and her whole face appeared to have completely lost its tension, taking on a seriousness and depth that was not there previously.
She felt very alive and sexual.

During the last few sessions I focused on
completely eliminating the biting from her
mouth and vagina. During one session her
pleasurable pelvic sensations became
blocked. This led to a violent explosive anger
at everyone, including me. She shouted and
kicked and hit. "I want to be well! I don't
want therapy any more!"

As she gave up her attachment to me, she
slowly relinquished her oedipal ties to her
father. She became capable of staying open
sexually and achieving genital gratification.
Correspondingly, her relationships with men
changed. She began to select men, not out
of neurotic motives or fantasies, but on the
basis of whether or not they provided genuine
satisfaction of her needs. Therapy lasted 215
sessions.

**Discussion.**

A precise understanding of the structure of
the armor, both from a characterological as
well as a biophysical standpoint, which pre-
sumes an accurate biopsychiatric diagnosis,
is essential for the successful treatment of
any patient. Since the major armoring of this
patient was in the pelvic segment with the
secondary source of armor in the oral segment, this patient was a hysteric with an oral
unsatisfied block. Her pelvic armoring was
manifested by the fact that a primary aspect
of her neurotic character was a constant push
toward genital contact with simultaneous
running from her sexual feelings because of
anxiety. . . . (Fenichel, 1945). The end result was that she was left chronically unsatisfied.

Complicating her basic structure was her
severe pregenital (oral) block. Her mouth
was genitalized and served as a substitute to
fulfill her sexual desires. Unlike the simple
hysteric who runs at the first sign of a sexual
encounter and/or sexual feelings, this patient
would cling tenaciously to any man with
whom she became involved. During the
course of therapy, constant mobilization of
her oral block was therefore essential. Prior
to loosening up a deeper level of armoring,
the therapist repeatedly had to return to the
oral segment and release the particular emotion that was being held.

In attempting to understand the treatment
of this patient, it will be helpful to follow
logically, step by step, the layering of the
armor from the most superficial to the deepest
expressions.

Psychologically one traces the layering
from the patient's most superficial character
traits through the deeper emotions which underlie the Freudian unconscious (or, in orgonomic terms, secondary drives) to the successful resolution of the oedipal conflict
(Fenichel, 1945). From the biophysical aspect one passes through the segmental layering of the armoring, from the most superficial features in the upper segments (eyes,
facial expressions, etc.) down through the
cervical, thoracic, diaphragmatic, abdominal, and finally into the pelvic segment where
the oedipal conflict is thoroughly dealt with.

The therapist's skill depends on his or her
being able to perceive which aspect of the
armor is closest to the surface and therefore
requires immediate attention. To begin with,
this patient's glib, indifferent facial expression covered the most superficial layer of her
fear of showing feelings. She would get
"kicked in the face" if she did. Expressing
this fear brought out her spiteful anger, primarily directed at her mother for controlling
her and interfering with her life. Exposing
this anger immediately brought out a deeper
layer, her present-day distrust of men based
on a fear of rejection by them. This fear made
her behave like a nice, sweet little girl, and

turned her into a "receptacle" to be used by any man. Working through this distrust brought out sneers and other angry faces. This anger, in turn, revealed a deeper fear of abandonment on an oral dependent level directed toward her mother. "Don't leave me the way Daddy did" is what she felt at this point. Until now the primary focus of attention was in her first and second segments (the ocular and oral), but as her emotions became deeper, she began to block in her throat. Facing her fear of maternal abandonment brought out angry biting, expressing her rage at being deserted by the mother. It was at this time that the patient first had fleeting oral-genital sensations with quivering of the lips. This rage was followed by deeper fear of abandonment by the father, which slowly gave way to profound rage toward him, and therefore toward all men. She felt the source of this rage primarily in the upper part of the abdominal segment. Expression of this hatred was followed by a deeper fear of longing (fear of being hurt), which began from her lower abdomen. This fear was based on her feeling that her father would leave her if she expressed any feeling toward him. This was followed by a profound sorrow and longing (localized in the lower part of her abdomen) for her father. Correspondingly, she began to lose weight (gave up the incorporated father in her abdomen), which was followed by sensations in her pelvis and thighs. This gradually produced preorgastic sensations, and the crystallization of the incest wish and castration anxiety (sexual taboo for longing for her father and the revival of her fear of punishment for seeing him naked). This in turn gave way to very powerful biting from her mouth and vagina based on her impulse to bite off and swallow her father's penis. Finally came the total mobilization of her jaw: her organism gave in with clonisms of the jaw and pelvis, which led to the orgasm reflex and orgasm anxiety (fear of dying). Tolerating these feelings soon produced strong feelings of genital excitation and the establishment of genitality.

# SUMMARY

Early in his analytic career, in the late 1920s, Wilhelm Reich moved down from behind the couch to sit beside the patient and look at him or her and to allow the patient to see him. He thus made contact with the individual behind the neurosis he was treating. He began to observe patients physically as well as listen to their words and emotions. With release of affect, he noticed changes in bodily attitudes, expressions, posture, and so forth. These accompanied changes in character traits such as arrogance, spite, compliance, and others. He intuitively made a connection between the two—that the neurosis had a somatic concomitant (or was "functionally equivalent," to use his phrase). This led (in the early to mid 1930s) to an important innovation in therapeutic technique, that of attacking neuroses somatically. At the same time he began to question the outcome of psychoanalysis—finding that only successful analysands had developed a satisfactory sex life with a specific type of orgastic response. He further studied orgastic function in conjunction with his new therapeutic techniques. He found that as people got well and lost their character, and physical, armor, they eventually developed a physiological spontaneous reflex of the body, which Reich called the "orgasm reflex" and which signified (and was validated by patient reports) the ability to discharge orgastically in a specific way—the "orgastic potency." Here were physiological criteria for cure. Psychoanalytic theories of psychosexual development and characterology were valid for Reich, as well as the concepts of libido and psychic energy. Orgonomists, however, unlike the Freudians, do not use "psychic energy" as a metaphor. Reich saw indirect evidence for a real energy in terms of tense muscles that became soft after emotional release, of dull eyes that sparkled thereafter.

Reich demonstrated that this energy had a physical, objective existence, and called it "orgone." The orgasm, to Reich, was the great regulator of this energy, and if orgastic potency existed, there was no libido stasis—therefore, no symptoms, and the individual had a healthy sex economy.

Orgonomic psychiatric technique currently uses a combination of physical (breathing and direct work on muscles) together with character-analytic methods. Character is thus specific blocking of the flow of orgone energy and therapy has as its goal the unblocking of this energy so that it might flow freely through the organism, signifying a state of health.

Reich's insights have led us to a new and deeper understanding of human functioning, as well as profound innovations in therapeutic theory and technique.

## REFERENCES

Baker, E. F. *Man in the trap*. New York: Macmillan, 1967.

Baker, E. F. Orgone therapy. *Journal of Orgonomy*, 1978, **12 (1,2)**, 41–54, 201–215.

Konia, C. Orgone therapy: A case history. *Psychotherapy: Theory, Research and Practice*, 1975, **12 (2)**, 192–197.

Nelson, A. Orgone (Reichian) therapy in tension headache. *American Journal of Psychotherapy*, 1976, **30 (1)**, 103–111.

Raknes, O. *Wilhelm Reich and orgonomy*. New York: St. Martin's, 1970.

Reich, W. *The function of the orgasm*. New York: Farrar, Straus, 1970.

Reich, W. *Character analysis*. New York: Farrar, Straus, 1971.

# CHAPTER 45

# *Personal Construct Psychotherapy*

FRANZ R. EPTING and PATRICIA A. BOGER

*There are several pairs of chapters in this book: two on Feminist Psychotherapy, two on Brief Therapy, and two on George Kelly's Personal Construct Theory. This chapter deals with a broad range of topics related to Kelly's Personal Construct Psychotherapy. The chapter by Adams-Webber is on Kelly's Fixed Role Therapy.*

*After reading Kelly, enthusiasts of Personal Construct Theory are often satisfied to give up other personality theories. Kelly has such a complex yet logical way of thinking that once you come to understand this system, you feel that he well may be absolutely correct. Kelly asks only that you suspend your conceptions of persons temporarily and give his a try. If it does not work out, you can always go back to your former system. Although Kelly has been traditionally classified as a cognitive theorist, this chapter, emphasizing emotional and nonverbal components, allows us a slightly different view of his construction of reality. Other chapters in this book are also concerned with how we construe the world (Camilla Anderson's, for example). Kelly's view is complex, encompassing, and rather complete.*

*The amazing ingenuity of the doctors of the mind to develop unusual methods of dealing wih the human soul is seen once again in this chapter by Franz Epting and Patricia Boger, who show how Kelly's theory can be applied to psychotherapy in a rather innovative manner.*

Personal construct theory and its methods of psychotherapy were first published in 1955 by George Kelly. Both theory and therapy propose the model of the person as scientist. The individual develops a theory about the world to achieve some level of understanding and to enhance personal predictive abilities regarding future events. The venue for this understanding and prediction is the system of personal constructs.

Personal constructs are bipolar meaning dimensions a person uses to understand life events. In psychotherapy these meaning dimensions are focused on interpersonal relationships and are usually characterized by such labels as outgoing—shy, kind—cruel, friendly—unfriendly, and so forth. Constructs are empirically tested, using events

from the world, for predictive efficiency and long-term usefulness. Based on the test results, one's construct system is modified. Philosophically, Kelly described his theoretical position as constructive alternativism—the world may be construed in various ways, all views subject to revision or replacement.

Since the investment in Personal Construct Psychotherapy is in the continual process of developing better construct systems, the therapist encourages experimentation and testing of new hypotheses by the client. The psychotherapy session serves as a testing ground with the therapist acting as the validator. As validation and invalidation begins to occur in both the therapy sessions and in the outside world, one's construct system changes. Constructive change represents the goal of Personal Construct Psychotherapy. Thus the therapy is a model of the theory, in that it views the person in therapy as a scientist, involved in hypothesis formation, in experimentation, and in change or revision of original ideas.

## HISTORY

Although Kelly mentioned various philosophers and psychologists in his writings, he seldom specified any particular influence. Rather, he simply mentioned them in the context of his work. For example, Shakespeare is noted as often as any of the philosophers. The sheer range of persons mentioned by Kelly hints at his educational background. He studied not only psychology but engineering, economics, speech pathology, and cultural anthropology—to name but a few areas.

His philosophical position is constructive alternativism, yet Kelly had no intention of developing this position into a complete philosophical system. He made clear his belief that one's interpretation of reality is always subject to revision and replacement. People are free to construe the world in different ways; no one should become a "victim of his biography." According to Kelly we are both free and determined. We are free to reconstrue our circumstances and thus not to be governed by them. However, we are determined by the range of our own construct systems; for the system limits our ability to reconstrue. Thus we set the boundaries of our freedom by the nature of our construct systems. If we develop broad-based systems, we allow outselves more freedom of movement in the world.

Constructive alternativism can be compared with other philosophical systems to gain a clearer perspective regarding Kelly's position. He saw his theory as essentially monistic and viewed the person and the construct system as wholes, not as independent units. Aligning himself to Spinoza, Kelly stated that he was willing to apply the plur-

alistic aspects of monism if it would serve the purposes of the theory. Personal construct theory could also be called empirical and pragmatic. Kelly's conceptualization of "the person as scientist," striving to predict, to control, and to offer sequential explanation of phenomena, thus attaining understanding, illustrates the empirical underpinnings of the theory. He mentioned John Dewey as an influence, but one would imagine that Immanuel Kant, Charles Peirce, and William James should also be given credit for their effect on Kelly's theoretical position regarding the anticipatory nature of the person.

Two other influences deserve mention: Hans Vaihinger, a philosopher; and J. L. Moreno, a psychologist. Kelly felt that Vaihinger's (1925) philosophy of "as if" had something to offer the field of psychology. Kelly applied the "as if" philosophy to his language of hypothesis by proposing an alternative use of language—the invitational mood—as a way of orienting thoughts toward the future, thereby setting the stage for prediction. The invitational mood allows for the existence of alternative constructions or interpretations of reality. This type of hypothesis formation is a necessary part of discovery because it allows the individual the freedom to explore new avenues without asserting them as truths.

Another safe method of exploration of change is utilized by Kelly in his Fixed Role Therapy process (see Chapter 24). The client is given an alternate personality sketch and invited to act as if he or she were the person characterized by the sketch. Using role-playing techniques, client and therapist work together in formulating new hypotheses and testing them in the therapy session and in "safe" real-life situations. Kelly was intrigued by Moreno's (1934) writings on psychodrama, which make heavy use of role-acting techniques. Moreno, however, took psychodrama back to the classical personality implied in Greek drama, whereas Kelly went only as far back as the development of extemporaneous theater in Europe after World War I. Doubtless he was also influenced by the period he spent as a drama coach at a junior college in Iowa.

Kelly began his career as an academic psychologist at Fort Hays Kansas State College in the depression years of the early 1930s. During this period of growth, challenge, and exploration of theoretical underpinnings the State of Kansas began funding one of Kelly's projects: traveling psychological clinics to serve the entire state.

World War II interrupted Kelly's career as associate professor of psychology, and he became a naval aviation psychologist in charge of a training program for pilots until 1945. After serving on the faculty of the University of Maryland, Kelly became director of the clinical psychology program at Ohio State University, a program he was to build to one of national standing.

During his years at Ohio State Kelly's theory of personal constructs reached fruition. His first few years were primarily devoted to the organization and administration of the clinical program. Later on he had more time to spend with his students, discussing ideas relevant to the theory he was developing. The end product of his efforts was the two-volume work, *The Psychology of Personal Constructs,* published in 1955.

Although Kelly published less than many other well-known psychologists, he was active in his field, serving as president of both the Clinical and Consulting Divisions of the American Psychological Association. In 1965 Kelly left Ohio State University for Brandeis University, to take the Riklis Chair of Behavioral Science. This new position would have allowed him complete freedom to concentrate on his academic interests. However, in March 1966 he died at the age of 62.

## CURRENT STATUS

Although Personal Construct Psychotherapy has not yet inspired the formation of an independent institute dedicated solely to the purpose of training construct therapists, its influence should not be underestimated. During his years at Ohio State University Kelly found himself at the center of an active, intellectual group of graduate students. Working with these students, Kelly developed his personal construct theory, which coalesced into his two-volume work (1955) on the subject. Kelly's enthusiasm and belief in his theory is clearly demonstrated through the research efforts of this dedicated group of graduate students and the European scholars who came to Ohio State for postdoctoral study years. Their subsequent research efforts were inspired by Kelly's explorations of the nature of personal construct psychology. As his students graduated from Ohio State and established themselves at other universities, a second generation of Kelly students began to reach maturity. Thus it is from the efforts of the students of George Kelly that this theory is gaining in popularity.

In 1976 the First International Congress on Personal Construct Theory in conjunction with the Nebraska Symposium on Motivation was held in Lincoln, Nebraska. The congress represented the first official gathering of students of construct theory from all over the world. They came from the United States, Canada, and England primarily, but there were also representatives from the Netherlands, New Zealand, Hong Kong, South Africa, and other countries far enough away to make one realize that the words of George Kelly were more pervasive than many psychologists had heretofore imagined. A second international congress was held in 1978 at Oxford University with over 200 participants; a third took place in the Netherlands in 1979 and was also well attended. The fourth congress is planned for Brock University in Canada for 1981. Soon after the first congress, Al Landfield and Franz Epting became co-coordinators of the Personal Construct Theory Clearing House. The clearing house was originally formed by Landfield to prepare a yearly list of references but has since expanded its functions to include lists of membership, newsletters, information regarding research interests of members, new training programs in personal construct psychology, and brief notes of the international congresses.

A number of different approaches to Personal Construct Psychotherapy have developed since Kelly's original formulation. An example is the work of Donald Bannister and his colleagues in the area of schizophrenic thought processes. Kelly had suggested that schizophrenic thought processes might be described as loose constructions. (A loose construct is defined as one that may lead to varying predictions.) Bannister (1963) described thought-disordered schizophrenics as having low correlations between constructs and between patterns of relationships of constructs. Since their thought patterns appear to be random, the question occurs, "How did they get that way?" Kelly stated that change in the construct system occurs as a result of validation or invalidation of one's predictions. Bannister hypothesized that the thought-disordered schizophrenic was a product of "serial invalidation," or repeated invalidation of construct predictions. He postulated that the loosening process is a strategy employed to avoid having predictions fail. By loosening, the schizophrenic successfully avoids further invalidation but the price is a rather meaningless existence.

In addition, Bannister's research has led him to some important discoveries relating to the process of moving from a "normal" construct system to the loose system of the thought-disordered schizophrenic. He conducted experiments in which normal subjects were serially invalidated; he found that those who were successively invalidated did not loosen relationships between constructs but rather changed the patterns of interrelationship to cause distorted linkages. Case histories of thought-disordered schizophrenics showing frequent paranoia and delusions also indicate that distortions in content may precede the actual loosening. The formation of new patterns, distortion of content, and subsequent loosening result in a system so unique that validation becomes increasingly unlikely.

The logical treatment approach formulated

by Bannister and his colleagues was serial validation (Bannister et al., 1975). The staff attempted to anticipate events in the way the patient did to provide validation. If this validation was successful, then the patient should begin to develop a core of related constructs that eventually would be strong enough to withstand some invalidation. The experiment met with mixed results; it was impossible to achieve enough control over the environment to insure serial validation. Interactions with other patients and family members often cancelled out careful validation by staff. However, this attempt was important because it paved the way for future research in the area of serial validation within the hospital setting.

Another example of developments in Personal Construct Psychotherapy is found in Landfield's approach to the suicidal person (Landfield, 1976). Based on Kelly's (1955) choice and organization corollaries, Landfield hypothesized that the "instigating context" of suicide is the imminent breakdown of the construct system. Thus the act of suicide can be seen by the construct theorist as an attempt to prevent any further invalidation of one's system or, conversely, as the *final* validation of a useless, constricted system that no longer facilitates predictions of the world.

Kelly's choice corollary states that one chooses alternatives that will enhance the possibility of elaborating the construct system. One alternative is constriction, which makes for clearer definition of terms and more certainty. The person whose system is rapidly becoming more and more constricted may make the ultimate choice of a certainty—death. Landfield described suicidal behavior as occurring in the context of disorganization and constriction. He is interested in exploring the context of suicide (imminent failure of the construct system) and its purpose (validation or invalidation of one's life). It may be that in understanding the context, self-destructive behavior could be prevented by rechanneling the purpose of the suicide.

Landfield's subjects were classified as a

serious suicidal group, a gesture group, an ideation group, a group of premature terminators from long-term therapy, and a control group of better adjusted students. Using a combined score of the measures of social conceptual disorganization, constriction in the context of constructs, and constriction in the application of constructs, Landfield found that the serious suicidal group had significantly higher average scores than the other groups. This exploratory research is a step in the direction of predicting suicidal behavior. Subsequent work in this area concentrates on reconstruction of the severely constricted system of the suicidal person so that alternatives to suicide can be considered viable.

## THEORY

Kelly's theory of personality differs from most other personality theories in several important ways. First, personal construct theory was formally and systematically laid out by Kelly in the form of a fundamental postulate and 11 corollaries. Although research may have led to varying interpretations, the assumptions of the theory remain easily recognizable today. Second, construct theory is reflexive—it includes itself in its explanation of events. Kelly was very careful to insure that his theory would be flexible enough to be applied to "the person as scientist" and also to the scientist who experiments on the person. It would appear that he succeeded; the theory can be used to describe itself and its author. The third distinction lies in the level of abstraction at which the theory was written. Kelly had in mind a broad range of convenience for his personal construct theory. He was comfortable with it being described as a metatheory and admitted he had intended as much. The final factor that distinguishes construct theory is Kelly's clear definition of measurement and assessment techniques: the Role Construct Repertory Test (rep-test) and the self-characterization and their application in therapy. Both the tools and the therapy are built upon the cen-

tral assumptions of the theory. In the rep-test the person is asked to list out a set of personal constructs, in bipolar form, using the triad procedure described below. The self-characterization is a procedure wherein the person is asked to write a short narrative describing him- or herself. Construct dimensions are then extracted from the narrative.

Personality was never explicitly defined by Kelly. It has generally been assumed that the construct system should be accepted as the essence of the personality. Each person uses his or her own system of constructs to categorize events and determine behavior; in short, to understand the world. Constructs are finite in number, dichotomous in nature, and hierarchically arranged. Each one has two poles—the construct and the contrast, for example, outgoing—shy. The minimum number of elements necessary for the formation of a construct is three. These might be three friends, John, Mary, and Tom. Two of the elements are seen as being similar (for example, John and Mary are seen as being outgoing); they form the *construct end*. The third (Tom) is seen as being different from the other two (shy); this difference is the *contrast end*. A construct gains meaning from both the similarity and the contrast. In the rep-test a person is presented with a list of different triads of people, and is asked to produce separate construct dimensions for each triad grouping.

Even more important to the notion of personality than the constructs themselves is the manner in which they are organized. Each person sets up a hierarchical system of constructs in which some are seen as more important than others. If one construct subsumes another, it can be called superordinate; the other becomes subordinate. In the example above, the construct dimension outgoing—shy might be subsumed by the superordinate construct of "sensitive to feelings of others versus insensitive to others" in such a way that the person sees *shy* as implying sensitivity, whereas being *outgoing* involves a level of insensitivity. Kelly stated that the unique arrangement of the system characterized the individual's personality to a greater extent than the constructs alone. It becomes clear that in organizing constructs into a personal system, interrelationships among constructs are defined. Once arranged, the system is not static but is continually evolving and being refined. Thus the personality is always in a state of flux. Just as it is defined, it may be redefined. The process of therapy is a means of helping with this reconstruction of the system.

Kelly did not deal extensively with the topic of personality development. He explained how constructs are formed—through the process of construing replications of events. He discussed the types of constructs that are present—permeable, impermeable, superordinate, subordinate, verbal, preverbal, and so on. But he was never explicit about the circumstances that would facilitate the initial formation of one or the other type of construct. There are no developmental stages laid out in personal construct theory that the individual must progress through to reach maturity. Preverbal constructs are developed in infancy and many of them are related to physiological processes. The construction process from infancy to childhood to adolescence to adulthood is basically continuous. The personal construct system is modified along the way to maintain its predictive efficiency.

It has been suggested that construct usage becomes more abstract and differentiated with age. Children who develop in a healthy environment will become more cognitively complex with age, will have a larger system for interpreting events, and the system will tend to be open to modification. Although Kelly never addressed the developmental factors leading to the content or structure of the system, there have been some recent attempts in this direction (Salmon, 1970).

Constructs are simply methods of anticipating events; as the person successively construes the replication of events, the constructs are modified to make the system more useful. This action is not determined by motivation, reinforcement, or consistency. Kelly rejected these notions. The individual is seen as being constantly in motion. Thus, the process of motion is built into the theory and need not be explained by drives. Only the direction of the motion needs explaining—the direction of personal change.

In describing personality within Kelly's system, it is important to include some discussion of the nature of change. Kelly saw the individual in a continual state of change. The principle of elaborative choice describes the directions the change may take—extension or definition. Generally the person is assumed to move in the direction of extension, increasing the range of convenience of the system. However, there are times when it seems that extension is neither possible nor desirable and the person makes the elaborative choice by the constricting move to define the system in greater detail.

What determines the extent to which the person will make the choice of extension or of definition? Kelly described three conditions favorable to the formation of new constructs, that is, personality change. The first condition is the *use of fresh elements* "relatively unbound by old constructs." Care should be taken to insure that the new constructs are developed on contexts that do not involve the self or family members. The "protected environment" of therapy is an ideal place to begin. The therapist is a new person to the client and can serve as a fresh element for the development of new constructs.

A second key condition is the *existence of an atmosphere of experimentation*. Without this, the role playing and characterizations would fall short with most clients. Kelly felt that psychotherapy is another form of experimentation. New constructs (hypotheses) are formed, tested, and modified in the session. The key to the process is the invitational mood; constructs are "being tried on for size" and may be altered without any lasting consequences for the client outside the session. The constructs are not yet solidified, rather they are viewed propositionally. This permissive atmosphere allows the client maximum freedom for experimentation.

The third condition necessary for the formation of new constructs is the *availability of validating data*. A construct is unlikely to be changed if no results on its predictive validity are available. Invalidation may also lead to change when presented in the supportive atmosphere of therapy. The therapist must be alert to which constructs are being experimented with and attempt to make available data relevant to those constructs. Role playing allows the client to try out new constructs with immediate access to validating data.

The goal of Personal Construct Psychotherapy is to promote change—reconstruction of the system. The therapist, however, must be careful not to *demand* change of the client. The client's needs must be accepted even when they involve a restatement of the old self and a concomitant shying away from further experimentation. Kelly recognized that the prospect of change in core constructs would prove difficult.

## METHODOLOGY

Personal construct theory, unlike some other theories, does not espouse a particular therapy technique to be used unfailingly with all clients. Kelly (1969) described his psychotherapy as "a way of getting on with the human enterprise and it may embody and mobilize all of the techniques for doing this that man has yet devised" (Kelly, 1969, p. 221). There is no central technique; rather the psychotherapist works to incorporate many therapeutic devices. Therapy is a joint venture, a cooperative effort, of client and therapist. There are, nevertheless, several techniques that might serve to characterize a Personal Construct Therapy. The techniques to be considered here are enactment, group psychotherapy, and the pyramid procedure. Fixed Role Therapy is omitted since Adams-Webber deals with that technique in Chapter 24.

Enactment, as it is used in individual psychotherapy, is similar to informal role-playing techniques suitable for a therapy session, with client and therapist enacting the parts. The therapist may structure the situation by elaborating the roles in advance or allow the enactment to develop spontaneously. In addition, the therapist may influence the direction of the situation through the playing of his or her part. The purpose of the enactment is to allow for the elaboration of the client's construct system. By experimenting within the safety of the therapy session, the client is protected from involving core constructs prematurely and is encouraged to view the problems in perspective. Enactment should be seen as a method of discovery of alternatives, not as a rehearsal of old constructions.

The purpose of using enactment in therapy is to provide material that the client can consider with some measure of detachment. Kelly delineated five points when using enactment in therapy. First, the therapist should remember that a lot may happen on a nonverbal level. Second, the sketch should be kept brief—anywhere from two to 15 minutes, with the average being about five minutes. Next Kelly emphasized changing parts. This allows the client to learn from the therapist's portrayal and serves to equalize matters if the client feels the therapist has had the better part during the session. Fourth, the therapist must be ready to use the enactment to protect the client if he or she gets into trouble. Last, the therapist should use judgment in selecting scenes from the client's reports of incidents. By using reported incidents, the enactment becomes more immediately useful for the person as contrasted with Fixed Role Therapy, where scenes are used to anticipate future events and are more experimental.

Kelly also suggested a model for group therapy to facilitate clients' predictions of others. He saw group psychotherapy as a procedure that could stand on its own—not only for use in conjunction with individual therapy. The function of group therapy is similar to that of individual therapy; it assists individual members in developing more effective constructs for anticipating events. Kelly discussed several advantages of group therapy. First, it gives the client a broader base for experimentation and development of the new role. Other members provide the opportunity for more variety in experimentation and thus allow for a more comprehensive role to be formulated. The group allows individuals to discover which constructs are permeable (easily applied to group members) and which are impermeable.

Another advantage of the group is that it provides a means of "shaking out" preemptive constructs (rigid constructs). In sharing other group members' mother or father figures, the client has an opportunity to make discriminations and generalizations along dimensional lines previously overlooked. Group psychotherapy is also more effective than individual in dealing with another form of rigidity—the problem of stereotypes of constellatory constructs. A client who feels that all men are logical and unemotional may find out in the course of the group that men are not so easily construed. The group situation provides a greater variety of validational evidence; events involving several people are more complex and hence more fertile. Advantages from the therapist's point of view include dispersion of dependency and economical use of time.

Landfield and his colleagues have developed a special group therapy procedure based on the concept of sociality in construct theory known as the interpersonal transaction (IT) group (Landfield, 1979). The IT group is designed to facilitate interpersonal relations. Dyadic interactions are used in a rotation system so that each member can learn to understand the others. Following the dyad experiences, group members are brought together for group interaction. Topics of discussion are general in nature to allow greater freedom. Members are instructed to share as much or as little as they wish and are urged to listen carefully and avoid value judgments. Landfield feels these characteristics reduce anxiety and threat, thereby improving the group experience. Mood tags are used at the beginning and end of each two-hour session to introduce personal feelings into the interactions and provide an index of mood change throughout the group. The mood tag is a short description of the participant's emotional state that is attached to each group member's clothing. IT groups have been used to evaluate change that occurs in alcohol groups, death education classes, and student groups.

Landfield also introduced the pyramid procedure, another personal construct methodology with therapeutic and diagnostic uses (Landfield, 1971). The therapist asks the client to describe the most important characteristic of a friend (the construct) and then elicits a contrast. In further descriptions of the initial construct and contrast, two additional levels (the pyramid) of constructs are generated by asking the client to elaborate on the meaning of the original construct dimension. A maximum of two pyramids are completed in one session. The pyramid procedure is proposed as an alternative to the rep-test in that it allows the therapist greater opportunity to study the client's language framework early in therapy. The pyramid procedure also works to make the client more aware of his or her language framework and how it is used.

Other methods derived from personal construct theory that can be used in therapy are rep-test methods, self-characterization, and self-other monitoring techniques. The rep-test can be used as a means for clients to explore ways they see themselves and others. To be an effective tool, the therapist must be able to design a rep-test with relevant role figures and analyze patterns of interrelationships. Self-characterization is employed in Fixed Role Therapy but also has a more general use in Personal Construct Psychotherapy. It can be used to monitor changes in the client's perceptions of self throughout therapy or to get at themes and key constructs in the client's system. Methods for exploring self-other relationships include the self-characterization used first to describe the client and then another person. Predictions of how the partners will describe one another can also be used (Mair, 1970).

## APPLICATIONS

For Kelly, the focus of convenience of personal construct theory is psychotherapy. In volume 1 of the *Psychology of Personal Constructs,* Kelly (1955) outlined the technique of Fixed Role Therapy. This technique has come to be associated in the minds of many as the only therapeutic intervention proposed by Kelly. On the contrary, in volume 2 Kelly discussed several other techniques appropriate for Personal Construct Psychotherapy. He devoted a chapter to methods for loosening and tightening a client's construct system, which include the use of dream interpretation, relaxation, chain association, summarization, and other techniques. Kelly also devised a personal construct strategy for group therapy (as described in the "Methodology" section) and for the training of personal construct psychotherapists. It becomes clear that Kelly intended Personal Construct Psychotherapy to be an extensive system with a broad range of treatment possibilities.

Fransella (1972) has pioneered one aspect of personal construct theory and its corresponding treatment strategies for the stutterer. The construct theory approach to the problem focuses on the person's construct system rather than the stuttering behavior. It is postulated that the way the world is construed leads to the behavior. Thus Fransella hypothesized that the stutterer has an elaborate subsystem built around stuttering in contrast to having few constructs relating to the act of fluent speech. For the client, it is in the context of him- or herself as stutterer that predictions are easily formulated and validated. It is possible that the stutterer has few possibilities for construing events other than those related to stuttering. When faced with an event difficult to construe, the stuttering occurs to achieve control over the situation, thus creating a cycle of stuttering

behavior. It is important to realize that stuttering is not seen as deviant when examined using the personal construct approach. It is a skill in its own right; it allows the person the greatest possibility for the anticipation of events.

Fransella's treatment approach emphasizes her belief that fluency can be achieved through the process of reconstruction. It must be kept in mind, however, that this proposed change in behavior will be seen as anxiety provoking for the client. The therapist must exercise caution in moving toward the goal of fluent speech. Fransella acted as therapist for a group of 20 stutterers in an attempt to operationalize her theoretical formulations regarding the necessity for reconstruction of one's self as a fluent speaker. An integral part of the treatment was concentration on the person's moments of fluency, produced through a series of experiments in which the client enacted the part of a fluent speaker and construed the fluency. Following this treatment clients were better able to construe themselves as nonstutterers, whereas prior to treatment they construed themselves more easily as stutterers. Rates of speaking and reading increased significantly during treatment. Perhaps the most critical ramification of Fransella's work is the possibility created for expanding her treatment approach to other areas such as the lisper, smoker, drug user, and people employing other neurotic behaviors.

Rowe (1978) employed personal construct theory as one of the elements of study in her work on depression. In day-to-day life people become secure in their constructions of reality, forgetting how changable life can be. When some unimagined or unexpected event does occur, the person is consumed with anxiety and fear and struggles to reconstrue (or deny) the event in an effort to regain security. The depressed person has construed him- or herself as being separated from the world and the people in it, which makes it very difficult for change to occur since change is usually implemented as a result of interaction. The depressed person has severely limited possibilities for interaction and the subsequent reconstruction. Rowe also noted that many depressed people have adopted some variation of the construct "suffering is virtuous."

Rowe began her study of depression with the rep-test grid form* as her primary exploratory tool. The rep grid provided a way of measuring change in the client and a method of analyzing the client's relationships with significant others. Rowe feels that understanding the language of depression is essential to understanding the phenomenon. The grid is easily applied to this quest for knowledge. It provides a starting point for conversation between client and therapist, using the client's constructs, which can be taken directly from the grid. As the therapist comes to understand how each person's constructs serve to isolate him or her, the therapist can begin to facilitate change.

Personal Construct Psychotherapy has also been applied to couples by Ryle, who developed the double-dyad grid method. The grid involves both partners and their relationships with each other, with parents, and with other couples. Each partner completes two versions: one for self and one as the other would have completed it. Ryle and Breen (1972) used the double-dyad grid to compare seven "maladjusted" couples with seven control couples to see if it would distinguish the two groups and would facilitate understanding among couples with problems. Individuals in maladjusted couples tended to view themselves as a child and their partner as parent more than did the control group. When the relationship was going very badly, the maladjusted couples saw themselves as becoming more childlike, with the partner acting less like a parent—a situation Ryle termed doubly depriving. The double-dyad grid is used as a therapy tool for delineating problem areas in a relationship—for example, areas of similarity and difference, and misperceptions of the other.

Morris (1977) has employed the construct theory approach to group therapy with psy-

chiatric outpatients. The group consisted of six outpatients (after dropout) and two therapists. They met weekly for over 50 sessions and followed Kelly's recommendations for group therapy. Role enactments and a conversational model (Mair, 1970) were also used. Assessment was made via rep grids given to clients and therapists at the beginning and end of therapy and by therapist's predictions of ideal and actual outcome for clients. Interviews structured around the grid were also given to clients and therapists. Rank ordering of group members on degree of change, degree of improvement, and need for more treatment made by Morris and the therapists provided another outcome measure. Results showed fairly accurate therapist predictions in nine of 12 cases, with the inaccurate ones being members who had terminated prematurely. Five of the eight group members had retest grids that conformed to their ideal outcomes and were said to be conforming to therapists' expectations. The results, therefore, were positive and represent a multidimensional analysis of change occurring during therapy.

Ravanette (1977) is representative of the group who have extended Kelly's theory to encompass psychotherapy and grid work with children. Pictures are frequently used in construct elicitation with young children as they yield a richer sample of constructs. Ravanette developed four specific techniques for use with children: the delinquency implication matrix, elaboration of personal troubles, elaboration of complaints, and perceptions of troubles in school. He feels that these techniques allow children a chance to think seriously about themselves and to make sense of things in their own way. The techniques also give the therapist an opportunity to view the child's construct system as it is applied to the problem situation and to other areas of life.

## CASE EXAMPLE

This case example is taken from Fransella's (1972) work with a group of 20 stutterers

---

*In the grid form each construct produced is used in rating a list of personal acquaintances.

described in the previous section. To be included in the treatment group the stutterers had to (1) be over 17 years old; (2) have no psychiatric disorders or history; and (3) have stuttered for as long as they could remember. At the onset of therapy two rep grids were completed: one with the self as a stutterer and the second as a nonstutterer. Fransella's description of therapy with "Luke" will be the focus of this discussion. Fransella worked with Luke off and on over a period of four years. She chose him to tape record and include in her book because she felt he would provide a "good test" of personal construct theory.

Luke was 26 years old at the beginning of therapy. Fransella described him as a typical "obsessional scientist," interested in facts and figures. He seemed incapable of loosening his construct system. Initially he could not provide a single construct for the nonstutterer grid as he could not see himself as a nonstutterer. The most significant clusters relating to him, as a stutterer, were those related to self (all evaluatively good) and those that Fransella related to his stuttering self (being liked, respected, having status, constructs regarding aggression). These latter constructs appeared over the years of therapy as recurrent themes. Following an experience of perfect fluency, a second nonstutterer grid was completed and several constructs emerged. They were found, however, to be closely linked with the central construct of respect.

Luke was a particularly difficult client because his interpersonal relationships were inadequately construed. His social competence, nevertheless, did improve over the course of therapy. Fransella helped him achieve this by concentrating on the "implicative networks surrounding certain constructs" and by "examining the evidence he used to validate his predictions" (Fransella, 1972, p. 225). Luke often found his evidence (in a hostile manner) by extorting it when it did not exist. By working on the implicative networks (which construct dimensions imply the presence of others), Fransella hoped to introduce invalidation gradually so as to

eventually facilitate modification of the entire system.

At the end of the seventeenth session, Luke was truly beginning to envision himself as a fluent person. He began to hypothesize about the following: will he chatter, will his speech be refined, will he be able to accept himself? It was predicted that a relapse would occur as a result of the threat produced by the notion of being fluent. At the next session it became clear that the relapse had occurred. Luke had been comparing himself with other fluent speakers and realizing what a difference there was. Fransella attempted to reduce the threat by being careful not to force him to proceed too quickly along the path of reconstruction. The threat appeared to diminish, as Luke's speech improved over the next weeks. During session 21 he introduced the idea that he could be resisting cure.

Progress was satisfactory, with some expected setbacks, for the next 20 sessions. In session 42 Luke had an insight into his experiences of perfect fluency. He realized that he could not expect to be fluent in every situation; knowing this, he could be fluent in the "easy situations" and not be upset by relapses in the more "difficult situations." The next 20 sessions he continued to improve, and concerns centered more on the implications of fluency for his interpersonal relationships. Fransella summarized three different levels of construing regarding fluency that Luke moved through. The most subordinate level deals with the implications for mechanisms of speech (tone, emphasis). The next level concerns subjects of conversation and how to keep a conversation going. The highest level is concerned with the ramifications for relationships with other people—his core role constructs. Following one relapse six months after session 85 (about three years into therapy), Luke has continued to increase his fluency.

The long treatment period should not be viewed as a function of the therapy procedures. Most of the original group improved markedly in a matter of months. Luke's weak system of interpersonal constructs accounted for his extended treatment. Fransella saw her therapy as progressing beyond the simple reduction of stuttering to the point at which Luke had a strong enough construct system regarding himself and others to make "reasonably accurate predictions." One important point Fransella made is that, due to the nature of her research, only those topics broadly related to stuttering were discussed. It is possible that therapy could have been shortened if Luke had concentrated more on role relationships rather than on fluency. Hindsight showed that after a point, fluency increased every 16 weeks even when only two sessions were held in that period.

## SUMMARY

Personal Construct Psychotherapy is based on an understanding of the client and the nature of the therapeutic relationship using bipolar construct dimensions as the unit of analysis. The therapy involves a cognitive (conceptual) appreciation of the content of the client's language and the structure of the client's thought. It takes into account the feelings and mood-states in order to locate those areas most important for therapeutic concern because they indicate transition (change) in the person's system. It makes extensive use of the behavioral involvement of the client through the use of role enactment both inside and outside the therapy hour. In summary, Personal Construct Psychotherapy involves the cognitive, affective, and behavioral components of the client's basic meaning dimensions (the personal constructs) to facilitate the client's ability to get on with life projects in a spontaneous manner. The therapist, in this tradition, feels free to appropriate any number of different techniques that enable the client to progress toward optimal functioning.

This system of psychotherapy has been applied to a wide range of problems encompassing schizophrenic thought-disorder, marital counseling, speech disorders, depression, and alcoholism, to name but a few. The application of Personal Construct Psycho-

therapy to these areas has been often accompanied by an empirical investigation of the procedure. This has been largely due to the fact that Kelly provided assessment tools that were integrally related to the psychotherapeutic enterprise.

Expanding on the original writing of George Kelly (1955), Jack Adams-Webber (1979), Donald Bannister (1975), Franz Epting (forthcoming), and A. W. Landfield and L. M. Leitner (1980) provide updated and detailed accounts of this psychotherapeutic system at work. Personal Construct Psychotherapy is best seen as an adventure for both the client and the therapist. It takes the position that new meanings are created by the client, with the therapist serving as a research advisor. These new meanings provide the basis for the client's behavior change and increased understanding of life situations. As a system of psychotherapy, it is constantly being modified by clinical and experimental data provided by investigators in the area.

## REFERENCES

Adams-Webber, J. R. Personal construct theory: Concepts and applications. New York: Wiley, 1979.

Bannister, D. The genesis of schizophrenic thought disorder: A serial invalidation hypothesis. British Journal of Psychiatry, 1963, 109, 680–686.

Bannister, D. Personal construct theory psychotherapy. In D. Bannister (Ed.), Issues and approaches in the psychological therapies. New York: Wiley, 1975.

Bannister, D., Adams-Webber, J., Penn, W. and Radley, A. Reversing the process of thought disorder: A serial validation experiment. British Journal of Social and Clinical Psychology, 1975, 14, 169–180.

Epting, F. R. A personal construct approach to counseling and psychotherapy. New York: Wiley, forthcoming.

Fransella, F. Personal change and reconstruction: Research on a treatment of stuttering. New York: Academic Press, 1972.

Kelly, G. A. The psychology of personal constructs (2 vols). New York: Norton, 1955.

Kelly, G. A. The psychotherapeutic relationship. In B. Maher (Ed.), Clinical psychology and personality: The selected papers of George Kelly. New York: Wiley, 1969.

Landfield, A. W. *Personal construct systems in psychotherapy.* Chicago: Rand McNally, 1971.

Landfield, A. W. A personal construct approach to suicidal behavior. In P. Slater (Ed.), *Explorations in intrapersonal space,* vol. 1. New York: Wiley, 1976.

Landfield, A. W. Exploring socialization through the interpersonal transaction group. In P. Stringer and D. Bannister (Eds.), *Constructs of sociality and individuality.* New York: Academic Press, 1979.

Landfield, A. W. and Leitner, L. M. (Eds.). *Personal construct approaches to psychotherapy and personality.* New York: Wiley, 1980.

Mair, J. M. M. Psychologists are human too. In D. Bannister (Ed.), *Perspectives in personal construct theory.* New York: Academic Press, 1970.

Moreno, J. L. *Who shall survive? A new approach to the problem of human interrelations.* Washington, D.C.: Nervous and Mental Disease Publication, 1934.

Morris, J. B. The prediction and measurement of change in a psychotherapy group using the repertory grid. In F. Fransella and D. Bannister (Eds.), *A manual for repertory grid technique.* New York: Academic Press, 1977.

Ravenette, A. T. Personal construct theory: An approach to the psychological investigation of children and young people. In D. Bannister (Ed.), *New perspectives in personal construct theory.* New York: Academic Press, 1977.

Rowe, A. *The experience of depression.* New York: Wiley, 1978.

Ryle, A. and Breen, D. A comparison of adjusted and maladjusted couples using the double dyad grid. *British Journal of Medical Psychology,* 1972, **45,** 375–382.

Salmon, P. A. A psychology of personal growth. In D. Bannister (Ed.), *Perspectives in personal construct theory.* New York: Academic Press, 1970.

Vaihinger, H. *The philosophy of "as if."* New York: Harcourt, 1925.

# CHAPTER 46

# *PLISSIT Therapy*

JACK S. ANNON

*I take a particular pride in this chapter because I had to convince Jack Annon, the author, that his system of Permission-Limited Information-Specific Suggestions-Intensive Therapy (PLISSIT) was indeed a general system of psychotherapy, one not limited to the treatment of sexual problems.*

*This chapter indicates that Annon's ideas of a four-step process is a kind of equivalent to the theory of medical triage, a most commonsense way of operating. My late teacher Rudolf Dreikurs often told his students that many psychiatrists had probably harmed their patients through an insistence on a thoroughgoing analysis, when perhaps all they needed was a bit of advice.*

*Annon indicates how to operate systematically in practically any situation in order to deal realistically with client problems. Because of this, this chapter should have meaning for all who practice psychotherapy.*

*In my judgment, one of the major problems with practitioners is that they have been programmed to operate practically unthinkingly in one procedure, and they don't use common sense in handling clients. Annon's PLISSIT approach is the acme of common sense, and it should be of value especially to new therapists.*

The PLISSIT approach to therapy is a conceptual scheme for approaching presenting client problems regardless of the clinician's particular therapeutic orientation. The PLISSIT model or, more accurately, P-LI-SS-IT, provides for four levels of approach to each client concern. Each letter or pair of letters designates a suggested method for handling such concerns. The four levels are: Permission-Limited Information-Specific Suggestions-Intensive Therapy.

The first three levels may further be grouped under the heading of Brief Therapy, as contrasted with the fourth level, Intensive Therapy. Brief Therapy in this approach means that it is time and problem limited. Time limited means that client contact may range from one session, lasting anywhere from 15 to 60 minutes, to possibly three to

five such sessions. Problem limited means that the brief approach is best suited to the client with one or two presenting problems as contrasted with a client with multiple areas of concern.

In the PLISSIT model, Intensive Therapy is seen as highly individualized treatment that is necessary because standardized treatment was *not* successful in helping the client reach his or her goals.

## HISTORY

The psychological treatment of client problems has often been costly and time-consuming; and, in the past, often the prognosis for change was not too promising, particularly with problems that have long been known to be resistant to most forms of treatment, such as sexual problems. With the advent of the psychological learning model, some successful therapeutic results were efficiently obtained. However, there was also a clear need for a broad-spectrum approach that allowed the clinician a wide range of therapeutic procedures for implementing a particular treatment strategy. On the other hand, use of a particular procedure just because it was available was obviously not automatically theoretically or therapeutically justified. Careful assessment of relevant factors in the client's life, history, and environment should dictate which treatment procedure to use for which aspect of the client's problem in a given social setting.

Initial assessment should have a direct relationship to the treatment procedure used. Many clinics that do a comprehensive and exhaustive initial assessment still have their clients all go through the same therapy program! In such standardized programs it is difficult to see what purpose an initial intensive assessment serves.

The current stress by many therapists on a broad-spectrum approach to therapy has no virtue unless there is some theoretically based plan for the ordering and selection of appropriate treatment techniques from among the various interventions available. Without such a plan, broad-spectrum treatment is not much different from the shotgun approach of using the same procedures for all client problems.

In response to this situation, it was considered of practical as well as theoretical value to design and carry out a study to investigate various methods of assessment and treatment, particularly in the sexual area, because of the prevalence of such problems and the difficulties associated with their resolution.

Such research was carried out (Annon, 1971) with the goal of developing, testing, and refining a conceptual scheme for the ordering of sexual problems and their treatment from within a psychological learning theory framework. A conceptual scheme for the ordering and treatment of such problems eventually emerged that, when tested in clin-

ical practice, indicated that the approach was highly effective, resulting in positive outcomes, particularly with sexual problems of long duration (e.g., fetishistic, pedophilic, transsexual). Then, as others began to use this approach in different settings with different problems, it became apparent that the scheme was not always appropriate. For example, the system was not particularly suited in settings where the client could not be seen on an ongoing, possibly long-term basis, if needed. Effective use of the system was also restricted to those clinicians who had a thorough knowledge of psychological learning theory together with relevant training and experience in the application of learning theory to client problems. Finally, even those with suitable training and experience who had sufficient time available to devote to the therapy reported that it was often not necessary to use the scheme to treat some of the more common problems presented.

It seemed that the conceptual scheme was appropriate for those problems requiring Intensive Therapy, but not for those that could profit from a brief therapy approach. What was needed was a flexible and comprehensive scheme that could be adapted to many settings and to whatever client or clinician time available. To be most effective such a plan should also be able to be used by a wide variety of people in the helping professions and allow for a range of treatment choices geared to the level of competence of the individual clinician. Ideally, such an approach would also need to provide a framework for screening out and treating those problems that would be responsive to brief therapy approaches from those that might require Intensive Therapy. It would also be helpful if such a scheme could provide a framework for conducting evaluative research. Finally, for those involved in teaching or training therapists, such a model should also offer a method for providing training that could be geared to the level of competence of the individual trainee.

After several years of devising and testing a number of different plans in diverse settings with a variety of sexual problems, a conceptual scheme for treatment that looked promising was finally developed. This tentative scheme was then shared and taught to others, and, after further refinement, the final model emerged. Initially this model was seen as only applicable to treatment in the sexual area. However, extensive use of this scheme has shown that it is equally applicable to a wide range of problem areas, as well as to research and training. Since then this model has been passed on to others via lectures, courses, consultations, workshops, and training programs, as well as through audio tape cassettes (Annon & Robinson, 1977; Hindle, 1978), articles (Annon, 1976b; Pion & Annon, 1975), and books (Annon, 1975, 1976a).

## CURRENT STATUS

A number of people with diverse training in the helping professions have found the PLISSIT model to be useful in their particular area of concentration. For example, it is currently being offered to and used by psychologists (Annon, 1975, 1976a, 1980(a)) as well as physicians (Annon & Robinson, 1980(b), 1981(a); Croft, 1976), and specialists such as obstetricians, gynecologists, and urologists (Hindle, 1978; Pion & Annon, 1975). In addition, others in different areas of specialization, such as social workers (Gochros, 1978; Hirayama, 1979; King, 1977); rehabilitation specialists (Annon & Robinson, 1981(a); sex therapists (Annon & Robinson, 1978, forthcoming (c); Fischer & Gochros, 1977); and family life and human sexuality teachers (Daniel, forthcoming) have also found the conceptual scheme helpful.

The model seems also to be applicable to different populations, such as college students with a variety of majors (Annon & Robinson, 1980, (b); Kelly, 1979), parents of the mentally retarded (Hirayama, 1979), and institutionalized adolescents (Annon & Robinson, (a)).

In addition to the model being used to assist individual clients and couples with a wide range of sexual concerns, it has also been applied to women's groups (Morton & Pion, 1976) as well as to groups of heterosexual couples with various sexual dissatisfactions (Baker & Nagata, 1978).

Finally, the PLISSIT scheme has also been shown to be equally applicable as framework for conducting research and training, and as a guide in the use of vicarious learning principles through audio and visual media in clinical treatment settings (Annon & Robinson, 1978, 1981g; Robinson, 1974a,b).

It is hoped that future applications of the PLISSIT model by different helping professionals with divergent populations presenting varied clinical problems will further define the extent of the scheme's usefulness as well as its limitations.

## THEORY

The research that supplied the impetus for the development of the PLISSIT model was designed to formulate, test, and refine a conceptual scheme for the ordering of sexual problems and their treatment within a psychological learning theory framework. As the research progressed, various inadequacies of then existing schemes of assessment became apparent. When the A-R-D system suggested by Staats (1968) became available, this approach was incorporated into the research. Staats advanced the concept of a human motivational system, which he refers to as the Attitude-Reinforcer-Discriminative (A-R-D) system. He suggested that the same stimulus may have multiple functions in relation to both classical and operant learning. The A-R-D system stands for the three functions that a stimulus may serve. An attitudinal stimulus is defined as a stimulus that has come to elicit an emotional response through the principles of classical conditioning. This same stimulus will also then function as a reinforcing stimulus for operant situations, as well as serve as a discriminative stimulus that may elicit overt behavior. This system has many important implications for the treatment of complex disorders as well as for theoretical considerations of how various behaviors and attitudes may be learned. However, space restrictions do not permit more than this brief background presentation; a more detailed explanation of the system in general (Staats, 1975) and particularly in regard to human sexual behavior (Annon, 1975) is available elsewhere.

The major conclusion of the research was that an initial analysis of a client's sexual problem from within the A-R-D framework, followed by a careful evaluation of relevant behavioral repertoires, offers the most promising conceptual scheme for the ordering of sexual problems and the development of appropriate treatment procedures.

This conclusion was based on a number of considerations. The use of the scheme offered a plan for simultaneously considering the full range of circumstances that might be related to the client's problem. Such an approach also allowed for the ordering of priorities for intervention and provided guidance for the timing of multiple interventions. Finally, the use of such a conceptual scheme was not tied to any particular behavioral technique or procedure, but fostered the development of efficient procedures based upon theoretical analysis.

For the reasons described earlier, a second scheme was then developed to provide a brief therapy approach for clinical concerns, and subsequently the two approaches were combined into the PLISSIT model.

A visual presentation of the proposed model may help clarify how it may theoretically be applied in a variety of clinical settings. Let each line in Figure 1 represent the different presenting concerns that a particular clinician encounters over time. Depending upon his or her setting, profession, and specialty, these problems may represent what he or she meets in one day, one month, one year, or even one professional lifetime. For reasons previously discussed, it would ob-

A Proposed Conceptual Scheme

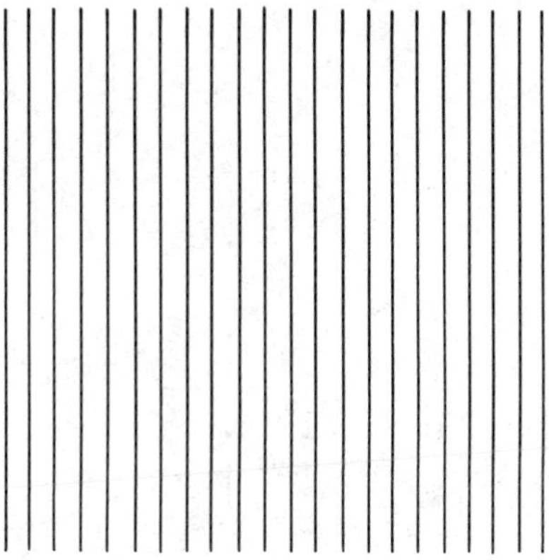

Figure 1    Presenting sexual concerns over time.

viously be inappropriate to attempt to assess and treat each presenting concern in exactly the same way.

Figure 2 depicts the theoretical application of the PLISSIT model to these presenting concerns. As the figure further illustrates, the first three levels can be viewed as Brief Therapy as contrasted with the fourth level, Intensive Therapy.

This model has a number of distinct advantages. It may be used in a variety of settings and adapted to whatever client time is available. Theoretically, each descending level of approach requires increasing degrees of knowledge, training, and skill on the part of the clinician. Because each level requires increasing professional experience, the model thus allows individuals to gear this approach to their own particular level of competence. This also means that therapists now have a plan that aids them in determining when referral elsewhere is appropriate. Most important, the model provides a framework for discriminating between those problems that require Intensive Therapy and those that are responsive to Brief Therapy.

How many levels of approach clinicians will feel competent to use will directly depend upon the amount of interest and time they are willing to devote to expanding their knowledge, training, and skill of each level.

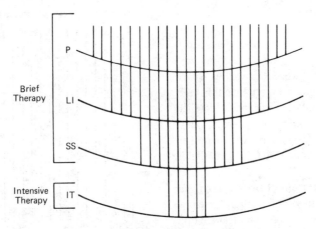

Figure 2   Application of the PLISSIT model.

## METHODOLOGY

While the PLISSIT model may be applied to a wide range of problems, for the sake of consistency it will be described primarily in reference to sexual concerns on the part of a client.

*Permission*   Sometimes all that people want to know is that they are normal, that they are not "perverted," "deviated," or "abnormal." Mostly they would like to find this out from an authority. Many times such people are not bothered by the specific behavior they engage in, but by the thought that there may be something "wrong" or "bad" with what they are doing. Frequently clients just want a professional to act as a sounding board for checking out their concerns. In such cases, the clinician can let them know that they are not unusual and that many people share such concerns. Reassurance that they are normal and permission to continue doing what they have been doing is sufficient in some cases to resolve what might become a major problem. *Permission giving* can be seen as a preventive measure as well as a treatment technique. Permission giving will certainly not solve many problems, but it will resolve some, as Figure 2 suggests. Permission takes minimal preparation on the part

of the clinician. Finally, it may be used to cover a number of areas of concern, such as thoughts, fantasies, dreams, and feelings, as well as overt behaviors.

*Thoughts, Fantasies, and Dreams.* Concerns over sexual thoughts and fantasies are common. It is not unusual for a man or woman to have sexual thoughts or fantasies about people other than their partners, or about people of the same sex, or even about their own parents, or brothers and sisters, or sons and daughters. Such occasional thoughts are quite common. Letting the client know this may relieve some anxiety or guilt feelings about being "abnormal." Only when such thoughts or fantasies become persistent or interfere with other areas of functioning do they create a problem.

Permission giving may also be appropriate for handling dream concerns. It is not unusual for people to have occasional dreams involving sexual activity with a wide variety of people. Reassurance that such dreams are entirely within the normal range and that they are not unusual or indicative of "abnormality" is usually sufficient to relieve anxiety or guilt. Often permission giving is sufficient to stop a recurring sexual dream associated with anxiety, just as it can alleviate persistent thoughts or fantasies.

*Feelings.*   It is not uncommon for people to respond with anxiety when they experience sexual arousal to what they consider inappropriate stimulation. Many such concerns arise from failure to discriminate between arousal resulting from sexual thoughts and fantasies and arousal from direct tactile stimulation.

*Behaviors.*   The degree to which a clinician feels comfortable in giving permission to a client to engage in certain behaviors will be determined by a number of factors, to be discussed shortly. Such permission giving may be applied to a wide range of sexual behaviors that the clinician recognizes as common and normal but that the client does not.

Many sexual concerns can also be handled by giving the client permission *not* to engage in certain sexual behaviors unless he or she chooses to.

The permission-giving approach has a number of advantages. Adaptable to almost any setting, it takes relatively little time or preparation on the part of the therapist. It can resolve a wide range of concerns, and it may prevent new ones from evolving. In addition, it may also be applied in conjunction with all other levels of approach in the PLISSIT model.

*Limitations.*   It may appear that the basic assumption underlying the permission-giving approach is that the therapist may sanction whatever sexual thought, fantasy, or behavior that a consenting adult wishes to privately engage in or engage in with other mutually consenting adults. In a general sense this may be correct; however, there are some definite limitations to such an assumption. While it is ultimately up to the individual client to choose whatever behavior he or she wishes to engage in, "blanket" permission given by the therapist may not be appropriate if the client is not making an informed choice. It is the clinician's responsibility to inform the unaware client of possible adverse conse-

quences that may result from engaging in certain thoughts, fantasies, or behaviors.

Further limitations of the permission-giving approach are set by legal considerations (e.g., sexual activity with children, rape). The extent to which therapists feel comfortable with and are willing to use the permission-giving approach will generally depend upon their breadth of sexual knowledge, their theoretical orientation, and their value system.

The more knowledge clinicians have of sexual behavior in their culture and in others, the more comfortable they may feel in applying this level of treatment. The therapist's particular theoretical or professional orientation may place limits on how appropriate permission giving may be for a particular thought, fantasy, dream, feeling, or behavior. For example, clinicians with a psychoanalytic background may wish to withhold permission for recurrent sexual dreams, preferring to work through such material with the client. Obviously, that is the individual clinician's choice. It is not the intention of this chapter to persuade professionals of any one orientation to change their viewpoint to that of a learning-oriented approach. It is assumed that clinicians will only use suggestions they feel appropriate to their frame of reference, but it is hoped that they may be willing to experiment a little.

Ideally, therapists will not intentionally impose their value system on their clients. In practice, however, this is sometimes difficult to achieve. This does not mean that therapists give up their own personal value systems. There may be times when the client's goals come into direct conflict with the clinician's value system. When this happens it is the clinician's responsibility to clearly inform clients of this and refer them elsewhere where appropriate.

A final important point is self-permission. Clinicians should also be able to give permission to themselves not to be experts. They must not be afraid to say that they do not know the answer when they do not. No one person is a complete expert in this or any other field. Theory, research, and practice in clinical areas are so far-ranging that no one individual or group of individuals can be expected to know or keep abreast of even a sizable fraction of the area. Clinicians do what they can for their clients based on their own knowledge and experience. In some cases, the most important thing that clinicians have to offer is themselves—someone who will listen, who can communicate interest, understanding, and respect, and who will not label or judge the client. If permission giving is not sufficient to resolve the client's concern, and the therapist is not in the appropriate setting or does not have sufficient time or relevant knowledge and skills, then it is the time to refer the client elsewhere. On the other hand, if therapists do have the appropriate setting, knowledge, and skills, then they can move on to the second level of treatment.

## Limited Information

In contrast to permission giving, which is basically telling clients that it is all right to continue doing what they have been doing, *limited information* is seen as providing clients with specific factual information directly relevant to their particular concern. This may result in their continuing to do what they have been doing, or it may result in their doing something different.

Limited information is usually given in conjunction with permission giving. While they may be used as separate levels, there obviously may be overlap between the two. Furthermore, both can also be used in conjunction with the remaining two levels of treatment. However, because each descending level of treatment usually requires more time, knowledge, experience, and skill on the part of the clinician for most effective application, each level is presented and discussed separately.

In giving limited information, it is important for the clinician to do just that, provide "limited" information directly relevant to

the client's concern. Robinson (1974a,b) has provided evidence indicating that even presenting three hours of a broad range of sexual information has little influence on changing a client's attitude or behavior associated with a specific sexual problem; however, presenting limited information *directly* related to the client's problem can effect significant change in relevant attitudes and behavior.

*Limitations.* The extent to which clinicians are willing to use the limited information approach in handling sexual concerns depends on their breadth of knowledge in the sexual area. How clinicians offer such information to their clients will depend on the individual style they feel most comfortable with. For example, with a conservative-appearing, middle-aged couple who hesitantly ask if anal contact is "normal" or "perverted," one may reply, "Such activity is not generally considered unusual or abnormal. A recent national survey of married males and females under 35 indicated that half of them experienced manual anal foreplay, and more than 25 percent had experienced oral-anal foreplay." On the other hand, with a young couple who casually ask if it is possible to transfer germs through oral-genital contact, one may respond, "Yes, it is possible. The mouth has a very high bacteria count."

As with permission giving, the degree to which clinicians feel comfortable with and are willing to use the second limited-information-giving level will also generally depend on their breadth of knowledge, their theoretical orientation, and their value system. The limitations imposed by these factors discussed in the first level of treatment apply here equally as well.

As seen in Figure 2, use of this second level of treatment may resolve some concerns not handled by the first level of treatment, permission, alone. If giving limited information is still not sufficient to resolve the client's concern, therapists have two further options available. They may refer the client for treatment elsewhere, or, if they have the appropriate setting, knowledge, skills, and experience, they may proceed to the third level of treatment.

## Specific Suggestions

Before therapists can give *specific suggestions* to a client, they must first obtain certain relevant specific information. It would not be appropriate to offer specific suggestions without first obtaining necessary information about clients and their unique set of circumstances. If therapists were to immediately launch into a number of suggestions after hearing the client's initial description of the problem (not their ''label'' of the problem), they may not only waste the client's time (e.g., offering suggestions that the client has already tried), but they may further compound the problem. By suggesting inappropriate and possibly useless treatment procedures based on insufficient data, they may overlook other more necessary and appropriate treatment such as medical evaluation and therapy.

*The Problem History.*   What the clinician needs is a problem history. The model proposed here assumes that a comprehensive history is not relevant or necessary at this level. As suggested in Figure 2, the application of the specific suggestion approach may resolve a number of problems that filtered through the first two levels of treatment; but, needless to say, it will not successfully deal with all such problems. If the third level of approach is not helpful to the client, then a complete history may be a necessary first step for Intensive Therapy.

Guidelines for taking a problem history deemed necessary for a brief therapy approach to treatment are outlined in Table 1. The therapists' setting and amount of time available dictates the amount of detail in any problem history. The format suggested in Table 1 is easily adapted to five minutes or five hours.

It is not relevant to the purpose of this chapter to provide further information on the

**Table 1.   The problem history**

1. Description of current problem.
2. Onset and course of problem.
   a.   Onset (age, gradual or sudden, precipitating events, contingencies).
   b.   Course (changes over time: increase, decrease, or fluctuate in severity, frequency, or intensity; functional relationships with other variables).
3. Client's concept of cause and maintenance of the problem.
4. Past treatment and outcome.
   a.   Medical evaluation (specialty, date, form of treatment, results, currently on any medicaton for any reason).
   b. Professional help (specialty, date, form of treatment, results).
   c. Self-treatment (type and results).
5. Current expectancies and goals of treatment (concrete or ideal).

sexual problem history. Those interested in a more detailed explication of the taking of such a problem history along with illustrative case examples may refer to Annon (1976a). Once therapists are familiar with the guidelines and feel comfortable and at ease in obtaining the problem history from clients, they are then ready to apply the third level of treatment.

In contrast to permission and limited information giving, which generally do not require clients to take any active steps to change their behavior unless they choose to, *specific suggestions* are direct attempts to help clients to change their behavior to reach stated goals. Within a brief therapy framework, this means that the approach is time and problem limited. Many suggestions can be given by a therapist who has only a relatively brief period, say 10 to 30 minutes, for a client interview. Specific suggestions may also be used in those situations where the clinician is only able to see the client on one or several occasions at the most. Obviously, these minimum time limits may be expanded and adapted to whatever time that the clinician has available. However, this level of approach is mainly intended for use within the brief therapy framework proposed.

If the suggestions are not seen as helpful within a relatively brief period of time, then Intensive Therapy is probably more appropriate.

As with the previous levels cf treatment, specific suggestions may also be seen as a preventive measure as well as a treatment technique.

Providing clients with specific suggestions directly relevant to their particular sexual problem is designed to help them achieve their stated goals. This level of treatment is particularly effective for dealing with problems concerned with arousal, erection, ejaculation, orgasm, or painful intercourse. The specific suggestions given (e.g., redirection of attention, graded sexual responses, sensate focus techniques, dating sessions, alternate sessions, interrupted stimulation, squeeze technique, vaginal muscle training, etc.) depends on the information obtained in the sexual problem history.

*Limitations.*   Efficient use of this third level of treatment in the PLISSIT approach will largely depend on the therapists' breadth of knowledge in the behavioral and sexual area, their skill and experience, and their awareness of relevant therapeutic suggestions. The limitations discussed previously apply here equally as well. It is not within the province of this chapter to offer specific suggestions covering sexual problems. A detailed description of the application of such suggestions to the more prevalent heterosexual problems is available elsewhere (Annon, 1976a).

As Figure 2 illustrates, this third level of approach concludes the presentation of the brief therapy approach of the PLISSIT model. A number of sexual concerns may successfully be treated by such an approach, but a number of problems not solvable by this approach will filter through. At this point therapists may refer the client for appropriate treatment elsewhere, or if they have the requisite time, knowledge, experience, and skills, they may apply the fourth level of treatment.

## Intensive Therapy

It is not within the scope of this chapter to describe or even to attempt to outline an intensive therapy approach to the treatment of sexual problems. For well-trained therapists, this is the appropriate time to initiate such treatment. For the clinician interested in a psychological learning approach to the intensive treatment of sexual problems, refer to Annon (1975).

## APPLICATIONS

Many in the helping professions have found the PLISSIT model to be useful. It is currently being employed by a wide range of people such as clergymen, nurses, paraprofessionals within a range of disciplines, physicians from diverse specialties, practical nurses, psychiatrists, psychologists, school counselors, social workers, rehabilitation specialists, sex therapists, institutional workers, and teachers, among others.

The approach has also been applied to children, adolescents, and adults with a variety of presenting conditions ranging from mental retardation and physical handicaps to sexual concerns and bedwetting.

Because the PLISSIT model is a conceptual scheme and not a form of psychotherapy, its limitations primarily reside in the use to which it is put by the particular practitioner. Limitations of each level within the model have been described previously.

## CASE EXAMPLES

### Permission

In the case of *feelings*, it has been noted that it is not uncommon for people to respond with anxiety when they experience sexual arousal to what they consider inappropriate stimulation. For example, it is quite normal for a mother who is breastfeeding her baby to occasionally experience some degree of sexual arousal due to the direct tactile stimulation of her breasts rather than to any latent incestuous desire. Another example is the father who experiences an erection when playing with his little boy on his lap. This is not due to latent homosexual tendencies, but due to direct physical stimulation of his penis. Reassuring the client that these are normal, quite common involuntary responses to tactile stimulation may reduce unnecessary anxiety and prevent a minor event from escalating into a major concern. Similar permission giving for such feelings can also apply for horseback and motorcycle riding; tree and rope climbing; the use of tampons, douches, and enemas; or any other behavior that involves tactile stimulation of the breast, genital, or anal areas.

In the area of overt *behavior*, take the case of the couple who read in their favorite magazine that the average frequency of sexual intercourse for people of their age and education is approximately two and a half times a week. Their personal frequency may be eight times a week or eight times a year, but now they begin to worry whether they are "normal," "oversexed," or "undersexed." A response by the clinician that in essence gives them permission to continue with their own preferred frequency may be all that is necessary to relieve their anxiety. There are other numerous examples, such as the man who really likes the "woman on top" position, but remembers reading somewhere that this was indicative of latent homosexual tendencies; or the young couple who "secretly" enjoy mutual oral-genital contact, but they have read or heard somewhere that this is considered "perverted" or "abnormal" or the symptom of "homosexual tendencies." The list could go on indefinitely, but by now the major point should be clear: Many of these types of sexual concerns may be resolved by a permission-giving approach.

As an example of the use of permission *not* to engage in a particular behavior, take the case of the young woman who is receiving pressure from her partner to experience "multiple orgasms" or who has read or heard

that it is every woman's right to "expect and demand them," yet she is very satisfied with the one orgasm that she experiences with her partner and does not really care whether she is multiorgasmic or not. If a professional counselor gives her permission not to experience multiple orgasms unless she chooses to, it may be very helpful to her. Conversely, in the case of the woman who would really like to experience multiple orgasms but is fearful or hesitant that she might then become a "nymphomaniac," permission to be multiorgasmic, if she chooses to, might be a helpful approach. Permission giving is most appropriate and helpful when used in direct relation to the client's goals. Keeping this in mind will make it easier for the clinician to decide what form of permission giving will be most beneficial for a particular client concern.

The limitations of permission giving have been described previously; however, it might be helpful to take an example where permission giving may *not* be helpful because it is given without informed choice. For example, a number of popular books have "given permission" by extolling the joys and harmless fun to be had for indiscriminate use of any sexual fantasy that a person may desire while engaging in masturbation or sexual behavior with a partner. Learning theory suggests, and clinical evidence substantiates (Annon, 1973), that systematically associating thoughts and fantasies with sexual activity is a very powerful means for conditioning arousal to almost any stimuli. This fact has been used to therapeutic advantage. However, in certain circumstances, engaging in such activity by the uninformed may have undesired results. For example, a woman who consistently uses fantasies of dogs while engaging in self-stimulation may eventually find that she is aroused by actual dogs in the environment. Fortunately, such conditioning does not usually take place unless the client systematically uses the same fantasy over an extended period of time. Informing clients of the possible consequences of their behavior and leaving the ultimate choice up to them seems more appropriate than "blanket" permission giving in such cases.

## Limited Information

An illustration of the use of this level of treatment is the case of a young man whose major concern was a feeling of inadequacy because he considered his penis too small in comparison to other males. He had withdrawn from any social contact, was depressed over his situation, and was contemplating trying to obtain surgery to correct his "deficient" penis. He was provided with the usual information that can be given in such cases (e.g., the foreshortening effect of viewing his own penis as compared to looking across at other males; no correlation between flaccid and erect penis size except the tendency for the smaller flaccid penis to become longer in the erect state than the longer flaccid penis; that the average length of the female vagina is usually three to four inches and that there are very few nerve endings inside the vagina). A few minutes of such relevant information giving was sufficient to change his outlook, and within two months he was socially popular and involved in a close sexual relationship with a young woman to whom he eventually became engaged. Of course, it is impossible to predict what might have happened had he not been given such relevant information, but it seems likely that his situation might have progressively deteriorated.

As with permission giving, providing limited information may also be seen as a preventive measure as well as a treatment technique. Also, in the situation described, the client was given permission to have his concern and to accept his own body, but he was not directly given permission to avoid or seek out sexual contact with women. By supplying relevant information, he was provided with an opportunity to change his behavior if he chose to do so.

Providing limited information is also an excellent method for dispelling sexual myths, either specific ones such as those pertaining to genital size or more general ones such as on the average, men and women differ markedly in their capacity to want and to enjoy sexual relations and in their fundamental capacity for responsiveness to sexual stimulation.

General myths, such as the one mentioned above, are quite common in our culture, despite the fact that there is a great deal of evidence to indicate that men and women are far more similar in their capacity for, and experience of, sexual responsiveness than they are dissimilar. Numerous cross-cultural studies from such fields as anthropology and sociology consistently reveal that cultures that are free and encourage women to be free in sexual expression produce sexually responsive women who are uninhibited and as responsive as males. Cultures that encourage and expect women to experience orgasm yield women who do experience orgasm, and vice versa.

Other examples of common areas where limited information can be most helpful are sexual concerns related to breast and genital shape, size, and configuration; masturbation; genital intercourse during menstruation; oral-genital contact; and sexual frequency and performance. It is not within the scope of this chapter to provide extensive information for each of the many possible areas of sexual concern that may be handled by this level of treatment. Such readings are available elsewhere (e.g., Annon, 1976a).

## Specific Suggestions

It may be recalled that, as with the previous levels of treatment, specific suggestions may also be seen as a preventive measure as well as direct treatment.

For example, suggesting to a woman specific ways to avoid experiencing pain associated with genital intercourse may prevent her from eventually experiencing vaginismus. Or direct treatment of ejaculation concerns with a male may prevent the eventual occurrence of erection problems. Also, this level of treatment may easily and advantageously be combined with the previous two levels.

Two common sayings are often quite helpful in applying this particular level of approach. These sayings may be passed directly onto the clients depending on their particular situation. One that is particularly beneficial for clients with concerns about a particular feature of their body is: "It is what you do with what you have rather than what you have that counts." Use of this saying in conjunction with specific suggestions on "what they may do with what they have" can be very effective in promoting attitude and behavior change in a particular client's area of concern.

The second saying has even broader application. Many clients who come in with sexual concerns relating to failure in arousal, erection, orgasm, or ejaculatory control tend to see each sexual contact with their partner as their "final test." If the man again ejaculates too soon, or again does not obtain an erection, he often feels as though he has lost his last chance. Similar concerns are reported by women in search of orgasms. Thoughts such as "Will it happen this time? It's got to happen this time or I'll die!" are not conducive to success in experiencing such goals. Helping the client to learn to say, and to believe "There is always another day," or "There is always another time," or "There is always another occasion" can do a great deal to relieve some of the self-defeating, grim determination that many clients have in trying to overcome their particular sexual problem. In general, it might be helpful to consider such suggestions as falling into three categories: suggestions to the male alone, suggestions to the female alone, and suggestions to the couple. Quite often the clinician is seen by a client with a heterosexual problem who has no immediate partner available. In such cases a number of suggestions can be made regarding self-stimulation procedures (Annon, 1973) that may be helpful to the client until a partner is available. Often, too, clinicians may see a client who is in a relationship with a second person who has a problem, but the second person is not able, or willing, to come in for consultation. Assuming that the second person is looking for suggestions, it is important for clinicians to obtain as much of a problem history as they can in such a situation. Depending on the information that they receive, they can then give whatever suggestions that they feel might be appropriate under the circumstances. However. the most helpful suggestions are usually those that can be made to both partners together. If at all possible, the client should be encouraged to have the partner come in also. If the couple comes in together and if they are willing to cooperate with the treatment suggestions, there is always a higher probability that they will achieve their goals than when one comes in alone. It is always risky in working with one person on a problem that involves two people in such an intimate situation, and the clinician should definitely attempt to see both people involved if at all possible.

*Readings.*   Specific readings may also be suggested by clinicians for a number of reasons. They may be used as another means of providing permission or limited information pertaining to a certain sexual area of client concern. Also, they may be used to supplement specific suggestions that clinicians have made or to promote new client-initiated procedures. Finally, because of time limitations, either on the therapist's or the client's part, readings may be suggested in lieu of any other specific suggestions. It is assumed that clinicians will not suggest any readings to clients until they are first well acquainted with their content and feel comfortable with recommending them.

## Intensive Therapy

Space limitations prevent giving examples of the use of this level of treatment; however, therapists interested in a detailed psychological learning approach to the Intensive Therapy of a number of sexual problems should refer to Annon (1975).

## SUMMARY

The possible advantages of employing the PLISSIT model have been described earlier and will not be repeated here. For those involved in teaching or training sexual therapists, this model may offer a framework for providing training that can be geared to the level of competence of the individual trainee. For clinicians, it is hoped that the model may provide a framework within which they can continue to develop and expand their knowledge, experience, and skills.

Clinicians will naturally have to adapt their use of the PLISSIT model to their particular setting, the amount of time available to them, and their particular level of competence. It is also important to emphasize that while the Brief Therapy part of the model is not intended to resolve all sexual problems, it may handle many.

Gambrill (1977) believes that one of the important aspects of the PLISSIT model is that it insures that clients will receive therapy that is suited for them as well as insuring that a problem that can be altered by Brief Therapy is not treated by an expensive and time-consuming program.

It is this writer's firm opinion, based on an increasing amount of clinical and research evidence, that it is unethical to involve clients in an expensive, long-term treatment program without first trying to resolve problems within a brief therapy approach. As the schematic presentation in Figure 2 implies, a number of sexual concerns may successfully be treated by a brief approach if the clinician is willing to apply it. On the other hand, as the model also indicates, a number of problems that cannot be solved by this approach will filter through. There will be times when the specific suggestions that may work for many others will not be effective for a particular client's problem, whether the clinician has suggested one or a dozen. There will also be times when interpersonal conflict may prevent many of the suggestions from being carried through. When this happens, and when clinicians feel that they have done as

much as they can from within the brief therapy approach, then it is time for highly individualized Intensive Therapy.

Kelly (1979) used this distinction of the PLISSIT model to draw a comparison between *sex counseling* and *Sex Therapy*. He pointed out that sex counseling concentrates more on the permission and limited information levels, and sometimes includes the specific suggestion level. He sees Sex Therapy as concentrating more on the specific suggestion and intensive therapy levels.

In the PLISSIT model proposed here, Intensive Therapy does not mean an extended standardized program of treatment. By their very nature such standardized programs will not be of help to some people, or they may not even be necessary. Many of the essential elements of some of the current standardized programs may be successfully utilized within a brief therapy approach. In the PLISSIT model, Intensive Therapy is seen as highly individualized treatment necessary because standardized treatment was *not* successful in helping clients to reach their goals. In the present framework, Intensive Therapy requires that a careful initial assessment of the client's unique situation and experiences be performed to devise a tailor-made therapeutic program unique to particular individuals and to their life circumstances. This is particularly important, because what is available to the client beyond the fourth level of treatment?

## REFERENCES

Annon, J. S. The extension of learning principles to the analysis and treatment of sexual problems. Ph.D. dissertation, University of Hawaii, 1971. Reprinted in *Dissertation Abstracts International*, 1971, **32 (6-B),** 3627. (University Microfilms No. 72-290, 570)

Annon, J. S. The therapeutic use of masturbation in the treatment of sexual disorders. In R. D. Rubin, J. P. Brady and J. D. Henderson (Eds.), *Advances in behavior therapy*, vol. 4. New York: Academic Press, 1973. (Also in J. Fischer and H. L. Gochros [Eds.], *A handbook of behavior therapy with sexual problems, vol. 1. General Procedures*. New York: Pergamon Press, 1977)

Annon, J. S. *The behavioral treatment of sexual problems: Intensive therapy.* Honolulu: Enabling Systems, 1975.

Annon, J. S. *The behavioral treatment of sexual problems: Brief therapy.* New York: Harper & Row, 1976a.

Annon, J. S. The PLISSIT model: A proposed conceptual scheme for the behavioral treatment of sexual problems. *Journal of Sex Education and Therapy,* 1976b, **2 (1),** 1–15. (Also in J. Fischer and H. L. Gochros [Eds.], *A Handbook of Behavior Therapy with Sexual Problems, vol. 1. General Procedures.* New York: Pergamon Press, 1977)

Annon, J. S. and Robinson, C. H. *The plissit approach to sex therapy.* Tape cassette E-7, Washington, D.C.: AASECT, 1977.

Annon, J. S. and Robinson, C. H. The use of vicarious learning in the treatment of sexual concerns. In J. LoPiccolo and L. LoPiccolo (Eds.), *Handbook of sex therapy.* New York: Plenum Press, 1978.

Annon, J. S. and Robinson, C. H. Sexual disorders. In A. E. Kazdin, A. Bellack and M. Hersen (Eds.), *New perspectives in abnormal psychology.* New York: Oxford University Press, 1980 (a).

Annon, J. S. and Robinson, C. H. The behavioral treatment of sexual dysfunctions. In A. Sha'Ked (Ed.), *Human sexuality in rehabilitation medicine.* Baltimore: Williams & Wilkins, 1981 (a).

Annon, J. S. and Robinson, C. H. A practical approach to day to day sexual problems. In D. A. Shore and H. L. Gochros (Eds.), *Sexual problems of adolescents in institutions.* Springfield, Ill.: Charles C Thomas, 1981 (a).

Annon, J. S. and Robinson, D. H. Sex therapies—peer and self-counseling. In W. E. Johnson (Ed.), *Sex in life.* New York: William Brown, 1981 (b).

Annon, J. S. and Robinson, C. H. Sexual disorders. In A. E. Kazdin, A. Bellack and M. Hersen (Eds.), *New perspectives in abnormal psychology.* New York: Oxford University Press, 1980 (a).

Annon, J. S. and Robinson, C. H. Treatment of common male and female sexual concerns. In J. M. Ferguson and C. B. Taylor (Eds.), *Comprehensive handbook of behavioral medicine, Vol. 1: Systems intervention,* New York: SP Medical & Scientific Books, 1980 (b).

Annon, J. S. and Robinson, C. H. Video in sex therapy. In J. L. Fryrear and B. Fleshman (Eds.), *Videotherapy, in Mental Health,* Springfield, C. C. Thomas, 1981 (b).

Baker, L. D. and Nagata, F. S. A group approach to the treatment of heterosexual couples with sexual dissatisfactions. *Journal of Sex Education and Therapy,* 1978, **4 (1),** 15–18.

Croft, H. A. Managing common sexual problems: A multilevel treatment model. *Postgraduate Medicine,* 1976, **60 (5),** 186–190.

Daniel, R. S. *Methods and materials for the human sexuality and family life professions. Vol. 1, An annotated guide to the audiovisuals.* Forthcoming.

Fischer, J. and Gochros, H. L. (Eds.). *A handbook of behavior therapy with sexual problems. Vol. 1, General procedures.* New York: Pergamon Press, 1977.

Gambrill, E. D. *Behavior modification: Handbook of assessment, intervention, and evaluation.* San Francisco: Jossey-Bass, 1977.

Gochros, H. L. Personal communication, 1978.

Hindle, W. H. The brief management of sexual problems. In *Female Emotional Problems.* Tape cassette, vol. 25 (12). Los Angeles: Audio-Digest Foundation, 1978.

Hirayama, H. Sex education training for parents of the mentally retarded: Trainer's guide. Unpublished manuscript. Memphis, Tenn.: University of Tennessee, 1979.

Kelly, G. F. *Sexuality—the human perspective.* Woodbury, N.Y.: Barron's Educational Series, 1979.

King, N. J. Handbook of human sexuality. Unpublished manuscript. Victoria, Australia: Preston Institute of Technology, 1977.

Morton, T. L. and Pion, G. A sexual enhancement group for women. *Journal of Sex Education and Therapy,* 1976, **2 (1),** 35–38.

Pion, R. J. and Annon, J. S. The office management of sexual problems: Brief therapy approaches. *The Journal of Reproductive Medicine,* 1975, **15 (4),** 127–144.

Robinson, C. H. The effects of observational learning on the masturbation patterns of preorgasmic females. Paper presented at the annual meeting of the Society for the Scientific Study of Sex, Las Vegas, November 1974a.

Robinson, C. H. The effects of observational learning on sexual behaviors and attitudes in orgasmic dysfunctional women. Ph.D. dissertation, University of Hawaii, 1974b. Reprinted in *Dissertation Abstracts International,* 1975, **35 (9-B).** (University Microfilms No. 75-5040, 221.) (b)

Staats, A. W. Social behaviorism and human motivation. Principles of the attitude-reinforcer-discriminative system. In A. G. Greenwald, T. C. Brook and T. M. Ostrom (Eds.), *Psychological foundations of attitudes.* New York: Academic Press, 1968.

Staats, A. W. *Social behaviorism.* Homewood, Ill.: Dorsey Press, 1975.

# CHAPTER 47

# *Poetry Therapy*

ARTHUR LERNER

*There is something unusual about proponents of various psychological systems and therapies. They tend to become obsessed with the value of their work and frequently are blind to the values of other points of view. My own experience with several dozen therapy innovators and initiators, including some in this book, bears this out. But there are exceptions, and Arthur Lerner is one of these. Modest and unpretentious, a thoroughly well-grounded individual (with, among other things, two doctorates, one in psychology and one in literature), he is an enormously hard worker and strong proponent of Poetry Therapy, but at the same time he is aware of the limitations of this technique, seeing it as an ancillary procedure rather than the method to end all methods.*

*I believe that the person who wishes to be a truly complete therapist should understand the value of each of the modalities covered herein and should experiment with those that he or she feels comfortable with. Poetry, whether reading it or composing it, should help some individuals to understand themselves better and learn how to fit into the world.*

Poetry Therapy is an operational term for the use of poetry in the therapeutic experience. The therapeutic experience may involve a one-to-one relationship, a group process, and/or both. Poetry in the therapeutic experience is, therefore, an eclectic and adjunctive phenomenon that can be used to complement any prevailing psychotherapy.

## HISTORY

### Precursors

Song, prayer, and poetry as healing agents have been used by shamans, witch doctors, and medicine men since earliest times. Along with this, the holy books of all societies contain poetic statements and poetry that act as healing/counseling/therapy supports.

In ancient Greek mythology, Apollo was thought of as the god of light, the god of reason, and the god of poetry. His son Asclepius was the god of healing. Thus, in one family, poetry and healing were united. Reason and emotion were the two major life elements with which the Greeks grappled. Their poetic drama addressed itself to deep life forces and the price paid in not attending to emotional blind spots. Their concern was to find an even keel, a balanced view—everything in moderation.

Aristotle (384–322 B.C.) in his *Poetics* observed literature very much in the fashion of a naturalist or scientist. He believed strongly in the concept of *psychagogia*, the leading out of the soul through the thrust and power of art, and pointed out that poetry was deeply rooted in two aspects of human nature that he regarded as instincts, imitation and a combining of harmony and rhythm (or meter). It is interesting to note how in contemporary psychological theory cognates of Aristotelian thought can be found in such concepts as modeling, integration, life style, closure, and a host of other terms.

Aristotle also believed that poetry was a form of knowledge, having a positive moral effect on the psyche. He went on to use the term *katharsis,* a purgation of the emotions through pity and fear. It is well to remember that Aristotle's frame of reference in the *Poetics* is Greek tragedy, the form and spirit which are always poetic.

The process involved in Aristotle's concept of *katharsis* includes both a controlling and directing of emotions, reminiscent of William Wordsworth's lines in "Intimations of Immortality":

To me alone there came a thought of grief;
A timely utterance gave that thought relief,
And I again am strong.

## Beginnings

At this time of writing there is no definitive history of Poetry Therapy. However, certain events and literary contributions pinpoint the beginnings of the field.

Poetry Therapy has been used at the Pennsylvania Hospital for almost 200 years and is still part of its Milieu Therapy. Jones (1969) indicated that Pennsylvania Hospital began to publish a newspaper, *The Illuminator,* in 1843 in which the mental patients did the writing (including poetry), editing, and hand copying.

In an essay in 1908 entitled "The Relation of the Poet to Day-Dreaming," Sigmund Freud observed that the imaginative writer is close to the daydream and that the poet's work was the daydream or wish. Carl Jung (1933) believed that in a psychoanalytic frame of reference a great work of art is like a dream. He felt a poem touched something in man that dealt with the problem of human existence, not necessarily from a personal point of view.

An essential work, *The Poetic Mind* (1922) by Prescott, was ignored for many years. Eventually it was reprinted in 1959. Prescott,

a professor of English, concerned himself with two aspects of poetry, unconscious determinants of inspiration and the phenomenon of dream life with its relevance to poetic expression. He also based some of his thinking on the tenets advanced by an Anglican clergyman, the Reverend John Keble, who 18 years prior to the birth of Freud set off the Oxford movement with his sermon on July 14, 1833 at St. Mary's Church in Oxford. Keble believed that literature was disguised wish fulfillment and that poetry provided an outlet and a catharsis that prevented madness.

Blanton, author of *The Healing Power of Poetry* (1960), indicated the breadth of a psychiatrist's use of poetry in 40 years of practice.

A major thrust in the growth of Poetry Therapy was due to the efforts of Eli Greifer (1902–1966) and Jack Leedy, a psychiatrist. Greifer, trained as a lawyer and pharmacist, found refuge and relief in poetry. He published, filed, and catalogued poems to meet specific ailments in the same fashion as a prescription. In *Poetry Therapy* (1969) Leedy informed us that Greifer was a volunteer in treating the emotionally ill through poetry under psychotherapeutic supervision. Greifer went to the Cumberland Hospital in Brooklyn in 1959 where, along with Samuel Spector and Leedy, poemtherapy evolved into Poetry Therapy. The Association for Poetry Therapy was organized in 1969 and has since sponsored world conferences.

In 1971 Julius Griffin, a psychiatrist, established the Calabasas Neuropsychiatric Center in California. A believer in replacing the custodial care concept with a therapeutic one, Griffin invited Arthur Lerner, a poet and psychologist, to be poet in residence and poetry therapist at the newly formed installation. This was a novel event in psychiatric history at a proprietary mental health setting. Later, under new management, the name of the center was changed to Woodview Calabasas Hospital. Abrams (1978) provides a vivid account of the poetry therapy program at Woodview, making it clear that poetry can easily be incorporated into the treatment program of a psychiatric hospital.

Another event of importance in the development of Poetry Therapy was the founding of the Poetry Therapy Institute in Encino, California, in 1973. The Institute, concerned with education, research, and therapy, offers workshops in cooperation with colleges, universities, hospitals, clinics, schools, and community mental health centers. In the summer of 1979, it co-sponsored the First National Conference on Poetry Therapy with Immaculate Heart College in Los Angeles.

## CURRENT STATUS

In addition to the Poetry Therapy Institute in Encino, California, other organizations offer courses and/or training programs in Poetry Therapy. These include the New School for Social Research in New York City; St. Elizabeth's Hospital in Washington, D.C.; the Institute for Sociotherapy in New York City; the American Academy for Poetry Therapy in Austin, Texas; the Association for Poetry Therapy in Columbus, Ohio; the Poetry Therapy Outreach Program in Fort Lauderdale, Florida; and the Louisville Poetry Therapy Institute in Louisville, Kentucky. This list is by no means complete.

In *The Therapy of Poetry* (1972) Molly Harrower argued that poetry is therapy and is vitally related to normal personality development. She offered many of her poems to point up her rationale. In doing this she has encouraged many individuals to focus on their own poetry as part of their normal developing process.

Leedy, as editor of *Poetry the Healer* (1973), expanded the scope of poetry as a therapeutic modality. In *Psychopoetry* (1976) Schloss reflected the influence of J. L. Moreno, the father of Group Psychotherapy and Psychodrama, and credited Moreno with using the term "psychopoetry" long before the current usage of Poetry Therapy. Schloss and Grundy (1978) also developed

this psychodramatic orientation by illustrating diverse psychopoetry techniques.

In *Poetry in the Therapeutic Experience* (1978), Lerner indicated that Poetry Therapy is groping for a basic rationale and is in need of carefully defined and refined research. Though there is evidence of the power of poetry as a healing agent in therapy, Lauer (1978) is of the opinion that Poetry Therapy is not altogether harmless.

Some practitioners have agreed that since Poetry Therapy is an ancillary modality, only specially trained individuals (facilitators and aides) with supervised experience and background in basic courses in psychology and human dynamics should be judged qualified to employ it. Others argue that only the bonafide professional—that is, psychiatrist, psychologist, counselor, and the like—should be involved in Poetry Therapy.

As of this writing, there is no evidence that any accredited college or university offers a specific curriculum with Poetry Therapy as a major, leading toward an undergraduate or graduate degree. Courses in Poetry Therapy are offered at various schools from time to time under diverse headings, such as Creative Arts Therapy or Expressive Arts Therapy. As of now, one "learns" Poetry Therapy by attending sessions where the process is taking place and then finds volunteer or paid work while under supervision. No state at present certifies poetry therapists per se.

In the appendixes of *Using Bibliotherapy: A Guide to Theory and Practice* (1978) Rubin lists points of information regarding certification and training for various programs, including among others Poetry Therapy.

## THEORY

One way of looking at Poetry Therapy is as a "merging" of two fields, poetry and therapy. It is important to note that poetry has been around longer than therapy and to remember that the rationale for the two fields is based on different experiences and assumptions. Rothenberg (1973) pointed out the similarities and differences of poetry and therapy in terms of the process of poetic creation and psychotherapy. He is most circumspect in his assumptions and draws conclusions from three sources involved in the creative process, namely, interview studies, manuscript studies, and experimental studies. One of the key points Rothenberg makes is to remind us that the poetic process as such does not involve a helping relationship. Though some poets may view themselves as helpers, their role is not intrinsic to the total therapeutic process.

In spite of difficulties certain guidelines of operation are beginning to emerge that may eventually lead to a refined theory of Poetry Therapy. The following are not all inclusive, not given in any order of importance, and will be familiar to psychologists within their own frame of reference.

1.  The use of poetry in a therapy milieu is an ancillary tool and can be employed on a one-to-one basis, group basis, and/or both.

2.  The emphasis in using poetry in therapy is upon the reaction of the person; in poetry workshop, the accent is on the poem.

3.  The poem may act as (a) a catalyst through which emotions are filtered, (b) an interpretation, (c) a projective instrument, and (d) even be considered as a dream.

4.  The basic power charge of the poem is metaphor and simile.

5.  A poem is most effective when geared to the level of feeling and understanding of the individual. This, of course, is a tenet of sound education based on proven laws of learning.

6.  The same poem that may be meaningful to person A at one point in time may not be at another. Likewise, a poem may be "effective" with person A and not be effective with person B, who may have a similar problem. At present there is no evidence that one can prescribe poems for specific ailments with assurance that effective healing will result.

7.  The use of a poem in therapy may enable the person to facilitate his or her own understanding of feelings, life styles, and preferences.

In addition to the interacting and reflecting that accompanies the communication process, the use of poetry in the therapeutic experience involves verbal and nonverbal phenomena. Meerloo (1969) has pointed up the idea that rhythm is essential in life and expresses feelings that were formerly repressed. Each of us is involved in repetition of archaic patterns of behavior. Beginning with our intrauterine life, biological rhythm is a vital part of the human condition. Through rhythm we can bring up forgotten memories. Often the rhyme and rhythm of poetry have a greater effect on our personality than the actual meaning of the words.

Additionally, the way we perceive things does not necessarily provide a "correct" picture of our observations. Ansell (1978) has suggested that we live each day experiencing speech and behavior through a network of illusions. Underneath it all lurks the possibility that Walt Whitman has so poignantly expressed:

Of the terrible doubt of appearances,
Of the uncertainty after all, that we may be deluded

*Leaves of Grass*

It has also been suggested that, like all the arts, poetry provides an aesthetic experience when it is introduced as part of the healing process. However, in Poetry Therapy, again as in all the healing arts, the aesthetic experience itself is often involved with personality dynamics and unique personal patterns in the development of growth and behavior. Some point to the possibility of a self-hierarchy pattern. Edgar (1978), making use of a Jungian frame of reference in Poetry Therapy, reported an evolutionary and sequential pattern of growth as part of the epiphany of selfhood.

This writer's own experience is that a poem used in therapy enables an individual to enlarge the scope of awareness, retreat from situations, decry, meet a newer concept that has just emerged, or not be affected at all. What is emphasized here is that since all theories of psychotherapy can include poetry in the therapeutic situation, the dynamics of each postulate are operating. Hence, it is to the poetry therapist's interest to have a wide acquaintance with theories of personality and psychotherapy in order to use poetry as an effective ancillary tool.

The use of poetry in therapy often evokes primary processes that go beyond the written and spoken word, and that activate fantasy and archetypal images deeply buried within the psyche. Affects aroused via poetry, primarily through simile, metaphor, and/or rhythm, can in the hands of an able therapist lead to wholesome self-expression and creativity, the raising of personal esteem, and help in developing insight on the part of the patient.

What then may be the goal as the process of Poetry Therapy unfolds? Regardless of the therapist's frame of reference, Stainbrook (1978) clearly indicates the significance of the joining of forces of poetry and therapy when he states:

Finally, and perhaps most important, there exists the possibility that in its optimum potential the merger of poetry with therapy may result in the revitalizing and remoralizing of the self by providing a wholeness of consciousness—an integration of emotion, cognition, and imagery—with which to create and maintain personal meaning. (p. 11)

The above statement provides room for the wide variety of processes as reflected in current psychotherapies and for the many elements of theory considered in current personality constructs.

## METHODOLOGY

The poetry therapist's goal during the first session, whether individual or group, is to enable the participant to "feel right" about being present. A person coming to therapy for the first time generally has feelings of anxiety and frustration, to say the least. This state is often compounded when poetry becomes the catalyst through which emotions and feelings will be expressed.

The setting in a group session is usually in a fairly large room with people sitting around in a circle. There are no tables or other obstructions to hide members from each other. Poetry books are found on the floor within the circle or copies of poetry may be on the seats as people enter; or copies may be handed out. In addition, group members bring in their own poems. Paper and pencil are also available. There may be a record player and/or a tape recorder in the event music is played and poems are read aloud.

Patients are usually professionally referred in a hospital setting. In other settings, such as clinics, counseling centers, and the like, the selection may be the same or it may be modified to fit the philosophy and schedule of the organization. It is important to let the participants know from the beginning that they are not involved in a poetry workshop. Otherwise, well-meaning individuals, often highly talented, will expect to gain kudos for their own poetry. In addition to being a human need, this expectancy may be vitally tied in with personality factors.

Along with the therapist there are one or two poetry therapy facilitators. Their roles are made clear to the group during the initial session. They assist the therapist in all ways, except that the final therapeutic responsibility rests with the therapist.

The element of applying the arts to therapy, particularly a verbal art such as poetry, often evokes feelings suggestive of a "high." Euphoria may be part of a therapeutic experience, but in and of itself it is not therapy.

Poetry in therapy has been discussed in

this chapter with the assumption that a bona fide therapist is involved in the experience. There is no carefully defined ongoing research program at this time concerned with selection, participatory experiences, process, content of poetry therapy sessions, and the like. What we do find is "Poetry Therapy" in hospitals, clinics, private settings, prisons, jails, mental health centers, schools, community centers, gerontology centers, and a host of other places. Included are varied ages, personalities, problems, ethnic groups, and so forth.

In some instances poetry in the settings mentioned above is featured under such headings as "growth through poetry," "communication through poetry," and others. At the other end of the spectrum are therapists and aides or facilitators working under supervision of a trained therapist and engaging in the practice of Poetry Therapy with individuals who have been assigned by their primary therapists. Following each session entries are made in charts and the primary therapist has a chance to review these so as to gain a fuller understanding of an individual's total progress. Facilitators also attend case conferences and thus have an opportunity to discuss mutual professional problems.

It has been this writer's experience that *closure* of each group session is most important. There is a *warmup*, of course, varying all the way from introduction by name and "How do you feel?" to "Let's say anything that comes to our minds." The closure generally involves either sitting or standing up and forming a circle with arms around each other and going around the room stating feelings. Every therapist soon learns that there are some individuals who do not like to be touched or have their arms around each other. While this is to be respected, it is also to be considered in light of the person's individual history and dynamics.

Intuitive experience is a vital part of poetry in the therapy; the therapist soon finds poems to deal not only with the material that has been brought up but finds a host of poems

that touch upon questions of personal behavior patterns. Poetry often acts as a "softening up" process for deeper interpretations, and represents a compelling challenge to facilitator, therapist, and participant, who form an important trinity.

## APPLICATION

One of the basic ingredients of all poetry therapy sessions, individual or group, is the genuine feelings that poems are able to tap. The atmosphere in Poetry Therapy must, therefore, be honest. What one does not say, the poem does say. Each is revealed as a person who hurts, enjoys, hates, smiles, and feels. The therapist is no exception and cannot hide for long behind knowledge, degrees, status, or whatever. One of the poems that has been used most effectively in uncovering feelings and laying open many defenses is entitled "A Poison Tree" by William Blake. The first four lines seem to do the trick. It reads:

> I was angry with my friend:
> I told my wrath, my wrath did end.
> I was angry with my foe:
> I told it not, my wrath did grow.

The poem opens up many vistas of feelings that touch upon theoretical approaches of psychotherapy and personality.

Groups are either closed or open, depending upon a host of circumstances. They are composed of both sexes as a rule, with a wide range of problems. Sometimes adolescents, young adults, and adults are together. Sometimes they are in separate groups. The addition of poetry to the therapeutic experience does not change the theoretical vantage point of the therapy or the therapist. Questions related to theory and practice still remain.

In general, most individuals, except the acting-out, the medicated and depressed who are "out of it," the extremely disturbed person who can't sit still or won't stop talking (and even they in some instances), can avail themselves of the healing potential inherent in Poetry Therapy. This writer has also conducted poetry therapy sessions, individual and group, with the blind, physically handicapped, mentally handicapped, and illiterate; it has been found to be an effective healing modality.

Because poetry is involved with metaphor and simile, primary processes are easily activated. Thus the skill of the therapist involves not only proficiency in therapy but a wide acquaintance with all kinds of poems—classical, modern, universal, good, and bad. Since the therapist may not have the background in the area of poetry, poetry therapy facilitators can help in the process of effecting a sound program. In this context, therapists can learn a new modality and can also concentrate more fully on the treatment aspect of their concern.

Finally, a word of caution. Poetry in therapy is a most seductive challenge in the nature of things. Each therapist sooner or later learns the importance of being aware of limitations. To illustrate, the poem ''Knowing Pains,'' written after a disturbing group session, enabled the writer of this chapter to cope with his own blind spots.

> I studied parts
> of a flower
>
> to understand
> its flowering.
>
> I learned much
> about my limits.
>
> I had forgotten
> Earth and climate.

## CASE EXAMPLE

The case example presented is a segment from a group session. This is offered in light of exploratory possibilities. The emphasis is on process and how poetry moves this process within the framework of a therapeutic milieu.

In this example, Martin R is singled out as the focal point around which the group enters into the poetry therapy situation. Each session was an hour in length. Meetings were held weekly. This was an open group. Each week there was generally one or two new people, while one of the old members was discharged. All the members mentioned had been together from the initial session and had stayed together throughout an eight-session experience. The group was composed of 10 members (only eight for the final session), a facilitator, and the poetry therapist.

Martin R, a 39-year-old male, had been institutionalized off and on for some 12 years. He was married, had a five-year-old son, whom he ''dearly loved'' and who was a source of ambivalent feelings. Martin was diagnosed as a person who suffered from chronic depression.

Both of Martin's parents were alive. Martin was the eldest of four children (two sisters and a brother). He had dropped out of college in his third year, after realizing that ''accounting was not for me.'' His vocational history included all kinds of odds and ends such as maintenance, tour guide, gardener, truck driver, news vendor, and messenger. He also had spent three years in the service, primarily as a clerk-typist, and received an honorable discharge. As far as could be ascertained, he had had no history of hospitalization while in the service.

Throughout his formative years he was close to both parents and ''got along fairly well with others.'' He claimed his troubles began when ''I began to feel too much pain in my head.'' And that started, as he remembered, when his brother, who was still a high school junior, came home one day and told his parents he had gotten a job as an usher in a theater. Martin, four years older than his brother, felt ''like he'd been hit with a ton of bricks.'' He became consciously aware of feeling inferior to his brother and sisters. ''I remember feeling as if the world had caved in. My younger brother had gotten a job and it made me feel like he had pulled me down.'' In the poetry therapy session, the third he had attended, he wrote these lines:

I remember my brother as a hustling man
Who got a job and made me feel
Like an also-ran.

The group began to question his "also ran" description, and it became quite evident that he felt hostile toward his brother. This can be seen in the following lines he wrote during the session:

My brother Pete is a good soul
Who knows his place and goal
My brother Pete I love and hate him so
But my hatred steals the show.

Since this session was about to come to an end, it was suggested that Martin think about what he had said and had written and comment upon them at the next session. He agreed to do so. At the beginning of the following session, which was the last, he addressed the group by reading:

This is a brief note to all of you.
I really felt last week
I had been gotten to. So I'll
tell you, it ain't easy to
be true, to reach
inside and get something
out which is new and
you don't know how to
put into words. You're
shaky at first, but then
it all fits
and falls into place.

There were eight people at this session; segments of the interaction process follow.

ALICE   (a 48-year-old mother of three, diagnosed as hypochondriacal and depressive):   Martin, everytime I hear you talk, it's like I'm hearing myself. We're both playing broken records—like we're losers.

MARTIN:   I don't know about that.

FACILITATOR:   Martin, what don't you know?

MARTIN:   I don't know—maybe.

JIM   (a 52-year-old male, father of two, diagnosed as borderline schizophrenic):   I agree. Maybe you don't know. But you sound like me and I sound like Alice just said. I sound like both of you. I wrote this over the weekend:

Martin wrote some lines which hurt me
Real bad. I'm glad to hear them
Again and again. I'm no longer sad.
Martin may have planted the truth
Which will help me grow healthy fruit.

POETRY THERAPIST:   I hear you saying, Jim, that Martin's lines began to have a big effect upon your feelings, particularly over the weekend. Maybe others in the group felt the same or had other reactions.

JERRY   (a 49-year-old widower, father of five, diagnosed as chronic alcoholic):   Yes, I felt something too. It seems I hear lots of honesty at times and then run, unless someone says, write, or I read about my situation.

FACILITATOR:   What do you feel right now, Martin?

MARTIN:   This group does funny things to me. When I'm in the group I learn a lot I don't understand. But I know I'm learning. And it seems to get to me too when I'm on the ward—in my room. It's like the group's fault I'm writing. Here is what I wrote about an hour ago. Here are my lines:

Whenever I'm angry, I feel inferior
Whenever I feel inferior, I'm angry
They both go hand in hand
I often wonder why I'm angry
I haven't learned to be
Totally me and free to be.

FACILITATOR:   Martin, have you discussed how you feel with your own therapist? It looks to me that you say some things in here that you find tough to share with others.

JIM:   Martin! How does this grab you? I picked it up from somewhere. I thought it was deep stuff, but the more I read it the easier it becomes. It's a line from Shakespeare, so they tell me: ''Things growing are not ripe until their season.'' Maybe you're coming into your own now. What do you say?

MARTIN:    This line you've read reminds me of what the Bible says about there being a season to everything—I guess my season is here. I still find it hard to communicate easily.

FACILITATOR:    Getting well inside often comes in slow stages.

MARTIN:    I guess that's so. Getting well on the outside also comes in slow stages.

POETRY THERAPIST:    What do you mean? I'm not quite clear what you're saying.

MARTIN:    (hesitatingly) I'm saying—I guess I am—that many times my head and body were telling me to avoid something or say no. I found myself saying yes and not meaning it. What a price to pay. I needed a lot of strength to keep my body from showing I was lying.

TONI    (a 25-year-old divorcee diagnosed as chronic depressive):    Martin, I know what you mean. I suffer too, like you. We both need psychological tune-ups.

POETRY THERAPIST:    Toni! What is a psychological tune-up?

TONI:    It's keeping your mind, body, and heart in close—well, I mean all these three should feel right with each other. I wrote these lines and I think they fit. Here:

> When my mind, body, and heart feel right
> I'm at my best with all my might.
> When all three are out of whack
> I feel I'm going to crack.

MARTIN:    Right! I agree! It takes time. Like the talking about the seasons before—

POETRY THERAPIST:    It seems to me, you haven't been able to express this before. Do you feel what you're saying? How do you feel it?

MARTIN:    This is the last session. I'll just say I feel what we're talking about will take time. I've just got to learn more patience. By the way, I've kept a notebook and diary—I don't have them with me. But I remember a line I've written goes like this:

> patience is a tough school
> in learning self-rule.

The session ended shortly after and all group members, including Martin, were discharged in a few days.

## SUMMARY

Poetry in the therapeutic experience is used as an adjunctive tool. Poetry can be used in therapy on a one-to-one basis and/or group basis. Furthermore, the accent in Poetry Therapy is on the person, unlike a poetry workshop where the accent is on the poem. Poetry Therapy is an eclectic experience. Theories of personality and psychotherapy underlying the field can be found in current psychotherapy and personality constructs.

The use of poetry in therapy is based on an assumption of openness, self-awareness of one's body and feelings, and acceptance of here-and-now life experiences. Inherent in this experience, as in all therapy experiences, are educational and spiritual elements that make for conditions of focusing on personal capacities for growth and creativity. The fact that a poem is saying what a person may be feeling acts like a Greek chorus in moving the drama along.

Poetry in therapy is being introduced in a wide variety of milieus at the present time and is greatly aided in its growth by especially trained facilitators who are knowledgeable in poetry and supervised in therapy. At present there are not many therapists versed in poetry. Thus the facilitator acts as a positive factor in the poetry therapy process.

Because process and psychotherapy movement are closely related, the use of poetry in therapy has carryover affects when individuals are away from their sessions. Often this reflects itself in poetry reading and/or writing by members.

Poetry Therapy can be employed with the young and the old of all sexes, races, beliefs, and educational levels. Illiterates are not excluded, since people will often gesture and utter in their idiosyncratic manner their essential feelings. The same holds true for individuals who do not speak or write the native language of the group but are acquainted with their own.

Poetry Therapy is not a cure-all and makes no claims as such. There are contraindications for its use and for those who are involved in its practice. At present, the evidence for many of the tentative observations and conclusions is in need of further research and data.

Poetry Therapy is involved in developing a central rationale out of its diverse experiences, practical reports, and observations. The field is really at its beginnings, though it may be considered as an old-new discipline.

At present, too, there are psychotherapists who are averse to the use of poetry or any of the arts in therapy. Also there are poets who believe that their field is being bastardized. Nevertheless, while there are numerous questions of a controversial nature that need to be addressed and answered, Poetry Therapy is proceeding at its own pace.

A healthy skepticism, an open mind, and respect on the part of poets and therapists for one another's frame of reference will smooth the road of poetry in therapy. At the same time conclusions drawn here point in the direction of the metaphor and simile as kinfolk in the healing experience.

# REFERENCES

Abrams, A. S. Poetry thereapy in the psychiatric hospital. In A. Lerner (Ed.), *Poetry in the therapeutic experience*. Elmsford, N.Y.: Pergamon Press, 1978.

Ansell, C. Psychoanalysis and poetry. In A. Lerner (Ed.), *Poetry in the therapeutic experience*. Elmsford, N.Y.: Pergamon Press, 1978.

Aristotle. Poetics. In R. McKeon (Ed.), *The basic works of Aristotle*. New York: Random House, 1941.

Blanton, S. *The healing power of poetry*. New York: Crowell, 1960.

Edgar, K. The epiphany of the self via poetry therapy. In A. Lerner (Ed.), *Poetry in the therapeutic experience*. Elmsford, N.Y.: Pergamon Press, 1978.

Freud, S. The relation of the poet to day-dreaming. In E. Jones (Ed.), *Collected papers*, vol. 4. London: Hogarth Press and the Institute of Psycho-Analysis, 1949.

Harrower, M. *The therapy of poetry*. Springfield, Ill.: Charles C Thomas, 1972.

Jones, R. E. Treatment of a psychotic patient by poetry therapy. In J. J. Leedy (Ed.), *Poetry therapy*. Philadelphia: Lippincott, 1969.

Jung, C. G. *Modern man in search of a soul*. New York: Harcourt, 1933.

Lauer, R. Abuses of poetry therapy. In A. Lerner (Ed.), *Poetry in the therapeutic experience*. Elmsford, N.Y.: Pergamon Press, 1978.

Leedy, J. J. (Ed.). *Poetry therapy*. Philadelphia: Lippincott, 1969.

Leedy, J. J. (Ed.). *Poetry the healer*. Philadelphia: Lippincott, 1973.

Lerner, A. (Ed.). *Poetry in the therapeutic experience*. Elmsford, N.Y.: Pergamon Press, 1978.

Meerloo, J. A. M. The universal language of rhythm. In J. J. Leedy (Ed.), *Poetry therapy*. Philadelphia: Lippincott, 1969.

Prescott, F. C. *The poetic mind*. New York: Macmillan, 1922. (Reissued, Ithaca: Cornell University Press, 1959.)

Rothenberg, A. Poetry and psychotherapy: Kinships and contrasts. In J. J. Leedy (Ed.), *Poetry the healer*. Philadelphia: Lippincott, 1973.

Rubin, R. J. *Using bibliotherapy: A guide to theory and practice*. Phoenix, Ariz.: Oryx Press, 1978.

Schloss, G. A. *Psychopoetry*. New York: Grosset & Dunlap, 1976.

Schloss, G. A. and Grundy, D. E. Action techniques in psychopoetry. In A. Lerner (Ed.), *Poetry in the therapeutic experience*. Elmsford, N.Y.: Pergamon Press, 1978.

Stainbrook, E. Poetry and behavior in the psychotherapeutic experience. In A. Lerner (Ed.), *Poetry in the therapeutic experience*. Elmsford, N.Y.: Pergamon Press, 1978.

# CHAPTER 48

# *Primal Therapy*

ROBERT F. A. SCHAEF, DENNIS O. KIRKMAN, and BARBARA UNGASHICK

*Perhaps the best known of all the innovative psychotherapeutic approaches is Primal Therapy. I imagine that it is one of the most frequently referred to systems in this book. After searching for the most qualified person to write this chapter, I was lucky enough to be able to tap the combined experience of Robert Schaef, Dennis Kirkman, and Barbara Ungashick, all of the Denver Primal Center.*

*Primal Therapy is certainly innovative, even though study of the history of psychotherapy indicates it has close parallels with the first of the modern group psychotherapists, Anton Mesmer, and with the work of the founder of modern group psychotherapy, J. L. Moreno, in both theory and operation. Primal Therapy closely resembles Aqua-Energetics, Creative Aggression, New Identity Process, and Z-Process, which are covered within this book. It is also similar to Moreno's Psychodrama and Perls's Gestalt Therapy.*

*The reader is in for an intellectual treat in this chapter, which provides a compact, authoritative statement of the theory and practice of Primal Therapy.*

Primal Therapy is an educative process based on the individual's natural movement toward fulfilling his or her vast potential as a human being. The emphasis is on the experiencing and expression of earlier blocked feelings and on their integration into total life functioning. We believe consciousness and physiology are a product of organism–environment interaction from the moment of conception. Traumatic interactions create a maladaptiveness that continues into adulthood. Therapy consists of guiding the client to the inner body systems (brain/mind, muscular, proprioceptive, etc.), which carry the memory of earlier, usually painful, events or states that were denied full awareness at the time because of their devastating character. These events or states are fully experienced, usually over a series of sessions, and reintegrated into the body and consciousness so that the client may fully function in the present with greatly expanded awareness.

## HISTORY

Arthur Janov was a practicing psychotherapist with 17 years of experience when during a session one of his patients told the bizarre story of Ortiz, an entertainer, who wore diapers, drank milk from a bottle, and cried out, "Mommy!" and "Daddy!" until he vomited into a plastic bag. Janov, seeing his patient's fascination with the act, encouraged him to call out "Mommy! Daddy!"

Suddenly, he was writhing on the floor in agony. His breathing was rapid, spasmodic: "Mommy! Daddy!" came out of his mouth almost involuntarily in loud screeches. He appeared to be in a coma or hypnotic state. The writhing gave way to small convulsions, and finally, he released a piercing, deathlike scream that rattled the walls

We wish to acknowledge these people for their contribution toward the development of the concepts contained herein: Jules Roth, Helen Roth, and Warren Baker.

of my office. The entire episode lasted only a few minutes, and neither Danny nor I had any idea what had happened. All he could say afterwards was: "I made it! I don't know what, but I can *feel!*" (Janov, 1970, pp. 9–10)

Early associates of Janov describe him as being a critical observer whose ideas developed both from what he saw and what his patients told him they were experiencing. Janov did not develop a cognitive, interpretive structure to describe the phenomena but recognized these events as important in and of themselves, allowed them to run their course, and then through feedback from the patient determined what had taken place. Eventually he saw people as reliving old, forgotten, and painful experiences in a pattern that the individual's nervous system demanded, not one that was consciously directed. There appeared to be a neurological sequencing of activity that was not intellectually controlled by the patient.

From these surprising beginnings, Janov began formulating a theory that would become known as Primal Therapy and that he would later claim to be "the cure for neurosis." In 1970 he published the first book of his theories and observations, *The Primal Scream,* which possibly was read by more people than any other in its field.

In the early days of his new practice, it has been reported he worked largely with young adult patients. They had experience with drugs and hallucinogens, probably had less intact defense systems, and may have been attracted to an antipsychiatry philosophy that allowed enormous individual freedom of expression and seemed to encourage a certain condemnation of the establishment. (Yoko Ono and John Lennon were two of the early patients of this genre.) So it is possible that these young patients contributed greatly to the early development of the therapy because they were more willing, open, and perhaps adventuresome than the average clinician's clientele.

It is further reported that Janov was very excited by what he was learning and approached his colleagues in the psychological community in California. His ideas were met with rejection and sometimes even ridicule. Janov was challenging some precepts long held sacred among the professionals—he was attempting to overthrow traditional concepts concerning the nature of human beings. He was redefining psychotherapy, and perhaps that was threatening to the traditionalists. (Historically, of course, this is a familiar response when revolutionary ideas are introduced.) His critics claimed that he emphasized the sensational aspects of his success, did not report his failures, and adopted a theatrical approach to treatment.

He later took complete control of Primal Therapy by having the name trademarked so that only he could use it legally. (This has since been challenged in court by the International Primal Association, which won, although Janov is appealing the decision.)

Additionally, he states in his writings that only a therapist with his certification may practice Primal Therapy.

Probably as a result of Janov's attitude in *The Primal Scream* toward professionals and the deceptive simplicity of the concepts, many nonprofessionals established themselves as primal therapists. Ill trained and lacking in experience, many outright charlatans and quacks, along with the benevolent ignorant, rode the crest of the primal popularity of the early seventies.

Primal Therapy had become more than an exciting contribution to the body of human knowledge, it had become "the in thing," replacing the encounter movement of the sixties in general public appeal. But aside from the dilettantes and those attempting to establish a new life style away from a world that rewarded nonfeeling, there were many who saw it as legitimately offering hope after a lifetime of suffering.

Janov attempted to define the therapy as being very precise and predictable with techniques that, once learned, could be used on anyone and produce the desired results. For example, he expected the therapeutic process to be naturally chronological. It seemed reasonable that the patient should start with some feeling in the present and work his way backward, into childhood events, and eventually to preverbal, even prenatal occurrences. This linearity did not bear itself out in practice.

Philosophical disagreements erupted from time to time at the Primal Institute. One major schism took place in 1974 when many of the staff and patients left. The Denver Primal Center was formed out of this separation and operates on the premise that the therapy, far from being precise and linear, is actually extremely individualistic. Janov's original belief was that the *method*, once perfected, would help all "neurotics." This is not true. Everyone simply does not fit Janov's model of technique. While there are similarities among patients, the overriding factor is that each person has a peculiar "track" or succession of neurological events; even more particular to the individual is the meaning of those events.

There was a wane of interest in Primal Therapy in the mid seventies as the fashion died out and most of the psychotherapeutic establishment still staunchly refused to consider the validity of Janov's claims. But now, over a dozen years since that first "primal," it seems that Primal Therapy has, after all, survived as a radical new way to understand the human process of life.

## CURRENT STATUS

The seat and recognized authority on Primal Therapy is Arthur Janov and his institute in Los Angeles, The Primal Institute. Primarily an outpatient clinic, Janov treats patients in his traditional approach to Primal Therapy, which begins with a three-week intensive therapy program and includes follow-up sessions over a period of one year. There are probably about 200 therapists and/or centers practicing Primal or a Primal-type Therapy around the world. These are concentrated mainly in the New York City area, California, the Great Lakes region, and Toronto.

The Denver Primal Center is the second largest center for Primal Therapy and offers a variety of programs for clients.

Primal Therapy has made an impact not only in the United States, but in many other countries as well. There is considerable interest among the lay population in particular in Australia, Canada, northern Europe, and especially West Germany, where there are not enough trained therapists to treat those who desire Primal Therapy. Waiting lists are long, so affluent West Germans often seek the therapy in the United States.

Training is difficult to come by, as Janov trains only people that have been patients at his institute for some time. Once trained, these therapists are defranchised should they leave the Primal Institute to practice on their own (1976). The Denver Primal Center will train the interested professional and encourages such interest. (There are probably many more practicing psychotherapists using some primal techniques than we are aware of who have never had any formal primal training or experience but who are attracted to the philosophy.)

Courses that include the discussion of Primal Therapy are and have been offered at the university and graduate level for several years. Some of these go under unfortunate titles such as "Fad Therapies" (University of Colorado Medical School), and "Pop Psychotherapy" (Metropolitan State College of Denver). Still other universities, particularly those with psychology departments that have a humanistic orientation, include Primal Therapy in their general overview of psychotherapies.

Janov is the only person who has written anything significant in volume and exposure on the subject. To date he has published five books (1970, 1971, 1972, 1973, 1975). He also publishes the *Journal of Primal Therapy*. The Denver Primal Center publishes the *Denver Primal Journal*. There have been a limited number of articles in the general literature. Many of these have been written from a critical stance as we continue to see the close association of Primal Therapy with

Arthur Janov reduce the objectivity of these reports. Most articles react negatively to what they consider an oversimplistic and sensational presentation of a rather complex theory in his first book *The Primal Scream* (1970).

From the beginning Janov had made efforts to prove his theories. He has his own research institute—The Primal Foundation, headed by Michael Holden, M.D., a neurologist. The bulk of his research attempts to show that there are significant and permanent physiological changes that occur as a result of having "primals." Such manifestations of tension reduction as lowered body temperature, lower blood pressures, and alterations in brain-wave patterns are being shown to be a direct result of "primaling." Janov published many of these studies in his most recent book, *Primal Man, The New Consciousness* (1975).

Independent research is starting to develop around such areas as the effects of prenatal and natal experiences on later personality development. While not primal per se, they do support some of Janov's basic contentions that very early trauma can be responsible for neurosis and psychosis. One well-known example is Frederick Leboyer (1975), who has been a pioneer in the gentle birthing movement. Preliminary follow-up studies done by Rapoport (1975–76) show that children who had Leboyer births were at age three and four more well adjusted, that is, happier, more tranquil, more relaxed children than their counterparts who had had standard hospital births. In addition, the infant is a far more sensitive organism than the pain-barrier theories of psychoanalysis allow. The exciting research on endorphins and the recent development of "infant psychiatry" at the Menninger Clinic all fit and support primal theory, however little this work attributes to it.

In 1972 in Montreal, the International Primal Association was formed. It had been active mainly on the East Coast. Some published material is available, and an annual convention is held.

Those interested in finding a psychother-apist who practices Primal Therapy may contact the local psychological association in their city, the International Primal Association, and, at this writing, the Los Angeles Information and Referral Service, a private organization that has names and information on those doing primal in this country.

## THEORY

Primal theory of personality started with observations of the process of psychotherapy and has grown within the pragmatics of the therapist-client interaction. Theory construction of this sort provides a series of assumptions that are intimately tied to and guide therapeutic practice. Such assumptions usually cover the genesis, development, and modification of organismic malfunctioning. However, since therapists have some goal for their clients, a theory of wellness develops alongside the theory of "neurosis."

Some primal assumptions are firmly validated; those more recently generated from the cutting edge of practice are more tenuously held. Others have not held up because new data have proven them false. What follows are general statements of theoretical beliefs and a summary of the basic assumptions of Primal Therapy.

One's notion of reality is based on how he or she selects and processes incoming data (Spinelli & Pribram, 1967). How input is selected and processed is a function of the structure of the individual's nervous system (Festinger et al., 1967). This, in turn, determines the quality of the individual's consciousness (Sperry, 1951). The structure of the nervous system is a result of genetic determinants evolving over millions of years, in a dialectic relationship with the environment—from the conception of the organism, through ontogeny, and continuing for the life of the organism. An organism is structurally determined by an interaction of what it is and what environment it lives in. In response to a highly acidic or low-oxygen environment, a paramecium will manufacture specific proteins to accommodate and survive. These become actual physical modifications to structure and further affect how the animal will function. This is ever-continuing and is a process of growth for living organisms. The higher up the phylogenetic scale, the more pronounced are the effects of inadequate environments (Simeons, 1960). That is to say, the more advanced the animal, the more profound are the effects of developmental deficiencies.

For many humans the *in utero* environment can be inadequate and stressful. The fetus responds to and is affected by physical and psychobiological events in the mother. The responses range from mild irritation to actual damage, depending upon the amount of deviation from life-supporting norms. Improper nutrition, disease, and the use of drugs, cigarettes, and alcohol obviously will have an effect, but what has not been generally considered is the "psychological" environment—experienced as physical. It makes sense to us, and is backed by research (Ferreira, 1969) that a psychological variable— for example, maternal anxiety, can mediate an excess of adrenal alkaloids to the child and will induce a stress state in the same way a physical variable such as excess smoking can. The infant responds viscerally to all stimuli via the autonomic nervous system, and this may form the child's characteristic style for responding to later stress. As the cortex develops, the capacity for repressing, somaticizing, and symbolizing those early events increases. These trauma will later manifest in dreams, personality structure, and symptomatology. It has been traditional to regard the *in utero* environment as a neutral experience, with the baby emerging as a tabula rasa. But the logic of our biological development and our own clinical observations tell us that often those early times can be truly "at the root" of our problems.

As the infant matures and his or her needs continue to be unfulfilled, the situation begins to compound in seriousness. The infant will pass through a number of important developmental stages for which he or she is inadequately prepared. These are physiologically triggered events meant to correspond, by reason of evolution, with a cumulation of physical and emotional readiness for their occurrence. These stages happen whether or not that individual is prepared for them. If, because of severe trauma, a current hostile environment, or previous assaults on its developing mechanisms, the child is not ready for the next stage, we may find an individual whose behavior and attitudes reflect either an arrest at a certain developmental stage of an incomplete development (Pearce, 1977). For example, a child should be ready at around age 10 months to leave the mother and begin to explore more independently the surrounding world. However, the child will need to return frequently to assure himself that mother is still there and has not left. If past experience has taught the child to doubt that mother will be there when he returns, he may opt to never "leave." This child may eventually become the overdependent adult, unable to make decisions, passive-aggressive, asthmatic, and so forth. On the other hand, another child may have learned as an infant that his or her signals for attention and to have needs met were ignored. Adapting to this limited nourishment, this child formed an attitude of independence—"I can do it myself"—long before the appropriate age. His or her personality is molded with not only independence, but a withdrawal from closeness and intimacy and an inability to form significant attachments.

In Primal Therapy we feel that it is not enough just to discuss these arrested or inadequate levels of development. In the therapeutic setting it is also necessary for the client to return not only to the memory, but also the feelings associated with it.

Our Western culture encourages the suppression of feelings and praises those who refuse to display their emotions. For example, Jacqueline Kennedy was lauded for her "strength" and "courage" at not weeping during the harrowing events in 1963. Little boys are taught that it's not manly to cry, while aggressive or assertive tendencies in little girls are discouraged in favor of coy and affectionate responses.

This deep cultural behavior goes against what is basically human, and causes conflict in an organism whenever an emotional response is called for but cannot be felt or expressed. The individual who is cut off from his or her feelings loses a basic organic avenue for existence—one which provides the color, texture, pleasure, and appreciation of life—and is condemned to live in a flatness not ever biologically intended. Those who remain connected to their feeling selves may learn to reproach themselves and feel guilty for being incapable of "achieving" a level of functioning that society demands. In losing this connectedness to our central selves, we cannot ever truly be connected to each other, and so we form a world that can incubate violence, cruelty, and terrible insensitivity to life.

In summary, the assumptions of primal therapists are as follows:

1. Experiences are stored in the organism from the moment of conception on. This notion runs counter to most psychological and medical belief that the embryo, fetus, and even the newborn are insensate (Ferreira, 1969). Witness the way circumcision is performed on the neonate.

2. Because the organism is dependent on the environment to have survival needs met and because, gratuitously or otherwise, they are not always met, some of its experiences are traumatic.

3. The earlier in the development of the organism a traumatic experience occurs, the more profound the effect.

4. Experiences of a hostile environment or of events that are life-threatening or traumatic are blocked from full impact or awareness and distort straight-line growth. Cells modify shape or structure, body parts lose sensibility, events are forgotten or not perceived by the senses, and so forth.

5. Fragments of blocked experiences continue into adult life. A seemingly unconnected numbness in the left hand of an adult may later be associated with repeated slapping of the left hand while learning to write as a child.

6. Experiences stored in the organism are retreivable. That is, they can be felt again.

7. Defenses that interfere with growth are jettisoned by the client at his or her own pace.

8. Feeling and integrating earlier blocked experiences and expressing previously unexpressed feelings is of therapeutic benefit.

9. Our culture supports the suppression of both the expression and memory of negative feelings.

10. Education is necessary to identify feelings and the sensations that signify feelings, especially those that are remnants of early trauma.

11. Feeling *is* the basic material and modus operandi of change.

## METHODOLOGY

The application process in Primal Therapy consists of writing an autobiography, giving a history, having a physical examination, and then having a preliminary and final interview. Upon acceptance clients are matched with a therapist at a full staff meeting and given a starting date.

The full program involves a three-week intensive during which the client, who devotes full time to therapy, is seen daily for a session lasting up to three hours. The therapist is on call twenty-four hours a day and additional emergency sessions may be scheduled. Each client is seen twice by a therapist of the opposite sex from the primary therapist and may attend up to six group sessions in addition to the regular sessions. At groups the client becomes familiar with the other therapists. After the three weeks the client has the choice of individual or group sessions with the therapist(s) of his choice.

Others may choose to begin therapy with only one or two weeks of intensive therapy and follow-up sessions. Also, there are those who begin with weekly individual sessions and forego the intensive. We recommend an 8- to 12-month period be committed to therapy.

The setting in which we do our work is somewhat unusual. The center has two group rooms and a number of small individual rooms. There are no windows. The floors and walls are padded and soundproofed. Pillows, blankets, and tissues are the only furnishings. Sessions are usually carried out in dim lighting. The facility is open 24 hours so that clients can "feel" on their own, or with another client who will sit for them, or can meet as a group at any time without a staff member present. Another important modification of usual psychotherapeutic practice is that the rooms are scheduled for three hours per session. Sessions run from one to three hours.

In every session there is an emphasis on feelings never before felt, never before spoken, about things that hurt—words, looks, deeds. Memories are uncovered; neglect is reexperienced in a physical way. Need becomes not just a psychological concept but a gaping wound that has been covered up for survival's sake—a physiological deficit that has required a deviation around the potential development of the organism. These are factors in the client's development that, while they are disintegrating or traumatic in and of themselves, are compounded or "overlaid" by later events, usually within the family. The lack of connection within the organism is increased when the attempts to "run off" the pain or attempts to reintegrate are blocked; what is natural expression to the person is denied. It is this natural expression that therapy attempts to reestablish.

An example of this dynamic is Carl, whose application and interviews provided us with most of the following information. He started drinking when he was 19. Previous to that he had been diagnosed as a catatonic schizophrenic. For three years, from age 16 to 19, he had been unable to find the impetus to get out of a chair. Sitting, he would watch the hands of the clock spin, as time flew by. Although he came from an affluent and well-educated family (mother a biology professor), Carl was unable to work for more than three months at a time, couldn't apply himself in any endeavor, and gravitated toward the life style of an inner city hardcore wino. Carl came into therapy not because of difficulty in feeling, but because of a great excess of pain occurring beyond his ability to assimilate. He was unable to function and described feelings of imminent dying and blackness. His appearance was unkempt and disheveled, and he vascillated between expressions of apathy and great fear. Carl was accepted for therapy and began with a three-week intensive.

During his intensive he talked predominantly about his mother; particularly that she was constantly undermining and criticizing him. Carl described a scene when he was seven where his mother had made an especially cutting remark (a useful tool in Primal Therapy is developing a scene; this involves helping the client piece together in as full a fashion as possible the details surrounding an earlier, significant event):

T:    What would you say to her when she'd hurt you like that, Carl?

C:    Oh, I could never say anything. I'd just withdraw farther into myself.

T:    Tell her now. Just look right at her and tell her how it feels.

Confronting the feeling so directly, Carl was rarely able to get out more than a few words before he would fall upon the floor, writhing and nearly convulsing, arch his back, with his head against the padded wall, and appear to have great difficulty in breathing. After going through this sequence many times and approaching it from different aspects of his life (how he felt his father had died trying to save him from his mother, losing his ability to play basketball, circumstances around the beginning of his catatonia), he began to piece together what it seemed his body was attempting to resolve.

In these sessions Carl revealed details of an especially traumatic birth and difficulties early in his life. He reported that as a child he always wanted to be active—very active. He wanted, in fact, never to sit still. This behavior represented a way for him to deal with the early pain he had incurred. It served to "run off" the excess, to keep the channels to direct expression open. However, as so often happens in this culture, spontaneity, rambunctiousness, and unorthodox behaviors were not suffered gladly in Carl's family. Directives like "straighten up," "be still," "behave yourself" presented familial and social demands for him to deny primal impulses, however symbolic, and to start jelling into the cultural mold. What opportunity he had for integration was thrown away by the imperative to deny that opening. The care and environment Carl required as a child, *particular* to his *in utero* trauma, were not there. In fact, as is usually the case, the opposite was true.

Primal therapists assume that there are etiologic components to trends of thought—that language, how it is used and its content, is symbolic of experience. The experience is what we are after, since it is its neglect and its expression that is most often at the roots of disintegrity. The therapist attempts to guide the client underneath the hubris of his or her own symbolization process to the "heart of the matter." This guiding ranges from merely providing safety, to the mechanics of the therapy, to intuitive grasps of what we call "openings." An opening is an opportunity whereby the person, either of his or her own accord or with some help (as with Carl), will begin what looks like a neural sequence. In psychoanalysis, the client may go from thought to thought with occasional affect. The analyst is in the position of knowing what the patterns and content of those meanderings might mean (in conjunction with transference, resistance, dreams, etc.). But primal therapists believe when the client is given the safety to not have to symbolize, or verbally defend, his body will begin to

*experience*, the meaning of which is his interpretation alone.

"Tracking" is another word used to describe what looks like an autonomous neural process. Steven Rose in *The Conscious Brain* (1973) describes a neuronal pathway model for memory, learning, and information processing:

In transversing a particular sequence of memory traces, the brain proceeds from state to state along the different individual traces in an ordered manner. The phenomenon is analogous to synaptic conduction or axonal firing—all of these processes are unidirectional. One state must "fire" another almost irreversibly. So the individual brain states associated with memories must presumably be linked by synaptic logic into a sequence in which one follows almost inevitably from another. It is as if the arrow of time is located at the synapse, at least so far as memories are concerned. (p. 210)

The task of the therapist is to guide the person into ever more *specifics* of what causes what feelings. This is an ideal, whereby the client proceeds in what looks like and sounds like an autonomous neural sequencing. This is the organism healing itself. There are times when not even one word is required from the therapist. On the other hand, there are times when the pain is so great, psychological damage so extensive, defensive structure so tight or intricate that it is not initially possible for one's own natural healing processes to emerge. It is at times like these when it is up to the therapist to become a catalyst, so to speak.

"Sequencing" is an ideal of the healing process aimed for where the organism is healing and integrating itself in a way and at a pace that is intrinsic to it, rather than by taking on additional effluvia of a therapist. It can begin by the therapist picking up on an "opening," that is, where feelings may be ascending. These are exemplified below:

B:   You know, I'm really scared right now. My arms and legs are tingly.

T:   What are you scared of?

B:   Oh, I don't know. I guess that I'm not

going to do this right, that you're not going to approve.

T:   Have you ever known this before?

B:   Oh yeah, every time I get up to give a presentation at the office all I can think of is how the other architects are going to respond. You know, really negative. It nearly incapacitates me and my stomach goes into knots like this.

T:   Ben, as much as you can now, focus on those sensations and let your body express them in whatever way that matches the feeling.

B:   (trembles and sobs for a few minutes) Something just occurred to me about this. I remember being in a school play when I was five and my mother and uncle were in the audience. It seems like I fucked up what I was supposed to do and afterward I was really ashamed and upset. When I saw my mother and uncle coming backstage, I wanted to run to her and cry but I saw this look on her face. She and my uncle were laughing. She thought what had happened was funny! She was laughing at me (begins to sob deeply)! Don't laugh at me, goddamn it! Don't laugh at me! Mommy! Mommy! . . .

From here Ben reexperienced a time even younger when his mother misread or missed what he needed. When he was not appeased he would continue to fret and cry. Out of frustration, she would scold and punish him.

It became apparent in subsequent postsessions* that Ben learned from his mother that his feelings and what he needed were not "right," they were something to be ashamed of. He also realized the summation of those hurts became symbolized at the time when he was in the play. In later situations in which he was called on to perform, he would suffer debilitating anxiety because of what the sit-

uation provoked and meant to him: that he would not be seen and be made to feel worthless. With the removal of societal inhibitions Ben was able to retrieve a part of himself he had had to disown. His body resolved it in an orderly, sequential fashion. The same feeling was traced from a present situation to a previous situation, to a memory, to a prior memory until the initial causal matrix was discovered. Those memories had an emotional charge to them. Because he could not experience or express those early hurts, he was driven to symbolize and generalize in his attempt to integrate himself.

Group sessions vary in format and structure. One form follows a workshop model in that one therapist might meet with the same four to six clients for several hours on a continuous periodic schedule (daily or weekly). These groups may be directed at a special area such as sexuality or creativity, and the purpose is to focus on problems clients have in those areas. The drop-in group is a regularly scheduled group open to any and all clients. They sign in on arrival, before the group starts. They indicate, from the list posted, which therapist they want to work with and which room they will be in. They go into that room and allow whatever feelings emerge while they are waiting for the therapist to come.

The therapists who are working go over the sign-up sheet and divide the clients about equally, each one taking several clients. (Group size has ranged as high as 50 clients with 10 to 12 therapists. However, they tend to be smaller now, with usually two or three therapists working each group.) Therapists then visit their clients twice during a two-hour period, about 15 minutes each time.

Postgroup* is announced in all the rooms, and then clients and therapists assemble in the large group room. Lights that have been dimmed are now brightened. During the hour or two that follows, one or two therapists lead the group; they are the focus toward

---

*The latter portion of a session is given over to what we call a postsession. This time provides an opportunity for the client to integrate what he or she has just experienced into full awareness and present life's functioning.

*Postgroups and postsessions have very similar functions.

whom comments, questions, and feelings are directed and from whom the majority of responses come.

Postgroup allows for the clients to: continue feeling what was started in the preceding two hours; talk about what they have been feeling, thus giving cognitive structure to what might otherwise be vague feeling experiences; deal with other persons in the room who have, by their presence or in more direct ways, triggered feelings in them and to work through those feelings; talk about what is happening in their present life. Clients learn from this that others feel in their own unique way and at their own pace and do get better. This helps them to accept themselves and their own process.

The aim of therapy is to provide the environment for gradual movement toward becoming a person who experiences feelings and expresses them appropriately in everyday life as they are evoked, and who also has a process for dealing with an upsurge of feeling that threatens to disrupt or warp functioning. In moving toward this goal, many clients go through one or both of the following steps:

1. Coming to the center and "feeling" on their own. To this end the center is open 24 hours, and over the years has come to be considered a safe place to lie down and express deep feelings at any time of the day or night.
2. A "buddy" system in which one client will "sit" for another as he or she has feelings. The presence of another can facilitate feeling expression for some who cannot do it alone.

At some point, the client will begin to move out and away from the therapeutic environment—will rely less and less on formal sessions. The need to release or run off strong feelings becomes less frequent and diminishes in intensity. Some clients will terminate therapy for months at a time and return occasionally. Others may continue using the facilities on their own or with "buddies" for several years before they have integrated

enough material to completely disengage themselves from the security of the center. It is important to us to respect a client's own special timing and intervene only when growth seems to be impeded. Above all else, we value every individual's sense of rightness and truth within himself and will nourish and encourage that awareness to flower so that eventually he can live from that wonderful place inside himself.

## APPLICATIONS

When humans fail to live up to the standards imposed by our culture, they are deemed and often consider themselves maladaptive or pathological. What they are actually failing to adapt to is a cultural set that is dehumanizing and of itself maladaptive. Their defenses are inadequate, failing to help them adjust to the rigors of day-to-day life. These people are failing to live in an integral fashion; at the same time, they are caught somewhere between the values and expectations of family and culture, and the long-denied and feared primal impulses and expressions they sense in their bodies. Not being able to go in either direction completely, they suffer "nervous breakdowns" or "anxiety attacks" and are vulnerable to labels and diagnoses such as paranoid schizophrenic or manic-depressive, which are in reality all descriptions of symptoms or an organism's attempts to move toward integration, toward healing itself.

These people are in pain—psychologically and often physically—and worse, they have to deny the experience and its expression. While the organism may be attempting reintegration symptomatically and symbolically, those defenses the body has taken on, out of necessity and acculturation, need to be addressed.

Many people who seek out Primal Therapy are "failures" at other types of therapy. They have not been able to grow and change in the ways they want to—the blocks to a complete and comfortable life seem indissoluble.

Many have been functioning effectively when they come to the center but report diffuse dissatisfaction with their lives: They want to become more aware of themselves so they may achieve a more fulfilling existence. Others have specific symptoms such as phobias, depression, or drug dependency. Still others have been institutionalized and seek a more humane, pertinent, and individual counseling than they had known.

The information in this section describes clients who have had the full program, the core of which is the three-week intensive. In 1978/79 we experimented with variations on this program to the extent that we now take some clients on a once- or twice-weekly basis. In time we will have data on this new group.

## Self-Selection

The typical applicant for our full program has been contemplating entering Primal Therapy for more than a year (some as many as seven years). He or she has usually read *The Primal Scream** (Janov, 1970) or other primal literature and searched out our center, many coming from as far as Australia and Germany. Often a usually nonfeeling person will describe having and experiencing deep feelings while reading primal material. Some describe a deep "inner knowing" that this process will help. They then set about planning their lives so they can take the time out for the commitment the therapy requires. At this time many of our applicants have been referred by former clients.

By the time they apply, they are usually highly motivated to become involved in, if somewhat fearful of, the process. However, since they have only a dim perception of the depth and extent of their pain, it is in the first six months that the 2.5 percent who will have dropped out leave. The bulk of these leave during the first month.

---

*Some applicants have been led to have high false expectations that have to be dealt with in the initial enquiring interview.

*A Further Description of Our Client Population.* As a group† our clients when contrasted with national norms have:

1. Greater birth traumas (premature and postmature, breech, caesarean section, twin, over 10 pounds at birth, especially long or short labor, birth defect, or injury).
2. More trouble with the law, previous psychotherapy and hospitalizations (mental), suicide attempts, "mental illness" in the family, drug and alcohol dependency or heavy usage.
3. More siblings.
4. Fewer marriages: with an average age of 29 years, in this sample 53 percent have never been married (national norm 18 percent).
5. Greater unemployment: 42 percent (national norm 8 percent) are unemployed. This is colored by the fact that a number of people come from distant places and give up their jobs just to do the therapy.

Of the more recently treated 180 clients of the 250 on whom the data were available, 95 percent had multiple psychophysiological disorders. The highest incidence (range = 21 to 81 percent) were in following systems: muscular/skeletal, gastrointestinal, respiratory, special senses, and cardiovascular.

It is our impression that our clients have had more childhood abuse (psychological, sexual, and physical) than the population of patients seen in clinics and by independent psychotherapy practitioners.

While we do not use clinical diagnostic categories in reference to our clients, it is also our impression that our population has included persons whose primary diagnosis would fall into the psychoses, neuroses, personality disorders, psychophysiologic disorders, and special symptoms as defined in the *Diagnostic and Statistical Manual of Mental Disorders* (DSM II, 1968).

---

†These data are based on 250 consecutively treated clients.

In summary, then, we have a multiply handicapped client group who have experienced extreme problems in living and are highly motivated to change their life patterns.

***Who Benefits Most.***    As with most therapies, a highly motivated client committed to enduring the pain and discomfort of the struggle to be real is likely to change for the better. However, there are several types for whom the process is especially suitable.

Persons who are in touch with their bodies seem to move into the process and benefit more easily from Primal Therapy. This stems from the fact that during the therapy session we focus on the body, facies, gestures, large movements, and sensations. Since we are after the recovery and expression of feeling, and feelings start in the body, it is important to move to that level as soon as practicable.* We also think that physical data are more reliable of what is happening in an individual than are cognitive data. This again leads us to consider it more efficient to work with body manifestations.

People who are in touch with their bodies may show it in several ways. One such group are those who somatize their pain. This may range from the severe asthmatic or arthritic to the person who carries tension in parts, or all, of his or her body. When they come to therapy, they already have body manifestations of their underlying pain and are easily directed to these entrances of channels into their feelings.

A second group are in touch with their bodies in another fashion. Even though they have learned, for the most part, to ignore body messages (for example: "You're tired, it's time to stop" in favor of some more pressing internalized environmental message: "Quitters never amount to anything"), they are still aware that the body is saying something. With a little help in focusing they begin to find their own "track" into their

past history. Persons in this group are often easier to work with than most.

Another group who benefit are people who "can't get anything done." They seem to combine the traits of neurasthenic neurotic, asthenic, and inadequate personality. They are often on welfare or Medicaid.† They spend much of their early therapy dealing with feelings that stem from birth and pre-birth trauma. The positive changes that occur in this group are generally slower in coming than the second group mentioned above. There is a long period of slow growth followed by a blooming in which they take a place in the world consistent with their chronological age. One reason for the slowness in movement with these people seems to be that, in addition to feeling their feelings in therapy, they must also learn to do things in the real world they never learned as children—they must develop coping mechanisms that other persons have in their repertoire even though they may not be using them efficiently or at all.

## CASE EXAMPLE

This study will be a continuation of Carl, who was described in the previous section on methodology. His is not an unusual case, although it does run counter to a general misconception of what Primal Therapy does—to take away defenses and to regress people into nonfunctional states.

Carl came in in a state of "overload." By way of how he looked, moved, what he said, and how he said it, it could be seen that his nervous system was having to process too much pain. He did not have the internal mechanisms to push the pain down, that is, defend, "pull himself out of it." At the same time, his access to what all this meant was quite remote, he was disconnected, and he could not integrate the whole, great mass of feeling at once. The task, then, was twofold:

---

*General rules for guiding the therapist are to move from the present to the past; general to the specific; cognitive to physical.

†We have been unofficially commended by Medicaid for our record in getting patients off their rolls.

First was to help him lower the level of pain he was living in so that what was experienced could be integrated a tolerable bit at a time. Second was to help him develop access to the lower levels of his psyche/body in a sequential fashion.

Based on this, an opening was taken that represented the level at which he could integrate; that is, experience a feeling, know it was a feeling, and understand where it came from and what it meant to his life. In this case, he could cry about a Joan Baez song he had heard that day. He was allowed and encouraged to cry as much as possible to drain some of the emotional load he carried. He talked about what she said, what it meant to him, and how it made him feel. From there it went to how rock and roll had affected him as a teenager, how it seemed that music was the one thing he could allow in. He proceeded to go into what he would later describe as a birth sequence, which was described earlier. Almost immediately he began to fragment. At this point the therapist addressed the base he had established for himself from when he was a teenager. They talked more and the therapist gradually moved the focus more toward the present, but always with the base Carl established as a reference point. This was to be the tenor of the rest of our meetings: building on what he was able to integrate, lowering the overall pain level, and allowing him to experience ever further the physical trauma he was born and lived in.

Obviously, from what has been said the task with Carl (and what happens often) was to integrate the meaning of what was already happening and to indeed help him develop some internal "stops." His emerging self-acceptance became evident as he found it within himself to not only face and resolve his internal hell, but that other areas of his life were appearing to be within his capacity to change also.

The therapist continued to meet with Carl after the initial "intensive" on a twice-weekly basis for four months and then once a week for four months. The sessions averaged one and one-half to two hours in length. Integrating what he was feeling into his present life enabled Carl to make simple yet profound changes. His attitude that he only deserved to live at a minimal level began to change to where he moved from the inner city (he lived in a bare room in a flophouse) and took an apartment near a park. This was to be the beginning of his development of "defenses" that enabled him to function but that did not impose on his growing integrity. Of the more significant "breakthroughs" was Carl's anger that for so long had imploded and been directed into self-hatred and immobility. Once the intense rage around his biological birth, and later periods, started to be discharged, he no longer depended on large amounts of caffeine for stimulation; in fact, an aliveness began to glow from within that was nurtured and encouraged in his relationship with the therapist. After one especially explosive session, Carl discovered that he could actually see more clearly and had to have the prescription changed on his glasses.

Since Carl enjoyed working with his hands and being out of doors, he became gainfully employed as a carpenter, whereupon he immediately furnished his apartment with a stereo. ("Long live rock 'n roll," he had said.) Carl's relationship with women was one of great frustration for him, as it contained such strong elements of fear and need. However, once with a woman he was seeing and was attracted to, he revealed to her what he considered his infantile need and told her he was afraid she would reject him because of it. The fact that she was open to Carl's just saying what was true for him and giving him the space to explore the feeling in a real context proved of enormous benefit to Carl's "barrier" to women.

He still drank heavily occasionally, when his "depression" recurred, but it manifested more as a function of extreme pain (i.e., he knew it was symptomatic of feelings) and happened periodically rather than as a life style. The last contact with Carl was 10 months after he began therapy. He seemed confident and very encouraged by his breaking his lifelong "failure" syndrome. At that time he was going to live in the foothills to work on and live in a cabin.

## SUMMARY

Primal Therapy in its theory and methodology has its roots in the humanistic movement. It is primarily client-centered, yet it attempts to synthesize with the "supportive, human" approach a rigorous methodology based on a developmental psychology and the biology of human existence. Underlying the theoretical structure is an implicit belief in the organismic "rightness" of the individual. Each person carries within his or her own healing process that will emerge given the proper therapeutic environment. Each neurological and biochemical individuality is a variation on the theme: disintegrity wrought by unfelt pain. This theme is given a further dimension by a model of neurological functioning that makes Primal Therapy one of the few, if any, systems to have underpinnings in an operational description of neuropsychology. With the theme as a reference point, each individual's variation provides the guidelines for how his or her growth process will proceed. In this way theory may follow from experience and practice—and not vice versa. Since it is basically an open system, information from other fields of thought such as embryology, anthropology, ethology, and so forth, are readily assimilated, providing for a holistic approach, which seems only proper given the complex and interactive nature of human existence.

Primal theory postulates that very early traumatic events and/or negative environmental influences provide the basis for later neurosis and psychosis; memory of these events and circumstances are stored physically in the organism; later retrieval and integration is possible by allowing and encouraging the individual not only to elicit unconscious material cognitively but to actually *go through* the feelings and physical sensations that could not be fully experienced at the time they happened. Maladaptive behaviors are motivated by earlier trauma. One's present life is influenced by earlier behavior patterns formed throughout childhood and adolescence but also during infancy, perinatal, and prenatal times. Attention is finally given to the first nine months of life in the womb as being significant in the development of the personality of the individual.

It is the particular contribution of Primal Therapy to extend our understanding of human functioning to include the prenatal months as important in the therapeutic process. This extension is not mere theoretical formulation but has come out of practice and observation; it has become clear that early events are not only available to us but are most apparent in the symptomatic behavior of all of us. It is these symptoms that bring people into therapy.

The primal approach has been used successfully with a wide variety of symptoms. For example, the lost abilities to think clearly, read and study effectively, and speak directly have been found again after getting in touch with old feelings. Formerly institutionalized patients start to function again in the outside world. Unavoidable impasses between husband and wife, and parent and child, have found alternative resolution through the choice to feel old feelings rather than act out against them.

Psychophysiological disorders have been highly responsive to this regimen. Persons with bad backs who have been treated with traction, surgery, and prosthetic devices have dramatically improved after deep feelings have been felt and body tension permanently reduced. High blood pressure, constant over many years and through many kinds of "remedy," has lowered significantly and permanently in the same way. Skin conditions, treated for years, have vanished during the course of therapy. Progressively worsening arthritis reversed its trend for the first time in 27 years in the crippled body of a 45-year-old woman.

Reclaiming repressed feelings may be a most difficult alternative, although for some it is the only one with any real promise. From the uncommon experiences of those we have been guiding, including ourselves, we feel urged to say to behavioral scientists, to medical practitioners, to parents, to philosophers and other thinkers, to teachers and lawmakers, "Look at this. See what's happening here."

## REFERENCES

Ferreira, A. J. *Prenatal environment*. Springfield, Ill.: Charles C Thomas, 1969.

Festinger, L., Ono, C., Burnham, C. A. and Bamber, D. Efference and the conscious experience of perception. *Journal of Experimental Psychology*, 1967, **74,** 1–36.

Gardner, H. *The shattered mind*. New York: Vintage Books, 1974.

Janov, A. *The primal scream*. New York: Vintage Books, 1970.

Janov, A. *The anatomy of mental illness*. New York: Putnam, 1971.

Janov, A. *The primal revolution*. New York: Simon and Schuster, 1972.

Janov, A. *The feeling child*. New York: Simon and Schuster, 1973.

Janov, A. *Primal man: The new consciousness*. New York: Crowell, 1975.

Janov, A. and Holden, M. Levels of consciousness. *Journal of Primal Therapy*, 1973,**1.**

Leboyer, F. *Birth without violence*. New York: Knopf, 1975.

Maclean, D. D. *A triune concept of the brain and behavior*. Toronto: University of Toronto Press, 1973.

Melzack, R. *The puzzle of pain*. New York: Basic Books, 1973.

Pearce, J. *Magical child*. New York: Dutton, 1977.

Rapoport, D. The Rapoport Survey. *Bulletin de Psychology* (Paris), 1975/76, **29,** 8–13.

Rose, S. *The conscious brain*. New York: Knopf, 1973.

Simeons, A. T. W. *Man's presumptuous brain*. New York: Dutton, 1960.

Sperry, R. Neurology and the mind-brain problem. *American Scientist,* 1951, **40,** 291–312.

Spinelli, D. N. and Pribram, K. H. Changes in visual recovery functions and unit activity produced by frontal and temporal cortex stimulation. *Electroencephalography and Clinical Neurophysiology*, 1967, **22,** 143–149.

# CHAPTER 49

# Primary Relationship Therapy

GENEVIEVE PAINTER and SALLY VERNON

*Robert Postel, the man who developed this form of therapy, was a strange and lonely person. A former student of mine at the Alfred Adler Institute, he was a true original, a person who had a unique view of life. It is indeed a shame, as Genevieve Painter and Sally Vernon state in this chapter, that Postel died before he ever wrote anything about his system. Some years ago, when I was editor of the* Journal of Individual Psychology, *I asked Postel to contribute to it. Characteristically, he never even answered—and yet some time later we had a wonderful breakfast meeting at which time he poured out to me his belief that Primary Relationship Therapy was absolutely and fundamentally the most correct way of treating certain kinds of problems: certain deprived people must reexperience their childhood but now in a positive manner with loving "parents."*

*It is surprising that so distant and unapproachable a person as Bob Postel could have wrought such a loving and tender type of therapy—and I am most pleased that this is the very first published presentation of this potentially very important mode of psychotherapy.*

Primary Relationship Therapy (PRT) is a reparenting form of individual psychotherapy for the person who felt strongly rejected by one or both parents, or who lost parents at an early age. This in-depth therapy was devised in the 1960s by the late Robert Postel and is based upon Adler's theory that both the pampered and neglected child manifest a life style that is not adequate for the solution of social problems.

Of the neglected child, Adler stated: "Such a child has never known what love and cooperation can be. . . . He has found society cold to him and will expect it always to be cold" (1958, p. 11). As an adult he usually is plagued with feelings of loneliness, unworthiness, bitterness, and hostility, and lacks the ability to form prolonged close, meaningful relationships.

PRT is effective with the client who is unable to experience a wide range of emotions because he or she fears facing the an-cient hurts of his or her life. A lifelong necessity for covering feelings leads to a developmental lack of emotional recognition.

PRT involves the client in an open, close, personal relationship with a mother therapist and subsequently with a father therapist. An average of 30 sessions with each therapist have been found to be necessary. The therapist acts as a warm, nurturing, teaching parent. In role plays the client receives cuddling, hugging, play, stories, games, and art activities. Clients also participate in guided fantasies that either change a negative childhood memory to a positive one or give them an experience they wish they had as a child.

As progress is made through "adolescence," the focus is more on real-life issues—sexuality, values, and career plans. In experiencing the parent therapist as an adult model who discloses feelings honestly, the client unscrambles past and current confusions and deprivations and builds the missing foundations he or she never had. Finally, after passing into adulthood and independence, therapy is terminated.

## HISTORY

Primary Relationship Therapy was devised in the 1960s by Robert Postel. It is regrettable that when Postel died in 1978 he had not yet written about his innovative therapy. He had been an Adlerian psychologist working in the Chicago practice of the late Rudolf Dreikurs when he was asked by a hospitalized schizophrenic if he would only hold and cradle her. He found that she improved markedly and thus was born a new technique within the Adlerian framework. In continuing his investigation of clients disordered enough to be hospitalized, Postel found that most of them had felt either neglected, rejected, or abused as children and that a form of warm, nurturing, experiential therapy was most effective. He extended this therapy to nonhospitalized clients who had felt early rejection.

In writing of the neglected child, Adler (1958) stated:

Such a child has never known what love and cooperation can be; he makes up an interpretation of life which does not include these friendly forces. It will be understood that when he faces the problems of life he will over-rate their difficulty and under-rate his own capacity to meet them with the aid and good will of others. . . . Especially he will not see that he can win affection and esteem by actions which are useful to others. He will thus be suspicious of others and unable to trust himself.'' (pp. 17–18)

Adler had written more about the pampered than the neglected child, but he believed that both were ill prepared to function cooperatively in the world:

From the beginning of his life the neurotic manifests the pampered style of life, which is not adequate for the solution of the social problems of life. And the potentially neurotic child later,

when confronted by a difficult situation, often becomes the neurotic patient. . . . This style of life can be found occasionally in cases where we cannot speak with any justification of pampering, but where on the contrary, we find neglect.

Adler went further in this direction, stating that:

This pampered style of life is found almost more frequently in neglected children or in those who feel themselves neglected. . . . A person with a pampered style of life is one who wants to be pampered rather than necessarily one who actually has been pampered.'' (Ansbacher & Ansbacher, 1964, p. 242)

Robert Postel left Dreikurs's practice to further refine his techniques in reparenting. He called his new approach Primary Relationship Therapy and trained others in his own practice. Later he gave classroom instruction for therapists. In these classrooms the senior author of this chapter was trained in Primary Relationship Therapy by Postel.

## CURRENT STATUS

Postel trained people working in hospital settings, mental health agencies, and private practices. Psychiatrists, psychologists, social workers, counselors, teachers, and the clergy were represented in his classes. Because this training was done in Chicago, more therapists practice Primary Relationship Therapy in that area than elsewhere. Some of these people moved to other parts of the country and are continuing to do this work; they can be found in the Midwest, in California, Oregon, and Hawaii.

As of this writing, training in Primary Relationship Therapy can be acquired in Chicago; Eugene, Oregon; and Honolulu, by therapists working in private practice.

One extension of this work in Honolulu has been in an agency setting with paraprofessionals working with abusive parents. The abusive parent was usually neglected, rejected, or abused as a child and now repeats the pattern with his or her own child. The agency was set up to enable a paraprofessional person to work with a client in a one-to-one supportive relationship. With the addition of Primary Relationship Training, the paraprofessional staff developed new insights into the parents' backgrounds and were able to be more nurturing in their supportive work.

In Hawaii Primary Relationship Therapy has also reached teachers and school counselors. Teachers and counselors, of course, do not have time to practice extensive individual psychotherapy. But an understanding of the techniques and issues involved helps them to deal more effectively with students who feel rejected or neglected. Essentially, PRT is reconstructive and when applied in schools can help counteract cold or over-solicitous attitudes of adults.

## THEORY

Adler and Postel differentiated the pampered from the neglected child, both of whom are unable to cope with the challenges of life as an adult. *Pampered* children grow up believing they deserve a continuation of the special treatment received from the parents. Since not much has been expected from them, as adults these people do not consider the ability to cooperate as an essential part of living. They are unable to carry on the tasks of life and are discontented, usually blaming others for the discontentment. They think they are right and that others are out of step. They are okay; it is others who are wrong. They frequently are willing to please others, but only if they get goodies (things, own way, sex, etc.) in return. They expect others to give to, and take care of, them.

On the other hand, *neglected* (rejected or abused) children also do not cooperate with the world but grow up believing that they themselves are always out of step. They believe that if only they try a little harder to please and become a little more perfect they will be acceptable or loved by others. They

always feel poorly about themselves and negatively different from other people. They do not trust self or others and, therefore, do not make close, lasting relationships.

## Etiology

The etiology of the neglected person syndrome stems from parents who were neglectful, abusive, or rejecting. The rejection may be true or only perceived by the client, because the parents may have loved the client. The feeling of rejection may be due to the following behavior by the parent: unable to express love in a way that fulfills the child's basic warmth and security needs; unable to give physical touching; love being conditional (I love you only if you are good, get good grades, do what I want); absent from the home so much the child is not able to depend on parent for meeting basic needs; distant and unresponsive; inconsistent in responding to the child, thus producing a lack of security; confusing as a role model (often schizophrenic); being so unhappy that the child is compelled to support the needy parent and thus receives no support for self; or not allowing the client to ever be a child.

## Indications for Use

Primary Relationship Therapy is beneficial for the neurotic or psychotic client who is afraid of physical or emotional closeness; has difficulty making lasting intimate relationships; is out of touch with many feelings because they are painful; has deep feelings of inadequacy and low self-esteem; feels unlovable; is depressed, pessimistic, or suicidal; continuously feels sad, hurt, or lonely; has difficulty expressing anger because of fear of rejection; has pervasive anxiety about ability to live up to expectations of self and others; is unable to play and enjoy life; or has physical symptoms (particularly digestive disorders and headaches).

*The rejected client* is seen weekly in a group to work on present adult situations. He or she is assigned to a weekly individual reparenting session to provide a bonding with the therapist and deep nurturing to bridge the gap from a love-barren childhood to present life.

*The pampered-rejected client* was not given unconditional love and nurturing as a child but was instead given material possessions, his or her own way, little order, or overprotection. This client feels rejected because love was denied or was conditional. This person seems to have even more difficulty adjusting to life's demands than the purely rejected person since he or she received a greater distortion of life's requirements and many double messages throughout the growing-up years. This client is seen in a group to work on present life poblems and in individual sessions for nurturing.

*The pampered client* does not need much reparenting since he or she was given much nurturing as a child. This client is usually seen only or mostly in a group to learn to cope with present adult problems. However, the reparenting therapy can be useful for a short time to work on understanding a wider range of emotions if the client is limited in emotional awareness.

Primary Relationship Therapy may be applied to anyone who deals with rejection (neglect, abuse), whether neurotic or psychotic, whether adolescent or adult. The outcomes of this process include increased feelings of self-love and self-worth, a significant lowering of anxiety level and depression, feelings of internal strength, and the development of social embeddedness that finally enable close, intimate relationships to develop.

## METHODOLOGY

### Diagnosis

The following questions are asked to determine if the client felt rejected as a child.

1. When you were four, five, or six years old and went to your mother for affec-

tion, how did she respond? Did she cuddle you? Could you climb into her lap? Would she hold you?

2. What kind of a person was your mother? Was she a warm person?

3. Did your mother withhold love if you were not good or if you did not achieve? Was her love conditional? Would she stay angry if you were not good?

4. How does that make you feel?

5. Could you find a way to gain her approval?

6. Ask the same questions for father.

7. How do you feel about your brothers and sisters? Did they receive more approval than you? How do you think they felt?

8. How well did you do in elementary, high school, college? (A rejected person usually did similarly throughout school because of trying to please or to be perfect. The pampered person often does better in elementary school than later when school becomes more difficult.)

9. When your parents fought, did you think it was your fault? How did you feel about their fights? (The rejected person often feels responsible for parental fights. The pampered person may feel unconcerned.)

10. Do you want to be best or perfect? (The rejected person wants to be perfect even if he or she says that no one is perfect. The pampered person wants to be best and outshine others.)

11. Do you ever feel sad and not know why?

12. Did you ever feel that there was something not good enough about you—too clumsy, the wrong sex, and so on? Do you at times feel that there is something unacceptable about you, that you are not as good as others and if someone got close to you they could tell? (The rejected person strongly identifies with this question and usually cries when

asked this because of a lifetime of this hurtful situation.)

13. Does it make you feel sad that you did not have mother's (father's) love?

14. Whose love did you want more, mother's or father's? (This question is asked if one parent was warm and nurturing and the other rejecting.)

15. There are six ways one can satisfy childhood needs for approval. Which one applies to you—to be good, to achieve, to become independent, to be sickly, to withdraw from others, to play the clown?

16. Were you a loner? Did you usually hide behind a wall? Did you sometimes hide behind a wall, then get lonely and make friends and then hide again?

The rejected person displays much sadness when asked these questions, feels one or both parents did not provide unconditional love, frequently had been or is a loner, tries to reach perfection and do well in school to gain approval, feels that he or she does not receive enough love as an adult, feels unworthy and unlovable. A parent dying or leaving the home is often felt as rejection.

After the diagnosis is made, the client is assigned to a weekly individual session with a mother or father therapist and to a group meeting weekly. Usually therapy starts with the "mother" since the first natural bonding, even before birth, is with the mother.

### Individual Sessions

In working with the mother or father therapist, the client requires the experience of a nurturing, teaching, parenting relationship. The need to be accepted and to build trust and bonding to another human being is the basis of the therapeutic process because the feelings of deprivation and nontrust are the common issue.

The therapist seeks the underlying feelings of anger and sadness to help the client acknowledge and handle these. The process involves the discharge of these feelings while accepting the warmth and nurturing that was missing or not perceived in childhood. The goal is to first establish the client's feelings of childhood dependency, then to move toward coresponsibility in the relationship, and finally to increase independence and decision making. Except in infancy, communication and awareness of feelings predominate as the theme of the therapy. Initially the therapist takes responsibility for acknowleding and communicating feelings for both of them until the client is trained to do it for him- or herself.

The client allows him- or herself to become vulnerable and open to feelings through the holding and cuddling experienced as a very small child; the silliness and fun of the preschooler; the adventure and organized play of the elementary school child; the questioning and reality seeking of the preadolescent; and the discussions, arguments, and identity search of the adolescent.

Throughout the process the therapist's honesty regarding all feelings (including anger and impatience) gives the client the willingness to accept his or her own feelings and the ability to start trusting self and therapist. The long-standing anger and sadness are gradually replaced by feelings of joy; the helpless behavior is transformed into an ability to cope with life situations.

Table 1 gives the picture of the issues, emotional needs, major feelings, and behavior exhibited at each emotional age during the therapy.

When the client completes the process with the mother therapist, regression again occurs with the father therapist. Usually the process with the second parent therapist is not as long-lasting. Occasionally the client goes back again to the mother therapist to complete some issues.

Tools and processes used in this therapy include some of the following:

1. *Ground rules:* In the first session the therapist will say to the client: "The trip you will be taking can be scary but not dangerous and I will be going on

**Table 1. Activity chart.**

| Emotional Age | Predominant Feelings | Behavior | Client Needs/Wants |
|---|---|---|---|
| Womb, fetal postion | Numb, safe | Hiding, withdrawn, out of touch | To be held and rocked as a baby; tactile touch (stroking); given permission to just be there; periods of holding in silence. |
| 1–2 years | anxiety, depression, confusion, pain, | Will put arm around P/T;[a] eyes will show warmth at times; seeks out P/T nonverbally in group; looks to P/T for approval | To feel warmth of P/T; to respond and be accepted by P/T; cuddling and holding; permission to cry; to have P/T feedback feelings of hurt and sadness. |
| 3–4 years | anger, hurt, pain, sadness, bittersweet[b] | Temper tantrums; verbalize hurts; crying, sobbing | Tickling, stories, unorganized spontaneous play; silliness, nursery rhymes; fantasies of P/T being with client on trips to park beach, playing at home; permission and demonstration to act out anger in therapy |
| 5–6 years | hurt, sadness, bittersweet | Begins to take self-control; continues to talk about hurts | Organized games and fantasies: go out for walk, buy ice cream cone, have a treat; cooperative art activities; stories including client's participation. |
| 7–8 years | Anger, sadness, warmth | Communicates anger; centers on source of anger (parent, therapist, significant other) | Roleplay (coping with problems, expressing feelings); awareness of identification with parent; fantasies to replace childhood memories, to try out a missing experience. |
| 8–10 years | Curiosity; cooperation enjoyment | Interested in friends; peer dependency; questions about life, values | Increased expression of feelings; sharing and discussing life; planning and doing activities; expressing ideas and opinions. |
| 11–12 years | Emotional ups and downs start again, rebellious anger | Interest in peer group, sports, organizations; talks about activities | wants P/T to listen; dependency on P/T lessens; expression of feelings toward P/T. |
| 13–14 years early adolescence | Tells P/T when angry; excitement; belonging unsure | Interested in dating, being with opposite sex; sexual fantasies; wants to cope with authority | Shares enjoyment of adolescence; discussion of religion, sex, philosophy; fun to be with. |
| 15–16 years middle adolescence | Wide variety of feelings; easily gets angry at P/T; disagrees openly | Knows what he or she wants from session; can handle things on own | Equality between P/T and client; information on sex and roles; money and goal planning; dealing with own children |
| 17–18 years late adolescence | Rebellion; independence | Wants to break therapy; no longer needs P/T | What kind of man or woman do I want to be? What are my moral values? How will I structure my life? What kind of life style do I want? |

[a] P/T: parent therapist.

[b] Bittersweet: client's sadness mixed with parent therapist's warmth.

the trip with you. My only expectation is that you be honest with your feelings as I will be with mine. All feelings are okay, including sexual feelings; little boys and girls may feel sexual with a parent. If it comes up we will talk about it, but we will not act on it.''

2. *Issues of suicide hospitalization:* These issues should be explored at the beginning of therapy. The client may have had these considerations in the past, and the fear and thought will surface in the therapeutic process.

3. *Fantasies:* Give client experiences with a parent that were missed in childhood; change negative memory to positive.

4. *Activities outside of the office:* Go for a walk, play, have a treat, have a meal or picnic.

5. *Phone calls as an assignment:* Give permission to a client who is afraid to phone the therapist or to limit a client who phones too often by setting limits for phone calls.

6. *Stories:* Read to client stories that fill the needs of the appropriate emotional age and that touch a client issue.

7. *Games:* Play impromptu and silly games, and noncompetitive and competitive games; these give the client spontaneity and assertiveness and deepen the relationship with the therapist.

8. *Role playing:* Therapist functions as parent and the client as a child. Client gets in touch with old situations and feelings, replays alternatives for old situations, adds experiences to childhood, assertively expresses new solutions and feelings in current relationships.

9. *Assignments:* Designed to clarify issues between therapy sessions and practice new behaviors.

10. *Therapist self-disclosure:* Enables the client to understand the surrogate parent emotionally and experientially by contrast, since client's parent was often emotionally closed or continually critical.

11. *Problem solving:* Experiences through role play and communication a variety of choices in childhood and adult issues. Earlier client often saw only "either/or" solutions.

12. *Art activities:* Work and play together for encouragement, spontaneity, cooperation, having fun, and deemphasizing perfection and competition.

13. *Significant others:* Have a session with significant person in client's life who can give support and understanding outside of therapy.

14. *Information:* Use available community resources to help client make work and educational decisions, such as vocational rehabilitation and educational institutions.

15. *Library:* Therapist and client build library of books, magazines, and other literature to promote understanding and awareness and to encourage reading (some clients' concentration has been poor since childhood). Books are made available that speak to the appropriate emotional age.

16. *Big You, Little You* (Kirste & Robertiello, 1975): Client separates his or her child from the adult state and dialogues with each, thus enabling him or her to handle hurtful and stressful situations.

17. *The demon:* The repressed devil or evil core the client sees in the self (screaming tiger, vulture, etc.) is acknowledged, named, and enjoyed by talking about it, drawing it, and putting the picture on the wall to admire.

18. *Parent study group:* Client studies *Children: The Challenge* (Dreikurs & Soltz, 1964) and participates in a parent study group as his or her own parent, discussing the behavior of self and siblings, understanding parents' position, and finally discontinuing parental blame.

## Group Sessions

The group is used to deal with present life situations—family and work relationships—and to experience the opinions of others. This type of group is honest with feedback, at times confrontive, and always supportive. Since one to four members usually work on in-group assignments, thus limiting their general participation, the group size is rather large—from 12 to 14 people. This allows about 10 people to participate in the general discussion.

Friendship and strong feelings of belonging are encouraged because most clients enter therapy feeling quite isolated and do not know how to make close relationships. Groups are held at noon or in the early evening for one hour, and members have lunch or dinner together to strengthen social ties.

The process of each group session is highly structured and divided into five sections: (1) *reactions* to the last session and weekly happenings; (2) *reports* on out-of-group assignments; (3) *introduction of new member* if a new person comes in (groups are ongoing and clients may enter at any time); (4) *presentation and discussion of problems* by two to four clients consecutively; (5) *end-of-group assignment*—some in-group assignments are done at the end, for example, giving each person a criticism by the client who is overly critical. Sections 1, 2, and 4 are done at each session; section 3 is done if a new person comes in; and section 5 occurs if someone has that form of assignment.

Feedback is given by therapist and group members during presentation and discussion of problems, and an assignment is suggested relating to the issue presented. Assignments help the client desensitize a fear, experience a new behavior, practice a nonfamiliar behavior, or overuse a negative behavior to eliminate it. Assignments are given for in-group or out-of-group practice.

Examples of in-group assignments are: (1) group host/hostess—gives a hug to each member upon arriving and leaving the session to help the client feel he or she belongs to the group; (2) group prince/princess—person is catered to by other members (given candy, gum, footstool, shoulder massage) to overdo his or her wish for pampering; (3) mask—client wears mask and reports feelings as session goes on to get in touch with feelings. The group continues with the discussion, tuning out the persons acting out their assignments.

Examples of out-of-group assignments are: (1) call group members or allow them to call you—for persons who feel isolated; (2) do clumsy and silly things—for the client who tries to be perfect; (3) ask people to do things for you (get you coffee, run an errand)—for the client who fears asking or is unable to receive from others; (4) be friendly but uncooperative—for the client who is nonassertive. Assignments last for six or more sessions, until the client learns the necessary lesson.

Through the use of the individual parenting and the group sessions, the client becomes more positive and optimistic about life, anger and sadness lessen, and coping skills increase.

## APPLICATION

A very wide range of behaviors and attitudes develops from being rejected as a child. Depending upon the degree of discouragement or nonadjustment, the client may fall into many categories of diagnosis—from the various neuroses to psychoses to character disorders. All of these can be treated in PRT.

### Neurosis

The neurotic client who consults us because of problems with family, work, friendship, or intimate relationships is placed in group and Primary Relationship Therapy if rejection (neglect, abuse) is an issue. The diagnosis may be any neurotic disorder—depressive, anxiety, hysterical, and so forth.

## Psychosis

The borderline to the severely psychotic client can be helped with a one-to-one, long-term, warmly nurturing therapy plus group therapy. For example, a 26-year-old female schizophrenic was sent to us by a psychiatrist, who said "Either you take her into PRT or I will have to send her to an institution for the rest of her life." The psychosis had prevailed throughout most of the client's life. Her mother was 45 and father 48 when she was born, and they were unable to accept her disturbance of their couple state. As a young child she had been very much aware of not being wanted. The client improved in this therapy and was able to leave her parents' home.

The less severely disturbed psychotic can also benefit from this therapy. Frequently this client is "borderline" psychotic. The warm, nurturing relationship with a parent therapist is usually the first time this person has been truly accepted by another person. The response finally emerges into the development of trust in the therapist.

## The Client Who Needs Hospitalization

In our practice we do not accept clients who are hospitalized. However, occasionally a client (psychotic or neurotic) becomes anxious or severely depressed after entering PRT. With the client's desires to escape present pressures and responsibilities, he or she may decide to go to a hospital for a while. We may or may not encourage this step, but once the client chooses this alternative we support it. As of this writing we have had only two clients (one neurotic and one psychotic) who made this decision; both stayed in the hospital three or four weeks. We were not involved in the hospital treatment but did keep in touch with the psychiatrist in charge and visited each client as a friend. Upon dismissal, the clients discussed their hospital experience with their therapy groups. They seemed to benefit from the experience by realizing that the hospital was only a tem-porary escape, that it was not the most pleasant place to be (although not unpleasant), and that it was up to them to take care of their responsibilities and to get well. Neither client returned to the hospital.

## Adolescents and Children

Although Primary Relationship Therapy is generally considered a psychotherapy for adults, we at times accept adolescents for a full-term therapy and children for a short time. This occurs occasionally when we have a parent in therapy who has been unable to give nurturing or support to his or her child, and the child is withdrawn, acting-out, or extremely rebellious. Since the child does not have a bonding with the parents, a nurturing therapist can lead him or her into learning to trust others and to accept self as a loving person. We generally accept adolescents into a teen group only. In the cases mentioned, though, there was severe depression in the adolescents stemming from feelings of rejection and the group did not suffice.

## Marriage and Family Counseling

At times a client who has felt rejected consults us for a marriage or childrearing problem. The client is unable to relate closely to his or her spouse, and the deep anger may lead to child abuse, especially if the client was abused as a child. The need for learning to cope with marriage and childrearing processes must be delayed until the client develops the ego-strength to cope with his or her own life. This is a very difficult situation for the entire family.

If one spouse is better able to handle the children, we ask that he or she do so until the client recovers. In one case a mother was assigned to PRT when she was unable to cope with her two children, one three and one four. She had quite seriously abused them. The father was unable to care for them, so they were sent to live with relatives for a year until the mother was able to handle herself and then the children. At that time (before she finished her own therapy) the mother was helped with problems of marriage and chil-drearing.

A wide range of behaviors develop from neglect, rejection, or abuse as a child. The degree of disturbance or nonfunctioning varies, and many types of the psychoses and neuroses are helped with Primary Relationship Therapy.

## CASE EXAMPLE

Joy, 26, a married woman, working as a tutor of children with learning difficulties, was ridden with anxiety but was a master at covering her feelings. She seemed self-assured, competent, and beautiful. Under the mask she felt shaky, incapable, unlovable, and ugly. She had been in other types of psychotherapy for many years.

Joy's mother was a perfectionist who treated her daughter, when young, as if she were a lovely doll. She dressed her beautifully, curled her hair, made sure she used the best manners. Her mother was also very critical because Joy was to be the perfect child—the child who could elevate the mother's position in life. Joy's mother herself had been raised by a strict mother and was not given warmth by either parent. She had not learned to be loving.

After several sessions in Primary Relationship Therapy and group sessions in which she mostly listened, Joy's facade was gone during one visit.

J:   I'm scared, I'm feeling like I'm floating above the ground.

T:   That is Okay. Come sit close to me on our floor pillow and I'll hold you. (Therapist cradles Joy as if she were a very little child.)

J:   My heart is beating fast.

T:   It will soon slow down (softly). Close your eyes; we are going on a lovely trip. See these big balloons with heavy ropes—one for you and one for me. Now I'm tying one around your waist and one around my own. And I'm holding on to you so you are per-

fectly safe. Aren't they lovely? They are Disneyland balloons. We're beginning to take off, here we go, just above the ground, and now a little higher. We're just above the rooftops of the small houses and going higher so we can just fly. Now we have cleared everything in the way, and we are up pretty high and just having a marvelous time. It is so beautiful up here, you and I both love it. Let's stay here for a while and just enjoy the beauty, peace, and quiet. (By now Joy is relaxed in the arms of the therapist silently enjoying it.)

T:   We're going to land now, just slowly down. We are enjoying the descent; it is easy. Coming down slowly, slowly, coming down. Here we are, down on the ground, feeling good. Joy, any time you feel that you are floating you can just remember to put the balloon rope around you and land yourself gently, just as we did now. How do you feel?

J:   I feel Okay. Not scared, and I'm not floating anymore.

*Comment.* The therapist joined in Joy's hallucination of floating and gently led her back to reality. It was the first time the therapist knew that Joy had psychotic tendencies. They showed again from time to time in which she either felt things were unreal or she was floating.

Joy remained feeling like a very little girl for some time. The therapist quietly cuddled her much of the time and also did other guided fantasies with Joy's assistance.

T:   Come let me hold you. Close your eyes. Can you see yourself as a little girl? How old are you?

J:   I'm one year old, just beginning to walk.

T:   Yes, you are my beautiful little girl, and you are just waking up this morning. I'm going to dress you.

J:   No (with alarm)! I don't want you to dress me in a beautiful dress.

T:   No, of course not. You are my beautiful baby girl, beautiful with no clothes on. I'm just going to put a diaper on you so you don't weewee all over the floor. You are lovable just as you are. You don't need a pretty dress.

J: That's better (more relaxed). I think I'm walking along a coffee table, looking at the things on the table.

T: Yes, you can look at those things. You really are curious.

J: Yes, I am. Won't you get mad that I'm touching things?

T: No, little girls can explore. There is nothing that will break anyway.

*Comment.* Joy is given the opportunity to be appreciated and loved just for being herself—with no clothes on. She is also given permission to be a very little girl and to enjoy her environment with a supportive surrogate mother.

As she began feeling older in therapy (five and six years old), Joy enjoyed doing artwork and showed a great deal of talent.

J: Sometimes I feel very strange, like there is someone or something else inside me that no one knows about.

T: Can you draw me a picture of the something inside of you? Joy, is that something bad, not Okay? Would you let me see it? What would it look like?

J: A scary, creepy thing like in a horror movie. It can pounce on you and make you scream. You won't like it.

T: Well, I think I can handle it. I would like to know this something. Maybe it just wants someone to know it exists. Is it really that awful?

J: Well, maybe if I draw it you can see. It chews up my insides sometimes. I feel like it is always feeding on me. Let's see, I think it is like a centipede.

T: With all those legs it would feel strange inside of you.

J: (engrossed in the face of the centipede) The eyes aren't right. She must be vicious.

T: She looks sad to me. I can almost see tears in her eyes.

J: She is sad. She is very sad.

T: If no one knows she is there, then she must also feel very lonely.

J: She isn't really mean, is she? She is lonely and sad. There, now you can see the tears. (Joy added tears to the face of the centipede.)

T: I would like to care about the centipede (putting arms around Joy). Would she let me be her friend?

J: She trusts you but she is scared. Yes, she wants you to be her friend. She's scared you will think she is ugly and awful and that you won't really care.

T: We'll have to be gentle with her so she will learn that she is not ugly and awful. Joy, can you accept the centipede and help me take care of her?

J: I want to.

*Comment.* The centipede represented to Joy the ugly place in her that was unacceptable. She did not want to see this ugly place and wanted to keep it hidden from the rest of the world. In encouraging her to name and draw her ugly place, we had acknowledged the hidden part of Joy that represented the hurts of rejection and sadness, of feeling unworthy of love. The picture was placed on the therapist's office wall, and Joy and the therapist played with the centipede. The sadness was replaced first by shyness and then a happy feeling.

At one point in her therapy Joy suddenly began sobbing and screaming.

J: I am in a black place and I can't get out. It's a black hole or cave.

T: Hold on to my hand; you are not alone. I am going to be with you.

J: I can't get out; there is no way out (sobbing).

T: I am not going to leave you. We will find the way out together. Let's walk slowly and see what is up ahead. This cave has a tunnel and I will not let go of you. I think I feel a turn coming; yes, the tunnel turns to the left. Hold on, it will be Okay. There is a faint light ahead; can you see it?

J:   Yes (still clinging to therapist).

T:   We will walk toward the light, there will be a way out. Yes, it is getting brighter. Oh, the light comes from the top of the tunnel. There are rocks we can climb on. Here, let me help you up. Are you Okay?

J:   Yes, I made it (no longer sobbing).

T:   Here I come. Can you make it through the hole?

J:   Yes, but I'm scared.

T:   I feel scared too but I'm not going to give up. Let's find out what is outside.

J:   You go first.

T:   All right. There I'm out. Give me your hand. We made it, we are out. See where we are. We are on top of a mountain.

J:   It isn't black anymore.

T:   Let's sit and rest for a while. We can climb down later.

J:   I feel safe (still being held by the therapist).

T:   Stay quiet and enjoy being safe. We have time to feel safe.

The following is a letter to the therapist written after five months of therapy:

Dear Genevieve:

I've had so many strong reactions to therapy. I want to connect with you. I don't feel comfortable calling at work as I know you are busy and I feel it unfair to take up your time in that situation. [Joy had been given permission to phone when she wanted to.]

Plus I know you're leaving sometime, and to be honest, I think I'd feel sad if a secretary told me you were out of town. So in a way, I prefer not opening it up too much. I guess I'm a little afraid of being overwhelmed by feelings—by reaching out to you.

After our last session I felt joy. Jumping up and down even. I also realized I was cautious about accepting the joy. Like it was on a deep level, but my conscious mind stayed in control.

I've become aware how constantly I desire acceptance from others. I sense my tension, watch it manifest and know exactly where it's coming from. It's difficult getting involved outside of myself, as I'm always watching other people or guarding myself.

For example, Tom [husband] was telling me about some ideas and I could see him only on the edge of my awareness. I was conscious mainly of desiring his acceptance. Not verbally. In a deeper way, like having my head on his lap. In a state like that I appear irrational, as any seemingly critical remark hurts my feelings or angers me, etc. Actually, it might simply be a statement of fact. I guess I'm watching for disapproval from Tom. Guarding myself is the word!

Also, whenever I feel overwhelmed by anything (mental conflicts, like decisions or even ambivalent feelings) I'm usually sad. I know this because this a.m. I stopped trying to decide what to do today in an anxious way and when I paused I regressed and felt small and sad.

I like knowing all this. It helps me to understand myself. It makes dealing with colleagues and outside acquaintances easier. (I'm not trying for their approval as much.) It's made dealing with closer friends and Tom clearer, but not easier. In fact, more difficult. I'm so aware of my deep desire to be loved and accepted by them that I don't know what to do. Like having a tea party in a thunderstorm.

About you. I feel a consistent warmth. I only feel secure when you are especially sending me your love (focusing on me). When you're thinking about an idea (just being you) I don't feel secure. Then it's like with friends—I desire to have that feeling of closeness, and get your full attention. Rationally, I know that it's absurd to take all your attention. The truth is my hunger is so great I have difficulty focusing on anything else.

As far as therapy goes, I basically feel positive and warm. My only fear is that I can never be filled. Filling a well with a measuring cup is my analogy.

Till Wednesday
Joy

P.S. In a way, it's never been easier living with myself. Now I don't fear what's inside, so I feel less out of balance. My difficulty comes when I fight the sadness, or fear the enormity of it.

Joy remained in therapy for one year. Her therapy had not actually been completed when she left with her husband, who had been transferred. Once she got over the infant stage her therapy went faster. She went up and down in age and emotions. By the time she left she felt comfortable in leaving the therapist, who assured her that she was able to handle her life on her own. Initially Joy had greatly feared pregnancy and motherhood. By the time she was settled in her new home, she was looking forward to motherhood and was determined to become pregnant. She later sent the therapist a picture of her baby and parents, and assured the therapist that she already had a close relationship with her daughter.

## SUMMARY

Primary Relationship Therapy (PRT) is a form of psychotherapy for the person who feels strongly rejected by one or both parents. Robert Postel, who evolved the therapy in the 1960s, died before he had written about PRT. Postel's new approach is based on Alfred Adler's theory that the neglected child has never known love and finds society cold, believing that it will always be cold.

The therapy involves the client in a warm, nurturing, supportive relationship with first a mother therapist, and then a father therapist, to work on childhood issues of neglect, hurt, anger, fear, and so forth. The client is also assigned to a therapy group to work on present adult concerns.

The therapy is useful to both neurotic and psychotic clients—anyone who has the issue of rejection (neglect, abuse) to deal with. The outgrowths of this process include increased feelings of self-love, self-worth, a significant lowering of anxiety level and depression, feelings of internal strength and the development of social embeddedness, which finally enable close, intimate relationships to develop.

Since this process is experiential more than verbal or insight oriented, it seems to produce a deep and lasting change in the client.

## REFERENCES

Adler, A. *What life should mean to you*. New York: Capricorn Books, 1958.

Ansbacher, H. and Ansbacher, R. *The individual psychology of Alfred Adler*. New York: Harper Torchbooks, 1964.

Dreikurs, R. and Soltz, V. *Children: The challenge*. New York: Hawthorn Books, 1964.

Kirsten, G. and Robertiello, R. *Big you, little you*. New York: Dial Press, 1975.

Montagu, A. *Touching: The human significance of the skin*. New York: Perennial Library, 1972.

# CHAPTER 50

# *Provocative Therapy*

FRANK FARRELLY and SCOTT MATTHEWS

*Undoubtedly this chapter will not only inform the reader about Provocative Therapy but will also provoke him or her to amazement—laughter—disbelief. Certainly, PT is one of the more innovative of psychotherapies in current use, and apparently it violates many of the commonly accepted preconceptions of courtesy and the dignity of the therapist-client professional "relationships."*

*Developed by Frank Farrelly, PT employs humor as one of its major tools. It also uses the "Leaning Tower of Pisa" approach to exaggerate and make worse various situations, to lead the client to see the humor and nonsense of his or her well-established position. Other forms of humor are found in O'Connell's Natural High Therapy, and similar confrontation techniques are seen also in Albert Ellis's Rational Emotive Therapy.*

*I imagine that Farrelly's rationale is that his system works best for him, and that he will employ many forms of humor including exaggeration, mimicry, ridicule, distortion, sarcasm, irony, and just plain jokes for the patient's benefit by deliberately violating the shibboleths of conventional thinking. This leads to the central issue of this book: Should a therapist employ such shock tactics even if they are personally distasteful to him or her? Should one at least know that such an approach can work with some people at some time? Should mordant humor become part of the complete therapist's armamentarium?*

*Among the interesting elements of this therapy is that it was developed in the context of that most courteous and gentle of all therapies—Carl Rogers' Client-Centered Therapy. This too can be seen as client-centered—with an ironic, humorous twist. PT deserves careful study.*

Provocative Therapy is a system of working with clients* developed by Frank Farrelly in the early 1960s, primarily while working with psychotic people in a state mental hospital; it has also been used successfully for almost two decades on a wide range of clients in outpatient settings. The therapeutic focus is on clients' false ideas, erroneous assumptions, painful feelings, and self-defeating behaviors. Clients are humorously and perceptively provoked or challenged to continue

*Note: The words "client" and "patient" are used in this chapter. A client is a nonhospitalized person; a patient is a hospitalized person.

in their misery-seeking ways to mobilize their own resistances and defenses against themselves for change. To effect this change, a strongly affective experience is deliberately established by the therapist, who uses nonpredictable behavioral responses that place clients in an altered state of consciousness, creates in them the felt experiencing of being deeply understood on multiple levels, irritates and amuses them, and rapidly connects them to their own personal power. The most outstanding characteristic of this system of psychotherapy is its effective and unusual use of humor to motivate clients to positive and growth-producing actions.

# HISTORY

One of Frank Farrelly's early goals was to enter the priesthood to help people. As a member of a devout Irish Catholic family, he grew up listening to the nuns and priests and to his father's Irish folktales and humor, all of which set a stage for what was to come as he began his studies in social work. It was his clients, however, who played the most influential part in the eventual development of Provocative Therapy as a system.

The history of the development of Provocative Therapy centers around a series of client-provoked experiences. Early in his career Farrelly read Carl Rogers's *Client-Centered Therapy* (1951) and was impressed with the verbatim interview samples. As Farrelly remembers: "This is the way it really is, with a broken sentence structure, the 'uhs,' the fractured grammar, the misunderstandings and efforts to correct them, and all" (Farrelly & Brandsma, 1974). He especially was impressed with Rogers's attempt to understand his clients from *their* internal state of reference.

The next important client influence was "the case of the malingering nut" (p. 10).* One day Farrelly "threw therapy out the window" and became furious at a client for writing obscene and frightening letters to a young hospital secretary. He threatened to "lock him in seclusion and throw away the key." "You can't hold me responsible—I'm mentally ill," replied the patient. Farrelly's conclusion was that the "mentally ill" have not all lost contact with reality, but that they know perfectly well what they are doing in most instances and are, in a sense, clever social systems analysts.

Through the inadvertent development of "open-fly therapy" (Farrelly's pants fly was open and obviously influenced an interview with a woman from whom he had to get a confession of sexual infidelity to her husband), he learned to laugh at himself and to

*From this point forward, all citations are to Farrelly & Brandsma, 1974.

share his "bloopers" with colleagues and clients.

In the "Clem Kadiddlehopper" case, he treated the patient who, indeed, looked and acted like the Red Skelton character, Clem Kadiddlehopper—a man with a shock of red hair standing four inches straight off his head and with his false teeth missing, two squinty little pig eyes, a bulbous tomato nose, and a ludicrous tone of voice. As soon as he saw the man, Farrelly began to laugh until tears streamed down his face. The psychologist co-therapist told him, "That's no way to treat a patient." The patient interrupted, "No, it's Okay, that's been the trouble. I try to make people laugh, then they laugh sometimes when I don't want them to, and I get hurt and mad and into trouble." Farrelly learned that "radical congruence, held constant, was very helpful to the patient." Laughter toward the patient's idiotic ideas and behavior did not inevitably demean their dignity (p. 13).

In the "case of the dangerous psychopath," Farrelly, after listening to an obviously well thought out speech by a patient about why he should be discharged from the hospital, stated, "Well, I think it's the slickest con job I've ever had pulled on me." After an excited tirade of anger and disjointed emotional behavior, the patient asked Farrelly to be his therapist. When asked why, he replied, "Cause you don't give me no shit off the wall." Farrelly concluded that confrontation and emotional honesty can quickly build a relationship of trust (p. 14).

In the "case of the slutty virgin," a young woman in group therapy who acted promiscuously but protested she was still a virgin was told, "Well, you talk like a slut; you dress like a slut; you walk like a slut; and you look like a slut. It's not what you are objectively, kid; it's the image you create in other people's minds." The patient tearfully remarked that she "wasn't that kind of girl." The group helped her develop more appropriate behaviors, she became a model patient, and was soon discharged. Several basic lessons were learned from this case. First, people can change dramatically and maintain their new behaviors and attitudes. Second, they can change in a relatively short period of time. Third, a vicious circle of negative feelings, attitudes, and behaviors can be changed to a beneficial reaction of positive behavior reinforced by praise and positive feedback, which leads to further changed feelings and attitudes. Farrelly concluded that the group is a powerful therapeutic tool and that people react to a person according to the subjective image they have of him or her in their "heads and guts." If this is true, the therapist's task is to aid the patient to attend to and not ignore the feedback that others, including the therapist, are communicating toward the patient and to help the patient act on this feedback (p. 17).

To a young male patient who bellowed, "You sound just like my father," the reply was, "Then your father and I would get along famously, buddy!" Farrelly discovered early that in his "countertransferrence," or strong reactions toward the patient, he often was highly accurate and learned that expressing these responses was more helpful than if he had suppressed them. In their book *Critical Incidents in Psychotherapy* (1959), Standal and Corsini describe case after case in which the therapist abandoned the standard response patterns and vented some long pent-up feelings toward the patient, with surprisingly consequent patient improvement.

In 1963 a woman being discharged from the mental hospital shared her worry that "my family is going to be watching my every move." Farrelly agreed with that observation and helped her utilize this insight to effect a community adjustment. Often patients' observations and formulations are more accurate than ours are (p. 21).

The specific interview in which Provocative Therapy was discovered occurred in July 1963, while Farrelly was participating in Carl Rogers's research project with chronic schizophrenics at Mendota State Hospital.

In the ninety-first interview with Farrelly, who was using a client-centered approach, the patient was still insisting that he was worthless and hopeless, and averred that he

was doomed to be perpetually psychotic. Farrelly had been reiterating that the patient was worthwhile, of value, and could change. Finally tiring of arguing with the patient, suddenly Farrelly humorously began agreeing with the patient's negative self-concept. Almost immediately the patient began to explode with laughter and to protest that he was not *that* bad or *that* hopeless, and to say the therapist had been of great help to him. The therapist disagreed humorously and declared that if he had been of any help to the patient and the patient was showing any kind of progress, he was moving with all the speed of a turtle encased in concrete. Within six interviews, the patient rapidly improved and was discharged (p. 27).

Each of these isolated experiences cemented together an experientially based theory that Farrelly later christened Provocative Therapy. Each therapist reaches his own "moment of discovery". Albert Ellis (1962) discussed the particular interview in which he discovered Rational Emotive Psychotherapy. Carl Rogers (1961) described the critical interview he had with the mother of a failure case. Blanchard (1970) has stated:

It is a convention in the scientific world to report the emergence of new theory as though it emerges slowly and inevitably from the analytical throttling of data. The scientist is pictured as plodding through his method, discovering some discrepancy until he stumbles over the doorstep of theory. Actually, far more often than not, the theory springs into the scientist's vision as a wild surmise, and he spends most of his time searching for facts to fit it. (p. 10)

And so it was with the discovery of Provocative Therapy.

## CURRENT STATUS

Provocative Therapy now is used in a wide variety of settings in both private and institutional work. Practitioners of psychology, clinical social work, psychiatry, psychiatric nursing, guidance and counseling, and others in the mental health field have been trained in and are currently using Provocative Therapy as their primary identifiable mode of treatment.

Currently the only center for training in Provocative Therapy is through the Madison Psychotherapy Associates in Madison, Wisconsin. Training is available in various forms, including: (1) PT supervision by telephone, (2) PT telephone seminars, (3) in-service training, and (4) individual training in Provocative Therapy.

Farrelly gives workshops throughout the country, which last from one to three days and include a lecture on Provocative Therapy, interviews with workshop members, "therapist-client" feedback session, group discussion, role playing of clients difficult for the therapists, experiential training, and so forth.

In PT supervision by telephone Farrelly is called by therapists across the nation for consultation on specific cases: for help when they are "stuck"; to broaden their perspectives about their work, themselves (both professionally and personally), and the systems within which they operate; as well as to increase their therapeutic response repertoire.

PT telephone seminars are provided to universities, agencies, and training centers; usually there is a two-hour "live" lecture on Provocative Therapy with case illustrations, comparisons with other psychotherapies, and wide-ranging discussion with embarrassing questions invited.

With in-service training, professionals in a variety of therapeutic settings work with both voluntary and involuntary clients. In-service training provides an opportunity for in-depth discussions on a wide variety of topics, including mental health delivery systems and system maintenance needs; predictable community and psychological pressures with specific client populations; meeting the needs of professionals to obviate "burnout"; you, sex, and the client; and others.

In addition to the above modes of teaching, individual supervised training in Provocative

Therapy is offered which has been dubbed "the parapatetic school of Provocative Therapy." This is an intensive experience for one or two mental health professionals or trainees for one week, tailored to their goals and individual schedules; this program includes direct therapeutic encounters in individual, family, and group treatment; PT interviews with trainee, audiotapes, readings, and so forth.

There are several publications, both written and audiotaped. *Provocative Therapy* (Farrelly & Brandsma, 1974), the major text, is a personal and detailed account of the system. The book includes a history and theory of Provocative Therapy as well as chapters on humor and Provocative Therapy, the four languages of Provocative Therapy, and the role of the provocative therapist.

"The Code of Chronicity" (Ludwig and Farrelly, 1966) and "The Weapons of Insanity" (Ludwig and Farrelly, 1967) are papers that develop the theoretical stance that is taken in Provocative Therapy.

"Provocative Therapy" (Farrelly, 1977) is a series of twelve audio cassette tapes in which Farrelly talks about the PT system and then demonstrates it with a series of interviews with patients ranging from the seriously delusional mental hospital patient to a confused college student.

The American Academy of Psychotherapists Tape Library tape number 58 is *Provocative Therapy* (Farrelly, 1971). This tape includes a lecture on Provocative Therapy and a demonstration with a hospitalized suicidal adolescent.

Richard Bandler and John Grindler analyze Frank Farrelly's demonstration of Provocative Therapy in an audio *Digest* tape entitled "Analyzing the Analyst—Identifying Effective Interventions" (Farrelly, 1978).

## THEORY

There is an old tale of the five blind Indian fakirs who are led to an elephant—one touched the trunk, another the ear, still another the leg, another the belly, and the last was given the tail to touch. Each, of course, experienced the elephant differently, then came to his own conclusions about his experiencing of this object. Much as the Indian fakirs did, each theory of psychotherapy is based on its own set of assumptions and hypotheses—a mental framework that utilizes specific techniques.

There are 10 assumptions and two hypotheses upon which Provocative Therapy is based (pp. 36–52). The assumptions are:

*"People change and grow in response to a challenge."* In Provocative Therapy, the client is carefully challenged so that he or she is forced to cope with rather than run from problems and the therapist. The therapist will pursue the client and not tolerate avoidance on the client's part. In contrast to many therapies where the attempt is to maintain the calm, cool, and smooth interview, the provocative therapist is attempting to create a healing energy vortex.

*"Clients can change if they choose."* In the Old Testament of the Bible, Adam and Eve were given free will. They were not helpless pawns, and neither are today's clients. "Few people other than therapists really believe that man is not responsible for what he does, that he does not choose but is driven." Instead of accepting the client's "I can't change," the provocative therapist firmly believes the client can change but humorously agrees and echoes the helplessly despairing "I'm trapped" messages of psychological determinism that the client asserts, in order to provoke the client into perceiving that his or her nonfunctioning is because he or she will not, rather than cannot, change.

*"Clients have far more potential for achieving adaptive, productive, and socialized modes of living than they and most clinicians assume."* Although clients believe they are helpless and hopeless, the greatest tragedy occurs when the therapist seriously agrees with the self-evaluation and says, "If I can't cure them, they're incurable." Furthermore, for the therapist to believe this is to perform an inappropriate psychological

alchemy whereby the therapist's failure is transformed magically into a *fact* residing in the client.

*"The psychological fragility of clients is vastly overrated both by themselves and others."* Although most clients and therapists see the client as someone similar to Humpty Dumpty, the ill-fated egg that fell off the wall, who will crack, break, or fall apart at the slightest provocation, the provocative therapist sees the client as having many strong, positive traits that form the basis of the emergence of the new person. For the provocative therapist it is not such a miracle that most people survive growing up and becoming adults without going crazy. The provocative therapist deliberately and humorously overfocuses on what is "wrong" with the client to provoke him or her into offering what is 'right" with him or her, to reaffirm strengths, and to actualize operationally personal power.

*"The client's maladaptive, unproductive, antisocial attitudes and behaviors can be drastically altered whatever the degree or severity of chronicity."* There is ample clinical evidence (cf. research on self-fulfilling prophecy) that supports the contention that people will change and respond to the belief of their significant others. If others believe the client can get well, the client often gets well, not by any miraculous process, but by the multiple ways in which the client is treated by others perceived as important by him or her. Finally a frequently significant phase in the process is when the client *chooses* to get better.

*"Adult or current experiences are as at least if not more significant than childhood or previous experiences in shaping client values, operational attitudes, and behaviors."* This is essentially the assumption underlying all views of psychotherapy as a corrective emotional experience capable of reversing years of maladaptation and generalizing to other relationships outside therapy. Every effective therapist operationally believes that the client is capable of changing, and that the experiences the client is

having with the therapist are capable of being transferred by the client to life outside the hospital or the therapist's office.

*"The client's behavior with the therapist is a relatively accurate reflection of his habitual pattern of social and interpersonal relationships."* Even though the client will act and react much as he or she acts outside the therapy room, the therapist presents a much different stimulus configuration. The therapist frequently (1) presents the client with an evaluation as significant others might perceive him or her and react to him or her; (2) negatively models social situations that will humorously demonstrate the negative social consequences that follow with a high degree of probability from the client's attitudes and behaviors; and (3) refers to the behavioral shaping and feedback available to the client from the matrix of his or her social relationship. ([T leaning forward, places his hand gently on C's forearm, says in a warm, "supportive" voice] "Look, dummy, you have got about the craziest picture of yourself I have ever seen, but then nobody is perfect. Even with your own distorted perception, I bet you can hear what others are telling you. But go ahead and ignore them, then you will really have a reason to be depressed.")

*People are relatively easy to understand—especially when we have the relevant data.* The provocative therapist, believing firmly in the necessity to obtain this data to achieve depth and breadth of understanding, will immediately approach those areas that the client shows he or she wants to avoid. In effect, the provocative therapist develops "red-green color blindness." When the client signals "Stop!" (blushing, hesitancy, avoidance, or outright resistance to discussing a topic), the therapist charges ahead.

*The judicious expression of "therapeutic hate and joyful sadism" toward the client can paradoxically markedly benefit him or her.* The reason that the mentally ill often feel rejected and unloved is because they *are* often rejected and unloved—for their rejectable and unlovable behaviors. The provoc-

ative therapist would rather offer genuine rejection for a given client behavior than a phony constrained acceptance. Consider this 18-year-old functionally illiterate female patient. Very combative and assaultive, she stabbed three people with pencils and threw a TV at a pregnant woman.*

P:  (Snarling) I am going to kick your goddamn teeth down your fucking throat.

T:. (Looking levelly at the patient) Yeah? And what do you think I am going to be doing while you're kicking my goddamn teeth down my fucking throat?

P:  (Taken aback; pauses, muttering sulkily) You'll bite my foot off at the ankle.

T:  (Nodding and smiling) You got it, you bitch. (Farrelly & Brandsma, 1974, p. 49)

In another example, a large family came in for therapy. Their house was in a constant state of chaos and the educationally sophisticated mother felt angry, guilty, and ready to collapse. She was asked for one concrete example of how she could be helped by the children in this situation. She decided that things would be measurably easier for her if the children would pack away their own clothes after being laundered.

T:  I am going to teach you how to be joyfully sadistic.

C:  What's that?

T:  How to inflict pain on others and get to love it. (Farrelly & Brandsma, 1974, p. 50)

In front of the children and with much humor and persuasion, the therapist convinced her to offer her children no food until their clothes were put away and to adopt the biblical injunction "If you don't work, you don't eat." With only five meal deprivations scattered among 10 children in two days, each and every child was cooperating beautifully. Often in therapy, distinction must be made between short-term cruelty with long-

---

*In the following dialogues, T stands for therapist, P, for patient, C, for client.

term kindness versus short-term kindness and long-term detriment.

*"The more important messages between people are nonverbal. It is not what is said, it is how it is said that is crucial."* Since often the provocative therapist transmits very negative verbal feedback (to sensitize or desensitize, set limits, provoke reality testing, etc.), he or she must also counterbalance that with highly positive nonverbal messages (for support, to make more palatable the rather bitter pills all of us must swallow at times, etc.). The provocative therapist frequently and deliberately appears to be incongruent by communicating one thing at one level with words, but quite the opposite with body language, tonal inflection, and other significant nonverbal qualifications. The therapist is communicating at different levels simultaneously, thereby creating ambiguity and a consequent altered state of consciousness within the client, a period of heightened suggestibility and receptivity during which the client can receive the nonverbal suggestions far more easily.

T: (Smiling, laughing warmly, leaning forward, gently patting the C.'s knee) Me like you? You have to be kidding. (T leans back, gazes quizzically at far corner of ceiling as though mental vistas are opening to him; slowly, in a puzzled, low tone, as though to himself.) Actually . . . I will confess to a scientific curiosity in *his* (gesturing nonchalantly toward C) case.

C: (Exploding with laughter) Well, I guess you've got poor judgment then, Scott.

T: ("Coming out of trance") Huh?!

There are two central hypotheses upon which Provocative Therapy is based. The first concerns the client's self-concept: If provoked by the therapist (humorously, perceptively, and within the client's own internal frame of reference), the client will tend to move in the opposite direction from the therapist's definition of the client as a person. The second hypothesis focuses on the client's overt behavior: If urged provocatively (humorously and perceptively) by the therapist to continue his or her self-defeating, deviant behavior,

the client will tend to engage in self- and other-enhancing behaviors, which more closely approximate the societal norm. These hypotheses are subject to proof and disproof with each new client.

In addition to the assumptions and hypotheses, the four different stages of process for the client in Provocative Therapy merit inclusion here. Although not sharply defined and somewhat impressionistic, they occur with sufficient frequency to be discernable.

*First Stage.* Typically in the first interview, the client is often left astonished and incredulous, uncertain, and humorously provoked. A typical response might be "I don't understand how you can help people this way, I've never had anybody talk to me like that." Or "I don't know why I'm laughing at what I've said. . . . I can't help it, what I've been doing seems so funny." Almost invariably the client returns for subsequent interviews (more than 90 percent return).

*Second Stage.* The client begins to realize that the therapist is accurate, and it is the client, not the therapist, who must change. Often there is a transitory sulkiness in the client's responses: "I don't like it, but you are right about me." A reduction and even at times total absence of psychotic defenses (when they have been present) is a mark of this stage.

*Third Stage.* This stage is characterized by the client becoming more rational and attempting to prove the therapist wrong. The client marshals and displays specific, concrete, and easily observable behaviors as evidence to disprove the therapist's definition and description of him or her.

*Fourth Stage.* Here the client will refer to his or her former self, or "The way I used to be." Often the client is able to laugh at his or her old self and laugh when he or she "goofs up" with new behaviors. This is an integrative and terminating stage in Provocative Therapy.

## APPLICATIONS

Because of the powerful tactics and strategies inherent in this system and the wide variety of behaviors that it allows the therapist to engage in to enhance communication skills in the interview, it has been successfully employed with clients ranging in age from preschool to geriatrics, with hospitalized and nonhospitalized clients, with psychotics from mute catatonics to manic-depressives in the manic phase, with character disorders and neurotics, with clients ranging in intelligence levels from the mentally retarded (educable level) to genius, as well as with all the major racial and ethnic groups in the United States and with people of other nationalities. Perhaps because of the provocative therapist's determination to and delight in crossing boundaries (class, sex, ethnic, racial, educational, religious, etc.), no major group, either diagnostic (with the exception of organic disorders) or sociological, has been found to date with which Provocative Therapy has not been successful. Additionally, as with other therapeutic orientations it has been especially successful with the YAVIS client (young, attractive, verbal, intelligent, successful) who (1) see talking over problems as helpful; (2) have an inner felt disturbance rather than an overt, acting-out behavioral disturbance; and (3) who are willing to engage in extensive self-exploration. Finally, it has been used with different client system sizes: individuals, couples, families, and group therapies.

However, it should be emphasized that therapy systems do not directly help clients. Instead therapy systems help therapists organize the kalidescopic ideational, affective, and behavioral phenomena that individuals bring to therapists to treat. Again, therapy systems do not help people; people help people.

And here is perhaps the significant, albeit puzzling, limitation of Provocative Therapy: Why should it aid and facilitate the therapist in helping one client while, with another highly similar client (in diagnosis, age, social background, etc.), the system apparently fails the therapist to be equally helpful? No research study of Provocative Therapy has been made to date to examine questions such as this, but preliminary evidence from provocative therapists across the country suggests that the therapist's energy level and investment with unsuccessful clients were not as high as with the puzzlingly similar clients who enjoyed successful outcomes. Was the decrease in energy investment a function of the specific relationship between the therapist and this particular client, or did the client counterprovoke the therapist to the degree that the therapist's initial energy investment was counterconditioned or extinguished? Is Provocative Therapy—in point of fact, all healing endeavors—basically a transfer to, release of, or increase in energy magnitude? And when the therapy was unsuccessful, was this because the energy level of the therapist (healer) was not sufficiently high or was blocked or short-circuited in some undefined way by either the client or the therapist so that the transfer, release, or increase of energy failed to occur?

## METHODOLOGY

Provocative Therapy is described as a "broadly based procedure applying many techniques and a wide range of freedom in responding for the therapist" (p. 55). Bandler and Grindler in *Frogs into Princes: Neuro-Linguistic Programming* (1979) state "Frank Farrelly, who wrote *Provocative Therapy,* is a really exquisite example of requisite variety." The intent within the variety afforded the therapist allows the therapist access to the totality of his or her experiences to increase empathic understanding and caring for the client, to employ tactics and strategies counter to those of the client in an effort to help the client change at multiple levels and to have fun and avoid burnout while doing therapy. The therapist's behaviors that distinguish this form of therapy from other approaches are the degree of directness and the use of confrontation, contradictory and equivocal communication style, the systematic use of both verbal and nonverbal cues, the eschewing of professional dignity, and the deliberate use of humor and clowning.

The stated goal is "to provoke the client to engage in five different types of behaviors":

1. To affirm his self-worth, both verbally and behaviorally.
2. To assert himself appropriately both in task performances and relationships.
3. To defend himself realistically.
4. To engage in psycho-social reality testing and learn the necessary discriminations to respond adaptively. Global perceptions lead to global, stereotyped responses; differentiated perceptions lead to adaptive responses.
5. To engage in risk-taking behaviors in personal relationships, especially communicating affection and vulnerability to significant others with immediacy as they are authentically experienced by the client. The most difficult words in relationships are often "I want you, I miss you, I care about you"—to commit oneself to others (p. 56).

In many forms of psychotherapy, the therapist is often expected to play according to the rules of Hoyle, while the client can employ any form of street fighting imaginable. In Provocative Therapy, the therapist can "lie," deny, rationalize, invent phony "research data," "cry," and think and act "crazy." The provocative therapist acts as a devil's advocate and sides with the negative half of the client's ambivalence toward self, signficant others, and his or her goals and values. At times the therapist will voice the client's worst thoughts and fears about him- or herself. The therapist will "express the unutterable, feel the unfeelable, and think the unthinkable" (p. 58). He or she often will volunteer idiotic rationalizations for the client's behavior. This has the effect of short-circuiting the client's own excuse-generating mechanisms and often leads clients to laugh

at themselves for the rationalizations they have been developing. Often the therapist will overemphasize the negative, thus forcing the client to emphasize the positive aspects of his or her life. Also, there is no such thing as a taboo subject and often feedback is immediate. Example: An obese patient enters the office.

P: May I speak with you, Mr. Farrelly?
T: My God, the Goodyear blimp has slipped its moorings! (p. 61)

There are several techniques that are specifically used to assist the client in reality testing. (1) *Reductio ad absurdum* (reduction to absurdity) is the carrying of the client's negative statements about him- or herself to the logical extremes until the client rejects them. A typical response to this is "Even *I* don't believe I'm *that* bad." (2) Often the therapist marshals idiotic "instant data or research" to humorously support the client's contentions that he or she is indeed either helpless or bad. (3) The therapist all too readily accepts the contentions that the client is no good and "gives up exhaustedly" with a smiling "What hope is there for someone so bad off as you?" (4) The therapist will directly challenge the client to "prove it." (5) One of the more frequently used tools that the provocative therapist uses to help the client focus specifically on himself is listing. For example:

T: (Sighing laconically) Give me three good reasons, sweetheart, why anyone would want to go out with you. Hell, you're either a ducker, a spitter or a swallower.

In using negative modeling, the therapist acts like the client. If the client acts in a staring and detached way, he or she may suddenly find the therapist acting just as "crazy." Often the client will laugh at this behavior, and if the client doesn't laugh, he or she at least must try to decode the therapist's "psychosis."

It is important to note here that the therapist and his or her role as well as the client often receives the butt of the joke.

c:   (Withdrawn and whining) Well, Scott, I thought you might be able to help me. . . . (Plaintively) Won't you help?

T:   (Plaintively protesting loudly) Help!? Who said anything about help? . . . Time I can give you . . . uh . . . I'm not smart enough to work miracles anymore. (Sadly) I lost my magic wand last year. (Puts head in hands as if crying.)

Neither the client nor the therapist's role is immune to lampooning.

The provocative therapist will often send contradictory messages to the client. Even though clinicians agree that this is one outstanding characteristic of schizophrenogenic families, the provocative therapist differs radically from these pathology-inducing familial constellations in that the goal in sending these powerful messages is to provoke independence rather than dependence, and they are also sent within an easily decoded context of caring, warmth, and support for the essential personhood of the client. If double messages have the power to drive people crazy, then they also have the power to drive people sane. The client is forced to choose between either the therapist's verbal messages, which agree with the client's predictions of doom and gloom, or with the strongly supportive, easily decodable, nonverbal messages that the client is lovable and worthwhile, can change, and has the power and knowledge within himself to take charge of and direct his own life. Provocative Therapy *releases* the client from powerlessness and places him or her in touch—often quite rapidly—with his or her own power; hence it is centrally and diametrically opposed to the schizophrenogenic, pathological dependency inducing type of messages that *bind*.

The provocative therapist's utilization of humor is central to his or her work. Among the several discernible forms of humor used are (1) exaggeration, (2) mimicry, (3) ridicule, (4) distortion, (5) sarcasm, (6) irony, and (7) jokes.

With *exaggeration* the provocative therapist either over- or understates the client's view of him- or herself. The therapist's artistic hyperbole, done with a twinkle in the eye or a sly smile, provokes the client into a more balanced perspective.

The therapist *mimics* the client in two ways. One way is by role playing the client's self-defeating behaviors. For example, the client who has fits of pique may find the provocative therapist suddenly rising out of a chair "ranting and raving," much as the client does. The impact is immediate. Since behavior is controlled by its perceived consequences, the client perceives quickly with embarrassment and laughter how he or she affects others negatively, which tends to lead to the extinction of the client's self-defeating behaviors.

The provocative therapist does not *ridicule* the client but rather the client's screwball and idiotic behaviors in an effort to extinguish or countercondition them. It should be emphasized that the therapist's role and "professional dignity" are also open to caricature. Since clients do not easily distinguish between themselves and their behaviors ("Love me, love my deviant behaviors"), ridicule is a tactic to be sparingly and skillfully used. As with any powerful tool, it can be used for better or for worse, so the provocative therapist invariably pairs warmth and obvious caring with ridicule of the client's inappropriate ideas and behaviors. Within a given social-psychological context, ridiculous thoughts and action merit ridicule.

In using *humorous distortion,* the therapist deliberately "misunderstands" the client or gives wild or plausibly distorted "psychological explanations" for the client's behavior or others' behavior toward the client. In the same vein, in order to provoke the client's reality testing and self-affirmation, the therapist will lampoon the client's expectations of the therapist's traditional role. For example: A middle-aged, female patient knocked almost inaudibly at the office door; when the therapist opened it:

P: (Querulously) May I see you, Mr. Farrelly?

T: (Loudly) Of course, gorgeous. (He strides back to his desk and sits down.)

P: (Coming into the room timorously) Where do you want me to sit?

T: (Pointing at chair next to his desk; the patient begins to sit down in the chair) Sit right there. (In a gruff tone; loudly) Hold it! (Pointing to a chair at the opposite wall) Sit over there.

P: (Shuffles over to the chair at which the therapist is pointing)

T: (In a commanding tone: looks around the office) No, wait a minute. . . . (He pauses, looks uncertain) I've got it! Sit over there (pointing to a chair near the door).

P: (Suddenly straightening up, frowning; loudly and forcibly) Aw, go to hell! I'll sit where I want! (She plumps herself in a chair.)

T: (Throwing up his arms as though defending himself; plaintively) Okay, okay, you don't have to get violent!

P: (Bursts out laughing) (p. 181)

*Sarcasm* must be accompanied by nonverbal warmth, caring, and acceptance if it is to have the humorous and therefore therapeutic effect on the client that the therapist wants. Sarcasm is a powerful communication modality frequently highly effective in sensitizing and desensitizing clients to certain perceptions and behaviors, but it needs to be used with discretion to achieve the desired therapeutic effect. As in the following example:

P: (Promiscuous patient coming into therapist's office, holding her hand out in a "halt" gesture) Now before you say anything, I want you to know I got a job.

T: (Suspiciously) Where did you get it?

P: (Triumphantly) In a laboratory.

T: (Sarcastically) As what, a specimen?

P: (Annoyed but grinning in spite of herself) Oh, you think you're so goddamn funny.

T: (Suspiciously and with a sarcastic tone) Oh yeah, how did you persuade him to hire you, sweetheart?

P: (Flushing) It wasn't like *that*. (p. 110)

There are three types of *irony* used in Provocative Therapy:

(1) By using Socratic irony, the therapist is assuming the pretense of ignorance so that by adroit questions, the client's nonuseful conceptions are made conspicuous. (2) Another form involves the use of words to express something other than the literal meaning of those words. (3) Dramatic irony involves making evident the incongruity between the actual situation versus the described situation. (p. 110)

Example: A combative female who has just been locked in the hospital seclusion room is standing near the grill in the door shouting obscenities at the hospital staff for putting her there for assaulting a fellow patient.

T: (Sidling up to the grill, in full view of the patient; chortling loudly) Atta girl! You have got 'em on the run! They're scared shitless of you now, the sonuvabitchin' bughousers and that crazy freak! Keep it up, don't let 'em break you (through clenched teeth) *No matter what! No matter how long they keep you in there!*

P: (Laughing in mid shout) Aw, go to hell, Frank! You ain't locked up in here. It's easy for you to say that. You try it, if you like it so goddamn much.

T: (Cringing, looking furtively up and down hall, drops his voice to a conspiratorial whisper) Not me! They broke my spirit long ago, but I always have hopes that they'll finally meet somebody they can't break. (Suddenly glaring furiously, raising his voice in a fanatical shout) *No matter what tortures they—*

P: (Laughing: interrupting in a conversational tone) Careful, they'll put you in here, next. Aw, piss on it, I'm shapin' up and shippin' outa here. (p. 110)

There are many truly funny things that clients say or do that can be used to provoke laughter. There are many more times when the provocative therapist is reminded of an appropriate *joke* that parallels the client's present situation. Laughter has the powerful effect of reversing the context of the conversation or freeing up the client's frame of reference, so that the client can see his or her life in a new, hopeful, and more healthful light.

A final note. In using humor, the provocative therapist speaks four different languages, which are explicated at length in *Provocative Therapy* (1974, p. 74). Space limitations here permit only the enumeration of these. The four languages are: (1) a religious-moral language, (2) locker-room, or a language of the street, (3) a body or kinesthetic language, and (4) professional jargonese. Each of these is used humorously.

## CASE EXAMPLE

### Herbert the Virgin

This excerpt is from Herbert's twelfth session. Approximately the first five minutes are presented to demonstrate the continuity and present a flavor for the provocative style. Shorter samples from the same interview follow the first long excerpt to highlight various techniques the provocative therapist uses.

Herbert (pseudonym) is a highly intelligent, good-looking university student. He is in his early twenties, heterosexual, and painfully shy, avoiding women like the plague.

Therapist and client walk into the office and sit down.

C:  Too bad Susan can't be here (ruefully).

T:  You'd like to have Susan here, huh?

C:  Yuh (with a chuckle).

T:  So would I (matter-of-factly). Sure would relieve the boredom, I'll say that. (Turns to tape recorder) Let the record show that he is referring to Susan ———, a graduate student of mine. Just a dynamite person and brilliant and also just the mere view of her is enough to make strong men weak (with lustful enthusiasm). (Turning to client) Now which was it, her strength, her brilliance, or the fact that she looked like certified gorgeous?

C:  (Well, I wouldn't put any of those quite so strongly but it was all of them put together (chuckling). She was very nice . . . gracious.

T:  Ya, she's very gracious to creeps (nonchalantly).

C:  (Laughing, and then sighs) Oh, I think she kinda liked me—actually.

T:  Oh, ya, she did have a certain positive attraction to your psychodynamics (puzzled, "disgusted").

C:  (Mumbles softly)

T:  Oh ya, what (challenging)? Are you muttering? Your lips are moving: Either that or my hearing aid battery has run out.

C:  Well, I'm not even mumbling this time (defensively, humorously).

T:  (Laughing) Well! (To tape recorder) Students, you've heard of counterconditioning. He used to mutter and mumble, now he just moves his lips.

C:  You really ought to turn that intimidating tape recorder off (laughing quietly).

T:  Agh, what are you talking about (feigned irritation)? The audience—this thing—Christ, nobody is going to listen to *our* tape. Some of them *might* listen. I say, "Here is some boring stuff. You oughta listen to this stuff because you'll find a lot of boring clients in the clinical field. Every once in a while you run across a jazzy one that perks your interest, but you got to learn how to deal with the boring ones too."

C:  I bet I was boring last Sunday night (slyly).

T:  Uh what? (fumbling for the right word) Wait a minute, I'll get this question right. . . . I'm supposed to respond by saying. . . . How were? . . . No, wait a minute. . . . Who? . . . to . . . (Gives up) No, that just slipped my mind.

C:  (Interjects) Well? . . .

T:  I thought there was a response called for there (with a grin).

C:  Well, there was (smiling). You were supposed to say something like, "Well, what happened last Sunday night? (chuckling)"

T:  Well, not what *happened* Sunday night (laconically). I don't like to say something like that because that means that something fell from out of the sky. I usually prefer to say, "What did you *do*, creep?" . . . or "*didn't* do?" Something like that, see? Not "What *happened*?" Should I say, "What did you do Sunday night?'' or ''What did you *not* do to make you boring?''

C:  Something like that. . . . (with a knowing grin).

T:  (Overriding and still fumbling for the ''right'' words) . . . Or ''With *whom* were you boring?''

C:  Well, I . . .

T:  (Comically fumbling) Or ''What were you *doing?*'' or ''What *weren't* you doing?'' or . . .

C:  Oh, never mind (smiling, exasperated)!

T:  (Interrupting again) Well, it's Tuesday morning and . . . I can't seem to . . . Well, I feel a response is called for (professionally).

C:  Well, I didn't want to plunge into the tale (grinning knowingly).

T:  Well, you want to ease your way into it. That's typical. Okay, with your glacial slowness.

C:  I want to be made to know that someone wants to hear me tell this fascinating tale (with insight, grinning).

T:  You want to know whether I'm fascinated. (Bored sigh) How do I know, maybe it's going to be a boring story. You've already said you were boring Sunday night.

C:  (Laughs)

T:  I'm supposed to be fascinated with your boredom.

C:  Actually it's kinda dry, but anyway . . . (with wry sense of humor).

T:  You are? (Interrupting and acting ignorant) The story is? . . . or . . .

C:  Everything, just everything (laughing out loud and giving up procrastinating).

T:  Everything is a drag.

C:  Anyway, I went up to this concert with this girl.

T:  With a real live girl (sarcastic enthusiasm)!

C:  And, uh . . .

T:  Let the record show that the creep nodded (talking sarcastically to tape recorder). All right, we have to do that (talks to client, explaining) You see, we're going to get vi-deotapes and so we'll be able to see your lips working, nods, and stuff.

C:  (Laughs and adds cooperatively) . . . And body writhings.

T:  Really (enthusiastically)!

C:  (Continuing) Get some closeups and show my perspiration. (Laughing)

T:  Ya (more enthusiasm and joining in). Head shots and armpit shots to show the sweat. . . . All those nonverbal cues.

C:  And my nervous leer.

T:  Ya (agreeing with a laugh). I like the choice of the word ''leer.''

C:  Instead of merely grimace of something like that (smiling proudly and nodding agreement). Well, anyway, we went up to this concert. She had a boyfriend so I really didn't expect much and I got even less than what I expected. So did she. It was a boring conversation.

T:  Oh, Lord (moaning).

C:  It was a good concert, but . . .

T:  Oh, Jesus (still moaning his words).

C:  But the conversation before and after was forced labor.

T:  Uh (playing dumb)?

C:  Awkward.

T:  Oh, shit (moaning again).

C:  We just couldn't think of much to say.

T:  Agonizing, excruciating silences (moaning in agreement).

C:  Naw, well, she talks when there are silences, but we sure didn't interrelate much.

T:  Interrelate!? (incredulous)

C:  Or whatever. We didn't hit it off.

T:  I was going to say you were starting to sound like a frigging social worker or therapist (relieved). (Turning his head as though holding a conversation with another person and voicing both responses) ''I can't interrelate to ice cream.'' ''Huh?'' (Both laugh) I can't relate to that . . . you didn't hit it off . . . like oil and water, you didn't mix. . . . Well, is she a queen? You keep going after those queen types. I've told you to take out other people.

C:   Well, let's not get on this again (assertively). As a matter of fact she's not a queen.

T:   Is she a frump?

C:   What's a frump? Is that a dog?

T:   Well, first cousin to a dog, except . . . more disheveled.

C:   No, she wasn't a frump either. She's fairly attractive. Actually sorta cute, charming face, a mildly dumpy body but nothing to be offended by.

T:   Oh, that Ichabod Crane body of yours (wincing). Hell, you shouldn't be too choosy and picky. Really, you don't look like Baretta.

C:   I'm just running up against an insuperable genetic barrier (humorously and with a big grin, agreeing with therapist).

T:   All right, I like it (laughing uproariously). You *know,* you're a bright guy. There's no-o-o question about it. . . .

C:   Oh, gee, thanks (grinning with gratitude).

T:   . . . You just act stupid (finishing sentence).

C:   That makes my day (feigning a crestfallen attitude, laughing) [End first excerpt]

Second sample: later in the interview they discuss some girls that C met.

T:   So you danced with a couple of gals but you didn't get their names or telephone numbers so you could know how to call them or how to get in touch with them.

C:   Frank, I don't think that girls like to get hustled (protesting).

T:   No, one has to proceed slowly, especially if everything is riding on it (mocking seriousness with a grin). You know these are pretty crucial kinds of maneuvers and, yuh, there's a great deal riding on them. (C laughs) What are you saying there?

C:   Well, all right (agreeing calmly). In the long run there isn't much riding on this. Well, I mean I *could* be embarrassed (more seriously).

T:   Well, *horrors* (sarcastically and smiling)! 'Course that's your continual state anyhow. What difference would it make? But I can see what you're saying, you know. It continually embarrasses you so that you can barely tolerate it. I mean you are neck deep in embarrassment and acute, kinda self-conscious awareness.

C:   Right, I don't want it to become acute (agreeing humorously). It's chronic but I don't want it to become acute so that's where it hurts. And I don't want it to hurt. [End of excerpt two]

Third excerpt; they talk about alternatives to meeting girls.

C:   Well, the night before I sat around and fantasized (interrupting).

T:   Well, yes, a lot of guys do, and there's no harm in that (agreeing facetiously). A lot of guys fantasize—they're not making a lot of moves, but they are having a whole hell of a lot of good picture-time-shows in their heads. It's a lot safer. You can't get crotch rot from your fantasies; research shows that *conclusively!*

C:   Ya, well, also (explaining). . . .

T:   (Interrupting) And you can't get a girl in trouble either, and you avoid risk of embarrassment: *You could be rejected.*

C:   As I'm filming the whole show myself I can just . . . you know (humorously playing along with T, smiling).

T:   Exactly (agreeing)!

C:   I'm the director and producer.

T:   Script writer (nodding). . . . You can make it turn out anyway you want.

C:   And I do (with a laugh).

T:   Fantasies many, many times with interpersonal relationships, especially heterosexual, are infinitely to be preferred than the actual thing, which is frequently a bummer (philosophically and ponderously).

C:   You mean you're saying I should just lay in bed all the time . . .

T:   (Interrupting) You just lay there with a smile on your face and beatin' your pud and just singing (Bursts into song) "Dream along with me, I'm on my way to the (T makes obvious mistake) st—uh, girls."

C:   (Laughs)

T:   Sure, hum a little tune.

C:   It doesn't work (thoughtfully).

T:   It certainly *does* (protesting with a twinkle in his eye).

C:   It does *not* (protesting more loudly).

T:   (Giving in a little) Well, it doesn't work to get a lot of embarrassment—or do your fantasies turn out embarrassing too?

C:   All right (giving in)!

T:   All right, then, by God, don't tell *me* it doesn't work (loudly). (T and C break up in laughter) And aren't they all dolls and queens in your fantasies?

C:   Well, just this morning I was fantasizing about Betty, sweet Betty, from moonlight bay. . . .

T:   Did it turn out right this time?

C:   Oh, it sure did (enthusiastically).

T:   Oh, God, thank God, sweet Jesus, thank the Lord (sarcastically and then with great enthusiasm)! See there? Don't tell me it doesn't work. It works a hell of a lot better than the real thing. (C laughs through this whole sentence) Shit, I know a guy who screwed a gal on moonlight bay—she got sand in her vagina and he was rubbing his cock back and forth and damn near abraided the thing down to a pencil size. (Instructively) See what I mean? The reality is *not* as good as the fantasy.

C:   (Laughing in mock agreement) . . . And I know some guys who have been hit by comets from outer space. But I mean that thing doesn't happen very often. [End of excerpt three]

## SUMMARY

When clinicians observe or listen to a provocative therapist at work, they are immediately struck by the quality of creative play inherent in the therapist's approach ("My God! Therapy can actually be fun!"), by the amount of energy the therapist invests, and by the concomitant energy response or release from the client. The serious work of therapy is being conducted at multiple levels by both participants in a spontaneous atmosphere of warmth and playfulness and humor, which energizes both. To their astonishment observers also hear the hallmark of provocative therapy: laughter. In spite of themselves, they invariably begin to laugh with the client and therapist. Fisher (1970) caught this flavor of PT interaction when he wrote:

Among the several possible models (e.g., healer) for the psychotherapist, consider the court jester. This figure, we are told, made playful comments about the king his followers, and affairs of state; he punctured pretensions, took an upside-down look at human events. Now the patient, it might be said, suffers from gravity. To him life is a burden, his personality a riddle; yet viewed from outside, he may seem altogether obvious and his problems nothing much. Indeed, just because he hurts and has a dreadful sense of failure, eventually he must find laughter in the midst of his accustomed tears and glimpse his own absurdity. Without irreverence both he and the therapist stay mired in earnestness.

In psychotherapy the therapist deals with human pain and suffering, problems that often have tragic consequences for the client and his or her significant others. However, the tragic mask alone really does not adequately symbolize the human condition; the provocative therapist holds that the addition of the comic mask is necessary to more completely reflect the entirety of our lives and struggles. And laughter is the sound of victory.

## REFERENCES

Bandler, R. and Grindler, J. *Frogs into princes: Neuro-Linguistic Programming*. Moab, Utah: Real People, 1979.

Blanchard, W. H. Ecstacy without agony is baloney. *Psychology Today,* 1970, **3 (8),** 8–11.

Ellis, A. *Reason and emotion in psychotherapy.* New York: Lyle Stewart, 1962.

Farrelly, F. Provocative therapy (# 58). Philadelphia: American Academy of Psychotherapists Tape Library, 1971. (audiotape)

Farrelly, F. Provocative therapy. Chicago: Human Development Institute, 1977. (audiotape)

Farrelly, F. Analyzing the analyst—identifying effective interventions. *Audio Digest, Psychiatry,* 1978, **7 (15).** (audiotape)

Farrelly, F. and Brandsma, J. *Provocative Therapy.* Cupertino, Calif.: Meta, 1974.

Fisher, K. A. The iconoclast's notebook. *Psychotherapy: Theory, Research, and Practice,* 1970, **7,** 54–56.

Ludwig, A. M. and Farrelly, F. The code of chronicity. *Archives of General Psychiatry,* 1966, **15,** 562–568.

Ludwig, A. M. and Farrelly, R. The weapons of insanity. *American Journal of Psychotherapy,* 1967, **21 (4),** 737–749.

Rogers, C. R. *Client-centered therapy.* Boston: Houghton-Mifflin, 1951.

Rogers, C. R. *On becoming a person.* Boston: Houghton-Mifflin, 1961.

Standal, S. W. and Corsini, R. J. (Eds.). *Critical incidents in psychotherapy.* New York: Prentice-Hall, 1959.

# CHAPTER 51

# *Psycho-Imagination Therapy*

JOSEPH E. SHORR

> One of the most energetic and successful proponents of the use of imagination in therapy is Joseph Shorr, the author of this chapter, who takes an existential/phenomenological point of view and who uses imagery as his main modality for personality change.
>
> Psycho-Imagination Therapy is one of the purest of systems. It is essentially an autochthonous system unsurpassed in charm and elegance by any of the systems in this book. And in my judgment it provides a process that all therapists should understand and be able to use. Like role playing, the interview, and analysis of early recollections, Psycho-Imagination is a technique of general value.

Psycho-Imagination Therapy is a phenomenological and dialogical process with major emphasis on subjective meaning through the use of waking imagination and imagery (Shorr, 1967). Emphasis on the therapeutic interaction itself has to do with the question of one's identifying oneself and separating one's own view of oneself from the attributed self as defined by the significant others in one's childhood.

First developed by this writer, a clinical psychologist, in 1965, the use of Psycho-Imagination Therapy is growing at the present time. Theoretically it is related to the interpersonal school of psychoanalysis that stems mainly from the work of Harry Stack Sullivan.

## HISTORY

Human beings have always been intrigued by their imagination, although historically it has variously been granted prominence or relegated to insignificance. The concept of imagination has served as an explanation of human behavior; as an agent of causality; as a source of physical, emotional, and mental disease—even death.

In the history of psychotherapy, imagination has played many roles with diverse implications. Eighteenth-century thought ranged from ascribing the effects of Anton Mesmer's hypnotic technique to imagination, through Italian Lodvico Muratori's concept of imagination being comprised of dreams, visions, delusions, *idées fixes,* and somnabulism.

During the nineteenth century, actions once attributed to imagination were deemed the products of suggestions or auto-suggestion. Sigmund Freud (1959), however, as early as 1892 attempted a "concentration technique" that utilized the patient's imagery.

I inform the patient that . . . I shall apply pressure to his forehead, and I assure him that all the time the pressure lasts, he will see before him a recollection in the form occurring to him, and I pledge him to communicate this picture or ideal to me, whatever it may be. . . . Having said this,

I then leave go and ask quietly, as though there were no question of a disappointment: ''What did you see?'' or ''What occurred to you?''

This procedure has taught me much and has also invariably achieved its aim. Today I can no longer do without it. (Breuer & Freud, 1953, p. 270)

My expectations were fulfilled; I was set free from hypnotism. . . . Hypnosis had screened from view an interplay of force which now came in sight and the understanding of which gave a solid formation to my theory. (Freud, 1959, p. 29)

Despite much enthusiasm, Freud later abandoned the concentration technique for free association. Jerome L. Singer (1971) suggests:

Freud may have erred in not insisting on imagery alone rather than allowing patients to shift to free verbal association. He might have gotten more powerful uncovering more rapidly from his earlier technique. Undoubtedly individual practitioners have sensed the importance of fostering greater emphasis on concrete imagery by patients and have found themselves impatient with the apparent glibness of defensiveness that often characterizes verbal free association. (p. 9)

One can only imagine what changes would have occurred in the field of psychotherapy if Freud had proceeded with ''free imagery.'' However, Carl Jung's concept of ''active imagination'' had an important influence on European intellectual thought.

The twentieth century saw a resurgence of interest in imagery in Europe. Carl Jung and Sandor Ferenczi redefined and revitalized imagination and imagery. But in the United States the use of imagination and imagery as psychotherapeutic tools followed a difficult path. Although E. B. Titchener worked with problems related to imagination and introspection, J. B. Watson, America's first major proponent of behaviorism, turned the mainstream of psychological investigation away from a concern with man's inner images—his daydreams, dreams, and fanciful ruminations—toward concepts of conditioning. The psychoanalysts of the period viewed fantasies and dreams as relevant areas of analytic in-

vestigation, but the free use of imagination was not encouraged since, to many, it reeked of resistance.

Freud believed fantasy and imagination were essentially limited to the person's defenses. The adaptive function of imagination was largely ignored except for Heinz Hartmann in 1958. Neither Hartmann's work nor an earlier emphasis by Erich Fromm (1955) was given much attention. Fromm voiced a plea for moving beyond the conventional free-association procedure into therapist-initiated situations. He advised analysts to make fullest use of their own imagination and suggested the use of active imagery methods to improve the flow of the patients' free associations.

By and large, however, American psychologists have tended to regard reverie and imagination as unproductive, impractical, and completely unempirical.

The return of the image in American psychology has, oddly enough, been given impetus by the same theoretical framework that delayed its emergence—behaviorism. The behaviorists' emphasis on visual imagery during systematic desensitization is such an example. T. G. Stampfl and D. J. Leavis (1967), for example, used powerful negative imagery in their Implosive Therapy. Although the behaviorists have helped reintroduce imagery in therapy, they do not show a keen interest in the patients' inner experiences or fantasies, and they generally leave unconscious processes uninvestigated.

Gestalt therapists use imagination in conjunction with dreams, but have limited the interpretive value of images and have shown disinterest in the imagination as it relates to past experience.

European psychotherapists draw heavily from the work of Robert Desoille, Hanscarl Leuner, Carl Happich, Roberto Assagioli, Andre Virel, Gaston Bachelard, and others, investigators who share an interest in using imagery and imagination in the psychotherapeutic experience.

Desoille stands above all others in the psychotherapeutic use of imagery. His pioneering work was influenced by E. Caslant (1927). From Caslant's original notion, Desoille (1965) developed the *rêve éviellé*, Guided Affective Imagery Technique. This served as a point of reference for nearly all psychotherapeutic developments employing imagery as a prime modality. His method suggests that many problems can be ameliorated by means of the symbolic combat, or transformation, that takes place in imagery.

The philosophical roots of psychoanalysis are uniquely Freud's—the concept of psychic determinism and the matrix of the triplicity of the ego, id, and superego. Jung, too, provided his own philosophical base—the collective unconscious. A comparable philosophical base emphasizing imagination and imagery was offered by a nonpsychotherapist, the phenomenologist Gaston Bachelard (1964). He broke with the more traditional psychological method of introspection by calling attention to man's innate capacity for generating imagery and symbolism.

With the increased awareness of imagination and imagery, the last decade has also seen a growing emphasis on phenomenology—the study of how a person sees his or her world. This writer believes that phenomenology requires that a person use his or her imagination as a vehicle by which to ready the self for all that he or she uniquely perceives, anticipates, defends, and acts upon. The person imagines how things will be, thereby preparing for whatever action may result. The integration of phenomenology with the concept and use of imagination is a palpable necessity. Our world of images reflects and represents our being-in-the-world, and we can only understand man as an individual, and as a part of mankind, when we grasp the imagery of his experience.

R. D. Laing (1965, 1971) helped to formalize and concretize the phenomenology of self-other concepts originally developed by H. S. Sullivan. By integrating this stream of thought with the European studies of imagery through a natural bridge—psychotherapeutic imagery productions—this writer has organized a systematic and comprehensive theoretical framework to provide a viable and innovative psychotherapy.

I find that the intensive use of imagery in psychotherapy heightens therapist motivation and involvement because of the interesting and dramatic nature of the material that is elicited. The probability is high that the vividness and intensity of the patient's imagery productions serve as a catalyst to his or her own therapeutic motivations.

## CURRENT STATUS

The Institute for Psycho-Imagination Therapy (IPIT) was founded in Los Angeles in 1972 by this writer. I had already spent close to 10 years developing the theory and methodology of Psycho-Imagination Therapy. Some of the basic work and theoretical structure was presented originally in several journal articles.

My first book, *Psycho-Imagination Therapy,* was published in 1972. My second book, *Psychotherapy Through Imagery* (1974b), contained new material developed during clinical and research work with Psycho-Imagination Therapy. My third book, *Go See the Movie in Your Head* (1977b), added material relating to self-image imagery.

Since its inception the institute has constantly expanded its field of influence. Seminars are held several times a year at the University of California at Los Angeles, Immaculate Heart College, California School of Professional Psychology, and the University of Southern California. Ten- and 20-week training sessions for professionals are offered in the theory and methodology of Psycho-Imagination Therapy. In addition I have given workshops at International Mental Imagery Congresses in France, Sweden, Germany, and Japan.

The Shorr Clinic was opened in 1976 to provide affordable therapy to a broad segment of the population. The staff members of the clinic have a minimum of four years training in Psycho-Imagination Therapy.

In 1974 the institute published the *Shorr Imagery Test* (SIT). This projective test using imagery yields both a quantitative conflict score and a qualitative personality analysis. The SIT is individually administered and has been used in numerous educational institutions and hospitals throughout the United States. It is also used in several branches of the Veterans Administration and at the Great Lakes Naval Station. In 1977 the Group Shorr Imagery Test (GSIT) was published. The GSIT makes it possible to administer the SIT to any number of persons simultaneously.

The Supplementary Shorr Imagery Test (SSIT) (1978) is another projective test using imagery, which provides both a quantitative conflict score and an in-depth qualitative personality analysis. It can be used independently or as an adjunct to the SIT to yield additional information.

The *Shorr Parental Imagery Test* (SPIT) (1979b) focuses on conflicts between parents and children and is used for diagnosis and treatment in counseling.

Current research projects have been done with the various Shorr imagery tests in research projects. David Tansey (1979) found confirmation for the thesis that there is a "criminal personality" and is researching the ability of the SIT to predict recidivism among felons convicted of violent crimes.

Jack A. Connella (1978) used Psycho-Imagination Therapy with groups of chronic benign intractable pain patients. He used the SIT pre- and posttherapy to evaluate the efficacy of the imagery treatment. Due to Connella's findings, the City of Hope Hospital in Duarte, California, regularly incorporates Psycho-Imagination Therapy procedures into their treatments and uses the SIT for patient evaluation.

Pennee Robin, used the SIT to do in-depth personality analyses of persons interviewed for the book *Sexual Jealousy* (forthcoming) written with Shorr.

Gail Sobel (1979) employed the GSIT as a tool in a test-retest situation to measure the degree of conflictual level reduction as a re-sult of participating in a course entitled "Group Dynamics."

Clifford Morgan (1979) has adapted the SIT for use with disabled persons and with the personnel who treat and/or deal with the disabled.

In 1976 the Institute for Psycho-Imagination Therapy was the initiating force in founding the American Association for the Study of Mental Imagery, which held its first annual conference in Los Angeles in 1979. The proceedings of this conference are published by Plenum Press (Shorr et al., 1979).

## THEORY

Psycho-Imagination Therapy is a phenomenological and dialogical process with major emphasis on subjective meaning through the modality of waking imagery and imagination.

The basic phenomenological proposition of Psycho-Imagination Therapy recognizes the individual's need to become aware of how he defines himself in relation to others, and how he feels others define him. For example:

How I see myself
How I see you
How I see you seeing me
How you see me seeing you

This phenomenological "in-viewing" is a synthesis of the self-other personality development theories of R. D. Laing and Harry Stack Sullivan. Sullivan (1953) believed that personality consists of the characteristic ways in which a person deals with others in his or her interpersonal relationships. In order to abolish anxiety—which is always the direct result of interpersonal interactions—a person must develop security operations. When those security operations are maladaptive, they produce the wide variety of interpersonal warps, emotional discomforts, and behavioral maladjustments that constitute psychiatric symptoms and psychiatric illnesses.

The two basic premises of Psycho-Imagination Therapy are: (1) everyone needs to make a difference to someone, and (2) everyone seeks confirmation or acknowledgment of the self. These needs occur cotemporaneously. When not fulfilled, the child develops false positions. If one is not confirmed for one's true self, the person then develops strategies to secure confirmation for a false self. The security operations one involves oneself in serve to maintain one's identity even in the absence of true acknowledgment.

My major emphasis in the therapeutic interaction is on separating one's own view of oneself from the attributed self as defined by the significant others in one's childhood. Ideally, the "true" identity is helped to emerge while the "alien" identity is eliminated.

Interpersonal and intrapersonal interactions, as well as the individual's strategies within the self-other relationships, are best seen through systematic use of waking imagery. A person's imagery can show how he or she organizes the world, his or her style of action, and marked individual differences to which the therapist should be attuned. Imagery provides a primary avenue through which thoughts, wishes, expectations, and feelings can be most effectively reactivated and reexperienced.

Imagery, unlike other modes of communication, ordinarily has not been punished in the past and is, therefore, less susceptible to personal censorship in the present. Thus imagery provides a powerful projective technique resulting in a rapid, highly accurate profile of the individual's personality and conflicts.

Imagination is viewed as the central kernel of consciousness and an important means of access to the uniqueness of the individual's world. The active introduction and conscious use of imaginary situations provides a stimulating investigative tool, an avenue to action possibilities. It allows the patient to explore more safely and openly, to differentiate, to experiment with and to integrate fantasy and reality, all within the context of a cooperative therapeutic alliance and encounter.

Psycho-Imagination Therapy puts the individual, through imagery, into a particular situation that can evoke a set of interactions useful in revealing major problems in the significant areas of life, and that also permit the individual to relive experiences. J. L. Singer (1974) writes: "Shorr uses an almost infinite variety of images geared very much to the specific characteristics of the patient and to specific developments in therapy."

I emphasize subjective meaning by recognizing that the patient's images are uniquely his or hers, coming from each individual's own storehouse of knowledge and experience. In the process of describing his or her image, the imager begins to relate it to something of meaning in his or her life. Hidden meanings of the events, attitudes, feelings, and motivations attached to the image are then used to explore further the interpersonal implications.

I have systematically categorized over 2,000 imaginary situations to reveal specific information about the patient's personality, world view, self-definition, areas of conflict, and style of defenses. Other categories are specifically for focusing on change and for facilitating the process. Responses to the categorized imagery usually elicit hidden or repressed material more efficiently than direct questioning by the therapist. In addition, the imagery bypasses the conscious censor and is less liable to denial by the imager than imprecise verbal statements.

The major categories of imagery employed (Shorr, 1978a), with examples, follow.

***Spontaneous Imagery.*** These images are generated by suggesting that the patient report the flow of imagery as it occurs, or report the next five consecutive images that occur, then another five, and so forth. In either sequence, certain images usually become affect laden and then will serve as the vehicle for dialogue or release of feeling.

*Directed Imagery.* At times a spontaneous flow of images seems to go on endlessly without theme or apparent coherency. Directed imagery can be then used to control the flow and bring coherency and integration to the production. My experience validates those of Horowitz and Becker (1971, who say that the specificity of instructions for reporting visual images increases the tendency to form, as well as to report, images.

*Self-Image Imagery.* Each of us has a self system—a set of attitudes about ourselves and by which we define ourselves (Shorr, 1979a). This system is inextricably bound to our perception of how others see us. Imaginary situations that help reveal this self system include:

*Imagine there are two of you. Imagine kissing yourself (sitting on your own lap, looking at yourself through a keyhole).*

*Dual Imagery.* Inner conflicts are caused by the opposition of two strong and incompatible forces, neither of which can be satisfied without exacting pain, fear, guilt, or some other emotional penalty (Shorr, 1976).

A remarkable phenomenon occurs when a person is asked to imagine two *different* animals, dolls, forces, impulses, and so forth. In the majority of reported imageries there is some degree of polarization. The contrast becomes more evident when the imager is asked to assign an adjective to each of the two images. The opposition is further enhanced when the patient imagines statements and replies from the two images. The complimentary opposites within experience are thus revealed.

These dual images frequently represent two parts of the self in conflict—self vs. self, or conflict between self and another. The dialogue that is a natural outgrowth of this imagery helps the patient become aware of the conflicts and their meanings.

*Body Imagery.* Empirical evidence indicates that people can sense the body-part core of their identity. They can also identify in which part of the body their anger (fear, guilt, joy) resides. These images provide clues to self-image, body image, and areas of conflict (Shorr, 1973).

Furthermore, introjection of parental figures is evidenced when persons are asked to imagine in what part of their body their parents reside. If, in the developmental process, a person has been falsely defined, the false definition may take on a body locus. The mother or father who "resides" in a part of the patient's body (chest, heart, guts, limbs) and appears hostile is, in reality, the false identity or the neurotic conflict internalized. When the patient "exorcises" the bad parental figure, the way is open to a healthier, more independent identity.

*Sexual Imagery.* Clinical experience reveals that people who say they do not have images will respond when asked to imagine or recall sexual scenes. Sexual themes are among the most powerful and most frequently occurring images. Many are related to the strategies of interaction between the sexes that anticipate acceptance or rejection.

Imaginary situations that are most productive in revealing attitudes and feelings about sex include:

*Imagine an animal that comes out of a penis and an animal that comes out of a vagina. Then imagine that both animals go down a road together.*

*Parental Imagery.* Parental imagery is a highly specialized category of imagery relating to the interactions of parents and children, or individuals and/or significant others. One example is:

*Whisper into your mother's (father's) ear. Have her (him) whisper something back to you.*

**Depth Imagery.** Images that reveal depth or unconscious forces almost always elicit profound reactions. These highly emotionally charged situations should be employed with caution and with the therapist's awareness of what the patient is ready to face. One example is:

*Imagine you are a child and you are crying. Now imagine your mother (father) licking away your tears.*

**Unconscious Imagery.** Although this material can emerge in any imaginary situation, those categorized as unconscious imagery achieve their purpose more readily. One of the most useful is:

*Imagine reaching into a cave three times, each time reaching deeper than the last. What do you do, see, and feel?*

**Task Imagery.** Task imagery may reveal the patient's internal conflicts, style and manner of approach, defenses and fears; it also serves as a vehicle for focusing for a changed self-concept in the "working through" of the imaginary task (Shorr, 1975).

An important ingredient following the initial flow of imagery is to redo or reexperience the imagery in a manner that leads to a healthy conflict resolution. But the patient must be *ready* to focus for change. The elements determining this readiness are the patient's awareness of his or her internal conflicts, the release of feeling connected with contributory traumatic incidents, cognizance of the undermining strategies of behavior of significant others, and recognition of his or her own counterreaction strategies.

Examples of task imagery include:

*Imagine building a bridge across a gorge. You are in a tank of the foulest liquid. How does it feel? Imagine getting out of it.*

**Cathartic Imagery.** Imaginary situations in which the patient is asked to imagine the "bad" parent in front of him and openly

define himself in a positive manner can substitute for actual face-to-face confrontations. Obviously this kind of focusing procedure requires a supportive therapist aligned on the side of the patient, and, equally important, a readiness on the part of the patient to liberate himself from a false identity.

In addition to the finish-the-sentence approaches such as: *I am not _____; I am __; Never refer to me as _____;* and so forth, the therapist can suggest general, special, or group therapy imagery.

**General Imagery.** These images cannot be classified as specifically dual images, task images, or others, yet they plumb a vast area of the imagination and often lead to meaningful dialogue and awareness. They are often the stimulus for focusing and change. Examples include:

*Imagine an image of a molecule of you (your conscience, paradise). What do you do and see and feel?*
*Stare into a fire. What do you do and see and feel?*

**Special Imagery.** These images defy ordinary categorization. They have proven to reveal enormous amounts of information about layers of personality, core conflict, and sexuality. Examples include:

*Imagine three boxes, large, medium, and small. Imagine something inside each box.*
*Imagine three doors (left, center, and right). Open each door. What do you see, do, and feel?*

**Group Therapy Imagery.** Psycho-Imagination Group Therapy emphasizes the patients' self-definition and the degree to which their self-concept permits or constricts behavior vis-à-vis the other group members. Group interaction crystallizes each member's awareness of how others in the group define him or her. In addition, the group becomes an arena for reenactment of old family interactions that molded the patient's false positions and negative self-images.

The overall purpose of interaction within the group is to help each patient become aware of his or her conflicts and then take the risks inherent in focusing for change. While nearly all of the imagery approaches suggested for individual therapy can be utilized in group therapy, several factors must be considered. First, groups involve interaction between men and women. Some patients find it considerably easier to express feelings and imagery to members of the same sex. Difficulties in revealing such material to members of the opposite sex is especially prevalent among persons with problems relating to exposure of sexual inadequacy. Overcoming this kind of reluctance, permitting oneself the free flow of imagery and emotional expression without the feeling that one is weird, is a barometer of the patient's growth.

Second, the factors of peer competition and belonging, while not always evident in one-to-one therapy, may surface in group contact. Disclosing such feelings and coping with them are part of the group process. Also, basic trust of authority figures and basic trust of one's peers are areas that may be subjected to considerable emotion and conflict within the group setting. Co-patients often afford the conflicted group member a chance to develop and nurture the courage for new alternatives by example, by identification, by stimulating one another, and by giving increasingly free play to their fantasies, dreams, imagination, and unconscious productions.

Group sessions are not so structured that only imagery is involved. Anything may be brought up at any time—a particularly traumatic situation or decision; carryover reactions from previous sessions; thoughts and feelings people have about others in the days between group meetings. Awareness and feelings patients have gleaned from individual sessions may be brought up in group situations. Nothing, certainly, should deter spontaneous behavior unless that behavior is used as a cover-up for some difficult internal conflict. A fine goal for any group therapist is to keep the structure and the spontaneity of the group unfettered.

## METHODOLOGY

Psycho-Imagination Therapy uses four techniques, namely: (1) imaginary situation (IS), (2) finish-the-sentence (FTS), (3) self-and-other question (S&O), and (4) most-or-least question (M/L).

The infinitely varied waking imagery elicited through the imaginary situation is the essence of the phenomenological method. This method involves asking the patient to relax, close his eyes, and trust his images. The therapist then suggests the appropriate imaginary situation to elicit the desired material. The patient's responses are the basis of the dialogical aspects of the therapeutic process. These responses suggest what the patient is opening for examination, what he is willing to face, where he is going, what he is ready for, what he appears to deny.

It is not wise to push the patient to image if none are forthcoming after a long interval. One may prefer to go either to other imaginary situations or perhaps to discuss current concerns. The patient must be assured that material is always available to him for awareness and meaning whether or not he is involved in imagery.

The patient's responses to certain structured situations often accurately bring into the "here-and-now" states of feeling that have their roots in the past. The therapist then stresses the *situation* and *interpersonal interactions* with the patient and encourages him in his *choice of action* within the situation. This ultimately helps him in greater choice of action in his external reality.

Clinical experience demonstrates that the finish-the-sentence technique can uncover the more complex emotional blockages. However, its effectiveness depends on its being woven into the fabric of the therapeutic dialogue at the appropriate moment. Consider the case of a young man who, when asked for the body-part core of his identity, replied: "My hands. . . . I am only what I'm doing. . . . If I am not doing anything, then I have no identity." The therapist can follow through by asking the patient to finish a sentence such as: "But for my father (or mother) I would have been _____." "My identity will suffer if I go toward _____." "I feel most hostility toward _____."

Both therapist and patient may be surprised by the response to the question "I deprive my wife (husband, father, mother, boss, or other significant person) of the satisfaction of _____." A variant of the latter refers to any other two significant persons in the patient's life: "My father deprives my mother of the satisfaction of _____."

Patients who are amnesic about their childhood and who may have difficulty with an imaginative situation often respond well when asked to supply 10 different endings to the sentence: "I strongly resent _____." After the patient selects the item he or she feels most strongly about, the therapist can use dialogue to stimulate awareness.

An important way to elicit the patient's conflict areas is by the use of existential, or self-and-other, questions. An existential question elicits how a person views the self and how he feels others define him. It is an effective tool when used in conjunction with the imaginary situation.

The manner of presenting these questions is of the utmost importance. Timing is critical, and under no circumstances should they be asked routinely or as a series of test items. This weakens the desired therapeutic effect. Nor should they be posed with predetermined answers in mind. Do not try to fit the patient in advance into any dogmatic theory or system of thought.

For example, with one patient it may be appropriate to ask: "How do you make yourself aware to others when in group therapy?" The answer will probably reveal the patient's inner consistency in functioning with others in a way that is unique to his or her self-system. If the therapist is following a pre-conceived theory, he may unwittingly try for a "desired" response and miss the way the patient really sees himself in relation to others.

Furthermore, judgment must be used to decide whether the patient has the ego strength to handle certain questions at a particular time. There is no substitute for the skill that comes from experience. In sessions where the patient requires much therapeutic support, they may have to be eschewed completely.

Following are some examples of self-and-other questions:

*To whom are you accounting?*

*Never refer to me as _____.*

*Did (Do) you make a difference to anyone?*

*Did (Does) anyone acknowledge your existence?*

*How do (did) you make people aware of you?*

*Were (Are) you ever believed?*

*What qualities did your parents deny in you?*

*How would you drive somebody out of their mind?*

The most-or-least question sharpens awareness of a person's self-image and the concept of his basic attitudes and values. Typical of this category is "What is the most immoral thing you can think of?" or "What is the least exciting part of your body?"

Often a person will assume a false identity ascribed to him through the unconscious strategy of his parents. This can lead in two directions. The first is what Karen Horney (1945) refers to as "the idealized image" in which the person is constantly trying to live up to his image and needs the world to concur with it. The other direction is when a parent, or significant other, confers a despised image. The person may continuously strive unconsciously to throw off this false self and live up to his true potential.

To assist the patient to become aware of his own despised image or the rigid need to sustain the idealized image, and to try to change it, the following questions are helpful:

*What is the biggest lie you have ever told?*
*What was the most unfair demand put on you?*
*What was the most often repeated statement made to you by your mother (father)?*

If the answer to the latter question has been a continual harping on the child's shortcomings, this will become the despised image that may haunt him as intolerable all his life.

The most-or-least question is an excellent tool to reveal a person's guilt. Inevitably either of the aspects of false identity is locked into guilt. If someone identifies with the despised false image, then he or she feels guilty; if someone falls short of the idealized image, the guilt will be compounded.

Questions such as "What did your mother (father) despise in you the most?" and "What is the most distasteful thing about you?" are guides to the dimensions of a patient's guilt. Also important in this context are: "What is the most shameful day of your life?" or "What is the most humiliating thing that ever happened to you?" In a sexual connotation an effective question is "In whose presence would it be most (least) difficult to have sexual thoughts?"

These four techniques enhance each other as they are combined and interwoven. Singly they can be valuable, but in combination the whole can be much greater than each of its parts. The integration of all the specific approaches within the framework of the individual's phenomenology, so that he can achieve greater awareness of himself, opens the door to possible ways of change. Here, for example, are some possible ways that each of the four techniques can be utilized to make the patient aware of a single feeling reaction:

1. Finish-the-Sentence (FTS): Never call me _____.

2. Self-and-Other (S&O): What image of yourself can you not allow?
   Imaginary Situation (IS):
   (a) Picture yourself on a blank screen in a position in which you detest yourself.
   (b) You are walking down a street and a person your own age accuses you of something. What does he accuse you of, and why?

3. Most-or-Least (M/L): What is the most detestable thing anyone can say about you?

As patients become accustomed to this kind of therapy it is less and less necessary to make interpretations for them. With specific cross-checking of the four modalities, it is possible to help focus patients to greater awareness where they are forced to face the truth *for themselves*.

## APPLICATIONS

Psycho-imagination therapy is applicable to a wide range of problems and situations. It has been used successfully in treating neuroses, emotional maladjustment, marriage and family problems, sexual dysfunction, psychosomatic problems, extreme jealousy, anxiety, and maladaptive behavior patterns.

Psycho-imagination therapy techniques have been useful in breaking impasse situations that arise in conventional therapy. A verbatim transcript of a patient/therapist interview concerning an impasse situation is included in Shorr (1972).

Clinical experience has shown that obsessive/compulsive patients are helped to cut down on meanderings and repetitious verbalizations when they are attending to their imagery productions. The imagery helps to focus attention on the root causes of the obsessive behavior and to aid in opening up new avenues to behavioral change.

Anxiety, depression, and other neuroses respond favorably to imagery techniques. In addition, the imagery productions accurately reflect the degree of conflict resolution and the changes made in therapy. For example, the imagery productions of depressive patients become more positive—for example, bare trees begin to show leaves, and scenes are more light and pleasant. I have found that psychodramatic confrontation through imagery often leads to conflict resolution and the lifting of anxiety.

When used in conjunction with psychodrama, imagery, especially dual imagery, has been of catalytic value and has had a highly therapeutic effect on institutionalized psychotic patients.

One of the most dramatic applications of Psycho-Imagination Therapy is in group therapy, where the interactions of the members through the modality of imagery can be highly therapeutic.

Since sexual conflicts deal with the most vulnerable, the most tender, the most shame-inducing, and the most guilty feelings, they are the most difficult to disclose to oneself and to others. The use of imagery bypasses the censorship and offers a vehicle for dialogue and possible conflict resolution.

The *Shorr Imagery Test* (1974a), the *Group Shorr Imagery Test* (1977a), the *Supplementary Shorr Imagery Test* (1978c), and the *Shorr Parent Imagery Test* (1979b), which have been developed and utilized primarily for diagnostic purposes, are the direct outgrowth of the theoretical structure of Psycho-Imagination Therapy. It must be emphasized that the tests are able to verify the concepts of Psycho-Imagination Therapy. Few systems of psychotherapy can utilize a test for verification.

## CASE EXAMPLE

The following is a report of a patient, Jim, in group therapy.*

JIM:  I don't really remember too well what actually happened. I know that I had been

*In this case example Shorr was the therapist. Other names refer to other group members.

suffering from extreme stomach pains for two days. Everything had been going extremely well in school for three weeks. Karen and I had just had the best two weeks of our relationship. For the first time in my life, I felt productive, social, myself, and in love with Karen at the same time. My fantasy of a "sunshiny winter afternoon" was going very well, except, for some unknown reason, my neck and shoulders were tightening up harder than steel—more than I had ever known.

Back to the stomach pain. At first I thought I had the flu. But I had extreme pains that were very high in my stomach. At the same time, I felt like vomiting, but I couldn't. I even stuck my finger down my throat and I couldn't, I wouldn't vomit.

Tuesday morning, I went to work. I talked to Helen (our friend) before I left and she said it sounded like I had an ulcer. Right then I got extremely depressed, angry, tearful, and alone. I went home and I was really angry. I felt shitty (guilty) for having an ulcer. I felt shitty that I was still so uptight and fighting and unproductive as to have an ulcer. I was also really mad and untrustful of group and my last two years in it. I went back and forth, between guilt and anger.

Then I called Bill (group member). The one thing I remember from the conversation was him saying, "I care that you are in such pain" and "I really like being around you and Karen when you're happy." When I got off the phone, I was wide open. I cried by myself and for myself without hesitation. For the first time, I let my guts hurt and I cried without any thoughts or judgments. I then felt like I wanted to cry "mommy." I wanted someone to love me and take care of me. I wanted a mother. But I knew I didn't want my mother. And it made me angry to realize I never had a mother.

When Karen came home, I was very aware of not wanting to show her my feelings. But I had called and asked her to come home. That was pretty hard to ask for. If I ever let it out to my mother, she used it for false motherings, and to shrink my cock and consume my balls.

By the time I got to group, my stomach was really hurting and I explained that everything was good but I was dying of pain.

SHORR:    What part of you hurts?

JIM:    My stomach. Right in the middle of my guts.

SHORR:    Can you hand that part to someone?

JIM:    When Dr. Shorr asked that, all I could do was cry. He asked me several times and it seemed impossible. It seemed it would be giving the vulnerable and dearest part of me away.

GWEN:    No wonder it hurts so much. It always hurt you and you were always alone with it.

JIM:    What bothers me is that I never got anything with my pain, and I'm not now.

JOHN:    You must have gotten something.

JIM:    Yes, I got to stay home. I didn't have to go to school and compulsively achieve. I got protection against my father. I didn't have to feel alone at school with the kids. I felt like I got some love. Even though it was being used to manipulate me into taking care of her. She had a way in, through my pain, and I had a way in with my pain.

SHORR:    Who does your stomach belong to? [self-other question]

JIM:    To me. It's a good stomach. Good color on the outside. But the inside is all jumbled.

SHORR:    Give that part a name. [imaginary situation]

JIM:    Me.

JOHN:    How does the rest of your body feel?

JIM:    Fine. It's all mine.

JOHN:    Then your stomach must not be yours.

JIM:    No, it's not. It's the shit part of me.

SHORR:    In what body part does your mother reside in? [imaginary situation]

JIM:    In my stomach.

JOHN:    Isn't it true that you still want a mother, and you want to call for her?

JIM:    Yes, no—I want a mother, but I don't want mine.

SHORR:    Reach in and grab her out.

JIM:    She's in there with tentacles. It is all around me of . . . (pause) . . . all through my meat.

SHORR:    Rip her out. She's scared of you. [imaginary situation]

JIM:    That's really true. That makes a difference. She's goddamned scared of me. I scream at her and she shrinks like a sea urchin. I'm not really the scared one, she is. (I remembered the dream where I jacked off on my mother and then I screamed I was going to kill her.) I pulled her out with my right hand, and held her there and talked about her. She was like a huge, sickly cancer cell. I talked a lot about her, and the more I talked, the more she was back in my stomach and the more my stomach hurt.

SHORR:    Rip her out and throw her in the fire (a dream I had about the ending of the world). Scream at her and tell her to get out. [imaginary situation]

JIM:    For a long time I didn't feel like I could. I just couldn't reach in and get her out. I decided to stand up and try it. I had to. My stomach hurt so bad. I couldn't let her stay in. Thinking of her as scared of me helped. But I still couldn't do it.

GROUP MEMBERS:    You won't be alone—we're all here.

SHORR:    I'll be right here.

JIM:    I know you all love me and you'll be here. But I'm afraid once I scream, I won't be able to call for you any more when I really need you. (This feeling is the same feeling when I get sick and am scared that I'm all alone and I wouldn't get any help if I really needed it.)

SHORR:    You won't have to call for me. I'll be right here with you, anyway. (That did it.)

JIM:    AND THEN I SCREAMED. I SCREAMED WITH ALL MY MIGHT. WITH ALL MY PAIN FOR MY WHOLE LIFE. WITH ALL MY ANGER FOR

MY WHOLE LIFE. WITH ALL MY GUTS. I SCREAMED FOR HER TO GET OUT. I SCREAMED FROM MY GUTS. WITHOUT ANY HESITATION. I SCREAMED FOR MYSELF. 'CAUSE I WANT TO LIVE FOR ME. 'CAUSE I DESERVE FOR ME. AND SHE GOT OUT. YOU'RE DAMN STRAIGHT SHE GOT OUT. AND SHE CAN NEVER GET BACK IN. SHE'S SCARED. I KNOW NOW. I KNOW IN MY GUTS. I KNOW WHO I AM. I KNOW MY STRENGTH, AND I KNOW HER WEAK, SADISTIC, INHUMAN GAME. I DON'T NEED IT. I DON'T NEED YOU. I'LL NEVER NEED YOU. SHE'S GONE.

As soon as I screamed, I bent over and clenched my fists. I felt like I was screaming to hell and back. Dr. Shorr straightened me up and told me I didn't have to bend over. She couldn't get back in now. He hugged me and protected my stomach with his belly. It felt good. I really needed the warmth. I don't really remember what happened after that. I was shaking a lot and Dr. Shorr stayed next to me and hugged me and sat down next to me. He really cared. And he was really there. And I didn't have to call for him. And I looked up and people really looked human and warm. And especially the women looked different. I guess not so much like my mother. They looked human and fleshy. My stomach actually felt like it had a wound in it. But it was a clean, fleshy wound. And now it can grow back together with me. It's mine.

Several months have passed since that group session. Jim has shown considerable change; he is much calmer and most of all, there has been a marked decrease in his strong suspiciousness. His own conclusion, verified in time, strongly suggested that he accounted his behavior to his mother according to her standards and felt great guilt if he did not. Since she was "inside" him, the accounting system was acute and ever-present. Just as the paranoid person is defined by nearly everyone he meets, this man on a lesser scale was defined by his mother and mother substitutes.

## SUMMARY

Psycho-Imagination Therapy (PIT) believes that any method of psychotherapy should be firmly rooted in a systematic theory of personality. PIT is operationally based on existential concepts and phenomenological foundations blended with the interpersonal developmental theories of Harry Stack Sullivan and R. D. Laing. The therapeutic emphasis is on the integration of imagination with existential phenomenology and the centeredness of the individual—imagination in the service of awareness and of the possibility for change.

While other types of psychotherapy use imagery as a modality, only Psycho-Imagination Therapy uses imagery systematically according to a well-defined theoretical stance. In addition, PIT uses other modalities, such as finish-the-sentence, self-other questions, most-or-least questions, and dialogue within the same interpersonal theoretical framework.

A person's imagery, more than any other mental function, indicates how he or she views the world. The use of systematically categorized imagery opens up the inner world to both patient and therapist. Imagery helps the patient to recognize and cast off the conferred "alien" identity and to redefine himself. It also aids the patient in becoming aware of strategies developed to maintain false positions and then supports him or her in focusing for change, resolving conflicts, and overcoming resistances.

Perhaps the most important factor of imagery is its ability to bypass the usual censorship of the person. Lowenstein (1956) made the point that the patient, through hearing himself vocalize, may control his own reactions to his thoughts. In short, one is verbally editing, and in so doing attempting to control the reactions of the therapist. Because one cannot usually tell in advance what effect or meaning the imagery will have, the patient may reveal in imagery what would not ordinarily be revealed in verbal conversation. Imagery has a prime value in that it can help break resistances usually found in verbal transactions.

The verbal process can be commingled with imagery to yield a cohesive logic and internal consistency to the psychotherapeutic process.

A further function of imagery in psychotherapy is that images can be transformed, reexperienced, and reshaped in line with a healthier self-concept. The patient's growing awareness of internal conflicts is one of the most important products of imagery in therapy.

In the long run it is not enough for a person to be aware of inner conflicts; a change must be made in self-definition. Resolution of a conflict is more important than mere solution. Sleeping pills offer a solution to insomnia, a vacation offers a solution to an unpleasant situation, but in neither case is the actual problem resolved. Superficial solutions are easily conceived and prescribed, but the therapist must ignore such temptations and deal constructively with the problem itself, however difficult it may be to liberate a person from a neurotic conflict resolution.

The focusing approaches of Psycho-Imagination Therapy are designed to free the patient from a deadlocked position in his or her psychological life. Suppression, avoidance, distortion, and withdrawal provide avenues to sustain conflict and escape from resolution. PIT approaches depend upon the self-definition. It is essential that the patient be assisted in changing his self-image, thus combating the inclination to let others define him falsely. Psycho-Imagination Therapy mobilizes the patient's constructive forces to work for liberation from an alien identity. The goal is to be what we are all striving to be—more human, namely, ourselves.

# REFERENCES

Breuer, J. and Freud, S. *Studies in hysteria.* London: Hogarth Press, 1953.

Caslant, E. *Method of development of the supernormal faculties.* Paris: Meyer, 1927.

Connella, J. A. The effects of psycho-imagination therapy on the treatment outcome of chronic benign pain patients. Ph.D. dissertation, CSPP, 1978.

Desoille, R. *The directed daydream.* Monograph No. 8. New York: The Psychsynthesis Research Foundation, 1965.

Freud, S. *An autobiographical study.* In J. Strachey (Ed.), *The standard edition of the complete psychological works of Sigmund Freud,* vol. 12. London: Hogarth Press, 1959.

Fromm, E. Remarks on the problem of free association. *Psychiatric Research Reports 2.* American Psychiatric Association, 1955.

Hartmann, H. *Ego psychology and the problem of adaption.* New York: International Universities Press, 1958.

Horowitz, M. and Becker, S. S. The compulsion to repeat trauma: Experimental study of intrusive thinking after stress. *Journal of Nervous and Mental Disease,* 1971, **153,** No. 1.

Laing, R. D. *The divided self.* New York: Penguin Books, 1965.

Laing, R. D. *The self and others.* New York: Pelican Books, 1971.

Lowenstein, R. M. Some remarks on the role of speech in psychoanalytic techniques. *International Journal of Psycho-Analysis,* 1956, **37,** 460–467.

Morgan, C. O. Disability through imagery experience. In J. Shorr et al. (Eds.), *Imagery: Its many dimensions.* Proceedings of the First Annual Conference of the American Association for the Study of Mental Imagery. New York: Plenum, 1979.

Shorr, J. E. The existential question and the imaginary situation as therapy. *Existential Psychiatry,* 1967, **6 (24),** 443–462.

Shorr, J. E. *Psycho-imagination therapy: The integration of phenomenology and imagination.* New York: Intercontinental Medical Book Corp., 1972.

Shorr, J. E. In what part of your body does your mother reside? *Psychotherapy: Theory, Research and Practice,* 1973, **10 (2),** 31–34.

Shorr, J. E. *Shorr imagery test.* Los Angeles: Institute for Psycho-Imagination Therapy, 1974a.

Shorr, J. E. *Psychotherapy through imagery.* New York: Intercontinental Medical Book Corp., 1974b.

Shorr, J. E. The use of task imagery as therapy. *Psychotherapy: Theory, Research and Practice,* 1975, **12 (2),** 207–210.

Shorr, J. E. Dual imagery. *Psychotherapy: Theory, Research and Practice,* 1976, **13 (2),** 244–248.

Shorr, J. E. *Group Shorr imagery test.* Los Angeles: Institute for Psycho-Imagination Therapy, 1977a.

Shorr, J. E. *Go See the Movie in Your Head.* New York: Popular Library, 1977b.

Shorr, J. E. Clinical categories of therapeutic imagery.

In J. L. Singer and K. Pope (Eds.), *The power of human imagination*. New York: Plenum, 1978a.

Shorr, J. E. Imagery as a projective device. *Imagery Bulletin of the American Association for the Study of Mental Imagery*. 1978b, **1** (2).

Shorr, J. E. *Supplementary Shorr imagery test*. Los Angeles: Institute for Psycho-Imagination Therapy, 1978c.

Shorr, J. E. Imagery as a method of self observation in therapy. *Imagery Bulletin of the American Association for the Study of Mental Imagery*, 1979a, **2** (2).

Shorr, J. E. *Shorr parental imagery test*. Los Angeles: Institute for Psycho-Imagination Therapy, 1979b.

Shorr, J. E. Discoveries about the minds ability to organize and find meaning in Imagery. In Shorr, J. E., Connella, J. A., Robin, P. and Sobel, G. (Eds.). *Imagery: Its many dimensions and applications*. Proceedings of the First Annual Conference of the American Association for the Study of Mental Imagery. New York: Plenum, 1979c.

Singer, J. L. Imagery and daydream techniques employed in psychotherapy: Some practical and theoretical implications. In C. Spielberger (Ed.), *Current topics in clinical and community psychology*, vol. 3. New York: Academic Press, 1971.

Sobel, G. A study of group dynamics at Los Angeles City College. In J. Shorr, et al. (Eds.), *Proceedings of the 1st Annual Conference for the Study of Mental Imagery*. New York: Plenum, 1979.

Stampfl, T. G. and Leavis, D. J. Essentials of implosive therapy. *Journal of Abnormal Psychology*, 1966, **72,** 496–503.

Sullivan, H. S. *The interpersonal theory of psychiatry*. New York: Norton, 1953.

Tansey, D. The use of the Shorr imagery test with a population of violent offenders. In J. Shorr, et al. (Eds.), *Imagery: Its many dimensions and applications*. New York: Plenum, 1979.

Shorr, J. E. The Psychologists Imagination and Sexual Imagery. In *Imagery: Its many dimensions and applications*. Vol II (Eds.) E. Klinger and M. Anderson, N.Y., Plenum Press, 1981.

# CHAPTER 52

# Psychosynthesis

MARTHA CRAMPTON

*This chapter was the first one contracted for and the last one received. Between the first author contacted and the final author, no fewer than six other individuals promised—and did not deliver—an account of Psychosynthesis. So from Honolulu to California to Massachusetts I contacted psychosynthesist after psychosynthesist; finally Martha Crampton delivered. I bring this up because the typical reader may believe all an editor has to do is write and ask—and the chapter comes in. Not at all. But this is an unusual chapter—well worth waiting for and agonizing over.*

*In my judgment, Dr. Roberto Assagioli, the developer of Psychosynthesis, like Trigant Burrow and many other giants in this field, has not received his full credit. Consequently, it is a pleasure to be able to introduce Psychosynthesis to a larger audience. As I was developing a list of therapies to include in this book, I informally questioned many therapists; it became clear that few knew much about Psychosynthesis. The reason will be evident on reading this complicated chapter, which, due to rigid space limitations, I had to cut considerably. More than most complex systems, Psychosynthesis stresses value; it is therefore similar to Formative Spirituality, Mutual Need Therapy, and others with a strong value orientation. In these respects Psychosynthesis is also similar to Alfred Adler's Individual Psychology. In view of the richness and complexity of Psychosynthesis, it is hoped the typical reader will further explore Assagioli's enormous vision.*

Psychosynthesis refers to the theory and practice of a perspective on human development first articulated by Italian psychiatrist Roberto Assagioli.

The approach is based on unifying one's personality expression with a deeper source of purpose in and direction to life, the transpersonal Self, which is seen as the integrating principle of the personality and as a source of wisdom, inspiration, unconditional love, and the will to meaning and service. The term "psychosynthesis" is also applied to the process of personality integration occurring within this framework, either through the individual's own efforts or with the assistance of a psychosynthesis practitioner.

## HISTORY

The foundations of Psychosynthesis were laid in the second decade of the twentieth century by Roberto Assagioli, whose work was far ahead of its time. Assagioli was one of those rare persons who can truly be called a sage. His wisdom, his radiant love, his down-to-earth simplicity were appreciated by all who knew him. Psychosynthesis, for him, was not merely an abstract doctrine but a practical philosophy that he applied in his daily living. Assagioli died in 1974 at the age of 86.

When Psychosynthesis spread to North America in the 1960s, it attracted many people who had a background in the new therapies and growth disciplines such as Gestalt, the abreaction therapies, Transactional Analysis, and so forth. Some aspects of these therapies enriched Psychosynthesis as it is currently practiced in North America. Many people within the human potential movement found in Psychosynthesis a framework comprehensive enough to include what they had found of value in other approaches and that provided an orientation for deciding which methods, among the vast spectrum of available ones, were best suited to particular people in particular situations.

Assagioli's thought had its roots in many Western and Eastern traditions. He knew Freud, was active in the early psychoanalytic circles, and was one of the first Italians to introduce psychoanalysis in his country. The Freudian conception of the unconscious was included within his framework, but he felt it was incomplete. He expanded his own conception of the unconscious to include what has since been called by Maslow "the farther reaches of human nature" (1972), and he distinguished between the primitive or lower unconscious—the repository of our basic biological drives and our unresolved complexes—and what he called the superconscious—a realm that he postulated as being above or beyond our normal level of conscious awareness.

Assagioli agreed with the view that an important goal of therapy is to "make the unconscious conscious," to extend the frontiers of our consciousness into areas that were formerly unconscious. He differed from the psychoanalytic position in that he believed we must have a "height" psychology as well as a "depth" psychology—that we must go "up" as well as "down" in the psyche. Therefore he developed techniques for evocation of the superconscious that helped people to contact directly latent positive and constructive energies within themselves. Contact with the superconscious often gave people the strength and inspiration to deal with disturbing aspects of themselves. At least for those persons who wished to undertake a

spiritual Psychosynthesis, he also considered it necessary to look "upward" toward the transpersonal Self as a source of direction and meaning in their lives.

Emphasizing the need to assume conscious responsibility for the contents of the unconscious, he did not agree with the assumption of most depth psychologies that making the unconscious conscious was sufficient to effect change. He believed that awareness was only part of the picture and that awareness had to be balanced with will for the personality to become effectively integrated. Unless his clients established a connection with the source of will within themselves, he found that their insights would tend to get lost and be wasted. There was a need to rouse the person's motivation to take responsibility and to help the person "ground" the insights achieved through active techniques applied in the course of day-to-day living.

Assagioli's insights into the nature and training of the will are perhaps his greatest contribution to modern psychology. His understanding of the will is both profound and radically different from most previous conceptions. Viewing the will as an expression of the I or the Self, depending on its level, he saw the intimate connection between the will and the source of identity. He realized that the will was an unpopular topic in psychology, attributing this in part to the Victorian misconception of the will as a harsh taskmaster that forces us to do things we do not really want to do. Therefore he endeavored to show that the true will is serene and unstrained, that it enables us to choose what is in harmony with our own deepest needs.

## CURRENT STATUS

The various centers and institutes of Psychosynthesis that have emerged in the Western world have all taken their point of departure in Assagioli's teaching. No orthodoxy has been established, however, and each center has interpreted theory and practice in its own way as well as adding to it. It was Assagioli's wish that the institutes remain autonomous and, to use his metaphor, relate to each other as the stars in a constellation rather than as satellites revolving around a central sun. He saw Psychosynthesis as needing to change and evolve with the times, as well as to adapt to the needs of different cultural settings. Founded in this spirit, the movement has avoided more than most therapeutic systems the tendency toward ossification. Psychosynthesis is practiced by an increasing number of human service professionals in North America, Europe, and South America. Areas of application include psychotherapy, counseling, medicine, education, religion, management and organizational development, and creative problem solving in a variety of fields.

Practitioners have generally been trained in one or more of the training centers that have been established in these countries. Training programs in Psychosynthesis vary somewhat from one institute to another, according to the particular emphasis of the center and the needs of the student. In the United States there are several training centers in California and Massachusetts, with other centers in Seattle, Washington; Lexington, Kentucky; Redding, Connecticut; and in Walpole, New Hampshire. The centers in Boston, Massachusetts, and Walpole have a particular emphasis on educational applications of Psychosynthesis, while the others focus more on psychotherapy and personal growth counseling. In addition, individual practitioners are working in most areas of the country and sometimes offer training as well as counseling and consulting services. In Canada the major center is in Montreal.

The basic reference sources on Psychosynthesis are the two books by Assagioli: *Psychosynthesis: A Manual of Principles and Techniques* (1965) and *The Act of Will* (1975). A new book, *The Realization of the Self: A Psychosynthesis Book*, written by James Vargiu (1980) is in press at the time of this writing.

## THEORY

Although Assagioli was a psychiatrist, his model of the human being was not based exclusively on the data of the psychiatric couch. He believed it was necessary to study the functioning of healthy individuals, including the most self-realized members of the human race, to gain a complete understanding of the full range and potentials of human nature. He deplored the tendency of diagnostic psychiatry to equate people with their illness. Instead, Assagioli viewed the person as a whole and considered pathological manifestations to be simply one aspect of the total person. As his perspective was one of growth, he tended to view symptoms not so much as something undesirable to be "gotten rid of" but rather as an indication of an energy blockage that needed to be explored. His emphasis was on releasing the constructive forces, on development of the person's positive resources, which he found would often cause symptoms to fall away.

Assagioli summarized his view of the human psychological constitution in Figure 1, which has come to be called the "egg diagram."

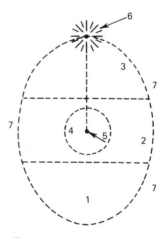

Figure 1    The egg diagram. 1. Lower unconscious; 2. middle unconscious; 3. higher unconscious or superconscious; 4. field of consciousness; 5. "I" (center of consciousness or Personal Self); 6. Self (Transpersonal Self or Higher Self); 7. collective unconscious.

The area within the central circle is the field of consciousness, at the center of which is the "I," or personal self. The "I" is the point of pure awareness and will, which is the subject of our field of consciousness and the integrating center of our personality.

In the egg diagram the "I" or personal self is connected by a dotted line to a point above it—the higher or transpersonal Self. This transpersonal Self, like the personal self, is a center of consciousness and of will; however its domain is more inclusive. The transpersonal Self extends its awareness to include the whole realm of the personal unconscious as well as the more limited field of consciousness. It is the center around which integration takes place at the stage of the transpersonal or spiritual psychosynthesis.

The area of the egg diagram that falls within the oval represents the personal unconscious, or that part of the unconscious that relates specifically to the individual, to his or her life experience, and to the unfolding of his or her inner qualities. The personal unconscious is divided into three levels: the lower unconscious, the middle unconscious, and the superconscious. The middle unconscious contains those elements that are similar to our normal waking state of consciousness.

A variety of "maps" are used in Psychosynthesis to help us understand and describe what is going on in a person. In discussing these, it is important to bear in mind that a map is only useful if it happens to fit the situation. The skillful psychosynthesist will be careful not to impose a preconceived conceptual system on the person he or she is working with, and will attempt to sense the unique reality of a particular individual rather than distorting the person to fit a rigid mold.

## The Subpersonality Map

We are all familiar with the many inner voices that clamor for our attention, often bearing messages that contradict one another. There may be a voice, for example, saying,

"I am really worn out; I think I will take a week off at Christmas and go to Florida." Another voice will reply, "But it costs too much; I can't afford to go." And yet another will be saying, "I really ought to buckle down during the holiday and finish fixing the kitchen so my wife will stop nagging me." This may be answered by a voice that says, "I don't care what she wants; I'm tired of her always telling me what to do anyway!" This kind of inner dialogue, which occupies so much of our energy, is going on within most of us a good deal of the time.

Psychosynthesis uses the term "subpersonalities" to refer to these "small I's" that speak for the part rather than for the whole. The subpersonalities are generally named. We might say that the person has a "pleaser" subpersonality that wants to ingratiate his wife, a "rebel" subpersonality that resents this, possibly a "striver" subpersonality that causes him to work too hard and become exhausted, and perhaps a "martyr" subpersonality that will not allow him to indulge in the expense of a vacation. Of course, we would have to know the person well to identify the subpersonalities accurately.

We can describe subpersonalities as being structured constellations or agglomerates of attitudes, drives, habit patterns, and belief systems, organized in adaptation to forces in the internal and external environment (Vargiu, 1975). They are similar to the "complexes" of psychoanalysis or the "games" of Transactional Analysis in that they contain crystallized energy that is "split off" from the whole of the personality.

When the child is unable to satisfy his basic needs and drives in a healthy, direct way, because of his own inadequacies or those of "significant others," he develops indirect and covert means to satisfy these needs. These means are the best available to protect his psyche from injury at the time, given his lack of experience, the immaturity of his organism, his internal dynamics, and the limitations of his environment.

An example to illustrate the process of subpersonality formation is the child who becomes the "good boy." Such a child is usually praised for obedient behavior and threatened with loss of love for expressing his own will. To obtain love, he learns to conform to the wishes of his parents. He develops a desire to please, to do what others want him to do, even when this means ignoring his own needs, because it is the only way he knows of gaining acceptance. The same child may later develop a "rebel" or "bad boy" subpersonality, as subpersonalities often develop in pairs of opposites, with the tendencies of one balancing out the tendencies of the opposite pole. The child who is experiencing an inner compulsion to submit to authority will suffer from this restriction and may try to counterbalance this by a provocative and rebellious attitude, or by acting-out a tough, daredevil role. One "good boy" I worked with—a man in his thirties—still played an abjectly servile role toward his mother but attempted to create a more "manly" image for himself by "tough" behaviors such as car racing and heavy drinking. Each subpersonality has some valuable qualities that are important to preserve in the process of personality transmutation.

## The "Personality Vehicles" Map

The term "personality vehicles" refers to the body, the emotions, and the mind. These three components, which make up the personality, are like "vehicles" for the Self because they are its media of manifestation on the material plane. It is important that each vehicle be adequately developed and coordinated with the others so that the personality expression is balanced and harmonious. Some people are so identified with one of the personality components that they are cut off from other aspects. Such a split is most common between the mind and the emotions. A person who has been rewarded in life primarily for mental performance may be very mistrustful of his or her emotions, thinking that they are dangerous and would completely take over if given a chance. A

mentally identified person will need help in accepting and in educating the emotional side of the personality. People who are strongly identified with their emotions, on the other hand, may reject the mind and fear that mental activity would eliminate the vitality of their emotional life. Such people are likely to be flooded with uncontrolled emotionality and will need help in accepting the mental side of their personality.

## The "I"-Self Map

Psychosynthesis posits that the process of synthesis requires an integrating center around which the synthesis can take place. Two such centers are postulated within the human psyche: the "I" and the Self. The "I" is considered to be a projection within the field of consciousness of the Self and functions as its deputy at the personality level. Both centers have the dual functions of will and consciousness. They are capable of awareness within their particular domain and of action upon it.

The psychosynthetic process can be considered as involving two stages that are successive but not rigidly separated: the personal Psychosynthesis and the transpersonal Psychosynthesis. In the personal Psychosynthesis, the "I" serves as the integrating center around which the process takes place. During this stage, the subpersonalities and personality vehicles are harmonized and integrated so that the person becomes able to function effectively in the realms of work and personal relationships and develops a relatively well-integrated personality.

During the transpersonal Psychosynthesis, the focus of personality integration gradually shifts from the "I" to the transpersonal Self. The "I" continues to collaborate in the process, but the transpersonal Self increasingly assumes a primary role, becoming the new center around which integration takes place. The "I" is like the mayor of a city who at first believes that he has full power and autonomy in his area of jurisdiction. He happily proceeds in the governing of the "citizens" (the various elements of the personality that require integration) until one day he discovers that many of the laws of his city are determined by the policy of the federal government.

During the transpersonal Psychosynthesis, the "I" has the task of aligning the personality with the more inclusive purpose of the transpersonal Self, with which it has now entered into conscious relationship. The personality sometimes rebels and struggles to maintain its autonomy. It must learn that in cooperating with the greater whole, in harmonizing and blending its energies with those of the transpersonal Self, it will achieve greater fulfillment than in seeking to maintain the illusion of independence. For it is through our connection with the transpersonal Self that we experience real purpose and meaning in life, that we transcend the boundaries of our small ego and discover our deeper relatedness to the universe.

The psychosynthesis guide aims at helping the client experience the reality of the "I" as early as possible, since the "I" plays such a central role in the therapeutic process. It is particularly important to cultivate and reinforce this experience when dealing with issues of will, of inner direction, and of identity to help people gain a sense of their own worth and identity, of their human dignity, and of their capacity to take responsibility for the direction of their own lives. Without this awareness of the "I," we are like a ship adrift upon a stormy sea without a rudder to guide its course.

Once the client's identity with the "I" is firmly established, the personality is gradually harmonized and integrated through the will of this organizing center. In the course of the process, the consciousness of the "I" is expanded, the area in which its will is active is correspondingly increased, and the "I" moves "up" or closer to the transpersonal Self, eventually to reunite with its parent entity. The expansion of the "I's" field of awareness is analogous to what occurs when a mountain climber approaches the top of a mountain. With each step upward, broader vistas appear and one can see the surrounding areas more clearly and comprehensively. To pursue the analogy, we could say that the closer a person's "I" is to the Self, the more full and enlightened will be that person's perspective on the total context of his or her life, with more understanding and acceptance of the past, and more strength and inspiration in approaching the future.

An interesting point is that as the individual's field of consciousness expands more into the "heights," he or she is thereby enabled to descend further into the "depths," when there is a need to do so. As the energies of the superconscious are increasingly contacted, the ability is gained to approach the confusion, the pain, and the distortions of the past with clearer vision and with greater compassion and understanding.

This point is illustrated in the stages one goes through in working out the relationships with the parent figures. As will be discussed later in the section dealing with emotional release, a client will often go through a period of expressing strong primal emotions, such as rage and pain. The field of consciousness at this stage of the work is relatively restricted, as the person is identified with his or her own strong feelings and is unable to see the parents' point of view. Later, when the person is more in touch with transpersonal energies, it becomes possible to disidentify with the "hurt child" attitude, to empathize with the situation of the parents, and to forgive them. At a still higher level of consciousness people can integrate more fully the experiences of their childhood, moving beyond simple forgiveness of and reconciliation with the parents to an understanding of deeper meaning and purpose in the fact that they were born to those particular parents. They become reconciled with their life as a whole. They are then able not merely to accept but actively to embrace their own destiny. They can see how even the most difficult and painful experiences have contributed to the development of cherished qualities and have prepared individuals for the part they are called upon to play in life.

# METHODOLOGY

## The Personality Assessment

Assessment of the client's personality, needs, and existential situation is the first step in Psychosynthesis after the initial contact has been established. It is an ongoing process that has value not only in terms of guiding the initial direction of the work but also for evaluating the progress and needs at various stages of the Psychosynthesis.

Unlike diagnosis, which is often something "done to" the client by an authority, the psychosynthesis assessment respects the client's perceptions of his or her own needs and goals. It also has a therapeutic value in that the ongoing aspect of the assessment process helps to keep the client's will aligned with the work that needs to be done.

## Unfolding of the Process

The real guide of the psychosynthesis process is the client's higher Self that, at any particular time, is directing the person's attention in certain directions. With this in mind, the external guide, whose role is to support the client's inner process, is attentive to what seems to "want to happen" in the session.

The actual sequence in which the issues emerge may come as a surprise. It is important that the guide refrain from imposing preconceived structures on the situation, remaining open to allow the client's process to *unfold from within*. For one client the most urgent need may be to get more in touch with powerful emotions; for another client the need will be to step back from emotional reactions so that he or she can perceive them more clearly and better understand what they are expressing. One client will need to explore intra-psychically a conflicted relation-

ship, while another will need to work this out at the interpersonal level. Sensitivity to timing and to the level at which particular issues can best be resolved at a particular time is crucial.

## Identification and Disidentification

The concept of disidentification is a central one in Psychosynthesis, and it is probably one of the most important contributions made by this theory to psychological thought.

Disidentification can be understood best in relationship to its polar opposite: identification. We are identified with something when we are unable to separate ourselves from that thing, when our sense of identity is bound up in it. Some men are so identified with their cars that, should the car be scratched, they experience it as though they had been personally defaced, as though they were diminished by the fact that their car was scratched. A woman who is identified with the appearance of her body may feel that her worth as a human being is lessened if she develops wrinkles on her face or gets gray hairs. It is as though these people believed "I am my car" or "I am my body."

In the work of integrating our subpersonalities, disidentification plays an important role. We must be able to "stand back from" our subpersonalities in order to see them more clearly and to find the vantage point from which we can do something to transmute them. A man who was identified with a manipulative "salesman" subpersonality always aroused defensive reactions in people until he was able to disidentify from the need to sell himself. When he saw what he had been doing, he found it very comical and felt motivated to change his way of relating to others. When he realized that he could now choose not to play this role, he experienced a great sense of relief and inner freedom.

In addition to the various forms of unconscious and blind identification with some partial aspect of the personality, there is a process of voluntary or conscious identification. At certain points in the psychosynthetic process, the guide may encourage a client to voluntarily identify him- or herself with some particular element of experience to achieve a specific purpose.

A basic principle is that we must "own" our experience: We must be aware of what is there and recognize it as part of ourselves, before we attempt to disidentify from it. Paradoxically, we are often able to be more in contact with our feelings when we are not identified with them. The ability to step back from our feelings into an observer position makes the feelings less threatening, allowing us to explore them more fully.

## Activation of the Will

The will is one of the central themes in Psychosynthesis, and it plays a pivotal role in the psychosynthetic process.

The psychosynthesis guide must patiently seek out and support the will of the "I." The guide presents the client with many choices during the session to determine what issues he or she is ready and willing to explore, and to develop in the client the sense of being able to choose one's own direction.

The process of eliciting and reinforcing the client's experience of intentionality creates vitally important side effects or "incidental learning." The fact that someone is interested in the client's choices and respects them gives the person a sense of being valued as a human being and helps to build feelings of self-worth and dignity.

A client's motivation to work at the beginning of a session often comes from a subpersonality rather than from the "I." This may take many forms. A striver subpersonality may be trying to elicit the guide's support to eliminate a "lazy" subpersonality, or a "superman" subpersonality may be seeking to eliminate the person's "weakness." A dependent client may passively wait for the guide to do something to make things better, or a controlling client will try to push the session in a preset direction,

rather than being open to his or her own process or to the guide. The most obvious motive of many clients at the beginning of their work is to get rid of some pain or symptom rather than to explore the meaning of the pain. When the motivation of the client in coming to the session is not in line with what really needs to happen (i.e., the purpose of the Self for that session), the guide must find a way to help the person sort out the various strands of conflicting motivation and find the way back to center. When the fog lifts in the process of coming to center, the person can see more clearly what is happening and is in a better position to make wise choices.

Another important aspect in working with the will is the role of "grounding," or putting into practice the insights that have been achieved. Psychosynthesis utilizes a variety of methods to facilitate the grounding process. Within the session itself, guides often use role playing to help the client practice new attitudes or behaviors. If the work is done in a group setting, group members can provide an opportunity for trying out new ways. Writing is also a useful means of anchoring insights that come in a session. Most important of all is the application in the client's daily life, which the guide will attempt to keep informed of, giving extra grounding help to those persons who have trouble applying their insights in action.

## Abreaction or Emotional Release

With many persons, since they bind so much of the person's energy, there is a need early in the therapeutic process to release strong emotions that have never been fully expressed. These emotions are usually related to painful relationships with the parent figures or to other traumatic situations in the person's life. At the stage when strong emotions of pain and anger are being expressed, the work may appear similar to Primal Therapy or other abreaction therapies. The philosophy of emotional release is different in Psychosynthesis, however, as the expression of hatred, pain, and anger is considered just a first step and not the ultimate goal. It may be a necessary step if a person's feelings in these areas are blocked, but one must move beyond the negative feelings so that the energy bound in hatred and resentment can be released for creative purposes. Real healing only occurs when forgiveness and reconciliation take place.

## Multiple Techniques

Many techniques are employed in Psychosynthesis, as no one technique fits all purposes or all persons. Some clients may work very well with certain techniques and not at all well with others. This depends both upon the psychological type and the level of development. A therapist who wishes to be fully responsive to the needs of a particular client must therefore be able to use a variety of approaches. It is important to bear in mind as well that new methods and techniques are constantly being developed in Psychosynthesis. Techniques are made to fit the person rather than the person being made to fit the techniques. Often the most effective approach is one that the guide develops on the spur of the moment to meet the needs of a particular situation.

## A Holistic Approach

Psychosynthesis can be considered a holistic approach concerned with balanced development of the various aspects of human experience: physical, emotional, mental, and spiritual (related to essence, purpose, values, will). In choosing techniques the therapist will bear in mind the development of these dimensions, stimulating those that are underdeveloped, using those that are well developed as entry points, and attempting to orchestrate them all in an integrated way.

## The Processes of Integration and Synthesis

The process of Psychosynthesis, as the name implies, is one in which the conflicting and disharmonious elements of the personality undergo a process of harmonization, integration, and synthesis. In the course of this they are brought into alignment with the person's higher Self, so that the personality becomes an instrument or channel through which the Self can manifest in the physical world.

Many polarities within the personality require integration. The exact nature of these varies from one individual to the next. Most can be related to the polarities the Chinese call *yin* and *yang*.

The entry points for therapeutic intervention can be at physical, emotional, or mental levels. In addition, the ''I'' or the Self can serve this purpose. This can be summarized in Figure 2.

Most current therapies tend to focus on the link between two of the three dimensions on the points of the triangle. Approaches like psychoanalysis, TA, and Rogerian Therapy emphasize the mental-emotional link; methods such as Gestalt, Bioenergetics, and Primal Therapy utilize primarily the link between the body and the emotions; and approaches like the martial arts, the Alexander technique, and the Feldenkrais method are based on the link between the mind and the body. Psychosynthesis recognizes all these links and uses whichever seem most appropriate to the situation. In most cases, there is an attempt to complete the circuit and to have the person work through the material at all levels, regardless of the entry point. Psychosynthesis differs from several other current therapies in that it values the

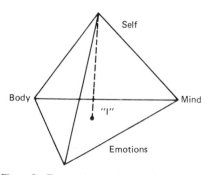

Figure 2   Entry points for therapeutic intervention.

role of mental understanding. Though a client may work through an issue primarily in a physical or emotional mode, it is important to understand the patterns and dynamics involved to be able to generalize from this experience and to ground it in daily living.

## The Technique of Guided Imagery

The technique of guided imagery consists in having the client utilize visual and auditory imagination to get in contact with an inner world of fantasy. It is assumed that the images encountered in this way are symbolic expressions of dynamic patterns within the client's personality.

The client is instructed to relax and allow the imagery to unfold on its own, just as though watching a film on the mind-screen.

The guide may suggest that the client attempt to do certain things, such as establish communication between different elements in the imagery, identify with a particular person in order to experience his or her emotions more deeply, or explore particular aspects of the imagery in more detail. This method allows one to work directly on the symbolic contents of the psyche, exploring the qualities and interrelationships of the various elements, and attempting to bring a greater degree of harmony and integration among them. The guided imagery technique is able to reveal unconscious material in the same way as night dreams do, while it offers the advantage of permitting the person's consciousness and will to interact with this material. Thus it creates a bridge between the conscious and unconscious levels of the mind.

The role of the guide in a guided imagery session is to help the traveler maintain contact with the flow of his or her inner process, keep a productive focus, deepen the emotional connections, clarify issues when necessary, and "ground" the experience or relate it to the client's everyday life.

## Evocation of Inner Wisdom

Various techniques may be used to help clients get in touch with their inner wisdom.

Usually these methods involve dialogue (imagined visually or acted out) with a figure that is designated as a source of wisdom. The figure may be imagined in human form, such as an elder or spiritual teacher, or it may be a sacred animal, an element in nature, or an abstract symbol. The guide will usually suggest that clients allow their own symbol to appear spontaneously. When outer dramatization is used, it has the advantage of "spacializing" the different positions so that the clear place of the client's wisdom figure may be more easily kept separate from the subpersonalities with their distorting lenses. This technique is based on disidentification and often yields amazing results. The wisdom figure is invited to comment on various aspects of the client's life or to respond to particular questions or fears the person may have. It is reassuring and uplifting for clients to discover that they have within themselves sources of wisdom that they can readily tap. The major counterindication to this technique is when clients with a harsh super-ego take on the role of a judge rather than that of a compassionate sage.

## Kinesthetic Imagery

A helpful technique is focusing on the kinesthetic sense of what is happening in the psyche, along with the feelings that are associated with the body-sense. Gendlin (1978), in his book, *Focusing,* speaks of contacting a "felt sense." The felt sense, which includes both a feeling and a bodily sensation, is first experienced and then translated into words or imagery. This technique is more effective than guided imagery with clients who tend to intellectualize, and it is a valuable foundation for most inner process work.

## The Spirit Behind the Methods

The essence of Psychosynthesis lies beyond a particular set of techniques. New methods are evolving with the times, and they differ from one practitioner to the other. Far more important than technical knowledge is the practitioner's own level of consciousness and his or her ability to be with a client from a place of clarity, wisdom, and unconditional love.

## APPLICATIONS

Psychosynthesis appears to be an effective approach for relating to a wide variety of human conditions. Its flexibility and lack of attachment to particular techniques or terminology allow it to respond to the needs of widely different clients and situations.

Persons trained in Psychosynthesis have applied this perspective to working with most kinds of clients in the mental health field—from ''normal neurotics'' to persons who are severely disturbed and who demonstrate antisocial behavior. The approach must, of necessity, be adapted to the individuals concerned. The most widespread field of application for Psychosynthesis to date has been in counseling persons who are relatively healthy. Such persons utilize the approach to facilitate their personal and spiritual growth and to enhance their creativity.

Psychosynthesis offers a perspective of particular value to individuals or groups who are seeking to orient their lives around a deeper sense of purpose and meaning, and who experience a need to include a spiritual dimension in their lives. It is also particularly effective in working with persons in ''existential crisis'' whose distress signals the need for reorientation to new, more inclusive values and/or new forms of life expression. Persons in transition, either in their careers or personal lives, benefit from the contact Psychosynthesis provides with deeper sources of identity and life direction. There is a special need at such times of outer flux for the experience of inner stability and contact with one's own creative process. Persons faced with the need to make life choices may be helped by the psychosynthesis approach to open up a place of inner clarity from which to discern the path of greatest life meaning and growth.

Psychosynthesis has also been applied in the field of education, particularly in teacher training and in the development of curricula, often in such neglected areas as self-understanding, imagination, creativity, intuition, and volition. Educational applications of this kind offer a significant opportunity for preventive mental health work. Other fields of application include religion, management and organizational development, interpersonal relations, and the facilitation of creative process in a variety of fields.

## CASE EXAMPLE

Jeanne, a young woman in her late twenties, was referred to me by another therapist who had become discouraged by her refusal to speak in therapy sessions over a period of several months. Heavy-set and overweight at the time, with an expressionless face, Jeanne was a secretary and was functioning well on her job while supporting herself in a bachelor of arts program in psychology, which she had almost finished. She had been married for a short time to an abusive man and was now living alone. She had been raised in an orphanage by nuns since the age of three, when her father had abandoned her mother. Jeanne's mother, later institutionalized as psychotic, was unable to take care of her and saw the girl only a few times while she was in the orphanage. Jeanne never saw or heard from her father again after he left home. She consulted a therapist because of depressive symptoms.

In our first session, Jeanne adopted the same stance as with her previous therapist. She sat in silence throughout, immobile as a statue, staring into space. At first I made some unsuccessful attempts at communication, both verbal and nonverbal, and finally realized that I needed to let go of the place within myself that wanted to ''make something happen'' in order that our communication could take place at another level. I needed to trust that, in allowing the deeper center within both of us to direct the process, what was needed would happen in its own way. And so I too sat in silence and simply chose to open myself to experience Jeanne's presence and to allow her to experience mine. As I did so, I became aware of her higher Self as a very bright light and felt that it was trying to break through in her life at this time. I was also aware of painful memories from the past that needed to come forward into consciousness to be healed. As I sat with Jeanne, I experienced her inner beauty and felt a deep love for her. At the end of our session, I told her that I sensed the presence of a very beautiful person inside her who wanted to emerge and that I believed I would be able to assist in the process. I also told her that I was powerless to do it alone and needed her cooperation for this to happen. I informed her that I did not have the skills to help her unless we could talk and that I felt it would be a waste of our time as well as of her money to continue meeting unless she were willing to speak to me. As she still did not respond verbally, I suggested that she go home and think about it, and that she call me for another appointment if she was willing to meet me halfway. My intuitive sense was that an inner contact had been established and that Jeanne's will was beginning to mobilize for the work, which was shortly confirmed.

At our next appointment, Jeanne's behavior was very much different. She was still stiff and fearful, but willing to communicate. In the interval between sessions, she had done some imagery work by herself, which had gotten her in touch with some previously repressed memories of her early childhood. The fact that she did this on her own suggested that she felt a need to demonstrate her power and autonomy in this way. Though she had consented to speak to me, she maintained her sense of personal control by unlocking the memory bank alone. Jeanne reported the work she had done on her own with a sense of pride and agreed to let me guide her imagery process where she had left off. She immediately went back to the image of herself as a small child huddled in the corner of a room while her father, who had

been drinking, was beating up her mother so viciously that he almost killed her. Jeanne recalled that this was the event that had precipitated her being sent off to spend the rest of her childhood in the orphanage.

She got in touch with the feelings of fear and anger and pain that she had had at that time. She expressed anger to both parents for abandoning her and not caring about her feelings. Having done this, she got in touch with the feelings of love she had for her father and expressed resentment toward her mother for being jealous of this love and trying to keep her away from her father. She felt her father's warmth, but sensed that he was placing impossible demands upon her to fill a vacuum in his own life. She felt the burden of having to meet the strong emotional needs of her father and expressed resentment at having been used in this way. The father figure in her imagery said that he was sorry—that he didn't realize what he was doing to her and that the reason he left home was not that he didn't love her. She started to feel more warmly toward him, but still had some residual anger, the reason for which did not emerge until our next session.

Jeanne came to our next session feeling quite agitated, with a sense that she still had to uncover something more. She was aware of anger toward her father but felt that something was stuck in her throat when she tried to express it. I asked her to let an image come that would help her get in touch with what it was that was blocking her. She then saw an erect penis and recalled having been sexually abused by her father. This released the energy and she was able to complete the expression of anger toward him.

The following session was the turning point for her in terms of the transmutation of her anger. In this session, we took as a starting point a dream she had reported in which she was in a room that had a door covered over with wallpaper. I had her imagine that she was going through this door. She followed a tunnel leading down to a room in which several old men were seated. One of these men, who appeared to be very wise, came over to her and told her that she had a firm foundation now and no longer needed to be angry. She was at first unwilling to accept this, as she still felt resentment at having been pushed around by so many people in her life. He explained to her that it was natural for her to have had these feelings when she was small and powerless, but that she was strong now and it was no longer appropriate. He told her that to continue holding on to her anger would only be a waste of energy. He then showed her some sort of plan or model that demonstrated to her that she really did have a strong foundation. As she opened herself to this realization, she felt that she could love without fear. She felt that she could trust other people now that she was able to trust herself. After that she was able to forgive her father and no longer saw him as a threat. Jeanne's process illustrates the usual progression in working with the parental "images" from expression of negative feelings through to reconciliation and forgiveness. The Self, or integrating center of the personality (symbolized by the wise old man figure in the imagery), seems to know when the stage of expressing anger is completed and can guide the person to the next stage.

After this stage in our work had been completed, Jeanne was a changed person. She was much more warm and open, and her depression lifted. She began to ask herself what she really wanted to do with her own life and developed a much stronger sense of her own worth. We were only able to have a few sessions together after this because unexpected commitments on my own part necessitated transferring Jeanne to another therapist. The work that we did during this period was focused on her own life direction and the exploration of possible alternative futures. She felt that she needed more time to find out what she really wanted to do and took some positive steps to explore various areas of interest. She also changed her job to work for an agency where the values were more in line with her own. After a period of work with another therapist, she decided that

she wanted to lose weight and within three months had lost 40 pounds. Shortly thereafter she met a very nice man with whom she fell in love, and at the time of this writing is happily married and waiting for her first child.

Jeanne's case is of particular interest because of the rapid and dramatic changes that occurred. This seems to be a result of several factors: her ripeness for this work, the good contact she was able to establish with her transpersonal Self, and the strength of will she had developed through coping with the challenges of her difficult life alone. Just as she used her powerful will in a distorted way at first to remain mute, she was able to move forward with surprising alacrity when she chose to align her will in a positive direction.

## SUMMARY

The psychosynthesis approach is founded on the basic premise that human life has purpose and meaning and that we participate in an orderly universe structured to facilitate the evolution of consciousness. A corollary is that each person's life has purpose and meaning within this broader context and that it is possible for the individual to discover this.

Psychosynthesis postulates that the sense of meaningful relationship to a greater whole is mediated through a transpersonal or spiritual center of identity, called the Self. It asserts that in learning to cooperate consciously with this deeper source of our being, we experience the fulfillment of human life. The Self is seen as having attributes of consciousness and creative, loving will, which seek expression through service in the world. Thus the Self finds consummation as we develop our gifts and discover our particular mode of contributing to the needs of the planet—our "calling," or unfolding vocation.

In line with this perspective, much of the work in Psychosynthesis is directed toward experiencing and expressing the life source from which one's most profound sense of identity is derived. Much of a client's therapeutic experience involves learning to discern when one is "coming from" the "source" experience and when one is coming from a false sense of identity with a distorted self-image, or "subpersonality." To facilitate the client's experience of this deeper center, it is important for the guide to stay inwardly connected to the client's essence and to avoid being taken in by the games or facades. A kind of "bifocal" vision is maintained in which the guide is simultaneously aware of the client's creative potentials and of the personality distortions that block their expresion. In seeing through the client's outer shell of defenses to the place of inner strength and wisdom, the guide "holds up a mirror" that reflects to the client his or her hidden resources and helps to evoke them. This understanding of the subtler dimensions of the helping relationship is an important feature of Psychosynthesis.

In addition, the many techniques developed to facilitate the source experience represent a significant contribution to the field of therapy. In the early phases of work, the therapist's focus is on helping the client to differentiate the "I" (which is considered to be a "spark" of the Self operating at the personality level) from the various pushes and pulls within the personality and from the environment that the person tends to confuse with the "I." Techniques that are useful at this stage include: inner dialogue to gain understanding of and distance from the subpersonality patterns; healing of memories that have distorted the self-image; learning to attune to one's organismic sense of what is right; and direct evocation of the source experience through suggestions involving the creative imagination and/or the will. Later, when the foundations of personal autonomy have been laid, the person begins to come into conscious relationship with the Self and issues of a different order emerge. The process of alignment with the Self generally stimulates various crises of spiritual awakening, which the therapist must be equipped to handle. The person's illusions at this stage

tend to revolve around fears of power or of the lack of power. The client is commonly afraid of such things as visibility, being alone or different, being criticized, making a wrong choice, or losing control, and may project the image of a harsh, judgmental, or controlling parent onto the Self. Work at this level may require the withdrawal of such projections when they exist. The major focus, however, is on helping the client have access to a place of inner knowing where wisdom, healing, and life direction are available. Psychosynthesis is one of relatively few therapies that offer some understanding and practical tools for intervention at this stage of development.

In the long run, it is perhaps for its innovative and profound understanding of the human will that Psychosynthesis will be best remembered in the annals of history. First, it has helped to clarify the nature of the will and to free it from various misconceptions that have given the topic a bad name in modern psychology. It asserts that true will is an expression of the "I," or the Self, and as such is a unifying and enjoyable experience. The imposters of will such as harsh discipline, self-flagellation, "should's," perfectionistic striving, and the bulldozer approach are considered by Psychosynthesis to be subpersonalities—an expression of inner division rather than of creative will.

Second, Psychosynthesis proposes a particularly useful developmental model for understanding the stages of will maturation. It suggests that the first stage in will development is learning to differentiate oneself from "mass consciousness" as a separate individual with an internal locus of valuation and responsibility for one's own life. When this stage of "individual consciousness" has been reached, the person is ready to relate to the collective or more universal dimension without getting lost in it. He or she can then learn to cooperate with others in a common purpose and to cooperate with the transpersonal Self without losing the sense of individual identity. Thus the full flowering of spiritual maturity requires the integration (not the surrender) of one's hard-won individuality within a more inclusive and transcendent pattern. The term "co-creation" is an appropriate one to describe a person's experience at this stage. At first there is a sense of creating one's destiny in partnership with a deeper life source that provides the pattern and direction. Later, as the center of identity shifts from the "I" toward the Self, the person is increasingly in touch with the creative will of the Self and experiences the personality as his or her vehicle of expression.

One feature in the psychosynthesis approach to the will that deserves special attention is its balanced appreciation of the role of both conscious and unconscious levels of motivation. Psychosynthesis acknowledges, on the one hand, the importance of taking conscious responsibility for one's life and of attempting to actualize one's highest values. It recognizes, on the other hand, that unconscious dynamics exist that a person must come to terms with. These are seen to include both unresolved material from the past and emerging patterns from the superconscious that point to the person's next step. While the value of "positive thinking" and of conscious efforts to reprogram "old tapes" is recognized, Psychosynthesis does not make a simplistic assumption that this approach alone is sufficient. Thus it avoids the imbalances common to many systems that tend at one extreme to emphasize a passive, receptive attitude toward the unconscious or, at the other extreme, to focus on conscious control while they neglect the role of the unconscious.

In summary, the uniqueness and special contribution of Psychosynthesis might be said to lie in its radically integrative view of the human being. Its unifying perspective offers a theoretical framework and a practical methodology for reconciling many traditional pairs of opposites: conscious/unconscious; individual/collective; inner/outer; awareness/action; spirit/matter. As such it provides a point of view that can assimilate new findings from diverse sources as we move toward a more inclusive understanding of human nature and destiny.

## REFERENCES

Assagioli, R. A. *Psychosynthesis: A manual of principles and techniques.* New York: Hobbs-Dorman, 1965.

Assagioli, R. A. *The act of will.* New York: Viking, 1973.

Bucke, R. M. *Cosmic consciousness, a study in the evolution of the human mind.* New York: Dutton, 1923.

Carter-Haar, B. Identity and personal freedom. *Synthesis,* 1975, **2,** 56–91.

Crampton, M. The use of mental imagery in psychosynthesis. *Journal of Humanistic Psychology,* 1969, **2,** 139–153.

Crampton, M. Psychological energy transformations: Developing positive polarization. *Jounal of Transpersonal Psychology,* 1973, **2,** 39–56.

Crampton, M. *An historical survey of mental imagery techniques in psychotherapy and description of the dialogic imagery method.* Montreal: Canadian Institute of Psychosynthesis, 1974.

Crampton, M. Answers from the unconscious. *Synthesis,* 1975, **2,** 140–152.

Gendlin, E. *Focusing.* New York: Everest House, 1978.

Haronian, F. The repression of the sublime. *Synthesis,* 1975, **1,** 125–136.

Maslow, A. H. *Religions, values, and peak experiences.* New York: Viking, 1970.

Maslow, A. H. *The farther reaches of human nature.* New York: Viking, 1972.

Miller, S. Dialogue with the higher self. *Synthesis,* 1975, **2,** 122–139.

Ouspensky, P. D. *In search of the miraculous.* New York: Harcourt, 1949.

Vargiu, J. Subpersonalities. *Synthesis,* 1975, **1,** 51–90.

# CHAPTER 53

# Radical Psychiatry

CLAUDE STEINER

*By now the reader may be fatigued by my use of the word "innovative," but I daresay that after finishing this chapter every reader will agree that the concepts of Claude Steiner are totally different from those described in any other chapter of this book. Even the title of the chapter indicates the radical approach this bold author and social critic takes.*

*Steiner's point of view is quite simple: He believes the world has gone mad, and the so-called maladjusted are the victims of a crazy society. Instead of attempting to cure the victims of society, we should change society. Don't we all know that crime is a function of social inequality? That insanity depends on social stresses? While most of us recognize the validity of these arguments, still we do little about the causes: We keep mopping up the floor because the sink is overflowing. But Steiner says we should turn off the water. In other words, he goes to the root of the problem—therefore he takes a radical approach.*

*Whether one agrees or disagrees with the views presented in this chapter, they are worthy of careful consideration. Were we to generate a factor analysis of the points of view in this book (a good idea for someone) Steiner's chapter would probably lie in a dimension of its own. Paradoxically, I would guess it would be close to O'Connell's, van Kaam's, and Lair's views, which on superficial reading may appear to be as different from Steiner's position as possible. This is a chapter that will challenge all readers.*

Radical Psychiatry holds that all functional psychiatric difficulties are forms of alienation resulting from the mystified oppression of people who are isolated from each other.

People's alienation is the result of power abuse and is therefore a political matter. Any person in the practice of psychiatry (soul healing) becomes involved in the personal politics of those he or she attempts to help, either as an ally or as an oppressor; there is no possibility of neutrality for a person with power in an oppressive situation. In order to be helpful any person who claims to practice psychiatry needs to become an ally against the oppressive influences in the lives of those he or she is attempting to help.

Radical Psychiatry is a political theory of psychiatric disturbance and a political practice of soul healing.

## HISTORY

I first heard the term "Radical Psychiatry" at the 1968 American Psychiatric Association meeting in Miami, Florida, where a group of young residents, outraged by the ways in which the psychiatric profession was aiding and abetting the Vietnam War, called for a Radical Psychiatry as an alternative to their profession.

At the time, I was a clinical psychologist attending the psychiatric convention with

Eric Berne and others to present a panel discussion about Transactional Analysis.

Prompted by a growing awareness of psychiatric power abuse and by some crystallizing, radicalizing experiences in Florida, I returned to Berkeley, California, where I was practicing Transactional Analysis, and began to teach a course called Radical Psychiatry at the Free University at Berkeley. This course resembled in format a number of other courses being taught at the Free University, all of which dealt with the patterns of power abuse in industry, the arts, commerce, the healing sciences, the law, institutions, the media, and so on. The radical psychiatry course focused on the oppressiveness of the practice of psychiatry, psychology, psychotherapy, and allied "helping" professions. Over the next year I taught several of these courses to small groups of Berkeley students and residents.

In September 1969 a coalition of women, homosexuals, mental patients, and others who felt oppressed by psychiatric practice organized to disrupt the American Psychiatric Association's conference meeting in San Francisco. I prepared the Radical Psychiatry Manifesto, which follows, to be distributed at the conference.

## MANIFESTO

1. The practice of psychiatry has been usurped by the medical establishment. Political control of its public aspects has been seized by medicine and the language of soul healing ($\psi v \chi \eta + \iota \alpha \gamma \rho \epsilon \alpha$) has been infiltrated with irrelevant medical concepts and terms.

*Psychiatry must return to its nonmedical origins since most psychiatric conditions are in no way the province of medicine. All persons competent in soul healing should be known as psychiatrists. Psychiatrists should repudiate the use of medically derived words such as "patient," "illness," "diagnosis," "treatment." Medical psychiatrists' unique contribution to psychiatry is as experts on neurology, and, with much needed additional work, on drugs.*

2. Extended individual psychotherapy is an elitist, outmoded, as well as nonproductive form of psychiatric help. It concentrates the talents of a few on a few. It silently colludes with the notion that people's difficulties have their sources within them while implying that everything is well with the world. It promotes oppression by shrouding its consequences with shame and secrecy. It further mystifies by attempting to pass as an ideal human relationship when it is, in fact, artificial in the extreme.

*People's troubles have their course not within them but in their alienated relationships, in their exploitation, in polluted environments, in war, and in the profit motive. Psychiatry must be practiced in groups. One-to-one contacts, of great value in crises, should become the exception rather than the rule. The high ideal of I-Thou loving relations should be pursued in the context of groups rather than in the stilted consulting room situation. Psychiatrists not proficient in group work are deficient in their training and should upgrade it. Psychiatrists should encourage bilateral, open discussion and discourage secrecy and shame in relation to deviant behavior and thoughts.*

3. By remaining "neutral" in an oppressive situation, psychiatry, especially in the public sector, has become an enforcer of establishment values and laws. Adjustment to prevailing conditions is the avowed goal of most psychiatric treatment. Persons who deviate from the world's madness are given fraudulent diagnostic tests, which generate diagnostic labels that lead to "treatment" that is, in fact, a series of graded repressive procedures such as "drug management," hospitalization, shock therapy, perhaps lobotomy. All these forms of "treatment" are perversions of legitimate medical methods, which have been put at the service of the establishment by the medical profession. Treatment is forced on persons who would, if let alone, not seek it.

*Psychological tests and the diagnostic labels they generate, especially schizophrenia, must be disavowed as meaningless mystifications, the real function of which is to distance psychiatrists from people and to insult people into conformity. Medicine must cease making available drugs, hospitals, and other legitimate medical procedures for the purpose of overt or subtle law enforcement and must examine how drug companies are dictating treatment procedures through their adver-*

*tising. Psychiatry must cease playing a part in the oppression of women by refusing to promote adjustment to their oppression. All psychiatric help should be by contract; that is, people should choose when, what, and with whom they want to change. Psychiatrists should become advocates of the people, should refuse to participate in the pacification of the oppressed, and should encourage people's struggles for liberation.*

**Paranoia is a state of heightened awareness. Most people are persecuted beyond their wildest delusions. Those who are at ease are insensitive.**

**PSYCHIATRIC MYSTIFICATION IS A POWERFUL INFLUENCE IN THE MAINTENANCE OF PEOPLE'S OPPRESSION.**

**Personal liberation is only possible along with radical social reforms.**

**PSYCHIATRY MUST STOP ITS MYSTIFICATION OF THE PEOPLE AND GET DOWN TO WORK!**

During 1969 I joined the Berkeley Free Clinic, an organization started by a group of Vietnam paramedics and antiwar medical professionals to start a psychological counseling section, the Rap Center (Radical Approach to Psychiatry). We offered drug, welfare, and draft counseling services, group psychotherapy, and some individual one-to-one therapy to the young people who were crowding the streets of Berkeley. Many of these "street people" were involved in the student revolt and participated in the riots against the Vietnam war and in support of People's Park that took place in Berkeley during that period.

In the course of that year a number of people joined the Rap Center, notably Hogie Wyckoff and Joy Marcus, who soon added their imprint on our work. It can be said that Radical Psychiatry today is a product of my initial impetus plus the many contributions of a large number of people who have practiced and taught Radical Psychiatry in the last decade. Rebecca Jenkins, Darca Nicholson, Beth Roy, and Robert Schwebel deserve special credit for their extensive involvement and contributions.

## CURRENT STATUS

Important in the development of Radical Psychiatry was the publication, starting in 1969, of the magazine *The Radical Therapist*, which encouraged our early writings by publishing them. Eventually the workers of *The Radical Therapist* repudiated our point of view. Therefore, we started another publication, *Issues in Radical Therapy*, to publish papers that shared with Radical Psychiatry the belief that psychotherapy is a valid political activity.

There are currently between one and two thousand people in the U.S. and Europe who call themselves radical therapists and about 20 who, by virtue of their training, can legitimately call themselves radical psychiatrists.

A radical psychiatrist is a person who has been personally, intensively trained by another radical psychiatrist and who currently belongs to a radical psychiatry collective. Intensive training is unfortunately almost completely unavailable at this time. People who live in the San Francisco Bay Area, who are able to support themselves while being trained, and who feel that they have a lifetime commitment to the Radical Psychiatry point of view are good candidates for training. In addition such a person would have to impress a trained radical psychiatrist with his or her interest and talent, since radical psychiatrists tend to feel that training someone requires a loving, committed, serious, emotional five-year relationship, akin in intensity to an intimate friendship. Any talented person regardless of background is qualified to be trained, and at this time (1980) we are especially interested in training people of color, people from the working class, older people, and gay people. There is a yearly Radical Psychiatry Institute weekend and periodic six-week training courses in the San Francisco Bay Area aimed at providing people with a working knowledge of our theory. In addition, Radical Psychiatry is strongly represented at the yearly Midwest Radical Therapy Conference on Memorial weekend.

# THEORY

At the core of Radical Psychiatry is a theory of alienation drawn from the writings of Karl Marx, Wilhelm Reich, Herbert Marcuse, Franz Fanon, and R. D. Laing.

## The Theory of Alienation

People are, by their nature, capable of living in harmony with themselves, each other, and their environment. To the extent that they succeed in this ideal, they feel, and are, powerful; to the extent that they fail, they are alienated. People's potentials are realized according to the conditions that they are born into and continue to find during their lives.

Clearly, different people have different innate strengths and weaknesses; however, these do not, by and large, account for the differences in well-being we find among people. Rather, the material conditions of their lives explain these differences.

Conditions of oppression directly affect people's power, and since conditions vary immensely for different people across the world, it follows that the development of people's potential will vary greatly as well. To the extent that a person's potential for a harmonious life is not realized, his or her state of being can be considered to be alienation, or powerlessness; to the extent that it is realized, the state is one of power in the world.

Karl Marx used the term "alienation" when he spoke of people being separated from their human nature, especially when they became estranged from a major aspect of their lives: their work and the products of their work.

The term "alienation" is used in a similar manner in Radical Psychiatry. We have observed that alienation tends to affect certain specific sources of individual power: our hearts, our minds, our hands, and our bodies. It also affects collective power, that is, people's capacity to live, love, and work together.

*Alienation From Our Hearts, or From Love.* We become alienated from our hearts, or from our capacity to relate to each other in a satisfying way. Our natural tendencies to love, appreciate, cooperate, and help each other are thwarted from early on. We are taught the rules of the Stroke Economy, which effectively reduce the amount of strokes or positive human interaction that occurs among people.

The Stroke Economy is a set of rules supported by strong social sanctions that seek to reduce the exchange of "strokes" between young and old, married and unmarried, men and men, women and women, and so on. In addition, it enjoins people not to give strokes that they want to give, not to ask for or accept strokes they want, not to reject unwanted strokes, and not to give themselves strokes.

As a consequence, we feel unloved and unlovable, incapable of loving, sad, isolated, and depressed. We don't love humankind and fail to act in each other's behalf. We learn that we cannot allow someone else to become close or to trust others with our hearts, and we fail to learn how to deal with the normal ups and downs of our relationships.

*Alienation From Our Minds, or From the Capacity to Think.* We all have the capacity to understand the facts and workings of our world, to predict the outcome of events, and to solve problems. This capacity has been developed to a large degree by some people but has become unavailable to others who, in their alienation from their minds, are incapable of thinking in an orderly way. Because of the way people are treated from early childhood on, some grow up unable to use their minds effectively. They cannot keep thoughts fixed in their consciousness long enough to combine them with other thoughts so as to derive logical conclusions. At the same time, they cannot exclude from their minds chaotic ideas and thought patterns. Complete confusion and the utter terror of mental breakdown are the extreme form of this kind of alienation, which tends to be diagnosed by the psychiatric establishment as "schizophrenia." Those who suffer from mind alienation are singled out for the harshest and most unjust treatment. Tranquilizing medication, shock therapy, imprisonment, padded cells, straitjackets, hot and cold water treatments, forced feeding, experimentation with dangerous drugs, and brain surgery have all been applied over the last century on people who have shown extreme forms of alienation from their minds. These methods, whose principal effect is to terrorize people into submission so that they will temporarily conform to the expectations of their helpers, have proven, one by one, to be totally ineffectual in anything but sweeping the problem under the rug.

Alienation from our minds is a result of systematic, lifelong lies and discounts. A discount occurs when another person denies the content of our experiences. If in addition to being told that our experiences aren't valid we are also fed false information in the form of lies, the combined effect is an interference with our thinking functions, which eventually can lead to total mental breakdown. One particular well-known form of alienation is called by establishment psychiatry "paranoid schizophrenia"; here the natural intuitive perception of the facts of our persecution, which some become keenly aware of, are systematically discounted by others who also often lie to explain away their oppressive behavior. People's budding perceptions of oppression, persecution, and abuse are most often effectively squelched and ignored; but for others, they evolve into large-scale obsessions that develop into systems that, when elaborated, become fantastic and unreal, at which point they are called "paranoid delusions." Radical Psychiatry holds that "paranoid delusions," no matter how fantastic, are always based on a kernel of truth, and that is why we say that "paranoia is a state of heightened awareness." Consequently, we encourage the expression of people's paranoid fantasies and seek their validation by willingly searching for the grain of truth in them.

*Alienation From Our Bodies, or From Our Feelings.* Our intimate relationship with ourselves, that is, with all parts of our bodies, is interfered with by a number of alienating influences. We are told that our minds or spirit are separate from our body or flesh and that our body is, in some manner, the lesser of the two. We are told that those who use their minds are the ones who deserve power. We are encouraged to ignore our body's perceptions of dis-ease resulting from abuse, especially at the workplace, and to deal with them through powerful drugs that temporarily eradicate the symptoms of dysfunction. We are told that bodily pleasures are a dangerous evil. We learn to deny our bodily experiences that include our emotions, whether they be positive or negative. We eat adulterated food without nutritional value and are told to ignore its side effects. Eventually this systematic attack creates an alienation that puts our body's function and its experiences beyond our conscious control. Our bodies, which are the vessel, the matrix of our aliveness, become complete strangers to us and seem to turn on us through illness, addictions to harmful amounts and kinds of foods and drugs, and to unexplained and seemingly perverted needs over which we have no control. We feel that we are dead, or that everyone around us is dead, or that we deserve to die. We commit slow or sudden suicide.

*Alienation From Our Hands, or From Our Work.* People have a natural desire for and capacity to enjoy productive labor. The pleasures of productive activity are taken from us in two major ways. We are separated from the products of our labor when we are forced to work at a small, seemingly meaningless portion of the product that we are creating. In addition, we are separated from the value of the product that we are helping to create by those who employ us and who eventually profit disproportionately from their own participation in the product's creation. Being separated from our products and from their value causes us to hate our work and to despise what we have produced. Our labor, or the creative and productive capacity of our hands, is lost to us, and we come to feel that we are unproductive, bored, without goals in life, lazy, and worthless failures.

The major source of labor alienation in our world is corporate monopoly capitalism, which treats workers as replaceable cogs in a profit-making machine. Within this system, labor is divided to the point that the worker doesn't have any involvement in the final product and may not even know what it looks like. Furthermore, the value of what he or she produces is taken largely by the employer. And to add insult to injury, some of those profits are used to further separate the worker from products and the means to produce them. This is done through strike breaking, automation, and the creation of multinational corporations that import and exploit third world labor and set worker against worker.

The result is a population-wide hatred of work, lack of productivity, job-related illness and accidents, and a loss of awareness of the joys of work that are people's birthright. Consequently, people resign themselves to being unhappy at work and seek pleasure through recreation, which has in itself been taken over by an exploitative industry, bent on further separating the worker from his or her money.

These four forms of alienation account for all of the expressions of human unhappiness described in the psychiatric texts as "functional" psychopathology. Neurosis, psychosis, addiction, depression, character disorder—in general, all "mental illness"—are forms of alienation. Alienation, as described in the above examples, is always the result of some form of oppression, combined with a set of lies and mystifications that supposedly legitimize that abuse. Oppression and mystification combine with physical and personal isolation of people from each other to create alienation:

$$\text{ALIENATION} = \text{OPPRESSION} + \text{MYSTIFICATION} + \text{ISOLATION}$$

## Oppression

The oppression that is a prime cause of alienation comes in the form of various systems that attack specific subgroups of people: the poor, workers, people of color, women, old people, children, gay people, fat people, short people, and so on. As a rule, oppression, and therefore alienation, is greatest for people who are most dispossessed.

Workers, more often than not, are oppressed by their employers. People of color are oppressed by white people. Women are taken advantage of by men. The rights of young and older people are usurped by and taken away by the middle-aged. We live in a society in which competition and the use of power is taught and valued as an ideal. Most people automatically will take advantage of their positions of power, whether it be based on their wealth, their ownership of land or a business, or whether their power is based on their race, their gender, their age. People almost unwittingly infringe on the rights of those who are less powerful, with full sanction of those around them.

Oppression is accomplished through a wide variety of manipulative power plays that are taught to people, ranging from the very crude, physical ones to the very subtle, psychological ones. Power plays are designed to cause people to do what they would not do of their free will. Power plays can be detected, analyzed, and classified. The study of power and power plays is an essential aspect of understanding oppression and alienation.

## Mystification

The perpetration of abuse and oppression upon others is usually accompanied by some kind of explanation, which supposedly justifies it. Corporations explain their abuse of workers by pointing out that the corporation (or its owners) did, after all, invent the process or own the machinery or pay the overhead that is essential for the manufacture of their product. Rich people take advantage of poor people while asserting that everyone has equal opportunities in this land of plenty, so that those who don't succeed are responsible for their failures. Landowners mystify peasants by claiming divine or private property rights to the land. White people claim that people of color are less intelligent, less creative, less productive, lazy, and slow, and thereby try to explain their own unequal access to privilege. Men justify their privilege over women with sexist arguments. Children are told that they are not complete human beings, and that they must obey grownups who know best. Old people are mystified with notions of aging and loss of vitality and productivity. Gay people are told they are depraved and sick. Single people are made to feel that their singlehood is neurotic. Each system of oppression has a set of mystifications that justify the power abuse perpetrated on its victims.

Eventually the oppressed actually come to believe the lies used to justify their oppression. When a person has incorporated in his or her own consciousness the arguments that explain and make legitimate his or her oppression, then mystification and alienation are complete. People will no longer rebel against oppression, but instead will blame themselves for it, accept it, and assume that they are the source and reason for their own unhappiness. In addition, they will apply their internalized oppression to everyone around them and enforce other's oppression along with their own.

This is where establishment psychiatry traditionally comes into the picture: to reinforce the mystification that is the source of alienation. Any person who holds him- or herself out as a soul healer and is offered the power of giving counsel to an alienated person has one of two choices: (1) demystifying the real causes of alienation: sexism, racism, class prejudice, and all the other oppressive systems and institutions; or (2) reinforcing mystification of oppression and alienation by ignoring these oppressive influences and looking for the reasons of the alienation *within* the person, whether it be through Psychoanalysis, Transactional Analysis, Gestalt Therapy, Primal Therapy, or any other conventional system of psychotherapy.

The portion of our mind that accepts the mystifications of our oppression is called, in Radical Psychiatry, the "Pig" or the "Enemy." The Enemy is like a prison warden who stands guard over our actions and feeds us messages to bolster and reinforce our alienation. The Enemy tells us that we are not okay: that we are bad, stupid, ugly, crazy, and sick and that we deserve, and are the cause of, our own unhappiness. The Enemy is an internal obstacle toward the achievement of people's power and the recapturing of our capacities to work, love, think, and be at home in our bodies. It is the internalization of oppression and its mystifications.

## Isolation

Being separated from, and unable to communicate with, each other is essential to alienation. By ourselves, without the aid of others who are in similar circumstances, we are powerless to think through our problems or do anything about them. It is part of the American Dream that people should achieve and do what they must do as individuals in isolation. Only those achievements that we can claim entirely for ourselves are thought of as being worthy. As a consequence, we erect barriers of competition, secrecy, and shame between each other. When we are together we do not trust each other, we do not share our thoughts and feelings with each other, and we go at the tasks of our lives as separate individuals, each one with separate projects, living quarters, transportation, and nuclear families. The cult of individualism is an important source of our isolation and alienation.

## METHODOLOGY

The opposite of alienation is being powerful in the world. The task we as radical therapists set for ourselves is to aid people in reclaiming their alienated human powers. This is accomplished by fighting each element of alienation in turn. It is because of this that we say that *power* in the *world* equals *contact* to deal with *isolation, awareness* to deal with *mystification,* and *action* to deal with *oppression:*

POWER = CONTACT + AWARENESS + ACTION

### Contact

To combat isolation it is necessary for people to join hands and gain the power of working together and supporting each other in their common goals through cooperation. The concept of cooperation is central to the methodology of Radical Psychiatry. We seek to establish cooperative relationships by establishing a cooperative contract with everyone we live or work with. The cooperative contract specifically defines a relationship in which everyone has equal rights and which is free of (1) power plays, (2) lies and secrets, and (3) Rescues.

By no lies or secrets we mean not only that we do not lie to each other by omission or by commission, but also that we do not keep hidden any of what we feel or fail to ask for all of what we want. We share our feelings and paranoid fantasies.

By not Rescuing each other we mean that we do not give or do more than what is fair and that we do not do anything we don't want to do. The concept of Rescue refers to one of three alienated game roles that people tend to alternate between. The three roles are Rescuer, Persecutor, and Victim, and by remaining in one of these three constricting roles people never deal with each other as equals in a spontaneous, intimate, or aware manner.

By not using power plays we mean that we do not coerce others into doing what they would not otherwise do.

In this manner we ask for what we need without being Victims, we help others without being Rescuers, and we express our feelings of anger without being Persecutors.

Only when we work cooperatively in an organized, coherent effort is it possible for us to make true progress in the fight against alienation. No one person can accomplish power in the world as long as he or she stands by him- or herself, whether alone or in a crowd. That is why Radical Psychiatry focuses so intensely on group process.

The practice of radical psychiatry occurs primarily in three types of groups: problem-solving groups, bodywork groups and mediations.

A problem-solving group is a group of seven or eight people, all of whom have an individual problem-solving contract and all of whom share a "cooperative contract" as defined above. The group works with a trained radical psychiatrist as a facilitator; additionally, there may be one or two observers in training. The group meets weekly for two hours, and whenever a vacancy occurs it is filled with a new person.

A bodywork group is a group of five or more people, led by a radical psychiatrist trained in bodywork, who come together once or regularly on a weekly, every other week, or monthly basis for two or more hours with one assistant for every two or three people. Bodywork is designed to break down the person's alienation from the body and its feelings. This is accomplished through relaxation exercises, deep breathing, and other techniques designed to bring about emotional release and centering.

A mediation is a meeting of two or more people who have experienced conflict with each other in their working or personal relationships, and who come together with a trained radical psychiatry mediator to explore their difficulties and make agreements aimed at resolving their conflicts.

## Awareness

The expansion of consciousness, especially one's understanding of the manner in which oppressive influences operate to diminish our power, is the essence of Awareness. Consciousness raising is the accumulation of information about the world and how it functions, and it is an important continuing task in expanding one's power in the world. Awareness of the function of class oppression, racism, sexism, ageism, heterosexism, coupleism, and so on is an essential aspect of consciousness raising.

Constructive criticism is a vital consciousness-raising technique. In the constructive criticism process, people will offer information to those who want to hear it concerning their behavior and how it affects others. In addition, a person may offer suggestions of how another person's behavior may be changed and corrected for the benefit of all. Constructive criticism is greatly aided by self-criticism and assumes willingness in all who participate to accept and learn from other people's critical analyses.

## Action

Action is the process whereby our awareness of things that need to be changed is put into effect. Contact alone, or Contact and Awareness, can lead to strong, increased, subjective feelings of power. However, objective power in the world is different from subjective feelings of power and cannot result from Awareness or Contact alone. Awareness and Contact must be translated into some form of Action that changes the actual conditions in a person's life. Action implies risk, and when a person takes risks, he or she may need protection from the fears and actual dangers that can result from that action. Potent protection in the form of actual alliances for physical or moral support are needed in effective Action and are an essential aspect of Contact. Action, Awareness, and Contact together are the elements that make it pos-

sible for people to reclaim their birthright and become powerful in the world.

## APPLICATIONS

Radical psychiatry problem groups have been attended by about a thousand people, between the ages of 16 and 70, almost exclusively white and of all social strata except the rich or very rich. It has been especially effective with problems of depression and the difficulties that people have in their relationships. People who have problems with alcoholism and drug abuse and those who have been psychotic have benefited from the method as well. On the other hand, Radical Psychiatry seems to have no particular effectiveness with problems of smoking and overeating. In the 10 years that Radical Psychiatry has been practiced, there have not been any cases of suicide or of a serious malpractice allegation or suit. On the other hand, the majority of the people who have worked in problem-solving groups and participated in mediations and bodywork seem to be pleased with the effects and recommend it highly to others. Because practitioners of Radical Psychiatry are politically aware and socially conscious people, the fees charged for problem-solving groups are modest and affordable by most. The majority of the people seeking help from Radical Psychiatry are referred by satisfied users of our services. We rarely have referrals from mental health professionals.

## CASE HISTORY

Initially, John and Mary contacted me to do a mediation for their deteriorating marriage of seven years. I made sure that each one of them was interested in the mediation, by speaking to each of them separately. In this conversation I checked the reasons for their interest and asked them to think about any held resentments and paranoid fantasies that each one had for the other as well as any Rescues that they may have been engaged in. We met, and in the process of trading held resentments, paranoid fantasies, and Rescues it became clear that Mary resented how John reacted to her feelings of anger and hurt and that she had been having sex with him when she really didn't want to. She had a suspicion (or paranoia) that he was unfaithful to her; he confirmed that her suspicion had a grain of truth by acknowledging that he had seriously considered having an affair with a neighbor. On the other hand, John was hurt and angry about Mary's lack of desire for sex and felt victimized by her emotional outbursts. We then agreed on a contract for the mediation: namely, we would make some agreements that would reestablish communcation between them.

My initial observations of the couple were as follows: John and Mary have two children, 8 and 10. John, a probation officer, smokes, drinks, and eats too much, seems unhappy at home, does not show Mary any affection, and is continually harassing her for sex. Mary works part time as a clerk, is depressed, cries a lot, feels guilty about yelling at her children and being "frigid," has trouble sleeping, and often thinks of suicide. She made one suicide attempt with sleeping pills but immediately called Suicide Prevention afterward. John and Mary spend most of their time in a polite superficial harmony punctuated by violent arguments, which often end up with Mary crying hysterically and John leaving the house and coming back drunk. Both of them are concerned and would like to change the situation. They feel that they still love each other, and both of them have tried various methods of psychotherapy including some marriage counseling.

During the initial part of the mediation I observed that John repeatedly interrupted Mary and discounted her feelings and that Mary had outbursts of anger and crying that caused John to become afraid, cold, and parental. Only through strict control of their transactions was I able to prevent their discussion from continually escalating into outbursts, accusations, and subtle insults on both parts.

I explained that I thought the problem between them was that they were deeply immersed in a repetitive of interaction pattern in which John discounts Mary's feelings, tries to dominate her behavior, and is unwilling to react to her feelings with sympathy, and in which Mary terrorizes and tyrannizes John with outbursts of emotion, which she sees as the only way she can get the faintest resemblance of what she wants from John. I explained my belief that this behavior on both of their parts is founded on stereotyped sexist roles that cause John to avoid feeling and to abuse power to get what he wants from Mary, especially sex, while Mary finds herself unable to verbalize what she wants, ask for it, and take steps to get it. Instead, Mary lashes out at John with her emotions. I explained that her depression and wishes to commit suicide were probably the result of stroke deficit and that John's abuse of alcohol, cigarettes, and food were all attempts to improve his bodily experience, which was one of emptiness, loss, and fear. I explained how their relationship is a faithful reproduction of society's role expectations of people and how John's lack of feelings, sexual obsession, and substance abuse and Mary's lack of control over her feelings and her depression were all the result of the oppression of men and women. I recommended that Mary join a women's group and that John enter a mixed group with me. Over the next year and a half John and Mary participated in problem-solving groups, and their situation was discussed at the radical psychiatry collective in which I and Mary's group leader participate. Mary learned how to get John to account for her feelings and how to speak clearly, how to ask for what she wanted, and how to implement her desires. She learned how to deal with John's interruptions, and she stopped adapting sexually. Her participation in the women's group gave her a sense of support and confidence that she was able to bring to the relationship and that gave her a sense of power so that she no longer allowed John to push her around. Soon she was no longer depressed or suicidal. John slowly came to the realization that he was not able to adequately express his feelings other than anger for Mary's emotional outbursts and sexual denial. In bodywork he was able to contact some of his other emotions and to allow himself emotional release of sadness, fear, and joy. He developed a good level of emotional literacy, which made it possible for him to understand and respond to Mary's feelings as well as express his own in the relationship. He learned to stop interrupting and discounting, and he learned to stop imposing himself sexually on Mary. Instead he learned to accept her affection and return it and to wait patiently for her desire for sexual intercourse to develop, and to find satisfying alternatives to intercourse in the meanwhile. He made and kept a contract to stop drinking altogether, eventually stopped smoking, and is currently working on life changes including more physical exercise, a change of job, and a change of diet. Separately John and Mary have changed dramatically from how they were when they entered therapy. Their relationship has improved, but it is not clear at the moment whether they will or will not stay married. They have spoken seriously about a separation and a possible divorce in the future but are presently reasonably happy with each other. They have opened up the marriage to allow John to express his desires for strokes from other women, but this is only in an experimental stage. Mary is fundamentally disinterested in a sexually open marriage at the time. At present they are both considering stopping therapy, as they both feel they have accomplished quite a bit for themselves even though the status of their relationship is still not clear. Both of them seem happier, more hopeful, healthier, and more alive. They speak very highly of the process of problem-solving groups and have incorporated into their daily lives the principals and guidelines of cooperation, which they use in their relationship with each other, their children, and their friends. They no longer fight, and their relationship is cordial. Though they do not necessarily feel that they are going to remain an intimate couple for the rest of their lives, they love each other and know that they will remain friends and helpmates in raising their children.

## SUMMARY

Radical Psychiatry is a theory of human emotional disturbance and a method designed to deal with it that is being practiced by a small group of trained radical psychiatrists, all of whom belong to collectives in which their work is scrutinized, encouraged, and criticized. The theory of Radical Psychiatry holds that people's problems are the result of oppressive influences and institutions that are mystified and with which the person colludes, thereby creating a state of alienation and powerlessness. The notion that emotional disturbance is externally caused is not new in psychiatry, but it is certainly not a popular one at this time and is not generally accepted by the psychiatric establishment. Yet Radical Psychiatry is gaining many adherents across the country and abroad as a theory and practice of psychiatry. Radical Psychiatry is not only a system of psychotherapy; it is also a world view applicable to institutions and communities, and it represents and proposes a cooperative style of life that is in sharp contrast with the style of the dominant culture. We feel it is conducive to well-being and power in the world.

## REFERENCES

Berne, E. *Beyond games and scripts*. New York: Grove Press, 1976.

Berne, E. *Transactional analysis in psychotherapy*. New York: Grove Press, 1961.

Fanon, F. *The wretched of the earth*. New York: Grove Press, 1968.

Karpman, S. Script drama analysis. *Transactional Analysis Bulletin*, 1968, **7**, 26–29.

Laing, R. D. *The politics of experience*. New York: Ballantine, 1967.

Laing, R. D. *The politics of the family and other essays*. New York: Pantheon, 1969.

Marcuse, H. *Eros and civilization*. New York: Vintage Books, 1962.

Marx, K. *Karl Marx, early writings*. New York: Ballantine, 1969.

Reich, W. *The function of the orgasm*. New York: Farrar, Strauss, 1961.

Steiner, C. *Readings in radical psychiatry*. New York: Grove Press, 1975.

Steiner, C. *Scripts people live*. New York: Grove Press, 1974.

Szasz, T. *Law, liberty and psychiatry*. New York: Collier, 1968.

Wolff, R. P. Barrington, M. and Marcuse, H. *A critique of pure tolerance*. Boston: Beacon Press, 1969.

Wyckoff, H. *Love, therapy and politics*. New York: Grove Press, 1974.

Wyckoff, H. *Solving problems together*. New York: Grove Press, 1981.

## CHAPTER 54

# *Radix Neo-Reichian Education*

ELAINE WARBURTON, Training Director, Radix Institute

*Perhaps, overall, the most important general innovation in psychotherapy of recent years has been an increasing emphasis on what may be called Body Therapy. This is discussed in several chapters in this book, especially in the chapter by Baker and Nelson entitled "Orgone Therapy" and the chapter by Green entitled "Body Therapies."*

*In this chapter, Elaine Warburton presents a clear explanation of an offshoot of Wilhelm Reich's thinking and procedures. Radix Neo-Reichian Education is similar to (and yet different from) other procedures that issued from Reich's work, such as Bioenergetics. The relatively well-established theory and procedure focuses on nonverbal processes leading to instances of intense emotionality, such as are featured in Primal Therapy, Primary Relationships Therapy, and Aqua-Energetics, among other systems covered in this book.*

*Essentially, Radix Education reestablishes balance of thoughts and feelings. It is a total therapy operating mainly through affect and behavior but affecting cognitive functions as well.*

Radix Education is a process developed by Charles Kelley from the work of Wilhelm Reich. It is an educational, personal growth process, both individually and group oriented, that endeavors to free the capacity for feeling and aliveness through gradual loosening of what Reich (1961) called "muscular armor," chronic muscular contractions that inhibit the free flow of radix (life force) through the body, hindering the full expression and awareness of feeling and limiting the availability of energy needed to live fully. Radix Education has a direct, nonverbal approach to deep emotional release and includes techniques for integrating freed capacity for feeling and energy. Radix Education strives not to restore the feeling capacity of the child, who is a victim of his or her feelings, but to develop a new capacity for choice in terms of when to express feeling and where to direct energy. Armor is seen as the mechanism of volition, and, as such,

valuable and not to be destroyed. The student is not taught what to feel but how to release feelings that are already there. Those coming into Radix work are not considered sick and so are not led to expect a "cure." It is recognized that all people are blocked to some degree in their capacity to feel and to experience aliveness, and each has to decide whether he or she wishes to learn to change life patterns. Education is understood as an ongoing, lifelong process; so there is no point at which one "has it" or is "there." The work is strongly body-oriented. As the student reclaims his or her body, self-concept (through improved body image) and the ability to get needs fulfilled (due to increased awareness of what those needs are and available energy to get them met) are improved. There is continuing respect for the individual's process; students are not advised, evaluated, or judged, so each must assume responsibility for how much of the work he or she wishes to do and how to utilize the changes.

## HISTORY

Radix Education has its roots in the works of Wilhelm Reich and the ophthalmologist William H. Bates. It was developed by Charles R. Kelley, who was for 13 years Chief Scientist and Laboratory Director for Dunlap and Associates, Inc., one of the country's major human factors consulting firms. Kelley was for four years Assistant Professor and Director of the Division of Applied Vision Research, Department of Psychology, North Carolina State College, and has been an adjunct associate professor at New York University and a NATO lecturer before major scientific institutions in Europe. In 1970 he served as the George A. Miller Visiting Professor at the University of Illinois.

Kelley was taught the Bates method of vision improvement by Margaret Corbett and practiced as a Bates teacher for two years. Intrigued by the emotional component of vision problems, as discovered by Bates (e.g., that people tend to become myopic when apprehensive), he found in Reich's work the answer to the question "why were some people able to improve their vision while others were not?" He became a student of Reich's and during Reich's life contributed to his journals; since Reich's death he has participated in the development of Reich's theories.

Kelley's work with Reich in the 1950s was mainly of a scientific and research nature. He was especially interested in Reich's theories of orgone energy and their applications in physics as well as psychology. He underwent Orgone Therapy and became interested in the effects of muscular armor.

In 1960 the Interscience Research Institute (since renamed the Radix Institute) was founded by Kelley to carry forward Reich's work, particularly in the effort to discover the origin of muscular armor and properties of orgone energy. From 1961 to 1965 the institute published *The Creative Process*, at that time America's only scientific periodical dealing with Reich's work. Kelley's goal at the time was to understand Reich's work in the context of earlier research concerning "life energy," such as the work of Anton Mesmer and Karl von Reichenbach. He also hoped to further the correlation of physiological changes with emotion, as had Reich.

In 1968 and 1969 Kelley's interest turned to applications of the work of Bates and Reich, and he started his first educational groups working with vision and feeling (Kelley, 1976). The objective of these groups of nearsighted people was vision improvement. The procedures included a synthesis of Reichian work plus techniques of vision improvement drawn mostly from the work of Bates. Kelley discovered that the vision work contributed greatly to freeing the feelings. All the students in these first groups changed both emotionally and in their vision. In assessing the significance of the work, however, the students agreed that the emotional changes they went through were more significant to them than was the improved vision. In 1970 the institute offered classes, workshops, and individual instruction in vision improvement and neo-Reichian emotional release work. Afterward Kelley became more interested in specific programs in education in feeling for the general populace, and also in training others to become competent practitioners in emotional release and vision improvement techniques. In 1974 the name of the organization was changed to the Radix Institute. Vision improvement continues to be one objective of Radix work, though not its primary objective. "Radix" is a rare word that means *root, source, primary cause*. Kelley sees the radix as a force somewhat different from Reich's concept of orgone energy. He does not see it as an energy but as the substratum from which energy, feeling, thought, movement, and so forth, all arise.

The Radix Institute continues today offering programs in education in feeling, self-direction, and vision improvement, with an extensive program for training Radix teachers throughout the world.

## CURRENT STATUS

The Radix Institute is centered in Ojai, California. In addition to the training program, Radix Education is available in both traditional and innovative formats.

1.  *The Concentrated Program for Individuals* offers up to three weeks of concentrated experiential work in any Radix Education Program. This is an intense individualized program composed of 10 sessions per week, mostly individual, some in a small group.
2.  *Segment One* combines didactic and experiential workshops. These are nonresidential week-long programs that include theory sessions in the morning and experiential sessions in the afternoon.
3.  *Santa Barbara Workshops*, week-long experiential combinations of group and individual work, are offered by the institute each June and July.
4.  *Individual Sessions* can be arranged on a regular basis.
5.  *Five-Day Workshops for Small Groups* are periodically available in various locations, throughout the United States and in Europe.

Qualified Radix work is done by Radix teachers and teacher trainees affiliated with the Radix Institute whose practice is governed by the provisions of the Radix Teacher's Code. All have been or are currently being trained by the Radix Institute and its training staff. Certified teachers have received three years of experiential work and two years of training, including seminars, practice teaching, and training workshops. The Radix Institute regulates all training and certification

in Radix Education. There are four levels of Radix teacher trainees, defined by length of training, amount of personal Radix work, and competency in their teaching.

Radix teachers and trainees are located throughout the United States, and in Canada, Mexico, Europe, and India. Soon Radix Education will be available in Australia.

In addition to its education in feeling programs and its teacher training programs, the Radix Institute offers a didactic program covering radix concepts and theories. This program is called Radix Segment One and is designed primarily for professionals who already have a practice involving personal growth and who wish to enhance their knowledge in the neo-Reichian area without committing themselves to the one- or two-year training programs.

Currently publications on Radix Education by Charles Kelley are available through the institute. They include:

1.  *The Radix Journal:* Published quarterly. In-depth articles by Kelley on Radix Scientific Processes and Radix Education.
2.  *Orgonomy, Bioenergetics, and Radix: The Reichian Movement Today* (1978): Compares the Reichian programs of Elsworth Baker (Medical Orgonomy), Alexander Lowen (Bioenergetics), and Charles Kelley (Radix), and describes eight major first- and second-generation Reichians not associated with these three programs.
3.  *Education in Feeling and Purpose* (1974): Deals with: (a) the origin of muscular armoring; (b) education in feeling: the Radix intensive; concepts; issues; (c) the learning of self-direction (purpose): an evening of education in self-direction; the responsibilities of purpose; and (d) reconciling feeling and purpose.
4.  *The Creative Process* (Charles Kelley, Editor, *Bulletin of the Interscience Research Institute* (1961–1965). Complete

set of five volumes, spiral bound, reprinted with a new introduction (1974). Devoted to the discovery and communication of knowledge about the creative process in nature as that process was described by Wilhelm Reich. Contains over 60 articles and reviews. Reich's physical orgone research; apparatus; weather control; Karl von Reichenbach; orgonomy and art; armoring; orgonomy since the death of Reich; and so forth.

5. "Post Primal and Genital Character: A Critique of Janov and Reich," *Journal of Humanistic Psychology,* 1972, **12, (2).** Includes a discussion of the medical versus the educational model of growth processes. Criticizes Reich's "genital character" and Janov's "post-primal" concepts.

6. "What Is Orgone Energy?" from *The Creative Process,* 2(2,3), (1962).

7. *Mysticism and Mechanism* (1975): Discusses "the two intellectual forces that have dominated human thought since the decline of primitive animism" and the character structures of the mystic and the mechanist.

Information on Radix training, individualized programs, group workshops, and publications can be obtained by contacting the Radix Institute, P.O. Box 97, Ojai, CA 93023.

## THEORY

The theory of Radix Education is rooted in two major discoveries of Wilhelm Reich. The first is muscular armor, the chronic patterns of tension in the body that correlate with blocked emotion. The second is the life force, existing tangibly in the body, the bridge between the armor and the emotion that is blocked. The muscular armor is objective, socially observable, physical, "body"; the emotion is subjective, not so-cially observable, "mind." The flow of the life force in the body is experienced as feeling, as emotion, and expressed in the body's spontaneous movements. The muscular armor dams the flow of the life force and, because of this, blocks the emotion. Reich never discovered the origin of the muscular armor; to him it was an inexplicable anomaly of the animal man, about which he puzzled unsuccessfully for much of the latter portion of his life. At the Radix Institute, we believe that armor is readily understandable in how it develops and in its twofold purpose and function.

As children we are victims of our feelings and impulses. The child in pain must cry; the child with anger must express it; the child with a need must have it fulfilled. As we grow up, dependent on our home environment and caretakers (usually parents), we learn which emotions are acceptable, which emotions are expected to be suppressed, which needs will be fulfilled. We learn by observing which emotions are responded to positively and which negatively. If a child receives negative responses to his tears a number of times, he learns that crying is not acceptable. How does he learn to stop crying? He must stop the flow of the life force from his gut to his eyes, and so block the feeling. This is done by slowing the breathing, constricting the throat, "swallowing" the tears, and tensing the eyes. As this process repeats over time these tensions and patterns will recede into the child's unconscious and become chronic patterns of tension (armor), and he will no longer be able to cry when he feels he wants to or needs to. This is one expression of the armor.

The other is the armor functioning as a mechanism of volition in human goal-seeking activity. We must as a matter of survival: plan, make goals, conceptualize the future, and, at times, be able to curb our impulses and our emotions. We must learn to by-pass an immediate "reward" for a later one of value (that we have chosen). If we have a goal, we plan, study, and practice at times instead of going to a movie, party, or to sleep. Purposive activity and volition are important; so, then, is armor—but not in the way that humans have become armored en masse. Armor as a mass development is not the result of purpose per se, but of purpose in an early and partial form. The compulsive struggling for goals that are not really the individual's own, that have instead been impressed on him or her by others, without being clearly understood, is the most deadening armor-producing form of goal seeking. People go through their lives without really understanding why they do what they do. Their purpose doesn't develop out of connection with their own wants and needs. So a major goal of Radix Education is to develop a capacity within the person to express emotion when he feels he wants/needs to and evaluates the situation to be appropriate; to develop the capacity to choose, to no longer be a victim of his feelings *or* his armor. Then the person is able to channel his wants and needs by his own will, able to delay fulfillment when necessary, and also able to enjoy it when that is right.

Radix theory of character centers around chronic patterns of blocks to emotions. Eight basic feelings are blocked in antithetical pairs: pain/pleasure, longing/fulfillment, anger/love (joy), and fear/trust. When an "unpleasant" emotion is blocked, there is also a block to the "pleasant" emotion in the pair. That is, if you are blocking pain, you can't fully experience pleasure; if you are blocking anger, you can't fully experience love; and so on. Most people block all these basic emotions to some degree, but usually they primarily block one pair. So when talking of radix character structure, we speak of a *pain blocker* (meaning he is blocking primarily pain, understanding he is blocking pleasure also), or a *fear blocker*, or sometimes combine two, a *pain/anger structure*. Our understanding of which feeling is being blocked is not based on the subjective experience of the student, but on an objective understanding of the body and body structure. As mentioned before in regard to crying, chronic patterns of tension develop in relation to any

feeling being blocked. Basically, the same body parts and groups of muscles *used* in the expression of a feeling will be the ones that also *block* the expression. For instance, when one expresses fright the eyes become wide, the voice raises in pitch, the shoulders are pulled up as if to avoid a blow, and (as Bates discovered) the eyes often become myopic (nearsighted). When fear is blocked these same features will be observed as chronic tensions.

The energy level and general focus of energy are also indicators of the feeling structure. Generally, high-energy, active, or hyperactive individuals whose energy is concentrated in the periphery of the body are blocking primarily anger. They generally have good strength and good contact with the environment. Their skin tends to be firm and ruddy. A problem with an anger blocker is that he has poor contact with his own center. His energy is directed toward the environment, and he is often out of touch with his own needs and wants.

The opposite, the person with low energy, is often sedentary. The energy is concentrated in the center, and this person has poor contact with his environment. The skin will often be pale and lifeless, and it will be difficult for this person to sustain activity. The low-energy person is usually blocking fear.

The goal in Radix Education is to establish a balance. A person only in touch with the environmental reality is handicapped, as is the person only in touch with his internal reality. A person in touch with both his needs and wants and the requirements for survival in the environment is better able to make choices for himself. The person with energy scattered in his periphery may be busy "doing" without accomplishing; he needs to learn to "center" and focus his energy to reach his goals. A person with energy drawn in will have trouble mobilizing himself for action and may be in contact with his needs, but lacking drive and volition to meet them.

Underlying this functional approach to character structure is Reich's theory of the segmental arrangement of the armor. The life force, radix, flows through the body longitudinally. It flows up the back, forward over the head, down through the front, forward in the direction of locomotion, the orientation of the sense organs, the orientation of the arms. This basic longitudinal flow of the radix underlies feeling. The flow of the radix and the feeling that is an expression of the radix are limited, blocked, and channeled by the muscular armor. Reich discovered that armor was arranged segmentally through the body. He identified seven horizontally divided segments: the ocular, oral, cervical, thoracic, diaphragmatic, abdominal, and pelvic. These segments can express emotion independent of each other when the flow of radix is limited by armor. So, for instance, a person can be clenching his fists in anger while sobbing. This lack of integration within the body and expression of emotion creates problems. Unless an emotion is expressed congruently throughout the body, it is never fully expressed and remains locked in the armor. The result is often experienced as confusion by the individual. What Radix teachers work for is integrated expression of feeling—that is, expressing the same emotion throughout all segments of the body. When this occurs, not only can the feeling be expressed, but the individual feels integrated, feels more in touch with his body, and thereby more alive. As his body image improves, a natural matter of course is for his overall self-image to improve. Often it is difficult for people to accept their emotions—they want to label them and judge them; they fear them. Learning to have choice and control over one's emotions enables the individual to better accept his feelings, accept himself. Feeling in charge of oneself is a very powerful and positive feeling. When a person has the ability to choose whether to allow an emotion, to accept his emotions, he can then accept his feelings and learn to evaluate and choose which emotions he can act on. An important concept to learn is that all feelings are okay, but acting on some is not okay. It's okay to be angry enough to want to kill someone; it's not okay

to do it. When a feeling can be fully expressed and accepted, an individual can understand that he doesn't need to act on the ones that would be harmful.

## METHODOLOGY

In Radix Education we work directly with the body and with the flow of the radix (life force) through the body. We work with the pulsation of the radix. All things pulsate. A pulsation is a rhythmic contraction and expansion; the heart as it beats expands to allow blood in one chamber, then contracts to force it out. Respiration is a pulsation, the major pulsation we work with in Radix Education. By developing and deepening the breathing pulsation, the body charges with more radix. As this charge develops two important things occur. First, the blocks to the flow of the radix in the body become accentuated. Often the blocks will redden in contrast to the pallor of the undercharged areas the flow has not yet reached. These blocks are active and are called *counterpulsations;* that is, another pulsation moving in opposition to the natural flow and pulsation of the radix. The second thing that happens is that the capacity for discharge (emotional release) is increased. The charge develops a capacity for action and for feeling, and discharge is the process by which the capacity is utilized.

The clearest illustration of this process is human sexuality. The radix charge develops relatively slowly at first, with only vague subjective sensations of restlessness and tension. The charge increases as one becomes increasingly "horny." There is a pleasurable tension and swelling in the genitals and a heightened interest in sexual experience. During foreplay the pulsation deepens and the charge increases and focuses at the genitals. In the sexual act the charge is increased rapidly as the respiratory pulsation deepens further, finally synchronizing with voluntary movements, pressing toward convulsion. Then movements become involuntary, the will is suspended, and the whole body surrenders to the convulsive pleasure of the orgasm.

The basic sequence was described by Reich as: tension-charge-discharge-relaxation. We now believe that charge leads to the tension, not vice versa, and the formula we use is charge-tension-discharge-relaxation. This basic sequence occurs in other deep emotions. The deepest expression of grief, rage, and terror involve a similar surrender to an overpowering and involuntary convulsion of the whole body.

Reich worked in this way through the segments from the top down, that is, beginning with the ocular segment. In Radix, we work from this top-down direction also, and in addition from the outside in (developmentally, then, we are working from more recent to early issues and blocks). The arms, hands, legs, and feet are seen as separate segments that are functionally connected to the ocular segment. Eyes, hands, and feet are the main contacts with the external world. It is with the eyes, hands, and feet that we contact reality. We see with our eyes, have a grasp of things, and have our feet firmly on the ground. So we work first with the ocular segment, hands and feet, working with freeing the armor and the feeling held in the armor; when there is some freeing here we will work with the oral segment, freeing armor there and integrating the emotion in this segment with that of the ocular segment. As we progress down the body we always return to the previous segments to facilitate integration. A person expressing anger with the whole body, but shut off in the eyes and mind, will not integrate the experience with the here and now, and so will not integrate the experiences into his or her life.

The central method in Radix Education for freeing the feelings is the Radix Intensive. An intensive is an individually focused body session, whether done in a private session or a group setting. The student lies on a mat and the teacher will kneel or sit at his or her side in order to have free access to the student's body. The student is invited to deepen breathing and center awareness in his or her body core. As the pulsation and breathing deepen, blocks/counterpulsations will develop. The teacher may work with the student's body to facilitate whatever process is occurring and to facilitate the movement of the radix through the blocks. The student is asked to surrender to whatever happens, not to force feeling or fantasy or to predetermine what ''should happen.'' The student is encouraged to surrender to the process; if he or she chooses to do so, the process will often move to discharge of the radix, freeing of contraction (armor) and felt as emotion. When this occurs there is usually awareness of the emotion being expressed as well as content associated with it. This is very much different from working with fantasy, or forcing the feelings by ''playing emotional scenes in the head,'' which will not free blocks, even though it may force discharge. Content that comes into awareness through the Radix Intensive comes through expression from the body, which has recorded the individual's emotional history. The person is never taught what to feel, but how to open his or her capacity and the opportunity for choice in feeling.

The fundamental form of the Radix Intensive is the small, supportive group. Being present as others open into feeling and giving to them emotionally is a highly important part of the work. The Radix Intensive is also an effective way to work with couples, allowing them to experience their relationship on the deepest emotional level, whatever that is for them. One of the innovations of Radix work is the development and synthesis of group techniques from many sources to deepen and support the intensive experience. Body awareness exercises, Feldenkrais exercises, encounter techniques, bioenergetic stress positions, Branden sentence completions, gestalt techniques, and other exercises are integrated with Reichian body work and used along with the intensive to deepen and expand the feeling capacities of the student. Many of the exercises are designed to help integrate the student's expanded feeling capacities into his or her life and actions.

# APPLICATIONS

Radix students are asked to read and sign a "Statement of Risks of Radix Education," adapted from "Risks of the Intensive" in *Education in Feeling and Purpose* (Kelley, 1974). This statement reads:

Radix Education poses two kinds of risks to students. The first, the short-term risk, is usually overestimated, while the long-term risk—the truly serious risk of Radix Education—is apt not to be appreciated.

*The short-term risk* is greatly exaggerated by the fear of loss of control and surrender to involuntary emotion that is common to civilized man. To give in to involuntary feeling is sometimes terrifying to those who have lost the capacity for surrender. Especially before one has learned to trust the guidance of the skilled instructor—and the inherent wisdom of one's body—the surrender to involuntary feelings can be very frightening.

The object of the fear may be unknown, or it may be felt that one will go berserk, will injure others or oneself, or will lose his grip on reality. For any normal person, there is little objective basis for such fear. No-one has injured himself or others in our work, although there have been many spontaneous and furious outpourings of rage. No-one has ever gone into shock or psychosis, although many have experienced moments of terror. The possibility of such an event occurring is like the possibility of a heart attack as a result of vigorous exercise; it is small but not entirely negligible.

If he decides to go ahead with Radix Education, it is important that the student go into it wholeheartedly, without reservations. The student who holds back actually increases the very risk he fears. The build-up of body energy and feeling that is an integral part of Radix Education will intensify his fear and increase his holding, and because he holds back he will have little chance to obtain the spontaneous discharge of energy and feeling that he needs. One should go into Radix Education with the determination to follow through, to neither force nor block, but to surrender as fully as one possibly can, to give in without reservation to one's involuntary feelings. This is not only the way to get the most from the program, it is the way which minimizes the risk.

*The long-term risk* is a far more serious one, because it concerns a much more likely consequence of Radix Education. This risk is a result of the very growth in the capacity for feeling that the program is designed to bring about. Education in feeling, purpose, and visual perception has an effect—often a profound effect—on students' lives, on their experience of themselves and on their relation to others.

To come alive in feeling can make one's work, marriage, and way of life each more significant, full and deep, and much more rewarding. It can also make any or all three of these unendurable. When one learns to open his eyes emotionally, he may or may not like what he sees. To come alive in feeling in an emotionally deadened world can be painful and disorienting. Mechanical work and superficial human relationships are no longer adequate. A student may no longer fit into the life pattern he has established and yet not be ready to establish another. The problem is felt most poignantly at the dawning of the realization, before one is sure of the true nature and extent of the problem, and so cannot reasonably take action on it.

It is also true that if a student has started opening up in feeling and decides he does not want to go ahead doing it because it is too painful, he may not easily be able to go back. There is no knowing where the freeing of feeling will lead. It is a chance for each to understand and weigh for himself. (Kelley, 1974, p. 17)

In light of the risks of Radix Education, any student wishing to participate must be willing to be responsible for him- or herself. The Radix teacher does not assume a role of caretaker or doctor, and students are expected to care for themselves and be responsible for their own actions.

It is important that students of Radix Education be in charge of the environment in which they live, as they may find that they need to make changes in life, work, relationships, and so forth. Therefore Radix Education is not generally suited to children, except in modified form, since they are not in a position to be able to alter their environment and relationships as they may feel it is necessary. A common criticism of Radix Education is that we do not do enough integrative-verbal work. People vary in their need for cognitive structure in which to integrate their experience in Radix Education.

Since our primary focus is with the body and feelings, when more verbal-oriented therapy is needed we will often suggest the student do it separately or concurrently. Someone wishing a cognitively based approach to personal growth would be dissatisfied with Radix Education.

The Radix Institute accepts all kinds of people with all kinds of problems for Radix Education. The work can benefit people in every walk of life, and the age range has been from 18 to 80. A concentrated week in Ojai gives the housewife an opportunity to explore her needs and wants away from responsibilities of taking care of children and husband and household tasks. She can explore who she is as a person independent of being mother and wife. The busy professional mental health worker or psychiatrist, especially those who work in a verbal mode, spends the week not only exploring and discovering him- or herself in a new way but is freed from taking care of others. The one requirement for all who undertake Radix work in regular settings is that they be functional. We have not, however, had sufficient experience in working with particular categories such as alcoholism, drug addiction, or psychosis to be able to evaluate what limitations might be in terms of working with those particular problems. Radix teachers who have private practices and are qualified as counselors, clinical psychologists, and other mental health professionals combine their Radix expertise with their work in the abovementioned categories.

## CASE EXAMPLE

The young woman lying on the floor looks very vulnerable. She is on her back, knees up with feet flat on the floor; her eyes are very brown, and sometimes they look frightened, sometimes they look angry. Her mouth is shaking. Her breathing is rapid but trying to regain rhythm and depth. She is trying to say something. I ask her to get up, onto her feet, erect so that she looks at me. I am male

or female; it doesn't matter at this point. But it does matter that I am an adult; my face is an adult face and my posture is an adult posture. At first she is shaky on her legs and needs support, but gradually she "feels" her legs, feels herself supported by them; she stands her own ground. She takes a deep breath now, looks me in the eye, and her mouth forms the words "My opinion matters." Softly at first. But as she is encouraged to deepen her breathing, "feel her ground," and repeat the words, they gain in intensity. A glitter comes into her eyes, she starts clenching her teeth and her fists, and we switch to her saying "My anger matters" and then to "My anger is important."

This young woman, Lisa, is shorter than I am, but as her intensity builds her voice gets louder, her eyes challenge mine, and she appears to grow several inches taller. As her excitement builds with the words and with the body language, the tone changes subtly. The challenge becomes a statement, and progresses into a quiet assertion. And there it is. There is nothing more either of us need to do except celebrate quietly, connected only through the eyes. Her opinions matter, and her anger is important.

Lisa has lain on the mat on the floor many times in the last months in order to reclaim parts of herself. Often there have been no words at all, but sometimes there were sentences such as "Listen to me," "Please see me," "Please notice me," "Please give me some attention." When the words were not expressed, there were sounds—cries, screams, sobs—or there was total silence.

Lisa had supported and defended herself in the world for several years, since running away from home at age 15. Pretty, intelligent, and proud, she set out to prove that she could do it even if her parents had negated her every action and opinion. And she had done it, but at cost. Her body reflected the struggle; neck and shoulders tense so that they moved almost as one piece; adult shoulders carrying adult burdens; jaw stubborn, and grinding her teeth most nights; little-girl defiance reflected in her locked knees and arched back, and yet her eyes were appealing, soft, nearsighted. She had trouble establishing, let alone maintaining, an intimate relationship because she couldn't trust; she got scared as soon as anyone tried to get close to her.

So here she was, a child-woman who knew only that she was not as happy as she should have been and that her body hurt where it shouldn't have hurt. At least she was aware of these things and did not accept them in herself. And here is the first important step: to become aware that we can be happier, less hurting and more fulfilled, and that we don't need to go around with permanently stiff necks in order to function.

Wilhelm Reich put the body into psychotherapy more than 50 years ago when he began investigating the *manner* in which his clients told their stories. Traumatic emotional incidents in their lives would be told with blank faces, matter-of-fact voices, stolid backs, or limp legs. Lisa's voice, for instance, used to develop a resigned quality and her breathing would almost cease; she didn't need to say the words ''What's the use?''; her body said it for her. She was partially dead—and this was a perfectly normal human being by anyone's standards.

As Reich's work with bodies and emotions became more refined, he was able to correlate particular sets of muscles with particular emotions and behaviors. So when Lisa increased her breathing volume, mobilized muscles in the ribcage, made her shoulders raise and lower, permitted her heart feelings to show in her eyes, then she experienced the feeling of resignation as something alive, something she could do something about. Her voice gave it a sound, and it developed into the racking sobs of deep hopelessness.

Lisa's deep surrendering to and acceptance of the hopelessness that brought up the convulsive sobs further loosened her structure and her diaphragm swung freely, allowing the pulsation to deepen into the belly. The work progressed from this point to allowing and contacting the mourning that she had never done. Over the next few months she grieved in her sessions for what was and what had not been; she grieved for herself and the way she had deadened herself and had not experienced life as fully as possible. Throughout this process her musculature was loosening and energy was flowing more freely. When the mourning ended and she gave up her expectations of the past, the pulsation was turned around and the energy flowed from her center to the periphery, coming out her eyes, hands, and grounding in her feet. The rage could then pour out. Reich had said that, in every individual, when the expression of life has been blocked a rage develops since the organism is prevented from expanding in its natural biological way. This was true for Lisa. Since her structure had been loosened and her eyes could accept a strong flow of energy, she was able to allow the anger to pour out. The anger was experienced and owned as *her* anger.

The work with Lisa was done over a two-year period. She is now married and able to commit herself to an intimate relationship with her husband. She functions as a professional and has progressively developed her career. Her life is not without problems, but she has the confidence in herself that enables her to handle whatever comes along.

## SUMMARY

Students who commit themselves to a program of Radix Education embark on a journey of self-discovery. They will be taught how to deepen and expand their capacity for feeling and aliveness, and will be facilitated in integrating this capacity into their life. Their own unique, individual process will be respected; this will enable each to gain tolerance and understanding of the self as well as others. They will learn to focus their energies so that they can accomplish the goals they set for themselves and be able to be aware of their wants and needs and how to go about fulfilling them. Opening the capacity for feeling and aliveness does not promise a nirvana, but with the deepened experiences of anger, sadness, and fear that accompany the deepened experiences of love, pleasure, and trust will come an appreciation for the experience of being alive.

Kelley (1978) makes the following important distinctions in *Orgonomy, Bioenergetics, and Radix:* The area of dependency/autonomy/transference is handled differently in Radix than in other personal growth programs. Radix places a degree of responsibility on its students that they often seem unequipped and unready to handle. We live in a society in which most individuals are rendered weak and dependent, ready to accept being taken care of by someone who seems stronger and more "together" than they do. In Radix Education, we do not see individual autonomy being served even by temporary transference-based relationships. Radix work is therefore offered as a personal service given by and to responsible individuals. The service does include support during difficult emotional changes, but this support is adult:adult, rather than parent:child in its dynamic. Because of this, the changes the individual makes become even more pro-found and powerful in that each person knows it was truly his or her own decision, power, and will that has been the impetus to the coming together of his or her life. The individual was assisted by a program of deep emotional release work, but no one did anything to the student, told him or her what to do, or judged his or her decisions to be good or bad. What individuals have done they have truly done for themselves, and that is autonomous, responsible functioning.

# REFERENCES

Kelley, C. R. *Education in feeling and purpose.* Ojai, Calif.: The Radix Institute, 1974.

Kelley, C. R. *New techniques of vision improvement.* In D. Boadella (Ed.), *In the wake of Reich.* London: Coventure, 1976.

Kelley, C. R. *Orgonomy, bioenergetics, and Radix: The Reichian movement today.* Ojai, Calif.: The Radix Institute, 1978.

Kelley, C. R. *The Radix Journal,* 1978–1979, **1 (1–4)**.

Reich, W. *The function of the orgasm (The discovery of the orgone, vol. 1).* New York: Farrar, Straus, 1961.

# CHAPTER 55

# *Rebirthing*

EVE JONES

*This chapter is unique in several ways and so deserves careful reading. I imagine it will disturb many readers. It is written by Eve Jones, a graduate (as I am) of the doctoral clinical psychology program at the University of Chicago, a clinician well trained and quite experienced. She is a member of a group known as Theta, which employs as their major method of therapy two main techniques: a system of connected breathing and a system of affirmations.*

*Like Arica, est, PSI, Mind Control, and Scientology, Theta belongs to a kind of psychotherapeutic underground. Started by a nonprofessional, it is part transpersonal, part mystical, part metaphysical, and, I am sorry to say, part "unscientific."*

*Theta, as you will read, has had many apparent successes as a psychotherapeutic method, and also seems to be growing rapidly. If what Dr. Jones writes is correct, many changes in our thinking and procedures are called for. This is why the chapter should disturb readers. Another important aspect of this chapter is that the author reports her own experiences as the case example. I found, and I think you will too, her account to be touching and impressive.*

Rebirthing is a holistic healing method that Leonard Orr originated on the West Coast in the mid 1970s. It is based on a simple breathing rhythm, without pauses between filling and emptying the lung space. By breathing in this connected manner for a few minutes to approximately an hour, clients find their consciousness involuntarily leaving the focus of connecting their breaths and moving to review events in their own individual past. The breathing exercise is done in the company of a trained Rebirther until the client can breathe fully and freely in a connected manner for an hour or more.

Rebirthing also utilizes another tool known as "affirmations," or statements of desired changes in current real-life experience, which are repeated by being written, spoken out loud, and even listened to.

A regressive method that produces psy-

chotherapeutic effects, this holistic healing technique also produces powerful and immediate physical therapy, as well as profound experiences characterized by most clients as spiritual. The Rebirth is thus physical, mental, emotional, and spiritual.

## HISTORY

### Precursors

The use of breathing rhythms to produce regression into past experience is not new to Leonard Orr's Rebirthing. Reichian and Primal therapies, for example, both utilize breathing techniques to facilitate the regression of patients into early childhood experiences, including birth. Rebirthing differs sharply from these and other regressive therapies, however, in its way of handling the experiences emerging into consciousness as a result of the successful regression.

The use of affirmations and visualizations to alter conscious thinking patterns is also, of course, not new to Orr's method. Indeed, not only behavior modification methods but even common prayer and supplication within most formal religions depend in part on the use of affirmations and visualizations. Rebirthing assigns a radically different role to these, however.

Most important, established psychotherapies did not form the foundation for Orr's Rebirth theory and practices. Instead, its sources lie almost entirely outside the framework of medically oriented psychology. Rebirthing was a result of efforts by Orr to evolve his own higher consciousness; its roots are metaphysical, mainly yogic traditions and fundamentalist Christian beliefs.

## Beginnings

Rebirthing had its beginnings, formally, in 1968 when Leonard Orr entered what he refers to as the "self-improvement business." Before that he had had no academic or professional experience or training in psychotherapy methods, nor was he heavily involved in consciousness raising or growth movements.

As an experiment in 1968, Orr decided to try to become wealthy by doing what he wanted to do, namely, stopping full-time work in a sales capacity and, instead, spending at least half a week for a month at home, reading metaphysical books. He actually tripled his income. Several of his clients became so interested in the ideas he was exploring that they paid him to stay home and read more, so he could tell them what he had learned so that they could, therefore, also improve the quality of their thoughts.

Over the next six years, Orr conducted numerous seminars on prosperity consciousness, self-analysis, and living relationships. The thoughts that he discussed with his followers and audiences were ones he arrived at as he sought, increasingly, to eliminate from his own consciousness all ideas or feelings that were negative in nature. He sought to do that because his readings in metaphysics had convinced him that our thoughts are the source of our environment and our being, our existence.

His readings in the field of psychology had convinced him that the only limitations to our thoughts are belief systems established during early development, so he sought to rid himself of the residue of such early traumatic experiences by attempting self-analysis. Because the earliest possible source of trauma in this lifetime is the birth experience itself, Orr sought to simulate birth conditions in the effort to reexperience his own birth and thus be free to eliminate the negative belief systems he had established at that time. Consequently, he spent a great deal of time immersed in a hot bath, frequently even breathing underwater with a snorkel, in the effort to recreate his prenatal experience so he could go from it, through birth, and into his conscious reality. In this, he succeeded: He reexperienced his birth.

Initially Orr assumed that the crucial element of his being able to recapture his birth experience was that he was in a simulated intrauterine environment. Not until several years later did Orr and his associates recognize that the crucial aspect leading to this result was the connected breathing they developed as they relaxed in the warm water. The original technique, known as the "wet Rebirth," is still used, but infrequently. Most Rebirthing is conducted out of the water, in ordinary surroundings.

Approximately three years passed while Orr worked on his birth experiences before he invited 15 of his seminar associates to enter a hot tub and attempt to relax sufficiently so as to go backward in time and to reexperience their own births. They were aided in achieving such relaxation and trust by having had long discussions previously about their fears, especially concerning their parents and the prospect of death. During that evening in March 1974, several people other than Orr experienced the Rebirth phenomenon.

Shortly after, Orr and a group of his close associates formed a community living in a Victorian mansion in San Francisco. They continued to wet Rebirth frequently, and they continued to evolve the concepts that form the theoretical basis for Rebirthing. An account of these early activities and conclusions was published in 1977 (Orr & Ray). The house was named Theta House because Orr used the Greek letter theta—$\theta$—as a symbol of Infinite Being manifesting on a material level. Theta seminars were headquartered in this building until the Rebirthing movement spread away from San Francisco to other parts of the United States and then to Europe and India. Various Theta Houses, Rebirth Centers, and state and local organizations came into being as a result of this quick-growing grassroots movement.

Starting in 1976, special advanced trainings have been held annually at the Jubilee gathering of all Rebirthers. At these trainings, several Rebirthers have received the unanimous approval of all other trainees, and thus became designated "Certified Rebirthers."

Several of these Certified Rebirthers, including Leonard Orr, were the main stimulators of the grassroots Rebirthing movement as they moved about the country leading training sessions and seminars. Since early 1978 there has been an International Rebirth Training Center, the Theta Growth Center of the High Sierras, located on 680 acres at Campbell Hot Springs, California.

Other Rebirthers have also contributed to spreading knowledge of Rebirthing as a result of their participation in a project launched by Orr in January 1979, called "Rebirth America." This program involves having 50 different Rebirth trainers or teams of trainers travel in rotation to each of the 50 states in the United States, conducting Rebirth trainings and leading seminars, as well as being available for Rebirthing sessions and consultations.

Since fall 1979 a similar plan, "Rebirth Europe," has been under way. Headquarters for Rebirth America and Rebirth Europe are located at Campbell Hot Springs.

## CURRENT STATUS

As of fall 1979 approximately 2,000 people have been functioning as professional Rebirthers in the United States, Europe, and India. Among these Rebirthers are several hundred professionally trained individuals who are using Rebirthing in their practices. These include nurses, nurse-midwives, nurse-practitioners, general-practice physicians, psychiatrists, respiratory therapists, social workers, teachers, and clinical psychologists. Professional training in one of the healing sciences is not a prerequisite to taking the week-long Rebirth training.

Orr and the other Certified Rebirthers agree that the qualities that enable a person to be a successful Rebirther and Rebirth training leader are those that automatically emerge as the individual lets go negative associations in thought, image, and feeling. Standards for certification and registration are upgraded continually.

The Rebirth training is a week-long intensive in the use of the connected breathing technique and of affirmations; it also includes participation in several seminars on various viewpoints that comprise the Rebirthing philosophy. Because scholarships are easily available, many clients and trainees are people without good financial means who seek to clean up their negative Money Cases by Rebirthing. A typical week-long training includes three Rebirthing sessions and admission to three seminars.

Rebirthers who have attended at least one week-long Rebirth training led by one of the Certified Rebirthers and who are sponsored by one can become "Registered Rebirthers," if they meet other broad qualifications. All Affiliated Rebirthers, Registered Rebirthers, and Certified Rebirthers are members of Rebirth International, whose headquarters are at Campbell Hot Springs.

At the time of this writing, the Rebirth America project has regular training programs occurring in approximately half the states and has about a dozen Rebirth America trainers traveling the training circuit.

More than 10,000 people have been Rebirthed and many more have participated in seminars.

All people who join and commit themselves to attend monthly seminars for 12 months belong to Theta International, which coordinates the one-year seminar (OYS) program. Being a Rebirther is not a requirement for membership in a OYS, though most members have been Rebirthed. Several dozen OYS's are currently operating.

People seeking to obtain information regarding available seminars or training programs or to locate a trained Rebirther for a private session can contact Theta International or Rebirth International, as well as local Rebirth or Theta Centers and organizers.

The International Journal of Rebirthing began publication in the spring of 1979. Its aim is to provide a forum for professional communication about Rebirthing.

Books and cassette tapes about Rebirthing cover such topics as self-analysis, prosperity consciousness, loving relationships, parental disapproval, physical immortality, spiritual psychology, and improvement of health and habits.

## THEORY

Rebirthing views personality as resting on the belief system or set of imprints regarding the self and reality established during the birth experience itself. These fundamental concepts established during and immediately before and after labor and delivery become guiding principles, referred to as "personal laws," that limit reactions to all events later in life that are similar in form or content.

To the extent that later childhood events reflect the perinatal circumstances, these later events also contribute additional negativity. Less importance is attributed to these psy-

chological traumata than to the birth, however.

The Rebirthing view of the determinants of personality may be regarded in one sense as an ultimate extension of ordinary psychoanalytic views: Freud regarded personality as the consequence of the solution of the Oedipal conflict; later Freudians saw personality as heavily determined by preoedipal events, especially those surrounding weaning and toilet training; and other psychoanalytically oriented theorists regarded the major determinant as the birth trauma. Thus, at first glimpse, Orr's viewpoint does not seem unique, although he attributes more importance to the birth per se than do others.

Orr's theories *are* unique, however, in that they assume the individual is responsible for the birth process itself, and they lay the groundwork for methods that depart totally from most accepted psychotherapies.

Seeing birth as the major personality determinant allows Rebirthing to explain why apparently identical childhood traumata may appear to have significantly different effects on two different individuals. For example, if the mother becomes ill and is removed to the hospital during the first year of a baby's life, one child may become severely depressed; another may simply become transitorily fretful. The first child's birth may have been the standard hospital delivery: The infant is separated from the placental support systems abruptly when the umbilical cord is clamped before the baby begins breathing independently; he is kept away from the mother while he is cleaned, weighed, measured, identified, and given neonatal medications; and he no sooner is finally reunited with the mother than he is removed again, to be placed in a newborn nursery, only to join her again for limited, infrequent feeding times. The second child may have had the good fortune of having been put to nurse and of being allowed to begin independent breathing *before* the umbilical cord was clamped, and to have had a continuing bond with his mother, staying near her continuously during the first few days following birth.

Rebirthing also explains why different children reared in almost identical ways within a single family, for example, may have radically differing attitudes toward life. For example, the first child, typically born after a longer labor than later children of the same mother, may establish the basic belief system that he has to struggle to get anything or that no one helps him get anywhere; a later child, often born almost precipitously from a uterus accustomed to the delivery, may establish the belief system that he doesn't have to work very hard for anything—indeed, he may not even know how to muster his energies for himself—or that he never has time to figure out what's happening.

Rebirthing also explains why even a very accomplished person who has achieved great success may carry around an extremely negative concept of self. He may have established the personal law that no matter what he does, he can't please anyone, if he absorbed some minor disappointment on the part of the mother when she learned she had a boy, not a girl, even if she never again feels or reveals such an attitude.

The prime concept in all Rebirthing theory is: Thought is creative, and we are the thinkers. Thus reality is regarded as a continual manifestation of our thoughts. Each of us constructs the universe in which we exist, obeying the personal laws we hold on to. If some aspects of that universe appear to be ones we resist, they must be regarded as manifestations of some negative thought that has not yet been released. Thus the quality of our lives reflects the quality of our thoughts. The thing to do when something goes wrong in our lives is to let go of whatever negativity in our thoughts appears to be creating the disturbance. This is primarily controlled by the belief system established in the perinatal period.

As clients reexperience their birth in the course of the Rebirthing session, they become free to examine their personal laws, and to choose to let them go or amend them more realistically. The clients' thoughts thus become different, and they are thus able to change their lives almost effortlessly.

They become able to let go of their personal laws as they breathe—simply breathe. Abreaction, catharsis, and even verbal expression are all regarded by Rebirthers as being as unproductive and as nontherapeutic as most traditional therapists regard mere acting-out. Rebirthing claims that therapy results *only* from letting go old grievances, and letting go is most easily accomplished by the connected breath and by replacing old negativity with affirmations.

Rebirthing theory argues that, if thought is creative, the individual's thought must have been responsible for having created the very circumstances of his or her birth that gave rise to the negative thoughts he or she established as personal laws at the time of birth. With such reasoning, Rebirthing theory departs from psychology proper and enters realms usually considered in metaphysics and theology. This position can more easily be presented after other Rebirthing concepts are considered.

Rebirthing's manner of dealing with the past interchanges between child and parent is radically different from most psychotherapies. The client is *not* urged to admit and express negative feelings about parents or to accept that parents had negative feelings about him or her. As stated previously, catharsis and abreaction are not encouraged. Instead, Rebirthing focuses on letting go grievances; blame is not attached to anyone. The connected breath allows clients to let go the negativity attendant upon their ignorant treatment of their parents and the parents' ignorant treatment of clients. As a consequence, clients are free to reexperience the total love and trust they initially felt as infants toward the parents, whatever else may have occurred later on.

Again, as with the circumstances of birth, clients assume responsibility for having created any so-called negative relationships with the parents.

Specific hardships, injuries, illnesses, and so forth, also leave a heritage of negativity that emerges during the Rebirth session. Since all such events must be regarded as manifestations of the individual's thought at the time, they must be regarded as having been desired by the individual. And since it is further assumed that the person does not want to inflict self-harm, these past so-called negative events must have been chosen by him or her so that a specific lesson about relationships could be learned. The focus therefore turns to determining what that lesson is, surrendering to it, and thus discovering the positive perfection of the lesson.

Thus within Rebirth theory there are no victims. Individuals have created all that has happened to them, created it by their thoughts. They have created a perfect universe in which they are totally free to release all negativity, to receive the support of that universe, and to receive exactly what they need as soon as they acknowledge such need. This concept is highly similar to concepts found within yogic and Hindu traditions. It leads to the formulation of a variation of reincarnation theory: Certain lessons are to be learned by the individual during the course of a lifetime, and the individual is continually constructing the situations in which these lessons can be learned; if not learned, such lessons will be presented in future lifetimes. Once all negativity is released and the lesson of Universal Love is learned, the individual experiences a continuous state of Bliss.

The healthy, mature individual who has let go all negativity is continuously centered in the here and now, having let go all ties to the past and trusting self and universe to be safe for all the future.

The breath is seen as the "rainbow bridge" between subjective and objective reality. Through the inhale, individuals reestablish a continuous connection with Infinite Manifestation, Infinite Intelligence, and Infinite Love. Through the exhale, individuals reestablish a trusting, supportive relationship with the universe they themselves have created.

The person who has eliminated the negativity associated with what are called "the Five Biggies"—(1) birth, (2) first breath and the life-death struggle, (3) parental disapproval, (4) specific negatives, and (5) past

lives—thus is in a total choice position about every and any event of his or her existence, including even such events as aging and dying. Hence, physical immortality is a possible consequence of full acceptance of personal responsibility.

Although such ideas as physical immortality and reversal of aging by thought are initially very upsetting to most people, these concepts become very acceptable and ordinary to people who persist with Rebirthing until they experience the basic clearing-out of birth trauma. Rebirthing as a process and as a formulated set of ideas is, of course, extremely young; so there has not been much changing of the basic ideas set forth by Leonard Orr and his early associates.

The remarkable friendliness between Rebirthers and the sense of shared community does not come about because of a theoretical position. Rather, these appear to be natural expressions of the deep love felt more and more continuously as Rebirthing continues.

The distance that is traditionally regarded within Western religions as existing between Man and God is totally eliminated within Rebirth theory. Just as the breath is regarded as the rainbow bridge between subjective and objective reality, the breath is also regarded as the bridge between one's unique individuality and one's godhead. The Rebirthee totally immersed in the breathing process experiences an identification with God. Indeed, the simple acknowledgment that thought is creative automatically leads to the necessity of acknowledging that we are all One and each of us is God.

## METHODOLOGY

The workings of Rebirthing are extremely simple and can be accomplished wherever there is time and place for the trained Rebirther to guide the client in a relaxed, safe atmosphere. Most of the time Rebirthing takes place in a quiet room, with the client lying on the floor, receiving additional support from pillows placed under parts of the body raised off the surface, and with blankets nearby so he or she can be covered if desired and can be as relaxed as possible. Every effort is made to provide comfort so that no negative influences are present during the Rebirthing session. It should be noted, however, that it is also possible though not especially desirable to accomplish Rebirthings while sitting up during commercial airline flights, while riding in cars, or while sitting up or lying down in the midst of noisy rooms where seminars or other activities are taking place.

Before the session, the client has had the opportunity to attend a Rebirth seminar covering the basic concepts on which Rebirthing rests. If he or she has not attended such a seminar, the trained Rebirther will review this material on a one-to-one basis prior to the session.

Rebirthing operates on a money-back guarantee basis, so clients typically pay for a session before it begins, assured that they will receive a full refund without delay if they are dissatisfied at the conclusion of the session. This enables the client to be free of any obligations at the conclusion too. In this regard, most Rebirthers only schedule appointments one in advance so that future commitments can be easily renegotiated if, for example, the client wants to work with another Rebirther.

Before the connected breathing starts, the Rebirther may discuss the client's current life situation with the aim of determining appropriate affirmations to correct aspects of the real-life situation the client seeks to change. Statements of problems by clients are taken at face value. Often the affirmation merely involves taking responsibility for the situation. For example, a client complaining about a boyfriend may be given the affirmation "My relationship with my boyfriend is exactly what I want."

Most Rebirthers establish a verbal contract with the clients at the beginning of the session regarding the length of the session. Usually it is agreed that both will keep consciousness on the client's connected breathing for at least an hour or until a Rebirth cycle is complete. Such a contract serves to permit the Rebirther to maintain a schedule of sorts, and it also serves to help the client know when to continue. Most sessions last approximately an hour or two, but sessions have been known to go for as long as five to seven hours and many sessions are completed in only a matter of 20 or 30 minutes. If the Rebirther chooses to let the client go without any preset limits, sessions are usually limited one to the morning, one to the afternoon, and one to the evening.

The client also usually agrees to continue to work with the Rebirther until the client achieves a breathing release—that is, until the client has reexperienced taking the first breath following birth. After that the client can breathe easily and fully without reminders to do so and can Rebirth him- or herself as desired. Rebirthers who travel to lead trainings and seminars make arrangements to have a client continue Rebirthing with a local Rebirther until the breath release is accomplished.

After the session starts, the Rebirther coaches the client and requests whatever changes in breathing pattern may be necessary to maintain the connected breath. Often the Rebirther breathes noisily to demonstrate the rhythm or pattern desired. He may want the inhale longer, deeper, slower, fuller, and so forth all in the effort to eliminate any blocks that seem to impede the full expansion of the entire chest during the inhale and the relaxed collapse of the chest wall during the exhale.

The Rebirther may or may not choose to touch the client, whether to reassure or to reposition. He is guided by intuition, not rules. Frequently the Rebirther intuitively experiences in his own body sensations that the client is simultaneously experiencing. This sharing is established by open-ended questioning. Care is taken not to make suggestions put in the form of questions.

Little attention is given to the transitory phenomena the client reports at the beginning of the session, such as dryness of the mouth or nostrils, clogging of the nostrils, itching, and feelings of pressure. The client is reassured that these will change as the breathing continues. The client is urged to refrain from moving, yawning, talking, or even trying to hold on to whatever thoughts, images, or feelings emerge; instead, the client is urged to keep his or her consciousness on the breath. These thoughts, images, and feelings are all regarded as merely old negativity coming to the surface of consciousness as they are about to be released with the exhale. Occasionally the Rebirther intuitively recognizes the value of permitting the client to talk or move; but the client is usually reminded that the work of Rebirthing is accomplished by breathing, not by dramatizing or by reporting old garbage that's about to be thrown out.

Rebirthing is *not* hyperventilation. The client ideally places emphasis on the inhale, deliberately enlarging the inhalation by relaxing the abdomen, shoulders, back, and pelvis. The exhale is the result of just totally letting go all constraint, so the ribcage and diaphragm collapse. The client does not make any effort to blow out or empty the lungs. Thus he or she is not lowering blood concentrations of carbon dioxide and thereby causing changes in blood calcium, as happens with hyperventilation. Thus, quite in contrast to hyperventilation, Rebirthing is a hyperoxygenation of the bloodstream without a concomitant increase in either the production of or the release of carbon dixoide. (It may be noted that most people experience a feeling of immense well-being when jogging or swimming long distances, and these positive feelings are highly similar to those produced in the course of the Rebirth. The height of the elation produced by such physical activity is not as extreme as with the Rebirth, however, because the exercise itself is producing wastes, so the breath is occupied with releasing newly made negativity and cannot therefore be releasing old.)

People new to Rebirthing may not trust the universe simply to accept the exhale; they may instead either guard it, letting it trickle out slowly, or they may deliberately blow out on the exhale, tensely *trying* to let go, not just letting go. It may take people who breathe in a measured, cautious manner several sessions before they can feel safe enough in the situation to begin to abandon their constraint. People who exhale effortfully usually experience symptoms of hyperventilation.

The hyperventilating client is reminded that the tingling, numbness, tetany, and spasm he or she may be experiencing are all transitory and will dissipate as soon as the Rebirthing breathing pattern of drawing in the inhale consciously and letting the exhale go effortlessly is returned to. Since the client is only exhaling effortfully because he or she is afraid of experiencing the Rebirth (afraid that the Rebirth will kill him or her), the Rebirther may remind the client that he or she survived birth.

In Rebirthing theory, pain is the effort of clinging to a negative thought. The client experiencing pain is therefore asked to affirm that he or she is breathing and thus losing negativity: "Every breath I take increases my aliveness and decreases my negativity," or "Every breath I take allows me to let go the negativity stored in my body, my mind, my heart, and my soul."

Clients who begin to reexperience later childhood events involving a lot of the parental disapproval syndrome (PDS) are urged to recognize that these are simply old feelings being felt as they are being released; such clients may move, cry, or yell if they want to so long as they maintain the connected breathing pattern. Several different affirmations are useful in expediting letting the PDS go: "I now forgive my parents for their ignorant treatment of me"; "I now forgive myself for my ignorant treatment of my parents"; "I am not my mother"; "I am not my father"; and "The more I am myself, the more I feel the love between me and my parents."

After approximately an hour's breathing, the client loses awareness of being in the here and now—not to reexperience some old negativity but rather to go into another condition of consciousness. It is during this time, often a time when breathing is suspended for minutes, that clients report all sorts of transcendental experiences, including being out of the body, being in other forms, experiencing interactions with mythological, archetypal figures, recalling recent dreams, or performing detailed behavior in settings that are totally familiar and recognizably from a former age. It is also during this time that people experience cosmic feelings of total bliss in which they are bathed in a continual flow of loving energy, often so intense that it is orgasmic.

The Rebirther makes no effort to stimulate the client's breathing if it has been suspended during this rapture, even if the breath is stopped for several minutes. Intuitively the Rebirther recognizes this is different from the stoppage seen early in the session. Frequently there is a remarkable awareness by other people that the crisis is happening. If conditions of the actual birth were unusual, it is not uncommon for those same conditions to be re-created to accompany the Rebirth. Thus a client born in the hospital corridor during the height of the postwar baby boom might, as he or she approaches going back to birth, draw people totally extraneous to the Rebirthing consultation right into the Rebirthing room—people who explain that they didn't know a Rebirth was in progress but that they felt impelled to enter that particular room.

Gradually, just as the connected breathing released any preceding agony and passion, the connected breathing now causes a subtle change in the feeling of ecstasy, so that the client feels satisfied, relaxed, and bouyant—free of negativity, full of peace and contentment, and ready to go about ordinary business, the same person he or she always was, but newly Reborn and different.

Because powerful effects are produced in a very short time, a few clients may experience some discomfort between sessions. They are usually advised to complete more breathing so they can move from that position of discomfort. They may also be advised to affirm "I am safe to complete my Rebirth process with every breath I take."

Rebirthees are urged to continue practicing the connected breathing pattern for at least an hour a day, every day, until all major aspects of their lives work to their satisfaction. They are also urged to take 20 connected breaths whenever they notice any tension or negativity. An ideal is to maintain the connected breath throughout the day so the person is continuously healing the self of negativity and is continuously in a conscious choice position regarding immediate reality.

## APPLICATIONS

No formal studies about types of clients seeking Rebirthing have been concluded as of fall 1979. But the structure of the post-Rebirth Seminar in which all people who have recently been Rebirthed share their experiences, both during and after the session, allows for a great deal of informal communication about problems that have been solved and also about the nature of the sessions themselves.

It appears that the vast majority of people who Rebirth report extremely positive effects. These effects persist—they are independent of length of time a person has been Rebirthing.

Claims that a particular form of therapy produces successful results with every sort of problem are generally regarded with suspicion and scorn by the professional. Yet the personal testimony of several hundred people who have Rebirthed is impressive in its consistency. Comments are highly positive, whether the problems had appeared to be physical or mental or emotional or spiritual. And positive comments are frequently provided by amazed and gratified family, friends, or associates, not just by the client.

Of course, this is to be expected if the theory is correct: An ill person who gives up the negativity causing the illness can then proceed to use his or her connection with Infinite Intelligence to heal the self. One problem is no harder to heal than another.

In this writer's experience Rebirthing hundreds of clients and participating, either as trainee, trainer, or organizer in dozens of week-long trainings, only one client has asked for a return of the session payment and only one trainee has asked for a refund of the training fee. During that time I have witnessed the apparently complete amelioration of an extreme variety of behavioral, psychological, psychosomatic, or medical conditions. Rebirthing appears to have been effective in "curing" people who, prior to treatment, had been depressed; anxious; paranoid; impotent; frigid; addicted to drugs, including alcohol, nicotine, caffeine, and refined carbohydrates; suffering from extremely low self-esteem, suicidal; violent; homosexual; criminal; asthmatic; obese; phobic; lazy; epileptic; lonely; unsuccessful; ostracized; arthritic; overwhelmed; obsessed; sterile; catatonic; or paralyzed following a stroke or injury, among many others. It also has had the effect of "curing" the therapy act that patients who had previously been in other forms of therapy tend to put on—lots of emotional acting-out by former primal patients, lots of detailed talk about motives for past behavior from former patients in most talk therapies, or lots of self-disciplinary behavior from patients who have undergone behavior modification techniques.

Its major limitations are not with the method or its results, but only with the way in which it challenges conventional scientific rationalism as this has been typically understood in the Western world. Research studies of Rebirthing, seeking to characterize the neurophysiological and physiological changes that occur during the session, for example, need to be concluded and their results published. And long-term studies need to be conducted to determine the stability of the almost magical successes so far induced in most Rebirthees.

## CASE STUDY

My primary reason for going to see Leonard Orr and signing up for his course was just plain professional curiosity about how he got back into birth so easily, compared to Primal Therapy with which I had been intensely involved for seven years. I also had the thought in the back of my mind that I might meet someone who wasn't a college student of mine or a patient of mine or a friend of one of my grown children.

Everything in my life was fine: My kids and I loved each other and enjoyed the time we spent together, I truly enjoyed playing house just for myself, I liked everything I did professionally, I gained lots of rewards for my work, I was healthy and strong, and I got a lot of pleasure out of living.

If anyone had asked me what could be better, I would only have said that I got tired of incessantly having to care for my roses, which were prone to rust and other diseases, I never really had had a good car since my '52 Dodge, and I'd had even worse luck with men. I granted that I had been loved by men more intensely perhaps than any woman my age and had loved them back. But, no matter how long we stayed together, eventually the marriage or love affair would end with beatings and betrayals of my love. Usually the man left when he came so close to killing me that he became afraid he might succeed and then would have to stand trial for murder. Even then I would generally forgive him, and we'd go through the whole number over and over before—his choice—the relationship would be over and I'd fall into the next.

Living alone without any man in my life, I felt a little surprised over the waste of me, but I wasn't lonely. I had a lot of fun with everyone I knew, but I wanted very much to change the pattern in me that caused me to be unable to turn away from anybody in need. I had an enormous capacity for getting into relationships in which I was giving—giving, not just professionally, but financially and emotionally as well. I knew I was strong enough to go on doing that, but I resented not having anyone take care of me, even a little, and not getting what I wanted if I finally did ask.

My Rebirther asked me some questions about that, not at all complicated, and then suggested that I might want to work with an affirmation that I serve myself first and as well as I serve others, and also that the more I serve myself, the more others serve me. I was very skeptical to learn about affirmations from her, since I thought it was very simpleminded; but I was polite about it and wrote her words down.

Then I started breathing the way she asked me to.

Although I usually didn't sweat, even on hot days, I found myself soaked through with perspiration after a few minutes. She said I was letting go toxins and that was good. I continued to breathe, occasionally getting very interested in a thought that crossed my mind and then being surprised to hear her ask me to breathe. Suddenly, I reexperienced my birth, in much greater detail and with more convincing a quality of being real, of happening right then and there, than I had ever experienced in Primal. The smell of blood, the sensation of falling, the lovely squeezing and sliding up and down were all there. Everything was fine, and then, even more suddenly, I was totally immersed in a feeling of vast disappointment and sorrow. All I could do was sob and weep for minutes. I finally felt relieved. I was surprised to realize that more than an hour had passed to that point. I assumed we were done, so I got up. My clothes, including my heavy jeans, were so wet I was dripping on the floor, and I was shaking with cold.

When I went back to the meeting, Leonard said, "Good," after I stood up in my wet, clinging clothes and told what had happened. I thought everyone was supposed to reexperience birth, so I didn't understand why the people behind me got sort of upset by my not making much of that part. I was impressed, but wondering "So What?"

My second session went much like the first initially. I was lying in a sleeping bag and I got it so wet with my tears and the drool that seemed to stream out of my mouth that I found myself sliding back and forth with each breath. It was very pleasant, just like sliding back and forth in the bathtub when

I was a little girl—a favorite way to end my daily bath.

After about an hour, I suddenly reexperienced my birth again, except that this time I felt really pleased to be out of the closeness and heat and into being able to unfold and to get a little cool. Then abruptly I was flooded with disappointment. Sorrow was drowning me. I was wrong, somehow, but I didn't want to be. I realized that these disappointed feelings weren't coming from me but from my mother who had hoped I would be a boy, not another girl.

My mother was a very loving woman who was tender and demonstrative when I was very little, spoiling and overprotecting me. But I had always felt the desire to make up to her for something, I didn't know what. And I'd often feel an almost alien sadness engulfing me, somehow tied to my feeling that I had to take care of others all the time to earn my right to be alive.

My Rebirther had me make an affirmation about forgiving myself and my parents for the ignorant ways in which we treated each other. And immediately I found that I was breathing really fully and that I felt very triumphant because I had never felt it was reasonable for me to be depressed, and yet there it was. Knowing that I had simply absorbed my mother's feelings made it easy for me to choose to throw away that existential guilt. I felt I was a self, all my own.

My third session wasn't at all the same. I started crying in deep anguish immediately upon lying down. I felt that no one had ever wanted me to be alive and that the only way I could possibly satisfy everyone would be to die. In fact, I realized that I felt and had always felt that I would immediately please the entire world if I would just stop being so selfish and interested in staying alive and would instead give up and die. I didn't want to die, but I wanted approval—and that would require my giving myself up.

While I was crying, I was holding my breath as the pain in my throat and chest got worse and worse, until I truly thought I would die. My Rebirther kept telling me to breathe and to stop the drama. At times I held my breath so long that I almost forgot that I knew how to breathe. I felt torn apart and hurting all over, both on the surface and in my joints, especially my shoulders, which have always had a tendency to dislocate easily.

I suddenly located the feeling, again outside of me. The doctor! He must have been plenty fed up if my mother was screaming for three days before I got born, and I know she was a screamer. I know *I* was having a good time, being squeezed. *I* wasn't in distress. But she was and he was, all because of me. Suddenly I was being moved out and I was sputtering, with that blood smell in my nostrils and that panicky dread in the pit of my belly that I associate with drowning or falling or dying. I wondered if he didn't just decide to get the old forceps on me and impatiently drag me out. I remembered as a child holding my breath until I blacked out when I couldn't get what I wanted.

My Rebirther kept telling me to breathe and to remember I was safe. Finally I realized that I had a right to want to stay alive and that I wasn't being wrong and selfish for not cooperating with that impatient force that seemed to want me to die already so it could leave. My breathing became full and easy again, and I felt very elated and extremely hungry.

Those first three sessions were so revolutionary in my experience that, without hesitation, I sought to Rebirth all my old patients and my friends and family. I even Rebirthed my pregnant daughter, calling her immediately after I heard Leonard remark that mothers pass on birthing patterns to their daughters during the birth and that the only way to get rid of a family birth pattern was to have the daughter Rebirth before she delivered.

My then-pregnant daughter, my second child, had been delivered 28 days after I went into labor for two days on her due date, and even then, a month postmature, the membranes didn't burst on their own and my cervix didn't dilate until I'd been back in hard labor all night and all day, a total of 24 hours.

So I had every desire to have her have an easier time and to have her child receive the benefits.

They did—her labor lasted about six hours and her daughter started to nurse as she took her first breath, all before the umbilical cord was clamped and cut by Daddy. Like other children born to mothers who Rebirthed before or during pregnancy, my granddaughter is amazingly quick at development, walking totally independently at less than nine months of age, for example. When she gets upset, she does what she can to get what she wants, and then afterward she connects her breathing and does the Rebirthing breath for a few minutes. Then she reaches the climax, relaxes, and everything's fine. Apparently she's letting go the negativity as soon as it builds up—or as soon afterward as possible.

I've finally understood the bizarre physical cruelty in my life since I moved away from my mother to attend college at 16 and get married a year later. I knew, of course, that it couldn't be due to my parents, for they practically never hurt me. Yelling, yes, my mother yelled. But they didn't beat their children or treat us cruelly. Yet every man I've been intimately involved with in a love relationship—brilliant, intellectual men who had never even had fist fights with other boys as children—became a raging, impersonally brutal creature, choking me, throwing me around, kicking me, all accompanied by saying, "Why don't you die already?"

And I would forgive them. What else? I already loved them. To stop loving them because they were hurting me would be to tear a piece of myself out of my being, and, anyhow, I knew they really didn't hate me. Something about me just drove them crazy, and it had something to do with my wanting to have what I wanted, even though I didn't want much and not often. But I was so urgent and unable to tolerate any delay when I finally did want something that everything would get crazy.

My own children were all born after long, hard labors, where my cervix didn't dilate until after many, many hours of half-minute contractions, a minute apart. That's hard labor. Then, inside of only a few minutes, the cervix would let go, the baby would crown, I would give the last convulsive squirt of the baby out of me, and then the afterbirth would be delivered. The whole second and third stages of labor would take less than a quarter of an hour. My fastest first stage of labor was an entire day, but that included more than six hours of having a constant drip of Pitocin to expedite labor.

And I was there, conscious. An early convert to natural childbirth. Ready to look at my children taking their first look at the world. Surprised to see that they didn't need to cry.

Let's assume that something similar happened with my mother with me. I feel confident that it did because my mother would often comment that I took three days to get born and I never had known when to stop bothering her.

Let's assume that my mother and the doctor and my father were all pretty fed up with me by the time I finally came on out. Maybe I popped on out by myself, in a hurry like my own children, with everything okay except for my absorbing my mother's terror over being "torn apart" and her disappointment over my being a girl.

Or maybe the doctor couldn't stand listening to my hysterical mother anymore—and I bet she yelped a lot, since they certainly couldn't have kept her knocked out for that long. Maybe he reached in and gave me a yank, possibly even hurting my shoulder in the process. Maybe he just had to slap me hard to get me to start breathing.

Who knows?

Sondra Ray, one of the Certified Rebirthers, said when she looks at me she gets the image of my being beaten up by the doctor during my birth.

I don't know. The doctor's dead. My mother's dead. The hospital burned down.

It actually doesn't matter. I know that in former therapies, including years of psychoanalysis, then later some more time with a psychoanalytically oriented psychotherapist and then later with Primal, some things didn't change. I'd recall lots of times my shoulder was injured in freak accidents—but my shoulder would still hurt, after all the crying and associating was done. I'd recall the few times my father was angry with me—but my menfolk would still use me for punching practice. And I'd beg my mother to forgive me for everything I could imagine she might ever have resented about me—but still I'd be a moral masochist, a sucker, an easy touch for every down-and-out bum to try to hustle. None of that therapy had changed me in those regards.

Then I Rebirthed and affirmed that I forgave myself and the doctor for any way we may have harmed each other during my birth. And everything changed. Since the day I first Rebirthed, I haven't been attacked or beaten! That's the absolute longest I've gone since the day I left my mother when I was 16. A stranger once even attacked me on the train an hour after I had said good-bye to my mother. It's all over. Magically, no one is hurting me.

For a few months I used to be verbally attacked at seminars—someone would stand up and start yelling at me and just dumping their whole hate trip on me. Then one day I Rebirthed and made the affirmation that everyone loved my presence and I forgave anyone who had ignorantly ever objected to me. Even the verbal attacks stopped!

My shoulder is fine: I gave up all the last tension in it after a long wet Rebirth in which I relived lots of bizarre accidents involving my shoulder, where it was dislocated in order to save me—same story as I suspect happened during my birth.

I'm not at all the same sucker, and no one abuses the privilege when I do share my abundance. Anyhow, the Rebirth Community genuinely respects my generosity and energy. Every dollar I spend comes back to me multiplied.

I have had awesome, transcendental, magical Rebirth experiences; I have also had ones where I merely breathe for an hour and feel cleaner. The ones I like the best are the ones that confirm that what Leonard writes and speaks about, however freaky it sounds at first, is really true. I've felt and now acknowledge my own divinity. I've experienced being an enduring consciousness that's separate from the self-awareness, the thinker I've always known as me. I've experienced very early fetal life and I can accept some dreams as visits back into previous lives. People have unexpectedly shown up to take care of a problem that has just arisen—over and over I experience a universe that totally supports me. I have experienced many sorts of extrasensory perceptions. I make money even more easily and enjoyably than I used to. I've watched people change, almost overnight—even faster sometimes. I look and feel great and I get into clothes I was wearing when I was a graduate student, long, long ago. My skiing is getting good. I have a deep love for everyone I've ever been associated with in a training or seminar, and by now that's almost 600 people. I've had the joy of hearing my son say that he feels as close to people in trainings as to his dearest friends or family, so I can tell him I feel that way too, and I know he isn't jealous. I look forward to being physically immortal, along with my children and everyone I love.

Even my three problems are taken care of: My roses haven't had rust for two years now; a fellow Rebirther was an automotive engineer for the company that manufactured my car and he's quite agreeable to helping me keep it in good repair; and I've had a man in my life for the past 14 months and we get along very well. We Rebirth each other or separately often enough to keep the negativity out of the relationship most of the time, except when we need it to go into a whole drama so we can learn some lesson. We don't stay crazy for very long. Our last argument lasted exactly an hour.

Most important, I'm finally really doing what I wanted to do in the first place when I became a psychologist: People continually heal themselves and others as they Rebirth in my presence.

## SUMMARY

The advantages of Rebirthing are many: It's simple, safe, effective, and enjoyable. It can easily be learned by people of any background. It can be taught to people who are from widely different cultures, not even sharing a spoken language. It can be practiced without any supervision after only a few sessions with a trained Rebirther. It can be carried on almost anywhere, anytime.

Its disadvantages are few: Not much is known about the neurophysiological and physiological events transpiring during the Rebirth, so people who want to be convinced of its goodness don't yet have scientific reports they can examine. It's spooky, strange, and difficult for the scientific rationalist to accept because it makes a mockery of all the cause-and-effect relationships science has struggled for centuries to establish. In the place of a limited universe with dwindling supplies, a scarcity consciousness, regrettably but stoically accepted by the linear logic of the rationalist, Rebirthing presents a limitless, expanding universe constructed continuously by thought—wishes do come true—and there's no limit to what can be manifested. Its Pollyanna idea that everything is perfect is an affront to those who have lost their innocence and are afraid to hope anymore, who are so worried about appearing to be foolish that they prefer remaining fools.

The great thing about it is that life is just as contagious as disease, and the epidemic of love is spreading fast. BREATHE!

## REFERENCES

Orr, L. and S. Ray. *Rebirthing is the new age*. Millbrae, Calif.: Celestial Arts, 1977.

# CHAPTER 56

# Reevaluation Counseling

GEORGE LOCKWOOD

*When I first began planning this book, I wrote to my friend Albert Ellis, with whom I generally check out everything that has to do with psychotherapy, since he is probably the single most knowledgeable person I know of in this field. I asked him to tell me what were, in his opinion, the most important innovative systems. To my surprise, one of the systems he mentioned was Reevaluation Counseling, which I had heard of only vaguely.*

*When I investigated, I realized that this system had quietly spread and had generated a good deal of interest in various communities. Practically everyone I talked with had good things to say about Reevaluation Counseling. However, when I looked for someone to write about it, I ran up against a blank wall. Neither its founder and developer, Harvey Jackins, nor any other well-qualified person was available. And so I turned to my friend George Lockwood to see if he would investigate and report on this important system. In my judgment he has done an outstanding job in explaining this approach.*

*The reader should prepare to learn about something important and different in the field of psychotherapy.*

Reevaluation Counseling, developed by Harvey Jackins in the 1950s, is a growing theory of human behavior and set of procedures for eliminating human irrationality. It views human beings as basically intelligent, happy, loving, and powerful. It assumes, however, that these qualities have, until now, for most people been largely obstructed by the harmful effects of distressing experiences that begin early in life. It is possible for this unfortunate result to be corrected by an inborn recovery mechanism that operates spontaneously under certain conditions in the aftermath of emotional or physical trauma. However, this innate curative capacity is usually blocked by social conditioning processes that encourage children to inhibit the discharge of emotions. The recovery mechanism can be liberated and the repressed intelligence, happiness, love, and power regained through the reestablishment of a

special kind of relationship. This relationship can be unidirectional or, more advantageously, it can be a peer relationship that involves two people, each alternately taking on the role of a counselor who is caringly attentive toward the other. This attentiveness triggers a discharge of painful emotion and a subsequent reevaluation of the contents of past distressing experiences on the part of the individual acting as client.

## HISTORY

### Precursors

Early in the history of Reevaluation Counseling (RC), Jackins made a decision to avoid borrowing from previous theories and to make a fresh start. This was because he felt none of the existing approaches seemed to work well enough to warrant endorsement. RC theory developed, therefore, directly out of the firsthand experiences of Jackins and his associates. Once they had built up a sufficient base of successful practices, a theory was gradually constructed to explain the results. Jackins claims that this process was rigorously scientific and empirical in the sense that no conclusions were accepted unless supported by actual observations and behavioral data. Subjective "studies" and opinions of people based on past experience are said to have been avoided. Development progressed in this inductive fashion until the early 1960s, at which point a parallel structure was created based on deductive logic. This structure consisted of 24 postulates whose intent was to assure logical consistency among the conclusions arrived at earlier, as well as clarify the basic set of assumptions upon which RC theory was based. In addition, the postulates served as a new source of theorems. Hypotheses derived from and consistent with them were deduced and then checked against reality. As this deductive structure grew, RC practitioners continued to work inductively. Insights arising out of practice and supported by empirical evidence were formulated so as to be consistent with the deductive structure. The two systems worked in a complementary fashion, one ensuring logical consistency and the other guaranteeing empirical validity.

Throughout the development of RC, Jackins has been hostile toward eclectic practices in which well-meaning individuals have attempted to mix RC with other approaches. Even though there may be superficial similarities, Jackins maintains that RC works from an entirely unique set of assumptions. Randomly incorporating such theories and practices without checking to be sure their assumptive base is consistent with RC leads to internal contradictions, which in turn may generate harmful results. Eclecticism is also seen as interfering with the generalizability of outcome. The criterion for selection of a given practice is often based simply on its having worked at one time in a specific setting for a certain group. RC, on the other hand, attempts to develop an approach that works consistently for all people.

## Beginnings

After receiving a bachelor of arts degree in mathematics, Jackins spent a number of years as a labor organizer. During this period he was active politically and became known as a poet and inventor.

In the early 1950s accidental circumstances confronted him with the problem of distressed human behavior. Jackins had a friend whose business partner, unbeknown to Jackins, had been under psychiatric care for months and had deteriorated to the point where he had been consigned to a state institution for life. Jackins's friend asked him to rescue his partner before the authorities arrived. Jackins took the man to his home and, in an effort to interrupt his wild behavior, began to ask him questions. The man began to cry. At first Jackins attempted to get him to stop but, after many attempts to question him always brought tears, he decided that perhaps the man needed to cry. The man cried for many hours as Jackins listened and encouraged him. After two days of this, there was a noticeable improvement in rationality and competence. This improvement continued through a week of crying. Many hours of shaking followed the tears. At the end of two weeks the man was back at work, functioning well, and thinking clearly.

Jackins found the results so startling he tried to duplicate them with others. He experienced enough success within a few months to attempt a generalized explanation. He concluded that humans became less disturbed when they were allowed to discharge accumulated distress. There was no need for interpreting, analyzing, or other such authoritarian tactics. Given the right conditions the mind seemed to have a capacity to heal itself. Apparently all the helper needed to do was pay warm attention in a way that facilitated the individual's discharge; the rest was a spontaneous process.

This seemingly natural capacity for recovering intelligent functioning, capacity for love, and zestful enjoyment of life caused Jackins to hypothesize that these may actually be people's true natures and that only through emotional and physical hurts are they obscured. Environmental factors became the assumed cause of all human dysfunction.

Crucial in the early development of RC was the implementation of what is termed co-counseling. Jackins found that over a period of time counselors would fail to gain in effectiveness unless their own levels of distress were lowered. In addition, they became eager to obtain the results observed in their clients. Their effectiveness was increased and the desired results obtained by having counselor and client regularly reverse roles. This peer or co-counseling relationship proved so effective it has become the main mode of RC.

RC achieved an encouraging degree of success with its permissive approach, yet certain patterns of distress (distress patterns are viewed as the unfortunate results of hurtful experiences responsible for rigid and compulsive behavior) seemed to persist. The underlying difficulty was clarified sometime in 1955 when the difference between chronic and latent distress patterns was first noticed. Latent patterns were triggered in certain settings, while chronic patterns seemed to be engaged continuously, permeating all behavior. In the case of chronic patterns Jackins found it necessary to go beyond the permissive approach to become much more active and directive.

## CURRENT STATUS

In 1952 a research and development organization called Personal Counselors Inc. was founded in Seattle for the purpose of permitting full-time exploration of Reevaluation Counseling as well as to provide teaching and counseling services. For about 20 years it was the main vehicle for the development of RC theory and practice. During this period many series of RC classes were taught to the public in an attempt to train people to become co-counselors. From the students in these classes eventually developed what are now called "RC Communities." These communities are currently established in 28 countries and are distributed widely throughout the U.S. and Canada.

Membership continues to climb. In recent years considerable numbers of clinical psychologists, psychiatrists, and other professional mental health workers have been among the new participants. New members come primarily from Fundamentals Co-Counseling Classes, in which the elementary theory and techniques of RC are taught through 16 weeks of weekly two and one-half hour meetings. Admission to the classes is selective—only those who can be expected to become proficient counselors in a relatively short period are accepted. In some communities Fundamentals Classes are attended indefinitely and serve as a continued source of theoretical and practical development. Other communities offer advanced classes beyond the Fundamentals Class to serve this function.

The entire network of RC communities is led by an International Reference Person. An Area Reference Person is chosen for each locality and is in charge of its development as well as making decisions regarding policy. There is a Reference Person leading international liberation efforts for each of the following groups as well: Blacks, Asians, Latinos, young persons, elders, Jews, women, physically different, Gays, Native Americans, and the working class. In addition, there are international reference persons for areas of special interest, such as for educational change, university and college faculty, and men.

Rational Island Publishers, the publishing firm of RC, has produced a variety of books, pamphlets, videotapes, and audio cassettes on the theory and practice of RC. Publication began with several forerunners of what is now entitled the *Fundamentals of Co-Counseling Manual* (Jackins, 1962). This contains a description of elementary counseling techniques used in beginning classes. *The Human Side of Human Beings* (Jackins, 1965) was written shortly afterward, and provides a succinct introduction to RC. A collection of essays and articles on RC appearing between 1962 and 1973 appear in *The Human Situation* (Jackins, 1973) and, together with the two publications mentioned above, round out the basic theoretical knowledge necessary to become a functioning member of an RC community. Important theoretical developments that appeared between 1973 and early 1977 are contained in *The Upward Trend* (Jackins, 1978). In addition, separate RC journals and periodicals are published for the following populations: scientists, teachers, college and university workers, teachers of RC, those in health work, wage workers, young RCers, Jews, Asians, Blacks, parents, the handicapped, elders, Native Americans, men, Latinos, priests and nuns, Gays, mental health workers, women, and those interested in social change. Important means of communicating recent developments in theory have been the journals *Present Times,* a quarterly publication read by most all community members, and the *Reevaluation Counseling Teacher,* geared toward those teaching RC classes.

Books, journals, and related materials may be purchased through an RC teacher or may be ordered directly from Rational Island Publishers in Seattle. Theoretical and practical knowledge of RC, outside of beginning classes, is generally spread by means of one-to-one communication. Someone who is experienced discusses it with or offers a session to an interested individual. Sole reliance on written communication is discouraged, because Jackins has found that all too often the message is unwittingly distorted by the receiver. One-to-one communication seems to afford a personal touch that cuts through much of the potential distortion and enables the remaining false conceptions to be cleared up quickly.* Theoretical and practical

---

*It was partly for these reasons that Jackins refused to write this chapter and hoped I would refrain from doing so as well. In addition, he objects to RC being bracketed with schools of psychotherapy or human growth movements, believing strongly that it is distinctly different from any of these.

knowledge is also imparted through RC workshops. Several hundred, from a weekend to two weeks in length, are held each year over much of the world, particularly in the United States.

Similarities between RC and other approaches to counseling and psychotherapy have been discussed by Somers (1972). Among the approaches dealt with are Psychoanalysis, Gestalt Therapy, Existential Therapy, learning theory, and behavioral therapies. Schiff (1972) has discussed some of the social implications of RC. In particular, he notes that the current problems arising out of dependence on professional experts for psychotherapy, such as high cost and limited accessibility, could be circumvented since RC trains lay people to provide help for one another.

Experimentation in RC has primarily taken the form of action research. RC is characterized by its practicality and direct relevance to the counseling situation as well as its flexibility. Few of the studies have as yet been formally recorded. Furthermore, little in the way of true experimental research has been done since on-the-spot innovations have been favored over rigid controls.

## THEORY

### Human Nature

Basic to reevaluation counseling theory is its definition of human intelligence, which is seen as the ability to create, on the spot, new and rational responses that meet exactly the demands of each situation encountered (Jackins, 1965). This ability is assumed to be the trait that distinguishes humans from all other animals. When a new situation is encountered, the incoming information is compared to the existing store. Memories of successful responses in similar contexts are recalled and modifications are made to allow for differences. These elements are then used to construct the new response. Concomitantly, an evaluation process goes on during which incoming information, including feedback. from the results of the new response, is broken down into usable bits, categorized, and then filed away in the memory bank to be used in the generation of future responses.

RC makes a number of other assumptions about human nature. It maintains that people are born with a far greater capacity for intelligent behavior than anyone currently demonstrates. RC assumes that individuals considered to be geniuses have simply managed to avoid the damaging circumstances that have obstructed this capacity in others. RC also asserts that successful people innately take a keen pleasure in living and view life, with all its uncertainties and problems, as an exciting and challenging process rather than an anxiety-ridden or depressing struggle. Furthermore, it holds that humans have an inborn desire to cooperate as well as to love and be loved. Thus conflicts of interest are not seen as inevitable, but rather as events that could be entirely eliminated if people were free to live according to their true nature. Any deviation from this rational, happy, cooperative, and loving mode of functioning is viewed as a distortion of human nature and the result of some harmful experience.

At the core of Reevaluation Counseling's theory and practice is the distinction made by the above set of assumptions between people's intelligent or rational essence and irrational aspects added to it. This distinction rests upon the posited criterion for rational behavior—*flexibility*. Rational behavior is typified by its responsiveness to the environment. It is continually changing and adapting to fit the subtle nuances of each new situation that arises.

## Human Dysfunction

Irrational responses seem to be most reliably characterized by their rigid, preset character. A behavior is irrational when it is repeated over and over in the same manner regardless of changes that arise in the environment and regardless of unfortunate results that may ensue. Jackins noted that an activity taking place unawarely is not necessarily indicative of irrationality. A great deal of rational behavior takes place at an unaware level.

RC theory asserts the sole cause of human dysfunction to be the residual rigidity left by an experience of physical or emotional distress generated by a traumatic event. During such times one's ability to think rationally is suspended and incoming information, which is usually analyzed and filed away, remains unevaluated. It becomes lodged in the mind as an undigested mass consisting of a complete literal recording of everything that occurred during the distressing episode. This literal recording is termed a "distress pattern." When part of this pattern is referred to, the entire unit is recalled, and this in turn generates a fixed, predetermined pattern of behavior. Because of this all-or-none process, there is no way for a relevant bit of information to be combined with others to form an entirely new response. The net result is an overall decrease in intelligence and a predisposition to function inappropriately in certain settings.

This unevaluated or mis-stored unit of information generates rigid behavior whenever a new situation is met that is similar enough to the distressing episode to trigger its recall. Once triggered, it is as if one is compulsively forced to reenact the original experience. A destructive cycle is established because the information from the second situation also goes unevaluated, enlarges the distress pattern, and consequently leaves the individual predisposed to acting even more irrationally in the future.

When a particular set of mis-stored information is restimulated enough times, it becomes chronic and tends to fade from conscious awareness. Chronic distress patterns result in fixed attitudes and emotional tones and become manifest in such features as bodily tensions, tone of voice, posture, or facial expressions. The bulk of the irrational forces that impinge on people are said to be due to these chronic patterns.

The chronic patterns are carefully distinguished from latent patterns, which become evident only under certain conditions. For instance, an individual may exhibit compulsive anger only when confronted with inefficiency in others. On the other hand, an individual may seem to hold a grudge against the world, as would be the case for a person exhibiting a chronic pattern associated with anger. Even though similar in origin and effect, the overcoming of chronic patterns requires a great deal more initiative, skill, and persistence on the part of the counselor.

The loss of human potential due to this repression of flexible intelligence is extensive. Jackins believes that most adults judged "successful" by current cultural standards seldom operate at better than about 10 percent of their inherent capacity for intelligent joyful living. In other words, he believes that about 90 percent of such people's behavior is tied up in nonadaptive patterns of thinking, feeling, and responding. RC theory does not view this as a permanent loss. Flexible intelligence is said to simply retreat and lie dormant in a perfectly preserved state ready to be actualized under more favorable conditions.

As stated earlier, all distress experiences are seen as resulting from some unfavorable aspect of the environment. Society serves as a source of much trauma through irrational practices such as exploitation, prejudice, and war. However, the most significant factor in the transmission of human disturbance is asserted to be the distress well-meaning parents beset upon their children. Healthy behavior on the part of the infant may trigger a distress pattern in the adult, which in turn serves as a source of distress for the child. The human infant is particularly vulnerable to this insult due to a lack of physical and cognitive development and a prolonged dependency upon adults. In addition, dysfunction produced in this way is perpetuated by a social conditioning process in which individuals learn to avoid the discharge necessary for its removal. For instance, children are taught to choke back emotions and to alternatively act "brave" or "grown up." Physical or even chemical force may be resorted to as children are beaten or given drugs to "calm them down."

## Recovery

Perhaps the most significant assertion of RC theory is that humans have an inborn capacity to recover their occluded intelligence. This process is available immediately upon the termination of trauma or injury and automatically leads to a complete retrieval if allowed to operate.

Recovery consists of two major processes termed "discharge" and "reevaluation." Discharge consists of a release of tension, characterized by a series of emotions that proceed in a specified order beginning with what is viewed as the most severe of all emotions—grief. The discharge of grief is evidenced by tears and sobbing. After repeated release such discharge will eventually give way to the trembling, shivering, and cold perspiration that typify the release of fear. Intense laughter will follow, and is considered to be a lighter type of fear discharge. The expression of anger then comes to the fore as loud words or sounds, violent movements, and then laughter are exhibited. Following this, reluctant and then interested talking are engaged in to release the painful emotions associated with boredom (Jackins, 1962). Throughout the process of discharge a spontaneous recall and review of mis-stored information takes place. The individual may or may not be aware of this.

Physical hurts are also believed to involve a storing up of tension that seeks discharge. The tension associated with physical discomfort, however, is assumed usually to be surrounded by emotional distress that must be let go of before the underlying physical discomfort is available for release. Discharge of physical distress is outwardly manifested by yawning and sometimes stretching and scratching.

Jackins asserts that a great deal of firsthand experience with RC shows that this exact series of discharges occurs for virtually all humans, with possible exceptions being when the order is obscured or a certain means of release is blocked through conditioned resistance to a particular form of discharge.

During and following discharge an automatic rational evaluation of mis-stored information takes place. This reevaluation entails an analysis of distressing material from a logico-empirical vantage point. As analysis progresses the mass of unevaluated information is broken into usable bits, categorized, and stored away to be utilized in the creation of rational behavior. Jackins maintains that the degree to which distress patterns can be reevaluated in this manner is directly dependent upon the degree to which the preceding discharge process has been completed.

As a whole, the recovery process can be seen essentially as one of attaining a more and more accurate picture of reality as distorted notions are reevaluated and irrational beliefs given up. With a clearer view of reality it is assumed that one will become more consistently zestful, loving, and intelligent.

*Necessary Conditions for Recovery.* The necessary and sufficient condition for the initiation of the recovery process is said to be "the division of the client's free attention approximately equally between the distress on which discharge is being sought and material contradictory to the distress" (Jackins, 1973). Throughout both discharge and reevaluation the mere presence of an attentive counselor is often a significant factor serving to contradict the distress pattern. The effectiveness of the counselor's presence can be enhanced if he or she expresses caring for and validation of the client. This attitude is achieved to the extent that the counselor has discharged his or her own distress, has assimilated RC theory, and has made a decision to wholeheartedly commit him- or herself to the client's reemergence.

RC emphasizes that the attention given by a counselor should establish a special type of relationship. When counselors present themselves as authorities and attempt to analyze, understand, and in other ways do the client's thinking for them, this interferes with the process of recovery. The recovery process must involve a relationship between

peers—in which the client is essentially self-directing and has as full a possession of the theory as possible. Such a peer relationship is fostered by the co-counseling mode of RC in which counselor and client regularly reverse roles.

Additional elements are added to the relationship as the counselor begins to confront the client's chronic patterns. He or she becomes more active in identifying problem areas and helping the client achieve a direction of thought and action that will lead to discharge. Jackins discovered that such a direction needs to contradict exactly the contents of the chronic pattern and to be maintained vigilantly both in and out of sessions if the pattern is eventually to lose its grip.

RC contends that basing all of one's actions on reason rather than emotion is another necessary condition for overcoming the influences of past afflictions. That is particularly evident in the case of chronic patterns that, if one is to successfully overcome them, require the experiencing of much discomfort and a sense of continually going against the addictive pull of distress.

## METHODOLOGY

The foundation upon which all reevaluation counseling methodology is built is the caring and interested attention of the counselor. It is said to make up about 90 percent of good counseling and is transmitted first of all by listening well. This in itself is often enough to produce significant gains in rationality. Asking questions is the second primary mode of paying attention. It is not done for the usual purpose of gathering data but to assure the client of the counselor's interest and to guide his or her awareness back to the appropriate balance between the distress pattern and material contradictory to that pattern.

The techniques discussed below describe the practice of RC in only the most general way. The real essence of its methodology lies in creating, on the spot, a specific technique for each moment with a given client. While the theory and general guidelines for technique are important, they are no substitute for the continual vigilance required to treat each client and moment as totally unique entities.

## Spectrum of Techniques

An ever-present danger to the counseling process involves the restimulation of a pattern so significant that it engulfs all the client's free attention, leaving none available to observe the painful material from a secure and objective framework. Even though the client often appears outwardly calm at such a time, no further progress is possible. This danger is avoided by working within what is referred to as a spectrum of techniques. One begins at the end of the spectrum, using methods that demand very little of the client's free attention, and works toward techniques that demand progressively more. If overstimulation seems imminent one retreats to the previously effective method.

One of the first methods in the spectrum involves guiding the client's awareness to various aspects of the environment. It is believed that attention freed up in this way becomes available for rational thought with a resultant increase in the client's well-being. Next in the hierarchy are a series of remembering techniques also geared toward lighter material. The client is initially asked to recall successful or pleasant memories. He or she is then asked to move quickly through a series of types beginning with ordinary memories and continuing on to those of rational activity and then back to those of successes or pleasant experiences. This change in topics is suggested to avoid too much free attention from being soaked up by deeply distressing events that may be recalled. As more and more free attention is accumulated, the counselor moves on to a procedure in which the client is asked to randomly recall mildly upsetting events in a rapid fashion. This process prompts further releases of tension. When a sufficient accumulation of free attention is gained, it is possible to move on to a tech-

nique in which the client is asked to recall the earliest memory of a specific type and to progressively recall later ones of similar content up until the present. This process is repeated many times, during which time the client adds additional experiences to the list as he or she remembers them. A point will be reached when it may prove difficult for the client to remember the series of experiences any longer due to the discharge and reevaluation taking place and progressively freeing the memories from the grips of a particular distress pattern.

Some memories, rather than fading, become more and more vivid. These experiences involve a great deal of tension and necessitate the use of thorough discharge techniques that differ from the above in that discharge usually involves greater amounts of painful emotion and is persisted in for longer periods. To accomplish this the counselor waits for clues from the client that indicate whether or not emotionally charged material is being discussed. The client's attention is then redirected to this point and discharge is encouraged. Encouragement may be provided simply through the counselor's aware attention and a warm direct gaze, or by holding the client's hands in a warm and relaxed manner. After a time the client's attention will tend to stray. It is up to the counselor to persistently bring it back to the particular thought or phrase that prompts release until no more discharge is left.

A client may compulsively, but unintentionally, block discharge from occurring. These blocks are referred to as *control patterns* and consist, in part, of observable behavior at the time of resistance. Since such blocks are employed in a repetitive and fixed way, one means of breaking through them is to ask the client to act in a manner that interferes with the patterned aspects of their behavior. For instance, if a client is slumped low in a chair and exhibits a deep frown indicative of a depressive control pattern, one might ask him or her to sit upright and look as if he or she were enthusiastic about life.

As he or she discusses the experience of doing this, discharge is likely to follow.

The techniques described so far have been those useful in overcoming latent distress patterns, with the counselor guiding part of the client's attention to the distressing material. Chronically restimulated patterns require the counselor to direct enough attention away from such material for the client to establish a rational and secure vantage point from which to work. In addition, chronic patterns necessitate going beyond the permissive methods described above and becoming a good deal more active and directive.

When a pattern becomes chronic an individual may no longer see it as a problem or as an entity separate from him- or herself. Consequently the counselor needs to take an active role in watching for and identifying them as foreign elements. Identification is accomplished by noticing rigidities such as a monotone voice or fixed facial expression. The next task for the counselor is to develop a counterdirection—a way in which the client can challenge and contradict the pattern at all times. For instance, countering a chronic depressive pattern might involve one forcing the client to become more active, speak in more positive terms, and challenge the negative thoughts that arise. Once such a course of action is established and the counselor is able to get the client to commit him- or herself to it, it must still be implemented.

The chronic pattern persistently pushes the client to forget the proper course of action or creates confusion. Such hindrances derive from the chronic pattern's tendency to soak up the client's free attention and leave none with which to obtain an objective vantage point. The counter to this force, and part of all counterdirections, is an effort to think rationally at all times. The role of the counselor during this phase is to join the client in ruthlessly attacking the pattern while at the same time providing him or her with love and support. The client needs to be reminded often of the direction against the pattern. Special aids may be used such as written reminders or publicly announcing the chosen course of action. To further counter the pattern's tendency to cause confusion and forgetting, the client is encouraged to draw up a set of clearly spelled-out goals. These goals are designed to guide a course of action affecting all levels (self, family, mankind, etc.) and are both immediate and long-range.

Among the many possible counterdirections are several that have proven to be close to universal directions for countering all patterns of distress. One involves a process of unconditional self-validation. This direction is particularly effective in the battle against a chronic pattern's ability to confuse and distort because it is clearly defined, well mapped out, and can be understood logically prior to a commitment to it. The distinction between the person, wholesome and good in every respect, and the pattern parasitic upon that person clarifies that the real person behind the smokescreen of irrationality is unreproachable.

The details of this ameliorative procedure involve the client expressing unlimited self-approval in word, tone of voice, posture, and facial expression to him- or herself and others. Doubts as to the validity of the statements are inevitably triggered, at which point the client is encouraged to persist in spite of his or her feelings. When actual self-invalidating thoughts are encountered, the client is to force him- or herself to examine them and contradict them aloud. This in itself may effectively challenge the validity of the negative thought; however, the client usually needs to continue on to compute the exact opposite of the statement. For instance, an individual might catch him- or herself thinking he or she is hopelessly slow and inefficient. This thought would then be turned around by declaring oneself to be remarkably efficient and quick. Discharge frequently follows such declarations.

Whether working against a chronic or a latent pattern, the key danger for client as well as counselor is suspension of critical thought. Once thinking stops RC assumes one is likely to succumb to old patterns.

Maintaining the required critical thought demands continual vigilance and the tolerance of much discomfort. Jackins notes, however, that there is satisfaction despite the discomfort in knowing one is approaching a highly valued goal.

The primary method for relieving physical distress is to focus efforts upon discharging the associated emotional tension. Guiding the client's attention directly to the somatic pain is to be avoided since it may simply increase it. A complete release of emotion will automatically lead to the yawning indicative of physical discharge, at which point the counselor should continue to direct the client's attention to the thought or phrase that triggered the yawning, perhaps for hours, until it has been persisted with as long as possible.

RC makes use of group counseling as an adjunct to co-counseling. Groups function by giving each member an equal amount of time in front of the rest to do whatever brings emotional release. Discharge and reevaluation is accelerated in this context, possibly because the effectiveness of the attention of each member combines with others in an additive fashion.

Co-counseling classes are an integral part of the RC approach as well. Through regular attendance, co-counseling pairs are able to sustain a high level of motivation and an effective direction. Without it, perspective is often lost and distress patterns begin to form the basis for decisions leading counselor and client into a dead end. It has also been found that these classes, and in turn individual co-counseling sessions, are enhanced when they exist within a strong local RC community organization. The community setting within which RC operates has proven to be an important aspect of its method.

## APPLICATIONS

It is the long-range objective of Reevaluation Counseling to reach everyone, including the most distressed individuals. At present, however, resources are insufficient to deal with severe disorders. In an effort to establish the necessary assets, RC communities are limiting membership to those who can become effective co-counselors with a relatively small investment of time and energy. Within this limitation, the effectiveness of RC has transcended national and cultural boundaries.

RC has found an important application in assisting individuals in their fight against social oppression. It does so by helping them emerge from rigid ways of responding and thereby becoming more effective in their struggle. Jackins was first led to his support of liberation groups when he realized that release from the harmful effects of one's past was not enough. It became clear to him that so much distress was being acquired anew each day due to the irrational ways of society that these forces would have to be faced as well.

The first major inroad for an application of RC principles in this area came when Jackins discovered that the maintenance of all oppression seemed to be rooted in one particular distress pattern. He said its content consists of the view that "situations which oppress us are beyond our powers to change and . . . we must 'adjust' to them" (Jackins, 1978, p. 25). This belief is said to obscure people's natural inclination to take the initiative and seek solutions to life's difficulties. With the discovery of this view, it became clear to Jackins that the route to liberation from socially oppressive forces was through individual liberation from patterned helplessness.

RC theory and techniques have also been successfully applied to the classroom learning situation. Along with assuming a vast untapped amount of intelligence, RC posits an inborn thirst for learning that is also blocked by environmental distress. In most classrooms these qualities remain obscured because no provision is made for discharge. Students arrive in a depressed, anxious, or hostile state and often remain this way with little free attention left to digest new information. Worse yet, many teachers place new distresses upon those already present by failing to recognize the difference between the student, with his or her natural desire to learn, and the pattern that throws up a resistance. Consequently the externally visible pattern is met with attempts to manipulate and control, while the real student behind them goes unnoticed.

According to RC, the key job of the teacher is to get students to the point where they are relaxed and feeling good. It is believed that this can only be accomplished through effective use of the discharge and reevaluation process. It should be noted that a severely distressed student cannot be handled in the classroom. However, if time is set aside for those who can, students spontaneously will begin to seek out new information.

A good deal can be accomplished in terms of promoting the necessary affect during the learning process itself. For instance, chronic feelings of loneliness can be disputed through a teacher's warm touch and caring gaze. Common sources of distress, such as invalidation, can be avoided by making students feel loved for who they are and by drawing them out on their strong points rather than instructing through criticism. Furthermore, it is recommended that grading systems be significantly revised or, better yet, entirely done away with. Grades are viewed merely as additional sources of invalidation. The message of grades to those who don't excel is that they are defective in some way. Low grades also imply that their recipients are responsible and therefore blameworthy for their shortcomings. RC asserts that motivating students through such a system of honors and demerits is unnecessary since more than enough inducement is provided by the learning situation itself.

Education can be further expedited by having learners teach learners. Just as counseling works best when there is a relationship between peers, learning seems to thrive in a similar context.

RC is also involved in the area of relationship counseling. Initially progress is more difficult with this application due to the complexity of the interaction that may develop. Instead of one distress pattern, there are now two or more to keep track of, which at times set one another off, creating a chain reaction that is difficult to diffuse. It is frequently necessary to employ a neutral party, acting as a buffer against such mutual restimulation. This can be accomplished by enforcing certain rules, such as having participants direct potentially restimulative comments to this neutral person, or by obtaining a commitment from each to hear the partner out. The use of a neutral party is viewed as a temporary phase to be ended as soon as the participants have discharged enough to successfully avoid mutual restimulation in the future. At this point the regular rules of co-counseling are followed. Marital partners who have learned to co-counsel effectively in this manner can begin to include their children. Small group sessions in which members express unlimited appreciation of one another are often effective in this situation.

A further application of RC can be made in relation to chemical dependency. RC assumes the roots of such dependency to be no different from those of any other form of rigid and compulsive behavior. During ingestion of the chemical the body is hurt. As with experiences of emotional trauma, the information coming in at the time remains unevaluated and is stored as a complete literal recording of everything that went on at the time. This recording of distress compels an individual to reenact the distress experience when stimulated by circumstances similar to the original hurtful situation. In this way the alcoholic or the heroin addict is compulsively forced to continue intake of such substances.

What leads those dependent upon chemicals to begin ingestion in the first place is the same factor that leads to addictions unrelated to chemicals, such as compulsive procrastination or aggressive outbursts. In response to the pain of successive restimulation of distress patterns, one is pushed to seek out anything that can provide an immediate deadening of the painful feelings, regardless of the long-term consequences. Chemicals often provide such a short-term "escape" along with the damage they instill. Since chemical dependency both arises from and is maintained by processes similar to those involved with other types of dysfunction, their treatment is handled in similar ways.

Jackins also discovered that RC may be utilized as a type of first aid for physical injuries. Typically any somatic disturbance acquires a shell of emotional tension that must be discarded prior to the commencement of any physical discharge. This, however, is not the case for a certain period shortly after an injury has been received. Apparently it takes some time for a layer of emotional distress to form. Before this occurs it is possible to focus attention directly on the physical discomfort as well as a review of the actual circumstances of the injury and thereby initiate discharge. If one refocuses upon this material a sufficient number of times and experiences it fully enough, there ensues a total and permanent elimination of pain as well as a hastening of the healing process (Jackins, 1962).

## CASE EXAMPLE

The following case history is adapted from a firsthand report. Identifying data are altered.

The client (C) was a young woman whose father (F) had been hospitalized repeatedly for manic depression and for attempted suicide over a period of 13 years. F was first hospitalized when C was seven years of age. At this time C began to feel guilty for not having prevented his "illness." In addition, she grew to hate her father and eventually lost all respect for him. C became increasingly inhibited in her self-expression for fear of releasing painful emotions that had welled up inside. She suspected that if she did so she too would be labeled crazy.

When first exposed to Reevaluation Counseling's optimistic view of human nature, C became hopeful of being freed from some of her pain by acquiring a new, more rational view of her father and of her past experiences with him. She started co-counseling and for the first time began to express a great deal of anger and grief over her father's condition. As this process continued she began sharing experiences about F with old friends, which she had previously been afraid to do.

Counseling eventually led to a clarification of a chronic pattern whose content generated in C a sense of powerlessness. Even though she had opened up a great deal, she was continuously worried that at some point her discharges would be so heavy she would be labeled as too "sick" to remain in the RC community. As more and more of her intellect became free for rational thought, C began to understand the roots of this chronic fear and its relationship to her complete rejection of her father. She came to see that her fear of being labeled crazy came out of a reaction to culturally oppressive forces that tend to leave people feeling hopelessly stuck as "sick" individuals once labeled as such. This fear also led her, in an effort to affirm her sanity to herself and others, to maintain a view of her father as a destroyed person.

Through RC group counseling she encountered others who had experienced the "mental breakdown" of a parent and consequently became less ashamed of it and increasingly willing to face the associated distress and to share it with others. During one of these sessions a counterdirection was discovered through which she could contradict her view of her father as a sick man as well as her fear of complete disclosure. It involved validating and accepting so-called "sick" individuals in thought and action and working to view them as essentially good and wholesome humans who have been victimized by deeply distressing experiences.

Shortly after committing to this direction, the client received word that her father had become disruptive in his current place of residence and was being asked to move. This meant a possible return to the hospital and restimulated in C fears of another suicide attempt by F. Furthermore, she desired to be close and at the same time feared being drawn into F's irrationality. With her co-counselor she was able to discharge some of her fear of his failing again, and to plan for an effective means of being supportive of F, while maintaining the previously committed to direction. This meant that C would have to continually look for and validate the real father that lay behind the patterns. Rather than criticize, she would need to draw him out on his strengths as well as act against her desire to take responsibility for his well-being, since this too was seen as a form of invalidation by reinforcing a belief in his inadequacy.

C's counselor decided to offer additional support by going along during her first visit with F. During this meeting the counselor's insights and comments at times disrupted C's tendency to do too much for her father and at other times validated the way in which C was supporting and appreciating her father. Through this process the client came to see her father in a new light. She noticed his genuine interest in people and the environment, how well he had done in managing to survive and get support, and came to believe more in his capacity to free himself from his distress. F, in turn, began to feel safe enough to disclose facts about himself he had not mentioned to his daughter before.

With the support of his daughter, F has managed to avoid rehospitalization and is now living on his own and caring for himself. In the meantime, C has continued to distinguish person from pattern and keep the father she loves in sight. As a result she has been able to maintain an unconditional acceptance of F and his life style; this in turn has left her feeling more accepting of herself. In addition C has since become socially active in combating oppressive forces associated with mental illness.

## SUMMARY

Jackins maintains that reevaluation counseling theory is a scientifically rigorous system. It grew inductively with conclusions being drawn only from the results of firsthand experience. In addition, a deductive structure was developed to ensure logical consistency among the basic assumptions of RC. It takes a dim view of eclecticism through which individuals often gather techniques and theorems without regard for logical consistency, firm empirical checks, and subsequent generalizability. RC is not interested in developing a theory and practice that works for a certain subset of the population. RC is attempting to develop an approach that will be effective with all humans, in all situations, at all times.

One of RC's most important assumptions involves its view of human nature. People are said to be born with vast amounts of intelligence, a feeling of zest, and a desire to love and be loved. Dysfunction is not seen as a bad side, but rather as a foreign element parasitic upon an essentially wholesome being. This foreign element is different in origin and nature from all human qualities. It originates from experiences of emotional or physical hurt that cause the information being received at the time to be deposited in the form of a rigid pattern. The nature of all emotional dysfunction, of every type and degree, consists essentially of the effect produced when one is compulsively forced to meet a new situation with fixed and compulsive behavior generated by this rigid pattern of information. A compulsive reenactment occurs when a new situation is encountered similar to the original one.

RC also maintains that people do not have to turn to "authorities" for cures or answers. The processes necessary for recovery are all part of their innate makeup. The only place for outside assistance is in setting up the proper conditions so that curative powers can spontaneously take over in the form of discharge and reevaluation. The client remains in full control of the process, doing his own thinking and arriving at his own solutions. The counselor relates to the client as a peer. The counselor may be directive only in relation to the dysfunctional entities, never toward the person behind them.

By viewing all forms of irrationality as foreign to man's nature and having definite causes and cures, one is led to another important assumption in RC. Dysfunction, in any form or degree, is not something people must learn to accept as part of life. It is believed that such misfortune can be completely and permanently overcome.

RC is distinct in the range of responsibilities it has taken on. Involvement is not limited to personal liberation, and fundamental changes needed in society are not viewed as a distant or impossible goal. It sees personal growth and profound social change as integral parts of the same process, and is actively promoting progress in both arenas. Furthermore, Jackins believes that RC may have the tools to conquer all human irrationality and to bring about one of the most fundamental revolutions that has ever occurred.

## REFERENCES

Jackins, H. *Fundamentals of co-counseling manual.* Seattle: Rational Island Publishers, 1962.

Jackins, H. *The human side of human beings.* Seattle: Rational Island Publishers, 1965.

Jackins, H. *The human situation.* Seattle: Rational Island Publishers, 1973.

Jackins, H. *The upward trend.* Seattle: Rational Island Publishers, 1978.

Schiff, T. Reevaluation counseling: Social implications. *Journal of Humanistic Psychology,* 1972, **12,** 58–70.

Somers, B. Reevaluation therapy: Theoretical framework. *Journal of Humanistic Psychology,* 1972, **12,** 42–57.

# CHAPTER 57

# *Self-Image Therapy*

CAMILLA M. ANDERSON

*I have a special fondness for this chapter, not only because it was the first one to come in, but because the writer, unknown to me except through her writings and her letters, seems to be a most unusual person. She deals courageously and sensibly with many problems in life, including a retarded daughter, about whom she wrote a book.*

*The ideas that Camilla Anderson expresses form a complete theory of personality and psychotherapy. The reader will have an opportunity to become immersed in an in-depth system of thought developed over many years.*

*One can feel Anderson's repressed anger at a world that just doesn't appear to value her contributions, her simple and obvious approach to life, her very logical explanation of the human condition and how distortions can be dealt with. Her ideas seem to follow those of another great woman, Karen Horney, who also, in my judgment, has been unfairly treated by the "psychological establishment." What struck me strongly was Anderson's view that people with so-called feelings of inferiorities really are people with grandiosity—a simple truth, but one that I had personally never grasped until I read the following exciting and extremely wise chapter.*

Self-Image Therapy is a simple yet comprehensive system of psychodynamics applicable to any person throughout a lifetime. It accounts for the development of the person's self-image and shows the role of the self-image in all behavior and feelings. A person's self-image begins to be developed soon after birth and is the product of surviving despite helplessness. From the beginning, interpersonal operations are paramount and are an integral part of all assumptions developed and, therefore, of all behavior.

The system encompasses the becoming of an individual as well as his or her being. The threat to survival associated with helplessness is the factor that leads to development of one's moral value system, and this, in turn, becomes one's "road map" for living. Surviving is accomplished with the help of others, and the value system is evidence that

all assumptions, all actions, all feelings, all values are developed in an interpersonal setting with survival as the goal.

A person's unique psyche is his or her reservoir of moral value judgments set up by experience in the interpersonal world. Psyche and self-image are synonymous and relate to security-insecurity experiences. It is that with which one identifies. Any threat to one's value system is experienced as threat to survival.

Because the self-image is bigger than life—grandiose—being cut down to size is experienced as threat to survival, and it sets the stage for anxiety and stress symptoms. Reconstitution—healing—means either removal of the stress or acceptance of the new and deflated but more realistic self-image. The business of living encompasses establishing or becoming, living out, protecting, defending, enhancing, and reconstituting one's self-image.

## HISTORY

Self-Image theory and Therapy was not developed or written "forthright and out of hand," but took many years aborning.

I came into psychiatry in New York in 1931, a time when there was a near religious fanaticism and fervor in the espousal of Freudian psychodynamics. To deviate from the "true religion" represented a foolhardiness that amounted to defiance of God. In 1934 I moved from New York, the heart of Freudian territory, to Pennsylvania, where there were other gods. Up to that time I had scarcely been aware that there were competing faiths. Gradually I developed a sense of my right to question, to doubt, and to challenge. Before then I had believed that, had I been more competent, I would surely find that my deviant impressions showed lack of maturity, and the Freudian system would be vindicated. No longer, however, did I have to be apologetic over disagreeing.

In 1941 I married, and this was, without doubt, the beginning of my personal growth and emancipation. The stresses I felt and the symptoms I developed as a result did not seem to follow the dynamics I had been taught, and they did not respond to the techniques I had used faithfully on my patients. I became aware that whereas resentment, stemming from frustration of felt entitlements, was an important factor in my case, Freudian literature did not even mention this.

This period marked the beginning of my professional growth, when I dared openly to challenge and disagree with those who had been accepted authorities. I still had no thoughts or expectations of developing any "system," but was content to note whatever I observed. I continued to be amazed at how many of my patients were like me, caught in a web of resentment and frustrated entitlement, and fortunately, this provided a framework for relieving their stresses, but it had nothing to do with developing a system.

My first clear move toward presenting a new framework was in 1950, when I published a paper (Anderson, 1950a) and later the same year a book (1950b) that recognized that assumptions were derived from experiences in a two-party system, and that the foundation of all behavior is interpersonal assumptions. A new concept was emerging that was reflected in all I was seeing clinically and in my psychotherapeutic efforts.

I no longer made any pretense of being Freudian, and I found that I seemed to understand patients as well or better than most other therapists I knew. I had good results in psychotherapy through using my concepts of structure and function (two-party assumptions) as laid down early in life, and through dealing with entitlements and resentments as they showed up.

Through the years when Self-Image Therapy was growing and developing, I knew of no way that I could hasten the process or steer it in its course. I simply used the insights I developed, with no idea of whether there would be a next step or where it might lie or where it would take me. It was obvious to me that all assumptions regarding behavior had an actor and a reactor component—they were interpersonal phenomena—and that, therefore, disturbances were possible in either the area of the action or the reaction (1950a). Sometimes as I watched myself I would be the actor; other times, I would be the reactor.

It was not until later, in the 1960s, that it dawned on me that while I had accumulated a host of the components of a system or theoretical framework, I had only dealt with the mechanics. The final detail left out was the dynamics, which would hold the components together and make it all into a single piece.

Then I made the discovery—startling to me—that the central core or the dynamic drive in all behavior was simply the drive to survive and to maintain oneself. This was the integrating as well as the dynamic factor in the whole picture. It was involved in the formation of the psyche or self-image; it was the theme in the daily application of the system in real life; it was clearly operative in the occurrence of stress feelings and symptoms, when surviving was threatened; and it related to psychotherapy when a model was needed to help in the face of an unrealistic and malfunctioning self-image. It became a tool to use when there was need for exploration and understanding, no matter at what stage of development or type of functioning or malfunctioning one had. Understanding the survival drive was as important when dealing with the psyche as when dealing with the soma.

An interesting aspect of this long and leisurely search and exploration was that I had less and less need for what is commonly known as "the eclectic aproach," because there was contained within the self-image system itself the basis for guiding and comprehending. It provided me with a North Star. Once seeing this, everything else followed automatically; it eliminated any confusion.

There were, however, areas that clearly had to be omitted from inclusion in its applicability, for there were people who did not develop any comprehensible or dependable psychic structure; they did not behave in a manner compatible with a belief in the overall guiding presence of a psyche or a value system; nor was it possible with them to utilize the schema I had elaborated in doing psychotherapy. But such people were in the minority, and fortunately for me and my continued growth and practical operations, I was familiar with the total picture of MBD (minimal brain damage or dysfunction), an organically determined deficit that is far more common than most people have been led to believe (Anderson, 1963). Those who have suffered this handicap, which shows up in all areas—the physical, the intellectual and the emotional—do not follow the usual patterns of behavior, and it is impossible in dealing with them to make use of the concepts I had developed for doing psychotherapy.

Fortunately, it is possible to understand the nature of MBD and to make fairly accurate observations and predictions, so one is not at the mercy of guesswork, and one can stand on solid ground even here. Anyone who proposes to work in a therapeutic manner with patients needs to be familiar with MBD—its history of development, its characteristic symptomatology, and its usual nature (Anderson, 1972a)—so as to avoid the frustration of trying to do analytic psychotherapy with a person incapable of carrying out the details of such therapy—that is, integrating.

I have come to view all behavior as either an expression of the psychodynamic self-preservation drive or an expression of the neurologic inadequacies of MBD. One must have different expectations of the two, and the manner of "doing therapy" with the two groups is widely different.

During the 1970s there was little or no change in the nature of the theoretical framework (Anderson, 1971) of the self-image system, but clinical experience has reinforced the validity of my concepts. I feel no need to search further, but rather I use what is already obvious. The system now seems to be completed. Everything one needs for understanding and dealing with behavior is here. Others may add to the mechanics from time to time, but the dynamics are provided.

## CURRENT STATUS

As far as I know, no one else is using Self-Image Therapy. This, in my estimation, does not derive from any significant theoretical defect, but from a combination of factors that I will attempt to make clearer. To do this I must share a number of personal experiences.

During the 1950s I was a member of an active teaching community (University of Utah College of Medicine and University of Utah School of Social Work, 1948–1957). I was making good strides in elaborating my system, trying to develop enough interest in it to promote its use for critical checking. As I began saying openly that my system and Freudian theory differed (Anderson, 1950), I was literally shut out from the Department of Psychiatry and told I could not return until I was willing to concede that my concepts were not unique and that there were no differences between my concepts and the Freudian system. Students were no longer assigned to me, opportunities for teaching were deleted, and in every possible way I was excluded.

Because at that time (1957) the University of Oregon Medical School was looking for a new person to head their Department of Psychiatry, and because Oregon was my school, I placed my name before their faculty appointing committee as a candidate. After waiting for months I finally called the chairman of the committee (who also happened to be a classmate of mine in medical school), asking when I might expect a response to my letter. He replied, "Camilla, we would not even consider appointing a woman." That ended my hope that I could develop this position into a place for presenting and testing my theory.

After almost 10 years in Salt Lake City, in 1958 I accepted a position as Director of the Outpatient Department of the Oregon State Hospital. It was a very comfortable position. While I continued to explore, write, and publish, it was obvious that to promulgate new ideas one must be tied into a "machine," that is, to a teaching institution that has sufficient clout so that it would be easy to get publishers, and there would be enough momentum in the machine for both push and reinforcement. No matter how good—or bad—ideas are, unless they see the light of day, they haven't much chance to survive.

Oregon State Hospital was a teaching hospital, but it was in the backwater. Few people associated with it were making any great waves, and the new head of the Department of Psychiatry at the University of Oregon Medical School was so involved in his own progress and programs that he had no time either to listen or to push someone else's ideas. I had a couple good critics on my staff, but no one was capable of assisting in getting my ideas before the public.

Nine of my papers were published by the *Journal of the American Medical Women's Association*, but it was not a good place to publish if one were looking for acceptance by the national psychiatric community, for it is not expected that this journal will present anything new or significant in the field of psychodynamics.

The emptying of the state hospitals and closing the state's clinics was the direct cause of my leaving Oregon. My next clinical experience was in California, where I had accepted the position of Chief Psychiatrist at the California Institution for Women at Frontera, then the largest prison for women in the world. It was a good place to expand my insights into criminal behavior and to share my concepts with staff, but it was remarkably isolated and this obstructed wider acceptance of my concepts. Nevertheless, I continued to write and to teach wherever there was an opportunity, and it is quite likely that there are still some individuals using my concepts, without being aware that these are new or different.

In 1971 I published a brief summary of my psychodynamic concepts. Since that time most of my published works have dealt with MBD or with the current status and plight of psychiatry (Anderson 1972a,b, 1973a,b, 1974).

In 1966 I wrote a chapter, "Assumption-Centered Psychotherapy," for a book on various systems of psychotherapy (Anderson, 1973b). In 1977 a priest living in San Diego wrote a doctoral thesis entitled "The Self-Esteem Theory of Human Motivation" (Campbell, 1977), and he wrote me that I had arrived at the same conclusions his research had led him to. From time to time individuals have been impressed with the validity and usefulness of my concepts, but no one in a position of influence has made self-image theory a useful tool for teaching or for therapy. Also, psychiatry has had minimal interest in psychodynamics for many years, while it has been busy developing new drugs to change behavior.

In 1978 I requested permission to present a formal course to be titled "An Alternative System of Psychodynamics" to any interested members of the American Psychiatric

Association at its annual meeting in Chicago, May 1979. My request was rejected. If my concepts fall by the wayside, "at least" I tried. It could be that my presentation has not been adequately clear, or that my concepts are so different from those psychiatrists are used to that they find it difficult to tie them to anything familiar. The problem of Self-Image Therapy is not its complexity but rather its simplicity.

## THEORY

I am seemingly as oblivious of "personality" in my theoretical formulations as I used to find Freudian theory oblivious of such things as "entitlements" and resulting "resentments." What replaces personality is "self-image," the total construct an individual uses to guide and determine behavior and reactions.

Each person's self-image is as unique, as detailed, and as faceted as the physical self-image. Like the body, the self-image is made up of an endless array of organized parts called assumptions, which relate to both action and reaction; that is, they are always two-party. They concern every conceivable aspect of behavior a person can be involved in (Anderson 1950, 1957).

By the time children start school they have accumulated enough beliefs—assumptions—to have a reasonably complete road map for living. They are the things people take so much for granted that they are unaware of their existence. Nevertheless, these assumptions about self, others, and life guide people in their choices and selections; they determine what will and will not be done, what people anticipate from others, what provides security and what is seen as dangerous. People acquire these concepts and conclusions out of their own experiences, just because they were there.

Because of self-image each individual operates almost unconsciously or automatically in all familiar settings. A person's total functioning, like his or her assumptions, is or-ganized into consistent and reliable patterns that are so completely identical with self that for all intents and purposes self-image *is* the self. People now can count on the person as well as on his or her behavior to be according to that structure. Part of the therapist's task is to become aware of repetitive patterns (structures) the patient operates according to, and to help him or her see them and thus to see the self.

Whatever concepts the person takes for granted—what he or she believes—was not arbitrarily or even casually laid down or incorporated into his or her self-image; rather it was the product of that person's experiences in his or her particular world. Likewise, every assumption is associated with a value judgment, determined by experiences in a world of significant people, and each experience was given a value depending on the security/insecurity or danger/well-being factor that resulted. For example, in my world, eating heartily was associated with parental approval—*good;* cleaning my plate—*good;* waste of any kind—*bad;* working hard—*good;* carrying my own weight—*good;* being a nuisance or bother—*bad;* having good posture—*good;* carrying gossip—*bad.*

Assumptions are the building blocks of a person's makeup and therefore of behavior. Included are reactions or responses to everything seen or done. Assumptions guide the individual, determine what he or she will and will not do. They determine what the person expects or anticipates from self and others in any situation. They also establish attitudes.

Every action is associated in the person's mind with some degree of good or bad, right or wrong. One develops a hierarchy of value judgments that derive from experiences. Values tell one that certain behaviors and things are good and others are bad. Behaviors and things, however, are not merely black or white, but more or less good or bad according to one's particular value schema. This is of great importance in determining choices and attitudes and in warding off guilt.

Of major importance in all behavior is a

hierarchy of values schema, which determines one's *at least*'s. A person may do things ordinarily not acceptable to one's value system *provided* one is sure to do or not to do something worse in one's schema than the prohibited thing; for example, I may have done *this* bad thing, but "at least" I did not do *that*. One feels no guilt as long as one's *at least*'s are intact. One may ward off guilt by following a code—by adhering to compulsive *have to*'s; by keeping at least's ready and available; by moving from the role of actor to the role of reactor, and thus feeling justified. Preventing guilt is a constant and major occupation of everyone (Anderson, 1950, 1957).

Everything a person experiences is classified into actions and reactions, or the role he or she or others is playing at any moment. If one does a bad thing as an actor, it is occasion for guilt, but when one does the same thing as a reactor—in response to someone else's behavior—it is assessed as justified.

Another way of making classifications, and therefore knowing what to do, is by *role*. Everyone falls into a variety of groups (Anderson, 1957) determined by age, sex, relationship, physical state, occupation, incidental activities, in-group or out-group status, religion, political persuasion, and so forth. There are an infinite number of these possible roles. Every role implies a whole constellation of related assumptions that determine how others must behave and what is expected.

Assumptions regarding role behavior are acquired early and are the basic determinants of behavior in similar situations. Even young children know what is to be done in all manner of interpersonal situations. Autistics are the only people who apparently do not have such a handy reference guide available to them. This deficiency appears to be due to their inability to retain concepts, which makes classification impossible.

Every assumption concerning role behavior is associated with a moral judgment. *Right-wrong, good-bad* labels are attached to every action and reaction, and the degree of rightness or wrongness is fairly clear to the person. People characteristically behave in ways accounted by them as right or justified, because that was the safe way for them to behave as children. It was safe because significant people approved of it—there was no pain or penalty—and they were "good." Past approbation is the basic reason why most people approve of themselves and feel satisfied with their manner of functioning. Attitudes and values do not change readily.

Contrary to common belief, *no person has a poor self-image!* Shedding this assumption is of major importance if we would do psychotherapy. We never need to build up a good self-image, because everyone already has one. It is never a poor self-image that causes people to behave inappropriately. On the contrary, it is our grandiose self-image—our bigger-than-life self-concept—that leads to difficulties. To help the person understand this is part of the goal of the therapist.

We have our grandiose self-image because of several factors: When our self-image was forming—in our infancy, when we were most helpless—we were the center of attention for important people. We were adept at controlling them and we took our power for granted. We cried and they came running. The fact that we survived is evidence of our success. Next we are the beloved children of very important people, and this alone was sufficient to make one believe in one's importance. Third, when our self-image was forming, everything we did was accounted special, both by ourselves and by the people significant to us whose opinions we valued.

Finally, we have still another basis for our private sense of specialness. We have arrived at value judgments remarkably akin to those of our significant people, and accounted *by them* as right values. The more right one's opinions, judgments, and values are, the greater is one's right to high self-esteem. It is the threat of low esteem from significant others that forces children to adopt "right" values and makes them acceptable in their specific interpersonal world. The conclusion from all this is that our self-image inevitably has a high value; it is *never* low.

When people insist that they have low self-esteem, the truth is they really have excessive expectations of themselves. Others may have faults and blemishes, but they do not permit themselves to have any. What looks at first like low self-esteem is actually grandiosity: *I must be perfect—without blame or defect (i.e., God) or I cannot tolerate myself. I may look only at my inadequacies, never at my assets. I must never let myself see that this is what I am doing. I may not see how I am playing God by striving for perfection, but only that I failed.*

It is common for us to attribute to others a low self-esteem because we see them as inferior, and we think they have reason to have low self-esteem. The fact that people attribute to others low self-esteem does not bring about such self-devaluation on their part. Instead it brings resentment. The devaluated person feels he is being short-changed, that he is not getting what he is entitled to, such as appreciation or recognition of quality. Everyone has his or her own private values, and these give each person the "right" to think well of him- or herself. Whenever one finds resentment, there cannot be a poor self-image.

Consequently, people at all levels—socially, intellectually, economically—have a good self-image. This is the basis of all our interpersonal operations. It dictates our functioning, our assertiveness, our self-pity, and our reluctance to be challenged. We hesitate to allow ourselves to be "put on the line." We avoid situations in which we might not show up well; we isolate ourselves from competition, or we find other ways of preserving our *amour propre*. Everything we do is calculated to preserve our pride system intact, to maintain our grandiose self-image. The primary driving force in life is preserving this grandiose self-image.

In the Orient this is called "saving face," and is seen as basic and essential. When pride is threatened and our grandiose self-image

is endangered, we feel anxious, and the experience is stressful. Anxiety results whenever one feels a threat to one's self-image. Hurt pride is anxiety provoking, and such tensions frequently result in occurrence of psychological and physical symptoms. Whenever one finds decompensation symptoms, one can assume that there has been threat to the person's self-image, that is, to his or her pride.

Several well-defined feelings are possible in any situation. If people have been following their code regarding behavior, they will tend to feel comfortable with their behavior. This is the usual way for everyone to feel. If they have followed their code, their value system, but did not get the anticipated interpersonal results, they may feel confused and helpless. Helplessness is the "mother" of rage or depression. They may also feel resentful of those who let them down.

It not infrequently happens that a person's assumptions set him or her up for trouble—for example, smug arrogance, clear assumptions regarding entitlements, when the appropriate attitude would be awareness of "contingent privilege." The therapist needs to be perceptive of such grandiose assumptions and help bring them to the light of day, even before they have given discernible trouble or symptoms. Many comfortable people are, in fact, "sick"—that is, quite unrealistic.

Since neither the patient nor the therapist deals with total pictures at any time, but only with segments or partials, there is never a need or even a possibility to see "the whole." It is sufficient in therapy to see that part with which we are dealing, and this implies only that one discovers—or uncovers—the specific and limited assumptions each person needs to deal with in this particular situation, which lie at the root of the present discomfort. The better one understands one's assumptions, the better able one can be to change behavior and thus avoid trouble.

The self-image therapist deals with the here and now. The therapist is aware that present actions or feelings are always determined by past experiences, when asumptions were first laid down. The whole of this interplay is generally not clearly visible to the patient, so the therapist deals always with less than conscious elements. We may label this past material unconscious, and so it is, but Self-Image Therapy has no need for such device as "an unconscious." Everything not in conscious awareness is unconscious at the moment, but conscious awareness is constantly changing.

There are no specific determinants of what is unconscious, such as the Freudian system postulates. It is not pain, or nonacceptability that determines the status, but rather the age at which the experience occurred, the clarity of the original impressions, the degree or extent to which words were attached to it then—and later—and the frequency or recency of repetition. Words usually help to fix and to clarify an experience, and to make one's status more accessible to conscious and critical awareness.

What makes patients uncomfortable relates to their failure to see the self accurately and the interpersonal situation realistically. The patients need to see how their natural, spontaneous, and semiautomatic behavior in response to what has been perceived is making life difficult for them. Patients must question whether their actions are necessary and realistic or whether they are merely behaving in accordance with habit and in the service of pride. If they assume that to behave in some other fashion would seriously impair their self-esteem, the therapist needs to explore this assumption, as well as to see if each patient's self-esteem is as essential as he or she has always assumed. If patients' pride has been injured, they need to understand that loss of self-esteem is truly not tantamount to death, as they may have thought.

Alterations in the patterns of one's behavior are almost always necessary in successful therapy. Such patterns have come about because they provided the best way to remain safe—they protected one's pride, one's grandiose self-image. People routinely assume they "have to" do this or that; that other

people "have to" behave in specific ways toward them, or their world "isn't right." When pride no longer is the most important factor, then it becomes possible to be aware of other factors and other needs and possibilities, and to have fewer *should*'s, *must*'s, and *have to*'s.

Probably the least important thing in the mind of the average person is a realistic regard for and protection of one's own welfare. People are so busy enhancing their self-image—often by inflating or deflating someone else—or doing whatever it is that makes them feel good about themselves that their real welfare never occurs to them. This must change if therapy is to be successful. Nothing good can be accomplished if the therapist not only condones but assists in disregarding the patient's real self and real needs; in one's eagerness to "look good," be accepted, please others, avoid hurting feelings, one may "go along" with situations detrimental to the patient's real welfare.

What are a person's real needs? Perceiving the extent of one's grandiosity, increasing meaningful communication, taking time to listen to oneself, becoming more realistically independent, being more honest, spending more time working and planning and less time hoping, being more assertive—or less—being less concerned about being "pretty" or perfect in behavior than being practical and realistic, being more caring of one's own welfare, having increasing respect for the selfhood of other people; these are some possibilities to explore.

Whatever changes need to be made should be made in the light of the fact that keeping one's pride intact serves no useful purpose. Life must be lived in such fashion as will best foster growth rather than vanity. Growth in a variety of ways is a realistic goal for everyone, and contentment is the usual accompaniment of growing.

Whereas the need for people is indeed realistic, even this must be carefully assessed to see whether it represents a neurotic dependency or a healthy interdependence that can foster growth. Learning that other people's lives and feelings are important must be evaluated against the possibility that acquiescing may mean giving in to the neurotic demands of other immature people. People no longer can be "just blobs," there for the neurotic and narcissistic convenience of the patient, but as individuals to know, to touch, and to let be free.

To be aware of all these possibilities minimizes the tendency to repeat old patterns and removes the tendency to have resentment, because one will have ceased to expect too much. Disappointment will be minimal to nonexistent, and depression will vanish because one no longer insists on doing the impossible, namely, changing the other person or becoming perfect oneself. After all, people are here for their own goals and not for my—or your—narcissistic designs.

Self-Image Therapy clearly relies minimally on predetermined goals and patterns. By constantly giving heed to unrecognized assumptions, the therapist gets into the world of the patient—the patient's orientation and values—and does not foist or project his or her own preconceptions on the patient.

## METHODOLOGY

Whereas every patient needs to tell his or her story without too much interruption, in employing Self-Image Therapy, therapists should not plan to have patients carry the sessions or determine their direction or even their content. The sessions are not freewheeling. The medical model offers the best plan for limited structure and adequate information. The therapist stays on course with the goal of getting a comprehensive history as early as possible. This will include *chief complaint, history of present illness, personal history,* and *family history.*

Several things must be clarified before formal therapy can begin. The therapist must assess whether the patient is capable of analytic therapy, or whether he or she is impaired in the ability to integrate—to make connections and to see relationships. Did the patient come for help for him- or herself, or is the patient primarily interested in changing someone else? Is the patient willing—and able—to give up drugs? Are drugs regarded as preferable and more helpful than psychotherapy, or does the patient want both? Does the patient regard his or her situation as desperate, and is hospitalization required—if so, briefly, or on a longer term basis?

The therapist must be a good listener, but not merely a friendly neighbor. He or she must listen critically and discover how the patient's difficulties arose and how they fit into the patterns of his or her life. When the therapist notes a repetitive pattern, what is heard should be verbalized. The therapist does not attempt to establish rapport, because it is assumed that the patient will behave toward the therapist as he characteristically does toward people whom the therapist represents to him or her—women, older people, people in a position of authority or control, or other categories (transference phenomena). It must also be assumed that not until the relationship is a truly helpful one should the patient trust or have a positive feeling for the therapist. If the patient's reaction is premature, this should be noted and verbalized.

There is no specific time for introducing observations or tentative insights; they are mentioned as the therapist becomes aware of them, always tentatively, but therapists should not wait until they are absolutely sure they are right. Insights may be phrased as: "Do I hear you saying . . . ?" "Am I correct in hearing you say . . . ?" "Are you saying that your opinions are . . . ?" or "Do I hear you have always . . . ?" It is not important to be right, but it is important to listen perceptively. It is also possible to have heard wrong, and the patient's help and cooperation should be enlisted.

The sooner the patient participates, the sooner we walk along together, rather than one of us being higher and the other lower. Equality gets the patient into the role of critical participant rather than merely feeling or reacting. Whereas the therapist should listen attentively, he or she should never worry about having missed something. If it is important, it will come up again.

In addition to looking for repetitive patterns, evidence of stress should be noted: strong feelings, such as helplessness, resentment, guilt, rage, depression, hopelessness, anxiety, vindictiveness, or physical symptoms. Evidences of smug self-satisfaction, pride, arrogance, impatience, or contempt should also be noted. These two main types of strong feeling indicate either that threat has already been felt or that the self-image has not yet been in danger. In either case what is noted may be mentioned. When a strong feeling emerges, therapists should assess whether it makes sense to them, given what is known of the patient, their beliefs and assumptions. When it does not make sense to the therapist, it is used as further grist for the mill. Therapists must understand, for otherwise it is doubtful whether the patient will move beyond where the therapist is (Anderson, 1973).

As an increasingly comprehensive picture of the patients in everyday functioning is gained, repetitive patterns as they move in and out of a variety of situations are watched for. These, together with the sense of *must* or *have to*, tell the therapist how each patient functions, what the patient regards as important and what is seen to be dangerous. All situations that bring anxiety are obviously important and need clarification. *What is the patient fearful of doing, or seeing, or realizing? What is absolutely essential? Are the patient's goals realistic?*

The therapist does not set traps for the patient or play games. In my practice I do not try to be clever or smart; I am more of a prosaic plodder than a hot shot. I don't try to test patients and I don't try to impress them. I just move along, one foot ahead of the other, always ready to go back over material, ready to take time for patients' reactions. I see that we keep in step. We may spend time on dreams, but this is rare, for routinely they take too much time and they can provide too many pitfalls in interpretations.

There is no schedule regarding how often or how long to see patients. In the past I saw patients more often than I do now. Sessions are usually an hour long. Less than once a week is probably too infrequent for most patients needing help. Rarely are patients seen more than twice a week, although when anxiety is high, this may be necessary for a time. When sessions are too close together, it is easy to overemphasize the importance of both therapist and therapy.

Many problems do not require protracted treatment. Sometimes even a single session suffices, but in any such short-term therapy, what goes on must be consistent with the overall design of the system. I do not mix personal and professional activities. I am not clever enough to wear two hats successfully. To remain helpful through being objective, I must protect us both from personal involvements.

Since self-image theory maintains that stress is the result of threat to one's grandiose self-image, we can say that the patient comes for help when threatened with being cut down to size, so the therapist must look for hurt pride. Those things associated with a sense of "inner have to" are noted. Such compulsions are always directed toward maintaining an intact pride system. They are also trustworthy earmarks of a neurotic trait, and are never in the service of reality.

Symptoms are of two general types: either longstanding ways of behaving and of life, or "decompensation" reactions, of shorter duration, in response to current stress. Common symptoms are paranoid thinking, distortion in perception, anxiety, depression, confusion, compulsions, phobias, physical symptoms, hyperreactions, sexual aberrations, or life pattern disturbances without other notable symptomatology.

Symptoms such as perseveration may also be an expression of organic handicap. The therapist needs to keep this possibility in mind to make correct decisions. The therapist ought not to get sucked into trying to do the impossible, or into an "interminable analysis," when what the patient needs is competent diagnosis and perhaps medical attention.

Often in therapy things are noted long before they are understood, but it is useful to mention them "out loud" even though understanding may be far away. The therapist does not need to wait to mention something until he or she is sure of the answer; to do so tends to increase the patient's sense of being in the hands of a superior person. It is acceptable for the therapist to be uncertain or not to have an answer; one can be uncertain without being lost. If the patient finds it hard to accept such uncertainty, this is grist to the mill. Another reason therapists may fail to acknowledge things of some importance is that they are in agreement with the therapists' own frame of reference and with the things *we* take for granted. Doing psychotherapy is a good way to become aware of our own neuroticisms.

Since so much of psychiatric symptomatology is derived from "hostility" (Anderson, 1957), it is essential to understand the term. There are three kinds of feelings covered by this term: First there is a longstanding feeling derived from the feelings and reactions of other people—almost a character trait, in that it is incorporated early and it stands ready to be utilized or expressed. For lack of a better term, I call it "essential hostility." Second there is the feeling that results from helplessness to do what must be done. It is related to the here and now, is always rooted in felt helplessness, and is called "rage." The third kind of feeling is "resentment," and this is quite different from the other two feelings. It stems from a sense of frustrated entitlement. It is useless to try to treat "hostility" without a clear understanding of the three separate implications of the term.

No matter what the presenting symptoms, the therapist's goal is to see how the patient's assumptions contribute to his or her distress, then see how the assumptions can be challenged and replaced by different assumptions that are more functional or realistic, and finally, to help the patient see how exclusive

attention to maintaining his or her self-image is destructive to the need to live peacefully and productively.

Neurotics' felt need is always to preserve their grandiose self-image, whereas their real need is to discover and give attention to their true welfare. With proper concern for their own welfare, they can begin experimenting and growing. They will no longer be hampered by their need to keep "safe" from injury to their pride system. They need to find out that hurt pride is not tantamount to destruction. The danger of failing to grow and to behave realistically is a greater danger than the danger of being cut down to size. When one no longer has to spend energies protecting pride, there will be energy available for experimentation and for growing. A simple rule to follow is that if the best reason one can find for doing something is that it bolsters and enhances one's pride, it is doubtful it should be done.

## APPLICATIONS

The people best suited for Self-Image Therapy are those old enough to have established a relatively stable value system or self-image; they will be beyond adolescence, but not be old in the sense of being rigid. They need to be able to entertain the possibility that their value system may need altering. Sometimes old people can see what is going on, but they would rather not be troubled with changing.

Regarding those people who suffer from minimal brain dysfunction, Self-Image Therapy works best with those who are only minimally affected, as therapy calls for the ability to make comparisons, see relationships, and integrate observations and facts. When there are problems with integration, as there are in MBD, progress will be minimal; this lack of progress should be attributed to factors outside the therapeutic system.

Even people who are very comfortable may be candidates for treatment, because the theory is applicable to everyone regardless of whether he or she has decompensated and responded with symptoms to a stressful situation. Stress remains the basic indicator for treatment. We all operate according to the same rules, but whether we are comfortable or we are having some degree of distress, we can all become more aware of our operations.

Anxiety or stress symptoms always are the result of felt threat to one's self-image, and, therefore, if the person has symptoms we need to understand what has threatened him or her and what he or she fears. The patient needs to learn that threat to the pride system is not the same as threat to the self. The self-image is always grandiose and fearful of being cut down to size, whereas the real individual, the true person, is not so easily damaged. Seeing why the self-image is bigger than life and bigger than it needs to be in any situation is part of the therapeutic process.

It is easy to develop the erroneous notion that, once having seen this, this understanding will remain constant in one's mind. Nothing could be further from the truth. We are forever forgetting our humanity and then repetitiously thinking and acting as though we were God, expecting too much of ourselves, demanding too much from others. All in all, we behave as though we have no true limitations—or at least as if we believe we should not have any. There seems to be no end to the *should*'s, *ought*'s, and *must*'s we place on ourselves and on others.

When we finally see our grandiosity, it is a major therapeutic event. Life can never be quite the same again, for we have seen, even momentarily, how ridiculous we are. But we cannot keep our minds focused on this new awareness; we get busy with living and doing and reacting and feeling, and before we know it, we are off and running again. The moment we do this we bring our grandiosity back into the picture and act as though this is a reasonable point of view. Therefore we have every reason to expect things to be according to the old grandiose pattern. But once having seen the shape of things and experienced the truth—that our grandiosity is always ready to be implemented again—it is easier to make

further realistic adjustments without great effort or expenditure of time. Insights are lost again and again, but regaining them is no longer a major undertaking.

True insight is an emotional experience, and therefore it needs to be in the present tense. One may look at events of the past, consider their meaning and their implications, and see for the first time how they are illustrative of the very things one has been talking about. This is insight of a certain kind, but it lacks the emotional factor present when one can see the self performing in the here and now, and it suddenly dawns on one that here one is, doing the same old thing again!

Self-Image Therapy provides a most useful framework for understanding and treating a wide spectrum of psychiatric patients: the usual and normal symptoms deriving from efforts to maintain the status quo, the selective inattentions so familiar to us, the compulsive and obsessive patterns people have carried around with them for years, the rigidities that interfere with easy living and all kinds of pleasurable experiences are all appropriate areas for treatment with this system; so are the decompensation symptoms that indicate there has been more stress than the patient has been able to adjust to.

There is just enough difference in patients with psychotic symptoms that it is not appropriate to expect them to be able to make use of this system. Occasionally they will benefit from Self-Image Therapy, but one ought not expect it. It is customary for therapists to think of people as having their usual patterns and symptomatology, or as having decompensated from their usual way of being. Determinations have to be made in each case regarding whether treatment of a psychological nature is indicated, and when is the appropriate time for such intervention.

Probably the most nearly unique as well as the most useful aspect of Self-Image Therapy is its emphasis on getting into the patient's frame of reference—getting acquainted with, or recognizing, his or her assumptions rather than projecting our own or some authority's assumptions on to the patient. This insight is always important, but it becomes even more important when we consider that travel is normal—movement of cultures and individuals is an everyday occurrence. This system minimizes the use of projection. All of us need some assurance of protection from bias, and this system seems to provide a good starting point.

## CASE EXAMPLE

A 52-year-old woman, Mrs. Y, came for help because she was depressed to the point where she felt she might have to go to a mental hospital. She also had gained too much weight because she eats when she is depressed. She had developed a bad memory in the past year, and her husband said she could not remember anything for two minutes; she has to write notes to herself to be sure anything gets done.

Until a year ago, she had never been depressed. At the first signs of depression, she went to a community mental health center in a nearby town and said she thought the problem was her husband. After therapists saw and talked to her, they told her that Mr. Y was not the problem; *she* was the problem. She felt better after she knew it was not her husband and she had been feeling well until recently, when the depression returned.

They are living in this area, some 300 to 400 miles from their home, because the husband wants to be helpful to his son (Mrs. Y's stepson), who lives here and is in some agribusiness venture. He needed a piece of equipment and Mr. Y borrowed $47,000 to get it for him. The son is supposed to pay it back, but Mrs. Y doubts he can; however, she likes him because he is a good worker. She really did not want to come here, but she felt she should be with her husband, and she hates dreadfully to be alone. Before they came, Mr. Y called his son every day on the phone, and Mrs. Y thinks this was an unnecessary expense. However, it seemed to be helpful to the son as well as to Mr. Y.

The only person Mrs. Y seems to express a great deal of hostility toward is her daughter-in-law, whom she sees as conniving, always going through large sums of money quickly, and having too much to do with lawyers, so she cannot help but feel suspicious of her intentions. Besides that, the daughter-in-law is a Mormon, has too clean a house, and is always ready to be critical of others. Mrs. Y fully expects her daughter-in-law to leave her husband within a year or two. The two women avoid one another carefully, having little or nothing to do with each other.

Mrs. Y had been married for 26 years to her first husband, and she remembers nothing but good about this marriage; there were two children, who are now married and doing well, and two grandchildren ages six and three. They live in another state and she sees them only once or twice a year. Her first husband died suddenly of a heart attack nine years ago, and Mrs. Y had a very hard time adjusting to the loss. For two years she practically hid from people; she never went out. Then she began working in a shop, and while there she met her present husband. They were married five years ago. He too had been married before; his wife had become mentally ill and lived in a mental hospital. They were finally divorced and Mr. Y was alone for 15 years before he met and married Mrs. Y. He had always said he would never marry again. His first wife is still living, and she is working in a shop. Mrs. Y maintains she doesn't see the first wife as a threat.

Mrs. Y's first marriage was happy; she and her husband worked hard, but they did it together. She inherited the ranch she and her husband had struggled so hard to buy, and she wants to give it to her children, but Mr. Y does not want that. He likes the ranch and wants to live on it.

When at home, she had many friends with whom she frequently did things. Now, however, so far from home, there is nobody to do things with. Mr. Y used to drink a lot before they were married, and he played cards, but now he has not been drunk for two to three months. She has no complaints about him now; he is "fun," he kids her a lot, teases her, but he does not annoy her about her weight gain even though he does not like it. He says she takes what he says too seriously, and perhaps she does, because she is a very serious-minded person.

She has always had little in the way of outside interests or activities. Her family has been her entire life. She crochets a lot and gets pleasure out of this. She reads little, but enjoys a number of quiet television shows. She sleeps well with the aid of bedtime medication, but she wakes up feeling tired.

Mrs. Y has a number of mild medical problems: She had thyroid trouble and has taken radioactive iodine, and she takes medication for her thyroid gland twice a day; she had a goiter before the iodine treatment; she has not menstruated for 10 years but she still has hot flushes. Her mother had two nervous breakdowns, and then developed Parkinson's disease plus some other nerve disease. Mrs. Y has migraine headaches and she feels she has "bad nerves." Recently she had a blood clot in her leg. Her husband has shingles on his shoulder and was in the hospital for bilateral hernia last year, but he seems to be in good health now. He is 64 years old, and she sees him as too old to be carrying his son's burdens or working so hard.

Mrs. Y's story suggests that despite her relatively good adjustment up until a year ago, she has marginal nervous system stability. Her family history of nervous disorder, plus gradual onset of memory failure, migraine headaches, and emotional instability suggest that there may be both an organic and a psychodynamic factor in her difficulties. I contacted her local physician and learned that he saw her as having an early aging process. However, there were numerous problems that clearly were of psychodynamic origin; I thought we could profitably explore and deal with these.

I suggested that Mrs. Y enumerate all the problems that she was aware of, and she came up with the following list: her daughter-in-law; her husband's kidding her; the money

they have borrowed to give to his son; her weight gain: her having to take medication; her memory failure; the mental health center's assurance that her husband played no part in her depression (therefore the entire weight of her problem rested on her own shoulders). She was also troubled because she had not done what her husband wanted her to do in regard to the property. She objected to the time and money her husband spent on his son, particularly when he interfered with her desire to give money to her own children, money that some people would rightfully say belongs to them anyway.

We talked of the "good old days" when life was quite simple; when she was sure of her husband's love, and there was nothing to figure out or wonder about. We talked of the expectations this created in her—for acceptance of herself and her children, and how difficult it must be to live with someone who does not see eye to eye with her or have the same goals. We talked of her patterns of dependency and what pitfalls this leads one into—for example, letting the mental health center decide for her what role her husband plays in her problem. We talked about the possibility that part of the problem may also well be herself, in the way she was raised to look at things and to expect.

We talked about depression and its relation to a sense of helplessness, and I wondered if she could put her finger on the things that caused her to feel helpless. She decided there were many things. Her daughter-in-law was a major problem; Mrs. Y felt totally incapable of understanding, liking, or trusting her. Mrs. Y doesn't like the way the daughter-in-law has tried to shut Mrs. Y out of her life. She has never before had anything to do with a Mormon, and she doesn't know how to deal with her. Added to this is the problem of what to do with her guilt toward her daughter-in-law. She has strong unacknowledged destructive feelings toward her, feelings she cannot recall having toward anyone before. We talked of how hard it is to stand any guilt.

There were other sources of a sense of helplessness—her husband, for one. She doesn't know how to cope with him. She isn't sure he really cares for her, and sometimes she wonders if he will divorce her if she has to go to a mental hospital. She wishes he didn't like her ranch so much. I encouraged her to feel it isn't occasion for too much guilt if she does not comply with his every wish. I thought there might well be some compromise and urged her to think of other possibilities besides those she had mentioned.

I wondered if she had ever thought of consulting a lawyer, to get help in making suggestions and working out details that she alone could not come up with. We talked about her mistrust of people who consulted lawyers. I indicated she might feel better if she were not totally dependent on her husband, but had some clear property rights of her own, particularly if such rights were fair and considerate of all people involved —herself, most of all, her children, and her husband. Things usually are not all one way, but compromises.

I suggested that her memory failure problem made it even more imperative that she be helped to give herself a fair deal, for she could not depend on her own efforts to support herself, and therefore she needed a financial cushion of some kind. I volunteered that the sooner she acted to protect both herself and her children's interests, the sooner she would get over her feeling of helplessness, and this would contribute to her sense of well-being. Uncertainty, confusion, and vacillation are no big help, so eliminate them as soon as possible. At this time I saw no reason why she would resist living on the ranch with her husband, provided ownership was secured for herself and the children.

We talked a good bit about securing a competent attorney, and I offered to put her in touch with someone who would help her select one. I also suggested she bring her husband to meet me; perhaps the openness implicit in such a meeting would help her feel comfortable with the idea. It took several discussions about this before she agreed it was probably best to keep things open, and

how much better that might be than suffering from guilt. She mentioned that her husband had been opposed to her seeking help both from the mental health center and from me, because of the expense involved.

We talked about the center and the role it played in her problems. Although it may have contributed to her discomfort, she had to realize that she is not tied to it. She does not have to accept its verdicts, but may come up with some answers of her own. I encouraged her to express her feelings about her husband, and as she talked she had less feeling of being caught, and more belief that it might be possible to work out a number of things that previously she had assumed had to be just one way or another. I also urged her to try standing a little more guilt than she had in the past—in other words, she should experiment with trying to be more fair to herself. She had been afraid Mr. Y would divorce her, and being alone again seems almost unbearable to her. I urged her to consider that things are not all that fragile, and that somehow with her own strength and the help of others she no doubt would weather whatever storms might come; however, I emphasized that I did not expect any notable storms to arise.

We talked about her reaction to her daughter-in-law's Mormon heritage. I had spent 10 years in Salt Lake City and so had abundant impressions and firsthand knowledge of this segment of our population. I reassured Mrs. Y about the Mormon culture and values, and suggested we take it a step at a time with relation to the daughter-in-law. I was hopeful it might work out to be an interesting and broadening experience, and I was ready to stand by and react to her reports, just as I would when she was confronted by any other new or possibly threatening experience.

The biggest step was taken when Mrs. Y agreed she had not only the right but the obligation to do whatever she did for her own welfare, rather than out of a belief about how people should behave. If she suffered a little guilt in moving in that direction, she had to learn to live with it. Her life would never be good so long as she was afraid to stand a little guilt. She would, no doubt, live her life in such a fashion as would largely preclude both resentment and helplessness, but her prime obligation was to maintain her own welfare rather than be concerned about how she looked to others, or what feeling she had at any moment.

The last time I heard from Mrs. Y, a number of months ago, she was functioning rather well.

## SUMMARY

Compared to Self-Image Therapy, it would be difficult to imagine a system of psychodynamics more complete or more simple. Learning how to recognize and to think about assumptions seems formidable and foreign to the average therapist—particularly if he or she is accustomed to the usual psychodynamic jargon—until it becomes automatic. Then the therapist wonders why it ever seemed to pose a problem and why he or she was unable to think in this manner. There are essentially no new terms to learn in Self-Image Therapy, certainly none of a complex or "scientific" nature, and the basic concepts and patterns are completely familiar to us; they always have been.

Given the need to survive, with helplessness there from the start, the fact of surviving has to be related to caring and helpful people, and this interpersonal aspect is woven into the fabric of all a person's basic assumptions about functioning. The "will to live," or the survival drive, makes interpersonal operations a natural and a must.

Some systems describe what takes place—they offer the mechanics—but they do not offer any dynamics. Self-Image Therapy offers both. Recognizing that the survival drive is basic in a psychological as well as in a physical framework brings harmony into the entire picture of human functioning. The moment we grasp the fact of the psychological self-image and recognize that grandiosity is an inevitable part of it, we have the means

for understanding how and why people behave as they do, both in sickness and in health. Surviving implies living out and maintaining one's grandiose self-image, because that is the only image the person has. It is all he or she has to work with.

The person is not compensating or overcompensating for inferiority feelings; he is just being himself and actualizing his image.

Originally, threat to survival occurred because of helplessness; resolution of the threat occurred through the assistance of others; this fostered the development of assumptions regarding danger and source of help. This in turn brought about the development of the person's value system—which is the result of the threat of nonsurvival and the experience of surviving—in the days, weeks, and months that follow the first and earliest state of danger. "Right" turns out to be that which promotes security, and "wrong" is that which brings insecurity. Moral values turn out to be the techniques for surviving, and they act as a guide as well as determinant of behavior and feelings. People do only what their code permits or dictates.

The goal of living is to continue to survive, and psychological survival implies survival of one's grandiose self-image, with the aid of one's value system.

Minimizing anxiety may be seen as one goal in therapy; feeling safe and surviving comfortably is no small achievement. A higher level goal is to make such realistic alterations in one's assumptions that self-maintenance takes a secondary place to protecting and enhancing one's welfare. This is the way to go if one wishes to promote growth and to experience "the good life." It cannot be done until the person can distinguish between vanity and welfare. The natural goal is enhancement of one's vanity or pride. Good therapy helps one see pride for what it is—a barrier to growth, to necessary relationships, and to realistic living.

The need for eclecticism vanishes, for Self-Image Therapy includes everything one needs—not only a dependable base, but a North Star and a compass. Therapists no longer feel lost, for they know what they are looking for and where they have to go. The greatest problem is with the people who are new to the concepts; because of prior commitments to other beliefs, they commonly find it difficult to see what is there to be seen.

# REFERENCES

Anderson, C. M. The anatomy, physiology and pathology of the psyche; a new concept of the dynamics of behavior. *American Practitioner and Digest of Treatment,* 1950a, **1,** 400–405.

Anderson, C. M. *Saints, sinners and psychiatry.* Philadelphia: Lippincott, 1950b.

Anderson, C. M. The self image, a theory of the dynamics of behavior. *Mental Hygiene,* 1952, **36,** 227–244.

Anderson, C. M. *Beyond Freud.* New York: Harper, 1957.

Anderson, C. M. *Jan, my brain-damaged daughter.* Portland, Ore.: Durham Press, 1963.

Anderson, C. M. The self image, a theory of the dynamics of behavior (updated). *Mental Hygiene,* 1971, **56,** 365–368.

Anderson, C. M. *Society pays; the high cost of brain damage in America.* New York: Walker, 1972a.

Anderson, C. M. Minimal brain damage. *Mental Hygiene,* 1972b, **56.** 62–66.

Anderson, C. M. Perspective. *Journal of the American Medical Womens' Association,* 1973a, **28,** 402–414.

Anderson, C. M. Assumption-centered psychotherapy. In Ratibor-Ray M. Jurjevich. (Ed.), *Direct psychotherapy, 28 originals.* Coral Gables, Fla.: University of Miami Press, 1973b.

Anderson, C. M. The brain-injured adult: An overlooked problem. In R. Weber (Ed.), *Handbook on learning disabilities.* Englewood Cliffs, N.J.: Prentice-Hall, 1974.

Anderson, C. M. and Plymate, H. B. Management of the brain-damaged adolescent. *American Journal of Orthopsychiatry,* 1962, **32,** 492–500.

Campbell, R. Private communications, 1977.

# CHAPTER 58

## Sex Therapies

DIANNE GERARD

*Although clinicians have been dealing with sexual problems for many years, recently a number of advances have been made in the direct treatment of such common sexual problems as impotence, frigidity, and premature ejaculation.*

*Essentially, as Dianne Gerard explains in this chapter, the big difference now is that the problem is dealt with directly on a here-and-now basis, rather than seeing the sexual difficulty as part of the total problem of the total individual. In this way, the systems mentioned in this chapter represent a kind of symptom removal rather than psychotherapy in the inclusive sense.*

*However, a good rationale would be an analogy: If you go to a doctor's office because you have a bit of sand in your eye or a splinter in your finger, the usual procedures of taking temperature, blood pressure, and a history may not be worthwhile: why not solve the problem as quickly and with as little fuss as possible? So too, if a short-term solution may work out for, say, premature ejaculation (a problem the new Sex Therapies have good success with), why not proceed immediately with the cure?*

*Symptom removal may be the equivalent to psychotherapy, and indeed some advocates of some kinds of Behavior Modification (of the Skinnerian variety) do think that this is what psychotherapy is all about.*

*This chapter is a survey of current thinking and methodology in various Sex Therapies. For a fuller exposure to a system concentrating on sexual problems, refer to Annon's chapter on PLISSIT Therapy.*

Sex Therapies are treatments designed to deal with specific barriers to sexual functioning. Sexual dysfunctions are attitudinal, behavioral, or emotional factors that hinder people from engaging in or enjoying sexual activities. The aims of Sex Therapies are to provide accurate sex education, to increase erotic pleasure by overcoming anxiety about sex, to improve communication between sexual partners, and to improve techniques so that maximal satisfaction is attained.

Sex Therapies focus primarily on symptom removal rather than personality changes. Attention is directed generally to the "here and now" and to specific barriers to current sexual functioning. Deeper, more intrapsychic or interpersonal conflicts are addressed only when they interfere with treatment progress.

There are three main types of Sex Therapy: (1) William Masters and Virginia Johnson's two-week intensive Behavioral Sex Therapy, (2) Helen Kaplan's combination of behavioral plus Psychodynamic Sex Therapy, and (3) Group Sex Therapy as employed by McGovern, Kirkpatrick, and LoPiccolo (1978). Couples typically are treated conjointly by one or two therapists; however, some therapists accept individuals without partners.

# HISTORY

Sex Therapies have come of age primarily with the publication of *Human Sexual Inadequacy* by William Masters and Virginia Johnson (1970). The authors described explicitly their short-term behavioral model of Sex Therapy plus data regarding its effectiveness. Earlier roots in this area, however, reach back perhaps 200 years. Sir John Hunter, an eighteenth-century British physician, reported a technique for treating impotence that anticipated that of Masters and Johnson (cited in Comfort, 1967). He used paradoxical intention by advising an impotent patient to go to bed with his lover for six nights in succession but not to have intercourse. The patient reported that he was so preoccupied with fears of having too much desire that he no longer was afraid that he could not perform.

Little progress beyond personal attitudes and beliefs about sexuality occurred until the 1940s, with the collection and publication of Alfred Kinsey's data (Kinsey, Pomeroy, & Martin, 1948, 1965) on the sexual behavior of men and women. This was a large-scale collection of sociological data on sexual functioning. Kinsey relied completely on self-reports; thus the subjectivity of the reported findings became a major criticism. The data presented a picture of the variety and frequencies of sexual activities of males and later of females but said little about psychological or physiological aspects of sexual response.

In the 1950s Masters and Johnson began to study scientifically the physiological sexual responses of men and women in a laboratory setting. They reported data on nearly 10,000 sexual acts, such as coitus and masturbation under a variety of conditions. Subjects were all volunteers. Sex therapy clients were not used for this data. However, this experimental process led to theories regarding sexual response and also served to generate ideas for treatment. They published their data and conclusions after following up treated couples for five years.

John Money and Anke Erhardt at Johns Hopkins University furthered knowledge by studying gender-identity formation and the role of hormonal influences on sexuality. Helen Kaplan (1974) added the psychoanalytic/psychodynamic components of Sex Therapy by examining the psychological roots underlying sexual dysfunctions and marital conflict. Behavior therapists identified the ways in which sexual dysfunctions were acquired and reinforced through focusing on factors in the current sexual situation of affected individuals that impair functioning; they also added innovative techniques for treatment such as combining dating sessions with sexual home assignments (Annon, 1974) and maintaining diaries of sexual thoughts and activities (LoPiccolo, 1978).

Sex Therapy with individuals began in the mid 1970s with the realization that not all people with sexual difficulties had current partners. This approach is controversial when surrogate partners are employed. Masters and Johnson have discontinued this practice. Martin Williams (1978) treats sexually dysfunctional men using "body-work therapists" at the Berkeley Sex Therapy Group; no figures are cited regarding treatment success rate. Lonnie Barbach (1975) devised a group treatment plan for what she calls "pre-orgasmic" (anorgasmic) women based on the Lobitz and LoPiccolo (1972) masturbation program for females. This method proved highly successful (93 percent of women became orgasmic after five weeks of treatment) and gained popularity across the country. Drawbacks centered on problems with transfer of learning; women might become orgasmic with self-stimulation but remain unable to experience orgasm with a partner.

Group treatment is used to reduce costs, provide opportunity for emotional support among couples and a modeling effect, and to serve a wider range of clientele. There appears to be promise in this approach, but as in all aspects of Sex Therapies there is a lack of controlled research. Relative effectiveness of one treatment over another is simply not known.

## CURRENT STATUS

An increase in interest in sexuality research and therapy has occurred since the pioneering work of Masters and Johnson. Numerous self-help books are available to improve people's understanding of sexuality and to help them to solve their sexual problems (Barbach, 1975; Heiman, LoPiccolo, & LoPiccolo, 1976; McCary, 1973; Pion, 1977). Journals such as the *Journal of Sex & Marital Therapy, Journal of Sex Education and Counseling, Archives of Sexual Behavior, Journal of Sex Research,* and *Medical Aspects of Human Sexuality* also have been started to keep pace with emerging research and theory.

A national organization, the *American Association of Sex Educators, Counselors and Therapists* (AASECT), begun by Patricia Schiller, has provided an impetus to the regulation of sex therapists. Currently no state regulates sex therapists, and thus anyone with or without training can claim to be qualified. AASECT currently certifies three subspecialists in this field: sex educators, sex counselors, and sex therapists. The standards are rigorous and are a step toward consumer protection. AASECT publishes annually the *National Register of Certified Health Service Providers in Sex Education and Sex Therapy,* with the names and addresses of all currently certified professionals.

Many graduate programs in medicine, social work, counseling, and psychology now offer courses on human sexuality and many teach sex therapy techniques. A number of postgraduate programs provide intensive training in Sex Therapy and sex education, including the Masters and Johnson Institute in St. Louis, the Sex Therapy and Education Program of the Payne Whitney Psychiatric Clinic of the Cornell University—New York Hospital Center, the Marriage Council of Philadelphia, and the Human Sexuality Program at the University of California Medical Center. This is not a complete list of training programs.

Sex Therapies draw professionals from a variety of disciplines. Physicians, ministers, educators, and psychotherapists all use various theories and techniques to help their clientele. This chapter deals with the treatment of sexually dysfunctional clients by professionals who specialize in the field. Because there is insufficient research data to specify which aspects of the treatment are crucial, there is little in the way of standardization. Much more research is needed to clarify the essentials for effective treatment. Douglas Hogan (1978) has made a start by reviewing the literature and recommending outcome studies that consider the interaction of client variables, treatment components, and modes of therapy using factorial designs.

## THEORY

To understand the etiology of sexual dysfunction, Kaplan (1974) examined the immediate and remote causes. Immediate causes are those factors that create an "antierotic" environment, anything in the present moment that ruins the sexual responsivity between the partners. Kaplan states that sexual response is a "complex series of autonomically mediated visceral reflexes which can only work successfully if the person is in a calm state and if the process is 'left alone,' i.e., not impaired by conscious monitoring processes" (p. 121). The person must be able to abandon him- or herself to the erotic sensations. Kaplan groups the immediate causes of sexual dysfunction into four categories:

1. Sexual ignorance and failure to engage in effective behavior.

2. Performance anxiety and fear of failure. There is often an excessive concern for pleasing the partner, which stems from an underlying fear of rejection.

3. Spectatoring—a term introduced by Masters and Johnson that refers to self-observation of one's sexual performance rather than total participation in it. This is a defense to bind the anxiety that sexual contact elicits. Another defense is

a perceptual one in which the person denies or fails to perceive erotic sensations.

4. Failure to communicate openly and without shame about sexual wishes, likes, and dislikes.

Much of the time in Sex Therapy, the above causes of sexual conflict can be addressed and alleviated via experiential rather than cognitive insight methods with a resulting disappearance of the symptom. If this cannot be accomplished, the remote causes of the conflict are explored in the psychotherapeutic sessions. Remote causes may be classified as either intrapsychic or interpersonal. Kaplan (1974) borrowed from psychoanalytic theory especially with the concepts of unconscious motivation of behavior and the importance of childhood experiences in shaping the adult personality.

Psychoanalytic theory explains sexual disorders in terms of repression of oedipal sexual urges and fixation at certain early stages of development (oral, anal, or phallic-oedipal). However, Kaplan states that an unconscious conflict can cause sexual dysfunction "only if it evokes disorganizing anxiety at the moment of lovemaking or mobilizes perceptual and obsessive defenses against arousal" (p. 145).

Childrearing practices that associate guilt and shame with sex are culprits in the etiology of sexual conflict as well. Our culture enforces a discontinuous type of learning about sexuality; that is, we are encouraged to learn as little as possible about sexual functioning until we are culturally sanctioned to express our sexual feelings in marriage. Conflict results from the backlog of suppression and from the notion that sex equals sin. Many children still are taught that masturbation is sinful, that sexual thoughts are as bad as sexual behavior, and that sexual experimentation prior to marriage is forbidden. These are not easy messages to undo. In fact, Kaplan (1974) remarks that "it speaks for the strength of the sex drive and the inherent potential towards mental health that many

persons who come from a restrictive background escape sexual problems" (p. 149).

Relationship variables also create deeper sources of sexual conflict. Lack of trust and power struggles create a destructive atmosphere and inhibit the abandonment necessary for full sexual responsivity. It makes sense that satisfying sexual expression often disappears when the couple's interpersonal system is rejecting, dehumanizing, or fraught with hostility. Thus, the sexual system—the relationship—assumes a central role in Sex Therapies.

Research does indicate that concentration on communication difficulties, marital conflict, and psychopathology without specific attention to sexual interaction have much less success in symptom reversal (citations in Marks, 1978). A major difference between Sex Therapies and psychotherapy or Marital Therapy is that they are not comprehensive; their focus is a narrow one. Traditional psychotherapy aims toward personality reconstruction; Marital Therapy attempts to reverse interpersonal conflict, increase harmony, and improve communication and understanding between the couple. Because the scope of Sex Therapies is limited, there are certain prerequisites. The couple needs to be committed to working on their difficulties, to viewing it as a joint problem rather than as involving one partner only, and to be willing to suspend for the duration of treatment (especially in the two-week intensive therapy) any preoccupation with past hurts and angers. A "here and now" orientation is encouraged.

Further assumptions are made. Sex is viewed as a natural function. The urge for orgasmic release is as natural as the other biological needs to breathe, eat, or defecate. However, the sexual urge is the only one that can be suppressed at will without harmful effects. It operates under two separate systems of influence: the biophysical and the psychosocial. Either or both can create sexual dysfunction. Past learning, misconceptions, fears of performance, anxiety regarding rejection, and sexually embarrassing or traumatic incidents constitute usual psychosocial barriers to satisfying sexual functioning. Drug abuse, alcoholism, diabetes, physical injuries, and certain endocrinological imbalances are biophysical causes of sexual dysfunction. Until recently it was assumed that upwards of 90 percent of sexual dysfunction was psychosomatic. More refined instrumentation has permitted study of physiological barriers to erection via use of the nocturnal penile tumescence monitor; this provides information on the diagnosis and prognosis of impotence (Karacan, 1970).

## METHODOLOGY

Sex Therapies are behavioral treatments designed to relieve impediments to satisfying sexual relations. As a treatment method, the therapies focus on relief of specific sexual symptoms via analysis of the etiology of the problem and the communication patterns of the couple; specific behavioral suggestions in the form of graduated sexual tasks are given to the couple, which they then experience together in privacy before reporting back to their therapist(s). Unlike analytic psychotherapies, Sex Therapies use a directive approach to modify the attitudes and atmosphere in which sex takes place. Communication exerises and graduated sexual experiences confront clients with their sexual anxiety and facilitate its resolution. Therapy establishes the attitudes and erotic atmosphere necessary for the natural physiological sexual responses to occur; these cannot be taught (Brecher, 1969). The rapid-treatment approach initiated by Masters and Johnson (1970) adds an environmental factor in that the couple is removed from their home situation and spends two weeks exclusively focused on their sexual relationship. Research to date, however, has not proved that this is necessary for treatment success. The method developed by Kaplan relies more on psychodynamic intervention than does the Masters and Johnson model, which focuses on the behavioral and communication aspects of the couple's dysfunction.

Masters and Johnson (1970), Hartman and Fithian (1972) and Kaplan (1974) begin with a detailed chronological history including sexual functioning, family-of-origin experiences, dating and marital adjustment. A thorough physical examination with appropriate lab tests is conducted. Annon (1974) diverges from this approach; he takes a history primarily of the sexual problem (description, onset and course, client's understanding of causation, past treatment, and goals). With completion of the history, the therapist(s) decides on the feasibility of treating the couple with the sex therapy method, then discuss the findings with the couple. This includes reflecting back in a "mirrorlike" manner the backgrounds of each partner, how certain variables created the sexual conflict, and aspects of the current sexual system that serve to maintain the dysfunction. Masters and Johnson (1970) refer to this as the "round table" session; goals are promotion of neutrality between the couple, encouragement of open communication (sharing oneself as accurately as possible), and increasing motivation for active participation by the couple in the treatment. Once the couple understands the likely etiology of their difficulty, the methods that will be used to reverse the dysfunction, and commits themselves to ongoing therapy, the first sexual tasks are assigned.

Sensate focus is typically the first assignment. The couple is instructed to choose a time when they are relaxed and receptive to one another; they are to take turns caressing each other in a gentle, nondemanding manner. Genitals, breasts, and intercourse are off limits. The "receiver" of the sensual touch has but one responsibility: to protect the partner from hurting him or her during the touching. Sensate focus is uniquely designed to increase each partner's sensitivity to sensual touch and to eliminate any need to perform or to watch oneself. The experience is discussed in the next psychotherapy session. If both partners report pleasure and are able to suspend their performance fears, they are asked to try the experience again with a modification: the receiving partner places his or her hand on the giver's hand to nonverbally show the kinds of strokes and pressures that are desired. As Sex Therapy progresses, the couple learns more effective communication about their specific sexual wishes.

Touching of the breasts and genitals in a light, teasing, and nondemanding way is the next step. Caresses that lead to orgasm are encouraged only when the couple feels relaxed, experiences erotic pleasure, and when spectatoring has been eliminated. Variations in the treatment method for different types of dysfunction begin at this point.

A brief description of the major types of sexual dysfunction and treatment strategies is necessary. Each may be classified as primary, when the dysfunction has been present at every sexual opportunity, or secondary, when there was at least one sexual experience without the sexual symptom. Male sexual dysfunctions include impotence, premature ejaculation, and retarded ejaculation. Female sexual disorders include general sexual dysfunction, orgasmic dysfunction, vaginismus, dyspareunia, and sexual anesthesia. As with male dysfunctions, these may be viewed as either vasocongestive disorders (general sexual dysfunction, vaginismus, and perhaps dyspareunia) or orgasmic phase disorders. Kaplan (1974) conceptualizes sexual response as biphasic: vasocongestion and orgasm. This contrasts with the concept of four phases of sexual response developed by Masters and Johnson (1966): excitement, plateau, orgasm, resolution.

### Premature and Retarded Ejaculation

Disorders of ejaculation include premature and retarded ejaculation (or ejaculatory incompetence, a term Masters and Johnson prefer). Difficulty arises in defining precisely what constitutes prematurity. Masters and Johnson (1970) generated the following definition: If a man cannot control his ejaculation for a "sufficient length of time during intravaginal containment to satisfy his partner in at least fifty percent of their coital experiences" (p. 92), then he is a premature ejaculator. Rather than pronouncing a specific length of time in which ejaculation is

delayed as the criterion, they define it in the context of the sexual system. Of course, if the female never experiences orgasm during vaginal penetration, this definition falls apart. For premature ejaculation, the stop-start or squeeze technique is suggested. The penis is manually stimulated to the point of ejaculatory inevitability; then the partner either ceases stimulation or squeezes the penis directly under the coronal ridge. Both techniques result in a decrease of arousal, loss of the urge to ejaculate, and sometimes partial loss of erection. This is repeated three or four times before ejaculation is permitted; thus, high levels of arousal are experienced without ejaculation. When the male experiences more voluntary control over ejaculation and can focus on his erotic sensations, he attempts penetration without thrusting. Gradually thrusting is initiated with stops to control ejaculation.

Ejaculatory incompetence is the absence of ejaculation during coitus; ejaculation may or may not occur at other times, such as during masturbation. For treatment the male is stimulated to ejaculation with his penis outside the vagina. Next, as he is stimulated to high levels of arousal, rapid penetration is attempted in the female-superior position. Vigorous thrusting until ejaculation occurs then. If this fails, manual stimulation is employed. Certain drugs may affect this phase of sexual response by causing retrograde ejaculation; certain antipsychotic and anti hypertensive medications occasionally cause this. Ejaculatory incompetence is a rare sexual dysfunction, while its opposite, premature ejaculation, is very common.

### Impotence

In the treatment of impotence, gentle manual caressing of the penis is used in a stop-start manner too; however, the purpose is to reassure the man that he can attain, lose, and regain his erection. Once confidence is reestablished and he experiences partial or full erections, he penetrates the woman, who is in the female-superior position. She controls the insertion process to avoid distracting him, and slow, nondemanding thrusting is initiated. There appear to be more organic causes of impotence than for any other type of dysfunction. However, this may simply reflect the current state of knowledge and the difficulties inherent in detecting physiological components.

## Vaginismus

Vaginismus occurs when the vaginal muscles involuntarily spasm and prevent penile penetration. Arousal and orgasm may be experienced in the presence of the spasm. Graduated dilators (or fingers) are used to treat vaginismus. Dilators are inserted by the woman or her partner and remain in place for several minutes to several hours. Masters and Johnson (1970) report that much of the involuntary spasm can be eliminated in three to five days. Coitus is attempted when the largest dilator can be tolerated without pain. Masters and Johnson suggest that a pelvic exam in which the involuntary spasm of the vagina is demonstrated to both partners is another important factor in symptom resolution; this relieves the belief that vaginismus represents a conscious rejection of the partner.

## Dyspareunia

Dyspareunia is painful intercourse. It may be caused by lack of arousal, which impairs or prevents vaginal lubrication. Other causes include gynecological disorders, entometriosis, vaginal infection, or herpes simplex. Usually there is no difficulty with orgasm. In treating dyspareunia, a thorough gynecological exam is vital to rule out physiological factors that cause pain during coitus. If insufficient lubrication is the cause, lack of arousal is suspected and the couple is instructed in sensate focus and genital pleasuring. Sterile vaginal lubricants may facilitate penetration. In older women, hormonal replacement therapy may help senile vaginitis and reduce dyspareunia. Also the use of the female-superior position in coitus enables the woman to regulate the depth and angle of penetration, thus avoiding pain from deep penetration. This may be the most viable solution when dyspareunia is caused by physiological impediments that cannot be reversed.

## General Sexual Dysfunction

General sexual dysfunction is characterized by inhibition of desire and arousal; the woman reports being uninterested and unexcited by sexual contact. She fails to lubricate although on occasion she may be orgasmic. This is somewhat analogous to sexual anesthesia in which the woman "feels nothing" when her genitals are touched, but may fully enjoy the cuddling in sexual contact. Kaplan (1974) defines this phenomenon as a hysterical conversion symptom rather than a true sexual dysfunction in that it seems more a psychoneurotic defense than a psychosomatic symptom.

For general sexual dysfunction, therapy relies on sensate focus, genital pleasuring, and nondemanding intercourse in which thrusting is controlled by the woman. Throughout the sexual tasks, her desires determine the pace and variety of caresses. This helps her both to focus on her own erotic sensations and to assume responsibility for her sexual pleasure.

## Orgasmic Dysfunction

Orgasmic dysfunction, the failure to reach orgasm during a sexual experience, may occur situationally, randomly, or absolutely, in which orgasm is never experienced under any condition. Having dispelled the myth of two kinds of orgasm (vaginal and clitoral) Masters and Johnson (1966), using laboratory data, report that orgasm has both vaginal and clitoral components. The clitoris registers most of the sensory input, and the orgasm is expressed via vaginal muscle contraction. A lack of solid data exists on the incidence of women who experience orgasm during coitus without concurrent clitoral stimulation. Controversy exists in that this has been held as the standard for normal female sexual functioning. Kaplan (1974) and Hite (1976) report differing figures: Kaplan approximates 50 percent of orgasmic women, Hite suggests 30 percent. An emphasis on sexual pleasure rather than how an orgasm occurs seems more valuable a measure.

In treatment for orgasmic dysfunction, self-stimulation is sometimes suggested to reduce the woman's fears of boring her partner by taking too much time and because masturbation provides a direct sensory feedback system. She immediately knows which types of caresses provide the most intense pleasure; this facilitates high levels of arousal and orgasm. Once orgasm is experienced during genital pleasuring with her partner, coitus with concurrent clitoral stimulation is tried. Kaplan (1974) suggests that this be used as a transition in which the man stimulates his partner's clitoral area until she feels close to orgasm; rapid thrusting is then begun until she reaches orgasm.

A new classification of sexual dysfunction is being addressed concurrently: disorders of sexual desire. Because of its psychological complexity, desire-phase dysfunction may require alternative forms of treatment. Kaplan (1977) is publishing in this area.

Masters and Johnson (1970) strongly emphasize that it is the relationship that is being treated rather than one partner or the other. Conjoint therapy is considered an absolute requirement by many sex therapists, although there are no solid data to back up this contention (Marks, 1978). For maximum transfer of learning, it seems important that the untreated partner at least be committed to the relationship and open to modifying sexual techniques and atmosphere.

## APPLICATIONS

Sexual therapy techniques are most useful when an intact couple reports having a specific sexual problem, when there is commitment between the partners and motivation to seek help for their sexual relationship, and where there is no severe psychopathology in either partner. Exceptions to this seem to be those couples who experience vaginismus or premature ejaculation. Kaplan (1974) states that the prognosis for treatment outcome for these dysfunctions appears independent of marital or individual pathology.

Contraindications for Sex Therapies include severe marital stress and hostility, severe psychopathology, and, for many therapists, the nonparticipation of one partner. Typically these impediments to treatment cannot be overcome by rapid symptom-removal treatment such as Sex Therapy. Kaplan (1974) lists a number of factors that predict a poorer prognosis when applying this model: excessive vulnerability to stress (such as in some cases of absolute ejaculatory incompetence and primary impotence), drug addiction and alcoholism, severe depression and/or anxiety, lack of commitment by one partner, and the contingency that the success of failure of the relationship depends on the outcome of therapy.

Dysfunctions with the best prognosis using the two-week intensive therapy model are premature ejaculation, vaginismus, primary orgasmic dysfunction, and secondary ejaculatory incompetence; primary and secondary impotence and situational orgasmic dysfunction are more resistant to the rapid-treatment model. Overall, during the two weeks of intensive treatment at Masters and Johnson Institute (formerly the Reproductive Biology Research Foundation) (1970), there was only a one-in-five failure rate. In the five-year follow-up, the overall failure rate (a combination of the initial failure rate and reappearance of the symptoms reported on five year follow-up) remained the same: 20 percent. Premature ejaculation was successfully treated in 97.3 percent ($N = 186$) of cases. No other researchers or therapists currently cite long-term success and failure rates for the treatment of sexual dysfunction. This is not unusual, as there are few statistics to prove the efficacy of any model of psychotherapy.

Basically, either the two-week intensive treatment method or the traditional once or twice a week outpatient method of Sex Therapy is appropriate and very successful in the reversal of sexual dysfunction. Approximately 80 percent of cases can be successfully treated. Of course, the more long-standing the problem, the presence of dysfunction in both partners, and the degree of relationship conflict and psychopathology all affect prognosis.

## CASE EXAMPLE

Mr. and Mrs. A were seen by this writer in nine sessions on a weekly basis. Mr. A was 33 years old, had been divorced once, had two young children who lived with his ex-wife, and reportedly had experienced rapid ejaculation since his first coital experience. He was a factory foreman with a high school education. Mr. A appeared shy and embarrassed; he had difficulty verbalizing his feelings, especially the specific details of his sexual life. His wife, on the contrary, was quite open, talkative, and psychologically-minded. She had prior psychotherapy during her divorce proceedings from her first husband. Mrs. A was 35, had custody of two young teenage daughters, and worked part time as a teacher's aide. She reportedly was regularly orgasmic with clitoral stimulation and had been orgasmic in coitus with other partners. This couple had been married for one and one-half years.

During the initial session it became clear that Mrs. A was quite angry toward her husband because of his premature ejaculation. Their sexual life had developed to the point where there was little kissing or caressing prior to penetration, little thrusting during intercourse, and ejaculation usually occurred in one minute or less. Mrs. A felt so frustrated and resentful that she would not want additional caressing after her husband's orgasms. He felt guilty, believed he was a failure as a lover, and tried to avoid sexual contact and foreplay for fear of becoming

stimulated to ejaculation before penetration. This, in fact, had happened several times.

Historically, Mr. A was given little information about sex from his parents. Reared mostly by his mother because of parental divorce when he was 11, he believed he had to learn about sex from peers and personal experience. During his teen years, he dated sporadically and began experimentation with petting at 16. His first coitus occurred at 17 in his girl friend's living room. The two were interrupted by her father; Mr. A recalled a feeling of panic. This seemed to have had a lasting effect on him and perhaps was his first association between anxiety, guilt, and coitus. In his first marriage, there was infrequent intercourse allegedly because his wife was unable to enjoy it or to achieve orgasm. I thought it likely that his prematurity was exacerbated by the infrequency of sexual contact. His masturbatory pattern was similar to coitus; he spent as little time as possible to reach orgasm.

Mrs. A grew up in an intact family with a father whom she described as tyrannical and alcoholic. She was frightened of him during childhood because of his temper outbursts and tendency to break things in the home when he was angry. She grew to have a wary attitude toward men; she desired a lot of nurturance and reassurance yet believed angrily that she would never get it. Her first marriage was to a man who helped her fulfill these expectations. She was pregnant at the time of the marriage. Despite the frustrations of her marriage, she was regularly orgasmic with clitoral stimulation and during intercourse. Sex was the major mode for her to feel loved in that relationship.

During courtship and marriage, this couple experienced the frustrations of their sexual problem but attributed it to the stress of forming a "reconstituted family" and believed that the premature ejaculation would diminish once they became better adjusted. After one and one-half years of marriage, they felt more compatible as a couple and with their step-parent roles; however, their sexual life had almost ended and both felt quite dissatisfied with this. At the time of therapy, there was substantial commitment to the marriage, a desire for Sex Therapy, and much half-concealed resentment in Mrs. A toward her husband.

A conjoint session occurred initially in which the history of the sexual problem and some history of the relationship was elicited. The following two were individual sessions with Mr. A and Mrs. A; the emphasis was on personal histories, sexual functioning prior to and during this marriage, and feelings toward the spouse. The fourth session was a "round table" session in which the dynamics of the problem and the possible treatment strategies were shared. Mr. A became more aware of his high anxiety level and how that along with infrequent sexual contact increased his chances of premature ejaculation. Also focusing his mind on nonerotic thoughts during intercourse only alienated him from the erotic experience. Mrs. A began to acknowledge her resentment and feelings of being cheated by men in general and by her husband in particular. These feelings did not disappear at this stage of therapy, but she had more cognitive insight. She was told that the beginning stages of treatment would focus on her husband and that she might find little erotic satisfaction during this time; this was clearly specified in an attempt to ward off her resistance. Sensate focus was assigned.

Both reported erotic arousal with sensate focus. Mrs. A was particularly pleased because she felt given to and loved without the usual frustrations of brief intercourse. Mr. A was surprised that he could touch and be touched without ejaculating. All was not rosy, however. Mr. A's job required a shift change so that he would be working all night. This left little time for sex.

Sensate focus plus the squeeze technique were suggested. Mrs. A was instructed to manually stimulate her husband's penis until he signaled that ejaculation was imminent. She then would squeeze his penis under the coronal ridge for approximately 10 seconds; when he lost some of his erection, stimula-

tion was to begin again. Mr. A was to direct his attention solely to his erotic sensations, to refocus them if he became distracted, and to let his wife know when he felt the sensations of ejaculatory inevitability. He was not to attempt to control his ejaculation in any way. After three or four stimulation-squeeze sequences he could be stimulated to orgasm. This process was to be repeated until he had a clear sense of ejaculatory inevitability.

This phase lasted for three weeks because of unavailability of time to practice (some avoidance was clearly noted) and Mrs. A's resentment during this procedure. She felt bored and used. Mr. A became aware of her resentment and had difficulty keeping his focus on his erotic sensations. At one point Mrs. A was seen individually to further explore her resistances; the anger she felt toward men as well as her hurt about not being loved enough were discussed. It was suggested that they spend additional time alone together so that she could satisfy her needs for love and attention in alternative ways. This seemed helpful. Also it was suggested that she be caressed by Mr. A at times other than their squeeze-technique sessions.

Coitus was initiated when Mr. A was able to clearly identify his point of ejaculatory inevitability, when he could sustain an erection for 10 minutes (an arbitrary figure) without ejaculation, and when he could rely on the cessation of stimulation rather than the squeeze to delay ejaculation. Mrs. A was instructed to take the female-superior position while Mr. A guided her thrusting with his hands on her hips; this put Mr. A in control of the speed of thrusting. When he reached the point of ejaculatory inevitability, he would signal her and she would stop moving. This technique was successful in enabling Mr. A to delay his ejaculation until he voluntarily chose. With additional intercourse, Mrs. A was able to experience high levels of arousal and orgasm.

Therapy was terminated at this point. The couple was instructed to continue to use the stop-start techniques as needed during coitus, to continue sensate focus and genital plea-suring, and to focus on Mrs. A's specific desires for foreplay and coital thrusting. Fol-low-up was not done.

## SUMMARY

Sex Therapies are treatment of behavioral, attitudinal, or emotional barriers to satisfying sexual functioning. Such barriers include male dysfunctions of impotence, premature ejaculation, and ejaculatory incompetence, and female dysfunctions of vaginimus, or-gasmic dysfunction, and general sexual dys-function. Sexual anesthesia and dyspareunia are sexual disorders that are typically not considered to be psychosomatic and so are classified separately. Disorders of sexual de-sire are new areas of classification.

Sex Therapies developed out of research on sexual behavior. This began with Kinsey's (1948, 1965) collection in the 1940s of so-ciological data on the sexual activities of males and females and continued with Mas-ters and Johnson's collection and publication of their data on the physiological components of sexual response in *Human Sexual Re-sponse* (1966). Since then techniques have been generated to successfully treat sexual dysfunctions. In *Human Sexual Inadequacy* (1970), Masters and Johnson describe a be-havioral treatment plan consisting of sexual and communication tasks for couples. In *The New Sex Therapy* (1974) Helen Singer Kaplan added a psychodynamic focus. Group therapy is being used for more cost-effective treatment and for the emotional support it offers clients (McGovern, Kirkpatrick & LoPiccolo, 1978; Barbach, 1975). Sex ed-ucation and self-help books for the public as well as research and treatment journals on sexuality have become popular.

Sexual dysfunctions are caused by im-mediate and remote conflicts that serve to create tension and an "anti-erotic" atmos-phere between sexual partners. Such con-flicts may be due to misinformation about sex, hostility between the partners, failure to engage in erotically stimulating activities, fears of rejection, fears of performance and failure, and spectatoring (watching one's sexual performance). Anxiety from previous sexual trauma, an overall destructive rela-tionship between the sexual partners, fears of intimacy and abandonment, faulty sexual learning, and unconscious conflicts may un-derlie the immediate causes of dysfunction.

Treatment usually involves both members of the couple and one or two therapists, al-though some clinicians work with groups of couples and some with individuals without partners. Therapy occurs in a two-week in-tensive style (Masters and Johnson) or tra-ditional outpatient format once or twice a week. The immediate rather than remote causes of the dysfunction are emphasized. If the couple can relax, give up their spec-tatoring, and create a warm, erotic ambience, they are removing the barriers to satisfying sexual responsivity. The deeper roots of sex-ual conflict are examined when therapy prog-ress becomes blocked. Major emphases are on facilitating open communication between partners and their experiences with a series of graduated sexual tasks (sensate focus, gen-ital pleasuring, and coitus). Couples who are committed to their relationship, have limited marital conflict or psychopathology, and who feel motivated to work on their sexual prob-lems have the best prognosis with this treat-ment.

Sex Therapies are intended for the rapid treatment of sexual dysfunction. They are not a panacea for marital conflict, personal un-happiness, or psychopathology. In terms of overall psychological benefits accrued from successful treatment, the results are mixed. Kaplan (1974) reports that "removal of the sexual symptom which had been plaguing the patient for years usually engenders an initial feeling of euphoria but this response is of relatively brief duration in most cases" (p. 446). It is rather quickly replaced by a "take-it-for-granted" attitude. Some couples report profoundly positive changes in their overall relationship; others report few changes. Neg-ative feelings typically emerge in two areas:

when couples expect that successful Sex Therapy will change their lives and when they experience an upsurge of anxiety just prior to symptom reversal. Sex Therapies are designed to expect and to cope with this anxiety and the defenses that emerge to mask it.

The field is young. There is little other than the uncontrolled Masters and Johnson (1966, 1970) data to support the claims of its efficacy; there are limited data to specify which factors in the treatment are necessary. There is a strong need for controlled research and outcome evaluations, a need to compare one style of treatment with another, and to delineate which clients and which specific problems benefit most and least from this treatment modality.

# REFERENCES

Annon, J. S. *The behavioral treatment of sexual problems*. Honolulu: Enabling Systems, 1974.

Barbach, L. *For yourself: The fulfillment of female sexuality*. New York: Doubleday, 1975.

Brecher, E. M. *The sex researchers*. Boston: Little, Brown, 1969.

Comfort, Alex. *The anxiety makers*. London: Thomas Nelson, 1967.

Hartman, W. E. and Fithian, M. A. *Treatment of sexual dysfunction*. Long Beach, Calif.: Center for Marital and Sexual Studies, 1972.

Heiman, J., LoPiccolo, L. and LoPiccolo, J. *Becoming orgasmic: A sexual growth program for women*. Englewood Cliffs, N.J.: Prentice-Hall, 1976.

Hite, S. *The Hite report*. New York: Dell, 1976.

Hogan, D. R. The effectiveness of sex therapy: A review of the literature. In J. LoPiccolo and L. LoPiccolo (Eds.), *Handbook of sex therapy*. New York: Plenum, 1978.

Kaplan, H. S. *The new sex therapy*. New York: Brunner/Mazel, 1974.

Kaplan, H. S. Hypoactive sexual desire. *Journal of Sex and Marital Therapy*, 1977, 3(1), 3–9.

Karacan, I. Clinical value of nocturnal erection in the prognosis and diagnosis of impotence. *Medical Aspects of Sexuality*, April 1970, 27–34.

Kinsey, A. C., Pomeroy, W. B. and Martin, C. E. *Sexual behavior in the human male*. Philadelphia: W. B. Saunders, 1948.

Kinsey, A. C., Pomeroy, W. B., Martin, C. E. and Beggard, P. H. *Sexual behavior in the human female*. New York: Pocket Books, 1965. (Originally published 1953.)

Lobitz, W. C. and LoPiccolo, J. New methods in the behavioral treatment of sexual dysfunction. *Journal of Behavior Therapy and Experimental Psychiatry*, 1972, **3**, 265–271.

LoPiccolo, J. Direct treatment of sexual dysfunction. In J. LoPiccolo and L. LoPiccolo (Eds.), *Handbook of sex therapy*. New York: Plenum, 1978.

McCary, J. L. *Human sexuality*, 2nd ed. New York: Van Nostrand, 1973.

McGovern, K. B., Kirkpatrick, C. C. and LoPiccolo, J. A behavioral group treatment program for sexually dysfunctional couples. In J. LoPiccolo and L. LoPiccolo (Eds.), *Handbook of sex therapy*. New York: Plenum, 1978.

Marks, J. Behavioral psychotherapy of adult neurosis. In S. Garfield and A. Bergin (Eds.), *Handbook of psychotherapy and behavior change*. New York: Wiley, 1978.

Masters, W. H. and Johnson, V. E. *Human sexual response*. Boston: Little, Brown, 1966.

Masters, W. H. and Johnson, V. E. *Human sexual inadequacy*. Boston: Little, Brown, 1970.

Pion, R. *The last sex manual*. New York: Wyden Books, 1977.

*National Register of Certified Health Service Providers in Sex Education and Sex Therapy*. Washington, D.C.: American Association of Sex Educators, Counselors and Therapists.

Williams, M. H. Individual sex therapy. In J. LoPiccolo and L. LoPiccolo (Eds.), *Handbook of sex therapy*. New York: Plenum, 1978.

# CHAPTER 59

# Social Influence Therapy

JOHN S. GILLIS

*If any readers are partial to humanistic systems of psychotherapy, viewing the client as being worthy of respect and seeing the therapist always dealing with the client on an equal basis, prepare for a surprise. As John Gillis forthrightly states, "The approach is forthrightly manipulative."*

*Perhaps we therapists tend to deny the therapeutic influence of matters such as doctoral degrees, diplomas on walls, double doors, soft chairs, attractive receptionists, expensive furniture—but we can be sure that such matters that have nothing to do with a therapist's effectiveness will nevertheless have some effect on the client.*

*Gillis, in my judgment, is correct in his statement that Social Influence Therapy can be applied to all systems of psychotherapy. However, it must be recognized that some practitioners will reject purposefully employing such tactics.*

*This is one of those chapters that actually cuts across all theories—as do the chapters on Feminist Therapy, Crisis Intervention, and Sex Therapies—and should greatly interest all who practice our arcane arts.*

Social Influence Therapy is an approach to treatment that attempts to change a client's attitudes or perspective by (1) having the therapist establish a position of ascendancy and (2) then using this position to implement attitude-change strategies. The system borrows freely from other disciplines those persuasive techniques of demonstrated or potential value, such strategies deriving mainly from social psychology. Thus the therapist attempting to maximize influence incorporates ideas and methods from such areas as attitude change and interpersonal attraction. The literature on placebo effects in medicine also serves as a frequent source of tactics.

The approach is forthrightly manipulative. Influence attempts are the primary strategies of treatment and are initiated and controlled by the therapist. It is, in fact, the position of those sympathetic to this view that most contemporary therapies involve strong com-

ponents of influence; social influence therapists simply attempt to identify these and then maximize their efficacy through careful pretherapy planning.

## HISTORY

Awareness of the significance of social influence factors in treatment is certainly not new. The importance of influence, placebo effects, and so-called "nonspecific" factors have been recognized in medicine since ancient times. While acknowledgment of their role in psychotherapeutic practice is more recent, Jerome Frank's classic, *Persuasion and Healing*, summarized a body of speculation and empirical work concerning such factors as early as 1961.

The past several years have witnessed both an increased awareness of influence pro-

804

cesses and an exploration of the manner in which they work in therapy. *Psychotherapy and the Psychology of Behavior Change,* by Goldstein, Heller, and Sechrest (1968), has a good deal to say about strategies of influence. So do a series of studies by Strong and his colleagues (Strong, 1968; Schmidt & Strong, 1970; Strong & Matross, 1973) and by other investigators (Harari, 1972; Dell, 1973). It is now not uncommon to view therapy in terms of demand characteristics (McReynolds & Tory, 1972), manipulation (Krainin, 1972), suggestibility (Lang, Lazovik, & Reynolds, 1965), and the intentional manipulation of client expectancies (Klein et al., 1969). Torrey (1972) has pointed out the (to many) distressing similarities between witch doctors and therapists; the bulk of these commonalities involve various means by which influence is exercised.

While many investigators have acknowledged the importance of such processes, few would regard themselves as influence therapists. The difference lies primarily in the readiness of the social influence therapist to elaborate the tactical possibilities of this position. This writer highlighted this pivotal difference in the 1974 *Psychology Today* article that brought the system to public attention. In that paper I urged that the strategic implications of the influence position be taken seriously. I then described a series of techniques by which this could be accomplished. No claim was made that therapists *should* employ such methods; it *was* argued that they should be aware of their potential efficacy in treatment. I elaborated my theme in my 1979 monograph. Here I attempted to (1) bring together the diverse theoretical and empirical writings concerning influence; (2) identify those areas of literature, both scientific and anecdotal, that might serve as sources of useful therapeutic tactics; and (3) illustrate the means by which such tactics could be generated and implemented.

In my 1974 and 1979 works I outlined a broad framework for conceptualizing influence in therapy. In the years between their publication a number of specific tenets of the

system were assessed empirically. Several of these studies are listed below in the "Current Status" section.

## CURRENT STATUS

A number of psychologists, some of whom would not consider themselves "social influence therapists," are acquainted with strategic approaches to maximizing influence. Some who are most familiar with the tactical approaches to be discussed are listed below. None of these individuals necessarily uses the tactics described or necessarily espouses the views presented herein. All, however, are knowledgeable regarding the assumptions, purposes, and applications of Social Influence Therapy. These psychologists include Michael Berren, Ph.D., Phoenix, Arizona; Keith Blevens, Ph.D., Richmond, California; Robert Childress, Ph.D., Tucson, Arizona; James C. Megas, Ph.D., Brownsville, Texas; S. W. Patrick, Ph.D., Houston, Texas; and Michael Sherrod, Ph.D., Knoxville, Tennessee.

Workshops and seminars on Social Influence Therapy, although offered on no regular schedule, have been presented at various locations throughout the country in the past few years. Two workshops were offered in 1979 in the Portland, Oregon, area. Any individuals or groups interested in attending or initiating such functions should contact this author.

I have recently published several papers that either outline the social influence position (Gillis, 1974, 1979) or lend empirical support to one of its tenets.

Five works lend empirical support to Social Influence Theory: (1) A 1977 study by Childress and Gillis points up the capacity of pretherapy role-induction interviews to enhance the client's expectations of benefit; (2) a 1976 report by Venzor, Gillis, and Beal shows the diverse range of therapeutic styles that clients accept as helpful; (3) a 1979 paper by Gillis and Patrick demonstrates that this tolerance of therapeutic styles extends even to approaches in which virtually every remark of the client is negated or challenged; (4) a 1977 paper by Friedenberg and Gillis (1977) demonstrates the effectiveness of videotaped lectures for enhancing clients' self-esteem; and (5) a 1978 study by Byrd, Osborn, and Gillis demonstrates the therapeutic effects of desensitization, even when the hierarchy employed is not appropriate to the problem.

In addition to evaluating the adequacy of their own propositions regarding therapeutic change, influence therapists refer to the empirical literature in a wide range of areas, particularly social psychology, to generate tactics. An individual attempting to learn to maximize influence might thus be directed to review the work in such areas as interpersonal attraction, placebo effects, coercive persuasion, and hypnosis.

## THEORY

Most of the theory underlying Social Influence Therapy concerns the nature of social interactions, particularly those interactions that have as their goal some change on the part of one or all of the participants. In this respect the theoretical base is narrow: Little concern is given to the origins and development of personality. Indeed, there is no explicit theory of maladjustment, other than the position that satisfaction with oneself and one's situation owes little to the objective realities of those situations.

Although Social Influence Therapy offers no detailed theory of personality or psychopathology, it is generally accepted that an individual's attitudes in therapy are critical for success. In this regard, Social Influence Therapy is in agreement with a number of theories—Albert Ellis's rational-emotive approach, the cognitive behavior therapies—that stress the fundamental importance of one's thought processes in adjustment. This being the case, the primary goal of Social Influence Therapy is to alter the patient's attitudes or perspective toward him- or herself and his or her situation. Although it is

obviously helpful if things change objectively for a client, behavioral changes are neither necessary nor sufficient for the critical cognitive alterations that must take place. Many influence tactics function, in fact, to convince the client that certain desired changes are already beginning to develop, and that he or she can already regard things as having changed for the better. Social influence therapists are certainly not opposed to behavior change, but it is apparent that people who are depressed about their failures or who are concerned about hostility are often no more extreme in these regards than the bulk of individuals who are not at all concerned about them. The task for the influence therapist is thus to alter individuals' view of things and not necessarily the behaviors themselves. This is, of course, precisely what happens when "self-acceptance" is realized by client-centered or other approaches. Empirical evidence on therapeutic outcomes indicates, in any case, that psychotherapy seems best able to achieve the objective of changing the individual's subjective state. To some extent, then, the goals of Social Influence Therapy are simply those that can be most reliably attained.

The probability of these goals being realized is largely dependent on the manner in which the therapist exercises influence. It has been found useful to consider the exercise of influence in therapy as a three-stage process. The first stage involves the enhancement of the client's expectation of benefits; the second, establishment of a position of influence by the therapist; and the third, use of this position to implement change. It is during this third stage that the actual content of treatment, the "healing ritual" as Jerome Frank (1974) calls it, is implemented. It is also possible to speak of a fourth stage, wherein any changes that have occurred are solidified. The tactics appropriate to this last purpose generally overlap those in stage 3 however and the two are treated together here.

The theory of change underlying Social Influence Therapy has some important similarities with Schein's (1971) model of persuasion. Presently held maladaptive beliefs must be "unfrozen"; new views must be inculcated. Clients are seen as seeking treatment because their approaches to the world, particularly the manner in which they conceptualize the social environment and their place in it, are not successful. "Not successful" here means that they do not get from others the responses—affection, recognition, respect—they would like. The number and severity of their objective problems may be no different from those of many persons who are reasonably satisfied with their situations. They are however, in Frank's (1974) terms, "demoralized." If they are to benefit from treatment, this demoralization must be combated. An altered view of circumstances, a differing way of assessing themselves, a new framework or belief system must be realized.

Significant change in a basic attitude is not easily accomplished. Nevertheless, such changes are realized in many extratherapeutic situations (religious conversions, advertising, political indoctrinations), and the social-psychological literature has much to say about the variables that are instrumental in these circumstances. It is clear, for example, that an important initial condition has been satisfied simply by the client's present perspective being unsatisfactory ("disconfirmed," in Schein's [1971] terms). Of the remaining factors involved in major alterations of attitude or beliefs only a few can readily be controlled by the change agent, in this case the therapist. The best that the therapist can do is to assure that (1) a different and plausible alternative perspective is presented; and (2) the conditions of its presentation are such that they maximize the likelihood of the client adopting it. These conditions are best accomplished by the therapist attending to the possibilities that his or her position allows, that is, attending to the tasks of maximizing expectations of gain, gaining a position of power, and conducting a plausible, persuasive healing ritual. The alternative perspective offered by the therapist can be as complex as a psychoanalytic or behaviorist view of human beings or as simple as the message that "you have pos-

itive qualities as well as distressing ones." The most important characteristic of the new perspective is not its objective validity but its usefulness to the client. An explanation of one's current difficulties in terms of the frustrated rage of childhood (and the performance of a therapeutic ritual designed to vent this rage) may be a valuable proposal for a client even if there is little evidence to support it.

The theory underlying Social Influence Therapy might be most succinctly summarized as follows: (1) Clients seek treatment because their view of life and themselves is unsatisfactory; (2) the purpose of psychotherapy is to induce the client to adopt a more benign perspective; (3) this can be accomplished only if the therapist maximizes his or her control over the variables conducive to change; and (4) most of these variables involve the establishment and use of interpersonal influence.

## METHODOLOGY

Even a casual perusal of the psychotherapy literature of the past 25 years reveals ample awareness of the role of influence processes. Social Influence Therapy is alone neither in its primary goal—altering the client's perspective—or in its stress on the primacy of cognitive factors in adjustment. What does give the approach some uniqueness is its emphasis on developing specific strategic maneuvers to maximize influence. It is one thing to recognize the contribution of a client's expectations to the eventual outcome of treatment. It is quite another to advocate that the therapist develop an array of tactics specifically intended to raise those expectations and to suggest that appropriate tactics might be borrowed from such nontherapeutic enterprises as advertising and attitude change. Social Influence Therapy, then, to the extent it offers something unique to the therapy researcher or practitioner, does so by its unabashed advocacy of tactical planning and its willingness to suggest the sorts of maneuvers that might be employed.

The three-stage influence process mentioned in the "Theory" section was developed largely as a framework for generating influence tactics. It can also serve as a convenient scheme for organizing the discussion of these procedures. It should be remembered as these methods are described that Social Influence Therapy is very much an open system as far as tactics are concerned. Indeed the major contribution of the approach may be to draw attention to some sources of tactics heretofore neglected by therapists. By reviewing such areas—interpersonal attraction and attitude change, for example—with the purpose of identifying items that might generalize to therapy, practitioners will doubtless be able to develop an impressive variety of innovative methods on their own. The suggestions raised by the social influence approach merely serve as examples of the kinds of tactical possibilities that abound in areas seemingly remote from therapy.

With this caveat, several specific procedures that might be employed to maximize influence can be described. These will, as noted, be organized in terms of a three-stage influence process. Due to space limitations only one or two illustrative strategies will be given for each stage. A more elaborate listing can be found in *Social Influence in Psychotherapy* (Gillis, 1979).

### Stage 1. Building Expectations. 

The first phase of therapy involves enhancing expectations of benefit. (This stage might also be thought of as maximizing placebo effects.) There are two aspects to this: increasing the client's faith in, and commitment to, psychotherapy itself and increasing his or her faith that the therapist is an especially adept practitioner of the art. The first objective might be accomplished in any of several ways.

First, the client's commitment to treatment (or need to believe in therapy) can be enhanced by introducing severe "initiation rites." Many therapy systems and treatment communities already practice this: Drug treatment groups may require prospective members to shave their heads and perform menial tasks for a time prior to receiving full status in the program; candidates for Primal Therapy spend a couple of days isolated in a motel room, refraining from sex, cigarettes, and alcohol. In more typical clinical settings the severity of one's initiation, the price he or she has to pay to gain admission to therapy, might be increased by having the client complete an exhaustive screening routine, perhaps involving repeated administrations of lengthy personality inventories. Inconvenient appointment times might be scheduled for initial sessions; clients might be made to spend some time on a waiting list; the therapist—because of a busy schedule—might have to arrive late for a few weekend appointments that the client made some sacrifices to attend.

Second, forced-compliance studies in social psychology suggest that under certain conditions persons will come to adopt attitudes that they have used to persuade others, even if these attitudes are contrary to their initial positions. Clients who have been in treatment for only a short time might therefore be asked to tell still newer clients, perhaps those awaiting their first contact with the therapist, about the benefits and promise of treatment.

Third, a commitment-enhancing gambit of a different order has been referred to as the "pseudo-free choice" maneuver. Here the therapist, preferably after one or two sessions, informs the client that two alternative forms of treatment are employed. One of these involves rather direct confrontation. While relatively stressful, it often yields strongly positive outcomes for the client who can cope with it. The alternative is more benign and less stressful, but also more superficial. The therapist adds that he doesn't typically give people a choice of treatment strategies, but that the client seemed to be one who could indeed handle the more challenging approach if he or she should choose it. The dice are, of course, loaded; clients invariably choose the more difficult approach (if there are any doubts that the client might not select this procedure the tactic should not be used). By virtue of this maneuver the client makes a commitment to a certain way of proceeding. His or her investment in the treatment's effectiveness, and belief that it will work, is increased. He or she has selected it precisely for these reasons. In presenting the choice to the client in this way the therapist is also sending a clear message: This is a client with obvious strengths who will indeed profit from therapy.

Increasing the client's faith in the personal merits of the therapist can be accomplished with similar maneuvers. The common theme of these practices is giving the client positive information about the therapist but doing so in a manner that is not suspect. To this end the therapist might arrange to have the client overhear certain persons (former clients or possibly confederates) discussing the merits of the therapist. This is most easily accomplished in the clinic waiting room. A second possibility is the "busy schedule" gambit. Here the client is told, most conveniently by the clinic receptionist or by a colleague during a role induction interview, that Dr. X is precisely the therapist he or she needs. Dr. X is in considerable demand, however, a very full schedule being displayed to substantiate this point. After considerable negotiations about scheduling problems the client is eventually assigned to Dr. X.

A variety of additional tactics designed to build expectations have been described (Gillis, 1979). I also consider the *maintenance* of credibility through the use of a series of statements ("no miss" interpretations) that are likely to be viewed as perceptive and insightful by a high proportion of clients. It is perhaps appropriate here to restate the position that "Social Influence Therapy" originated as an attempt to offer an alternative view of treatment. "No-miss" interpretations, for example, were seen as statements that were offered as comments on a client's situation with great frequency. Giving them tactical status therefore amounts to little more than claiming that therapists should recognize what they are doing. If such practices

increase the effectiveness of treatment, however, the therapist may wish to use them strategically rather than leave their occurrence to chance.

***Stage 2. Gaining Ascendancy.*** "Ascendancy" in psychotherapy has some overlap with the concept of "power" in social psychology, but the two are not identical. To gain ascendancy in therapy is to achieve a status where one's remarks are "taken account of" by the client. Such status is necessary, we would argue, since the essential messages the therapist delivers are not substantially different from those given the client by others. The therapist's communicating of the message (e.g., "you *can* control your anger"; "you are an adequate person") is often effective where other's doing so was not, however, because the therapist presents it (1) in terms that the client has never before encountered or, more likely, (2) from a uniquely authoritative and powerful position.

Tactics for gaining such a position can be usefully classified under two broad headings: command power and "friendship" (or referent) power. The former can be, and is, achieved with a number of traditional practices. These include the use of powerful arguments in which the therapist clearly has the advantage; the use of esoteric jargon and interpretations in which the client has no choice but to defer; and the "audience-performer" strategy, in which the client's task is essentially to present his or her case while the therapist comments on the meaning and appropriateness of this verbal performance. The research literature suggests a myriad of additional procedures for establishing command power. Schmidt and Strong (1970), for example, have empirically determined a set of characteristics by which clients define "expertness" in therapists; these include such items as hand shaking, sitting postures, and a confident tone of voice. Torrey (1972) advises on the construction of a persuasive "edifice," the foundation of which is the display of the accoutrements of authority and knowledge.

"Friendship" power is perhaps more often sought by present-day practitioners. Effective tactics here induce allegiance of client to therapist, usually because the latter has established himself as an attractive, decent, caring person whose friendship and approval the client wishes to maintain. Cohesive links can often be fashioned (and likely are) in therapy by the use of the "ingratiation" tactics described by Jones (1964). These include such practices as expressing liking for the client (making it difficult for him to dislike you), flattering him (by commenting on his positive characteristics or his ability to handle confrontation), stressing the similarities between the two of you ("I know what it's like being under those kinds of pressures"), and stating your own strengths in a noncompetitive manner. Even admitting one's weaknesses or regrets about not having sufficiently helped a client can beget cohesion when used at appropriate times. Most therapists employ some or all of these practices unwittingly. Social Influence Therapy points up the possibility of using them strategically. The value of obtaining a positive affective response from the client, one of liking and respect, cannot be overstated. In the extreme, one might argue as I (1979) have, that once one has induced a patient to feel positively about the therapist and therapy itself, *nothing else* need be accomplished in order for the treatment to be regarded as successful.

A range of other strategies can be used to bring about a cohesive relationship between client and therapist. These might include:

1. The disclosure of personal difficulties by the therapist
2. The initiation of unexpected or "disinhibiting" experiences in which both parties participate (George Bach's birth scenarios and constructive aggression exercises probably accomplish this, as do some psychodrama formats)
3. The introduction of an external enemy (e.g., an impersonal society, tyrannical parents, materialistic employers) against whom client and therapist can unite.

Each of these tactics has a basis in social psychological research. Any number of similar strategies can be derived from that literature or from the therapist's experience *outside* of the clinic.

*Stage 3. The Healing Ritual.*   The third segment of treatment involves the carrying out of a therapeutic ritual. If the initial stages—building expectations and establishing ascendancy—have been successfully negotiated, this segment, while it appears to be the focus of therapy, should present few problems. The task of the therapist is to select a set of procedures that the client can accept as plausible. The client, that is, should view the activities of the therapeutic hour—discussing childhood experiences, venting intense emotions, reenacting one's birth, meditating, repeating positive statements about oneself—as being somehow related to the source of his or her disorder and to its alleviation. The concerns of the therapist here are two: determination of a treatment method that the client will find believable (meditation or exploration of one's dreams may not seem, to a ghetto resident, as the answer to his or her problems) and competent performance of that ritual. An important point here is that the client who expects to benefit will accept a wide range of therapeutic rituals or styles. Part of the therapist's task is thus to simply avoid the totally implausible ritual (such as the meditation-ghetto client combination). If selection is carefully made, however, a ritual likely to have maximum influence power with each specific client can usually be identified.

In addition to encouraging a thoughtful selection of treatment methods, the therapist interested in exerting influence might consider the following two methods: (1) The therapist may provide the client with evidence that he or she is indeed changing as treatment progresses. This can be accomplished with techniques as elaborate as charting response rate changes over time, or as simple as selectively commenting on anything that might be remotely construed as change. Used in this way, such feedback is a vehicle to *induce* change. Used in this way, such feedback is a vehicle to *induce* change rather than a recognition of change already accomplished. The therapist might also consider adding a description of the altered behavior so that the client will know specifically *how* to change.

(2) The therapist may direct the client to behave differently—that is, *tell* him or her to change. If authority has been effectively established, many clients require nothing more than an order to change and a clear description of what the new responses should be.

These, then, are some of the methods that can be used to enhance the effectiveness of treatment. There are countless others, of course, limited only by the ingenuity (and perhaps the role-playing ability) of the individual therapist. The therapist interested in social influence will consider some such maneuvers as adjuncts to his or her customary, perhaps more traditional, methods.

## APPLICATIONS

It is difficult at this juncture to map the limits of influence tactics. It was originally thought that the tactics would be most readily applicable with patients who (1) were not severely ill, (2) were highly susceptible to suggestions, (3) did not have highly circumscribed symptoms, and (4) were somewhat vague about their own desired outcomes from treatment. Neurotics, particularly hysterics, and those with relatively moderate personality disorders were obvious possibilities. These persons would have much in common with the clients whom Frank (1974) labels as "demoralized." Influence maneuvers would thus be most efficacious for those who were anxious and depressed, had lost hope that things might improve, and felt that they didn't measure up to either their own or other's expectations.

Fortunately or not, the greater proportion of clients seeking psythotherapy would seem

to qualify as appropriate under these guidelines. What such individuals require is not a major change in situation or behavior but a fresh perspective; a perspective that will give them a feeling of control over their destiny, a feeling that life and they themselves can be understood and enjoyed.

Influence tactics have proven, in fact, to be applicable to a much broader spectrum of patients than these. They have been successfully employed with some psychotic patients. Influence strategies have also been adapted for use in group, marital, and family therapies. The principal patient sample for which they are relevant, however, remains those who are "demoralized." The techniques have thus been most often employed with outpatients and college students having vague complaints of depression, social isolation, and alienation.

## CASE EXAMPLE

Social Influence Therapy is most usefully considered as an adjunct to other systems (although it can be maintained that the substantive aspects of these systems have little to do with their effectiveness). Citing a case in which the method was successful, then, is most readily done by identifying a case in which a special conscious effort was made to maximize influence, regardless of which other techniques—the healing rituals—were employed. One case is familiar to this writer, however, in which influence tactics constituted almost the sole approach to treatment. This case was meant to demonstrate the power of providing patients with concrete feedback that they have indeed changed even before this change is fully realized.

The client was a 21-year-old female with a phobia for injections; a phobia of such severity that, a few months previously, she had postponed her wedding in order to avoid a blood test. She was unable to receive an injection without fainting or, at the very least, engaging in considerable histrionics. She came in for treatment when she learned that within the next three weeks she would have to receive a "shot" for an allergy. After discussing the problem, the therapist assured her that dealing with the phobia would be no problem and that they would be using a behavioral technique that had proven very successful in the past. The "treatment" consisted of handling a toy syringe every evening for 10 minutes. The prospect of this task did not arouse any anxiety in the client and it was decided that she would return in one week for another interview. The therapist then handed the syringe to the client, and wished her good luck (in a manner analogous to Dorothy of the *Wizard of Oz* being sent off to kill the wicked witch).

The client reported back the following week to participate in a 10-minute session with the therapist. This meeting consisted of therapist and client squirting each other with the toy syringes. It was explained that this was a very important aspect of treatment. At the end of the session the client was told once again to handle the syringe every evening and then to report back in one week. At the next session the client was presented with a "certificate of improvement," awarded with no small degree of ceremony.

For the first few minutes, therapist and client again squirted each other with the syringes. The therapist then asked if handling the syringe at home had been upsetting. The client reported that it was not (which was expected, since the toy version of the feared object had aroused little reaction initially). The therapist then announced that treatment was completed and congratulated her on such a speedy recovery. He told the client, that, as good as he thought the method was, he had never seen anyone go through it quite so smoothly and with such dramatic changes. The therapist then reported that his supervisor had been watching the previous week's sessions through a one-way vision screen (this was the case) and that he too was amazed at the rapidity with which the client recovered. Indeed he was so impressed that he thought it appropriate that she be presented with some formal recognition of the change. The ther-

apist then gave the client an impressive-looking "certificate of change" signed by the supervisor (and identical to that given introductory psychology students for participation in departmental experiments). It was explained that this was very rarely done but, considering the fact that her progress had been exemplary, he and the supervisor thought it appropriate here. The therapist then shook her hand, congratulated her, and told her that she was now ready to receive her injection.

The client immediately made an appointment at the student health center. Unfortunately her allergy had cleared up and she did not require an injection. She then asked the physician to give her any shot at all because she wanted to prove that it really wouldn't bother her. The physician refused. Acting on the client's request, the therapist made arrangements with the health center for her to return for an injection of a saline solution. The client received the injection and reported only minor fearful anticipation. The certificate, she reported some weeks later, was still hanging on her bedroom wall.

It is not suggested that improvement in this case was traceable solely to the presentation of the "certificate of change." One can argue, for example, that the simple handling of the toy syringe might have served as a form of systematic desensitization for the client. Neither is the case meant to suggest a tactic that is appropriate to a large number of clients. Indeed such a transparent gambit is likely to evoke suspicion, if not outright derision, in most patients. The therapist must select tactics with the specific client in mind. What the case *is* intended to illustrate is the use of feedback to induce change and to solidify change once it has occurred. The specific procedures by which feedback is implemented to this end will vary with each patient. Such methods can be used as an adjunct to any method of treatment, including a more formalized systematic desensitization. More generally, this case report is meant to serve as a demonstration of the use of influence strategies with a patient who had formerly proven resistant to change. The reader interested in other case reports from influence therapy should consult my 1979 monograph, particularly the accounts of the use of "friendship power" with psychotic patients.

## SUMMARY

It has long been recognized that certain aspects of therapeutic interaction, apart from the techniques themselves, may contribute to the effectiveness of treatment. Such nonspecific factors are sometimes seen to be common to all effective therapeutic systems. The central tenets of Social Influence Therapy are that (1) within such nonspecific factors are contained the essential curative elements of therapy; and (2) these essential ingredients can be most usefully conceptualized as methods by which the therapist exerts influence over the client. Social Influence Therapy thus attempts to identify and analyze the many ways in which influence operates in therapy.

This approach was originally intended to offer an alternative perspective on existing systems of therapy. The initial goal of the system was to determine if all forms of therapy could be translated into a common set of terms—most likely those derived from social psychology. Because of a focus on the specific maneuvers used to exert influence, the influence perspective has come to be increasingly viewed as a strategic guide to therapeutic practice. In a broad fashion it may be said to possess the rudiments of a system of therapy: It includes a view of the client and his or her source of distress; a view of the therapist's role and task; a view of the interaction between the two; and suggestions as to the procedures that might make that interaction most efficacious. Because of these characteristics, it is probably possible to use Social Influence Therapy as one's major approach to practical treatment problems. It is this writer's belief, however, that Social Influence Therapy is still best considered an alternative conceptual scheme that can be applied to *all* systems of psychotherapy. So too are its tactical possibilities most usefully considered as adjuncts to more traditional systems.

Influence pervades all human interactions, therapy included. It can be enhanced by thoughtful planning, should the therapist decide to do this. It can be ignored, perhaps to the jeopardy of the encounter, only if some of the realities of human interaction are ignored.

## REFERENCES

Byrd, G. R., Osborn, S. and Gillis, J. S. Use of pseudodesensitization in the treatment of an experimentally produced fear. *Psychological Reports*, 1978, **43**, 947–952.

Childress, R. and Gillis, J. S. A study of pretherapy role induction as an influence process. *Journal of Clinical Psychology*, 1977, **33**, 540–544.

Dell, D. M. Counselor power base, influence attempts, and behavior. *Journal of Counseling Psychology*, 1973, **20**, 399–405.

Frank, J. D. *Persuasion and healing*. Baltimore: Johns Hopkins Press, 1961.

Frank, J. D. Psychotherapy: The restoration of morale. *American Journal of Psychiatry*, 1974, **131**, 271–274.

Friedenberg, W. P. and Gillis, J. S. An experimental study of the effectiveness of attitude change techniques for enhancing self-esteem. *Journal of Clinical Psychology*, 1977, **33**, 1120–1124.

Gillis, J. S. Therapist as manipulator. *Psychology Today*, December 1974, 90–95.

Gillis, J. S. *Social influence in psychotherapy: A description of the process and some tactical implications*. Counseling and Psychotherapy Monograph Series, No. 1. Pilgrimage Press, 1979.

Gillis, J. S. and Patrick, S. W. A comparative study of competitive and social reinforcement models of interview behavior. *Journal of Clinical Psychology*, 1980, *36*, 277–282.

Goldstein, A. P., Heller, K. and Sechrest, L. *Psychotherapy and the psychology of behavior change*. New York: Wiley, 1980, *36*, 277–282.

Harari, H. Cognitive manipulations with delinquent adolescents in group therapy. *Psychotherapy: Therapy, Research and Practice*, 1972, **9**, 303–307.

Jones, E. E. *Ingratiation: A social psychological analysis*. New York: Appleton, 1964.

Klein, M. H., Dittman, A. T., Parloff, M. B. and Gill,

M. M. Behavior therapy: Observations and reflections. *Journal of Consulting and Clinical Psychology*, 1969, **33**, 259–266.

Krainin, J. M. Psychotherapy by counter-manipulation. *American Journal of Psychiatry*, 1972, **129**, 749–750.

Lang, P. J., Lazovik, D. J. and Reynolds, D. J. Desensitization, suggestibility, and pseudotherapy. *Journal of Abnormal Psychology*, 1965, **70**, 395–402.

McReynolds, W. T. and Tori, C. A further assessment of attention-placebo effects and demand characteristics in studies of systematic desensitization. *Journal of Consulting and Clinical Psychology*, 1972, **38**, 261–264.

Schein, E. H. *Coercive persuasion*. New York: Norton, 1971.

Schmidt, L. D. and Strong, S. R. "Expert" and "inexpert" counselors. *Journal of Counseling Psychology*, 1970, **17**, 115–118.

Strong, S. R. Counseling: An interpersonal influence process. *Journal of Counseling Psychology*, 1968, **15**, 215–224.

Strong, S. R. and Matross, R. Change process in counseling and psychotherapy. *Journal of Counseling Psychology*, 1973, **20**, 25–37.

Torrey, E. F. What western psychotherapists can learn from witch doctors. *American Journal of Orthopsychiatry*, 1972, **42**, 69–76.

Venzor, E., Gillis, J. S. and Beal, D. G. Preference for counselor response styles. *Journal of Counseling Psychology*, 1976, **23**, 538–542.

# CHAPTER 60

# Stress Management

HARRY A. OLSON and JOAN ROBERTS

As Harry Olson and Joan Roberts state in their chapter on Stress Management, theirs is a therapy for the well, used to bring well-functioning people higher up the scale of functioning. This is a well-known approach found in the so-called growth centers such as Esalin, and is dealt with in a number of chapters in this book, such as those by Joseph Hart, Nira Kefir, Jesse Lair, and Will Schutz.

The point that Olson and Roberts make is that most successful people could be even more successful if they would relax and take it easy. In a sense, this is the opposite position taken by George Gazda, who stresses the importance of below-par people learning new skills. Olson and Roberts say, in effect, that whatever skills you do have can be better employed if you learn to take it easy. Or, as a business saying goes, "Learn to work smarter, not harder."

Stress Management is aimed at the so-called Type A personality—hard drivers, typically executives who agonize over decisions, who are always pushing forward and are at high risk for a variety of psychosomatic diseases.

It seems highly probable that as time goes on, programs such as the one developed in this chapter will become increasingly common to modern businesses, to help people simultaneously to relax and yet be more successful. For a fuller account, this chapter should be read together with Forgione and Holmberg's chapter, "Comprehensive Relaxation."

Stress Management is a relatively new psychotherapeutic intervention process that draws from a number of well-established techniques including Biofeedback, hypnosis, the behavior therapies, and insight-oriented approaches. Its goal is to alter the individual's subjective experience of both psychological and physiological stress as well as to lower such physiological indices of stress disorders as hypertension, cardiovascular disorders, diabetes, gastrointestinal disorders, and others. The program is multimodal. A variety of techniques are employed including hypnosis, cognitive restructuring, and an educational component embracing nutrition as well as exercise. In this manner the individual is helped to change his or her physical response pattern and to modify the beliefs and behaviors that produced the stress response in the first place.

## HISTORY

Attempts to understand the role of stress and psychological factors in disease date back to Hippocrates. Moving into modern times, nineteenth-century scientific methods fostered a specialization and emphasis on organic factors that excluded psychological speculation. Sigmund Freud, Ivan Pavlov, and Walter B. Cannon were the prime movers of modern Stress Management (Wittkower, 1977). Freud's contribution revolved around his discovery of the unconscious and fundamental psychodynamics. In contrast, Pavlov's introduction of the "conditioned reflex" provided both a method for inducing stress as well as for measuring the associated emotions. Cannon noted that situations evoking fear or rage in the individual could produce important bodily changes (fight or flight reactions). The concept of "homeostasis" was developed as part of his description of the individual's physiological equilibrium. As a result of these three separate developments, the twentieth century began with both psychological and neurophysiological models available as well as techniques providing access to unconscious processes.

Psychoanalytic theory played a leading role in early formulations and treatment of stress disorders. In postulating that bodily changes have a symbolic meaning, Freud paved the way for psychoanalytic treatment of psychosomatic disorders. Both Felix Deutsch and Melanie Klein developed theoretical models that provided analytic explanations for the stress diseases. Franz Alexander (1950) explained psychosomatic disorders in terms of three key variables: (1) inherited or acquired organic vulnerability; (2) psychological conflict and defense mechanisms; (3) precipitating life situations. In 1930 he founded the Chicago Psychoanalytic Institute, where systematic psychoanalytic treatment of these disorders was carried out. Specific psychological patterns were found to be related to a number of diseases including ulcerative colitis, bronchial asthma, dermatitis, and duodenal ulcer. In general, early psychoanalysts saw psychosomatic symptoms as regressive physiological responses related to the underlying psychological regression. Psychoanalytic treatment for management of stress disorders became increasingly less and less popular, and because they were often not amenable to this approach and the treatment was not always cost effective. There has also been a gradual shift from treatment to prevention in Stress Management.

## CURRENT STATUS

A number of trends are outstanding when the current literature on Stress Management is reviewed. First there is a move toward prevention and an openness to experimentation and "creative interventions." Many individuals and firms are providing "stress reduction" programs. However, missing from many of these programs are consistency and ongoing evaluation. As with hypnosis and Biofeedback, two important treatment techniques, overexposure and inflated promises have led to negative reactions on the part of many individuals as well as the professional community. "Stress Management" may be in for the same type of experience as other programs that proliferate like "mushrooms after the rain." It remains the responsibility of mental health professionals to control the quality of programs and to evaluate outcome. The techniques utilized in Stress Management run the gamut of practical *how to*'s such as "time management" or "priority setting" to more traditional types of psychotherapeutic interventions, biofeedback, and hypnosis.

Insight-oriented individual or group psychotherapy programs are an outgrowth of the analytic tradition, but often are problem focused. Rosenman and Friedman (1969) have identified a personality (Type A) with a high risk of coronary disease and a low-risk personality (Type B). Some of the chief characteristics of the Type A person are considerable aggressiveness, competitiveness, impatience, and an extreme sense of time urgency. Studies show that while the Type B person goes about his or her basic life tasks in a far less driven, more relaxed fashion, he or she often gets more accomplished. Rosenman and Friedman point out that "Type A" behaviors are encouraged by our contemporary Western civilization and that there are even "Type A settings." For these reasons, it is difficult for this "driven" personality to change even in the face of increased health risks. Responsibility and work pressure play a key role in maintaining this life style. Studies of individuals in especially responsible or demanding positions, such as air traffic controllers, have a high risk and earlier onset of hypertension and peptic ulcers than did the control group of airmen (Cobb and Rose, 1973). Roskies has doncuted groups for postcoronary males focusing on behavioral change in an attempt to modify "Type A" patterns (Roskies et al., 1978). In general, the postcoronary patients have fared well in these group experiences. Additional evaluation and research is ongoing. The techniques focus on increasing the individuals awareness of "Type A" patterns and changing them with the help of the social support of the group. There are still many questions, however, regarding the meaning of the "Type A" syndrome and the most effective interventions into this constellation of behavior.

Frankel (1973) and Field (1979) are involved in Stress Management of disorders through hypnosis. Frankel distinguishes between "mild hypnosis" or relaxation, symptom removal, and hypnotherapy. The hypnosis literature abounds with single case studies of stress disorders, but there is little discussion of hypnosis in prevention programs or in groups for stress control. Group processes have tended to rely on systematic relaxation as the method for returning individuals to homeostasis.

Biofeedback continues to be an effective technique for Stress Management but is generally tied to a laboratory setting. The problem is one of helping individuals generalize from the calm of the lab to the "chaos" of a busy, demanding work setting. However, a growing number of portable, small-scale instruments provide feedback regarding blood pressure and cardiac function. We prefer to see them used as adjuncts to a program rather than utilized solely by themselves.

In considering the variety of stress management techniques utilized by management consultants and health care providers, we designed our own multimodal approach to Stress Management.

## THEORY

In designing a stress management program suitable for industrial groups or individual clients, we attempted to integrate techniques from the most current approaches to stress. Consideration was given to psychobiological studies, psychological variables, and sociological findings. The resulting program provides three main features: (1) Reduction of physical tension through hypnosis; (2) cognitive restructuring of high-stress situations; (3) education and the learning of improved coping skills.

Research findings and our clinical experience indicated that individuals in high-stress situations would need to learn a method of relaxing themselves that could be applied "as needed." Training in autohypnosis proved most efficient in terms of time and degree of response in contrast to systematic relaxation or Biofeedback. Individuals unable to enter trance have nevertheless reported deep relaxation. Biofeedback equipment is included in the program more as a demonstration tool than as a clinical intervention. Individuals report that they reach a state of physiological homeostasis rather early in our program; the challenge is for them to maintain this state. For this reason, we offer a cognitive restructuring component to the program and follow-up over a two-year period. Intensive follow-up and ongoing assessment are especially important in view of the limited systematic field research.

The cognitive restructuring techniques range from specific management techniques such as problem solving or setting priorities to raising central philosophical issues and establishing individual life goals. This scope is particularly helpful for the workaholic, or "Type A" individual, who often participates in efficiency-oriented programs to learn how to be a better "Type A." Even in presenting routine concepts such as time management techniques, we point out that the goal is to "work smart" rather than "work hard." By allocating "time to think" rather than jumping into relentless activity, the individual saves considerable effort in the long run. The "hurry syndrome" is discouraged at every turn. For persons who deny the reality that they have a lopsided life style with close interpersonal relationships getting "short shrift," we introduce them to the "wheel of life." The key areas included are: work, friendship, love or intimate ties, religious-philosophical issues, leisure, and self. The emotions associated with each dimension are discussed at length, and it is noted that if even one part is missing, one is probably in for a bumpy ride. Research such as Lynch's (1977) work on cardiovascular disease suggests that the "bumpy ride" eventually results in increased physical vulnerability.

Another important issue raised by our program is humor. Any of the stress carrier's victims (commonly known as associates and employees) will attest to his or her lack of a sense of humor in the face of an absurd task. High-stress people are so competitive that they can't laugh at themselves or the situation when appropriate. In conjunction with humor and keeping life in some reasonable perspective, the program introduces some basic rational-emotive principles from Albert Ellis's theory (1962). Various irrational ideas common to Western society are presented with emphasis on the need to be perfect, have everyone love you, and so forth. It is suggested that while it would be "nice" to be successful at every undertaking with full staff cooperation, it isn't "absolutely necessary" for feeling stress free. It is not events themselves that make us unhappy, frustrated, or stressed but what each individual tells him- or herself about a given event that produces the dysphoric feeling. Often if you "use it" instead of letting it "use you," it is possible to take advantage of a "failure."

Just as high-stress individuals seek perfection in themselves, they often demand it in others. They exert a degree of controlling behavior at work and home that undermines relationships and productivity. We emphasize that you can only "control yourself"

and that imperfectly at best. There is no way to "make" others perform. The effective manager learns how to engage others in creative cooperation. The emphasis is shifted from an ego orientation (will I succeed or fail?) to a task orientation (how can I get this job done?).

Another issue important for "Type A" managers is aggression. Often we find that these persons are not sufficiently assertive in delegating tasks or explaining overall goals to staff. They then become overwhelmed and feel that they "never get any help"; frustration builds, and they "blow up" at staff. For this reason some assertiveness training is built into the program, although these are hardly passive, dependent clients.

In contrast to the cognitive restructuring portion of the program, the educational component involves little discussion. The emphasis here is on holism and health maintenance. Managers are presented with information and statistics geared to get them to reevaluate their own health "probabilities." The data presented includes the incidence of disease as related to recent life changes, the importance of a balanced life and close personal ties for general health as well as weight reduction, exercise, and smoking control. Since this program involves a variety of personal contracts, these individually designed plans may incorporate the behavior modification plan for each individual. It is not unusual to meet up with a middle-age overweight client having one or more stress-aggravated disorders (e.g., hypertension, peptic ulcer, etc.) who also smokes and works over weekends. In this type of situation, one begins the modification plan in the life area in which (1) the individual is most willing to work on and (2) has a high likelihood of success. By the time one has completed the basic program and initial follow-up, both long- and short-term goals are outlined.

The assessment of individual change and program effectiveness is central to the stress program. Firms have frequently complained to us that some management programs come in, share some good concepts, and leave. Positive changes last a few weeks, fading gradually. For this reason, our follow-up extends for a two-year period with confidential contact of participants. Counseling and referral to outside resources is included in the program.

## METHODOLOGY

While stress management programs exist in a variety of formats on location for business and industry and for the general public, the intervention process to be described here is the individual program. It is designed for the person who wishes to correct a particular problem or manage life pressures more effectively. Such a person may not require or desire a more traditional psychotherapeutic treatment. The individual program is a time-limited (16 visit) psychoeducational experience designed to train the client in cognitive management skills and in techniques for physiological control. The program as described is flexible enough to reflect clinicians' individual theoretical orientations. The following discussion emphasizes an Adlerian approach.

After opening introductions, the initial interview serves to gather essential background information and to orient the client as to what can be expected during the course of the 16 sessions. A fact sheet is completed with such information as age, occupation, income level, members of the nuclear family, parents' occupations, and place in the family of origin. A brief medical history is then taken, which also includes the client's own report as to how he or she handles stressful situations. Since appropriate and rapid screening is a necessary part of this program, such information is taken in detail; the therapist immediately processes several questions: *Is the client appropriate for this program? What are major life-style issues in the client's background? How functional is this client right now? What goals are likely to arise?* The next area of inquiry focuses upon the client's stated concerns—why he or she is there. As part of the assessment this information provides useful life-style information and often an estimate of the client's level of hope and degree of activity.

At this point clients are usually informed that the "problems" of which they complain are their strategies for coping with life's tasks; that difficulties such as anxiety and depression, for example, are actually creative endeavors turned toward unproductive goals and portray their level of discouragement. The emphasis from the beginning is on each client as an active, creative agent, not as a passive victim; and that together we will tap his or her well of creativity and use it to solve problems. This approach reinforces the client's owning of his or her personal responsibility and is explicitly stated.

If the client volunteers a "symptom" as part of the problem, the Dreikurs question is asked: "If you did not have this symptom, how would your life be different?" (1954). If the client is able to give a relatively concrete answer, it is likely that the area indicated in the answer—for example, improved sexual relations—is the very area he or she is trying to avoid by producing the symptom. The reader is referred to Dreikurs (1954) for a full explanation.

The stress battery is administered next. This is a compilation of short scales including a modification of the Holmes life-change inventory, Type-A behavior questionnaire, the FIRO-B, and an exercise called the Wheel of Life. On the Holmes scale, the client is asked to indicate which of the life events on the scale he or she experienced in the past year. Research (Holmes & Rahe, 1967) has found that there is a correlation between the number of life changes and the probability of contracting severe physical illness. While a person cannot alter past life events, he or she can alter reactions to present ones and thus reduce stress. The scale serves as an index of the external stresses the individual is experiencing.

The FIRO-B (Schutz, 1966) is an indicator of the client's preferred behaviors in the areas of social relations, affection/love, and independence/decision making, and thus provides a measure of assertiveness and the degree of social interaction and encouragement.

The Wheel of Life provides the client an opportunity for self-assessment regarding six life tasks: *occupation,* the area of work and productive endeavor; *friendship; intimacy,* the area of sex and love; *leisure,* the area of the use of free time; *spiritual,* the area dealing with religious, moral-ethical issues, and the meaning of life; and *self,* which covers self-esteem and self-development activities. The client is given a paper with a circle on it divided into six equal sectors, one for each life task. The tasks are areas in which life makes demands on us just by the nature of our existence. After the tasks are defined, each client is asked to develop a subjective formula of time times energy that he or she devotes to each task. The client then fills in the portion of each sector that he or she determines best represents the amount of investment placed on each task. Clinicians and philosophers have known for years that for life to be fulfilling and meaningful, it must be relatively balanced among the various tasks. Most of our clients, however, end up with wheels that are quite skewed. A common profile is high investment in occupation with scant investment in intimacy. The Wheel of Life technique shows us areas of overinvestment and deficit.

Life goals are a major emphasis in the program, and they are conceptualized in terms of the six life tasks. While most people set short-term goals for certain activities, relatively few people think in terms of developing goals for their lives apart from the obvious area of occupation. We have found that setting life goals in the other areas as well, even if the goals should change, helps provide cohesiveness and meaning to existence, and sense of increased control and determination, with a resultant lowering of overall stress. Clients often need reorientation from the outset in this area, which reinforces their own power to determine major aspects of

their future. As the first interview draws to a close, the client is instructed to write out some tentative life goals based on the six tasks during the week before the next session. Heart rate, blood pressure, and weight are recorded. The client is then oriented to the process of the remaining sessions. The stress battery and physiological measures are repeated at the end of the program. Heart rate, blood pressure, and weight are monitored more frequently if specific problems in these areas are found.

At the close of the first session, the client is instructed to obtain a physical examination from the family physician. While the primary purpose of the physical is to detect any problems, for the purpose of the program both the client and we must be informed if there are any restrictions or requirements regarding exercise or diet. In addition, the possibility of an organic cause for any physical complaint must be checked.

During the second session feedback from the stress battery is provided. The client's written life goals are examined, refined, and modified if necessary by mutual discussion. These goals are then formalized and serve as a basis, along with the stress data and physical examination, for the stress management/health maintenance prescription, which is the core of the program. This prescription sets forth the operational goals mutually developed by the client and the therapist toward which the client will direct his or her efforts throughout the program. The prescription is flexible and open to change if the client deems necessary. It is also possible that the client will not complete work on the goals during the program, but in the case of broader goals, this is quite permissable. Life is a process of growth and development that continues from birth to the grave; what is important is that the client develop and incorporate new and effective skills and attitudes into his or her attitudinal/behavioral repertoire. Once a solid foundation is laid, the client can, and is most likely to, continue on his own. The prescription organizes an action plan under the following headings: family, interpersonal, occupation, hypnosis, nutrition/exercise, other, and is set up on a form that also allows for recording a formal progress review every fourth session.

During the second session, if time permits, the client is introduced to hypnosis. First hypnosis is discussed to clarify any myths. Then the client is given a hypnotic induction and scene visualization and/or other suggestions to induce relaxation. The client is also trained at that time in self-hypnosis. Self-hypnosis is a standard part of the program, and clients are instructed to practice it daily. Deep relaxation is the basis from which all other specialized suggestions are developed, and hypnosis is the primary tool used to teach clients to modify their physiological responses. Later in the program hypnosis is integrated into specific problem-solving and creativity-tapping techniques. The effects of guided fantasy and covert rehearsal are often magnified via hypnosis. Each week the client usually spends some time in hypnosis, and new suggestions and skills are taught to be practiced at home. Skills and suggestions included depend on the client's needs and goals; no two clients will have the same program of hypnotic interventions.

The importance of self-hypnosis cannot be overstressed. Hypnosis is a powerful tool during and after which people often experience notable, if not profound, results. In addition, in the minds of most laymen, hypnosis has a magical quality. Many, unless instructed otherwise, believe that under hypnosis they are under the therapist's control. Even some knowledgeable clients believe that the hypnosis is somehow ''better'' if it is done by the therapist rather than self-induced. All of these conceptions can lead to excessive dependence on the therapist when hypnosis is involved. When self-hypnosis is used from the outset, this tendency is minimized. Dependent behaviors toward the therapist must be discouraged as they contradict the basic actor-creator role of the client.

Two other ancillary aspects of the pre-scription are exercise and nutritional recommendations. These recommendations are negotiated with the client, but the overriding determinant is whether the client's physician has indicated any limitations or requirements. Within the framework of such limitations, if there are any, it is recommended that the client engage in fitness activities that exercise the cardiovascular and respiratory systems. Such exercise will raise heart rate momentarily and lower blood pressure over time. The positive effects of exercise also helps to lower stress. The exercise program is tailored to the individual and may consist of jogging, active sports, calisthenics, or other activities that exercise the heart-lung-artery systems.

Nutritional recommendations, if needed, usually revolve around a balanced diet. No weight-reduction emphasis is included unless this becomes a program goal. Then the focus switches to initial calorie counting on a nutritionally balanced calorie-restricted diet and specific hypnotic and behavioral suggestions focusing on developing a new body image and altered eating habits. The emphasis here is not only on losing weight, but keeping it off.

While the overall framework of the program is structured, the content agenda for each session depends mainly on the goals and issues determined by the client. The major portion of each session involves cognitive restructuring techniques and consists of instruction by the therapist and discussion and skill practice with the client. The week's progress is checked, and new suggestions and homework assignments are given. Homework assignments vary with client needs but are designed to help inculcate new learnings through hypnosis and direct behavior, reinforce new skills through practice, and to help the client move toward his or her goals by successive approximation. Homework is assigned and self-hypnosis is reinforced each session.

Over the course of the program, clients are instructed in the nature of stress and stress reduction, how they can lower or intensify stress via self-indoctrination, and how to spot negative thoughts and mistaken ideas with specific techniques for disputing them or altering one's attention. Particular emphasis is placed upon problem solving, developing creative alternatives, and in redefining problems as opportunities. At every turn the client is challenged to create, re-create, and explore, renouncing by action and definition any mistaken perception of his or her victim role. We also encourage the individual to make greater use of, and commitment to, existing sociocultural support systems such as clubs and organizations, and kindle a reawakened interest, where necessary, in spiritual-philosophical issues, religion, and family or ethnic traditions, as well as an increased and more philosophical sense of humor and perspective on life.

## APPLICATIONS

As stated in the previous section, the client for whom this particular program is most applicable should be verbal and relatively well-functioning. Since we all suffer from chronic human imperfection, all of us face stress in our daily lives, and we all react both physically and emotionally to those stresses whether we are consciously aware of it or not. Most, if not all, of us could learn to manage our stress more effectively and expand into more meaningful and fulfilled lives. The stress management program, then, is a kind of "therapy for the well."

The approach thus far outlined dovetails very well with traditional American values of self-control and achievement, and thus is consonant with the beliefs of the average American businessperson and worker. Yet in Stress Management those values are reorganized away from their limiting and stress-producing aspects. For example, while "self-control" may mean not showing your emotions, it healthier to view it as not being a victim, but rather one who can actively plan and coordinate one's own life experi-

ences in a more useful and beneficial light. The attempt is to fine-tune the human engine, working out the rough spots for smoother functioning.

The program, therefore, is best suited for "average people" who feel the pinch of pressure or stress and want to achieve a greater sense of relief or control over their life. These people are usually not experiencing major traumas in their daily life, but the little, everyday stressors build. Most of the people for whom this program was designed identify their major stresses as coming from their jobs, and most of the problems here boil down to strained relationships, with high work demands a close second. Such people can be found in almost all occupational fields and strata. Housewives and especially the dual-career woman (housewife plus work outside the home) are appropriate candidates for this approach. Since the program is flexible in content, it can reach a great variety of human needs, and do so without the stigma often associated with going to a mental health professional.

The people most likely to benefit from the program also may have mild or circumscribed "hang-ups" that may interfere to a greater or lesser degree with some, but not all, areas of their life. They may also have particular worries or fears that limit their potential in some way but that are not overly debilitating.

Specific symptom populations such as minor arthritics, hypertensives, gastrointestinal patients, cardiac patients; headache and low-back pain patients, on the other hand, often require more long-term and intensive therapy because of the neurotic underlay usually associated with a chronic pain problem.

Severe neurotics are a special case. Our same procedures work very well with neurotics in the context of longer-term therapy. The severe neurotic experiences the symptom as ego-alien—that is, at a conscious level the person wishes to be rid of the symptom, yet the symptom actually serves such a compelling purpose for him or her that, unconsciously, the person cannot conceive of letting it go so easily. In fact, the neurotic symptoms may be deeply ingrained in the fabric of the life style. These clients, as well as psychotics, would be seen in longer-term therapy and our stress program would be contraindicated.

The greatest hindrance to this program, as for all therapy, regardless of client disorder, is the lack or the lag of development of a therapeutic alliance. While the stress program is a highly educational/mutual contract approach, it possesses all the interpersonal dynamics of any brief psychotherapy. Given the short-term nature of the program, rapport must be well established very early.

As time goes on, more and more emphasis nationwide is being placed on prevention and holistic health maintenance, and it is in this area where Stress Management has its greatest utility. There is also a need to move such programs out of the confines of the therapist's office into naturalistic settings where the people are, especially into business and industrial locations. In fact, the program described here had its origin in a small-group followup for a program the Stress Management Institute carries out for executives. As awareness in the business sector is increasing regarding stress and holistic health maintenance, more and more companies are desirous of effective programs of a preventive nature.

What is needed now, however, is a rapproachment between the work setting and the laboratory. Each is often suspicious of the other. Businesspeople may charge that the scientists' results are irrelevant or do not generalize to the complexities of the work environment, and the scientists seeing the same complexities may argue that it is impossible to isolate necessary variables. The rapproachment can be achieved through long-term research follow-up of participants in training and other kinds of health-maintenance programs. In the final analysis, this is the best way to determine program effectiveness. Analogue studies and the traditional "smiles report" ("Did you like the program?") often obtained as "evaluation" directly after a conference or workshop are equally ineffective at assessing a program's or technique's effectivenss in a naturalistic setting.

## CASE EXAMPLE

Ted is a 32-year-old white male assistant accountant in his second marriage. He first married at age 22, but the marriage was stormy. He was tense and uptight most of the time and claimed that his wife constantly had to have her own way and achieved it through hysterics. He put up with it for three and one-half years and then divorced her at age 25. At age 30 he remarried. He has two children by his first marriage who reside with his former wife and is stepfather for two children, age 12 and 11, from his present wife's first marriage. He describes his second marriage as good.

Ted is the younger of two children. He claims to have been anxious most of his life, and reports three blackouts due to anxiety in childhood and severe migraine headaches through his teens until the end of his first marriage, after which he had only one migraine. Ted was easily given to guilt and had excessive desires to please others and meet their expectations regardless of his own wants. He became anxious in the face of conflict and was generally nonassertive and became "nervous"( sweating palms, fast heart, tingling in hands, lightness in head) at the slightest provocation. He was also depressed and judged himself as perfectionistic. While in the service (1968) he had very high blood pressure.

Eight months before entering the stress management program, he had a severe anxiety attack, with dangerously elevated blood pressure, chest pains, and pounding in his head. He was hospitalized until his blood pressure was brought under control and then treated by his family physician with Hygroton (50 milligrams a day). At the time Ted entered the program, he was on medical leave from his job because of elevated blood pressure. He was under great strain at work, having just trained his own supervisor, who then dumped most of his (supervisor's) work on Ted. Ted felt helpless to complain because the supervisor was in a favored position.

During the first interview, Ted indicated his goals as being able to cope and manage his anxiety. His average score on the Type A Behavior Questionnaire was 2.8 out of a possible 4, indicating a decidedly Type A personality. His Holmes score was 199.

During the second interview, he was hypnotized for deep relaxation, including scene visualization and dialogue with his inner self for assets discovery. A progressive muscular relaxation exercise was also included. His blood pressure before hypnosis was 167/67; afterward in the same session it was 141/61. Ted was instructed in self-hypnosis.

In the third interview, Ted was shown how he used anxiety to push himself into assertive action, that anxiety was his "old friend," a tool he used to act on his own when he otherwise did not give himself permission to act without having to wait to get anxious. He was instructed in his rights and taught step by step how to develop assertive behavior.

During the sessions that followed, the focus in hypnosis was on deep relaxation, patience, and self-control, and positive assets and assertiveness. Progressive scene visualization and direct suggestion were most commonly employed.

In progressive visualization, the client keeps revisualizing the same scene, making modifications until he is comfortable with the outcome. On one occasion we analyzed a dream hypnotically in which Ted was able to confront his boss on the boss's ineptitude. Cognitive and behavioral work was on specifics of handling stress in the office, positive assets, and analysis of his ultimate purposes behind anxiety. He also discovered his negative self-references and was taught to reprogram himself with positive self-talk. Significant emphasis was placed on the development of assertive behaviors through role play, discussion, scene visualization,

and homework contracts to practice; making decisions regarding his vocational growth; and gaining a broader perspective and sense of humor, especially about daily stressors. An exercise program was negotiated including weight-lifting and the Apollo Exerciser fitness routine.

At one point Ted reported feeling anxious when riding the bus to work. He was instructed to make himself even more anxious when riding the bus, a process that in a week caused his anxiety to dminish considerably.

Ted was seen for 17 sessions. His coworkers, he reported, noted a considerable degree of calm and control in his behavior. He no longer gets anxious in his car pool and has mastered his anxiety on the bus. Occasionally he feels mildly anxious about the bus, and he has been told that this is his way of toying with the past. When he is ready to let go of his former game, he will give up that anxiety. His wife notes a remarkable change at home, first in calmness, but also in assertiveness. Ted can now effectively insist on his rights without undue anxiety or anger, and is able to get proper action. Indeed, Ted is liberated.

At the end of the program, his blood pressure was 138/62, which we attributed to program gains because the medication was held constant over the course of the program. Significantly, Ted's termination average score on the Type A Questionnaire was 1.8, down from the prior 2.8, showing a marked reduction in Type A characteristics. Ted is easier on himself, has lessened his perfectionism, and is imbued with much greater self-confidence. While he uses the self-hypnosis on an as-needed basis, he has incorporated most of the cognitive principles and techniques into his daily life.

Ted's case demonstrates the effectiveness of a short-term, encouragement and goal-directed individual stress-reduction program on both cognitive style and physiological symptom control, in this case hypertension. Anxiety and depression, often treated by much longer therapies, also were significantly reduced. It is important to note, however, that while Ted had chronic problems with anxiety, he was highly motivated for change and not too neurotically entrapped in secondary gain to require a much greater therapeutic time frame. The initial impetus that drove him to seek help was his hypertension, and Ted is typical of many who enter treatment for such a specific symptom disorder.

## SUMMARY

While "stress" is becoming a household word, Stress Management itself is not a fad in spite of the fadlike nature of the popular emphasis on stress today. Stress research and programs for stress reduction and control will be with us for some time to come as quality interventions serve a basic human need. In our view, Stress Management was the missing link on the path to developing a holistic, health maintenance, preventive approach to medicine and mental health. An appreciation for the function and impact of stress and the development of specific stress management techniques allows one to move parsimoniously beyond limiting and partial explanations of the human predicament as originally offered by such theories as the sickness or disease model, traditional psychodynamics, instinctual drives, and conditioning. A holistic approach demands an integration of biological, intrapsychic, social-environmental, and ecological concerns impacting on a socially imbedded individual and mediated by his ability to make choices within limits Holism and the final authority of individual action and choice are cornerstones of the program described in this chapter.

The continual reference to our interventions as "programs" rather than a "therapy" is highly intentional; we eschew the model of "cure" and the traditional implications that accompany that concept. Another reason for the term "program" is that in this manner the intervention is delivered on a contract basic with individuals or corporations.

Because of the multifarious components of "stress," a multimodal approach is essential. While we cannot claim to do everything, our programs involve the three basic areas of physiological control, experiential cognitive restructuring, and direct educational activities with homework.

Two related areas of concern are of prime importance as we approach stress or any other popular topic. The first is research. Intervention strategies need to be based squarely on sound scientific and clinical findings, and new techniques must be thoroughly tested and evaluated in terms of outcome before one can in clear conscience declare them efficacious for the general populace. Much more research needs to be done in such settings as the home and office. The second area is ethics and protection of the public. With any popular topic there is market demand, and almost any new gimmick will attract attention and provide short-term gains. Although one cannot deny the economic aspects of addressing popular concerns, the first issue should be the production of desired and beneficial long-term changes in the client and the commitment to follow through as much as possible to insure client success. We must be prepared to service what we sell as professionals, and we must maintain high standards of program development and performance.

## REFERENCES

Alexander, F. *Psychosomatic medicine: Its principles and applications*. New York: Norton, 1950.

Cobb, S. and Rose, R. Hypertension, peptic ulcer and diabetes in air traffic controllers. *Journal of The American Medical Association*, 1973, **224,** 489–492.

Dreikurs, R. The psychological interview in medicine. *American Journal of Individual Psychology*, 1954, **10,** 99–122.

Ellis, A. *Reasons and emotions in psychotherapy*. New York: Lyle Stuart, 1962.

Field, P. Stress reduction in hypnotherapy of chronic headache. Paper presented at the Annual Meeting of The American Psychological Association and The Society for Clinical and Experimental Hypnosis, 1979.

Frankel, F. H. The effects of brief hypnotherapy on a series of psychosomatic problems. *Psychotherapy and Psychosomatics*, 1973, **22,** 264–275.

Friedman, M. and Rosenman, R. H. *Type A behavior and your heart*. New York: Fawcett, 1974.

Holmes, T. H. and Rahe, R. H. The social readjustment rating scale. *Journal of Psychosomatic Research*, 1967, **11,** 213.

Lynch, J. The broken heart. New York:Basic Books, 1977.

Roskies, E., Spevack, M., Surkis, A., Cohen, C. and Gilman, S. Changing the coronary-prone (Type A) be-havior pattern in a non-clinical population. *Journal of Behavioral Medicine*, 1978.

Schutz, W. C. *The interpersonal underworld*. Palo Alto, Calif.: Science and Behavior Books, 1966.

Wittkower, E. D. Historical perspective of contemporary psychosomatic medicine. In Z. J. Lipowski, R. Lipsitt and P. C. Whybrow( Eds.), *Psychosomatic medicine: Current trends and clinical applications*. New York: Oxford University Press, 1977.

# CHAPTER 61

# *Structured Learning*

ROBERT P. SPRAFKIN, N. JANE GERSHAW, and ARNOLD P. GOLDSTEIN

*The various therapies in this book can be classified in a number of ways. One classification may refer to the complexity of the system. For example, my own system of Immediate Therapy has a single dimension and is relatively easy to understand, but it is seriously limited relative to population. Other systems, such as Functional Psychotherapy or Multimodal Therapy, have very broad aims, wide-ranging theories, and ambitious aspirations. Structured Learning by Robert Sprafkin, Jane Gershaw, and Arnold Goldstein is of this latter variety: It is a total, complex, complete system.*

*The logic of this method seems impeccable, and its genius probably lies in the fact that it is a total system that includes in a rational order four sets of processes. The other system in this book most like this one is Nira Kefir's procedure of Impasse/Priorities.*

*One of the interesting aspects of Structured Learning is the absence of any cognitive-phenomenological concepts. It is a kind of no-nonsense, engineering, behavioristic, complete system for curing human problems.*

*I believe that the message these authors provide should be well listened to by all readers. Their concept is grand—and even a bit frightening.*

Structured Learning is a behaviorally oriented, psychoeducational skill training approach for teaching a variety of interpersonal, planning, and stress management skills to a wide range of clinical and nonclinical populations. It combines four behavior change procedures in its basic training/treatment sequence: (1) modeling, (2) roleplaying, (3) performance feedback, and (4) transfer of training. Groups of trainees are: (1) shown numerous, specific, detailed examples (live, on audiotape, videotape, filmstrip, or film) of a person (the model) performing the skill or behaviors to be learned (i.e., modeling); (2) given considerable opportunity and encouragement to practice or rehearse the behaviors that have been modeled (i.e., roleplaying); (3) provided with positive feedback, social reinforcement, and corrective suggestions regarding their enactment of role

plays of the modeled behaviors (i.e., performance feedback); and (4) exposed to procedures that increase the likelihood that the newly learned behaviors will be applied in an effective manner at home, at work, or elsewhere in the person's real-life environment (i.e., transfer of training).

## HISTORY

### Precursors

Structured Learning, like most behaviorally oriented treatments, owes its philosophical allegiance to the tradition of John Locke and the British empiricists. Within that framework, and consistent with much of academic psychology, behavior is viewed primarily as a product of the organism's experiences, and human behavior is considered to be subject to the laws of learning. Structured Learning shares with other behavioral approaches its affinity for the Lockean notion that concepts develop in a hierarchical fashion from experience, and that effective learning also takes place in an incremental, hierarchical manner (cf. Rychlak, 1973).

Another important philosophical influence on Structured Learning and many other behavioral approaches is American pragmatism. William James, John Dewey, and other pragmatists emphasized empiricism, facts, action, consequences—the practical use value of activities. James characterized this basic point of view of pragmatism, so compatible with later behavioral orientations in psychology: "The attitude of looking away from first things, principles, 'categories,' supposed necessities; and of looking towards last things, fruits, consequences, facts" (1960, p. 33).

Structured Learning, like most other behavioral forms of treatment or training, developed in the context of American psychology. A primary concern of American psychology since its formal inception in the late nineteenth century has been the understanding and enhancement of the learning process. This readiness to center upon learning processes took major therapeutic form starting in the 1950s, as psychotherapy practitioners and researchers alike came more and more to view treatment in learning terms. This joint learning–clinical focus gave birth to the behavior modification movement, with its emphases on laboratory-derived procedures, specified and specifiable treatment goals, and frequent employment of the change agent or therapist as a teacher/trainer. Behavioral approaches to treatment have clearly presented a major challenge to the more firmly entrenched medical model treatments in a variety of institutional and non-institutional psychiatric settings.

Another historical challenge to the established medical model of treatments for institutionalized psychiatric patients, which also appears as a spiritual precurser of Structured Learning, was the moral treatment movement that began at the start of the nineteenth century. It was characterized by its humane concern for patients' welfare and its emphasis on the environment in shaping normal and abnormal behavior. The particular aspect of moral treatment that bears the closest affinity to Structured Learning was its use of a variety of formal and informal educational methods for bringing about appropriate "mental discipline" (Sprafkin, 1977).

Yet another movement serves as an important historical antecedent to Structured Learning and other psychoeducational skill training approaches. This movement was called by different names at different times; generally it sought to influence the development of interpersonal, social, and moral behavior through the use of parenting manuals, self-improvement books, religious tracts, and a variety of other educational methods. Best known among these educational methods were Character Education, popular in the 1920s, and methods that sought to use pedagogic techniques for teaching ethical interpersonal behavior, leadership skills, group decision-making skills, and self-control. Even though that particular movement faded by the 1930s, the formal involvement of professional educators with the development of appropriate or prosocial behaviors has persisted under new forms and titles: moral education, affective education, human relations training, confluent education, and identity education. While their methods and rationales vary considerably, these approaches all share the goals of helping to foster the growth, development, and appropriate behavior of their various trainees.

## Beginnings

The developers of the Structured Learning approach, Arnold P. Goldstein, Robert P. Sprafkin, and N. Jane Gershaw, each brought a unique set of interests and experiences to their collaborative effort. Arnold P. Goldstein, senior author and moving force behind the development of the approach, received his degree in clinical psychology from Pennsylvania State University, where he was most strongly influenced by Donald H. Ford and William U. Snyder and their interest in psychotherapy research. He began to develop his own view of psychotherapy research, which took into account social psychology, as well as clinical variables. His first book, *Therapist-Patient Expectancies in Psychotherapy* (1962), written while he was at the University of Pittsburgh Medical School, reflected his growing concern with the importance of social psychological factors in the psychotherapeutic endeavor. Shortly thereafter he began collaborating with Kenneth Heller and Lee B. Sechrest on their encyclopedic review of social psychological research relevant to the understanding of psychotherapeutic practices. This resulted in the publication of *Psychotherapy and the Psychology of Behavior Change* (1966), which cast psychotherapy research squarely within the mainstream of empirically based investigation, and emerged as a standard text for psychotherapy researchers. Goldstein (1971) has long been concerned with the problem of making psychotherapy more relevant, attractive, and available to those who tend to underutilize such services. This preoccupation culminated in the publication of *Structured Learning Therapy: Toward a Psychotherapy for the Poor* (1973), which presented the theory, research support, and basic components of the structured learning approach.

Robert P. Sprafkin worked on his doctorate in counseling psychology at Ohio State University, where he was attracted to the teaching of Harold B. Pepinsky, then engaged in a series of investigations concerning social influence processes operating in dyadic and group communications, including psychological treatments. After completing his doctoral research (Sprafkin, 1970), he moved to Syracuse University and then to the Syracuse Veterans Administration Hospital as Coordinator of the Day Treatment Center, a day-long treatment facility for chronic psychiatric patients. There he became concerned

with providing relevant treatment and training to his clientele, who typically had fared poorly in traditional, verbal, psychotherapeutic endeavors in the past.

N. Jane Gershaw was a student of Goldstein's at Syracuse University and through his teaching developed a special interest in methods of group psychotherapy. In her first position after receiving her doctorate, she began supervising psychology interns and psychiatric residents at Hahnemann Medical College and Community Mental Health Center in Philadelphia in directive and skill-training-oriented groups with psychiatric patients.

In 1973 Goldstein obtained a research grant from the National Institute of Mental Health to develop concrete training techniques that paraprofessional and professional mental health workers could use in implementing Structured Learning Therapy with institutionalized psychiatric patients. At the same time Sprafkin was using some of the behavioral components of Structured Learning Therapy, in a less systematic fashion, in his Day Treatment Center program. And Gershaw was beginning to use some components with her own patients at the VA Mental Hygiene Clinic. The situation was ideal for a collaborative effort aimed at the development of specific, systematic techniques for teaching staff to work with psychiatric patients using the major components of Structured Learning Therapy. Goldstein, Sprafkin, and Gershaw agreed to embark in such a collaborative effort, which culminated in the systematic presentation of the Structured Learning Therapy approach.

## CURRENT STATUS

As indicated by the title of Goldstein's book, *Structured Learning Therapy: Toward a Psychotherapy for the Poor* (1973), his aim was to develop a therapeutic approach that would be appropriate for those persons served inadequately by traditional, verbal, insight-oriented psychotherapies, which tend to be middle class in orientation. The structured learning approach, developed for use primarily with institutionalized psychiatric patients (who tend to come from low-income backgrounds) was presented in a systematic fashion in Goldstein, Sprafkin, and Gershaw's *Skill Training for Community Living: Applying Structured Learning Therapy* (1976). This approach has been adopted widely and is currently in use in several hundred inpatient, transitional, and outpatient psychiatric treatment facilities.

It appears to be the natural history of any psychotherapeutic treatment approach that once it is used successfully with one population and/or problem area, it is rapidly applied to other populations and behavior configurations. Such was certainly the case with the attempts at the application of psychoanalysis to populations never envisioned by Freud; certainly Gestalt Therapy, Transactional Analysis, and numerous other treatment approaches have been applied to all types of persons and problems far beyond the scope of their initial usages.

So, too, appears to be the emerging pattern with Structured Learning Therapy. As the writers presented talks and training workshops to various groups, explaining the appropriateness of Structured Learning with institutionalized, low-income psychiatric patients, questions invariably arose concerning the possible application to other clinical and nonclinical populations. "What about delinquents?" "Why not use it with geriatric patients?" "How about us 'normals'?" "Can only low-income people benefit from the techniques?" The answer to these kinds of questions is obviously "Yes, try it." But the "yes" must be a qualified one. The specific techniques, methods of presentation, and the like must be prescriptively appropriate to the population with which it is used. Rather than insisting that the therapy "works" regardless of where it is used, and that clients, trainees, or patients should be shoe-horned into the existing therapy, we take the opposite approach. That is, rather than saying, "Make the patient fit the therapy," we have attempted to modify the therapeutic offering

to meet the particular characteristics of different populations: "Make the therapy fit the patient." Attempts at modification and application should, in our view, always be tied to empirical investigations (e.g., Goldstein & Stein, 1976; Goldstein et al., 1979).

## THEORY

Structured Learning views behaviors as having been learned during the individual's developmental history. Major concern is with the social determinants of behaviors, which have been learned through direct or vicarious experience. As a behavioral approach, Structured Learning is not concerned with positing "inner causes"—needs, drives, or impulses. The behaviors that have been learned by an individual are more or less adaptive in enabling that person to meet life's demands and to achieve personal satisfaction. Thus, Structured Learning, as a therapy, training, or teaching method seeks to: (1) identify the ways in which behaviors have been and may be learned and in which the individual is deficient; (2) identify the behaviors or skills that, if acquired, would enable the individual to achieve personal satisfaction; and (3) systematically apply effective learning principles to the task of teaching desirable behaviors.

Structured Learning views behaviors as skills acquired through learning. An individual may be more or less proficient in using these skills in meeting life's challenges. Thus the goal of Structured Learning is to help people acquire and perfect skills. The individual's behavioral repertoire is described in terms of skill proficiencies and deficiencies, rather than using more abstract diagnostic categories. And, as a system concerned with the development of behavioral proficiencies, primary emphasis is placed upon effecting behavior change, rather than bringing about self-attitude change. Many approaches to psychotherapy focus primarily on helping the individual change self-attitudes—self-image, self-concept, and so forth—with the assumption that once one's attitudes about one's self change, then one's behaviors will change. By contrast, Structured Learning sees the goal of treatment or training as bringing about behavior change, which will then affect self-attitudes. Evidence suggests that the latter approach is more rapid and more likely to bring about the desired changes.

The first target population for Structured Learning Therapy was low-income, institutionalized psychiatric patients. Historically such patients have faired poorly in traditional, verbal, psychodynamic psychotherapies whose goals are generally to achieve self-attitude change and insight antecedent to any hopes for behavior change. We have argued (Goldstein, 1973; Goldstein et al., 1976) that the roots of preferences for these differing approaches may be in differing childrearing practices in middle- versus lower- or working-class homes. Middle-class childrearing and life styles, with their emphases on intentions, motivation, self-control, inner states, and the like, provide excellent early training for traditional, verbal psychotherapies, should the person require such treatment in later life. Lower- (and working-) class childrearing practices and life styles, with their emphases on action, behavior, consequences rather than intentions, reliance on external authority and a more restricted verbal code, ill prepare a person for appropriate participation in traditional, verbal, insight-oriented psychotherapy aimed at explorations of self-attitudes. A therapy more responsive to the stylistic characteristics of such lower- or working-class childrearing practices would have to be brief, concrete, behavioral, authoritatively administered, require imitation of specific overt examples, teach role-taking skills, and provide early, frequent, and continuous reinforcement for the performance of appropriate behaviors.

We wished to develop a psychotherapy that capitalized upon the learning style characteristics and preferred channels of accessibility of the abovementioned target population, so that the therapy could prescriptively "fit the patient," instead of

vice versa. Thus the four major components of Structured Learning—modeling, role playing, social reinforcement, and transfer of training—were combined in an attempt to meet this prescriptive goal. Structured Learning has also been applied to other populations, with modifications in the treatment and training procedures to meet the particular stylistic requirements of each population.

Modeling, or learning by observation and imitation, has been demonstrated as an effective method for learning new behaviors. Such behaviors as self-assertion, self-disclosure, helping others, empathic behavior, plus literally dozens of others, have been learned through modeling. In addition to being a powerful technique for teaching new behaviors, research has demonstrated that already learned behaviors can be strengthened or weakened through modeling.

Laboratory research has identified a number of characteristics of modeling displays that make it likely that the modeled behavior will be imitated by the observer. These "modeling enhancers" include characteristics of: (1) the model, (2) the display itself, and (3) the observer or learner.

1. Greater modeling has been shown to occur when the model is: highly skilled; of high status; friendly; of the same sex, age, and socioeconomic status as the observer; and is rewarded for the behavior in question.

2. Concerning the modeling display, to increase modeling effects the behaviors to be imitated should be shown clearly, with little irrelevant detail, in order from least to most difficult behaviors, and with several different models performing the behaviors to be learned.

3. The observer or learner characteristics that serve to enhance modeling are complementary to those described under the category of model characteristics. Greater modeling tends to occur when the observer is told to imitate the model, likes the model, is similar to the model

in background or other important characteristics, and is rewarded for imitating the modeled behavior.

If modeling is so effective, why go beyond modeling to other training procedures? Albert Bandura (1977) states that the learning effects of modeling can be enhanced through procedures that allow the learner to rehearse or practice what has been observed. In addition, many modeling effects are only short-lived. Perry (1970) and Sutton (1970), among others, have demonstrated that modeling effects that occur immediately after training often disappear in a very short time. For learning to be lasting, the individual must be exposed to procedures that enable him or her to practice what has been modeled, receive feedback on this practice, and, most important, encourage use of the newly learned skills in real-life situations.

Role playing, the second major component of Structured Learning, is defined as practice or behavioral rehearsal of a skill for later real-life use of that skill. Research evidence supports the value of role playing in order to effect behavior as well as attitude change. Several role-play enhancers have been identified that make learning through role playing more likely and make the effects of such learning more lasting. These enhancers include: choiceful participation by the role player, role player commitment to behavior or attitude being enacted, role player improvisation of enactment, and reinforcement of the role player following the enactment.

Research has demonstrated the effectiveness of role playing in training such attitudes and behaviors as assertion (McFall & Marston, 1970), empathy (Staub, 1971), moral judgment (Arbuthnot, 1975), and a variety of interpersonal skills (Rathjen, Heneker, & Rathjen, 1976). However, several studies have added a note of caution to the research on role playing. Lichtenstein, Keutzer, and Himes (1969) found in three studies that the effects of role playing on reducing smoking behavior were only short-lived. Hollander (1970) found no change in a number of patient psychotherapy interview behaviors as a function of role playing. Thus, as with modeling, role playing alone appears to be insufficient to effect lasting behavior change. Role playing provides the learner with practice but does not provide a good example or demonstration of the behavior to be learned prior to such practice. This example can be provided through modeling (e.g., Bandura, 1977). But even these procedures, taken together, do not provide the learner with the motivation or incentive to behave differently. This incentive component is the third major procedure of Structured Learning.

Performance feedback involves providing the learner with information following the role-play enactment of the skill. It may include social or material reinforcement, criticism, reteaching, or other instruction. We have placed heaviest emphasis on social reinforcement as a useful form of feedback. Such reinforcement is provided as the trainee's role-play behavior becomes more similar to the skill behaviors modeled earlier.

Research highlights a number of rules of reinforcement that determine the potency of the effect of reeinforcement. We have learned that: the type of reinforcement (material, social, etc.) should be flexible and consistent with the needs and reinforcement history of the trainee; reinforcement should follow immediately after the desired behavior; the contingent relationship between the desired behavior and the reinforcement should be clear to the trainee; generally, the larger the reward the greater the likelihood of a positive effect on performance; the desired behavior should occur with sufficient frequency that opportunity for reinforcement is provided; and reinforcement that is provided intermittently is more resistant to extinction than reinforcement provided every time the desired behavior occurs.

Modeling, role playing, and reinforcement, when taken together, comprise a powerful skill-training program. When one adds to this the fourth component of Structured Learning, transfer of training, a critical element of training is added. This element deals with real-life use of what has been learned in the training setting. Transfer of training consists of a set of procedures designed to encourage such real-life use. These transfer-enhancement procedures or principles include providing the trainee with: sufficient opportunity to practice correct use of the skill so that the new response will be more available or, in effect, overlearned; a training setting having many identical elements or characteristics shared with the application setting; stimulus variability or a variety of interpersonal stimuli in the training setting that will later serve as cues for the desired behavior outside of the training setting.

These four behavioral techniques—modeling, role playing, performance feedback, and transfer of training—comprise the structured learning approach.

## METHODOLOGY

Generally, a group of 6 to 12 patient/trainees, selected on the basis of shared skill deficits, led by two trainers, are presented first with live or recorded modeling displays of the skill to be learned. Each skill is broken down into a series of behavioral steps, or "learning points." Each modeling display depicts a model successfully performing a skill by enacting various behavioral steps. Content for the modeling displays should be relevant to the trainees' lives, so that they can identify with the situation being modeled. In the modeling displays, repetition is relied upon to maximize learning. Ideally the actors who serve as models are as similar as possible to the patient/trainees in terms of age, sex, apparent socioeconomic status, as well as other relevant dimensions. In each modeling display the model is depicted as successful in using the skill and receives social reinforcement for such effective skill use.

Once the patients/trainees have been exposed to the modeling displays, the trainers stimulate discussion of the modeled skill. Also, each trainee in the group is given a

chance to enact the skill via content relevant to his or her own life. Other trainees in the group will play the roles of significant others in the main actor's life. To maximize transfer of training, a great deal of emphasis is placed upon "setting the stage" in the role play. Here the trainer asks the main actor to describe in detail the persons and places involved in his or her real-life problem situation. In keeping with the transfer principle of identical elements, trainees are encouraged to use any props or equipment to help simulate the application setting. Such setting of the stage is also helpful in assisting trainees who think concretely to begin to engage in the rather difficult activity of role taking. Once the stage is set, the trainees enact the skill. The main actor, co-actor, and observers are given cards on which are written the behavioral steps of the skill being enacted. The observers, usually consisting of the trainees who are not involved in the role play, are asked to attend to how well the main actor follows the steps and performs the skill. The trainers provide any added instruction or prompting required by the actors.

After each role play, the main actor receives for social reinforcement and performance feedback comments from the observing trainees and co-actors on how well he or she executed the role play. The trainers also provide the main actor with feedback on the performance. Trainees are instructed to keep a behavioral focus during this phase of the group. If indicated, a particular scene may be re-role played after corrective feedback is given. In a forthright effort at transfer of training as the last step in each group session, the trainer provides each trainee with an opportunity to practice the newly learned material in his or her real life environment. With the aid of a variety of homework forms, trainees who have role played are asked to sign a written contract to practice the new skill at a particular time and with a particular person before the next group session. Having done this, trainees complete the rest of the form, indicating the outcome of their efforts, and report back to the group at the next meeting. After the assignment of homework, the group session ends.

We recognize that unless there is some real-life reward to the trainee for using his or her new skill—unless the people with whom the trainee tries the skill respond in a positive way—it is unlikely that the new behavior will be sustained. Therefore it is often helpful to enlist the aid of outside people—family members, ward personnel, teachers—and to instruct them in how to respond when the trainee initiates the new behavior in the real-life situation.

Not all significant others in trainees' lives are willing or able to provide the necessary social reinforcement to help make the trainee's new behavior become established, however. Persons with whom trainees work and live may even actively resist trainees' efforts of behavior change. For these reasons, it has been shown to be useful to include in later transfer-of-training procedures a method through which trainees can learn to be their own independent self-rewarders. That is, following initial role play and home-

work efforts, a program of self-reinforcement can be instituted. Trainees can be instructed in the nature of self reinforcement and encouraged to "say something and do something nice for yourself" if they practice their new skill well.

## APPLICATIONS

In Structured Learning behaviors are viewed as skills, and individuals may be described as more or less proficient in their use of these skills. In developing a comprehensive set of skills for adult psychiatric patients, an attempt was made to include those skills cited in the professional literature as well as by practitioners and psychiatric patients themselves as important for daily functioning in the community. The final list was thus derived from research findings plus surveys of mental health workers and of psychiatric patients. Subsequent to administration and compilation of these materials, the list of Basic Skills found in Table 1 was developed.

**Table 1.   Structured Learning basic skills for adults.**

Conversations: Beginning Skills
1.  Starting a conversation
2.  Carrying on a conversation
3.  Ending a conversation
4.  Listening

Conversations: Expressing Oneself
5.  Expressing a compliment
6.  Expressing appreciation
7.  Expressing encouragement
8.  Asking for help
9.  Giving instructions
10.  Expressing affection
11.  Expressing a complaint
12.  Persuading others
13.  Expressing anger

Conversations: Responding to Others
14.  Responding to praise
15.  Responding to the feelings of others (empathy)
16.  Apologizing
17.  Following instructions
18.  Responding to persuasion
19.  Responding to failure
20.  Responding to contradictory messages
21.  Responding to a complaint
22.  Responding to anger

Planning Skills
23.  Setting a goal
24.  Gathering information
25.  Concentrating on a task
26.  Evaluating your abilities
27.  Preparing for a stressful conversation
28.  Setting problems priorities
29.  Decision making

Alternatives to Aggression
30.  Identifying and labeling your emotions
31.  Determining responsibility
32.  Making requests
33.  Relaxation
34.  Self-control
35.  Negotiation
36.  Helping others
37.  Assertiveness

Each skill is broken down into its constituent behavioral steps. These steps are based upon behavioral analysis and experimental evidence from the literature. Trainers and/or trainees can assess (via checklists or behavior observation methods) trainees' observed or felt proficiencies or deficiencies in the various skills. The skills, their behavioral steps, and related information appear in Goldstein, Sprafkin, and Gershaw (1976). Examples of behavioral steps are found in Table 2.

Structured Learning has been used to teach a variety of interpersonal, aggression-control, planning, and stress management skills to adolescents in both regular schools and residential treatment settings. While some of the skills developed for adult psychiatric patients were used, a substantial number of new skills had to be added. In some instances the wording and complexity of the behavioral steps were modified. Skills developed for use with adolescents are listed in Table 3.

In addition to altering the list of skills to be taught, other procedural modifications were made to prescriptively meet the training needs of adolescents. One such change was in the mode of presentation of the modeling displays. While adult psychiatric patients are typically passive and able to attend to audiotaped modeling displays, youngsters seem to require more action, more vivid examples, including visual as well as auditory cues.

Table 2.   **Typical behavioral steps.**

Starting a Conversation
Learning points:
1. Choose the right place and time.
2. Greet the other person.
3. Make small talk.
4. Judge if the other person is listening and wants to talk with you.
5. Open the main topic you want to talk about.

Negotiation
Learning points:
1. State your position.
2. State your understanding of the other person's position.
3. Ask if the other person agrees with your statement of his or her position.
4. Listen openly to his or her response.
5. Propose a compromise.

Thus an attempt was made to present active models live, on videotape, or on filmstrip.

Another modification used with teenagers attempts to capitalize on the power and attractiveness of natural peer leaders. Such peer leaders clearly have much more influence and sustained contact than any adult could hope for. It is often possible to take advantage of the peer leader's influence by having the (adult) trainer employ the peer leader as a co-trainer in some structured learning sessions. The peer leader must, of course, be trained, follow the sequence of procedures, and be relatively competent in the particular skill being taught. The specific techniques developed for use with teenagers are described in detail in *Skillstreaming the Adolescent: A Structured Learning Approach to Teaching Prosocial Skills* (Goldstein et al., 1980).

The structured learning approach also has been applied to training police officers. The complexity of police work is only slowly coming to public awareness. With this awareness comes the recognition of the need for training in such difficult interpersonal tasks as handling family disputes, hostage negotiations, and crisis intervention. Structured learning techniques have been used to train police officers in these areas (Goldstein et al., 1977; Miron & Goldstein, 1978). Geriatric patients have been a recent target population for the application of Structured Learning. Sensitized to the interpersonal skill deficits of institutionalized geriatric patients by practitioners working with such patients, Lopez and associates (1980) conducted a series of studies to see how much repetition in role playing was optimal for facilitating skill acquisition. These studies demonstrated the prescriptive application of the structured learning approach, whereby the manner of presentation of the components is modified to meet the needs of the population.

We have also recently modified the manner of presentation of the structured learning components so that general audiences seeking to improve their social skillfulness might do so by using Structured Learning on a self-help basis (Goldstein, Sprafkin, & Gershaw,

**Table 3.    Structured Learning skills for adolescents.**

Beginning Social Skills
 1.  Listening
 2.  Starting a conversation
 3.  Having a conversation
 4.  Asking a question
 5.  Saying thank you
 6.  Introducing yourself
 7.  Introducing other people
 8.  Giving a compliment

Advanced Social Skills
 9.  Asking for help
10.  Joining in
11.  Giving instructions
12.  Following instructions
13.  Apologizing
14.  Convincing others

Skills for Dealing with Feelings
15.  Knowing your feelings
16.  Expressing your feelings
17.  Understanding the feelings of others
18.  Dealing with someone else's anger
19.  Expressing affection
20.  Dealing with fear
21.  Rewarding yourself

Skill Alternatives to Aggression
22.  Asking permission
23.  Sharing something
24.  Helping others
25.  Negotiation
26.  Using self-control
27.  Standing up for your rights
28.  Responding to teasing
29.  Avoiding trouble with others
30.  Keeping out of fights

Skills for Dealing with Stress
31.  Making a complaint
32.  Answering a complaint
33.  Sportsmanship after the game
34.  Dealing with embarrassment
35.  Dealing with being left out
36.  Standing up for a friend
37.  Responding to persuasion
38.  Responding to failure
39.  Dealing with contradictory messages
40.  Dealing with an accusation
41.  Getting ready for a difficult conversation
42.  Dealing with group pressure

Planning Skills
43.  Deciding on something to do
44.  Deciding what caused a problem
45.  Setting a goal
46.  Deciding on your abilities
47.  Gathering information
48.  Arranging problems by importance
49.  Making a decision
50.  Concentrating on a task

1979). In this adaptation, *modeling* is presented through written examples that illustrate effective skill use; *role playing* is self-administered (e.g., tape recorded) or accomplished with the help of a trusted friend; *feedback* is accomplished through self-critique, observed reactions of others, and/or requested evaluations from friends; and *transfer* is effected using a variety of practice assignments, contracts, and self-reward systems.

In addition to the populations listed above, Structured Learning also has been used with child-abusing parents, with the goal of helping them develop self-control, parenting, marital, and peer relationship skills; with managers in industry, with the aim of developing effective supervisory skills (Goldstein & Sorcher, 1973); and, most recently,

in teaching interpersonal skills to youngsters with learning disabilities and to youngsters and adults considered to be mildly to moderately retarded.

## CASE EXAMPLE

The following case is intended as a composite illustration of the application of the structured learning approach with an adult psychiatric patient. The person described is fairly typical of those individuals who have developed a "revolving door" career of frequent psychiatric hospitalizations, inpatient stays ranging from a few days or weeks to several months, and only limited success at community tenure.

Frank W is a 48-year-old single man, the

second of three children in a working-class family. He grew up in a medium-sized city in the northeastern part of the United States. Frank's teachers described him as withdrawn and fearful. He quit high school during eleventh grade to go to work. Schoolwork never appealed to him, he had no friends, and money was needed at home. After taking a couple of unskilled jobs, he enlisted in the army. Following an honorable discharge from the service, Frank took a job on a factory assembly line in another part of the country. He lived in furnished rooms, had no friends and no outside hobbies or interests. He quickly lost contact with his family, except for occasional letters from his older brother.

After two years of fairly steady employment, economic conditions changed and Frank found himself out of work. He became more seclusive and felt confused and overwhelmed by various problems. He was hospitalized for the first time in a state psychiatric facility. In the 20-odd years that have passed since that first hospitalization, Frank seldom spent more than a year outside of a state or Veterans Administration psychiatric hospital. Typically he would become overwhelmed by a variety of environmental stresses—financial problems, conflicts with landlords, run-ins with shop foremen—and he would seek hospitalization. Generally he was given the diagnosis of "schizophrenia, chronic undifferentiated." When hospitalized, Frank would usually receive psychotropic medications and custodial treatments; he had not done well with a few attempts at verbal, insight-oriented psychotherapies.

Frank was seen at a Veterans Administration Day Treatment Center, having been referred upon discharge from an inpatient psychiatric facility. The referral information from the hospital indicated that Frank had been an inpatient for three months, tended toward withdrawal and seclusiveness, but no longer needed inpatient care. Frank was accompanied to the day treatment center by his older brother, with whom he was living until other arrangements could be made. The brother indicated that he was Frank's only remaining family, but that he and his wife

could not keep him indefinitely. The brother also stated that he managed Frank's money, and that both he and his wife had come to accept Frank's "illness" and tried not to put too many demands on him.

During the initial interview at the center, Frank's brother did most of the talking. Questions directed at Frank were answered by yes or no. He avoided eye contact with the interviewer. The interviewer explained the day treatment center program to Frank and his brother (e.g., Sprafkin, Gershaw, & Goldstein, 1978). The program was set up using a psychoeducational training model, with a variety of classes in social skills and self-management areas. Frank passively agreed to a schedule of classes, which included several ones in Structured Learning.

Before Frank and his brother left the center, one of the structured learning trainers met with them to explain what would be going on in the structured learning classes. The trainer asked both Frank and his brother to indicate which skills each thought Frank needed help with. While Frank was shown the rest of the center, the trainer explained further to the brother how he (the brother) and his wife might be helpful in fostering Frank's anticipated progress in the classes. The brother was given some written descriptions of the program and an open invitation to remain in contact with the trainer.

Frank was placed in a structured learning class with seven other trainees who were all, by their own and others' reports, deficient in "Basic Conversational Skills." During the first class session the new members of the class were introduced and were then acquainted with the structured learning procedures. The trainer suggested that the class get right to work on practicing the skill of "Starting a Conversation." He then played several audiotaped modeling vignettes, each depicting actors starting conversations successfully by following a series of behavioral steps, or "learning points." The trainers then opened up a discussion of the taped examples, and a few members of the class volunteered that a couple of the situations reminded them of when they had had difficulty in initiating conversations. The trainer asked

Frank if any of the modeling displays reminded him of situations that were problematic for him, and Frank admitted, reluctantly, that he was very uncomfortable starting conversations with certain clerks in stores. The trainer then proceeded to lead the various trainees in role plays of some of the situations they had described. After the role plays, the trainees were provided with feedback, and, finally, those who had been the main actors were given specific "homework assignments" for real-life practice of the skill.

During the second meeting of the class Frank was given an opportunity to role play. He was extremely hesitant and anxious at first, but with encouragement from the trainer and other trainees he assented. He chose another trainee who reminded him of a clerk in his neighborhood grocery store. With a good deal of coaching from the trainer, he completed the role play and received helpful, favorable feedback from the other trainees. As his homework assignment he agreed to start a conversation with the actual clerk, which he did that very day. Fortunately, the clerk was very helpful, and Frank returned to his next class eager to report on his accomplishment.

After practicing a number of other conversational skills, with increasingly more active participation on Frank's part, the class addressed the skill of "Making Requests." In the discussion following the modeling displays, Frank said that he found it extremely difficult to make requests of others, and in particular to make requests of his brother, who, after all, "took care of him." He stated that he would like to ask his brother to allow him to manage his own money, as he now felt competent to do so. As he was eager to deal with the problem, he was the first to role play this skill. He chose as a co-actor another trainee whom he felt resembled his brother. He proceeded to role play "Making a Request," with the content dealing with his money management. While Frank's performance was quite adequate, he did not yet feel confident enough to try the skill with his brother. Rather, as a homework assignment

he agreed to make a request of the secretary of the center, a person and situation he felt to be less threatening. During the next class he reported that his encounter with the secretary had been successful, and that perhaps he was ready to try the skill with his brother. The brother, who had maintained contact with the center and was generally aware of Frank's growing desire for financial independence, responded to Frank's attempt in a guardedly positive way, much to Frank's delight.

Frank continued to attend structured learning classes at the center for several months following the incident described above. During that time he was able to begin discussing with his brother his desire to live independently and secure employment, at least on a part-time basis. After several months Frank was in fact able to master the skills necessary to find a job and to move into his own small apartment. At that point his contact with the center tapered off to occasional social visits.

## SUMMARY

Structured Learning is a psychoeducational, skill-training approach for teaching a range of interpersonal, planning, and stress-management skills to a variety of clinical and nonclinical populations. Its roots lie both in education and psychology, with a clear commitment to the incorporation of sound, empirically based principles of learning into training methods that are readily comprehensible to different types of trainees.

Structured Learning is basically a group technique whose major components are modeling, role playing, performance feedback, and transfer of training. While each of these components individually appears to be necessary for learning to occur, their use in combination has been shown to greatly enhance the likelihood of the acquisition and performance of new behavioral skills.

Structured Learning is not conceived of as a static entity, which once described must remain unchanged. The approach began as a psychotherapy tailored to the treatment needs of chronic, institutionalized, low-income psychiatric patients and, in relatively few years, has been adapted and applied to a number of other groups of trainees. It is the authors' hope that the structured learning appraoch will be creatively and prescriptively adapted to the particular training needs and learning styles of each target population.

The other major goal that remains in the development of Structured Learning is to increase the likelihood that what is learned in the training setting will in fact transfer effectively to real-life applications. Much research has yet to be done in this regard, although much progress has already been made. The challenge lies, however, in helping a variety of trainees to learn *and* to *apply* the skills they feel they need in order to live productive, satisfying lives.

# REFERENCES

Arbuthnot, J. Modification of moral judgment through role playing. *Developmental Psychology,* 1975, **11,** 319–324.

Bandura, A. *Social learning theory.* Englewood Cliffs, N.J.: Prentice-Hall, 1977.

Goldstein, A. P. *Therapist-patient expectancies in psychotherapy.* New York: Pergamon, 1962.

Goldstein, A. P. *Psychotherapeutic attraction.* New York: Pergamon, 1971.

Goldstein, A. P. *Structured learning therapy: Toward a psychotherapy for the poor.* New York: Academic Press, 1973.

Goldstein, A. P. and Sorcher, M. *Changing supervisor behavior.* New York: Pergamon, 1973.

Goldstein, A. P. and Stein, N. *Prescriptive psychotherapies.* New York: Pergamon, 1976.

Goldstein, A. P., Heller, K. and Sechrest, L. B. *Psychotherapy and the psychology of behavior change.* New York: Wiley, 1966.

Goldstein, A. P., Sprafkin, R. P. and Gershaw, N. J. *Skill training for community living: Applying structured learning therapy.* New York: Pergamon, 1976.

Goldstein, A. P., Monti, P. J., Sardino, T. and Green, D. *Police crisis intervention.* New York: Pergamon, 1977.

Goldstein, A. P., Sprafkin, R. P. and Gershaw, N. J. *I know what's wrong, but I don't know what to do about it.* Englewood Cliffs, N.J.: Prentice-Hall, 1979.

Goldstein, A. P., Sprafkin, R. P., Gershaw, N. J. and Klein, P. *Skillstreaming the adolescent: A structured learning approach to teaching prosocial skills.* Urbana, Ill.: Research Press, 1980.

Hollander, T. G. The effects of role playing on attraction, disclosure and attitude change in a psychotherapy analogue. Ph.D. dissertation. Syracuse University, 1970.

James, W. What pragmatism means. In M. R. Konvitz and G. Kennedy (Eds.), *The American pragmatists.* New York: Meridian Books, 1960.

Lichtenstein, E., Keutzer, C. S. and Himes, K. H. Emotional role playing and changes in smoking attitudes and behaviors. *Psychological Reports,* 1969, **23,** 379–387.

Lopez, M. A., Hoyer, W. J., Goldstein, A. P., Gershaw, N. J. and Sprafkin, R. P. Effects of overlearning and incentive on the acquisition and transfer of interpersonal skills with institutionalized elderly. *Journal of Gerontology,* 1980, *35,* 403–409.

McFall, R. M. and Marston, A. R. An experimental investigation of behavior rehearsal in assertive training. *Journal of Abnormal Psychology,* 1970, **76,** 295–303.

Miron, M. and Goldstein, A. P. *Hostage.* New York: Pergamon, 1978.

Perry, M. A. Didactic instructions for and modeling of empathy. Ph.D. dissertation. Syracuse University, 1970.

Rathjen, D., Heneker, A. and Rathjen, E. Incorporation of behavioral techniques in a game format to teach children social skills. Paper presented at the Association for Advancement of Behavior Therapy, New York, 1976.

Rychlak, J. F. *Introduction to personality and psychotherapy.* Boston: Houghton, 1973.

Sprafkin, R. P. Communicator expertness and changes in word meanings in psychological treatment. *Journal of Counseling Psychology,* 1970, **17 (3),** 191–196.

Sprafkin, R. P. The rebirth of moral treatment. *Professional Psychology,* 1977, **8 (2),** 161–169.

Sprafkin, R. P., Gershaw, N. J. and Goldstein, A. P. Teaching interpersonal skills to psychiatric outpatients: Using structured learning therapy in a community-based setting. *Journal of Rehabilitation,* 1978, **44 (2),** 26–29.

Staub, E. The use of role playing and induction in children's learning of helping and sharing behavior. *Child Development,* 1971, **42,** 805–816.

Sutton, K. Effects of modeled empathy and structured social class upon level of therapist displayed empathy. Masters thesis. Syracuse University, 1970.

# CHAPTER 62

# *Triad Counseling*

PAUL B. PEDERSEN

*How does one train counselors to deal with counselees from different cultures? How does one effectively treat counselees who not only have the usual resistances but also special resistances due to the circumstances of different classes or different cultures? A well-intentioned and well-prepared counselor who faces hostile, fearful, resistant, and non-communicative individuals from different-from-himself/herself ethnic, social, cultural, economic groups with radically different values and lifestyles often faces what appears to be insuperable communication and relationship problems. As a former prison psychologist and as one who has worked in social agencies, etc., I am well aware of the extent of this professional dilemma.*

*The triad model developed by Paul Pedersen is a genuinely novel approach to this kind of problem, and calls for a re-evaluation of traditional assumptions and procedures with such groups. The invention of the 'anticounselor' is in my judgment a significant innovation not only for training but also for treatment with fearful, suspicious or alienated clients frequently met in various social agencies such as mental hospitals, clinics, student centers and the like. Prepare for a brand new perspective on counseling and psychotherapy.*

The triad model of counseling is specifically designed for effective cross-cultural counseling and is seen as a three-way interaction between the counselor, the client, and the problem. Its special features, which include an "anticounselor," are intended to reduce the well-known problem of client resistance, a problem that is generally stronger when the counselor and client come from different cultural backgrounds, whether they be "caste" or "class" differences. The greater the cultural difference, the less likely it is generally for a counselor to form an effective coalition with the client against the problem. When the social psychological perspectives of coalition formation in a triad are applied properly, the counselor is guided toward adjusting his or her power influence effectively to maintain a "willing coalition" format.

In the training of people to become cross-cultural counselors, the counselor, client, and a third person—the "anticounselor"—interact, with the "anticounselor" providing continuous immediate feedback relative to the power flow, thus sharpening the counselor's perceptions and skills.

## HISTORY

The triad model grew out of a graduate seminar in 1965 at the University of Minnesota conducted by Clyde Parker and Donald Blocher, where the class assignment was to

This chapter was prepared through support from the National Institute of Mental Health Grant No. IT24 MH 15552-01.

840

develop an original idea in counseling. Having just returned from three years counseling in an Indonesian university, this writer was intrigued by how Asian clients generally conceptualized personal problems differently from U.S. clients. Problems were seen as both good and bad, and not as simply bad. Each problem was viewed by clients as having rewarding and valuable as well as undesirable features, thereby presenting a dilemma to the client. A problem was viewed as a complex entity, as a personality is, and not limited to the client's presenting symptom. The problem was viewed as actively changing in an almost "demonic" configuration with a "mind" of its own, not passively accepting client or counselor controls. In the counseling relationship a problem sometimes resembled a personified enemy, having a secret strategy of its own with concrete and specific manifestations of control over the client much as a malevolent person might control the client against the client's best interests, through implicit threats and promises.

To better understand the client's problem in cross-cultural counseling, I (1976b) experimented with using a third person from the client's culture in a simulated cross-cultural counseling interview. The third person was called the "anticounselor," to describe that person's function in the interview, using cultural similarity with the client to sharpen the counselor-client cross-cultural coalition.

The use of three persons in therapy is not new. Bolman (1968) was probably first to suggest that at least two therapists, one representing each culture, be used in cross-cultural therapy to provide a bridge between the client's culture and the therapist. Triads were also advocated by Slack and Slack (1976) by involving a third person who had already coped effectively with the client's problem in the counseling relationship. Triads have been applied to Family Therapy as examples of pathogenic coalitions (Satir, 1964), with the therapist employing mediation and side-taking judiciously to replace pathogenic re-

lating. Counseling thus becomes a series of negotiations in which all three parties vie for control. Zuk (1971) described this approach as a "go-between" process in which the therapist catalyzes conflict in a crisis situation in which all parties can take an active role.

Historically, it is well accepted that counselors who differ from their clients in race, culture, or social class have difficulty effecting constructive changes, while counselors who are most similar in these respects have a greater facility for appropriate intervention. A common example is that alcoholics apparently are best helped by other alcoholics. Barriers of language, class-bound values, or culture-bound goals have a tendency to weaken the counselor-client coalition and disrupt the counseling relationship. In working with clients from other cultures, there is a great danger of mutual misunderstanding; imperfect understanding of the other culture's unique problems; an ingrained prejudice that destroys rapport, leading to increased negative transference toward the counselor and presenting the danger of confusing a client's appropriate cultural response with foreign constructs such as "neurotic transference" (Pedersen, 1976a).

The culturally encapsulated counselor might disregard cultural variations among clients in a dogmatic adherence to some "universal" notion of technique-oriented truth.

The usual system of selecting, training, and certifying counselors reflects and even reinforces culturally encapsulated bias. There is evidence that even well-trained counselors are not generally prepared to deal with individuals who come from racial, ethnic, or socioeconomic groups whose values, attitudes, and general life styles are different from middle-class norms (Pedersen, 1976a).

Therapists unable to adjust their own attitudes, beliefs, and style of behavior to those of another culture are likely to substitute their own criteria of desired social effectiveness for alternative criteria more appropriate to the client's environment.

## CURRENT STATUS

Most of the current work on Triad Counseling has been done in a training mode rather than in a direct service to clients in therapy situations, but, paradoxically, training of counselors becomes therapy for the trainees.

Research among students using Triad Counseling showed they achieved statistically significantly higher scores on a multiple-choice written test designed to measure counselor effectiveness; they demonstrated a lower discrepancy between real and ideal self-description; and they chose a greater number of positive adjectives in describing themselves as counselors than previous semester students who did not use the triad model. In addition, there were significant increases from pretest to posttest on videotaped cross-cultural interviews rated for empathy, respect, and congruence. In addition, pretest training videotapes, when rated on the seven-level Gordon scales measuring communication of understanding of affective meaning, showed that students had increased their skill levels significantly (Pedersen, Holwill, & Shapiro, 1978).

After a one-day in-service training workshop with 39 Asian-American counselors working with transient mainland youth, participants responded to a questionnaire: Did the training help them anticipate client resistance? (28 yes, 4 no, 7 no response) Did it help to articulate the problem? (25 yes, 6 no, 2 somewhat, 6 no response) Did they want additional training with the model? (22 yes, 8 no, 1 maybe, 8 no response) When asked what values they had gained as a result of using the model, 12 emphasized better understanding of cultural differences, 8 emphasized improved in-service training for counselors, 5 emphasized the value of a third person (anticounselor) in simulated counseling interviews. Responding to a similar questionnaire, 40 other counselors were also positive: Did the training help them anticipate client resistance? (32 yes, 1 no, 1 maybe, 4 somewhat, and 2 no response) Did this training help articulate the problem? (30 yes, 2

no, 5 somewhat, and 3 no response) Did they want additional training in the model? (28 yes, 1 no, 1 maybe, and 10 no response)

In 1977 Fahy Holwill-Bailey (1979) compared a traditional mode of teaching human relations/intercultural skills to counselors with a design similar to Kagan et. al., (1965). "interpersonal process recall" method and a triad model design. As dependent measures she used Ivey's counselor effectiveness scale, the Revised Truax Accurate Empathy scale, the Revised Carkhuff Respect and Genuineness scale, the Shapiro Adjective Checklist, and the Bender Tolerance and Ambiguity Scale. In a three-way analysis of covariance, all tests were found significant between the control group and the treatment group. In a preliminary analysis of her data no significant differences were found between the measures of the triad and the dyadic training design, however, suggesting that both approaches were approximately equally effective but both seemed superior to the traditional counselor education approaches.

Ivey and Authier (1978) discuss the triad model in "the cultural-environmental-contextual implications" of microcounseling as a training approach. Ivey and Authier (1978) indicated that "The most powerful and direct method for cross-cultural training appears to be that of the cross-cultural triad model of Pedersen" (p. 215). At the same time he pointed out that the triad model would not be appropriate for all trainees; naive trainees might "wilt" under the pressure of the anticounselor. Ivey suggested further that trainees would benefit most from the triad model after having learned basic microcounseling skills of counseling.

The Institute of Behavioral Sciences in Honolulu, Hawaii, is sponsoring an intercultural mental health training program. The program will provide in-service training on cross-cultural counseling skills, annual conferences on cross-cultural counseling, and an evaluation component to monitor the effectiveness of the training methods. Derald Sue (1979) is collecting data comparing the effectiveness of triads with an anticounselor and triads using a "procounselor."

A procounselor is a resource person from the client's culture whose task is to facilitate the counseling experience, emphasizing the positive aspects of the interaction just as an anticounselor emphasizes the negative aspects. The procounselor needs to help the counselor do a better job without taking over the client or disrupting the counseling process. The procounselor role requires more skill than an anticounselor role, as the resource person must not only identify the mistakes being made but reinterpret and redirect the counselor's intervention to minimize the negative and maximize the positive impact. Having a procounselor ally from the client's culture is often reassuring to the counselor, although an insensitive procounselor may take over the interview and become extremely threatening to the insecure counselor.

Additional experiments with Triad Counseling have resulted in six alternative training designs: (1) the anticounselor, in which the client's partner role plays the negative feedback; (2) the procounselor, where the client's partner role plays the positive feedback; (3) the interpreter, where the client's partner facilitates accurate communication between client and counselor with both positive and negative feedback; (4) a third-person-hostile, where the client's partner role plays a close friend or relative hostile to counseling; (5) a third-person-friendly, where the client's partner role plays a close friend or relative friendly to counseling; and (6) a quartet of both the hostile and friendly partner to the client interacting with the counselor.

Further modifications seek to specify the training and therapy skills in greater detail, adapt the triad model design to verbal and nonverbal, confronting and nonconfronting cultures, and collect data on the specific impact of the direct and immediate feedback from a client during the simulated cross-cultural interview. This writer has compiled previously published materials on the triad model in a book, *Basic Intercultural Counseling Skills* (1979a), in connection with further research development and teaching that incorporates the model.

## THEORY

Counseling can be described as an interaction of push and pull factors in which the counselor seeks fulfillment in being helpful, the client seeks to reconcile internalized ambiguity, and the problem loses its control over the client. The counseling force field suggests a triad of stress, response to it, and ameliorative intervention, all three of which are potentially subject to being culturally mediated. The counselor-client interaction is basically a social interaction following the same laws and principles as other social interactions. This writer (1968, 1973) has described this force field as a dynamic interaction of contrary forces in the mode of social power theory and in the context of an equilibrium between the counselor seeking coalition with the client against resistance by the problem (Caplow, 1968). The counselor-client coalition requires identification of action in accord with a shared goal. Just as the client has called in a counselor for assistance, the counselor must also depend on the client for knowledge about the problem. Negotiating a coalition between the client and counselor describes the task functions of counseling, subject to frequent maintenance and modification.

Figure 1 outlines a schematic for describing the relationships between the counselor, client, and problem as a triadic interaction. This figure describes counseling as competition for influence between a client-counselor coalition on the one hand and the problem on the other. The figure assumes that we are able to estimate differences between high and low levels of power or influence as a general descriptor for measuring client progress. Counseling, then, becomes a process whereby a client's contribution of power or influence is increased and, as an inverse function of this process, the problem's capacity

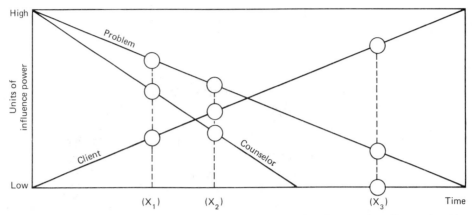

Figure 1   A schematic description of the ratio of power influence over time for counselor, client, and problem with three (X₁, X₂, X₃) points in the counseling process indicated.

for power or influence is decreased. The client is expected to move up the slope from having less power to having more power as the desired outcome. The desired outcome is that the problem is expected to move down the slope to having less power. The counselor is expected to intervene to encourage client progress through a client-counselor coalition that isolates and weakens the power of the problem. At any given point along the time dimension, the power of a successful counselor plus the power of the client should be approximately the same as the power of the problem (Co + Cl = P). The unequal and dynamic distribution of power requires the effective counselor to vary the intensity of intervention accordingly. If the counselor assumes too much power, the client will withdraw from counseling, preferring to have the problem, since it will be seen as less threatening or dominating than the counselor. If the counselor assumes too little power, the problem will dominate through a continued coalition with the client.

Three situations (X₁, X₂, X₃) are indicated in Figure 1. In X₁, the client has little power and is dominated by the problem. Situation X₂ shows the client able to exert enough power so that the counselor may become the weaker member of the triad, transfering more responsibility to the client. Situation X₃

shows the client able to manage the problem independently, needing little help from the counselor. A "low-power" client statement might be "I feel bad and I don't know why." This might be matched by a more intense counselor interpretive statement such as "Perhaps the reason you feel bad is thus and so." A higher power client statement might be "But that's not at all how I feel." This might be matched by a less intense counselor reflection such as "You don't feel thus and so it is a problem for you." Clients who are reasonably effective in dealing with their problem require minimal intervention by the counselor. Good counseling will help clients be more effective.

The units of high- and low-power influence are relative and not absolute points; thus it is necessary to distinguish between a relatively effective client facing a difficult problem and a relatively ineffective client facing a mild problem. Counselors need to coordinate their own intervention according to the variable rate and direction of the client's movement to maintain the client-counselor coalition. Counselor interventions toward the left side of Figure 1 tend to be confronting and interpretive, while interventions toward the right side of the figure tend to be reflective and nondirective. The counselor needs to monitor accurately and attend to client feelings, otherwise interventions are likely to be inappropriate. When the client comes from a culture different from that of the counselor, however, it is extremely difficult to interpret client communications accurately.

The "anticounselor" is similar to the alter ego in psychodrama or Gestalt Psychotherapy, except that the anticounselor is not neutral or helpful but is deliberately subversive, attempting to disrupt the counseling interview. The counselor, therefore, is pulling in one direction toward a solution, while the anticounselor is pulling in exactly the opposite direction, attempting to maintain the problem. The client chooses which alternative, the cross-cultural counselor or the same-culture anticounselor, offers the most meaningful ally. A client/counselor coalition against the anticounselor becomes the vehicle of effective counseling, while ineffective counseling results in a client/anticounselor coalition isolating and rendering ineffective the counselor. While the strategies of a counselor and the role expectations for a client are familiar to us, the notion of an active, back-talking anticounselor at first seems bizarre and strange. The problem, represented by the anticounselor, develops its own unique strategies.

The role of the anticounselor is distinguished from the role of a person with a problem. The anticounselor role carries negative function, just as the counselor's role implies positive function in the counseling relationship, thereby polarizing these two roles. The client is "wooed" by both the counselor and the anticounselor. The anticounselor's intention might be to contain counseling at a superficial level; to confuse, distort, distract, discredit, complicate, or otherwise frustrate the counselor. Most anticounselors make themselves attractive to same-culture clients, not being constrained by rules of logical consistency and with private cultural access to the client. The anticounselor provides negative feedback that would not be appropriate coming from the client even in role play, thereby articulating

the resistances that would otherwise be symbolically ambiguous.

Triad Counseling combines insights from a wide range of theories. The principles of psychodrama and sociodrama have long advocated the use of role play to illustrate clearly the otherwise ambiguous elements of a complicated relationship. The role playing of interviews for counselor training has been standard procedure for many years, although not with the same negative and positive structures described in this chapter. The insights of social psychology are applied in the literature about coalition formation in a triad; the illustrations of force-field theory and analysis of push/pull factors of a relationship are evident in the triad model in the tension between pro- and anticounselor perspectives. Kelly and Thibaut (1978) review the social psychology literature about interdependence in dyads influenced by the social environment. The triad model has adapted theories of social psychology to the counseling dyad partners in their various configurations in their interdependent relationship to one another.(Revich & Geertsma 1969; Salomon & McDonald, 1970; Stroller, 1967).

## METHODOLOGY

The first step in setting up a triad model is to locate a suitable resource person. He or she must be matched with the client as a team. It is essential that the teams of resource persons be culturally similar to one another and communicate well enough to anticipate what the other would be thinking and feeling. Often, having located one resource person, it is best to let that person select the other. Whether as an anticounselor, interpreter, or procounselor, the client's partner needs to provide accurate insight into what the client is really thinking and feeling for the model to work. The resource team needs to be articulate enough to provide feedback to the counselor that would be understood even by an outsider to that culture; additionally, the feedback must be authentic to the basic values of the culture. The resource team should also be comfortable giving positive and/or negative feedback to the counselor.

The second step is in training the resource persons to perform in a triadic situation. The resource persons are instructed to give positive feedback exclusively *or* negative feedback exclusively, with the client's partner providing one or the other but *not* both. In this way the counselor working with a culturally different client will enter the interview knowing unambiguously that the resource person is either an "enemy" or a "friend." The counselor gains facility in differentiating positive from negative feedback in a culturally different setting by focusing on them separately without initially having to disentangle them during the interview itself. The triad model can be demonstrated through previously videotaped interviews showing the simulated interaction between a counselor and a client with an anticounselor, procounselor, interpreter, or one other adaptation. If videotaped models are not available, simulated role plays might help the resource persons understand the interaction process. It is important for them to watch a model of the interaction to clarify what will be expected of them later. They will then be able to practice role playing the triad model, if possible reviewing their interviews on videotape for debriefing. Where resource persons are reluctant to provide negative feedback, it might be useful to involve several persons in the anticounselor role simultaneously to take the pressure off the resource person as an individual. It is important for resource persons to be well trained so that they understand what will be expected of them.

The resource persons should be instructed to give continuous and immediate feedback to the counselor about what is working and what is not working. They may provide this feedback verbally or nonverbally, but the cues should accompany the good or bad counselor interventions as immediately as possible, as unmistakably obvious as possi-

ble, and continuously throughout the interview. The counselor, having identified the good or bad intervention, can then recover or correct the intervention immediately. Gradually the counselor is expected to become more sensitive to subtle positive and negative cues from the client/resource person team and take immediate corrective action to anticipate negative feedback even before it is given.

The third step in using the triad model is in selecting the problems to be studied. In an actual setting where the resource person will be used in direct therapy, the problems would be provided by the client. The task of the anticounselor, procounselor, or interpreter would be to accurately reflect and understand the problem from the client's point of view. To perform effectively, the resource person would have to be extremely skilled and sensitive to the client's unique perspective. In a training setting the client/resource person team would be able to identify a series of problems familiar to both of them and likely to be unfamiliar to the counselor trainee. The problems should be selected for their training potential so that they would be complex rather than simple and with no easy solution, reflect the client's cultural values wherever possible, and fairly frequently encountered as serious and meaningful issues in the client's culture. Often the resource team might be helped in selecting the problems for training by asking them to model their problem on the actual problem of someone from their culture. It is extremely important that the resource team *not* use a serious problem in which one of them might themselves be seeking therapy; this would confuse the training situation with direct counseling and could result in the resource person's injury.

Once the resource persons have been selected, trained, and appropriate problems have been selected, the team is ready to work in a direct service, in-service, or preservice setting. While there is some data from using the model for in-service or preservice training, there is no data from using the model in direct service therapy. Extreme caution should therefore be used especially if an adaptation of the anticounselor is used in direct service therapy.

## Direct Service Therapy

The use of a third person in therapy is not new. In many non-Western cultures the role of the go-between or third person as broker of advice and help has been the standard mode of "counseling." Often the client will bring a third person into the interview who is positively or negatively disposed toward the counseling process. Even when there is only the counselor and the client alone in the interview, however, the triad model hypothesizes that positive and negative advice from the client's environment continue to influence the client's response and is heard much more clearly by the client's "inner ear" than by the counselor as a cultural outsider. Much of counseling is spent articulating these sources of "*anti*counseling."

If the counselor is experiencing an impasse either because of language problems or some other source of client resistance that may be culturally related, the counselor may request an interpreter or third person to assist in the interview. To some extent counseling through a translator resembles an adaptation of the triad model, especially insofar as the culture as well as the language needs to be translated. Even when there is no language problem, however, a third person may be required to help the counselor work more sensitively and effectively in another culture. Such a third person might further reduce the client's anxiety, especially if the client has a role in selecting the third person, and facilitate the counseling interview. The third person's role would have to be clarified to the client in detail, especially if the third person emphasized negative feedback to the counselor.

Another adaptation of Triad Counseling currently being used in marriage counseling asks the husband and the wife each to bring an advocate to the session who would argue for their point of view. Then a videocamera focuses on the four persons (husband, wife, prohusband, prowife) and the counselor leaves the room while the four persons are videotaped discussing together the disagreements of the husband and the wife. After a period of time the counselor returns to the room and watches the videotape with the husband and wife, and they discuss the issues of disagreement that came out in the earlier quartet. Again, the otherwise ambiguous and obscure positive and negative feedback are made articulate by the resource persons in ways that the client, or in this case clients, were unable to deal with explicitly.

Even in an interview alone with the client, a counselor may wish to "hypothesize" the problem as a third "presence" there in the room working against the counselor, counseling process, and ultimately against the client as well. In helping the client to see the influence of this problem as anticounselor, the client might be helped to articulate many of the otherwise implicit negative feelings about being in counseling.

## In-Service Training

Generally in in-service training two teams are trained. Ten to 15 counselors are assembled in a meeting room with a video monitor. Following an introduction and presentation of a video demonstration tape of Triad Counseling, the facilitator answers questions while one of the counselors leaves the room with a client/anticounselor team to make the first videotape. The counselor and team return to the group after having produced a 10-minute videotape of a simulated counseling interview and a 5-minute videotape of the three participants debriefing one another. This 15-minute videotape is then shown to the larger group for comments and discussion. While the first tape is being viewed and discussed, another counselor leaves the room with the second client/anticounselor team to produce a second videotape. Throughout the day there is always one counselor and team making a tape and another videotape being viewed or discussed, until all counselors have had a chance to produce a videotape and receive feedback on their performance. Each counselor thereby misses the viewing and discussing of one colleague's videotape. The advantages of immediate feedback on videotaped counseling interviews are that stimulating discussion on the variety of cultures and presenting problems on counseling relationships is provoked. The videotapes produced during such a workshop can also provide a valuable resource (Pedersen, 1976b). In larger groups the videotaping might be less appropriate than role-played interviews in small groups of about 10 counselors plus a resource team.

### Preservice Training

The triad model can also be adapted for use in the classroom. In one trial 30 graduate counseling students were randomly paired with other classmates from the opposite sex and/or different ethnic group. Each pair made two videotapes of simulated counseling interviews, switching roles for the second tape, as a premeasure of cross-cultural counseling ability. These tapes and a similar series of posttraining tapes were scored to measure changes in skill resulting from training. The 30 students were then assembled into triads so that each triad contained two subjects of one sex and the third member of the opposite sex. Five of the 10 triads were also cross-cultural in ethnic composition. The objective was to have triads where two persons were much alike and one person was as different as possible, using sex role and ethnicity as indicators of differences. During the first phase of training, one student in each triad was assigned to the counselor role, one to the client role, and one to the anticounselor role. The triads met for three hours in the same roles, simulating and discussing three different cross-cultural interviews. During the second phase of the training one week later, the students rotated roles in the triad and the three-hour procedure was repeated. During the third phase in the third week of

the project, students again rotated their roles for a third three-hour session. Afterward each student had experience in each of the roles, for a total of nine hours, using the triad model with feedback on nine cross-cultural interviews (Pedersen, Holwill, & Shapiro, 1978).

Adaptations of these training designs have been used in a wide variety of workshop or classroom situations. The triad model seems to work best when (1) there is positive as well as negative feedback to the counselor; (2) all three persons interact with one another rather than there being just counselor and client interaction; (3) the client/anticounselor team is highly motivated and feels strongly about the issue under discussion; (4) the anticounselor has a high degree of empathy for and acceptance by the client; (5) the anticounselor is articulate and gives direct, immediate verbal and/or nonverbal feedback to the counselor; (6) the client has *not* selected a real problem from his or her current situation where counseling might be appropriate; (7) the discussion is spontaneous and not scripted; (8) the counselor has a chance to role play the model and receive feedback three or four times in sequence; (9) the client feels free to reject an inauthentic anticounselor; and (11) the facilitator introducing the model and leading the discussion is well acquainted with how the model operates.

## APPLICATIONS

Triad Counseling has been used to train counselors working with welfare clients, alcoholics, the handicapped, foreign students, prisoners, and other identity groups where there is likely to be a difference in values between counselors and clients.

We know that cultural backgrounds influence a counseling relationship, but we do not know how. We know that counselors have a cultural bias, but we are not able to evaluate it. We know that the appropriate matching of problems and solutions differs from one culture to another, but we don't know why. There are several reasons why a cross-cultural training program for counselors is valuable.

1. Traditional systems of mental health services have a cultural bias favoring dominant social classes, which can be counterproductive to an equitable distribution of services.
2. Various cultural groups have discovered that indigenous modes of coping and treatment that work better for them may also be usefully applied to other groups.
3. Community health services are expensive when they fail, and cross-cultural training might prevent some programs from failing.
4. Training methods that directly include indigenous people as training resource persons have not been widely used in counselor education.
5. The constructs of healthy and normal that guide the delivery of mental health services are not the same for all cultures and might cause the culturally encapsulated counselor to become a tool of a particular political, social, or economic system.
6. Increased interdependence across national, ethnic, and social-cultural boundaries requires direct attention as part of mental health training.
7. Most therapists come from dominant cultures, while most clients do not and are consequently not likely to share the same perspectives.

Triad Counseling seems to offer numerous advantages that complement other training approaches.

1. It provides an opportunity for people of different ethnic groups to role play critical incidents likely to arise in cross-cultural counseling.
2. The use of an anticounselor makes the cultural problems and value issues specific and concrete to the counselor trainee.

3. Inappropriate counselor intervention is immediately and obviously apparent through feedback from the anticounselor.
4. The counselor trainee becomes very much aware of the unspoken thoughts and feelings of the client from another culture through feedback from the anticounselor.
5. Videotaped simulations between the counselor, client, and anticounselor can be used to analyze specific ways in which cultural differences affect counseling.
6. Counselor trainees can learn to generalize insights from simulated cross-cultural interviews to direct contact with culturally different clients.
7. A careful analysis of the transcripts of simulated interviews with a culturally different client/anticounselor team will identify explicit skills for development with specific cultures.

In their anecdotal comments about the triad model, counselors emphasize the importance of "dealing with feelings" as well as content in the interview, "learning to deal with feelings of helpless frustration" from culturally different clients in a nondefensive mode, learning "how to be in two cultures at the same time," and learning "the cues a client from another culture uses to communicate feelings."

Coached clients report that "the questions you (counselor) ask don't stick in my head as well as what he (anticounselor) says," that "the anticounselor forces me to express myself more totally than I would otherwise," that "having the problem objectified helped lay it out objectively from an outside point of view," and that the problems of working with a counselor from another culture who didn't understand the cues, hints, understatements, or omissions become painfully clear.

Coached anticounselors found that "they could defeat the counselor by carefully attending to feelings," described themselves as "the personalized, hidden self out in the open exposing all the contradictions, value conflicts, fears, expectations that are not supposed to come out," detailed how the model "allows a counselor and client to cut through pretense and the defenses they both have erected against the other" and how to "intensify the client's anxiety and fortify the cultural barriers to communication," which might otherwise escape detection.

## CASE EXAMPLE

Four skill areas for counselors have emerged from working with the triad model in simulated cross-cultural interviews. These skill areas are (1) articulating the problem from the client's cultural perspective, (2) recognizing resistance from a culturally different client in specific rather than general terms, (3) diminishing counselor defensiveness when confronted by an anticounselor, and (4) learning recovery skills for getting out of trouble when making mistakes counseling culturally different clients. Excerpts from interviews will demonstrate how the triad model brings to surface otherwise implicit messages from a culturally different client.

### Articulation

All of us perceive the world from our own culturally biased points of view. To the extent that a client does not share our cultural background, the client is equally unlikely to share our point of view. In the first example from a simulated counseling interview between a white male counselor, a black female client, and a black male anticounselor, notice how the three-way interaction helps the counselor "articulate the problem."

CLIENT:    . . . Like I am a College of Liberal Arts major and a lot of times most of the classes are a lot of white kids, there aren't that many black kids on campus. And not in General College, you know, so the ones I do know I have to go elsewhere to meet, to talk to them and stuff.

COUNSELOR:    Is it white gals you have problems relating to and white guys or . . . ?

CLIENT:    Well, . . .

ANTICOUNSELOR:    Right now, the question is can you relate to *him* (pointing to counselor)? (pause) Yeah, what are you doing here?

CLIENT:    Well, umm . . . you got a good question there. I mean . . .

COUNSELOR:    Do you have difficulty relating to me now? I'm white, you're black.
. . .

ANTICOUNSELOR:    Remember all those things that happen when white folks deal with black folks. . . .

There is a clear division of responsibility between the counselor, client, and anticounselor in explicating the problem, with the client acknowledging what the anticounselor says as true but being reluctant to say the same things herself. It is as though the client can rely on the anticounselor to bring out the negative, embarrassing, and critical aspects of the problem, which would otherwise be left implicitly ambiguous. Although those negative aspects might not have been brought out explicitly, they would nonetheless be there and, even unexplained, would have a profound effect on the interview.

### Resistance

It is important to recognize resistance in specific rather than general terms as it relates to cultural differences between a counselor and a client. When resistance arises in an interview, it is important to identify and deal with it before proceeding toward controlling the problem dimension of the interview. It is important to listen to the anticounselor and determine whether the client is accepting and thereby validating the anticounselor's statements. The counselor may then modify interventions to accommodate the resistance in specific rather than general terms. An excerpt from the same interview with a white male counselor, a black female client, and a black male anticounselor illustrates this point.

ANTICOUNSELOR: We've been here five or six minutes and how much trust do we have in him? What has he done so far that can make us say that we can trust him to deal with the whole situation? You heard him hesitate. You heard him stumble around, we've heard him take the uniqueness out of the problem. . . .

COUNSELOR: Terry . . .

ANTICOUNSELOR: We've heard him say deal with the jokes. How much trust can we put in this man?

COUNSELOR: Terry, why don't you ah . . . try to, ah . . . eliminate (pause) . . . Not eliminate, certainly not eliminate . . .

ANTICOUNSELOR: I'm beginning to think trust is getting less and less.

COUNSELOR: I asked you a question on . . .

CLIENT: Well, it's like the questions you are asking don't stick in my mind as well as what he is saying to me. It's like he can relate with what I'm, you know, the thing I'm going with and you gave me a lot of stuff about how a lot of black people are approaching the same problem. But the thing is what I want to know is how do I deal with it?

There is a buildup of data where counselor mistakes contribute toward an overall loss of counselor credibility. In all therapy sessions, the client is likely to move toward a conclusion that is either positive or negative. However, the counselor would be less likely to get that explicit feedback in a cross-cultural interview without the anticounselor. Somehow the counselor is going to have to work through the specific resistance before counseling can result in an acceptable outcome for the client; before the counselor can do that, he or she will have to know clearly the mistakes being made.

## Defensiveness

The cross-cultural interview is frequently ambiguous for the counselor and can easily cause even a skilled counselor to become less

sure of him- or herself, leading to defensive behavior. It is important for the counselor in any interview to avoid the distraction of defensive behavior and focus more directly on the client's message. If the counselor is distracted by becoming defensive, the rapport with a client is likely to diminish. If a counselor is ever going to be defensive, it is more likely to occur in the presence of an anticounselor who is seeking to sabotage the interview. The triad model allows counselors to examine their own latent defensiveness and raise their threshold for nondefensive counselor responses. An excerpt from a simulated interview with a U.S. male counselor, a Latin-American female client, and a Latin-American female anticounselor demonstrates how counselor defensiveness can become a distraction.

CLIENT: Yeah, you see this thing, these things for me are very intense for me right now because I just came here. I've been here for only a month.

COUNSELOR: Would you feel better if I got back behind the desk and we sort of had that between us?

CLIENT: No, then you remind me of my father.

COUNSELOR: Okay, I don't want to do that (laugh). . . . Okay, is this more comfortable?

CLIENT: Yeah, it is.

COUNSELOR: Okay (pause).

CLIENT: Then you make me feel like you are rejecting me. You are not rejecting me?

COUNSELOR: I'm in a box here. On the one hand I want to do the things that will make you comfortable, and on the other I don't want to get too distant and make you feel like I'm rejecting you.

ANTICOUNSELOR: He's manipulating you little by little till he gets to a point that he's going to say that you got to be just like American girls. That's the best way.

COUNSELOR: How do you feel now as opposed to when you came in?

CLIENT: Well, I'm kind of feeling uncomfortable. It was okay for a while and now I feel like, I don't know . . . I feel like I want to go.

The counselor is trying to deal with his own discomfort as well as the client's discomfort and is scrambling to establish a comfortable rapport. The harder he struggles to regain the client's confidence, the more anxious the client becomes. As the resistance increases the anticounselor consolidates her position and the counseling intervention is further blocked. Perhaps if the counselor had dealt more with the client's feelings and less with his own defensive responses the rapport could have been restored.

### Recovery

Skilled counselors make perhaps as many mistakes as unskilled counselors; however, skilled counselors are able to get out of trouble and recover from mistakes with increased rather than diminished rapport. The function of training is then perhaps not to teach counselors how to avoid making mistakes but rather to help those who make mistakes to recover effectively. If a counselor working with a culturally different client is not making mistakes, then he or she may very well not be taking enough personal risk in the interview. The triad model provides opportunities for the counselor to make mistakes and experiment with various recovery strategies. The counselor who feels confident that he or she can recover from mistakes is likely to be less apprehensive about making mistakes in the first place. Another interview excerpt with the U.S. male counselor, the Latin-American female client, and the Latin-American female anticounselor will illustrate the point.

ANTICOUNSELOR: You know what he is trying to do? He is going to try to get everything out of you and then convince you that you have to be the way Americans do and just screw around. . . .

COUNSELOR: Well, I'm just thinking that you . . . I don't understand much about your

country. . . . What you have been used to. . . .

ANTICOUNSELOR: . . . And you know what will happen when you go back home.

COUNSELOR: So I need to find out first of all what you have been used to and what pleases you, and then I can help you learn how to get men to respond to you in that same way here. It is not necessary, you see, that you respond as they demand. It is perfectly possible, and I guess you have to take this kind of on faith. . . . This is, I might say, a problem not just foreign girls have; American girls have this problem too.

CLIENT: No! You know, *they* don't have that problem! They seem to enjoy that type of thing and they don't seem to have a problem with it!

COUNSELOR: I don't want to argue about that. What we want to do is deal with your problem.

CLIENT: That's right.

In the process of exploring the client's problem, the counselor tries to generalize the problem to include American girls as well as foreign girls. Both the client and the anticounselor totally reject that generalization and obviously resent being lumped together with American females in this instance. The counselor could have defended his statement; he could have gotten into a discussion with the client on the topic; he could have argued or apologized; but he did none of these. Instead he brought the focus directly back to the client and the client's problem and very neatly avoided what could have been a serious misunderstanding.

Through simulated cross-cultural counseling interviews the culturally implicit element becomes visible through the interaction of a counselor, client, and anticounselor within the safety of a role play. Separating the roles of client and anticounselor makes the problem less diffuse and abstract to counselor trainees, with the negative feedback being both more direct and specific, appropriate to the role of the anticounselor. Inappropriate counselor intervention is apparent immediately, and the counselor can adjust his or her approach immediately. The members of a client culture become resource persons for learning to counsel persons from those same cultures in a mutualistic exchange of knowledge; consequently, the client culture has more invested in the success of those counselors they have trained. Finally, the triad model illustrates the balance of power between the counselor, the client, and the anticounselor, reminding trainees that ultimately the determination of success or failure lies with the client and not the counselor (Pedersen, 1978).

## SUMMARY

Triad Counseling is a conceptual framework for viewing the interaction between a counselor, a client, and the problem that brings them together. The greater the cultural difference between counselor and client, the more ambiguous the problem element and the more difficult the task of appropriate counselor intervention. The triad model therefore is also a training design for developing interculturally skilled counselors by matching the counselor trainee with a coached client/client-partner team from the same other culture. The three-way interaction between the client, counselor, and the client's partner will provide immediate and continuous feedback to the counselor on the otherwise implicit dynamics of the counseling interview. The client's partner may interact as an anticounselor, procounselor, interpreter, third-person-hostile or third-person-friendly, depending on the appropriate constraints on each training situation.

In each case the culturally different resource persons (anticounselors) become the training authority for helping the counselor learn to articulate the problem from the client's cultural perspective, recognize resistance in specific rather than general terms, diminish counselor defensiveness, and learn

recovery skills for getting out of trouble. The counselor learns about counseling in a simulated cross-cultural interview where the otherwise implicit and generalized principles of counseling become explicit and specific. The use of videotape in recording the simulated interviews further enhances the power of the training through detailed debriefing of the interview.

Thus far little research has been completed on Triad Counseling, although several research studies using the training design are in progress. The triad model is being used in a variety of programs to train counselors to work with culturally different clients. There is interest in using Triad Counseling to train counselors working with clients who are culturally similar but differ from the counselor according to age, sex role, socioeconomic status, physical handicap, life style, or other affiliations important to the client's identity. (Pedersen, 1977)

There is a serious bias among most counselors that favors the cultural assumptions of a very small minority labeled the "dominant culture" in our society. Counseling will need to develop conceptual and training models that will assist counselors to learn a variety of approaches appropriate to our pluralistic society. Triad Counseling is one attempt to suggest an eclectic approach to understanding counseling that might adapt to a variety of cultural environments. (Pedersen, 1974)

## REFERENCES

Bolman, W. M. Cross-cultural psychotherapy. *American Journal of Psychiatry*, 1968, **124**, 1237–1234.

Caplow, T. *Two against one: Coalitions in triads.* Englewood Cliffs, N.J.: Prentice-Hall, 1968.

Holwill-Bailey, F. Personal communication, 1979.

Ivey, A. E. and Authier, J. *Microcounseling: Innovations in interviewing training.* Springfield, Ill.: Charles C Thomas, 1978.

Kagan, N., Krathwohl, D. and Farquhar, W. *Interpersonal process recall.* East Lansing, Mich.: Michigan State University, 1965.

Kelley, H. and Thibaut, J. *Interpersonal relations: A theory of interdependence.* New York: Wiley, 1978.

Pedersen, P. B. A proposal: That counseling be viewed as an instance of coalition. *Journal of Pastoral Care,* 1968, **22,** 139–146.

Pedersen, P. B. A conceptual system describing the counseling relationship as a coalition against the problem. Paper presented at the meeting of the American Psychological Association, Montreal, 1973.

Pedersen, P. B. Cross-cultural communications training for mental health professionals. *The International and Intercultural Communication Annual,* 1974, **1,** 53–64.

Pedersen, P. B. The field of intercultural counseling. In P. Pedersen, W. Lonner and J. Draguns (Eds.), *Counseling across cultures.* Honolulu: University Press of Hawaii, 1976a.

Pedersen, P. B. A model for training mental health workers in cross-cultural counseling. In J. Westermeyer and B. Maday (Eds.), *Culture and mental health.* The Hague: Mouton, 1976b.

Pedersen, P. B. The triad model of cross-cultural counselor training. *Personnel and Guidance Journal,* 1977, **56,** 94–100.

Pedersen, P. B. Four dimensions of cross-cultural skill in counselor training. *Personnel and Guidance Journal,* April 1978.

Pedersen, P. B. *Basic intercultural counseling skills.* Honolulu: DISC, 1979a.

Pedersen, P. B. Counseling clients from other cultures: Two training designs. In M. Asante and E. Newmark (Eds.), *Handbook of intercultural communication.* Beverly Hills, Calif.: Sage, 1979b.

Pedersen, P. B., Holwill, C. F. and Shapiro, J. L. A cross-cultural training procedure for classes in counselor education. *Journal of Counselor Education and Supervision,* 1978, **17,** 233–237.

Revich, R. and Geertsma, R. Observational media and psychotherapy training. *Journal of Nervous and Mental Disorders,* 1969, **148,** 310–327.

Salomon, G. and McDonald, F. J. Pretest and post-test reactions to self-viewing one's teaching performance on videotape. *Journal of Educational Psychology,* 1970, **61,** 280–286.

Satir, V. *Conjoint family therapy.* Palo Alto, Calif.: Science and Behavior Books, 1964.

Slack, C. W. and Slack, E. N. It takes three to break a habit. *Psychology Today,* February 1976, 46–50.

Stroller, F. M. Group psychotherapy on television: An innovation with hospitalized patients. *American Psychologist,* 1967, **23,** 158–163.

Sue, D. W. Preliminary data from the DISC Evaluation Report #1. Hayward, Calif.: California State University, 1979.

Zuk, G. *Family therapy: A triadic based approach.* New York: Behavioral Publications, 1971.

# CHAPTER 63

# Transcendence Therapy

ADRIAN VAN KAAM

*Prepare for a difficult chapter—perhaps the most difficult one in this book. Adrian van Kaam, a Catholic priest and psychologist, has his own language, and a good many terms and concepts may puzzle you—and this after my inducing him to simplify his writing.*

*While I am enthusiastic about a good many of the chapters in this book for a variety of reasons and think they are important enough to merit close reading, none of them affected me so strongly as this one on Transcendence Therapy, possibly because of my own early Catholic upbringing.*

*Van Kaam has what is probably the most ambitious of all of the programs in this book. His idea that conventional religion and psychotherapy will some day merge is quite possible, and indeed we do see evidence of this occurring already; but to me van Kaam's program seems much better organized and already realized than any other of its kind. This important chapter should be read carefully. Getting past the difficult language will be well worth the effort. Recourse to the Glossary is recommended.*

Transcendence Therapy is the formative assistance of persons involved in an implicit or explicit transcendence crisis. Therapy is given in the light of the formative tradition persons are committed to and sustained by the relevant insights and data of directive and incarnational sciences.

Transcendence is the act of "going beyond." Transcendence Therapy is intended to help people surpass past ways of life wholesomely and is based on the discipline of holistic formation called Formative Spirituality. Transcendence means to be raised beyond the form a person has given to life so far. Self-formation is to be deepened in a way that will free one from historical, vital, and functional determinations. Such a transition is usually accompanied by a crisis. Many people can handle this crisis by themselves. Others need assistance to bring the crisis to a head and to work it through meaningfully.

Assistance during this crisis helps a person to clarify and deepen life direction within the religious or humanistic formation one is committed to.

Transcendence Therapy can be effective only if participants are already committed to basic formative insights and if the therapist can experientially grasp individuals' traditions in their formative aspects and can sympathize with their attempts to transcend to a more congenial form of life in light of this wisdom.

## HISTORY

In the late 1950s and early 1960s this writer, a Catholic priest and psychologist–therapist, was increasingly consulted by people committed to and formed by a religious or humanist tradition. Their problems generally were not of a neurotic or psychotic nature.

Mainly they manifested symptoms of what was later identified as a transcendence crisis. In their often unconscious aspiration for a more transcendent life style, these people experienced, among other problems, difficulties in integrating their formative tradition with their newly emerging form of life. While the manifest symptoms often seemed similar to those originating from neurotic conflicts, the usual therapeutic approaches proved helpful only to a point. This experience stimulated this writer to complement these standard approaches with a special formation therapy based on my formative theory of personality.

While almost all of the basic principles of Transcendence Therapy can be utilized with some modification by any of the great formation traditions, I paid special attention to the formative tradition of Christianity.

Up to 1963 my research, teaching, and publication in this field was within the psychology department of Duquesne University in Pittsburgh. By 1963 this approach was sufficiently developed to warrant the foundation of a separate graduate institute at the same university. Initially called Institute of Man, its name was changed to the Institute of Formative Spirituality in 1978.

## CURRENT STATUS

The Institute of Formative Spirituality offers master's and Ph.D. degrees in Formative Spirituality mainly within the formative tradition of Christianity. It has graduated about 140 students, some of whom occupy leading positions in spiritual formation in a wide variety of Formation Institutes in many countries. Besides its own students, students of other schools and departments, such as the theology and psychology departments and of education and nursing, take courses at the institute.

The groundwork of this approach is laid in its steadily expanding body of knowledge as developed so far by faculty and students.

Its principles, assumptions, and methods are explained in approximately 30 books and over 150 articles published by faculty members. Furthermore it is developed to date in 15 volumes of *Humanitas,* in 160 issues of *Envoy,* and in the more than 125 theses by institute graduates. It is also contained in the tape library of courses, lectures, and films given within and outside of the university and in theses and dissertations at other universities in the United States, Canada, and Rome. The publisher of Dimension Books has invited graduates to prepare their theses and dissertations for book-length publication in a special series entitled Studies in Formative Spirituality.

The institute holds seminars, symposia, and workshops in the following countries besides the United States: Australia, Barbados, Canada, Colombia, Curacao, Egypt, England, France, Germany, Ghana, Guyana, Hong Kong, Ireland, Italy, Jamaica, Japan, Mexico, the Netherlands, New Zealand, Nigeria, the Philippines, Portugal, Puerto Rico, Surinam, Taiwan, Thailand, and Trinidad.

## THEORY

### Holistic Formation of the Human Person

The principles of formation are based on two essential characteristics of human life. The first one is "form-ability," referring to the human ability to give form in some measure to one's life.

The second is the dynamic of ongoing self-formation. The human being is always trying, mostly implicitly, to give form to his or her life. This formation process is *holistic* because it tends to give a unifying form to life as a whole. Holistic formation is based on the unique capacity of the human being to rise above his or her separate, particular experiences in an appraising and integrating overview, a capacity we call spirit. Holistic formation can, therefore, also be called spiritual formation.

## Unfolding and Formation

People, like plants and animals, unfold spontaneously. People, however, are able to reflect on their unfolding, to observe the direction of their development. Animal life unfolds spontaneously, programmed by instinct and drive. Animals do not complement their spontaneous development by self-awareness or spiritual formation. But human life is marked by a tension between spontaneous self-unfolding and transcendent formation that must shape that unfolding. At certain crucial moments that tension can grow to a crisis of self-direction. Because the solution of that crisis implies a "going beyond" the form life has assumed so far, what develops is a transcendence crisis; the therapy concerned with it has been called Transcendence Therapy. This crisis is generally known as an *identity crisis*. Transcendence therapists prefer the term *transcendence crisis,* because it emphasizes the transcendent core of human identity.

Human development thus implies two poles: spontaneous self-unfolding and formation. If either of these two poles is neglected, human growth will be hampered or falsified.

## Differentiation and Integration

The holistic formation of human life implies two mutually complementary dialectical movements: differentiation and integration. Differentiation underlies the disclosure and implementation of new life directives in response to new life experiences. In self-formation our life becomes increasingly differentiated in a variety of modes, giving rise to new directives of self-formation. Integration complements this differentiation; it reintegrates the differentiating life form.

Formative integration depends on our transcendent view of life, our rising beyond disparate experiences and observations. This transcendent view is colored by our unique personality and the way in which this unique personality assimilates, usually implicitly, the formation traditions of the culture.

## The Vitalistic View of Self-Unfolding and Formation

There is a spontaneous movement of growth in every human being. Holistic formation should always communicate with this spontaneous self-unfolding. Formation is an ongoing dialogue or a creative tension between our transcendent self-dimension as formative and our spontaneous self-unfolding. A purely biological view of human unfolding would deny that tension between unfolding and formation. In this view anything new in human development is not due to formation but is simply the result of an unfolding of a kind of blueprint laid down in our biological organism. This theory of unfolding would not deny that the environment of the child has something to do with his growing up. But in the biological view the environment is utilized by the unfolding organism only in accordance with its innate biological blueprint. The environment merely offers useful matter for the preestablished unfolding organism.

Holistic formation holds that the innate laws of the organism do have a basic influence on the unfolding of the person. One certainly utilizes the environment in service of organismic needs and perceptions. But the environment also contains values. Cultural values and traditions do have a directive influence on the life of the person. In dialogue with the biological influences, they become formative of the person as a whole in both his biological and transcendent abilities.

If self-unfolding were only a question of autochthonous biological growth, it would be impossible to give any form to this growth from a cultural value perspective. The biological perception of self-unfolding in the human person is deduced from the organic growth seen in vegetative organisms. A plant's unfolding can only be influenced partially; by manipulating temperature, light, and humidity we can affect the plant's growth. Such influences cannot change *essentially* the basic form that plant will assume once the growth process has taken its course. The holistic view of formation holds that we can find a unique form of life that goes beyond biological determinations. Biological determinations of development are always there; we must respect them and take them into account; but the way in which we do so depends on the cultural values we accept to form our lives holistically.

If growth or unfolding were only a biological process, no formative aid would be possible. As certain behavior therapists argue, the only meaningful aid to growth would be the effectuation of favorable conditions that facilitate the already predetermined form the human organism should assume. However, this kind of help would only be of minor importance. It would not offer any real formative assistance to the process of biological unfolding; it would remain exterior to the process. The only assistance such a behaviorist could offer the unfolding organism would be care, protection, and sustenance of the growth process. There would be no direction for any formation in the holistic sense described above.

### Transcendence Crisis

Transcendence is one of the fundamental dynamics of human formation. Each person approaches his or her full potential by transitions from lower to higher forms of life. Each transition is accompanied by a transcendence crisis.

When the climate for formation is favorable, crises of transition begin early in life, and stages of development succeed one another gradually and smoothly. Such gradual succession is unlikely in cultures that neglect spiritual formation. In these cultures during the first half of life, people have little time or space for reflection. In midlife, however, some people come to acknowledge the limits of their vital and functional powers. Because of the earlier denial or unconcern for such

limits, the crisis of transcendence may find them unprepared. Striking psychological problems may result from this delayed breakthrough of a first experience of contingency.

The resulting panic in a number of people has made the transcendence crisis—for the first time in history—an object of study for sciences other than formative spirituality. Anthropologists, medical researchers, psychologists, sociologists, and other specialists have added their insights to those of people engaged in formation and usually refer to this phenomenon as the "midlife crisis." But the midlife crisis is only one of many possible transcendence crises that foster human formation in depth. Midlife crises have emerged in our Western cultures in such intensity—and have become thus an object of psychological concern—because of the reasons mentioned above. The midlife crisis serves as a paradigm of all transcendence crises: It demonstrates the dynamics of transcendence in formation as a whole.

### Crisis: Danger and Opportunity

Crisis, from the Greek *krineo*, literally means "a parting of the ways." The transcendence crisis denotes a parting of life directions. A person's options lie between a less or more transcendent direction of self-formation. Crisis implies stress and uncertainty. A transcendence crisis may make us tense and anxious: It means the loss of a life form we felt at home with and the option to grow into another form foreign to us.

The Chinese have two characters for the word crisis. One character means danger, the other opportunity. A transcendence crisis gives rise to many dangers. First, there is the danger of becoming fixated, out of fear, on a no longer functioning level of life, or the reverse, the danger of overreacting against the former formation period, leading to a rejection of its authentic gains for our formation. Second, there is danger of opting for a false form of life. Third, there is danger of past unsolved problems and neuroses reappearing. Fourth, there is danger either of defensive overactivity or of withdrawal to escape the crisis.

Yet any transcendence crisis means also opportunity: the opportunity to become truly human, to discover our unique self, to integrate increasingly our life, to grow in wisdom and inwardness, to come more in touch with our deepest self.

## Main Questions of a Transcendence Crisis

*What does life mean? Where am I going? What form should I give to my life? Can I find help for my life direction in the formation tradition I am committed to?* These questions express human aspirations for meaning, direction, formation, belonging. When worked through effectively, they become thematic in a transcendence crisis.

To give form to our life we need to know in what direction we should go. To find that direction we should find out what life means to us and what we can learn uniquely from our chosen formation tradition about the meaning of life in general. Logically, therefore, questions concerning the meaning of life should come first; those of direction, formation, and formative tradition should follow.

In practice, the questioning of the direction arises first in a transcendence crisis or during Transcendence Therapy. We look into the past. *Where have we gone? What direction did our life take? Why is this direction disrupted?* We look toward the future. *How should we direct our life from now on?*

## Detachment Crisis

Detachment is indispensable in self-formation; it can be passive and external, or active and internal. Passive detachment involves the deprivation of something sufficiently significant in our current life form to affect its strength and structure. This is structural deprivation. Active detachment is a personal giving up of the inner attachment to what we have been deprived of and that cannot be regained realistically. This is called formative deprivation.

The transcendence crisis is initiated by unavoidable deprivations due to radical changes in life. Letting go of active detachment is a necessary condition for an effective solution of a transcendence crisis; it demands a working through of our feelings about structural deprivations. Working through on our own, sustained by Transcendence Therapy, consists of a phase of mourning; a phase of redirection of our thoughts, feelings, and perceptions; and a final phase of reintegration of relevant former and present life directives into a new form of life.

Transcendence Therapy, therefore, implies a facilitation of inner detachment from invincible structural deprivations. Because we may have invested years of self-exertion in the formation of our current and periodic self and thus found security in this form, detachment may be difficult; it often leads to conflicts that give rise to temporary psychic and psychosomatic symptoms. The formative detachment process during therapy entails a detachment from emotional investments. It involves a divesting that sets us free for a deeper investment to more transcendent values and realities.

## Direction Crisis

The direction of our life is partly chosen, partly imposed. Many life directives are imposed by our culture which limit possibilities of self-formation. Our capacities are also limited, and they pose another restriction on us, one of re-formation. Initially we tend to be unaware that our life follows directives. They are implicit as we interact daily with people, events, and things that constitute our life situation. As long as effective directives flow spontaneously over into daily living, things are unproblematic. Deeper reflection on where we are going seems a hindrance rather than a help in our normal living. As Socrates said, the unexamined life is not worth living. Yet most people do not examine their lives.

A special source of life direction are the directives communicated by parents, teachers, preachers, friends, colleagues, political parties, school acquaintances, neighbors, and the media. They present a fund of sedimented cultural directives. We have, as it were, a stock of culturally transmitted life directives at hand. Out of this stock we fashion spontaneously our daily life activities. Each time we meet a challenge, we fall back on this stock of directives to help us meet life's crises. Every time a directive meets the situation encountered effectively, it is confirmed as part of our life direction.

Sooner or later, however, we will meet problems we cannot solve with these confirmed directives. The taken-for-granted effectiveness of our life direction is interrupted; the unproblematic now becomes problematic. If this questioning of our life direction is accompanied by stress and deprivation, it may give rise to a transcendence crisis. Shocked by the insufficiency of our guidelines, we may turn to others for help. Transcendence Therapy can be helpful for people in this situation, especially when they cannot find wise and sympathetic listeners to relieve their lonely search for appropriate directives.

The problem of a halted life direction can be solved only by taking a stand that transcends both the familiar stock of directives already available and the stress and deprivation of the crisis situation.

We must distinguish between the "raw material" out of which the transcendence crisis is made and the "formative objective" of this crisis. The various deprivations and stresses comprise the "raw material." The turning to a more transcendent form of life is the formative objective of this crisis. It can thus never be solved satisfactorily by isolated solutions to each distinct stress that accompanies each structural deprivation. We would be dealing with symptoms instead of with the crisis itself. What is needed is an integrated, holistic solution.

## Continuity Crisis

The reorganization of our current life form does not mean that our previous life direction will be eradicated. Our core remains intact.

To explain: There is a distinction between our lasting "core self" and our "periodic self." A well-formed life is an integrated structure of various dimensions and articulations of human living. We call them the historical-cultural/vital/functional/and transcendent dimensions. They are differentiated in various substructures or articulations. These structural dimensions and their articulations do not develop equally all at once. Each attains to a fuller development at a different period of our life. These periods of special development and dominance of a specific structure are "temporal dimensions" of our selfhood, and they are distinguished from structural ones.

In a transcendence crisis the dominance of past periodic forms of life is more radically questioned. As a result, our periodic and current selfhood may be strikingly transformed. Yet our core self stays relatively the same. We may come, however, to a deeper awareness than we had previously of our core self.

The collapse of a periodic and current life form leads to a temporary loss of balance. Hesitantly, in the midst of trial and error, a new self begins to emerge. The self is differentiated; then a process of integration sets in. Wholeness is slowly restored. Our new life form—more transcendent in nature—is gradually integrated with the sediments of our former forms of life. These sediments enriched our continuous core self, provided they were compatible with our unique life direction. In the course of this process of reintegration, we become more at home with that deeper core.

Aspects congenial to our unique life form gained in former periods of growth are thus not necessarily abandoned; they receded temporarily in the background. When the new dimension—or any one of its articulations—has been sufficiently formed in us, the residues of the former dimensions and articulations emerge again to be reintegrated into the new deeper dimension. They will now be subordinated more explicitly to the transcendent dimension of human life.

The task of Transcendence Therapy thus implies a relativizing of former periods of self-formation; the acceptance of detachments such relativizing entails; the appraisal of our current life direction; the decision to deepen certain aspects of that direction while abandoning others; the appraisal of the task of self-formation in the future; and the reintegration of past and present congenial directives. Much now present in the current direction of life may have to be abandoned during and after therapy. Still, there is much that can be retained as a basis for the formation of a new form of life. In case no Transcendence Therapy is needed, much of this process evolves spontaneously and preconsciously without logical deliberation, illumined mostly by the implicit wisdom of our transcendent self.

### Idealized Life Directives Crisis

Our transcendent self is a self of aspirations, just as our functional self is a self of ambitions. Aspirations stimulate us preconsciously long before they appear in the foreground of our formation efforts. Early in life our innate aspirations manifest themselves in our inclination to set up ideal life directives. Our tendency to idealize is a symptom of our congenital transcendency.

An ideal life directive is a wished-for event. This wish reveals a hidden awareness that we should not be satisfied with any current or periodic form of life as ultimate. A vague sense of being called to an ever more transcendent life direction gives rise to an idealized vision of what we should become. The dynamism of our transcendent aspirations—as such still unknown to us—lends color, excitement, and elation to our ideal directives. The functional realistic dimension of our human life is still underdeveloped in our youth. At that time the preconscious transcendent aspirations can give rise to idealized or even "idolized" life directives, for they are not yet modulated by the sense of concrete incarnation in daily life. A realistic appraisal of idolized directives is one of the functions of a transcendence crisis and of Transcendence Therapy. This appraisal should not paralyze idealism but should harmonize it both with the unique life form we are called to unfold and with the demands of daily life. If idealized life directives are not made consonant during Transcendence Therapy, they may simply die, and with that dies our sense of aliveness and purpose.

As children, we may be misled by our innate but untested aspirations. We believe that we can make things come true by our wishes alone. This magical deformation of childhood aspirations is partly remedied by the incarnational aspect of human life, which asserts itself during the periods of more functional self-formation. Ideal directives are tempered by the demands of reality.

A transcendence crisis—and respectively Transcendence Therapy—tends to radically purify our idealized or idolized directives. Our formation attempts are then increasingly released from their magical component. In therapy we observe often that this rebirth is preceded by a temporary regression, marked by a feeling of insecurity. Control of life seems lost. Praise or blame of the therapist does not help. Praise is easily taken as a reassurance that the participants can still realize their unrealistic life directives. Blame may tell the opposite—that clients should feel guilty because they cannot live up to their exalted self-expectations.

### Crisis of Appearances

The self-in-formation must adapt itself to its surroundings, for we live not only with ourselves but with others. This adaptation implies a guarded yet relaxed self-revelation—guarded in the sense that our inmost self is vulnerable and easily misunderstood. If manifested unwisely, it might evoke disbelief, irritation, envy, ridicule, and suspicion. Moreover, an unnecessarily powerful manifestation of our uniqueness may overwhelm others, hurting their independence and self-reliance.

There must thus be a difference between who we are for ourselves and what we look like to others. Our apparent self should not reveal totally our deepest self. Each current life form we develop maintains this "apparent selfhood,'' the way we are genuinely present to others, the limited but true face we show in daily life.

In Transcendence Therapy participants become more aware of the appearances they developed in their interaction with others. They look at them more critically, realizing that some impressions they make are deceptive. They then seek to drop or replace them. In other words, they try to overcome the separation between apparent self, current self, and inmost self.

Therapeutic teaching and dialogue about their crisis makes them gradually aware that a congenial ''apparent self'' is a selective expression of only those true aspects of a person's life direction relevant to the situation at hand.

The beginning of Transcendence Therapy is often a period of ambivalence and uncertainty. Ambiguous about their inner turmoil and desirous to hide it from themselves and others, participants may begin to wear masks foreign to who they are. This trying out of false masks is part of the process of finding appearances that fit the more congenial life form that emerges during this crisis. If the therapy fails, participants may spend the rest of their lives in tiring attempts to keep up false appearances. Others, distraught by the disclosure of their deceptive appearances, go through a period of neglect of appearances; they may look sloppy, unsettled, unreliable, eccentric, and out of touch with daily reality. In a later phase of therapy many begin to try out new considerate ways of presence to others faithful to the more syntonic life form that emerges.

## METHODOLOGY

### Principle of Clarification of Dialectics and Dynamics

Group therapy should help clarify the common elements of formation and how they are responded to in the formation tradition the group is committed to. The sessions should help participants to discover experientially

how a personal assimilation of these foundations can be facilitated by an effective utilization of the relevant contributions of the arts and sciences. The therapist then assists the group in making explicit the implicit dialogue between these fundamentals of their psychologically enlightened formation tradition and their personal formation.

Clarification implies a ''conscientization'' of the dynamism of each individual's current form of life. The dynamism of the self is co-constituted by pulsations, impulses, ambitions, and aspirations; these can be in harmony or disharmony with one another. The self is historical, vital, functional, and transcendent at the same time. It becomes clear to group members how the historical dimension gives rise to pulsations, the vital to impulses, the functional to ambitions, the transcendent to aspirations. Participants should be helped to see how their current life form modulates these dynamic orientations, their hierarchy and interaction, and why a particular modulation can become problematic in a transcendence crisis. They should realize experientially that any modulation of the dynamism of the self can be congenial or uncongenial; it is congenial in the measure that the modulation is in harmony both with the unique life form they feel called to and with the current form their life must assume here and now. They should discover and accept the fact that nobody attains perfect congeniality, that they themselves and their therapist can only strive to be on the way to congenial living.

Subsequently participants are encouraged to clarify the cause of possible uncongeniality in their present life. This cause is self-alienation; it ensues from the structural deprivations that initiated their transcendence crisis and brought them to therapy. Reflection on alienation should make them question any excessive dominance of pulsations, impulses, ambitions, or aspirations. By implication the structure of their current self—its underlying attitudes, perceptions, feelings, and motivations—can become the subject of therapeutic clarification.

Clarification should be deepened by transcendent reading therapy. The group is exposed to classical and contemporary formative writings of their own tradition. Reading therapy introduces them, in a contemporary and personally meaningful way, to the formative wisdom accumulated by generations.

## Principles of Resourcing and of Relief of Accretion Anger

A number of participants discover that their humanist or religious directives of formation are more a result of acculturation than of a personal assimilation of the sources of their formation tradition. Correspondingly they realize that the life directives obtained this way contain accidental cultural accretions. Certain accidental accretions—now seen to be at odds with their unique formation call—were formerly communicated as essential. Sometimes such quasi-foundations of formation were imposed under threat of punishment and failure of life. This imposition gave rise to false guilt feelings and to a deepseated anger, often repressed and denied. This anger tends to come to awareness during the therapy sessions. So do the deformations such false guilt and repressed anger gave rise to.

Transcendence Therapy deals with this guilt and anger by the application of its principle of formative resourcing: an experiential going-back to the very sources of the formative tradition and a working through, in this light, of false guilt feelings and accretion anger. There is an intimate link in this approach between reading and resourcing therapy.

## Principles of Resistance-Resonance Identification and of Their Appraisal

Therapy sessions must develop the art of resistance-resonance recognition. They should heighten the sensitivity of the participants to their own reactions to the communications of therapist, group members, and formative readings. Participants learn to appraise the inner sources of their resistance and resonance reactions and what meaning they may have for their life direction. The therapeutic method suggests that they write down those experiences and their subsequent reflections on them. If a directive keeps drawing them and if appraisal has purified it from excessive one-sided determinants, they should be encouraged to try this directive out in daily life and to discuss the consequences of their attempt.

The spontaneous resistance or resonance reaction may be vivid or faint, depending on the temperament of the participant. What matters is the final effect of the appraisal: The sure and lasting impression that a certain directive seems significant for this unique person at this moment of his life while in harmony both with the fundamental wisdom of his chosen formation tradition and the uniqueness of his personality. Individuals should learn to accept that they may not yet fully grasp the meaning of a directive that touches them. They must allow the directive to disclose itself further in its own good time and in its own unique way.

## Principle of Illusion Identification

The therapist dialogues with the group about the danger of illusionary resonances. Group members should become aware how self-alienating pulsations, impulses, ambitions, and aspirations may lead them to pretend that they experience the same resonance they admire in the therapist or other members of the group. It can lead to the adoption of willful life directives that make them the captives of an anxious web of *do*'s and *don'ts*; not formation but obsessive-compulsive deformation may be the result. Because the false self-image is a product of the ambitious ego, it may lead to envious formation competition. Such image envy usually betrays itself in the group discussion, creating an opportunity to work this problem through by means of experiential dialogue.

## Principle of Facilitation of Self-Direction

The atmosphere fostered by the therapist can facilitate or stifle the participants' self-direction. Participants are always treated with dignity; they are considered people attempting to find and unfold their own form of life. The therapist's attitude communicates itself in subtle ways and is perceived preconsciously by participants; it fosters the unfolding of self-direction more than anything else the therapist does. The transcendence therapist should aspire to be a facilitator of the unique transcendence process in the participants. He or she should respect their path of inmost self-becoming. At times the therapist unfortunately may fall back into that "gray area" that includes respect and goodwill but also a tendency to impose on others certain aspects of one's own personal expression of the formation tradition shared with group members. Insofar as this is the case, the solution of participants' transcendence crises will be delayed.

The therapist should work through personal flights from transcendence and point out to the participants what is personal in his or her communications and what is universal and foundational in their shared tradition.

## Principle of Clarification of the Fusion Impulse

During Transcendence Therapy, a desire for fusion with therapist or group members may manifest itself. This impulse is a distortion of an emergent aspiration for union with transcendent values, symbols, and realities. Hence the participant's striving to lose the self in the idolized therapist, group member, or group. Some may seek desperately for the legendary guru who will save them at once from the emptiness the crisis entails. To avoid friction and to foster fusion, participants may flow with every thought and feeling of the therapist or the group without regard for their own direction. Unconsciously they try to fit their emergent life form into the contours of the life form of the therapist

or of significant group members. Their praise entices them to still greater compliance; their blame signifies a break in fusion that they patch up by greater submission. This distortion of the aspiration for transcendent union explains the magic hold of certain cult leaders on young people driven by our one-sided functionalistic culture into a transcendence crisis they cannot cope with yet.

If the fusion impulse is deep-seated or reinforced by such cult leaders, the person should work this distortion through in private Transcendence Therapy before being allowed to continue group sessions.

One means to lessen the fusion impulse is the use of sessions guided by different therapists, each representing a different style of transcendent life. This may counteract the tendency to identify transcendence with the unique mode of transcendence characteristic of only one of the therapists.

## APPLICATIONS

### Principle of Clarification

The principle of clarification can be applied effectively if group members overcome their self-deceptions. A too-direct attack on their illusions may enhance their defenses and entrench them more deeply in their outmoded forms of life. Sensitive to their defensive self-perceptions, the transcendence therapist begins where the participants are, allowing ample time for dialogue and questions. The therapist may establish a question box in which participants can deposit anonymously their questions and objections. In service of right timing, the therapist reads carefully progress notebooks and integration papers entrusted to him or her. It is essential that participants know the therapist realizes what they are going through; the therapist must manifest an understanding of their feelings, an empathy with their guilt, anger, resistance, anxiety, and uncertainty. The therapist unveils as much or as little of their illusions and deformations as they seem able to bear at any given moment. He or she does not compel the admission of their deceptions; admissions may come long after the session, in later sessions, or in between sessions. The therapist's formative role consists mainly of creating opportunities for awareness of the real and illusory facets of participants' self-formation.

As we have seen, the first step toward the solution of the transcendence crisis is an awareness of an alienation from one's current form of life. When this principle is applied, this discovery is unsettling for many. The pain of momentarily losing one's bearings cannot be prevented, even by the most understanding therapist. It may express itself in tears, angry resistance, patterns of fight or flight, veiled attacks, or hostile questions to catch the therapist or to make him or her feel uncomfortable.

Paradoxically, all these eruptions of open hostility may be signs of progress. They signify that the implicit crisis has become explicit, that the first phase of awareness has been initiated. The therapist's behavior at this time should be marked by respect, equanimity, compassion, and empathy. The therapist should understand that the attacks are not directed at him or her but at what he or she symbolizes: the inexorable demands of the unique life form to be disclosed and implemented.

## Principles of Transcendence Therapy and Resistance

The concrete application of the method runs, of course, into the problem of resistance. Resistance is due not only to the defensive self-perception, just mentioned, but also to the newly emerging transcendent aspirations. Transcendence implies not only an aspiration to union with transcendent values, symbols, and realities but also to the aspiration to live them uniquely. This appeal to transcendent uniqueness can be distorted by the still-dominant functional ego into a striving after absolute independence. This distortion manifests itself in a stubborn resistance to any

appeal of the transcendence teacher. Resistance often reveals itself in slightly veiled hostile questions, in aggressive one-upmanship, or in withdrawal. It may also lead to a defensive inner focusing on any idiosyncrasy of the therapist that seems to justify the rejection of painful self-insight engendered by his or her communications.

A participant, for example, may defend himself against change by making himself feel so upset by the therapist's *way* of saying things that he becomes unable to hear *what* the therapist tries to communicate. He keeps himself busy upbraiding the therapist inwardly so that he may protect himself against any challenging directive that may announce itself. He becomes caught in internal scolding. He confuses transcendent self-direction and ego-direction, transcendent uniqueness and ego uniqueness. Experiential dialogue during the sessions should foster the insight that there is only one way to preserve and enhance ego strength while at the same time growing to union with the transcendent and its manifestation in self, people, world, and nature. That way is to analyze one's resistances and to disclose how they are rooted in a still too exclusive dominance by the historical, vital, and functional dimensions of the self.

A special resistance may be expected from anyone in the group who has been liberated from the effects of brainwashing by cults they belonged to. The same resistance can be found in group members who have been shocked by the dire effects of cultic brainwashing they observed in others. The sessions should clarify the nature of authentic solutions of the transcendence crisis. Such solutions grow slowly from relaxed self-insight fostered by therapeutic dialogue about one's self and about the foundations of one's formation tradition. They should be distinguished from changes that are the result of manipulative words and actions of certain cult leaders that play on affective needs (love bombing), false guilt feelings, and distortions of transcendent aspirations. Their manipulations are based on a too-limited special or personal spirituality instead of being based on one that is foundational.

## Resistance-Resonance Identification Principle

An effective application of this principle of identification presupposes that the participants come to recognize any affinity reaction they may experience during their therapy. The resistance or resonance reaction is due to an experienced affinity between, on the one hand, the communications of the therapist, of the group or the formative readings, and, on the other hand, the directives or needs for directives that play a role in one's life. The affinity reaction can be negative or positive.

The negative reaction points indirectly to one's affinity insofar as it is a defense against any directive that is rightly or wrongly experienced as a threat to one's current or deeper life direction. The need for affinity makes people yearn for affirmation in the communications of the therapist. When it does not come forth, frustration and resentment will be felt. Resistance results.

Positive reaction is the result of an experienced affinity—rightly or wrongly—felt between therapeutic communications and emergent selfhood. The participants should be helped to move from reaction to response. The affinity response may be different from the original affinity reaction that gave rise to it, for it has been transformed or affirmed by the therapeutic process of appraisal.

## Formative Appraisal Principle

A responsible application of the appraisal principle requires attention to the various dimensions of appraisal namely: fundamental, adaptive, situational, vital, functional, and transcendent appraisal.

Fundamental appraisal discerns if the negative or positive affinity reactions point to a fundamental affinity, an attunement to what the person is basically called to become. Adaptive appraisal discerns how the direc-

tive—that the person does have a fundamental affinity—can be adapted to the empirical self he has already developed in life. Situational appraisal ponders how the new current self that emerges can most effectively appear in the concrete life situation here and now. Vital appraisal evaluates the organismic. Functional appraisal estimates the practical implications of the emergent form of life. Transcendent appraisal discerns which transcendent values, symbols, and/or realities can serve effectively as ultimate, integrating motivation for the new form of life.

This prolonged process of appraisal fostered during the dialogical sessions enables the participants to grow from a blind affinity reaction to an enlightened, free affinity response.

## Formation Exercises

The practical application of Transcendence Therapy includes the keeping of a progress notebook and a "formative reading notebook," and the writing of experiential play papers and personal integration papers as additional means to self-direction. These notebooks and papers enable the therapist to take into account the needs of the participants. They warn the therapist when some participant needs personal contact with him- or herself or another transcendence therapist. It makes the therapist aware, moreover, of symptoms of pathology necessitating other kinds of therapy.

## Idolizing and Demonizing of the Transcendence Therapist

When the phase of the explicit experience of alienation from the current form of life is worked through, a phase of anxious search for a new form follows. Initially the participants look for this form as embodied in living persons after whom they can model themselves. The transcendence therapist often becomes the target of this search. Some may identify the therapist as *the* embodiment of transcendent living, *the* model of the "ideal" form of life. Such idolizing cannot be maintained indefinitely. The devotees are bound to discover the limitations of the therapist's way of presence. Disappointed, they may fall into the opposite exaggeration and demonize the therapist, one-sidedly stressing the flaws of his or her style of transcendence. This phase of the process liberates them from their binding to the therapeutic teacher and creates more room for self-direction.

The therapist should realize that different participants may be at different stages of the transcendence crisis. Accordingly, he or she may be the target of a variety of projections. Some newcomers, for example, try to keep their crisis at a safe distance by attending the sessions in a state of affable, intellectual interest. They may reduce their perception of the therapist to that of an amusing, interesting, or arrogant teacher. Others, already beyond this stage, begin to experience an explicit alienation from their current form of life; they may feel lost and desperate, tearful, and anxious. They alternately hate and love the therapist for what he or she does to them. A number of them will resist the therapist stubbornly to maintain the life form they were at home with before the crisis. Those who enter the next stage of a positive search for a more transcendent form of life may idolize the therapist, while the ones who move beyond that initial enthusiasm may perceive him or her as a fake who disappointed their expectations, a person with feet of clay who cannot live up to what is communicated.

When participants grow beyond these latter idolizing-demonizing stages of the crisis, they begin to recognize that both they and their therapist are limited, unique persons called to grow by a succession of increasingly transcendent forms of life, none of which will grant perfection to either them or the therapist. Once this stage is reached in therapy, the positive work of disclosure and implementation of the new current form can progress unhindered. Defenses and projections that prolonged the crisis no longer stand in the way.

The therapist should learn how to lessen the intensity of the feelings projected by the participants. By discussing the transcendence crises of people in general, he or she may make them ready for these experiences. By pointing out from the beginning his or her own limitations (as only a person also always in ongoing formation), the therapist may lessen the intensity of the positive and negative projections.

## Therapeutic Reading Principle

The practical application of reading therapy demands that readings selected have proven to be helpful to persons in a transcendence crisis. The group is initiated in the art of formative reading, taught to ask themselves questions that do not emerge from literary or intellectual criticism but from the aspiration for transcendent illumination. Questions might include: Is there something in this text relevant to the crisis I find myself in? Do I feel reactions of negative or positive affinity, of resistance or resonance, when reading reflectively? How do I appraise these feelings in accordance with the kinds and rules of appraisal discussed in the sessions? How can a text that touches me be assimilated uniquely so that it begins to direct my emergent form of life?

Fostering the reading of classical formative writings, such as Thomas À Kempis's *Imitation of Christ, The Confessions* of St. Augustine, and Pascal's *Pensées,* lessens the danger that the person in crisis becomes the victim of passing fads, the devotee of incidental cults, or the captive of totalitarian movements. The transcendence teacher introduces the participants to the classical texts. He or she fosters an attitude of inner availability to any word of the writer that may be potentially relevant to the search for personal transcendence and a readiness to appraise such words in careful reflection. Participants are asked to note such texts in their reading notebook, along with their experience of resistance or resonance, and to add their own reflections. Therapeutic teaching makes them see that writing as a mode of self-expression tends to clarify and deepen the experiences they have to cope with as a result of both the teaching and the readings. They are encouraged to reread such notes; this may reawaken in them reverberations of the original experience and give rise to deeper understanding of why the struggling self is this way. These personal reading notes, like those in the progress notebook, provide a kind of log of the inner journey of the participants, helpful to them and the therapist.

One important task of the formation sessions is to help the participants to shift from informative speed reading to formative reading slowed down and interspersed with pauses of reflection. They are taught to read with ease of mind, to dwell on the text leisurely, to muse about it—not to become strained, tense, or willful but to keep quietly open to hints, sudden associations, flashes of insight. They are encouraged to maintain the inner freedom to close the book when a thought strikes home and to take time to dwell on it, sitting quietly or walking in nature. Soon the participants experience that true formative reading mellows the ego, not by sapping its strength but by diminishing its arrogance, its false exclusiveness, its pretense of ultimacy. Any diminishment of the ego's arrogance makes the participants more available to the transcendent life direction hidden in formation writings. The power of this direction does not depend on how much but on *how well* the participants read. One page of a book that really speaks to them, dwelt upon reflectively, perhaps dialogued about with the therapy group, gives more inner direction than whole chapters devoured eagerly but in a superficial manner. A page that resonates for a participant may be of such profundity at this moment of his crisis that he keeps receiving light and direction every time he dwells on it. The therapist's experience—nourished constantly by personal interaction with the participants and by the reading of their notebooks and papers—enables him or her to advise them on literature that may be especially relevant for them at certain stages of their crisis. The

formative directives disclosed this way are not necessarily new and bright ideas. The ideas may be familiar. What is new is that they light up in a personal way because of the dynamics of the transcendence crisis at work in the participants.

## Coping with Vital Tensions

Effective application of this approach requires that the participants lessen excessive bodily strain while reading or attending the sessions. Strained functional reading, listening, or discussing does not occur just in the brain of the participants; it establishes itself in muscles. This tautness reinforces in turn the tension already present in their minds. Tight lips, clenched teeth, frowning forehead, or rigid posture may betray how tense and achievement oriented people are while reading, listening, or discussing. When tense and taut, they cannot dwell on the written or the spoken word; they are not ready in gentle equanimity for any directives relevant to their struggle. Hence dialogue is encouraged about how to engage in progressive bodily relaxation, in gradual emptying of the mind so that they may unwind and feel comfortable and at ease. Participants are asked at the same time to keep in mind any text they have found to nourish their emergent self-direction. The deeper their relaxation and receptivity, the emptier their heart and mind in regard to things unrelated to this personal transcendence, the closer they will be to the disclosure of directives that may carry them beyond their crisis.

## Therapeutic Limits

Transcendence Therapy has been developed to bring to a head a transcendence crisis, to facilitate the solution of its conflicts, and to heal in this process its psychic and psychosomatic disturbances. Transcendence Therapy does not solve serious neurotic and psychotic conflicts; it presupposes their solution for its own final effectiveness.

For example, a second generation of Moslems growing up in the West—without symptoms of neurosis or psychosis—may manifest psychic and psychosomatic distress that upon examination cannot be traced to a character neurosis but only to an intensified transcendence crisis.

Fiercely committed to the formation tradition of their people, averse to humanist or Christian traditions in the realm of self-formation, they still experience at a later age a conflict between the formative customs of their families with their accidental cultural accretions and their need for a cultural and personal adaptation to Western ways of formation. The structural deprivations later in life deepen their need for a more transcendent outlook on reality, but they cannot find it in family customs whose accretions veil their deeper formative meaning. When such problems seem unsolvable and the disturbances unbearable, they may find relief in a transcendence therapy group with others who share similar needs, conflicts, crises, and traditions. In the therapy sessions they are encouraged to return creatively to the formative foundations implied in the Koran and elaborated experientially as wisdom of living in the formative writings of the Moslem tradition, such as the Sufi classics. Relevant insights of the arts and sciences help them to integrate the rediscovered foundations of their tradition with their cultural and personal formation demands.

In case their Moslem tradition as such has become a question, Transcendence Therapy by itself alone cannot answer it. Other professionals, such as theological, philosophical, and spiritual counselors, are the experts to be consulted then. Similarly, if serious neurotic or psychotic conflicts are the main source of their disturbances, other kinds of therapy must solve these problems before Transcendence Therapy can be effective.

## CASE EXAMPLE

The following case example presents some data on one specific group. To protect its anonymity, all indications that could lead to an identification of the group or its participants will be avoided.

The group under consideration consisted of 12 participants cared for by three collaborating transcendence therapists, each one conducting two successive periods of about three and one-half months coinciding with the two semesters held during the academic year of the university employing the therapists. To enhance the probability that the participants were at least in an implicit or potential formation crisis—instead of suffering mainly from deep neurotic or psychotic disturbances—they were selected by means of personal interviews by each of the staff members. These interviews were given after the staff discussed the detailed, lengthy essay required from each applicant, which explained why he or she wanted to participate in the sessions. In this essay they were asked to tell as much about themselves as they could: family; personal and professional history; educational background; current work and future task orientation; personal motivation for coming to the sessions; and how they felt this therapy could be meaningful at this moment of their life. After the personal, separate interviews by the three staff members, a follow-up discussion by the staff of the results of the interviews led to a decision to accept or reject their application. By means of this method some serious cases of neurosis or psychosis were eliminated; these people were advised to look for other kinds of therapy. In two cases in this group, therapists failed to detect severe neurotic problems before acceptance.

In other accepted participants, as usual during the therapy sessions, when the potential transcendence crisis became acute, minor traumatic and neurotic problems of the past reemerged and were intense enough in five of the participants for them to be referred for appropriate treatment to a psychiatrist. This outside treatment did not interrupt but complemented their participation in the group therapy. Because of this experience it has become standard procedure to inform the participants of the availability of outside therapists and to encourage them to contact them the moment they feel the need for this assistance.

Because of the therapeutic work of integration of one's formation tradition with one's unique formation history, participants of a group are selected on the basis also of their sharing in the same tradition. For this specific group, people committed to a Christian formation tradition were chosen. The results of the therapy were mixed: the two wrongly admitted, seriously disturbed people needed prolonged private therapy after finishing the sessions; from the 10 remaining participants two avoided therapeutic change by fixation on a past ineffective form of life; two others entered but did not surpass the negative phase of the transcendence crisis, as became clear in a yearly follow-up meeting of former participants. Six participants were able to bring their implicit transcendence crisis to a head and to initiate an effective solution during the therapy.

In follow-up studies a few years later resistant participants who did not reach a full crisis awareness and its solution during the therapy admitted to having learned "a lot." It is not impossible that these lasting impressions may play some role later, in case life makes it difficult for them to avoid the transcendence crisis entirely. Staff experience with successive groups and with the failing, resistant participants in the yearly follow-up meetings increased their skill in selection and therapeutic approach. While the effectiveness of the therapy—dependent also on the free cooperation of the participants—can never be 100 percent, the number of successful participants may increase over the years.

In this group the main obstacles against a therapeutic awareness and solution of the transcendence crisis were a lack of contact with their own experiential life; a failure of personal experiential penetration of the theological and ethical abstractions of their religion, combined with unfamiliarity with its formation tradition; a postponement of the solution of adolescent authority problems; an overdependency on affection, praise, and assurance by significant others; and self-alienation due to a somewhat hysterical or compulsive identification with social-religious slogans in regard to contemporary social or political issues.

The writing of so-called play papers about a life experience in *their* own words and the dialogue about these papers made participants aware of their experiential estrangement. One tragic case was that of a participant who had an extensive professional knowledge of psychology and had complemented that expertise with theological studies. He was so totally alienated from his own experience that it was impossible for him to report on any personal experience in his own words. If he could not use general psychological or theological categories, he panicked. The patient experienced the same blocking in the keeping of an experiential progress and reading notebook and had to be referred to private therapy.

When participants were able to come in touch with their own experience, they went through a crisis, facing for the first time feelings and conflicts they had always covered up with theological, ethical, or psychological abstractions and generalities. Part of this crisis could be solved by bringing them in touch with the more experiential writings of their tradition, until then unknown to them, and encouraging dialogue about them. Another result of this first experiential self-awareness was a becoming conscious of an authority conflict not solved in adolescence and expressing itself now in an emotional negativity, slightly veiled in "rational" complaints about the therapists. On the other hand, their need to maintain a childlike affective dependency made them try to seduce the therapists to parental manifestations of warmth, love, acceptance, praise. When the therapists were able to resist this seduction, some insecure participants became hostile and angry. In some failed cases, this childlike hostility syndrome would remain, as became clear in the yearly follow-up meetings. The more anxiety was evoked through the emergence of the crisis, the more some participants tried to escape change by flight into intellectual discussions. The more intellectual and academic the participant, the more often he was tragically alienated from his experiential life. When finally the intellectualistic defensiveness would break down, the "learned" participant would often become the victim of severe sexual problems. Having repressed his experiential life for so long, he did not know how to cope wisely within his formation tradition with urges he had been so long unaware of.

An anxious clinging to a religious-social slogan was for some a last defense against facing themselves and their formation crisis. To avoid this confrontation, they would try stubbornly to replace the discussion of the inner problematics with a discussion of social problems and their solutions. It was also threatening for them to face themselves as responsible for their own choice of life instead of blindly following a slogan that pointed to a valuable social enterprise but one perhaps not valuable for them in terms of their own uniqueness. By wise application of the methods described earlier, at least six members of the group were able to break through their compulsion for praise and affection, their self-alienating social slogan identification, and their intellectualistic defenses; to grow in openness to their experience and to the deeper life meanings of their tradition; to make explicit their formation crisis; and to find a solution of this crisis in a more mature and open form of life.

## SUMMARY

Transcendence therapy is a group process that attempts to assist individuals involved in a transcendence crisis. Its roots are in a new discipline known as Formative Spirituality. The underlying theory of group transcendence therapy depends on the concept of the holistic formation of the human person and involves the notion of spontaneous unfolding in contrast to the vitalistic view of self-unfolding and formation. People in a transcendence crisis are in a transition from a lower to a higher form of life, and in such a transition a number of subcrises occur; these include detachment, need for direction, the issue of continuity, and a movement toward idealized life directions.

The therapeutic process relates to the clarification of dialectics, understanding the dynamics of the crises, the resourcing processes that the individual in the process of formation goes through, and the relief the individual experiences with the casting off of the accretions that have alienated him from the sources of his formative tradition.

In transcendence therapy, several other processes generally occur, such as anger about these accretions, resistance experiences, and identification of illusions.

In this system, participants tend to react strongly to the therapist, idolizing or demonizing him or her. The therapist has the task of helping participants deal with these attitudes and helping them cope with these vital tensions during the sessions and also during the readings.

## REFERENCES

Agnew, U. Originality and spirituality: The art of discovering and becoming oneself. Master's thesis. Duquesne University, 1974.

Gratton, C. Some aspects of the lived experience of interpersonal trust. *Humanitas*, 1973, **9**, 273–296.

Muto, S. A. *Approaching the sacred: An introduction to spiritual reading*. Denville, N.J.: Dimension Books, 1973.

Muto, S. A. *A practical guide to spiritual reading*. Denville, N.J.: Dimension Books, 1976a.

Muto, S. A. *Steps along the way: The path of spiritual reading*. Denville, N.J.: Dimension Books, 1976b.

Muto, S. A. *The journey homeward: On the road of spiritual reading*. Denville, N.J.: Dimension Books, 1977.

Muto, S. A. *Renewed at each awakening: The formative power of sacred words*. Denville, N.J.: Dimension Books, 1979.

Sharpe, M. J. Life form and its transforming influence upon the person. Master's thesis. Duquesne University, 1971.

van Kaam, A. *Religion and personality*. Englewood Cliffs, N.J.: Prentice-Hall, 1964.

van Kaam, A. *The art of existential counseling*. Denville, N.J.: Dimension Books, 1966.

van Kaam, A. and Healy, K. *The demon and the dove: Personality growth through literature*. Pittsburgh, Pa.: Duquesne University Press, 1967.

van Kaam, A. *Existential foundations of psychology*. Denville, N.J.: Dimension Books, 1969.

van Kaam, A. *On being yourself*. Denville, N.J.: Dimension Books, 1972.

van Kaam, A. *In search of spiritual identity*. Denville, N.J.: Dimension Books, 1975.

van Kaam, A. *The dynamics of spiritual self-direction*. Denville, N.J.: Dimension Books, 1976.

van Kaam, A. (Ed.). Originality and conformity. *Humanitas*, 1977(a) **12.**

van Kaam, A. (Ed.). Aging gracefully. *Humanitas*, 1977(b) **13.**

van Kaam, A. Dynamics of hope and despondency in the parents of handicapped children. *Humanitas*, 1977, **13,** 307–317.(c)

van Kaam, A. *Living creatively*. Denville, N.J.: Dimension Books, 1978.

van Kaam, A. *The transcendent self: Formative spirituality of the middle, early and later years of life*. Denville, N.J.: Dimension Books, 1979.

van Kaam, A. Provisional Glossary of the Science of Foundational Life Formation. *Studies in Formative Spirituality*. Pittsburgh, PA: IFS, Duquesne University, 1980, I (1), 137–155; (2), 287–304; (3), 449–479 and 1981, II (1), 117–143.

## CHAPTER 64

# Twenty-Four-Hour Therapy:
# A Personal Renaissance

EUGENE E. LANDY and ARNOLD E. DAHLKE

*Eugene Landy's Twenty-Four–Hour Therapy well meets the criteria of being theoretically sound and quite innovative. It is, on reflection, a perfectly logical system. When hearing of it for the first time, one is likely to say, "Well, it is common sense. . . ." Unfortunately, common sense is not so common and things look so much clearer on the basis of hindsight.*

*As is the case with any really effective method that moves in new dimensions, from those readers whose ideas have crystallized and who may object to the complete patient takeover by the therapist—which is indeed a bold and brilliant move—we can expect outraged cries. I am particularly impressed by the apparent internal contradictions involved in this system—a person is led to autonomy through extreme dependency.*

*This chapter by Eugene Landy and Arnold Dahlke contains many important theoretical elements relating to family life and parenting, proper roles of therapists, and the whole mental health movement. I for one enjoyed reading this stirring account of an unusual and potentially important system. It should be read along with Painter and Vernon's Primary Relationship Therapy and Rosen's Direct Psychoanalysis.*

Twenty-Four–Hour Therapy is a unique, intensive, team approach to therapy developed by Eugene E. Landy in the late 1960s and early 1970s. Unlike traditional therapy, where the patient has limited contact with the therapist in an office setting, or institutional therapy, where the patient is placed in a controlled, artificial environment, Twenty-Four–Hour Therapy maintains total contact with patients, 24 hours a day, in their own environment. The goal of this intensive approach is the patient's attainment of adequacy within the context of his or her natural problem-provoking environment, whether it be home, work, or play.

Twenty-Four–Hour Therapy is based on the central theme that people behave in ways that mask their inadequacies, whether real or imagined, as they function in the world.

They do so by creating facades and external support systems, while engaging in interpersonal power games to get what they want. Focusing on those "secret" inadequacies that patients keep hidden from others (and even from themselves), Landy and his associates totally disrupt the privacy of their patient's lives, gaining complete control over every aspect of their physical, personal, social, and sexual environments. Employing a variety of behavioral strategies, Landy and his team confront patients with the secrets of their real and imagined inadequacies and then teach them how to develop a strong

The writers express their gratitude to Audrey Levy, Dana Longino, Sara Hardman, Nancy Fuller, and the staff of the F.R.E.E. Foundation for their invaluable critique and assistance in the preparation of this chapter.

sense of self-sufficiency and control over their lives, which Landy defines as adequacy.

## HISTORY

### Precursors

In the early 1960s, Landy was invited to join Frederick H. Stoller, the father of Marathon Therapy, who had just completed his innovative work with "swing groups" at Camarillo State Hospital (Stoller, 1967). While working with Stoller in marathon groups, Landy was struck by the importance of the time factor in dealing with patients. He became aware of the number of hours it takes for people to drop their facade, or, as T. S. Eliot (1936) says, "to prepare a face to meet the faces you meet. . . ." He concluded that if therapists stay with patients long enough, the patients eventually drop their facades and grow more authentic. Then, dealing more authentically with environmental circumstances, they develop feelings of adequacy and confidence about their ability to handle themselves with other people. They begin to make decisions without resorting to their old facades.

Landy noted a significant problem, however, with the marathon approach. When patients left the protective environment of the marathon and returned to their natural environment, authenticity faded and facades reappeared. The relatively short-term marathon experience simply did not allow enough time for sufficient practice of new behaviors. Landy recognized that what was needed was a more prolonged therapeutic experience situated within the patient's normal daily environment. This conclusion was an important precursor to the development of Twenty-Four–Hour Therapy.

Landy further developed methods for application to prolonged therapeutic experiences at the University of Oklahoma in the mid-sixties as a consultant to Job Corps training and Community Action programs funded by the Office of Economic Opportunity (Landy, 1967; Landy, 1970; Landy & Steele, 1967).

He developed close friendships at the university with W. Robert Hood, Director of the University of Oklahoma Institute of Group Relations, from whom he learned the integration of psychopharmacological techniques with traditional therapy and the sociological skills of manipulating contingencies in natural environments (Sherif et al., 1954; Hood & Sherif, 1955), and with Arnold Dahlke, Associate Director of the institute, who stressed the importance of applying the rigorous thinking of experimental methods to clinical settings (Kelley et al., 1965; LaCharite & Dahlke, 1975; Jones, Dahlke & LaCharite, 1978).

### Beginnings

The initial application of Landy's earlier ideas occurred in 1968, when he was Director of the Adolescent Program at Gateways Hospital and Community Mental Health Center in Los Angeles. During this period he was strongly influenced by the dynamic, interpersonal philosophies of Solon D. Samuels (1971, 1976), an early associate of Eric Berne. Landy considers Samuels to be his most significant influence, both personally and professionally.

Working primarily with drug-addicted adolescents, Landy first attempted to set up a hospital environment similar to the street environment of his patients. His intention was to get at the process that made these adolescents so unable to handle normal circumstances of living that they resorted to substance abuse (including alcohol), which he collectively referred to as "dope." His observations led him to distinguish between dope used for entertainment and dope used to cover up feelings of inadequacy.

Landy further observed three major types of "dopers": those who used "uppers"—amphetamines—appeared to be withdrawn and experiencing difficulties accepting themselves as adequate; those who used "downers"—barbiturates—hypnotics, and sedatives evidenced a great deal of anger and lack of self-control; and those who used psychedelics were more intellectualizing and existentially despairing.

The more Landy observed the adolescents in the hospital setting, the more he noticed that they tended to separate themselves socially into the uppers, downers, and psychedelic groups. He decided to move them all together into a large house, forcing them into close interaction with one another. In a very short time, arguments and loud physical fights broke out. Landy then brought in staff members to be with them at all times. These staff members continuously provided him with feedback on the daily habits of the adolescents. He became aware of his patients' inabilities to function without the aid of some medicine: The downers adolescents (angry and lacking self-control) were continuously antagonizing everybody; the uppers adolescents (withdrawn and scared) were constantly looking for rescue and approval; and the psychedelic adolescents (intellectual "head-trippers") were bored and depressed. It was this feedback that led him to speculate that they were using drugs to cover their feelings of inadequacy.

From the hospital program, Landy developed a large drug-user, adolescent private practice. He wrote *The Underground Dictionary* (Landy, 1971), a unique compendium of drug and subculture language, still widely used today as a standard reference by law enforcement, legal, medical, and social service agencies. The book attracted many parents seeking assistance for their drug-abusing children.

Within the context of this practice, Landy expanded and developed several of the basic notions underlying Twenty-Four–Hour Therapy. Through arrangements with parents, he blocked all of the normal routes that the adolescents had for covering up their inadequacies. They then had to earn their rights and privileges by accomplishments. Their lives were thus organized into the pursuit of adequacy goals.

To facilitate these adolescent accomplish-

ments, Landy established the Center for Adjunctive Therapeutic Activity (CATA). CATA was a unique program that applied principles of occupational therapy to "real-life" settings. The center's program consisted of a wide array of arts and crafts, such as drama classes, leather work, and candle making. The typical patient entered both individual and group therapy and was assigned to a variety of classes. Landy met with his therapists and instructors periodically to assess the progress of his adolescent patients and to structure new experiences for them.

CATA operated on the assumption that one of the dynamics of drug-abusing adolescents is their inability to postpone gratification in the pursuit of long-range success experiences. The classes were therefore structured to give them a variety of immediate success experiences. Operating under the old adage that "nothing succeeds like success," Landy thus created an environment that enabled his patients to develop a generalized sense of confidence in their own adequacy.

At this point (early 1970s), Landy began applying his total-environment approach to individual patients in his private practice. He continued to refine and expand his methodology in applications with a variety of patients from all walks of life. With the assistance of key staff members, he has trained and continues to train professionals and paraprofessionals in the techniques and strategies of Twenty-Four–Hour Therapy.

## CURRENT STATUS

Since the early 1970s, over 50 patients have benefited from Landy's full approach. Close to 200 others have had Twenty-Four–Hour Therapy focusing on more specific problem areas of their lives, such as weight and substance control, relationships, and career-associated difficulties.

In addition, staff members who trained with Landy on earlier cases are currently applying his techniques to cases of their own in various parts of the country, while training still other staff in similar applications. Landy established the F.R.E.E. Foundation (Foundation for the Rechanneling of Emotions and Education), a community counseling center in Beverly Hills. Interns at F.R.E.E. are using his approach on a partial basis with patients plagued by specific areas of inadequacy.

With his associate Arnold Dahlke, Landy is currently completing a book on Twenty-Four–Hour Therapy. Landy discussed his approach at the 1973 American Psychological Association Convention in Montreal where he participated in a symposium with Joseph Wolpe and Harold Greenwald (Landy, Wolpe, & Greenwald, 1973). More recently he shared his ideas in conversation hours at the Western Psychological Association meeting in Honolulu, Hawaii (1980a) and the American Psychological Association meeting in Montreal, Canada (1980b).

Landy's patients have come from all over the world and from all walks of life, from adolescent drug abusers and their parents, to executives, to Hollywood superstars. His successful use of this approach with Brian Wilson of The Beach Boys, rock star Alice Cooper, and actors Rod Steiger and Richard Harris (to mention only the few that have publicly acknowledged in print their participation in Twenty-Four–Hour Therapy) have made him a controversial psychologist. Landy's approach involves developing complete patient dependency on the therapist and total therapist control of the patient's life. Most people outside of the patient's immediate circle are fearful of a person upon whom so much dependency is placed and who exercises such extreme control.

## THEORY

*Adequacy* is the central concept of Twenty-Four–Hour Therapy. An adequate person is one who both feels and is capable of getting what he or she wants from the world. People who feel adequate *know* they are capable of accomplishing something, even if they don't

have the skills at the moment; those who feel inadequate often say "I could never do that!"

The roots of a person's adequacy (real or imagined) begin in earliest childhood. Landy sees the newborn child basically as a "raw little animal" that brings with itself a quest for life, a continuation, a survival, because it has no knowledge whatsoever. Either it was well nurtured in its intrauterine environment, becoming a healthy newborn, or it is born unhealthy and faces an intense struggle to survive physically.

From the very beginning, the child is socialized. The first thing that it feels is a strange environment. It doesn't know what hunger is—it simply has a physical response. It cries. Someone puts a bottle in its mouth and the life-long learning process begins to take place; the child quickly finds that specific behaviors elicit specific responses.

The most important feature of this life-long learning experience is a person's social environment. First there is the earliest, close family constellation, then the extended family, then peers, and then a variety of other significant figures such as teachers and employers. At each stage along the way, every participant in this social environment is continuously giving "evaluative" feedback (Rogers & Roethlisberger, 1952). The child is praised when it learns how to use eating utensils, when it says its first words, and when it defecates at the right moment in the right place. It meets with disapproval when it throws its food on the floor, when it doesn't speak properly, and when it wets its bed after it has been toilet trained.

Part of this continuous evaluative feedback leads to the development of fears. We fear that we have displeased our parents. We are afraid that we won't be able to pass an exam. We are anxious about doing our job well.

The life-long learning process shapes our definition of our own adequacy. We all evolve into adulthood with varying levels of self-confidence in our ability to get what we want from the world. Some of us believe we are adequate and can do anything. Others of us feel inadequate and doubt our ability to accomplish even the simplest task.

We continuously compare ourselves to our society's norms. All of us find ourselves "better" on some things and "worse" on others. Thus, each of us ends up with little pockets of inadequacies; these inadequacies become our secrets that we hide as we prepare our face to face the world.

We develop facades to keep others from seeing our secrets and thus avoid the possibility of others evaluating us negatively. We become skilled at manipulative, interpersonal games designed to cover up our feelings that we are basically inadequate. For Landy, the discovery and exorcising of these secret inadequacies is the focal task in all therapy, and especially in Twenty-Four–Hour Therapy.

An important component of adequacy is *emotional control*. Adequate persons are capable of making adaptive decisions to get what they want under the most adverse circumstances. They are capable of making rational decisions even while they are experiencing extreme emotional states such as intense fear.

Inadequate persons, on the other hand, are victims of their emotions. They generally make their decisions out of fear. Whether it is fear of succeeding at a task or fear of the disapproval of significant others, they act out of their emotions rather than from logical thinking. Compared to adequate people who take actions out of conscious choice, inadequate persons are not aware of their capability to choose.

Landy is not arguing that we are capable of doing away with our emotions. Emotions are like perspiration: When the hot sun beats down on us, we will sweat. The question is not whether we can stop ourselves from sweating, but rather what we choose to do about it when it happens. Similarly, we will never stop ourselves from having emotional responses to our environment. But we can train ourselves, as adequate individuals, to choose what is best for us when those emotional situations do occur.

Since our estimate of our own adequacy is a *learned* stance toward our lives, we are capable of reeducating ourselves. Thus therapy can be viewed as a process of reeducation. In therapy we do not *unlearn* the dysfunctional behaviors that grow out of our inadequacies; we simply learn additional alternative behaviors and, further, we learn that we have the capability to choose an action that serves us best in any specific instance.

## METHODOLOGY

The strategies and techniques that make up Twenty-Four–Hour Therapy are all conducted in the service of one central goal: the development of adequacy. To attain that goal, the therapy must be all-encompassing. The therapist, assisted by a team of professional and paraprofessional staff members, disrupts every aspect of the patient's life. The staff size varies at times from three to 30 and always includes a psychiatrist to determine possible medical needs.

All patient contacts with other people are monitored and controlled. Through face-to-face interactions with the patient, extensive use of telephones with staff members, and the use of both video- and audio tapes, the therapist is aware of everything the patient does. In many instances staff members as well as family members are told, verbaitum, by the therapist, how to respond to specific actions and verbalizations of the patient. Situations are set up in advance (or on the spot in response to a patient action) to teach the patient some principle or provide him or her with an important experience. The therapist, in effect, choreographs a very complex fabric of activities, 24 hours a day, much like the conductor of a large symphony orchestra; and the music that is played is called *education*.

Each patient is taken through a unique, individually designed program of Twenty-Four–Hour Therapy. Individual programs last anywhere from a week to a year or more. Each program consists of eight major phases: (1) initiation; (2) discovery; (3) inadequacy; (4) preadequacy; (5) self-adequacy; (6) self-functioning; (7) adequacy; and (8) termination. A summary of the activities that occur in the eight phases is shown in Table 1.

The length of each phase is a direct function of patient progress at any given point in time. Although the phases are sequential, they do overlap: The therapist, for example, might uncover some inadequacies in phase 4 that call for some of the strategies used in phase 3; and while patients might be in phase 5 in one category, they could be in phase 3 in another simultaneously. The entire process is a fluid, dynamic orchestration of the patient's life directed toward the patient's attainment of adequacy in his or her own environment.

**Phase 1: Initiation**

Many patients entering Twenty-Four–Hour Therapy are brought in by a family member who has chosen to do so as a last resort because nothing else worked. Others enter because they want to work on some specific problem area but then soon find that their difficulty is tied to a much deeper thread;

they decided to totally immerse themselves in the program.

The initial contact with the patient and his or her family is very significant, because the therapist identifies not only what face the patient wants to present to the world but how the family wants the patient to be seen. This provides keys for the therapist in unlocking a picture of the patient's support system.

Three important conditions need to be agreed upon between the patient, family, and therapist. First, the patient must be cut off from all possible financial resources for the duration of the therapy. The success of Twenty-Four–Hour Therapy rests on the extent to which the therapeutic team can exert control over every aspect of the patient's life. When patients have access to any form of financial resources, they can easily use them to engage in the cover-up of inadequacies that the therapist regards as dysfunctional for their progress.

The second important condition is total cooperation from every member of the patient's support system, usually the family.

**Table 1. Summary of phases in Twenty-Four–Hour Therapy.**

| | | |
|---|---|---|
| 1. | Initiation | Patient and family present themselves; patient cut off from all financial resources; total family cooperation agreed upon; therapist established as absolute authority. |
| 2. | Discovery | Delineation of patient inadequacies and total patient support systems; complete therapist takeover of patient support system; creation of total dependency on therapist. |
| 3. | Inadequacy | Therapist and team withdraw support, allowing patient to experience total inadequacy; patient sees choice and makes decision to become adequate (get what he or she wants) or continue inadequacy (do without). |
| 4. | Preadequacy | Patient learns that there are other ways for getting what he or she wants; therapist sets up contingencies that make learning of new ways easier than doing without; patient learns that he or she is capable of learning. |
| 5. | Self-Adequacy | Focus on patient taking care of self and developing sense of self-sufficiency; patient learns the concept of giving to self; therapist begins diminishing patient dependency on therapist/team. |
| 6. | Self-Functioning | Expansion of adequacy-learning beyond self-care to function in and getting what he or she wants from the world; increased socializing and sexual functioning; further diminishing of patient dependency. |
| 7. | Adequacy | Gradual withdrawal of therapy team and increased one-to-one contact with therapist; patient learns to integrate adequacy functions toward becoming more self-sufficient in the world, living without therapy team. |
| 8. | Termination | Patient achieves complete self-sufficiency, lives by self or with nontherapy team roomate; therapist becomes friend and advisor. |

If cooperation cannot be obtained from some individuals, then they must not be allowed any contact with the patient. An uncooperative family member can easily sabotage the therapy by responding to the patient as being incapable or inadequate, thus retarding the patient's progress.

The third important condition is that the therapist be established as the supreme authority. This means, for example, that if a patient wants something and turns, as usual, to a family member for help, that family member is told to respond with "I'll be happy to help you if the doctor agrees." In this way the family member remains an ally and has not deserted the patient while reinforcing the authority of the therapist.

These three conditions are necessary before Twenty-Four–Hour Therapy can begin, because the therapist must move very quickly to establish patient dependency. It is the dependency that provides the therapist with the necessary authority to reshape the patient's responses to situations that typically elicited the cover-up of inadequacies.

**Phase 2: Discovery**

The second phase of the therapy begins with a delineation of the patient's inadequacies and the identification of all of the major and minor figures in the patient's support system. Every person identified in that system is contacted and interviewed extensively, to develop a complete "history" of the patient from the viewpoints of each key individual in the patient's life. All interviews are taped and transcribed. The history is then carefully examined for the purpose of uncovering as many of the patient's inadequacies as possible.

Once the key individuals in the patient's support system are identified, the therapist takes over the system. As agreed on in phase 1, the therapist instructs each individual how to respond to specific actions and verbalizations of the patient. In addition, a staff member moves in with the patient; the therapist arranges to have staff members with or observing the patient every moment of the day.

The therapist is constantly informed of everything the patient is doing and continually feeds staff responses to the patient.

At this point, then, the therapist has created total patient dependency on the therapeutic team. The therapy cannot proceed to the next phase until this happens.

**Phase 3: Inadequacy**

During the third phase, a pivotal one, patients are compelled to face their secret inadequacies. They suddenly find themselves without the usual financial or family support systems to help them deal with their inadequacies. Since they are now completely dependent on the therapeutic team, they turn to that team for the assistance that was formerly supplied by family and friends. When they say to a staff member, "Help me, I don't know what to do," the staff member replies only with "Think!" or "I have confidence that you can work it out" or "I know you can deal with this." Then the staff member waits to assist the patient with the logic needed to reach a conclusion or a decision. Previously, family and friends "rescued" the patient in order to expedite action, or out of their own lack of patience; as a result, the patient never learned to do for him- or herself.

Thus, during this phase patients find themselves in a vulnerable position: With all of their normal supports withdrawn, they are faced with either not getting what they want by staying with their inadequacies or getting what they want by learning new, adequate behaviors. Many patients panic at this point. Without the accustomed support of family and friends, they come to recognize that they are really not functionally adequate on their own. With that recognition comes the realization that they have a choice: "I stay inadequate and do not get what I want or I learn new ways of getting what I want."

Landy believes that patients must fully experience inadequacy before the therapy can proceed. He compares this phase to going to the dentist: The dentist must drill to the root of the tooth before reconstruction can begin.

## Phase 4: Preadequacy

In the preadequacy phase, patients learn that there are other ways for getting what they want. The therapist sets up contingencies in their environment that literally make the learning of new ways easier than doing without (remaining inadequate).

Patients begin to learn by not being told how to do something. They now must find out for themselves. In the process of finding out for themselves, staff members are available to provide information, staff are instructed by the therapist not to rescue, only to respond to patient questions that ask for specific information—information designed to light up alternative solutions.

The significance of this phase is *not* the information learned by the patients, but rather the concept that they are *capable* of learning. Once they *know* they *can* learn, they also know they have a *choice* to learn. As inadequates, they did not experience that choice. Thus, in this phase they take an important step toward adequacy.

## Phase 5: Self-Adequacy

The focus now turns to structuring the patients' environments toward teaching them self-care. Many patients who come into Twenty-Four–Hour Therapy have abandoned themselves; they are so used to being dependent on significant other persons that they have never really learned self-sufficiency. Many of them must be taught how to function by themselves, including such specifics as personal hygiene, taking pride in their appearance, securing and holding a job, planning a budget within which they can survive and get what they want (while avoiding constant debt), and knowing how to get around the city. They are, in essence, learning a whole new concept of giving to themselves. This is in contrast to their past experience, where they were "psychologically anorexic," working so hard getting someone else to give to them that they never learned how to give to themselves.

## Phase 6: Self-Functioning

Once patients evidence the capability of self-care, they are ready to move into the sixth phase of Twenty-Four–Hour Therapy. In this phase they expand their learning beyond themselves to functioning in the world around them. They learn to socialize and then to sexualize, which, in turn, leads them to seek and form relationships. Self-functioning means the ability, in spite of the normal feelings of strangeness that we all experience in a new situation, to walk into strange places, such as a bar, social gathering, or a classroom, not knowing anybody, and yet be able to meet and interact with people.

During this phase patient dependency on the therapist markedly diminishes. Patients learn to increase their ability to function and develop more effective and creative ways of utilizing their talents and skills.

The therapist allows them to become reinvolved with members of their former support system, only now patients act from a place of self-sufficiency rather than dependency. Family and friends, meanwhile, have been educated in the process, either through contact with the therapeutic team or through independent therapy set up for them by the therapist.

An important skill that patients learn during this phase is that of time structuring. In the previous two phases they learned how to develop routines aimed at self-care; now they are dealing with other peoples' schedules besides their own. They learn how to develop a comfortable looseness and flexibility in their interactions with others.

## Phase 7: Adequacy

As they move into the seventh phase of therapy, patients have learned methods for making accommodations to the world; they have learned to put themselves first, while still maintaining concern for others. During this phase, the therapist begins to withdraw staff members from the case. Where staff members were previously with the patient 24 hours a day, the patient begins to adequately function alone more often.

At the same time the patient begins to have regular, more traditional individual and group sessions with the therapist. In earlier phases patients interacted primarily with staff members. At that time they felt inadequate in dealing with the therapist with anything other than appeasement or withdrawal. By the time they reach phase 7, however, they have developed enough adequacy to be able to confront the therapist, even in the midst of a disagreement or anger.

**Phase 8: Termination**

In the final phase of Twenty-Four–Hour Therapy, patients are completely self-sufficient, functioning from a position of a strongly felt sense of adequacy. Their dependency on the therapist is no more than any normal patient-doctor relationship, yet there exists a sense of closeness after having been through so much together.

During this phase, patients live alone or with roommates of their choice. Contact with staff members is minimal, much as a busy person has with friends. Patients are now practicing everything they have learned.

Their contact with the therapist settles down to infrequent meetings, arranged at their own request, to deal with specific problems. The therapist has thus moved from being a strong authority upon whom the patient is dependent to becoming a friend and advisor, a person who can be trusted to be objective.

**APPLICATIONS**

Landy maintains that Twenty-Four–Hour Therapy is applicable to all diagnostic categories as long as patients can be treated in their natural environments. This is an especially important requirement for mentally retarded patients or for patients with chronic psychotic reactions, who have had long or multiple hospitalizations. The hospital setting provides them with very limited physical and social mobility. More important, almost everyone who interacts with them, from doctors and nurses to relatives, usually treats them as though they are not capable of taking care of themselves and not adequate at functioning in the normal world. Hence, since they are treated as incapable and inadequate, they come to believe and accept that they are. As long as they are in the artificial environment of the hospital, they will continue to be reinforced as inadequate. For Twenty-Four–Hour Therapy to be successfully applied to them, it must be implemented in their natural nonhospital environment.

Age is no limit. Although Twenty-Four–Hour Therapy has been used most often with adults, it has also been very successfully applied to adolescents and some children. In those cases the basic strategies and phasing of the therapy are the same, but the goals and some of the specific procedures differ.

Time is also no limit. Some patients, working in specific problem areas, have gone through Twenty-Four–Hour Therapy in as little as one week; one patient was fully involved for two years. Whether it be one week or two years, patients experience a far more intense and concentrated *renaissance* than in more traditional therapies.

Because of the strong therapist control exerted in Twenty-Four-Hour Therapy, family and friends often react to specific therapeutic moves with angry resistance. Therapists must be strong enough in their convictions and secure enough under intense stress to not personalize such reactions, which should be recognized as fearful responses to the breaking of patients' dependent, manipulative ties with their former support systems. Twenty-Four-Hour therapists, in other words, must not allow these unavoidable encounters to influence their function and decision making with their patients. They must be willing to absorb the inevitable anger that will be directed at them.

Currently, Twenty-Four–Hour Therapy is very costly because of the intensive time commitment required of a large number of professional staff members. Landy and his associates, however, have been experimenting with cutting costs through the utilization of psychological interns who rotate on a part-time basis in various cases as a part of their internship training program at the F.R.E.E. Foundation. Additional attempts at cost reduction in other training institutions and academic settings, supported by grants from federal, state, and local social service agencies, are envisioned.

## CASE HISTORY

Robert came into therapy when he was 27 years old. He had been in therapy on and off since the age of 16, first with a psychoanalyst (who had diagnosed him as a chronic undifferentiated schizophrenic) for about four years and then with a psychiatrist for over six years.

After graduating from a public high school, Robert attended one semester of college and then went to work for his father. He entered into a brief marriage at the age of 19, which ended in annulment a few months later. He married again at the age of 21 and fathered two children; his second wife left him when he was 26.

Robert was adopted at the age of one week and raised as an only child by a successful, upper-middle-class businessman, whose wife had not been able to have children. He was desired by both parents and raised as their own son until the age of eight, when his parents told him that he had been adopted.

### Phase 1: Initiation

The initial contact with Dr. Landy, the therapist in the case, was made by Robert's father. At the time of presentation, Robert was functioning marginally. He was working as the manager of a store that his father bought for him because of his concern with Robert's inability to function in the world.

Upon meeting Robert's father, Landy informed him of the conditions under which he would be willing to take the case: financial control, complete family cooperation, and the therapist's position as an absolute authority with Robert.

Several days later, as prearranged with Robert's father, Landy visited the store as a customer to observe Robert functioning. He saw him basically "busy keeping himself busy." Robert spent his time talking with employees, but from what Landy could observe, he was not really performing any serious managerial or store function. He would spend periods of 15 to 20 minutes in this kind of activity, walking around briskly, picking up things, looking at them, and then leave the store to go to a local bar, where he would nurse a beer for a half hour or so. Then he would return to the store. Robert thus alternated between his store and the bar throughout the day.

At the bar, observed and taped by Landy (who was unknown to Robert), he lamented to the bartender, telling her how underpaid he was, how busy he was, and what a toll the whole thing was taking on him. Listening to him, one would assume that he had been wronged by his father, who he saw as "the rat-fink of all times." (In fact, since he was unable to provide for himself, his father paid him a salary of $35,000.00 a year, made all the payments on his sports car, and paid all his bills, including rent, utilities, credit cards, and insurance.)

Shortly after the initial observation, Robert's father told him of Landy, and Robert agreed to meet with the therapist in his office. Robert's father agreed to all of Landy's conditions. Landy suggested the conditions be written and the papers be signed in front of Robert.

At the meeting, with Robert's father present, Robert complained about his very difficult life. Landy asked Robert about his feelings concerning his father. Robert looked puzzled and didn't answer. Landy told him what he had heard in the bar. Robert denied everything. Landy played a tape of the bar conversation (in Twenty-Four–Hour Therapy everything is taped). Robert appeared surprised and embarrassed and began to cry. He said he would rather be in therapy with his last therapist, who never made him feel as bad as Landy just had. Landy told Robert it was not his intention to make him feel bad; but if what he was saying was true, Landy would assist Robert by getting his father to stop being such a critical, discounting person. Robert continued to cry.

At that point Robert's father informed him that Landy now had control of any money he would spend on Robert, and that if Robert needed anything he would have to deal through Landy's office and Landy; he then signed a document stating so in the presence of Robert, Landy, and a notary public.

**Phase 2: Discovery**

Landy immediately formed a therapy team to develop a complete history of Robert and to delineate all of the key figures in Robert's support system. He rented a two-bedroom apartment and a staff member moved in as Robert's roommate. From then on a staff member was either with Robert or in a position to observe him throughout the duration of therapy. Landy also initiated a series of meetings with significant family members and friends, instructing them how to respond to Robert so as not to become hooked into "rescuing" him when they interacted with him. Robert, they were told, was a professional "victim."

Landy told Robert that he was willing to allow him to continue functioning in the store, as long as he did not make any purchase-order decisions without first clearing them with Landy. Robert agreed to the conditions and left his session with Landy, disbelieving that his father was "doing this to him."

Robert tested his father's position and the therapist's authority within three days when he ordered close to $15,000.00 worth of material for his store. Landy (since he had direct lines of communication with everybody associated with Robert, his father, and the store) was immediately informed. He

called Robert into his office and told him he was unhappy with the fact that he had broken his agreement. Robert replied that he was sorry. Landy, in turn, said that he too was sorry, but he would now not allow Robert to place any future orders until a complete inventory was taken in the store.

Robert, upset by this turn of events, threatened his father with a knife. When his father attempted to talk to him, he threatened to harm himself. Landy assured Robert's concerned parents that, in his professional opinion, Robert would not harm himself or any others. Landy told Robert that he would close the store if Robert did not start and complete the inventory immediately.

Robert again tested his father and Landy's authority by sending a letter of resignation to his father. Much to his surprise, his father accepted the resignation (at Landy's direction). Robert suddenly found himself no longer employed and penniless. He panicked, complaining that he had "made the business what it was today," in spite of the fact that the business was losing thousands of dollars per month because of mismanagement. Robert had never learned how to read the cash register receipts and employees stole money openly. Robert also had to hire a manager to deal with business affairs he didn't understand. Landy sent a staff member to collect all of his company credit cards and keys for the store.

**Phase 3: Inadequacy**

Robert was caught off-guard by the suddenness of Landy's actions. In the past, Robert's threats with people had been quite successful, because he convinced them he meant what he said and they didn't know how to deal with him, other than to appease him. He rapidly discovered that Landy would not respond to threats.

Previously, while working in his store, Robert had covered up his inadequacies through his assumed position as manager. This gave him all of the status and social contacts he needed. When Landy withdrew this support, Robert came face to face with the fact that he had no friends or involved relationships in his life. It also became apparent to him that he was no longer able to use his threats as influence with his family or with any of the people who had worked for him.

Because Robert saw Landy's action as punitive, he spent close to four months in the inadequacy phase, demonstrating his inadequacy over and over again. For example, because he did not get a job, he was evicted from his apartment and lost his car.

Landy placed him in a board-and-care home. As Robert began to feel safe in his new environment, he slowly realized that his fellow residents were physically and emotionally handicapped, unable to take care of themselves. After a while, he was given a job in the facility for $5.00 a day, three days a week. This, in effect, was the first real job he had ever held. He worked very hard at it, outperforming everyone else.

He became so comfortable and successful in his new position, the first such success he had ever had, that Landy withdraw all financial support, in order to stimulate his moving beyond this first position. The board-and-care home then refused to keep him. Landy offered him another board-and-care facility in a distant and unfamiliar part of the city, but Robert found that too threatening. Instead, he looked for a job to pay his own way, which signaled his emergence from the inadequacy phase.

### Phase 4: Preadequacy

Robert began the preadequacy phase applying for jobs around the city at various locations, but he hesitated to take any of them. Landy expected that he would probably be fired from the first several jobs, and advised Robert that it didn't matter which job he chose, because getting this first job and working was only an "exercise." He used staff members to show Robert how to fill out job applications and how to respond to job interviews.

Since Robert did not have transportation of his own, he had to learn how to use the bus system, which he had never used before. This was a painful experience for him. At one point, stranded several miles from his residence, he sat on a bench for five hours (with a staff member nearby who would not rescue him), before he decided he could help himself by contacting the bus company and getting the information that would tell him how to get home.

Slowly Robert came to accept the reality that no one was going to rescue him at this stage in his life and that his only hope for survival was for him to become self-sufficient.

### Phase 5: Self-Adequacy

Robert began to take more care with his appearance and learned how to dress in a suit and tie. He learned how to develop and operate within the limits of a budget.

At this point, Landy assisted him in buying a car with the stipulation that it be a stick shift, which Robert had avoided how to drive. At first Robert felt himself incapable of learning how to drive it, and he regressed into inadequacy: He simply left the car at a curb and eventually it was towed away. After riding buses for a while, however, Robert finally told Landy that he would like to learn how to drive the stick-shift car. Robert made arrangements and slowly and painfully accomplished that task.

Having been through more than a half-dozen different jobs, Robert finally landed a sales job at a major department store. Once he overcame the fear that he would not be able to learn how to handle the computerized cash register, he began to prosper. He increasingly formed new social relationships with people that he encountered at the store. He worked there for almost a full year.

### Phase 6: Self-Functioning

Landy moved Robert and a staff member into an apartment located in a very social, singles complex. Again Robert slipped back into some inadequate behaviors, withdrawing and refusing to participate socially; recognizing this pattern of "three steps forward and two steps back," Landy withdrew and waited. Robert then began to socialize, because it was the only way Landy would respond.

Gradually Robert developed new competencies. He came to the realization that spending a great deal of time in getting nothing accomplished and feeling bad about it was not a very effective way for him to deal with the world. He realized increasingly how good he felt after accomplishing something. He began to expand his time horizon, by making more long-range plans.

## Phase 7: Adequacy

At this point Robert moved into the adequacy phase. He was able to hold a job successfully; he developed friendships; and gradually he became more comfortable with women.

He determined that he would like to return to school, but could not afford it. Since earning a minimal living and going to night school at the same time appeared to be too great a task, he decided to join the Army for financial support while he obtained an education. He chose to do this to be independent of his family and because, looking to the future, he could put to use his service education after his discharge.

## Phase 8: Termination Phase

Robert went off to basic training. When he realized that he was now 28 years old, in with a batch of 18-year-olds, all of whom were in better physical shape than he was, he began to regress again. He was threatened by the possibility of discharge because of his inability to function satisfactorily.

Landy advised Robert's sergeant on how to deal with Robert constructively, suggesting strategies that would facilitate continued development of Robert's adequacy. Even though it took an additional two weeks, Robert successfully completed basic training and was sent off to Korea, skilled in electronics.

Robert is still in the Army. He now relates to women with far less fear. He has formed social and sexual friendships. He is looking forward to returning to university life after military service, supported by the G.I. Bill.

Since Robert had been accustomed to "having," after recognizing his own ability he decided to "get for himself"; he would not settle for a secure, minimal-paying job as a salesman in a department store with little responsibility. He therefore chose the Army as a way of starting to get what he wanted: to have all the good things he had before, but this time he wanted to get them (and more) for himself. He is now aware of the difference in value between "having been given to" for most of his life and the greater enjoyment experienced when he gives to himself.

## SUMMARY

Landy compares Twenty-Four–Hour Therapy to a large chess game; the patient makes a move and the therapist responds with a move, which, in turn, elicits still another patient move. The intent in this process is for the patient to learn a lesson from everything that happens; to undercut the patient's manipulatory games; and to structure events in the patient's environment that facilitate the occurrence of spontaneous success experiences, continuously and in every aspect of the patient's life.

Landy believes that most traditional therapy is superficial and limited because therapists, in their relatively brief encounters with their patients, are too respectful and courteous of the patient's privacy. This means that therapists rarely get to the bedrock secrets of inadequacy upon which all of their patient's manipulative and acting-out behaviors are based. Only by getting to those secrets as quickly as possible can a therapist be a successful facilitator of change for the patient.

An important feature of Twenty-Four–Hour Therapy is its application in the patient's natural environment. As early as the 1920s, J. L. Moreno argued that patients should be treated *in situ* (Moreno, 1927).

Lewis Yablonsky, known for his work with psychodrama (Yablonsky, 1976) and an associate of Landy's since the early 1960s, recalls assisting Moreno in his treatment of a female psychotic patient who he had moved into a house where staff members served as "auxiliary egos," entering her fantasy world and then slowly bringing her back to reality (Yablonsky, 1980).

Landy questions why it is that patients don't get the same total treatment as football players: If players break their diet or stay out late, they are fined; they receive special kinds of treatment, special meals, special kinds of rubdowns, special kinds of education, and special kinds of exercises. All of this happens just because they are athletes. Patients are entitled to be given the same good advice, help, and total emotional structure that we afford our gladiators.

Landy's concepts of extreme dependency and total authority are parallel to the "governing principle of direct analysis" developed by John N. Rosen (1953), who specified that the therapist must act as the patient's "omnipotent protector." Twenty-four–hour therapists have as much ethical and professional responsibility to create and exert extreme dependency and authority as they do in preserving patient confidentiality.

Rosen agrees with Landy that patients should be treated in a pleasant therapeutic milieu outside of the hospital setting (Rosen, 1980); Landy, however, goes a step further, proposing that patients are most effectively treated in their own natural environment, those same environments that caused the initial problem. Also, while Rosen and his associates spend a great deal more time with the patient than traditional therapy, Landy extends this concentration to a total twenty-four–hour day involvement.

Jacqui Schiff (1970), in what she calls "reparenting," also extends her involvement to 24 hours. But, as Levy (1978) pointed out, Schiff's reparented patient is still placed in an artificial setting. Further, Schiff's patients are literally spanked and treated as children; Landy emphasizes the facilitation of ade-

quacy through the use of adult choice, logical thinking, and natural consequences rather than punitive parent-therapist responses.

Adequacy, the central concept of Twenty-Four Hour–Therapy, is similar to Albert Bandura's concept of "efficacy expectation," which refers to the extent to which a person expects to be successful at executing behaviors required to produce specific outcomes (Bandura, 1977). The strength of people's efficacy expectations determines whether they will attempt to handle difficult situations. For Landy, self-efficacy is an important ingredient of adequacy: Adequate people hold strong efficacy expectations. He adds, however, that an adequate person knows that he or she has the choice of behaving efficaciously or not; adequate people are willing to attempt an action, even though they might fail. Handling failure is a part of life for successful people. Additionally, they have learned how to be successful at getting what they want, without losing concern for others.

In applications of Bandura's social learning theory, currently being applied to 10-day, intensive workshop settings (Bandura, 1980), therapists model and guide patients through threatening activities, even performing behaviors jointly and with physical assistance, if necessary. Landy, however, does not go for the success experiences until after the patients have fully experienced inadequacy during the third phase of therapy. This experience polarizes the choice between two extreme alternatives: staying inadequate or developing adequacy. In the past that choice was not clear for patients because they were so successful at covering their inadequacy through the facades involved in manipulating members of their support system. This also means that the choice to learn is now theirs and not that of the therapist.

Patients emerge from their intensive, round-the-clock experience with a very clear choice. There are the old facades and interpersonal manipulations that they previously could not live without, because they used them to cover up the secrets of their inadequacies. Now there are the new, self-sufficient behaviors that they, as adequate persons, know they are capable of using to get what they want from the world.

Eugene Landy's Twenty-Four–Hour Therapy thus provides patients with an opportunity to transform their lives into a Personal Renaissance.

# REFERENCES

Bandura, A. *Social learning theory*. Englewood Cliffs, N.J.: Prentice-Hall, 1977.

Bandura, A. Personal communication. June 1980.

Eliot, T. S. *Collected poems, 1909–1935*. New York: Harcourt, 1936.

Hood, W. R. and Sherif, M. Personality oriented approaches to prejudice. *Sociology & Social Research*, 1955, **40**, 79–85.

Jones, M., Dahlke, A. E. and LaCharite, N. A. *An empirical examination of the helping relationship in a crisis intervention setting*. Washington, D.C.: American Institutes of Research, 1978.

Kelley, H. H., Condry, J. C., Jr., Dahlke, A. E. and Hill, A. H. Collective behavior in a simulated panic situation. *Journal of Experimental Social Psychology*, 1965, **1 (1)**, 20–54.

LaCharite, N. and Dahlke, A. E. *Improving information gathering for hotlines*. Washington, D.C.: American Institutes for Research, 1975.

Landy, E. E. Sex differences in some aspects of smoking behavior. *Psychological Reports*, 1967, **20**, 575–580.

Landy, E. E. Attitude and attitude change toward interaction as a function of participation vs. observation. *Comparative Group Studies*, 1970, **1**, 128–155.

Landy, E. E. *The underground dictionary*. New York: Simon & Schuster, 1971.

Landy, E. E. Twenty-four–hour therapy: Return from the land of Oz. Paper presented at the Western Psychological Association, Honolulu. May 1980a.

Landy, E. E. and Dahlke, A. E. Twenty-four–hour therapy: A personal renaissance. Paper presented at the American Psychological Association, Montreal. September 1980b.

Landy, E. E. and Steele, J. M. Graffiti. A function of population and building utilization. *Perceptual Motor Skills*, 1967, **25**, 711–712.

Landy, E. E., Wolpe, J. and Greenwald, H. Directive versus non-directive modes of therapy. Symposium presented at the American Psychological Association, Montreal. September 1973.

Levy, A. A comparison of reparenting techniques. Paper presented at the F.R.E.E. Seminar, June 1978.

Moreno, J. L. *Theatre of spontaneity*. New York: Beacon House, 1927.

Rogers, C. R. and Roethlisberger, F. J. Barriers and gateways to communication. *Harvard Business Review*, 1952, **30**, 28–35.

Rosen, J. N. *Direct analysis*. New York: Grune & Stratton, 1953.

Rosen, J. N. Personal communication. June 1980.

Samuels, S. D. Games therapists play. *Transactional Analysis Journal*, 1971, **1 (1)**, 95–99.

Samuels, S. D. On using our brains again. *Transactional Analysis Journal*, 1976, **6 (3)**, 245.

Schiff, J. L. *All my children*. New York: Evans, 1970.

Sherif, M., Harvey, O. J., White, B. J., Hood, W. R. and Sherif, C. W. *Experimental study of positive and negative intergroup attitudes between experimentally produced groups: Robbers Cave study*. Norman, Okla.: University of Oklahoma, 1954.

Stoller, F. H. Extending group functions by focused feedback with video tape. In G. Gazda (Ed.), *Basic innovations in group psychotherapy and counseling*. Springfield, Ill.: Charles C Thomas, 1967.

Yablonsky, L. *Psychodrama: Resolving emotional problems through role playing*. New York: Basic Books, 1976.

Yablonsky, L. Personal communication. June 1980.

## CHAPTER 65

# *Verbal Behavior Therapy*

HUGH A. STORROW

*Some therapies in this book could be classified as unimodal (e.g., Ego-State Therapy and Focusing) while others are multimodal, combining two or more approaches (e.g., Nondirective Psychoanalysis and Structured Learning). Going back to the pioneers in the field, we find that both Jung and Freud were essentially unimodal whereas Adler was a multimodal theorist/therapist.*

*Which way will therapy go in the long run? My own guess is that the final complete therapist will be truly eclectic. This is in no way intended to disparage any of the unimodal methods. Personally I would rather go to a capable person using a single method than to one not so capable who combines methods. But in the long run, I believe the final trend will be a combination.*

*In Hugh Storrow's chapter we find an interesting combination of apparently contradictory theoretical elements: (1) an appeal to the "mind" via words and (2) an underpinning of behaviorism that denies the importance of cognition. It appears to me that this approach of combining apparently contradictory elements (as in I. H. Paul's Nondirective Psychoanalysis) is a step in the final direction. It is close to the position of such systems as Functional Counseling and Multiple Impact Therapy. Storrow's combination of seemingly contradictory aspects is a well conceived and logical system for dealing with a wide variety of human psychological problems.*

Verbal Behavior Therapy is a form of behavioral psychotherapy. Theoretically it rests on the principles of classical and instrumental conditioning expanded and enriched by Bandura's social learning theory (1977) in order to deal more adequately with the complexities of human behavior. It is technically eclectic, drawing interviewing and relationship management methods from traditional insight approaches and many of its specific techniques from Behavior Therapy. From Behavior Therapy also comes its emphasis on precise delineation of target problems and goals as well as careful follow-up of treatment results. Perhaps the most innovative aspect of this approach is its blending of disparate elements into what is hoped will be a harmonious and effective whole.

## HISTORY

### Precursors

Since Verbal Behavior Therapy is technically eclectic and can incorporate any technique shown to be effective or promising, its ancestors could theoretically include all lines of development in the entire field of psychotherapy. A few streams of influence stand out, however.

The techniques of minimal directiveness that are emphasized in Verbal Behavior Therapy's interviewing are clearly in the psychoanalytic tradition. The history of this movement has been clearly traced many times in the past and will not be covered again here. Carl Rogers (1951) and his many associates have shed light both on interviewing and on methods for fostering therapeutically effective relationships with patients.

John Dollard and Neal Miller, with their seminal *Personality and Psychotherapy* (1950), provided the impetus that began the development of Verbal Behavior Therapy. They helped me to shift from the purely psychoanalytic orientation of my training years into behavioral channels. Their work took psychoanalytic principles and redefined them in terms of Hullian learning theory. Its impact on me was electric; what had been muddy was suddenly clear. I think that what happened illustrates in a minor way what Kuhn (1962) talks about when he discusses paradigm shifts—either for individuals or for entire disciplines. The impact of the new paradigm is often esthetic as well as purely scientific; it feels better as well as seems to explain more. And, at the time it is accepted, there may be no certain proof that it does the latter. The behavioral paradigm certainly feels better to me; it provides me the best peg I've yet found to hang my therapeutic hat on. But I still can't prove that it explains more or predicts more than the theories I was taught earlier.

The behavioral movement from Watson (1913) to Wolpe (1958) stands out as an obvious precursor to the approach of Verbal Behavior Therapy. After a few early—and often successful—attempts to explain and treat mental disturbances along behavioristic lines, the behaviorists retired to the laboratory until Wolpe dragged them back to the clinic. This long-lasting clinical inferiority complex is difficult to explain. It was probably due primarily to the overwhelming but apparently temporary success of psychoanalysis during the first half of the twentieth century.

Another line of influence leading toward Verbal Behavior Therapy comes from the earlier cognitive therapists. They emphasized conscious thought in the form of beliefs, value systems, expectations, and hypotheses about cause and effect as independent variables with important effects on behavior.

Furthermore they suggested that efforts to control thinking often led to changes in behavior. Among these cognitive therapists those with the most impact on me were Kelly (1955), Phillips (1956), Anderson (1957) and Ellis (1962).

When Verbal Behavior Therapy first appeared, its theoretical groundwork and techniques were already available or in the process of development. My contribution was mainly to organize these elements into a systematic treatment approach. In this I think my contribution is not much different from that made by many other "innovative" psychotherapists. But I think I'm more honest than at least some of them.

## Beginnings

Verbal Behavior Therapy grew out of personal interests similar to some of the streams of influence described above. First to appear in print was an attempt to apply cognitive reeducation to psychotherapy (Storrow, 1963–64). A year later came an early attempt to put together a psychotherapeutic system, primarily based on learning theory, but already technically eclectic (Storrow, 1965). In this paper the label Verbal Behavior Therapy appeared for the first time. The most complete account of the system was published in book form in 1967 (Storrow, 1967).

The past 15 years or so have, of course, seen further developments in all the precursor areas described above. These changes have brought the methods of many therapists closer to the position advocated here. Garfield and Kurtz (1976) found American psychologists showing increased interest in Behavior Therapy and in eclectic practice. Although these were not the only trends noted, they were prominent. It seems clear to me that at least two other trends have been gathering adherents among psychotherapists. One of these is increasing interest in the cognitive therapies. Albert Ellis has continued to attract disciples. Other cognitive systems have appeared; they stand on the same basic assumptions but vary from Ellis's to a greater or lesser degree in theory, practice, or both (Beck, 1976; Greenwald, 1973; Mahoney, 1974; Maultsby, 1975; Meichenbaum, 1977).

The other significant trend I have noted among psychotherapists is a tendency toward rapprochement between behavior therapists and those of a cognitive persuasion (Mahoney, 1977). Most of the cognitive therapists cited above use behavioral techniques to some extent. Behavior therapists are also beginning to see the value of cognitive methods (Goldfried & Davison, 1976). At first glance such a joining of forces seems odd. In order to base their work on reliable and repeatable observations, behavior therapists have traditionally avoided inferences about internal processes such as perceptions, thoughts, and affects. Cognitive therapists, on the other hand, begin by violating this sacred behaviorist commandment.

What has happened? Both groups of therapists have had considerable success treating patients suited to their methods. As both groups have tried to handle a broader variety of cases, difficulties have arisen. "Narrow-spectrum" behavior therapists have had trouble handling complex human problems. They have also found simple cases becoming more complex when closely examined. Cognitive therapists have begun to learn the same lessons patients have been trying to teach insight therapists for years: A person can learn all the correct words without changing his or her behavior at all. Because of these troubles, the cognitive and the behavioral points of view have begun to merge. A halfbreed has been spawned: Cognitive-Behavior Therapy.

Verbal Behavior Therapy was one of the first of these cognitive-behavioral blends. As time has passed, it has developed further and now attempts to deal with other facets of behavior as well.

## CURRENT STATUS

Verbal Behavior Therapy bears kinship to a number of currently popular active-directive therapies. In line with the convergences described above, most of the "cognitive" therapies and most of the "broad-spectrum" behavior therapies share important basic assumptions and points of view while emphasizing theoretical and technical differences that have not yet been shown to have a great deal of impact on effectiveness. Consequently, training in approaches similar to these can be obtained in a variety of university centers and training institutes.

Some of the elements of Verbal Behavior Therapy—particularly the assessment procedures and forms—have been used by other therapists. These have usually been professionals employing behavioral methods.

Verbal Behavior Therapy as a system has not been extensively taught or promoted. Usually elements of the methods have been presented with clear acknowledgment of their behavioral or cognitive ancestry. For these reasons the system as a whole can still be studied only by reading my publications on it—see references—or by working with me at the University of Kentucky College of Medicine in Lexington. *Introduction to Scientific Psychiatry* (Storrow, 1967) remains the most complete account; although it is now out of print, a revision is planned. A brief account that covers different ground from this one was published in 1973 (Storrow, 1973).

## THEORY

I will begin each paragraph in this section with an assumption, assertion, or hypothesis basic to the theory underlying the system and will amplify it in the sentences that follow. The most fundamental principles are those of behavioristic learning theory: classical and instrumental conditioning. I employ, however, a broader definition of behavior; I also use many of the principles of Bandura's version of social learning theory (1977).

The goal of psychotherapy is behavior change. This notion is, of course, fundamental to all behavioristic psychotherapies. It provides an anchoring point that has been invaluable to the clinician—in choosing and changing treatment tactics—and to the investigator—in trying to learn what tactics work best with which problems.

Behavior can be either overt or covert. Overt behavior—speech, actions, and physiological changes—is, in principle at least—publicly observable, either directly or through instrumentation. Overt behavior is the sole focus of change for the "narrow-spectrum" behavior therapies. It is not, however, the only behavior of interest when one deals with humans. Covert or subjective behavior—perception, imagery, thinking, emotions—is of equal or greater interest: as a target of, or an instrument for, change. The two kinds of behavior differ only in accessibility to observation. Overt behavior can be observed and described by anyone with the necessary training; observations can thus be checked for reliability and accuracy. Covert behavior can be observed only by the person behaving; it is not now possible to check such observations in the same fashion. In outpatient practice, however, even this distinction often breaks down; much of the time all we have to work with is the patient's report, whichever kind of behavior is the focus of interest.

Although the human organism always behaves as a whole, for practical purposes it is useful to consider behavior as falling into a number of more or less well-defined categories. We can then check each of these categories as we go about our assessment and treatment planning tasks. The categories I use are:

1. Overt or objective behavior
   a. Actions
   b. Speech
   c. Physiological activity
2. Covert or subjective behavior
   a. Perception
   b. Imagery
   c. Thinking
   d. Emotions

Each of these categories—facets, modalities—of behavior can be, and often is, influenced by one or more of the others. A person's actions, for example, can be a function of speech, physiological activity, perception, imagery, thinking, and/or emotions. Similar equations can be written for the other modalities.

When a given facet of behavior is abnormal or maladaptive, corresponding abnormalities appear in one or more of the other categories. This means that a therapeutic program can be set up to change a given facet of behavior by changing another modality of which it is a function. For example, depressed patients often describe patterns of withdrawal from customary activities coupled with almost obsessional ruminations about personal worthlessness and inability to cope with overwhelming demands. The depressive mood—even when accompanied by the physiological changes we call vegetative signs—may lift in response to a therapeutic attack on the withdrawal (actions) and on the depressive ruminations (thinking).

If a behavioral abnormality is accompanied by corresponding abnormalities in several other facets, a treatment program aimed at multiple facets may produce more lasting change than one aimed at a single facet. This is Lazarus's (1976) multimodal hypothesis. Although I consider it reasonable enough to serve as a general guide for therapeutic planning, it has yet to be proven.

All categories of behavior are strongly influenced by the current environment and can be molded through the well-known processes of simple learning: classical or respondent conditioning and instrumental or operant conditioning. The many successes of behavioral treatment programs based on these principles—for example, token economies—adequately illustrate this point.

In the case of human beings, however, the more complex processes of vicarious learning and cognitive control provide what is usually a safer and more rapid route to new behavior. A child usually doesn't have to experience the aversive experience of being struck by a car in order for the behavior of "running in front of cars" to be suppressed. Often a strongly worded explanation will suffice (cognitive control). Certainly a child's future behavior will be strongly influenced if he or she ever sees another child struck (vicarious learning). A more commonly seen example of vicarious learning is the role-reversal technique in assertiveness training where the patient takes the role of the menacing authority figure while the therapist stands up to him in the role of the patient. Both these processes—vicarious learning and cognitive control—are discussed extensively by Bandura (1977).

Finally, what about the problem of determinism versus free will? This has plagued psychotherapy system builders for many years—although many system builders have elected to ignore it. The trouble is that a therapist must accept some form of determinism in order to believe that his or her efforts can have an impact on another person; at the same time he or she must accept some form of free will in order to explain why patient improvement so frequently occurs only in the company of patient behaviors labeled as "trying" or "making an effort." Bandura (1977) handles the dilemma in the neatest fashion I have encountered—by advancing the notion of "reciprocal determinism." Behavioral causality is a two-way street. A person is influenced by his or her physical and social environments, but the person's behavior also influences the environments. The obvious fact that a person exerts a considerable degree of control over his or her own acts need not be ignored in order to be "scientific"; it can be explained. Reciprocal determinism also provides a rationale for the "self-control" procedures that have become so important a feature of current behavioral psychotherapies.

## METHODOLOGY

Verbal Behavior Therapy—similar to a number of other systems of psychotherapy—can be usefully viewed as divided into three somewhat overlapping phases: opening, middle, and closing.

The opening phase of treatment sets the therapeutic stage by accomplishing a number of preliminary tasks associated with helping the patient become accustomed to his or her role in therapy and with the clinical assessment of the problems. The tasks needing attention—though not necessarily in this order—are: adaptation, diagnostic investigation, and negotiating the therapeutic contract.

Adaptation means giving the patient a chance to become accustomed to the therapeutic setting before demands are made on him or her. It also involves establishing the therapist as a source of reinforcement. As the patient begins to like the therapist and to desire to please him or her, the therapist's approval can begin to be employed as a reinforcer for effortful activities required of the patient, such as completion of homework assignments. The tasks of the adaptation period are accomplished primarily by establishing an empathic, warm, and authentic therapeutic climate and by making demands on the patient only as he or she is clearly ready to handle them. It is also helpful if the therapist can provide a bit of immediate relief for patient discomfort—by prescribing a minor tranquilizer, for example.

The diagnostic investigation involves a complex set of tasks that are the keystone of the entire treatment. Here's what needs to be done:

1. Inventory symptoms and problems
    a. Personal Data Form
    b. Case Study Form
2. Identify symptoms and problems
3. Identify central symptom or problem
4. Pinpoint therapeutic targets
    a. Central symptom or problem
    b. Other important therapeutic targets
5. Gather baseline data
6. Functionally analyze therapeutic targets
    a. What intensifies problem behavior?
    b. What alleviates problem behavior?
    c. Stimulus antecedents of problem behavior
    d. Consequences of problem behavior
7. Specify goals for each therapeutic target

I continue to label this phase the diagnostic investigation even though I know that diagnosis is a red-flag word for many therapists. I wish to emphasize the notion that here we are attempting a task similar to what confronts the physician in daily practice: the search for functional relationships that will aid our efforts to relieve the patient's complaints. At the outset we don't know whether we are dealing with the symptoms of a disease process or what has been called "problems of living." In many cases we won't know the answer to that question until research yields us more answers.

The inventory of symptoms and problems involves collecting a data base covering the patient's complaints and describing his or her functioning in the various areas of living. I use two forms to aid me in the search. The Personal Data Form is completed by the patient, and the Case Study Form guides and structures the diagnostic interview or interviews. Both may be found in *Introduction to Scientific Psychiatry* (Storrow, 1967).

In spite of the apparent objectivity of behavioral approaches, when treating outpatients we must still depend primarily on the patient's report even in the case of behaviors that, under ideal conditions, could be directly observed. We should therefore try to use interview techniques that inject the least possible bias into what our patient tells us. These seem to be interventions that involve minimal therapist activity, interventions such as those taught generations of insight therapists. These points are dealt with in detail in my book (Storrow, 1967).

Data gathering should aim at discovering all the problems that could possibly merit attention and then winnowing the list to those that will be the focus of treatment. Central symptoms or problems—if they are discovered—always merit attention. These are problems that appear early and appear to be the core around which other problems develop. If they are treated effectively, entire problem complexes often improve with them. Other important therapeutic targets are distressing symptoms or problems that appear to have a life of their own and thus need to be treated separately.

The functional analysis is then focused on the therapeutic targets. It involves looking for environmental antecedents and consequences just as in a strictly behavioristic functional analysis. Beyond this, however, we look for problems in behavioral categories, other than the target, that precede, accompany, or follow the target behavior. These other problems may then be treated along with a direct attack on the target. For example, an anxious patient often thinks frightening thoughts as he begins to panic. A good treatment plan may be to couple a direct attempt to reduce the anxiety with relaxation training and an attack on the harmful thought patterns with cognitive reeducation.

We should next try to formulate reasonable goals for each target problem. How will the patient behave when our task is complete? The goal may be complete cure or something short of that. Deciding upon a reasonable goal involves considering a number of different factors, such as how long the problem has been present, the nature of the problem, the accessibility of relevant treatment variables, availability of proven techniques for the problem under consideration, and so forth.

Negotiating a therapeutic contract usually completes the opening phase of treatment. The therapeutic contract expresses the goals and conditions of treatment as well as the rationale for each and asks for the patient's agreement to each point. Each item should be presented and negotiated, not imposed. This helps to insure patient cooperation as treatment proceeds.

Treatment conditions are both general and problem-specific. General conditions are those that seem to favor success regardless of the specific treatment measures being employed. I ask patients to make commitments to be honest with me and to take responsibility for their behavior, both during the interviews and between them. Problem-specific conditions are just that: tailored to specific problems, goals, and treatment plans. For example, many of my treatment plans involve homework assignments to practice relaxation, to ask for a date, to speak up in class. I outline what will be expected and ask the patient to commit him- or herself to the requirements.

Treatment planning in Verbal Behavior Therapy—as in other behavioristic psychotherapies—is much more difficult than in more traditional approaches. Instead of one treatment for every problem there are many problem-specific methods. Most of these were devised by behavior therapists, but some—and commonly used ones at that—come from the cognitive therapy tradition. As time goes on, we shall probably employ promising maneuvers from Gestalt and the experiential therapies.

I shall not try here to outline the details of specific therapeutic techniques. The verbal behavior therapist must be catholic in choosing and learning techniques to employ. Most of the common behavioral methods may be found in Goldfried and Davison (1976). Methods for using homework assignments, which I strongly favor, are covered thoroughly in Shelton and Ackerman (1974). For cognitive reeducation, which I find myself using more and more frequently, I prefer Beck (1976) and his Socratic approach to Ellis (1962) and his strident argumentation.

I have one caveat for therapists wishing to move in the directions I advocate. Don't try to incorporate a new technique until you have made every effort to learn it thoroughly. Read about it carefully, try to obtain some competent supervision, and practice it. Otherwise it will probably fail to perform as advertised, and you'll give up on something that could have been useful. The essence of Verbal Behavior Therapy lies in its structure, in its emphasis on a growth-promoting therapeutic climate—rare in the behavioral tradition—and in its approach to assessment. Its essence does *not* lie in a specific bagful of technical tricks.

Selection of therapy tactics depends to a considerable degree on the kind of problem being treated. For "behavior surplus" prob-

lems where we wish to decrease the frequency and/or intensity of some behavior—such as anxiety—there are extinction and counterconditioning techniques, such as flooding and desensitization. For "behavior deficit" problems where we wish to increase the frequency and/or intensity of some behavior—such as assertiveness—such techniques as role playing and positive reinforcement can be employed. Complex methods, such as cognitive reeducation and homework assignments, can be applied to both kinds of problems.

The question of whether specific target problems can be treated effectively and efficiently by concentrating directly on the problem alone or perhaps on one other behavioral category of which the target is a function cannot be settled with data at present. Lazarus (1976) would say we should perhaps treat the entire "BASIC ID," that is, all the behavioral categories where abnormalities can be found corresponding to the target problem. My own solution is to treat central symptoms as intensively as possible and to do the same with other symptoms and problems that prove to be treatment resistant. I'm likely to treat other problems in a simpler and more direct manner.

In the middle phase of treatment the therapeutic plan is implemented with most of the attention focused on the central symptom or problem, if one has been identified. Progress—or the lack of progress—is monitored by continuing to keep logs of problem frequency or intensity and comparing the new data with baseline findings. If improvement can be demonstrated, its presence serves as a reinforcement for continued effort on the part of both patient and therapist. If no improvement occurs in a reasonable period of time, this serves as a signal to recycle the data to see if there has been an error in assessment, treatment planning, treatment application, and/or patient cooperation. Opportunity is thus available for another try with the error or errors corrected.

As target behavior changes approach the levels specified in the goals, termination should be considered. This brings us to the closing phase of treatment. I like to think of treatment termination as proceeding through four stages: the preclosing stage, the confrontation, the closing stage, and the postclosing stage.

The preclosing stage begins during the middle phase of treatment. As treatment proceeds I try to keep the patient's attention focused on all the hours between treatment sessions. This helps to prevent him or her from valuing the sessions so highly that it will be difficult to give them up. Both of us review events between sessions, focusing on both successes and difficulties. One of the reasons I favor homework assignments so highly is that they help to keep emphasis on those hours of daily life between sessions. I thus strive to prevent my patient from construing our sessions as a way of life. Termination is then much easier when the time comes.

The confrontation comes when I decide that termination may be in order and raise the question with my patient. At this point the notion is "for discussion only." If the patient accepts the notion, we move to the closing stage. If he or she objects, we take time to discuss what our new goals may be, should we decide to continue. I try not to drift aimlessly, although with some patients that's hard to do.

The closing takes a month or so after the patient has accepted—or even first mentioned—the idea. It provides time to discuss what may happen should we actually stop seeing each other. Even patients who at first seem eager to close may have second thoughts later. This stage gives us an opportunity to discuss them.

The postclosing stage continues indefinitely after closing. I make clear to the patient that no known form of treatment for mental disturbance insures against relapse or the development of new problems. I say that I will be happy to communicate with him or her later, should the patient feel it is necessary. We can then decide if further treatment is in order.

## APPLICATIONS

When Verbal Behavior Therapy was initially developed during the early 1960s, systematic desensitization stood out as a behavioral treatment effective for phobic patients and applicable in outpatient as well as inpatient settings. Its full range of application was not known, however, and is still not completely known today. At that early time other behavioral therapies were developing—many of them based on the operant model—but they flourished best in inpatient units where readymade opportunities were available for the careful observation and recording that characterized these procedures.

As a psychiatrist interested in treating neurotic outpatients, I wondered if a system were available to extend behavioral techniques to all such patients, rather than to phobics alone. It seemed at that point that I would have to devise one myself. If patients could be relied upon to make their own behavioral observations and if the biases in self-reports could be minimized through good interview technique, it seemed possible. Thus Verbal Behavior Therapy was born.

As one might expect from this thumbnail sketch, the system seems best suited to neurotic outpatients. It requires a good deal of voluntary cooperation on the part of the patient, though, and works less well with less responsible patients. But then, no form of psychotherapy works particularly well with such individuals; they often won't even take medication as directed. As other behavioral methods, it seems to handle best those patients whose problems can be precisely defined—such as phobics and obsessive-compulsive persons—and perhaps less well for those patients whose problems defy precise definition—such as patients with existential angst. This latter distinction, however, seems less clear-cut now that the scope of the method has been extended with increased attention to covert forms of behavior.

Patients with personality disorders respond poorly to all forms of psychotherapy. They are likely to be uncooperative and to drop out prematurely. Although Verbal Behavior Therapy doesn't solve these problems, its no-nonsense emphasis on present problems and on behavior change probably gives these patients a better shake than do the traditional insight psychotherapies.

My own conviction is that much of the behavior that falls in the psychotic spectrum is not treatable with psychotherapy alone. Some problems that occur in psychotic patients—such as social skills deficiency—can be helped with psychotherapy, however. These difficulties, in my opinion, clearly respond better to behavioral interventions than to traditional therapies.

And finally, a clear limitation: the patient who enters treatment expecting to be helped toward insight. This patient is usually widely read along self-help lines and is sometimes familiar with some of the technical psychotherapy literature. To use Verbal Behavior Therapy with this patient requires a careful and ample explanation of its rationale, an explanation that often amounts to salesmanship. Otherwise he or she is likely to drop out of treatment without announcing that intention. Then he or she goes elsewhere.

## CASE EXAMPLE

When Mrs. Morse began her treatment with Verbal Behavior Therapy, she was a 33-year-old married woman with one small child. For the previous five years she had been almost continuously tortured with frightening and guilt-provoking obsessions. She had been hospitalized twice and had received several electroconvulsive treatments about three years previously during the first period of hospital care. These treatments had altered her clinical condition hardly at all. She had also previously received a great deal of fairly traditional insight-oriented psychotherapy with little impact on her symptoms.

At the time Verbal Behavior Therapy began, the patient was taking rather large doses of a medication containing both a tricyclic antidepressant and a major tranquilizer. She

began therapy about a week after discharge from the hospital for the second time. She stated she was feeling "a bit better," but her clinical condition was essentially unchanged from that illustrated in the brief history given above.

At this point the following diagnostic investigation was recorded, and the problems listed below were identified:

Problem 1.   Obsessions. Frightening and guilt-provoking thoughts intrude on the patient's consciousness in spite of almost constant attempts to exclude them.

Problem 2.   Agoraphobic syndrome. The patient is frightened of leaving home unless accompanied by her husband or her child. She has not left home alone for two years. Although she has a driver's license, she has not driven a car, either alone or accompanied, for almost three years.

Problem 3.   Deficit in assertiveness. Patient describes herself as shy and unable to defend her rights.

The obsessional thoughts were of two kinds clearly distinguished by the patient. First were "bad thoughts," thoughts of causing harm to her child, usually by strangling or stabbing him. Second were "fear thoughts," thoughts about being harmed by someone else, about her symptoms becoming worse, about becoming completely incapacitated, and so forth. Both kinds of thought were accompanied by guilt, intense apprehension, and painful muscle tension involving usually the back of the neck, the shoulders, upper back, and upper arms.

The apprehension and the mobility deficit that characterized the agoraphobic syndrome arose out of concern that her fright might increase, at almost any time, to the point that she would lose all control of herself. If such a crisis should occur when she was away from the safety of her home, something disastrous might happen. *What* might happen was unknown.

The deficit in assertiveness was a problem of lesser importance. The patient had found it difficult to stand up for herself "all my life." She did not appear to be greatly disturbed by this problem, and its intensity did not seem to vary in relation to the other two.

### Identification of Central Symptom or Problem.

Although this patient's deficit in assertiveness was of lengthy duration and meets the central symptom criterion of first appearance, its onset and fluctuation apparently were unrelated to the two problems that bothered Mrs. Morse the most. It was therefore not a central symptom. Since Mrs. Morse was not particularly concerned about this problem, it would not be the focus of treatment efforts at this point.

The obsessional thinking antedated the agoraphobic syndrome. Furthermore, the two problems appeared intertwined. The patient, for example, thought that fear of leaving home could be "punishment" for the "bad thoughts." It appeared that the obsessional thinking was a central symptom and that it should have the top priority for treatment. Note: Even though Mrs. Morse clearly distinguished two kinds of obsessional thoughts, they were treated as one problem because they clearly varied together and because available treatment methods were the same for both.

### Pinpointing Therapeutic Targets.

Our therapeutic targets were: (1) Obsessions—the central symptom; and (2) agoraphobic syndrome—also very troublesome to the patient.

### Gathering Baseline Data.

After we had defined the behavior illustrative of the two therapeutic targets as carefully as we could, Mrs. Morse started keeping a frequency log for both. She kept her counts in a pocket spiral notebook that she carried with her at all times. One week of data keeping showed obsessional thoughts to occur at the rate of 35 to 40 times per day. The behaviors we chose as indices for the intensity of the agoraphobic syndrome occurred at the following rates per day: Leaving house alone—0, Driving car alone—0, Driving car while accompanied by a family member—0.

Note that since the rates of all behaviors of interest were reasonably stable, one week's recording seemed adequate for a baseline. If the rates were more variable from day to day, a two-week recording period would have been employed.

### Functional Analysis of Therapeutic Targets.

The obsessional thinking was intensified when the patient was alone and "taking it easy." The worst time was when she was sitting at the kitchen table drinking her midmorning coffee. The problem was alleviated when stimuli for competing responses were present, when she had "something else on my mind" or when she had "something else to do." The stimulus antecedents appeared to be a relative lack of stimuli that might be expected to lead to competing behavior. The immediate consequences were aversive affects such as guilt and apprehension. The only positive consequences I could identify were the conversations she had with her husband about these thoughts. These conversations occurred almost nightly.

Note that obsessions leading to what appear to be aversive affects are difficult to explain in operant terms. I believe that patients subject to these problems are unusually concerned about hostile thoughts. They watch so closely that they attend to thought fragments that most of us ignore.

The agoraphobic syndrome consisted of both aversive affects—primarily fear—and inhibition of action—failure to leave home, to drive, and so forth. The action inhibition was always maximal; the patient never left home alone. The apprehension, however, varied and was intensified whenever an occasion to leave the house arose—for example, when groceries were needed. The feelings were alleviated under the opposite circumstances. The consequences of staying home were obvious; Mrs. Morse's husband helped her shop for groceries and took over many other responsibilities that usually are handled by homemakers.

Behavior in another category was also related to the components of the agoraphobic syndrome. When apprehension was high, the patient was aware of thinking: "I'll get out, and I won't be able to get back. I'll be trapped."

***Goals for Each Therapeutic Target.*** Our goal for the obsessional thoughts was to reduce their frequency to zero. This was probably a bit ambitious, considering the usual prognosis for such problems. The goal for the agoraphobic syndrome was also somewhat grandiose: The patient would be able to go comfortably anywhere she chose.

The treatment plan made the primary focus the obsessional thinking. The first step was to deprive the behavior of the positive reinforcement that might be coming from discussing it with the husband. The patient was asked to discuss these problems only with me. The next step was an effort to reduce the frequency of the problem behavior with self-administered aversive stimulation. Mrs. Morse was instructed to "shout" the word *stop* to herself each time she became aware of either a "fear thought" or a "bad thought." If this measure failed to interrupt the thinking sequence after being employed three times, another measure was to be used. The patient was to go to a preselected place in the home and to think the obsessional thought over and over until she could do so no longer. This procedure is designed to make the symptomatic behavior itself aversive and thus reduce its frequency.

A separate therapeutic plan was designed for the agoraphobic syndrome. This was a graded series of homework assignments. Mrs. Morse was instructed to walk a greater distance from her home each day and to keep a careful log of her performance. A similar series of assignments was later applied to driving the family car. The negative thoughts connected with fear of leaving home were also carefully considered in an effort to alter them. The patient agreed that, in actuality, she was rarely "trapped," that she could almost always return home if panic should occur.

Mrs. Morse agreed to the treatment plan and to the general conditions for treatment. Throughout our work together she completed her assignments faithfully. This was probably one of the primary reasons for the success we attained.

As treatment progressed, the only additional measure employed was relaxation training to counter the muscle tension the patient experienced when she was frightened.

*Obsessional Thinking.* There was a gradual reduction in this problem behavior over a period of four months. One major interruption in this decline occurred when the patient was called upon to participate in a relative's wedding. At the end of this period Mrs. Morse needed the treatment measures only occasionally, and the obsessional thoughts were noted on an average of once or twice per week. This degree of improvement has been maintained for one year. Medication has been discontinued.

*Agoraphobic Syndrome.* There was gradual improvement over a period of about five months. At the end of this period Mrs. Morse was able to drive alone for all ordinary household errands. Distance from home was no longer a problem, although she still avoided heavy traffic and crowded shopping center parking lots. She could shop in crowds, however, if someone else drove her to the shopping center. She was satisfied with this degree of improvement and did not wish to work on the problem further. Improvement has been maintained for a follow-up period of one year without medication.

## SUMMARY

Since psychoanalysis began to lose its hold—some say stranglehold—on the discipline of psychotherapy in the middle 1950s, the field has become progressively more chaotic and confusing. If there is a single principle of therapeutic importance that has been settled beyond dispute, I'm not aware of it. These are exciting times, but they are also difficult times for both therapists and patients.

Verbal Behavior Therapy represents one therapist's attempt to bring some order to the field. It has several virtues. Although it rests on the firm foundations of a consistent theory, it has the flexibility of technical eclecticism. It has the highly structured qualities of the behavioristic psychotherapies plus the breadth that comes from a broadly conceived definition of "behavior."

Designed for outpatients and tested mainly with them, this approach recognizes the reliance that must be placed on patient reports. It therefore strives to incorporate systematic assessment procedures that reduce the bias often found in such reports.

Today's practitioner of psychotherapy must make choices from a supermarket of competing theories and techniques. He or she must do so with very little hard data to go on. My recommendation would be that he or she look for an approach that is systematic but flexible, and that has room for new developments as they come along. Verbal Behavior Therapy is such a system.

# REFERENCES

Anderson, C. M. *Beyond Freud: A creative approach to mental health.* New York: Harper, 1957.

Bandura, A. *Social learning theory.* Englewood Cliffs, N.J.: Prentice-Hall, 1977.

Beck, A. T. *Cognitive therapy and the emotional disorders.* New York: International Universities Press, 1976.

Dollard, J. and Miller, N. E. *Personality and psychotherapy.* New York: McGraw-Hill, 1950.

Ellis, A. *Reason and emotion in psychotherapy.* New York: Lyle Stuart, 1962.

Garfield, S. L. and Kurtz, R. Clinical psychologists in the 1970s. *American Psychologist,* 1976, **31,** 1–9.

Goldfried, M. R. and Davison, G. C. *Clinical behavior therapy.* New York: Holt, 1976.

Greenwald, H. *Decision therapy.* New York: Wyden, 1973.

Kelly, G. A. *The psychology of personal constructs.* New York: Norton, 1955.

Kuhn, T. S. *The structure of scientific revolutions.* Chicago: University of Chicago Press, 1962.

Lazarus, A. A. *Multimodal therapy.* New York: Springer, 1976.

Mahoney, M. J. *Cognition and behavior modification.* Cambridge, Mass.: Ballinger, 1974.

Mahoney, M. J. Reflections on the cognitive-learning trend in psychotherapy. *American Psychologist,* 1977, **32,** 5–13.

Maultsby, M. C. *Help yourself to happiness.* New York: Institute for Rational Living, 1975.

Meichenbaum, D. *Cognitive behavior modification.* New York: Plenum, 1977.

Phillips, E. L. *Psychotherapy: A modern theory and practice.* New York: Prentice-Hall, 1956.

Rogers, C. R. *Client-centered therapy.* Boston: Houghton, 1951.

Shelton, J. L. and Ackerman, J. M. *Homework in counseling and psychotherapy.* Springfield, Ill.: Charles C Thomas, 1974.

Storrow, H. A. Learning, labeling, general semantics and psychotherapy. *General Semantics Bulletin,* 1963–64, **30, 31,** 84–86.

Storrow, H. A. Psychotherapy as interpersonal conditioning. In J. H. Masserman (Ed.), *Current psychiatric therapies,* vol. 5. New York: Grune & Stratton, 1965.

Storrow, H. A. *Introduction to scientific psychiatry: A behavioristic approach to diagnosis and treatment.* New York: Appleton, 1967.

Storrow, H. A. Verbal behavior therapy. In Ratibor-Ray M. Jurjevich (Ed.), *Direct psychotherapy.* Coral Gables, Fla.: University of Miami Press, 1973.

Watson, J. B. Psychology as the behaviorist views it. *Psychological Reviews,* 1913, **20,** 158.

Wolpe, J. *Psychotherapy by reciprocal inhibition.* Stanford, Calif.: Stanford University Press, 1958.

# CHAPTER 66

# Z-Process Attachment Therapy

ROBERT W. ZASLOW

*Around 1955, when we were both graduate students at the University of California in Berkeley, Bob Zaslow was known as an innovator. And so it was no great surprise for me to learn that he had developed a new system of psychotherapy known as "Rage Reduction." When I heard that in this method, patients were held down physically and tickled, I remember thinking, "Yup, that's Bob, all right."*

*However, until I received this chapter, my only knowledge of Z-Process was from informal conversations and items from the popular press and news magazines. But what I had learned was enough for me to realize that this was a significant, controversial, innovative psychotherapeutic technique.*

*On reading this chapter I was pleasantly surprised to learn that Z-Process has a most meaningful rationale, and that the process that offends most people on first learning about it gets to make sense after one understands its rationale.*

*On a number of points the theories of Freud and Zaslow seem to be complete opposites. On those points where they conflict, it seems to me that Freud was wrong and Zaslow is right: Freud is wrong in considering the major cause of maladjustments to be conflicts between sexual drives and social sanctions. It is rather lack of attachment and separation that are at the heart of maladjustment. The problem of psychotherapy is to help individuals form new attachments. As an Adlerian, I find Zaslow's system fascinating in terms of its agreement with individual psychology theory.*

Z-Process* Attachment Therapy is a system of human bonding applicable to disturbances in the attachment process throughout the life cycle, from infancy to adulthood. Functional psychological disorders, ranging from the less severe behavior and personality problems to the major psychoses, are viewed fundamentally as attachment disturbances in face-to-face relationships that result from anger, rage, and resistances, the negative core behaviors of psychopathology. The face is seen as the focal area of human bonding and is responsible for the integration of perceptual, cognitive, emotional, and sensorimotor behavior necessary for behavioral equilibrium. Z-Process Attachment Therapy is designed to reduce pathological resistances, to facilitate attachment and growth, and thus to liberate the individual. It is a comprehensive high-energy therapeutic system in which high arousal is activated to a peak of full rage. The assumption is made that the therapeutic effectiveness of the rage reaction is maximized with face-to-face and eye-to-eye contact under the control of the therapist while the person's body is securely held. Z-Process is effective in reducing resistances to therapeutic progress and, in so

---

*Z-Process was originally known as Rage Reduction. Z in ancient Greek means "he is alive."

doing, dramatically transforms behavior and attitudes.

The system was developed by Robert W. Zaslow with the assistance of Marilyn Menta.

## HISTORY

### Precursors

One may go back to the Bible and view the bonding of Isaac for sacrifice by Abraham as an early example of the resolution of destructive aggression through the handling of resistances. The test was to not resist God's command to sacrifice Isaac and to not resist God's command to stop the sacrifice. Through a resolution of his resistances arising from repressed rage, Abraham demonstrated his trust in God, and an enduring attachment was formed between Abraham and his son Isaac.

According to Nathan Ausubel (1948), exorcism is illustrated in Jewish medieval tales. People afflicted by physical or mental illness were brought into the synagogue and surrounded by a *minyan,* or 10 men required for religious services. The group would surround the afflicted one and then provoke him into extreme anger. The demon would then find that body uncomfortable and be forced to leave. The affliction would vanish following the rage reaction.

According to Robert Harper (1959) Sandor Ferenezi, a psychoanalyst, was an early pioneer in the therapeutic holding of people. He held patients on his lap in an attempt to treat them like children to resolve their childlike conflicts. He thus hoped to generate a feeling of trust, love, and affection. However, he discontinued this process because much anger and hostility would emerge that he could not handle in a one-to-one situation.

Lester Witmer (1922) described a treatment of an apparently autistic boy who went into intense rage while being held. The boy eventually learned that Witmer was in control. Once the bonding was established, the process of learning and socialization could then begin.

In the education of Helen Keller by Anne Sullivan as portrayed in *The Miracle Worker* (Gibson, 1973), Helen is depicted as a wild and uncontrollable creature who only relates to people on her own terms and whose temper tantrums could not be handled. Only by literally fighting it out through a persistent and intense confrontation was Sullivan able to establish the bond from which the "miraculous" growth experience occurred. The reduction of Helen's rage was achieved through conditions of persistant contact, physical control, and the pursuit of a specific issue (folding a napkin and sitting at the table).

Both Witmer and Sullivan were unencumbered by complex theory. They engaged in a natural act of attachment with these children, for they could see a temper tantrum for what it was. They controlled it in a constructive and appropriate manner. Without a theory, their results were somewhat incomprehensible to other professionals, so that this approach was not carried on by others. An observer may see these encounters as a wild scene and not appreciate the significance of the high-arousal behavior as a release of energy to form attachment bonds.

A recent precursor is an intrusive method of therapy developed by Nora Waal (1955), a Norwegian child psychiatrist. She describes her treatment method as involving physical holding, body stimulation, manipulation of tense limbs, and hugging in both a soothing as well as a provocative manner. Waal also uses rhythmical tickling, touching, stimulation of the eyes, and the encouragement of looking and peeking games. Screaming, weeping, anger, biting, and kicking are verbally accepted and supported by the therapist until the child's reactions change to positive responses. Z-Process is also similar to the Will Therapy of Otto Rank (1947), in which the negative will of the patient is confronted and resolved by the positive will of the therapist.

The ideas of Charles Darwin (1965), who commented on the use of rage to overcome grief, and Konrad Lorenz (1963), who stated that the more aggressive species bond best, also support Z-Process theory.

## Beginnings

The first Z-Process holding took place in August 1966 with a five-year-old normal child, Ted, who was not toilet trained. This writer thought the boy should be held like a baby because he acted like a baby by resisting toilet training. I fully expected Ted to go into rage when held, as a sign of his immaturity, anger, and resistance. The incident was precipitated by the parents' sense of urgency because Ted was soon to enter kindergarten and previous therapeutic attempts had failed.

Ted's mother was aware and accepted the fact that a new procedure would be tried. Ted was asked, "Why are you here [in my office]?" Ted responded, "Because I go in my pants." He was asked, "Who goes in their pants, big boys or babies?" Ted answered, "Babies," so he was told he would be held like a baby. Ted said, "You're kidding." I replied, "I'm not kidding," and quickly lifted him onto my lap, face upward, holding him tightly.

The "good" boy went into a rage reaction, a temper tantrum. Mother was reassured that no harm was being done. Ted was asked to answer one simple question before being let go. "What do you want to be, a big boy or baby?" Instead of answering, Ted continued to rage. Finally Ted quieted down and said, with his eyes blinking, "I want to be a big boy." But his voice was full of protest and he moved his body in an irritated fashion. At this point I felt justified in adding a new condition, namely that the statement should be made with full face–eye contact with no motor reactions revealing conflict.

Ted was asked to repeat "I want to be a big boy" every time he moved his foot, coughed, closed his eyes, raised his eyebrows, or moved. Finally Ted looked fully into my eyes and said, "I want to be a big boy" in a comfortable, calm manner with good body equilibrium. Ted was then released.

I then wanted to change Ted's immature, indirect expressions of rage and resistance into more direct aggressive behavior. I told Ted to show anger like a big boy by hitting the palms of my outstretched hands. Ted began to do this and then broke into a grin, saying, "I don't want to do it any more." Following this sequence of controlled aggression I found that Ted and I felt close. I spontaneously said, "I love you," and the boy replied, "I love you," and we hugged each other.

I then tested Ted's resistance to being controlled by telling him to sit on a chair. Ted started for the chair, then changed his mind and ran to his mother. He was held again and he raged again for just a few minutes, then settled down and gave a good response to me. Then he got up and sat in the chair.

Mother received counseling, mainly to treat the boy like a five-year-old and encourage him to show appropriate aggression. The next day, to my amazement, the mother reported that Ted went to the toilet without resistance. A six-month follow-up revealed that Ted remained toilet trained, was doing well in school, and had changed from a passive boy to an assertive one.

Several months later another child was held, four-year-old Sylvia, who had a history of asthma, allergies, hyperactivity, and temper tantrums. I requested that the child be taken off allergy medication and used the same procedure that had worked for Ted. Sylvia went into a temper tantrum immediately. She also showed her rage by yelling, "I want to get a knife and stab you." And then later, "I want to burn your house down." After handling Sylvia's rage by prolonged holding, she became calm and peaceful and said, "I want to be a big girl," with full face–eye contact. Prior to the holding she was offered a chocolate chip cookie which would normally give her an asthma attack. Sylvia had fearfully rejected the cookie. After the session she was again offered the cookie and she popped it into her mouth with a smile. The expected asthma attack never occurred. The child was seen and held once a week for a month. The immediate results, supported by a four-year follow-up, revealed that all the presenting symptoms disappeared and no medication was necessary since the first holding.

I realized that the effects achieved in the two therapeutic processes just described were significant for behavioral science. Holding seemed to be a very powerful therapeutic technique that might be beneficial in a variety of psychological and psychosomatic disorders. *Activated resistance and rage could be therapeutically beneficial when controlled and reduced by holding with face–eye contact.* I discovered that each therapeutic issue and the resistances surrounding it had to be resolved before the next issue could be dealt with effectively.

The therapeutic knowledge gained concerning attachment was applied in holding and interview settings to wide range of psychological disorders in children and adults. A period of creative excitement prevailed from 1966 to 1972. During this period, over 200 children and adults underwent Z-Process Attachment Therapy. Surprisingly effective results were achieved in a short period of time. Well over 1,000 holding sessions were administered by this writer and by parents of children with no harmful effects.

## CURRENT STATUS

The teaching of Z-Process Attachment Therapy is centered at San Jose State University in California where specific courses in Z-Process were developed by 1970. Courses have been taught at the University of California at Santa Cruz and San Diego. Graduate students at San Jose State University have done much of the work with the Z-Process with respect to research, clinical application, training, professional presentations, and published articles.

Donald Saposnek (1972) reported significant improvement of autistic children who underwent Z-Process Therapy. Menta (1972), in a psycho-educational research project for the Los Angeles City school system, showed significant social, behavioral, and educational improvement with autistic and schizophrenic children treated with Z-Process. John Allan (1977) used reactions to touching and holding as diagnostic indicators of resistant behaviors in autistic children. Allan (1976) also published an article on correcting problems with difficult babies through the use of holding. Cremer (1973) showed the positive effects of Z-Process in reducing hyperactivity in children using mothers as holders. Schreiber and Pirtle (1979) made a formal analysis of Z-Process with the aim of developing psychotherapeutic programs.

Replication of the Z-Process approach to adolescent schizophrenia was done by James Carpenter (1976). Robert Freidman (1970) adapted Z-Process holding as a diagnostic technique for young children. Freidman (1978) also demonstrated parent effectiveness training using the holding technique in the treatment of omnipotent and behavior problem children. His results of 75 percent successful treatment approximates the 80 percent effectiveness I obtained with children having similar problems.

Foster Cline (1978) reported the successful use of Z-Process with nonpsychotic children to the American Association for the Advancement of Science.

Menta and I have co-authored three books on Z-Process: *The Psychology of the Z-Process* (1975), *Face to Face with Schizophrenia* (1976) and *Rage, Resistance, and Holding* (1977). These books were based upon an earlier volume by this writer, *Resistances to Growth and Attachment* (1970).

## THEORY

The attachment process continues throughout life; that is, the primary bond of the infant to the mother grows into attachments between family members, peers, children, spouse, country, home, religion, and all aspects of life. The attachment bond is the basic foundation for social behavior, psychological growth, and development and must continue to evolve into significant relationships in life.

The basic premise of Z-Process attachment theory is that psychopathology is fundamentally a disturbance of attachment (Zaslow, 1970; Zaslow & Menta, 1975). More specifically:

The face is the essential and focal area of social interaction. Human attachment is primarily achieved through face-to-face orienting reaction. . . . *all functional behavior disorders are the result of disturbances of attachment to the face.* Major resistances to human attachment is centered upon the face. (Zaslow & Menta, 1975, p. 10)

John Bowlby (1977) came to the same general point of view.

Attachment theory conforms to the ordinary criteria of a scientific discipline. Advocates of attachment theory argue that many forms of psychiatric disturbance can be attributed either to deviations in the development of attachment behavior or, more rarely, to failure of its development. Persons, including the therapist, may be being influenced and perhaps seriously distorted by the experiences which he had with his parents in the past. While especially evident during early childhood, attachment behavior is held to characterize human beings from the cradle to the grave. (p. 201)

Bowlby, however, does not propose any specific therapy based on attachment principles to deal with these disorders. Essentially he relies upon conventional therapies. Z-Process attachment theory focuses upon the role of aggression as it either facilitates or disrupts human attachment. Freud's (1933) libido theory postulated two primary drives, sex and aggression, but did not adequately deal with aggression and its components of rage and resistance.

Gregory Zilboorg (1941) quotes Ludwig Jekels: "his great need for love was an obstacle to Freud . . . because he discovered so late that in the development of man, hate is the forerunner of love." Zilboorg also quotes Freud: "It may be that this is the meaning of William Steckel's contention that hate and not love is the primary emotional relationship between men. At that time that Steckel wrote this, it seemed to me inconceivable."

In psychoanalytic thinking, transference is considered to be a resistance and a form of neurosis. The negative phase of transference is thought to be indispensible for therapeutic progress. Negative transference is a resistance characterized by heightened anger, negativism, and a general hostility of the patient toward the therapist. Both positive and negative transference may then be considered as an expression of the attachment process, with the negative phase being therapeutically important in correcting the distortions or disturbances of attachment bonds. Z-Process Therapy dramatically and rapidly goes through the transference cycle, thus speeding and facilitating the entire course of therapy.

A theory concerning aggression must concern itself with two important behavioral characteristics. The first are the negative emotions of hate, anger, and rage, and the second are the *resistances* that are dynamically linked to these emotions. When we are angry, our resistances and negativism increase. Resistance frequently appears in the form of overt aggression. On the battlefield, the aggressors and resistors of aggression are both locked in combat committing acts of aggression, but their behavior is indistinguishable by an observer. When rage and anger are covert, repressed, or inhibited, aggression ceases to be a bold biological act in constructive or destructive forms. Instead, repressed anger and rage generate stress that appears in the form of feeling hurt, suffering, grief, and a general negative attitude toward life. Repressed hate and hostility now appear in insidious forms, as psychological disturbances, since they are not openly faced and resolved through constructive assertion. Many clinical symptoms represent an indirect way of showing hostility and anger to people. In Z-Process Therapy, we say to a suffering client, "hurt hides hate." Bowlby (1960) states: "It is my belief that there is no experience to which a young child can be subjected more prone to elicit intense and violent hatred for the mother figure than that of separation. . . ." It is common for broken, deep attachments to produce rage. Bowlby (1961) also writes: "Looked at as a means that in other circumstances aids the recovery of the lost object and the maintenance of union with it, the anger characteristic of mourning can be seen to be biologically useful." He claims that after an initial positive bond is formed between mother and infant at about six months of age, the infant reacts to the loss of his mother in three characteristic stages: (1) Protest (crying and rage) that serves to bring the mother back; (2) if this is not successful, a period of despair follows characterized by withdrawal, depression, and a decrease in activity; (3) detachment characterized by unresponsiveness to people.

A key theoretical assumption in Z-Process is that individuals suffering from various degrees of protest, grief, despair, and detachment must be brought to an active state of protest to develop adequate biological energy to form attachment bonds. Protest in the Z-Process theory is rage and resistance, and it is by holding a person in a state of face-to-face protest that positive attachment can develop and broken attachments repaired.

The ethologist Konrad Lorenz (1963) has noted that bonding between young and mother is much stronger in the aggressive species. One may infer that the stronger the aggression is in a species, the stronger is the expression of hate, anger, and hostility when attachment bonds are threatened or disrupted.

Breger and I (1969) state:

The stress to relaxation cycle may be considered the basic unit of comforting. The greater and more intense the initial stress reaction, the greater the relaxation at the end of the sequence. An insufficient number of such holding experiences may lay the foundation for weak and early disrupted

relationships which may, in time, prove a precursor to autism and other disturbances in childhood. (p. 252)

The critical experiments of Harlow (1958) with baby monkeys and mannikin mothers vividly demonstrates that when adequate holding interactions do not occur, detachment and behavioral disturbance result.

The development of Z-Process attachment theory for treating psychopathology began with the challenge presented by the extreme form of detachment of an autistic child. This child, who was not separated from the mother, was not conceived by authorities to have an attachment problem, even though the child was obviously detached from people. The positive results that this approach achieved in attaching this autistic child became the basis for a general theoretical model for the treatment of attachment disturbances applicable to a wide range of psychopathologies.

The human face is the focus of the dual emotional expressions of love and hate, nurturance and aggression. It is the focal center of human communication and human bonding. Consequently a theory of aggression centers on face-to-face interactions, in contrast to Freud's emphasis upon the genitals and his avoidance of the face in therapy. Z-Process interprets the face as a *face*, important for attachment, and a primary area of the expression of aggression and love.

Ronald Laing (1960) reports that schizophrenics are fearful of looking into someone's eyes because they might be "turned into stone. . . . a sense of being in danger from the gaze of the other. . . . to the schizoid individual, every pair of eyes is in a Medusa head which he feels has a power actually to kill or deaden."

The Oedipus myth is best understood with respect to a disruption of early attachment and unresolved rage. When all was revealed, Oedipus took his *eyes* out, instead of castrating himself. This act reflects the importance of the eyes as a focal point of attachment to the face. Thus the Medusa complex emerges as more fundamental than the Oedipus complex. The mother of Oedipus becomes the Medusa that he could not face, for if his eyes remained intact, Oedipus would psychologically turn to stone. The ultimate pathological example of the Medusa complex are autistic children who show the most extreme avoidance of face–eye contact and go into stress and rageful resistance when attempts are made to force them to look at the human face. They stare through you in a manner that implies that they have psychologically turned to stone.

Z-Process incorporates specific attachment principles into a therapy system. These principles consist of holding, rage, and resistance.

*Holding* is an important attachment behavior for it continues the fetal condition being held in the womb externally and allows the development of comfortable body contact through handling. From this is formed a positive bond essential in the development of basic trust that Erik Erickson (1950) claims occurs in the first year of infancy, a period of frequent holding and frequent infant high arousal.

The *rage* reaction is the most powerful unified reaction that an individual can mobilize. Although basically it evolved as an attack behavior to counter physical or psychological threat, this great biological energy has therapeutic value. It has a special quality of being conflict- and resistance-free; thus, under the proper conditions, negative hostile behavior is transformed into positive loving behavior when done face-to-face. The psychobiological effects of the rage reduction is similar to that of the sexual orgasm in that it reaches a peak and then produces relaxation and closeness.

*Resistance* is a necessary organismic act for autonomy. Frequently this is seen as a negative reaction leading to a negative form of autonomy. It also may lead to premature autonomy in which a child acts omnipotent, like a baby. A viable autonomy is a system balanced between positive and resistant behaviors, all of which support growth and positive attachment. Negative resistances

prevent the formation and growth of attachment bonds that may result in disorganization of behavior and eventually result in emotional disturbances. Positive resistances, as in immunization, protect and facilitate growth.

When resistances are to intimate physical and face-to-face contact, then the attachment bonds are more severely disturbed, resulting in the severe psychoses of the schizophrenias. Resistances frequently appear as inappropriate or incorrect responses to a question. They may be conscious or unconscious and may appear on the verbal, emotional, or body-movement levels of behavior. They are derived from a chronic anger that must be exploded as rage to reduce resistance. Covert resistances do not manifest the underlying anger and rage supporting them. Z-Process activates resistances, which, in turn, makes the anger and rage manifest. When the rage is resolved, the resistances *collapse*. As a consequence, the energy locked into the unresolved angers and resistances is now freed for productive integrative growth. Through the handling of rage and resistances, attachment bonds are repaired, strengthened, and revitalized to continue the evolution of the self. Z-Process allows this to occur safely and securely for the therapist as well as the client. This is schematically shown in Figure 1.

## METHODOLOGY

The basic method of Z-Process treatment is a holding session, and the conditions vary depending on age level. A young child requires one adult holder, an older child may require two to four holders, and an adolescent or adult may require six to twelve holders. Following is a general model of Z-Process applicable to adolescents and adults.

### Preparation

The prospective client or client's parent has one or two interviews prior to the session. During these interviews case history material

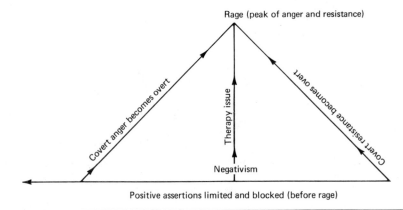

Rage (peak of anger and resistance)

Covert anger becomes overt

Covert resistance becomes overt

Therapy issue

Negativism

Positive assertions limited and blocked (before rage)

All energy now used for positive assertion (after rage)

is collected and the process is fully described, for the purpose of informed consent. Frequently prospective clients are shown a film of the treatment process. Clients are also told that they must give their permission to be held for a certain number of hours, even though they may want to get up. They are told they are expected to actively resist since the process depends on activated resistances to get good results. The client is informed that tactile stimulation (tickling) of the ribcage could be used in the therapy.

Written consent is obtained from the client, parents, or legally responsible adult, and a medical statement is obtained to assure the client has good physical health.

## Procedure

The client is held by a group of individuals composed of a head holder and body holders. The head holder holds the head region and engages in face-to-face verbal and tactile interactions with the individual held. The body holders hold the individual and apply counterpressure to tense or thrusting body parts. The holders provide information about body reactions (which may be resistances), thus giving feedback information to the head holder. The head holder, in whose lap the subject's head rests, coordinates and interprets information provided by the holders and generally directs the progress of the session.

During the holding session, tactile stimulation on the ribcage by the head holder or helper continue throughout the interactions, basically to maintain a biorhythm and to intensify the communications. Some Z-Process therapists choose not to use tactile stimulation and obtain good results. Tactile stimulation on the ribcage has the following functions:

1. The hand and finger can move lightly on the ribcage as a form of touch contact.
2. Tactile stimulation may be used to emphasize the verbal communication of the therapist with a rhythm of minor intensities.
3. In deep resistances such as found in psychosis, tactile stimulation may become intense at times and is found to be necessary in overcoming deep resistances. Bruising may occur as a side effect.

The amount of time spent in a single session may vary from 10 minutes with infants, two hours for children, and five hours with adults. The session is entirely under the supervision of a chief therapist, who guides other head holders, whether they be parents, role players, or trainees. These intermediary head holders perform certain roles as required, such as male or female, mother or father, husband or wife, sister or brother, or peers. Family members are part of the holding team and also act as head holders. This permits dealing with problems as they relate to the entire family. The Z-Process holding technique provides the conditions for control of the body and head, without which therapeutic change does not occur.

The holding session begins when the therapist asks the individual, "Do I have your permission to hold you?" The response is almost always affirmative; if not, the session does not take place. Adults lie down voluntarily and so do the great majority of children. Psychotics, unable to make proper judgments, may be held without their consent, providing legal consent is obtained.

## Reactions to Holding

It is a sign of basic trust when an individual can lie down and be secure when held. Young children sometimes start screaming and resist holding in a primitive, infantile manner, indicating that they have yet to learn basic trust. Some schizophrenics become very excitable when held, bouncing up and down in an agitated rhythm, reflecting their inner tensions. For them basic trust in being held is an alien experience with which they are not comfortable. Most individuals lie down feeling secure and comfortable until they are confronted with their problems. The holding session can be divided into three phases, as is chess, with its beginning, middle, and end game. The following are the phases of a single session.

*Phase 1.* The goals of this phase are:

1. Reviewing the client's problems in a conversational manner. The client's reactions and resistances are noted during this period.
2. Resolving the "Who's boss?" issue.
3. Evaluating and correcting body and verbal resistances of the client.
4. Eliciting expression of love—hate, yes—no, good—bad in varying degrees of intensity, and evaluating resistances to these expressions.

5. Establishing a comfortable body equilibrium within the subject as he or she responds to the therapist or head holder.

The first phase begins when the client has adjusted his or her body comfortably to the holding, and the holders have been given instructions as to how to hold and what their roles are. The session begins with a conversation between the therapist (head holder) and the client. The therapist explains the criteria or fundamental rule concerning *sensorimotor overflow:* When the subject blinks the eyes, looks away, sticks out the tongue, raises the eyebrows or closes the eyes, twitches any part of the body, extends the toes, becomes rigid, holds the breath or coughs, and so forth, these reactions will be considered a conflict and resistance, whether they occur prior, during, or after a response. If resistance behavior appears, then the therapist is to repeat the question or statement until the person can make the correct response to the face without resistance. This procedure establishes a good body equilibrium in the held individual.

The first issue is: *"Do you want to be a baby or a person your age?"* This issue is designed to measure the intention of the person to become *age-appropriate* and is used to determine the resistance one has to growth change. The answer as well as the signs of motor overflow are indicative of the degree of resistance to be expected in the session. This issue also defines the major purpose of the session.

The second issue is: *"Who's boss?"* The therapist, similar to the captain of a ship or pilot of an airplane, has a certain function to perform, which is reasonably accepted by the average individual. Bosses are a part of the human condition, and the therapist must be a good boss by helping the person resolve problems. The question is asked: *"I am being your boss so you can be a better what of yourself?"* The answer, of course, is *boss*.

This issue is the first significant confrontation between the therapist and the subject. It deals with the issue of mature autonomy versus premature autonomy. Premature autonomy refers to the tendency to blindly resist all attempts to be controlled, just as a child might with respect to a parent. This issue is a key one because many individuals have not been appropriately controlled or "bossed," which in turn makes it difficult for them to be self-controlled and be a good boss of themselves. *Positive control is a basic organismic need, which, if absent, produces emotional disturbance. The more severe the disturbance, the greater the resistance to control.*

The next issues relate to cognition and affect. The cognitive dimension deals with the capacity to say yes or no. Many people are evasive when it is important to give a definitive response of yes or no. The affective dimensions are expressions of love and hate and feelings of "good" and "bad." This procedure enables the individual to express a range of feelings and to be clear and certain about them.

When these polarities are locked in and well defined, one is less ambivalent and more capable of using a range of expressions that lie between them. When the cognitive and emotional dimensions are clarified, the individual becomes more integrated and communication is more effective.

*Phase 2.*    The goals of this phase are:

1. Explore family dynamics.
2. Explore and clarify the individual's self-concepts.
3. Confront and change negative attitudes toward family and self.
4. Further refine and stabilize the client's body equilibrium.

This phase takes up half of the session time. In her thesis, Menta (1972) showed that four autistic children made dramatic progress over a year's time.

While the first phase is fairly structured, the second phase tends to be somewhat fluid. To the casual observer it may even appear

wild at times because of the intensity generated and the rhythms of interaction. However, the therapist trained in Z-Process has a flexible but precise control over the situation. As the principles of the process are learned, one becomes aware of the high degree of logic, precision, and direction required to effect change.

During the middle phase the most dynamic confrontation of resistance occur, and it is in this phase that the client makes the most dramatic transformations. It deals with the specific dynamics meaningful for the individual with respect to family and to significant others. They are the same issues that commonly occur in individual and family therapy.

Specific issues that are frequently dealt with are sexual identity issues (which always includes asking the person *"Are you a man or a woman?"*), and early feelings of love and hate toward their primary family members, especially mother and father. This area includes a detailed exploration into childhood issues of love—hate, control, and attachment. The client must report at least one positive and one negative incident that occurred with each parent when the client was a child. After this is done and feelings about the client's present relationship with the primary family are explored, the person may be asked: *"What do they do now that makes you angry?"* There is a discussion about appropriate angers and how to express them constructively and what the appropriate feelings of love are.

Not only are the resistances of the held person taken up, but the resistances of any family member, such as father and mother, are also confronted during the session. If, for example, a teenager is being too controlled by his father and not permitted to exercise an appropriate amount of autonomy, the father's resistances on this issue are confronted. This is done while the teenager is being held by the father or a bodyholder. A child learns resistance from the parents; that is, there is a symbiotic tie-in of resistances between parent and child. Parents may resist, act stupid, or say they "don't know" in the same manner that the child does. It is easier to change the child's negative resistances after the parent's resistances have been confronted and handled.

*Phase 3.* The goals of this phase are:

1. Generally conversational to gain insight, explore and resolve residual issues and conflicts.
2. Discussion of future goals and follow-up work.
3. Demonstration of close feelings.

Whereas the second phase had much negativism and resistance, the third phase is characterized by cooperation, reasonableness, and productivity. The client has now gone through a confrontation of the critical issues and resistances that produce conflict in phases 1 and 2. He or she is more comfortable, integrated, acts more mature, thinks and communicates clearly and has a friendly, positive attitude to self and others.

A holding session is followed by a series of family or individual therapeutic interviews within two weeks in which the issues covered in the holding sessions are discussed and the progress of the client is evaluated. If necessary, one or more additional holding sessions may be required depending on the severity of the pathology.

## Therapeutic Principles

1. The therapist must be comfortably unafraid of the client's rage, which reassures the client that the therapist is in control; this reduces the client's omnipotent feelings that are reinforced by rage reactions. The therapist must be masterfully loving and not get into a verbal fight with the client.
2. Each issue and its resistances must be systematically resolved before a new issue is considered. Unresolved resistances are like cancer cells; they grow and block therapeutic progress.

3. The therapist must communicate clearly, precisely, and unambiguously to clarify the thinking and the feeling of the client and to prevent the client from resisting by exploiting ambiguity. The client has many answers that can be teased out by the proper use of questions.
4. The therapist must take the responsibility of adequate dominance and control in order to reduce the client's dependency by developing the client's self-control for mature, liberated autonomy.
5. The therapist must be capable of generating interaction rhythms of intensity between periods of relaxed conversation. Pathological resistances are reduced first by the dominating rhythm of the therapist and later by the use of verbal logic. The therapist must dominate the rhythm of interaction to develop the momentum of the session in a controlled direction for therapeutic goals. A basketball team that develops sufficient intensity develops a momentum that wins the game.
6. The therapist must generally maintain face–eye contact and attend to motor overflow in a holding session as well as in sitting in face-to-face interview.

## APPLICATIONS

Since attachment extends from birth throughout the life cycle, Z-Process Attachment Therapy is effective with a large group of disorders throughout the life cycle. The application of Z-Process is far-reaching. Many cases have been successfully treated, including:

1. The schizophrenias, such as early infantile autism, childhood schizophrenia, adolescent and adult schizophrenia
2. Depression
3. Neurotic disorders
4. Family and marriage problems

5. Growth experiences
6. Identity problems
7. Childhood disorders, such as colic, temper tantrums, hyperactivity, sleeping and eating problems, enuresis, and educational problems
8. Psychosomatic reactions such as asthma and allergies

## Early Infantile Autism

Z-Process Therapy was born out of an attempt to correct the attachment disturbances of autistic children. The behaviors of this child are compatible with attachment theory as an attachment deficit at the infancy level. Significant treatment successes have been achieved with such children. Of the three cases reported by this writer and Breger (1969), two of the autistic children progressed to essentially normal levels of behavior and are now in public schools. The third child's treatment was interrupted and did not progress. In her thesis Menta (1972) shows that these two children made intellectual and social progress over one year's time.

## Colic

Colic is a frequent disturbance in infancy. A special adaption of Z-Process Therapy has been used to handle colic successfully through the use of compression techniques that have the effect of initially increasing the intensity of the crying, but then reducing the crying and stress of the infant. Three two-minute applications of the technique over a 10-minute period have been found to be sufficient to transform the baby into a happy, peaceful, playful infant.

## Temper Tantrums

Temper tantrums have been called the normal psychosis of childhood. In a full-blown temper tantrum, a child is obviously in rage. In a classic temper tantrum, the child will fall on the floor, screaming and beating hands and feet on the floor. The temper tantrum is a diffuse immature rage, while the adult uses rage as a focally directed attack behavior or face-to-face confrontation.

One may use the holding technique for two purposes: First it may be used merely to control the child adequately, and second, if held in the Z-Process holding position, on the lap with face up, the child will feel closer to the adult when the rage subsides, and the energy displayed will be used for attachment rather than uselessly dissipated.

## Asthma

Asthma is viewed as a stress reaction of the respiratory system that is incompatible with a rage reaction. Z-Process holding in high-arousal rage reduces the stress of this system by making the individual's energy reach a uniform level throughout the body, thus reducing the focus of energy and stress in the bronchial system. The stressful inhalation of air in asthmatic breathing is replaced by the intense inhalation of air during the rage reaction. Significant success with asthmatic clients are achieved by Z-Process when medical conditions permit its use.

## Growth Experience

The following revealing self-report of a 21-year-old married student describes the general subjective effect of Z-Process application.

Life began for me only a month ago. Having a rage reduction [Z-Process] was the turning point between mere existence and the rewards of a fuller life. All my life I had been building a wall around myself, isolating myself from others as a defense against the projections of my personality that I attributed to others. As day after day passed, the wall grew higher, wider and more impenetrable. I know that I could trust no one; my mother and father had proven this to me. Nobody could understand the sensitive feelings that were so entangled in my heart and soul.

I know that I was not like anyone else. I fooled myself into believing that I really didn't want to belong or be like others, though I was constantly aware of my self-deceit. The wall I was erecting for my protection soared over my head, overwhelming and trapping me in a snare of my own design. I tried to rescue myself, but the walls were too high and thick and pressed too close to my body to allow me to make any movements other than squirming. I was depressed, lonely, and helpless.

I screamed for help several times. I could feel psychologists with conventional tools futilely gnawing at the outside of the impenetrable wall. I knew that my problem was unique and that I could not trust them and, unwillingly, I repaired what portion of the wall they had begun to penetrate. I felt so depressed and even more lonely during the next three years that I became desperate for help.

Every moment of the rage reduction was an eternity and after it was over, it seemed to have lasted only a few short moments. I had never had a boss and would not accept one willingly. I had to be convinced. After a short period of time I decided to have a boss of my eyes and mouth but would not accept a boss of my mind. Silly little games that I was playing seemed so disproportionately important. I exploded into a slight rage. I alternated rage with relaxation and waited for any of my holders to relax their grip so that I could break loose. Here I thought I was going beyond my knowledge.

I felt really secure knowing that I was in good hands and could not hurt anyone or myself when I lost control. I felt rather powerful, but not omnipotent, knowing that at times I was straining eight or nine holders in my rage. I found that I became most frustrated when the holders verbalized to me the nature of the games I was playing as a defense or resistance. I tried to vomit as a resistance but was thwarted when a chorus of holders verbalized my motivation. I tried every move, game, and resistance I could think of, with only negative results to show for my efforts.

I also raged when they hit me with characteristics of my psychological conflicts. I knew I wanted to be a man, that my physical structure was that of a man, but I didn't feel like one. Nor did I feel like a woman. I knew what I wanted to be, but not what I was. When the holders verbalized my ambivalence, it made me angry and put me into rage.

I was using my wagging tongue as a resistance until the holders caught on. As long as we were conversing aimlessly, I was able to put up with the annoyances such as the tickling and heckling. When verbalization became a one-way interaction between myself and a wall of silence, I became frustrated over losing this important crutch. This was a very effective technique on their part.

The morning following the rage reduction I awoke to prepare for class. I felt similar to a time when I was sitting on a rock below a cypress tree with the salt spray of crashing waves showering me, making me feel completely in tune with the natural environment. I felt completely relaxed and comfortable, being able to feel and coordinate every part of my body in an unfamiliar but pleasing way.

This "rebirth" that I mention began with the release of the static energy that had been building up inside of my mind and body for many, many years, freeing at least 95 percent of the anxiety and guilt feelings that had been obstructing my *normal* social, intellectual, physical, and emotional capabilities. Standing before my reflection in the mirror, I was a new and beautifully human face. It was as though I had been blind before and had miraculously been given back my sight. My face was so relaxed that I had my first and only close, smooth shave of my life. I looked at my naked body in the mirror and rejoiced over the wonderful, powerful feeling I felt knowing that I was indeed a man. Not a stereotyped James Bond, Hercules, or Paul Newman, but a real, everyday-type male specimen.

My relations with my employer have changed now that I accept him as a boss. I can now see through the ego games played by others and am no longer the sensitive victim of their play. I have found that everyone is plagued by psychological problems and that my problems are the same as many other people's (especially males, as I observed in a number of sessions). My problems were not as unique as I once believed them to be. Simply put, this realization has put me more in tune with the human race, making me feel that I am one of the many, an integral and important part of the race we call the human species.

I have also been able to confront both of my parents with the information and feelings that were uncovered in the rage-reduction sessions without emotional conflict. I no longer "cry over spilled milk" or search for the life I had longed for as a child and had missed. I am now living in the present, the reality, and am setting realistic goals for myself. I am more aware of my capabilities and my limitations, and it seems that I am no longer hostile and jealous of the success of others.

## CASE EXAMPLE

The case of Ana, a schizophrenic adolescent girl, is taken from *Face to Face with Schizophrenia* (Zaslow & Menta, 1976). Ana is one of a number of successfully treated cases documented by psychiatric and hospital reports as well as by videotapes of the Z-Process treatment with follow-up interviews.

In 1972 this writer and Menta were asked by Foster Cline, a psychiatrist in Colorado, to direct a Z-Process treatment program for a 16-year-old patient, Ana, who was hospitalized for a year with the diagnosis of schizophrenia. Ana had not responded to treatment, which included drugs, psychotherapy, and reparenting. About a year before her hospitalization she had become increasingly withdrawn from friends and family and adopted a wooden stick figure with a face, which she called her friend Green Eye Beam. She developed delusional systems with schizophrenic speech, called herself a "penguin," classified people in terms of pica or elite (picas being the inferior), burned her body with cigarettes, and claimed that she had died.

Her early history revealed that her biological father had been accidentally electrocuted when Ana was two. She obviously had been affected by this incident, for when she was requested to draw a person, she drew one in the form of an electric grid. All of these signs indicated that a strong process of detachment and depersonalization had developed. After her father's death, her mother became depressed and was separated from Ana for a period of one year.

Ana was a quiet and good child. When Ana was six years old, her mother remarried a man who had several children of his own. When Ana was 12 years old, her mother obtained a divorce and later remarried when Ana was 14 years of age.

Ana was affected by the two stepfathers, who had conflicts about showing feelings and affection toward her because of ambivalence concerning their own children. Another important factor was the symbiotic relationship between Ana and her mother. There apparently had been a continuing alienation within Ana, which developed as a schizophrenic break. This occurred shortly following the new marriage and was probably a reaction to it. Ana's developmental history was characterized by a series of broken attachments in which the only constant figure was her mother.

### Treatment Program

Ana was given a series of four-hour Z-Process sessions over a period of a month. Family Therapy, Peer Group Therapy, and an active physical program (such as swimming) was developed for a period of a month, after which Ana went with a tour group to Mexico City.

### Presession Behavior

Prior to her first session, Ana crouched between a chalkboard and wall and had to be led out of the room. She was asked to make several drawings, write a sentence, and have a conversation with the therapist. Her drawings were bizarre; the sentences incomprehensible to everyone but herself; and her conversation was illogically argumentative in defense of bizarre notions, such as that she was a penguin, she was dead, she was not born on the planet earth and, touching would burn her and lead to murder. Her initial attempt at lying down on the laps of the holders consisted of crossing her legs in the yoga position, a posture frequently observed at the hospital. Ana had poor face–eye contact in the presession interview.

### First Session

***Goal: Establish Communication, Face–Eye Contact, and Begin Affective Bonding.*** In the holding position, Ana was passive, but tension was obvious in her face. She closed her eyes and made strenuous attempts to turn her head away from the therapist, who gently but firmly applied counterpressure on the sides of Ana's face to maintain face contact. When asked a series of questions, such as "What is your name?" she said "Pykit." When tactile stimulation began on the ribcage, to break through the schizophrenic resistances, she erupted with, "Would you stop putting I P rays into me!" She was then shown the finger that was stimulating her and was asked, "What is this?" Ana at first insisted it was an "I P ray," but as the stimulation became intense, she called it a finger. After further stimulation she said her name was Ana. This was the beginning of normalizing communication and establishing identity. *The power of the tactile stimulation was critical in overcoming these first resistances.*

Later in the session when the female therapist was holding her head, Ana began to raise her voice and show intense anger. (We felt that a tremendous amount of hidden rage had become frozen in her flat affect.) Her anger developed in intensity, and she was confronted on her resistances in an escalating rhythm of verbal and tactile interactions. Ana became very angry as we pursued her resistances. Rage and intense hate surged out toward the female therapist when the issues began to focus on her feelings about being female and about her mother. She went into "burning" rage, screaming and verbalizing her inner feelings of hatred for her mother. She was encouraged and supported for her expressions of anger, loss of alienation that had been buried inside of her. By showing these feelings, Ana became *alive* and *real*. Following this rage reaction her delusional system began to collapse and her speech became calm and relevant with good face–eye contact. When she got up she was open and capable of receiving affection from others. Ana now repeated the presession tasks in a normal manner and was able to touch and be touched. The next day at the hospital Ana cheerfully showed us around and then packed her belongings to go home.

## Second Session

*Goal: To Reattach Ana to Mother Through the Direct Expression and Resolution of Rage in Face-to-Face Confrontation with Mother.* Our goal was, in effect, to resolve the Medusa complex. Two days later Ana came with her parents for the second session. Mother reported positive changes in Ana's behavior and agreed to hold Ana's head during the session. Guided by the therapists, mother confronted Ana about her feelings. Ana erupted into an even more intense rage and expressed her intense hate direct to her mother's face. Mother, who was at first fearful, was encouraged and shown how to *face* Ana's anger, yell back at her with intensity and take *positive control* over her daughter. This interchange enabled Ana and mother to become *reattached*. They began to feel close and loving toward each other, as demonstrated by full hugs and smiles. (With the expression of Ana's great rage toward her mother, the core of her psychosis was resolved—we had broken through Ana's rage barrier.)

The Medusa complex was revealed when Ana told her mother "I'll cut your head off." (Allan Brauer, a psychiatrist, had a schizophrenic patient who, in a holding session, said, "I'll tear your eyes out!" to her mother.) Love and hate feelings were resolved and affectionate bonding developed. She returned to school and became reunited with her peer group, some of whom participated in her sessions.

After a month's treatment, Ana went with a group of peers to Mexico and returned to high school, where she received excellent grades. At the end of the school year she was selected to be an exchange student in Sweden. Upon her return home she was upset to find a vivacious Latin American student occupying her room. Ana's sensitivities in this situation combined with her unresolved attachment problems and anger toward her stepfather resulted in her developing the symptoms of anorexia nervosa. Her psychiatrist began treatment, but her condition became severe.

Z-Process therapists were again called in to consult on Ana's new problem. Ana was unable to have a holding session because of her weak physical condition. We therefore modified the Z-Process approach for conventional Family Therapy. Six home visits of about three hours each were made during which time issues were confronted in a face-to-face sitting arrangement. The previous holding sessions had sufficient effect on Ana and her father to be a positive factor in the success of this further therapeutic effort. The climax of the therapy was a resolution of the angers between Ana and her father. Ana recovered from anorexia nervosa.

A few weeks later Ana was raped. This event did not hinder her positive progress. Ana thus demonstrated that she could deal with stress in a crisis situation. She became righteously angry and wanted justice. With the support of her father she took the rapist to court and he was found guilty.

A seven-year follow-up report revealed that Ana had no remissions and was adjusted to normal life. She is now working in an art gallery and has an additional job as a writer for a local newspaper.

## SUMMARY

Z-Process Attachment Therapy has taken on the challenge of handling rage, the missing link in psychotherapeutic systems. In a time when aggression, not sex, is the major problem, our ability to control this great biological force is a major survival task of our time. People have always been afraid of the destructive force inherent in rage, for the loss of control makes for two possible disasterous consequences: killing or going insane, and sometimes both.

The harnessing of this great force poses problems akin to those of atomic energy. Atomic explosions are not desirable, but controlled reactors are. A great fear of psychotherapists has been the potential rage reactions in their clients. Primarily therapists avoid evoking rage, thus compromising therapeutic aims. When therapists learn to face the rage of their clients in a safe and controlled manner, they may use their psychodynamic or behavior-modified skills to become dramatically more effective in handling a great range of therapeutic problems.

High-arousal–activated rage may be understood within the context of attachment theory as a form of protest behavior that occurs upon separation—the loss of or a threat of breaking the attachment bond. However, activated rage not only overcomes conditions of grief and detachment, but it also provides the psychobiological energy necessary for rapid and effective reunion, behavioral change, and attachment. When rage is properly handled, affectionate bonds develop to stabilize behavior.

Some professionals find it difficult to accept the widespread beneficial results of Z-Process because they think of rage in Newtonian rather than Einsteinian terms. To convert the biological energy of the rage reaction into positive constructive behavior through the reduction of resistances, rage must be brought to full peak to reduce negative resistance.

Many therapies have been influenced by this writer's early work in rage reduction, but the screaming therapies—Primal Scream and Scream Therapy—have failed to develop full rage reactions to the human face, which resolves the rage and the emotional problems positively.

For a number of years, extensive work on Z-Process Therapy has demonstrated that it is theoretically elegant and therapeutically beneficial.

## REFERENCES

Allan J. The identification and treatment of "difficult babies": Early signs of disruption in the parent-infant attachment bond. *The Canadian Nurse*, 1976, 11–17.

Allan, J. The use of holding with autistic children. *Special Education in Canada*, 1977, **51 (3)**, 11–15.

Ausubel, N. *Treasury of Jewish folklore*. New York: Doubleday, 1948.

Bach, G. and Goldberg, H. *Creative Aggression*. New York: Doubleday, 1974.

Bowlby, J. Processes of mourning. *International Journal of Psychoanalysis,* 1960, **42,** 317–334.

Bowlby, J. Separation anxiety. *International Journal of Psychoanalysis,* 1961, **41,** 89–113.

Bowlby, J. The making and breaking of affectional bonds. *Journal of Psychiatry,* 1977, **130,** 201–210.

Carpenter, J. C. Single case study change in a schizophrenic adolescent as a result of a series of rage-reduction treatments. *Journal of Nervous and Mental Disease,* 1976, **162,** 58–63.

Champion, R. A. *Learning and activation.* New York: Wiley, 1969.

Cline, F. W. Z therapy may aid non-psychotic, antisocial children. *Clinical Psychiatry News,* 1978, **5,** 50.

Cremer, J. Effects of a two week Z-process treatment program with hyperkinetic children. Master's thesis. California State University, Long Beach, 1973.

Darwin, C. *The expression of the emotions in man and animals.* Chicago: University of Chicago Press, 1965.

Erickson, E. H. *Child and society.* New York: Norton, 1950.

Freud, S. *New Introductory Lectures on Psychoanalysis.* New York: Norton, 1933.

Freidman, R. A rage-reduction diagnostic technique with young children. *Child Psychiatry and Human Development,* 1970, **1,** 112–125.

Freidman, R., Dreizen, K., Harris, L., Schoer, P. and Shulman, P. Parent power: A holding technique in the treatment of omnipotent children. *International Journal of Family Counseling,* 1978, **6 (1),** 66–73.

Gibson, W. *The miracle worker.* New York: Bantam, 1973.

Guirand, F. *Greek mythology.* Trans. D. Ames. London: Paul Hamlyn, 1963.

Harlow, H. F. The nature of love. *American Psychologist,* 1958, **12,** 673–685.

Harper, R. A. *Psychoanalysis and psychotherapy.* Englewood Cliffs, N.J.: Prentice-Hall, 1959.

Laing, R. D. *The divided self.* New York: Pantheon, 1960.

Lorenz, K. *On aggression.* New York: Harcourt, 1963.

Menta, M. Psycho-educational project utilizing Z-Process Therapy. Master's thesis. San José State University, California, 1972.

Rank, O. *Will therapy and truth and reality.* New York: Knopf, 1947.

Reich, W. *Character analysis.* New York: Noonday Press, 1965.

Saposnek, D. An experimental study of rage reduction treatment in autistic children. *Child Psychiatry and Human Development,* 1972, **1,** 50–52.

Scheiber, E. and Pirtle, R. The Z-process approach to psychotherapy: A formal analysis toward theory and integration. Master's thesis. Fresno State University, Fresno, California, 1979.

Waal, N. A. A special technique of psychotherapy with an autistic child. In G. Caplan (Ed.), *Emotional problems of early childhood.* New York: Basic Books, 1955.

Witmer, L. Orthogenic cases, Don: A curable case of arrested development due to a fear psychosis, the result of shock in a three-year-old infant. *Psychological Clinic,* 1922, **13,** 97–111.

Zaslow, R. W. *Resistances to growth and attachment.* San Jose, Calif.: San Jose State University Press, 1970.

Zaslow, R. W. and Breger, L. A theory and treatment of autism. In L. Breger (Ed.), *Clinical-cognitive psychology: Models and integration.* Englewood Cliffs, N.J.: Prentice-Hall, 1969.

Zaslow, R. W. and Menta, M. *The psychology of the Z-process.* San Jose, Calif.: San Jose State University Press, 1975.

Zaslow, R. W. and Menta, M. *Face to face with schizophrenia.* San Jose, Calif.: San Jose State University Press, 1976.

Zaslow, R. W. and Menta, M. *Rage, resistance, and holding: Z-process approach.* San Jose, Calif.: San Jose State University Press, 1977.

Zilboorg, G. *A history of medical psychology.* New York: Norton, 1941.

# Glossary

| | |
|---|---|
| ACTION THERAPY | A democratically oriented method of group psychotherapy, using psychodramatic techniques for diagnosis, treatment, and training. Its goals are openness, self-disclosure, and the giving and receiving of feedback with mutual cooperation, incorporated into Natural High Therapy. |
| AFFINITY RESPONSE | The free and insightful ratification of an affinity reaction after it has been appraised as congenial and congruent. |
| AFFIRMATION | A short positive statement repeatedly used to introduce new beliefs and patterns. |
| AFFIRMATIVE OPPOSITE | A recycled admonition. Example: Love is the affirmative opposite of hate. |
| AFFIRMED FORMATION DIRECTIVE | A formation consciously and rationally opted for or ratified. The affirmation is based on insightful appraisal of one's life experiences seen in light of the foundations of one's formation tradition. Not only the life experiences but also the experiential foundations of the formation tradition and their accidental accretions are raised to the level of focused consciousness and distinguished from one another. After the process of appraisal and subsequent affirmation, the affirmed direction is allowed to sink into the preconscious life attention and to remain operative there until the life situation calls for its reappraisal. |
| AIKIDO | An oriental martial art based on subduing an opponent through harmony rather than opposition. |
| ALEXANDER | A method for retraining the body to eliminate parasitic, unnecessary, inefficient movements. Originated by F. Mathias Alexander, an Australian actor. |
| ALIENATION | The condition of being separated from one's potentialities for work relationships, thought, or feelings. The consequence of mystified oppression in isolation. |
| ALPHA FEEDBACK | The feedback of alpha rhythm to the patient. The alpha rhythm can be as slow as 8 cycles per second or as fast as 13 cycles per second. Standard electrode placement is over the occipital lobes. |
| ANCHORING | Establishing a memory trigger through physical contact connected with a desired feeling or behavior. |
| ARMORING | The total expression of the individual of holding back. Armoring is characterized by pulled back shoulders, a pulled up thorax, a rigidly held chin, shallow respiration, an arched lower back, a retracted and "dead" pelvis, and stiffly stretched out legs. |

| | |
|---|---|
| ASSERTIVENESS TRAINING | A process whereby the client is taught to speak up whenever he or she believes an injustice is done. |
| ASSETS-DISCOVERY | A process, regardless of which technique is used to bring it about, of identifying one's inner resources and strengths, and learning how to capitalize on them in everyday life. |
| AUTOGENIC STANDARD FORMULAS | Suggestions made to induce warmth, heaviness, reduced breathing and heart rate, cool forehead, and so forth. |
| AWARENESS | Consciousness, information, and understanding about the facts of oppression. |
| BATACAS | A pair of rubberfoam (pillowlike) "encounter-bats" with which intimate opponents—for example, couples—can hit but not hurt each other during rule-governed hostility rituals in Creative Aggression. |
| BELTLINES | Tolerance limits for physical and verbal assaults by which foul fighting behavior is differentiated from fair during Creative Aggression procedures. |
| BILATERAL EMG | An electomyographic technique in which the muscle tension of the left side of the face is measured simultaneously with the tension of the right side of the face by two instruments. Sensors are placed on the temple and masseter of each side. With this measure tension can be studied during bite and swallow. |
| BODY ARMOR | Chronically tense musculature sensitive to pressure that impedes breathing and the flow of life energy. Holding the breath by constricting the musculature is the process by which emotion is repressed and body armor is formed. |
| BOUND FLOW | Body movement that appears tense or restricted because of increased opposition between agonist and antagonist muscles. |
| CABBIE POSITION | A sitting position in which the weight of the body rests in the pelvis, the arms are lying loosely across the thighs, hands are not touching, the head is slightly forward. |
| "CALLING CARDS" | The presenting complaints of clients as they seek psychological help. |
| CHAKRAS | An Indian spiritual term designating a center or vortex of energy. There are seven main chakras said to lie in the center of the body from the perineum to the center of head. |
| CHAOTIC MEDITATION | A type of meditation in which participants experience a period of total catharsis—screaming, jumping, pounding—and a period of quiet contemplation. |
| CHARACTER ARMOR | The sum total of the character attitudes that an individual develops as a defense against anxiety, resulting in character rigidity, lack of contact, "deadness." Functionally identical with muscular armor. |
| COEX SYSTEMS | A specific constellation of memories consisting of condensed experiences and related fantasies from different life periods of the individual. The memories belonging to a particular COEX |

system have a similar basic theme or contain similar elements and are associated with a strong emotional charge of the same quality. The deepest layers are derived from infancy while more superficial layers involve memories of similar experiences from later periods of life.

COGNITIVE RESTRUCTURING TECHNIQUES — Any psychotherapeutic technique aimed at having the client reassess through rational processes his attitudinal set or belief system regarding a specific situation or problem, or, more generally, regarding his self-image. Inner dialogue, assets-discovery, and covert rehearsal are all cognitive restructuring techniques, as is the challenge for the client to redefine problems as opportunities.

CONGENIAL TRANSCENDENCY — The surpassing and subsequently the modulation and integration of one's nuclear life form, of past current life forms, and of the historical, vital, and functional determinants of one's life in a way that fosters increasing disclosure and realization of one's uniqueness as a person in the light of the foundations of one's chosen formation tradition.

CONGRUENT TRANSCENDENCY — The surpassing and subsequently the modulation and integration of the nuclear life form, of past current life forms, and of the historical, vital, and functional determinants of one's life in a way that ensures the highest integration of the current life form with one's life situation without diminishing the essential congeniality of this life form.

CONNECTION — A process in which the client experiences a meaningful bond.

CONNECTED — Being in touch with and/or aware of thoughts, emotions, and body reactions that help create a sense of meaningful involvement.

CORE OR NUCLEAR LIFE FORM (CORE OR NUCLEAR SELF) — The relatively enduring ground form of life formed during the period between birth and early adulthood. In later life it is usually not changed fundamentally, but is continuously modulated by the succession of current life forms.

CONSCIENTIZATION — The bringing to focused awareness of formation directives that actually give form to life, be it on a pre-, infra-, or supraconscious level.

CONTACT — Validation feedback protection and strokes that come from a mutual support group.

CONTIGUITY MEDIATIONAL MODEL — Albert Bandura's explanation that observational learning follows the verbal and imaginal coding of the interaction of the model with the environment.

CONTRACT — A mutually agreed upon statement of the changes a person wants to accomplish in therapy.

CONTRACT SESSION — The initial meeting between psychotherapist and client. This session is for the exchange of expectations and giving of information.

COSMIC SHADOW — Carl Jung's concern in his later years, that God, being incomplete, relies on the individuation of humans for the energy necessary for divine completion.

| | |
|---|---|
| COVERT EXTINCTION | Imagining a response to be decreased and then imagining the reinforcement maintaining that response is not presented. |
| COVERT MODELING | Imagining observing a model performing a behavior and then imagining particular consequences. |
| COVERT NEGATIVE REINFORCEMENT | Imagining an aversive stimulus and then imagining the response to be increased immediately after imagining the aversive stimulus to be terminated. |
| COVERT PROCESSES | Unobservable behavior labeled as thoughts, images, and feelings, or physiological processes that take place beneath the skin. |
| COVERT REHEARSAL | An imagery technique in which the client is asked to imagine himself effectively handling a difficult situation. He may repeat the visualization over and over, incorporating different alternatives each time. |
| COVERT REINFORCEMENT | Imagining a response to be increased, followed by the image of a pleasant scene. |
| COVERT RESPONSE | Same as convert processes. |
| COVERT RESPONSE COST | Imagining a response to be decreased and then imagining the loss of a reinforcement. |
| COVERT SENSITIZATION | Imagining responses to be decreased and then imagining an aversive stimulus. |
| CREATIVITY-TAPPING TECHNIQUES | Any technique that assists a client in reassessing a familiar situation in new ways or actualizing latent creative potentials. Such techniques may focus on thinking or actual performance. An example is to imagine oneself solving an algebra problem in the fashion in which a famous mathematician would approach it. |
| CURRENT LIFE FORM | The transitional form that life assumes in reaction and response to a life situation and/or to a new disclosure of a person's uniqueness. This change usually implies a modulation of the nuclear form of life and offers an opportunity for a more nuanced disclosure of the uniqueness of one's personality. |
| DEATH AND TRANSFORMATION WORKSHOPS | Weekend didactic-experiential groups, focusing on the ultimate death and/or diminishment of participants and their significant others. Exercises revolve around action therapy, active imagination, and art and music therapy. |
| DEFORMATIVE ATTACHMENT | A clinging to worn out formation directives no longer relevant and effective in a period or situation of life and/or no longer congenial in view of new disclosures of the uniqueness of the personality. |
| DEFORMATIVE DETACHMENT | The ratification of deprivations undesirable in a new period or situation of life. |
| DEMANDMENTS | Internalized sentences, often unconscious, having an arbitrary, "must" quality that lead to discouragement. |
| DEMONIZING | The absolute rejection and condemnation of an absolutized (idolized) life form when one experiences disappointment in regard to this form. |

| | |
|---|---|
| DIAGNOSTIC BASELINE | A base level of psychophysiological parameters usually obtained under conditions of rest or standard stimulus conditions. These recordings are obtained before treatment and provide a basis of comparison with other patients and normals. |
| DIRECTEDNESS OF FORMATION | The overall pattern of formation that life follows as a result of the interaction of various formation directives operative in the person. |
| DIRECTIVE DISCIPLINES | Disciplines such as the history of ideas, spirituality, philosophy, theology, ethics, and the study of formation traditions that can enlighten people in their appraisal of formative directives. |
| DISCOUNT | A transaction that invalidates another person's experience. |
| DISSIPATIVE STRUCTURES | An open nonequilibrium system characterized by a high degree of energy exchange with the environment, which creates instabilities or fluctuations that drive the system toward high entropy productions within a new, dynamic regime that creates a new state of complexity. |
| DOUBLES | Psychodramatic technique used to guess at another's thoughts, feelings and purposes. |
| DYSTONIC LIFE FORM | The life form insofar as it is uncongenial with one's emergent uniqueness and incongruous with one's life period and life situation. |
| EFFORT/SHAPE SYSTEM OF MOVEMENT ANALYSIS | A system of describing qualitative change in body movement in terms of exertion of energy and body adaptations in space. |
| EGO CONSTRICTIONS | The process or result of diminishing one's innate self-esteem and social interest, in favor of gaining power or influence from others. Such thoughts, feelings, and actions become ego-addictions, part of any identity other than the self-identity of actualization. |
| EGO-NOISE | Putting one's psyche above or below others in an attempt to gain interpersonal power and ego-esteem. |
| ELECTROMYOGRAPH | An electronic instrument that can detect and amplify electrical potentials generated within muscles. The potentials measured are on the microvolt level. |
| EMOTIONAL CHARGE | A build-up of emotions, especially anger, rage, or hurt, stored in the body/psyche. Analogous to the build-up of electrical energy in a capacitor. |
| ENEMY | The "Big Parent" or the portion of the personality that enforces externally imposed oppression. |
| ENERGY FLOW SYSTEMS | Systems for working with the electromagnetic vital energy that runs through the body. This energy is called "Chi" or "Ki" or "Prana" and runs along paths known as meridians or "nadis." |
| ENVELOPE | A psychophysiological term used to refer to tracings that lie within limits of certain values. |

| | |
|---|---|
| EXPERIENTIAL | The "lived" sensed, and felt aspect of one's presence to the formative meaning of people, events, and things that constitute formation situations for self, others, and world. |
| EXPERIENTIAL PLAY PAPER | A prescientific description of the spontaneous experiences of certain directives that play a formative role in one's own life and the lives of others in order to gain access to these experiences and their formative influence. Such play papers are a remote preparation for prescientific and scientific reflections on the formative experience disclosed this way. |
| EXTINCTION | Extinction takes place when a response no longer occurs because the reinforcer that has been maintaining the response is removed. |
| FALSE KNOWLEDGE | Incorrect belief structures about Reality. |
| FASCIAL TISSUE | Connective tissue that surrounds muscles and muscle groups. A collaginous, protective tissue. |
| FEEDBACK | Sharing of thoughts, feelings, and purposes without labeling or demanding changes. Rational, objective information. |
| FELDENKRAIS | A method of functional integration of the body through training the nervous system to be aware of all the options available to it. |
| FOCUSING | The placing of attention on a particular point of interest such as a thought, an emotion, or a body reaction. |
| FOLLOW THE FLOW | An intuitive empathic ability and behavior of the therapist who "goes along" in his feelings and thought with the words, actions, and feelings of the client. |
| FORMATION | Unconscious process of realization of a characteristic form each living being, event, or thing is tending toward in accordance with its nature and conditions. |
| FORMATIVE ATTACHMENT | A commitment to formative directives relevant and effective in the present period or situation of life and congenial with the present awareness of the uniqueness of the person. |
| FORMATIVE DETACHMENT | The ratification of privations appraised as desirable in a new period or situation of life seen in the light of one's emergent uniqueness and chosen formation tradition. |
| FORMATION DIRECTIVE (OR LIFE DIRECTIVE) | An ideal life form or aspect thereof that operates preconsciously as one of the guiding principles of the unique formation of one's life. |
| FORMATION REACTION | Any reaction insofar as it is related to the formation of one's life. |
| FORMATIVE READING | A slowed-down, reflective way of reading whose primary focus is not information but transformation of one's life. |
| FORWARD CONDITIONING | The conditioned stimulus followed by the unconditioned stimulus. |
| FOUNDATIONAL CONSTITUENTS | Those primary constituents of a core or current life form that sustain all secondary manifestations of this life form and prevent their structure from tending toward dissolution. |

| | |
|---|---|
| FOUNDATIONAL DIRECTIVE DISCIPLINES | Primary constituents of a formation tradition or other directive discipline that support all the secondary aspects of the formation model it proposes. |
| FOUNDATIONAL SPIRITUALITY | A formative theory of personality that distinguishes between the foundations of the formative spirituality a person is committed to and the accidental additions to these foundations. |
| FREE FLOW | Body movement that appears loose or relaxed because of minimal opposition between agonist and antagonist muscles. |
| FRONTALIS (EMIG) FEEDBACK | Feedback of electromyographic potentials obtained from electrode placement on the forehead (frontalis muscle) directly above each eyebrow. It is customary to refer to the electrode placement as a frontalis placement so as not to imply that frontalis activity alone is fed back. |
| FUSION | A blind, identification with another person's life form at the expense of one's own congenial and congruent self-formation. |
| GSR (BIOFEEDBACK) | The Galvanic Skin Reflex is a change in the electrical properties of the skin. In biofeedback, GSR responses are presented to the patient as information about his own physiological activity. |
| HAIRCUT | A ritualized one-way dressing down, by permission, for fouls and other hurtful offenses, optionally followed by a "Doghouse-release"—a technique that facilitates forgiveness and making up. |
| HAMSA MANTRA | The natural vibration of the Inner Being, the Self, which occurs spontaneously with the incoming and outgoing of the breath. The literal translation is "I am That." |
| HEALTH SWEEP IMAGERY | Imagining that a liquid or other substance is flowing through one's body, starting from the head and going down to the toes, cleansing the body of all disease and pathology. |
| HUMORDRAMA | A group method to teach and learn the sense of humor based on a psychodramatic format. Participants soliloquize their thoughts and feelings while playing their stressful situations. Doubles then use such techniques as brief sudden swithches, employing verbal condensations, understatements, and overstatements to generate the humorous attitude. |
| IDEALIZING | The uncritical exaltation of a potential life form without excluding totally, as in idolizing, the worth of other forms of life. |
| IDIOPANIMA | Empathy relative to another's feeling for one's self. *What I think you think of me*. |
| IDOLIZING | The irrational absolutizing of the value of a life form to the exclusion of any other life form as equally valuable, including one's own potential form of life. |
| ILLUSIONARY RESONANCE | The affirmative reverberation of a potential formation directive in experience not due to a real but to an imagined congeniality and congruity. |

| | |
|---|---|
| IMAGE ENVY | The distress experienced when appraising another's potential or actual life form as more desirable for oneself than one's own potential life form. |
| IMPLOSIVE THERAPY | Imagining an intense anxiety-producing situation for long periods of time without escaping. This procedure is assumed to extinquish the avoidance response maintaining anxiety. |
| INCARNATION | The process of gradually fleshing out (carnis: flesh) in all dimensions and articulations of the personality the directives of one's life formation. |
| INCARNATIONAL DISCIPLINES | Disciplines such as psychology, psychiatry, anthropology, sociology, psychobiology, psychotherapy, medicine, and other arts and sciences that can enlighten people in their appraisal of effective means of fleshing out in all dimensions of their life their directives of self-formation. Both directive and incarnational disciplines are considered necessary auxiliary disciplines of the discipline of formation. |
| INNER DIALOGUE | A technique in which the client is instructed to teach, demand, or in any way hold a conversation with him or herself or the subconscious, or inner self or mind. This technique may be used to challenge troubling or limiting beliefs, or to argue the case from a different point of view than he or she usually espouses. The possible variations are legion, and the technique may be done in or out of the hypnotic state. |
| INSTRUMENTAL SETTINGS | Support groups for the actualization of persons, using levels I, II, and III of Natural High Therapy. Opposed to institutional settings that lead to ego-esteem for the few, constriction for the many. |
| INTERACTIONAL TRAINING LAB | A research and treatment process that specializes in small-group exercises and interactions to teach patients social responsibility. |
| INTERNALIZED PSYCHODRAMA | A psychodrama in which the participant interacts with parental figures and other important persons in his background as they appear in one's fantasy rather than having these parts played by other participants. |
| INTROJECTS | The individual's past as it appears in his present fantasies, including all of the persons and circumstances that were important in his development. |
| KINESPHERE | The area of space around the body in which one can move the whole body or a body part while remaining in one place. |
| KO HAM | "Who am I?" The question asked by the psyche from birth. |
| KUNDALINI | An energy symbolized as a coiled snake that lies sleeping at the base of the spine. When awakened, it rises slowly up the spinal canal to the top of the head. This marks the beginning of enlightenment. |
| LEVEL I | The basic viewpoint of Natural High Theory. The "skills" of constriction of self-esteem and social interest are elaborated. |

| | |
|---|---|
| LEVEL II | The 12 steps of active social interest for practice on the transactional mode of actualization. Level I competency is a prerequisite for this dyadic development. |
| LEVEL III | The latest and final dimension of Natural High Therapy. After a person has experiential knowledge of the previous two dimensions, contact with the expansive, numinous growth symbols of this transpersonal focus can proceed. Level III is blocked by ego constrictions. |
| MAIN-TENT | Willard Beecher's term for the prime issues of responsibility in life. Opposite of the side-show, the production of ego-noise, on the peripheral symptomatic side of life. |
| MBD | Minimal brain damage. |
| MANTRA | Sacred words or sounds |
| MAYA ILLUSION | In terms of eternal reality, the world we see and the self we believe we are are illusory. |
| MERIDIAN | Pathway for electromagnetic energy to flow in the body. Associated with Chinese acupuncture system. |
| MINDRAPE | A creative Aggression exercise (negative practice) to recognize and to control the tendency of intimate partners to impose on one another feelings and thoughts in brainwashing fashion. |
| MISHIRABE | Meditative introspection as practiced by a subsect of Buddhist priests. |
| MODELING | Learning by observing other individuals interacting with their environment. |
| MODULATION | Those changes of the core or current life form that do not affect their foundations or basic structure. |
| MYSTIFICATION | The process whereby a person's oppression is explained away and becomes acceptable. |
| NAIKANSHA | The client in Naikan Therapy, a retrospective meditative treatment form. |
| NATURAL FLOW | Getting in touch with one's real self, namely, those aspects of self that are spontaneous rather than defensive and/or adaptive. |
| NATURAL HIGH | An optimistic action-oriented approach to living which emphasizes here-and-now self-responsibilities. |
| NATURAL HIGH LAB INTERVIEWS | Part of the dyadic structure of didactic-experiential workshops. Early in the labs, participants interview each other around a main topic, using steps of encouragement, as a mode of learning through practice and overcoming isolation. |
| NEGATIVE LOVE | Conditional "love". "Love" that comes from ego mechanisms, such as "giving to get," or "I love you, I hate you. . . ." |
| NEGATIVE PATTERN/ PROGRAM | Belief structures in contradiction with Reality and the Inner Being. Negative modalities of behavior usually learned from parents in prepuberty years. |
| NICHIJO NAIKAN | Daily Naikan meditation. Reflecting morning and evening on what was received from and returned to others and what trouble was caused them both in the past and during that day. |

| | |
|---|---|
| OCULAR ZONE | One of the segments of the body; considered an erogenous zone in orgonomy in addition to those recognized in psychoanalysis. |
| ONE-POINTING | In Natural High Therapy, one of the first benefits of meditation. Clients are thereby able to clear the psyche of ego-noise, in a state of alert relaxation. |
| OPERANT PARADIGM | The learning model that assumes most relevant human behavior is controlled by the consequences. |
| ORDER THROUGH FLUCTUATION | The achievement of a new level of complexity of organization through the non-random fluctuations of an open nonequilibrium system which possesses many degrees of freedom for change. |
| ORGASM ANXIETY | Anxiety produced by final and complete surrender of the organism giving in to its involuntary convulsion. Seen in the final stages of therapy. In the final analysis, orgasm anxiety is behind all armored manifestations. |
| ORGASM REFLEX | The unitary involuntary contraction and expansion of the total organism seen when the organism is at rest and energy flow is uninhibited. Also seen at the acme of the sexual act, suppressed in most humans. |
| ORGASTIC POTENCY | The capacity for complete surrender to the involuntary contraction of the organism and complete discharge of sexual excitation in the acme of the sexual act. It is always lacking in neurotic individuals. |
| ORGONE | Primordial cosmic energy, universally present and demonstrated visually, thermically, electroscopically, and with the Geiger-Muller counter. In the living organism it is biological energy. |
| ORGONOMY | The natural science of orgone energy and its functions. |
| PASSIVE CONCENTRATION | The concentration of the observer, Nongoal oriented without concern to outcome. Noncompetitive. |
| PERIODIC FORM OF LIFE (PERIODIC SELF) | That aspect of the current life form in a reaction and response to situational changes and uniqueness-disclosures resulting from a specific developmental period such as infancy, adolescence, mid-life, old age. |
| PERTURBATION | The quality of a dissipative structure to cause fluctuations in an open nonequilibrium system. |
| PHALLIC NARCISSISTIC TYPE (CHARACTER) | An early genital stage where development may be arrested. |
| PHASIC ACTIVITY | Physiological activity which is either spontaneous or in response to external stimulation and usually rapid in nature. This type of activity occurs upon a slowly shifting background of activity known as tonic level. |
| POWER PLAY | A transaction designed to coerce others into doing what they would not otherwise do. |
| POW WOW | A family gathering for the purpose of conducting a "fair fight" session. |
| PRANA | Life energy that flows throughout the body being directed by the breath. Wilhelm Reich termed this *energy orgone* and indicated that its flow was blocked by the presence of body armor. |

| | |
|---|---|
| PRECONSCIOUS | Preconscious patterns of attention and inattention that influence in some measure the perceptions and rational processes marking the direction of focused awareness and attention. |
| PRESENCE | The overall direction and quality of one's global attention to the formative meaning of people, events, and things that constitute the formation situations for self, others, and world. |
| PROGRESSIVE RELAXATION | Identifying the tense areas of one's body by deliberately tensing and relaxing muscles throughout the body. |
| PULSATIONS | The formative forces that move significantly in any current history and that affect a person's formation in the way and measure of his sharing in this movement of history. |
| QUADRINITY PROCESS | (formerly called FISCHER-HOFFMAN) An intensive program designed to clear up unfinished issues with parents. Originated by Robert Hoffman. |
| RECIPROCAL INHIBITION | The inhibiting of a response by the substitution of an antagonistic response, for example, inhibition. |
| RECYCLING | Term used in the Quadrinity Process to denote the turning of a negative belief pattern into a positive affirmation, for example, "You'll never make anything of yourself" becomes "I am successful and competent." |
| REFRAMING | The process in which a previously unpleasant event is viewed from a different perspective. |
| REICHIAN ORGASM | An involuntary convulsive pleasurable movement throughout the entire body that accompanies sexual climax in individuals who are relatively free of body armor. The full discharge of sexual energy is experienced as melting, flowing, and dissolving in the universe and is followed by a sense of rebirth and renewal. |
| REINFORCEMENT SURVEY SCHEDULE | A self-report inventroy designed to discover reinforcing experiences in an individual's life. |
| RESCUE | Doing more than one's share or doing what one doesn't want to do. |
| RESISTANCE-RESONANCE RECOGNITION | The acute awareness of one's spontaneous repulsion or attraction—rightly or wrongly—when exposed to potential formation directives. |
| RESONANCE | The affirmative reverberation evoked in experience by a potential formation directive when it is spontaneously felt—rightly or wrongly—to be congenial with one's uniqueness and congruent with one's formation situation. |
| RESOURCING THERAPY | The fostering of the healing and integrating power of personal, experiential assimilation of the sources of a formation tradition one is freely committed to. |
| RESPONDENT CONDITIONING | Synonymous with the classical conditioning procedure of Pavlov. |
| ROLFING | A method of structurally integrating the muscles and fascia to realign the body to be compatible with the field of gravity. Originated by Ida Rolf. |

| | |
|---|---|
| SATORI BUDDHIST ENLIGHTENMENT | The ability to accept reality "as it is." |
| SCENE VISUALIZATION | Any visual imagery technique where one is instructed to visualize a certain geographical location or spatial surroundings. |
| SE | Abbreviation for self-esteem, the unconditional sense of worth beyond the circumscribed roles, goals, and controls of ego-esteem. |
| SEDIMENTED CULTURAL DIRECTIVES | Directives for possible life formation that are contained in the language, customs, traditions, expressions and monuments of the culture in which a person lives and that influence at least preconsciously the direction of his life formation. |
| SEI NO YOKUBO | The innate desire to survive and actualize one's potential. |
| SEIKATSU NO HAKKENKAI | Morita therapy mental health organization. |
| SEISHIN KYOIKU | Training of the mind. Literally, "spiritual education." |
| SEIZA | A form of meditative sitting in Japan. Literally, "quiet sitting." |
| SELF-ALIENATING PULSATION | A formative movement in any current history that affects one's own life formation but is at odds with one's emergent uniqueness, one's life situation, and one's chosen formation tradition. |
| SELF-CONTROL TRIAD | Procedure developed by Joseph Cautela to decrease an undesirable response such as anxiety or temptation to perform a maladaptive approach response. The client is instructed to imagine a sequence, say "Stop" to him or herself, inhale deeply, relax while exhaling, and then imagine a pleasant scene. |
| SELF SYNCHRONY | Correlation among one's own body rhythms, including vegetative rhythms (breathing, heartbeat, etc.), and rhythms of movement in various body parts. |
| SEX ECONOMY | The body of knowledge that deals with the economy of the biological energy in the organism, with its energy household. |
| SHINKEISHITAU | Broad category of neurosis; characterized by perfectionism, idealism, self-centeredness, and a strong desire to get rid of symptoms. |
| SI | Abbreviation for social interest. In Natural High Theory social interest is expanded to Adler's original meaning of a general universal connectedness. |
| SINISTER-CIRCLE | A descriptive term for the inner ego movements of constriction which diminish our innate social interest and self-esteem. |
| "SMILES" REPORT | Colloquial term for any all-too-typical evaluation form filled at the end of conferences to attempt to measure the effectiveness of the conference or workshop. Such a method generates information on what the participants thought of the program and instructor but cannot in any way measure effectiveness. |
| SO HAM MANTRA | Literally, "I am that." The natural vibration of the self, which occurs spontaneously with each incoming and outgoing breath. |
| SOMATIC ARMOR | The muscular armor, functionally equivalent to the character armor. |

SPIRITUAL FORMATION
An initially conscious process of realization of a unique human form of life guided by directives, of self-formation opted for or—if already operative—ratified in relative freedom on the basis of insightful appraisal of the directives concerned.

STROKE
The unit of positive recognition or love.

STROKE ECONOMY
A set of rules limiting the exchange of strokes between people.

STRUCTURAL DEPRIVATION
A loss of situational opportunities for formative interaction on which the structural integrity and strength of one's current life form depend.

SYNTONIC LIFE FORM
The life form insofar as it is congenial with one's emergent uniqueness and congruent with one's life period and situation.

SYSTEMATIC DESENSITIZATION
Imagining being exposed to a phobic stimulus, proceeding in gradual steps starting from those situations that produce minimal anxiety to those producing maximum anxiety.

TABLE WORK
Term used in body therapy to denote the use of a massage table for application of technique.

T'AI-CHI
A Chinese moving meditation. Originally a martial art, now also used widely for centering, grounding, and balancing the body.

TAIJIN KYOFUSHO
A common type of neurosis found in Japan. Anthropophobia or social phobia. Literally, "other-person phobia."

TANTRIC FUSION
The first phase in tantric union during which the two individuals experience ego loss and dissolve into each other, becoming one being.

TANTRIC UNION
The end result of a yoga procedure in which a couple meditates while having intercourse. Lying completely motionless and relaxed, they experience the flow of life energy between them and gradually surrender their egos and merge into one being. In this process the individual selves transcend time and death and share in the immortal being of the Divine Self.

THETA FEEDBACK
Rhythms that fall within 4–7 cycles per second and occur in the normal person associated with decreased tension in the somatic musculature.

THOUGHT-STOPPING
Imagining hearing the word "Stop" whenever an undesirable thought occurs.

TRAGER MENTASTICS
A method of freeing the body of tensions and aberrations through shaking movements. Originated by Milton Trager.

TRANSCENDENCE
The process of "going beyond" a current life form that has been congenial and congruent in a specific life period or situation.

TRANSCENDENCE CRISIS
A period of basic insecurity due to the structural weakening of a no longer effective life form and deepened by the uncertainty about appropriate directives for a new current life form more congruent with the changing life period or situation and more congenial with one's unique personality as it increasingly discloses itself.

| | |
|---|---|
| TRANSCENDENT LIFE FORM | That aspect of the life form that goes beyond and at the same time liberates, modulates, and integrates the determinants of the historical, vital, and functional dimensions of the life form. Same as transcendent self. |
| TRANSITION STATES | The mutatory transitions in an open nonequilibrium system that generate the conditions for renewed high entropy production within a new regime. |
| TYPE A | A personality pattern characterized by a chronic sense of time urgency, competitiveness and hostility, insecurity regarding status, and a quest for numbers. This pattern is conducive to cardiovascular disease. |
| TYPE B | A personality pattern characterized by easygoingness and relaxation. |
| VALIDATION | The recognition that a person's perceptions and feelings have validity. |
| VESUVIUS | A time-limited cathartic ritualized verbal hostility outburst—by permission of attending spouse, friend, co-worker, or family member. |
| VICTIM | The recipient of Rescuing or Persecution. A person who feels powerless. |
| VITALISM | The vital dimension of the life form, in the formation theory of personality, representing the formative influence of the organism and its impulses on the life form of the person. |
| WHEEL OF LIFE | A graphic technique in which program participants plot the degree of time/energy they invest in each of six life tasks: occupation, friendship, intimacy, leisure, spiritual, and self. |

# *APPENDIX*

## Sources

In their original manuscripts, a number of authors included names and addresses of institutions and individuals that readers could contact for further information about training and therapy. After rigorously excising all such information from the manuscript, I decided to include this appendix in consideration for the reader who might want such information. I sent a notice to every senior author asking for such information for this appendix. This list of all places and persons to reach for further information is the result.

## Actualizing Therapy

Institute of Actualizing Therapy
2200 E. Fruit St., Suite 206
Santa Ana, CA   92701
(Dan Montgomery, Ph.D.,
Everett L. Shostrom, Ph.D.)

## Aesthetic Realism

Aesthetic Realism Foundation
141 Greene Street
New York, NY   10012
(Martha Baird,
Arnold Perey, Ph.D.,
Ellen Reiss,
Rebecca Thompson)

## Aqua-Energetics

Paul Bindrim, Ph.D.
2000 Cantata Drive
Los Angeles, CA   90068

## Art Therapy

Myra F. Levick, M.Ed.
Hahnemann Medical College and Hospital
7601 NCB, 15th and Vince Streets
Philadelphia, PA   19102

## Body Therapies

Aston-Patterning Consultants
Box 114
Tiburon, CA   94920

Feldenkrais Guild
1776 Union Street
San Francisco, CA   94123

Institute of Psycho-structural Balancing
1122 Fourth Avenue
San Diego, CA   92101

New England School of Acupuncture
5 Bridge Street
Watertown, MA   02172

Polarity Institute—Alive Fellowship
Star Route Box 86
Olga, WA   98279

Rolf Institute
Box 1868
Boulder, CO   80306

Trager Association
110 Tiburon Boulevard
Mill Valley, CA   94941
(Betty Fuller)

University for Humanistic Studies
420 Ash Street
San Diego, CA   92101

## Biofeedback Therapy

Biofeedback Society of America
4200 East Ninth Avenue
Denver, CO   80262

## Brief Therapy

Darryl L. Gentry, M.S.W.
1200 Glade Street
Winston-Salem, NC   27101

Lynn Segal, L.C.S.W.
Mental Research Institute
555 Middlefield Road
Palo Alto, CA   94301

## Cognitive Behavior Therapy

John P. Foreyt, Ph.D.
Diet Modification Clinic
6535 Fannin, M.S., F 700
Houston, TX   77030

## Comprehensive Relaxation Training

Alan C. Turin, Ph.D.
19 Muzzey St.
Lexington, MA   02173

## Conditioned Reflex Therapy

Andrew Salter
903 Park Avenue
New York, NY   10021

## Conflict Resolution Therapy

E. Lakin Phillips, Ph.D.
George Washington University
718–21st Street N.W.
Washington, D.C.   20052

## Creative Aggression

Luree Nicholson
Family Counseling Center
6329 East Forest City Road
Orlando, FL   32810

Roger Carl F. Bach, Ph.D.
Bach Institute
9071 Nemo Street
West Hollywood, CA   90069

George R. Bach, Ph.D.
Center for Creative Aggression
8437 Hollywood Boulevard
Los Angeles, CA   90069

Edward Bourgh, Ph.D.
California School Professional Psychology
56 Ross Circle
Oakland, CA

## Crisis Intervention

Southwestern Academy of Crisis Interveners
8609 NW Plaza Dr.
Suite 440A
Dallas, Texas
(Sharon Levitan,
James L. Greenwood)

## Dance Therapy

Diane M. Duggan, M.S.
149 West 4th Street
New York, NY   10012

American Dance Therapy Association
2000 Centry Plaza
Columbia, MD   21044

## Direct Psychoanalysis

John N. Rosen, M.D.
Direct Psychoanalytic Institute
155 East Oakland Avenue
Doylestown, PA   18901

## Ego State Therapy

Helen H. Watkins
Center for Student Development
John Watkins
Department of Psychology
University of Montana
Missoula, Montana   59803

## Eidetic Psychotherapy

Akhter Ahsen, Ph.D.
International Imagery Association
22 Edgecliff Terrace
Yonkers, NY   10705

Anees A. Sheikh
Department of Psychology
Marquette University
Milwaukee, Wisconsin   53233

## Encouragement Therapy

Lew Losoncy, Ed.D.
Institute for Personal and
    Organizational Development
2904 State Hill Rd, 7-12
Wyomissing, PA   19610

## Feminist Therapy

National Feminist Therapy Association
Box B 1302
San Diego, CA   92112

Blue Sky Consultants
4135 Bagley N.
Seattle, WA   98103

Association for Women in Psychology
114 W 85 St. # 8B
New York, NY   10024

## Focusing

Focusing Group
Chicago Counseling and Psychotherapy
  Research Center
5711 South Woodlawn Avenue
Chicago, IL   60637

Eugene T. Gendlin, Ph.D.
University of Chicago
5848 University Avenue
Chicago, IL   60637

Elfie Hintekopf, Ph.D.
Focusing Institute
5637 Kenwood
Chicago, IL   60637

## Holistic Education

Center for Holistic Studies
Antioch University West
650 Pine Street
San Francisco, CA   94108

## Impasse/Priority Therapy

Nira Kefir, Ph.D.
Alfred Adler Institute
Tel Aviv, Israel

## Integrative Psychotherapy

Walter J. Urban, Ph.D.
1097 South Genessee Avenue
Los Angeles, CA   90019

## Morita Therapy

*See* Naikan Therapy

## Multimodal Therapy

Multimodal Therapy Institutes
28 Main Street
Kingston, N.J.   08528

1385 York Ave.
New York, NY   10021

33 Chestnut Hill Ave.
Philadelphia, PA   19118

Southgate Medical Arts Building

21100 Southgate Park Blvd.
Maple Heights, Ohio   44137

## Multiple Family Therapy

John Raasoch, M.D.
Mowadrock
Family and Mental Health Service
331 Main St.
Keene, NH   03431

## Multiple Impact Training

George M. Gazda, Ed.D.
408 Aderhold Hall
University of Georgia
Athens, GA   30602

## Natural High Therapy

Walter E. O'Connell, Ph.D.
Veterans Administration Center
2002 Holcombe Boulevard
Houston, TX   77211

## Primary Relationship Therapy

Genevieve Painter, Ed.D.
Associates for Human Development
750 Amana Street, Suite 205
Honolulu, HI   96814

## Naikan Therapy

David K. Reynolds, Ph.D.
Department of Anthropology
University of Houston, Central Campus
Houston, TX   77004

## New Identity Process

Casriel Institute
47 East 51st Street
New York, NY   10022

## Personal Construct Therapy

A. W. Landfield, Ph.D.
Personal Construct Clearinghouse
University of Nebraska, Lincoln
Lincoln, NE   68588

Franz R. Epting, Ph.D.
Personal Construct Clearinghouse
Department of Psychology, University of Florida
Gainesville, FL   32611

## Plissit

Jack S. Annon, Ph.D.
Queen's Physicians' Office Building
1380 Lusitana Street
Honolulu, HI   96813

## Primal Therapy

Denver Primal Center
323 South Pearl Street
Denver, CO   80209
(Dennis O. Kirkman,
Robert F. A. Schaef, Ph.D.,
Barbara Ungashick, MA)

## Psycho-Imagination Therapy

Joseph E. Shorr, Ph.D.
Institute for Psycho-Imagination Therapy
580 South San Vicente B1
Los Angeles, CA   90048

## Psychosynthesis

Martha Crampton, M.A.
Psychosynthesis Training Institute, Holodynamics
218 Black Rock Turnpike
Redding, CT   06896

Ed Turner, Ed.D.
Psychosynthesis Training Center
311 W. McGraw
Seattle, WA   98119

Edith Stauffer, Ph.D.
Psychosynthesis Training Center
647 N. Madison Ave
Pasadena, CA   91101

Dorothy Firman
Synthesis Center
Box 575
Amherst, MA   01004

## Radix Neo-Reichian Education

Elaine Warburton, M.Ed.
Box 97
Ojai, CA   93023

## Rebirthing

Eve Jones, Ph.D.
140 South Norton
Los Angeles, CA   90004

Rebirthing Center of the High Sierras
Campbell Hot Springs
Box 224
Sierraville, CA   96126

Roberta Rigney
301 Lyon Street
San Francisco, CA   94117

Theta House
301 Lyon Street
San Francisco, CA   94117

## Sex Therapies

Dianne Gerard, M.S.W.
400 Hobron Lane
Honolulu, HI   96815

## Social Influence Therapy

John S. Gillis, Ph.D.
Department of Psychology
Oregon State University
Corvallis, OR   97331

## Stress Management

Stress Management Institute
313 Main Street
Reisterstown, MD   21136
(Harry A. Olson, Ph.D.,
Joan Roberts, Ph.D.)

## Structural Learning

Structural Learning Associates
129 Nottingham Rd.
Syracuse, NY   13210
(Robert P. Sprafkin, Ph.D.,
N. Jane Gershaw, Ph.D.,
Arnold P. Goldstein, Ph.D.)

## Triad Therapy

Paul B. Pedersen, Ph.D.
East-West Culture Learning Institute
1777 East-West Road
Honolulu, HI   96848

## Z-Process Attachment Therapy

Robert W. Zaslow, Ph.D.
Department of Psychology
San Jose State University
San Jose, CA   95192

# Author Index

# Subject Index

Encouragement Therapy, 286–297
  applications of, 294–295
  case example of, 295–297
  current status of, 288–289
  history of, 286–288
  methodology of, 292–294
  theory of, 289–292
    encouraging confidence, 291
    encouraging responsibility, 290–291
    origins and dynamics of discouragement, 290
    process of encouragement, 291–292
"Encouragement Therapy" (Losoncy), 286–298
*Encouragement Therapy: A Positive and
  Practical Approach to Developing
  Responsibility, Confidence, and Courage*
  (Losoncy), 292
Encouragement Training (ET), 288
*Encouraging Children to Learn* (Dinkmeyer &
  Dreikurs), 287
Energy
  in Integrative Therapy, 418–419, 423–425
  in Radix Education, 740–741
  *See also* Life energy
*Energy* (Stone), 98
"Energy and Character" (bulletin), 98
Energy-flow balancing, 97, 101, 103
Enlightenment
  Aqua-Energetics and, 33–35
  Meditation and, 473
Eosinophiles, 574
Epilepsy, Covert Conditioning for, 197, 198
Equal Rights Amendment (ERA), 305
Equilibrium equation, Aqua-Energetics and, 39,
  40
Erogenous zones, in orgonomy, 601, 604
Ethics
  Aesthetic Realism and, 21
  Meditation and, 476
Euphoria, Poetry Therapy and, 644
Evolution, Aqua-Energetics and, 38–39
Exaggeration, in Provocative Therapy, 687
Excitation
  Conditioned Reflex Therapy and, 163–167
  Pavlov's concept of, 160, 161
Excitatory reflex, 163
Excitatory training, 167
Exercise, Stress Management and, 821
Exercise effect, in Functional Psychotherapy, 367
Exhibitionism
  Aqua-Energetics and, 45
  covert response cost for, 196
Existential anxiety, Aqua-Energetics and, 32, 37,
  38, 43
Existentialism, Encouragement Therapy and, 287
Existential neurosis, Encouragement Therapy for,
  295
Expectation of benefit, enhancing, 808–809
Experiencing
  Focusing and, 345–350
    defined, 347
    states of experiencing, 348–351
  Gendlin's concept of, 345–347
Experimental psychology, psychoanalysis and,
  177

*Face to Face with Schizophrenia* (Zaslow and
  Menta), 903, 913
Facial talk, 166
"Facial touch" exercise, 8–9
False knowledge, in Psycho-Structural Balancing
  theory, 99, 102–103
Family
  Aesthetic Realism and, 26
  Art Therapy and, 56–57
  behavioral-interactional view of problems in,
    108
  in double-bind theory, 108
  Twenty-Four-Hour Therapy and, 878–879
Family counseling, Primary Relationship Therapy
  for, 673
Family therapy
  Brief Therapy, 122
  Creative Aggression in, 213
  triads in, 841
  *See also* Multiple Family Therapy; Parent-
    Child Therapy
Fantasies, in Primary Relationship Therapy, 671
Fear(s)
  in Actualizing Therapy, 6
  Interpersonal Process Recall and, 447
  two-factor theory of, 190
Feedback
  alpha, 81–82
  in Structured Learning, 827, 832, 833, 836
  *See also* Biofeedback
Feeling polarities, in Actualizing Therapy, 1–10
Feeling-talk, 165
Feeling Therapy, 369, 371
Feldenkrais Guild, 97
Feldenkrais technique (or exercises), 97, 102, 103
  in Holistic Education, 379
Felt sense, 344–351
  *See also* Focusing
Feminism, 299
"Feminist Psychotherapy II" (Forisha), 315–332
Feminist Therapy, 299–330
  applications of, 307–309, 326–328
    depression, 308–309
    power, 307
    sexuality, 307–308
    victims of violence, 308
  assumptions of, 299
  case example of, 309–311, 328–330
  current status of, 301–302, 318–319
  history of, 300–301, 316–318
    humanistic psychology, 317–318
    marginality of women, 316–317
    Women's Movement, 318
  humanist psychology and, 315, 317–318
  male therapists, 301
  methodology of, 305–307, 324–326
    assertiveness training, 306
    life planning, 306
    sex-role analysis, 306–307
  social change and, 305–307
  theory of, 302–305, 319–324
    anger, 321, 322
    changes, 304–305
    diagnosis, 304

Psychology and Psychiatry in Courts and Corrections: Controversy and Change
*by Ellsworth A. Fersch, Jr.*

Restricted Environmental Stimulation: Research and Clinical Applications
*by Peter Suedfeld*

Personal Construct Psychology: Psychotherapy and Personality
*edited by Alvin W. Landfield and Larry M. Leitner*

Mothers, Grandmothers, and Daughters: Personality and Child Care in
Three-Generation Families
*by Bertram J. Cohler and Henry U. Grunebaum*

Further Explorations in Personality
*edited by A. I. Rabin, Joel Aronoff, Andrew M. Barclay, and Robert A. Zucker*

Hypnosis and Relaxation: Modern Verification of an Old Equation
*by William E. Edmonston, Jr.*

Handbook of Clinical Behavior Therapy
*edited by Samuel M. Turner, Karen S. Calhoun, and Henry E. Adams*

Handbook of Clinical Neuropsychology
*edited by Susan B. Filskov and Thomas J. Boll*

The Course of Alcoholism: Four Years After Treatment
*by J. Michael Polich, David J. Armor, and Harriet B. Braiker*

Handbook of Innovative Psychotherapies
*edited by Raymond J. Corsini*